Get started with your Connected Casebook

Redeem your code below to access the **e-book** with search, highlighting, and note-taking capabilities; **case briefing** and **outlining** tools to support efficient learning; and more.

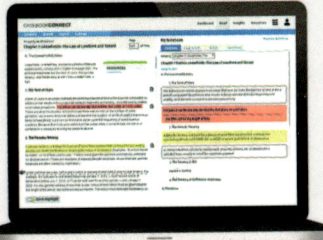

1. Go to www.casebookconnect.com
2. Enter your access code in the box and click **Register**
3. Follow the steps to complete your registration and verify your email address

If you have already registered at CasebookConnect.com, simply log into your account and redeem additional access codes from your Dashboard.

ACCESS CODE:
Scratch off with care.

Is this a used casebook? Access code already redeemed? Purchase a digital version at **CasebookConnect.com/catalog**.

If you purchased a digital bundle with additional components, your additional access codes will appear below.

"I liked being able to search quickly while in class."

"Being able to highlight and easily create case briefs was a fantastic resource and time saver for me!"

"I loved it! I was able to study on the go and create a more effective outline."

PLEASE NOTE: Each access code can only be used once. Access codes expire one year after the discontinuation of the corresponding print or bundle title and must be redeemed before then. CCH reserves the right to discontinue this program at any time for any business reason. For further details, please see the CasebookConnect End User License Agreement at CasebookConnect.com/terms.

For technical support, please visit http://support.wklegaledu.com.

The Law of Armed Conflict: An Operational Approach

EDITORIAL ADVISORS

Rachel E. Barkow
Segal Family Professor of Regulatory Law and Policy
Faculty Director, Center on the Administration of Criminal Law
New York University School of Law

Erwin Chemerinsky
Dean and Jesse H. Choper Distinguished Professor of Law
University of California, Berkeley School of Law

Richard A. Epstein
Laurence A. Tisch Professor of Law
New York University School of Law
Peter and Kirsten Bedford Senior Fellow
The Hoover Institution
Senior Lecturer in Law
The University of Chicago

Ronald J. Gilson
Charles J. Meyers Professor of Law and Business
Stanford University
Marc and Eva Stern Professor of Law and Business
Columbia Law School

James E. Krier
Earl Warren DeLano Professor of Law
The University of Michigan Law School

Tracey L. Meares
Walton Hale Hamilton Professor of Law
Director, The Justice Collaboratory
Yale Law School

Richard K. Neumann, Jr.
Alexander Bickel Professor of Law
Maurice A. Deane School of Law at Hofstra University

Robert H. Sitkoff
John L. Gray Professor of Law
Harvard Law School

David Alan Sklansky
Stanley Morrison Professor of Law
Faculty Co-Director, Stanford Criminal Justice Center
Stanford Law School

ASPEN CASEBOOK SERIES

THE LAW OF ARMED CONFLICT: AN OPERATIONAL APPROACH

Second Edition

Geoffrey S. Corn
Vinson & Elkins Professor of Law
South Texas College of Law Houston

Victor Hansen
Professor of Law
New England Law—Boston

Richard B. Jackson
Adjunct Professor
Georgetown University Law Center

Chris Jenks
Professor of Law
SMU Dedman School of Law

Eric Talbot Jensen
Professor of Law
Brigham Young University

James A. Schoettler, Jr.
Adjunct Professor
Georgetown University Law Center

Copyright © 2019 CCH Incorporated. All Rights Reserved.

Published by Wolters Kluwer in New York.

Wolters Kluwer Legal & Regulatory U.S. serves customers worldwide with CCH, Aspen Publishers, and Kluwer Law International products. (www.WKLegaledu.com)

No part of this publication may be reproduced or transmitted in any form or by any means, electronic or mechanical, including photocopy, recording, or utilized by any information storage or retrieval system, without written permission from the publisher. For information about permissions or to request permissions online, visit us at www.WKLegaledu.com, or a written request may be faxed to our permissions department at 212-771-0803.

To contact Customer Service, e-mail customer.service@wolterskluwer.com, call 1-800-234-1660, fax 1-800-901-9075, or mail correspondence to:

> Wolters Kluwer
> Attn: Order Department
> PO Box 990
> Frederick, MD 21705

Printed in the United States of America.

2 3 4 5 6 7 8 9 0

ISBN 978-1-4548-8088-2

Library of Congress Cataloging-in-Publication Data

Names: Corn, Geoffrey S., author. | Hansen, Victor M., 1962-, author. | Jackson, Richard B. (Lawyer), author. | Jenks, Chris (Law teacher), author. | Jensen, Eric Talbot, author. | Schoettler, James A., Jr.. author.
Title: The law of armed conflict : an operational approach / Geoffrey S. Corn, Vinson & Elkins Professor of Law, South Texas College of Law, Houston; Victor Hansen, Professor of Law, New England Law, Boston; Richard B. Jackson, Adjunct Professor, Georgetown University Law Center; Chris Jenks, Professor of Law, SMU Dedman School of Law; Eric Talbot Jensen, Professor of Law, Brigham Young University; James A. Schoettler, Jr., Adjunct Professor, Georgetown University Law Center.
Description: Second edition. | New York : Wolters Kluwer, [2019] | Series: Aspen casebook series
Identifiers: LCCN 2018032175 | ISBN 9781454880882 (hardcover)
Subjects: LCSH: War (International law) | LCGFT: Casebooks (Law)
Classification: LCC KZ6355 .L39 2019 | DDC 341.6—dc23
LC record available at https://lccn.loc.gov/2018032175

About Wolters Kluwer Legal & Regulatory U.S.

Wolters Kluwer Legal & Regulatory U.S. delivers expert content and solutions in the areas of law, corporate compliance, health compliance, reimbursement, and legal education. Its practical solutions help customers successfully navigate the demands of a changing environment to drive their daily activities, enhance decision quality and inspire confident outcomes.

Serving customers worldwide, its legal and regulatory portfolio includes products under the Aspen Publishers, CCH Incorporated, Kluwer Law International, ftwilliam.com, and MediRegs names. They are regarded as exceptional and trusted resources for general legal and practice-specific knowledge, compliance and risk management, dynamic workflow solutions, and expert commentary.

Summary of Contents

Contents	ix
Foreword	xxiii
Acknowledgments	xxv
Introduction	xxvii
Iraq Scenario	xxxvii

Chapter 1:	Legal Bases for Use of Force	1
Chapter 2:	History, Sources, and Principles of the Law of Armed Conflict	37
Chapter 3:	Triggering the Law of Armed Conflict	93
Chapter 4:	Classification and Status of Persons	141
Chapter 5:	Belligerent Detention	169
Chapter 6:	Civilian Protection Law	213
Chapter 7:	Targeting	247
Chapter 8:	Weapons and Tactics	285
Chapter 9:	Wounded and Sick	319
Chapter 10:	Occupation, Termination of Hostilities, and Transition	357
Chapter 11:	Naval Warfare and Neutrality	421
Chapter 12:	Air, Space, and Cyber Warfare	477
Chapter 13:	War Crimes	537
Chapter 14:	Command Responsibility and Compliance Mechanisms	595

Glossary of Terms	641
Table of Cases	649
Index	651

Contents

Foreword	*xxiii*
Acknowledgments	*xxv*
Introduction	*xxvii*
Iraq Scenario	*xxxvii*

Chapter 1: Legal Bases for Use of Force ... 1

- I. Introduction ... 1
- II. Historical Background ... 3
- III. The United Nations Charter Paradigm ... 4
  - A. General Assembly ... 5
  - B. Security Council ... 7
    - 1. Chapter VI—Pacific Settlement of Disputes ... 7
    - 2. Chapter VII—Action with Respect to Threats to the Peace, Breaches of the Peace, and Acts of Aggression ... 9
  - C. International Court of Justice ... 13
- IV. The Use of Force ... 15
  - A. Consent ... 18
  - B. Security Council Authorization ... 19
  - C. Self-Defense and Other Uses of Force ... 20
    - 1. Self-Defense ... 20
      - a. Principles ... 21
        - (1) Necessity ... 21
        - (2) Proportional Response ... 22
        - (3) Timeliness ... 22
      - b. "Inherent Right" of Self-Defense ... 23
        - (1) No Action Before Armed Attack ... 24
        - (2) Anticipatory Self-Defense ... 24
        - (3) Interceptive Self-Defense ... 24
        - (4) Preventive Self-Defense ... 25
      - c. Collective Self-Defense ... 26

		d. Armed Attack	26
		e. "Until the Security Council Has Taken Measures"	27
	2.	Other Uses of Force	28
		a. Protection of Nationals	28
		b. Humanitarian Intervention and the Responsibility to Protect	29
D.	Some Contemporary Challenges		31
	1.	Non-State Actors	31
	2.	Drones	33
	3.	Cyber Operations	34
Study Questions			35

Chapter 2: History, Sources, and Principles of the Law of Armed Conflict — 37

I.	The LOAC Tradition	38
II.	Historical Foundations	42
III.	LOAC Principles	46
	A. Importance of Principles	47
	B. Defining the Principles	49
	1. Military Necessity: The First Principle of Authority	50
	2. Humanity: The First Principle of Restraint	53
	3. Distinction: The Essential Requirement for Lawful Targeting	55
	4. Proportionality: The Balancing Principle	57
	5. Precautions: The Precondition for All Combat Operations	59
IV.	Treaty Law	61
	A. Hague Law	61
	B. Geneva Law	64
	C. Additional Protocols of 1977: Merging of Hague and Geneva Law	68
	D. Other LOAC Treaties	70
	1. Cultural Property	70
	2. Weapons	72
	E. Treaties Outside the Scope of the LOAC	73
V.	Customary International Law	76
VI.	Other Sources of the LOAC	82
	A. Decisions of Courts and Tribunals	82
	B. "Soft Law"	84
	C. Statutes, Regulations, and Policies Affecting LOAC	86

		1. Laws and Executive Orders	87
		2. Military Doctrine	87
		3. Rules of Engagement	89
	Study Questions		91

Chapter 3: Triggering the Law of Armed Conflict — 93

I. Introduction — 94
II. Origins of the Conflict Classification Paradigm — 95
III. The 1949 Geneva Conventions and the Advent of a Law Trigger — 99
    A. The Triggers—Common Articles 2 and 3 — 99
    B. The Existence of an Armed Conflict — 103
    C. The Nature of the Armed Conflict — 113
IV. The 1977 Additional Protocols to the Geneva Conventions: Clarifying or Confusing the Law Applicability Assessment? — 120
V. A Few Wrinkles — 127
    A. External Intervention in an Internal Armed Conflict — 127
    B. Transnational Armed Conflicts? — 132
VI. Conclusion — 137
    Study Questions — 137

Chapter 4: Classification and Status of Persons — 141

I. Combatants and Civilians — 143
    A. A Problem of Definition — 143
    B. Civilians — 144
    C. Combatants — 145
    D. Presumptions — 147
II. Prisoners of War — 148
    A. Historical Development — 148
    B. Civilians Accompanying the Force — 150
    C. Retained Personnel — 150
III. Additional Protocol I — 151
IV. Unlawful Combatants — 152
    A. Historical Development of the Terms — 152
    B. A Gap in Coverage? — 154
    C. Habeas Corpus Litigation — 155
V. Non-International Armed Conflicts — 157
VI. Organized Armed Groups — 158

VII.	Civilians Directly Participating in Hostilities	161
	A. The ICRC Interpretive Guidance	162
	B. An Alternative Definition of DPH	164
	C. Human Shields	165
	D. Detention	166
VIII.	Conclusion	166
	Problems	167

Chapter 5: Belligerent Detention — 169

I.	Introduction to Detention	171
II.	Authority for Detention	173
III.	International Armed Conflict Detainee Categories	175
	A. Prisoners of War and Civilians	175
	B. Unprivileged Belligerents	177
IV.	Detainees in Non-International Armed Conflict	178
V.	What Process Is Due	180
	A. Article 5 Tribunals	180
	B. Procedural Safeguards in the Civilians Convention	183
	C. Detention Process in Non-International Armed Conflict	184
	D. Supplemental Standards for Detention Review: Contemporary U.S. Practice	186
	E. Ongoing Enhancement of "Law of War Detention" Process	189
VI.	Standard of Treatment	190
	A. Prisoners of War	190
	B. Civilians	196
	C. Treatment in Non-International Armed Conflict	197
VII.	Interrogation	198
	A. Interrogation in International Armed Conflict	198
	B. Interrogation in Non-International Armed Conflict	199
	C. Historical Limitations on Interrogation	200
	D. Interrogation in the War on Terror	202
	Study Problems	212

Chapter 6: Civilian Protection Law — 213

I.	Introduction	215
	A. The Concept of Civilian	218
	B. Who Is a Civilian Within the Meaning of LOAC?	219
II.	LOAC Shields of Protection for Civilians	220

		A. Shield from the Harmful Consequences of Attack	221
		B. Shield from Maltreatment at the Hands of a Party to the Conflict	221
		C. General Shield of Protection for Civilian Populations	225
		D. Shield of Special Protection for Especially Vulnerable Civilians	227
		E. Maximum Shield of Protection: Protected Persons	227
		1. Protected Persons in the Territory of Their Enemy	230
		2. Protected Persons in Occupied Territory	230
		F. Shield of Protection for Private Property	232
		1. Destruction of Private Property	232
		2. Taking Possession of Private Property	234
		G. Shield of Protection for Interned Civilians	236
		1. Basis for Civilian Detention	236
		2. Civilian Detention Treatment Protections	237
		3. Civilian Detention Review and Release Protections	240
	III.	The Role of Human Rights Law	240
	IV.	Conclusion	243
		Study Questions	244

Chapter 7: Targeting — 247

I.	Introduction	249
II.	The Targeting Process	249
III.	Applying the General Principles in Targeting	252
	A. Military Necessity	252
	1. Distinction	252
	a. Persons	253
	(1) Combatants	254
	(2) Civilians	254
	(3) Unprivileged Belligerents	256
	(4) Other Protected Persons	257
	(a) Persons Who are "*Hors de Combat*"	257
	i. Persons in the Power of an Adverse Party	257
	ii. Persons Who Have Clearly Expressed an Intention to Surrender	258
	iii. Persons Who Have Been Rendered Unconscious or are Otherwise Incapacitated by Wounds or Sickness, and Therefore are Incapable of Defending Themselves	258
	(b) Medical Personnel	258
	(c) Auxiliary Medical Personnel of the Armed Forces	259
	(d) Medical Transport	259

(e) Relief Societies 259
(f) Chaplains 259
(g) Civilian Medical and Religious Personnel 259
(h) Personnel Engaged in the Protection of Cultural Property 260
(i) Journalists 260
b. Objects 261
(1) Military Objectives 261
(a) Nature 262
(b) Location 262
(c) Purpose 263
(d) Use 263
(e) "Make an Effective Contribution to Military Action" 264
(f) "Offers a Definite Military Advantage" 264
(g) Examples 265
(2) Civilian Objects 267
(3) Protected Objects or Places 267
(a) Undefended Places 268
(b) Hospitals or Safety Zones for the Sick or Wounded 268
(c) Cultural Property 268
(d) Works and Installations Containing Dangerous Forces 269
(e) Objects Indispensable to the Survival of the Civilian Population 270
(f) Natural Environment 270
2. Proportionality 272
3. Current Controversy 275
a. Money and Revenue-Generating Objects 275
b. Targeting Individuals Who Are Outside "Areas of Active Hostilities" 276
c. Application of Targeting Principles to NIAC 277
B. Humanity and Unnecessary Suffering 278
IV. Review of Targeting Decisions 279
V. Non-Lethal Targeting 280
VI. Rules of Engagement 280
VII. The Legal Advice 281
Study Questions 281

Chapter 8: Weapons and Tactics — 285
- I. Introduction to Means and Methods of Warfare — 286
  - A. Humanity — 287
  - B. Chivalry — 288
- II. Legal Reviews of Weapons or Weapons Systems — 289
  - A. The Requirement for Legal Review — 289
  - B. Unnecessary Suffering — 290
  - C. Illegal Use in Customary Law and Treaty Law — 291
- III. Specific Prohibitions on Weapons and Ammunition — 293
  - A. Exploding Bullets — 293
  - B. Expanding Bullets — 294
  - C. Convention on Certain Conventional Weapons — 294
    1. Plastic Fragments and Incendiaries — 295
    2. Blinding Lasers — 296
    3. Anti-Personnel Land Mines — 296
  - D. Biological Weapons — 299
  - E. Chemical Weapons — 299
  - F. Riot Control Agents — 300
- IV. Specific Weapons — 301
  - A. Cluster Munitions — 301
  - B. Shotguns — 302
  - C. Small Arms and Small Arms Ammunition — 302
  - D. Edged Weapons — 303
  - E. .50 Caliber Rounds — 303
  - F. Explosive Munitions — 304
  - G. Depleted Uranium — 304
  - H. Snipers — 305
  - I. Silencers — 305
  - J. Non-Lethal Weapons — 306
  - K. Cyber Weapons — 307
- V. Employment of Weapons — 307
- VI. Methods of Warfare — 308
  - A. Ruses — 309
  - B. Perfidy — 310
  - C. Assassination — 310
  - D. Espionage — 312
  - E. Reprisals — 312
  - Study Problems — 318

Chapter 9: Wounded and Sick — 319
    I. Background — 320
    II. International Armed Conflict — 324
        A. Wounded and Sick — 324
            1. When Are Individuals Wounded or Sick? — 326
            2. How Are the Wounded and Sick Protected? — 328
                a. Respect and Protect — 328
                    (1) Respect — 328
                    (2) Protect — 328
                b. Obligation to Search and Collect — 329
                c. Obligation to Provide Medical Care — 330
                d. Obligations to the Dead — 332
                e. Obligation to Provide Information — 333
        A. Care Providers, Equipment, and Facilities — 334
            1. Personnel Aiding the Wounded and Sick — 336
                a. Exclusively Engaged Medical Personnel and Staff of the Armed Forces, Chaplains, and Members of National Relief Organizations — 338
                b. Auxiliary Medical Support Personnel of the Armed Forces — 340
                c. Members of Societies from Neutral Countries — 341
            2. Medical Units, Establishments, and Transportation — 342
                a. Facilities and Vehicles — 342
                b. Medical Aircraft — 345
    III. Protecting the Wounded and Sick in Non-International Armed Conflicts — 349
    IV. Violations — 351
    V. Conclusion — 351
        Study Questions — 352

Chapter 10: Occupation, Termination of Hostilities, and Transition — 357
    I. Introduction — 360
    II. Triggering the Law of Belligerent Occupation — 362
        A. Essential Criteria — 362
        B. Other Types of Operations — 363
        C. Relationship to Non-International Armed Conflict — 365
    III. Terminating Hostilities: Transition to Occupation — 367

IV.	Features of Occupation	370
	A. Commencement	370
	B. Direct and Indirect Control	372
	C. Is There an Obligation to Take Control?	373
	D. Distinguishing Invasion from Occupation	374
	E. Occupation vs. Annexation	375
V.	Implications of Being an Occupying Power	375
VI.	Applicable Law	377
	A. 1907 Hague IV	378
	B. 1949 Geneva Convention Relative to the Protection of the Civilian Population	379
VII.	Fundamental Obligations of the Occupying Power	383
	A. Ensuring Public Order and Safety	383
	B. Obligations Not Balanced with Military Necessity	384
	C. Protection of Basic Human Rights	386
	D. Protection of Property	386
VIII.	Restoring Order	387
	A. The Duty of Obedience	387
	B. Use of Existing Personnel to Continue Public Services	388
IX.	Addressing Threats to Security	390
	A. Preventive Detention	390
	B. Procedural Requirements for Detention	391
	C. Treatment Standards for Internment	392
	D. Assigned Residence	395
	E. Generally Applicable Treatment Standards	396
	F. Prohibited Treatment	397
X.	Meeting the Needs of the Civilian Population of the Occupied Territory	397
XI.	Governing the Occupied Territory	400
XII.	Managing the Property of the Occupied Territory	403
XIII.	Transformational Occupation: Expanding the Permissible Scope of an Occupation	410
XIV.	Transition to Post-Conflict Phase and Termination of Occupation	412
	A. Conflict Termination	412
	B. Cessation of Occupation	415
	Study Questions	419

Chapter 11: Naval Warfare and Neutrality — 421
- I. Introduction — 423
- II. Sources of the Law Applicable to Naval Warfare — 426
- III. The Law of Sea — 427
  - A. The Division of the World's Waters — 427
  - B. The Exercise of Maritime Freedoms in National and International Waters — 430
    1. National Waters — 430
    2. International Waters — 433
  - C. Status of Vessels and Aircraft Under International Law — 434
- IV. The LOAC Applicable to Naval Warfare — 436
  - A. Sources — 436
  - B. Rights to Engage in Warfare at Sea — 439
  - C. General Rules Regarding Attacks on, or Captures of, Vessels — 440
    1. Vessels Subject to Attack — 440
    2. Vessels Subject to Capture — 442
  - D. Disposition of Crews and Passengers — 444
  - E. Blockade — 445
  - F. Zones and Control of Immediate Area of Naval Operations — 447
  - G. Submarine Warfare — 450
  - H. Mines and Torpedoes — 451
  - I. Protection of Persons *Hors de Combat* in Naval Operations — 454
- V. The Law of Neutrality — 459
  - A. Sources of the Law of Neutrality — 459
  - B. Rights and Obligations of Neutral States — 461
  - C. Rights and Obligations of Belligerents Regarding Neutrals — 464
  - D. Rules Governing Neutral Shipping — 466
  - E. Neutrality and Non-International Armed Conflicts — 469
- Study Questions — 472

Chapter 12: Air, Space, and Cyber Warfare — 477
- I. Introduction — 478
- II. Air Warfare — 480
  - A. Sources — 480
    1. General International Law — 480
    2. Customary and Treaty LOAC — 482
  - B. General Framework — 486

	1. Definition of Airspace	486
	2. Types of Aircraft	486
	3. Rights and Obligations of Belligerents and Neutrals	491
	a. Areas Open for Air Operations by Belligerents	491
	b. Neutral Airspace	492
	4. Methods of Warfare	493
	a. Conduct of Hostilities	493
	b. Interception and Capture	498
	i. Enemy Aircraft	498
	ii. Neutral Aircraft	500
	iii. Destruction of Captured Aircraft	502
	c. Other Air Operations	502
	5. Air Warfare in a Non-International Armed Conflict	505
III.	Space Warfare	506
	1. Space Warfare Legal Framework	508
	a. Where Does Space Begin?	508
	b. Treaty Obligations Regarding Outer Space	508
	c. LOAC Applicable to Hostilities Involving Outer Space	514
	2. LOAC Issues in Space Warfare	515
	a. Dual Use Space Objects	516
	b. Collateral Effects Resulting from Attacks on Space Objects	518
IV.	Cyber Operations	521
	1. Defining Cyberspace	522
	2. Legal Paradigms	522
	a. Domestic Law	522
	b. International Law	523
	3. *Jus ad Bellum*	523
	a. Armed Attack	524
	b. Use of Force	525
	c. Prohibited Intervention	526
	d. Sovereignty	527
	4. *Jus in Bello*	528
	a. LOAC General Principles	528
	i. Distinction	529
	ii. Proportionality	530
	b. Precautions in the Attack	531
	i. Constant Care	531
	ii. Military Objective	531
	iii. Indiscriminate Attacks	532
	c. Precautions Against the Effects of Attacks	532
	d. Neutrality	533

		e. Non-State Actors	534
		f. Conclusion	534
	V.	Emerging Technologies	534
		Study Questions	535

Chapter 13: War Crimes — 537

- I. Introduction to War Crimes — 538
  - A. Why Follow the LOAC? — 539
  - B. What Is a War Crime? — 541
  - C. Historical Background — 542
- II. Sources of Contemporary War Crimes — 545
  - A. Geneva Conventions and Grave Breaches — 546
    1. Duties of Signatory States — 547
    2. IAC Trigger — 551
    3. "Simple Breaches" — 552
  - B. Common Article 3 as a Source of War Crimes — 553
  - C. Customary Law — 555
  - D. Other Sources and Other Laws — 556
    1. Aggression — 556
    2. Genocide — 557
    3. Crimes Against Humanity — 558
    4. War Crimes Codified by Specialized Tribunals — 559
    5. War Crimes Codified by the ICC — 560
  - D. *Nulla Crimen sine Lege* — 564
- III. Jurisdiction — 565
- IV. Recent Developments in War Crimes Prosecutions — 568
  - A. Use of Specialized Tribunals — 568
  - B. Blurring the Lines of IAC and NIAC — 569
- V. The U.S. Approach to War Crimes Prosecution — 571
  - A. A Subject Matter Jurisdiction — 571
    1. Uniform Code of Military Justice Structure — 571
       a. Punitive Articles — 572
       b. Article 18 Jurisdiction over War Crimes — 573
    2. The War Crimes Act — 576
       a. Punishable Offenses — 576
       b. Modifications by the DTA and MCA — 578
- VI. Personal Jurisdiction — 580
  - A. Jurisdiction over Soldiers — 580

	B. Jurisdiction over Former Soldiers	581
	C. Jurisdiction over Civilians	582
	D. Jurisdiction over Enemies and Former Enemies	583
VII.	Defenses to War Crimes	584
	A. Obedience to Superior Orders	585
	B. Duress	585
	C. Self-Defense	586
	D. Lack of Mental Responsibility	587
	E. Head of State and Official Acts Immunity	587
VIII.	Emerging LOAC Issues	588
	A. Applicability of the Law of War to Non-State Actors	589
	B. Accountability Norms	591
	Study Questions	593

Chapter 14: Command Responsibility and Compliance Mechanisms   595

I.	Introduction	596
	A. The Role of the Commander	596
	B. A Commander's Involvement or Complicity in LOAC Violations	597
II.	Command Responsibility	599
	A. Definition	599
	B. Pre-World War II History of Command Responsibility	601
	C. World War II War Crimes Tribunals: The Doctrine Evolves	602
	1. The Yamashita Military Tribunal	603
	a. Scope of Authority	605
	b. Mens Rea of Command Responsibility	605
	c. Actus Reas of Yamashita Command Responsibility	606
	d. Causation	606
	e. Imputed Liability	607
	2. *In re Yamashita*	607
	3. Other World War II Tribunals	608
	D. International Developments after the World War II Tribunals	611
	1. Additional Protocol I	612
	2. Implementing Command Responsibility: Contemporary International Criminal Tribunals	615
III.	U.S. Practice and the Accountability of Responsible Commanders	620
	A. Accountability of U.S. Commanders	620
	1. My Lai and Command Responsibility	622

		2. Article 92 Dereliction of Duty	623
		3. Gap in U.S. Military Law	624
	B.	Accountability of Enemy Commanders	625
IV.	Other Compliance Mechanisms	628
	A.	Investigating War Crimes	628
		1. Investigation Procedures: The Army Example	629
		a. Commander's Inquiry	630
		b. Investigations Under Army Regulation 15-6	631
		c. Criminal Investigations	632
		d. Inspector General Investigations	633
		2. Investigation Oversight and Review	634
	B.	Ensuring Compliance with the LOAC	635
	Further Reading	637
	Study Questions	638

Glossary of Terms	*641*
Table of Cases	*649*
Index	*651*

Foreword

Like all of the co-authors of this text, I devoted almost the entirety of my professional life to service as an Army officer. My career began as an infantry officer in the storied 82nd Airborne Division following my graduation from the United States Military Academy in 1985. At that time, the role of law and lawyers in military operations was usually imperceptible to junior combat leaders like me, focused on preparing for high-intensity conflict against the Soviet threat.

My role in the Army changed dramatically when, in 1990, the Army selected me to attend law school and become a Judge Advocate (military attorney). When I returned to the 'operational Army' as a Judge Advocate in 1993, the increased significance of law and legal advisors during military operations was apparent; the radical change in the strategic environment that occurred during those three years led commanders at every level to become increasingly aware of the indelible connection between law, legitimacy, and mission accomplishment.

In the years that followed, I served as a legal advisor at every level of command, in many different theaters of operations. My career culminated with the honor of serving as the legal advisor to General Marty Dempsey, the Chairman of the Joint Chiefs of Staff. As I reflect back on my experience, one constant was the value military commanders placed in legal advisors who were not only expert in law, regulations, and policies but who also remained cognizant of the complex military operational context within which their 'clients' functioned.

I believe that to fully understand the law of armed conflict (sometimes referred to as the "law of war" or "international humanitarian law"), one must study not only the law, but also how that law is interpreted, applied, and assessed in the context of military operations. Given that, I consider THIS text unique and valuable. While there are other sources that describe this law, no other source provides students and other interested readers with not only a comprehensive explanation of the law, but also an opportunity to work through operational hypotheticals to gain an appreciation for the challenge commanders confront when striving to ensure legal compliance while navigating complex operational situations.

This comprehensive text covers the landscape of the law of armed conflict: how it regulates hostilities; protects victims of war like the wounded or sick combatant or the prisoner of war; mitigates the risk to innocents amid the ambiguity and brutality of armed hostilities and combat; and provides the foundation for discipline and accountability of those who engage in conflict. The operational scenarios and study problems tie the topics together and exposes the reader to the reality that—no matter how certain the law may appear—military operational decisions are often made in chaotic, complex, and time-sensitive situations, where the stakes are literally life and death.

THE LAW OF ARMED CONFLICT: AN OPERATIONAL APPROACH provides an opportunity to develop an understanding of this complexity. Each of the authors shared my experience of many years of military service, and all served as military legal advisors. Indeed, I have worked side by side with most of them. The text they produced is consistent with my high expectations—a reflection of the fact that they are able to leverage their unique expertise as both legal scholars and military operational practitioners. They use a scenario-based approach to provide readers not only the means to develop expertise in the law of armed conflict, but also the opportunity to appreciate how it is applied in the chaos of combat.

Throughout the text, OPERATION IRAQI FREEDOM provides the perfect vehicle for case studies because it covers—in a short time period—most of the thorny legal issues that have become nearly standard in military operations from Grenada in 1983 to Iraq, Syria, and Afghanistan today. These include assessing when the law applies, targeting, weapons and tactics, treatment of the wounded and sick, detention, rules of engagement, post-hostilities security operations, naval warfare, war crimes and accountability issues, and other nuanced topics that implicate law, policy, and the military mission. This scenario-based approach ties together all the chapters and illuminate the law and how it is applied, both in theory and in practice.

Military legal advisors, as the authors can personally attest, have extraordinarily difficult jobs in military operations. They share the dangers and privations of other soldiers and practice law amid the chaos and confusion of combat. They routinely offer advice on matters that have direct and immediate mortal consequence, and their advice profoundly impacts mission accomplishment and the perception of legitimacy. Their advice is not always perfect, but their presence demonstrates the commitment of our Nation and our allies to the law of armed conflict.

There can be no doubt, therefore, that both this topic and this book are important to enhance the understanding of a body of law that will only become more significant in the years and decades to follow. In its Second Edition, it will undoubtedly continue to be a valuable resource not only for students of the law of armed conflict, but also for all who want to comprehend the difficulties—and criticality—of its practical application.

Richard C. (Rich) Gross, Brigadier General (U.S.A. Retired)
Former Legal Counsel to the Chairman of the Joint Chiefs of Staff

Acknowledgments

The authors express their collective gratitude to all the great leaders who contributed to their professional development as officers and military attorneys throughout their many years of military service. The opportunities to study, practice, and ponder the complex legal issues related to the planning and execution of military operations and learn from the very best in the business laid the foundation for this entire project.

We would also like to thank the many research assistants who contributed to both the original and this second edition, and whose dedication is woven through every chapter of this book. These current and former students are Peter Chickris, Esq., Christopher Davidson, Ryan Fisher, Joel Glover, Alan Hickey, SueAnn Johnson, Clinton Long, Jessica Poarch, Esq., Ryan Sylvester (now himself a U.S. Navy JAG officer), Robert Thomson, and Brigham Udall, Andrew Culliver (now himself a U.S. Army JAG officer), Robert Smallwood, and John Wooldridge. Thanks also go to Mark Newcomb, Commander, U.S. Navy (Retired), for his valuable input on issues of naval warfare, and to Richard Whitaker, Colonel, U.S. Army (Retired) for sharing his experiences as a legal advisor to a combat unit during the first Gulf War. Finally, special thanks to Brigadier General (Retired) Richard Gross for providing the Forward for this second edition.

The authors also wish to thank James Lambert, Jr. for providing the photos used throughout the book.

We also collectively thank our families, whose support through our professional careers has been a true "force multiplier." Special acknowledgment is owed to Colonel Ed Haughney (Chris Jenks' Grandfather), U.S. Army (1917-2012). Soldier, judge advocate, and professor, Colonel Haughney was a consummate operational law attorney—before there were operational law attorneys—and an icon of legal education whose impact on generations of law students we can only hope to emulate. We also acknowledge Major James A. Schoettler, M.D. (1931-2012), who served in the U.S. Air Force Medical Service from 1958 to

1968, before entering a long and successful career in private medical practice; and Colonel Robert L. Corn, M.D., who served in the U.S. Army Medical Corps from 1956 to 1958, and again from 1987 to 1993, with his active service divided by an equally devoted career in private medical practice. Both men throughout their lives exemplified the humanitarian ideals of all the military and civilian medical personnel who serve our country in various capacities during peacetime and in war. Further acknowledgement goes to Lieutenant Colonel Blaine P. Jensen who enlisted as a U.S. Marine and then served more than twenty years as a U.S. Army aviator (1958 to 1978) including two combat tours in Vietnam, and who served his country with the same commitment and energy he served his family, Church and community.

Finally, we devote this new edition to all the patriotic men and women who choose to accept the challenge and responsibility of serving as leaders in our armed forces, to include family members like First Lieutenant Owen Corn, U.S. Air Force, and our many exceptional former students who volunteered to serve as JAG officers. We hope that as students and other readers consider the hypothetical challenges woven through this text, they recognize, as we do, that there will always be some for whom the law and principles in this text will not only be learned, but lived.

Geoffey S. Corn
Victor Hansen
Richard B. Jackson
Chris Jenks
Eric Talbot Jensen
James A. Schoettler, Jr.

August 2018

Introduction

The second edition of *The Law of Armed Conflict: An Operational Approach* includes three substantial changes from the original text. First, we added relevant updates to the laws and policies addressed in each chapter. Second, we reorganized some chapters to better align the text with operational practice. Third, we have created a new operational scenario focused on the 2003 Iraq conflict.

Of course, a comprehensive understanding of the law of armed conflict (LOAC) remains the ultimate objective of the text and the courses we hope will rely on the text. For this collection of co-authors, "comprehensive" requires more than an understanding of the law itself, but instead an understanding of how the law influences the planning, execution, and critique of military operations. It is this context we believe is essential to truly appreciate the LOAC, which is why we chose to present the law through the lens of an actual military operation.

The focus of this text, the LOAC, is the modern incarnation of what was prior to 1949 characterized as the law of war or the laws and customs of war. This body of law traces its roots deep into the history of international law itself. The contemporary trend in international law to focus on interests related to the individual and not only the state has influenced an increasingly common trend to characterize this body of law as international humanitarian law, or IHL. However, while debates over the "proper" or "best" term to use to denote this body of law continue, it is important to note from the outset that the terms LOAC, IHL, and laws of war all refer to the same substance: the law the applies during armed conflicts to regulate hostilities, protect victims of war, and provide for international legal accountability for those who violate the law.

Respect for and compliance with the LOAC is today a primary touchstone for assessing the legitimacy of military operations. This is a manifestation of the reality that the very notion of legitimacy is no longer a secondary consideration for professional armed forces, but a central tenet in the equation of strategic and operational success. This is manifested both explicitly and implicitly in U.S. military operations. The explicit manifestation takes the form of the inclusion of legitimacy as a principle of war in U.S. military doctrine, alongside traditional principles such as objective, offensive, and economy of force. According to Joint Publication 3-0, *Joint Operations,* "Legitimacy is based on the legality, morality, and rightness of the actions undertaken. Legitimacy is frequently a decisive element . . ."[1] U.S. military doctrine acknowledges that *legitimacy* will often be a decisive element in military operations. The implicit manifestation takes the form of the critical role of military legal advisors—called Judge Advocates or JAGs in U.S. practice—in every phase of military operations. It is therefore unsurprising that the LOAC has become a growth area in legal and political science education.

The significance of this law is, however, nothing new for military commanders and the lawyers who advise them. Battle command is the art of leveraging all available resources and power to achieve a defined objective, or "end state." Inclusion of the principle of legitimacy among these core principles is profoundly significant. It reflects the reasoned judgment of our highest level military commanders and most insightful strategists that compliance with law in the execution of military operations is as important as achieving the intended effects of leveraging the nation's immense combat power. Law and the LOAC more specifically impacts every aspect of U.S. military operations.

Brigadier General Mark J. Martins, the Commanding General of the Rule of Law Field Force-Afghanistan, Joint Task Force 435, eloquently emphasized this imperative when he accepted the honor of receiving the Harvard Law School Medal of Freedom. Martins, a JAG officer, served as the first Commander of this unit and at the time of the speech had been selected by President Obama (his former Harvard Law School classmate) as the Chief Prosecutor for the Military Commissions. Martins noted:

> The question [rule of law in Iraq and Afghanistan] urges inquiry into how law has constrained, enabled, and informed our own military operations since September 11th, 2001, even as it also causes us to mull whether and how an abstract concept we all approach with a multitude of assumptions arising from our own experiences can possibly help oppose ruthless and diverse insurgent groups halfway across the globe. The case I will briefly sketch here today is this: your armed forces heed and will continue to heed the law, take it seriously, *and in fact respect it for the legitimacy it bestows* upon their often violent and lethal—necessarily violent and lethal—actions in the field.[2]

Contributing to decisions that ensure military operations are planned and executed in accordance with applicable domestic and international legal obligations is now, has been, and will always be a core function of JAGs. But these officers, enlisted paralegals, and civilian legal advisors must not only study the

---

1. JOINT CHIEFS OF STAFF, JOINT PUB. 3-0, JOINT OPERATIONS, (AUGUST 11, 2011) at A-4.
2. Speech by Brigadier General Mark J. Martins, Harvard Law School, July 5, 2011 (emphasis added), *available at* http://www.youtube.com/watch?v=g6zBLMpU6Ew.

LOAC, they must be prepared to put the law into practice, often in extremely demanding situations.

The study of any law loses value without an understanding of the context of its application. For the LOAC, this loss of value is exponential, for it is the context of application that has always influenced the development of the law. That context is war, or what military lawyers call armed conflict. During war, military lawyers may provide critical advice, but military commanders make the critical decisions. The LOAC provides the international legal framework for the conduct of the military operations these commanders are tasked with executing. It is a body of law with roots deep in the history of war and international law, constantly evolving to meet the challenges of the contemporary battlefield, and reflected in a variety of sources. The application of the LOAC is sometimes straightforward, more often complex, but today more than ever absolutely central to the credibility of the forces engaged in these operations and the causes for which they fight.

Interest in the LOAC increased when the United States initiated the military response to the terrorist attacks of September 11, 2001 and characterized the conflict against terrorism as a "war." Literally overnight the authority granted and the limitations imposed by the LOAC became central to the debate over the nature and extent of the U.S. response to the terrorist threat—a debate that continues to this day.

The LOAC related implications for the now 17-year long U.S. conflict against al Qaeda, associated terrorist groups, and the Islamic State (ISIS) are myriad. The justification for the use of military force, the long-term military detention of captives, the treatment, interrogation and prosecution of those captives, the use of combat power to attack terrorists alleged to be enemy belligerents targetable anywhere in the world, the risk of collateral damage to civilians as result of this transnational war, the inter-operability of U.S. legal theories with other countries whose view of the LOAC differed from that of the United States, and obligations under the LOAC that followed from the intervention of U.S. and coalition forces in countries where operations were being conducted provide just a sampling of such LOAC-related issues. Complicating these issues is the reality that the U.S. and other states continue to apply rules that were developed primarily in response to large scale state versus state conflict to conflicts that increasingly involve contests between states and non-state groups.

During this "post-September 11th" era, military and civilian international law experts continued to provide advice to their commanders and high level political leaders according to long-standing military understanding of U.S. obligations under the LOAC. Unlike their academic counterparts, the role of these lawyers extended well beyond debate and contemplation, normally culminating with a need to provide opinions to contribute to decisive action where lives were in the balance. These lawyers understand intuitively that the context of LOAC practice is fundamentally different than that of mere study. Expertise in the law is essential to that practice, and the increasing academic interest in this field has contributed to important insights into the complexities of the law. Indeed, like all international law, the works of distinguished scholars have and will continue to significantly influence the evolution of the LOAC. Ultimately, however, it is the ability to apply the law to the problems presented during military operations that defines success, and an appreciation of the complexity of this intersection of law and operations will contribute to positive developments in the law.

This text is designed to offer an opportunity to gain a better appreciation of this context without compromising the substance of the law. While it is impossible to replicate the challenge confronted by legal advisors involved in actual military operations, and perhaps even more so the commanders they advise, we believe that providing operational context will substantially enhance your understanding of the law. Accordingly, we have designed our text around an operational scenario. Your journey will begin in each chapter with an overview of a military operation, providing enough background to allow you to consider how the law you will learn is contextually relevant to "the fight." Each chapter will then provide an overview of a distinct LOAC topical area, followed by study questions linking you back to the military operation. You will then have the opportunity to apply the law to the type of operational problems JAGs and their commanders confront on a routine basis, not only from the perspective of a military lawyer, but also from that of civilians within and outside of government.

We have chosen as our contextual vehicle Operation Iraqi Freedom, the 2003 U.S. and coalition invasion of Iraq, and the operations that followed defeat of conventional Iraqi resistance in the effort to facilitate the restoration of a civilian-led democracy in Iraq. Many aspects of the scenario and many of the study questions are drawn from the actual events. However, for purposes of improving its value in a classroom environment, we have adopted certain embellishments and modifications. This is necessary to produce the range of issues we believe provide a comprehensive journey through the military operational legal landscape. We will highlight for you those aspects of the scenario and problems that deviate from the actual history. We will also ask you to consider how the issues related to Operations Iraqi Freedom might be presented and resolved in the context of other contemporary military operations, such as those currently ongoing in Iraq, Syria, and Afghanistan.

Our goal is not to rehash the policy debates over the wisdom of this military action; military commanders don't have that option. Instead, we want the focus to be on the law. Operation Iraqi Freedom involved an unsurprisingly wide array of LOAC issues, and is therefore ideal as our battlefield scenario, while the post-conflict stability effort, undertaken in collaboration with Iraqi authorities, reveals the complexity of transitioning from active hostilities to the stability needed for disengagement. And, while our treatment of the LOAC is primarily focused on U.S. practice, the text will also address the inter-operability complexities inherent in "coalition warfare." This is essential to expose the reality that not all nations, and sometimes not even our closest allies, interpret and apply the law as does the United States. Understanding the challenge of LOAC compliance in a multi-national coalition context is therefore important to understanding how U.S. practitioners operating in a coalition command will apply this law.

We cannot take you to a tactical operations center on a battlefield or sit you around a table in the Pentagon to wrestle with LOAC issues. What we can do is offer for you the type of problems we collectively confronted in our own practice in order to illuminate for you not only the black letter LOAC, but the challenge of applying that law to resolve complex issues during actual military operations. We hope you enjoy the journey.

Where You Fit in Our Operation

To navigate through our operational journey, you must have a sense of who you are and where you fit into this equation. We want you to learn this law through the lens of a junior JAG officer participating in the operation. In most problems, you will be in that role—advising your commander or his or her staff on legal issues related to the planning and execution of a wide array of combat and post-combat operations. The following very cursory overview of U.S. military structure is provided to facilitate your understanding of this pedagogical context.

National Defense Organization

Department of Defense: The President is the Commander-in Chief of all military forces. The three military branches are the Army, Air Force, and Navy; the Marine Corps falls under the Department of the Navy.[3] All of these forces are managed by the Department of Defense (DoD). The DoD is responsible for providing the military forces needed to deter war, and protect the security of the United States. The Secretary of Defense exercises authority, direction, and control over the Department which includes the Chairman of the Joint Chiefs of Staff, the three Military Departments, and the Unified Combatant Commands.

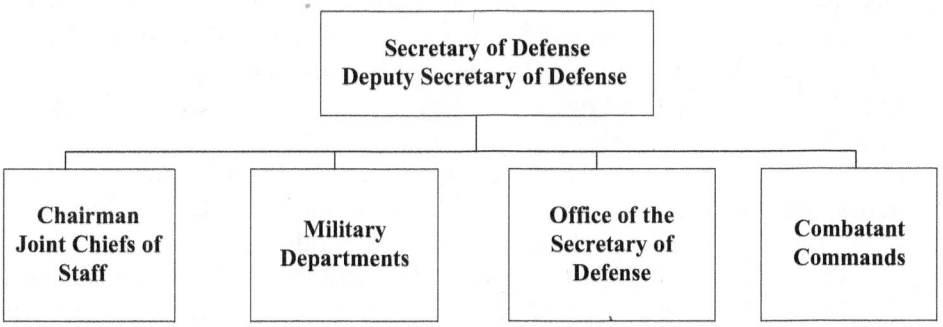

---

3. The U.S. Coast Guard is a separate uniformed service with both law enforcement and military missions that during peacetime is part of the U.S. Department of Homeland Security and in wartime can be integrated into the DoD.

The Chairman of the Joint Chiefs of Staff is the senior ranking military member of the Armed Forces and is the principal military advisor to the President. He is not, however, in command of U.S. military operations, nor are any of the Service Chiefs. When the United States conducts actual military operations, they will always fall under the command of a Combatant Commander. These are 4-star generals or admirals in command of operational organizations that bring together forces from all the services to execute specific operational missions. These "joint" operational commands were created to mitigate inter-operability problems between forces from the different services and maximize the efficiency and effectiveness of U.S. operations. When allied forces are added to the mix, the term "combined" is added to "joint."

One way to understand this it to imagine Combatant Commands as warfighting headquarters with very few forces assigned when they are not conducting operations. When, however, an operation is ordered, the different Services provide forces to execute the operation.[4] These forces are essentially "plugged into" the Combatant Command based on existing or ad hoc plans, and execute the operation under the chain of command established by the Combatant Commander. The Military Service Chiefs of each Service are not in the operational chain of command. The Military Service Chiefs perform two primary functions. First, as the Chief of their respective Service they are responsible for the training and management of that Service and to provide forces for use by the combatant commanders. Second, the Service Chiefs all serve as their Service's representative on the Joint Chiefs of Staff. As members of the Joint Chiefs of Staff, they offer advice to the President, Secretary of Defense and the National Security Council (NSC) on military matters.

Operational Chain of Command

When the President, through the Secretary of Defense, orders the execution of an actual military operation, the mission is conducted under the authority of the operational chain of command. The operational chain of command in the U.S. military proceeds from the President to the Secretary of Defense to one of the six Combatant Commanders. There are six regional combatant commands that divide the world into six geographic regions. The six combatant commands are: United States Northern Command (USNORTHCOM), which includes Mexico and North America; United States Southern Command (USSOUTHCOM), which includes Central and South America; United States Pacific Command (USPACOM), which includes China, India, Southeast Asia, and Australia; United States European Command (USEUCOM), which includes Europe and Russia; United States Central Command (USCENTCOM), which includes the Middle East and Egypt; and United States Africa Command

---

4. These forces can include active duty (i.e., full-time) and reserve (i.e., part-time) units and personnel, as well as the National Guard, which constitutes the organized militia of each State of the United States and is under both State and Federal government control.

(USAFRICOM), which includes all of the African continent other than Egypt. In addition, there are three commands that have functional rather than regional responsibilities. They are the Special Operations Command, Strategic Command, and Transportation Command.

Each combatant command is a joint military command that is composed of forces from two or more of the military services. The combatant commands have a broad and continuing mission within their respective areas of operation. The mission of the combatant command is to provide effective command and control of all U.S. forces operating in their area of responsibility. To do so, they normally form subordinate joint and/or combined task forces to conduct and execute the missions they have been tasked to accomplish.

Joint Task Force

At the point of actual mission execution, it is the task force that will command and execute operations. The task force concept allows military units to be task organized on an ad hoc basis to accomplish a specific military objective or function. This task force structure allows for greater operational flexibility and ensures that all of the necessary capabilities are included within the force package and all units fall under a clear chain of command.

A Joint Task Force (JTF) executes most major military operations. A JTF is a force composed of assigned and attached elements of the Army, Navy, Marine Corps, and the Air Force, or two or more of these Services. A JTF is typically established by order of the Secretary of Defense or by the Commander of a Unified Command. A JTF often contains a ground force, an air component, and a naval commander. In addition to Joint Task Forces, there are also Combined Joint Task Forces (CJTF). A CJTF is a task force that is comprised of elements of more than one service and more than one nation.

The operational chain of command flows from the President to the Secretary of Defense, to the Combatant Commander, and then to the Commander of the task force. Some task forces are relatively permanent such as Joint Task Force North (formally, JTF-Six), which provides military support to state, and federal counterdrug operations. Other task forces are of short duration and are disbanded once the specific operation is completed.

A JTF or CJTF conducting ground operations will almost always include Army and Marine Corps assets. Since our scenario involves sustained ground operations, many of the problems you analyze will be in response to questions presented by Army or Marine Corps commanders. Remember, however, that while these commanders may be in command of primarily Army or Marine Corps personnel, they are part of a broader JTF or CJTF. Nonetheless, both the Army and the Marine Corps organize their forces to maximize their effectiveness when "plugged into" a Combatant Command. For the Army, this is reflected in the Brigade Combat Team (BCT) structure. For the Marine Corps, this is reflected in the Marine Air Ground Task Force (MAGTF) structure. Both of these are what are called "combined arms" units, in that they include within the organic command structure all elements of ground combat power (infantry, artillery, engineers, support), as well as air support (combat helicopters, and for the MAGTF combat fixed wing aircraft). A colonel normally considered among the top 10 percent of his professional peer group commands each. One, and oftentimes more than one, dedicated JAG officer will support each of these commanders.

The following summary of each military service completes this overview.

Army

Army Mission: The Army's mission is to fight and win our nation's wars by providing prompt, sustained land dominance across the full range of military operations and spectrum of conflict in support of Combat Commanders.

Force Structure: The major war fighting elements of the Army are the Corps, Division and Brigade Combat Teams (BCT). These are all modular units and are task organized to make the most effective use of the functional skills and specialized equipment that each unit brings to the fight. The Army also maintains a number of Special Operations Units (Special Forces Groups, Ranger Regiments).

There are currently four modular corps headquarters in the Army. A 3-star General (Lieutenant General) normally commands a Corps. There are currently 18 modular divisions in the Army (10 Active and 8 National Guard). A 2-star General (Major General) normally commands a Division. The primary fighting unit in the Army is the Brigade Combat Team (BCT). A Colonel normally commands the BCT. BCTs are task organized to be self contained, highly deployable units. A BCT will include infantry, armor, artillery, engineer, and combat support units. The maneuver BCTs will either be infantry, armor, or Stryker brigades.

A brigade contains approximately 3,000-4,000 soldiers. Within the brigade there are several battalions of approximately 500-1,000 soldiers. Within each battalion there are a number of companies of approximately 100-200 soldiers. Within each company there are a number of platoons of approximately 30-40 soldiers.

Marine Corps

Marine Corps Mission: The Marine Corps' primary mission is to provide fleet marine forces of combined arms, together with supporting air components, for service with the fleet in the seizure or defense of advanced naval bases and for the conduct of such land operations as may be essential to the prosecution of a naval campaign.

Force Structure: The Marine Corps is organized into four categories: Headquarters, Operating Forces, Reserves, and the Supporting Establishment. The Marine Corps is part of the Department of the Navy and includes three combat divisions, three air wings, and other land combat, aviation, and air services as may be organic therein.

The Marine forces are organized into mission-oriented Marine Air-Ground Task Forces (MAGTF). The MAGTF is the principal organization for the conduct of all missions. The MAGTF may be of varying sizes and composition, depending on the mission. In each case, there will be a command element and ground combat element, an aviation combat element, and a combat service support element.

A Marine Expeditionary Force (MEF) is a "standing MAGTF" and exists in both peace and war. It is can range in size from 20,000-90,000 Marines and sailors. The MEF is normally commanded by a Lieutenant General (3-star). A Marine Expeditionary Brigade (MEB) is an intermediate-sized MAGTF and ranges in size from 3,000-9,000 Marines and sailors. A Brigadier General (1-star) normally commands the MEB. An MEB can operate independently or as part of an MEF. It is normally composed of an infantry regiment, a Marine Air Group and a Brigade Service Support Group.

A forward deployed Marine Expeditionary Unit (MEU) can provide a quick reaction response to crises. The MEU is typically embarked aboard amphibious shipping within a naval expeditionary strike group. An MEU includes approximately 2,000 Marines and sailors, and is commanded by a colonel. The overriding requirement for any of these MAGTFs is the ability to rapidly plan and execute contingency operations.

Air Force

Air Force Mission: The mission of the U.S. Air Force is to defend the United States and protect its interests through air and space power.

Force Structure: The Air Force organizes, trains, and equips air forces through its Major Commands (MAJCOM). MAJCOMs are subdivided into Numbered Air Forces, wings, groups, and squadrons. MAJCOMs are commanded by a general. Numbered Air Forces (NAF) are the senior war-fighting echelon of the Air Force. The NAF conducts combat operations with assigned and attached forces. When participating in joint operations, the NAF serves as the Joint Forces Commander's Aerospace Expeditionary Task Force. The NAF is commanded by a lieutenant general or a major general.

A wing is the next element and it contains all of the assets required to accomplish the organizational function. There are four main groups within a typical wing: the operations group; the maintenance group; the mission support group; and the medical group. A wing is normally commanded by a colonel. The squadron is the basic fighting group. They are not designed to conduct independent operations. They interact with other squadrons to provide effective air and space operations. Squadrons are normally commanded by a lieutenant colonel.

Navy

Navy Mission: The mission of the Navy is to maintain, train and equip combat-ready Naval forces capable of winning wars, deterring aggression and maintaining freedom of the seas.

Force Structure: There are two primary types of Naval power projection. They are the Carrier Strike Group (CSG), and the Expeditionary Strike Group (ESG).

The CSG generally consists of an aircraft carrier, its embarked airwing of approximately eighty aircraft, a cruiser, two destroyers, a replenishment ship, and a submarine. A CSG is normally commanded by a rear admiral. An ESG generally consists of an amphibious assault ship; its embarked Marine Expeditionary Unit and its aviation combat element, two smaller amphibious ships, a cruiser, and a submarine.

Iraq Scenario

Scenario

This book is divided into chapters addressing different topical areas of the law of armed conflict (LOAC). Each chapter ends with a series of study questions requiring analysis of the application of this law to issues arising during different phases of a fictional military operation. The focus of the text is to provide more than an understanding of black letter law; it is to provide the student with military operational context by using examples and problems that will help students see how the law influences the planning, execution, and assessments of military operations. The authors collectively believe that without such context, understanding of the LOAC is incomplete.

While professors and instructors may use their own examples and scenarios drawn from history or current events, the questions following each chapter all relate to one overarching military operation in order to provide consistency in the student's exploration of the LOAC as applied in an operational context. This operation is the 2003 invasion of Iraq by the U.S., U.K. and other "coalition" forces, followed by an occupation of Iraq until mid-2004 and ultimately a transition to an elected government. The following scenario summarizes those events and emphasizes points that the authors believe are relevant to the material in the textbook. In using this scenario, however, the student should apply the LOAC that is currently in force, and not the law as it existed in 2003-04.

A. Introduction

The year is 2003. Added to the many national security challenges confronting the United States, including Operation Enduring Freedom in Afghanistan, is the threat the United States believes to be posed by Iraq. U.S. leaders have concluded that Iraq's chemical, biological, and nuclear weapons, long-range missile capabilities, and support for terrorism represent a direct threat against the

United States and its allies. Twelve years prior, in what is known as the First Gulf War, or Operation Desert Storm, the U.S. military, along with a broad international military coalition operating under several U.N. Security Council Resolutions, conducted major combat operations against Iraq in order to eject Iraqi forces from Kuwait, which Iraq occupied in August of 1990. To adequately understand the United States' actions and justifications for its invasion in 2003, it is important to provide some background on this first military campaign against Iraq.[1]

B. The First Gulf War and its Aftermath

In 1990, a rocky relationship between Iraq and Kuwait became even more difficult when Iraqi President, Saddam Hussein, accused Kuwait of oil overproduction and stealing oil, which Hussein declared as "economic warfare." Historically, Iraq had maintained that it had a right to Kuwait and the oil dispute became the justification that Hussein used to try to rectify the perceived wrong. In July, Hussein threatened military action, and in August Iraqi forces invaded Kuwait and declared the country the 19th province of Iraq. The U.N. Security Council condemned the invasion and demanded that Iraqi forces withdraw from Kuwait.

In November of 1990 the U.N. Security Council, in Resolution 678, asserted that Iraq had until January 15, 1991 to withdraw from Kuwait or the U.S.-led coalition of 34 nations would be authorized by the Security Council to take "all necessary means" to expel Iraq from Kuwait. By December, the United States, United Kingdom, and France had all deployed troops to the Persian Gulf region. With no action from Iraq, Operation Desert Storm commenced at 3 a.m. Baghdad time on January 17, 1991. The objective was to expel occupying Iraqi forces from Kuwait, restore Kuwaiti sovereignty, and thereby implement a range of U.N. Security Council resolutions.

The first month of the campaign involved relentless air and missile attacks against Iraqi targets in Kuwait and Iraq, with only very limited special operations ground incursions to identify high value targets. On February 22, 1991, President George H.W. Bush issued an ultimatum against Hussein—withdraw from Kuwait or face a full-scale land war. Iraq's failure to comply with this ultimatum led to the "100 hour" ground war, which saw U.S. and coalition forces close with Iraqi forces in Kuwait through both a direct invasion of Kuwait and a sweep through border areas of Iraq to Kuwait. These coalition forces defeated Iraqi forces decisively. This led to a mass retreat of Iraqi forces from Kuwait. By February 26, Iraqi troops had fully withdrawn from Kuwait, and on February 27 President George H.W. Bush declared Kuwait liberated.

---

1. For a detailed overview of U.S. operations in the Gulf War, *see* U.S. Dep't Defense, Conduct of the Persian Gulf War: Final Report to Congress (1992).

Combat operations came to a close when, in a traditional surrender ceremony, Iraq agreed to a military ceasefire in Safwan, Iraq on March 3, 1991 pursuant to U.N. Security Council Resolution 686. The decision for the United States and coalition to not invade further into Iraq and overthrow Hussein was controversial. General H. Norman Schwarzkopf, the American representative for the Iraqi Surrender, made it clear that the meeting was not a negotiation, rather the terms of the agreement were set, and Iraq had to comply.[2] Soon thereafter, in Resolution 687, the U.N. Security Council called for a formal ceasefire between Iraq, Kuwait, and the coalition States, subject to Iraq's meeting a number of conditions. Those conditions included, among other things: (1) the prohibition of development and removal of all chemical weapons, biological weapons, and ballistic missiles, and (2) not committing or supporting any act of international terrorism or allowing any organization that participated in terrorism to operate within its territory.

Along with the above conditions, U.N. Security Council in Resolution 688 took note of the Iraqi government's repression of various groups in Iraq, causing a massive flow of refugees that threatened international peace and security. The Security Council demanded that Iraq "ensure that all the human and political rights of all Iraqi citizens be respected" and allow access by international humanitarian organizations to the refugees. On the basis of Resolution 688, as well as the accords signed in Safwan, which prohibited Iraqi fixed wing aircraft to interfere with coalition air operations over Iraq, the United States, France, and the United Kingdom created two "no-fly zones" to prevent Hussein from using aircraft to attack Iraqi minorities, including the Kurds in northern Iraq and the Shiite Muslims in the south. Iraqi forces could fly helicopters in the no-fly zones for administrative purposes as long as the helicopters were not used for any combat reasons.[3] Along with the no-fly-zones, Iraq was not permitted move ground forces into a protected enclave of the zone so that Iraqi Kurds would be protected there.

Between 1991 and 2003, Hussein violated the no-fly zone on a number of occasions, and on at least one occasion, in 1996, Iraq briefly moved ground troops into the protected enclave. From the perspective of the United States and others, Hussein's actions showed a history of non-compliance with the U.N. Security Council Resolutions.[4]

---

2. http://www.nytimes.com/1991/03/04/world/after-war-cease-fire-meeting-hard-faced-schwarzkopf-sets-terms-desert-meeting.html.

3. http://articles.chicagotribune.com/1991-04-07/news/9102010009_1_iraqi-president-saddam-hussein-gunships-president-bush.

4. For a discussion of the no-fly zones and other matters related to dealings with Iraq after the Persian Gulf War, *see* Alfred B. Prados, *Iraqi Challenges and U.S. Responses: March 1991 through October 2002* (Congressional Research Service report RL31641)(Nov. 20, 2002) *available at* http://www.au.af.mil/au/awc/awcgate/crs/rl31641.pdf (last visited June 23, 2016).

> ### *Kurdish Conflict within Iraq*
>
> During the period after the end of the Gulf War, the Kurds—a large ethnic group that inhabits a mountainous region where Iran, Iraq, Syria, and Turkey intersect—were able to achieve a measure of autonomy due to the no-fly zone. Subsequently, the Kurds joined an opposition group—the Iraqi National Congress—backed by the United States, which then operated from Kurdish territory. A provisional parliament was established, which pushed for a federated state within Iraq rather than full independence. Tension between rival factions led to armed clashes, and one group sought help from the central government in Iraq to take control of Irbil, the regional capital, and control of the region of Iraqi Kurdistan was divided between the factions.
>
> In 1998, the United States brokered reconciliation between the factions as part of its effort to build up an opposition to the Hussein regime, and the Kurdish Parliament reconvened in 2002. The Kurds prepared for possible war between the United States and Iraq, with the hopes of greater independence.[5]

Saddam Hussein's non-compliance with U.N. Security Council resolutions on disarmament resulted in several military strikes by the United States during the period after the end of the Gulf War. For example, in January 1993, the United States launched cruise missiles against the Zaafaraniyeh industrial complex in Baghdad in response to U.N. inspectors' suspicions that it was involved in producing uranium enrichment equipment and missile components. Further, in December 1998, the United States and the United Kingdom conducted four days of airstrikes in "Operation Desert Fox" to retaliate against Iraq's failure to fully cooperate with U.N. weapons inspectors.[6] Iraq's noncompliance also led to greater calls for "regime change" in Iraq, particularly within the United States.[7]

C. The Opening Salvos for War

By 2001, the United States was involved in fighting the terrorist group al Qaeda in Afghanistan and Congress had enacted a Joint Resolution for the "Authorization for Use of Military Force" (AUMF), which authorized the President to "use all necessary and appropriate force against those nations, organizations, or persons he determines planned, authorized, committed, or aided the terrorist attacks that occurred on September 11, 2001, or harbored

---

5. *See* Kenneth Katzman, *The Kurds in Post-Saddam Iraq* (Congressional Research Service report RS22079 (Oct. 1, 2010); *Iraqi Kurdistan profile - timeline*, bbc.com, Aug. 1, 2015 available at http://www.bbc.com/news/world-middle-east-15467672 (last visited July 1, 2016).

6. Transcript: President Clinton explains Iraq strike, cnn.com, Dec. 16, 1998 *available at* http://www.cnn.com/ALLPOLITICS/stories/1998/12/16/transcripts/clinton.html (last visited July 1, 2016).

7. Kenneth Katzman, *Iraq: U.S. Regime Change Efforts and Post-Saddam Governance* (Congressional Research Service report RL31339), at CRS-13 (Oct. 22, 2004).

such organizations or persons...." President George W. Bush signed the resolution into law on September 18, 2001.[8]

In 2002, as the United States was fighting al Qaeda, U.S. and allied concerns over the risk that Iraq might provide international terrorist groups with weapons of mass destruction led U.S. leaders to focus on forcing Iraq to comply with all disarmament obligations. On November 8, 2002, the U.N. Security Council enacted Resolution 1441 in response to the determination that Iraq was in material breach of the disarmament obligations imposed by Resolution 687. The Security Council declared that Iraq had 45 days to resume mandatory inspections allowing "immediate, unimpeded, unconditional and unrestricted access" to any place in Iraq so that the inspectors could remove or destroy any restricted weapons. During the meeting of the Security Council, representatives from the United States noted that, "While primary responsibility rested with the Council for the disarmament of Iraq, nothing in the resolution constrained any Member State from acting to defend itself against the threat posed by that country, or to enforce United Nations resolutions protecting the world peace and security."[9]

In 2002 and early 2003, President Bush and U.K. Prime Minister Blair asserted the necessity of coalition action to compel Iraq to completely disarm, including the use of force if necessary.[10] Their legal rationale for using military force against the Hussein regime was twofold. First, President Bush reasoned that the United States could act in preemptive self-defense because Iraq had weapons of mass destruction (WMD). According to President Bush, the alleged weapons development, coupled with Hussein's hatred and declared "jihad," or holy war, against the United States, and the ties between Iraq and al Qaeda created a threat, "whose outlines are far more clearly defined, and whose consequences could be far more deadly. Saddam Hussein's actions have put us [, the United States,] on notice, and there is no refuge for our responsibilities."[11] Second, Iraq materially breached the conditions in U.N. Security Council Resolution 687, thereby violating its ceasefire obligations. This breach, according to the United States and the United Kingdom, provided authority to use force as a measure consistent with Security Council Resolution 678's authorization for States to "use all necessary means to uphold and implement

---

8. Pub. L. 107-40, 50 U.S.C. § 1541 note (2001).

9. Press Release, Security Council, Security Council Holds Iraq in 'Material Breach" of Disarmament Obligations, Offers Final Chance to Comply, Unanimously Adopting Resolution 1441,' U.N. Press Release SC/7564 (Nov. 8, 2002).

10. For example, in a March 2003 press conference held by Prime Minister Blair and President Bush jointly with the prime ministers of Portugal and Spain, Prime Minister Blair said: "But the truth is that without a credible ultimatum authorizing force in the event of noncompliance, then more discussion is just more delay, with Saddam remaining armed with weapons of mass destruction and continuing a brutal, murderous regime in Iraq." The President's News Conference With Prime Minister Jose Manuel Durao Barroso of Portugal, President Jose Maria Aznar of Spain, and Prime Minister Tony Blair of the United Kingdom in the Azores, Portugal, 1 PUB. PAPERS 267, 269 (Mar. 16, 2003).

11. Address to the Nation on Iraq From Cincinnati, Ohio, 2 Pub. Papers 1751, 1756 (Oct. 7, 2002).

Resolution 660 (1990) and all subsequent relevant resolutions and to restore international peace and security in the area."[12]

On September 12 2002, President Bush called upon the United Nations General Assembly to confront Iraq.[13] In spite of the proverbial "full court press" made by the United States, including sending Secretary of State Colin Powell to present the U.S. case for a new use of force authorization at a meeting of the Security Council in February 2003,[14] it was clear that France and Russia were unwilling to support such authority until weapons inspectors were afforded more time to complete their efforts in Iraq. As a result, the United States and the United Kingdom withdrew their March 7, 2003 proposal to the Security Council for a use of force resolution authorizing military action to completely disarm Iraq.[15] Instead, the United States asserted that the Resolution 678 provided sufficient authority to take military action against Iraq,[16] and assembled what it characterized as a "coalition of the willing" that garnered its support from approximately 50 different nations (although only a small number agreed to commit military forces to engage in combat operations).[17]

During this same period, President Bush also pursued a new use of force authorization from Congress to provide solid constitutional authority for initiating military action against Iraq. On October 10, 2002, Congress granted that authority when it enacted a new Joint Resolution authorizing the use of force against Iraq, declaring that, "The President is authorized to use the Armed Forces of the United States as he determines to be necessary and appropriate in order to—(1) defend the national security of the United States against the continuing threat posed by Iraq; and (2) enforce all relevant United Nations

---

12. Address to the Nation on Iraq, 1 Pub. Papers 277, 278 (Mar. 17, 2003) (hereinafter "March 17 Address to the Nation") ("Under Resolutions 678 and 687, both still in effect, the United States and our allies are authorized to use force in ridding Iraq of weapons of mass destruction. This is not a question of authority. It is a question of will.") The material breach argument was the central rationale offered by both the United Kingdom and the United States when they commenced operations against Iraq in March 2003. See Permanent Representative of the United States of America to the United Nations, Letter dated 20 March 2003 from the Permanent Representative of the United States of America to the United Nations addressed to the President of the Security Council, U.N. Doc. S/2003/351 (Mar. 21, 2003); Letter dated 20 March 2003 from the Permanent Representative of the United Kingdom of Great Britain and Northern Ireland to the United Nations addressed to the President of the Security Council, U.N. Doc. S/2003/350 (Mar. 21, 2003).

13. Address to the United Nations General Assembly in New York City, 2 Pub. Papers 1572, 1576 (Sept. 12, 2002).

14. Press Release, Security Council, Briefing Security Council, US Secretary of State Powell Presents Evidence of Iraq's Failure to Disarm (Feb. 5, 2003).

15. Press Release, Security Council, Importance of Humanitarian Aid for Iraq Stressed, as Security Council Members Voice Different Views on Disarmament Process, SC/7696 (Mar. 19, 2003) ("Divergent views were expressed by the representatives of the United States, United Kingdom and Spain, which had tabled a further resolution on the situation on 7 March containing a deadline of Monday, 17 March, for Iraq's full compliance. Failing to win the necessary support for the draft in the Council and amid the threat of a veto by a permanent member, the three announced on Monday that they would not put it to a vote.") See also President of the United States, A Report in Connection with Presidential Determination under Public Law 107-243, H.R. Doc. 108-50, at 7 (2003).

16. Id., at 10.

17. Stephen Carney, Allied Participation in Operation Iraqi Freedom, 5 (2011) [hereinafter Allied Participation in OEF].

Security Council resolutions regarding Iraq."[18] On December 21, 2002, President Bush approved the deployment of 200,000 U.S. military personnel to conduct the offensive against Iraq. These forces would join military forces from the United Kingdom, Australia, Poland, Spain, the Netherlands, and several other countries.

D. Invasion of Iraq

Despite the inability of the United Kingdom and the United States to obtain a Security Council resolution to support the invasion, the United States and its coalition partners remained determined to take action. On March 17, 2003, President Bush issued an ultimatum to Saddam Hussein informing him that he and his two sons had 48 hours to leave Iraq or there would be severe consequences.[19] Hussein refused to leave and offensive operations against Iraq began.

Initial air strikes where followed by a ground offensive into Iraq via Kuwait and by airborne operations in Northern Iraq. The U.S. V Corps and I Marine Expeditionary Force headed north toward Baghdad, while U.K. forces were tasked with securing the southeastern city of Al Basrah. At the same time, U.S. Marines, British forces, and Polish commandos were tasked with taking over Umm Qsar, a port city near the Iraq-Kuwait border.[20]

As the invasion commenced, President Bush announced to the American people that U.S. forces were again involved in combat in Iraq and asserted that the military operation would be a "broad and concerted campaign."[21]

All multinational armed forces that participated in Iraq were under the command and control of General Tommy R. Franks, the commander of U.S. Central Command, or CENTCOM. The coalition's opposition included the Iraqi Army which consisted of the regular army, the Republican Guard, and the Special Republic Guard. Irregular forces, called the Fedayeen Saddam, also began to conduct operations against coalition forces.

The Iraqi regular army had an estimated troop number of between 300,000 and 350,000 men, which were organized into five corps and 17 divisions. There were 11 infantry divisions, three mechanized divisions, and three armored divisions. Approximately two-thirds of the soldiers that composed the regular army were enlisted compulsorily, and the United States believed that the regular army would quickly surrender because of its lack of military training and modern weapons. The Republican Guard was estimated to include between 60,000 and 70,000 men, and was controlled by Saddam's son, Qusay. This group

---

18. Authorization for Use of Military Force Against Iraq Resolution of 2002, Pub. L. 107-423, 116 Stat. 1498 (2002).
19. March 17 Address to the Nation, *supra* note 10, 278 ("All the decades of deceit and cruelty have now reached an end. Saddam Hussein and his sons must leave Iraq within 48 hours. Their refusal to do so will result in military conflict, commenced at a time of our choosing.")
20. ALLIED PARTICIPATION IN OEF, *supra* note 15, at 9; *See also* CENTER FOR MILITARY HISTORY, 2 AMERICAN MILITARY HISTORY 481-490 (2010) (summarizing events of the invasion).
21. Address to the Nation on Iraq, 1 PUB. PAPERS 281 (Mar. 19, 2003).

was organized into six divisions and consisted of mainly career soldiers who had better training and weapons then the regular army. In addition, the Special Republican Guard, who were well trained in urban combat, contained between 15,000 and 25,000 men, and was located in central Baghdad. The Special Republican guard was responsible for guarding the president and other high value individuals and had its own heavy armored brigade and air defense command unit.[22]

The Fedayeen Saddam was an Iraqi paramilitary group, composed of between 30,000 to 40,000 men, who attacked coalition forces in southern Iraq with guerilla-style attacks.[23] The group was created in 1995, and its members were handpicked from loyal tribal areas. By 2003, the group was led by Saddam Hussein's eldest son, Uday Hussein.[24] While experts on Iraqi military were aware of the Fedayeen Saddam, they underestimated what a force the group would be against the coalition.[25] Among other acts the Fedayeen Saddam is thought to be the perpetrators of some of the regime's most brutal attacks, including the beheading of more than 200 women as part of an alleged anti-prostitution campaign.[26]

The United States correctly predicted that the regular Iraqi army would not put up much opposition to the invasion, but far fewer soldiers surrendered than anticipated. Instead, most discarded their uniforms and returned to their homes and mixed back into the civilian population.[27] By April 9, 2003, the coalition forces had overwhelmed the Iraqi Army and Saddam Hussein's regime was overthrown, symbolized by the toppling of a huge statute of the man who ruled the country for a quarter of a century. *The Wall Street Journal* estimated that approximately 3,160 Iraqi soldiers were killed and 13,800 were captured by the coalition during this phase.

On May 1, 2003, President Bush arrived on the U.S.S. Abraham Lincoln, located off the coast of San Diego, and announced that the United States was at the end of major combat operations in Iraq. In back of President Bush waved a banner reading "Mission Accomplished" as the President congratulated Operation Iraqi Freedom as "a job well done" and declared that "In the battle of Iraq, the United States and our allies have prevailed. . . . Because of you, our nation is more secure. Because of you, the tyrant has fallen and Iraq is free."[28]

---

22. *See* Sharon Otterman, *IRAQ: Iraq's Prewar Military Capabilities*, Apr. 24, 2003 [hereinafter "Iraqi Pre-War Capabilities"], *available at* http://www.cfr.org/iraq/iraq-iraqs-prewar-military-capabilities/p7695 (last visited July 1, 2016).

23. *Id.*

24. *See* Sharon Otterman, *IRAQ: What is the Fedayeen Saddam?*, March 31, 2003, *available at* http://www.cfr.org/iraq/iraq-fedayeen-saddam/p7698 (last visited July 1, 2016).

25. *Id.*

26. *Id.*

27. Saddam Hussein's resistance to the invasion also relied on guerilla-style attacks, which consisted of "mounting hit-and-run attacks by small groups of armed men; dressing soldiers as civilians; setting oil fires and burning oil wells; dispatching suicide bombers, faking surrenders; and using civilians as human shields." Iraqi Pre-War Capabilities, *supra* note 20.

28. Address to the Nation on Iraq From the U.S.S. Abraham Lincoln, 1 Pub. Papers 516 (May 1, 2003).

E. Occupation of Iraq and Transition to New Iraqi Government

Once concerted Iraqi military resistance was overcome, coalition operations transitioned into an occupation of Iraq, managed by the coalition Provisional Authority (CPA), a governing body headed by L. Paul Bremer, who was appointed by the United States to serve as CPA Administrator. However, the exact legal basis for the CPA is unclear, "as there is no formal document—whether statute, United Nations Security Council resolution, or other organic document—that plainly establishes the CPA or provides for its formation. . . . The earliest public reference to the CPA appears in General Franks' April 16, 2003 Freedom Message to the Iraqi People. In that message, General Franks, in his capacity as Commander of the coalition Forces, announced the formation of the CPA as the body that would exercise the temporary powers of government in Iraq."[29] While this statement would suggest that the CPA was created by the United States, the CPA is referred to in a joint letter submitted to the UN Security Council by the U.K. and U.S. governments, which states:

> [T]he United States, the United Kingdom and coalition partners, acting under existing command and control arrangements through the Commander of coalition Forces, have created the coalition Provisional Authority, which includes the Office of Reconstruction and Humanitarian Assistance, to exercise powers of government temporarily, and, as necessary, especially to provide security, to allow the delivery of humanitarian aid, and to eliminate weapons of mass destruction.[30]

On May 16, 2003, Administrator Bremer issued coalition Provisional Authority Regulation Number 1, which provided, *inter alia*, that:

(1) The CPA shall exercise powers of government temporarily in order to provide for the effective administration of Iraq during the period of transitional administration, to restore conditions of security and stability, to create conditions in which the Iraqi people can freely determine their own political future, including by advancing efforts to restore and establish national and local institutions for representative governance

---

29. United States ex rel DRC, Inc. v. Custer Battles, LLC, 376 F. Supp. 2d 617, 620 (E.D. Va. 2005). The court noted further that:

> While the substantial majority of the positions in the CPA were filled by United States citizens, many of whom were also United States government employees, an average of 13% of CPA personnel came from other coalition partners, including Australia, the Czech Republic, Denmark, Italy, Japan, Poland, Romania, Spain, the United Kingdom, Ukraine, and others.

Id. at 623.

30. Letter from the Permanent Representatives of the United Kingdom of Great Britain and Northern Ireland and the United States of America to the United Nations addressed to the President of the Security Council, U.N. SCOR, U.N. Doc. No. S/2003/538 (May 8, 2003).

and facilitating economic recovery and sustainable reconstruction and development.
(2) The CPA is vested with all executive, legislative and judicial authority necessary to achieve its objectives, to be exercised under relevant U.N. Security Council resolutions, including Resolution 1483 (2003), and the laws and usages of war. This authority shall be exercised by the CPA Administrator.
(3) As the Commander of Coalition Forces, the Commander of U.S. Central Command shall directly support the CPA by deterring hostilities; maintaining Iraq's territorial integrity and security; searching for, securing and destroying weapons of mass destruction; and assisting in carrying out coalition policy generally.[31]

In a little over a year, the CPA issued 100 "orders" which were "binding instructions to the Iraqi people that create penal consequences or have a direct bearing on the way Iraqis are regulated, including changes to Iraqi law."[32] The orders included instructions on the management of property, copyright law, weapons control, banking, securities, traveling for educational purposes, and prohibited media activity.[33] Along with the "orders," the CPA also released "memoranda" that expanded on the "orders" and "regulations" and "public notices" that communicated the intentions of the CPA to the public.[34]

In December 2003, Bremer signed a statute establishing the Iraqi Special Tribunal for Crimes Against Humanity. The Tribunal was created to prosecute individuals in Iraq who were accused of genocide, war crimes, and crimes against humanity between 1968 and 2003. The Tribunal was in charge of the trial of Saddam Hussein along with other senior officials under his regime.

The Iraq Governing Council had signed an interim constitution on March 8, 2004 and by June of that year the United Nations Security Council had unanimously approved Resolution 1546 to end the formal occupation of Iraq at the end of June and transfer "full sovereignty" to an interim Iraqi government. In October of 2004, 70 percent of registered Iraqi voters turned out to a general election and were able to elect a new national assembly of 275 members. The election created a transition government until a permanent constitution and government could be elected at the end of 2005.

---

31. Coalition Provisional Authority, Coalition Provisional Authority Regulation Number 1, Sec. 1, May 16, 2003, *available at* http://www.iraqcoalition.org/regulations/20030516_CPAREG_1_The_Coalition_Provisional_Authority_.pdf (last visited July 1, 2016).

32. The Coalition Provision Authority (website), *CPA Official Documents*, http://www.iraqcoalition.org/regulations/index.html (last visited July 1, 2016) (listing 100 "orders").

33. *Id.*

34. *Id.* (listing 17 memoranda and 12 public notices).

F. Key Military Operations During and After the Occupation through 2004

1. Search for Saddam Hussein

In the months after the invasion of Iraq, one of the largest military objectives of the coalition was to find and capture Saddam Hussein and his sons. Hussein had fled the capital city of Baghdad at the beginning of Operation Iraqi Freedom and the intelligence community spent months locating him. After months of hunting by focusing on Hussein's family network, as well as on "High Value Targets," there was finally a lead that came from the Al-Muslit brothers, who were both members of Hussein's inner circle of bodyguards. On December 13th 2003, the United States captured Ibrahim Al-Muslit, who reported directly to Hussein, and during interrogation, Al-Muslit revealed where Hussein was hiding. Operation Red Dawn quickly commenced with special operations focusing on two farmhouses, and found Hussein in a concealed manhole. On December 14, 2003, approximately ten months after the invasion of Iraq, Saddam Hussein was captured.[35]

2. Combating the Insurgency

While the Bush administration believed that operations were coming to a close because the Iraqi Army was subdued in May of 2003, there were still clashes around the country with remnants of the Iraqi Armed Forces and with groups unaffiliated with the Iraqi Army. Defense Secretary Donald Rumsfeld categorized the lawlessness and skirmishes around the country as acts of desperate "dead-enders." The administration believed that the resistance groups were going to be easily subdued.[36]

Twenty-three days after President Bush's May 1, 2003 speech on the U.S.S. Abraham Lincoln, the head of the Coalition Provisional Authority in Iraq disbanded the Iraqi army and intelligence services.[37] This decision sent hundreds of thousands of military-trained men into the streets with few employment prospects and an increasingly building anger towards coalition forces. Within one month of President Bush declaring the end of major combat operations, this move proved to be a windfall for an emerging insurgency. In the month that followed, what originated as seemingly uncoordinated and random violence quickly evolved into an organized resistance against the United States and coalition forces, which posed a major challenge to the coalition's ability to stabilize Iraq.

---

35. See USAICoE Command History Office, *Operation RED DAWN nets Saddam Hussein*, Dec. 6, 2013, https://www.army.mil/article/116559/Operation_RED_DAWN_nets_Saddam_Hussein (last visited July 1, 2016).

36. *Rumsfeld blames Iraq problems on 'pockets of dead-enders'*, USA Today, June 18, 2003, http://usatoday30.usatoday.com/news/world/iraq/2003-06-18-rumsfeld_x.htm (last visited July 1, 2016).

37. Coalition Provisional Authority, Coalition Provisional Authority Order Number 2, Dissolution of Entities, May 23, 2016, *available at* http://www.iraqcoalition.org/regulations/20030823_CPAORD_2_Dissolution_of_Entities_with_Annex_A.pdf (last visited July 1, 2016).

By 2004, the armed opposition was threatening Iraq's stability. Though somewhat disparate in nature and varied depending on the geography, the various groups included remnants of the Iraqi Army, organized Sunni militias who were supported by Iran, Baathists who were supportive of Saddam, ultra-Iraqi Nationalists, and even elements of al Qaeda. The insurgency was composed of almost 20 different groups that had differing rationales for fighting against the coalition. Some of the insurgency groups were secular in nature, former Iraqi military and other nationalists, and other groups were more religiously motivated.[38]

Many of these groups also were using the instability to engage in sectarian violence against civilians and each other, motivated by longstanding resentments that had been suppressed by the Hussein regime.

Some of these groups were responsible for the deadliest and most destructive attacks in Iraq. For example, on August 19, 2003, a suicide bomber destroyed the United Nations headquarters in Iraq killing Sergio Vieira de Mello, a U.N. special representative, as well as 22 members of his staff. This attack led the United Nations to withdraw all nonessential employees from Baghdad.

---

38. *Iraq's Numerous Insurgent Groups*, www.npr.org, June 8, 2006, http://www.npr.org/templates/story/story.php?storyId=5468486 (reproducing an excerpt from by AHMED S. HASHIM, INSURGENCY AND COUNTER-INSURGENCY IN IRAQ (2006)). The groups included: (1) The Fedayeen Saddam, also known as Saddam's Men of Sacrifice; (2) The Al Quds Army, a volunteer civilian group composed of men and women who were trained in basic combat and participated in guerrilla attacks outside of Baghdad; (3) The Mehdi Army, a paramilitary force supporting Iraqi Shi'ite cleric Moqtada al-Sadr; (4) The General Command of the Armed Forces, Resistance and Liberation in Iraq, likely composed of former Iraqi military; (5) Popular Resistance for the Liberation of Iraq, which called for all in the Arab and Islamic world to fight against the United States in Iraq; (6) Iraqi Resistance and Liberation Command, which desired "jihad until the liberation of Iraq"; (7) The Al'Awdah (The Return), composed of "former security-service members and Iraqi armed forces personnel organized into cells distributed throughout cities such as Baghdad, Mosul and Ramadi"; (8) Harakat Ra's al-'Afa (Snakes Head Movement), which had links to Sunni Arab tribes; (9) Thuwwar al-'Arak—Kata'ib al-Anbar al-Musallaha (Iraq's Revolutionaries—Al-Anbar Armed Brigades), an anti-Saddamist group; (10) General Secretariat for the Liberation of Democratic Iraq, an anti-Saddam group who criticized the coalition for not proving proper security and services to Iraqi civilians; (11) Higher Command of the Mujahideen in Iraq, which was one of the most active insurgent groups. It is unclear if the group was working in tandem with other groups who were affiliated with former Iraqi armed forces, or if its mission was unrelated to any former regime and was focused on establishing an Islamic State; (12) Munazzamat al-Rayat al-Aswad (Black Banner Organization), which called for the sabotage of the oil industry in fear of the West obtaining control of the industry; (13) Unification Front for the Liberation of Iraq, an anti-Saddamist and anti-Ba'thist that called for all Iraqi forces to fight the U.S. occupation; (14) National Front for the Liberation of Iraq, which included Republican Guards and Islamists; (15) Jaish Ansar al-Sunnah, one of the largest and deadliest groups known for terrorist attacks against the Kurdish in the north and the executions of 12 kidnapped Nepalese hostages and 17 Iraqi contractors working for the U.S. military; (16) Mujahideen al ta'ifa al-Mansoura (Mujahideen of the Victorious Sect), which included non- Iraq Sunni Islamist elements and Sunni fundamentalist elements; Kata'ib al Mujahideen fi al-Jama'ah al-Salafiyah fi al-"Arak (Mujahideen Batalions of the Salafi Group of Iraq), a Sunni Islamist group; Jihad Brigades/Cells, which called for guerilla warfare and threated to execute those who were believed to collaborate with the U.S. occupation; (17) Armed Islamic Movement of Al Qaeda Organization, Fallujah Branch; little is known about this group except for the fact that it claimed several attacks on U.S. forces; (18) Jaish Muhammad (Army of Muhammad), composed of five different Brigades and allegedly specialized in the targeting of foreign institutions; Islamic Army of Iraq, made up of Iraqi Salafists which may have had ties to Osama Bin Laden.

Another example happened in August 2004 when fighters loyal to a Shia cleric, Moqtada al-Sadr, shot down a U.S. helicopter in fierce clashes in the Shia city of Najaf. Not only were U.S. lives lost, but the uprising also threatened to unravel a June 2004 agreement to end an uprising by the militant cleric that had killed hundreds. In August of 2004, Sadr, who had become a "symbol of resistance for foreign occupation,"[39] ordered his militia to end attacks on the U.S. and Iraqi government forces but continued to be vocal about his dislike of the U.S. occupation. Sadr continued to fight against the U.S.-led occupation and election process by using both force and political influence during the 2005 elections.

The Sunni insurgency became an especially difficult problem for the coalition, particularly because a branch of al Qaeda, al Qaeda in Iraq ("AQI"), emerged as a major component of this threat. These insurgents targeted both American troops and the Shia population. In March of 2004, members of AQI conducted a wave of suicide bombings against Shi'ite holy sites, killing hundreds of people, including four U.S. contractors who were burned, and hung from a bridge. Shiite neighborhoods where also targeted and thousands of Shiite civilians were abducted and murdered. The Shia fought back through its own militia attacks and murders.

The coalition (which now included Iraqi security forces and a reconstituted Iraqi Army[40]) needed to overcome insurgent control in these cities in order to provide enough stability to allow Iraqi elections to commence—a critical objective in the overall effort to create a new government in Iraq. In late September 2004, coalition forces attacked the insurgent stronghold in Samarra. The city was mainly controlled by Sunni Arabs but Baathists, al Qaeda operatives and other insurgent groups quickly flocked to the city to help defeat the coalition. The rebels in Samarra attacked coalition forces with guerrilla-style warfare, but the city was quickly taken, and more than 100 rebels were killed.[41]

Given the political objective behind the battle for Samarra (known as Operation Baton Rouge), the attack required cultural and religious sensitivity. Samarra had a population of about 200,000, composed mostly of Sunnis, but the city also has significant historic and religious significance for Shias.[42] During the battle for Samarra, insurgents used the Golden Mosque (and other protected objects) as cover, which, as noted by a U.S. Army account of the battle, "posed a unique challenge" to commanders on the ground:

> Preferring to have Iraqis enter the religious shrine, ... [a U.S. brigade commander] tasked the soldiers of the Iraqi 36th Commando Battalion to force their way into the mosque and eliminate the enemy threat. At around 1100

---

39. http://www.bbc.com/news/world-middle-east-12135160.
40. Donald P. Wright & Timothy R. Reese, On Point II: Transition to the New Campaign 433-438 (2008) *available at* http://usacac.army.mil/cac2/cgsc/carl/download/csipubs/OnPointII.pdf.
41. *Id.* 43-44. Military success in Samarra yielded mixed results, however, as insurgents returned after the battle and continued to pose a military and political challenge for coalition forces and the transitional Iraqi government, which "highlighted the difficulties in forging lasting changes in those communities where the insurgents chose to contest the coalition." *Id.* at 344.
42. *Id.* at 338.

that morning, . . . the Commandos blew open the front doors of the main building and secured the site, detaining 25 insurgents in the process. The 36th Commando Battalion would later capture 50 suspected insurgents while securing the city hospital.[43]

Shortly after taking Samarra, U.S. forces shifted their attention to the town of Fallujah. On November 8, 2004, U.S. forces began Operation AL FAJR (New Dawn) to overthrow the insurgent regime. The operation was the largest combat operation in Iraq since April 2003.[44] The following is a U.S. Army account of the key part of the battle:

> The decisive assault that began on 8 November was led by two US Marine Corps regimental combat teams, reinforced by two US Army mechanized battalions, multiple Iraqi Army battalions, and numerous fire support platforms. This formidable force met the determined resistance of approximately 4,500 insurgents defending a fortified Fallujah that had been in their hands since April 2004. AL FAJR came to epitomize the type of full spectrum operations the US military had gradually learned to conduct in response to the insurgency. As a broad-based operation, AL FAJR included shaping actions that relied heavily on the use of IO, violent combined arms operations that defeated the insurgents in Fallujah, and stability operations that returned the city to normalcy and reasserted Iraqi authority.[45]

3. Detention Operations

The invasion of Iraq and the subsequent insurgency resulted in detention of a large number of individuals. Among the detention facilities operated by the U.S. Army was Abu Ghraib, a prison 20 miles outside of Baghdad. An article published in *The New Yorker* magazine in May 2004 revealed instances of mistreatment of detainees in late 2003 by members of the U.S. Army, illustrated with photographs of some of the incidents.[46] According to a report written by Major General Antonio M. Taguba, there were "numerous incidents of sadistic, blatant, and wanton criminal abuses . . . inflicted on several detainees."[47] The abuses included:

> Punching, slapping, and kicking detainees; jumping on their naked feet; Videotaping and photographing naked male and female detainees; Forcibly arranging detainees in various sexually explicit positions for photographing; Forcing detainees to remove their clothing and keeping them naked for several days at a time; Forcing naked male detainees to wear women's underwear; Forcing groups of male detainees to masturbate themselves while being photographed and videotaped; Arranging naked male detainees in a pile and then

---

43. *Id.* at 343.
44. *Id.* at 345.
45. http://www.globalsecurity.org/military/library/report/2008/onpoint/chap08-07.htm.
46. Seymour M. Hersch, *Torture at Abu Ghraib*, NEW YORKER, May 10, 2004 available at http://www.newyorker.com/magazine/2004/05/10/torture-at-abu-ghraib.
47. https://fas.org/irp/agency/dod/taguba.pdf.

jumping on them; Positioning a naked detainee on a MRE Box, with a sandbag on his head, and attaching wires to his fingers, toes, and penis to simulate electric torture; Writing "I am a Rapest" (sic) on the leg of a detainee alleged to have forcibly raped a 15-year old fellow detainee, and then photographing him naked; Placing a dog chain or strap around a naked detainee's neck and having a female Soldier pose for a picture; A male MP guard having sex with a female detainee; Using military working dogs (without muzzles) to intimidate and frighten detainees, and in at least one case biting and severely injuring a detainee; and Taking photographs of dead Iraqi detainees.[48]

The events at Abu Ghraib led to the conviction of seven lower ranking soldiers for torture and humiliation of the detainees. Although no senior officials faced criminal prosecutions, the fallout from the debacle was far more extensive, with many experts convinced that the resentment it triggered substantially emboldened the Iraqi insurgency, and led many Iraqis to join the anti-coalition cause.

In April 2003, the Mujahedin-e Khalq (MeK), an exiled Iranian cult dissident group, requested a ceasefire during combat between the group and coalition forces. In May 2003, the ceasefire agreement was accepted, and approximately 3,800 members of the MeK were disarmed and detained at Camp Ashraf. Coalition forces did not determine the legal status of these detainees for over a year, during which time U.S. policy of not applying the Fourth Geneva Convention (which governs the status of civilians in an occupation) to foreign terrorists fighting in Iraq was adopted.[49] During this time, the MeK alleged that it had not engaged in combat with coalition forces, a claim which was accepted by officers responsible for detaining the group, irrespective of the fact that there was at least one Special Forces casualty stemming from the fight between the coalition and the MeK. In June 2004, without review by a tribunal as required by the Fourth Geneva Convention, U.S. Secretary of Defense Donald Rumsfeld, designated the detained members of the MeK as civilian "protected persons" under that Convention. This decision created considerable controversy stemming from the selectivity of granting this protected status to one designated terrorist organization, but not to others.[50]

In January 24, 2004 the Bush administration admitted to the world that it was mistaken about Iraq having any weapons of mass destruction. The top U.S. weapons inspector reported to Congress that the United States was wrong in believing there were extensive stockpiles of chemical, biological, and nuclear weaponry in Iraq. By March of 2005, a Presidential Commission had also concluded that there was no prewar intelligence regarding weapons of mass destruction.

---

48. https://fas.org/irp/agency/dod/taguba.pdf.

49. "Protected Person" Status in Occupied Iraq Under the Fourth Geneva Convention 18 Op. O.L.C. 35 (2004) *available at* https://www.justice.gov/sites/default/files/olc/opinions/2004/03/31/op-olc-v028-p0035.pdf.

50. Jeremiah Goulka, Lydia Hansell, Elizabeth Wilke & Judith Larson, The Mujahedin-e Khalq in Iraq: A Policy Conundrum xii-xiv (2009), *available at* http://www.rand.org/content/dam/rand/pubs/monographs/2009/RAND_MG871.pdf (last visited July 2, 2016).

The Law of Armed Conflict: An Operational Approach

1 | LEGAL BASES FOR USE OF FORCE

The Secretary of State walked into the Legal Advisor's office. "I just met with the President and the Vice President and they are contemplating taking action against Saddam Hussein." It was the Fall of 2002. The events of September 11, 2001 had triggered a significant military response in Afghanistan that was still increasing in size and scope. A new political leadership had been installed in Kabul, but resistance was still strong, and military forces seemed no closer to capturing or killing Osama bin Laden than they had in the early days of the military operation. Al Qaeda was still a significant threat to the security of the United States and their influence and connections seemed to be spreading. In fact, recent intelligence reports had drawn possible connections between al Qaeda and the rogue Iraqi regime headed by Saddam Hussein.

"The Vice President is urging military action against Iraq immediately and the President is seriously contemplating it," the Secretary continued. "I need you to look at all the facts and provide me with a thorough legal analysis of the international law regarding using force. I have to be able to clearly articulate the legal rationale and objections to taking action against Iraq under the current circumstances."

"We'll get right on it," the Department of State Legal Advisor responded, and picked up the phone to make a call as the Secretary walked out of his office.

I. Introduction

Using force against another State or sovereign is a significant decision and one that requires the leader of a nation to carefully weigh many important factors. In addition to political, diplomatic, and economic factors, legal factors also play a substantial role in the decision. States generally want to be perceived as complying with the law and will often go to great lengths to ensure their actions have legal legitimacy.

The legal issues involve both international and domestic law. This chapter will focus on the applicable international law, but it is important to note that for the United States there are vital constitutional law and national security law aspects to making the decision to satisfy national objectives through the use of force. These issues include both constitutional separation of powers issues and statutory issues such as the War Powers Resolution. For example, the Constitution expressly gives Congress the authority to define and punish piracy and other felonies on the high seas, and offenses "against the law of nations;"[1] declare war, and make rules for capturing the enemy;[2] raise, support and regulate military forces and militias;[3] and the Senate has the responsibility to provide advice and consent to Treaties, and confirm ambassadors and other Executive branch officials.[4] As compared to these express grants of authority, the Constitution only speaks in generalities with respect to the Executive. The President is the commander-in-chief;[5] makes Treaties with the advice and consent of the Senate;[6] and appoints and receives ambassadors.[7] Implicit in these enumerated powers is the primacy of the President with regard to foreign affairs.[8]

Unlike other areas of the Constitution, known for establishing a system of separation of powers, with respect to national security, the system is more one of shared powers. And over two centuries of interaction between the President and the Congress have created a "gloss"[9] that now colors the understanding of those shared powers between the two political branches of government. While the President and Congress have clashed regularly on how these powers should be shared, neither has been anxious to take the question to the Judiciary for resolution. On the few occasions where those questions have made it to the courts, the courts have generally avoided providing an answer through claiming some judicial doctrine such as ripeness, standing, or the political question doctrine. A few notorious examples exist where the courts have stepped in with respect to national security and war powers. One recent example is *Hamdan v. Rumsfeld*[10] where the Supreme Court ruled that the President's application of international law was incorrect with respect to the treatment of detainees in the war on terror.

The resolution of these questions undoubtedly has a significant impact on the use of force by the United States. However, those questions are left for another course such as national security law. This book will focus on international law

---

1. US Constitution, art I, sec. 8, cl. 10.
2. US Constitution, art I, sec. 8, cl. 11.
3. US Constitution, art I, sec. 8, cl. 12-16.
4. US Constitution, art 2, sec. 2, cl. 2.
5. US Constitution, art II, sec. 2, cl. 1.
6. US Constitution, art II, sec. 2, cl. 2.
7. US Constitution, art II, sec. 2, cl. 2; sec 3.
8. *See* generally Harold Hongju Koh, Why the President (Almost) Always Wins in Foreign Affairs: Lessons of the Iran-Contra Affair, 97 YALE L.J. 1255 (1988).
9. Youngstown Sheet and Tube Co. v. Sawyer 343 U.S. 579, 610-611(1952) where Justice Frankfurter, in his concurring opinion, writes "In short, a systematic, unbroken, executive practice, long pursued to the knowledge of the Congress and never before questioned, engaged in by presidents who have also sworn to uphold the Constitution, making as it were such exercise of power part of the structure of our Government, may be treated as a gloss on 'executive Power' vested in the President by sec 1 of Art. II."
10. Hamdan v. Rumsfeld, 548 U.S. 557 (2006).

and its application to the use of force by nations. The legal bases for the use of force have strong historical roots. The current paradigm arises out of the experiences of World War I and World War II and has continued to develop through State practice since that time. In the current international environment, every use of force is scrutinized. Articulating a clear and considered legal basis for using force is essential to sustaining support at home and gaining acceptance abroad.

II. Historical Background

As long as there has been conflict between peoples, there have been rules intended to limit the conduct of hostilities and the decision to resort to hostilities.[11] This chapter deals with the rules governing the legality of going to war, or *jus ad bellum*. The rest of the book will discuss the rules that apply once war has commenced, or *jus in bello*.

A complete history of the *jus ad bellum* is too long for this chapter. However, there are some significant theories that require a brief historical introduction. One of the most prominent early theories on the law governing the resort to war was the Just War Theory. This theory was practiced particularly throughout Europe between 335 B.C. and 1800 A.D. Under a Just War Theory, a resort to force was morally justifiable if the cause was "just." Over time, there were several different criteria for determining what "just" meant, but it was usually understood to include some form of a decision that was made by the sovereign based on his or her assessment of various moral or religious principles.

With the rise of the nation state and a more legalist/positivist approach to war making, "Just War" gave way to "War as Fact." During the nineteenth and early twentieth centuries, war came to be recognized as an instrument of national policy. Rather than determining the "just" nature of the sovereign's decision to use force against another sovereign, a more utilitarian approach was used. Sovereigns were free to use force as another means of foreign relations. There were, however, attempts to place some controls on the resort to force. For example, the 1899 and 1907 Hague Conventions required an official declaration of war before hostilities could commence.[12]

After World War I, many of the major powers, including many European countries, created the League of Nations. The League of Nations attempted to create a "collective security" system whereby each member State would guarantee the protection of other League States from aggression by coming to that State's

---

11. Ian Brownlie, International Law and the Use of Force by States (1963) (providing detailed discussion of the *jus ad bellum*'s history and development).

12. Convention for the Pacific Settlement of International Disputes, July 29, 1899, 32 Stat. 1779, T.S. 392, 1 Bevans 230; Convention Respecting the Laws and Customs of War on Land, with Annex of Regulations, Oct. 18, 1907, 36 Stat. 2277, 1 Bevans 631.

aid.[13] In 1928, most of these same nations signed the Kellogg-Briand Pact, which renounced the recourse to war.[14] However, the Pact lacked any enforcement mechanism and proved its impotence with the onset of World War II.

In the aftermath of World War II, the victorious allies were committed to attempt a more effective regime to control the resort to force. Article 6 of the Nuremberg Charter made "waging a war of aggression" a "crime against peace" for which there was individual criminal responsibility for a nation's leaders, and the Nuremberg Trials successfully convicted former Nazi leaders of this new crime.[15] The desire to deter nations, and individual leaders of nations, from engaging in aggressive wars underpinned the post WWII thoughts on collective security.[16]

III. The United Nations Charter Paradigm

After the failure of the pre–World War II attempts at regulating the use of force, the representatives of more than 50 countries convened at San Francisco from April 25 to June 26, 1945. Those delegates deliberated on the basis of

---

13. League of Nations Covenant, June 28, 1919, 225 Consol. T.S. 188, *available at* http://avalon.law.yale.edu/20th_century/leagcov.asp.

14. Treaty Providing for the Renunciation of War as an Instrument of National Policy art. I, Aug. 27, 1928, 46 Stat. 2343, 94 L.N.T.S. 57. ("Art. I. The High Contracting Parties solemnly declare in the names of their respective peoples that they condemn recourse to war for the solution of international controversies, and renounce it, as an instrument of national policy in their relations with one another.").

15. Agreement for the Prosecution and Punishment of the Major War Criminals of the European Axis Powers and Charter of the International Military Tribunal art. 6(a), Aug. 8, 1945, 59 Stat. 1544, 82 U.N.T.S. 279 ("Article 6. . . . The following acts, or any of them, are crimes coming within the jurisdiction of the Tribunal for which there shall be individual responsibility: (a) Crimes Against Peace: namely, planning, preparation, initiation or waging of a war of aggression, or a war in violation of international treaties, agreements or assurances, or participation in a common plan or conspiracy for the accomplishment of any of the foregoing; . . .").

16. The International Criminal Court (ICC) in Article 5 states that the crimes of genocide, crimes against humanity, war crimes, and the crime of aggression are subject to the Court's jurisdiction. Rome Statute of the International Criminal Court, art. 5, para. 1, July 17, 1998, 2187 U.N.T.S. 3, U.N. Doc. A/CONF.183/9. However, the second paragraph of Article 5 states the following with respect to the crime of aggression: "The Court shall exercise jurisdiction over the crime of aggression once a provision is adopted in accordance with articles 121 and 123 defining the crime and setting out the conditions under which the Court shall exercise jurisdiction with respect to this crime. Such a provision shall be consistent with the relevant provisions of the Charter of the United Nations." *Id.* at art. 5, para. 2. There has been significant scholarly discussion about the ICC's attempts to define aggression. *See, e.g.,* Michael J. Glennon, *The Blank-Prose Crime of Aggression*, 35 YALE J. INT'L L. 71 (2010); Major Kari M. Fletcher, *Defining the Crime of Aggression: Is There an Answer to the International Criminal Court's Dilemma?*, 65 A.F. L. REV. 229 (2010); Mark S. Stein, *The Security Council, The International Criminal Court, and the Crime of Aggression: How Exclusive Is the Security Council's Power to Determine Aggression?*, 16 IND. INT'L & COMP. L. REV. 1 (2005); Jennifer Trahan, *Defining "Aggression": Why the Preparatory Commission for the International Criminal Court Has Faced Such a Conundrum*, 24 LOY. L.A. INT'L & COMP. L. REV. 439 (2002); Theodor Meron, *Defining Aggression for the International Criminal Court*, 25 SUFFOLK TRANSNAT'L L. REV. 1 (2001-2002); Philippe Kirsch & John T. Holmes, *The Rome Conference on an International Criminal Court: The Negotiating Process*, 93 AM. J. INT'L L. 2 (1999).

proposals worked out by the representatives of China, the Soviet Union, the United Kingdom, and the United States at Dumbarton Oaks in August-October 1944. The result was the United Nations Charter. The Charter was signed on June 26, 1945 and the United Nations officially came into existence on October 24, 1945. The Charter is the current international legal paradigm for regulating the use of force.

One of the key goals of the Charter was to establish a presumptive prohibition on the use of force by States. It was clear that a complete prohibition was unworkable, but a presumption against the use of force, with specific exceptions, was thought to be more practical. The Charter was then organized with States agreeing to the presumption against the use of force, and the consensual bestowal of authority to authorize force in a representative council known as the Security Council, which was supported by other agencies and organizations.

Before discussing the details of the Charter regime for the use of force, a brief overview of these UN organs and agencies is appropriate. There are six primary organs of the United Nations: a General Assembly (UNGA); a Security Council (UNSC); an Economic and Social Council; a Trusteeship Council; an International Court of Justice (ICJ); and a Secretariat.[17] For the purposes of regulating the international use of force, the most significant three organs are the UNGA, the UNSC, and the ICJ.

A. General Assembly

Chapter IV of the Charter, comprising Articles 9-22, outlines the duties and responsibilities of the UNGA. The body is open to all member States and there are currently 193 members. There are also a number of organizations or entities that have been granted observer status who take an active role in the General Assembly. The UNGA provides a forum for the member States to discuss matters of international concern, including the use of force. Within the Charter, the UNGA's relationship to the use of force and the maintenance of international peace and security is specifically discussed. According to Article 10, the UNGA may "discuss any questions or any matters within the scope of the present Charter or relating to the powers and functions of any organs provided for in the present Charter, and, except as provided in Article 12, may make recommendations to the Members of the United Nations or to the Security Council or to both on any such questions or matters."[18] Additionally, Article 11 provides that the UNGA "may consider the general principles of co-operation in the maintenance of international peace and security" and "may discuss any questions relating to the maintenance of international peace and security brought before it by any Member of the United Nations, or by the Security Council, ... and, except as provided in Article 12, may make recommendations with regard

---

17. U.N. Charter art. 7.
18. U.N. Charter art. 10.

to any such questions to the state or states concerned or to the Security Council or to both."[19]

It is important to note that these paragraphs grant no additional authority to the UNGA other than the authority to "discuss" and "make recommendations." Further, even these roles are caveated by Article 12. The reference to Article 12 is illuminating. In describing the limits of the UNGA's competence, Article 12 states:

> 1. While the Security Council is exercising in respect of any dispute or situation the functions assigned to it in the present Charter, the General Assembly shall not make any recommendation with regard to that dispute or situation unless the Security Council so requests.
>
> 2. The Secretary-General, with the consent of the Security Council, shall notify the General Assembly at each session of any matters relative to the maintenance of international peace and security which are being dealt with by the Security Council and shall similarly notify the General Assembly, or the Members of the United Nations if the General Assembly is not in session, immediately [when] the Security Council ceases to deal with such matters.[20]

Although it is clear that the UNGA does have some competence in the area of international peace and security, it is completely subject to preemption and exclusion by the UNSC. It is the UNSC that bears the authority and responsibility for the maintenance of international peace and security as will be outlined below.

Despite the textual limitations of the UNGA with regard to international peace and security, during the height of the Cold War, and its resultant Security Council inaction, the UNGA passed the Uniting for Peace Resolution.[21] The resolution was passed during a time of UNSC deadlock and states that "if the Security Council, because of lack of unanimity of the permanent members, fails to exercise its primary responsibility for the maintenance of international peace and security in any case where there appears to be a threat to the peace, breach of the peace, or act of aggression, the General Assembly shall consider the matter immediately with a view to making appropriate recommendations to Members for collective measures, including in the case of a breach of the peace or act of aggression the use of armed force if necessary, to maintain or restore international peace and security."[22] The practical importance of this resolution is still unclear because it has not been applied to any particular international situation. The potential of the UNGA responding in such a situation and its importance has been discussed often among academics.[23] For example, Israel's Permanent

---

19. U.N. Charter art. 11.
20. U.N. Charter art. 12.
21. G.A. Res. 5/377, U.N. Doc. A/RES/5/377 (Nov. 3, 1950).
22. *Id.* ¶1.
23. HANS KELSEN, THE LAW OF THE UNITED NATIONS: A CRITICAL ANALYSIS OF ITS FUNDAMENTAL PROBLEMS 953-990 (1951) (Kelsen argues that either the General Assembly already possessed the power described in the Uniting for Peace resolution, or it represented an illegitimate attempt to amend the Charter); Amy E. Eckert, Comment, *United Nations Peacekeeping in Collapsed States*, 5 D.C. L.J. INT'L L. & PRAC. 273, 303 n.74 (1996) ("Even the limited authority that the Uniting for Peace resolution does confer is controversial, because the resolution contradicts portions of Article 11 of the United Nations Charter, which are cited above.").

Representative to the United Nations asserts in an article that Resolution 337 "has largely become moot," as a result of the ICJ's Advisory Opinion on *Certain Expenses of the United Nations.*[24]

In practice, the UNGA has taken some important actions with respect to the use of force and international peace and security. For example, the UNGA has asked for Advisory Opinions from the ICJ on several key use of force issues, including the use of nuclear weapons and Israel's building of a wall to separate Palestinians from Israeli areas as an anti-terrorist measure.[25]

B. Security Council

The UNSC is discussed in Chapter V of the Charter, consisting of Articles 23-32. The UNSC consists of fifteen members, five of which are permanent—China, Russia, France, the United Kingdom, and the United States—and ten of which are elected for two-year terms, based on geographical representation. Each member of the Council has one vote and nine votes are sufficient to take an action, but no resolution, except those of a procedural nature, can pass over the veto of one of the permanent five members.

The UNSC has the real power governing the use of force to maintain international peace and security under the Charter. Article 24 accomplishes this allocation of authority and responsibility by stating that "Members confer on the Security Council primary responsibility for the maintenance of international peace and security, and agree that in carrying out its duties under this responsibility the Security Council acts on their behalf."[26] In addition to conferring this responsibility, Article 25 provides, "The Members of the United Nations agree to accept and carry out the decisions of the Security Council in accordance with the present Charter."[27]

The meaning of these two articles is clear. The States that are members of the United Nations assign the primary responsibility for the international use of force and the maintenance of international peace and security to the UNSC and then commit to accept and comply with the UNSC decisions. Chapters VI and VII of the Charter then lay out how the UNSC accomplishes this mission.

1. Chapter VI—Pacific Settlement of Disputes

Chapter VI commits the State Parties to "seek a solution by negotiation, enquiry, mediation, conciliation, arbitration, judicial settlement, resort to regional agencies or arrangements, or other peaceful means of their own choice."[28] In response to such potential conflicts, the UNSC still plays a vital role. The UNSC can "call

---

24. Yehuda Z. Blum, *The Seventh Emergency Special Session of the UN General Assembly: An Exercise in Procedural Abuse*, 80 AM. J. INT'L L. 587, 588 (1986).
25. Legality of the Threat or Use of Nuclear Weapons, Advisory Opinion, 1996 I.C.J. 226 (July 8); Legal Consequences of the Construction of a Wall in the Occupied Palestinian Territory, Advisory Opinion, 2004 I.C.J. 136 (July 9).
26. U.N. Charter art. 24, para. 1.
27. U.N. Charter art. 25.
28. U.N. Charter art. 33, para. 1.

upon the parties to settle their dispute" by peaceful means,[29] investigate disputes,[30] and make non-binding recommendations on how to solve the dispute.[31]

In many ways, the UNSC's Chapter VI actions were the predominant means by which the Council responded to threats to international peace since the UN's inception through the post-Cold War thaw.[32] The UNSC was able to use Chapter VI to avoid superpower confrontation and still take action to preserve the peace.

Several recent examples highlight the UNSC's use of Chapter VI authority. In 2001, the UNSC passed a resolution addressing the concept of "conflict prevention." The resolution "[r]*eaffirms* [the UNSC's] role in the peaceful settlement of disputes and *reiterates* its call upon the Member States to settle their disputes by peaceful means as set forth in Chapter VI of the Charter."[33] Then, in 2003, the UNSC passed a resolution that explicitly stated it was acting under Chapter VI when it expressed support for the Secretary-General in his efforts to resolve the issue related to Western Sahara. The resolution called upon the parties to work with the United Nations and each other to implement the proposed peace plan, and called upon all parties and regional States to cooperate in the process.[34] While not explicitly referenced, the UNSC has recently relied on Chapter VI authority in Côte d'Ivoire,[35] Cyprus,[36] Afghanistan,[37] Georgia,[38] Ethiopia and Eritrea,[39] and Croatia.[40]

---

29. U.N. Charter art. 33, para. 2.
30. U.N. Charter art. 34.
31. U.N. Charter art. 36, para. 1.
32. David M. Morriss, *From War to Peace: A Study of Cease-Fire Agreements and the Evolving Role of the United Nations*, 36 Va. J. Int'l L. 801, 805 (1996). *See also* United Nations, *Repertoire of the Practice of the Security Council: Pacific Settlements of Disputes (Chapter VI)*, http://www.un.org/en/sc/repertoire/settlements.shtml (last visited Apr. 20, 2011), for an examination of the implicit and explicit references to Chapter VI by the UNSC.
33. S.C. Res. 1366, ¶9, U.N. Doc. S/RES/1366 (Aug. 30, 2001).
34. S.C. Res. 1495, ¶¶1-3, U.N. Doc. S/RES/1495 (July 31, 2003). In 1976, the UNSC also referenced Chapter VI in a preambulatory clause in a resolution concerning the conflict between Greece and Turkey. The resolution states that the Council "bears in mind" the principles concerning the peaceful settlement of disputes, specifically those provisions of Chapter VI of the Charter and urges the parties to reduce tensions and negotiate over their differences. S.C. Res. 395, ¶¶2-3, U.N. Doc. S/RES/395 (Aug. 25, 1976).
35. The UNSC in February 2003 endorsed the Linas-Marcoussis Agreement and called upon all Ivorian political forces to implement it without delay in relation to the conflict in Côte d'Ivoire. S.C. Res. 1464, ¶1, U.N. Doc. S/RES/1464 (Feb. 4, 2003). Thereafter the UNSC in May 2003 established the United Nations Mission in Côte d'Ivoire (MINUCI) to facilitate implementation by the Ivorian parties of the Linas-Marcoussis Agreement, complementing efforts by French and Economic Community of West African States (ECOWAS) forces. S.C. Res. 1479, ¶2, U.N. Doc. S/RES/1479 (May 13, 2003).
36. The UNSC in 2003 passed a resolution supporting the Secretary-General's plan for negotiations between the parties related to the situation in Cyprus and further expressed its support for his mission of Good Offices entrusted to him in resolution 1250 (1999). S.C. Res. 1475, ¶¶1, 4-5, U.N. Doc. S/RES/1475 (Apr. 14, 2003).
37. The UNSC in 2002 endorsed the establishment of a United Nations Assistance Mission in Afghanistan (UNAMA) and called upon all Afghan parties to cooperate with UNAMA in implementing its mandate. S.C. Res. 1401, ¶¶1, 5, U.N. Doc. S/RES/1401 (Mar. 28, 2002).
38. S.C. Res. 1287, ¶4, U.N. Doc. S/RES/1287 (Jan. 31, 2000); S.C. Res. 1393, ¶¶3-4, U.N. Doc. S/RES/1393 (Jan. 31, 2002).
39. S.C. Res. 1297, ¶7, U.N. Doc. S/RES/1297 (May 12, 2000).
40. S.C. Res. 1285, U.N. Doc. S/RES/1285 (Jan. 13, 2000).

In addition to more passive applications of Chapter VI, the UNSC also developed the idea of using "peacekeeping forces" to help maintain the peace between warring parties. The UNSC's use of peacekeeping missions is an interesting development because the Charter does not explicitly authorize or even mention peacekeeping missions as a tool for use by the UNSC.[41] These forces have traditionally been inserted by agreement of the previously warring parties, which is in contrast to the use of Chapter VII forces that will be discussed below. Examples of the use of peacekeeping forces include Cyprus,[42] India and Pakistan,[43] and FYROM.[44] The mission of these forces was not to intervene to maintain the peace, but merely to observe actions in the area and report incidents that might threaten peace.

Between making recommendations, calling for negotiations, and even consensually inserting forces to monitor and observe cease-fires, the UNSC has authority to take significant actions to prevent threats to international peace and security. However, as the former United States representative to the United Nations, John Negroponte, stated during a Security Council meeting in 2003 discussing the role of the Security Council in the pacific settlement of disputes, Chapter VI actions are designed to deal with disputes that may endanger the peace whereas Chapter VII actions are designed to restore it.[45] Therefore, it is to Chapter VII that one must look for a fuller view of the UNSC powers.

2. Chapter VII—Action with Respect to Threats to the Peace, Breaches of the Peace, and Acts of Aggression

Chapter VII vests the UNSC with the responsibility and authority to "determine the existence of any threat to the peace, breach of the peace, or act of aggression."[46] The UNSC, and only the UNSC, has this authority. It exercises this authority through the measures provided in Articles 39, 41, and 42.

In Article 39, the Charter provides a threshold determination that must be made by the UNSC in order to trigger the other provisions of the Chapter. Article 39 states:

> 39. The Security Council shall determine the existence of any threat to the peace, breach of the peace, or act of aggression and shall make recommendations, or decide what measures shall be taken in accordance with Articles 41 and 42, to maintain or restore international peace and security.

Once the threshold determination that a threat or breach of the peace or an act of aggression has occurred, the UNSC can then utilize the authorities granted to it in Articles 41 and 42.

---

41. Saira Mohamed, Note, *From Keeping Peace to Building Peace: A Proposal for a Revitalized United Nations Trusteeship Council*, 105 Colum. L. Rev. 809, 820 (2005).
42. S.C. Res. 186, U.N. Doc. S/Res/186 (Mar. 4, 1964).
43. S.C. Res. 307, U.N. Doc. S/Res/307 (Dec. 21, 1971).
44. S.C. Res. 983, U.N. Doc. S/Res/983 (Mar. 31, 1995).
45. U.N. SCOR, 58th Sess., 4753d mtg. at 17, U.N. Doc. S/PV.4753 (May 13, 2003).
46. U.N. Charter art. 39.

41. The Security Council may decide what measures not involving the use of armed force are to be employed to give effect to its decisions, and it may call upon the Members of the United Nations to apply such measures. These may include complete or partial interruption of economic relations and of rail, sea, air, postal, telegraphic, radio, and other means of communication, and the severance of diplomatic relations.

42. Should the Security Council consider that measures provided for in Article 41 would be inadequate or have proved to be inadequate, it may take such action by air, sea, or land forces as may be necessary to maintain or restore international peace and security. Such action may include demonstrations, blockade, and other operations by air, sea, or land forces of Members of the United Nations.[47]

The difference between the UNSC authority in Chapter VI and that in Chapter VII is the binding nature of Chapter VII actions. For example, after Saddam Hussein invaded Kuwait in August of 1990, the UNSC passed Resolution 660 condemning the invasion and demanding the withdrawal of Iraqi forces.[48] This resolution was mandatory and Iraq had an obligation to comply under Article 25 of the Charter. Iraq did not heed the UNSC, which then utilized its Chapter VII authority through subsequent UNSC resolutions (UNSCRs) to authorize military action that eventually expelled Iraq from Kuwait and defeated its forces. The key resolution was UNSCR 678, which said in part,

Acting under Chapter VII of the Charter, [the UNSC]

1. Demands that Iraq comply fully with resolution 660 (1990) and all subsequent relevant resolutions, and decides, while maintaining all its decisions, to allow Iraq one final opportunity, as a pause of goodwill, to do so;

2. Authorizes Member States co-operating with the Government of Kuwait, unless Iraq on or before 15 January 1991 fully implements, as set forth in paragraph 1 above, the above-mentioned resolutions, to use all necessary means to uphold and implement resolution 660 (1990) and all subsequent relevant resolutions and to restore international peace and security in the area;

3. Requests all States to provide appropriate support for the actions undertaken in pursuance of paragraph 2 of the present resolution;[49] . . .

In order to draw the contrast more clearly between Chapter VI and Chapter VII action, the UNSC resolutions regarding the situation in the Democratic Republic of the Congo (DRC) are instructive. The UNSC established the United Nations Organization Mission in the DRC (MONUC) in 1999 and a year later the Council approved another resolution that included several operative clauses that implicitly invoke Chapter VI (i.e., calling on the parties to fulfill their Ceasefire Agreement obligations, expanding MONUC personnel numbers, and defining the mandate of MONUC).[50] In that same resolution, subsequent to

---

47. U.N. Charter arts. 41-42.
48. S.C. Res. 660, ¶1, U.N. Doc. S/RES/660 (Aug. 2, 1990).
49. S.C. Res. 678, ¶¶1-3, U.N. Doc. S/RES/678 (Nov. 29, 1990).
50. S.C. Res. 1291, ¶¶1, 4, 7, U.N. Doc. S/RES/1291 (Feb. 24, 2000).

III. The United Nations Charter Paradigm | 11

those implicit Chapter VI clauses, in the eighth operative clause, the Council stated that it is acting under Chapter VII in deciding "that MONUC may take the necessary action, in the areas of deployment of its infantry battalions and as it deems it within its capabilities, to protect United Nations and co-located [Joint Military Commission] personnel, facilities, installations and equipment, . . . and protect civilians under imminent threat of physical violence."[51] This differentiation between the Security Council's more passive Chapter VI authorities and more forceful Chapter VII authorities is significant when considering the current *jus ad bellum* paradigm.

Another important example of the difference in Chapter VI and VII actions is highlighted by the recent formation of the "Intervention Brigade" as part of the United Nations Organization Stabilization Mission in the Democratic Republic of the Congo (MONUSCO). After taking many actions under Chapter VI, including the establishment of peacekeeping forces in accordance with those outlined above, the UNSC determined in UNSCR 2098 that those actions had been insufficient and the situation in the DRC "continue[d] to constitute a threat to international peace and security in the region." In response, the UNSC acted "under Chapter VII of the Charter of the United Nations," and "decide[d] that MONUSCO shall . . . include an "Intervention Brigade" consisting inter alia of three infantry battalions, one artillery and one special force and reconnaissance company . . . with the responsibility of neutralizing armed groups . . . and the objective of contributing to reducing the threat posed by armed groups to state authority and civilian security in eastern DRC and to make space for stabilization activities."[52] This action was the first of its kind and demonstrates the clear difference in the use by the UNSC of Chapters VI and VII, particularly the enhanced ability to use force in Articles 41 and 42.

Additionally, the specific authorities mentioned in Articles 41 and 42 of the UN Charter have, over time, come to be understood as illustrative, and not limiting. This was confirmed by the International Criminal Tribunal for the Former Yugoslavia (ICTY) in one of its first cases, *Prosecutor v. Dusko Tadic a/k/a "Dule"* (hereinafter *Tadic*). Defense attorneys for Tadic argued that the establishment of the ICTY by the UNSC in UNSC Resolutions 808 and 827 was not within the power of the UNSC. The question eventually made it to the ICTY Appeals Chamber, which issued its decision, determining the ICTY was properly constituted. In the process of doing so, the Tribunal discussed the UNSC's powers under Articles 41 and 42.

> 31. Once the Security Council determines that a particular situation poses a threat to the peace or that there exists a breach of the peace or an act of aggression, it enjoys a wide margin of discretion in choosing the course of action. . . .
>
> A question arises in this respect as to whether the choice of the Security Council is limited to the measures provided for in Articles 41 and 42 of the Charter (as the language of Article 39 suggests), or whether it has even larger

---

51. *Id.* ¶ 8.
52. S.C. Res. 2098, ¶¶ preamble, 9, U.N. Doc. S/RES/2098 (Mar. 28, 2013).

discretion in the form of general powers to maintain and restore international peace and security under Chapter VII at large. In the latter case, one of course does not have to locate every measure decided by the Security Council under Chapter VII within the confines of Articles 41 and 42, or possibly Article 40. In any case, under both interpretations, the Security Council has a broad discretion in deciding on the course of action and evaluating the appropriateness of the measures to be taken. The language of Article 39 is quite clear as to the channeling of the very broad and exceptional powers of the Security Council under Chapter VII through Articles 41 and 42. These two Articles leave to the Security Council such a wide choice as not to warrant searching, on functional or other grounds, for even wider and more general powers than those already expressly provided for in the Charter.

These powers are *coercive vis-à-vis* the culprit State or entity. But they are also *mandatory vis-à-vis* the other Member States, who are under an obligation to cooperate with the Organization (Article 2, paragraph 5, Articles 25, 48) and with one another (Article 49), in the implementation of the action or measures decided by the Security Council.

. . .

36. Logically, if the Organization can undertake measures which have to be implemented through the intermediary of its Members, it can a fortiori undertake measures which it can implement directly via its organs, if it happens to have the resources to do so. It is only for want of such resources that the United Nations has to act through its Members. But it is of the essence of "collective measures" that they are collectively undertaken. Action by Member States on behalf of the Organization is but a poor substitute *faute de mieux*, or a "second best" for want of the first. This is also the pattern of Article 42 on measures involving the use of armed force.

In sum, the establishment of the International Tribunal falls squarely within the powers of the Security Council under Article 41.[53]

Tadic makes it clear that although the UNSC's power and authority are not unlimited. They are very broad and when exercised, binding on the international community. The UNSC is permitted to define its own options under Articles 41 and 42 and not feel bound to only those mentioned in the articles. The use of analogy and reason guide the UNSC in determining what it can and cannot do when faced with a Chapter VII breach of the peace. While *Tadic* was decided under Article 41, a similar understanding applies to Article 42.

Immediately following Articles 41 and 42, Article 43 of the Charter states:

1. All Members of the United Nations, in order to contribute to the maintenance of international peace and security, undertake to make available to the Security Council, on its call and in accordance with a special agreement or agreements, armed forces, assistance, and facilities, including rights of passage, necessary for the purpose of maintaining international peace and security.

---

53. Prosecutor v. Tadic, Case No. IT-94-1-AR72, Decision on Defence Motion for Interlocutory Appeal on Jurisdiction, ¶¶26-28, 31, 36 (Oct. 2, 1995).

At the time of formulation, it was thought that the Security Council could use these dedicated UN forces to accomplish its resolutions and maintain international peace and security.

For several reasons, the "UN forces" never materialized. The onset of the Cold War as well as concerns about sovereignty and control were strong contributing factors to the almost immediate morbidity of Article 43. As will be illustrated below, the lack of Article 43 forces leaves the Security Council with the need to rely on "authorizing" States to apply force in response to breaches of international peace and security. This need for volunteerism severely affects the ability of the UNSC to fulfill its responsibilities, though in the post–Cold War era, the UNSC has become quite adept at authorizing the use of force.

There appears to be little doubt that the UNSC is the controller/authorizer of the use of force in international law. The nations who formulated the Charter envisioned such a system and the paradigm continues today, albeit with varying success.

C. International Court of Justice

The final organ of the United Nations with some competence over international peace and security is the ICJ, which is treated generally in Chapter XIV of the Charter. It is the principal judicial organ of the United Nations[54] and consists of 15 judges who are elected by separate vote of the UNGA and UNSC. Judges serve for nine years, and may be re-elected. Though not dictated by the Charter, it is generally accepted that each of the permanent five members of the UNSC will have one judge sitting on the court.

The Statute of the ICJ is an annex to the UN Charter. It provides for jurisdiction of contentious cases between States[55] and for the issuance of Advisory Opinions in particular cases.[56] It is important to note that only States can appear before the ICJ (this is in contrast to international criminal tribunals, which will be discussed in later chapters). Jurisdiction depends on the consent of the parties; consent may be express or implied in a treaty or other agreement between the parties. States may also accept compulsory jurisdiction, either unconditionally or on the condition of reciprocity on the part of other parties.[57] Under

---

54. U.N. Charter art. 92.
55. Statute of the International Court of Justice art. 36 (hereinafter I.C.J. Statute).
56. I.C.J. Statute art. 65.
57. I.C.J. Statute art. 36. The United States revoked its declaration accepting the ICJ's jurisdiction under Article 36(2) of the ICJ Statute in 1985, but nevertheless reaffirmed its "traditional commitment to international law and to the International Court of Justice in performing its proper functions." Department [of State] Statement (Oct. 7, 1985), DEP'T ST. BULL., Jan. 1986, at 67, *reprinted in* 24 I.L.M. 1743, 1744-1745 (1985). *See also* Statement of State Department Legal Adviser Abraham D. Sofaer to the Senate Foreign Relations Committee (Dec. 4, 1985), *reprinted in* 86 DEP'T ST. BULL. 67, 71 (Jan. 1986) (hereinafter Sofaer Statement). *See also* Heidi K. Hubbard, Note, *Separation of Powers Within the United Nations: A Revised Role for the International Court of Justice*, 38 STAN. L. REV. 165, 175-179 (1985) (discussing ICJ history of attempting to adjudicate use of force cases that have resulted in respondent governments having denied or revoked jurisdiction, refusing to appear, and balking at complying with court orders).

Article 59 of the ICJ Statute, "The decision of the Court has no binding force except between the parties and in respect to that particular case."[58]

Early in the ICJ's jurisprudence, the question was raised as to the Court's competence to hear cases concerning issues of international peace and security, particularly those of which the UNSC had already taken cognizance. This controversy is illustrated by the case of *Military and Paramilitary Activities in and Against Nicaragua* (hereinafter *Nicaragua*).[59] The *Nicaragua* case concerned military support given by the United States to rebels fighting against Nicaragua in response to Nicaragua's supplying rebels who were trying to undermine the government in El Salvador. During those proceedings in which the United States' support for insurgents in Nicaragua was the legal issue, the United States argued that, for several reasons, the ICJ had no jurisdiction over the situation. The ICJ determined that it did have jurisdiction and ruled against the United States.

After the verdict, the United States decided to terminate its acceptance of compulsory jurisdiction to the ICJ. Abe Sofaer, then Legal Adviser to the U.S. State Department, stated:

> Even more disturbing, for the first time in its history, the Court has sought to assert jurisdiction over a controversy concerning claims related to an ongoing use of armed force. This action concerns every state. It is inconsistent with the structure of the UN system. . . . In the Nicaragua case, the Court rejected without a soundly reasoned explanation our arguments that claims of the sort made by Nicaragua were intended by the UN Charter exclusively for resolution by political mechanisms—in particular, the Security Council and the Contadora process [initiated in January 1983 at a meeting of the foreign ministers of Mexico, Venezuela, Colombia, and Panama on Contadora Island in the Gulf of Panama, this was an effort to find a purely Latin American diplomatic solution to stabilize the Central American situation and prevent either military confrontation between neighboring states or direct military intervention by the United States]—and that claims to the exercise of the inherent right of individual and collective self-defense were excluded by Article 51 of the Charter from review by the Court.
>
> . . . It shows a Court majority apparently prepared to act in ways profoundly inconsistent with the structure of the Charter and the Court's place in that structure. The Charter gives to the Security Council—not the Court—the responsibility for evaluating and resolving claims concerning the use of armed force and claims of self-defense under article 51.[60]

Despite some States' contention that the ICJ has no role in adjudicating issues of international peace and security, the ICJ continues to do so through both advisory opinions and in contentious cases. Recent cases include the 1999 *Armed Activities on the Territory of the Congo (Democratic Republic of the Congo*

---

58. I.C.J. Statute art. 59.
59. Military and Paramilitary Activities (Nicar. v. U.S.), 1986 I.C.J. 14 (June 27).
60. Sofaer Statement, *supra*, note 57, at 70-71.

v. Uganda) and the 2003 *Advisory Opinion on the Legal Consequences of the Construction of a Wall in the Occupied Palestinian Territory*.[61]

In several of these cases, the ICJ has issued opinions directly opposed to UNSC resolutions and practice.[62] The UNSC has never taken action to resolve this potential conflict between the two UN organs, but debate continues to rage as to the competence of the ICJ in this area.

Having discussed the primary organs of the UN and their role in international peace and security, it is now important to look at the substantive provisions of the UN Charter system and their application in current practice.

IV. The Use of Force

The Charter, much like the Kellogg-Briand Pact before, prohibits the use of force by individual States, with the exception of three specific methods of lawful force. Article 2(3) states that "All Members shall settle their international disputes by peaceful means in such a manner that international peace and security, and justice, are not endangered." This provision is generally read in conjunction with the next article, Article 2(4), which states that "All Members shall refrain in their international relations from the threat or use of force against the territorial integrity or political independence of any state, or in any other manner inconsistent with the Purposes of the United Nations."

Article 2(4) has become the accepted norm restricting the use of force among States. However, universal acceptance does not mean universal understanding or universal application. Although the international community as a whole accepts Article 2(4) to be binding, nations have very different views on what the language actually means. For example, the prohibition refers to the "threat or use of force," as opposed to words such as "war" or "aggression." The Charter contains no definitions section, leaving each nation to determine what constitutes a "use of force."

One of the terms that has gained in acceptance and that will be used throughout this book in the discussion of the law is "armed conflict." Although this term is mostly applied to the rules governing war (which are the bulk of this book's topic) and is certainly not synonymous with a "use of force," the definition of armed conflict is helpful in analyzing what constitutes a use of force since it is assumed that armed conflict would involve the threat or use of force at its inception. In *Tadic*, the ICTY stated, "[W]e find that an armed conflict

---

61. These opinions can be found at the ICJ website, http://www.icj-cij.org.
62. Sean D. Murphy, *Agora: ICJ Advisory Opinion on Construction of a Wall in the Occupied Palestinian Territory: Self-Defense and the Israeli Wall Advisory Opinion: An Ipse Dixit from the ICJ?*, 99 AM. J. INT'L L. 62 (2005) (discussing the ICJ's Advisory Opinion, which states that although Article 51 of the Charter recognizes an inherent right of self-defense, Israel in this case had not made a claim "that the attacks against it are imputable to a foreign State" in comparison to UNSC practice, which "has repeatedly found that the conduct of nonstate actors can be a threat to international peace and security").

exists whenever there is a resort to armed force between States or protracted armed violence between governmental authorities and organized armed groups or between such groups within a State. International humanitarian law applies from the initiation of such armed conflicts and extends beyond the cessation of hostilities until a general conclusion of peace is reached. . . ."[63] It seems clear from this that activities that directly lead to an armed conflict may be a use of force.

Additional insight can be found in the 1970 Declaration on Principles of International Law Concerning Friendly Relations and Co-operation Among States in Accordance with the Charter of the United Nations[64] that was adopted by the UNGA. The Declaration states that:

> Every State has the duty to refrain from the threat or use of force to violate the existing international boundaries of another State or as a means of solving international disputes, including territorial disputes and problems concerning frontiers of States.
>
> Every State likewise has the duty to refrain from the threat or use of force to violate international lines of demarcation, such as armistice lines, established by or pursuant to an international agreement to which it is a party or which it is otherwise bound to respect. Nothing in the foregoing shall be construed as prejudicing the positions of the parties concerned with regard to the status and effects of such lines under their special regimes or as affecting their temporary character.
>
> States have a duty to refrain from acts of reprisal involving the use of force.
>
> Every State has the duty to refrain from any forcible action which deprives peoples referred to in the elaboration of the principle of equal rights and self-determination of their right to self-determination and freedom and independence.
>
> Every State has the duty to refrain from organizing or encouraging the organization of irregular forces or armed bands including mercenaries, for incursion into the territory of another State.
>
> Every State has the duty to refrain from organizing, instigating, assisting or participating in acts of civil strife or terrorist acts in another State or acquiescing in organized activities within its territory directed towards the commission of such acts, when the acts referred to in the present paragraph involve a threat or use of force.
>
> The territory of a State shall not be the object of military occupation resulting from the use of force in contravention of the provisions of the Charter. The territory of a State shall not be the object of acquisition by another State resulting from the threat or use of force. No territorial acquisition resulting from the threat or use of force shall be recognized as legal.[65]

---

63. Prosecutor v. Tadic, Case No. IT-94-1-AR72, Decision on Defence Motion for Interlocutory Appeal on Jurisdiction, ¶70 (Oct. 2, 1995).
64. Declaration on Principles of International Law Concerning Friendly Relations and Co-operation Among States in Accordance with the Charter of the United Nations, G.A. Res. 25/2625, Annex, U.N. Doc. A/RES/25/2625/Annex (Oct. 24, 1970).
65. *Id.*

IV. The Use of Force

This list is certainly not exclusive, but it does give some idea as to the types of activities that constitute uses of force and threaten the territorial integrity or political independence of another State.

Another helpful document is the UNGA Resolution 3314 on the Definition of Aggression. In this resolution, the GA determined that

> Any of the following acts, regardless of a declaration of war, shall, subject to and in accordance with the provisions of article 2, qualify as an act of aggression:
>
> (a) The invasion or attack by the armed forces of a State of the territory of another State, or any military occupation, however temporary, resulting from such invasion or attack, or any annexation by the use of force of the territory of another State or part thereof;
>
> (b) Bombardment by the armed forces of a State against the territory of another State or the use of any weapons by a State against the territory of another State;
>
> (c) The blockade of the ports or coasts of a State by the armed forces of another State;
>
> (d) An attack by the armed forces of a State on the land, sea or air forces, or marine and air fleets of another State;
>
> (e) The use of armed forces of one State which are within the territory of another State with the agreement of the receiving State, in contravention of the conditions provided for in the agreement or any extension of their presence in such territory beyond the termination of the agreement;
>
> (f) The action of a State in allowing its territory, which it has placed at the disposal of another State, to be used by that other State for perpetrating an act of aggression against a third State;
>
> (g) The sending by or on behalf of a State of armed bands, groups, irregulars or mercenaries, which carry out acts of armed force against another State of such gravity as to amount to the acts listed above, or its substantial involvement therein.[66]

States that want to abide by the Charter will want to ensure that their actions stay "below the threshold of force" understood to meet the Article 2(4) prohibition. Additionally, if an action is not against the "territorial integrity or political independence" of another State, it is not a violation of Article 2(4).

During the Charter negotiations, Brazil and several other States argued that actions other than military-type actions, such as economic pressure, ought to be contemplated under this prohibition, but that idea was specifically rejected.[67]

---

66. Definition of Aggression, G.A. Res. 29/3314, Annex, U.N. Doc. A/RES/29/3314/Annex (Dec. 14, 1974).

67. Doc. 215, I/1/10, 6 U.N.C.I.O. Docs. 559 (1945). *See* Doc. 784, I/1/27, 6 U.N.C.I.O. Docs. 334-35 (1945) (Summary Report of committee meeting at which the Brazilian amendment was discussed. The San Francisco Conference that drafted the United Nations Charter was considering the prohibition on the use of force that became Article 2(4) of the Charter; it rejected by a 26-2 vote an amendment proposed by Brazil that would have added to the prohibition on the threat or use of force the words "and from the threat or use of economic measures.").

However, with the increase of modern financial dependency, the calls for a prohibition on certain levels of economic pressure are being raised again.[68]

What about some more modern forms of force that were not contemplated by the Charter signatories, such as computer network operations, or actions in space such as those taken against another State's satellites? Some scholars have argued, particularly with reference to computer operations, that if the results resemble a kinetic use of force (or one using traditional weapons that rely on heat, blast, or fragmentation for their damage) then it is a use of force. However, this is not yet a generally accepted view.

The prohibition on the use of force in Article 2(4) is not absolute. As mentioned above, rather than a prohibition, Article 2(4) creates a rebuttable presumption against the use of force. The Charter allows for three lawful methods of resort to force outside a nation's own territory. The use of force by a State is presumed illegal unless it is based on one of these three exceptions. The first method is consent by the State within whose borders that force is being used. The second enhances the principle of collective security by vesting the control of the use of force and the responsibility for the maintenance of international peace and security in the UNSC. Third, the Charter preserves the inherent right of States to act in self-defense after an armed attack until the UNSC takes necessary measures to restore peace. Each of these methods and the institutions that govern them will be discussed below.

A. Consent

Article 2(7) of the Charter states that "[n]othing contained in the present Charter shall authorize the United Nations to intervene in matters which are essentially within the domestic jurisdiction of any state or shall require the Members to submit such matters to settlement under the present Charter; but this principle shall not prejudice the application of enforcement measures under Chapter VII." This explicit recognition of state sovereignty is important for two reasons. First, it recognizes that States have the right to put down insurrections or other internal threats to the existing government. Second, it confirms the basis for the use of force by consent. If a nation requests the aid of a fellow nation or ally, that fellow nation or ally is free to use force within the boundaries of the requesting nation.[69]

The recognition that States can continue to act within their own borders to ensure their own sovereignty against internal enemies is not in doubt. However,

---

68. Andre Beirlaen, *Economic Coercion and Justifying Circumstances,* 18 Revue beige de droit international 58, 67 (1984-85) ("Several GA Resolutions consider economic coercion as an intervention in domestic affairs."); Justin D. Stalls, Note, *Economic Sanctions,* 11 U. Miami Int'l & Comp. L. Rev. 115, 134-135 (2003).

69. Office of the White House, Report on the Legal and Policy Frameworks Guiding the United States' Use of Military Force and Related National Security Operations 8, 11 (Dec. 2016) at https://obamawhitehouse.archives.gov/sites/whitehouse.gov/files/documents/Legal_Policy_Report.pdf.

even a domestic use of force against an internal threat is still subject to some degree of UNSC intervention, as will be explained below.

A recent example of the use of force by one nation in the territory of another with the consent of the second nation is the United States operation in Iraq after the establishment of the Interim Iraqi government in June of 2004. At the end of the occupation by United States forces of Iraq, as signaled by UNSCR 1546, sovereignty transitioned to the new Iraqi government, who asked for the continuance of the multinational force to work toward stability and peace.[70] A similar request was renewed by then-Iraqi Prime Minister Nouri al-Maliki in November of 2006.[71] The authority for the U.S. military to use force in the sovereign nation of Iraq, was thus based largely on the consent of the Iraqi government. This is the same basis by which the United States is taking action in Iraq against the terrorist group Daesh.[72]

B. Security Council Authorization

The UNSC is granted "primary responsibility for the maintenance of international peace and security" and member States agree to "accept and carry out the decisions of the Security Council in accordance with the present Charter." When the Charter was originally written, an "on-call" force was envisioned that would be at the disposal of the UNSC as needed. Because of the onset of the Cold War, the agreements necessary to establish this force never came into being. However, this has not prevented the UNSC from taking action with respect to the use of force. UNSC practice has been to "authorize" the use of force and then for member States to volunteer forces.

The response to the 1990 invasion of Kuwait by Iraq is an example of UNSC practice. After the invasion on August 2, 1990, the UNSC passed Resolution 660, which condemned Iraq's actions and demanded a complete and unconditional withdrawal.[73] The UNSC followed up with UNSCR 661, which imposed sanctions on Iraq and then in UNSCR 678 authorized member States to use "all necessary means" to restore international peace and security and requested all States to provide appropriate support to do so.[74]

The UNSC has taken similar actions in a number of other situations across the world and it is now clear that the UNSC can authorize the threat or use of force in order to maintain or restore international peace and security.[75]

---

70. S.C. Res. 1546, ¶¶preamble, 1, 2, Annex, U.N. Doc. S/RES/1546 (June 8, 2004).
71. UN Renews Mandate for Iraqi Troops, BBC News (Nov. 28, 2006) at http://news.bbc.co.uk/2/hi/middle_east/6193880.stm.
72. Brian Egan, International Law, Legal Diplomacy, and the Counter-ISIL Campaign, Annual Meeting of the American Society of International Law, Washington DC, April 4, 2016.
73. S.C. Res. 660, ¶¶1-2, U.N. Doc. S/RES/660 (Aug. 2, 1990).
74. S.C. Res. 661, ¶3, U.N. Doc. S/RES/661 (Aug. 6, 1990); S.C. Res. 678, ¶2, U.N. Doc. S/RES/678 (Nov. 29, 1990).
75. Office of the White House, Report on the Legal and Policy Frameworks Guiding the United States' Use of Military Force and Related National Security Operations 8 (Dec. 2016) at https://obamawhitehouse.archives.gov/sites/whitehouse.gov/files/documents/Legal_Policy_Report.pdf.

Additional examples include Haiti in 1994 (UNSCR 940 authorized States to use all necessary means to facilitate the departure from Haiti of the military leadership and to effect the prompt return of the legitimately elected President); Kosovo in 1999 (UNSCR 1244 authorized an international security force to ensure peace); and Afghanistan in 2001 (UNSCR 1368, which condemned the September 11 attacks, called on all States to work together to bring the perpetrators to justice, to redouble efforts to suppress terrorist acts, and expressed the Security Council's readiness to take all necessary steps to respond to the attacks).[76] UNSCR 1368 was followed by UNSCR 1373, which decided that all States shall prevent and suppress the financing of terrorist acts, take the necessary steps to prevent the commission of terrorist acts, and deny safe haven to terrorists.[77] Note the use of the "all necessary means" language in UNSCRs.

C. Self-Defense and Other Uses of Force

1. Self-Defense

At the end of Chapter VII is Article 51, the provision on the exercise of self-defense. Article 51 states:

> Nothing in the present Charter shall impair the inherent right of individual or collective self-defense if an armed attack occurs against a Member of the United Nations, until the Security Council has taken measures necessary to maintain international peace and security. Measures taken by Members in the exercise of this right of self-defense shall be immediately reported to the Security Council and shall not in any way affect the authority and responsibility of the Security Council under the present Charter to take at any time such action as it deems necessary in order to maintain or restore international peace and security.[78]

The content of this provision has been often relied on to support military actions,[79] and even more often debated as to its meaning and continuing validity. For example, numerous State actions have been justified by reliance on Article 51, but received simultaneous condemnation as being unlawful.

There is clearly no common understanding of the application of this article to State actions. States who argue for a broad or expansive right of self-defense generally believe that it provides greater deterrence, international stability, and ultimately less uses of force. Opponents are concerned that a broader interpretation erodes the basic prohibition against the unilateral use of force. Despite

---

76. S.C. Res. 940, ¶4, U.N. Doc. S/RES/940 (July 31, 1994); S.C. Res. 1244, ¶5, U.N. Doc. S/RES/1244 (June 10, 1999); S.C. Res. 1368, ¶¶1, 3-5, U.N. Doc. S/RES/1368 (Sept. 12, 2001).
77. S.C. Res. 1373, ¶¶1-2, U.N. Doc. S/RES/1373 (Sept. 28, 2001).
78. U.N. Charter art. 51.
79. Office of the White House, Report on the Legal and Policy Frameworks Guiding the United States' Use of Military Force and Related National Security Operations 8 (Dec. 2016) at https://obamawhitehouse.archives.gov/sites/whitehouse.gov/files/documents/Legal_Policy_Report.pdf.

this disagreement, there is general consensus on the principles that apply to a use of force in self-defense.[80]

a. Principles

Three major principles are generally accepted as governing self-defense actions under Article 51: necessity, proportional response, and timeliness. When a nation claims to have responded in self-defense, it will often be questioned on the application of these principles. One such action was the United States' response to the April 5, 1986 bombing in Berlin, Germany that destroyed the "La Belle Disco" injuring over 200 and killing 2 people, including an American serviceman. Prior to the bombing, in December 1985, Abu Nidal terrorists conducted bombings at the Rome and Vienna Airports. The Berlin bombing occurred the day after communications were intercepted between the bombers and Libyan government officials in Tripoli, indicating the bombers were acting on orders from Libya. On April 15, the United States executed Operation El Dorado Canyon. U.S. air and naval assets struck targets in and around Tripoli, including an intelligence headquarters, military bases, airfields, and suspected terrorist training camps.

President Reagan announced, "These strikes were conducted in the exercise of our right of self-defense under Article 51 of the United Nations Charter. This necessary and appropriate action was a preemptive strike . . . designed to deter acts of terrorism by Libya. . . ."[81]

(1) Necessity

The principle of necessity in the context of exercising the right to self-defense requires the nation to have an objective necessity to respond with force to an attack or threat. A number of people criticized the U.S. attack on Libya as violative of the principle of necessity because one of the targets was Qaddafi's palace. The necessity of attacking such a target seemed dubious to many observers as the palace had no obvious military benefit.

In recent years, particularly in the modern era of terrorism and its link with ungoverned or semi-governed states, a debate has arisen on how the doctrine of self-defense, and particularly the principle of necessity, applies in states that are unwilling and unable to prevent harms that initiate within their territory. For example, during the last decade the governments of Somalia and Yemen, among others, have admitted an inability to control terrorist activities occurring within their boundaries. Some argue that in cases where threats arise from territory where the sovereign is unwilling or unable to prevent external harms,

---

80. Office of the White House, Report on the Legal and Policy Frameworks Guiding the United States' Use of Military Force and Related National Security Operations 9 (Dec. 2016) at https://obamawhitehouse.archives.gov/sites/whitehouse.gov/files/documents/Legal_Policy_Report.pdf.

81. Ronald Reagan, Letter to the Speaker of the House of Representatives and the President Pro Tempore of the Senate on the United States Air Strike against Libya, 1 Pub. Papers 478 (Apr. 16, 1986).

the harmed state can of necessity exercise extraterritorial self-defense without needing the consent of the uncontrolling state.[82]

In a recent statement by Brian Egan, Legal Advisor to the United States Department of State, he confirmed that the United States has accepted this view and stated "there will be cases in which there is a reasonable and objective basis for concluding that the territorial State is unwilling or unable to effectively confront the non-State actor in its territory so that it is necessary to act in self-defense against the non-State actor in that State's territory without the territorial State's consent . . . This 'unable or unwilling' standard is, in our view, an important application of the requirement that a State, when relying on self-defense for its use of force in another State's territory, may resort to force only if it is necessary to do so—that is, if measures short of force have been exhausted or are inadequate to address the threat posed by the non-State actor emanating from the territory of another State."[83]

(2) Proportional Response

The principle of proportional response, often referred to as proportionality, requires that the force utilized in self-defense must be limited in scope, intensity, and duration to that which is reasonably necessary to counter the attack or neutralize the threat. Therefore, if the need for self-defense was occasioned by a small armed band, responding with a nuclear weapon would be disproportionate.

(3) Timeliness

The principle of timeliness means that the response must happen within some reasonable proximity in time to the hostile act. The idea is that the passage of time also may work to minimize the threat and diminish the need for self-defense. Rather than self-defense, a delayed response may look more like revenge or a reprisal. The passage of ten days from the bombing in Berlin to the response led some to criticize the United States' reliance on self-defense based upon the principle of timeliness.

A similar event occurred in Iraq in 1993. On 14 April, Kuwaiti authorities thwarted a plot to assassinate former President Bush while he was scheduled to visit Kuwait. On 26 June, the United States launched 23 missiles at Iraqi Intelligence Headquarters from ships in the Persian Gulf and Red Sea. Then-Secretary of State Albright justified the actions by saying, "We responded directly, as we are entitled to do under Article 51 of the United Nations Charter, which provides for the exercise of self-defense in such cases. Our response has

---

82. Ashley Deeks, "Unwilling or Unable": Toward a Normative Framework for Extraterritorial Self-Defense, 52 VJIL 483 (2012).

83. Brian Egan, International Law, Legal Diplomacy, and the Counter-ISIL Campaign, Annual Meeting of the American Society of International Law, Washington DC, April 4, 2016; Office of the White House, Report on the Legal and Policy Frameworks Guiding the United States' Use of Military Force and Related National Security Operations 10 (Dec. 2016) at https://obamawhitehouse.archives.gov/sites/whitehouse.gov/files/documents/Legal_Policy_Report.pdf.

been proportionate and aimed at a target directly linked to the operation against President [George H.W.] Bush."[84] In both this case, and the Eldorado Canyon operation by President Reagan, it appears the United States' timeliness element incorporates elements of preventive self-defense, as will be discussed below.

This approach was confirmed in a recent U.S. government "Report on the Legal and Policy Frameworks Guiding the United States' Use of Military Force and Related National Security Operations". The Report noted, with respect to the timeliness of responses under article 51:

> When considering whether an armed attack is imminent under the jus ad bellum for purposes of the initial use of force against another State or on its territory, the United States analyzes a variety of factors. These factors include "the nature and immediacy of the threat; the probability of an attack; whether the anticipated attack is part of a concerted pattern of continuing armed activity; the likely scale of the attack and the injury, loss, or damage likely to result therefrom in the absence of mitigating action; and the likelihood that there will be other opportunities to undertake effective action in self-defense that may be expected to cause less serious collateral injury, loss, or damage." Moreover, "the absence of specific evidence of where an attack will take place or of the precise nature of an attack does not preclude a conclusion that an armed attack is imminent for purposes of the exercise of the right of self-defense, provided that there is a reasonable and objective basis for concluding that an armed attack is imminent." Finally, as is now increasingly recognized by the international community, the traditional conception of what constitutes an "imminent" attack must be understood in light of the modern-day capabilities, techniques, and technological innovations of terrorist organizations.[85]

This broadening of the doctrine of Timeliness would presumably apply not only to actions in advance of an attack, but also actions in response to an attack that would be necessary to prevent further attacks.

b. "Inherent Right" of Self-Defense

The language of Article 51 speaks of an inherent right of self-defense. Some have argued that by using this language, Article 51 incorporated and codified the preexisting right to self-defense as it was then understood. Others have argued that the right is no more than was granted in the Charter and must, therefore, be understood in conjunction with other Charter provisions limiting the resort to force. Still others argue that there remains some right to respond in self-defense outside the Charter.

These differing viewpoints are unresolved and have all been relied on in making arguments both for and against specific uses of force in self-defense.

---

84. U.N. SCOR, 48th Sess., 3245th mtg. at 3-9, U.N. Doc. S/PV.3245 (June 27, 1993) (speech by Madeleine Albright, U.S. Permanent Representative to the United Nations).

85. Office of the White House, Report on the Legal and Policy Frameworks Guiding the United States' Use of Military Force and Related National Security Operations 9 (Dec. 2016) (footnotes omitted) at https://obamawhitehouse.archives.gov/sites/whitehouse.gov/files/documents/Legal_Policy_Report.pdf.

A nation's position on this question has a significant effect on how it interprets the use of force in self-defense, particularly in advance of a known or suspected attack. The following sections detail some specific approaches to acting in self-defense under the Charter.

(1) No Action Before Armed Attack

The language of Article 51 states that a nation can act in self-defense "if an armed attack occurs." The definition of armed attack is controversial and will be discussed below, but some argue that the use of the word "if" means that in the post-Charter world, a nation can only respond in self-defense once the attack has occurred. It is the UNSC's job to maintain international peace and security and allowing nations to act in advance of an actual attack is really just a justification for aggression. Therefore, a nation cannot attack another nation in self-defense until it has been the object of an actual armed attack and then it can do so only until the Security Council takes some action.

(2) Anticipatory Self-Defense

Other States argue that there is no requirement to wait until the actual attack has occurred, but rather that if an attack is imminent, the potential victim can act in defense by anticipating that attack and taking action in advance of the attack. Anticipatory self-defense refers to the concept that self-defense is permissible in anticipation of an armed attack. The classic statement of the requirements for anticipatory self-defense was made by U.S. Secretary of State Daniel Webster in correspondence relating to the *Caroline* affair. In 1837, British troops crossed into the United States and seized the *Caroline*, a vessel suspected of being used in attacks into Canada. The ship was set ablaze and adrift on the Niagara River. The *Caroline* grounded, broke up, and its pieces went over Niagara Falls. In response to the event, Webster wrote to British Lord Ashburton concerning self-defense in anticipation of an actual attack. Webster's famous formulation is that anticipatory self-defense should be limited to cases that "show a necessity of self-defence, instant, overwhelming, leaving no choice of means, and no moment for deliberation."[86]

State practice since the *Caroline* incident has expanded the restrictive Webster formulation of the right. In addition to the U.S. bombing of Libya mentioned above, States have relied on the doctrine of anticipatory self-defense in a number of cases. It is certainly the most well accepted of the self-defense doctrines allowing for the use of force prior to an actual armed attack.

(3) Interceptive Self-Defense

Another theory of self-defense, originating with prominent Israeli scholar Yoram Dinstein, is the idea of interceptive self-defense. Under this theory, once

---

86. Letter from Daniel Webster, U.S. Secretary of State, to Henry Fox, British Minister in Washington (Apr. 24, 1841), *in* 29 BRITISH AND FOREIGN STATE PAPERS 1138 (1857).

an attacker has "committed itself to an armed attack in an ostensibly irrevocable way,"[87] the target has the right to use force in self-defense.

This theory can be illustrated by the situation of nuclear weapons during the Cold War. Both opposing sides had strategic missiles that carried nuclear warheads. Under this theory, once a missile was launched, but had not yet landed, one could argue that the armed attack had not yet occurred. However, the nation launching the missiles had triggered an action that could no longer be recalled. Therefore, the target nation's right of self-defense had accrued.

(4) Preventive Self-Defense

Preventive self-defense is perceived by many to push the limits of State action even further. When a State acts in preventive self-defense, it acts to prevent a potential attack before it is imminent or even capable of being launched. This theory of self-defense has only recently begun to receive acceptance. In 1981, Israel launched an attack against the Osirak nuclear facility south of Baghdad, Iraq. In justifying its attack, Israel claimed, "The atomic bombs which that reactor was capable of producing whether from enriched uranium or from plutonium, would be of the Hiroshima size. Thus a mortal danger to the people of Israel progressively arose."[88] When this attack occurred in 1981, the world generally condemned it as beyond the scope of appropriate self-defense.[89]

Twenty years later, President George W. Bush clearly articulated the doctrine of preventive self-defense, or preemption, in the U.S. 2002 National Security Strategy. The Strategy states:

> We must be prepared to stop rogue states and their terrorist clients before they are able to threaten or use weapons of mass destruction against the United States and our allies and friends. . . .
>
> We must adapt the concept of imminent threat to the capabilities and objectives of today's adversaries. . . .
>
> The United States has long maintained the option of preemptive actions to counter a sufficient threat to our national security. The greater the threat, the greater is the risk of inaction—and the more compelling the case for taking anticipatory action to defend ourselves, even if uncertainty remains as to the time and place of the enemy's attack. To forestall or prevent such hostile acts by our adversaries, the United States will, if necessary, act preemptively.[90]

Some have discussed this theory as applying at the last point at which a State can effectively intervene. Take, for example, a terrorist group meeting to get their final instructions before launching an attack, including details of how the coordinated attack is to transpire, and then will not meet together again until after the attack. Attacking the group at that point in time, even though the

---

87. YORAM DINSTEIN, WAR, AGGRESSION, AND SELF-DEFENSE 191 (4th ed. 2005).
88. Statement by the Government of Israel on the Bombing of the Iraqi Nuclear Facility (June 8, 1981).
89. S.C. Res. 487, ¶1, U.N. Doc. S/RES/487 (June 19, 1981).
90. U.S. National Security Council, *National Security Strategy* (Sept. 2002), *available at* http://georgewbush-whitehouse.archives.gov/nsc/nss/2002/nss5.html (last visited Apr. 25, 2011).

attack is far from imminent, might be the last time the target State can successfully intervene.

The international community is dramatically split on this notion of self-defense, but it is clear that some States have already justified the use of armed force against another State under this theory.

c. Collective Self-Defense

In addition to individual self-defense, Article 51 also recognizes the right to collective self-defense. Many mutual assistance treaties exist that enshrine the collective right to self-defense. Perhaps the most well-known is the North Atlantic Treaty. Article 5 states:

> The Parties agree that an armed attack against one or more of them in Europe or North America shall be considered an attack against them all and consequently they agree that, if such an armed attack occurs, each of them, in exercise of the right of individual or collective self-defence recognised by Article 51 of the Charter of the United Nations, will assist the Party or Parties so attacked by taking forthwith, individually and in concert with the other Parties, such action as it deems necessary, including the use of armed force, to restore and maintain the security of the North Atlantic area.[91]

However, the exercise of collective self-defense is not unlimited. In the ICJ's *Nicaragua* case discussed above, the Court refused to acknowledge the United States' claim to collective self-defense because El Salvador had not officially requested such help. The Court stated:

> It is also clear that it is the State which is the victim of an armed attack which must form and declare the view that it has been so attacked. There is no rule in customary international law permitting another State to exercise the right of collective self-defence on the basis of its own assessment of the situation. Where collective self-defence is invoked, it is to be expected that the State for whose benefit this right is used will have declared itself to be the victim of an armed attack.[92]

This ICJ case, as with every case, is only binding between the Parties, and the United States did not take part in the actual case, casting even greater doubt on the importance of the decision. However, many States accept the principle that the right of collective self-defense may only be invoked by the State experiencing the armed attack.

d. Armed Attack

As Article 51 clearly states, whatever right of self-defense a nation might rely on, a response involving the use of force is not triggered unless the attack is an "armed attack." Once again, there is no agreed definition of what equates to

---

91. North Atlantic Treaty art. 5, Apr. 4, 1949, 63 Stat. 2241, 34 U.N.T.S. 243, *available at* http://www.nato.int/cps/en/natolive/official_texts_17120.htm (last visited Apr. 25, 2011).
92. Military and Paramilitary Activities (Nicar. v. U.S.), 1986 I.C.J. 14, 195 (June 27).

an armed attack. There is discussion both as to what counts as "armed" and as to what constitutes an attack. For instance, could a computer network attack equate to "armed" or does it require heat, blast, and fragmentation? Despite this lack of clarity, States seem to agree that not all armed military actions equate to an armed attack. The ICJ confirmed this in the *Nicaragua* case. The ICJ decided that Nicaragua's provision of arms to the opposition in El Salvador was not an armed attack.[93]

Additionally, there are unresolved questions about the application of new technologies, such as cyber operations, to armed attack. It is still unclear what level of offensive cyber operations against a State will constitute an armed attack. Some scholars have argued that the decision should be based on the effects of the cyberattack,[94] but the law is still unclear and States have been hesitant to commit themselves to clear rules.

The United States has taken a somewhat unique approach to the definition of armed attack. Virtually all other nations think "armed attack" is different from a "use of force" that is prohibited under Article 2(4). In their view, an armed attack is more severe, creating a gap between the two types of actions. In other words, in this view, a state might commit a use of force that would be illegal under international law but not give rise to the right to self-defense if the use of force did not also meet the definitional requirements to be considered an armed attack as well. For actions in that "gap," the victim state would have to rely on the UNSC to take action or respond with countermeasures or other measures that did not amount to a use of force.

In the view of the United States, recently reiterated by then-Department of State Legal Advisor Harold Koh, "the United States has for a long time taken the position that the inherent right of self-defense potentially applies against *any* illegal use of force. In our view, there is no threshold for a use of deadly force to qualify as an "armed attack" that may warrant a forcible response."[95] In other words, the United States understands the terms "use of force" and "armed attack" to be synonymous. Under this view, there is no "gap." Rather, the United States will respond to any illegal "use of force" in self-defense.

e. "Until the Security Council Has Taken Measures"

As the text of Article 51 notes, a nation has the right to respond to an armed attack in self-defense "until the Security Council has taken measures necessary to maintain international peace and security." The meaning of this language in practice is still unclear. The plain meaning at least seems to remove

---

93. *Id.* ¶230.

94. Michael N. Schmitt, *Computer Network Attack and the Use of Force in International Law: Thoughts on a Normative Framework*, 37 COLUM. J. TRANSNAT'L L. 885, 915-916 (1999).

95. Remarks, Harold Hongju Koh, Legal Advisor U.S. Department of State, USCYBERCOM Inter-Agency Legal Conference, Ft. Meade, MD (September 18, 2012), available at http://www.state.gov/s/l/releases/remarks/197924.htm.

the authority granted to a nation under self-defense, once the Security Council has taken action that has effectively restored international peace and security.[96]

For example, it is certainly possible that once an armed attack occurs or is even threatened, the UNSC could pass a resolution notifying the target State that the UNSC is seized of the issue and that the State's ability to act under Article 51 has been preempted by the UNSC's authority under Chapter VII. Many States, including the United States, take the view that for the UNSC to remove the right of self-defense, it must take "effective" action, and that the right to self-defense would remain until peace had been restored.[97]

2. Other Uses of Force

Along with self-defense of the nation, there are other justifications for threatening or using force without consent or UNSC approval that are rooted in self-defense or defense of others but that are not necessarily accepted as part of one of the theories above.

a. Protection of Nationals

Nations have also claimed the right to exercise self-defense on behalf of their nationals abroad. Some modern views place this doctrine within the Article 51 right of self-defense. Others believe that since this right was exercised prior to the promulgation of the UN Charter, it is part of the customary "inherent" right that survives outside the Charter provisions.[98] Either way, there are numerous modern exercises of force based on the right of a nation to protect its own nationals, even when within the sovereign territory of another state.

As a matter of international law, the State in which the nationals reside has the primary responsibility for providing protection for all persons within its territory, and it would only be in cases in which that State was unable or unwilling to provide protection that another State would be justified in intervening. This normally arises in the context of hostage situations or general unrest in the host country where the nationals' security is no longer assured. Ostensibly, the threat or use of force to protect a State's nationals requires similar justifications as other customary forms of self-defense discussed above, but applied to individuals.

Often this use of force is exercised through a "non-combatant evacuation operation" or NEO. In an NEO, the host-nation government is usually collapsed or incapable of sustaining peace and order and the sending nation(s) determines that it needs to evacuate its non-essential nationals from the area. This is usually coordinated from the sending nation's embassy and is a voluntary evacuation for non-sending nation government personnel.

---

96. THE CHARTER OF THE UNITED NATIONS (Bruno Simma et al. eds.) 1401-02 (3ed 2012).
97. Tom Ruys, "Armed Attack" and Article 51 of the UN Charter: Evolutions in Customary Law and Practice 77 (2010).
98. U.S. Department of Defense, Law of War Manual (2015) (revised Dec. 2016), available at https://www.defense.gov/Portals/1/Documents/pubs/DoD%20Law%20of%20War%20Manual%20-%20June%202015%20Update%20Dec%2016.pdf?ver=2016-12-13-172036-190 (hereinafter DoD Law Manual (Dec. 2016)).

There have been many NEOs in the past two decades. One example is the NEO from Sierra Leone in 1997. As the security in Sierra Leone deteriorated in May 1997, the United States worked with other sending nations to evacuate their nationals. By the end of June 1997, the United States had moved over 450 U.S. citizens and more than 2,000 nationals of other States from Sierra Leone aboard the USS *Kearsarge* to Guinea for safety and repatriation. NEOs are generally well accepted in international law.

Sometimes, the exercise of protection of nationals is not as peaceful as a NEO. For example, in 1983, after the fall of the government of Grenada and the seizure of power by a military council, the United States and several other Caribbean nations sent troops to Grenada to restore peace and protect nationals that were currently in Grenada. The United States justified its actions by claiming that there was a real risk that a group of U.S. medical students who were studying in Grenada at the time could be taken hostage in the ongoing conflict. In order to protect its nationals, the United States used force in self-defense. In response, the UNGA passed a resolution by a vote of 108 to 9, with 27 abstentions, deeply deploring the "armed intervention" by the United States.[99]

b. Humanitarian Intervention and the Responsibility to Protect

Although not universally recognized, some States contend that there exists a right to intervene within the territory of another State (without that State's consent, and without UNSC authorization) in order to prevent certain large-scale atrocities or deprivations. The argument is that such intervention does not violate Article 2(4) because the purpose is not to affect the territorial integrity or political independence of the State, but rather to prevent a humanitarian disaster. This theory of use of force has gained greater adherence with the rise of human rights as a force in international law.

Because humanitarian intervention is based in human rights and not meant to affect the political independence or territorial integrity of the host nation, the intervening State bears the heavy burden of proving its "pure motive." Any aggressive perceptions or self-serving designs will undermine the legitimacy of the intervention.

The North Atlantic Treaty Organization's (NATO) actions in Kosovo supply a potential example of humanitarian intervention. While the United States has not adopted this reasoning, several other European States have accepted it as the basis for actions in Kosovo.[100] Beginning in 1997, violent clashes erupted between the Kosovars and the Serbians in Kosovo. The situation escalated, creating tens of thousands of refugees. Many international organizations involved themselves in the problem and urged both sides to seek peaceful solutions. By September 1998, the United Nations estimated that there were 200,000 refugees.

---

99. G.A. Res. 38/7, ¶1, U.N. Doc. A/RES/38/7 (Nov. 2, 1983).
100. William H. Taft IV, Legal Adviser, Department of State, *Role and Significance of International Law Governing the Use of Force in the New Global Context Confronting the United States After 9/11: remarks regarding the use of force under international law* (Oct. 27, 2004).

From the beginning of the Kosovo crisis, the UNSC was "seized" of the issue and passed numerous resolutions dealing with the situation in Kosovo. UNSCR 1199 in September 1998 was especially important and demanded an immediate cease-fire, withdrawal of military and paramilitary forces, complete access for humanitarian organizations, and cooperation on the investigation of war crimes in Kosovo.[101] Belgrade maintained that this was a purely internal matter under Article 2(7) of the UN Charter and that the international community should not get involved.

After no response to UNSCR 1199, NATO decided to take action. Though not specifically authorized by UNSCR 1199, NATO issued an ultimatum to Belgrade, which was followed by a partial withdrawal of Serbian forces and the insertion of UN representatives to verify compliance with the ultimatum. Belgrade continued to resist negotiation efforts, claiming that the conflict in Kosovo was an internal matter. In March 1999, NATO began a bombing campaign that lasted 11 weeks. By the end of the bombing, over 800,000 people were displaced and thousands had been killed. The UNSC issued Resolution 1244 in June, which created a multinational force to ensure the peace and provide an environment for reconstruction.[102]

Despite what some argue was a ratification of the actions of NATO's humanitarian intervention, the international community is still deeply divided on the legality of humanitarian intervention. In the aftermath of Kosovo, Canada (with backing from the UN) created the International Commission on Intervention and State Sovereignty. In 2001, the Commission issued a report that first coined the term "Responsibility to Protect" (R2P). Many see R2P as the theoretical successor of humanitarian intervention, though this view is not universal.

In 2004, the UN High Level Panel on Threats, Challenges and Change issued a report titled *A More Secure World: Our Shared Responsibility*, in which it stated that "there is a growing acceptance that while sovereign Governments have the primary responsibility to protect their own citizens from such catastrophes, when they are unable or unwilling to so do that responsibility should be taken up by the wider international community."[103] This finding was subsequently endorsed by the UN Secretary-General, adopted by the UN General Assembly in 2005,[104] and referred to approvingly by the Security Council.[105] However, acceptance of these documents does not equal either agreement as to its meaning or as to its applicability.

Generally, R2P[106] is based on three pillars: (1) The domestic State carries the primary responsibility for the protection of its population from mass atrocities;

---

101. S.C. Res. 1199, ¶¶1, 4, 13, U.N. Doc. S/RES/1199 (Sept. 23, 1998).

102. S.C. Res. 1244, ¶5, U.N. Doc. S/RES/1244 (June 10, 1999).

103. A More Secure World: Our Shared Responsibility, Report of the High-Level Panel on Threats, Challenges and Change, ¶201, U.N. Doc. A/59/565 (Dec. 2, 2004), *available at* www.un.org/secureworld/report.pdf.

104. 2005 World Summit Outcome, U.N. Doc. A/RES/60/1 (Oct. 24, 2005).

105. S.C. Res. 1674, U.N. Doc. S/RES/1674 (Apr. 28, 2006).

106. For an excellent discussion on R2P, *see* Carsten Stahn, *Responsibility to Protect: Legal Rhetoric or Emerging Legal Norm?*, 101 AM. J. INT'L L. 99 (2007).

(2) the international community has a responsibility to assist States in fulfilling this responsibility; and (3) the international community should use appropriate domestic, humanitarian, and other peaceful means to protect populations from these crimes. If a State fails to protect its populations or is in fact the perpetrator of these crimes, the international community must be prepared to take stronger measures, including the collective use of force as approved by the UN Security Council. Note that pillar 3 requires Security Council approval before a use of force. Some who see this as the successor to humanitarian intervention are not convinced that Security Council approval is necessary.

On March 17, 2011, in response to the situation in Libya, the UNSC passed Resolution 1973.[107] Based on a deteriorating situation where Libyan State forces were killing civilians who were attempting to overthrow the Qaddafi regime, the UNSCR authorized "all necessary measures" to "protect civilians and civilian populated areas."[108] The UNSCR further implemented a no-fly zone, an arms embargo, and an asset freeze.[109]

Many have claimed that this is the UNSC's first exercise of R2P. Given the language of the UNSCR, it seems very similar to the justification for humanitarian intervention used in Kosovo, and seems to comply with the three pillars analysis. To some, this raises questions about the overall validity of humanitarian intervention and R2P as acceptable uses of force, outside the Charter. Since the UNSC has authorized an R2P, does that now mean that such actions are only valid with UNSC authorization? Or does it mean that R2P is now viewed as a valid use of force, with or without UNSC authorization?

The answers to these questions are unclear as of now. However, the actions in Libya will undoubtedly be the cause of much discussion over the next few years before we know exactly what it all means for international law and the law of armed conflict (LOAC).

D. Some Contemporary Challenges

1. Non-State Actors

Contemporary issues surrounding the legal basis for the use of force have been especially prevalent since the attacks on September 11, 2001. One of the most interesting from the standpoint of this chapter is the use of force against non-state actors. After the September 11 attacks, the UNSC passed Resolution 1368, which connected self-defense under Article 51 to terrorist attacks from non-state actors.[110] This was followed by NATO nations invoking Article 5 of the NATO Treaty, allowing for collective defense from the terrorist attacks. Many governments and scholars understood these actions to be a clear confirmation that a State has a right to respond to armed attacks from non-state actors under

---

107. S.C. Res. 1973, U.N. Doc. S/RES/1973 (Mar. 17, 2011).
108. *Id.* ¶4.
109. *Id.* ¶¶6, 13, 19.
110. S.C. Res. 1368, U.N. Doc. S/RES/1368 (Sept. 12, 2001).

Article 51. The United States confirmed this approach in its recent Department of Defense Law of War Manual.[111]

However, the ICJ seemed to take a different approach. In two particular cases (both mentioned above), the 1999 *Armed Activities on the Territory of the Congo* and the 2003 Advisory Opinion on the *Legal Consequences of the Construction of a Wall in the Occupied Palestinian Territory*,[112] the ICJ held that an armed attack can only come from States or from State-sponsored armed groups. As stated above, this appears to directly contradict the UNSC and State practice. Recent actions against the non-state actor known as Daesh appear to confirm the view that States will act against non-state actors in self-defense. In particular, while U.S., French, and UK forces are attacking Daesh forces and equipment in Iraq with the consent of the Iraqi government, Syria has not given similar authority and the U.S., France, and the UK continue to conduct military operations within Syria's sovereign territory. In addition to the United States and the United Kingdom, several other nations have provided Article 51 letters to the United Nations Security Council explaining that their actions in Syria are taken in self-defense, including Australia,[113] Belgium,[114] and Germany.[115]

It is unclear how this will be resolved, but it seems unlikely that States will refrain from exercising their self-defense right merely because the attack comes from a non-state actor such as an armed terrorist group.

Another interesting consideration with respect to non-state actors, particularly global terrorist networks, is determining when the armed conflict has ended. This question has become more focused, given the continuing reliance as a matter of domestic law on the 2001 "Authorization to Use Military Force" by the United States to fight Daesh.[116] The United States has responded by saying:

> At a certain point, the United States will degrade and dismantle the operational capacity and supporting networks of terrorist organizations like al-Qa'ida to such an extent that they will have been effectively destroyed and will no longer be able to attempt or launch a strategic attack against the United States. At that point, there will no longer be an ongoing armed conflict between the United States and those forces.[117]

---

111. U.S. Department of Defense, Law of War Manual (2015) (revised Dec. 2016), available at https://www.defense.gov/Portals/1/Documents/pubs/DoD%20Law%20of%20War%20Manual%20-%20June%202015%20Update%20Dec%2016.pdf?ver=2016-12-13-172036-190 (hereinafter DoD Law Manual (Dec. 2016)).

112. These opinions can be found at the ICJ website, http://www.icj-cij.org.

113. Australia's article 51 letter states "These operations are not directed against Syria or the Syrian people, nor do they entail support for the Syrian regime. When undertaking such military operations, Australia will abide by its obligations under international law."

114. Belgium's Article 51 letter states "Those measures are directed against the so-called 'Islamic State in Iraq and the Levant' and not against the Syrian Arab Republic."

115. Germany's Article 51 letter states "These measures are directed against ISIL, not against the Syrian Arab Republic."

116. Office of the White House, Report on the Legal and Policy Frameworks Guiding the United States' Use of Military Force and Related National Security Operations 3-7 (Dec. 2016) at https://obamawhitehouse.archives.gov/sites/whitehouse.gov/files/documents/Legal_Policy_Report.pdf.

117. Office of the White House, Report on the Legal and Policy Frameworks Guiding the United States' Use of Military Force and Related National Security Operations 11-12 (Dec. 2016) at https://obamawhitehouse.archives.gov/sites/whitehouse.gov/files/documents/Legal_Policy_Report.pdf.

At some point in the future, the United States will declare the fight with "al-Qa'ida, the Taliban, and associated forces" is over, and that will provide more clarity on at least one view of this difficult issue.

2. Drones

One of the topics causing the most controversy recently has been the use of drones, both in and out of geographic combat areas. Since September 11, the United States has dramatically increased its use of drones in tracking but also attacking suspected terrorists. Many of these attacks have occurred within a recognized combat zone and the legality of these attacks will be discussed below in the chapter on targeting. However, many of these attacks have also occurred outside the active theater of combat, and have drawn criticism from both governments and scholars.

The basic issue is what authority the United States relies on to attack a terrorist in another sovereign country. Clearly, if that State consents, there is no problem. Additionally, if the UNSC authorized such attacks, they would also be legal. However, it seems clear that at least some of the attacks have not fallen within these two exceptions and the United States has relied on Article 51 to provide the basis for these attacks. The recent attack on Taliban leader Mullah Omar is such an example. It appears clear that Pakistan had not given its permission, but the United States took military action anyway.[118]

> Critics of these attacks argue, among other things, that responses to terrorism are better understood as law enforcement actions rather than military actions and that Article 51's authorization for using force is geographically constrained to only active theaters of operations. They further argue that the use of drones is disproportionate and also a poor policy choice as it creates more enemies than it kills.[119] However, after criticizing President Bush's methods in the war against al Qaeda, President Obama has actually increased the number of drone attacks during his administration and defends his decision as both legal and the best policy, including those executed without the consent of the territorial nation.[120] The current U.S. policy was again stated by Brian Egan, Department of State legal advisor, at a recent conference of the American Society of International Law. I'd also like to say a few words on how

---

118. Pakistan Says the U.S. Drone Strike That Killed Taliban Leader Violated its Sovereignty, theguardian (May 22, 2016) at https://www.theguardian.com/world/2016/may/22/pakistan-us-drone-strike-taliban-violated-its-sovereignty.

119. For exploration of these perspectives, *see* various readings and video recording of the debate as part of the Washington University Law, Whitney R. Harris World Law Institute Debate Series: Are U.S. Drone Attacks in the "War on Terror" Lawful? Do They Make for Sound Foreign Policy? (Oct. 8, 2010), *available at* http://law.wustl.edu/harris/pages.aspx?id=8325 (last visited Apr. 25, 2011).

120. Harold Koh, *The Obama Administration and International Law* (Mar. 25, 2010), *available at* http://www.state.gov/s/l/releases/remarks/139119.htm (last visited Apr. 25, 2011); Peter Baker, *Obama's War Over Terror*, N.Y. Times Mag., Jan. 4, 2010, *available at* http://www.nytimes.com/2010/01/17/magazine/17Terror-t.html (last visited Apr. 25, 2011) (over 50 drone strikes launched in 2009); Scott Shane & Eric Schmitt, *C.I.A. Deaths Prompt Surge in Drone Strikes*, N.Y. Times, Jan. 23, 2010, at A1, *available at* http://www.nytimes.com/2010/01/23/world/asia/23drone.html (last visited Apr. 25, 2011) (over 10 drone strikes in one month kill 90 people in Pakistan).

State sovereignty and consent factor into the international legal analysis when considering the use of force. President Obama has made clear that "America cannot take [drone] strikes wherever we choose; our actions are bound by consultations with partners, and respect for state sovereignty." This is true of our operations against ISIL as it has been true in our non-international armed conflict against al-Qa'ida and associated forces.

Indeed, under the jus ad bellum, the international legal basis for the resort to force in self-defense on another State's territory takes into account State sovereignty. The international law of self-defense requires that such uses of force be necessary to address the threat giving rise to the right to use force in the first place. States therefore must consider whether unilateral actions in self-defense that would impinge on a territorial State's sovereignty are necessary or whether it might be possible to secure the territorial State's consent before using force on its territory against a non-State actor. In other words, international law not only requires a State to analyze whether it has a legal basis for the use of force against a particular non-State actor—which I'll call the "against whom" question—but also requires a State to analyze whether it has a legal basis to use force against that non-State actor in a particular location—which I'll call the "where" question.

It is with respect to this "where" question that international law requires that States must either determine that they have the relevant government's consent or, if they must rely on self-defense to use force against a non-State actor on another State's territory, determine that the territorial State is "unable or unwilling" to address the threat posed by the non-State actor on its territory. In practice, States generally rely on the consent of the relevant government in conducting operations against ISIL or other non-State actors even when they may also have a self-defense basis to use force against those non-State actors, and this consent often takes the form of a request for assistance from a government that is itself engaged in an armed conflict against the relevant group.[121]

3. Cyber Operations

As alluded to earlier in this chapter, one of the most vexing issues in the area of legal bases for the use of force is the use of cyber capabilities. It is clear that most nations now have or are developing an offensive cyber capability and many non-state actors are also trying to do so. There are very few actual statements as to what various nations think about the use of cyber weapons and how they will be treated. The U.S. Department of Defense Office of General Counsel issued a statement in 1999 that is very vague and provides little actual guidance.[122] More recently, various members of the United Nations have begun meeting together to discuss the issue and gather input from States but the reports have been similarly unclear.[123]

---

121. Brian Egan, International Law, Legal Diplomacy, and the Counter-ISIL Campaign, Annual Meeting of the American Society of International Law, Washington DC, April 4, 2016.
122. OFFICE OF GENERAL COUNSEL, DEPARTMENT OF DEFENSE, *An Assessment of International Legal Issues in Information Operations* (Nov 1999).
123. *See* United Nations, Department of Economic and Social Affairs: World Summit on the Information Society in New York, United States (Dec. 14, 2010) (discussing the future of internet

In 2008, a group of experts was convened in connection with Estonia's Cooperative Cyber Defense Center of Excellence to write a Manual on International Law Applicable to Cyber Conflict. This Manual provides an analysis of the current international law with respect to cyber operations, mostly in situations of LOAC, but also talks briefly about the *jus in bello*. A similar group subsequently met in Tallinn and has produced a new manual that focuses almost exclusively on *jus in bello* rules. These Manuals provide interesting and helpful analysis but lack the power of actual statements by governments to create state practice.

As demonstrated in the Tallinn Manuals, scholars and practitioners will continue to debate what uses of a cyber weapon would actually constitute an attack or would remain below the threshold of a use of force. The predominant theory, best articulated by Michael Schmitt, is that if a computer network operation has similar consequences to other proscribed uses of force, then the computer operation is also likely a use of force.[124] Many States and non-state actors are already actively engaged in offensive cyber operations as evidenced by numerous recent events, including those in Estonia and Georgia.[125] However, until there is some international agreement on the issue or sufficient State practice to generalize a rule, this area remains unclear.

Study Questions

On the next page are some questions concerning the use of force. When considering these questions, assume the situation is as it is today with current law and technology.

---

governance); International Telecommunications Union, Plenipotentiary Conference in Guadalajara, Mexico (Oct. 4-22, 2010) (disagreement over whether the internet should be brought under the control of intergovernmental organizations); John Markoff, *Step Taken to End Impasse over Cybersecurity Talks*, N.Y. Times, July 17, 2010, at A7, *available at* http://www.nytimes.com/2010/07/17/world/17cyber.html?_r=1 (last visited Apr. 25, 2011); U.N. Secretary-General, *Note by the Secretary-General on the Group of Governmental Experts on Developments in the Field of Information and Telecommunications in the Context of International Security*, ¶7, delivered to the General Assembly, U.N. Doc. A/65/201 (July 30, 2010) (Fifteen countries, including the United States, China, and Russia, agreed to a set of recommendations aimed at improving international cooperation regarding cybersecurity and discussed use of offensive cyber warfare capabilities.); U.N. News Service, *Experts at UN-backed Meeting Lay Foundation for Global Cybersecurity Roadmap* (Oct. 8, 2007), *available at* http://www.un.org/apps/news/printnewsAr.asp?nid=24221 (last visited Apr. 25, 2011).

124. Schmitt, *supra*, note 94, at 911-916.

125. Eric Talbot Jensen, *Cyberwarfare and Precautions Against the Effects of Attacks*, 88 Tex. L. Rev. 1533, 1540-1541 (2010); Wing Commander Duncan Blake & Lieutenant Colonel Joseph S. Imburgia, *"Bloodless Weapons"? The Need to Conduct Legal Reviews of Certain Capabilities and the Implications of Defining Them as "Weapons,"* 66 A.F. L. Rev. 157, 182-183 (2010); Lieutenant Colonel Patrick W. Franzese, *Sovereignty in Cyberspace: Can it Exist?*, 64 A.F. L. Rev. 1, 4 (2009); Lieutenant Colonel Joshua E. Kastenberg, *Non-Intervention and Neutrality in Cyberspace: An Emerging Principle in the National Practice of International Law*, 64 A.F. L. Rev. 43, 45-46 (2009); Major Graham H. Todd, *Armed Attack in Cyberspace: Deterring Asymmetric Warfare with an Asymmetric Definition*, 64 A.F. L. Rev. 65, 91 (2009); Major Arie J. Schaap, *Cyber Warfare Operations: Development and Use Under International Law*, 64 A.F. L. Rev. 121, 124 (2009).

1. In the Scenario, subsequent to the meeting between the Secretary of State and his legal advisor, you were tasked to present the legal options for the Secretary's consideration concerning the use of force against Iraq.
   (a) Is there a legal basis for the United States to take action?
   (b) Which bases are most compelling?
   (c) What should the Secretary recommend?
2. Assume the President ultimately decides to go to the UNSC prior to taking action.
   (a) What are the UNSC's options?
   (b) What language should the United States try to get into a resolution?
3. Assume the President alternatively decides to take action under Article 51.
   (a) Under what theories can he justify his use of force?
   (b) Which are most likely to be accepted as legitimate?
   (c) Must the President take any actions with respect to the Security Council if he decides to act?
4. If the President determines to not use force, what actions might the President take that are "below the threshold" of a use of force?
5. Assume the President decides to not take action against the State of Iraq.
   (a) Can he still take action against elements of al-Qaeda inside Iraq?
   (b) If so, what is his best theory for action?

2 | History, Sources, and Principles of the Law of Armed Conflict

You are a military lawyer who has been assigned to the planning cell of the U.S. Army's V Corps to provide legal support as the military staff begins contingency planning for the invasion of Iraq. As you discuss the various courses of military action, you are asked to brief the cell regarding the international law that might apply to the operation and in particular the legal obligations of U.S. forces. In your view, these obligations could impose limitations on the conduct of the operation and need to be clearly understood up front to guide the development of potential courses of action to execute combat operations in Iraq.

The challenge before you is to present the law to your colleagues in a way that is most useful. The cell consists of military and civilian personnel with expertise in the planning and execution of combat and peacekeeping operations. The staff includes subject matter experts in a wide range of military skills, such as maneuver, fire support (e.g., artillery), combat air support, combat engineering, detention operations, intelligence, logistics, and medical support. None of them are lawyers, though all the military members have been briefed on the humanitarian goals of the law of armed conflict (LOAC) over the course of their military careers and are generally familiar with its principles. Their primary interest at this time is to understand the specific requirements applicable to this mission and to ensure that the plan they develop complies with all legal obligations and emphasizes those particularly relevant to specific tasks assigned to subordinate units.

You participated in the briefing to the commander on the general concept of the operation. You then immerse yourself in the planning process by meeting with each staff element responsible for planning the operation to better understand what issues will be raised during operational execution. Based on the "Warning Order" issued by higher headquarters, your commander envisions a rapid, intensive attack against the Iraqi targets, synchronizing the efforts of ground, air, and sea power to rapidly neutralize and destroy Iraqi military forces, followed immediately by operations to restore public services and participate in the military occupation of Iraq pending transfer to civilian authorities.

Because a significant element of the Iraqi military, including its leadership, are located in urban areas, the cell knows that there will be substantial risk of civilian casualties and damage to civilian property, which they must plan carefully to minimize. They also understand that opposing Iraqi forces may attempt to melt into the population to continue their opposition and to organize civilians into guerilla bands to resist U.S. forces. At the same time, because the cell is expecting U.S. forces to prevail, they anticipate taking prisoners, and holding them for some period after hostilities, as well as providing for the security and stability of Iraq. If necessary, violations of the LOAC, whether by Iraqi or Coalition forces, will need to be investigated and punished, and in any case, measures need to be taken in advance to ensure LOAC compliance by U.S. forces and the forces working with them.

You quickly conclude that because of the broad range of activities encompassed by this operation, you will need to brief the cell on the full range of U.S. legal obligations under the LOAC, while translating those obligations into practical terms that non-lawyers can appreciate and understand. As an initial matter, it will be important to stress the key principles of the LOAC, as well as the legal obligations applicable to the U.S. military operations under both treaty and customary law. It must be clearly understood that, while many obligations are expressed today in treaties, the treaties reflect core principles and customary law that may apply even in situations that do not fall squarely within the scope of the treaties. Therefore, your briefing must cover these principles as well. Further, you recognize that the guidance issued by commanders must be tailored to the operation, as reflected in "rules of engagement" that your team will help draft. Therefore, you need to clearly explain how the LOAC interacts with operational art in the preparation of these rules.

I. The LOAC Tradition

All civilizations have developed rules limiting violence in war, and we can trace such rules far back in human history. Up until the middle of the nineteenth century, these rules were based exclusively on tradition and custom, and they were respected for the following reasons:

- They reflected the requirements of military honor, embodied in chivalry codes that existed in various parts of the world;
- They had been recognized for generations;
- They were deemed necessary to prevent a drift toward unlimited violence in war; and
- They reflected religious tenets and were believed to comply with the orders of the divinity.

Such customary rules have existed for centuries, whereas the codification of the LOAC is, by comparison, a fairly recent process.[1]

---

1. François Bugnion, Director for Int'l Law and Cooperation Within the Movement, ICRC, Customary Int'l Humanitarian Law, Presentation to Council of Delegates, Seoul, Korea (Nov. 16-19, 2005), *available at* http://www.icrc.org/eng/resources/documents/statement/statement-customary-law-161105.htm.

I. The LOAC Tradition

As stated in the U.S. Army's seminal 1956 Field Manual on The Law of Land Warfare, the LOAC,

> ... is inspired by the desire to diminish the evils of war by:
> a. Protecting both combatants and noncombatants from unnecessary suffering;
> b. Safeguarding certain fundamental human rights of persons who fall into the hands of the enemy, particularly prisoners of war, the wounded and sick, and civilians; and
> c. Facilitating the restoration of peace.[2]

While today we have detailed rules for the conduct of hostilities and the protection of the victims of armed conflict, a systematic articulation of these rules into codes and treaties really did not begin until the nineteenth century. Prior to that time, rules to regulate the conduct of hostilities and the treatment of persons not participating in the fighting generally were found only in the customs and code of ethics followed by military professionals. However, as conflicts expanded in scope and violence in the nineteenth and twentieth century and armies expanded to include a greater number of conscripts, the need for written rules increased.

It is the purpose of this chapter to describe the sources that form the LOAC today, including its core principles. As you will see, these sources extend beyond simply a set of LOAC treaties, although treaties are a key part of the LOAC, and include basic principles and customary international law that apply to all armed conflicts and that may parallel treaty law (with the treaty being simply a tangible expression of the principle or tenet of customary law). The principles and customary law may apply the rules in a treaty to situations not explicitly covered by the treaty (for example, by applying a treaty rule that was written for international armed conflicts (IACs) to situations of non-international conflict (NIAC) as well).

The challenge for the practitioner is to take all these sources and apply them in a manner pertinent to the conflict or operation at hand. As discussed elsewhere in this book, the trigger for the LOAC is "armed conflict".[3] In practical terms, this means situations in which the dominant feature is the use of military force, either to target or detain someone, with little time for contemplation of alternatives or consultation with others. Therefore, the military practitioner needs to translate complex rules based on diverse sources into clear and understandable guidance for military forces. Similarly, those communicating with armed forces to advocate in favor of the application of humanitarian rules (such as human rights advocates) need to explain their position in clear terms, grounded in all applicable sources, if they are to be persuasive.

In short, it is important to keep in mind that the LOAC requires implementation by combatants on the ground, in the air (and in space), and on (and

---

2. U.S. Dep't of Army, Field Manual 27-10, The Law of Land Warfare para. 2(a) (18 July 1956) (hereinafter FM 27-10).
3. *See infra*, ch. 3.

under) the sea. These individuals typically are not lawyers, and therefore the rules need to be put into a context that they can easily understand. The following excerpt, taken from a U.S. military manual, provides a good example of how the core LOAC principles and rules have been translated into terms that military personnel will readily appreciate. It reflects the long tradition within the LOAC of regulating armed conflict through the use of straightforward and comparatively simple standards of conduct for armed forces to follow.

> The law of war principles . . . can be safely applied by Soldiers and Marines by adhering to the following ten basic rules:
> - Soldiers and Marines fight only enemy combatants.
> - Soldiers and Marines do not harm enemies who surrender. They disarm them and turn them over to their superiors.
> - Soldiers and Marines do not kill or torture enemy prisoners of war or detainees.
> - Soldiers and Marines collect and care for the wounded, whether friend or foe.
> - Soldiers and Marines do not attack medical personnel, facilities, or equipment.
> - Soldiers and Marines destroy no more than the mission requires.
> - Soldiers and Marines treat all civilians humanely.
> - Soldiers and Marines do not steal. They respect private property and possessions.
> - Soldiers and Marines do their best to prevent violations of the law of war.
> - Soldiers and Marines report all violations of the law of war to their superior.[4]

An Example from the Gulf War

In February 1991, Captain Rich Whitaker, a young 30-year-old U.S. Army JAG officer, was living in a dirt hole with a scrap of canvas pulled over it, like his fellow officers who manned the 327th Infantry Regiment Tactical Operations Center. The "TOC" was hidden along with the entire regiment of over 5,000 soldiers, only a kilometer south of the Iraqi border. Captain Whitaker thought of himself as a litigator, and knew little more about the LOAC than the non-lawyers who worked around him. However, he understood that they now relied upon his ability to quickly learn about this important body of law. Accordingly, he repeatedly read through his copies of the Hague Regulations and the four Geneva Conventions, along with a few Army publications that provided explanations and examples of how these rules were to be applied in the context of an international armed conflict.

Within a few days, the brigade would conduct the longest and most complex air assault (helicopter insertion) mission in the Army's history, and Whitaker understood that they likely would run into two Republican Guard Armored

---

4. U.S. Dep't of Army, Field Manual 3-24, Insurgencies and Countering Insurgencies para. 13-6-7 (13 May 2015) (hereinafter FM 3-24).

(Tank) Divisions. Like his buddies in the infantry, Whitaker thought the likelihood of death was very high, and he had even sent his wedding band home to his wife, under the pretense that he had lost so much weight he feared that it might fall off and get lost.

On the day before the attack, Whitaker's Brigade Commander, Colonel Tom Hill, called Whitaker into his tent and directed him to go out among the troops and teach blocks of instruction on the Third and Fourth Geneva Conventions. Whitaker told Colonel that he thought the soldiers had more important things to attend to as they prepared for battle. Colonel Hill interrupted him and explained that the soldiers needed to hear what their JAG had to say. Finally, he placed his hand on Whitaker's shoulder and said, "Rich, this is important stuff, as you will understand before you finish tonight."

Within about 30 minutes of departing Colonel Hill's tent, Whitaker arrived in the sand dunes that served as the temporary home for his unit and began a class on the Third Geneva Convention, the Prisoner of War Convention. Whitaker (who later retired as a colonel) recalled a feeling akin to embarrassment as he began his class. He thought the soldiers had more important matters to attend to at that late moment, such as cleaning the sand out of their protective masks and firearms, and going over the battle order just recently handed down by their company headquarters. Most importantly, given the threat these men collectively faced, they needed time to write the type of letters that Whitaker had already authored to his wife and family. He felt like a "lawyer-geek" talking about ivory tower concepts of law and justice, and was sure his class would not be welcomed by the soldiers.

To his surprise, as he looked out on the 160 battle-gear-clad men standing before him, he noticed that every eye was focused on him. These men were not fidgeting with their weapons or masks and they were not chatting among themselves as soldiers often do. Instead, they paid strict attention, and after Whitaker explained a legal concept they asked questions to ensure that they understood the rules about which Whitaker spoke. As he continued to speak, he considered what was going on around him; at first, he found it odd and almost inexplicable. Then suddenly, he understood what Colonel Hill had meant when he explained that "this stuff is important." These soldiers looked upon themselves as the good guys, who wanted to play by the rules and conduct themselves with honor. Whitaker understood that each solider wanted to grasp the key LOAC rules to ensure he could honorably fulfill his obligations once the attack began.

Whitaker completed that class and dozens more like it that night before returning to his hole for a few hours of sleep before the attack began. As he stood before his sleep hole, removing his gear, a lone figure approached him and asked, "Rich, do you get it now?" Whitaker replied, "Yes, sir," and Colonel Hill continued to walk, alone with his thoughts.

II. Historical Foundations

Since antiquity, organized military forces and groups have observed at least some rules in the conduct of hostilities, both with respect to actions on the battlefield and the treatment of prisoners, non-combatants, and civilians.[5]

Many of these rules were derived from major religious or philosophical traditions that called for restraint in war in at least some circumstances. In *Deuteronomy*, for example, Moses instructed the tribes of Israel to spare cities that surrender:

> When you draw near to a city to fight against it, offer terms of peace to it. And if it responds to you peaceably and it opens to you, then all the people who are found in it shall do forced labor for you and shall serve you.[6]

The *Old Testament* book of *2 Kings* describes an incident of a later era in which King Jehoram of Israel spared the vulnerable Syrian army, which had been blinded by God and led into Samaria. King Jehoram adhered to the insight of the prophet Elisha, and fed the Syrian army and sent them on their way. As a result, "the Syrians did not come again on raids into the land of Israel."[7]

The *Qur'an* also includes a passage advising kindness be shown to prisoners of war,[8] while the Hindu *Laws of Manu* contain prescriptions against the use of poison, or attacks on "one who looks without taking part in the fight" or on enemies who have surrendered.[9] More broadly, in the third chapter of the classic ancient Chinese text *The Art of War*, Sun Tzu notes:

> [i]n considering the complete art of war, it is preferable to capture a state . . . an army . . . a battalion . . . a company . . . whole rather than break it up. Using this principle, you can understand that winning a hundred victories out of a hundred battles is not the ultimate achievement; the ultimate achievement is to defeat the enemy without even coming to battle.[10]

In the first millennium, Christian leaders in the Holy Roman Empire, who originally rejected any form of warfare in accordance with their faith in Jesus Christ, adopted a "Just War" rationale, reconciling the faith with the need to

---

5. For a detailed and thoughtful analysis of the history of the LOAC, *see* LESLIE C. GREEN, ESSAYS ON THE MODERN LAW OF WAR 1-40 (2d ed. 1999).

6. *Deuteronomy* 20:10-12 (English Standard Version).

7. *2 Kings* 6:20-23 (English Standard Version).

8. Quran 47:4, *available at* http://quod.lib.umich.edu/cgi/k/koran/koran-idx?type=DIV0&byte=797085 (last visited Feb. 13, 2017) ("So when you meet in battle those who disbelieve, then smite the necks until when you have overcome them, then make (them) prisoners, and afterwards either set them free as a favor or let them ransom (themselves) until the war terminates.").

9. THE LAWS OF MANU (MĀNAVA-DHARMAŚĀSTRA) 16.3.11 (G. Bühler trans., 1886), *available at* http://www.cincinnatitemple.com/downloads/MANU_1.pdf (translating and including chapter 7, verses 87-98 of the Mānava-Dharmaśāstra).

10. SUN TZU, THE ART OF WAR 17 (James Trapp trans., Chartwell Books 2012). For a more complete discussion of these early traditions, *see* LESLIE C. GREEN, THE CONTEMPORARY LAW OF ARMED CONFLICT 26-36 (3d ed. 2008).

defend the Empire from vandals.[11] This rationale identified circumstances in which individuals could fight for the State based on the justness of the cause and the purity of the motives of the State in employing force. While this Just War tradition focused principally on regulating the resort to war, it also had beneficial effects for the conduct of hostilities, at least when the opposing forces were both Christians. Those effects were not as prevalent, however, where the war was conducted against non-Christians and the religious overtones of such a conflict could result in an increase, rather than decrease, in brutality, as was seen in the Crusades.

As the modern Western European nation-states emerged in the sixteenth and seventeenth centuries, and war was fought between nations rather than between leaders, the Just War tradition receded in favor of the use of war as an instrument of State policy.[12] Similarly, religion as the basis for limitations on war-fighting also receded in importance, and instead scholars identified a "natural law" basis for the applicable rules of international law. Among the leading scholars in this area was Hugo Grotius (1583-1645), whose work, *On the Law of War and Peace*, is considered to be a landmark in the development of the modern international law.[13] Grotius articulated many of the same principles that applied under the Just War tradition, but based them on his perceptions of natural law, rather than religious law.

None of the rules articulated during these periods provided a comprehensive set of guidelines for the conduct of hostilities. Indeed, most writers and theorists focused on the law applicable to a State's resort to military force against other States — the *jus ad bellum* — rather than the regulation of hostilities — or, the *jus in bello*. This may have been due, in part, to the fact that prior to the end of the eighteenth century, most European wars were conducted by professional soldiers who knew and passed on to their subordinates certain unwritten rules or conventions of chivalrous conduct. Further, while not always true, wars prior to the nineteenth century were fought by soldiers in open battlefields or by navies in the open sea, at a distance from the civilian population.

In the late eighteenth and early nineteenth centuries, the French Revolution and the Napoleonic Wars were fought with larger armies, including conscripts. Further, technological developments in the nineteenth century resulted in a marked increase in the lethality of weapons, the severity of wounds, and the extent of destruction of property. Still, States viewed war as a necessary, or at least unavoidable, component of their relationships with other States. Indeed, in the first half of the nineteenth century, Prussian Field Marshall Karl von Clausewitz's classic treatise, *On War*, characterized war as "not merely a political act, but also a real political instrument, a continuation of political commerce, a carrying out of the same by other means."[14] In that context, there was no effective

---

11. INT'L & OPERATIONAL LAW DEP'T, THE JUDGE ADVOCATE GEN.'S LEGAL CTR. & SCH., U.S. ARMY, LAW OF ARMED CONFLICT DESKTOP 12 (2016).
12. *See id.* at 12-13.
13. *Id.* at 12.
14. CARL VON CLAUSEWITZ, ON WAR 12 (J.J. Graham trans., 1873) (1832) (Clausewitz's *On War* was a posthumous publication).

restraint on war other than the political value or risk associated with pursuing it, and the physical costs associated with the suffering and destruction of war.

Three developments in the middle of the nineteenth century helped foster efforts in Europe and North America to articulate specific limitations on the conduct of warfare. First, in June 1859, a Swiss businessman named Jean-Henri Dunant traveled through Northern Italy to meet with Emperor Napoleon III of France. While on this journey, Dunant witnessed a massive battle at Solferino, Italy, between French and Sardinian forces on one side, and Austrian forces on the other. In less than one day, 6,000 soldiers were killed and another 35,000 wounded, many seriously. Dunant and other volunteers assisted the wounded and dying soldiers, an experience that inspired him to write and publish, in 1862, *A Memory of Solferino*,[15] in which he advocated for the creation of a neutral and impartial organization to protect and assist the wounded in war, the creation of voluntary relief agencies that could care for the wounded, and the adoption of an "international principle" that could be the basis for the work of these societies. His suggestions led to the formation of the International Committee of the Red Cross (ICRC) and the Red Cross movement; additionally, an agreement took form in 1864 — the first Geneva Convention for the Amelioration of the Condition of the Wounded in Armies in the Field[16] — which, among other things, provided for protection, collection, and care of wounded and sick combatants regardless of their national origin, as well as the medical personnel and civilians that care for them. The movement also established the "red cross" as a symbol for distinguishing hospitals, ambulances, and evacuation parties. Dunant's efforts, for which he received the first Nobel Peace Prize in 1901, were the starting point for the continuing efforts to ensure humane treatment of the victims of armed conflict.[17]

Second, during the American Civil War, Professor Francis Lieber of Columbia College wrote a detailed code of the rules to be followed by Union forces during the conflict with the Confederacy. The rules were intended to secure humane treatment of the population in occupied areas and prevent the already bloody conflict from devolving into unrestrained brutality. Commonly referred to as the "Lieber Code," Professor Lieber's "Instructions for the Government of Armies of the United States in the Field" were promulgated by President Abraham Lincoln as General Order 100 in 1863, and were followed by the U.S. Army well into the twentieth century.[18] As the following excerpt

---

15. *See, generally* HENRY DUNANT, A MEMORY OF SOLFERINO (1862), *available at* https://www.icrc.org/en/publication/0361-memory-solferino.

16. Geneva Convention for the Amelioration of the Condition of the Wounded in Armies in the Field, Aug. 22, 1864, 22 Stat. 940 (1864 Geneva Convention).

17. *See infra* pt. IV.B.

18. *See* General Order No. 100, Instructions for the Government of Armies of the United States in the Field (Apr. 24, 1863), *reprinted in* THE WAR OF THE REBELLION: A COMPILATION OF THE OFFICIAL RECORDS OF THE UNION AND CONFEDERATE ARMIES (Lieber Code), Series III, vol. 3, (GPO 1899) (hereinafter Lieber Code).The DoD Law of War Manual cautions that while "[m]any key law of war principles, such as the principle of military necessity were codified in the Lieber Code . . . parts of the Lieber Code reflect 19th century understandings of the law of war that have been modified by treaties that the United States has ratified or by subsequent customary international law." U.S. DEP'T OF DEF., LAW OF WAR MANUAL para. 19.3 (June 2015, updated Dec. 2016) (hereinafter DoD LAW OF WAR MANUAL).

shows, the Lieber Code articulated rules that are the heart of the core principles of the LOAC, such as necessity and distinction:[19]

> Art. 14. Military necessity, as understood by modern civilized nations, consists in the necessity of those measures which are indispensable for securing the ends of the war, and which are lawful according to the modern law and usages of war.
>
> Art. 15. Military necessity admits of all direct destruction of life or limb of armed enemies, and of other persons whose destruction is incidentally unavoidable in the armed contests of the war; it allows of the capturing of every armed enemy, and every enemy of importance to the hostile government, or of peculiar danger to the captor; it allows of all destruction of property, and obstruction of the ways and channels of traffic, travel, or communication, and of all withholding of sustenance or means of life from the enemy; of the appropriation of whatever an enemy's country affords necessary for the subsistence and safety of the army, and of such deception as does not involve the breaking of good faith positively pledged, regarding agreements entered into during the war, or supposed by the modern law of war to exist. Men who take up arms against one another in public war do not cease on this account to be moral beings, responsible to one another and to God.
>
> Art. 16. Military necessity does not admit of cruelty—that is, the infliction of suffering for the sake of suffering or for revenge, nor of maiming or wounding except in fight, nor of torture to extort confessions. It does not admit of the use of poison in any way, nor of the wanton devastation of a district. It admits of deception, but disclaims acts of perfidy; and, in general, military necessity does not include any act of hostility which makes the return to peace unnecessarily difficult.
>
> . . .
>
> Art. 20. Public war is a state of armed hostility between sovereign nations or governments. It is a law and requisite of civilized existence that men live in political, continuous societies, forming organized units, called states or nations, whose constituents bear, enjoy, suffer, advance and retrograde together, in peace and in war.
>
> Art. 21. The citizen or native of a hostile country is thus an enemy, as one of the constituents of the hostile state or nation, and as such is subjected to the hardships of the war.
>
> Art. 22. Nevertheless, as civilization has advanced during the last centuries, so has likewise steadily advanced, especially in war on land, the distinction between the private individual belonging to a hostile country and the hostile country itself, with its men in arms. The principle has been more and more acknowledged that the unarmed citizen is to be spared in person, property, and honor as much as the exigencies of war will admit.
>
> Art. 23. Private citizens are no longer murdered, enslaved, or carried off to distant parts, and the inoffensive individual is as little disturbed in his private relations as the commander of the hostile troops can afford to grant in the overruling demands of a vigorous war.[20]

---

19. *See infra* pt. III.
20. Lieber Code, *supra*, note 18, art. 14-16, 20-23.

Although the Lieber Code was intended only for the U.S. Army, it inspired two other nineteenth century attempts to draft international codes of conduct that ultimately became the basis for international conventions adopted in 1899 and 1907 to regulate hostilities.[21]

Third, responding to his country's development of a bullet that exploded on contact with human tissue, Tsar Alexander of Russia proposed that an international agreement be adopted to ban the bullet as an inhumane weapon of war. The result was the Declaration Renouncing the Use, in Time of War, of Explosive Projectiles Under 400 Grammes Weight, adopted by 17 countries in St. Petersburg, Russia in 1868.[22] Although the prohibition has been limited by State practice,[23] the St. Petersburg Declaration's example of an international convention banning a weapon of war, as well as the following articulation of the reasons for basis for adoption of the prohibition, continues to be relevant today:

> That the progress of civilization should have the effect of alleviating as much as possible the calamities of war;
>
> That the only legitimate object which States should endeavour to accomplish during war is to weaken the military forces of the enemy;
>
> That for this purpose it is sufficient to disable the greatest possible number of men;
>
> That this object would be exceeded by the employment of arms which uselessly aggravate the sufferings of disabled men, or render their death inevitable;
>
> That the employment of such arms would, therefore, be contrary to the laws of humanity. . . .[24]

III. LOAC Principles

Before turning to treaty law, it is important to review the fundamental principles that underpin all the LOAC and which are reflected in LOAC treaties. An enumeration of LOAC principles is a common feature of military manuals published by a number of nations that pride themselves on the professionalism and quality of their armed forces. For example, the United Kingdom's Ministry of Defence's Manual of the Law of Armed Conflict provides the following definition of what the United Kingdom considers the four LOAC principles:

> Despite the codification of much customary law into treaty form during the last one hundred years, four fundamental principles still underlie the law of armed conflict. These are military necessity, humanity, distinction, and

---

21. *See infra* pt. IV.A (discussing the Codes and Conventions comprising "Hague Law").
22. *See* Declaration Renouncing the Use, in Time of War, of Explosive Projectiles Under 400 Grammes Weight, Nov. 29, 1868, 138 Consol. T.S. 297 (hereinafter St. Petersburg Declaration).
23. DoD Law of War Manual, *supra*, note 18, para. 19.6.
24. St. Petersburg Declaration, *supra*, note 22.

proportionality. The law of armed conflict is consistent with the economic and efficient use of force. It is intended to minimize the suffering caused by armed conflict rather than impede military efficiency.[25]

Like the U.K. Manual, the U.S. Department of Defense (DoD) Law of War Manual devotes an entire chapter to enumerating and explaining these principles. At the outset of that chapter, the DoD Manual explains the importance of these principles:

> Law of war principles: (1) help practitioners interpret and apply specific treaty or customary rules; (2) provide a general guide for conduct during war when no specific rule applies; and (3) work as interdependent and reinforcing parts of a coherent system.[26]

As the DoD Law of War Manual indicates, LOAC principles serve important interests. They provide key guidance for interpretation of LOAC treaties and obligations, and provide LOAC standards where there are no specific treaty or customary law rules. This is particularly important when new weapons or tactics emerge and there are no treaty rules specifically applicable to them. Or, if there is no expressly applicable treaty to deal with a particular situation or conflict, lawyers can rely on the principles to draw conclusions about the legal rules that should apply in those circumstances.

A. Importance of Principles

The principles are extremely valuable to military lawyers and others engaged in the practice of the LOAC. By providing a common, consistent, and logical focus for understanding how the LOAC is applied, the principles facilitate training of military forces, and planning and executing military operations, thereby enhancing LOAC compliance and the evaluation of compliance by military forces. Furthermore, because the principles are readily translated into what are sometimes referred to as "soldiers' rules" — basic rules of conduct taught to soldiers from initial entry training through all phases of professional development — the principles help distill often complex LOAC concepts into generally understood standards of professional military conduct. The principles also contribute to planning and execution of military operations by non-lawyers, either in situations where the precise legal rules applicable to the mission are uncertain, or where there is limited time to sort out the rules with legal counsel, which is not an uncommon operational situation. While commanders and their staffs might not know exactly where their mission fits in the legal applicability continuum, they do know that following these LOAC principles will ensure legitimacy even in zones of uncertainty.

---

25. *See* U.K. Min. Def. Manual of the Law of Armed Conflict ¶ 2.1 (2004) (hereinafter UK LOAC Manual) (The U.K. Manual also provides an extensive definition of these principles.)
26. DoD Law of War Manual, *supra*, note 18, para. 2.1.2.

LOAC principles reflect lessons from hard-earned combat experiences with applying humanitarian protections in military operations. It is axiomatic that, in order to be implemented by military forces, the protection of humanitarian objectives must not preclude the ability of belligerents to accomplish their strategic, operational, and tactical objectives; otherwise, military forces will not comply with the law. Consequently, the contemporary LOAC principles reflect a carefully evolved balance between humanity and military necessity, which is a balance informed by the realities of war. Indeed, LOAC principles often are soldiers' first introduction to the symmetry the law seeks to achieve between the interests of military necessity and humanity.

The LOAC is replete with examples of this symmetry. A quintessential example is the prohibition against the infliction of superfluous—and therefore legally unnecessary—suffering. This prohibition was first codified in the St. Petersburg Declaration of 1868 described above, with roots that run deep in customary international law.[27] In the St. Petersburg Declaration, the parties agreed to renounce, in the case of war among them, the use of a particular weapon on the basis of their mutual agreement that "the employment of arms which uselessly aggravate the sufferings of disabled men, or render their death inevitable . . . [is] contrary to the laws of humanity."[28] By prohibiting the infliction of unnecessary or useless suffering (but, by implication, allowing for suffering necessary to achieve legitimate military objectives), humanitarian goals are advanced by recognizing that a legitimate military interest in achieving an objective against an enemy in armed conflict may justify the infliction of harm only to the extent necessary to achieve that objective. At the same time, by focusing on necessity, the prohibition of superfluous injury is consistent with sound military practice because it recognizes that avoiding *unnecessary* suffering, in addition to serving humanitarian interests, also serves military interests by avoiding the use of scarce resources to inflict suffering that is not needed to achieve an objective (e.g., by causing additional injury or harm to an enemy already rendered combat ineffective).

Ultimately, demonstrating to soldiers the symmetry between necessity and humanity can enhance LOAC compliance by showing that the LOAC is consistent with military operational logic and indeed may enhance it. Consider, for example, the importance of successfully protecting the civilian population from harm during a counterinsurgency operation; in such a case, compliance with the LOAC's restraints on attacks that have disproportionate impacts on civilians and civilian property fits well with military objectives of the State armed force's counterinsurgency strategy.

LOAC principles also serve military operational interests by contributing to the discipline and professionalism within military forces. Indeed, this contribution to professionalism has long been recognized as a rationale for the LOAC. For example, the 1880 Oxford Manual on the Laws of War on Land provides:

---

27. St. Petersburg Declaration, *supra*, note 22.
28. *Id.*

A positive set of rules . . . , if they are judicious, serves the interests of belligerents and is far from hindering them, since by preventing the unchaining of passion and savage instincts — which battle always awakens, as much as it awakens courage and many virtues — it strengthens the discipline which is the strength of armies; it also ennobles their patriotic mission in the eyes of the soldiers by keeping them within the limits of respect due to the rights of humanity.[29]

B. Defining the Principles

While military forces clearly benefit from compliance with LOAC principles, laying out the content and requirements of these principles can be challenging, in part because there is no single authoritative source defining exactly what the principles are. For example, military manuals and other sources do not agree on the list of principles themselves. As noted above, the U.K. Manual lists four "basic principles" — military necessity, humanity, distinction, and proportionality.[30] The DoD Law of War Manual adds the principle of "honor" to this list.[31] Meanwhile, the Canadian Forces' Joint Doctrine Manual on the Law of Armed Conflict lists a number of principles, including, as "primary concepts", the principles of military necessity, humanity, and chivalry; as "fundamental principles", the humanitarian principle, the principle of the Law of Geneva, and the principle of the Law of War (or the Law of the Hague); and, as "operational principles", the principles of distinction, non-discrimination, proportionality, and reciprocity.[32] In its LOAC manual, the Australian Defence Forces lists three core principles — military necessity, avoidance of unnecessary suffering, and proportionality — as well as a "related principle" of distinction.[33]

The lack of strict uniformity in military manuals aside,[34] the principles in all military manuals generally are variants of the "four cardinal principles of international humanitarian law [IHL]"[35] identified by the International

---

29. Inst. of Int'l Law, The Laws of War on Land preface (1880) (hereinafter Oxford Manual).

30. UK LOAC Manual, *supra*, note 25, ch. 2.

31. DoD Law of War Manual, *supra*, note 18, para. 2.1.2.3. The significance of the principles is reinforced by DoD's directive on the Law of War Program, which requires training on the LOAC principles by all the military branches. U.S. Dep't Defense, Dir. 2311.01E, DoD Law of War Program para. 5.8 (9 May 2006, current 22 Feb. 2011) (hereinafter DoDD 2311.01E) (directing the Secretaries of the military services to "[p]rovide directives, publications, instructions, and training so the principles and rules of the law of war will be known to members of their respective Departments").

32. Canada, Department of National Defence, Joint Doctrine Manual B-GJ-005-104/FP-021, *Law of Armed Conflict at the Operational and Tactical Levels* (Aug. 13, 2001), ¶ 202-04. (hereinafter Canadian LOAC Manual).

33. Australian Defence Force, Australian Defence Doctrine Publication 06.4, *Law of Armed Conflict* (May 11, 2006), ch. 2.

34. Of course, when a state's military manual or other national military policy defines applicable principles, that definition is binding on that nation's armed forces, even if those principles are articulated in a different manner than they are articulated by other nations' armed forces.

35. International Humanitarian Law (IHL) is synonymous with the LOAC, and the two terms are frequently debated and used in place with one another.

Court of Justice in its 1996 Advisory Opinion on the Use or Threat of Nuclear Weapons — military necessity, humanity, distinction, and proportionality.[36] While other principles may be listed in various manuals, these four unquestionably belong in any listing.[37] These four principles — plus one other principle, "precautions", which the authors of this text believe also to be of cardinal importance — are discussed below.

1. Military Necessity: The First Principle of Authority

The principle of military necessity is central to the basic function of military action during armed conflict, which is to use force, and most notably combat power, to impose one's will on the enemy. The LOAC principle of military necessity finds its origins in State practice that predates contemporary LOAC treaty law. For example, the Lieber Code provided that:

> Art. 14. Military necessity, as understood by modern civilized nations, consists in the necessity of those measures which are indispensable for securing the ends of the war, and which are lawful according to the modern law and usages of war.
>
> . . .
>
> Art. 16. Military necessity does not admit of cruelty — that is, the infliction of suffering for the sake of suffering or for revenge, nor of maiming or wounding except in fight, nor of torture to extort confessions. It does not admit of the use of poison in any way, nor of the wanton devastation of a district. It admits of deception, but disclaims acts of perfidy; and, in general, military necessity does not include any act of hostility which makes the return to peace unnecessarily difficult.[38]

As the law evolved from primarily customary rules to rules codified in treaties, the principle of military necessity remained prominent. For example, the Regulations annexed to the 1899 Hague Convention with Respect to the Law and Customs of War on Land (1899 Hague II), and to the 1907 Hague Convention Respecting the Laws and Customs of War on Land (1907 Hague IV), which provide for comprehensive regulation of hostilities in land warfare, prohibit destruction or seizure of enemy property, "unless such destruction or seizure be imperatively demanded by the necessities of war."[39]

However, military necessity is perhaps the ultimate manifestation that war — or more accurately, armed conflict — is not an unlimited license to inflict death, destruction, and suffering. Instead, the authority to cause harm during

---

36. *See* Legality of the Threat or Use of Nuclear Weapons, Advisory Opinion, 1996 I.C.J. 226, 257 (July 8).

37. A more comprehensive and generally accepted enumeration would add, for example, a precautionary measures principle. *See infra* pt. III.B.5 (regarding precautions).

38. Lieber Code, *supra*, note 18, art. 14-15.

39. Regulations Respecting the Laws and Customs of War on Land, annexed to Convention with Respect to the Laws and Customs of War on Land, Jul. 29, 1899, art. 23(g), 32 Stat. 1803, 1811 (hereinafter 1899 Hague II); Convention (IV) Respecting the Laws and Customs of War on Land and its annex: Regulations concerning the Laws and Customs of War on Land, Oct. 18, 1907, art. 23(g), 36 Stat. 2277 (hereinafter 1907 Hague IV).

conflict is limited and regulated. This axiom of conflict regulation is inherent in the contemporary notion of military necessity, which is defined by the DoD Law of War Manual as "the principle that justifies the use of all measures needed to defeat the enemy as quickly and efficiently as possible that are not prohibited by the law of war."[40] Accordingly, military necessity is both a license and a restraint, permitting only those harmful measures that are linked to bringing about the prompt submission of the enemy. Or, as explained by Napoleon's great maxim: "[I]n politics and war alike, every injury done to the enemy, even though permitted by the rules, is excusable only so far as it is absolutely necessary; everything beyond that is criminal."[41]

The U.S. view, as is expressed through the above excerpt from the DoD Law of War Manual, is that the principle of military necessity provides legal authority to employ the means necessary to defeat an enemy.[42] This includes authority to use combat power and to detain captured enemy combatants until the end of hostilities (or at least until they no longer present a threat).[43] In a number of cases, however, LOAC rules have been adopted that prohibit certain actions or weapons without regard to necessity. For these rules, the necessity principle no longer provides an independent authority to engage in the actions or to use the weapons banned by such rule.[44] In those cases, the absolute nature of the rule reflects a judgment among States that there are no situations where military necessity might justify the banned action or weapon, although the historical background of any absolute rule needs to be considered in order to carefully define the intentions of the parties when the rule was adopted in order to avoid an overbroad application.[45]

---

40. DoD LAW OF WAR MANUAL, *supra*, note para. 18, 2.2.
41. GEOFFREY BEST, WAR AND LAW SINCE 1945 242 (1994).
42. DoD LAW OF WAR MANUAL, *supra*, note 18, para. 8.1.3.1 (citing Hamdi v. Rumsfeld, 542 U.S. 507, 518 (2004) (plurality opinion)).
43. A recent U.K. court decision adopted a more restrictive interpretation of the LOAC to hold that U.K. armed forces did not have authority to detain a captured Taliban belligerent in Afghanistan for more than the period authorized by Afghan law. The U.K. court rejected the government's assertion that detention authority could be derived from customary international law, including the argument that a right to kill supports, *a fortiori*, a right to detain. Muhammed v. Sec'y of State for Defence, [2015] EWCA (Civ) 843 [251]-[253] (Eng.). Instead, the court concluded that absent positive implementation of this authority by treaty or statute (neither of which were present in that case), U.K. forces lacked legal authority to subject a battlefield captive to detention in the NIAC in Afghanistan beyond what was permitted by Afghan law.
It is clear that this interpretation contradicts the U.S. view of the military necessity principle as authority to detain, although in the case of detention of Taliban and al-Qaeda fighters, there arguably is U.S. statutory authority for detention by U.S. forces. *See* National Defense Authorization Act for Fiscal Year 2012, Pub. L. No. 112-81, § 1021(a), 125 Stat. 1298, 1562 (2011).
44. One example is the prohibition on the employment of poison or poisoned weapons in armed conflict, which is found, in Article 23 of both 1899 Hague II and 1907 Hague IV. 1899 Hague II, *supra*, note 41, art. 23(a); 1907 Hague IV, *supra*, note 41, art. 23(a).
45. *See, e.g.*, W. Hays Parks, *Open Tip Match: When a "Hollow Point" is Not a Hollow Point*, SMALL ARMS DEF. JOURNAL, http://www.sadefensejournal.com/wp/?p=1262 (last visited Feb. 19, 2017). W. Hays Parks argues that Sierra Bullets' "MatchKing" was mistakenly believed to fall within the scope of a multilateral ban on the use of expanding bullets because, in part, the weapon had been "judg[ed] ... based solely on its appearance" (which was possibly similar to the banned munitions) without testing to *see* if it fell within the intent of the multilateral ban, which was to prohibit bullets that are

Even a more expansive interpretation of military necessity does not provide a blanket justification for deviation from the LOAC, and it is clearly erroneous to assume that military necessity is a blank check of authority during armed conflict. This "blank check" approach to military necessity was rejected by the international community during the war crimes trials that grew out of World War II.[46] Instead, military necessity includes an inherent limitation on the exercise of military power that reflects the central LOAC balance between military and humanitarian considerations.

The Canadian Forces' LOAC manual provides an excellent explanation of the limitations on authority inherent in the principle of military necessity:

> 2. Military Necessity. Military necessity is related to the primary aim of armed conflict — the complete submission of the enemy at the earliest possible moment with the least possible expenditure of personnel and resources. The concept of military necessity justifies the application of force not forbidden by International Law, to the extent necessary, for the realization of the purpose of armed conflict.
>
> 3. The concept of military necessity presupposes:
>   a. the force used can be and is being controlled;
>   b. the use of force is necessary to achieve the submission of the enemy; and
>   c. the amount of force used is limited to what is needed to achieve prompt submission.
>
> 4. Military necessity is not a concept that can be considered in isolation. In particular, it does not justify violation of the LOAC, as military necessity was a factor taken into account when the rules governing the conduct of hostilities were drafted.
>
> 5. For example, military necessity is not the 19th Century German Doctrine of *Kriegsraison*, which asserted that war could justify any measures — even in violation of the laws of war — when the necessities of any particular situation purportedly justified it. War crimes trials after World War II clearly rejected this view. Military necessity cannot justify actions absolutely prohibited by law, as the means to achieve military victory are not unlimited. Armed conflict must be carried on within the limits set by International Law.[47]

The DoD Law of War Manual also emphasizes that military necessity does not authorize or justify violation of other prohibitory LOAC rules:

---

employed to uselessly aggravate suffering or wounding by expanding or opening easily when they strike the body. In reality, the MatchKing's open-tip design was employed for purposes of increased accuracy over the traditional full metal jacketed rounds. *Id.*

46. *See, e.g.*, The Hostage Case, 11 Trials of War Criminals (T.W.C.) 1255-56 ("It is apparent from the evidence of these defendants that they considered military necessity, a matter to be determined by them, a complete justification of their acts. We do not concur in the view that the rules of warfare are anything less than they purport to be. Military necessity or expediency do not justify a violation of positive rules."); The Krupp Case, 9 Trials of War Criminals (T.W.C.) 1340 (rejecting defense counsel argument that 1907 Hague IV and the regulations annexed to it, did not apply in cases of "total war").

47. Canadian LOAC Manual, *supra*, note 32, ¶ 202.

Military necessity does not justify actions that are prohibited by the law of war.

From the late 19th Century through World War II, Germany asserted that *military necessity* could override specific law of war rules (*Kriegsraeson geht vor Kriegsmanier*—"necessity in war overrules the manner of warfare"). This view was strongly criticized. Post-World War II war crimes tribunals rejected it as well.

Military necessity cannot justify departures from the law of war because States have crafted the law of war specifically with war's exigencies in mind. In devising law of war rules, States considered military requirements. Thus, prohibitions on conduct in the law of war may be understood to reflect States' determinations that such conduct is militarily unnecessary *per se*.[48]

Military necessity therefore provides a critically important justification under international law for actions falling within the scope of the "necessities of war," which are those actions belligerents must take to defeat an enemy. Further, LOAC treaty provisions may be expressly conditioned with reference to necessity.[49] But the absence of a reference to this principle in a prohibitory LOAC treaty rule also means that the rule categorically prohibits the action or weapon it regulates, no matter how "necessary" a belligerent may claim that such action or weapon may be to its war effort. In other words, where a LOAC rule prohibits an act or omission without reference to necessity, the "necessity" question has already been considered, and States adopting the rule have collectively determined that such actions (or omissions) or weapons are never necessary in armed conflict.

2. Humanity: The First Principle of Restraint

The principle of humanity provides an essential humanitarian limit on the brutality of war, to the benefit of civilians and belligerents alike. Further, because the principle of military necessity only allows for measures "not prohibited by the law of war," humanitarian limits under international law are inherently incorporated into the notion of necessity.[50]

The contours of the principle of humanity are difficult to define with precision, although the principle is central to the regulation of armed conflict. It includes within its scope the prohibition against inflicting superfluous injury or unnecessary suffering on an enemy (injury or suffering beyond that which is necessary to bring about the opponent's prompt submission), and the humane treatment obligation applicable to civilians and the wounded and sick, which will be addressed in detail in subsequent chapters. Like necessity, humanity applies to both IACs and NIACs. This is unsurprising, as the principle of humanity lies at the very core of the Geneva tradition of protecting victims

---

48. DoD Law of War Manual, *supra*, note 18, para. 2.2.2.1.
49. *See id.*, para. 2.2.2.2 (including a discussion of the various ways that necessity is incorporated into treaty rules).
50. *Id.*, para. 2.2.2.1.

of war, and there is virtually no logical basis to apply the principle differently based on the nature of the armed conflict.[51]

The principle of humanity provides the foundation for a modest yet important limit on the authority to employ combat power against an enemy—the prohibition against inflicting superfluous injury or unnecessary suffering. Indeed, this was one of the first rules codified in LOAC treaties,[52] and it was included in contemporary iteration through Article 35 of Additional Protocol I, which provides that "the right of the Parties to the conflict to choose methods or means of warfare is not unlimited."[53] Accordingly, participants in armed conflicts are "prohibited to employ weapons, projectiles and material, and methods of warfare of a nature to cause superfluous injury or unnecessary suffering."[54]

The influence of the principle of humanity is most pervasive in the protection of victims of armed conflict, including the wounded, sick, shipwrecked (as well as the facilities and personnel who provide medical and spiritual care for them), and detainees. Indeed, virtually every treaty and customary international law rule protecting victims is a manifestation of this principle. These rules include the prohibition against the use of any type of coercion against a prisoner of war or civilian internee; the obligation to search for and collect the wounded and sick and ensure that priority of medical care is based solely on medical considerations; the obligation to search for and collect the shipwrecked at sea; the obligation to provide notice of capture of enemy personnel to the enemy state through a neutral intermediary; the obligation to facilitate the efforts of neutral relief agencies; the extensive immunities from attack afforded to places engaged in medical functions; and even the obligation to maintain and record the location of interment of the enemy dead.[55]

This pervasive influence is not limited to IACs. Since 1949, Common Article 3 to the Geneva Conventions has been perhaps the most direct manifestation of the principle of humanity, mandating humane treatment of any person not actively participating in hostilities during NIACs.[56] Today, this rule is supplemented by

---

51. On the other hand, the treaty rules that implement the principle of humanity are far more detailed with respect to IACs.

52. *See, e.g.*, 1899 Hague II, *supra*, note 39, art. 23(e).

53. Protocol (I) Additional to the Geneva Conventions of 12 Aug. 1949, and Relating to the Protection of Victims of International Armed Conflicts, June 8, 1977, art. 35(1), 1125 U.N.T.S. 3 (hereinafter AP I). The United States is not a party to AP I, but the rule also is embodied in other treaties ratified by the United States. See 1907 Hague IV, *supra*, note 39, art. 20.

54. AP I, *supra*, note 39, art. 35(2). The principle behind this rule, too, is embodied in other treaties to which the United States is bound. *See* 1907 Hague IV, *supra*, note 39, art. 23(e).

55. *See infra* ch. 7 (discussing the rules regarding the wounded and sick), ch. 9 (discussing the rules regarding prisoners of war and other detainees).

56. *See* Geneva Convention for the Amelioration of the Condition of the Wounded and Sick in Armed Forces in the Field, Aug. 12, 1949, art. 3, 6 U.S.T. 3114, 75 U.N.T.S. 970; Geneva Convention for the Amelioration of the Condition of Wounded, Sick, and Shipwrecked Members of the Armed Forces at Sea, Aug. 12, 1949, art. 3, 6 U.S.T. 3217, 75 U.N.T.S. 971; Geneva Convention Relative to the Treatment of Prisoners of War, Aug. 12, 1949, art. 3, 6 U.S.T. 3316, 75 U.N.T.S. 972; Geneva Convention Relative to the Protection of Civilian Persons in Time of War, Aug. 12, 1949, art. 3, 6 U.S.T. 3516, 75 U.N.T.S. 973 (hereinafter Common Article 3).

Additional Protocol II,[57] and by customary international law.[58] Thus, no person should ever fall outside the protection of the principle of humanity.

The principle of humanity reflects an important normative premise: War is limited not only by necessity but also by the obligation to ensure that all individuals, even combatants, are entitled to respect as human beings. Thus, the principle of humanity is directly linked to the regulatory premise that while States may employ military force in an armed conflict to defeat their enemies, personal anger, animosity, or instinct for revenge never justify the violence associated with armed conflict.[59] Accordingly, these inherent but violent human instincts should never influence the treatment of individuals under the control of a party to the conflict or justify excess in the manner in which hostilities are conducted.

3. Distinction: The Essential Requirement for Lawful Targeting

Distinction is a vital LOAC principle for determining who or what can be targeted with lethal force in armed conflict, as explained in extensive detail in Chapter 7. Distinction imposes an obligation on belligerents to distinguish between persons, places, and things that can be made the lawful objects of attack, and those persons, places, and things that cannot.[60] Accordingly, it violates the principle of distinction to deliberately attack any individual or object that does not qualify as a lawful target pursuant to LOAC rules. Distinction is derived from military necessity, as it limits application of combat power to targets that contribute to an opponent's war-fighting capability.[61]

---

57. Protocol (II) Additional to the Geneva Conventions of 12 Aug. 1949, and Relating to the Protection of Victims of Non-International Armed Conflicts, June 8, 1977, 1125 U.N.T.S. 609 (hereinafter AP II).

The United States is not a party to AP II, but, as noted in the DoD Law of War Manual, "reviews have concluded that the provisions of AP II are consistent with U.S. practice," and various Administrations have supported ratification of AP II. DoD LAW OF WAR MANUAL, *supra*, note 18, para. 19.20.2.1; *see also* Ronald Reagan, Letter of Transmittal, The White House, Jan. 29, 1987, *available at* https://www.loc.gov/rr/frd/Military_Law/pdf/protocol-II-100-2.pdf; William J. Clinton, Letter of Transmittal, The White House, Jan. 6, 1999, *available at* http://www.loc.gov/rr/frd/Military_Law/pdf/GC-message-from-pres-1999.pdf; Press Release, White House, Fact Sheet: New Actions on Guantanamo and Detainee Policy (Mar. 7, 2011), *available at* https://obamawhitehouse.archives.gov/the-press-office/2011/03/07/fact-sheet-new-actions-guant-namo-and-detainee-policy.

58. *See* DoD LAW OF WAR MANUAL, *supra*, note 18, para. 17.1.3.2.

59. This same premise applies to all those participating in hostilities, even if not members of State armed forces. Most experts agree that even those who do not enjoy belligerent rights, do not violate international law by engaging in hostilities so long as they do not violate the LOAC. *See* Sean Watts, *Combatant Status and Computer Network Attack*, 50 VA. J. INT'L L. 391, 422 (2010).

60. *See* AP I, *supra*, note 53, art. 48. Article 48 states:

In order to ensure respect for and protection of the civilian population and civilian objects, the Parties to the conflict shall at all times distinguish between the civilian population and combatants and between civilian objects and military objectives and accordingly shall direct their operations only against military objectives.

Id.; *see also*, JEAN-MARIE HENCKAERTS & LOUISE DOSWALD-BECK, CUSTOMARY INT'L HUMANITARIAN LAW 3-8 (2009) (hereinafter CIL STUDY) (asserting, in Rule 1, that the principle of distinction is a norm of customary international law in all armed conflicts).

61. There is a debate over the contribution that an object must make in order to be a lawful military objective. The definition of "military objective" in AP I focuses on the contribution the object

Targets are simply those persons, places, or things made the object of deliberate attack by a military force. The target selection and engagement process begins with the military mission. Operational planners then determine how to best leverage the capabilities of their military units to achieve the effects deemed necessary to accomplish that mission. In operational terms, the principle of distinction focuses on how commanders and their subordinates should draw the line between what is and is not a lawful target.

Targeting effects need not be only destruction, but instead include, among other effects, deception, denial, degradation, delay, disruption, interdiction, and neutralization.[62] The process of selecting and engaging targets is defined by U.S. military doctrine, using a process followed by many armed forces.

Understanding the impact of distinction on the targeting process begins, of course, with the definition of the term "target." U.S. military doctrine defines a target as follows:

> a. A target is an entity (person, place, or thing) considered for possible engagement or action to alter or neutralize the function it performs for the adversary. A target's importance derives from its potential contribution to achieving a commander's objective(s) or otherwise accomplishing assigned tasks. These objectives must be consistent with national strategic direction and selected to accomplish the assigned missions and tasks. Targets nominated for attack may include the following:
>
> (1) Facility: a geographically located, defined physical structure, group of structures, or area that provides a function that contributes to a target system's capability.
>
> (2) Individual(s): a person or persons who provide a function that contributes to a target system's capability.
>
> (3) Virtual: an entity in cyberspace that provides a function that contributes to a target system's capability.
>
> (4) Equipment: a device that provides a function that contributes to a target system's capability.
>
> (5) Organization: a group or unit that provides a function that contributes to a target system's capability.[63]

U.S. doctrine also explains that targeting is fundamentally driven by the effect that the commander intends to achieve in support of the overall operational plan, and not simply on the nature of the target:

> Effects-Based. The art of targeting seeks to create desired effects with the least risk and least expenditure of time and resources.[64]

(which may include a place) makes to "military action". AP I, *supra*, note 53, art. 52(2). The United States contends that this includes objects that make an effective contribution to an enemy's "war fighting or war-sustaining capability." DoD LAW OF WAR MANUAL, *supra*, note 18, para. 5.7.6.2. However, academic experts believe this is too broad. *See, e.g.*, Yoram Dinstein, *Legitimate Military Objectives under the Current Jus In Bello*, 78 INT'L L. STUD. 139, 145 (2002) ("an American attempt . . . to substitute the words 'military action' by the idiom 'war-fighting or war-sustaining capability,' goes too far.").

62. U.S. DEP'T OF ARMY, FIELD MANUAL 3-60, TARGETING, para. 1-6 (7 May 2015).
63. JOINT CHIEFS OF STAFF, JOINT PUB. 3-60, JOINT TARGETING, at para. I-1-2 (31 Jan. 2013).
64. *Id.*, at viii.

Accordingly, under an effects-based standard, targets can include virtually any person, object, or place within the zone of military operations.

By contrast, the principle of distinction is based on a presumption that many persons, places, or things are not lawful targets. While military personnel, equipment, and facilities are presumptively lawful objects of attack, all other persons, places, or things are presumptively protected from attack. However, the presumption is rebuttable. For example, the presumption that military personnel are subject to attack does not apply where an enemy soldier, disabled by capture, wounds, or illness, is no longer engaged in hostilities, because attacking such a soldier is no longer justified by military necessity. On the other hand, a civilian who directly participates in hostilities loses the protection from attack for such time as he/she participates, for the equally obvious reason that disabling that civilian is necessary in order to protect friendly forces.[65]

A central component of the distinction principle is reflected in Article 51 of Additional Protocol I, which provides that "[t]he presence or movements of the civilian population or individual civilians shall not be used to render certain points or areas immune from military operations, in particular in attempts to shield military objectives from attacks or to shield, favour or impede military operations."[66] Pursuant to this rule, the presence of civilians or civilian property in or near a lawful target will not "immunize" the target from being attacked. However, the risk that the attack poses to civilians and civilian property is not irrelevant, even when an enemy deliberately exploits that risk in order to complicate the enemy attack decision. Whenever an attack is expected to expose civilians or civilian property to the risk of death, injury, or destruction, the law mandates that this risk be evaluated before an attack is launched. This evaluation is required by the complementary LOAC principles of proportionality and precautions, discussed below.

4. Proportionality: The Balancing Principle

Risk to civilians and civilian property would appear to be an inevitable consequence of armed conflict, which is, without question, one of the great tragedies of war. In fact, despite efforts to ensure greater precision and accuracy of combat power, civilians have been killed or injured during armed conflicts, not because they were deliberately attacked, but because of the incidental injury to civilians or collateral damage to civilian property that may result from an attack on a lawful military target. Because of this reality, something more than distinction is required to limit the risk to these innocent victims of war.

The principle of proportionality is a central component of this "something more", and qualifies the authority to deliberately attack a lawful target. Under this principle, once a target is assessed as lawful pursuant to the principle of distinction, proportionality imposes an additional obligation to forgo attack when

---

65. AP I, *supra*, note 53, art. 51(3). The United States defines the category of private persons who may be targeted more broadly. *See* DoD Law of War Manual, *supra*, note 18, para. 4.18.

66. AP I, *supra*, note 53, art. 51(7).

it is anticipated that the attack will cause loss of civilian life, injury to civilians, damage to civilian objects, or a combination thereof, which would be excessive in relation to the concrete and direct military advantage anticipated.[67] Any attack that violates the proportionality principle is considered indiscriminate and therefore unlawful.[68] This principle is customary international law, applicable to all armed conflicts.[69]

The term "proportionality" can be somewhat misleading. An attack does not become indiscriminate when the incidental injury to civilians or collateral damage to civilian property is slightly greater than the military advantage anticipated (as is suggested by the term "disproportionate"), but only when those effects are *excessive*. In this regard, it is important to distinguish the LOAC proportionality principle from the human rights notion of proportionality applicable to peacetime law enforcement activities, and to constabulary-type missions during armed conflict (such as maintaining law and order in an area subject to belligerent occupation) that might apply a law enforcement paradigm with respect to the use of force. In the law enforcement context, rules governing use of force are much more aligned with everyday notions of proportionality, allowing only the minimal amount of force necessary to subdue a threat (e.g., capture before wound, wound before kill).[70] Furthermore, in the human rights context, the obligation to use proportionate force protects the deliberate object of violence, and not only those proximate who are also put at risk. In the armed conflict context, by contrast, proportionality does not protect the lawful target, but only innocent civilians and their property that are endangered by the incidental or collateral effects of the attack.[71]

The LOAC principle of proportionality is therefore a balancing test, with excessiveness acting as the proverbial fulcrum. The two critical components of this balance in the LOAC are the anticipated military advantage to be gained by attacking the lawful target, and the collateral damage to civilian property and incidental injury to civilians anticipated from the attack. As a result, the principle plays no role in an attack on a combatant or military objective that does not expose civilians or civilian objects to risk.[72]

There are no established numerical equations or ratios for applying the proportionality balance.[73] Furthermore, application of the LOAC proportionality

---

67. *Id.*, art. 57(2)(a)(iii)-(2)(b); *accord* DoD LAW OF WAR MANUAL, *supra*, note 18, para. 5.12.

68. AP I, *supra*, note 53, art. 51(4)-(5). Under AP I, it is a grave breach to launch an attack affecting civilians or civilian objects in the knowledge that the attack will cause excessive loss of life, injury to civilians or damage to civilian objects, as prohibited by Article 57(2)(a)(iii). *Id.*, art. 85(3)(b).

69. *See* CIL STUDY, *supra*, note 59, 46-50 (asserting in Rule 14 that the principle of proportionality is a norm of customary international law in all armed conflicts); *accord* DoD LAW OF WAR MANUAL, *supra*, note 18, para. 17.7.

70. ICRC, THE USE OF FORCE IN ARMED CONFLICTS: INTERPLAY BETWEEN THE CONDUCT OF HOSTILITIES AND LAW ENFORCEMENT PARADIGMS 8-9 (Gloria Gaggioli ed., 2015), *available at* https://www.icrc.org/eng/assets/files/publications/icrc-002-4171.pdf.

71. *See id.*

72. DoD LAW OF WAR MANUAL, *supra*, note 18, para. 5.12.1.

73. Though, the U.S. Government employs a detailed process to estimate collateral damage. *See* CHAIRMAN, JOINT CHIEFS OF STAFF, INSTR. 3160.01, NO-STRIKE AND THE COLLATERAL DAMAGE ESTIMATION METHODOLOGY (13 Feb. 2009).

principle requires consideration of operational variables and therefore any evaluation of whether the principle was correctly applied must be made through the perspective of the attacking force at the time the attack decision was made. All facts and circumstances facing the commander at the time of the attack, including the pressures of time and the proverbial "fog of war," properly frame such decisions, and therefore must be considered when assessing compliance with the principle. Thus, the principle does not demand that an attack decision is always correct, but it does demand that a reasonable judgment about (i) the expected incidental injury and collateral damage, and (ii) the value of the military advantage expected to be achieved through the attacked as compared to the incidental injury or collateral damage. Launching an attack with the knowledge that the harm it will cause to civilians and/or civilian property is expected to be excessive compared to the military advantage it will produce, is simply unreasonable and a violation of the proportionality principle.

It is also important to recognize that if the anticipated harm to civilians and civilian property resulting from an attack on a military objective is not excessive compared to the anticipated military advantage, the attack is lawful, even if the attacking force knows civilians will suffer and civilian property will be damaged. This is a harsh reality of war: commanders may lawfully order attacks with knowledge that the likely outcome will include significant harm to the civilian population. Distinction prohibits the deliberate attack against civilians and/or civilian property; proportionality prohibits launching an attack on a lawful target when the anticipated collateral or incidental harm will be *excessive* compared to the advantage expected to be gained. Thus, compliance with the proportionality principle demands a good faith effort to anticipate the harm to civilians and damage to civilian property that will result from an attack. It does not require, however, that there be no harm or damage anticipated.

5. Precautions: The Precondition for All Combat Operations

Protecting civilians and civilian property from avoidable harm is facilitated by consideration of civilian risk mitigation measures in addition to proportionality considerations. These measures fall under a general principle known as "precautions in the attack" or simply "precautions." Precautionary measures are vital civilian risk mitigation tools.

While the precautions principle is considered to be part of customary law by some experts,[74] not all military manuals expressly adopt it as a principle. For example, although precautions in the attack are included in the DoD Law of War Manual,[75] there is no reference to a precautions principle in the Manual.[76] This is unfortunate, as precautionary measures complement, and in some ways facilitate, compliance with distinction and proportionality.[77] For example, the

---
74. *See, e.g.,* CIL STUDY, *supra*, note 59, at 51 (describing precautions as a principle).
75. *See* DoD LAW OF WAR MANUAL, *supra*, note 18, para. 5.11.
76. *See id.*, ch. 2 (*see*, specifically, the lack of a precautions principle).
77. *See, generally* Geoffrey Corn & James A. Schoettler, *Targeting and Civilian Risk Mitigation: The Essential Role of Precautionary Measures*, 223 MIL. L. REV. 786, 787-790, 832-837 (2015) (advocating the adoption of precautions as a LOAC principle).

obligation to gather the best available information related to the nature of a proposed target and the risk to civilians and civilian objects associated with an attack on that target is considered a precautionary measure, as it enhances the quality of distinction and proportionality judgments. Furthermore, a general obligation to take constant care to employ feasible measures to mitigate civilian risk advances the principle of humanity and contributes to an effective balance between military necessity and humanity.

Precautionary measures to mitigate civilian risk should, therefore, be considered a LOAC principle. This principle requires commanders and subordinates to integrate precautionary measures into every aspect of military operations whenever doing so is feasible. This feasibility qualifier is integrated into the treaty rules that enumerate the precautions obligation,[78] in recognition of the fact that in many circumstances, use of precautionary measures may compromise mission accomplishment. For example, a commander contemplating an attack on targets in an area with a civilian population should consider issuing a warning to the civilians, but if doing so will expose his forces to increased enemy risk, a warning might not be feasible under the circumstances.[79] Similarly, if a commander has multiple weapon system options to achieve the same attack effect, she should consider utilizing the option that poses the least risk to the civilian population.[80] But if the nature of the mission demands that she preserve certain weapon systems for other aspects of the operation, it may not be feasible to use the lowest risk system.[81]

As a general matter, the precautions principle includes both an active and passive component.[82] The active component includes the obligation to gather the maximum amount of information feasibly available, the obligation to constantly update target information, and the obligation to consider use of civilian risk mitigation measures such as warnings, evacuations, agreement on safety zones, timing of attack, weapon system selection, and tactic selection. The passive component is focused on measures that enhance civilian protection by facilitating the enemy's distinction process. These include refraining, where feasible, from locating military objectives in the midst of civilians, and refraining from tactics that blur the line between civilian and belligerent operative, such as fighting in civilian clothing. Ideally, good faith implementation of precautionary measures will enhance the ability to distinguish between lawful targets and protected civilians and civilian objects, and will substantially reduce anticipated risk to civilians and civilian objects resulting from an attack, thereby making

---

78. *See, e.g.*, AP I, *supra*, note 53, art. 57(2)(a)(i).

79. *Id.*, art. 57(2)(c) ("effective advance warning shall be given of attacks which may affect the civilian population, unless circumstances do not permit").

80. CIL STUDY, *supra*, note 59, at 56 ("Rule 17. Each party to the conflict must take all feasible precautions in the choice of means and methods of warfare with a view to avoiding, and in any event to minimising, incidental loss of civilian life, injury to civilians and damage to civilian objects.").

81. DoD LAW OF WAR MANUAL, *supra*, note 18, para. 5.11.3 ("As with other precautions, the decision of which weapon to use will be subject to many practical considerations, including effectiveness, costs, and the need to preserve capabilities for other engagements.").

82. *See* AP I, *supra*, note 53, art. 57-58.

the proportionality judgment far less complex than it would have been without the use of such measures.

IV. Treaty Law

Treaties — "international agreements concluded between States in written form and governed by international law"[83] — are arguably the most important source of LOAC rules. While the rules in treaties are binding only on the parties to the treaties, the most important LOAC treaties — the Geneva Conventions of 1949 — have been ratified (as of mid-2018) by 196 countries.[84]

A. Hague Law

There were two efforts in the latter half of the nineteenth century to produce international codes of conduct for warfare. Both codes contributed to the adoption of conventions around the turn of the twentieth century that still regulate battlefield conduct today.

In July 1874, at the invitation of Russian Tsar Alexander II, representatives from 15 States met in Brussels, Belgium to review a proposed international agreement regarding the laws and customs of war prepared by the Russian Government. The draft International Declaration concerning the Laws and Customs of War (Brussels Declaration)[85] was adopted by the delegates with minor changes, but their governments were not prepared to accept it as a binding instrument. Nevertheless, the draft, which addressed in detail subjects directly connected with the conduct of hostilities — including: (1) the lawful and unlawful means of injuring the enemy; (2) sieges and bombardments; (3) the military occupation of enemy territory; (4) spying and the treatment of spies; (5) prisoners of war; (6) the sick and the wounded; (7) armistices, capitulations, and related subjects; and (8) rules for neutral countries caring for interned and wounded belligerents — ultimately became a basis for binding international rules adopted in The Hague, Netherlands, at the end of the century.

Although the Brussels Declaration was not adopted, the Institute of International Law in Geneva, Switzerland, created a committee to study the Brussels Declaration and to submit its opinion and supplementary proposals on the subject to the Institute. The result was the Manual of the Laws and Customs

---

83. DoD Law of War Manual, *supra*, note 18, para. 1.7.
84. *Int'l Comm. Red Cross, State Parties to the Following International Humanitarian Law and Other Related Treaties as of 20-Jun-2018*, available at https://ihl-databases.icrc.org/ihl (hereinafter, State Parties List).
85. Project of an International Declaration Concerning the Laws and Customs of War, Aug. 27, 1874, 4 Martens Nouveau Recueil (ser. 2) 219.

of War adopted in Oxford, England in 1880.[86] The Oxford Manual addressed many of the same subjects as the Brussels Declaration, though it used different language. Like the Brussels Declaration, the Oxford Manual contributed to the rules adopted in The Hague in 1899 and 1907.

Two international "peace conferences" held in 1899 and 1907, primarily for the purpose of seeking terms to ensure "to all peoples the benefits of a real and last peace," resulted in the adoption of a comprehensive set of rules to regulate the conduct of hostilities. The Regulations and Annexes appended to the Convention (II) with Respect to the Laws and Customs of War on Land of July 29, 1899 (1899 Hague II),[87] and the Convention (IV) respecting the Laws and Customs of War on Land of October 18, 1907 (1907 Hague IV),[88] established foundational LOAC rules concerning: (1) the qualifications of lawful combatants; (2) prisoners of war; (3) lawful and unlawful means and methods of warfare; (4) the status and treatment of spies in wartime; (5) flags of truce, capitulations, and armistices; and (6) military occupation of enemy territory. As of mid-2018, there are 51 States party to 1899 Hague II, and 38 States party to 1907 Hague IV; but, the regulations appended to these treaties are identical in almost all respects, and 1907 Hague IV, at least, is binding on all States as customary international law.[89]

Among the most important provisions of the regulations appended to the 1899 Hague II and 1907 Hague IV are Articles 22 and 23:

> Art. 22. The right of belligerents to adopt means of injuring the enemy is not unlimited.
>
> Art. 23. In addition to the prohibitions provided by special Conventions, it is especially forbidden
>
> (a) To employ poison or poisoned weapons;
>
> (b) To kill or wound treacherously individuals belonging to the hostile nation or army;
>
> (c) To kill or wound an enemy who, having laid down his arms, or having no longer means of defence, has surrendered at discretion;
>
> (d) To declare that no quarter will be given;
>
> (e) To employ arms, projectiles, or material calculated to cause unnecessary suffering;
>
> (f) To make improper use of a flag of truce, of the national flag or of the military insignia and uniform of the enemy, as well as the distinctive badges of the Geneva Convention;
>
> (g) To destroy or seize the enemy's property, unless such destruction or seizure be imperatively demanded by the necessities of war;
>
> (h) To declare abolished, suspended, or inadmissible in a court of law the rights and actions of the nationals of the hostile party. A belligerent is likewise forbidden to compel the nationals of the hostile party to

---

86. *See, generally* Oxford Manual, *supra*, note 29.
87. *See, generally* 1899 Hague II, *supra*, note 39.
88. *See, generally* 1907 Hague IV, *supra*, note 39.
89. *See, e.g.*, FM 27-10, *supra*, note 2, para. 6 (noting that 1907 Hague IV's principles "have been held to be declaratory of the customary law of war, to which all States are subject").

take part in the operations of war directed against their own country, even if they were in the belligerent's service before the commencement of the war.

Taken together, these provisions account for today's most significant restrictions applicable to the conduct of military operations against other combatants.

In addition to 1907 Hague IV, the second Hague Peace Conference resulted in the adoption of the Convention (VIII) Relative to the Laying of Automatic Submarine Contact Mines,[90] and the Convention (IX) Respecting Bombardment by Naval Forces in Time of War (1907 Hague IX);[91] which, along with a 1936 Procès-verbal relating to the Rule on Submarine Warfare,[92] and the 1949 Geneva Convention for the Amelioration of the Condition of Wounded, Sick and Shipwrecked Members of Armed Forces at Sea,[93] are the key international conventions dealing with the conduct of naval warfare. The second Hague Peace Conference also produced several conventions addressing the rights and obligations of neutrals during wartime, which form the basis for the law of neutrality today.[94] These include the Convention (V) Respecting the Rights and Duties of Neutral Powers and Persons in Case of War on Land,[95] the Convention (VI) Relative to the Status of Enemy Merchant Ships at the Outbreak of Hostilities,[96] and the Convention (XIII) Concerning the Rights and Duties of Neutral Powers in Naval War.[97] Like 1907 Hague IV and its annex

---

90. Convention (VIII) Relative to the Laying of Automatic Submarine Contact Mines, Oct. 18, 1907, 36 Stat. 2332.

91. Convention (IX) Concerning Bombardment by Naval Forces in Time of War, Oct. 18, 1907, 36 Stat. 2351 (hereinafter, Hague IX).

92. Procès-verbal Relating to Rules of Submarine Warfare Set Forth in Part IV of the Treaty of London of 22 April 1930, Nov. 6, 1936, 173 L.N.T.S. 353 (this procès-verbal entered into force November 6, 1936).

93. Geneva Convention for the Amelioration of the Condition of Wounded, Sick, and Shipwrecked Members of the Armed Forces at Sea, Aug. 12, 1949, 6 U.S.T. 3217, 75 U.N.T.S. 971 (hereinafter GWS Sea). This treaty was preceded by another treaty from the second Hague Peace Conference. Convention (X) for the Adaptation to Maritime Warfare of the Principles of the Geneva Convention, Oct. 18, 1907, 36 Stat. 2371 (1907 Hague X). There also is a 1904 convention exempting hospital ships from certain "dues and taxes" in time of war. Convention for the Exemption of Hospital Ships, in Time of War, from The Payment of all Dues and Taxes Imposed for the Benefit of the State, Dec. 21, 1904, 197 Consol. T.S. 331.

94. The right of a State to remain neutral with respect to a particular conflict may be limited by that State's obligations under international agreements. For example, where the U.N. Security Council has taken action under Chapter VII of the U.N. Charter to authorize military operations with respect to a particular conflict, the State may be obligated to provide assistance to those operations and refrain from assisting the State(s) against which the operation is being conducted. *See* DoD Law of War Manual, *supra*, note 18, para. 15.2.3.2; U.S. DEP'T OF NAVY, NWP 1-14M, COMMANDER'S HANDBOOK ON THE LAW OF NAVAL OPERATIONS para. 7.2.1 (Aug. 2017).

95. Convention (V) Respecting the Rights and Duties of Neutral Powers and Persons in Case of War on Land, Oct. 18, 1907, 36 Stat. 2310.

96. Convention (VI) Relating to the Status of Enemy Merchant Ships at the Outbreak of Hostilities, Oct. 18, 1907, 205 Consol. T.S. 305 (the United States did not ratify this Convention).

97. Convention (XIII) Concerning the Rights and Duties of Neutral Powers in Naval War, Oct. 18, 1907, 36 Stat. 2415.

governing the conduct of hostilities on land, these conventions have not been adopted by all States, but largely reflect customary international law.[98]

The rules on the conduct of hostilities established by 1907 Hague IV and its annex have come to be known as "Hague Law" and remain directly relevant to military operations today. Attempts prior to World War II to supplement Hague IV with binding rules concerning the conduct of hostilities in the air and sea failed,[99] although there have been recent efforts to articulate rules of air warfare that constitute customary law.[100] However, since the end of World War II, there have been several additional treaties that regulate warfare.[101]

Also part of the Hague Law are provisions that ban specific weapons or methods of warfare. For example, Article 23 of 1907 Hague IV includes a specific prohibition against "poison or poisoned weapons,"[102] and a more generic provision against employing "arms, projectiles, or material calculated to cause unnecessary suffering."[103] In 1925, a protocol to ban first use of gas weapons was opened for signature, but many States (including the United States) did not adopt it until well after World War II.[104] In the years after World War II, however, a number of agreements have been concluded to limit or ban the use of certain weapons deemed to cause unnecessary suffering or otherwise to be incapable of being employed discriminately. This includes not only treaties to ban certain types of weapons of mass destruction, but also a discrete set of conventional battlefield weapons, such as anti-personnel mines.[105] The United States, however, has not signed or ratified all of these treaties.

B. Geneva Law

The 1864 Geneva Convention for the Amelioration of the Condition of the Wounded in Armies in the Field, inspired by Henri Dunant's *A Memory of Solferino*, was aimed to protect the wounded in war.[106] Conventions adopted at the first and second Hague Peace Conferences in 1899 and 1907, respectively, extended the protections for the sick and wounded to naval warfare.[107] In 1906, a new treaty, the Geneva Convention for the Amelioration of the

---

98. *See, generally, e.g.*, SAN REMO MANUAL ON INT'L LAW APPLICABLE TO ARMED CONFLICTS AT SEA (Doswald-Beck, ed., 1995) (hereinafter SAN REMO MANUAL) ("most" of Hague XIII considered to be "declaratory of customary law").

99. A manual on naval warfare was drafted in 1913, and a set of rules regarding air warfare was drafted in 1922-1923 but never adopted. Except to the extent indicative of customary law, neither are binding as a matter of international law.

100. *See infra* pt. V (discussing customary international law).

101. *See infra* pt. IV.C, D.

102. 1907 Hague IV, *supra*, note 39, art. 23(a).

103. *Id.*, art. 23(e).

104. Protocol for the Prohibition of the Use in War of Asphyxiating, Poisonous, or Other Gases, and of Bacteriological Methods of Warfare, June 17, 1925, 94 L.N.T.S. 65.

105. *See infra* pt. IV.D.

106. 1864 Geneva Convention, *supra*, note 16.

107. *See, generally* 1907 Hague X, *supra*, note 95.

Condition of the Wounded and Sick in Armies in the Field, was adopted;[108] and, in 1929, a third treaty, the Geneva Convention Relative to the Treatment of Prisoners of War, was adopted to address the treatment of prisoners of war.[109] These treaties became the foundation for what has come to be known as "Geneva Law", which seeks to protect those who are not actively engaged in hostilities, due to injuries, illness, or capture, as well as those who are responsible for their care.

Despite their advancements, there were a number of weaknesses in the pre-World War II Geneva Conventions. First, they only protected the forces of countries who were a party to the treaties, and the fact that the treaties were not universally adopted meant there were significant gaps in coverage during World War II.[110] Also, they only applied in cases where the parties acknowledged that they were at war, which at a minimum, required at least one of the parties to issue a formal declaration of war. This meant that the protection afforded by the treaties would not apply if neither party to a conflict was willing to recognize that a state of war existed. Further, because "war" was considered to be a conflict among States, none of the protections applied to internal conflicts, which, during the interwar period, included violent conflicts such as the Spanish Civil War. Finally, and perhaps most significantly in the context of World War II, none of the treaties dealt with the treatment of the civilian population generally, namely, outside the context of a military occupation.[111]

Weaknesses and ambiguities in the treaties, the atrocities suffered by civilians during World War II, and the success of war crimes tribunals in applying international law against the Axis powers, all led to a major postwar effort to revise the treaties comprising the Geneva Law, and further expand their coverage to include civilian populations. Ultimately, four Conventions were negotiated. In 1949 at Geneva, Switzerland, these new Geneva Conventions were opened for signature. They included:

- The Geneva Convention for the Amelioration of the Condition of the Wounded and Sick in Armed Forces in the Field (GWS);[112]

---

108. Geneva Convention for the Amelioration of the Condition of the Wounded and Sick in Armies in the Field, July 6, 1906, 11 L.N.T.S. 440.

109. Geneva Convention Relative to the Treatment of Prisoners of War, Jul. 27, 1929, 47 Stat. 2021. This Convention applied, *inter alia*, to U.S. military personnel held as prisoners of war by Germany during World War II.

110. Indeed, 1899 Hague II and 1907 Hague IV stipulated that the regulations annexed to each Convention would not apply if any State involved in the conflict was not a party, which meant that there was a significant risk that in a wider war, the regulations would not apply. Because the Hague Regulations are now considered to reflect customary law that is binding on all States, this limitation on the applicability of the regulations is no longer relevant. *See supra*, pt. IV.A.

111. 1907 Hague IV and its annexed regulations did address the military occupation context. *See* 1907 Hague IV, *supra*, note 39, § III.

112. Geneva Convention for the Amelioration of the Condition of the Wounded and Sick in Armed Forces in the Field, Aug. 12, 1949, 6 U.S.T. 3114, 75 U.N.T.S. 970 (hereinafter GWS).

- The Geneva Convention for the Amelioration of the Condition of Wounded, Sick, and Shipwrecked Members of the Armed Forces at Sea (GWS Sea);[113]
- The Geneva Convention Relative to the Treatment of Prisoners of War (GPW);[114] and
- The Geneva Convention Relative to the Protection of Civilian Persons in Time of War (GC IV).[115]

A number of key improvements in the LOAC were introduced by the 1949 Geneva Conventions. First, each Convention included a "Common" Article 2 — present identically in all four Conventions — that eliminated the necessity for a declared war in order for treaty application. Instead, Common Article 2 stipulated that each Convention was applicable, not only in the case of a declared war, but also in the event of "any other armed conflict which may arise between two or more of the High Contracting Parties, even if the state of war is not recognized by one of them."[116] Common Article 2 also provided that the treaty would apply in "all cases of partial or total occupation of the territory of a High Contracting Party, even if the said occupation meets with no armed resistance."[117] Thus, the applicability of the 1949 Conventions was potentially far broader than had been the case in the earlier treaties.

Second, each of the Conventions listed certain violations of the Convention's norms that were considered to be so serious as to be a universal crime — meaning that all countries were bound to search for and apprehend violators of these norms, and that any country could prosecute these crimes, even if its citizens were not involved in the crimes either as perpetrators or victims. If a country was unwilling to prosecute a violator, it was bound to hand the violator over to a country that was willing to prosecute. These provisions strengthened the potential legal basis for prosecuting serious violations of the LOAC and contributed to the development of an international criminal law.

Third, each Convention included a Common Article 1 that obligated all parties to the Conventions (called "High Contracting Parties") to "undertake to respect and to ensure respect for the present Convention in all circumstances."[118] This provision eliminated any requirement for reciprocity, so that a party's obligation under the Convention is absolute, regardless of whether other countries abide by their obligations.

---

113. GWS Sea, *supra*, note 93.
114. Geneva Convention Relative to the Treatment of Prisoners of War, Aug. 12, 1949, 6 U.S.T. 3316, 75 U.N.T.S. 972 (hereinafter GPW).
115. *See, generally* Geneva Convention Relative to the Protection of Civilian Persons in Time of War, Aug. 12, 1949, 6 U.S.T. 3516, 75 U.N.T.S. 973 (hereinafter GC IV).
116. GWS, *supra*, note 112, art. 2; GWS-Sea, *supra*, note 93, art. 2; GPW, *supra*, note 114, art. 2; GCIV, *supra*, note 115, art. 2 (hereinafter Common Article 2).
117. *Id.*
118. GWS, *supra*, note 112, art. 1; GWS-Sea, *supra*, note 93, art. 1; GPW, *supra*, note 114, art. 1; GCIV, *supra*, note 115, art. 1 (hereinafter Common Article 1).

Fourth, nations for the first time adopted a Convention that established a basic level of protection for civilians generally, not only in occupied territory,[119] but also in areas near active battlefields and in a belligerent's own territory.[120] In addition, the protection afforded to civilians in occupied territory was enhanced by this convention, and greater protection was extended to enemy civilians residing in the home territory of the opposing belligerent, such that, while in those territories, they are considered to be "protected persons" who are entitled both to be respected and protected by their nation's enemy during an armed conflict.[121]

Finally, the Conventions included, for the first time, a Common Article 3 addressing "the case of armed conflict not of an international character occurring in the territory of one of the High Contracting Parties."[122] These "non-international" armed conflicts were thought at the time to include rebellions and other internal wars and conflicts, such as the Spanish Civil War, that traditionally were outside the scope of the law of armed conflict except in unusual circumstances (i.e., where the rebels were able to achieve many of the attributes of a State and to conduct hostilities accordingly, such as in the American Civil War).[123] Since 1949, Common Article 3 has come to be viewed as a "minimum yardstick" of treatment in any armed conflict, and to apply to all individuals not participating in hostilities.[124]

A key element of the four 1949 Geneva Conventions is their focus on obligations to "respect" and "protect" the persons and property covered by each Convention. As the 1958 Commentary to GC IV explains:

> The word "respect" (*respecter*) means according to the Dictionary of the French Academy, "to spare, not to attack" (épargner, ne point attaquer), whereas "protect" (protéger) means "to come to someone's defence, to give help and support." These words make it unlawful to kill, ill-treat or in any way injure an unarmed enemy, while at the same time they impose an obligation to come to his aid and give him any care of which he stands in need.[125]

---

119. Which, as noted earlier, is addressed (albeit in less detail) in 1907 Hague IV. *See supra*, n. 113.

120. With the exception of certain generally applicable protections found in Part II of the treaty, the treaty's protections are directed principally to enemy civilians in territory under military occupation by a belligerent State or in the belligerent State's own territory, but some of these protections may apply more broadly as a matter of customary law in an IAC.

121. *See* GC IV, *supra*, note 115, art. 4.

122. Common Article 3, *supra*, note 56.

123. *See generally* INT'L COMM. RED CROSS, CONVENTION (I) FOR THE AMELIORATION OF THE CONDITION OF THE WOUNDED AND SICK IN ARMED FORCES IN THE FIELD. GENEVA, 12 AUGUST 1949: COMMENTARY OF 2016 paras. 197, 357-83, https://ihl-databases.icrc.org/applic/ihl/ihl.nsf/Treaty.xsp?documentId=4825657B0C7E6BF0C12563CD002D6B0B&action=openDocument.

124. *See* DoD LAW OF WAR MANUAL, *supra*, note para. 18, 8.1.4.1 (citing, *inter alia*, Hamdan v. Rumsfeld, 548 U.S. 557, 630-631 (2006).

125. COMMENTARY, GENEVA CONVENTION RELATIVE TO THE PROTECTION OF CIVILIAN PERSONS IN TIME OF WAR 134 (Jean S. Pictet ed., 1958).

The use of the terms "respect" and "protect" predates the Geneva Conventions, but a greater emphasis is placed on them in the Conventions (and in treaties since 1949) to underline the proactive nature of the humanitarian obligations imposed under these treaties.[126]

All countries in existence today have ratified the 1949 Geneva Conventions, and thus, they represent the minimum obligations of States in any IAC. As a result, Common Article 3 is applicable in all cases of conflicts "not of an international character." Countries remain free to withdraw from (or "denounce") the Conventions, but only by giving a one-year advanced notice; and furthermore, any such withdrawal would not apply to any armed conflict in which the denouncing country is involved at the time of denunciation.[127] Finally, as discussed below, arguments could well be made that the provisions of the Geneva Conventions have now matured into customary international law, and would be applicable notwithstanding the denunciation.

C. Additional Protocols of 1977: Merging of Hague and Geneva Law

The most significant LOAC treaties since World War II are the two supplemental agreements to the 1949 Geneva Conventions, which were negotiated during the 1970s and opened for signature in 1977:

- Protocol (I) Additional to the Geneva Conventions of 12 Aug. 1949, and Relating to the Protection of Victims of International Armed Conflicts (AP I);[128] and
- Protocol (II) Additional to the Geneva Conventions of 12 Aug. 1949, and Relating to the Protection of Victims of Non-International Armed Conflicts (AP II).[129]

AP I was intended to supplement the four Geneva Conventions, but it also included several innovations. First, Article 1(4) of AP I extended the full benefit of the Geneva Conventions, as supplemented by AP I, to "armed conflicts in which peoples are fighting against colonial domination and alien occupation and against racist regimes in the exercise of their right of self-determination."[130] Because these conflicts typically involve rebellions against States, rather than inter-state conflicts, AP I for the first time applied the full body of the LOAC to conflicts previously considered to be NIACs.

Second, Articles 8-34 of AP I extended the protection of GWS and GWS Sea, as supplemented by AP I, to civilian medical personnel, equipment, and

---

126. COMMENTARY, GENEVA CONVENTION FOR THE AMELIORATION OF THE CONDITION OF THE WOUNDED AND SICK IN ARMED FORCES IN THE FIELD 137 (Jean S. Pictet ed., 1952).
127. *See, e.g.*, GWS, *supra*, note 112, art. 63.
128. *See, generally* AP I, *supra*, note 55.
129. *See, generally* AP II, *supra*, note 57.
130. AP I, *supra*, note 53, art. 1(4).

supplies, and to civilian units and transports, and further developed the rules applicable to the protection of medical transportation.

Third, in addition to supplementing provisions of the protections of victims under the four Geneva Conventions, Articles 35-60 of AP I updated the rules governing the conduct of hostilities articulated in 1907 Hague IV and its annex, and set out in detail the rules applicable to the principle of proportionality, the definition of military objectives, the protection of the civilian population and civilian property against attacks, and the scope of the definitions of armed forces and combatants. Articles 61-79 added rules for the protection of civil defense organizations and relief actions; and, in Article 75, AP I detailed the protection to which any individual detained or otherwise in the power of a party to the conflict is entitled in an IAC, thus protecting those not expressly covered by GPW or GC IV.

Fourth, Article 85 of AP I sets out additional grave breaches of the LOAC, and Articles 86 and 87 addressed the responsibility of commanders, including for failure to act when a subordinate violates the LOAC.

AP II is a much shorter version of AP I and is intended to apply certain key provisions of AP I to NIACs, including the protections afforded to detained persons under Article 75 of AP I. However, the scope of NIACs covered by AP II is narrower than the conflicts covered by Common Article 3 of the Geneva Conventions, and includes only conflicts that "take place in the territory of a High Contracting Party between its armed forces and dissident armed forces or other organized armed groups which, under responsible command, exercise such control over a part of its territory as to enable them to carry out sustained and concerted military operations and to implement this Protocol."[131] Thus, AP II would not apply to conflicts between two non-State parties or internal conflicts where the non-State party does not control territory; however, even where AP II is not applicable, such conflicts are covered by Common Article 3.

For various reasons, neither AP I nor AP II has been ratified by the United States, even though as of mid-2018, 174 States are party to AP I and 168 States are party to AP II.[132] The wide international adherence to both treaties by U.S. allies can affect the interoperability of U.S. armed forces with allies in coalition operations.

---

131. AP II, *supra*, note 57, art. 1(1).
132. State Parties List, *supra*, note 84. The United States has ratified a third additional protocol that establishes the red crystal as a protective symbol on equal footing with the red cross and the red crescent. Protocol (III) Additional to the Geneva Conventions of 12 Aug. 1949, and Relating to the Adoption of an Additional Distinctive Emblem, Dec. 8, 2005, 2404 U.N.T.S. 1.

D. Other LOAC Treaties

1. Cultural Property

The regulations annexed to 1907 Hague IV (and its predecessor, 1899 Hague II) include two provisions intended to protect cultural property:

> Art. 27. In sieges and bombardments all necessary steps must be taken to spare, as far as possible, buildings dedicated to religion, art, science, or charitable purposes, historic monuments, hospitals, and places where the sick and wounded are collected, provided they are not being used at the time for military purposes. It is the duty of the besieged to indicate the presence of such buildings or places by distinctive and visible signs, which shall be notified to the enemy beforehand.
>
> . . .
>
> Art. 56. The property of municipalities, that of institutions dedicated to religion, charity and education, the arts and sciences, even when State property, shall be treated as private property. All seizure of, destruction or wilful damage done to institutions of this character, historic monuments, works of art and science, is forbidden, and should be made the subject of legal proceedings.[133]

These provisions make no distinction based on the cultural significance of the property they protect, and as the term "as far as possible" suggests, some of the protections they provide are subject to a possible override where military necessity requires. As the text of Article 27 notes, it only protects "buildings." Article 56 is possibly broader, because it protects "property"; but Article 56 is part of the provisions of 1907 Hague IV dealing with military occupation of enemy territory and is not expressly applicable in other combat situations (e.g., where control of territory is still being contested).

At the suggestion of Professor Nicholas Roerich, a treaty to protect cultural property was prepared by Georges Chklaver of the Institut des Hautes Études Internationales of the University of Paris and ultimately adopted by certain American States in the 1930s, including the United States.[134] The so-called Roerich Pact came into force in 1935. It provides for cultural institutions, as well as the personnel of such institutions, to be treated "as neutral and as such respected and protected by belligerents."[135] It also provided for a distinctive flag to indicate the protection afforded to these institutions, consisting of a red circle with a triple red sphere in the circle on a white background.[136] As noted, however, it only applies in certain North, Central, and South American States.

---

133. A provision similar to Article 27 of 1907 Hague IV was included in 1907 Hague IX regulating naval bombardment. See Hague IX, *supra*, note 91, art. 5. Unlike 1907 Hague IV, however, Hague IX also provided for the marking of cultural property (i.e., buildings) with special black and white panels to indicate that the property is protected. *Id.*

134. See, generally Treaty on the Protection of Artistic and Scientific Institutions and Historic Monuments, Apr. 15, 1935, 49 Stat. 3267.

135. *Id.*, art. 1.

136. *Id.*, art. 3.

IV. Treaty Law

Following the experience of World War II, in which Germany plundered many of the cultural properties of Europe, a more comprehensive treaty was negotiated and signed. The 1954 Hague Convention for the Protection of Cultural Property in the Event of Armed Conflict (1954 Hague Convention),[137] which entered into force in 1956, protects cultural property "of great importance to the cultural heritage of every people." The property protected by the 1954 Hague Convention includes not only institutions and monuments (i.e., "immovable" property), but also "works of art; manuscripts, books and other objects of artistic, historical or archaeological interest; as well as scientific collections and important collections of books or archives" (i.e., "moveable" property) as well as reproductions of the protected property.[138] It also protects buildings intended to exhibit or preserve the protected property, including "museums, large libraries and depositories of archives, and refuges intended to shelter, in the event of armed conflict," the protected property, as well as "centers" containing large amounts of the protected property.[139] But, as it is directed only at property "of great importance,"[140] not all the property protected by 1907 Hague IV would fall under the protection of the 1954 Hague Convention.

Under the 1954 Hague Convention, States are obligated to safeguard (e.g., by marking) cultural property in their own territory.[141] They also are obligated to respect cultural property in the territory of all contracting States, including their own territory, by "refraining from any use of the property and its immediate surroundings or of the appliances in use for its protection for purposes which are likely to expose it to destruction or damage in the event of armed conflict; and by refraining from any act of hostility directed against such property."[142] Thus, States are prohibited from attacking covered cultural property, except in the case of "imperative" military necessity, and also must "prohibit, prevent and, if necessary, put a stop to any form of theft, pillage or misappropriation of, and any acts of vandalism directed against, cultural property" and shall not take reprisals against cultural property.[143] A State occupying the territory of another State must "as far as possible support the competent national authorities of the

---

137. Convention for the Protection of Cultural Property in the Event of Armed Conflict, May 14, 1954, art. 1, 249 U.N.T.S. 240 (hereinafter 1954 Hague Convention). There are two protocols to this Convention that are worth noting. Protocol for the Protection of Cultural Property in the Event of Armed Conflict, May 14, 1954, 249 U.N.T.S. 358 (addressing the exportation of cultural property for occupied territories, including by requiring the return of such property); Second Protocol to the Hague Convention of 1954 for the Protection of Cultural Property in the Event of Armed Conflict, Mar. 26, 1999, 2253 U.N.T.S. 212 (seeking to update the 1954 Hague Convention to reflect provisions of Additional Protocol I, and to establish a regime for enhanced protection of cultural property that is more workable than the regime for special protection under the 1954 Hague Convention). The United States has not ratified either of the Protocols to the 1954 Hague Convention.

138. 1954 Hague Convention, *supra*, note 137, art. 1(a).

139. *Id.*, art. 1(b)-(c).

140. *Id.*, Preamble ("Considering that the preservation of the cultural heritage is of great importance for all peoples of the world and that it is important that this heritage should receive international protection....").

141. *Id.*, art. 3.

142. *Id.*, art. 4(1).

143. *Id.*, art. 4(3).

occupied country in safeguarding and preserving its cultural property," and "should the competent national authorities be unable to take such measures, the Occupying Power shall, as far as possible, and in close co-operation with such authorities, take the most necessary measures of preservation."[144] Importantly, and consistent with the fact that the 1954 Hague Convention applies to a State's own territory, as well as the territory of other States party to the Convention, the obligation to respect cultural property applies in a NIAC conflict as well as an IAC.[145]

2. Weapons

Another important post-World War II LOAC treaty is the 1980 Convention on Prohibitions or Restrictions on the Use of Certain Conventional Weapons Which May Be Deemed to Be Excessively Injurious or to Have Indiscriminate Effects (CCW).[146] The CCW provides a framework for the adoption of protocols banning or limiting certain weapons. To date, States party to the CCW have adopted protocols to ban: (1) weapons whose "primary effect" is to injure by means of fragments that cannot be detected by X-rays (Protocol I),[147] and (2) laser weapons "specifically designed, as their sole combat function or as one of their combat functions" to cause permanent blindness to uncorrected vision (Protocol IV).[148] Other protocols under the CCW limit, but do not ban: (1) certain land mines, booby-traps, and other explosive devices (Protocol II, as amended),[149] and (2) incendiary weapons (Protocol III).[150] An amendment adopted in 2001 extended all the terms of the CCW and its protocols to include

---

144. *Id.*, art. 5.
145. *Id.*, art. 19. The 1954 Hague Convention also includes a regime for registration of, and special protection for, (i) "refuges" to shelter movable cultural property, and (ii) centers "containing monuments and other cultural property of very great importance" and provisions for special protection of transports used exclusively to transfer cultural property under international supervision. *Id.*, art. 11-12. The 1954 Hague Convention also provides for a distinctive emblem that can be used to indicate that the property is protected and, when used in a group of three, that the property is subject to special protection. *Id.*, art. 8.
146. Convention on Prohibitions or Restrictions on the Use of Certain Conventional Weapons Which May be Deemed to be Excessively Injurious or to Have Indiscriminate Effects, Oct. 10, 1980, 1342 U.N.T.S. 137 (hereinafter CCW).
147. Protocol (I) on Non-Detectable Fragments, Annexed to the Convention on Prohibitions or Restrictions on the Use of Certain Conventional Weapons Which May be Deemed to be Excessively Injurious or to Have Indiscriminate Effects, Oct. 10, 1980, 1342 U.N.T.S. 137.
148. Protocol (IV) on Blinding Laser Weapons, Annexed to the Convention on Prohibitions or Restrictions on the Use of Certain Conventional Weapons Which May be Deemed to be Excessively Injurious or to Have Indiscriminate Effects, Oct. 13, 1995, 1380 U.N.T.S. 163.
149. Protocol (II) on Prohibitions or Restrictions on the Use of Mines, Booby-Traps and Other Devices, as Amended on May 3, 1996, Annexed to the Convention on Prohibitions or Restrictions on the Use of Certain Conventional Weapons Which May be Deemed to be Excessively Injurious or to Have Indiscriminate Effects, May 3, 1996, 2048 U.N.T.S. 93.
150. Protocol (III) on Prohibitions or Restrictions on the Use of Incendiary Weapons, Annexed to the Convention on Prohibitions or Restrictions on the Use of Certain Conventional Weapons Which May be Deemed to be Excessively Injurious or to Have Indiscriminate Effects, Oct. 10, 1980, 1342 U.N.T.S. 137.

NIACs.[151] A fifth protocol (Protocol V), with rules for addressing the location and disposal of "explosive remnants of war" (e.g., unexploded landmines), was opened for signature in 2003 and came into force in 2006.[152]

The United States is a party to the CCW and all of its Protocols. However, unlike the 1949 Geneva Conventions, neither the CCW, nor any of its Protocols or related agreements has achieved the universal acceptance of the Geneva Conventions. Therefore, in determining what law applies to a conflict, it is necessary to consider all the LOAC treaties ratified by each of the parties to the conflict, as there may be inconsistencies or even gaps in coverage. All necessary information to determine which countries are States party to the various treaties is available from various sources online.[153]

In addition to the CCW, there have been other arms control treaties that have been adopted since World War II. These include treaties to ban the production, development, stockpiling, and use of chemical and biological weapons,[154] and treaties to reduce stockpiles of nuclear weapons and to ban certain types of nuclear weapons testing.[155] (No treaty in force, as of yet, bans the use of nuclear weapons of any size, however.) The United States is a party to these treaties.

A treaty to ban the use of anti-personnel landmines was opened for signature in 1997 and entered into force in 1999,[156] and another treaty to ban the use of cluster munitions was opened for signature in 2008 and entered into force in 2010.[157] The United States, as well as other States that employ these weapons, such as Israel and Russia, have yet to sign these treaties and are unlikely to do so in the near future. However, as with the Additional Protocols, the fact that many U.S. allies have ratified these treaties while the United States has not, creates interoperability issues in coalition operations.

E. Treaties Outside the Scope of the LOAC

In addition to treaties regulating the conduct of hostilities, there are treaties that could have a direct or indirect impact on military operations and must be considered by LOAC practitioners. Primary among these is the UN Charter,

---

151. Amendment to Article I of the Convention on Prohibitions or Restrictions on the Use of Certain Conventional Weapons Which May be Deemed to be Excessively Injurious or to Have Indiscriminate Effects, Dec. 21, 2001, 2260 U.N.T.S. 82.

152. Protocol (V) on Explosive Remnants of War, Annexed to the Convention on Prohibitions or Restrictions on the Use of Certain Conventional Weapons Which May be Deemed to be Excessively Injurious or to Have Indiscriminate Effects, Nov. 28, 2003, 2399 U.N.T.S. 100.

153. *See, e.g.*, State Parties List, *supra*, note 84.

154. Convention on the Prohibition of the Development, Production, Stockpiling and Use of Chemical Weapons and on Their Destruction, Jan. 13, 1993, 1974 U.N.T.S. 317; Convention on the Prohibition of the Development, Production and Stockpiling of Bacteriological (Biological) and Toxin Weapons and on Their Destruction, Apr. 10, 1972, 1015 U.N.T.S. 163.

155. *e.g.*, Treaty Banning Nuclear Weapon Tests in the Atmosphere, Outer Space and Under Water, Aug. 5, 1963, 480 U.N.T.S. 43.

156. Convention on the Prohibition of the Use, Stockpiling, Production and Transfer of Anti-Personnel Mines and on their Destruction, 18 September 1997, 2056 U.N.T.S. 241.

157. Convention on Cluster Munitions, May 30, 2008, 48 I.L.M. 357.

which, *inter alia*, (1) requires all States to "refrain in their international relations from the threat or use of force against the territorial integrity or political independence of any state, or in any other manner inconsistent with the Purposes of the United Nations";[158] (2) grants to the Security Council the authority to "take such action by air, sea, or land forces as may be necessary to maintain or restore international peace and security";[159] and, (3) acknowledges "the inherent right of individual or collective self-defence if an armed attack occurs against a Member of the United Nations."[160] These provisions of the UN Charter, along with customary rights and obligation of States under international law, are the primary source of the law governing the resort to force (*jus ad bellum*) discussed in Chapter 1 as distinct from the LOAC (*jus in bello*).

However, there are other treaties and conventions dealing with specific matters under international law that potentially limit the scope of military operations even during armed conflict. These include treaties limiting or prohibiting military operations in the Antarctic,[161] as well as treaties regulating the use of space and space bodies.[162] In the case of naval operations, consideration should be given to the 1982 UN Convention on the Law of the Sea, which although it deals principally with the law applicable to claims of national sovereignty over, or economic rights to, areas in and under the oceans, is also potentially relevant to the rights of non-belligerents *vis à vis* military operations in neutral waters and on the high seas.[163]

It is controversial whether or has treaties related to international human rights are applicable in armed conflict. Such treaties include:

- the Convention on the Prevention and Punishment of the Crime of Genocide (1948);[164]
- the United Nations Convention Against Torture (CAT);[165] and
- the International Covenant on Civil and Political Rights (ICCPR) (1966).[166]

These treaties, which collectively form part of a body of law known as international human rights law (IHRL), provide international guarantees of many fundamental rights, including a right to be free from torture and inhumane treatment, as well as a right not to be arbitrarily deprived of life or liberty. In

---

158. Charter of the United Nations, Jun. 26, 1945, art. 2, para. 4, 59 Stat. 1031.
159. *Id.*, art. 42.
160. *Id.*, art. 51.
161. *See* The Antarctic Treaty, Dec. 1, 1959, art. 4(1), 402 U.N.T.S. 72.
162. Treaty on Principles Governing the Activities of States in the Exploration and Use of Outer Space, including the Moon and Other Celestial Bodies, Jan. 27, 1967, 610 U.N.T.S. 206.
163. *See infra* ch. 11 (discussing the provisions of the law of the sea affecting the LOAC).
164. Convention on the Prevention and Punishment of the Crime of Genocide, Jan. 12, 1951, 78 U.N.T.S. 277.
165. Convention Against Torture and Other Cruel, Inhuman or Degrading Treatment or Punishment, Dec. 10, 1984, 1465 U.N.T.S. 85.
166. International Covenant on Civil and Political Rights, Dec. 16, 1966, 999 U.N.T.S. 171.

many cases, they provide for international bodies to consider claims that the rights guaranteed by the treaties have been violated. Further, many of these treaties allow for derogations of State obligations in the case of war or national emergency, although under strict conditions and not with respect to the prohibitions of torture and inhuman or degrading treatment, slavery, *ex post facto* penal laws, and the arbitrary deprivation of life.[167]

The United States for many years has taken the position that, by their terms, many of these treaties are only applicable to Parties with respect to persons within their territory,[168] and in any case, key prohibitions, such as the prohibitions against torture, are already covered by provisions of LOAC treaties. Recently, the U.S. position on the relationship of the LOAC and IHRL has evolved, with an acknowledgement that while the LOAC may be controlling where it specifically addresses an issue, human rights treaties can be applicable in situations of armed conflict where the LOAC is silent. According to the DoD Law of War Manual:

> In some circumstances, the rules in the law of war and the rules in human rights treaties may appear to conflict; these apparent conflicts may be resolved by the principle that the law of war is the *lex specialis* during situations of armed conflict, and, as such, is the controlling body of law with regard to the conduct of hostilities and the protection of war victims.
>
> . . .
>
> On the other hand, during armed conflict, human rights treaties would clearly be controlling with respect to matters that are within their scope of application and that are not addressed by the law of war. For example, a time of war does not suspend the operation of the ICCPR with respect to matters within its scope of application. Therefore, as an illustration participation in a war would in no way excuse a State Party to the ICCPR from respecting and ensuring the right and opportunity of every citizen to vote and to be elected at genuine periodic elections.[169]

The U.S. position may conflict with the position of other countries in coalition with the United States, either because these other countries have a different interpretation of the application of human rights treaties or because they are subject to different treaties and treaty interpretations.[170] The International Court of Justice (ICJ) has on several occasions affirmed that IHRL is applicable in armed conflicts,[171] as has the European Court of Human Rights,[172] and the

---

167. *See, e.g., id.*, art. 4(1).
168. *See, e.g.*, Follow-Up Response to the Human Rights Committee by State Party, U.N. Doc. CCPR/C/USA/CO/3/Rev.1/Add.1 (2008), at 2-3.
169. DoD Law of War Manual, *supra*, note 18, para. 1.6.3.1.
170. *Id.*, para. 1.6.3.2.
171. *See* Michael J. Dennis, *Agora: ICJ Advisory Opinion on Construction of a Wall in the Occupied Territory: Application of Human Rights Treaties Extraterritorially in Times of Armed Conflict and Military Occupation*, 99 Am. J. Int'l L. 119, 120-22 (2005).
172. Al-Skeini v. United Kingdom, App. No. 55721/07, 53 Eur. Ct. H.R. 589 (2011) ("the United Kingdom, through its soldiers engaged in security operations in Basrah during the period in question, exercised authority and control over individuals killed in the course of such security operations, so as

U.N. Human Rights Committee.[173] The ICJ's approach is to treat the LOAC as a specialized law, or *lex specialis*, that either supersedes provisions of IHRL or provides the context in which a right that applies as a matter of IHRL is to be interpreted in an armed conflict.[174] For example, there is no deprivation of a right to be free of arbitrary deprivation of life under IHRL when a combatant is targeted in armed conflict because, under LOAC, a combatant is a legitimate military objective. As noted above, the U.S. government has made similar *lex specialis* arguments with respect to the relationship of LOAC and IHRL in recent years.

V. Customary International Law

Treaty law is not the only source of the LOAC. Customary law is an equally important source of law, and in the absence of treaty law (due, for example, to the lack of adherence of many States to a treaty), may be the only source to turn to in determining which law applies.[175]

According to Section 102 of the Restatement of the Law, Third, Foreign Relations of the United States, "[c]ustomary international law results from a general and consistent practice of states followed by them from a sense of legal obligation."[176] A seminal 1969 decision of the ICJ, which explored the concept of customary law in depth,[177] indicated that customary law has two elements: (1) a consistent practice of States (*usus*), and (2) a view that the practice is required, prohibited, or allowed, depending on the nature of the rule, as a matter of law

---

to establish a jurisdictional link between the deceased and the United Kingdom for the purposes of Article 1 of the Convention.").

In *Al-Skeini*, the European Court of Human Rights found the European Convention on Human Rights applied to allegations of violations of the human rights in situations of armed conflict. For example, in a case concerning six Iraqi civilians killed by U.K. forces during the occupation of Iraq in 2003-2004, the Court held that there had been a failure to conduct an independent and effective investigation into the deaths of five of the six civilians in violation of the right to life under the Convention. *See id.*

173. *See* General Comment No. 31, CCPR/C/21/Rev.1/Add.13 (26 May 2004).

174. Legal Consequences of the Construction of a Wall in the Occupied Palestinian Territory, Advisory Opinion, 2004 I.C.J. 136, 178 (July 9).

175. Treaty law and customary law are interrelated. Treaties often reflect codification of existing customary law norms, although the treaty may include nuances and detail that exceed the customary norm and thus do not amount to customary law, but rather are new rules, binding only on the treaty partners. Even where treaty provisions reflect new rules, rather than customary law, those rules may blossom into customary law if consistently applied by treaty parties to situations outside the scope of the treaty (e.g., a norm only applicable by treaty to an IAC that the treaty parties also apply to NIAC) or if applied by parties who are not treaty members out of a sense of legal obligation. Note, however, that to evolve into customary law, a norm must be applied outside the scope of the treaty out of a sense of legal obligation. Merely adopting a rule as a matter of policy does not suffice. For example, U.S. forces comply with numerous regulations, directives, field manuals, orders, and rules of engagement, but unless compliance is required as a matter of law or out of sense of legal obligation, it will be difficult to say that U.S. actions amount to the evolution of a customary international law principle.

176. Restatement (Third) of Foreign Relations Law § 102 (1987).

177. *See* North Sea Cont'l Shelf, Judgment, 1969 I.C.J. 3 (Feb. 20).

(*opinio juris sive necessitatis*).[178] Thus, the mere fact that States may engage (or not engage) in a practice is not enough to indicate that it is required as a matter of customary law. States also must consider the practice or its omission to be a legal requirement.

Although unwritten, customary LOAC undoubtedly exists.[179] Indeed, the premise of the Lieber Code was to set down in one code the rules of war as they then existed. The preamble to 1907 Hague IV (and its 1899 predecessor) acknowledges the existence of customary law:

> Until a more complete code of the laws of war is issued, the High Contracting Parties think it right to declare that in cases not included in the Regulations adopted by them, populations and belligerents remain under the protection and empire of the principles of international law, as they result from the usages established between civilized nations, from the laws of humanity, and the requirements of the public conscience.[180]

This preamble — the so-called "Martens Clause," named after the Russian diplomat who proposed the language — was intended to assure certain countries that the regulations could not be viewed as setting forth the only rules that would apply in armed conflict. Similar language is repeated in the four 1949 Geneva Conventions to make clear that even if a State denounces (withdraws from) one or more of the Conventions, that Party is still bound by "the obligations which the Parties to the conflict . . . remain bound to fulfil by virtue of the principles of the law of nations, as they result from the usages established among civilized peoples, from the laws of humanity and the dictates of the public conscience."[181] Article 1 of AP I similarly states that "[i]n cases not covered by this Protocol or by other international agreements, civilians and combatants remain under the protection and authority of the principles of international law derived from established custom, from the principles of humanity and from dictates of public conscience,"[182] while the preamble to AP II asserts that "in cases not covered by the law in force, the human person remains under the protection of the principles of humanity and the dictates of the public conscience."[183]

While customary law exists, the difficulty lies in identifying the content of that law with precision. Many believe that most or all of the provisions of AP I reflect customary law. The U.S. position is unclear. In a memorandum to

---

178. *Id.* at 44.
179. The U.S. Defense Department clearly accepts that customary law is part of the law of armed conflict. *See, e.g.*, JOINT CHIEFS OF STAFF, JOINT PUB. 1-0, DOCTRINE FOR THE ARMED FORCES OF THE UNITED STATES, at I-20-21 (25 Mar. 2013) ("The law of war . . . includes treaties and international agreements to which the United States is a party, as well as applicable customary international law."); DoD LAW OF WAR MANUAL, *supra*, note 18, 1.3.
180. 1907 Hague IV, *supra*, note 39, preamble.
181. *See, e.g.*, GWS, *supra*, note 112, art. 63.
182. AP I, *supra*, note 53, art. 1.
183. The preamble of the CCW also repeats the Martens Clause. *See* CCW, *supra*, note 146, preamble. Article 1 of the 1899 Hague II, 1907 Hague IV, and Article 4A of the GPW, define legitimate militias and armed groups as those who, *inter alia*, conduct their operations in accordance with "the laws *and customs* of war." *See* 1899 Hague II, *supra*, note 39, art. 1 (emphasis added); 1907 Hague IV, *supra*, note 39, art. 1 (emphasis added); GPW, *supra*, note 114, art. 4A (emphasis added).

President Reagan recommending that the United States not submit AP I to the Senate for ratification, Secretary of State Shultz acknowledged that certain provisions of AP I did reflect customary law:

> We recognize that certain provisions of Protocol I reflect customary international law, and others appear to be positive new developments. We therefore intend to consult with our allies to develop appropriate methods for incorporating these provisions into rules that govern our military operations, with the intention that they shall in time win recognition as customary international law separate from their presence in Protocol I. This measure would constitute an appropriate remedy for attempts by nations to impose unacceptable conditions on the acceptance of improvements in international humanitarian law. I will report the results of this effort to you as soon as possible, so that the Senate may be advised of our progress in this respect.[184]

However, the United States has never clearly identified which provisions of AP I are customary law. A speech given in 1987 by Michael Matheson, then-U.S. Department of State Deputy Legal Advisor,[185] is considered by some to be a statement of the official U.S. position regarding this issue. However, this has never been confirmed by the U.S. government.[186] In any event, given that the language used in AP I reflects negotiation and compromise, it may not be pos-

---

184. SEN. TREATY DOC. NO. 100-2 (letter of submittal from Secretary of State George P. Shultz, accompanying President Reagan's AP I letter of transmittal, dated 29 January 1987).

185. *See, generally* Michael Matheson, *Session One: The United States Position on the Relation of Customary International Law to the 1977 Protocols Additional to the 1949 Geneva Conventions*, 2 AM. U. J. INT'L L. & POL'Y 419 (1987).

186. For U.S. practitioners, identifying exactly what the U.S. government considers to be customary international law LOAC norms can be challenging, because there is no single written "summary" of this law to turn to. Typically, practitioners will look to military manuals and regulations, legal opinions from the Departments of Defense, Justice, and State, the military services and the legal staffs of the civilian departments that oversee these services, and statements from the White House. The difficulty with all these sources is that it is not always clear that they were intended to be expressions of a U.S. position on customary law. On the other hand, there are occasions when the administration will act with apparent intent to provide a basis to assert that a rule is binding as a matter of customary law. For example, a fact sheet circulated in early 2011 by the White House Press Office expressing support for Article 75 of AP I (a treaty the United States has never ratified) included language that suggests that the administration considers Article 75 to be part of customary international law applicable to IACs. Press Release, White House Office of the Press Sec'y, Fact Sheet: New Actions on Guantanamo and Detainee Policy (Mar. 7, 2011), *available at* https://www.whitehouse.gov/the-press-office/2011/03/07/fact-sheet-new-actions-guant-namo-and-detainee-policy.

One difficulty with expressions from Executive Branch officials regarding customary law (e.g., as may be found in teaching materials and other sources generated for internal U.S. government use) is that these officials rarely can claim the authority to speak authoritatively on behalf of the U.S. government as to what the U.S. government considers to be binding as a legal matter. Indeed, it could be that a provision of the Military Commissions Act of 2006 limits to the President the authority to speak for the Executive Branch as to what customary law is with respect to the 1949 Geneva Conventions. Section 6 of the Act includes the following:

> (3) INTERPRETATION BY THE PRESIDENT.—
> (A) As provided by the Constitution and by this section, the President has the authority for the United States to interpret the meaning and application of the Geneva Conventions and to promulgate higher standards and administrative regulations for violations of treaty obligations which are not grave breaches of the Geneva Conventions.

sible to say that the text itself is customary law. Rather, it is the broad principles that the language reflects that would be customary law.

In 2005, the ICRC published a study of customary international humanitarian law, seeking to identify the customary LOAC applicable in six key areas.[187] The study's methodology, which relied heavily on military manuals and other written materials as evidence of State practice that was required as a matter of legal obligation, was sharply criticized by the United States. In a letter to the ICRC from the senior legal counsel to the Defense and States Departments, the U.S. government noted:

> [T]he Study places too much emphasis on written materials, such as military manuals and other guidelines published by States, as opposed to actual operational practice by States during armed conflict. Although manuals may provide important indications of State behavior and opinio juris, they cannot be a replacement for a meaningful assessment of operational State practice in connection with actual military operations.[188]

The U.S. letter also emphasized that in determining customary law, what is at issue was State practice and the views of States as to whether that practice is a legal obligation. Thus, "the Study gives undue weight to statements by non-governmental organizations and the ICRC itself, when those statements do not reflect whether a particular rule constitutes customary international law accepted by States."[189] The U.S. letter also criticized the study for treating the practice of all States as having equal value:

> [T]he Study tends to regard as equivalent the practice of States that have relatively little history of participation in armed conflict and the practice of States that have had a greater extent and depth of experience or that have otherwise had significant opportunities to develop a carefully considered military doctrine. The latter category of States, however, has typically contributed a significantly greater quantity and quality of practice.[190]

    (B) The President shall issue interpretations described by subparagraph (A) by Executive Order published in the Federal Register.

    (C) Any Executive Order published under this paragraph shall be authoritative (except as to grave breaches of common Article 3) as a matter of United States law, in the same manner as other administrative regulations.

    (D) Nothing in this section shall be construed to affect the constitutional functions and responsibilities of Congress and the judicial branch of the United States.

Military Comm'n Act of 2006, Pub. L. No. 109-366, § 6(a)(3), 120 Stat. 2632, *codified at* 18 U.S.C. § 2441 note.

    187. *See, generally* CIL STUDY, *supra*, note 59 (The six areas are (1) the principle of distinction; (2) specifically protected persons and objects; (3) specific methods of warfare; (4) weapons; (5) treatment of civilians and persons *hors de combat*; and (6) implementation of the LOAC.).

    188. John B. Bellinger, III & William J. Haynes, II, *A U.S. Government Response to the International Committee of the Red Cross Study Customary International Humanitarian Law*, 89 INT'L REV. RED CROSS 443, 445 (2007).

    189. *Id.*

    190. *Id.* at 446.

The U.S. government on occasion has made clear the rules of customary law that it believes apply. For example, in April 2016, Brian J. Egan, the Legal Adviser of the U.S. State Department, in a speech to the American Society of International Law, outlined the following rules that the United States considers to be customary law in the conduct of hostilities in NIACs:

> I would like to clarify briefly some of the rules that the United States is bound to comply with as a matter of international law in the conduct of hostilities during NIACs. In particular, I'd like to spend a few minutes walking through some of the targeting rules that the United States regards as customary international law applicable to all parties in a NIAC:
>
> - First, parties must distinguish between military objectives, including combatants, on the one hand, and civilians and civilian objects on the other. Only military objectives, including combatants, may be made the object of attack.
> - Insofar as objects are concerned, military objectives are those objects which by their nature, location, purpose or use make an effective contribution to military action and whose total or partial destruction, capture or neutralization, in the circumstances ruling at the time, offers a definite military advantage. The United States has interpreted this definition to include objects that make an effective contribution to the enemy's war-fighting or war-sustaining capabilities.
> - Feasible precautions must be taken in conducting an attack to reduce the risk of harm to civilians, such as, in certain circumstances, warnings to civilians before bombardments.
> - Customary international law also specifically prohibits a number of targeting measures in NIACs. First, attacks directed against civilians or civilian objects as such are prohibited. Additionally, indiscriminate attacks, including but not limited to attacks using inherently indiscriminate weapons, are prohibited.
> - Attacks directed against specifically protected objects such as cultural property and hospitals are also prohibited unless their protection has been forfeited.
> - Also prohibited are attacks that violate the principle of proportionality — that is, attacks against combatants or other military objectives that are expected to cause incidental harm to civilians that would be excessive in relation to the concrete and direct military advantage anticipated.
> - Moreover, acts or threats of violence the primary purpose of which is to spread terror among the civilian population are prohibited.[191]

Often, however, in presenting rules applicable to military operations that are not clearly covered by applicable treaties, U.S. government officials are either silent as to the source of these rules, or present them as part of a "policy," without clarifying whether the rules reflect legal obligations or merely establish practice under particular circumstances (and hence variable in other circumstances).

---

191. Brian J. Egan, *International Law, Legal Diplomacy, and the Counter-ISIL Campaign: Some Observations*, 92 INT'L L. STUD. 235, 242-43 (2016).

For example, in an Executive Order governing the protection of civilians in U.S. operations involving the use of armed force in armed conflict or in the exercise of the United States' inherent right of self-defense, President Obama described the measures to protect civilians included in the Order as a "policy":

> Sec. 2. *Policy.* In furtherance of U.S. Government efforts to protect civilians in U.S. operations involving the use of force in armed conflict or in the exercise of the Nation's inherent right of self-defense, and with a view toward enhancing such efforts, relevant departments and agencies (agencies) shall continue to take certain measures in present and future operations.
>
> (a) In particular, relevant agencies shall, consistent with mission objectives and applicable law, including the law of armed conflict:
>
> (i) train personnel, commensurate with their responsibilities, on compliance with legal obligations and policy guidance that address the protection of civilians and on implementation of best practices that reduce the likelihood of civilian casualties, including through exercises, pre-deployment training, and simulations of complex operational environments that include civilians;
>
> (ii) develop, acquire, and field intelligence, surveillance, and reconnaissance systems that, by enabling more accurate battlespace awareness, contribute to the protection of civilians;
>
> (iii) develop, acquire, and field weapon systems and other technological capabilities that further enable the discriminate use of force in different operational contexts;
>
> (iv) take feasible precautions in conducting attacks to reduce the likelihood of civilian casualties, such as providing warnings to the civilian population (unless the circumstances do not permit), adjusting the timing of attacks, taking steps to ensure military objectives and civilians are clearly distinguished, and taking other measures appropriate to the circumstances; and
>
> (v) conduct assessments that assist in the reduction of civilian casualties by identifying risks to civilians and evaluating efforts to reduce risks to civilians.[192]

Further, the Executive Order makes clear that "[t]he *policies* set forth in this order are consistent with existing U.S. obligations under international law and are not intended to create new international legal obligations; nor shall anything in this order be construed to derogate from obligations under applicable law, including the law of armed conflict."[193] Thus, it is not clear which part of the Executive Order reflects legal obligations. This blurring of the line between policy and international law effectively prevents pronouncements, such as this Executive Order, from contributing directly to the creation of customary law. Moreover, it leaves open the door for possible modification or rejection of the "policies" by future Presidents.

---

192. Exec. Order No. 13,732, 81 Fed. Reg. 44,485 (July 1, 2016).
193. *Id.* (emphasis added).

VI. Other Sources of the LOAC

A. Decisions of Courts and Tribunals

The LOAC treaties agreed to in the nineteenth century and the first half of the twentieth century generally did not include provisions for enforcement of the obligations of the States party to those treaties, with the exception of Article 3 of 1907 Hague IV, which provides:

> A belligerent party which violates the provisions of the said Regulations shall, if the case demands, be liable to pay compensation. It shall be responsible for all acts committed by persons forming part of its armed forces.[194]

At the end of World War I, over the objection of the United States, the Treaty of Versailles provided that the "Allied and Associated Powers [could] publicly arraign William II of Hohenzollern, formerly German Emperor, for a supreme offence against international morality and the sanctity of treaties," and also that Germany would recognize the right of "the Allied and Associated Powers to bring before military tribunals persons accused of having committed acts in violation of the laws and customs of war."[195] As it turned out, the former German emperor was not tried because the Netherlands would not hand him over for trial. In addition, the German government proposed that war crimes trials be held in German courts, rather than in Allied military tribunals, and Germany conducted a number of trials of its own citizens under German law with mixed and unsatisfactory results.[196]

By contrast, given the scope of atrocities and crimes committed during World War II, the Allies established international tribunals and also conducted military tribunals to punish both German Nazis and Japanese militarists for crimes against peace, crimes against humanity, and war crimes. Separate international tribunals for the crimes committed in Europe,[197] and those committed in Asia were established.[198] The trials before these tribunals, and trials before military tribunals conducted by each of the Allies, produced a rich body of case law regarding criminal liability for violations of the LOAC that today form the

---

194. 1907 Hague IV, *supra*, note 39, art. 3.
195. Treaty of Peace with Germany (Treaty of Versailles), June 28, 1919, Art. 227, 11 Martens Nouveau Recueil (ser. 3) 323.
196. *See* Theodor Meron, *Centennial Essay: Reflections on the Prosecution of War Crimes by International Tribunals*, 100 AM. J. INT'L L. 551, 558 (2006). Attempts to provide for the trial of war criminals in peace arrangements with Turkey similarly did not yield fruit. *Id*. In the German cases, convictions were obtained in two cases that established precedent for dealing with the defense of superior orders. *See* Judgment in Case of Commander Karl Neumann: Hospital Ship "Dover Castle", June 4, 1921, and Judgment in Case of Lieutenants Dithmar and Boldt: Hospital Ship "Llandovery Castle", July 14, 1921, *reprinted in* 16 AM. J. INT'L L. 704-724 (1922).
197. *See, generally* Agreement for the Prosecution and Punishment of the Major War Criminals of the European Axis, Aug. 8, 1945, 59 Stat. 1544, 82 U.N.T.S. 279.
198. *See, generally* Charter of the International Military Tribunal for the Far East, Jan. 19 & Apr. 26, 1946, T.I.A.S. No. 1589, 4 Bevans 20.

basis for a body of law commonly referred to as international criminal law. These cases provided further detail regarding the scope and application of the LOAC, and also gave more meaningful weight to the LOAC as law. The success of these cases led to the inclusion of provisions in each of the Geneva Conventions (and subsequent treaties) regarding potential individual responsibility for violations of these treaties,[199] as well as State responsibility to repress violations.[200] These provisions, and the work of courts, governments, and academics in interpreting them, have helped define the scope of the LOAC since World War II.

After the World War II war crimes tribunals, the prosecution of violations of the LOAC was left to national courts until 1993, when, prompted by atrocities committed in the former Yugoslavia, the UN Security Council acted under Article VII of the UN Charter to authorize the creation of a tribunal to prosecute crimes committed in the former Yugoslavia.[201] A similar tribunal to deal with crimes committed in Rwanda was created by the Security Council in 1994.[202] The crimes that are subject to these tribunals are similar to those considered by the World War II tribunals, but the scope of the jurisdiction of these tribunals specifically includes NIACs. Like the World War II cases, these tribunals have produced significant decisions that in turn have helped further shape both the LOAC and International Criminal Law. For example, cases such as the ICTY's *Tadic* case,[203] have helped define the scope of State responsibility for armed groups, command responsibility, and the threshold for triggering the application of the LOAC.[204]

In addition to these tribunals, the ICJ has handed down a number of key decisions with implications for the application of the LOAC, including cases dealing with nuclear weapons,[205] support for insurgents in Nicaragua,[206] and the construction of a wall in Palestinian territory.[207] Decisions of national courts also may be a source of persuasive, if not binding, precedent as to the scope and application of the LOAC.[208]

---

199. *See, e.g.*, GWS, *supra*, note 112, art. 50 (acts considered to be "grave breaches" of GWS).
200. *Id.*, art. 49.
201. *See, generally* S.C. Res. 808, U.N. Doc. S/RES/808 (Feb. 22, 1993).
202. *See, generally* S.C. Res. 955, S/RES/955 (Nov. 8, 1994).
203. *See, generally* Prosecutor v. Tadic, Case No. IT-94-1-AR72, Decision on Defence Motion for Interlocutory Appeal on Jurisdiction, (Int'l Crim. Trib. for the Former Yugoslavia Oct. 2, 1995).
204. In addition to tribunals created for specific conflicts, the creation of the International Criminal Court (ICC) resulted in creation of a detailed "Elements of Crimes" pursuant to Article 9 of the Rome Statute that is an additional source of law regarding the scope and application of the LOAC. Rome Statute of the International Criminal Court, July 17, 1998, art. 9, 2187 U.N.T.S. 90.
205. Legality of the Threat or Use of Nuclear Weapons, Advisory Opinion, 1996 I.C.J. 226 (July 8).
206. Military and Paramilitary Activities (Nicar. v. U.S.), Jurisdiction and Admissibility, 1984 I.C.J. 392 (Nov. 26); Military and Paramilitary Activities (Nicar. v. U.S.), Merits, 1986 I.C.J. 14 (June 27).
207. Legal Consequences of the Constr. of a Wall in the Occupied Palestinian Territory, Advisory Opinion, 2004 I.C.J. 136 (July 9).
208. An Israeli court decision concerning targeting of terrorists by the Israeli military is worth noting. HCJ 769/02 Pub. Comm. against Torture in Isr. v. Gov't of Isr. 57(6) PD 285 [2005].

B. "Soft Law"

Four projects over the past several decades have sought to restate the law as it applies to certain issues under the LOAC. These "soft law" projects are not intended to establish new law, but rather to restate what the existing law is. The studies have proven controversial where States have perceived them as attempts by the organizations sponsoring them (such as the ICRC) to advance the state of the law outside the treaty making process. However, due to the detailed nature of these studies, they are important sources of information for practitioners even if their conclusions are disputed by some States.

Perhaps the least controversial of the four is the San Remo Manual on International Law Applicable to Armed Conflicts at Sea.[209] The San Remo Manual was prepared from 1988 to 1994 by a group of legal and naval experts participating in their personal capacity for the purpose of providing a contemporary restatement of international law applicable to armed conflicts at sea. According to the ICRC, "[T]he Manual includes a few provisions which might be considered progressive developments in the law but most of its provisions are considered to state the law which is currently applicable," and it was viewed as the "modern equivalent to the Oxford Manual on the Laws of Naval War Governing the Relations Between Belligerents adopted by the Institute of International Law in 1913."[210] The need for such a manual was driven by the lack of any substantial comprehensive treatment, in treaty law, of the law of armed conflict in naval operations since 1907 (with the exception of GWS Sea and a few provisions of AP I that impact naval operations).

In 2009, the Program on Humanitarian Policy and Conflict Research at Harvard University (HPCR) concluded a six-year effort to draft the Manual on International Law Applicable to Air and Missile Warfare.[211] The Manual was the first comprehensive study of the law applicable to air operations since the Rules Concerning the Control of Wireless Telegraphy in Time of War and Air Warfare drafted at The Hague from 1922 to 1923 by a Commission of Jurists (established by the Washington Conference on the Limitation of Armament).[212] Prepared by a group of experts participating in their personal capacities and funded primarily by the Swiss Federal Department of Foreign Affairs, the HPCR Manual addresses not only air and missile warfare, but also touches on subjects related to cyber warfare.

Possibly the most controversial of the recent studies is the Interpretive Guidance on Direct Participation in Hostilities Under International

---

209. SAN REMO MANUAL, *supra*, note 98.

210. *Int'l. Comm. Red Cross, San Remo Manual on International Law Applicable to Armed Conflicts at Sea*, 12 June 1994, ICRC, *available at* http://www.icrc.org/ihl.nsf/INTRO/560?OpenDocument (emphasis removed).

211. PROGRAM ON HUMANITARIAN POLICY AND CONFLICT RESEARCH (HPCR) AT HARVARD UNIV., MANUAL ON INT'L LAW APPLICABLE TO AIR AND MISSILE WARFARE (2009).

212. Rules concerning the Control of Wireless Telegraphy in Time of War and Air Warfare, Drafted by a Commission of Jurists at The Hague, December 1922-February 1923, Parliamentary Papers, Cmd. 2201, Misc. No. 14 (1924).

Humanitarian Law,[213] which was adopted by the Assembly of the ICRC in February 2009.[214] The purpose of the guidance is "to provide recommendations concerning the interpretation of international humanitarian law (IHL) as far as it relates to the notion of direct participation in hostilities."[215] The guidance examines the scope and implications of the concept of direct participation in hostilities (DPH) in connection with the question of when an individual loses his or her immunity from attack in an armed conflict. Conducted with the participation of a group of experts working in their private capacities, the guidance ultimately proved so controversial that it was published as the view only of the ICRC. The ICRC asserted that "the Guidance does not purport to change the law, but provides an interpretation of the notion of direct participation in hostilities within existing legal parameters."[216] A number of the experts who worked on the project challenged that claim, however.[217]

Perhaps prompted by the criticism it received, the ICRC included the following statement in the guidance:

> [T]he Interpretive Guidance is not and cannot be a text of a legally binding nature. Only State agreements (treaties) or State practice followed out of a sense of legal obligation on a certain issue (custom) can produce binding law.[218]

The same statement is true with respect to all of these soft law projects, which nonetheless remain highly persuasive due to the participation of experts in each project.

The fourth project is the Tallinn Manual on the International Law Applicable to Cyber Operations, was completed in 2013 (Tallinn 1.0),[219] and then updated in 2017 (Tallinn 2.0).[220] More akin to the San Remo Manual than the HPCR Manual or the ICRC's study of direct participation in hostilities, this project, which was sponsored by the North Atlantic Treaty Organization's Cooperative Cyber Defense Centre of Excellence in Tallinn, Estonia, has proven to be extremely influential on thinking about this new domain of warfare not only within academic and business circles, but also within governments. However, as with the other projects, the drafters of Tallinn 2.0 stress at the beginning that the Manual is not binding on States:

---

213. N. Melzer, Interpretive Guidance on the Notion of Direct Participation in Hostilities Under Int'l Humanitarian Law (2009) (hereinafter DPH Interpretive Guidance).

214. *See id.* at. 8-11.

215. *Id.* at 9.

216. *Id.* at 6.

217. *See, e.g.*, W. Hays Parks, *Part IX of the ICRC "Direct Participation in Hostilities" Study: No Mandate, No Expertise, and Legally Incorrect*, 42 N.Y.U. J. Int'l L. & Pol. 769, 783-784 (2010) (describing a controversy over a portion of the draft Study (dealing with the use of force) that was deemed legally incorrect by a number of the experts working on the project and that led them to withdraw when the ICRC refused to change it in the final version of the Study).

218. DPH Interpretive Guidance, *supra*, note 213, at 6.

219. Tallinn Manual on the Int'l Law Applicable to Cyber Operations (Michael N. Schmitt ed., 2013).

220. Tallinn Manual 2.0 on the Int'l Law Applicable to Cyber Operations (Michael N. Schmitt ed., 2017).

Ultimately, Tallinn Manual 2.0 must be understood only as an expression of the opinions of the two International Groups of Experts as to the state of the law.[221]

Further, while in drafting Tallinn 2.0, the experts solicited the views of governments through a process sponsored by the Dutch government (called the "Hague Process"), the drafters make very clear that Tallinn 2.0 "does . . . [not] reflect the position of any other organisation or State represented by observers or any of the States involved in the 'Hague Process.'"[222]

Despite these disclaimers, these soft law projects will influence the development of the LOAC, particularly if cited by courts or governments seeking to identify applicable legal rules. In addition, soft law can become the basis for future treaties, as was the case with the Oxford Manual of the Laws and Customs of War of 1880, which contributed to the provisions of the 1907 Hague IV and its 1899 predecessor.[223] In the future, it can be expected that States may want to look first to the results of soft law projects on emerging LOAC issues, such as Tallinn 2.0, to determine what future rules might look like, before engaging diplomatically on the creation of "hard" law, such as treaties.

Aside from these soft law projects are commentaries prepared by the ICRC and others to help explain these conventions and protocols, although these are scholarly works that do not constitute binding precedents.[224] Also helpful in this regard may be collections of the preparatory working papers and records of the proceedings during negotiation of the 1949 Geneva Conventions and the 1977 Additional Protocols, all of which can help provide insight into the reasoning behind the choice of language used in these treaties.[225]

C. Statutes, Regulations, and Policies Affecting LOAC

To be effective, the LOAC must be implemented in the domestic law of each State, so that it is clearly binding on, and enforceable against, the State's military forces and citizens. In some countries, international law is part of domestic law, so that ratified treaties create direct rights and obligations for the citizens of that country.[226] In the United States, while LOAC treaties are part of domestic

---

221. *Id.* at 4 (emphasis removed).
222. *Id.*
223. *See supra*, pt. IV.A (discussing the contribution of these soft law instruments to the regulations appended to 1907 Hague IV and its 1899 predecessor).
224. ICRC commentaries can be found on the U.S. Library of Congress's Military Legal Resources website, http://www.loc.gov/rr/frd/Military_Law/military-legal-resources-home.html (last visited Feb. 12, 2017), as well as on the ICRC's websites.
Another persuasive commentary on the two Additional Protocols of 1977 is MICHAEL BOTHE ET AL, NEW RULES FOR VICTIMS OF ARMED CONFLICTS: COMMENTARY ON THE TWO 1977 PROTOCOLS ADDITIONAL TO THE GENEVA CONVENTIONS OF 1949 (1982).
225. Many of these sources are also available on the Library of Congress website. *See supra*, note 224.
226. *See, e.g.*, Germany, Federal Ministry of Defence, Joint Service Regulation (ZDv) 15/2, *Law of Armed Conflict Manual* (May 1, 2013), ¶ 144 (hereinafter GERMAN LOAC MANUAL).

law, they are not self-executing, meaning that Congress must adopt a law to make the treaty enforceable in court. Enactment of legislation may actually be a requirement of the treaty. For example, all four of the 1949 Geneva Conventions require States to "enact any legislation necessary to provide effective penal sanctions for persons committing, or ordering to be committed, any of the grave breaches" of the four Conventions.[227] However, whether or not Congress has acted, a ratified treaty is binding on the United States in its relations with other countries. The lack of implementing legislation does not justify the United States' failure to comply with a LOAC treaty in its relations with others.

1. Laws and Executive Orders

For U.S. military practitioners, there are other sources that do not represent international law, but are nonetheless binding as a matter of domestic law. These include the War Crimes Act and the Military Commissions Acts of 2006 and 2009.[228] These, and other U.S. laws discussed in greater detail in later chapters, allow for the enforcement of the LOAC by the U.S. government.

2. Military Doctrine

The U.S. Department of Defense also has issued directives and regulations to implement U.S. obligations under the LOAC. One example is the DoD Directive (DoDD) 2311.01E, DoD Law of War Program, which requires compliance by the DoD with the law of armed conflict "during all armed conflicts, however such conflicts are characterized, and in all other military operations."[229] This is an extremely important policy statement. As discussed in Chapter 3, the body of international law applicable to a conflict will vary depending upon how the conflict is characterized. However, under DoDD 2311.01E, DoD personnel are to consider the full body of the LOAC to apply to all conflicts as a matter of policy, even if international law would not require its application.[230] In addition, DoDD 2311.01E requires all DoD organizations (including, but not limited to, U.S. military forces) to report and investigate allegations of violations of the LOAC.[231]

Another important example of binding rules for U.S. forces is Army Regulation 190-8, which is a multi-service regulation that implements U.S. legal obligations under the LOAC, including under GPW, with respect to "persons captured, detained, interned, or otherwise held in U.S. Armed Forces custody

---

227. *See, e.g.*, GPW, *supra*, note 114, art. 146.
228. War Crimes Act of 1996, Pub. L. 104-192, 110 Stat. 2104; Military Comm'n Act of 2006, Pub. L. No. 109-366, 120 Stat. 2600; Nat'l Defense Authorization Act for Fiscal Year 2010, Pub. L. 111-84, 123 Stat. 2190.
229. DoDD 2311.01E, *supra*, note 31; *see also, generally* U.S. Dep't Defense, Dir. 2310.01E, DoD Detainee Program (19 Aug. 2014) (originally issued in 2006 to establish minimum standards of humane treatment and accounting for any person detained by U.S. forces and other DoD components other than for law enforcement purposes (except where the United States is an occupying power)).
230. DoDD 2311.01E, *supra*, note 31, para. 4.
231. *Id.*, para. 4.4.

during the course of conflict."[232] Among other things, this regulation establishes the procedures for classification of persons detained in connection with military operations, as well as standards for their treatment while in detention.

Military manuals and doctrinal guidance also are important to U.S. military practitioners. Each of the U.S. military services engaged in hostilities has promulgated its own manual and has training programs in place to ensure military members and the civilians that accompany them in military operations are aware of the requirements of international law. First issued in 1956, with a 1976 update, the U.S. Army's Field Manual 27-10 is the leading example of this type of doctrinal document.[233] FM 27-10 organizes into discrete categories all of the U.S. LOAC treaty obligations in effect in 1956, and includes commentary that over time has come to be viewed as reflective of customary law.[234] FM 27-10 has been superseded by the DoD Law of War Manual, first issued in June 2015 and more recently amended in December 2016.[235]

Another recent example is the U.S. Navy's Commander's Handbook on the Law of Naval Operations, which was last revised in 2017.[236] This handbook seeks to summarize the key aspects of international law applicable to both peacetime and wartime naval operations. Other key U.S. doctrinal manuals of relevance to LOAC practitioners are those dealing with counterinsurgency,[237] interrogation,[238] and detention.

Other nations have promulgated manuals that are considered to be persuasive as to the interpretation of the LOAC. This includes the German Joint Services Regulation (ZDv) 15/2, which was promulgated in 1992,[239] and the Manual of the Law of Armed Conflict adopted by the U.K. Ministry of Defence in 2004.[240]

---

232. U.S. DEP'T OF ARMY, ARMY REGULATION 190-8: ENEMY PRISONERS OF WAR, RETAINED PERSONNEL, CIVILIAN INTERNEES AND OTHER DETAINEES 1-5 (1 Oct. 1997).

233. FM 27-10, *supra*, note 2.

234. *See id.*

235. DoD LAW OF WAR MANUAL, *supra*, note 18.

236. U.S. DEP'T OF NAVY, NWP 1-14M, COMMANDER'S HANDBOOK ON THE LAW OF NAVAL OPERATIONS (Aug. 2017) (This publication also is listed as a U.S. Marine Corps publication, MCTP 11-10B, and Coast Guard publication, COMDTPUB P5800.7A.).

237. *See, generally* FM 3-24, *supra*, note 4.

238. *See, generally* U.S. DEP'T OF ARMY, FIELD MANUAL para. 2-22.3, HUMAN INTELLIGENCE COLLECTOR OPERATIONS (6 Sept. 2006). According to Executive Order 13,491, FM 2-22.3 provides that "an individual in the custody or under the effective control of an officer, employee, or other agent of the United States Government, or detained within a facility owned, operated, or controlled by a department or agency of the United States, in any armed conflict, shall not be subjected to any interrogation technique or approach, or any treatment related to interrogation, that is not authorized by and listed in Army Field Manual 2-22.3 . . . ." Exec. Order No. 13,491, 74 Fed., which has since been updated Reg. 4,893 (2009).

239. An annotated version of the German manual was published in 1995, *see* THE HANDBOOK OF HUMANITARIAN LAW IN ARMED CONFLICTS (D. Fleck ed., 3d ed. 2013). In 2013, the German Federal Ministry of Defense issued a revised version of the manual. *See, generally* GERMAN LOAC MANUAL, *supra*, note 226.

240. *See, generally* UK LOAC MANUAL, *supra*, note 25.

3. Rules of Engagement

No understanding of the LOAC and its impact on the planning and execution of military operations would be complete without an examination of the LOAC's relationship with rules of engagement (commonly referred to as ROE). Although the LOAC and ROE are inextricably connected, they are not synonymous, and are two distinct sources of operational regulation.

As defined in U.S. military doctrine, ROE are "directives issued by competent military authority that delineate the circumstances and limitations under which United States forces will initiate and/or continue combat engagement with other forces encountered."[241] In other words, ROE are intended to give operational and tactical military leaders greater control over the execution of combat operations. Though not historically labeled ROE, the history of warfare is replete with examples of ROE-type tactical controls. The Battle of Bunker Hill provides an excellent example. Captain William Prescott imposed a limitation on the use of combat power by his forces in the form of the directive, "don't shoot until you see the whites of their eyes."[242] Given his limited resources against a much larger and better-equipped foe, he used this tactical control measure to maximize the effect of his firepower. This example of what was, in effect, an ROE is remembered to this day for one primary reason—it enabled the colonial militia to maximize tactical effects.

Another modern example of tactical controls on the use of force is the Battle of Naco in the fall of 1914. The actual battle was between two Mexican factions, but it occurred on the border with the United States.[243] In response to the threat of cross-border incursions, the 9th and 10th Cavalry Regiments, stationed at Fort Huachuca, Arizona, were deployed to the U.S. side of the border to ensure that U.S. neutrality was strictly maintained. As part of the Cavalry mission, "[t]he men were under orders not to return fire,"[244] despite the fact that the U.S. forces were routinely fired upon and "the provocation to return the fire was very great."[245] Because of the soldiers' tactical restraint and correct application of their orders—what today would be characterized as ROE—the strategic objective of maintaining U.S. neutrality was accomplished without provoking a conflict between the Mexican factions and the United States. The level of discipline reflected by the actions of these U.S. forces elicited a special

---

241. JOINT CHIEFS OF STAFF, JOINT PUB. 1-02, DEPARTMENT OF DEFENSE DICTIONARY OF MILITARY AND ASSOCIATED TERMS, 207 (8 Nov. 2010, amended through 15 Feb. 2016).

242. *See* JOHN BARTLETT, FAMILIAR QUOTATIONS 446, n.1 (Emily M. Beck ed., 14th ed., Little Brown & Co. 1968), *quoted in* Major Mark S. Martins, *Rules of Engagement for Land Forces: A Matter of Training, Not Lawyering*, 143 MIL. L. REV. 1, 34 (1994).

243. For more information regarding the fall of Naco, *see* Elizabeth A. Palmer, *Democratic Intervention: U.S. Involvement in Small Wars*, 22 PENN ST. INT'L L. REV. 313 (2003).

244. *See Buffalo Soldiers at Huachuca: The Battle of Naco*, BYU, http://net.lib.byu.edu/estu/wwi/comment/huachuca/HI1-10.htm (last visited Feb. 13, 2017).

245. *Id.*

letter of commendation from the President of the United States and the Chief of Staff of the Army.[246]

ROE have become a key issue in modern warfare and a key component of mission planning for U.S. and many other armed forces.[247] In preparation for military operations, the President and/or Secretary of Defense may personally review and approve ROE, ensuring they meet the military and political objectives.[248] Ideally, ROE represent the confluence of three important factors: Operational Requirements, National Policy, and the LOAC,[249] as illustrated by this diagram:

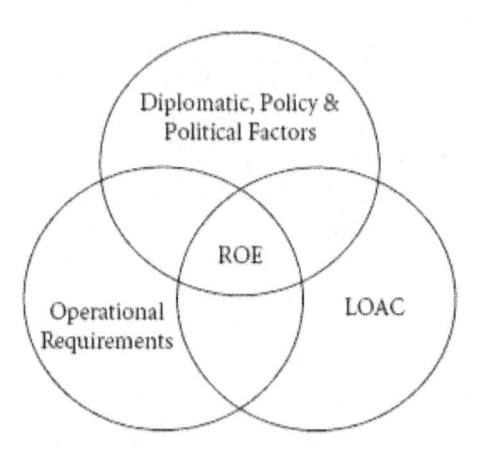

It is particularly important to note that while ROE are not coterminous with the LOAC, they must be completely consistent. In other words, while some aspects of the LOAC do not impact a mission's ROE, all ROE must comply with the LOAC. This is illustrated by the diagram above, which reflects the common situation where the authority provided by the ROE is more limited than would be consistent with the LOAC. For example, in order to provide greater protection against collateral injury to civilians, the ROE may require that the engagement of a clearly defined military objective in a populated area is permitted only when the target is under direct observation. Thus, ROE may impose

---

246. The commendation letter stated, "During the siege of Naco, Sonora, which was carried on for two and one-half months, the American troops at Naco, Arizona, were constantly on duty day and night to prevent the use of United States territory in violation of the neutrality laws. These troops were constantly under fire and one was killed and 18 were wounded without a single case of return fire of retaliation. This is the hardest kind of service and only troops in the highest state of discipline would stand such a test." *Id.*

247. *See, e.g.,* INT'L & OPERATIONAL LAW DEP'T, THE JUDGE ADVOCATE GEN.'S LEGAL CTR. & SCH., U.S. ARMY, JA 422, OPERATIONAL LAW HANDBOOK 81 (2015) (ROE serve three purposes: (1) provide guidance from the President and Secretary of Defense (SECDEF), as well as subordinate commanders, to deployed units on the use of force; (2) act as a control mechanism for the transition from peacetime to combat operations (war); and (3) provide mechanism to facilitate planning.").

248. Lieutenant Commander Dale Stephens, *Rules of Engagement and the Concept of Unit Self-Defense*, 45 NAVAL L. REV. 126, 126 (1998).

249. Richard J. Grunawalt, *The JCS Standing Rules of Engagement: A Judge Advocate's Primer*, 42 A.F. L. REV. 245, 247 (1997).

limits on otherwise lawful authority to engage enemy forces under the LOAC, but may never grant authority beyond that permitted by the LOAC. In fact, the preeminent U.S. ROE order explicitly directs U.S. forces that they "will comply with the Law of Armed Conflict during military operations involving armed conflict, no matter how the conflict may be characterized under international law, and will comply with the principles and spirit of the Law of Armed Conflict during all other operations."[250] Note that this directive applies to any "armed conflict," and not only to IACs.

To illustrate the interaction between ROE and the LOAC, consider an ROE provision that allows a soldier to kill an enemy. Although this provision is completely appropriate, it does not implicitly include the authority to kill an enemy who is surrendering because such conduct would violate the LOAC. Similarly, if the ROE allows for a pilot to destroy a bridge with a bomb, it does not relieve the pilot of his responsibility to terminate the attack if she believes it will cause disproportionate injury to civilians or civilian property.[251] ROE will also often contain provisions that remind soldiers that they may only engage the enemy (or other individuals that engage in defined conduct endangering soldiers or others), but not civilians who are not directly participating in hostilities. In this way, ROE are used to reinforce compliance with the LOAC.

Appreciating this interrelationship between the LOAC and ROE is vital to understanding why the violation of a constraint imposed by a specific ROE does not *ipso facto* establish a violation of the LOAC. Rather, to assess whether an ROE violation is a LOAC violation, it is necessary to determine whether the ROE constraint was coterminous with the LOAC, or more restrictive than the LOAC requires.

Study Questions

1. In preparing a presentation on the LOAC to other members of your cell on the conduct of military operations, you want to begin with a summary of the rules that apply to combat against the Iraqi armed forces, both those that will be encountered during the invasion and those located to the rear. Which treaties do you think are most relevant?
2. The United Kingdom and Australia are partners in the operations against the Iraqis. By checking the ICRC website (http://www.icrc.org), can you identify any treaties to which the United Kingdom and Australia, but not the United States, are a party? Under which of these treaties do you think there could be potential for significant conflicts between the members of a coalition, including all three countries arising from the LOAC rules governing conduct of hostilities against Iraqi forces? How could these conflicts be mitigated?

---

250. CHAIRMAN, JOINT CHIEFS OF STAFF, INSTR. 3121.01B, STANDING RULES OF ENGAGEMENT/STANDING RULES FOR THE USE OF FORCE FOR US FORCES, encl. A, para. 1d (13 June 2005).
251. *See* AP I, *supra*, note 53, art. 57(2)(b).

3. You have been informed that a preliminary survey of potential targets includes an Iraqi artillery battery located near a dam. You understand that there is a provision of AP I (Article 56) that specifically addresses the targeting of dams that may be potentially relevant. However, the United States is not a party to AP I. Does that mean that you do not need to consider Article 56? What does the DoD Law of War Manual say about situations to which Article 56 applies?
4. Your team would like to consider a computer attack on certain networks in Iraq that are used by Iraqi armed forces. You understand that there is no specific treaty on cyber warfare, but can you find any provision(s) in the 1907 Hague IV that you think you might have to consider as potentially applicable? How about in AP I? Are there other sources that you might consider in assessing what the LOAC requires?
5. DoDD 2311.01E requires U.S. forces to apply the LOAC in all military operations, including those abroad that do not qualify as armed conflicts. Why would the United States apply the law in situations in which it is not clearly required?
6. Your team begins working on plans for post-invasion operations in Iraq. In areas actually placed under the authority of coalition forces following the invasion, which LOAC treaties will likely be most applicable in developing guidance for coalition forces in their relationship with civilians and the civilian population in these areas? Are there non-LOAC treaties that you will need to consider? Does the fact that the United Kingdom is a coalition partner influence your answer to that last question?
7. Your team is drafting possible ROE for (i) the invasion of Iraq and (ii) the occupation that will follow. What proposals might you make for limitations to include in the ROE that go beyond what the LOAC requires? Would you propose different ROE for each phase of the operation? Please explain.

3 | Triggering the Law of Armed Conflict

Just navigating the Pentagon is the first challenge of your day. Recently assigned to the Office of the Judge Advocate General's International and Operational Law Division, this is your first participation in the Department of Defense Law of War Working Group (LOWWG). The LOWWG's function is to analyze and resolve law of armed conflict (LOAC) related questions for the Secretary of Defense and all subordinate commands. It is composed of representatives from all the Service Judge Advocates (Army, Navy, Air Force, Marines), the State Department, and the Chairman of the Joint Chiefs of Staff Legal Advisor. A senior lawyer serving as the LOAC expert for the General Counsel to the Secretary of Defense — the SECDEF's legal advisor, runs the LOWWG.

The meeting begins, as normal, with the General Counsel — the lawyer who advises the Secretary of Defense — presenting the group with the issue to be addressed:

> CENTCOM (United States Central Command — the joint (all services) Combatant Command responsible for executing all military operations in the Middle East and Southwest Asia (except Israel) received a warning order to execute an OPLAN (operations plan) to oust Saddam Hussein from power in Iraq and defeat all forces supporting his regime. CENTCOM is aware that behind-the-scenes diplomatic efforts are ongoing to persuade Hussein to step down from power and leave Iraq voluntarily, although this is not considered a likely scenario. Still, it is uncertain whether the U.S. forces will confront resistance when they initiate operations, or whether some type of interim government will be in power that may choose not to resist, or perhaps even cooperate with the intervention.
>
> CENTCOM requests a General Counsel opinion on how this range of potential situations will impact the legal characterization of the operation and applicable international law.

I. Introduction

Lawyers typically serve clients by identifying issues, determining applicable law, and recommending courses of action that enable the client to effectively and efficiently achieve objectives in compliance with that law. This method of legal analysis is no different for the general counsel of a corporation than it is for the General Counsel of the Department of Defense or any other attorney, military or civilian, providing legal support to military commanders. However, what is often different for military legal advisors is that their advisory process begins by assessing the controlling legal framework applicable to the operation. More specifically, when hostilities are anticipated, military attorneys must assess whether the operation will be subject to the law of armed conflict (LOAC), and if so, which provisions of that law are binding on U.S. forces.

What makes this method unusual? Quite simply, "law applicability analysis" is normally not a significant aspect in addressing civilian legal issues. Most lawyers operate in situations where the applicable law is quite clear, and they devote their analytical efforts towards the meaning and impact of that law. Legal analysis of the regulation of hostilities is different. In this context, it is critical to determine whether the LOAC, and more precisely what provisions of that law, apply to the military operation. This law applicability analysis is often referred to as "conflict classification." But even that characterization is somewhat misleading, for it assumes the existence of "armed conflict", the essential requirement for LOAC applicability. In fact, determining LOAC applicability first requires analysis of whether the military operation even qualifies an armed conflict. If the operation does qualify, the next step in the analysis is assessing the *type* of armed conflict — the true "conflict classification" step in the analysis.

Determining the legal framework that applies to military operations is complex and critically important. The use of armed forces — even for missions abroad — do not always trigger LOAC application. Perhaps more importantly, when the LOAC is applicable, it substantially expands the scope of legal authority to employ measures related to mission accomplishment.

To understand this dynamic, it is useful to begin with a very generalized comparison of the scope of "mission accomplishment" authority applicable during both peacetime and armed conflicts. In both contexts, government forces often seek to impose their will on those they encounter, which frequently takes the form of deprivation of property, liberty, or life. Outside the context of armed conflict, even when confronting significant civil unrest or criminal activity, individuals encountered by government forces (most commonly the police, although military forces may also participate in peacetime law enforcement activities) are *presumed* peaceful and law abiding. Accordingly, international law (specifically, international human rights law (IHRL)) places the burden of rebutting that presumption on the government agent, with all which that entails. On the other hand, an armed conflict involves a contest between members of opposing organized belligerent groups. In this situation, the peacetime/law enforcement presumption is effectively inversed, and individuals are *presumed* hostile based solely on their "status" as members of the organized enemy group. This is reflected in the LOAC's expanded grant of authority to kill, capture, detain, commandeer, and destroy. The following table summarizes the difference in incapacitation authority derived from these two distinct legal regimes:

Human Rights/Law Enforcement Framework	The Law of Armed Conflict Framework
Primary Objective: to Prohibit Arbitrary Treatment of Individuals by State Actors by Limiting Situations Requiring Resort to Force	Primary Objective: Regulate the Conduct of Hostilities Between States or Other Organized Armed Belligerent Groups by Limiting Violence to Only that Which is Necessary to Subdue an Opponent
Presumption that Individuals Act on Their Own Volition	Presumption that Hostile Group Members Act Pursuant to Leaders' Will
Presumes Individuals Normally Comply with State Authority and Are Therefore Inoffensive	Presumes Members of Hostile Groups Intend to Inflict Harm on Opponent and Are Therefore Presumed Offensive
Requires State Actor to Make Individualized Judgment to Support Deprivations of Life or Liberty (Conduct Based Deprivations)	Authorizes Deprivations of Life and Liberty Based on Presumption of Offensiveness (Status Based Deprivations)
Allows Minimum Force Necessary to Restore the Status Quo: Deadly Force is a Measure of Last Resort	Allows for Application of Overwhelming Force: Deadly Force as a Measure of First Resort
Proportionality: Protects the Object of Deliberate Violence from Application of Excessive Force	Proportionality: Protects Collateral Victims of Deliberate Violence from Excessive Collateral Suffering Resulting from Attack on a Lawful Target

The determination of the existence of armed conflict is therefore a critical threshold inquiry whenever states utilize military power. Determining that a situation qualifies as an armed conflict will provide the legal foundation for a range of measures otherwise incompatible with international, and in most cases domestic, law. This "conflict classification" analysis is at once simple and complex, but it is the genuine starting point in operational lawyering.

II. Origins of the Conflict Classification Paradigm

Law applicability analysis is a relatively new aspect of LOAC compliance. Prior to 1949, the law — known to that point as the laws and customs of war or, in the alternative, the laws of war — applied only during "war." This was not the result of any positive legal rule, but instead more of a self-evident proposition — the law developed to regulate the conduct of war logically applied only during war. But evolutions in international law — most notably the international legal efforts to prohibit war, explained in Chapter 2 — created uncertainty as to what was meant by "war." Was it to be interpreted pragmatically, to mean hostilities between states or perhaps between states and non-state groups? Or was the meaning strictly *de jure*?[1]

A pragmatic answer seemed logical: War should include any situation of armed hostilities manifesting the characteristics of violence traditionally associated with wars. However, war for purposes of international law war meant something quite different. In his classic treatise on international law, L. Oppenheim provided the seminal and authoritative international legal definition of war: "a contention between two or more States through their armed forces, for the purpose of overpowering each other and imposing such conditions of peace as the victor pleases."[2]

This definition imposed certain limitations on the situations to which the laws of war applied. First, the law applied only to inter-state contentions; no matter how widespread or intense hostilities between a state and a non-state enemy might be, it was not (with one exception) war within the meaning of international law. The one exception was the doctrine of belligerency, which allowed for certain conflicts between a state and a dissident entity to qualify for law of war regulation. Prior to the twentieth century, hostilities between two entities within a sovereign state vying for authority over the state — the classic civil war — would be addressed from a legal perspective through the doctrine of belligerency.[3] Pursuant to that doctrine, the belligerent non-state party would be treated as a state for purposes of international legal rights and obligations until resolution of the situation of internal uncertainty.[4] The American Civil War provides a classic example of application of this doctrine. Domestically, the federal government treated the rebellious Confederate states as belligerents, applying the *jus belli* to the hostilities between the two parties.[5] Internationally, other sovereigns recognized the Confederacy as a belligerent, extending accordant international status as a result.[6] As the distinguished international law scholar Professor Dinstein notes, this concept of belligerency somewhat offset the consequence of the "state centric" meaning of war.

The efficacy of the doctrine of belligerency — provision of conflict regulation during civil war — was essentially nullified by the evolving nature of

---

1. *See, generally* Yoram Dinstein, War, Aggression, and Self-Defense 5 (4th ed. 2005) (hereinafter Dinstein).

2. L. Oppenheim, II International Law 202 (H. Lauterpacht ed., 7th ed. 1952) (hereinafter Oppenheim).

3. *See* Dinstein, *supra*, note 1; *see also* Lieutenant Colonel Yair M. Lootsteen, *The Concept of Belligerency in International Law*, 166 Mil. L. Rev. 109 (2000) (hereinafter Lootsteen).

4. Lootsteen, *supra*, note 3, at 109.

5. *See* The Brig Amy Warwick (The Prize Cases), 67 U.S. (2 Black) 635 (1863); *see also* The War of the Rebellion: A Compilation of the Official Records of the Union and Confederate Armies (Lieber Code), Series III, vol. 3, 148-164 (GPO 1899).

6. Lootsteen, *supra*, note 3, at 114.

non-state conflicts. The politicization of external reactions to civil wars, and the proclivity of insurgencies where the non-state groups did not assert sufficient territorial control to qualify as belligerents, were common features of twentieth-century hostilities between states and non-state groups. The Spanish Civil War of 1936 to 1939 illustrates the first of these influences. Soon after the Nationalist opponents to the Republican government in Madrid launched their uprising, Spain divided between two political entities claiming authority over the state, the existing Republic, and the rebellious Nationalists. Instead of treating the rebellious Nationalists as a "belligerent," several nations supporting the rebellion—most notably Italy and Germany—recognized the Nationalist regime as the legitimate government of Spain. The Republic's main supporter—Stalin's Soviet Union—adopted the same position *vis à vis* the Nationalists.[7] But none of these external states treated either side to the conflict as a belligerent, and instead rejected assertions of international legal rights and obligations by the forces of the side to the conflict they did not support, (for example, both Germany and Italy treated Republican naval forces attempting to interdict their supply vessels as pirates).

Perhaps even more problematic for application of the doctrine of belligerency was the increasingly common situation involving insurgencies that did not assert territorial control or governance analogous to that associated with traditional civil wars. These insurgencies involved organized, non-state belligerent groups whose control of national territory was inconsistent. This, combined with the political reality that many of these movements were sponsored and encouraged by the Soviet Union (a fact that reduced the probability of other states recognizing the belligerent status of the rebels), resulted in conflicts that fell outside the scope of accepted international legal criteria for application of the laws and customs of war. As a result, the decline of reliance on the belligerency doctrine resulted in the common occurrence of armed hostilities with all the pragmatic characteristics of war, but with no legally required application of regulatory rules.[8]

This chasm between the pragmatic reality of hostilities and legal regulation was not, however, limited to hostilities between states and non-state belligerents. It also became an impediment to application of the laws and customs of war to hostilities between states.[9] Oppenheim's definition of war, which sets

---

7. James G. Stewart, *Towards a Single Definition of Armed Conflict in International Humanitarian Law: A Critique of Internationalized Armed Conflict*, 85 Int'l Rev. Red Cross 313, 317 (2003), available at http://www.icrc.org/Web/fre/sitefre0.nsf/htmlall/5PXJXQ/$File/irrc_850_Stewart.pdf (hereinafter Stewart); *see also* Lootsteen, *supra*, note 3, at 115-117 (analyzing the impact of the Spanish Civil War on the development of common Article 3).

8. *See* Chinese Civil War, http://www.dean.usma.edu/history/web03/atlases/chinese%20civil%20war/chinese%20civil%20war%20index.htm (last visited July 16, 2016); *see also* Lootsteen, *supra*, note 3, at 115-117.

9. *See, generally* Commentary on the First Geneva Convention: Convention (I) for the Amelioration of the Condition of the Wounded and Sick in Armed Forces in the Field (2nd ed., 2016), para. 192-350, *available at* https://www.icrc.org/applic/ihl/ihl.nsf/Treaty.xsp?action=openDocument&documentId=4825657B0C7E6BF0C12563CD002D6B0B. In 2016, the ICRC released an updated Commentary to the First Geneva Convention (GWS). This Commentary supplanted the

forth the requirement that hostilities be conducted "for the purpose of overpowering each other and imposing such conditions of peace as the victor pleases,"[10] along with other constituent elements of the "war" definition, provided states with theories to disavow the existence of a state of war. These theories would be based on claims that, *inter alia,* an opponent did not satisfy the formalities of declaring war, or that the opponent did not qualify as a legitimate sovereign state, or that hostilities were conducted for a defensive purpose. Some states advanced the argument that hostilities were not conducted with the intention to impose their will upon another sovereign state, and thereby did not qualify as war and did not require application of laws and customs of war. This method of "regulatory avoidance" is highlighted in the International Committee of the Red Cross (ICRC) Commentary to common Article 2 of the Four Geneva Conventions of 1949, the article (as will be explained below) developed to align law applicability with *de facto* situations of armed conflict:

> [N]either the 1899 and 1907 Hague Conventions nor the 1864, 1906 and 1929 Geneva Conventions specified under what conditions their application would be triggered. In the absence of any explicit indication, it was generally understood that these instruments applied only during a declared war, with recognition by the belligerents that a state of war existed between them.
> . . .
> In the 1930s, it became apparent that it would be useful to indicate precisely to which situations the 1929 Geneva Conventions on the Wounded and Sick and on Prisoners of War would apply. . . . At the same time, especially in the light of the Spanish Civil War, it became apparent that armed conflicts did not necessarily occur only between States and that the 1929 Conventions did not apply to 'civil wars'. In addition, the experience of the Second World War brought to light the need to apply the Conventions to all situations of military occupation.
> . . .
> [Furthermore,] [s]ince 1907, experience ha[d] shown that many armed conflicts, displaying all the characteristics of a war, . . . ar[o]se without being preceded by any of the formalities laid down in the 1907 Hague Convention (III).[11]

By the time of the outbreak of World War II, the laws and customs of war provided a relatively comprehensive package of international legal rules to regulate war. However, uncertainty as to when this law came into force produced what came to be regarded as an unacceptable lacuna in the regulation of armed hostilities. The solution would take the form of perhaps the most significant twentieth-century development in the international legal regulation of armed hostilities: an express law triggering mechanism.

---

original 1952 Commentary, the first of four similar Commentaries drafted from 1952 to 1960, that were published for each of the four Geneva Conventions. Because Article 2 of each original Commentary is identical — or *common* — to each Convention, the Commentary for these articles is also identical in each of the four Commentaries.

10. OPPENHEIM, *supra*, note 2, at 202.
11. Commentary, Convention (I), *supra*, note 9, para. 192, 197-98, 210.

III. The 1949 Geneva Conventions and the Advent of a Law Trigger

The post-World War II process of revising the 1929 Geneva Conventions culminated in 1949 with three revised Geneva Conventions and one completely new Convention (protecting civilians). In addition to this new "Civilians Convention," the revisions included many other advances in humanitarian protection. Still, the need for a provision aimed at preventing warring states from disavowing the existence of a state of war, and thereby denying the humanitarian protections to war victims, led to one of the most significant advancements in humanitarian law.[12]

The product of the international effort to mitigate the effects of conflict disavowal was the creation of two critically important articles. Articles 2 and 3 are referred to as the *common Articles*, as they are present and identical in all four of the 1949 Geneva Conventions. Each article defines situations to which the four Conventions apply; in other words, these common Articles provided the "trigger" for application of the humanitarian protections provided by the Geneva Conventions.[13] Responsive to the inherent uncertainty in law application that flowed from the international definition of war, these articles reflect a clear objective of ensuring application of humanitarian protections during a *de facto*, as opposed to *de jure* war.[14] As the ICRC Commentary emphasizes, the drafters' objective of ensuring that victims of war received the benefit of the Conventions necessitated an applicability criterion that remained unaffected by the participants' legal characterization of the hostilities, or the legal status of the belligerent parties to the conflict.[15]

A. The Triggers — Common Articles 2 and 3

Understanding the law triggering equation established by common Articles 2 and 3 requires appreciation of not only the background that led to their adoption, but also the dichotomy between the two categories of hostilities they addressed. When the Conventions were drafted, the regulation of inter-state hostilities remained the primary focus of the international community. The carnage of World War II highlighted the importance of obligatory humanitarian protections during armed conflicts, no matter how they might be legally characterized. Accordingly, included within these four treaties were hundreds of rules developed to regulate hostilities between sovereign states.[16]

---

12. *Id.* para. 202.
13. *See, generally id.* para. 192-907.
14. *See id.* para. 192-98, 357-83.
15. *See id.*
16. *See* Geneva Convention for the Amelioration of the Condition of the Wounded and Sick in Armed Forces in the Field, Aug. 12, 1949, 6 U.S.T. 3114, 75 U.N.T.S. 970 (hereinafter GWS); Geneva Convention for the Amelioration of the Condition of Wounded, Sick, and Shipwrecked Members of

Another important influence at that time was the collective international memory of the widespread humanitarian abuses associated with intra-state armed hostilities both immediately preceding and following World War II, most notably in the Spanish and Greek Civil Wars.[17] As will be explained in more detail below, there was no consensus that these armed conflicts should be subjected to a regulatory regime as comprehensive as that applicable to inter-state armed conflicts. However, there was consensus that the widespread suffering associated with these "non-international" armed conflicts necessitated the imposition of baseline humanitarian protections for victims of these "wars."[18] This necessity required articles indicating when relevant regulatory provisions applied *to both* inter and intra-state armed conflicts, culminating in the adoption of common Articles 2 and 3 of the four Geneva Conventions — the "law triggering" provisions of the Conventions.

Common Article 2[19] addressed situations that trigger the application of all provisions (except common Article 3) of the Geneva Conventions. Declared wars were unsurprisingly included within the scope of the article. However, responsive to the uncertainty as to when the law applied, the article included within its scope two important additional situations, each focused on the *de facto* nature of a dispute between two or more states:

> Art. 2. In addition to the provisions which shall be implemented in peacetime, the present Convention shall apply to all cases of declared war or of any other armed conflict which may arise between two or more of the High Contracting Parties, even if the state of war is not recognized by one of them.
>
> The Convention shall also apply to all cases of partial or total occupation of the territory of a High Contracting Party, even if the said occupation meets with no armed resistance.[20]

This emphasis on either the *de jure* or *de facto* nature of a dispute between states as a method of maximizing alignment between the need for humanitarian regulation and the actual situation was emphasized in the ICRC Commentary to common Article 2, which provides:

> The rationale ... is to extend the scope of application of the Geneva Conventions so that their provisions come into force even when hostilities between States do not result from a formal declaration of war. [T]his ... serves the humanitarian purpose of the Geneva Conventions by minimizing the possibility for States to evade obligations under humanitarian law simply by not declaring war or refusing to acknowledge the existence of an armed conflict.
>
> ...

---

the Armed Forces at Sea, Aug. 12, 1949, 6 U.S.T. 3217, 75 U.N.T.S. 971 (hereinafter GWS Sea); Geneva Convention Relative to the Treatment of Prisoners of War, Aug. 12, 1949, 6 U.S.T. 3316, 75 U.N.T.S. 972 (hereinafter GPW); Geneva Convention Relative to the Protection of Civilian Persons in Time of War, Aug. 12, 1949, 6 U.S.T. 3516, 75 U.N.T.S. 973 (hereinafter GCC) (collectively, hereinafter Geneva Conventions).

17. Commentary, Convention (I), *supra*, note 9, para. 365.
18. *See id.* para. 357-83.
19. *See* GWS, art. 2; GWS Sea, art. 2; GPW, art. 2; GCC, art. 2 (hereinafter common Article 2).
20. *Id.*

... Therefore, the determination of the existence of an armed conflict ... must be based solely on the prevailing facts demonstrating the *de facto* existence of hostilities between the belligerents, even without a declaration of war.[21]

The situations addressed by common Article 2, to include *de facto* interstate hostilities, are generally known today as "international armed conflicts." Situations of *de facto* armed hostilities, and not the *de jure* characterization of the dispute by the states involved, therefore became the focal point of this new law triggering standard. Further, because the objective of this new focal point was to maximize humanitarian protections for the individuals impacted by *de facto* hostilities, the limited duration, geographic scope, or intensity of hostilities in no way impacted the application of the law, a point noted by the ICRC Commentary:

> Article 2(1) itself contains no mention of any threshold for the intensity or duration of hostilities. Indeed, in the frequently cited 1958 commentary on common Article 2, Pictet stated: "Any difference arising between two States and leading to the intervention of members of the armed forces is an armed conflict within the meaning of Article 2, even if one of the Parties denies the existence of a state of war. It makes no difference how long the conflict lasts, or how much slaughter takes place." Furthermore, it makes no difference how numerous are the participating forces. . . .[22]

Like common Article 2, common Article 3 also established a triggering standard for application of humanitarian law. However, unlike common Article 2, common Article 3 triggered a much more limited body of law. Specifically, common Article 3 triggered only the humanitarian rules included within the Article itself. As a result, common Article 3 was characterized as a "Convention in miniature."[23] In simplest terms, this means that unlike common Article 2, common Article 3 was more than just a law triggering provision. Instead, common Article 3 included two components. The first (best understood as the triggering prong of the article) is the law applicability rule, which provides:

> In the case of armed conflict not of an international character occurring in the territory of one of the High Contracting Parties, each Party to the conflict shall be bound to apply. . . .[24]

The second (best understood as the humanitarian prong) is the actual law applicable to situations falling within the scope of the article: non-international armed conflicts.[25]

---

21. Commentary, Convention (I), *supra*, note 9, para. 202, 211.
22. *Id*. para. 236 *citing* Commentary, Convention (I) for the Amelioration of the Condition of the Wounded and Sick in Armed Forces in the Field, Geneva, 12 August 1949 (Jean S. Pictet ed., 1960), at 32, *available at* http://www.icrc.org/ihl.nsf/WebList?ReadForm &id=365&t=com (hereinafter 1952 Commentary, Convention (I)).
23. *Id*. para. 356.
24. GWS, art. 3; GWS Sea, art. 3; GPW, art. 3; GCC, art. 3 (hereinafter common Article 3).
25. *Id*.

Thus, both common Articles 2 and 3 function as "conduits" leading to rules that regulate two distinct categories of armed conflict. However, in 1949 there was little international appetite for adopting a robust regulatory regime for non-international armed conflicts. The consensus reached by the drafters of common Article 3 was a limited regulation of these conflicts, essentially through only a humane treatment requirement of individuals not actively participating in hostilities. Therefore, common Article 3 triggers only the humane treatment rules contained within the Article itself.[26] In contrast, common Article 2 serves as a conduit that leads to the application of every other rule codified in the Geneva Conventions — rules developed for the regulation of international armed conflicts.[27]

Understanding this "conduit" effect of common Articles 2 and 3 is facilitated by visualizing each law triggering article as a funnel. In order to reach substantive rules of conflict regulation, it is necessary to pass through one of these funnels: passing through the common Article 2 funnel leads to the numerous rules of the Geneva Conventions applicable to international (inter-state) armed conflicts; passing through the common Article 3 funnel leads to the far more limited humane treatment rule contained in common Article 3 itself. The figures below depict this 'conduit' concept:

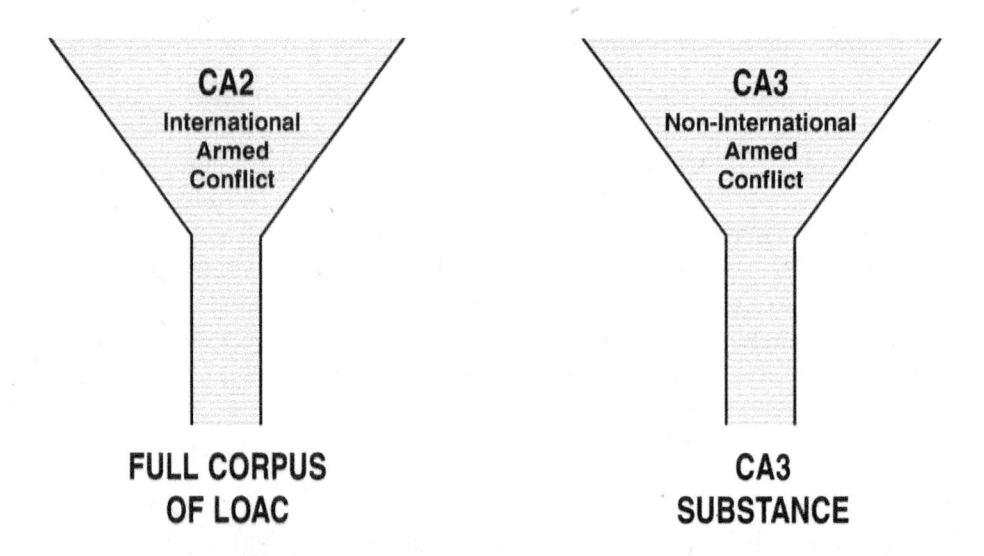

```
       CA2                              CA3
   International                   Non-International
      Armed                            Armed
     Conflict                         Conflict


   FULL CORPUS                          CA3
     OF LOAC                         SUBSTANCE
```

As the funnel visualization indicates, the original effect of these law triggering articles was limited to application of relevant provisions of the four Geneva Conventions. Although neither common Articles 2 or 3 purport to trigger any other law, these law triggering provisions rapidly evolved to produce such an effect.[28] Today, these two law triggering articles provide the principal standard

---

26. Commentary, Convention (I), *supra,* note 9, para. 357-59, 389.
27. *See* Common Article 2, *supra,* note 19.
28. *See, generally* INTERNATIONAL LAW ASSOCIATION, USE OF FORCE COMMITTEE, FINAL REPORT ON THE MEANING OF ARMED CONFLICT IN INTERNATIONAL LAW 33 (2010), *available at* http://www.

for assessing application of the LOAC writ at large, not just the Conventions. Pursuant to this evolution, LOAC application assessment focuses on two essential factors: first, the existence of armed conflict; second, the international or non-international character of the armed conflict.[29]

B. The Existence of an Armed Conflict

The existence of armed conflict is a central requirement incorporated into both common Articles 2 and 3. This requirement is logically derived from the purpose of these articles: to ensure regulation of armed hostilities. However, because the term "armed conflict" was not defined in the Conventions, there is no definitive test for assessing when a situation qualifies as an armed conflict. The ICRC Commentary associated with common Articles 2 and 3 did, however, provide useful insight into the intended meaning of this term, and is routinely relied upon as a guide for assessing the existence of armed conflict. According to the Commentary, several important factors, considered either individually or collectively, facilitate the armed conflict determination. There is, however, no single dispositive indicator of an armed conflict. Instead, these factors are assessed on a case-by-case "totality of the circumstances" basis, informed by the underlying purpose of common Articles 2 and 3: linking law applicability with the *de facto* existence of armed hostilities necessitating humanitarian regulation.[30]

It is not uncommon for states to be hesitant or unwilling to acknowledge the existence of armed conflict when hostilities break out, especially when the scope and duration of hostilities is limited. However, the existence of armed conflict is not contingent on acknowledgement by the states whose armed forces are engaged in hostilities. Any inter-state dispute resulting in hostilities between opposing armed forces qualifies as an international armed conflict, irrespective of how the states choose to characterize the action. This is an important aspect of common Article 2's armed conflict standard, as it emphasizes the *de facto* nature of hostilities and prioritizes it over official or *de jure* characterizations, thereby ensuring humanitarian protections apply when logically needed.

One example of this "short duration" armed conflict scenario was the 1982 incident involving a U.S. Navy pilot who was shot down by Syrian armed forces in the Bekaa Valley region of Lebanon. Although the United States never asserted it was involved in a "war" or a "conflict" with Syria, it demanded the pilot be treated as a prisoner of war (POW). Because POW status is contingent on the existence of an international armed conflict, in demanding such

---

ila-hq.org/en/committees/index.cfm/cid/1022 (hereinafter ILA FINAL REPORT ON THE MEANING OF ARMED CONFLICT).

29. *See* INTERNATIONAL AND OPERATIONAL LAW DEP'T, THE JUDGE ADVOCATE GENERAL'S SCHOOL, LAW OF WAR DESKBOOK 23-28 (Major Gregory S. Musselman eds., 2011).

30. Commentary, Convention (I), *supra*, note 9, para. 210-11, 416-21.

status, the United States implicitly acknowledged the incident fell within the scope of common Article 2.[31]

There may, of course, be incidents involving confrontations between armed forces of two states that do not qualify as armed conflicts because they do not result from a deliberate use of military force to address an inter-state dispute. Examples include situations where military forces of one state stray into the territory of another state and are subsequently detained. When this happens, such as the 2007 incident involving British sailors captured at gunpoint by Iranian forces, or the 2015 incident involving the detention of the crew of a U.S. Navy patrol boat that strayed into Iranian territory, the absence of the requisite "dispute between states" justifies the conclusion that no armed conflict exists.[32]

These incidents should not, however, be taken as indicating that the motive for inter-state hostilities is decisive when assessing the existence of armed conflict. Indeed, the Geneva Conventions appear to accord no significance to the motive or characterization of disputes between two states resulting in the capture of armed forces. Accordingly, characterizing even an arguably inadvertent cross-border incursion by armed forces as a criminal incident outside the scope of common Article 2 may contradict the objective of the treaties. Indeed, it may be logical to treat such captives as POWs for the short duration of their detention, shielding them from liability under the domestic immigration and criminal laws of the detaining state. In fact, a similar incident occurred in 1998 when four U.S. soldiers serving as part of a United Nations peacekeeping mission in Macedonia, allegedly crossed the border into Serbia without authority. After a brief firefight, these soldiers were captured by Serbian forces and imprisoned as illegal aliens. Although initially hesitant, the United States eventually demanded that Serbia extend POW status and protections to these soldiers.[33] Like the incident of the pilot shot down by Syrian armed forces, the United States considered the brevity and isolated nature of the event irrelevant for purposes of legal status of the incident and the captives.

Not all experts agree that duration and intensity of hostilities are irrelevant considerations when assessing when a clash between state armed forces qualifies as an armed conflict. An example of the contrary view is provided by the report of the committee established by the International Law Association (ILA) to analyze the meaning of the "armed conflict." This committee concluded that the existence of armed conflict requires a certain threshold of intensity:

---

31. Interview with Mr. W. Hays Parks, a senior attorney for the Defense Department and recognized expert on the law of armed conflict. Mr. Parks was personally involved in developing the United States position on the status of Lieutenant Goodman and indicated during the interview that the United States asserted prisoner of war status for Goodman as a matter of law due to the existence of an "armed conflict" between the United States and Syria within the meaning of Common Article 2.

32. Thomas Harding & George Jones, *Captured Britons may face show trial in Iran*, TELEGRAPH, Mar. 30, 2007, *available at* http://www.telegraph.co.uk/news/worldnews/1547122/Captured-Britons-may-face-show-trial-in-Iran.html; James Rothwell et al, *Iran parades U.S. sailors on state TV before releasing them unharmed*, TELEGRAPH, Jan. 13, 2016, *available at* http://www.telegraph.co.uk/news/worldnews/middleeast/iran/12096275/Iran-holds-two-US-Navy-boats-in-Persian-Gulf.htm.

33. Stephen Lee Myers, *Serb Officer, Captured by Rebels, Held by U.S.*, N.Y. TIMES, Apr. 17, 1999, at A6.

In May 2005, the Executive Committee of the International Law Association (ILA) approved a mandate for the Use of Force Committee to produce a report on the meaning of war or armed conflict in international law. The report was motivated by the United States' position following the attacks of 11 September 2001 that it was involved in a "global war on terror." In other words, the U.S. has claimed the right to exercise belligerent privileges applicable only during armed conflict anywhere in the world where members of terrorist groups are found. The U.S. position was contrary to a trend by states attempting to avoid acknowledging involvement in wars or armed conflicts.

. . .

. . . Plainly, the existence of armed conflict is a significant fact in the international legal system, and yet, the Committee found no widely accepted definition of armed conflict in any treaty. It did, however, discover significant evidence in the sources of international law that the international community embraces a common understanding of armed conflict. *All armed conflict* has certain minimal, defining characteristics that distinguish it from situations of non-armed conflict or peace. In the absence of these characteristics, states may not, consistently with international law, simply declare that a situation is or is not armed conflict based on policy preferences. The Committee confirmed that at least two characteristics are found with respect to all armed conflict:

1. The existence of organized armed groups
2. *Engaged in fighting of some intensity*

In addition to these minimum criteria respecting all armed conflict, [International Humanitarian Law (IHL)] includes additional criteria so as to classify conflicts as either international or non-international in nature.

. . .

. . . The Committee, however, found little evidence to support the view that the Conventions apply in the absence of fighting of some intensity. . . .[34]

This "intensity" requirement might be useful to address situations such as those involving the sailors from the U.K. and U.S. navies. However, the apparent motivation for this ILA interpretation risks undermining the original purpose of the term "armed conflict." As noted above, this term was incorporated into the Geneva Conventions in 1949 to maximize application of humanitarian protections.[35] Because the Convention drafters failed to include any "intensity" qualifier to the term, it seems they were not particularly concerned that the definition might result in LOAC application to situations of minimal or brief hostilities. Instead, application of the Conventions to such situations was more likely perceived as a benefit, as it could only result in enhanced humanitarian protections for war victims. Certainly, captives such as the U.S. Navy pilot shot down over Syria benefit from this expansive and unqualified definition of armed conflict.

Of course, history did not stand still after 1949, and by the time the ILA Committee set about its analysis, two fundamental developments altered the

---

34. ILA Final Report on the Meaning of Armed Conflict, *supra*, note 28, at 1-2 (emphasis added).
35. *See* Commentary, Convention (I), *supra*, note 9, para. 201-02, 210-11.

perceived effect of an unqualified notion of armed conflict. First, as noted above, the armed conflict trigger evolved into the standard for assessing applicability of not only the humanitarian protections of the Geneva Conventions, but also other LOAC provisions, including rules related to the conduct of hostilities.[36] Second, when the United States characterized its struggle against transnational terrorism as an armed conflict, it revealed the legal consequence of an expansive definition; namely, the invocation of broad authority to attack, capture, detain, and prosecute terrorist operatives.[37] Thus, the ILA Committee's motivation does not seem to have been to deny humanitarian protections to war victims, but instead to place an intensity based limitation on invocation of armed conflict-derived authority in response to unconventional non-state threats.

Ultimately, whatever motivated the inclusion of the intensity element, the practice of states seems to contradict this effort to qualify the meaning of armed conflict. Where inter-state hostilities are concerned, this practice suggests that an intensity threshold is not a legitimate or widely accepted requisite element for assessing the existence of armed conflict. Intensity of hostilities is, however, a more widely accepted aspect of determining the existence of non-international armed conflict: a contest between a state and a non-state belligerent group, or between multiple non-state belligerent groups.

As noted above, prior to 1949 these situations of hostilities fell outside the scope of the conventional (treaty) law (whether customary principles of the law applied in such situations prior to 1949 is a question of contemporary debate).[38] Common Article 3 altered this situation, injecting baseline humanitarian protections into the realm of non-international armed conflicts. However, while this reflects international agreement on the humanitarian imperative for extending protections to victims of these non-international conflicts, there was less consensus about when a situation triggered application of this new law.[39]

In 1947, the ICRC proposed that the Geneva Conventions apply to any armed conflict, international or non-international. This proposal would have eliminated the distinction between the two categories of armed conflict.[40] From a humanitarian perspective, this made perfect sense: Why should the nature of the contestants influence the humanitarian protection for those who suffer as the result? However, support never coalesced around the proposal;[41] states were simply unwilling to cede their sovereign prerogative to deal with internal armed challenges (the primary focus of the non-international armed conflict debate) by committing to extensive international legal regulation.[42] Central to

---

36. ILA FINAL REPORT ON THE MEANING OF ARMED CONFLICT, *supra*, note 28, at 33.
37. *Id.*
38. *See, generally* Geoffrey S. Corn, *Hamdan, Lebanon, and the Regulation of Hostilities: The Need to Recognize a Hybrid Category of Armed Conflict*, 40 VAND. J. TRANSNAT'L L. 1 (2007); *see also* Geoffrey S. Corn, *Taking the Bitter with the Sweet: A Law of War Based Analysis of the Military Commission*, 35 STETSON L. REV. 811 (2006).
39. *See* Commentary, Convention (I), *supra*, note 9, para. 357-83.
40. *See id.* para. 197-98, 862-63.
41. *See id.* para. 357-83, 862-63.
42. *Id.* para. 416.

this resistance was the concern that the ICRC proposal would legitimize efforts of non-state dissident groups seeking to break away from or overthrow their governments. In 1947, states were, and remain to this day, simply unwilling to extend the same extensive corpus of international legal regulation applicable to inter-state armed conflicts to non-international armed conflicts.[43]

In response to this resistance, a compromise emerged: require the humane treatment for any individual taking no active part in hostilities, whether because they are not participants in hostilities (such as civilians), or because they have been rendered *hors de combat* (out of the fight) as the result of wounds, sickness, or capture.[44] Common Article 3 is the provision of the four Geneva Conventions that codified this compromise, imposing a humane treatment obligation on "each party to the conflict." But this reference to parties to "the conflicts" indicates that, like common Article 2, only situations qualifying as armed conflicts trigger application of this obligation.[45] Of course, this agreement extended the humane treatment obligation to a new category of armed conflict: "non-international armed conflict," or NIAC. Obviously, assessing when this rule becomes applicable requires identifying what qualifies as an armed conflict outside the context of inter-state hostilities.

This was in 1949, and remains, to this day, a complicated question. This complexity is a consequence of two primary influences. First, the fact is that internal disturbances, and challenges presented to states by internal and external non-state actors, are rarely as binary in nature as interactions between the armed forces of two states. Second, there is a reticence of states to acknowledge that non-state challenges have reached a magnitude as to justify application of international humanitarian regulation.

Confrontations between state forces (both police and military) and non-state threats range across a wide spectrum of organization and intensity. This spectrum runs from low-level sporadic violence by random actors, to low level acts of violence perpetrated by emerging insurgent threats, to isolated but highly destructive actions by internal and transnational non-state actors. In some cases, these confrontations evolve into, hostilities between highly organized belligerent groups bearing all the traditional indicia of regular armed forces. Retired Brigadier General Kenneth Watkin, the Judge Advocate General for Canadian Forces from 2006 to 2010, lends further detail on this spectrum in his book, *Fighting at the Legal Boundaries*.

> As Lindsay Moir has identified, under classic international law, there were three stages of violence identified as being used against the established authorities "depending on the scale and intensity of the conflict: rebellion, insurgency and belligerency." Rebellion represented a sporadic and more modest challenge to the control over the population, "[p]rovided the uprising could be dealt with swiftly and effectively in the normal course of international security, the conflict remained fully domestic." As such the rebels had no recognition under

---

43. *Id.* para. 862-63.
44. Common Article 3, *supra*, note 24.
45. *Id.*

international law and remained punishable under municipal law. In contract, insurgency represented a more substantial challenge against the order of the State with "the rebelling faction being sufficiently organised to mount a credible threat to the government." This forced a form of acknowledgement of the existence of an insurgency, although it did not accord any belligerent rights. In contrast, the recognition of belligerency by the parent government or a third State "amounted to a declaration by the recognizing party that the conflict had attained such a sustained level that both sides were entitled to be treated in the same way as belligerents in an armed conflict."[46]

In the latter situation — normally involving some form of internal military rebellion — the existence of armed conflict is relatively obvious due to the traditional military organization and activities of the opposing armed forces — a situation that would generally be characterized as a civil war. However, insurgent and dissident doctrine routinely produces a progression of violence from criminal activity (in order to amass resources) to more organized challenges to government authority, or to all out hostilities against the full power of the challenged governing authority. Furthermore, this progression is rarely uni-directional; it is common for non-state insurgent forces to move up and down this continuum, depending on the relative success or failure of their efforts.[47] As a result, determining the line between internal disturbances falling below the NIAC threshold, and those that qualify as NIACs, thereby triggering common Article 3's humane treatment obligation, is a difficult process.

Defining this demarcation point between disturbances that did not qualify as armed conflicts and NIACs was, according to the ICRC Commentary, the key concern of the common Article 3 drafters:

> In situations of violence between non-State armed groups and government authorities or between several non-State armed groups, the fundamental question is at what point such violence becomes a non-international armed conflict subject to humanitarian law.
>
> . . .
>
> Pictet's 1952 Commentary on the First Geneva Convention, referring to the absence of a definition of the term 'armed conflict not of an international character', stated:
>
>> [M]any of the delegations feared that it might be taken to cover any act committed by force of arms – any form of anarchy, rebellion, or even plain banditry. For example, if a handful of individuals were to rise in rebellion against the State and attack a police station, would that suffice to bring into being an armed conflict within the meaning of the Article?

---

46. KENNETH WATKIN, FIGHTING AT THE LEGAL BOUNDARIES: CONTROLLING THE USE OF FORCE IN CONTEMPORARY CONFLICT 160-61 (2016) (hereinafter WATKIN).

47. See id. at 160-65; Hassan Hassan, Is the Islamic State Unstoppable?, N.Y. TIMES, July 9, 2016, available at http://www.nytimes.com/2016/07/10/opinion/is-the-islamic-state-unstoppable.html?_r=0

These concerns relating to sovereignty help to explain the higher threshold for the applicability of humanitarian law in non-international armed conflict than in international armed conflict.[48]

In spite of these concerns, proposals to provide an explicit definition of armed conflict were abandoned (the 1952 Commentary characterized this decision as "wise," almost certainly because of the risk that any explicit definition would be almost immediately over-broad and under-inclusive).[49] The Commentary emphasizes that no single factor dictates this demarcation point. Instead, armed conflict must be determined by a "totality of the circumstances" analysis that considers a number of proposed — although not exclusive — factors, considered in any combination or even individually.[50]

The ultimate question to be answered by the totality analysis proposed by the 1952 Commentary is when a situation rises from the level of internal disturbance falling outside the scope of LOAC applicability, into the realm of armed conflict subject to common Article 3 (and over time other LOAC rules). According to the 1952 Commentary:

> [T]hese different conditions, although in no way obligatory, constitute convenient criteria, and we therefore think it well to give a list of those contained in the various amendments discussed; they are as follows:
>
> (1) That the Party in revolt against the de jure Government possesses an organized military force, an authority responsible for its acts, acting within a determinate territory and having the means of respecting and ensuring respect for the Convention.
>
> (2) That the legal Government is obliged to have recourse to the regular military forces against insurgents organized as military and in possession of a part of the national territory.
>
> (3) (a) That the de jure Government has recognized the insurgents as belligerents; or
>
>   (b) that it has claimed for itself the rights of a belligerent; or
>
>   (c) that it has accorded the insurgents recognition as belligerents for the purposes only of the present Convention; or
>
>   (d) that the dispute has been admitted to the agenda of the Security Council or the General Assembly of the United Nations as being a threat to international peace, a breach of the peace, or an act of aggression.
>
> (4) (a) That the insurgents have an organisation purporting to have the characteristics of a State.
>
>   (b) That the insurgent civil authority exercises de facto authority over persons within a determinate territory.

---

48. Commentary, Convention (I), *supra*, note 9, para. 415, 417, *citing* 1952 Commentary, Convention (I), *supra*, note 21, at 49.

49. Commentary, Convention (I), *supra*, note 9, para. 373.

50. *See* Geoffrey S. Corn & Laurie R. Blank, *Losing the Forest for the Trees: Syria, Law and the Pragmatics of Conflict Resolution*, 46 Vand. J. Transnat'l L. 693, 731-45 (2013).

(c) That the armed forces act under the direction of the organized civil authority and are prepared to observe the ordinary laws of war.

(d) That the insurgent civil authority agrees to be bound by the provisions of the Convention.[51]

Some of these factors address what might best be considered, "traditional" civil war type contests. For example, combining the first and fourth factors produces a situation where a dissident force controls territory, exercises governing authority in that territory, and deploys forces organized and commanded in a manner consistent with a regular state armed force. However, these are not the only types of contests between states and non-state threats, or between non-state groups themselves, that qualify as armed conflicts. Indeed, while the world continues to witness the brutality associated with these type of "traditional" NIACs (such as the ongoing civil war in Syria), the adaptability and strategic and tactical agility of non-state threats means that other less traditional forms of organization and operational practices will cross the line from peacetime challenges to NIACs. So much was recognized in the first revision to the 1952 Commentaries, launched in 2016. According to this revised Commentary to common Article 3, today, other factors are increasingly significant when determining what situations qualify as NIACs:

> The Commentaries... published by the ICRC under the general editorship of Jean Pictet between 1952 and 1960 listed a number of 'convenient criteria' for assessing the applicability of common Article 3. As these Commentaries noted, the 'convenient criteria' were drawn from 'the various amendments discussed' during the 1949 Diplomatic Conference, considering that 'these different conditions, although in no way obligatory, constitute convenient criteria', which 'are useful as means of distinguishing a genuine armed conflict from a mere act of banditry or an unorganized and short-lived insurrection'.
>
> These 'convenient criteria' are merely indicative, however. . . .
>
> Over time, of the criteria enumerated in the Pictet Commentaries, two are now widely acknowledged as being the most relevant in assessing the existence of a non-international armed conflict: that the violence needs to have reached a certain intensity and that it must be between at least two organized Parties/armed groups. The existence of a non-international armed conflict thus needs to be assessed according to these specific criteria.[52]

Like its international armed conflict counterpart, the proposed Commentary factors were intended to ensure the applicability of humanitarian protection to any *de facto* situation of non-international armed conflict. Perhaps unsurprisingly, this *de facto* law triggering focus is widely accepted and emphasized in post-1949 practice, scholarly commentary, and jurisprudence. One of the most important affirmations of this approach to conflict assessment came in the initial decision of the then first international war crimes tribunal established since

---

51. 1952 Commentary, Convention (I), *supra*, note 21, at 35-36.
52. Commentary, Convention (I), *supra*, note 9, para. 419-21.

adoption of the 1949 Geneva Conventions, *Prosecutor v. Tadic*.[53] In that widely cited decision, the International Criminal Tribunal for the Former Yugoslavia (ICTY) — the ad hoc war crimes tribunal created by the UN Security Council to impose accountability following the breakup of the former Yugoslavia — concluded that the hostilities between the Government of the Republic of Bosnia and Herzegovina and dissident Bosnian Serb forces qualified as an armed conflict. According to the Tribunal's judgment, "[A]n armed conflict exists whenever there is a resort to armed force between States or protracted armed violence between governmental authorities and organised armed groups or between such groups within a State."[54]

The ICTY's definition of non-international armed conflict emphasized two considerations, which have come to be known as "elements": protracted hostilities and organized opponents (both of which are, as is indicated in the extract above, incorporated into the 2016 Commentary to common Article 3). The requirement of "organized opposition groups" seems consistent with the definition of international armed conflict — a contest between opposing state armed forces.[55] The requirement of protracted hostilities, in contrast, represented a break from the unqualified standard for assessing the existence of an IAC. The ICTY later interpreted this "protracted" requirement as encompassing both a duration *and* intensity assessment. In *Prosecutor v. Haradinaj*, the Tribunal concluded that the notion of "protracted armed violence" must be understood to include not only the duration of the violence, but also all aspects that would enable the degree of intensity to be evaluated.[56]

This "duration and intensity" consideration is unique to the NIAC assessment. However, it seems consistent with common Article 3, and clarifies the demarcation line between civil strife or other acts of general lawlessness and actual armed hostilities. This does not mean that states may act with impunity before a situation crosses that demarcation point, but only that LOAC regulation is inapplicable. In situations falling below this threshold, state actors must comply not only with domestic legal limitations on their power, but also with applicable human rights obligations, which also protect individuals from inhumane treatment (a point emphasized by the 1952 ICRC Commentary to common Article 3).[57]

Accordingly, this "duration and intensity" consideration is both an important aspect of NIAC assessment, and a consideration that distinguishes the

---

53. Prosecutor v. Tadic, Case No. IT-94-1, Decision on the Defence Motion for Interlocutory Appeal on Jurisdiction (Int'l Crim. Trib. for the Former Yugoslavia Oct. 2, 1995).

54. *Id.* ¶70.

55. *See* Prosecutor v. Limaj, Case No. IT-94-1, ¶94 (Int'l Crim. Trib. for the Former Yugoslavia Sept. 2007); Prosecutor v. Boskoski, Case No. IT-04-82, Judgment, ¶175 (Int'l Crim. Trib. for the Former Yugoslavia July 2008). These criteria have since been taken up by other international bodies. *See* Prosecutor v. Rutaganda, Case No. ICTR-96-3, Judgment, ¶93 (Int'l Crim. Trib. for Rwanda Dec. 6, 1999); International Commission of Inquiry on Darfur, Report Pursuant to Security Council Resolution 1564 of 18 Sept. 2004 (Jan. 25, 2005), ¶¶74-76.

56. Prosecutor v. Haradinaj, Case No. IT-04-84-T, Judgment, ¶49 (Int'l Crim. Trib. for the Former Yugoslavia Apr. 3, 2008).

57. Commentary, Convention (I), *supra*, note 9, para. 550-64.

definition of NIAC from IAC. However, these factors do not alter the "overall totality of the circumstances" for assessing the existence of NIAC. Instead, "duration and intensity" are important, although not dispositive considerations in this totality analysis, which considers:

> ...the collective nature of the fighting or the fact that the State is obliged to resort to its army as its police forces are no longer able to deal with the situation on their own. The duration of the conflict, the frequency of the acts of violence and military operations, the nature of the weapons used, displacement of civilians, territorial control by opposition forces, the number of victims (dead, wounded, displaced persons, etc.) are also pieces of information that may be taken into account.[58]

Ultimately, no formula can guarantee a perfect symmetry between the ground truth of armed conflict and recognition or acknowledgment of the same by the participants in the hostilities. Although the ICRC Commentary factors as subsequently interpreted and applied by states and international tribunals facilitate such recognition, the fact remains that states were in 1949 and seem still to this day reticent to acknowledge the existence of NIAC, especially within their own borders. This is almost certainly due to state concern related to the consequence of such recognition. The perceived detrimental consequence of acknowledging existence of a NIAC fall into two categories: first, concern that acknowledging applicability of common Article 3 will somehow constrain state authority to address the non-state threat; second, concern that acknowledging the existence of armed conflict will "legitimize" the non-state group challenging state authority.

The 1952 ICRC Commentary noted these concerns as potential impediments to the recognition of NIACs, and more specifically that these concerns impeded efforts to extend international humanitarian protections to this new realm of armed conflicts.[59] However, the Commentary also emphasized the invalidity of such concerns, and that a broad interpretation of non-international armed conflict and application of common Article 3 in no way compromises state efforts to respond to non-state threats:

> We think, on the contrary, that the Article should be applied as widely as possible. There can be no reason against this. For, contrary to what may have been thought, the Article in its reduced form does not in any way limit the right of a State to put down rebellion. Nor does it increase in the slightest the authority of the rebel party. It merely demands respect for certain rules, which were already recognized as essential in all civilized countries, and enacted in the municipal law of the States in question, long before the Convention was signed.[60]

---

58. Sylvain Vite, *Typology of Armed Conflicts in International Humanitarian Law: Legal Concepts and Actual Situations*, 91 INT'L REV. RED CROSS 69, 76 (Mar. 2009), *available at* http://www.icrc.org/eng/assets/files/other/irrc-873-vite.pdf.
59. *See, generally* 1952 Commentary, Convention (I), *supra*, note 21, at 50.
60. *Id.*

These considerations may explain why state authorities might resist acknowledging the existence of NIAC, and also why the ICTY interpreted NIAC as requiring a certain level of intensity. These considerations do not, however, justify diluting or compromising the objective of common Article 3: to maximize the applicability of humanitarian protections during *de facto* armed conflicts, which, when non-international, often involve a level of brutality that rivals or exceeds that associated with inter-state conflicts.

C. The Nature of the Armed Conflict

The existence of *de facto* armed conflicts is the first component of the common Article 2/3 law application equation. The second component is the nature of the armed conflict: international or non-international. This second component dictates the extent of LOAC regulation applicable to each respective "type" of armed conflict. As noted above, armed conflicts considered "international," pursuant to common Article 2, trigger the full corpus (all the rules) of the LOAC (all four Geneva Conventions and all other conventional and customary LOAC provisions developed to regulate both the conduct of hostilities and the treatment of war victims). In contrast, armed conflicts considered "non-international" pursuant to common Article 3, bring into force a more limited package of regulatory norms (common Article 3's humane treatment obligation, supplemented in some situations by additional treaty obligations established by Additional Protocol II, and by a limited (but increasing) number of customary norms that have "migrated" from the international armed conflict realm).[61]

The absence of an explicit definition of "international" or "non-international" in common Articles 2 or 3 produced its own uncertainty. However, this uncertainty has been far less problematic than the uncertainty associated with the meaning of armed conflict. The intent of the Convention drafters, explained by the ICRC Commentary, has been generally successful in guiding interpretation of these terms.[62] "International" within the meaning of common Article 2 is understood as essentially synonymous with inter-state; as noted above, any dispute between states that leads to the intervention of armed forces qualifies as an IAC.[63] It is the *de facto* nature of the dispute, and not the legal or formal characterization of the situation, which indicates an IAC, even if the states disavow the existence of a state of war (although such acknowledgment would obviously provide an almost conclusive indication of the requisite dispute).[64] Equally irrelevant is the fact that one state involved in the dispute refuses to recognize the opposing state, or that a military intervention by one state meets no

---

61. *See* Prosecutor v. Tadic, Case No. IT-94-1-AR72, Appeal on Jurisdiction, ¶70 (Int'l Crim. Trib. for the Former Yugoslavia Oct. 2, 1995).
62. *See, generally* Commentary, Convention (I), *supra*, note 9, para. 210-84, 384-502.
63. *Id.* para. 217-35.
64. *Id.*

military resistance by the other. As long as the use of armed force is the product of an underlying inter-state dispute, the situation is considered an IAC.[65]

This broad concept of "international" has not, however, eliminated all uncertainty as to whether the use of armed force by one state, in the territory of another state qualifies as an IAC. It may be that a state, using military force in the territory of another state asserts that the intervention of armed forces was not the result of a dispute between the two states.[66] This is an increasingly common situation, arising when one nation uses military force in the territory of another, without consent, in order to attack a non-state group located in that territory. In such situations, it is not uncommon for the intervening state to assert that because force was used against the non-state group, the use of force did not result from a dispute with the state whose territory was compromised. In other situations, the intervening state may assert that the dispute was with an illegitimate governing authority, but not against a legitimate government.

Each of these "hostilities without dispute" theories seems to conflict with the plain meaning and widely understood interpretation of common Article 2. Nonetheless, it is understandable why a state would disavow the existence of an inter-state armed conflict when the objective of a military action is carefully limited to the non-state opponent, even when the operation is conducted in the territory of another state. For example, in 2006 Israel launched a military action in the territory of Lebanon to attack Hezbollah forces. While neither Israel nor Lebanon asserted they were involved in an IAC,[67] the ICRC disagreed, concluding the hostilities fell within the definition of common Article 2.[68] An example of the "failed state" theory is provided by the 1992 U.S. military actions in Somalia. Based on the conclusion that Somalia was a "failed state" — essentially a state without any functioning government — the United States asserted that its use of military force could not have been the result of a "dispute between states," and therefore did not qualify as an IAC.[69] President Bush also asserted a similar failed state theory in 2001 when the United States began combat operations in Afghanistan. Although he later reconsidered and reversed this position, the United States initially asserted the intervention did not qualify as an IAC.[70] This theory remains controversial.

---

65. *Id.*
66. *See, e.g.,* Pierre Tristam, *The 2006 Lebanon War: Israel and Hezbollah Square Off*, About. com, *available at* http://middleeast.about.com/od/lebanon/a/me070918.htm (last visited July 12, 2016) (hereinafter Tristam).
67. *See id; see also Security Council Calls for an End to Hostilities Between Hezbollah, Israel, Unanimously Adopts Resolution 1701*, U.N. Security Council (Aug. 11, 2006), http://www.un.org/News/Press/docs/2006/sc8808.doc.htm (indication that Hezbollah and not Lebanon was responsible for the attacks).
68. Stewart, *supra*, note 7, at 313, 330.
69. *See, generally* Center for Law and Military Operations (CLAMO) and The Judge Advocate Gen.'s School, CLAMO Report: The Marines Have Landed at CLAMO (1998).
70. Memorandum from President George W. Bush to Vice President Richard Cheney, Humane Treatment of Taliban and al Qaeda Detainees (Feb. 7, 2002), *available at* http://www.pegc.us/archive/White_House/bush_memo_20020207_ed.pdf (hereinafter Bush Torture Memo).

The U.S. intervention in Panama in 1989 provides another interesting example of denying the existence of an IAC by asserting a military intervention was not the result of a dispute between states. When President George H.W. Bush informed the nation of his decision to order a large-scale military intervention in Panama, he emphasized that the *de facto* head of state, General Manuel Noriega, declared that Panama was in a "state of war" with the United States. However, he then used terminology indicating that the intervention was for the more limited purpose of protecting the lives of the 35,000 U.S. nationals in Panama, and neither the White House nor the Pentagon announced a position on the nature of the ensuing armed conflict.[71]

U.S. forces executed Operation Just Cause without a clear indication of the nature of the armed conflict. As the operation progressed, certain decisions, related to the status of captured PDF personnel and the responsibility to maintain law and order in Panama indicated that the United States did not consider the armed conflict to be international within the meaning of common Article 2.[72] Later, during the course of the litigation surrounding General Noriega's criminal prosecution in the United States, the government confirmed this position. According to government pleadings in that case, the intervention did not qualify as an IAC because the democratically elected President of Panama, who Noriega had prevented from taking office, requested the U.S. intervention to oust Noriega and neutralize his Panamanian Defense Force. As a result, there was no "dispute" between the two nations. Accordingly, the government asserted that the armed conflict was not international within the meaning of common Article 2. The federal judge, charged with adjudicating Noriega's claim to POW status rejected this argument.[73] However, Just Cause serves as a reminder that even the meaning of what appears to be an obvious international armed conflict is subject to interpretive debate.

In contrast, when adopted in 1949, the term "non-international" found in common Article 3 generated almost no uncertainty. At that time, and for decades thereafter, the term meant intra-state, or "internal." However, the meaning of non-international has evolved during the past two decades. Events such as the U.S. military response to the terrorist attacks of September 11, 2001, U.S. and coalition combat operations against the self-proclaimed Islamic State, and Israeli combat operations against Hezbollah in Southern Lebanon, all challenged the assumption that only "internal" armed conflicts qualified as common Article 3 non-international armed conflicts. As a result, the meaning of NIAC, and the accordant applicability of common Article 3, is no longer considered strictly limited to internal or intra-state hostilities. Indeed, debate over the proper scope of non-international armed conflicts is a focal point of contemporary LOAC applicability debate. This debate centers on the question

---

71. Geoffrey S. Corn et al, U.S. Military Operations: Law Policy and Practice 75-76 (2016).

72. *Id.*

73. *See* United States v. Noriega, 808 F. Supp. 791, 794 (S.D. Fla. 1992) ("However the government wishes to label it, what occurred in late 1989–early 1990 was clearly an "armed conflict" within the meaning of Article 2. Armed troops intervening in a conflict between two parties to the treaty.").

of whether the transnational geographic scope of military operations directed against non-state organized armed groups qualifies as a NIAC pursuant to common Article 3, or whether the "transnational" nature of such conflicts excludes them from this category.[74]

As noted above, common Article 3 represented the first treaty extension of international humanitarian regulation to non-international armed conflicts; without question it was a landmark humanitarian protection development. Responsive to the humanitarian abuses associated with the brutality of civil wars during the years between the two World Wars, common Article 3 sought to extend the protection of international law to any person not actively engaged in hostilities and subject to the power of any party to such conflicts.

This historical context for the development of common Article 3 — preventing humanitarian abuses during civil wars — contributed to the assumption that "non-international" was a synonym for "internal." When states such as the United States began to characterize military operations against transnational non-state enemies, such as al Qaeda, this assumption led to the assertion of the existence of armed conflict that fell into a proverbial gap between common Article 3 (regulating internal armed conflicts), and common Article 2 (regulating international inter-state armed conflicts). However, it is important to remember that common Article 3 does not include the term "internal" as a qualification to the notion of *non-international* armed conflicts. Instead, common Article 3 expressly applies to all "conflicts not of an international character."[75]

This plain reading of common Article 3 undermines the "internal" armed conflict interpretation of non-international. However, the text of common Article 3 also indicates that it applies to "conflicts not of an international character" that occur "within the territory of one of the High Contracting Parties."[76] Because in 1949 (unlike 2016), not all states were party to the Conventions,[77] this territorial qualifier provided an alternate basis to interpret non-international as meaning only "internal." The impact of this qualifier is highlighted by the following excerpt from a 2004 presentation by the ICRC legal advisor:

> Humanitarian law recognizes two categories of armed conflict — international and non-international. Generally, when a State resorts to force against another State (for example, when the "war on terror" involves such use of force, as in

---

74. *See* Kenneth Watkin, *Controlling the Use of Force: A Role for Human Rights Norms in Contemporary Armed Conflict*, 98 Am. J. Int'l L. 1, 3-4 (2004) (discussing the complex challenge of conflict categorization related to military operations conducted against highly organized non-state groups with transnational reach); *see also* Kirby Abott, *Terrorists: Combatants, Criminals, or . . . ?*, in The Measures of International Law: Effectiveness, Fairness, and Validity, Proceedings of the 31st Annual Conference of the Canadian Council on International Law, Ottawa, Oct. 24-26, 2002; *see also* Jennifer Elsea, Cong. Research Serv., Order Code RL31191, Terrorism and the Laws of War: Trying Terrorists as War Criminals Before Military Commissions 10-14 (2001) (analyzing whether the attacks of September 11, 2001 triggered the law of war).

75. *See, e.g.,* common Article 3, *supra*, note 24.

76. *Id.*

77. Geneva Conventions of 12 August 1949, http://www.icrc.org/ihl.nsf/WebSign?ReadForm&id=375&ps=P (last visited July 12, 2016).

the recent U.S. and allied invasion of Afghanistan) the international law of international armed conflict applies. When the "war on terror" amounts to the use of armed force within a State, between that State and a rebel group, or between rebel groups within the State, the situation may amount to non-international armed conflict. . . .[78]

Illustrative of the generally accepted pre-2001 interpretation of the situations to which the LOAC applies, this highlights the uncertainty produced by so-called transnational armed conflicts: conflicts that were neither internal, nor international within the meaning of common Article 2. According to this interpretation, there are only two possible characterizations for military activities conducted against transnational terrorist groups: international armed conflict (when the operations are conducted outside the territory of the state) or non-international armed conflict (limited to operations conducted within the territory of the state).

Over time, this interpretation of LOAC "triggers" began to shift to account for the reality of NIACs extending beyond state borders. The universal adoption of the Geneva Conventions meant that *any* armed conflict between a state and a non-state opponent would *ipso facto* occur "in the territory of one of the High Contracting Parties." Further, these conflicts often included "cross-border" operations into neighboring state territory but directed against non-state belligerents. However, it was the U.S. initiation of a military response to the terrorist attacks of September 11, 2001, that stimulated substantial reconsideration of the assumption that NIACs could only occur within the territory of the state engaged in the armed conflict with the non-state group.[79]

In November 2001, President Bush issued Military Order Number 1.[80] This order directed the establishment of a military detention facility and use of military commissions and authorized the use of detention and trial by commission for captured al Qaeda and Taliban personnel. President Bush characterized the ongoing struggle with al Qaeda as an armed conflict. In so doing, the President signaled the U.S. deterination that operations against al Qaeda qualified as an NIAC of international scope, a position that was manifested by the use of military force reflecting an invocation of the laws and customs of war (to kill as a first resort; to detain preventively without charge or trial; to try by military tribunal). Although these combat operations extended well beyond U.S. borders, the United States did not consider the armed conflict to be international within the meaning of common Article 2. Instead, because al Qaeda was not a state, the United States concluded the armed conflict did not qualify as inter-state, nor did it result from a dispute between states.[81]

---

78. Gabor Rona, *When Is a War not a War?—The Proper Role of the Law of Armed Conflict in the "Global War on Terror,"* International Action to Prevent and Combat Terrorism—Workshop on the Protection of Human Rights While Countering Terrorism, Copenhagen, 15-16 March 2004—Presentation given by Gabor Rona, Legal Adviser at the ICRC's Legal Division, *available at* http://www.icrc.org/eng/resources/documents/misc/5xcmnj.htm.

79. *See* ELSEA, *supra*, note 74.

80. Military Order of November 13, 2001, *Detention, Treatment, and Trial of Certain Non-Citizens in the War Against Terrorism*, 66 Fed. Reg. 57,833 (Nov. 16, 2001).

81. *See* Bush Torture Memo, *supra*, note 70, para. 2(c).

However, relying on the assumption that common Article 3 applied only to "internal" armed conflicts, the President also concluded that the transnational scope of operations against al Qaeda meant the conflict did not fall within the scope of common Article 3.[82] Thus, the United States was engaged in an armed conflict against a non-state enemy that fell into a gap between common Articles 2 and 3.

This interpretation of the common Article 2/3 law triggering equation, with the accordant determination that no provisions of the Conventions applied to the conflict, generated justifiable controversy—controversy that continues to this day. It also resulted in legal challenges that led to a U.S. Supreme Court decision rejecting the president's treaty interpretation in *Hamdan v. Rumsfeld*.[83] That decision addressed Hamdan's challenge to the legality of his trial by military commission. Hamdan argued that the procedures established for the commission violated the humane treatment obligation of common Article 3. This required the Supreme Court to address the meaning of "not of an international character" in the context of the common Article 2/3 law triggering equation. Rejecting the government's argument that common Article 3 applied only to internal armed conflict—an argument that prevailed before the D.C. Circuit Court of Appeals—the Supreme Court determined that:

> . . .[t]he Court of Appeals thought, and the Government asserts, that Common Article 3 does not apply to Hamdan because the conflict with al Qaeda, being "international in scope," does not qualify as a "conflict not of an international character." That reasoning is erroneous. The term "conflict not of an international character" is used here in contradistinction to a conflict between nations. So much is demonstrated by the "fundamental logic [of] the Convention's provisions on its application." Common Article 2 provides that "the present Convention shall apply to all cases of declared war or of any other armed conflict which may arise between two or more of the High Contracting Parties." High Contracting Parties (signatories) also must abide by all terms of the Conventions vis-a-vis one another even if one party to the conflict is a nonsignatory "Power," and must so abide vis-a-vis the nonsignatory if "the latter accepts and applies" those terms. Common Article 3, by contrast, affords some minimal protection, falling short of full protection under the Conventions, to individuals associated with neither a signatory nor even a nonsignatory "Power" who are involved in a conflict "in the territory of" a signatory. The latter kind of conflict is distinguishable from the conflict described in Common Article 2 chiefly because it does not involve a clash between nations (whether signatories or not). In context, then, the phrase "not of an international character" bears its literal meaning.[84]

This treaty interpretation—that any armed conflict not falling within the scope of common Article 2 *ipso facto* falls within the scope of common Article 3—trumped the president's interpretation of the Conventions and

---

82. *Id.*
83. 548 U.S. 557 (2006).
84. *Id.* at 630.

required application of common Article 3 to the armed conflict with al Qaeda. Accordingly, an armed conflict between the United States and non-state belligerent groups falls within the scope of common Article 3, even if that group operates transnationally.

This interpretation of common Article 3 and the overall notion of "transnational" armed conflict remains controversial. Many experts continue to reject the idea that a state can be engaged in a NIAC with no geographic boundaries. However, there is virtually no support for the suggestion that such operations qualify as IACs within the meaning of common Article 2, because those conflicts require an inter-state dispute.[85] Instead, the sporadic nature of terrorism leads many experts to assert that counter-terror military operations do not rise to the level of armed conflict.[86] Instead, these experts believe such operations are better characterized as international law enforcement, subject to international human rights law, but not triggering the LOAC.[87] As noted earlier, the ILA Committee that studied the meaning of "armed conflict" reached this exact conclusion.[88] The 2016 ICRC Commentary to common Article 3 addresses these concerns more carefully, instead proffering several examples where such armed conflicts of a transnational nature may exist:

> One type of armed conflict not confined to the borders of a single State that States appear to have accepted as 'non-international' in practice occurs when a State fighting an armed group on its territory is joined by one or more other States. Although such a conflict may occur within the territory of one State, other States use force extraterritorially, i.e., outside their own territory, as Parties to the conflict. In such cases, the conflict remains non-international in nature....
>
> Second, an existing non-international armed conflict may spill over from the territory of the State in which it began into the territory of a neighbouring State not party to the conflict. These are sometimes called 'spillover' non-international armed conflicts, although this is only a descriptive term and not a legal term of art....
>
> ...
>
> A third scenario of a non-international armed conflict not limited to the territory of one State is that of armed confrontations, meeting the requisite intensity threshold, between a State and a non-State armed group which operates from the territory of a second, neighbouring State. The armed confrontations could also be between two organized non-State armed groups. In such a scenario, the confrontations are of a 'cross border' nature....

---

85. *Cf.* David Glazier, *Playing By the Rules: Combating Al Qaeda Within the Law of War*, 51 WM. & MARY L. REV. 957, 991-1015 (2009).

86. *See, e.g.,* Mary Ellen O'Connell, *Defining Armed Conflict*, 13 J. CONFLICT & SEC. L. 393 (Winter 2008).

87. *See, e.g.*, WATKIN, *supra*, note 47, at 181, 610-17.

88. ILA FINAL REPORT ON THE MEANING OF ARMED CONFLICT, *supra*, note 28, at 33; *cf.* Brian Egan, Legal Advisor, U.S. Dep't of State, Keynote Address at the American Society of International Law Annual Meeting (April 2016), *available at* https://www.justsecurity.org/wp-content/uploads/2016/04/Egan-ASIL-speech.pdf (hereinafter Egan Address).

... [T]he question arises as to whether geographical considerations could play a minimal role with respect to non-international armed conflicts. For example, the question has arisen whether a non-international armed conflict between a non-State armed group and a State could exist, with or without having an anchor in a particular State as the primary or key theatre of hostilities. There are two possible scenarios. The first is the situation of an extended spillover conflict described above. In this scenario, the intensity and organization are sufficient for a conflict to arise and be classified as such in the primary theatre of hostilities and the only question remaining is how far the spillover may stretch. A second scenario considers the possibility of a conflict arising solely on the basis of the actions of a non-State armed group but where hostilities and the members of the armed group are in geographically disparate locations. In that scenario, the main question is whether it is possible to assess far-flung hostilities as a whole so as to conclude that there is one armed conflict between a non-State armed group and a State. Thus, while not abandoning the criteria of organization and intensity required for a non-international armed conflict to exist, this approach would accept that acts that may seem sporadic or isolated within the confines of each State in which they occur may be considered cumulatively as amounting to a non-international armed conflict.

...[T]he practice of States party to the Geneva Conventions in support of a global or transnational non-international armed conflict remains isolated. The ICRC has thus expressed the view that the existence of an armed conflict or the relationship of a particular military operation to an existing armed conflict has to be assessed on a case-by-case basis.[89]

However, at least for the United States, any assertion that the nation is engaged in an armed conflict must result in application of the law brought into force by either common Article 2 or 3.[90] Accordingly, military operations associated with such armed conflicts will always trigger some humanitarian obligations.

IV. The 1977 Additional Protocols to the Geneva Conventions: Clarifying or Confusing the Law Applicability Assessment?

In 1975, the ICRC convened a conference of state delegates to revise the 1949 Conventions. Two treaties emerged from that conference: the two 1977 Additional Protocols to the Geneva Conventions of 1949.[91] Additional Protocol

---

89. Commentary, Convention (I), *supra*, note 9, para. 473-82.
90. *Hamdan*, 548 U.S. at 557, 630.
91. Protocol Additional to the Geneva Conventions of 12 Aug. 1949, and Relating to the Protection of Victims of International Armed Conflicts, June 8, 1977, 1125 U.N.T.S. 3 (hereinafter AP I). Additional Protocol II (AP II) supplemented the law applicable to non-international armed conflicts. Although the United States has not ratified either of these treaties, as will be noted throughout this text, many of their articles are nonetheless considered by the United States to be reflections of binding customary international law.

I (AP I) supplemented the law applicable to international armed conflicts; Additional Protocol II (AP II) supplemented the law applicable to certain non-international armed conflicts.

The purpose of these two supplemental treaties was to enhance the substantive regulation of armed conflicts.[92] However, both treaties initially addressed their respective material fields of application — the situations to which they would apply. Accordingly, like the Geneva Conventions they supplemented, each Protocol included a law triggering article; and each of these articles added a new dimension to LOAC application analysis.

Article 1 of AP I defines situations to which it applies. Sub-paragraph 3 of Article 1 includes, within this scope of applicability, all situations already addressed by common Article 2 to the Geneva Conventions. Specifically, Article 1(3) provides that:

> 3. This Protocol, which supplements the Geneva Conventions of 12 August 1949 for the protection of war victims, shall apply in the situations referred to in Article 2 common to those Conventions.[93]

This was both a logical and uncontroversial law applicability provision. According to the associated ICRC Commentary, "[T]he wording of this paragraph did not raise any difficulties in itself. . . ."[94] The Commentary continues, however, to address how Article 1 expanded the scope of law applicability beyond what common Article 2 provided for, noting that "there was heated and lengthy debate regarding extending its scope to the conflicts referred to in paragraph 4."[95] This Commentary excerpt addressed sub-paragraph 4 of Article 1. This provision of AP I's law applicability article expanded the definition of IACs beyond that included in common Article 2, adding to situations qualifying as IACs armed conflicts that were, prior to 1977, considered NIACs. Specifically, Article 1(4) provides that:

> 4. The situations referred to in the preceding paragraph [international armed conflicts] include armed conflicts in which peoples are fighting against colonial domination and alien occupation and against racist régimes in the exercise of their right of self-determination, as enshrined in the Charter of the United Nations and the Declaration on Principles of International Law concerning Friendly Relations and Co-operation among States in accordance with the Charter of the United Nations.[96]

This provision of Article 1 significantly expanded the common Article 2 IAC definition, an expansion that was considered problematic by a number of

---

92. *See* Introduction to the Commentary on the Additional Protocols I and II of 8 June 1977, ICRC, http://www.icrc.org/ihl.nsf/COM/470-750001?OpenDocument.
93. AP I, *supra*, note 90, art. 1(3).
94. Commentary, Protocol (I) Additional to the Geneva Conventions of 12 Aug. 1949, and Relating to the Protection of Victims of International Armed Conflicts, June 8, 1977, 1125 U.N.T.S. 3, at 39 (hereinafter Commentary, Protocol I).
95. *Id.*
96. AP I, *supra*, note 90, art. 1(4).

states. This was because it was perceived as fundamentally inconsistent with the underlying purpose of common Article 2: to define IACs as inter-state armed conflicts and eliminate political considerations from the law applicability determination.[97] Contrary to this objective, Article 1(4) essentially re-characterized *de facto* NIACs into *de jure* IACs based on the motive for opposing state authority, and not on the nature of hostilities and the parties involved. The associated Commentary notes that contrary to the outcome of that conference, prior to 1977, the majority of states considered these so-called "wars of national liberation" as NIACs, and not IACs:

> During the various meetings of experts devoted specifically to the reaffirmation and development of international humanitarian law applicable in armed conflicts, whether these were consultations in groups with restricted participation or the Conferences of Government Experts or Red Cross experts, the majority of experts considered that wars of national liberation were conflicts not of an international character.[98]

Of course, the post-colonial era emergence of new states—many former colonies—produced a major influence on the development of the two Additional Protocols. Article 1(4) reflects that influence, and by the end of the drafting conferences sufficient consensus developed to anoint such wars of national liberation with some recognition of the legitimacy of the struggle for liberation. This legitimacy would be provided by characterizing these armed conflicts no differently than armed conflicts between states: as IACs. As the Commentary notes:

> Common Article 2 can, and should be interpreted as covering wars of liberation, since, although they do not take place between States, they are certainly of an international character, according to the United Nations; thus the term "Power" does not refer only to States, but also to non-State entities which enjoy the right to self-determination.[99]

As will be explained in Chapter 5, this expansion of the meaning of IAC significantly impacted POW qualification. By making armed groups fighting for liberation eligible for POW status by virtue of their involvement in newly designated IACs, AP I did, at least implicitly, legitimize their cause. Article 1(4) created this opportunity by including within the IAC definition armed conflicts conducted to challenge colonial domination, alien occupation, or a racist regime (CAR). Because of this expansion and legitimization, these so-called "CAR" armed conflicts became the focal point of controversy surrounding the AP I.[100]

Although many states objected to Article 1(4), proponents of this expansion ultimately prevailed. This led a number of states to enter reservations

---

97. Commentary, Protocol I, *supra*, note 93, at 41-55.
98. *Id.* at 47.
99. *Id.*
100. Gary D. Solis, The Law of Armed Conflict: International Humanitarian Law in War 123-125 (2010) (hereinafter Solis).

when they ratified the treaty, indicating a commitment to the original common Article 2 IAC definition.[101] In contrast, several states, including the United States, cited the combined effect of expanding the IAC definition and dilution of POW qualification requirements (explained in Chapter 5) as a justification for rejecting the treaty. Although President Carter authorized signature of both Additional Protocols, President Reagan subsequently notified the Senate that he would not submit AP I for advice and consent. In his letter transmitting AP II to the Senate for advice and consent, Reagan emphasized his objection to the politicization of the IAC definition:

> I have . . . concluded that the United States cannot ratify . . . [AP I], which would revise the rules applicable to international armed conflicts. Like all other efforts associated with the International Committee of the Red Cross, this agreement has certain meritorious elements. But Protocol I is fundamentally and irreconcilably flawed. It contains provisions that would undermine humanitarian law and endanger civilians in war. One of its provisions, for example, would automatically treat as an international conflict any so-called "war of national liberation." Whether such wars are international or non-international should turn exclusively on objective reality, not on one's view of the moral qualities of each conflict. To rest on such subjective distinctions based on a war's alleged purposes would politicize humanitarian law and eliminate the distinction between international and non-international conflicts. It would give special status to "wars of national liberation," an ill-defined concept expressed in vague, subjective, politicized terminology.[102]

Accordingly, AP I is not binding on the United States. Furthermore, the rejection by some treaty parties to the IAC expansion, coupled with the paucity of state practice applying Article 1(4), undermines any assertion that this "CAR" concept has evolved to customary international law status. While the United States does acknowledge that many other provisions of AP I are customary in nature, the United States is bound by these provisions only during armed conflicts falling within the original common Article 2 IAC definition.

In contrast to AP I, AP II received a much warmer reception by the United States. Substantively, AP II added much needed flesh to the bones of NIAC regulation.[103] However, like AP I, AP II also included an applicability article; and like AP I, this provision modified the broad common Article 3 conception of NIAC. Specifically, Article 1 of AP II provides:

> This Protocol, which develops and supplements Article 3 common to the Geneva Conventions of 12 August 1949 without modifying its existing conditions of application, shall apply to all armed conflicts which are not [international armed conflicts] and which take place in the territory of a High Contracting Party between its armed forces and dissident armed forces or

---

101. *Cf.* AP I, *supra*, note 90.
102. Ronald Reagan, Letter of Transmittal, The White House, Jan. 29, 1987, *available at* https://www.loc.gov/rr/frd/Military_Law/pdf/protocol-II-100-2.pdf (hereinafter Ronald Reagan, Letter of Transmittal).
103. *See, generally* AP II, *supra*, note 90.

other organized armed groups which, under responsible command, exercise such control over a part of its territory as to enable them to carry out sustained and concerted military operations and to implement this Protocol.[104]

This text seems to indicate that AP II does not modify common Article 3's NIAC definition. In fact, it established a more restrictive field of application, resulting in a two-tier NIAC definition: NIACs falling within the scope of common Article 3, and a more limited range of NIACs that also satisfy the more demanding requirements of AP II.

It is clear that Article 1's purpose was to restrict application of AP II to only a certain type of NIAC: a purely internal armed conflict in which the dissident forces establish and maintain control over a portion of the national territory. However, this is not a common Article 3 requirement, but instead just one factor to consider in the totality of the circumstances armed conflict assessment. The Commentary associated with Article 1 acknowledges the distinction between these two types of NIAC resulting from this new law applicability provision:

> At first sight the article seems to be based on complicated concepts. In fact, the Protocol only applies to conflicts of a certain degree of intensity and does not have exactly the same field of application as common Article 3, which applies in all situations of non-international armed conflict.[105]

The Commentary then explains the reasons for this restriction:

> Common Article 3 does not contain a definition of armed conflict. In the absence of clarity of this concept, it gave rise to a great variety of interpretations and in practice its applicability was often denied. To improve the protection of the victims of non-international armed conflicts it proved necessary not only to develop the rules, but also to find more objective criteria to determine whether they are applicable and to reduce the measure of discretion left to each government.
>
> Initially, two possibilities had been envisaged: either to establish a procedure for determining objectively whether an armed conflict existed, or to clarify the concept of non-international armed conflict, i.e., to select a number of concrete material elements so that, when these elements are present, the authorities concerned could no longer deny the existence of a conflict.
>
> . . .
>
> The ICRC proposed a broad definition based on material criteria: the existence of a confrontation between armed forces or other organized armed groups under responsible command, i.e., with a minimum degree of organization. . . . The three criteria that were finally adopted on the side of the insurgents, i.e.—a responsible command, such control over part of the territory as to enable them to carry out sustained and concerted military operations, and the ability to implement the Protocol—restrict the applicability of the Protocol to conflicts of a certain degree of intensity. This means that not all

---

104. *Id.* art. 1(1).
105. Commentary, Protocol (II) Additional to the Geneva Conventions of 12 Aug. 1949, and Relating to the Protection of Victims of Non-International Armed Conflicts, June 8, 1977, 1125 U.N.T.S. 609, at 1348 (hereinafter Commentary, Protocol II).

cases of non-international armed conflict are covered, as is the case in common Article 3.[106]

Like the expansion of the IAC definition in AP I, this more restrictive NIAC definition also generated opposition from the United States.[107] However, unlike the objection to AP I's scope provision, the objection to AP II focused on the way in which AP II constricted situations qualifying as NIACs. Both of these objections were consistent. According to President Reagan, AP I's expansion of the IAC definition contributed to a dilution of protection for the civilian population by encouraging dissident violence.[108] Similarly, AP II's constricted NIAC definition also diluted humanitarian protections by making application of AP II more limited than application of common Article 3. The following graphics illustrate the impact of these provisions: Article 1(4) of AP I expands the "funnel" that leads to the law applicable to IACs, while Article 1 of AP II constricts the "funnel" that leads to law applicable to NIACs:

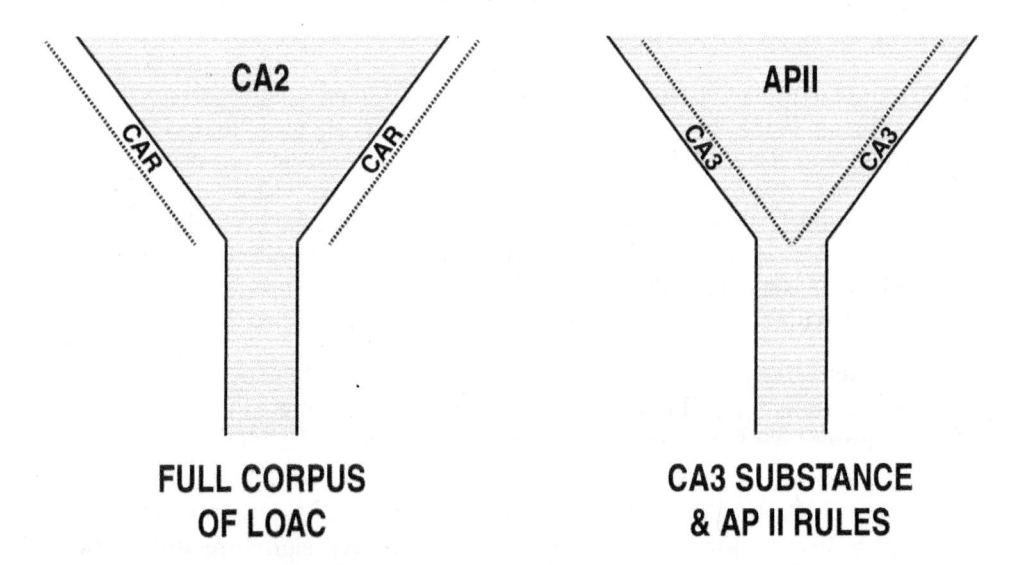

FULL CORPUS OF LOAC   **CA3 SUBSTANCE & AP II RULES**

Because, however, Article 1 of AP II specifically indicates that it did not alter the scope of law applicability pursuant to common Article 3, the United States found the provision less troubling than AP I's IAC expansion. As a result, U.S. opposition to the scope provision of AP II did not result in an outright rejection of the Protocol. Instead, President Reagan requested Senate advice and consent for ratification, but also emphasized that the United States considered the scope restriction unjustified and would therefore apply AP II to any NIAC falling within the scope of common Article 3. According to President Reagan's Letter of Transmittal:

---

106. *Id.* at 1348-1349.
107. SOLIS, *supra*, note 99, at 131-132.
108. Ronald Reagan, Letter of Transmittal, *supra*, note 101.

The final text of Additional Protocol II did not meet all the desires of the United States and other western delegations. In particular, the Protocol only applies to internal conflicts in which dissident armed groups are under responsible command and exercise control over such a part of the national territory as to carry out sustained and concerted military operations. This is a narrower scope than we would have desired, and has the effect of excluding many internal conflicts in which dissident armed groups occupy no significant territory but conduct sporadic guerilla operations over a wide area. We are therefore recommending that the U.S. ratification be subject to an understanding declaring that the United States will apply the Protocol to all conflicts covered by Article 3 common to the 1949 Conventions (and only such conflicts) which will include all non-international armed conflicts as traditionally defined (but not internal disturbances, riots and sporadic acts of violence).[109]

To date, the Senate has yet to provide the advice and consent needed to ratify AP II requested by President Reagan. President Clinton resurrected this request in 1999, emphasizing the U.S. desire for expansive application of humanitarian regulation to all armed conflicts:

Because the United States traditionally has held a leadership position in matters relating to the law of war, our ratification would help give Protocol II the visibility and respect it deserves and would enhance efforts to further ameliorate the suffering of war's victims — especially, in this case, victims of internal armed conflicts. I therefore recommend that the Senate renew its consideration of Protocol II Additional and give its advice and consent to ratification, subject to the understandings and reservations that are described fully in the report attached to the original January 29, 1987, transmittal message to the Senate.[110]

Like President Reagan's request, this request also failed to generate consent to ratify AP II. In fact, AP II continues to languish in the Senate.[111]

Still, unlike AP I, these presidential efforts indicate the United States continues to support the substantive content of AP II. The continued commitment to ultimate ratification of AP II also results in a more substantive consequence. Pursuant to international law, during the time between signature and ratification of a treaty, the signature state must refrain from any action contrary to the "object and purpose" of the treaty.[112] Accordingly, U.S. practitioners must assume that the content of AP II applies during NIACs, and that in accordance with presidential statements, these provisions apply to any NIAC within the scope of common Article 3.

There are other reasons why both the Additional Protocols play an important role in the planning and execution of U.S. operation even though the

---

109. Ronald Reagan, Letter of Transmittal, *supra*, note 101.
110. William J. Clinton, Letter of Transmittal, The White House, Jan. 6, 1999, *available at* http://www.loc.gov/rr/frd/Military_Law/pdf/GC-message-from-pres-1999.pdf.
111. The Obama administration also issued a press release in 2011 indicating strong support for the ratification of AP II. *See* Press Release, White House, Fact Sheet: New Actions on Guantanamo and Detainee Policy (Mar. 7, 2011), *available at* https://www.whitehouse.gov/the-press-office/2011/03/07/fact-sheet-new-actions-guant-namo-and-detainee-policy.
112. Vienna Convention on the Law of Treaties, art. 18, May 23, 1969, 1155 U.N.T.S. 331.

United States is not a party to either treaty. First, the United States considers many of the provisions of these treaties codifications of customary international law. Second, many potential U.S. coalition partners will be bound by the two Additional Protocols; as soon as a coalition partner joins the U.S. effort, these treaties may create significant inter-operability issues. As a result, it is essential that U.S. commanders and legal advisors consider the impact of these two treaties on their operations, and that legal advisors understand the various situations that bring the LOAC into force.

V. A Few Wrinkles

A. External Intervention in an Internal Armed Conflict

It is not uncommon for armed conflicts to involve participation by multiple states. Such situations often confuse conflict classification. This is especially true where one state intervenes in another state's territory, involving itself in an ongoing NIAC. Determining how such an intervention impacts the character of the initial NIAC requires a careful assessment of the party to the NIAC supported by the external state intervention. This assessment will dictate whether the intervention transforms the NIAC into an IAC, or merely adds another party to the pre-existing NIAC.

When a third state commits its armed forces to a NIAC to assist in another state in its struggle against a non-state organized armed group, the pre-existing armed conflict remains non-international. In such situations, the consent of the state on whose behalf the intervention is conducted indicates an absence of a dispute between states, which means there is no IAC.[113] In contrast, when a state commits its armed forces to an ongoing NIAC to assist the non-state forces in defeating the armed forces of the challenged state, the armed conflict transforms from a NIAC to an IAC. This is because the assistance to the non-state party to the NIAC indicates a dispute between the intervening state and the state engaged in the pre-existing NIAC.

Third-party interventions into ongoing NIACs often produce complicated questions beyond those of conflict classification. For example, what effect does the intervention have on the status of the original NIAC between the state and the non-state forces (NSFs)? One answer might be that the NSFs become "incorporated" into the armed forces of the intervening state, enabling them to qualify for status as lawful combatants (discussed in greater detail in Chapter 5). However, the intervening state may assert it is not intervening to assist the NSF, but for independent reasons. For example, when NATO launched its air and missile campaign against Serbia in 1998, it did so for the purpose of forcing the Serbian regime to cease the ethnic cleansing campaign in Kosovo. During that

---

113. *See, e.g.,* common Article 2, *supra*, note 19.

same time, the Kosovo Liberation Army (KLA), a NSF, was involved in an ongoing NIAC with Serbian armed forces. Although the NATO campaign certainly produced a major benefit for the KLA, NATO never accepted that it was in any way allied or connected with the KLA.[114] Instead, the NATO intervention created a distinct IAC between NATO member states and Serbia. As a result, there was no justification for KLA forces to assert that they were also engaged in an IAC, with the accordant legal consequences of such a conflict transformation.

The notion of two ongoing but legally distinct armed conflicts in the same territory is a relatively new aspect of armed conflict assessment and classification. This theory of "conflict bifurcation" has been significant in the U.S. classification of the ongoing armed conflicts with al Qaeda and ISIS.[115] For example, because the United States explicitly considers itself engaged in a NIAC with al Qaeda, execution of operations against al Qaeda in Afghanistan suggests that the United States considers the armed conflict with al Qaeda as distinct from the IAC originally launched against Afghanistan and the Taliban armed forces (an armed conflict that transformed into another distinct NIAC when the Taliban was ousted from authority in Afghanistan and operations supported the new Afghan regime).[116] It is unclear whether U.S. coalition partners in Afghanistan agreed with this bifurcated armed conflict interpretation. Instead, many of these states considered al Qaeda forces in Afghanistan to be part of the initial IAC against the Taliban government, and later part of the ongoing NIAC in support of the Afghan government against Taliban dissident forces.[117] In Syria, counter-ISIS operations may occur in Syrian territory, but the United States does not consider itself a party to an IAC with Syria, or a party to the ongoing NIAC in Syria.[118]

---

114. Stewart, *supra*, note 7, at 313, 315.
115. *See* Geoffrey S. Corn, *Making the Case for Conflict Bifurcation in Afghanistan: Transnational Armed Conflict, Al Qaida, and the Limits of the Associated Militia Concept,* International Law Studies (U.S. Naval War College), vol. 85, 2009 (republished in the Israeli Yearbook of Human Rights) (hereinafter *Making the Case for Conflict Bifurcation*).
116. *Id.*
117. *Making the Case for Conflict Bifurcation, supra,* note 113.
118. *See* Egan Address, *supra*, note 87. Specifically, Brian Egan articulated the U.S. position in Syria as follows:

> ...[T]he United States' armed conflict with ISIL is taking place in a complicated environment—one in which a non-State actor, ISIL, controls significant territory and where multiple States and non-State actors have been engaging in military operations against ISIL, other groups, and each other for several years. Unfortunately, this scenario is not unprecedented in today's world. Iraq and Syria resemble other countries where multiple armed conflicts may be going on simultaneously—countries like Yemen and Libya.
>
> In such complex circumstances, States can potentially find themselves in more than one armed conflict or with multiple legal bases for using force....
>
> ...
>
> ...As a threshold matter, some of our foreign partners have asked us how we classify the conflict with ISIL and thus what set of rules applies. Because we are engaged in an armed conflict against a non-State actor, our war against ISIL is a non-international armed conflict, or NIAC. Therefore, the applicable international legal regime governing our military operations is the law of armed conflict covering NIACs, most importantly, Common Article 3....

Another area of uncertainty is at what point the external state becomes a party to an ongoing NIAC as the result of its support to NSFs engaged in hostilities against the NIAC. An important authority related to this question is *Nicaragua v. United States*.[119] The *Nicaragua* decision arose out of Nicaragua's allegation that the United States had engaged in illegal aggression by planting mines in Nicaraguan harbors, conducting sabotage missions against Nicaraguan ports, oil installations, and a naval base, and by providing continued support to the *Contras* (an internal dissident group challenging the Sandinista government).[120] The United States challenged the jurisdiction of the Court to hear the case, and eventually terminated participation in the proceedings when the Court rejected that challenge. Prior to withdrawing, however, the United States proffered collective self-defense as a theory of legality for the activities directed against Nicaragua.[121] This theory was premised on an assertion that Nicaragua's support for the leftist insurgents in El Salvador amounted to unlawful aggression against that neighboring state, and therefore, the United States was legally permitted to engage in conduct in defense of El Salvador.[122]

The ICJ began by concluding that the United States was responsible for laying mines and the alleged acts of sabotage.[123] The Court then ruled that these actions did constitute acts of aggression in violation of customary international law.[124] In reaching this conclusion, the Court analyzed the relationship between the conduct and sponsorship of NSFs, and the definition of aggression triggering the right of individual and collective self-defense. First, the Court concluded that,

> [i]t may be considered to be agreed that an armed attack must be understood as including not merely action by regular armed forces across an international border, but also "sending by or on behalf of a State of armed bands, groups, irregulars or mercenaries, which carry out acts of armed force against another State of such gravity as to amount to (*inter alia*) an actual armed attack conducted by regular forces, "or substantial involvement therein."[125]

Accordingly, the decision supports the invocation of the inherent right of self-defense in response to an act of aggression by both regular armed forces of another state *and* paramilitary forces acting as an agent for or on behalf of a state.

The Court also addressed the level of state sponsorship of paramilitary activities necessary for the attribution of those activities to the state. This issue was relevant to both the assertion that the United States had committed acts of aggression against Nicaragua (by supporting the *Contras*) and the assertion that armed activities against Nicaragua directed or supported by the United States

---

119. Military and Paramilitary Activities (Nicar. v. U.S.), 1986 I.C.J. 14 (June 27).
120. *Id.* ¶21.
121. *Id.* ¶24.
122. *Id.* ¶48.
123. *Id.* ¶80.
124. *Id.* ¶226.
125. *Id.* ¶195.

were justified as collective self-defense in response to Nicaraguan aggression toward El Salvador (by supporting the FMLN leftist insurgents in El Salvador). The Court concluded that it,

> ... does not believe that the concept of "armed attack" includes not only acts by armed bands where such acts occur on a significant scale but also assistance to rebels in the form of the provision of weapons or logistical or other support. Such assistance may be regarded as a threat or use of force, or amount to intervention in the internal or external affairs of other States.[126]

Thus, the Court drew a demarcation line between the use of paramilitary (or irregular) forces as a state proxy, with their hostilities effectively directed by the state, and the provision of logistical support (including military logistics such as weapons and ammunition) to such forces. According to the Court, only the former category qualified as aggression triggering the inherent right of individual and collective self-defense.

Based on this demarcation, the Court concluded that U.S. support for the *Contras* rose to the level of aggression, because this support included "organizing or encouraging the organization of irregular forces or armed bands ... for incursion into the territory of another state."[127] In contrast, the Court rejected the assertion that Nicaraguan support for the FMLN in El Salvador qualified as an act of aggression. Specifically, the Court found that,

> ...between July 1979 and the early months of 1981, an intermittent flow of arms was routed via the territory of Nicaragua to the armed opposition in that country. The Court was not however satisfied that assistance has reached the Salvadorian armed opposition, on a scale of any significance, since the early months of 1981, or that the Government of Nicaragua was responsible for any flow of arms at either period. Even assuming that the supply of arms to the opposition in El Salvador could be treated as imputable to the Government of Nicaragua, to justify invocation of the right of collective self-defence in customary international law, it would have to be equated with an armed attack by Nicaragua on El Salvador.[128]

It therefore seems that, as a matter of international law, providing direction and direct assistance to a NSF may result in an external state becoming a party to an ongoing NIAC.

This issue again arose in relation to the various armed conflicts that broke out in 1992 following the breakup of the former Yugoslavia. The Serbian NSFs engaged in these conflicts received substantial support and sponsorship from Serbia. In 1995, the ICTY addressed the question of whether Serbian support for Serb NSFs in Bosnia resulted in Serbia becoming a party to an IAC against Bosnia. In *Prosecutor v. Tadic*, the Tribunal concluded:

---

126. *Id.*
127. *Id.* ¶228.
128. *Id.* ¶230.

It is indisputable that an armed conflict is international if it takes place between two or more States. In addition, in case of an internal armed conflict breaking out on the territory of a State, it may become international (or, depending upon the circumstances, be international in character alongside an internal armed conflict) if (i) another State intervenes in that conflict through its troops, or alternatively if (ii) some of the participants in the internal armed conflict act on behalf of that other State.[129]

The Tribunal then undertook the task of defining what "on behalf of that other state" means or, in other words, to "identify the conditions under which those forces may be assimilated to organs of a state other than that on whose territory they live and operate."[130] The test applied is one of control.[131] In *Tadic*, the Tribunal looked to the realities on the ground and actual control of the Federal Republic of Yugoslavia and its army (VJ) over the Army of Serbian Republic of Bosnia and Herzegovina (VRS). The Tribunal found that "the VRS and VJ did not, after May 1992, comprise two separate armies in any genuine sense."[132]

In reaching this conclusion, the Tribunal looked to the military objectives and command structure of the newly formed Yugoslavia People's Army (JNA). The Tribunal found that "[t]he command structure of the JNA and the re-designation of a part of the JNA as the VRS, while undertaken to create the appearance of the compliance with international demands, was in fact designed to ensure that a large number of ethnic Serb armed forces were retained in Bosnia and Herzegovina."[133] Additionally, the Tribunal found "extensive financial, logistical and other assistance" as well as an identical structure and rank system between the VJ and VRS.[134] This led the Tribunal to conclude that:

> It follows that in the circumstances of the case it was not necessary to show that those specific operations carried out by the Bosnian Serb forces which were the object of the trial (the attacks on Kozarac and more generally within opština Prijedor) had been specifically ordered or planned by the Yugoslav Army. It is sufficient to show that this Army exercised overall control over the Bosnian Serb Forces. This showing has been made by the Prosecution before the Trial chamber. Such control manifested itself not only in financial, logistical and other assistance and support, but also, and more importantly, in terms of participation in the general direction, coordination and supervision of the activities and operations of the VRS. This sort of control is sufficient for the purposes of the legal criteria required by international law [to render the conflict international].[135]

---

129. Prosecutor v. Tadic, Case No. IT-94-1, Judgment, ¶80 (Int'l Crim. Trib. for the Former Yugoslavia, Oct. 2, 1995).
130. *Id.* ¶91.
131. *Id.* ¶95.
132. *Id.* ¶151.
133. *Id.* ¶151(i).
134. *Id.* ¶151(ii).
135. *Id.* ¶156.

Whether extensive sponsorship and support is sufficient to establish control remains to be unclear. What is clear is that once control over proxy forces is established, the sponsoring state becomes a participant in the armed conflict.

B. Transnational Armed Conflicts?

When the United States initiated military action against al Qaeda in response to the September 11th terrorist attacks, both President Bush and Congress asserted that the United States was engaged in an armed conflict — an armed conflict of international scope against a non-state enemy.[136] Critics of this assertion raised two primary objections: first, the concern that the United States had impermissibly invoked LOAC authority to disrupt and disable transnational terrorist operatives (authority significantly more robust than peacetime law enforcement powers); and second, the concern that the determination that the armed conflict fell outside the scope of both common Articles 2 and 3, resulting in an armed conflict with no legally imposed limits.[137]

The characterization of the struggle as an armed conflict was not a mere hyperbole. Instead, it represented a clear indication that the United States adopted a "new" approach to the struggle against international terrorism. For the first time since the inception of the Geneva Convention law application equation, a state asserted it was engaged in an ongoing armed conflict of international scope with a non-state entity.[138] Because this was an armed conflict, the implication was clear: The United States would no longer limit its response to domestic and international law enforcement efforts. Instead, the nation would employ its full power — to include military power — against this threat.[139] In the months and years following September 11th, all three branches of the U.S. government endorsed efforts to disable the al Qaeda threat within the LOAC legal framework.[140] The most recent explanation of this theory came in a 2016 speech by the U.S. Department of State Legal Advisor, who noted that,

> The United States is engaged in an armed conflict with a non-State actor that controls significant territory, in circumstances in which multiple States and non-State actors also have been engaging in military operations against this enemy, other groups, and each other for several years. These conflicts raise novel and difficult questions of international law that the United States is called to address literally on a daily basis in conducting operations.[141]

---

136. *Cf.* Authorization for the Use of Military Force, Pub. L. No. 107-40, 115 Stat. 224 (2001) (hereinafter 2001 AUMF).

137. WATKIN, *supra*, note 47, at 352-356

138. *See* Bush Torture Memo, *supra*, *note* 70, para 2; *see also* Fact Sheet: Status of Detainees at Guantanamo, AM. PRESIDENCY PROJECT (Feb. 7, 2002), http://www.presidency.ucsb.edu/ws/index.php?pid=79402.

139. 2001 AUMF, *supra*, note 135.

140. *See id.; see also* Hamdan v. Rumsfeld, 548 U.S. 557 (2006).

141. Egan Address, *supra*, note 87.

Designating the struggle against a transnational terrorist organization and its members as an armed conflict seemed logical, at least at the military operational level. U.S. armed forces were directed to seek out and engage al Qaeda operatives with the type of combat power traditionally employed during armed conflicts. Further, captured terrorist operatives were to be detained without charge or trial to prevent their return to the "global fight."[142] However, a legal incongruity was almost immediately exposed: While these military activities implied a U.S. invocation of the most fundamental authorities associated with armed conflict, the transnational scope of the non-state enemy led to a determination that the conflict did not fit within the common Article 2/3 inter-state/intra-state law triggering equation. According to President Bush, because al Qaeda was not a state, the armed conflict did not trigger the full corpus of the law pursuant to common Article 2; and because the conflict was not confined to the territory of the United States, it did not trigger the baseline humane treatment obligation of common Article 3.[143]

On February 7, 2002, President Bush issued a directive on the status and treatment of captured al Qaeda and Taliban personnel. This directive fully articulated the theory that the armed conflict with al Qaeda fell outside the scope of either common Article 2 or 3.[144] President Bush explicitly disavowed any U.S. obligation to comply with the LOAC *vis à vis* al Qaeda detainees. According to the President, not even the humane treatment obligation of common Article 3 applied to these detainees (as a matter of law).[145] The "authority without obligation" theory was further exposed by President Bush's order to try al Qaeda operatives before a military commission for violations of the laws and customs of war.[146] The President's invocation of the LOAC as the source of authority to condemn the conduct of these operatives, coupled with the implementation of trial procedures arguably inconsistent with common Article 3, left no doubt that the United States considered the struggle against transnational terrorism as an armed conflict outside the scope of any legally mandated regulation.

As noted earlier, in *Hamdan v. Rumsfeld*, the Supreme Court rejected this LOAC interpretation when it held that common Article 3 applied to any armed conflict falling outside the scope of common Article 2.[147] For a majority of the U.S. Supreme Court, invoking the laws and customs of war for the authority to prosecute captured opponents, while at the same time rejecting LOAC obligations, conflicted with the underlying purpose of the Geneva law application concept.[148] The government's assertion of an armed conflict against al Qaeda, coupled with the Court's conclusion that it must fall within the scope of com-

---

142. Detention, Treatment, and Trial of Certain Non-Citizens in the War Against Terrorism, 60 Fed. Reg. 57,833, (Nov. 16, 2001).
143. *Hamdan*, 548 U.S. at 557, 630; Bush Torture Memo, *supra*, note 70.
144. *See* Bush Torture Memo, *supra*, note 70.
145. *See Id.*
146. Detention, Treatment, and Trial of Certain Non-Citizens in the War Against Terrorism, 60 Fed. Reg. 57,833, 57,833 (Nov. 16, 2001).
147. *Hamdan*, 548 U.S. at 557.
148. *Id.*

mon Article 3, upended the longstanding assumption that common Article 3 applied only to "internal" NIACs.

A similar reaction followed Israel's 2006 military incursion into South Lebanon to attack Hezbollah. Israel's use of combat power clearly indicated the existence of an armed conflict, but neither Israel nor Lebanon considered it to be an IAC. This "cross-border" NIAC was not the result of "spillover" from an ongoing NIAC in Israel, but instead a distinct external armed conflict in the territory of a neighboring state. Government and non-government critics of both Israeli and Hezbollah tactics consistently cited the LOAC to support their critique of the conflict. The international reaction to this military campaign quite logically demanded compliance with "rules" that regulate the application of combat power, protect innocent victims of the hostilities, and ensure the humane treatment of captured opponents.[149] The existence of *de facto* hostilities and the invocation of LOAC authorities indicates that the Lebanon War is best characterized as a transnational NIAC. Ongoing U.S. combat operations against ISIS in Syria seem to fall into the same category.

This notion of a "transnational" NIAC remains controversial. International law experts continue to struggle with the prospect of an armed conflict against a loosely organized enemy with no geographic boundaries or limitations. But it is not a concept that can be ignored, and may be a necessary evolution in response to the evolving nature of non-state threats. The 2016 ICRC Commentary revision makes a brief reference to the concept, but notes that it lacks substantial acceptance in the international community.[150] Still, the fact that the Commentary acknowledges the emergence of this theory reflects the evolution of LOAC applicability since 2001.[151]

There is some irony in the continuing hostility towards this transnational NIAC theory. Of all the LOAC advancements contained in those four treaties, the express rejection of interpretive law applicability avoidance was arguably the most significant. The purpose of the *de facto* armed conflict law trigger was to ensure that humanitarian protections came into force based on the pragmatic necessity for those protections, and not on legalistic definitions and interpretations of the term "war."[152] The term "armed conflict" was adopted to meet this necessity and denoted a situation of armed hostilities justifying the imposition of international humanitarian regulation.[153] Once hostilities existed, the humanitarian interests of victims required application of legal standards that prevented states from disavowing international humanitarian legal obligations.[154] Even in

---

149. *See* Tristam, *supra*, note 66; *see also Security Council Calls for an End to Hostilities Between Hezbollah, Israel, Unanimously Adopts Resolution 1701*, U.N. SECURITY COUNCIL (Aug. 11, 2006), http://www.un.org/News/Press/docs/2006/sc8808.doc.htm (indication that Hezbollah and not Lebanon was responsible for the attacks).
150. Commentary, Convention (I), *supra*, note 9, para 472-482.
151. *Id.*
152. *Id.* para 210-212.
153. *Id.* para. 201-216.
154. *Id.* para. 202.

the realm of intra-state hostilities, common Article 3 imposed basic humanitarian obligations on all parties.[155]

However, the drafters of the Geneva Conventions focused on the two types of conflicts that dominated the periods between World War I and World War II, and the post-World War II eras: inter-and intra-state armed conflict. As a result, the law application triggers they adopted became synonymous with these, and only these types of armed conflicts. This explains why this inter/intra-state equation was leveraged in the aftermath of September 11th to assert that the inapplicability of LOAC obligations to the "transnational" armed conflict with al Qaeda, even though the United States was invoking the authority of war to combat this opponent. Thus, the Bush administration lawyers based their "authority without obligation" legal interpretation on a plausible interpretation of this 1949 law triggering equation.[156]

This interpretation defied the underlying spirit of common Articles 2 and 3, and distorted the purpose of the law itself: to strike an efficient balance between the authority of military necessity and the constraints of the dictates of humanity. Rejection of this selective invocation of authority without obligation was central to the Supreme Court's interpretation of common Article 3.[157] But this was just the tip of the iceberg. Designating the struggle against transnational terrorism as an armed conflict necessitated a re-evaluation of the entire law triggering equation. The Supreme Court's interpretation of common Article 3 ensured the humane treatment of detainees—the issue the Supreme Court confronted in *Hamdan*—but common Article 3 provides little in the way of regulating the application of combat power.[158] As a result, the *Hamdan* decision did not address a broader, but equally important question: what rules regulate hostilities between state armed forces and transnational NSFs?[159] The Israel/Hezbollah conflict confirmed this by exposing the world to the reality that conflict regulation becomes essential when the first salvo is fired, and not just when opponents are detained.[160]

The great innovation of the 1949 law triggering equation was the recognition that armed conflict must dictate LOAC applicability, and this applicability must be based on a truly *de facto* assessment of ground truth. What is emerging in response to the reality of transnational armed conflict is the understanding that *any* armed conflict triggers a customary regulatory framework composed of LOAC principles and rules, many of which developed to regulate IACs. This

---

155. *Id.* para. 357-361, 550-564.
156. Jay S. Bybee, Memorandum for Alberto R. Gonzales, Counsel to the President, and William J. Haynes II, General Counsel of the DoD Re: Application of Treaties and Laws to al Qaeda and Taliban Detainees (Jan. 22, 2002), *available at* http://www.washingtonpost.com/wp-srv/nation/documents/012202bybee.pdf.
157. *See Hamdan*, 548 U.S. at 557, 630.
158. *See, e.g.*, common Article 3, *supra*, note 24.
159. *See Hamdan*, 548 U.S. at 557.
160. *See* Tristam, *supra*, note 66; *see also Security Council Calls for an End to Hostilities Between Hezbollah, Israel, Unanimously Adopts Resolution 1701*, U.N. SECURITY COUNCIL (Aug. 11, 2006), http://www.un.org/News/Press/docs/2006/sc8808.doc.htm (indication that Hezbollah and not Lebanon was responsible for the attacks).

regulatory framework is essential not only to ensure the humane treatment of captured and detained enemy personnel, but also to effectively regulate the conduct of hostilities and application of combat power. As a result, in addition to the humane treatment mandate, this framework includes LOAC principles addressed throughout this text: military necessity (which itself reflects an inherent balance between power and restraint by authorizing only those measures that are not otherwise forbidden by international law); distinction (limiting attacks to only lawful military objectives); proportionality (imposing an obligation to balance the advantage of an attack against the anticipated but non-purposeful infliction of harm to innocents); and a prohibition against infliction of unnecessary suffering (prohibiting the infliction of superfluous injury or suffering to lawful objects of attack).[161]

Acknowledging the need to ensure transnational armed conflicts are subject to LOAC regulation does not, however, resolve the even more difficult question of how to define these "internationalized" NIACs. Although this NIAC concept is based on the illogic of limiting the response to transnational threats to law enforcement authority, it is equally invalid to suggest all counter-terror operations qualify as armed conflicts. What is needed are logical and effective standards to distinguish between non-conflict and armed conflict uses of military force by states against transnational terrorist capabilities.[162] What this suggests is that contrary to the hyperbolic designation of a "global war," a much more precise analysis of the military component of this struggle is necessary.[163]

The "organization and intensity" test for assessing the existence of a NIAC is increasingly considered authoritative, although is itself potentially under-inclusive. One possible alternate indicator is the nature of the state response. The most fundamental distinction between law enforcement and armed conflict is the nature and extent of the authority for the use of deadly force.[164] At the most basic level, law enforcement allows the use of deadly force only as a measure of last resort. In contrast, armed conflict allows such use as a measure of first resort. This dichotomy provides a useful (although not necessarily conclusive) indication of *de facto* armed conflict; Armed conflict exists whenever a state employs armed force pursuant to authority that can only be derived from an armed conflict; to use deadly force against an opponent as a measure of first resort. This is intuitive to military professionals increasingly competent in the full spectrum of military operations. They understand that patrolling the streets in Kosovo or Bosnia is not armed conflict because their use of force authority is purely responsive. In contrast, whether engaging terrorist operatives in the mountains of Afghanistan, a base camp in Somalia, or the hills of southern Lebanon, it is the authority to engage an opponent with deadly combat power once that opponent is identified that defines such operations as armed conflict.

---

161. *See, generally* Geneva Conventions, *supra*, note 16; *see also* SOLIS, *supra*, note 99, at 250-285.
162. WATKIN, *supra*, note 47, at 604-610.
163. *See id.* at 604-617.
164. *See* Geoffrey S. Corn, *Mixing Apples and Hand Grenades: The Logical Limit of Applying Human Rights Norms to Armed Conflict*, 1 INT'L HUMANITARIAN LEGAL STUD. 52 (2010).

Depriving armed forces of this legal regulatory framework in such situations produces a distortion between the law and the nature of their operations. More problematically, it also deprives them of the framework developed to guide their conduct in the most brutal environments, an outcome that is not only inconsistent with the general perception of what is "right" or "moral," but also with the preservation of disciplined and morally based armed forces.

VI. Conclusion

The military component of the struggle against transnational terrorism will almost certainly continue to present complex challenges for the United States and other nations. But such complexity is not unprecedented in the history of warfare. Conducting military operations against highly organized NSFs has been an aspect of the strategic use of military force for centuries, and an aspect of the American military experience since the inception of the nation. What is new is the suggestion that, based on the transnational non-state nature of the enemy, these operations fall into a legal "black hole" permitting states to selectively invoke those LOAC principles that serve their interests. Such a suggestion fundamentally undermines the basic "charter" of a professional armed force, creates a dangerous risk of encouraging the darkest instincts of those called upon to "deliver" results, and corrodes the moral integrity of the men and women who serve this nation. Only a rejection of this proposition and an endorsement of the obligation to comply with a LOAC regulatory framework during *all* armed conflicts will preserve the appropriate balance between the dictates of necessity and the interests of humanity. Such an outcome is more than logical; it is a fulfillment of the most significant LOAC advancement produced by the 1949 Geneva Conventions: a categorical rejection of law avoidance through the common Article 2/3 law triggers. These triggers remain vital to the regulation of hostilities.

Study Questions

Suggested Research Focus

- GPW, Articles 2 and 3
- Commentary to Article 2 of the GWS
- Commentary to Article 3 of the GWS
- AP I, Article 1
- AP II, Article 1
- Commentary to Article 1 of AP I
- Commentary to Article 1 of AP II
- ILA Final Report on the Meaning of Armed Conflict in International Law

You are a member of the Department of Defense LOWWG at the meeting discussed in the opening vignette. How would you analyze the following questions?

1. Assume that in the months preceding the U.S. intervention in Iraq, there was an increasingly robust public opposition to the Saddam Hussein's regime. Media reports routinely showed scenes of mass demonstrations. Government policy allowed paramilitary-type police units to use harsh tactics to break up these demonstrations (tear gas, clubs, water cannons) while opposition political leaders continued to publicly denounce Hussein. During one meeting, the Department of State Working Group member asks the following questions:
    a. Are the paramilitary forces being used by Iraq to break up these demonstrations obligated to comply with LOAC humanitarian rules?
    b. If not, what law should the United States cite to condemn the heavy-handed government response?
    c. Is there any point at which the government response might violate LOAC? How do we know when that situation exists?
2. As the situation continues to deteriorate, there are increasing incidents of U.N. weapons inspectors being harassed by Iraqi forces, and several have been detained for short periods of time. Should the U.S. and the U.N. demand that detained U.N. personnel qualify as prisoners of war?
3. Many members of the Kurdish minority in Iraq have long sought creation of an independent Kurdish state, and consider themselves under the repressive authority of the Iraqi government. Assume that as it becomes increasingly clear to Iraqi Kurds in Northern Iraq that Hussein will be ousted by U.S. military action, opposition to Hussein gains momentum. Kurdish leaders decide the time is opportune to demand independence from Iraq. Sensing Iraqi military weakness, Kurdish political leadership proclaims independence. A small Kurdish Liberation Force is established, consisting of approximately 500 armed personnel organized into two "battalions." These forces wear camouflage tunics with a distinctive Kurdish headdress, and carry rifles seized from Iraqi military facilities in their area.
    a. Intelligence reports indicate that the Iraqi military is preparing to launch an operation to reassert control over Kurdish areas and disarm and disable the Kurdish forces. If hostilities break out between these two groups, what is the status of the situation? Would it matter if Iraq was a party to the 1977 Additional Protocol I?
    b. Kurdish leaders have approached U.S. diplomats requesting U.S. support in the event Iraq launches an attack. If the United States were to use military forces to support the Kurdish independence effort against a PDF response, how would that impact the status of the situation?
    c. What if the United States decides to provide "behind the scenes" support to the Kurds? If that support is limited to arms, ammunition, and communications equipment, will the United States be considered a

party to the NIAC between the Kurds and Iraqi forces? What if the United States provides military advisors to help train Kurdish forces? What if these advisors start plans of action to the Kurds to help prepare for a U.S. military invasion of Iraq?

4. In early December, the Working Group is notified of a potential U.S. military intervention in Iraq. The operational planners at United States Central Command (the military command responsible for planning and executing the mission) submit a number of questions to the Working Group for resolution.

   a. If Iraqi forces attack U.S. military staging areas in Kuwait, and U.S. forces respond in self-defense, will this trigger application of the LOAC?
   b. There is a possibility that opponents to Hussein may make a move to seize control of Iraq in order to avert a war with the United States. There is also a possibility the new leaders will request U.S. assistance in disabling Iraqi military and security forces loyal to Hussein. If this occurs, and the United States does intervene militarily to assist the coup effort, how will it affect the nature of the situation upon U.S. intervention?
   c. If the United States launches military action against Iraq with no request from dissident forces, but Iraqi armed forces choose not to resist the intervention, what is the status of the situation?
   d. The United States expects that a number of other nations will join in a coalition to oust Hussein from power, including the United Kingdom, Spain, The Netherlands, Australia, and South Korea. If armed forces from any of these nations join in the U.S. effort against Iraq, how, if at all, will this impact the status of the situation? Will it matter if they join prior to or after the initiation of operations?

4 Classification and Status of Persons

The V Corps Military Police (MP) Brigade deployed with the Corps Headquarters to Kuwait and prepared to conduct a variety of combat support functions on the battlefield, including battlefield mobility and checkpoint control, providing security in liberated areas (stability operations), criminal investigations, and prisoner of war detention and custody missions; a small number of MP planners were dedicated to transition planning, as Iraqi police forces were expected to remain in place after the invasion, for a rapid transition to Iraqi (largely expatriot) control over governmental functions. Although General Shinseki noted that hundreds of thousands of troops would be necessary to conduct stability operations after the combat phase was complete and the military police were responsible for much of the security and stability mission, insufficient MP resources were planned for these missions; as a result, it was difficult to maintain control over a newly liberated population who promptly looted government buildings and removed all evidence of the Saddam regime. The Time Phased Force Deployment List (TPFDL) included a reserve MP Brigade that was due to arrive in May 2003, at the end of the "combat phase" [which President Bush declared as complete on May 1, 2013].

The V Corps MP Brigade was assigned a Brigade Judge Advocate (Major) and an assistant (a less-experienced Captain), but they proved sufficient to assist the MP Battalion assigned to detain the vast numbers (over 13,000) of Iraqi military, who surrendered in droves; the other two MP Battalions were concentrated on the other combat support functions listed above. The reserve MP Brigade was staffed with a Lieutenant Colonel JAG, who was promptly assigned to Abu Ghraib prison, where the MPs established a Theater Detention Facility, along with a Joint Intelligence Center to process information from detainees. The majority of the Enemy Prisoners of War (EPWs) were promptly released, as the Coalition Provisional Authority disbanded the Iraqi military in June of 2003; as a result, very few Article 5 Tribunals, classifying Prisoners of War, were necessary before June of 2003.

Responsibility for the Coalition to detain Iraqis for imperative security reasons was included in UN Security Council Resolution, UNSCR 1483 (2003), which assigned occupation responsibilities to the Coalition forces and the U.S. and U.K. governments. In June of 2003 the Coalition Provisional Authority issued CPA Memo 3, which classified all detainees who were not Enemy Prisoners of War as civilian internees, who were to be classified and treated as "protected persons" under the 4th Geneva Convention (GC). A later Office of Legal Counsel (Department of Justice) Memo addressed those who were specifically excluded from protected person status, including unprivileged belligerents and nationals of third States who had maintained (or renewed) diplomatic relations with Iraq.

The JAGs at all forward-deployed Brigade headquarters and at intermediate detention centers (at the Brigade and Division level) began to receive questions from their supported commanders about battlefield status of different individuals, and they began to see all manner of detainees after the abolition of the Iraqi military (Saddam Fedayeen, "dead-enders," and "Former Regime elements"; members of insurgent groups not associated with the former State, from Iraq or infiltrating from Iran, Syria, and a variety of Arab countries; civilians involved in looting; other civilians committing crimes against the Coalition; and individuals suspected of crimes against the new Iraqi State and Coalition forces). They were simple questions when the opposition consisted of clearly identified Iraqi soldiers, but who was the "enemy combatant" now? Who can be targeted? Who was to be carefully protected from attack? What was their status when detained? How long could they be detained? And who should be prosecuted for their warlike acts (and under whose jurisdiction)?

The principle of distinction, discussed in Chapter 2, is critical to the balance between military necessity and humanity embodied in the laws of war. In order to exercise this principle, also called discrimination, the soldier must distinguish between combatants and civilians, between those to be protected and those to be lawfully targeted (subjected to deliberate attack).[1] Exercise of this principle is increasingly difficult on the asymmetric battlefield. No longer are wars fought on battlefields far from concentrations of civilians, nor do armies line up in distinct lines, wearing brightly colored uniforms as a source of pride, enabling distinction as a matter of course.[2] The soldier is faced with combatants masquerading as civilians, in order to take advantage of the humanity of the warrior, to use the law as a shield of protection against attack. And many modern combatants employ civilians in roles once reserved for the military, from combat to combat support roles, providing direct support to the warfighter, while ostensibly cloaked in the protections afforded to civilians. But,

---

1. *See* DoD Law of War Manual (hereinafter DoD LOWM), Para. 2.5.

2. This idealized form of warfare has rarely been part of the American experience. Compare the colonists who fought in the French and Indian Wars, or the Revolutionary War, and the American military that fought in the cities of Europe or the jungles of Vietnam, with the lines of Confederates and Yankees, fighting in the European style on the fields of Manassas or Gettysburg. Even during the Civil War, where the Zouaves wore brightly colored uniforms, Francis Lieber noted the presence of irregular forces, from guerrillas and partisans, to brigands and marauders. *See* FRANCIS LIEBER, GUERRILLA PARTIES CONSIDERED WITH REFERENCE TO THE LAWS AND USAGE OF WAR (1862).

even on this battlefield, to complete the military mission of defeating the ill-defined enemy, gaining the trust and confidence of the civilian population they are charged to protect, and preserving the ability to restore the peace, the warrior must retain his humanity and exercise the principle of distinction. At the core of the distinction principle is determination of "status," the legal category established under the LOAC for targeting or detaining an individual encountered on the battlefield.

Classification, or status determination of individuals on the battlefield, is the essential starting point for the legal analysis under the LOAC. The rights, duties and liabilities of each individual is determined by analyzing the relevant facts; and the class and category of individuals determines who may be the object of attack, who is protected from attack, who may be detained and for how long, who is entitled to Prisoner of War (POW) or "protected person" status, and who may be punished for their belligerent acts.[3]

I. Combatants and Civilians

A. A Problem of Definition

Combatants[4] and civilians are the most widely recognized terms for describing the actors on the battlefield, for establishing their legal status, and providing guidance to the soldier as to who may be lawfully targeted in armed conflict, or detained on the battlefield until the threat to the force is ended or the enemy has been defeated. Even the International Committee of the Red Cross (ICRC), in their Customary International Humanitarian Law Study, acknowledges that the terms are not precisely defined in all battlefield contexts; in referring to combatants, the study says, for the purposes of the principle of distinction, the term "combatant" is used in its "generic meaning, indicating persons who do not enjoy the protection against attack accorded to civilians, but does not imply a right to combatant status or prisoner-of-war status."[5] Combatants could be further subdivided into lawful and unlawful combatants; but these terms are not without controversy, as will be explained below. Lawful combatants retain the "combatant's privilege," which provides immunity from prosecution for warlike acts (killing or destruction of property), as long as they comply with the laws of war. Unlawful combatants may not claim that protective immunity and therefore remain subject to criminal sanction for the death and destruction they cause during hostilities (usually pursuant to the law of the capturing State).[6]

---

3. See DoD LOWM, para. 4.1.2.
4. Combatants are also called belligerents, throughout the relevant treaties and the literature. See, e.g., HR, arts. 1-3, and AP I, art. 43. See also DoD LOWM, para. 4.1.1.2.
5. J. Henkaerts & L. Doswald-Beck, Customary International Humanitarian Law, Volume I: The Rules (2005) [hereinafter CIL Study].
6. See DoD LOWM, para. 4.4.3.1.

In return for complying with the law of war and distinguishing themselves on the battlefield, the captured lawful combatant, or privileged belligerent, receives the status of a POW. A POW is entitled to respect and protection in accordance with the Third Geneva Convention, Relative to the Treatment of Prisoners of War (GPW).[7] Unlawful combatants will receive humane treatment, as a matter of law, and may be protected as a matter of policy, by GPW or the Fourth Geneva Convention, Relative to the Treatment of Civilian Persons in Time of War (GC).[8] Historically, only the representatives of sovereign governments were privileged belligerents, as they were asked to represent their government and charged with the responsibility of using lawful force on behalf of their nation to subdue the enemy. Unprivileged belligerents do not represent lawful (competent) State authority. With one exception,[9] civilians were obligated to refrain from participation in hostilities and would receive protection from the effect of combat. But how are these two categories defined?

B. Civilians

Although the concept of distinction between combatants and civilians is at the foundation of the law of war, GC contains no definition of who falls within the category of "civilian."[10] In fact, general protections for civilians, under Part II of GC, were not dependent upon the technical status of the individual, but rather these protections extend to "the whole populations of the countries in conflict," and they "are intended to alleviate the sufferings caused by war"[11] (in an almost hortatory fashion), without the technical requirements for determining status under either GPW or GC. As civilians became human shields, or were caught in the cross-fire in the post-colonial wars of the second half of the twentieth century, they were often seemingly unprotected by the conventions. By 1974, it was apparent that the lack of a definition of "civilian" in GC was inadequate and jeopardized the principle of distinction. As the ICRC Commentary to the Protocol Additional to the Geneva Conventions of 12 Aug. 1949, and Relating to the Protection of Victims of International Armed Conflicts (AP I)[12] notes, "As we have seen, the principle of the protection of the civilian population is inseparable from the principle of the distinction which should be made between military and civilian persons. In view of the latter principle, it is essential to have a

---

7. Geneva Convention (III), Relative to the Treatment of Prisoners of War, Aug. 12, 1949, T.I.A.S. 3364 [hereinafter GPW].

8. Geneva Convention Relative to the Treatment of Civilian Persons in Time of War, Aug. 12, 1949, T.I.A.S. 3365 [hereinafter GC].

9. *See* discussion on *levée en masse*, below.

10. GC, instead, defines the term "protected person," who is more narrowly defined as an individual in the "hands of" a party to the conflict or occupying power of which they are not nationals. GC, art. 4. Civilians, including "protected persons," are discussed in greater detail in Chapter 9.

11. GC, art. 13.

12. Protocol Additional to the Geneva Conventions of 12 Aug. 1949, and Relating to the Protection of Victims of International Armed Conflicts, June 8, 1977, 1125 U.N.T.S. 3. [hereinafter AP I].

clear definition of each of these categories."[13] However, "civilian" was not easily defined, particularly when the drafters of AP I were trying to extend POW status to individuals who did not comply with the generally accepted definition of combatants and would, therefore, place civilians at risk.[14] Accordingly, AP I, article 50, adopts a "negative" definition, including anyone not defined to be a combatant by the traditional standards of GPW (members of the armed forces or others who wear uniforms, carry arms openly, and operate under responsible command) or the more controversial standards of articles 43 and 44 of AP I (members of irregular forces who merely show their weapons immediately prior to the attack). Accordingly, a civilian is anyone who would not qualify for POW status if captured (with the exception of civilian employees who accompany the armed forces to perform non-combat functions). This was the most logical method of defining civilians as anyone *not* authorized to participate in hostilities. This methodology applied exclusively to international armed conflicts. Whether it should extend to non-international armed conflicts is a more complex question and will be addressed in more detail below.

C. Combatants

The definition of combatants corresponds to the definition of POW established in the 1907 Hague Regulations[15] and further refined and defined through several iterations of the Prisoner of War Convention, GC, as well as AP I.[16] Like civilians, however, it was not until 1977 that treaty law defined the term "combatant." That definition is found in Art. 43 of AP I, which incorporates by reference the GPW definition of POW as the benchmark for determining who qualifies as a combatant. Accordingly, the definition of POW and combatant are in many respects synonymous – at least at the core (although there are several categories of individuals who qualify for POW status who are excluded from Art. 43's definition of combatant). Combining the GPW with Art. 43 indicates that combatants include the following categories of individuals: members of the armed forces of a party to the conflict; members of militias and organized resistance movements belonging to a party to the conflict; members of regular armed forces belonging to governments not recognized by the Detaining Power; and inhabitants of non-occupied territory who spontaneously take up arms to resist invading forces (the so-called *levée en masse*).[17] Because all members of

---

13. Commentary on the Additional Protocol of 8 June 1977 to the Geneva Conventions of 1949 (AP I) 610 ¶ 1911 (S. Pictet et al. eds., 1987) [hereinafter Commentary, AP I].
14. Article 44(3) extends combatant status to individuals who are members of organized armed groups that carry their arms openly. AP I, art. 44(3). *See* further discussion of AP I, below.
15. 1907 Regulations Annexed to Convention IV Respecting the Laws and Customs of War on Land [hereinafter Hague Regulations].
16. *See* Hague Regulations of 1907, art. 1; Convention Relative to the Treatment of Prisoners of War, art. 1, July 27, 1929, 47 Stat. 2021, 118 L.N.T.S. 345; GC, art. 50. The latter, which has not been ratified by the United States, adds the controversial category mentioned above.
17. *See* GPW, art. 4(A)(6). In general, State practice has been to narrowly apply this provision to those who spontaneously react to an invasion, carry their arms openly, and comply with the laws of

the armed forces of a state party to the conflict are entitled to POW status based solely on their membership in the armed forces, they are lawful combatants, entitled to the combatant's privilege. This includes members of militias or volunteer corps that are a formal part of the armed forces.

Because the GPW provides POW status for members of other militias, volunteer corps, and organized resistance movements not formally associated with a State, these individuals also qualify as lawful combatants so long as they meet the requirements of the GPW. Extending POW and combatant protections to this category was considered extremely important based on the experience of World War II, which involved widespread hostilities between such 'unaffiliated' organized belligerent forces and regular State armed forces.[18] Examples of these groups include the French Resistance fighters and the Russian partisans of World War II. Similar status and protection was extended by the GPW to members of armed forces of a party to the conflict even when the authority they fought for is not recognized as legitimate by the other party.

Unlike membership in the regular armed forces of a state party, being a member of a resistance movement, or an "army in exile," is not itself sufficient to qualify for POW status. In order to obtain POW status, and combatant immunity, these groups: (1) must be involved in international armed conflict; and (2) must comply with the following four criteria:

- Being commanded by a person responsible for their subordinates;
- Having fixed distinctive insignia, recognizable at a distance;
- Carrying arms openly; and
- Conducting their operations in accordance with the laws and customs of war.[19]

The requirements for militia to establish their combatant status are essential to maintaining distinction on the battlefield. The requirement to be responsible to a senior commander enables the conduct of disciplined operations that comply with the LOAC to include a command structure that is capable of enforcing LOAC obligations through a chain of command responsible for training and supervision of operations. In addition, the requirement of a responsible chain of command implicitly provides a criminal enforcement mechanism, through the sanction attached to the theory of command responsibility.[20] The requirement for a fixed distinctive insignia, often called the "uniform requirement," is the key provision to enable distinction, which requires the soldier to distinguish himself in battle from civilians and combatants of the opposing side.[21] The requirement to carry arms openly is similar and closely linked to the uniform

---

war. *See, e.g.,* DoD LOW Manual, para. 4.7. The *levée en masse* has its origins in the Napoleonic Wars, where the entire population was exhorted to rise against invading forces, to defend the nation-state. LIEBER, GUERRILLA PARTIES, *supra*, note 1, at 15.

18. GPW Commentary, at 49.
19. These requirements are outlined in GPW, art. 4(A)(2).
20. Discussed in detail in Chapter 14.
21. For a discussion of the uniform requirement, *see Ex parte* Quirin, 317 U.S. 1 (1942) and Mohamadali and Another v. Public Prosecutor (Privy Council, 28 July 1968), 42 I.L.R. 458 (1971).

requirement. It does not require that the arms be carried visibly at all times, especially when otherwise identifiable as a member of opposing forces. Both of these requirements rest on the ability to recognize a combatant and distinguish him from the civilian population.[22]

The requirements in the preceding paragraph are not express prerequisites for POW status for regular members of the armed forces of a state party to a conflict, including those militias and volunteer corps that are a formal part of the armed forces. But all members of the armed forces and militia members are by implication required to satisfy these four conditions. Indeed, the very concept of "regular" armed forces implies compliance with these conditions. It would be counter-intuitive to require members of militia groups to meet these requirements while releasing members of regular armed forces from an analogous obligation.[23] Accordingly, regular armed forces must distinguish themselves by wearing a distinctive insignia, recognizable at a distance, and carrying their arms openly.

It must be noted, however, that these distinction provisions, so essential to distinguish between combatants and civilians on the battlefield, do not prevent soldiers from using effective camouflage, or prohibit special operations forces from wearing non-standard uniforms to associate themselves with the irregular forces they are advising.[24] Members of the armed forces of a party to the conflict are also presumed and expected to conduct their operations in accordance with the LOAC. Failure to do so may subject members of the armed forces to prosecution for LOAC violations (although not denial of POW status).[25]

D. Presumptions

Additional Protocol I includes a presumption of civilian status, "in case of doubt whether a person is a civilian, that person shall be considered to be a civilian."[26] The U.S. position appears to challenge that presumption due to the fog of war: "A legal presumption of civilian status in cases of doubt may demand a degree of

---

22. AP I changes this requirement in a significant way. Under GPW, a combatant is required to distinguish himself throughout military operations. AP I, art. 44(3) only obligates a combatant to distinguish himself from the civilian population "while they are engaged in an attack or in a military operation preparatory to an attack, or in any action carried out with a view to combat." COMMENTARY, AP I, at 527 ¶ 1691. *See also* further discussion, below.

23. *See, e.g.*, U.S. v. Lindh, 212 F. Supp. 2d 541, at 558 (E,D, Va. 2002).

24. Otto Skorzeny, the famous German commando leader, was tried after World War II for planning and conducting commando operations behind U.S. lines, during the Battle of the Bulge, where the commandos were instructed to wear U.S. uniforms to infiltrate the lines. He was acquitted, as the German commandos were instructed to remove the uniforms when they entered into combat with U.S. forces. *Trial of Otto Skorzeny and Others*, Law Reports of Trials of War Criminals, United Nations War Crimes Commission, Vol. IX (1949), at 90. Soldiers caught out of uniform, or even a "non-standard" uniform, behind enemy lines, who fail to distinguish themselves from the civilian population, are at risk of treatment as spies. AP I, art. 46. They would retain the minimum protections of GPW, art. 5, however. *See also* DoD LOW Manual, para. 4.5.2.1.

25. GPW, art. 86.

26. Art. 50(1), AP I.

certainty that would not account for the realities of war."[27] In practice, however, U.S. forces start with the presumption that a civilian or a civilian object is not targetable unless persuaded that the person or object is demonstrably contributing to military action "in light of the circumstances ruling at the time."[28]

II. Prisoners of War

A. Historical Development

In ancient times, the concept of POW was unknown and the defeated became the victor's "chattel."[29] Until the seventeenth century the captive could be killed, sold, or put to work at the discretion of the captor. One of the first agreements for the repatriation of POWs was an agreement between Spain and the Netherlands, signed at Westphalia on January 30, 1648.[30] The American Revolutionary War saw mistreatment of POWs on both sides, but the British did not try American belligerents as traitors and the Americans, at the insistence of George Washington, established POW camps and took steps to prevent abuse of prisoners.[31] One of the first treaties signed by the young United States, the 1785 Treaty of Friendship between the United States and Prussia, provided for POW treatment, should hostilities break out.[32] Over the next two centuries, the development of, and respect for laws relating to the protection of POWs was not without its problems. For example, the first recognized codification of the law of war, General Order No. 100 of the Lieber Code contained the following POW definition:

> Art. 49. A prisoner of war is a public enemy armed or attached to the hostile army for active aid, who has fallen into the hands of the captor, either fighting or wounded, on the field or in the hospital, by individual surrender or by capitulation. All soldiers, of whatever species of arms; all men who belong to the rising en masse of the hostile country; all those who are attached to the

---

27. DoD LOWM, para. 5.4.3.2.
28. *Compare* DoD LOWM, para. 5.4.3.2 and Gen. McKiernan, COMISAF Tactical Directive (30 Dec 2008), [directing utmost restraint in engaging civilian objects].
29. Commentary, Geneva Convention (III), Relative to the Treatment of Prisoners of War 45 (Jean S. Pictet ed., 1960) [hereinafter Commentary, GPW]. The International Committee of the Red Cross (ICRC) commentary on the GPW, edited by Jean Pictet provides general history and guidance for interpretation of the conventions.
30. Extract contained in *Documents on Prisoners of War* (Naval War College, Documents on Prisoners of War 5 (Howard S. Levie ed., U.S. Naval War College International Law Studies vol. 60, 1979) [hereinafter Levie, Documents on Prisoners of War]. This volume and Professor Levie's companion, *Prisoners of War in International Armed Conflict*, are indispensable references for any research on the history of prisoner of war legal issues. Howard S. Levie, Prisoners of War in International Armed Conflict (U.S. Naval War College International Law Studies vol. 59, 1978) [hereinafter Levie].
31. S. Fisher, The Struggle for American Independence Vol. II, pp. 104–105 (1908).
32. Levie, Documents on Prisoners of War, *supra*, note 30, at 8.

army for its efficiency and promote directly the object of the war, except such as are hereinafter provided for; all disabled men or officers on the field or elsewhere, if captured; all enemies who have thrown away their arms and ask for quarter, are prisoners of war, and as such exposed to the inconveniences as well as entitled to the privileges of a prisoner of war.[33]

However, article 60 of the code permitted Union commanders "to give no quarter, in great straits, when his own salvation makes it impossible to cumber himself with prisoners."[34] The Regulations Annexed to the 1907 Hague Convention IV provided the first codification of POW qualification requirements.[35] Using the term "belligerents," the Hague Rules established the four conditions adopted later by the GPW for militia and volunteer corps POW qualification discussed above, and noted that individuals satisfying these conditions became subject to the "laws, rights and duties" applicable to armies.

There was little change in those requirements until the revisions of the Geneva Conventions following World War II. Prior to these revisions during intervening conflicts, protection of POWs was inconsistent. For example, German officials refused to apply the Hague Regulations to Allied prisoners in World War I because all parties to the hostilities were not signatories to the treaty (which was a technical requirement for applicability of the obligations, known in international law as a *si omnes* clause).[36] The Japanese had a similar experience in World War II, having signed but not ratified the 1929 Prisoner of War Convention. By the end of World War II, however, the concept of protection for POWs and retained persons had advanced to the point that a number of German and Japanese officers were tried and convicted for murder or mistreatment of captured military and civilian personnel in their custody.[37] The summary execution of partisans and commandos by German forces caused the negotiators of the 1949 Geneva Convention for the Protection of Prisoners of War to address the "partisan issue" by adding art. 4(A)(3) of GPW;[38] this provision provided for irregular forces who were associated with a party to the conflict to be recognized as POWs as long as they comply with the four provisions mentioned above. The 1949 Geneva Conventions have attained universal

---

33. Francis Lieber, General Order No. 100, Instructions of the Government of Armies of the United States in the Field art. 49 (1863) [hereinafter Lieber Code].

34. *Id.*, art. 60.

35. HR, art. 1.

36. G.I.A.D. Draper, The Red Cross Conventions 11 (1958).

37. The Charter of the International Military Tribunal (IMT) in Article 6b included among war crimes "murder or ill-treatment of prisoners of war." *See, e.g.*, Trial of Martin Gottfried Weiss and Thirty-Nine Others (Dachau Concentration Camp Trial), XI U.N. Law Reports 5 (1945); Trial of Erich Killinger and Four Others (The Dulag Luft Trial), III U.N. Law Reports 67 (1945); Trial of Josef Kramer and 44 Others (The Belsen Trial), II U.N. Law Reports 1 (1945); *In re* Homma, 327 U.S. 759 (1946). Similarly, the Japanese garrison commander on Wake Island was tried and convicted of the murder of U.S. civilian heavy equipment operators captured in 1942 and forced to continue their work on behalf of the Japanese, then murdered shortly before U.S. armed forces recaptured Wake Island.

38. The issue of Hitler's "Commando Order," to kill all partisans and commandos captured behind the lines, was addressed in the "High Command Case," *Wilhelm von Leeb et al.*, 12 TWC 462.

ratification, enabling the application of POW status in all international armed conflicts.

B. Civilians Accompanying the Force

The 1949 Geneva Convention III also extends POW status to certain civilians and other non-combatants. It is common that many civilians are authorized by the government of a state party to an international armed conflict to accompany the armed forces in the field. Granting these civilians POW status continued the approach recognized in the Lieber Code of extending POW protections to "citizens who accompany an army for whatever purpose, such as sutlers, editors, or reporters of journals, or contractors."[39] Article 4 of GPW provides POW status for civilians accompanying the force such as: war correspondents, civilian contractors, civilian members of military aircraft crews, merchant marine and civil aviation crews, and other civilians accompanying the forces in the field. These civilians must have "received authorization from the armed forces they accompany."[40] Current examples include Department of Defense civilian employees, civilian contractors, civilian intelligence analysts assigned to an air crew, civilian merchant marine, and accredited journalists.[41] These civilians would not qualify for belligerent status in accordance with the Hague Regulations because they do not carry arms openly. Furthermore, these categories of POWs were explicitly excluded from the AP I Article 43 definition of combatant. Accordingly, individuals in this category do not enjoy combatants' privilege although they may act in individual self-defense from unlawful attack, for example a terrorist attack. Finally, foreign civilians who do not accompany the force, but may be hired in theater, would not be entitled to either the combatant's privilege or POW status.

C. Retained Personnel

The term "non-combatant" technically refers to non-combatant members of the armed forces: chaplains and medical personnel exclusively engaged in the care of sick and wounded.[42] When captured, these individuals are not POWs, but instead "retained personnel" in accordance with the Geneva Convention for the Amelioration of the Condition of the Wounded and Sick in the Field (GWS). This status is contingent on refraining from belligerent acts. Accordingly, like civilians who accompany the force, retained personnel do not have the combatant's privilege although they may use force to defend themselves, or their patients, from marauders who do not respect the law of war.[43] They are to be

---

39. LIEBER CODE, art. 50.
40. GPW, art. 4(a)(4)-(5).
41. See, e.g., DoD LOWM, para. 4.15.1.
42. See DoD LOWM, para. 4.1.1.1.
43. GWS, art. 22(1).

respected, protected, and retained with POWs to assist in ministering to their needs. But they are to be released as soon as they are not required to assist the prisoners.[44]

III. Additional Protocol I

Additional Protocol I (AP I) attempted to establish a legal system that recognizes only combatant or civilian status on the battlefield. The definition of combatants in Article 43 does not distinguish between regular armed forces of a state party and other armed groups or units, but defines all armed forces as groups and units which are under a command responsible to a party for the conduct of its subordinates as armed forces of that party. The AP I definition of armed forces and combatants does not mention the specific requirements for a "fixed distinctive insignia, recognizable at a distance." Furthermore, AP I requires combatants to "distinguish themselves [by carrying their arms openly] from the civilian population while they are engaged in an attack or in a military operation preparatory to an attack."[45]

As noted in Chapter 2, in one of the most controversial provisions AP I extended the treaty (and the law applicable to international armed conflicts) to "peoples fighting against colonial domination and alien occupation and against racist regimes."[46] The consequence of this extension was exacerbated by AP I's extension of combatant status and POW recognition to members of "organized armed groups," as long as they were under a responsible command, were subject to an internal disciplinary system enforcing the law of war, and carried their "arms openly" while visible to the enemy and "engaged in a military deployment preceding the launching of an attack."[47] This latter provision, particularly when coupled with the elimination of a "distinctive insignia" requirement, allows members of irregular armed groups to hide themselves amongst the civilian population, even while preparing for an attack, and still gain combatant status which in effect means POW status with its accordant lawful combatant immunity. As a result, the United States and several of its allies have refused to ratify AP I.[48]

---

44. GPW, art. 33.
45. AP I, art. 44(3).
46. AP I, art. 1(4).
47. AP I, art. 43(1) and art. 44(3).
48. This provision is the principal reason that the United States has not ratified AP I, as it places civilians at risk, because individuals will fail to identify themselves as fighters, abandoning "distinctive insignia," using civilians to shield their movements, and only carry their arms openly in the final attack. *See* A. Sofaer, *The Position of the United States on Current Law of War Agreements*, 2 AM. J. INT'L L. POL'Y 460, 463 (1987). Sofaer, the Legal Advisor to the State Department at the time, noted that the provision "grants combatant status to armed irregulars, even in cases where they do not distinguish themselves from non-combatants, with the result that there will be increased risk to the civilian population, within which irregulars attempt to hide." *Id. See also*, DoD LOWM, para. 4.6.1.2.

Commentary by Yoram Dinstein, the preeminent Israeli law of war scholar, typifies the widespread criticism of this extension of lawful combatant status to irregular belligerents: "[B]lurring the lines of division between combatants and civilians is bound to end in civilians suffering the consequences of being suspected as covert combatants."[49] Even many states that ratified AP I pushed back against the effect of this provision. Many of these States attempted through reservations and understandings to the treaty to limit the application of this provision to occupied territory, or the situations described in article 1(4), and clarified that their understanding of the term "deployment" includes "any movement towards a place from which such an attack is to be launched."[50] And State practice has not demonstrated any application of these controversial provisions in international armed conflict. One thing is clear: the United States does not and likely will not extend lawful combatant status to such irregular operatives. Instead, the GPW test for POW status will remain the benchmark for assessing who qualifies for the combatant's privilege.

IV. Unlawful Combatants

A. Historical Development of the Terms

For the last several years, controversy has raged over whether the LOAC permits defining certain belligerent operatives as "unlawful combatants," or "unprivileged belligerents" even though this term does not appear in any LOAC treaty.[51] For example, from the outset of the U.S. military response to the terrorist attacks of September 11, 2001, the United States has designated belligerent operatives who fail to meet the GPW definition of POW as unlawful enemy combatants or unprivileged belligerents. Furthermore, the Military Commissions Acts of 2006 and 2009 utilized both these characterizations, respectively, as being appropriate for al Qaeda, Taliban, and associated personnel, as well as those individuals who participated in hostilities against the United States or its allies, or who "purposefully and materially" supported those organized armed groups.[52] Critics of this characterization assert in response that the LOAC recognizes only two categories of individuals: combatants and civilians. Combatants are

---

49. Y. Dinstein, The Conduct of Hostilities under the Law of International Armed Conflict (2004).

50. *See, e.g.,* , Roberts & Guelff, Documents on the Laws of War 502 (2001) (Understanding of the Government of Canada). In the view of some commentators, as a practical matter, "the main issue involving armed members of resistance or liberation movements which may be anticipated in armed conflicts affecting such movements is whether the movement qualifies as a Party to an international armed conflict." M. Bothe, K. Partsch & W. Solf, New rules for Victims of Armed Conflicts PG 50 (1982).

51. *See* DoD LOWM, para. 4.3.1.

52. Military Commissions Act of 2009 (MCA 2009), 10 U.S.C. § 948a et seq.; Military Commissions Act of 2006 (MCA 2006), 10 U.S.C. § 948, et seq.

those individuals who satisfy the combatant definition of AP I; civilians are all others. These critics argue that individuals who fail to satisfy AP I's combatant definition but nonetheless participate in hostilities remain civilians, are subject to responsive action (attack or detention) based on their direct participation in hostilities. Because, however, they are civilians, they may not be subjected to the broad scope of attack and preventive detention authority applicable to combatants.

The issue highlighted by this debate is whether there is a gap, as a matter of law, between the *lawful* combatant defined by AP I (and by incorporation the GPW), and civilians, defined in AP I as all other persons. Are individuals who join a belligerent group and engage in belligerent conduct civilians simply because they fail to qualify for lawful combatant status? Or does their association with the belligerent group and their belligerent conduct indicate that they are *de facto* although not *de jure* combatants, subject to attack and preventive detention like any other combatant, but not entitled to the privileges accorded to lawful combatant? This could include members of non-State belligerent groups who cannot qualify for lawful combatant status because they are not engaged in an international armed conflict, or members of belligerent groups in the context of an international armed conflict who fail to comply with the four qualification requirements of the GPW. For example, members of an armed group fighting on behalf of a State who fail to wear a distinctive emblem and show no respect for the laws and customs of war would not qualify as lawful combatants.

This is not a new debate. Unprivileged belligerency was prohibited by the *jus militare* and the Just War Tradition, which required war to be "public war," authorized by the "right (competent) authority." Individuals engaged in unauthorized acts of war were acting outside the "faith and law of nations."[53] Lieber noted the presence of brigands and "free-booters," contrasting the lawful status of partisans and "free-corps," on the Civil War battlefield.[54] The "Lieber Code," in article 82, declared unprivileged belligerents who did not represent the organized hostile army as the equivalent of "highway robbers or pirates," who should be treated "summarily" (i.e., executed) and denied the "privileges of prisoners of war."[55] Of course, no one is suggesting summary execution for current "unprivileged belligerents." But it is nonetheless important to recognize that invoking this category of operatives was not an arbitrary action lacking historical foundation. Instead, it was a modern invocation of a longstanding recognition that belligerent status and POW status need not be synonymous, a recognition that finds endorsement in U.S. practice, both in the form of military history and judicial decisions.

For U.S. practice, the most significant authority on the validity of the unlawful combatant/unprivileged belligerent status comes from a World War

---

53. G.I.A.D. Draper, *The Status of Combatants and the Question of Guerrilla Warfare*, 45 Brit. Y. B. Int'l Law 173, 176 (1971).
54. Lieber, Guerrilla Parties, *supra*, note 1, at 10.
55. Lieber Code, *supra*, note #, art. 82.

II military commission case involving German saboteurs. The status of unlawful combatants was clearly defined, for the United States, prior to the Geneva Conventions, in the *Quirin* (German Saboteurs) case:

> By universal agreement and practice, the law of war draws a distinction between the armed forces and the peaceful populations of belligerent nations and also between those who are lawful and unlawful combatants. Lawful combatants are subject to capture and detention as prisoners of war by opposing military forces. Unlawful combatants are likewise subject to capture and detention, but in addition they are subject to trial and punishment by military tribunals for acts which render their belligerency unlawful.[56]

Although the crimes punishable at military commissions are beyond the scope of this chapter, the Supreme Court during World War II drew clear lines between lawful and unlawful combatants and peaceful populations. While it is true that the GC had yet to be adopted at the time of the decision, it seems relatively clear that the Court's *ratio decidendi* was not the absence of a clearly defined category for civilians who pose a security risk to the State, but instead that the captives were belligerent operatives of an enemy armed force who failed to meet the lawful combatant qualification by not wearing uniforms.

B. A Gap in Coverage?

When the Geneva Conventions were revised following World War II, the States' parties negotiating the treaties implicitly acknowledged the gap between GPW and GC – a gap occupied by unprivileged belligerents. The ICRC representative to the Diplomatic Conference made it clear that "although the two conventions might appear to cover all categories concerned, irregular belligerents were not actually protected."[57] The British representative was equally emphatic that "the whole conception of the [civilians convention (i.e., GC)] was the protection of civilian victims of war, and not the protection of illegitimate bearers of arms." Other delegations offered similar comments.[58]

Subsequent literature has acknowledged that unprivileged belligerents remained a recognized category of battlefield operatives, even after the modifications of article 4(A) of GPW. Then-Major Richard Baxter wrote a seminal article on the subject in 1951 that noted the category of "unprivileged belligerents," who, like spies and saboteurs, were not entitled to POW status and were not to be given the full status of civilians. Baxter noted that individuals who were fighting against the armed forces of the State, without qualifying as a member of the armed forces, or some other authorized group properly distinguishing themselves from the civilian populace captured on the battlefield prior

---

56. *Ex. Parte* Quirin, 317 U.S. 1, 30-31 (1942).
57. Vol IIA, Final Report of the Diplomatic Conference of Geneva of 1949, at 622.
58. *Id.*

to occupation, were unprivileged belligerents, not civilians protected by GC.[59] Yoram Dinstein has noted, "a person is not allowed to wear simultaneously two caps: the hat of a civilian and the helmet of a soldier."[60] Such individuals are "combatant[s], in the sense that [they] can be lawfully targeted by the enemy, but [they] cannot claim the privileges appertaining to lawful combatancy. Nor do [they] enjoy the benefits of civilian status."[61] While some non-governmental organizations and commentators dispute the existence of this category,[62] there is substantial support for the concept of unlawful combatants, or unprivileged belligerents, on the battlefield.[63]

Ironically, AP I also implicitly acknowledges the existence of "unprivileged belligerents." Article 44(4) provides that an individual captured by an adverse party who fails to comply with the requirement to distinguish himself from the civilian population, or fails to carry his arms openly during a military engagement and while deploying to that engagement, will forfeit his right to be a POW. It is significant that the treaty does not suggest that such captives shall be considered civilians subject to security detention. Instead, by indicating they shall be denied POW status, the article suggests they are combatants, albeit not lawful or privileged.

C. Habeas Corpus Litigation

Recognition of this category of battlefield operatives has been central to the U.S. response to our current al Qaeda and Taliban enemy. Because many of these captives have challenged their detention in U.S. courts, the law of battlefield status continues to develop in U.S. courts. Although *Hamdi v. Rumsfeld*[64] recognized the right of a belligerent State to detain unlawful combatants, as incident to the authority to use military force, *Boumediene v. Bush*[65] provided for habeas corpus review for those detained at Guantanamo Bay. As a result, the District of Columbia Circuit Court of Appeals and its constituent District Courts have been struggling to establish the parameters of Military Commission Act definition of "unprivileged belligerents" as implemented by the Executive Branch.

---

59. If captured during occupation, according to Baxter, they would be considered civilians, subject to detention for "imperative reasons of security," under GC, article 78. R. Baxter, *So-Called Unprivileged Belligerents, Spies, Guerrillas, and Saboteurs*, 29 BRIT. Y. B. INT'L LAW, 321, 328 (1951).
60. If so, DINSTEIN, *supra*, note 49, at 29.
61. *Id.*
62. *See, e.g.*, G. Rona, Director of Human Rights First, "Testimony at Hearing on the U.S. Detention Facility at Guantanamo Bay," Helsinki Commission 3 (2007).
63. *See* DoD LOWM, para. 4.2.3.3 et. seq.
64. Hamdi v. Rumsfeld, 542 U.S. 507, 521 (2004) ("we understand Congress' grant of authority [under the Authorization for the Use of Military Force (AUMF), Public Law 107-40 (2001)] for the use of 'necessary and appropriate force' to include the authority to detain for the duration of the relevant conflict, and our understanding is based on longstanding law-of-war principles.").
65. Boumediene v. Bush, 128 S. Ct. 2229 (2008).

On March 13, 2009, the government filed a brief in several District Court habeas cases to explain the Obama administration's detention policy.[66] The government relied heavily on Congress' Authorization for the Use of Military Force (AUMF),[67] using a standard of membership or providing "substantial support" to al Qaeda, the Taliban, and associated organizations, as the basis for unprivileged belligerent classification.[68] The memorandum provided for "substantial support" to be interpreted based on "various analogues from traditional international armed conflicts."[69] The administration relied on the distinction, drawn below, between "individuals who belong to armed forces or armed groups (who may be attacked and, *a fortiori*, captured at any time) and civilians who are immune from direct attack except when directly participating in hostilities."[70] Accordingly, the government asserted its explanation of who may be detained in armed conflict, consistent with the AUMF and informed by traditional LOAC detention principles.[71]

The Circuit Court responded, in its first appellate case on the issue, *Al-Bihani*, by rejecting the law of war as a sole basis for detention, instead relying on the language of the statutes. The court effectively modified the government's definition of a detainable enemy belligerent:

> The sources we look to for resolution of Al-Bihani's case are the sources courts always look to: the text of relevant statutes and controlling domestic caselaw [sic].
>
> Under those sources, Al-Bihani is lawfully detained whether the definition of a detainable person is, as the district court articulated it, "an individual who was part of or supporting Taliban or al Qaeda forces, or associated forces that are engaged in hostilities against the United States or its coalition partners," or the modified definition offered by the government that requires that an individual "substantially support" enemy forces. The statutes authorizing the use of force and detention not only grant the government the power to craft a workable legal standard to identify individuals it can detain, but also cabin the application of these definitions. The AUMF authorizes the President to "use all necessary and appropriate force against those nations, organizations, or persons he determines planned, authorized, committed, or aided the terrorist attacks that occurred on September 11, 2001, or harbored such organizations or persons." AUMF § 2(a).... Congress, in the MCA 2006, provided

---

66. *See generally* Respondents' Memorandum Regarding the Government's Detention Authority Relative to Detainees Held at Guantanamo Bay, In re Guantanamo Bay Detainee Litigation, Misc. No. 08-442 (TFH) (D.D.C. Mar. 13, 2009), *available at* http://www.usdoj.gov/opa/documents/memo-re-det-auth.pdf (last visited Feb. 21, 2011) [hereinafter Detention Memorandum].

67. Authorization for the Use of Military Force, Public Law 107-40, 115 Stat. 224 (2001) [hereinafter AUMF].

68. Detention Memorandum, at 3. Although the administration did not get into this point in the memorandum, it is arguable whether the "substantial support" prong justifies targeting; it does, however, clearly provide a reason for detention under article 78 of GC, which authorizes detention of civilians who may be interned (i.e., detained) for "imperative reasons of security." As this is a provision applying to an occupying power, the provision would be applied by analogy in the current conflict.

69. *Id.* at 2.
70. *Id.* at 9.
71. *Id.* at 11.

guidance on the class of persons subject to detention under the AUMF by defining "unlawful enemy combatants" who can be tried by military commission. MCA 2006, sec. 3, § 948a(1). The MCA 2006 authorized the trial of an individual who "engaged in hostilities or who has purposefully and materially supported hostilities against the United States or its co-belligerents who is not a lawful enemy combatant...."[72]

Despite the court's protestation about the applicability of the law of war to the discussion of who qualifies as an unlawful combatant, it is clear that the terms and principles of the LOAC infused and informed its analysis. This is especially true in light of the Supreme Court's characterization of the current conflict as a "non-international" in its *Hamdan* opinion.[73] Ultimately, *Al Bihani* and other Federal District habeas decisions appear to endorse the government's reliance on unprivileged belligerent status as a basis for wartime preventive detention. And the recent DoD Law of War Manual has retained the "unprivileged belligerent" category.[74]

V. Non-International Armed Conflicts

The concept of combatants and civilians in non-international armed conflicts are much more uncertain than in international armed conflict. Although neither common Article 3 to the Geneva Conventions nor Additional Protocol II (AP II) may be operative at a certain level of violence that is deemed "armed conflict," neither provides much guidance as to the status of individuals found on that battlefield. But given the prevalence of non-international armed conflict, definition of these terms is essential. Indeed, the historic risk to innocent civilians in this form of conflict, and the likelihood that these types of conflicts will continue to be dominant in the foreseeable future, indicate that a workable combatant/civilian framework is perhaps more important in this context than in the context of international armed conflicts.

Both common Article 3 and AP II, at least by implication, indicate that there is a division between combatants (or belligerents) and civilians, even in non-international armed conflicts. Common Article 3 refers to "parties" to the armed conflict, implying a contest between two organized belligerent groups. Article 13(2) of AP II provides that "civilians" should not be the object of attack, without defining the term. And combatants are not mentioned. Furthermore, AP II's scope provision (Article 1) also refers to the parties to the conflict, as the armed forces of the State and "dissident armed forces or other organized armed groups which [are] under responsible command."

---

72. Al-Bihani v. Obama, 590 F.3d 866, 871-872 (D.C. Cir. 2010).
73. Hamdan v. Rumsfeld, 126 S. Ct. 2749, 2795 (2006). Should this be: Hamdan v. Rumsfeld, 548 U.S. 557, 630 (2006).?
74. *See* DoD LOWM, para. 4.3.

This latter provision arguably provides a means to identify the lawful combatants, and unlawful combatants. These members of dissident armed forces or organized armed groups cannot qualify as lawful combatants because they are challenging the sovereign power of the State and do not represent a State. The sole criterion for their unlawful combatancy, therefore, is membership in the organized armed group, "under responsible command." The ICRC Commentary to Article 13 also provides a clue to the nature of combatants, "[T]hose who belong to armed forces or armed groups may be attacked at any time;"[75] combatants, albeit unlawful, are distinguished from the "civilians" who are the object of protection in Article 13.

Asserting that all non-State belligerent forces are merely civilians taking a direct part in hostilities is therefore inconsistent with the text and implications of the principle legal provisions applicable to such conflicts. Perhaps more importantly, it is also inconsistent with the operational realities of such conflicts. Insurgent, dissident, and other irregular forces challenging State forces in non-international armed conflicts operate analogously to organized enemy State forces in international armed conflicts, and should be treated no differently for purposes of attack and detention. Characterizing these belligerents as civilians would produce the perverse result of vesting them with greater protections than the regular armed forces they challenge in battle—the forces that routinely manifest greater compliance with the obligations imposed by the LOAC. Whether the FARC in Colombia, Hezbollah in southern Lebanon, the PKK in Turkey, or the Taliban in Afghanistan, the United States will almost certainly continue to characterize these forces as unprivileged belligerents for the indefinite future.[76]

VI. Organized Armed Groups

Within international armed conflicts or non-international armed conflicts, the armed forces of a State may engage in hostilities with organized armed groups. Although most international armed conflict involves hostilities between the armed forces of two or more States, situations can occur, such as during occupation, where such armed forces and other armed security forces of the State (including police forces) are engaged in combat with organized armed groups, or other persons who are not part of a State armed force.[77] Such a group can take a variety of forms, including an organized resistance movement that belongs to a state party but fails to meet the POW qualification requirements of GPW

---

75. COMMENTARY, ADDITIONAL TO THE GENEVA CONVENTIONS OF 12 AUG. 1949 AND RELATING TO THE PROTECTION OF VICTIMS OF NON-INTERNATIONAL ARMED CONFLICTS (Protocol II), Aug. 6, 1977, 1453 ¶ 4789 [hereinafter COMMENTARY, AP II].
76. *See, e.g.*, DoD LOWM, para. 4.18.4.1.
77. This does not include civilians who become part of a *levée en masse* under GPW, article 4A(6).

article 4A(2), or a terrorist organization such as al Qaeda that, without regard to compliance with any of the other requirements of the Geneva Convention, operates without any authorization or affiliation with a State and thereby outside of the GPW. These belligerent operatives—individuals formally or functionally part of an organized armed group that is engaged in hostilities—may be targeted at any time.[78] Unlike a true civilian directly participating in hostilities, however, the authority to attack such belligerent operatives is not the result of their direct participation in hostilities. Instead, it is their membership in armed forces/armed groups that results in a presumption of hostility and the authority to attack and subdue such a belligerent. Although the difference between this authority and the authority to attack a civilian directly participating in hostilities may be almost functionally analogous, it is important to emphasize the difference between status-based targeting of enemy belligerents, and the conduct-based targeting authority resulting from direct participation in hostilities.

Along with the factors discussed above, there are several relevant criteria to determine whether the person is part of the group, including but not limited to: evidence of formal membership in the group (e.g., evidence that an individual has sworn allegiance to the group); evidence of a person acting at the direction of the group or within its "command structure"; the extent to which an individual performs a function under a command structure of an organized armed group that is analogous to a function normally performed by a member of a State military; the extent to which the individual is taking a part in hostilities, including the frequency, intensity, and duration of such participation; and other similar criteria determined in the reasonable judgment of a commander in the field to demonstrate an individual's integration into the armed group.[79] While assessing belligerent group membership for irregular forces is obviously more difficult than for regular armed forces who wear distinctive uniforms, this difficulty in no way alters the ultimate outcome of the assessment in both case: status-based targeting authority.[80]

One of several possible indicia of integration into an organized armed group is whether a person is functionally part of the group. The ICRC Interpretive Guidance provides a more narrow definition of the functional membership test, requiring the individual to perform a "continuous combat function," tantamount to continuously carrying out a combat function in active combat.[81] For the U.S. forces, functional membership includes carrying arms, exercising command over the armed group, or carrying out planning related to the conduct of hostilities. Further, a combat function is not limited to applying force; it includes individuals who are performing tasks under a command structure of an organized armed group similar to those provided in a combat, combat support, or combat service support role in the armed forces of a State. Therefore

---

78. *See, e.g.,* COMMENTARY, AP II, *supra*, note #, at 1453 ¶ 4789 (regarding Article 13, "Those who belong to armed forces or armed groups may be attacked at any time.").
79. *See* DoD LOWM, para. 5.8.3.
80. *See* DoD LOWM, para. 4.18.4.1.
81. Nils Melzer, ICRC INTERPRETIVE GUIDANCE ON THE NOTION OF DIRECT PARTICIPATION IN HOSTILITIES UNDER INTERNATIONAL HUMANITARIAN LAW (2009), at 39 [Hereinafter ICRC INTERPRETIVE GUIDANCE].

Chapter 4 ■ Classification and Status of Persons

a person who, while being a member of an armed group, gathers intelligence, maintains communications, or provides logistics support (e.g., cooking or supply), can be targeted in the same manner as if that person carried out these tasks as a member of the armed forces of a State.[82] Carrying out such a function on a sufficiently frequent or intensive basis identifies a person as a member of an organized armed group.

Armed non-State actors may also, depending upon their level of organization and the types of operations being conducted, make use of civilians who are not members of the group to provide services that are not dissimilar to civilian contractors working with traditional armed forces. Depending upon what role those civilians play, they may be taking a direct part in hostilities. For example, if a civilian who is not a member of the group delivers ammunition to the front lines, he or she may be considered to be taking a direct part in hostilities.

Depending upon the nature and level of sophistication of a group, it may also have sections engaged in civilian activities (e.g., political or humanitarian). In such situations, targeting must be limited to the members of the armed wing of the organized armed group, rather than civilians who are exclusively engaged in humanitarian activities. However, where someone involved in other activities also engages in direct participation in hostilities, such as when a leader exercises command over the armed group, that person may be targeted.[83] The integration into an organized armed group also sets these participants apart from civilians who may merely be sympathetic to the goals of the organized armed group. Such sympathies do not make these civilians members of the armed group or otherwise direct participants in hostilities.

U.S. practice is such that only an authorized official should designate an organized armed group as hostile, and that its members qualify as direct participants in hostilities.[84] Absent such a designation, the determination of whether a civilian may be targeted depends on whether they are committing specific acts that amount to hostile acts or demonstrations of hostile intent, in accordance with the Chairman of the Joint Chiefs of Staff's Standing Rules Of Engagement.[85] In addition, individual conflicts may involve specific rules of engagement that incorporate direct participation in hostilities analysis.

In cases where a civilian has engaged in a continuous pattern of belligerent acts, he or she may be treated as taking a direct part in hostilities on an ongoing

---

82. See DoD LOWM, para. 5.8.3.2. See also BOTHE, PARTSCH & SOLF, supra, note 50 at 252 ("combatants" who are operating amongst the populace are obliged to distinguish themselves "when engaged in such military operations as recruiting, training, general administration, law enforcement, aid to underground political authorities, collection of contributions and dissemination of propaganda;" also, "military operations preparatory to an attack should be construed broadly enough to include administrative and logistic activities preparatory to such an attack").

83. See DoD LOWM, para. 5.8.4.

84. This approach is similar to and consistent with the "declaration of forces hostile" in rules of engagement. See CHAIRMAN, JOINT CHIEFS OF STAFF INSTRUCTION (CJCSI) 3121.01B, STANDING RULES OF ENGAGEMENT/STANDING RULES FOR THE USE OF FORCE FOR US FORCES, (Jun. 13, 2005).

85. Id.

basis, or essentially attaining combatant status through functional analysis.[86] This subjects the civilian to attack at any time, unless and until he or she has clearly renounced that participation through an overt and unambiguous act, or demonstrably ceased to engage in belligerent acts. Persons who are part of an organized armed group can be targeted until such time as they take concrete and verifiable steps to disassociate themselves from the armed group.[87] Whether such a person may be viewed as having ceased participation in hostilities—and is again protected from direct attack as an inoffensive civilian—is a determination based upon a reasonable assessment of the facts available at the time, including the amount of time that has passed since the individual has undertaken the function or conduct that made the individual a part of the group.[88]

When captured, members of organized armed groups that do not qualify for POW treatment are considered "unprivileged belligerents." They are to be treated humanely and may be given equivalent treatment to civilian status, as a matter of policy.[89]

VII. Civilians Directly Participating in Hostilities

It is, however, also true that actual civilians may at times engage in conduct that amounts to direct participation in hostilities. In response to this reality, and as a qualification to the protection from attack provided to civilians in both AP I and II, each of these treaties introduced provisions to establish when such conduct results in the forfeiture of protection from deliberate attack. Article 51(3) of AP I notes that civilians receive protection from direct attack, "unless and for such time as they directly participate in hostilities." The same concept is included in Article 13 of AP II, and is even reflected in Common Article 3, which provides protection for both combatants and civilians who are no longer taking an "active part" in hostilities. The two terms, "active" and "direct," are viewed by most commentators as synonymous.[90] Other than the civilian who, in accordance with national command, spontaneously takes up arms on the approach of an invading army (*levée en masse*), this qualification addresses the dilemma of responding to civilians who commit belligerent acts. What is their

---

86. *See* DoD LOWM, para. 5.8.3.2. Some States prefer to consider these individuals as civilians who are continuously directly participating in hostilities; the United States uses a functional membership approach to identify members of organized armed groups that may be targeted at any time. The effect is the same, through different reasoning. *Id.*, at para. 5.9.2.1.

87. *See* DoD LOWM, para. 5.8.3.3.

88. *Id.* Relevant factors in determining when an individual ceases to be a member of an armed group include the amount of time that has passed since the individual has undertaken the function or conduct that made the individual a member of the group in question, and whether there are concrete and verifiable facts or persuasive indicia that he or she has affirmatively returned to civilian life.

89. *See* U.S. Army Field Manual 27-10 (1956), *The Law of Land Warfare*, para 248. *See also* DoD LOWM, para. 4.19.

90. *See, e.g.*, DoD LOWM, para. 5.9.1.1.

status on the battlefield? They can certainly be attacked if they are directly participating in hostilities; but, if captured, are they civilians or POWs?

A. The ICRC Interpretive Guidance

There is no definition of "direct part in hostilities" in treaty law or customary international law. After six years, however, the ICRC completed a study of the meaning of this provision.[91] Government and academic experts participated in the study in an attempt to produce "Interpretive Guidance" by consensus, a goal that they failed to achieve.[92] But there are several very useful concepts that were developed in the Interpretive Guidance, the most important of which is the idea of "functional membership" in an organized armed group, which may be interpreted as taking individuals out of the "civilian" category and placing them firmly in the category of "combatants," discussed above:

> Membership in irregular armed forces, such as militias, volunteer corps, or resistance movements belonging to a party to the conflict, generally is not regulated by domestic law and can only be reliably determined on the basis of functional criteria, such as those applying to organized armed groups in non-international armed conflict.[93]

The Interpretive Guidance also provides some useful criteria for determining whether a civilian who is not a member of an organized armed group is directly participating in hostilities (DPH).

The ICRC creates three criteria for determining when a civilian is directly participating. The first criterion is the threshold of harm: "[T]he act [in question] must be likely to adversely affect the military operations or military capacity of a party to the conflict or, to inflict death, injury, or destruction on persons or objects protected against direct attack."[94] To meet this criterion, the action must create harm of some kind to the enemy or to civilians.

If the first criterion is met, the second criterion is to establish a direct link between the action and the harm. This second criterion is direct causation and requires that there must be a direct causal link between the act in question and the harm likely to result from that act, or from a concrete and coordinated military operation of which that act constitutes an integral part.[95] This does not include an indirect link, such as working in a munitions factory or an oil refinery that supplies the enemy's military with war sustaining capability. Rather, the action must be an integral part of a concrete military action.

---

91. ICRC INTERPRETIVE GUIDANCE, at 6.
92. The experts were unable to agree on many of the ICRC's statements. *See generally* Forum, *The ICRC Interpretive Guidance on the Notion of Direct Participation in Hostilities under International Humanitarian Law*, 42 N.Y.U. J. INT'L L. & POL. 637 (2010).
93. ICRC INTERPRETIVE GUIDANCE, at 25.
94. ICRC INTERPRETIVE GUIDANCE, at 47.
95. ICRC INTERPRETIVE GUIDANCE, at 51.

Finally, the third criterion requires a belligerent nexus, or that the act must be designed to directly cause the required threshold of harm in support of a party to the conflict and to the detriment of another.[96] Much of the criticism of this view centers on the threshold of harm requirement. For example, under this criterion, is the civilian who supplies parts to a bomb maker taking an action that will meet the test? What about a person who collects and transports goods or provides services to persons who directly participate? There is a point of attenuation on the activity that amounts to threshold of harm, but there is no general agreement where that point is.

Once a determination has been made that a civilian is directly participating, the question becomes for how long is he targetable. The language of AP I is "for such time" and the Commentary states that "[t]hus a civilian who takes part in armed combat, either individually or as part of a group, thereby becomes a legitimate target, though only for as long as he takes part in hostilities.. . . Once he ceases to participate, the civilian regains his right to the protection under this Section, i.e., against the effects of hostilities, and he may no longer be attacked."[97] As the commander contemplates targeting that individual, he may not be able to target him at the exact moment the individual takes direct part in hostilities. At what point and for how long does that individual remain targetable? On one end of the spectrum is the civilian who directly participates one time and then ceases his participation. Is he targetable until the end of hostilities? On the other end of the spectrum is the civilian who may not be a member of an organized group but each night carries out a continuous pattern of hostile acts against his foes. Is he only targetable while conducting the actual nighttime raid? This element of time is the second element of a civilian's participation in hostilities and is based on the phrase "unless and for such time."

To highlight this quandary, assume that once U.S. forces have arrived in Kosovo and the fighting has begun, an unknown person begins to launch mortars into both military and U.S. citizen housing areas.[98] These attacks have occurred three or four times within a week. The U.S. forces are able to locate the individual using radar tracking methods and send an unmanned aerial vehicle (UAV) to the area. The UAV identifies a civilian dismantling a mortar and loading the mortar base plate into the back of his truck. The civilian then begins to drive away. Because of the remoteness of the location from U.S. forces, and the congestion of the city, there is no way to adequately detain the individual. If the UAV was armed, could the pilot of the UAV launch a missile and kill the civilian? It is clear that the civilian has recently taken a direct part in hostilities but since he is no longer in the act of launching a mortar, has the time passed? What if the UAV gathers information on the truck but is unable to engage the truck at that time, but reacquires the same truck several hours later?

---

96. ICRC Interpretive Guidance, at 58.
97. AP I Commentary, at 618, para's. 1942-1944.
98. This scenario is loosely based on actual events that occurred in Kosovo in 1999.

The ICRC Interpretive Guidance argues that civilians lose protection against direct attack for the duration of each specific act amounting to direct participation in hostilities. This loss of protection only occurs during concrete preparatory measures, deployments to the location of its execution, and return from the location of its execution.[99] Responding to the often-raised "revolving door" problem where civilians are farmers by day, but become insurgents every night, the ICRC recognizes that these individuals should have an expanded window of targetability, but only if they are part of the armed wing of an organized armed group, which was discussed above.

B. An Alternative Definition of DPH

At a minimum, direct participation in hostilities encompasses actions that are belligerent *per se,* that is, by their very nature and purpose can be expected to cause actual harm to the enemy.[100] In general, the qualification of an act as direct participation in hostilities is a fact-dependent analysis that must be made after analyzing all relevant available information, in the circumstances prevailing at the time.[101] The U.S. approach "extends beyond merely engaging in combat and also includes certain acts that are an integral part of combat operations or that effectively and substantially contribute to the adversary's ability to conduct or sustain combat operations."[102] A totality of circumstances test is appropriate in determining whether an individual is taking a direct part in hostilities, taking some or all of the following considerations into account: whether the function performed is an integral part of combat operations; whether the function performed is likely to adversely affect the military operations or military capacity of an opposing party to the conflict, or is likely to harm persons or objects under the party's control; whether there is a direct causal link between the act in question and the harm likely to result; whether there is a nexus between the activity and hostilities (i.e., does the activity advance the interests of one party to the detriment of another); the discretionary nature of the activity (e.g., measuring the use of combat power and applying the law of war);[103] the civilian's

---

99. ICRC Interpretive Guidance, at 65.

100. The ICRC Commentary, AP I, page 619 para. 1944, states, "Thus 'direct' participation means acts of war which by their nature or purpose are likely to cause actual harm to the personnel and equipment of the enemy armed forces." The "actual harm" standard, in practice, has been demonstrated to be too narrowly focused on combat activities, while excluding conduct that, by a reasonable assessment, should amount to direct participation.

101. *See* 2004 U.K. Manual, ¶¶ 2.5.3, 5.32.10. *See also Prosecutor v. Tadic,* Case No. IT-94-1-T, Opinion and Judgment, ¶ 616 (May 7, 1997):

[I]t is unnecessary to define exactly the line dividing those taking an active part in hostilities and those who are not so involved. It is sufficient to examine the relevant facts of each victim and to ascertain whether, in each individual's circumstances, that person was actively involved in hostilities at the relevant time. *Id.*

102. *See* DoD LOWM, para. 5.9.3. *Compare* the definition of military objective, art. 52(2), AP I.
103. The Law of War imposes duties on combatants to apply the law of war in the use of force, in order to obtain lawful combatant status (e.g., Article 4, GPW). Unprivileged belligerents or civilians directly participating in hostilities who make such judgments lose their protection from direct

temporal or geographic proximity to active hostilities;[104] and/or the criticality of the act to the direct application of violence against the enemy.[105]

Certain activities, such as taking up arms, or otherwise trying to kill or injure enemy personnel or destroy enemy property, are widely regarded as sufficient to constitute direct participation in hostilities. In addition, a civilian who plans or implements a combat operation against military personnel or objectives, or against civilians or civilian objects, can also be considered to be directly participating in hostilities, even if he or she does not personally utilize weapons or otherwise employ destructive force in connection with the operation.[106] On the other hand, efforts by civilians to support the war effort, such as working in a munitions factory, or supplying food, lodging, and logistical support, are generally not considered direct participation.[107] While the line between direct participation and indirect support to military operations may be amorphous, seeking clarity (even if it appears artificial) is universally accepted as necessary to preserve the relevance of the principle of distinction.

C. Human Shields

Direct participation in hostilities also applies to civilians who, in an effort to protect lawful military objectives from attack, act as human shields by voluntarily placing themselves in or around the objective. Accordingly, these civilians lose their protection from deliberate attack for such time as they engage in such voluntary action.[108] However, decisions regarding targeting such an objective may be impacted by political or other factors. Furthermore, voluntary action by

---

attack. *Compare* Department of Defense Instruction (DoDI), *Policy and Procedures for Determining Workforce Mix*, No. 1100.22, at Encl. 4? (Apr. 12, 2010), *available at* http://www.dtic.mil/whs/directives/corres/pdf/110022p.pdf (last visited Feb. 21, 2011) (which requires civilians to refrain from decision-making in combat operations, to preserve discipline, command responsibility, and compliance with the law of war).

104. This list is neither a checklist, nor exhaustive. Rather than the formulaic "cumulative criteria" proposed by the ICRC Interpretive Guidance in section 2.B.V., one approach is to make a case-by-case determination considering the totality of the circumstances.

105. *See* DoD LOWM, para. 5.9.3.

106. In its commentary to AP I, art. 51(3), the ICRC acknowledges that it is not necessary to carry a weapon in order to directly participate in hostilities. Commentary, AP I, at 618-19 ¶ 1943.

107. This includes not only the general contribution made by civilians to the war effort (e.g., by virtue of their labor in factories that produce goods that are useful to the military) but also to the supply of food, lodging, equipment, or other logistical support to a country's armed forces. Civilians who work in military objectives, like munitions factories, may be at risk of death or serious injury when such a valid military objective is attacked. Supply of weapons and ammunition, whether to conventional armed forces or armed non-State actors, or assembly of weapons (or improvised explosive devices) in close geographic or temporal proximity to their use, however, would constitute direct participation. Any loss of protection from direct attack, or targeting criteria based on direct participation in hostilities, is not directly linked to the legality of the act; for example, providing shelter or supplies to insurgents may violate domestic law (like material support to terrorism), but would not necessarily subject an individual to targeting if they are not members of an organized group or otherwise directly participating in hostilities. *See* DoD LOWM, para. 5.9.3.2.

108. Voluntary human shields are not to be considered as civilian casualties for the purpose of proportionality calculations.

the civilian is a critical element of this direct participation conclusion. Civilians who are involuntary human shields remain protected from deliberate attack by their civilian status. This would not automatically prohibit attack against the target they are forced to shield. It would require analysis of whether the attack violated the targeting principle of proportionality.[109] The difficulty in distinguishing voluntary from involuntary shielding may limit the significance of this category of direct participation.

D. Detention

Direct participation in hostilities analysis determines whether an individual may be deprived of the protections afforded by civilian status. It is not determinative of detention status. For example, a civilian authorized to accompany the force would be afforded POW status, whether or not they had directly participated in hostilities. Because they are not privileged combatants they may be prosecuted under the law of the detaining State for their acts of hostility. A civilian who is otherwise directly participating in hostilities, without any State sanction or recognition, may be considered an unprivileged belligerent. Their treatment status may be that of a "protected person," in occupation (with certain derogations appropriate to security concerns),[110] or include only minimum humane treatment standards for those who qualify for neither POW nor "protected person" status. Detention and treatment standards for civilians are covered more extensively in Chapter 6.

VIII. Conclusion

The distinction between "combatant" and "civilian" on the battlefield is essential to the disciplined application of this cardinal LOAC principle, and central to the operational targeting process. Although this is complicated on the modern battlefield, rules of engagement that provide for "status-based" targeting are pretty straightforward. Once the soldier positively identifies a military objective he or she may engage the target. In non-international armed conflict, such designation of "hostile forces" is less common. In those situations, soldiers generally apply a self-defense rationale for targeting. But the evolving concepts of direct participation in hostilities, the renewed emphasis on the status of unprivileged belligerent, and definitions of each type of actor on the battlefield will undoubtedly have a significant impact on targeting authority and practice in the future. These designations are equally critical to the determination of status upon capture. As we shall see in subsequent chapters, the protections afforded

---

109. *See* DoD LOWM, para. 5.12.3.4.
110. Art. 5, GC.

VIII. Conclusion | 167

detainees, whether "unprivileged belligerents," civilian internees, combatants, POWs, Retained Persons, or civilian security internees depend upon the status determinations made at the time of capture, or during subsequent administrative or judicial proceedings. For the warfighter, however, determining who may be lawfully attacked, and what factors trigger that lawful authority, will always be the first question, for it is this question that holds truly life and death consequences.

Principal References

AP I, Arts. 1, 43-57, 75
AP II, Arts. 4-6, 13
GPW, Arts. 3-4
GC, Arts. 3-5
DoD LOW Manual, Chapters 4 and 5
ICRC, Interpretive Guidance on Direct Participation in Hostilities

Problems

Analyze the following individuals, encountered at the Brigade Temporary Holding Facility. Determine the status of each, under the law of war. Who are the actors on the battlefield, the combatants, who could be engaged, and who are the civilians to be "respected and protected" on this asymmetric battlefield? May some of the civilians be engaged for such time as they directly participate in hostilities? Does that make them combatants or civilians? Is there such a thing as an "unlawful combatant" or "unprivileged belligerent" on the battlefield, and if so, who may be attacked and detained? Justify your answer.

1. The members of the regular forces of the Iraqi Armed Forces (IAF), like the members of the vaunted Iraqi Republican Guard?
2. Reserve forces of the IAF, like Uday and Qusay, Saddam's sons, who held reserve rank in the armed forces and led special operations and intelligence forces of the IAF?
3. Members of the "Saddam Fedayeen," a group of erstwhile insurgents organized by Saddam to use tribal forces and criminals to attack Iraqi political opponents and oppose the invasion?
4. A paramilitary police unit of the IAF that was so effective in stamping out any domestic opposition?
5. Civilians who rise up to turn away the American invaders?
6. Civilians who claim they took up arms to assist the Americans, or defend their neighborhood from the ravages of the Saddam Fedayeen?
7. Former regime elements who faded into the populace, once the country was occupied by coalition forces?

8. During stability operations in the Iron Triangle, to attack Former Regime Elements, some al Qaeda members from Tunisia are engaged and detained in Iraq; what is their status?
9. Iranian Quds Force who are advising Sunni militias opposed to the occupation?
10. Common criminals and mental patients would be thrown into the mix, as Saddam opened wide the doors of his prisons and insane asylums. What is their status?

5 | BELLIGERENT DETENTION

Judge Advocate Captains, assigned to maneuver brigades all over Iraq, were given the additional duty of establishing "magistrate's reviews" (a one-man tribunal, similar to the Article 5 Tribunal conducted by many States under the GPW, used as a sorting mechanism to determine if further detention was warranted) for individuals detained during the initial phase of combat in Iraq and later, during the stability/counter-insurgency operation conducted to respond to a growing insurgency. Under U.S. policy [AR 190-8] and consistent with Article 5 of the GPW, the detainees held at Brigade and Division holding cells were treated as if they were Enemy Prisoners of War (EPWs), until their status could be reviewed at the Theater Detention Facility. You may recall from Chapter 4 that the majority of the EPWs were promptly released, as the Coalition Provisional Authority disbanded the Iraqi military in June of 2003; as a result, very few complete review tribunals were conducted at the Theater Detention Facility before June of 2003.

During the occupation phase of Operation Iraqi Freedom, in June of 2003, the Coalition Provisional Authority issued CPA Memo 3, which classified all detainees who were not Enemy Prisoners of War as civilian internees, who were to be classified and treated as "protected persons" under the 4th Geneva Convention (GC); this guidance continued to be applied throughout the coalition operations in Iraq. A memorandum of understanding between the acting Prime Minister of Iraq and Colin Powell, the U.S. Secretary of State, granting the continued authority and responsibility to the Coalition to detain Iraqis for "imperative security" reasons was appended to the UN Security Council Resolution, UNSCR 1546(2004). A later Office of Legal Counsel (Department of Justice) Memo addressed those who were specifically excluded from protected person status, including unprivileged belligerents and nationals of third States who had maintained (or renewed) diplomatic relations with Iraq.

The JAGs at all forward-deployed Brigade headquarters and at intermediate detention centers (at the Brigade and Division level) began to receive questions from their supported commanders about battlefield status and treatment of different individuals, and they began to see all manner of detainees after the abolition of the Iraqi military (Saddam Fedayeen, "dead-enders," and "Former Regime elements"; and members of insurgent groups not associated with the former State, from Iraq or infiltrating from Iran, Syria, and a variety of Arab countries). They were simple questions when the opposition consisted of clearly identified Iraqi soldiers, but who was the "enemy combatant" now? How were they to be treated, initially? Were there any limitations on their battlefield interrogation? What form of initial due process were they entitled to? How was their detention regulated and what form should it take?

The Joint Intelligence Center, which had been under the XVIIIth Airborne Corps in Afghanistan, was initially assigned to Abu Ghraib and came prepared to obtain intelligence from members of the Iraqi military. The intelligence officers had a "black, grey, white" list that provided information from local and national intelligence sources on many of the Iraqi officials, classifying each according to their function within the military and, later, according to their involvement with insurgent activities. And each detainee came to the camp with a "capture tag" that provided various quantities and qualities of information regarding the circumstances of capture. That information was provided to the Joint Intelligence Center to process and interrogate the detainees, to help spur the quickest possible end of the conflict.

The V Corps Military Police (MP) Brigade initially responsible for detainee activities had a number of different responsibilities. Detachments of the 1st Battalion conducted battlefield circulation missions and ran collection points, to consolidate detainees and speed them to the rear. The 2d Battalion was responsible for running the detention facility for "High-Value Detainees (HVDs)" at the Camp Liberty detention facility, a small detention facility established near Baghdad International Airport that eventually held Saddam Hussein and many of his associates until they could be prosecuted by the Iraqi War Crimes Tribunal. Finally, the 3d Battalion, augmented by several companies from the other two battalions, was responsible for Abu Ghraib, the designated Theater Detention Facility. All three units were trained as general support, Combat Support MP units, trained to perform all the Military Police tasks, from detention and POW processing, to battlefield circulation and combat functions. Within months, a brigade of reserve Military Policemen, specially trained to administer a detention facility, led by a Brigadier General, would be dispatched to relieve the V Corps MPs and assist in the growing mission.

As Abu Ghraib was closed, following the mistreatment allegations that arose in early 2004, the Joint Intelligence Center and the MP unit were re-constituted and Camp Bucca was established. From 2004-2005, until the "surge" in 2007-2009, Camp Bucca would occasionally swell to 20,000 detainees – including civilians rebelling against the coalition "occupation" and the new Iraqi government or providing assistance to rebels, lawful combatants (or members of the Iraqi forces), and "unprivileged belligerents" (insurgents, terrorists, and other irregular forces).

The same reserve Judge Advocate Lieutenant Colonel that was assigned to Abu Ghraib to assist in establishing an initial Theater Detention Facility was also tasked with setting up a more complete Theater Detention Facility at Camp Bucca, farther south in Iraq, in a more secure area, to handle the thousands of detainees that resulted from the growing stability/counter-insurgency operations. During *that period of growth and partially in reaction to the Abu Ghraib investigations, including the Taguba Report, Detention Operations and Camp Bucca would eventually be overseen by a Major General, though the individual camp commander would still be an MP Colonel, responsible for all detention operations within the camp. The same attorney who was assigned to provide advice to Camp Bucca was faced with a number of other issues. It was not just a question of who would be detained and how they would be classified. How were they to be treated? What processes were required? What standards would be applied? Did the CPA Memo 3 designation of non-EPWs as "protected persons" mean that the detention regime must be entirely consistent with the civilian internee approach detailed in Chapter 6? How long could they be detained? Could they be interrogated? And how?*

As the numbers grew, the Military Policemen struggled to provide adequate housing, food, water, latrines, and other facilities for the detainees. They were also challenged to provide security for the facility, with some hardcore fighters who did not want to give up the fight. Riots erupted in Camp Bucca on several occasions, prompting riot control measures and the use of deadly force to prevent escapes and detainee-on-detainee violence. At one point, Major General Miller, who was assigned as the Detention Operations Commander for the Multinational Corps, came out to look at Camp Bucca. He observed that idle detainees were causing unrest in the camp, continuing the fight "within the wire." He initiated methods to employ the detainees, educate them, periodically review their status with enhanced procedures, and increase security within the Theater Detention Facility. His efforts were successful in preventing further violence within the camps and, eventually, turning detention operations over to Iraqi control.

I. Introduction to Detention

For much of the last century, an individual's status as a prisoner of war or a civilian security threat to the force dictated the detention authority, standards, and procedures. Furthermore, detainees failing to qualify for either status were labeled "common criminals," subject to the law of the capturing State. The Geneva Conventions established status qualification criteria, with reciprocal effect for all State parties, even if the treaty itself did not require reciprocity—at least in theory.[1] Throughout the latter half of the twentieth century, internal armed conflicts and unconventional tactics stressed this Geneva equation. In the view of many, this stress culminated in what President Bush labeled the Global War on Terror. Detention and interrogation standards became easily the

---

1. *See* Article 2, common to all four Geneva Conventions, providing for application of the conventions, even if "one of the Powers in the conflict may not be a party." But, as Dieter Fleck points out in his HANDBOOK FOR INTERNATIONAL HUMANITARIAN LAW, 2D ED. (2008), at 689, "Soldiers must treat their opponents in the same manner that they themselves wish to be treated. Although humanitarian protection may not be made subject to reciprocity, the expectation of reciprocal behavior should be the driving force to motivate for better compliance."

most contentious LOAC issues associated with this conflict. Understanding this stress and the controversy associated with U.S. military detention of captured al Qaeda and Taliban operatives necessitates a solid understanding of the underlying LOAC principles related to detention and treatment of wartime captives—an almost inevitable incident of any military operation.

Pursuant to the LOAC, the status or classification of detainees and the nature of the armed conflict dictate treatment standards, to include the "process due" for determining the status of individual detainees. U.S. JAG officers often refer to this equation as the "right type of conflict/right type of person" analysis. As a matter of law, LOAC status and the process (and in many cases treatment) due to the detainee turns on the type of conflict (international armed conflict, belligerent occupation, or non-international armed conflict), and whether the individual detainee satisfies defined individual qualification requirements.[2] This may seem like putting the proverbial cart before the horse. But this equation is central to resolving critical operational questions: what is the authority for detention? How is the status of an individual determined? What process is involved? And what form of treatment is warranted for each class of individuals? And finally, the most important question about war on terror detainee treatment: what does this mean for interrogation standards?

The contemporary complexities of belligerent detainee status and treatment are, in large measure, the consequence of applying a legal regime developed to deal primarily with inter-state conflicts involving hostilities between uniformed belligerents, a world where armies wore uniforms and agreed to abide by the LOAC. Like so many other LOAC issues addressed in this text, applying this legal framework to the reality of conflict between States and increasingly decentralized non-state groups employing unconventional tactics and targeting 'soft' targets is like trying to squeeze a square peg into a round hole. What in one context is a generally straightforward question became increasingly complicated for U.S. forces operating in places like Panama, Somalia, Bosnia, Iraq, and Afghanistan. These forces confront fighters who shed distinctive insignia, routinely hid behind civilians or employed human shields, and often did not even represent a sovereign State. This not only stressed the efficacy of the legal standards for defining status and treatment, but also nullified the self-interest of reciprocity that always provided a foundational pillar for POW status. Today, soldiers fighting for the United States and other State parties to the Geneva Conventions routinely expect abuse, torture, and even beheading if captured, rather than the humane treatment they must extend to the captured insurgent. In such conflicts, is a "golden rule" based historically on a concept of reciprocity able to survive? If not, how and why will the principle of humanity be sustained?

---

2. *See* Chapter 4 on Classification and Status of Persons. *See also* DoD Law of War Manual (Dec. 2016) (hereinafter DoD LOWM), Chapter IV, Classes of Persons.

II. Authority for Detention

The LOAC does not normally authorize conduct; rather it has a "prohibitory effect." Army Field Manual 27-10 notes:

> The law of war [law of armed conflict] places **limits** on the exercise of a belligerent's power in the interests of [protecting both combatants and non-combatants from unnecessary suffering; safeguarding certain fundamental human rights of persons who fall into the hands of the enemy, particularly prisoners of war, the wounded and sick, and civilians; and facilitating the restoration of peace] (emphasis added).[3]

The LOAC also limits the kind or degree of violence [including capture and the level of force applied to captives] to that required by military necessity, with due regard for humanity and honor. These principles provide the foundation for military detention. Captives are detained pursuant to the principle of military necessity in order to prevent them from returning to hostilities or engage in activities threatening the security of the capturing force. Balancing this preventive detention authority is the obligation to respect and protect detainees, to include the obligation to treat them like human beings. These obligations are derived from the Geneva tradition and a tradition of reciprocal treatment. According to the ICRC Commentary before the Geneva Convention Relative to the Treatment of Prisoners of War (Prisoner of War Convention):

> The requirement that protected persons must at all times be humanely treated is the basic theme of the Geneva Conventions. The expression "humanely treated" is taken from The Hague Regulations and the two 1929 Geneva Conventions.
>
> The word "treated" must be understood here in its most general sense as applying to **all** aspects of life. With regard to the concept of humanity, the purpose of the Convention is none other than to define the correct way to behave towards a human being; each individual is desirous of the treatment corresponding to his status and can therefore judge how he should, in turn, treat his fellow human beings. The principal elements of humane treatment are subsequently listed in the Article.
>
> The requirement of humane treatment and the prohibition of certain acts inconsistent with it are general and absolute in character. They are valid at all times, and apply, for example, to cases where repressive measures are legitimately imposed on a protected person, since the dictates of humanity must be respected even if measures of security or repression are being applied. The obligation remains fully valid in relation to persons in prison or interned, whether in the territory of a Party to the conflict or in occupied territory. It is in such situations, when human values appear to be in greatest peril, that the provision assumes its full importance.[4]

---

3. Para. 3(a), DEPARTMENT OF THE ARMY, FIELD MANUAL 27-10, THE LAW OF LAND WARFARE (1956) [FM 27-10]. SEE ALSO DoD LOWM, para. 1.3.3.1.

4. Commentary, Convention (III) Relative to the Treatment of Prisoners of War. Geneva, 12 August 1949 (Jean S. Pictet ed., 1960), at 141 (hereinafter Commentary, Convention (III)). The DoD LOWM also emphasizes a baseline "humane treatment" standard; *see* DoD LOWM, para. 8.2.

The authority to wage war includes as a necessary incident the authority to detain opponents captured during armed conflict. Detention to prevent a captive from returning to hostilities is an incidental authority to the sovereign power to wage war. That power, which implies the power to wage war successfully, triggers the LOAC principle of military necessity, which includes all measures "indispensible for securing the complete submission of the enemy as soon as possible."[5] Accordingly, detention of captured enemy personnel is justified even absent express treaty authorization. It is axiomatic that preventing captured enemy belligerent operatives from returning to hostilities is necessary to bring about the enemy's prompt submission. It is equally axiomatic that the authority to attack and kill enemy operatives implies the authority to capture and detain them in order to prevail in armed conflict. Any other interpretation of the principle of military necessity would deny the State the authority to select the more humane method of disabling the enemy.

This authority to detain may also be derived, by implication, when the State invokes domestic authority to wage war, by whatever domestic process is required for such invocation. As Justice O'Connor noted in *Hamdi v. Rumsfeld*:

> The AUMF [Authorization for Use of Military Force] authorizes the President to use all necessary and appropriate force against nations, organizations, or persons associated with the September 11, 2001, terrorist attacks. There can be no doubt that individuals who fought against the United States in Afghanistan as part of the Taliban, an organization known to have supported the al Qaeda terrorist network responsible for those attacks, are individuals Congress sought to target in passing the AUMF. We conclude that detention of individuals falling into the limited category we are considering, for the duration of the particular conflict in which they were captured, is so fundamental and accepted an incident to war as to be an exercise of the necessary and appropriate force Congress has authorized the President to use. The capture and detention of lawful combatants and the capture, detention, and trial of unlawful combatants, by universal agreement and practice, are important incident[s] of war. The purpose of detention is to prevent captured individuals from returning to the field of battle and taking up arms once again.[6]

Accordingly, in U.S. practice, express statutory authorization to wage war (normally in the form of a joint resolution)[7] triggers the authority to preventively detain captured enemy belligerent operatives. This authority would also be triggered if the President authorized a military response to a sudden attack on the United States or its armed forces abroad, even without congressional action. In short, U.S. forces engaged in armed conflict—even against a non-state enemy employing irregular and unconventional tactics—rely on the customary

---

5. FM 27-10, *supra*, note 2, para. 3(a).
6. *Hamdi v. Rumsfeld*, 542 U.S. 507, at 517 (2004) [*Hamdi*].
7. *See also* 2012 National Defense Authorization Act (NDAA), §1022 (authorizing detention of "member[s] of, or part of, al-Qaeda or an associated force").

principle of military necessity as the legal basis to detain captured opposition personnel.[8]

Decisions by U.S. federal courts on *habeas corpus* petitions filed by al Qaeda and Taliban detainees held by the United States at Guantanamo Bay, Cuba, have also illuminated the source and extent of this authority. On March 13, 2009, the government filed an extremely important response to a consolidated group of *habeas* actions challenging the legality of continued detention of these captives. In that response, the Department of Justice explained the government's legal basis: detentions in the ongoing armed conflict against these two organizations were pursuant to the domestic authority provided by the Authorization for Use of Military Force (AUMF), as "informed by the laws of war."[9]

Subsequent appellate court rulings from the District of Columbia Circuit Court of Appeals have relied almost exclusively on this assertion of domestic statutory authority implicitly invoking the laws and customs of war, echoing Justice O'Connor's *ratio decidendi* from *Hamdi*.[10] These opinions indicate that when Congress authorizes a use of military force it need not explicitly authorize detention of captured enemy operatives. Instead, the invocation of national war powers implicitly triggers the inherent LOAC authority to prevent such captives from returning to hostilities. The LOAC, rather than authorizing detention specifically, "informs" that detention by providing processing and treatment standards for each category of detainee recognized in U.S. practice. Accordingly, in U.S. practice, whether an armed conflict is authorized by joint resolution, declaration of war, or unilateral executive decision, detention authority will invariably turn on two key questions: first, what is the nature of the armed conflict; second, what is the category of the captive?

III. International Armed Conflict Detainee Categories

A. Prisoners of War and Civilians

There are two primary categories of detainees in international armed conflict: prisoners of war and civilian internees. Whether these categories are exclusive is an issue of contemporary debate. However, there is no debate on the validity of these two categories, both of which are defined by a Geneva Convention.

Prisoners of war, defined by Article 4 of the Geneva Convention for the Protection of Prisoners of War (Prisoner of War Convention), include

---

8. *See* DoD LOWM, Para. 8.1.3.1.
9. *See generally*, Respondents' Memorandum Regarding the Government's Detention Authority Relative to Detainees Held at Guantanamo Bay, In re Guantanamo Bay Detainee Litigation, Misc. No. 08-442 (TFH) (D.D.C. Mar. 13, 2009), available at http://www.usdoj.gov/opa/documents/memo-re-det-auth.pdf (last visited Feb. 21, 2011) (Detention Memorandum) and discussion in Chapter 5.
10. *Al-Bihani v. Obama*, 619 F.3d 1, 8 (D.C. Cir. 2010) (en banc).

belligerents who qualify as lawful combatants, as well as civilians accompanying the force and military non-combatants (retained personnel defined by the Geneva Convention for the Amelioration of the Condition of the Wounded and Sick in the Field (GWS)). These individuals all qualify as "protected persons," as the respective Geneva Conventions vest them with special protections. Civilian internees, defined by Articles 42 and 78 of the Geneva Convention for the Protection of Civilians (Civilian Convention), are also "protected persons," a status technically limited only to civilians interned pursuant to the provisions of the Civilians Convention. According to Article 4 of the Civilians Convention, civilians qualify as protected persons only when they "find themselves, in case of a conflict or occupation, in the hands of a Party to the conflict or Occupying Power of which they are not nationals." Technically, this civilian "protected person" category does not include civilians of a neutral State that has diplomatic relations with a belligerent power and can, therefore, provide protection for its nationals via diplomatic relations with the detaining State.[11]

Civilians who are citizens of the enemy State may be detained in the home State of a nation at war if they "voluntarily demand internment" (presumably to be protected from the other residents of their State of domicile), or "if the security of the Detaining Power makes it absolutely necessary."[12] Civilians may also be detained by an occupying power if considered "necessary, for imperative reasons of security, to take safety measures concerning protected persons," according to Article 78 of the Civilians Convention. During belligerent occupation, civilian internees are also called "security detainees" or "security internees" by some nations.[13] Civilians suspected of engaging in activities hostile to the occupying power, to include espionage and saboteur activities, are included within this category. The other type of civilian internee most commonly seen in conflict or an occupation is the "criminal detainee."[14]

Additional Protocol I (Protocol I), while supplementing the Geneva Conventions, did not deviate from this bifurcated characterization of potential detainees in international armed conflict. Like the Conventions, Protocol I recognizes only two categories of individuals in international armed conflict: combatants and civilians. Combatants, as defined by Articles 43-45 of Protocol I, are entitled to prisoner of war status, under provisions for treatment and processing established by the Prisoner of War Convention. Protocol I treats all other detainees as civilians. Protocol I provides no revisions to the definition or status of civilian detainees from that of the Civilians Convention,

---

11. *See* discussion in Chapter 10. For a discussion of this issue in the War on Terror, *see* OFFICE OF LEGAL COUNSEL, DEPARTMENT OF JUSTICE, MEMORANDUM (18 Mar 2004), "'Protected Persons' Status in Occupied Iraq under the Fourth Geneva Convention," available at http://www.justice.gov/olc/2004/gc4mar18.pdf(last visited 22 Jan 2011). SEE ALSO CHAPTER 6 (CIVILIAN PROTECTION CHAPTER), INFRA.

12. Geneva Convention Relative to the Protection of Civilian Persons in Time of War, Art.42 (1949).

13. *See, e.g.,* Coalition Provisional Authority Memorandum 3, "Criminal Procedures," available at http://www.gjpi.org/wp-content/uploads/cpa-memo-3-og.pdf (last visited 17 Jan 2011).

14. *Id.*

with the exception of including within the scope of Article 75 "persons arrested, detained or interned, for actions related to the armed conflict."

B. Unprivileged Belligerents

Contemporary U.S. practice resurrected the significance of what the U.S. considers to be a valid (and longstanding) third category of international armed conflict detainee: the unprivileged belligerent. Many experts challenge this category, insisting that the LOAC recognizes only two categories of individuals: lawful combatants and civilians. However, Article 45 of Protocol I implicitly recognizes this third category of battlefield detainee, lending support to the U.S. position:

> Any person who has taken part in hostilities, who is not entitled to prisoner-of-war status and who does not benefit from more favorable treatment in accordance with the Fourth Convention shall have the right at all times to the protection of Article 75 of this protocol [discussed below].[15]

As this article implies, there is a third category of detainees: belligerent operatives who fail to qualify for lawful combatant status in accordance with the Prisoner of War Convention. Indeed, this article confirms the gap between the Prisoner of War Convention and the Civilians Convention highlighted in the *travaux préparatoires* to these Conventions—the gap that led several States to emphasize that belligerents who failed to qualify for POW status pursuant to the Prisoner of War Convention *were not* to be considered civilians protected by the Civilians Convention.[16] Furthermore, because international armed conflict is the exclusive context in which non-state belligerents may qualify for lawful combatant status (through association with State armed forces), this third category *ipso facto* covers all non-state belligerent forces in non-international armed conflicts.

It is this category of detainee that has generated the most controversy in relation to U.S. detention practice in the war on terror and recent transnational armed conflicts. This is a manifestation of two realities related to contemporary U.S. detention practice. First, the continued international opposition to this categorization; second, the lack of controversy surrounding detainee designations based on the well-settled POW and civilian internee categories. However, because it is unlikely the U.S. will abandon this interpretation of LOAC detainee categories (an interpretation likely to find increasing support by States fighting against non-state belligerent groups), it is essential to consider the process

---

15. Protocol Additional to the Geneva Convention of 12 August 1949, and relating to the Protection of Victims of International Armed Conflicts (Protocol 1), Art. 45 (1977).

16. *See, e.g.,* Internment of Unlawful Combatants Law, 5762-2002, SEFER HA-HUKIM [the official gazette], No. 1834, at 192 (5762-2002) (Israeli Unlawful Combatant Statute, detailing the status and due process applied to individuals who do not qualify for civilian or lawful combatant status, under the LOAC).

and treatment standards for all three categories of detainees: POWs, civilian internees,[17] and unprivileged belligerents.

IV. Detainees in Non-International Armed Conflict

Detainee categorization in non-international armed conflicts is much more complicated than in international armed conflicts. This is the result of several factors. First, LOAC treaty regulation in non-international armed conflict is far less comprehensive than in international armed conflict, necessitating reliance on more amorphous customary international law principles. Second, the law of non-international armed conflict has always reflected a greater deference to domestic law, for the simple reason that non-international armed conflict was historically a domestic contest. Third, as the result of these two influences, the law of non-international armed conflict never defined detainee status with anything close to the precision of the law of international armed conflict, leaving detainee status issues primarily to the State for resolution. Indeed, as Common Article 3 indicates, the primary focus of LOAC non-international armed conflict regulation has been the imposition of minimum humane treatment standards without attempting to define status. Finally, this combination of factors has led many international law experts to assert that the absence of express detainee status provisions in the law of non-international armed conflict indicates that there is no "status" in non-international armed conflict. According to this interpretation of the law, there are no combatants in non-international armed conflict; instead, there are only government armed forces (and police) and civilians. Hence, this approach dictates that non-state belligerents must be treated as civilians for all purposes.

The United States and other States that are now or have in the past engaged in protracted armed struggles against non-state belligerent groups reject this LOAC interpretation. While acknowledging that the applicable law is indeed less definite than the international armed conflict counterpart, these States rely on a simple but critical premise: all armed conflict must, at a minimum, involve a bi-lateral struggle between organized belligerent forces. Accordingly, members of organized armed groups or civilians taking up arms in a non-international armed conflict are not civilians. They are all unprivileged belligerents subject to preventive detention authority analogous to that applicable to a POW. However, unlike the POW, because they do not represent a government they may not qualify for lawful combatant status and immunity. Furthermore, when they are also rebellious citizens of a State, they are fully subject to the State's domestic law criminalizing dissident activities and hostilities against government interests. As a result, these unprivileged belligerents are almost always subject to

---

17. Process and treatment standards for civilian internees, generally, are covered in Chapter 6, Civilian Protection.

detention and prosecution by the detaining State for their warlike acts.[18] Even transnational non-state belligerents (like al Qaeda operatives), because they are unable to claim lawful combatant immunity, will often be subject to criminal sanction pursuant to long-arm statutes enacted by States they seek to harm.[19]

From the inception of the law for non-international armed conflict, Common Article 3 implicitly acknowledged a distinction between the general (inoffensive) civilian population, and organized belligerent forces. Indeed, the humane treatment obligation created by Common Article 3 applied explicitly to such belligerents and hostile civilians, by implying their previous active participation in hostilities when it extended the mandate to:

> "persons [no longer] taking ... active part in the hostilities, including members of armed forces who have laid down their arms and those placed *hors de combat* by sickness, wounds, detention, or any other cause ..."[20]

In contrast, the scope of Additional Protocol II seems broader than that of Common Article 3. Under the approach established for non-international armed conflicts by Additional Protocol II, in Article 5, "Persons whose liberty has been restricted," refers to "persons deprived of their liberty for reasons related to the armed conflict, whether they be interned or detained." This language seems to cover belligerents as well as civilians detained for security reasons. Persons detained in non-international armed conflict are provided minimal protection under the LOAC, however, because States are presumed to be applying their domestic human rights law to their citizens in internal armed conflicts, or rebellions, which are the bulk of the conflicts anticipated by Common Article 3.[21]

---

18. *See* Commentary, Convention (III), at 40. Pictet encourages States Parties, as a matter of policy, however, once the fighting reaches a certain magnitude and the insurgent forces meet the criteria of Art. 4(A)(2) of the GPW, to consider treating insurgent forces consistent with the GPW. Additional Protocol II encourages a similar approach by recommending the broadest possible amnesty for insurgent forces, in Article 6(5), when it says, "At the end of hostilities, the authorities in power shall endeavor to grant the broadest possible amnesty to persons who have participated in the conflict, or those deprived of liberty for reasons related to the armed conflict, whether they are interned or detained."

19. *See* DoD LOWM, Para. 4.19.

20. Geneva Conventions, Common Article 3.

21. Commentary, Convention (III), at 36, "... the Article, in its reduced form, contrary to what might be thought, does not in any way limit the right of a State to put down rebellion, nor does it increase in the slightest the authority of the rebel party. It merely demands respect for certain rules, which were already recognized as essential in all civilized countries, and embodied in the national legislation of the States in question, long before the Convention was signed. What Government would dare to claim before the world, in a case of civil disturbances which could be justly described as mere acts of banditry, that, Article 3 not being applicable, it was entitled to leave the wounded uncared for, to torture and mutilate prisoners and take hostages? No Government can object to observing, in its dealing with enemies, whatever the nature of the conflict between it and them, a few essential rules which it in fact observes daily, under its own laws, when dealing with common criminals."

V. What Process Is Due[22]

What is the nature of the armed conflict, and what is the category of the detainee? As noted above, these two questions will determine detainee status in virtually every situation, producing the axiomatic "right type of conflict/right type of person" analysis for assessing detainee status. However, no matter what the outcome of this status assessment process might be, it is a process, and as a result it is essential that JAGs understand the procedural rights afforded to each category of detainee, and how these rights are implemented in practice. Process established for POWs and civilian internees is the logical start-point of this understanding, for two primary reasons. First, and unsurprisingly, process will be best defined for the detainee categories comprehensively defined by treaty; second, the process established for these two categories of detainees will often, by necessity, provide a baseline from which to analogize when crafting process for less defined categories of detainees.

A. Article 5 Tribunals

Sometimes captives assumed to be POWs will challenge that designation in order to avoid preventive detention. The Prisoner of War Convention provides for a simple process to determine the status of an individual detained on the battlefield in international armed conflict. Article 5 of the Prisoner of War Convention provides:

> Should any doubt arise as to whether persons, having committed a belligerent act and having fallen into the hands of the enemy, belong to any of the categories enumerated in Article 4 [providing for POW criteria, discussed in Chapter 4], such persons shall enjoy the protection of the present Convention until such time as their status has been determined by a competent tribunal.[23]

Article 5 creates a limited particularized process, intended to sort individuals when any doubt exists as to their status.[24] The sole question for determination

---

22. *See* Jelena Pejic, "Procedural Principles and Safeguards for Internment/Administrative Detention in Armed Conflict and Other Situations of Violence," 858 *International Review of the Red Cross* (2005). Jelena Pegic, an attorney for the International Committee of the Red Cross in Geneva, surveys the requirements under the law of armed conflict for the procedural due process of detainees, noting the provisions required by law of armed conflict, as a matter of legal standards, and proposing supplemental measures, generally provided by analogy to Human Rights law or the law of the detaining power.
23. Geneva Convention Relative to the Treatment of Prisoners of War, Aug. 12, 1949, 6 U.S.T.3516, 75 U.N.T.S. 973, art. 5 (hereinafter GPW).
24. *See* Commentary, Convention (III), at 77. Pictet notes, "This [doubt] would apply to deserters, and to persons who accompany the armed forces and have lost their identity card." *See also* DoD LOWM, Para. 4.27.3.

is whether the captive meets the definition of POW in Article 4 of the Prisoner of War Convention.

Detainees typically arrive at a POW facility with a capture tag, explaining the circumstances of their capture. That information is supplemented with intelligence data garnered before, during, and after the conflict, including interrogation of the detainees. The composition and procedures of the tribunal are not described in Art. 5, or by the associated ICRC commentary.[25] Accordingly, composition and process is left to the capturing State (the detaining power in the terms of the Prisoner of War Convention).

During Operation Just Cause in Panama, for example, the United States captured many individuals of uncertain status. The Article 5 tribunal utilized to sort these captives consisted of an attorney from the Army Judge Advocate General's (JAG) Corps, an officer from the Joint Intelligence Center (JIC), and a representative of the Camp Commander (a Military Policeman, or MP). The tribunal conducted a review of the file, including any statement of the detainee, the capture tag, reports received on conduct and activities in the camp, the "black-grey-white" list (compiled before the conflict to define membership in the Panama Defense Force (PDF) and affiliations within the force), and other available intelligence. They then determined the status of the detainee and what category he or she belonged to—PDF, PDF auxiliary or militia, common criminal, or civilian.

Just Cause was, in a sense, a warm-up for Operation Desert Storm in 1991. Article 5 tribunals established at the many POW camps established by U.S. and coalition forces in Kuwait and southern Iraq processed thousands of captured Iraqi personnel. The Article 5 "best practices" used by U.S. forces in both these conflicts provided the foundation for a revised Army Regulation establishing procedures for dealing with captured, detained, and interned personnel. Army Regulation 190-8 is today the primary authority for implementing Prisoner of War Convention Article 5 (and Civilians Convention) procedural obligations. This regulation, applicable to all military services, established more formal procedures, with notice and an opportunity for the detainee to appear, a hearing in the presence of the detainee, and procedures to call witnesses who are reasonably available.[26]

The Article 5 tribunal is provided once, when there is doubt at the time of capture. There is no requirement in the Prisoner of War Convention for periodic review of POW status. Article 118 of the Prisoner of War Convention provides that prisoners of war "shall be released and repatriated without delay after the cessation of hostilities." This provision, along with the underlying purpose

---

25. Id. An earlier draft, allowing for a determination by a "responsible authority," was replaced by the current article, requiring a "competent tribunal." "This amendment was based on the view [of the drafters] that decisions which might have the gravest of consequences should not be left to a single person, who might be of subordinate rank."

26. *See* ARMY REGULATION 190-8, ENEMY PRISONERS OF WAR, RETAINED PERSONS, CIVILIAN INTERNEES, AND OTHER DETAINEES (1997), at 2 [AR 190-8].

for detention, provides the legal basis for interning POWs for the duration of the conflict.[27]

An Article 5 tribunal is required if there is doubt as to a captive's status, but what if the detaining power concludes there is no doubt? In such a situation, is an individual entitled to demand an Article 5 review of his status? This was precisely what occurred when the United States began detaining al Qaeda and Taliban operatives captured in Afghanistan in 2001-2002. President Bush, after consultation with the Department of Defense and the Office of Legal Counsel in the Department of Justice, determined there was "no doubt" that these captives failed to meet the POW qualification requirements of Article 4 (al Qaeda because they were not associated with a state party (wrong type of conflict); and Taliban because they failed to meet the Article 4 requirements for POW status (wrong type of person)).[28] The President, exercising his Commander in Chief authority, designated these detainees "unlawful combatants."[29] As a result, during the initial years of the war on terror, individuals captured in Afghanistan (and certain other locations) were not provided with Article 5 tribunals or any alternate status determination review. Instead, their status resulted from the classified decision to move an individual to Guantanamo Bay for further detention.[30]

Standing alone, Article 5 suggests no impediment to the approach adopted by President Bush. However, Article 45 of Protocol I supplemented Article 5, providing for a status review tribunal if the individual "claims the status of prisoner of war, or if he appears entitled to such status, or if the Party on which he depends claims such status on his behalf."[31] Protocol I therefore indicates that an Article 5 status determination is an individual right applicable to any captive who seeks to contest POW status. Based on U.S. practice, it does not appear the United States is bound by this supplement to Article 5. Although the United States did subsequently implement a status review process for all Guantanamo detainees, it emphasized this was done as a matter of policy and not in order to comply with Article 5—a provision the United States has never conceded applies to these detainees. Because the review process ultimately implemented was analogous to the AR 190-8 Article 5 process, the distinction may appear to be more form than substance, as it is unlikely the United States will return to the original no-review approach in the future. Nonetheless, the distinction remains significant, for it is based on the underlying conclusion that as unlaw-

---

27. Although the Geneva Conventions were signed by States that had just participated in a relatively short conflict, in World War II, some prisoners of war have been held for much longer. For example, a recent quarterly newsletter of the International Committee of the Red Cross showed a picture of a Spanish Air Force pilot, held by the Polisario Front of the Spanish Sahara for 20 years.

28. Memorandum, George W. Bush, to Vice President et. al., Subject: Humane Treatment of Taliban and al Qaeda Detainees (7 Feb 2002), available at http://www2.gwu.edu/~nsarchiv/NSAEBB/NSAEBB127/02.02.07.pdf (hereinafter Bush Memorandum).

29. *Id.*

30. LTC Jeff Bovarnick, "Detainee Review Boards in Afghanistan: From Strategic Liability to Legitimacy," *The Army Lawyer*, (June 2010), at 16, available at http://www.loc.gov/rr/frd/Military_Law/pdf/06-2010.pdf (last visited 16 Jan 2011) [hereinafter, Bovarnick].

31. Additional Protocol I, Art. 45.

ful combatants/unprivileged belligerents, these detainees may not claim the protections of the Prisoner of War Convention. While they may receive analogous status review process, the distinct legal basis for that process is linked to a distinct legal basis for their detention.

B. Procedural Safeguards in the Civilians Convention

As a matter of policy the procedures for review of "security detainees," including "unprivileged belligerents" and others detained because they have "engaged in hostile or belligerent conduct but who are not entitled to treatment as prisoners of war," are adopted for those who fail to qualify for POW status.[32] In addition, States have acknowledged that some form of periodic review is appropriate in non-international armed conflict.[33] In order to effectuate the authority for the internment of civilians who threaten the security of a party to an international armed conflict, the Civilians Convention includes certain internment procedures. However, like the Prisoner of War Convention, the process provided by the treaty is limited and relatively undefined. Article 43, which enumerates procedures for processing civilians detained in the territory of a party to the conflict, provides:

> Any protected person who has been interned or placed in assigned residence shall be entitled to have such action reconsidered as soon as possible by an appropriate court or administrative board designated by the Detaining Power for that purpose. If the internment or placing in assigned residence is maintained, the court or administrative board shall periodically, and at least twice yearly, give consideration to his or her case, with a view to the favorable amendment of the initial decision, if circumstances permit.[34]

It is apparent from the terms of Art. 42 that the Civilians Convention drafters expected civilians subjected to deprivations of liberty in the territory of an enemy State would retain access to the courts of the State. This, coupled with intervention by the Protecting Power (the neutral State or ICRC that represents the interests of persons protected by the Geneva Conventions), would operate to ensure compliance with the Civilians Convention.

The situation of civilians subjected to deprivations of liberty in their own territory by an occupying power is obviously quite different. Unlike their counterparts stranded in the territory of the enemy, these civilians will be subject to the military governing authority of an enemy State. Article 78 of the Civilians Convention establishes the authority and process for the internment of these civilians by an occupying power. Like Art. 42, Art. 78 provides that decisions regarding internment "shall be made according to a regular procedure to be prescribed by the Occupying Power in accordance with the present Convention,"

---

32. *See* FM 27-10, para. 247b. *See also* Coalition Provision Authority Memo 3 (18 June 2003), *available at* http://gjpi.org/wp-content/uploads/cpa-memo-3-og.pdf.
33. *See* DoD LOWM, para. 8.14.2.
34. Geneva Convention IV, Art. 43.

which is widely believed to be a reference to the provisions of Art. 43.[35] Article 78 also provides for review every six months, "by a competent body set up by the said Power." However, similar to Art. 5 of the Prisoner of War Convention, Art. 78 does not enumerate actual review procedures; and like Art. 5, States have been required to implement this process through operational practice.

Accordingly, the procedures for civilian internee administrative boards are very similar to those established for an Article 5 tribunal.[36] The trend in recent operations, however, has been to provide additional process, as a matter of policy, including the support of a "personal representative" to assist the civilian subject to internment prepare his case, and providing increased opportunities for the detainee's witnesses to appear from the point of capture, or their home village.[37] For example, the Multi-National Force Review Committee procedures, applied in Iraq under Coalition Provisional Authority Memorandum 3, and the Detention Review Boards instituted in Afghanistan (though not subject to Article 78) contain similar procedures. These enhanced procedures have been implemented in an effort to determine if the individual represents an ongoing threat justifying internment, while providing notice and an opportunity to respond to detainees and periodic review of internment determinations.[38] Although the procedures required by the LOAC are not very extensive, the provision of additional procedures, as a matter of policy, serves a number of purposes. They enhance legitimacy for the detention process, which is very important in counter-insurgency operations. They also provide a model for future host nation detention to ensure follow-on detention process affords process sufficient to comply with human rights obligations and the law of the detaining power.

C. Detention Process in Non-International Armed Conflict

Procedures for assessing the legality of detaining unprivileged belligerents and civilian security threats in non-international armed conflict are minimal compared to even the general standards applicable to international armed conflict. Preventive detention is explicitly acknowledged by Common Article 3, which applies to "[P]ersons taking no active part in the hostilities, including members of armed forces who have laid down their arms and those placed 'hors de combat' by sickness, wounds, *detention* . . ."[39] However, Common Article 3 did not include any express detention procedures or requirements (other

---

35. *See* Commentary, Convention (IV), at 368.
36. *See, e.g.*, reference to a "board of officers" in AR 190-8, at 19.
37. Bovarnick, at 22.
38. Compare the procedures discussed in Jeffrey Azara, "Is US Detention Policy in Iraq Working?" American Enterprise Institute for Policy Research (1 Jan 2009), available at http://www.aei.org/article/29134 (last visited 22 Jan 2011), with the procedures described by LTC Bovarnick, in the article on Afghanistan's Detainee Review Boards, at Note 32.
39. Common Article 3 (emphasis added).

than the requirement (contained throughout the Geneva Conventions and the Protocols) to refrain from making decisions based on "adverse distinctions founded on race, color, religion or faith, sex, birth or wealth, or any other similar criteria."). The sole procedural focus of Common Article 3 is the proscription against passing of sentences and carrying out executions, without previous judgment pronounced by a "regularly constituted court." While important in relation to criminal prosecution, this provision is unrelated to the preventive detention process.

Protocol II added little to the procedural requirements related to non-international armed conflict detention. Protocol II, like Common Article 3, acknowledges that preventive detention will occur in non-international armed conflict. However, like Common Article 3, Protocol II did not include explicit procedural obligations, instead addressing only peripheral issues. For example, Article 5 provides an oblique reference to due process, reminding parties to a non-international armed conflict that "[I]f it is decided to release persons deprived of their liberty, necessary measures to ensure their safety shall be taken by those so deciding."[40] And Article 6 (5) of Protocol II encourages parties to provide for a general amnesty at the end of hostilities to those who have been detained or interned for "reasons related to armed conflict."

This *lacunae* in the LOAC regulation of non-international armed conflict detention is, in the view of many, partially filled by operation of a provision developed to apply to international armed conflict. As noted earlier, Article 75 was included in Protocol I to expressly extend Common Article 3's humane treatment mandate to international armed conflicts. By its terms, therefore, Article 75 applies during this category of armed conflict. However, Article 75—or perhaps more precisely the principles reflected in Article 75—have evolved to be considered by most nations as a customary law recitation of minimum essential guarantees applicable during any armed conflict—in essence a supplement to Common Article 3.[41] This is especially relevant on the issue of non-international armed conflict detention procedures, because Article 75 provides:

> Any person arrested, detained, or interned for actions related to the armed conflict shall be informed promptly, in a language he understands, of the reasons why these measures have been taken. Except in cases of arrest or detention for penal offenses, such persons shall be released with the minimum delay possible and in any event as soon as the circumstances justifying the arrest, detention or internment have ceased to exist.

Although the U.S. is not a signatory to Protocol I, the U.S. detention policy and doctrine arguably complied with or exceeded the requirements of Article 75. Whether the Article was binding as a reflection of customary international

---

40. Geneva Convention IV, Art. 5.
41. *See*, e.g., Presidential Fact Sheet: New Actions, Guantanamo and Detainee Policy (March 7, 2011) (also providing the administration position on the application of Art. 75, AP I, "out of a sense of legal obligation," to all detainees in an international armed conflict), *available at* http://www.whitehouse.gov/the-press-office/2011/03/07/fact-sheet-new-actions-guant-anamo-and-detainee-policy.

law was, however, never squarely addressed. This led to a significant degree of controversy when the U.S. initiated detention operations at Guantanamo following the September 11, 2001 terrorist attacks. The Bush administration consistently asserted that, while the United States would extend humane treatment to detainees as a matter of policy (subject to the dictates of military necessity), Article 75 did not impose any binding limitation on detention operations. The controversy related to this position was effectively mooted when, in March of 2011, Secretary of State Clinton explicitly asserted that the United States would comply with Article 75 out of a sense of legal obligation during all operations, indicating the United States considers Article 75 a reflection of customary international law.[42]

D. Supplemental Standards for Detention Review: Contemporary U.S. Practice

Periodic review, an independent administrative board, and a chance to view all evidence submitted to the board are not included in these minimum procedural guidelines included within Article 75 of Protocol I. Nonetheless, in large measure responding to Justice O'Connor's plurality opinion in *Hamdi v. Rumsfeld*, the Department of Defense established detainee review boards—first at Guantanamo and later extended to Afghanistan—built upon these procedures. *Hamdi* involved a *habeas* action on behalf of a U.S. citizen detained by the United States based on a determination that he was a member of an enemy belligerent group. Hamdi argued first that the LOAC did not permit his detention, and second that if it did, the summary process utilized to conclude he was an enemy belligerent deprived him of due process.

Hamdi, as an American citizen, was an unusual case. Nonetheless, Justice O'Connnor concluded that his citizenship did not exclude him from the preventive detention authority established by the principle of military necessity which was implicitly invoked by the AUMF. The process used for making the detainability determination was, however, inadequate to comply with the dictates of due process. As a U.S. citizen, Justice O'Connor concluded that Hamdi was entitled, at a minimum, to notice of the basis for detention and a meaningful opportunity to challenge that basis before an impartial decision-maker. The unilateral Executive Branch decision did not come close to satisfying these requirements. Instead, Justice O'Connor suggested compliance with AR 190-8's procedures for conducting an Article 5 Tribunal would satisfy minimum constitutional process.

Although Hamdi was a U.S. citizen, the decision led to the implementation of a detainee review process for all captives transferred to Guantanamo. This process included the type of fundamental process Justice O'Connor indicated

---

42. Statement by Secretary of State Hillary Rodham Clinton, (March 7, 2011), available at: http://still4hill.wordpress.com/2011/03/07/secretary-clinton-reaffirming-americas-commitment-to-humane-treatment-of-detainees/.

would pass constitutional muster for a U.S. citizen; process which applied a domestic administrative due process standard for reviewing the status of alleged unlawful combatants (today called "unprivileged belligerents").

The *Hamdi* opinion is an illustration of blending domestic standards for detention with general LOAC obligations to produce a credible and effective review process. The result was the Combatant Status Review Tribunals (CSRTs), which looked in large measure like Article 5 tribunals, although clearly not created to assess POW status. The CSRTs provided extensive due process, greater than any battlefield tribunal established even pursuant to international armed conflict standards. CSRT procedures included personal representatives, an opportunity to testify before a board of officers, disclosure of unclassified evidence, and the ability to call "reasonably available" witnesses.[43] The CSRT procedures, applied to unlawful combatants detained in Guantanamo Bay, Cuba, were never designed to meet domestic law standards under *habeas corpus*. Accordingly, CSRTs (like other recently established administrative tribunals used to determine LOAC-based detention authority) did not provide legal representation to detainees and were not originally subject to judicial review. While the LOAC does not mandate that level of due process, it is essential for compliance with human rights law[44] and domestic *habeas corpus* rights. This domestic standard was, however, subsequently imposed on the Guantanamo detention process as the result of a *habeas* decision in *Boumediene v. Bush*.[45] In that decision, the Supreme Court held that the constitutional writ of *habeas corpus* ran to non-resident aliens detained by the United States in Guantanamo. The Court extended *habeas* review to these non-citizens, held pursuant to the LOAC, based on three factors: citizenship, the nature of the site of detention, and the practical obstacles to application of *habeas corpus* standards.[46] Justice Kennedy, writing for the majority, then explained that *habeas* review necessitated meaningful judicial review and assistance of counsel to challenge detention.[47]

Boumediene left unresolved the applicability of *habeas corpus* review to other non-resident aliens detained outside the territory of the United States pursuant to LOAC authority. The United States has historically treated LOAC-based detentions as beyond the scope of judicial review. It has also asserted that the only relevant law to assess the legality of such detentions—both substantively and procedurally—is the LOAC and not human rights law, which is more analogous to domestic judicial standards. The *Boumediene* opinion set up a conflict of law between this long-standing U.S. approach of *lex specialis*,

---

43. Deputy Secretary of Defense Memorandum, Subject: Implementation of Combatant Status Review Tribunal Procedures for Unlawful Enemy Combatants Detained at Guantanamo Bay, Cuba (14 Jul 2006), at 1.
44. *See*, e.g., Article 9, INTERNATIONAL COVENANT ON CIVIL AND POLITICAL RIGHTS (ICCPR); Article 9, however, may be derogated in national security emergencies, according to Article 4.
45. *Boumediene v. Bush*, 553 U.S. 723.
46. *Id.*, at 759-760.
47. *Id.*, at 777.

applying only LOAC standards on the battlefield,[48] and extraterritorial application of domestic law and human rights obligations.

One of the factors that complicates this issue is that the United States has always treated human rights treaties, like the International Covenant for Civil and Political Rights, as applicable only within the jurisdiction and control (or territory) of the party State not on far-off battlefields. The potential for extending, as a matter of law, *habeas*-type human rights process to areas of active armed conflict is inconsistent with the consistent "no extraterritorial scope" interpretation of the intersection between human rights law and the LOAC endorsed by numerous administrations. Indeed, this interpretation dates back to the origins of modern human rights law, when Eleanor Roosevelt emphasized this scope limitation during negotiations of the Universal Declaration of Human Rights.[49] Many of our closest allies have, however, abandoned this interpretation, and now concede that human rights standards apply to LOAC detentions.

Will the United States follow the interpretation of its European allies and concede applicability of human rights standards for detention in armed conflict,[50] or will the United States maintain a *lex specialis* approach of treating the LOAC as the exclusive legal regime applicable to wartime detentions? For the time being, at least, that question seems to have been resolved in favor of the traditional *lex specialis* approach. In *Maqaleh v. Gates*, a *habeas* case brought by three alien unlawful combatants detained at Bagram Air Base in Afghanistan, the D.C. Circuit Court ruled that the *Maqaleh* defendants were being held in a site where the practical difficulties of extending the *Boumediene* holding outweighed detainee interests. Accordingly, the court held that pursuant to the Supreme Court's *Boumediene* criteria, *habeas* access did not run to these detainees.[51] How future challenges will be resolved is unclear, but it does appear that the Court has drawn an important distinction between a "mature" detention facility far removed from ongoing and active military operations (Guantanamo), and a detention facility in close proximity to such operations (Bagram). This at least suggests that the military will need to continue to rely on the process of blending domestic and LOAC principles to ensure credible deten-

---

48. *See, e.g.,* Advisory Opinion of the International Court of Justice on the Legality or the Threat or Use of Nuclear Weapons (1996), at 240, available at http://www.icj-cij.org/docket/files/95/7495.pdf?PHPSESSID=0f41467697138187908622a2a94816f4 (last visited 22 Jan 2011), which provides that a conflict between the International Covenant on Civil and Political Rights (Art. 4) and the LOAC must be resolved in favor of the LOAC:

> In principle, the right not arbitrarily to be deprived of one's life applies also in hostilities. The test of what is an arbitrary deprivation of life, however, then falls to be determined by the applicable *lex specialis*, namely, the law applicable in armed conflict which is designed to regulate the conduct of hostilities.

See also DoD LOWM, para. 1.6.3.1 ("...the law of war is the *lex specialis* during situations of armed conflict , and, as such, is the controlling body of law with regard to the conduct of hostilities and the protection of war victims.").

49. Dennis, Michael J., *Application of Human Rights Treaties Extraterritorially in Times of Armed Comflict and Military Occupation*, 99, Am. J. Int'l. 119 (2005).

50. *See, e.g., Al Skeini v. The United Kingdom*, IV Eur. Ct. H. R. Rep. 99 (2011).

51. *Maqaleh v. Gates*, 620 F. Supp. 2d 51, at 77.

tion operations. Indeed, the extension of CSRT-type process to the Afghanistan detention operation is an indication that the United States recognizes that even absent judicial review, supplementing LOAC detention process is essential to such credibility.

E. Ongoing Enhancement of "Law of War Detention" Process

On March 7, 2011, President Obama issued an Executive Order directing the periodic review of detention of the Guantanamo detainees.[52] The periodic review board (PRB) procedures are not substantially different from those applied previously under the policy established by President Bush in 2004 and endorsed by Congress in the Detainee Treatment Act. This previous review framework included not only the initial Combatant Status Review Tribunal, but also an annual file review of the continuing necessity for detention, called an Administrative Review Board.[53] This review framework continued during the first two years of the Obama administration, pursuant to Executive Order 13492. Within the following year, and every three years thereafter, a review board consisting of senior officials designated by agency principals (Secretary of Defense, Attorney General) will review each case to determine if the detainee continues to pose a "significant threat to the security of the United States." The PRB will examine all the evidence available to the government, classified and unclassified, and hear from any witnesses requested by the detainees who are reasonably available to testify.

The PRB panels will provide the detainee notice of the hearing and any unclassified evidence, as well as an unclassified summary of classified evidence. The detainee will receive the assistance of a "personal representative" and/or a private attorney hired at no expense to the government. The detainee may testify before the board, present evidence, and be present for all unclassified sessions of the board. If the PRB is unable to achieve consensus, the case will be presented to the Principals Committee of the National Security Council (the actual principal directors of executive agencies that meet at the committee level[54]) for decision. In addition, a file review board will evaluate each case every

---

52. EXECUTIVE ORDER, PERIODIC REVIEW OF INDIVIDUALS DETAINED AT GUANTANAMO BAY NAVAL STATION PURSUANT TO THE AUTHORIZATION FOR THE USE OF MILITARY FORCE (March 7, 2011), *available at* http://www.whitehouse.gov/sites/default/files/Executive_Order_on_Periodic_Review.pdf.

53. Administrative Review Boards are annual proceedings (in contrast to Combatant Status Review Tribunals, which were conducted only once with regard to an individual detainee) used by the U.S. government to determine the necessity of continued detention of individuals held at the U.S. Navy facility at Guantanamo Bay, Cuba. The ARB is a paper review, and does not involve a hearing.

54. *See* National Security Presidential Decision Directive, SUBJECT: Organization of the National Security Council System, (February 13, 2001), available at: http://www.fas.org/irp/offdocs/nspd/nspd-1.htm, ("The NSC Principals Committee (NSC/PC) will continue to be the senior interagency forum for consideration of policy issues affecting national security, as it has since 1989. The NSC/PC shall have as its regular attendees the Secretary of State, the Secretary of the Treasury, the Secretary of Defense, the Chief of Staff to the President, and the Assistant to the President for National

six months, using procedures to be established by the Secretary of Defense. This administrative board will be required to provide notice to the detainee, review any additional evidence presented by the detainee, and refer the case to a PRB, if the evidence warrants release. The PRB process will also monitor transfers to ensure that detainees recommended for release are expeditiously transferred to their home country or a third country for further rehabilitation or release and ensure they are not tortured or otherwise mistreated. Procedures for conduct of the PRBs were published in 2017. These procedures are similar to previous iterations of administrative boards conducted at Guantanamo, with the changes noted above.[55]

VI. Standard of Treatment

Establishing a legal basis for detention of wartime captives is only one part of the detainee treatment process. Once detention commences, how the detainee is treated also implicates LOAC compliance. Indeed, as will be explained below, establishing treatment standards is the predominate focus of LOAC detention provisions. Like the legal basis itself, those standards will vary based on the nature of the armed conflict, and the category of detainee. It is also important to note that the LOAC is rarely the exclusive source of obligation in relation to detainee treatment. While the treatment of detainees in international and non-international armed conflict is primarily dictated by the LOAC, certain provisions of human rights law, and possibly domestic law, also influence it.[56]

A. Prisoners of War[57]

Prisoners of War must be respected and protected pursuant to the Prisoner of War Convention. Article 13 establishes the basic rule that they are to be humanely treated at all times:

> Any unlawful act or omission by the Detaining Power causing death or seriously endangering the health of a prisoner of war in its custody is prohibited, and will be regarded as a serious breach of the present Convention. In

---

Security Affairs (who shall serve as chair). The Director of Central Intelligence and the Chairman of the Joint Chiefs of Staff shall attend where issues pertaining to their responsibilities and expertise are to be discussed. The Attorney General and the Director of the Office of Management and Budget shall be invited to attend meetings pertaining to their responsibilities.").

55. Deputy Secretary of Defense, Policy Memorandum, Subject: "Implementing Guidelines for Periodic Review of Detainees Held at Guantanamo Bay per Executive Order 13567" (28 Mar. 2017), *available at* http://www.prs.mil/Portals/60/Documents/2017_PRB_Policy_Memo_Signed.pdf, (last visited 23 Feb. 2018).

56. With the exception of overlapping provisions of the Convention Against Torture [applied by the United States to this issue, as a matter of policy, extra-territorially], international human rights law generally has no application to the treatment of detainees.

57. *Compare* DoD LOWM, Chapter IX.

particular, no prisoner of war may be subjected to physical mutilation or to medical or scientific experiments of any kind which are not justified by the medical, dental, or hospital treatment of the prisoner concerned and carried out in his interest.[58]

Likewise, POWs must at all times be protected, particularly against acts of violence or intimidation and against insults and public curiosity. Measures of reprisal against POWs are also strictly prohibited. The following are some of the most important protections afforded to POWs by the Prisoner of War Convention:

- Non-Combatant Status (no longer subject to hostile action)
- Humane Treatment (treatment you would demand for your subordinates)
- Remove from Area of Immediate Danger
- Protection from Elements
- Provide Essential Food, Water, Medicine (respect religious considerations)
- No Medical or Scientific Experiments
- Protection from Insults and Public Curiosity (no parading in public)
- Notice of Capture
- Access to External Communications
- Equality of Treatment
- Free Maintenance and Medical Care
- No Reprisals against Prisoners of War
- Access to the Protecting Power and/or the ICRC
- No Renunciation of Rights
- Combatant Immunity (no criminal punishment for *lawful* pre-capture wartime conduct).[59]

In addition, according to Article 14 of the Prisoner of War Convention, POWs are "entitled in all circumstance to respect for their persons and their honor." Women prisoners must also be treated "with all the regard due to their sex," and may not receive less favorable treatment than men in similar circumstances. POWs may not be "unnecessarily exposed to danger, while awaiting evacuation from a fighting zone" (Art. 19). Along with these proscriptions, the Prisoner of War Convention provides the Detaining Power with extensive prescriptions, or guidance as to the treatment of POWs in captivity. The general prescriptions require POWs be provided the maintenance and medical attention "required by their state of health" (Art. 15). In addition, during their initial stages of captivity, POWs who are being evacuated should be provided "sufficient food and potable water, and with the necessary clothing and medical attention" (Art. 20). They should be evacuated, as quickly as possible, through transit camps, if necessary, to prisoner of war camps established in accordance with the Convention (Art. 48).

---

58. Geneva Convention III, Art. 13, et seq.
59. *Id. See also* Geoffrey S. Corn and Michael L. Schmidt, *"To Be or Not to Be, That Is the Question" Contemporary Military Operations and the Status of Captured Personnel*, 1999 ARMY LAW. 1, 8-14 (1999).

The Prisoner of War Convention provides detailed instructions on how to construct prisoner of war camps and how POWs are to be treated in those camps. The Prisoner of War Convention provides guidance as to the circumstances of detention, including housing, medical care, recreation facilities, food, and internal governance of detainees, as well as external relations, including mail and periodic visits by the Protecting Power and the International Committee of the Red Cross (ICRC). For example, POW housing should be the equivalent of that provided to the military forces of the opponent billeted in the same area; in no case can the conditions be prejudicial to the health of the POW—they must include minimum standards to protect them from dampness and provide adequate heat and light (Art. 25). The medical care should also be sufficient to maintain prisoners in good health, including preventive medicine or equivalent medical attention to that provided to the soldiers of the detaining power (Art. 29-32). POWs are generally provided communal living quarters and facilities that allow for intellectual, educational, and recreational pursuits, to allow them to maintain their physical health, mental health, and morale in extended captivity (Art. 22 & 38).

Operating a POW facility is fraught with challenges, not the least of which is maintaining order and discipline among the POW population. To that end, the detaining power may need to subject POWs to disciplinary or criminal sanction. The Uniform Code of Military Justice—the U.S. military criminal code—accounts for this necessity by subjecting POWs to its criminal proscriptions. This means that POWs are subject to trial by courts-martial for any conduct that violates the Code. This is common practice, and as a result POWs would normally be subject to the military law of the detaining power. The Prisoner of War Convention also addresses this issue by indicating that POWs shall be subject to the law and regulations of the detaining power, and through provisions regulating the use of disciplinary and criminal sanctions against POWs.

Disciplinary procedures, normally in response to failure to follow camp rules, are limited to administrative punishment (like fines, discontinuance of privileges, and close confinement (Art. 89)); penal sanctions, in contrast, should only be used for serious infractions for which administrative discipline will be insufficient. Thus, the Prisoner of War Convention clearly distinguishes disciplinary from penal measures, and expresses a clear preference for the former (Art. 99-108). Criminal procedures for POWs guarantee all judicial processes recognized by civilized peoples, including no *ex post facto* application of the law, representation by counsel, opportunity to cross-examine witnesses, the presumption of innocence, and appellate procedures. In a clear reference to the concept of reciprocity, the Prisoner of War Convention provides that criminal prosecutions should be conducted by a military court, and may only be conducted by a court following procedures identical to that provided under the law of the detaining power to its own service members (Art. 84). Thus, instead of enumerating all requisite criminal procedures, the Prisoner of War Convention attempts to ensure POWs receive fair process by requiring the same process the detaining power utilizes for its own personnel (whether this would always be the outcome is debatable, but certainly for U.S. practice trial by courts-martial would provide quite substantial due process). Finally, the Prisoner of War Convention provides that a POW who successfully escapes and returns to her forces, who is subsequently captured, is immunized for any offenses committed during the escape. However, if the escape attempt fails, the POW may be prosecuted for offenses committed during the attempt.

POWs may also be prosecuted for pre-capture offenses. This will normally be the case when evidence indicates the POW committed a war crime prior to capture. However, it may be that the POW violated the domestic law of the detaining power prior to the initiation of armed conflict. For example, at the time the United States intervened in Panama, General Noriega (and a number of his subordinate officers) had already been indicted for narcotics-related offenses in violation of U.S. federal law committed in the years leading up to Operation Just Cause. Although Noriega qualified for POW status, nothing about that status deprived the United States of exercising criminal jurisdiction on these indictments once Noriega was brought into U.S. jurisdiction. The Prisoner of War Convention does not limit the authority of the detaining power to prosecute for such offenses, or for pre-capture war crimes. However, Art. 86 of the Prisoner of War Convention provides that if convicted for such pre-capture offenses, POWs retain their status and all associated privileges. Accordingly, individuals like General Noriega may be sentenced to criminal confinement, but will be treated as POWs during the period of incarceration. Because the sentence to incarceration may very well extend beyond termination of hostilities, this means that the POW may be confined far longer than required to prevent return to hostilities.

POWs should be provided copies of the Geneva Conventions, as well as camp rules, in a language they understand, so they are informed of their standards of treatment and standards of conduct (Art. 41). Prisoners are under the internal discipline of their own commanding officer, who is charged with communicating to the camp authorities regarding the application of the Prisoner of War Convention (Art. 39). In the alternative, when no officers are present, the POWs may elect their representative (Art. 79). Through their chain of command, or their representatives, POWs may complain about their conditions of captivity; these complaints must be provided directly to the Protecting Power, or in its absence (which is the case in most post-1949 armed conflicts to the ICRC) (Art. 78).

Internal communications and relations with the exterior are intended to provide for internal governance of the prisoners and oversight of POW operations. Prisoners may communicate with relatives through the mail (subject to censorship for security reasons) and, increasingly, through electronic media; they may also receive relief parcels from the ICRC, home, or relief agencies (Arts 70-77). The Detaining Power is responsible for setting up a process for recording information on each POW and communicating that information, via a Protecting Power or the ICRC, to the individual's home country (Art. 122-124). The Protecting Power, or the ICRC, is charged with: receiving reports of detention and transmitting them to the prisoners' home country (Art. 123); providing relief supplies, aided by other relief agencies (Art. 125); and unrestricted visits to the prisoners, in order to ensure compliance with the convention (Art. 126). In turn, the ICRC will provide confidential reports to the detaining power and provide reassurance to POW families, offering its services to improve the treatment of POWs and connect them to their relatives at home. In some cases these services are provided by other relief agencies recognized as legitimate by the Detaining Power (Art. 125). For example, during Operation Just Cause, the Committee of the Green Cross provided many of these services (rather than the ICRC or a local Red Cross Society).

The detaining power may employ POWs for camp administration and improvement of their condition, as well as in domestic industries unrelated to the war effort. Work should be appropriate to the prisoners' age, sex, rank, and physical aptitude and provided "with a view, particularly, to maintaining them in a good state of physical and mental health" (Art. 49). Work in domestic industries cannot be of a "military character or purpose" (Art. 50) and should be regulated in accordance with the detaining power's national safety and employment standards (Art. 51). POWs may provide labor without additional pay to maintain the administration of the camp, improve their conditions, and construct additional facilities (Art. 50). POWs should be protected from humiliating or dangerous work, unless they truly volunteer (Art. 52); and they should be paid appropriately (Art. 54), provided medical care while working (Art. 55), and organized in labor detachments, under their camp leadership (Art. 56). Whether they are working or not, POWs are entitled to be paid by the Detaining Power, in order to provide additional funds for amenities and purchase of additional items at a "canteen"; modern practice, however, has been for the Detaining Power to provide all the amenities required by prisoners, rather than administering funds during captivity.

POWs may be transferred, retained, or released. Transfer may be made to other local camps, or facilities in the territory of the Detaining Power; but such facilities should maintain the same conditions noted above, in any case avoiding treatment that would expose them to greater risk, or be "prejudicial to their health" (Art. 46-48). They also may be transferred to a neutral country, for safekeeping, or medical care, so long as they are provided with equivalent treatment (Art. 109-116); the Detaining Power also retains responsibility, administered by agreement between countries, for the treatment of transferred POWs to allied powers (Art. 12). "Retained personnel," including medical personnel and chaplains, may remain with POWs, though not considered as POWs, and should be granted "all facilities necessary to provide for the medical care of and religious ministration to prisoners of war" (Art. 33). POWs may also be repatriated to their home country, prior to the end of the conflict, particularly if they are retained personnel who are no longer needed or wounded and sick whose health is "gravely diminished," or if the individuals are unlikely to recover within one year (Art. 110).

Art. 118 requires that "Prisoners of war shall be released and repatriated without delay after the cessation of hostilities." Note that the event that triggers the repatriation obligation is cessation of hostilities, *not* termination of the armed conflict. This was a deliberate choice of terminology intended to require repatriation upon dissipation of the necessity for preventive detention, even if a state of war or general tension between the parties in conflict continues. Facilitating repatriation is a key function of the ICRC, and may often involve the support of neutral powers (for example, to provide for transport of POWs). It is also often an important component of a cease-fire or armistice agreement. Even this unambiguous provision is subject to caveats, however; POWs may be retained to serve their judicial sentence, or be extradited to another country for criminal prosecution (Art. 119).[60]

One issue that may arise in relation to repatriation is how to deal with POWs who request not to be repatriated. Article 7 of the Prisoner of War Convention provides that "Prisoners of war may in no circumstances renounce in part or in entirety the rights secured to them by the present Convention..." The Commentary associated with this Article indicates that it was added to the Convention in 1949 "to ensure that prisoners of war in all cases without exception enjoy the protection of the Convention until they are repatriated. It is the last in the series of Articles designed to make that protection inviolable — Article 1 (application in all circumstances), Article 5 on the duration of application, and Article 6 prohibiting agreements in derogation of the Convention."[61] This article protects POWs from being influenced to renounce the protections of the treaty; in essence, they are agents of their State and as such have no individual authority to decide whether or not they want these protections. The article was also intended to protect POWs whose State ceases to exist as the result of armed hostilities by preserving POW status until the termination of all hostilities; and to protect POWs from being impressed into the military service of the detaining power, even if the POW appears to consent to such a change in loyalty.

But what if the POW seeks to renounce the right of repatriation based on a desire to remain in the territory of the detaining power? This situation can present a conflict between the desire to protect the interests of the individual POW and the non-renunciation rule. This conflict first arose at the end of the Korean War, when large numbers of North Korean POWs expressed their opposition to repatriation. Although the 1949 Prisoner of War Convention was not in force at the time the Korean hostilities terminated in 1953, the terms of the treaty were generally applied.[62] North Korea demanded strict compliance with the repatriation provision, and rejected the suggestion that individual POWs could block repatriation based on their individual desires. The United Nation's Command took the opposite view, asserting that general humanitarian principles trumped the repatriation obligation when an individual POW sought refuge in the territory of the detaining power.

While the ICRC Commentary emphasizes that the Korean experience should not be considered a precedent due to the fact that the 1949 Convention

---

60. *See General Manuel Antonio Noriega v. George Pastrana, Warden, FCI Miami, and Hillary Clinton, Secretary of State* (11th Cir., April 8, 2009) (Noriega was extradited to France, over 20 years after his apprehension in Operation Just Cause, after serving his criminal sentence related to drug trafficking in the United States; Noriega retained his POW status throughout his U.S. detention.)

61. Commentary, Convention (III), at 88.

62. *Id.* at 543.

did not apply to the conflict, it nonetheless indicates that exception to the repatriation obligation may be justified based on compelling humanitarian considerations—in essence, a recognition that a POW who can make a colorable claim of refugee status should not be forcibly repatriated against her will. However, the Commentary also emphasizes that extreme care must be taken to ensure that non-repatriation requests be carefully and critically assessed. Ultimately, the Commentary indicates that "[W]hile recognizing the possibility of recourse to general humanitarian rules, one should nevertheless make a rather strict appraisal of each case, since the Third Geneva Convention has certainly not established a system under which repatriation depends solely on the wishes of the prisoner of war concerned. Each case must therefore be dealt with individually, on its own merits. A decision against repatriation must be "reserved for exceptional cases where the dangers involved for the person concerned seems manifestly unjust and grave."[63] Army Regulation 190-8 addresses repatriation obligations and establishes repatriation procedures, but does not address the situation where a POW might request asylum. If such a case were to arise, it is likely that the request would be subjected to inter-agency review (to include the Department of Justice and Immigration and Naturalization). If the claim seems credible, it is doubtful the United States would forcibly repatriate the POW, although this is certainly not a decision that would be made at the tactical or operational levels of command, and would almost certainly require Department of Defense level approval.

B. Civilians

The Civilians Convention expressly protects civilians subjected to belligerent occupation (or who are stranded in the country of an enemy). Long-standing U.S. practice has been to treat those who have engaged in belligerent activities who are not protected by the POW Convention as if they qualified for "protected person" status, under the Civilians Convention (GC). As a matter of policy, for example, Coalition Forces extended "protected person" status to all who were detained for security purposes in Iraq, even after the termination of the occupation phase of the conflict.[64] The practice has also been to derogate from those treatment standards when a person "similarly not entitled to claim [protected person] rights and privileges under GC as would, if exercised in favor of such individual person, be prejudicial to the security of [the party to the conflict]."[65] This is a similar approach to the express derogation provided in Article 5 of the Civilians Convention, which allows a detaining State to withhold communication rights from detainees who are detained as a "spy or saboteur, or as a person under definite suspicion of activity hostile to the security of the Occupying Power." Practice in Iraq, Guantanamo, and Afghanistan was to segregate and

---

63. *Id.* at 549.
64. *See* Coalition Provision Authority Memo 3 (18 June 2003), *available at* http://gjpi.org/wp-content/uploads/cpa-memo-3-og.pdf.
65. U.S. Army, Field Manual 27-10 (1956), para. 248b.

withhold communications privileges for certain individuals who were continuing the conflict "within the wire," or who were believed to be recruiting jihadis for their insurgent activities.

C. Treatment in Non-International Armed Conflict

Individuals (*hors de combat,* or out of combat) detained in the context of non-international armed conflict must, in accordance with Common Article 3, be treated humanely, without any adverse distinction. Although not intended to be exhaustive, Common Article 3 explicitly prohibits the following:

(a) violence to life and person, in particular murder of all kinds, mutilation, cruel treatment and torture;
(b) taking of hostages;
(c) outrages upon personal dignity, in particular, humiliating and degrading treatment;
(d) the passing of sentences and the carrying out of executions without previous judgment pronounced by a regularly constituted court affording all the judicial guarantees which are recognized as indispensible by civilized peoples.

Protocol II, the treaty that supplemented Common Article 3, also explicitly prohibits certain conduct: violence to the life, health, and physical or mental well-being of detained persons; collective punishment; acts of terrorism; rape, enforced prosecution and any form of indecent assault; slavery and the slave trade; pillage; and threats to commit the foregoing acts (Art. 4). But there is precious little guidance as to treatment in either Common Article 3 or Protocol II.

The only treatment standards for detainees in Common Article 3 were indirect, by nature. Common Article 3 provided for medical care for wounded and sick, and oversight by the ICRC, subject to the consent of the state party. Like the prohibitions noted above, Protocol II also elaborated upon the minimum "humane treatment" standards of Common Article 3. Article 5 of Protocol II provides guidance as to "persons whose liberty has been restricted." Like the civilian internees, non-international armed conflict detainees must be given sufficient food and drinking water to maintain health and hygiene, and must be protected "against the rigors of the climate and the dangers of armed conflict." They must be allowed to receive individual or collective relief, practice their religion and receive spiritual assistance, and benefit from the same work standards as the local civilian population. Non-international armed conflict detainees should be segregated between men and women. They should be allowed to send and receive letters and cards (with censorship, as required), provided medical examinations, and protected from the dangers of armed conflict. Finally, penal prosecutions cannot violate the extensive due process provisions discussed above, in Article 75 of Protocol I, or the similar provisions in Article 6 of Protocol II.

A group of nations involved in extra-territorial non-international armed conflicts and peacekeeping operations released a series of "best practices" in 2012 for detention in international military operations after extensive consultations with 24 States and numerous international organizations.[66] These guidelines supplement the provisions of Common Article 3 and Additional Protocol II discussed above with practices which appear to be derived from the law of international armed conflict (e.g., periodic review of detention) and, according to the non-binding Commentary, are consistent with international human rights law.[67] The International Committee of the Red Cross has also led an effort to arrive at a consensus on treatment standards for non-international armed conflict. These efforts were largely rejected at the 2015 meeting of States Parties and representatives of the Red Cross and Red Crescent organizations, as the final resolutions urged further study and consultation with States.[68] By policy, the United States has adopted a "minimum humane treatment" approach that is consistent with all of these references for treatment of detainees in non-international armed conflict.[69]

VII. Interrogation

A. Interrogation in International Armed Conflict

POWs are also protected from any sort of cruelty or maltreatment in the course of interrogation, pursuant to Article 17 of the Prisoner of War Convention:

> Every prisoner of war, when questioned on the subject, is bound to give only his surname, first names and rank, date of birth, and army, regimental, personal or serial number, or failing this, equivalent information. If he willfully infringes this rule, he may render himself liable to a restriction of the privileges accorded to his rank or status. . . . No physical or mental torture, nor any other form of coercion, may be inflicted on prisoners of war to secure from them information of any kind whatsoever. Prisoners of war who refuse to answer may not be threatened, insulted, or exposed to unpleasant or disadvantageous treatment of any kind.

These proscriptions are clear and unequivocal.[70] They do not prohibit the interrogation of POWs, nor do they require any sort of "Miranda warnings" be provided to enemy combatants. But they do prohibit involuntary statements,

---

66. *See Copenhagen Process: Principles and Guidelines*, YIHL, Vol. 16 (2013), pp. 3-32.
67. *Id.*
68. 32d International Conference of the Red Cross and Red Crescent, *Strengthening International humanitarian Law Protecting Persons Deprived of their Liberty* (8-10 Dec 2015), *available at* http://rcrcconference.org/wp-content/uploads/2015/04/32IC-AR-Persons-deprived-of-liberty_EN.pdf.
69. *See* DoD DIRECTIVE 2310.01E, *DoD Detainee Program* (19 Aug 2014); *compare* DoD LOWM, Chapter VIII.
70. *Compare*, DoD LOWM, para. 9.8.

induced by any form of coercion or torture. And the provision banning "disadvantageous treatment of any kind" prevents interrogators from denying the standard of treatment applicable to all POWs to induce prisoners to provide information. Providing positive incentives for POW cooperation is, however, in no way prohibited. In fact, the ICRC Commentary to Art. 17 acknowledges that such practice is both customary and permissible.

The Civilians Convention protects Civilian Internees from the types of physical suffering or torture prohibited against POWs (Art. 32); in addition, no "physical or moral coercion shall be exercised against protected persons, in particular to obtain information from them or from third parties" (Art. 31).[71] This provision and a ban on reprisals against civilians, captives, and the taking of hostages prevent the use of other civilians as leverage to induce civilian internees to provide information.

Finally, coercive or abusive interrogation techniques would also violate the humane treatment mandate reflected in Common Article 3 as extended to international armed conflict explicitly by Art. 75 of Protocol I.[72] Accordingly, while POWs and Civilian Internees are expressly protected from such techniques by specific provisions of the Prisoner of War Convention and Civilians Convention (respectively), even a detainee who does not qualify for such status is protected from these techniques by the baseline humanitarian protections of the LOAC.

B. Interrogation in Non-International Armed Conflict

Common Article 3 protects detainees subjected to interrogation during a non-international armed conflict. As noted above (and throughout this text), this critically important LOAC provision prohibits violence to life and person, mutilation, cruel treatment and torture, hostage taking, and outrages upon personal dignity, including humiliating and degrading treatment. Protocol II adds proscriptions against violence to the health and physical or mental well-being of detained persons, any form of indecent assault, and threats to commit the foregoing acts. These proscriptions establish limitations on interrogation methods utilized during non-international armed conflict (in reality, any armed conflict): insurgencies, civil wars, and transnational armed conflicts. Most of these prohibitions need no elaboration or definition, but "outrages upon personal dignity" or "humiliating and degrading treatment" are less susceptible to easy definitions. For most professional armed forces, there is nothing especially remarkable about these limitations. Indeed, as will be explained below, imposing humanitarian limitations on permissible interrogation techniques has been a consistent feature of U.S. military practice for decades, if not centuries.

---

71. *See* DoD LOWM, para. 10.5.3.1.
72. *See* DoD LOWM, para. 8.2.1.

C. Historical Limitations on Interrogation

The standard for interrogation embraced by the U.S. Army throughout the post-World War II era is based on the Prisoner of War Convention prohibitions against POW coercion, as well as the proscriptions on assaults, cruel treatment, torture, and threats included in the Prisoner of War Convention, the Civilians Convention, and the UCMJ. In large measure a result of the debates surrounding "enhanced interrogation techniques" adopted for use against al Qaeda and Taliban detainees at the inception of the war on terror, the Army Field manual on interrogation that implements this protective standard has attained both iconic and statutory status. Field manuals establish Army doctrine, which is essentially a "how to" guide for subordinate forces developed after careful assessment of "best practices" developed over time. The interrogation FM provided doctrinal guidance to Army interrogators for decades and adopted the Prisoner of War Convention standard prohibiting the use of coercion during interrogation, also prohibiting mistreatment of all other detainees.[73] The 1987 version of the field manual also expanded on the prohibition against the use of force against detainees and proscribed "brainwashing, mental torture, or any other form of mental coercion, to include drugs."[74] The current version of this FM, modified in the face of allegations that U.S. military advisors condoned torture of prisoners during the civil war in El Salvador in the early 1980s, added the requirement that U.S. military advisors eschew "brutal methods" used by host country forces, remove themselves from the scene, and report in accordance with theater command directives.[75]

Another important source of authority related to non-international armed conflict interrogation arose out of the insurgency in Nicaragua that occurred at the same time U.S. advisors were operating in El Salvador. In *Military and Paramilitary Activities in and Against Nicaragua*[76] (the *Nicaragua* case), the International Court of Justice (ICJ) analyzed, *inter alia*, LOAC standards related to interrogation during non-international armed conflict. The court considered the legality of providing advice on how to conduct coercive interrogation contained in manuals allegedly provided by the United States to Contra rebels. The court concluded that the methods in these manuals were contrary to standards of customary "international humanitarian law [law of armed conflict]." The ICJ noted that Common Article 3 was the "minimum yardstick" of conduct for military activities conducted during a non-international armed conflict.[77] It also found that, under general principles of humanitarian law, the United States was bound to:

---

73. U.S. Dep't of Army, Field Manual 34-52, Intelligence Interrogation p. 1-1(May 1987) [hereinafter 1987 Interrogation FM].
74. *Id.*
75. *Id.* p. 9-5.
76. Military and Paramilitary Activities in and Against Nicaragua (Nicar. v. U.S.), 1986 I.C.J. 114, (June 27), *reprinted in* 25 I.L.M. 1023 (1986).
77. *Id.*, at para. 218 (June 27), *reprinted in* 25 I.L.M. 1023 (1986).

> ... refrain from encouragement of persons or groups engaged in the conflict in Nicaragua to commit violations of Common Article 3 of the four Geneva Conventions of 12 August 1949. The manual on "Psychological Operations in Guerrilla Warfare," for the publication and dissemination of which the United States is responsible, advises certain acts which cannot but be regarded as contrary to that article.[78]

The *Nicaragua* decision really just confirmed the practice of U.S. forces. There is no indication that the interrogation methods in the manuals provided to the Contras the ICJ assessed were ever utilized by the U.S. military. The decision did, however, have an important impact by confirming the customary international law status of the Common Article 3 humane treatment mandate, bolstering the Army FM approach to extending humanitarian protections to any detainee subject to interrogation. Universal application of this standard continued, especially after the largely conventional 1991 Persian Gulf War involving hundreds of thousands of U.S. forces engaged in an international armed conflict in Kuwait and southern Iraq. Detainee protection, and by implication limitations on interrogation techniques, was enhanced by several revisions of the U.S. Army Regulation for detention during the 1990s. The 1997 version of this regulation (AR 190-8), which as explained above applies to all military services, added several of the protections afforded by Article 75 of Protocol I and Article 4-6 of Protocol II. Accordingly, this joint service regulation — a source of binding authority within the military — provides equivalent "minimum humane treatment" standards consistent with those of Common Article 3, Protocol I, and Protocol II.[79] The mandate of this regulation, still in effect today, provides:

> **1–5. General protection policy**
> *a.* U.S. policy, relative to the treatment of EPW, Civilian Internee and RP in the custody of the U.S. Armed Forces, is as follows:
>
> (1) All persons captured, detained, interned, or otherwise held in U.S. Armed Forces custody during the course of conflict will be given humanitarian care and treatment from the moment they fall into the hands of U.S. forces until final release or repatriation.
>
> (2) All persons taken into custody by U.S. forces will be provided with the protections of the GPW until some other legal status is determined by competent authority.
>
> (3) The punishment of EPW, CI, and RP known to have, or suspected of having, committed serious offenses will be administered IAW due process of law and under legally constituted authority per the GPW, GC, the Uniform Code of Military Justice and the Manual for Courts Martial.
>
> (4) The inhumane treatment of EPW, CI, and RP is prohibited and is not justified by the stress of combat or with deep provocation. Inhumane treatment is a serious and punishable

---

78. *Id.*, at 129-130, paras. 254-256.
79. U.S. Dep't of Army, Reg. 190-8, Enemy Prisoners of War, Retained Persons, Civilian Internees and Other Detainees (October 1997) [hereinafter AR 190-8].

violation under international law and the Uniform Code of Military Justice (UCMJ).

b. All prisoners will receive humane treatment without regard to race, nationality, religion, political opinion, sex, or other criteria. The following acts are prohibited: murder, torture, corporal punishment, mutilation, the taking of hostages, sensory deprivation, collective punishments, execution without trial by proper authority, and all cruel and degrading treatment.

c. All persons will be respected as human beings. They will be protected against all acts of violence to include rape, forced prostitution, assault and theft, insults, public curiosity, bodily injury, and reprisals of any kind. They will not be subjected to medical or scientific experiments. This list is not exclusive. EPW/RP [Enemy Prisoners of War/Retained Persons] are to be protected from all threats or acts of violence.

Like U.S. military interrogation manuals of this same period, the minimum humane treatment standards for all detainees eschewed maltreatment and coercive interrogation techniques under all circumstances, irrespective of the legal status of the detainee. Events following September 11, 2001 would, however, expose that policy as ultimately malleable.

D. Interrogation in the War on Terror

It was only during the war on terror that interrogation standards were relaxed for "unlawful combatants" seized shortly after September 11, 2001, and then only for a brief period. The determination to obtain timely and accurate intelligence from captured terrorists drove this alteration of treatment standards from the fall of 2001 to late 2008. Ultimately, the Supreme Court, legislation, and policy developments restored traditionally followed LOAC standards for military's treatment and interrogation of detainees.[80] In the interim, the military essentially abandoned its long-standing reliance on LOAC treaties and principles as the baseline for the treatment of detained terrorists, in favor of a narrowly drawn legal position that allowed the U.S. government to selectively use aggressive interrogation and treatment techniques that did not comport with these time-tested standards.

The military legal community at every level resisted this deviation from the traditional application of LOAC standards to all detainees in all operational contexts. However, investigations conducted in response to detainee abuse at the U.S. detention facility in Abu Ghraib, Iraq concluded that some of the aggressive interrogation techniques adopted for unlawful combatants detained

---

80. President Obama's January 22, 2009 Executive Order applied the Army Field Manual standard, discussed *infra* at note 77 and accompanying text, which is based on an international armed conflict standard, to the Central Intelligence Agency's (CIA) interrogation action, withdrawing President Bush's Executive Order 13440. The CIA standard for interrogation is not the subject of this text.

at Guantanamo migrated to other theaters of operations and resulted in mistreatment of detainees in several instances despite the efforts of many Judge Advocates in the chain of command.

This deviation from the traditional LOAC-based approach to detainee treatment and interrogation began when President Bush issued Military Order Number 1 on November 13, 2001. That order mandated the following treatment of captured Al Qaeda terrorists responsible for the attacks on September 11, 2001, those who "aided and abetted," and those who "knowingly harbored" them (to include Taliban detainees):

> Any individual subject to this order shall be –
> (a) Detained at an appropriate location designated by the Secretary of Defense outside or within the United States,
> (b) Treated humanely, without any adverse distinction based on race, color, religion, gender, birth, wealth, or any similar criteria,
> (c) Afforded adequate food, drinking water, shelter, clothing, and medical treatment,
> (d) Allowed the free exercise of religion, consistent with the requirements of such detention,
> (e) And detained in accordance with such other conditions as the Secretary of Defense may prescribe.[81]

The order seems to adopt a Common Article 3 humane treatment standard. However, a subsequent determination made by President Bush indicated that the humane treatment mandated by this order was in fact not analogous to the minimum standards of Common Article 3 and paragraph 1-5 of Army Regulation 190-8. On 7 February 2002, President Bush issued a memorandum specifically addressing treatment of captured Taliban and al Qaeda detainees.[82] This memorandum included the President's determination that detainees captured during the war against al Qaeda and the Taliban did not qualify as POWs. As a result they were not protected by the Prisoner of War Convention, but instead must be treated "humanely and, to the extent appropriate and consistent with military necessity, in a manner consistent with the principles of Geneva." This memorandum was preceded and followed by memoranda from the Department of Justice Office of Legal Counsel (OLC)[83] and the White

---

81. Military Order of November 13, 2001 – Detention, Treatment and Trial of Certain Non-Citizens in the War Against Terrorism, 66 Fed. Reg. 57,833 (2001).

82. Memorandum, President George W. Bush, to Vice President et al., subject: Humane Treatment of al Qaeda and Taliban Detainees (Feb. 7 2002), *available at* http://www2.gwu.edu/~nsarchiv/NSAEBB/NSAEBB127/02.02.07.pdf.

83. *See* Memorandum, U.S. Dep't of Justice Office of the Legal Counsel, to Counsel to the President, subject: Status of Taliban Forces Under Article 4 of the Third Geneva Convention of 1949 (February 7, 2002) (authored by Jay S. Bybee, Assistant Attorney General), available at http://www.usdoj.gov/olc/2002/pub-artc4potusdetermination.pdf. (The OLC is charged with developing legal positions for the Executive branch. These memoranda were prepared to establish the administration positions on the status of captured enemy combatants in the fight against the Taliban and al Qaeda, as well as their treatment.) *See also* Draft Memorandum, John Yoo, Deputy Assistant Attorney General, U.S. Department of Justice & Robert J. Delahunty, Special Counsel, U.S. Department of Justice, to General Counsel, U.S. Department of Defense, subject: Application of Treaties and Laws to al Qaeda

House Counsel,[84] all of which justified this position and exploited the relaxed standards to provide a legal justification for harsh interrogation techniques. Some of these techniques were then adopted by the U.S. interrogators for limited application at Guantanamo Bay and in Afghanistan.

In August of 2002, John Yoo, a Deputy Assistant Attorney General at the Office of Legal Counsel (OLC) (writing for his immediate superior, Jay Bybee), provided an opinion to the General Counsel of the Department of Defense (DOD General Counsel (the legal advisor to the Secretary of Defense), William Haynes) on legally permissible interrogation techniques.[85] This infamous "Torture Memorandum," later repudiated[86] by Yoo's successors, provided broad latitude for the conduct of harsh interrogations. Yoo's opinion excluded unlawful combatant detainees from any LOAC protections, and concluded any violation of U.S. domestic law criminalizing torture (10 USC 2340A, the Torture Statute) requires proof of specific intent to violate the law, which would presumably not be present for U.S. officials that relied on his opinion.[87] In addition, Yoo concluded the "severe pain and suffering" provision of Torture Statute requires "serious physical injury so severe that death, organ failure, or permanent damage resulting in a loss of significant body function will likely result" or "severe mental pain" which exists only if there is "lasting psychological harm, such as seen in mental disorders like post-traumatic stress disorder."[88] Finally, Yoo posited that both "necessity" and "self-defense" would legally justify use of torture to determine key details of an impending al Qaeda threat to national security.[89] Because of the quasi-judicial function of the OLC (establishing the legal standards for the Executive Branch), this legal opinion, coupled with the President's prior findings and other classified legal opinions on specified techniques,[90] laid the foundation for proposed interrogation techniques for use by Civilian Internee[91] and military

---

and Taliban Detainees (Jan. 9, 2002), *available at* http://www2.gwu.edu/%7Ensarchiv/NSAEBB/NSAEBB127/02.01.09.pdf.

84. Memorandum, White House Legal Counsel to President George W. Bush, subject: Decision Re Application of the Geneva Convention on Prisoners of War to the Conflict with Al Qaeda and the Taliban, at 2 (Jan 25, 2002) available at http://www.washingtonpost.com/wp-srv/politics/documents/cheney/gonzales_addington_memo_jan252001.pdf.

85. *See* Memorandum, Assistant Attorney General, Office of Legal Counsel, U.S. Department of Justice, to Counsel to the President, subject: Standards of Conduct for Interrogation under 18 U.S.C. §§ 2340–2340A (Aug. 1, 2002) (authored by Jay Bybee and John Yoo) [hereafter Yoo Memorandum], *available at* http://www2.gwu.edu/~nsarchiv/NSAEBB/NSAEBB127/02.08.01.pdf.

86. Memorandum, Daniel Levin, Acting Assistant Attorney General, Office of Legal Counsel, U.S. Department of Justice, to Deputy Attorney General, subject: Legal Standards Applicable Under 18 U.S.C. §§ 2340-2340a (December 30, 2004) (authored by Mr. Goldsmith) *available at* http://www.usdoj.gov/olc/18usc23402340a2.htm.

87. Yoo Memorandum, *supra*, note 45, section 1.A.

88. *Id.*, section I.C.4.

89. *Id.*, section IV.

90. *See* Memorandum, Assistant Attorney General, Office of Legal Counsel, U.S. Department of Justice, to Acting General Counsel to the Central Intelligence Agency, subject: Interrogation of al Qaeda Operative (Aug. 1, 2002) (authored by Jay Bybee and John Yoo), *available at* http://www.fas.org/irp/agency/doj/olc/zubaydah.pdf.

91. Some of these techniques were, in fact, employed by CIA interrogators at undisclosed locations around the world. *See, e.g.,* Peter Finn and Jody Walsh, "Detainee's Harsh Treatment Foiled No Plots," *Washington Post* (29 Mar 2009), available at http://www.washingtonpost.com/wp-dyn/content/

interrogators that were facially inconsistent with the Geneva Conventions and the "minimum humane treatment" mandate of Common Article 3.

The Department of Defense subsequently considered a list of such techniques proposed for use at Guantanamo by a JAG officer assigned to provide legal advice to the detention facility commander. The request included three categories of techniques, each increasingly more aggressive: Category I included yelling at the detainee, techniques of deception, and false flag (interrogators claiming to be from a harsh allied regime); Category II included stress positions, use of false documents, and up to 30 days of isolation, deprivation of auditory stimuli, prolonged interrogations, removal of comfort items (including religious items), changing hot rations to MREs, removal of clothing, forced grooming, and exploitation of detainee phobias (e.g., fear of dogs); Category III would include use of scenarios threatening death to him or his family, exposure to cold weather or water, use of dripping water to induce "misperception of suffocation" (water-boarding), and use of "mild, non-injurious physical contact."[92] Military law of war experts involved in this study heavily criticized the proposal.[93] Nonetheless, despite objections from the military services, the DOD General Counsel recommended approval of several restricted techniques (which did not include Category III techniques of water-boarding or death threats, but did include "mild, non-injurious physical contact"), to be carefully controlled and personally approved by the Secretary of Defense.[94]

These techniques, approved by the Secretary of Defense in December 2002, were withdrawn in January 2003 after Alberto Mora, the General Counsel of the Navy, threatened to prepare a formal memorandum of non-concurrence for the DOD General Counsel after he was made aware of detainee abuse at Guantanamo (a Naval Base subject to his legal oversight).[95] Shortly thereafter, the DOD General Counsel convened a panel of legal experts to conduct another review of the interrogation techniques; but the committee was told to

---

article/2009/03/28/AR2009032802066.html. As noted above, however, CIA interrogation techniques are not the subject of this text.

92. Memorandum, Director, J-2 to Commander, Joint Task Force 170, subject: Request for Approval of Counter-Resistance Strategies (Oct. 11, 2002), *available at* http://levin.senate.gov/newsroom/supporting/2008/Documents.SASC.061708.pdf, (Tab 8).

93. *See, e.g.,* Memorandum. John Ley Chief, International and Operational Law Division, U.S. Army Office of The Judge Advocate General, to Office of the Army General Counsel, subject: Review – Proposed Counter Review Techniques *available at* http://levin.senate.gov/newsroom/supporting/2008/Documents.SASC.061708.pdf, (Tab 12). The Ley memorandum was attached to a November 2002 memorandum from the Assistant Deputy Chief for Operations and Plans to the Legal Counsel to the Chairman, Joint Chiefs of Staff available at http://levin.senate.gov/newsroom/supporting/2008/Documents.SASC.061708.pdf, (Tab 12).

94. William J. Haynes II, General Counsel, Memorandum for Secretary of Defense, Subject: Counter-Resistance Techniques (27 November 2002), *available at* http://levin.senate.gov/newsroom/supporting/2008/SASC.documents.061708.pdf. Secretary Rumsfeld approved the list of interrogation techniques Mr. Haynes recommended, noting, "I stand for 8-10 hours a day. Why is standing limited to 4 hours?"

95. Memorandum, Navy General Counsel to Inspector General, Department of the Navy, subject: Statement for the Record – Office of General Counsel Involvement in Interrogation Issues (July 7, 2004), at 3, *available at* http://www.newyorker.com/images/pdfs/moramemo.pdf [hereinafter Mora Memorandum].

confine their legal analysis to the contours of a re-issued Yoo memorandum[96] on the applicability of the law of war and humane treatment standards.[97] On 16 April 2003, less than two weeks after the Working Group completed its report,[98] the Secretary of Defense authorized the use of 24 specific interrogation techniques at Guantanamo. While the authorization included such techniques as dietary manipulation, environmental manipulation, and sleep adjustment, it was silent on many of the more aggressive techniques in the original request.[99] Secretary Rumsfeld's authorization did, however, indicate that "[I]f, in your view, you require additional interrogation techniques for a particular detainee, you should provide me, via the Chairman of the Joint Chiefs of Staff, a written request describing the proposed technique, recommended safeguards, and the rationale for applying it with an identified detainee."[100]

The techniques approved on 2 December 2002 were transmitted to Guantanamo for use only at that facility. However, the movement of interrogators between facilities at Guantanamo and others in Iraq and Afghanistan resulted in use of these techniques without authorization in these other operational theaters. The end result of this process contributed to abuses at all three locations.[101] At least one Guantanamo detainee, Mohammed Al Qahtani (the alleged "20th hijacker") was subjected to sleep deprivation for weeks on end, stripped naked, harassed by military working dogs and loud music, made to wear a leash and told to perform dog tricks.[102] Detainees in Afghanistan and Iraq suffered similar abuses.

Soldiers who conducted interrogations at the U.S. detention facility at Bagram Air Base in Afghanistan also claimed they had been authorized to

---

96. Memorandum, John Yoo, Deputy Assistant General Counsel, Department of Justice Office of Legal Counsel, Memorandum, to William J. Haynes, General Counsel, Department of Defense, subject: Military Interrogation of Alien Unlawful Enemy Combatants Held Outside the United States (March 14, 2003), *available at* http://ftp.fas.org/irp/agency/doj/olc-interrogation.pdf.

97. Testimony of Alberto Mora, Congressional Transcript, Senate Armed Services Committee Hearing on Aggressive Interrogation Techniques, Part One, at 145 (June 17, 2008) [hereinafter 17 June 2008 Senate Hearing].

98. Working Group Report on Detainee Interrogation in the Global War on Terrorism: Assessment of Legal, Historical, Policy, and Operational Considerations (April 4, 2003), *available at* http://www.defenselink.mil/news/Jun2004/d20040622doc8.pdf.

99. Memorandum, Secretary of Defense to Commander, U.S. Southern Command, subject: Counter-Resistance Techniques in the War on Terrorism (April 16, 2003) *available at* http://levin.senate.gov/newsroom/supporting/2008/Documents.SASC.061708.pdf, (Tab 23).

100. *Id.*

101. *See* FINAL REPORT OF THE INDEPENDENT PANEL TO REVIEW DoD DETENTION OPERATIONS 36 (Aug. 24, 2004) [hereinafter Schlesinger Report] *available at* http://fl1.findlaw.com/news.findlaw.com/wp/docs/dod/abughraibrpt.pdf. *See also* Major General Fay, Investigating Officer, *AR 15-6 Investigation of the Abu Ghraib Prison and 205th Military Intelligence Brigade*, at 20 (Aug. 25, 2004) [hereinafter Fay Report] *available at* http://www.dod.gov/news/Aug2004/d20040825fay.pdf. *See also* Major General Taguba, Investigation of the 800th Military Police Brigade (March 2004), *available at* http://news.findlaw.com/hdocs/docs/iraq/tagubarpt.html [hereinafter Taguba Report].

102. Bob Woodward, *Detainee Tortured, Says U.S. Official*, WASH. POST (January 14, 2009), *available at* http://www.washingtonpost.com/wp-dyn/content/article/2009/01/13/AR2009011303372.html?hpid=topnews (noting the conclusion of the Military Commissions Convening Authority, Judge Crawford, that Qahtani's charges must be dismissed, due to cumulative actions that amounted to torture).

provide "punishment blows" to detainees who were not cooperating with the interrogation.[103] When their abusive interrogation resulted in the death of a taxi driver (Nabibullah) and several other detainees, they were tried and convicted by court-martial.[104] The criminal misconduct by soldiers using unauthorized interrogation techniques or committing aggravated assault or murder was never linked directly to the policies adopted by the Secretary of Defense. The abuse resulted, at least in part, "from misinterpretation of law or policy" and "confusion about what techniques were permitted,"[105] all of which began with these policies.

All of the investigations of the abuses at Abu Ghraib that evaluated the involvement of the chain of command in the scandal, including the overarching Schlesinger Report, resulted in the same conclusion.[106] The first investigation, regarding alleged military police misconduct and conducted by Major General Antonio Taguba, concluded that there were numerous incidents of "sadistic, blatant, and wanton criminal abuses intentionally inflicted on several detainees from October to December 2003,"[107] and recommended criminal liability for soldiers who engaged in such misconduct. Major General George Fay, who investigated the involvement of military intelligence interrogators, concluded "most of the violent or sexual abuse occurred separately from interrogations and was not caused by uncertainty about law or policy. Soldiers knew they were violating approved techniques and procedures."[108] He also found that the Commander of the Joint Intelligence Center (JIC) at Abu Ghraib, Colonel Thomas Pappas [assisted by Captain Wood, who had previously worked at Bagram], consented to "clothing removal and the use of dogs" without proper authorization from higher headquarters; but those actions did not cause the violent or sexual abuse at Abu Ghraib.[109]

The military's use of "enhanced interrogation techniques" (with one exception, a carefully prescribed "separation technique") ceased after exposure of the detainee abuse at Abu Ghraib. Congress intervened in 2005 when it passed the Detainee Treatment Act (DTA).[110] The DTA proscribed torture, but also permitted certain techniques that pass a Fifth Amendment substantive due process test, which is based on balancing the importance of the governmental interest with the nature of the method used by government agents, prohibiting only conduct that "shocks the conscience." Incorporating this due process test in the

---

103. *See* Tom Lasseter, "Day 2: U.S. Abuse of Detainees Was Routine at Afghanistan Base," McClatchy Newspapers (June 16, 2008), *available at* http://www.mcclatchydc.com/detainees/story/38775.html; *see also* the documentary film by Alex Gibney, Taxi to the Dark Side (released 18 January 2008).
104. *Id.*
105. Fay Report, *supra*, note 56, at 22.
106. *See* Schlesinger Report and Fay Report, *supra*, note 56.
107. Taguba Report, *supra*, note 56, at 16.
108. Fay Report, *supra*, note 94, at 11.
109. *Id.*, at 22.
110. Detainee Treatment Act of 2005, Pub. L. No. 109-148, § 1005(e), 119 Stat. 2680, 2742-44 [hereinafter, DTA].

context of a dire threat to national security,[111] because the law was interpreted as being consistent with the Yoo memoranda, it had little effect on interrogation policy.

Ultimately, it was a Supreme Court decision unrelated to interrogation that resurrected the LOAC-based detainee treatment standard. In *Hamdan v. Rumsfeld*,[112] the Court considered the legality of trying an al Qaeda detainee by a military commission established pursuant to President Bush's Military Order Number 1. Resolution of this issue led the Court to consider applicability of Common Article 3 to unlawful combatants captured in the transnational armed conflict with al Qaeda. A majority of justices rejected the Bush administration's interpretation of Geneva applicability, and concluded that Common Article 3 applied in any armed conflict that does not qualify as an international armed conflict.[113] The implication of this decision on the interrogation debate was immediately clear: because the Court interpreted Common Article 3 to apply to the armed conflict with al Qaeda, even unlawful combatants were protected by this baseline humane treatment obligation.

Immediately following the *Hamdan* decision, Undersecretary for Defense Gordon England issued a memorandum to all elements of the Department of Defense, confirming that all existing Department of Defense orders, policies, orders and doctrine comply with Common Article 3 (other than the commission procedures that the *Hamdan* court found in violation), and directing that all Department of Defense personnel adhere to the humane treatment standards of Common Article 3.[114] This memorandum reconfirmed the "minimum humane treatment policy" of the Department of Defense Law of War Directive (2311.01E). The pre-September 11 practice of full compliance with all provisions of Common Article 3 and the General Protection Policy in paragraph 1-5 of AR 190-8, is, as a result, once again controlling.[115] Furthermore, on 6 September 2006, the Army released a revised Field Manual for interrogation operations, FM 2-22.3. This new interrogation manual elevated the standards from Common Article 3's "minimum humane treatment standards" to the more protective standard of Prisoner of War Convention, Art. 17, requiring compliance with the most protective international armed conflict standard during the interrogation of any detainee.[116] Congress endorsed this more protective

---

111. Michael Garcia, *U.N. Convention Against Torture (CAT): Overview and Application to Interrogation Techniques*, CONGRESSIONAL RESEARCH SERVICE (January 26, 2009), at 6, *available at* http://www.fas.org/sgp/crs/intel/RL32438.pdf.

112. 126 S. Ct. 2749, at 2795 (2006).

113. *Id.* at 2795 (2006).

114. Department of Defense Memorandum, "Application of Common Article 3 of the Geneva Conventions to the Treatment of Detainees in the Department of Defense" (July 7, 2006) *available at* http://www.defense.gov/pubs/pdfs/DepSecDef%20memo%20on%20common%20article%203.pdf (last visited Aug. 11, 2010).

115. U.S. DEP'T OF DEFENSE, DIRECTIVE 2310.01E , DoD DETAINEE PROGRAM, Enclosure A (Sept. 5, 2006) [hereinafter DoD DIR. 2310.01E].

116. U.S. DEP'T OF ARMY, FIELD MANUAL 2-22.3, HUMAN INTELLIGENCE COLLECTOR OPERATIONS (Sept. 6, 2006) [hereinafter FM 2-22.3].

approach by including in the DTA a provision indicating that the Army Field manual techniques are the exclusive techniques permitted for use by U.S. interrogators.[117]

The debate over the harsh interrogation techniques authorized for use against unlawful combatants, the process that led to that authorization, and responsibility for subsequent abuses continues to this day. Did these techniques qualify as torture? Should senior government officials, to include President Bush, be held accountable for criminal violations? Why were the concerns of military legal advisors dismissed? These are all important questions, but ultimately beyond the scope of this Chapter. What is clearly within the scope, however, is the transcendent lesson learned from this brief but significant deviation from the traditional approach of extending LOAC treatment standards to all detainees. It has never been established that an unbroken chain of orders and supervisory responsibility linked the abuses at Abu Ghraib to Secretary Rumsfeld's authorization for use of harsh interrogation techniques.

That authorization stands, however, as a clear leadership failure and, at a minimum, establishes moral responsibility for the corrosion of standards applied at Guantanamo, Bagram, and Abu Ghraib. Interpreting the LOAC to justify abusive treatment of wartime detainees perverted the underlying principles of the Conventions and distorted the logic of conflict regulation. It also produced a corrosive effect on subordinates who were empowered to make their own value judgments on whether a detainee in Iraq or Afghanistan was morally worthy of humane treatment. This is not a judgment soldiers should ever be entitled to make. Instead, offsetting the instincts generated by the brutality of armed conflict necessitates constant emphasis on the principle of humanity that must permeate all military policies and orders.

Military leaders have long understood this imperative, which was central to the Department of Defense policy of extending LOAC principles to all detention operations. Restoration with enhancement of this core ethos is perhaps the one beneficial outcome of the brief but significant deviation from this tradition. Contrary to the opinions relied on by Secretary Rumsfeld to authorize harsh interrogation techniques, no person subject to the absolute control of the military should be excluded from humanitarian protections—military necessity cannot justify "whatever it takes" to extract information from detainees. From the Lieber Code's categorical prohibition against the use of torture to extract information from prisoners (adopted at a time when the nation faced perhaps the greatest challenge ever to its survival), to the development of Common Article 3, Protocol II, and Art. 75 of Protocol I, to the adoption of the Department of Defense Law of War Directive and the extension of humane treatment to all military operations, U.S. military practice and international law have continuously evolved to stress the importance of this baseline treatment standard.

---

117. DTA, §1002(a).

Appendix 1: Detention in International Armed Conflicts

Type of Detainee	Basis for Detention	Justification for Detention	Detention Process	Duration of Detention	Limits on Location of Detention	Disciplinary Authority
POW	Prevent Return to Hostilities	Presumed Threat based on Status	Presumed based on Status; Art. 5 When Status in Doubt	Until Termination of Hostilities	Remove from Immediate Conflict Area	Subject to U.S. Military Criminal Code (UCMJ)
Civilian	Protect Friendly Forces from Imperative Security Risk	Actual Threat based on Conduct	Notice and Hearing; Periodic Review	Until Risk to Force Dissipates	May not Remove from National Territory	Subject to Domestic Law of Occupied Territory
Unprivileged Belligerent	Prevent Return to Hostilities	Presumed Threat based on Membership in Hostile Group	Policy: Notice, Opportunity to be Heard; Periodic Review	Until Termination of Hostilities	None	Military Commission Act
Criminal Convict	Punish for Criminal Misconduct	Actual Violation of Local Criminal Law	In Accordance with Local Law	Until Sentence is Complete	None, Unless Protected Civilians Remain in Territory	Local Criminal Law
Spy	Protect Friendly Forces and Prevent Transmission of Information	Espionage Activity Against Friendly Forces	Internment; Restricted from External Communication	Criminal Sentence or Until No Longer a Threat	None	Subject to Domestic Law of Occupied Territory

Appendix 2: Detention During Non-International Armed Conflicts

Type of Detainee	Basis for Detention	Justification for Detention	Detention Process	Duration of Detention	Limits on Location of Detention	Disciplinary Authority
POW	N/A	N/A	N/A	N/A	N/A	N/A
Civilian	Protect Friendly Forces from Imperative Security Risk	Actual Threat Based on Conduct	Contingent on Domestic Legislation	Until Risk to Force Dissipates	Removed from Immediate Threat of Hostilities	Subject to Domestic Law of Detaining Power
Unprivileged Belligerent	Prevent Return to Hostilities	Presumed Threat based on Membership in Hostile Group	Policy: Notice, Opportunity to be Heard; Periodic Review	Until Hostilities Terminate or No Longer Threat	Removed from Immediate Threat of Hostilities	Subject to Domestic Law of Detaining Power
Criminal Convict	Punish for Criminal Misconduct	Actual Violation of Local Criminal Law	In Accordance with Local Law	Until Sentence is Complete	None, Unless Protected Civilian Remains in Territory	Local Criminal Law
Spy	Protect Friendly Forces and Prevent Transmission of Information	Espionage Activity Against Friendly Forces	Contingent on Domestic Law of Detaining Power	Criminal Sentence or Until No Longer a Threat	None	Subject to Domestic Law of Detaining Power

Study Problems

You are the attorney assigned to Camp Bucca, to provide advice for the Joint Intelligence Center (JIC) and the MPs. How do you address the following issues?

1. The Commander of the JIC proposes to use the Category I-III interrogation techniques, discussed above. What is wrong with those techniques, from a law of international armed conflict or non-international armed conflict perspective?
2. Soon a myriad of individuals begin to pour into Camp Bucca: Uniformed Republican Guard, irregular Saddam Fedayeen, and, later, organized armed groups like al Qaeda in Iraq and Sadr's militia, unaffiliated civilians who were protecting their neighborhoods; criminals and others all begin to arrive. Who has the authority to detain them? How should the military sort them?
3. A year has gone by. What procedures should have been implemented in the interim? Is the process discussed above sufficient, over time? Is President Obama's Executive Order from 7 March 2011 sufficient for long-term detainees?
4. What are some of the most important standards of treatment for POWs? Do some of these standards appear "quaint" or anachronistic, as President Bush's White House Counsel once suggested?
5. Once the nature of the conflict changes and becomes a non-international armed conflict, how do the treatment standards change? Should detainee treatment standards change with the scope of the conflict? Is there another regime that is more appropriate?
6. What accommodations should be made for "jihadis" who present a continuing security threat during their detention? What use of force is permitted within the detention center to stop riots or prevent escape?

6 | Civilian Protection Law

It is early April, 2003, though you aren't exactly sure of the date. Since your unit participated in the invasion of Iraq in March, time has been measured by how many kilometers into Iraq you have advanced and how many times you have set up and then torn down and relocated your Infantry Division's Tactical Operations Center. You are a Judge Advocate in the U.S. Army and were just told to find and grab your gear (a rucksack and a duffle bag), and report to the newly established Civil Military Operations Center (CMOC), hastily established by your unit's Civil Affairs section. You learn that the CMOC is in the Iraqi town of al-Khalis, approximately 50 miles north of Baghdad and 40 miles west of the Iran/Iraq border. After several hours, your paralegal Non-Commissioned Officer, Sergeant Puzon, tells you he has good news and bad news. The bad news is that your duffle bag is amidst several hundred bags in a vehicle that no one seems to know the location of. The good news is that Sergeant Puzon has found several other members of the TOC who need to travel to al-Khalis and together you have enough vehicles to comply with the Division Tactical Standard Operating Procedure that unarmored vehicles must travel in at least a four-vehicle convoy. You arrive in al-Khalis and find the CMOC.

Almost as soon as you walk into the large tent that houses the CMOC, you are approached by U.S. Army Major Smith, the CMOC Officer in Charge (OIC), whom you have never met. Major Smith immediately asks if you are the lawyer and seems very glad that you've arrived. Over the noise of generators, she explains why she requested a military lawyer be sent to work on her staff. She updates you that while the intensity of the fighting continues to wane, questions and even accusations of misconduct during U.S. military operations are on the rise, and starting to receive media attention.

"We are getting all kinds of questions, from local Iraqis, governmental, non-governmental, and humanitarian organizations, media from all over. Heck, we are even getting questions from other parts of the U.S. government. We can answer some of them. But a lot of people are claiming our operations – and in

particular treatment of local civilians – are inconsistent with our international legal obligations. That's why I asked for you. Let me bring you up to speed on some of the events which seem to be behind a lot of the questions:

- *We have been set up for less than three days. But you name it, they have already been here. Women, children, the elderly, Iraqis, Iranians, Syrians, Jordanians, and whatever a Yazidi is. We only have three interpreters. Though we did have someone who speaks perfect English. He was waving an American passport and saying he was from West Chester, Pennsylvania. Why he is in the middle of a war zone I have no clue. Another guy looked like he may have been Iraqi Army, he was still wearing half a uniform. All saying they have rights and demanding protection from the U.S. forces.*
- *Several groups of Iraqis have approached us saying that their relatives were wounded or killed as a result of U.S. airstrikes or engagements between U.S. forces and the Iraqi Army. Some journalist just asked us to comment on 'U.S. War Crimes.'*
- *We just had a local Iraqi family come in, asking where they were supposed to live. They said the crew of a U.S. Army armored vehicle ordered them out of their house and then leveled it. When they asked why this was happening, the soldier in charge told them their house was 'in the way.' I have no idea whether that happened and if it did, whether it was one of our vehicles or some other units.*
- *Some civilians have claimed we destroyed their cars. I don't have a cell phone. These guys not only have phones — have you heard of a "GoPro" camera?[1] I'd never heard of it, but one of them has one and recorded a tank from our very own 2/64 Armor Battalion crushing a civilian car.[2] You can hear our guys saying the Iraqis were looting, which they deny.*
- *I'm receiving reports of some kind of camp outside of town that has thousands of Iranians in it. Camp has obviously been there for a while. Let me know which part of this is supposed to make sense to me: Iranians, living in a camp in Iraq, sent a note to the Americans demanding that we recognize and treat them as protected persons.*
- *Finally, and before you ask, the kid over there flex-cuffed to the tent is named Akram. Akram tried to grab some gear out of one of the Humvees, so we have him in time out till we figure out what to do with him. The Military Police have suggested that they build a detention facility for folks like Akram, though the Platoon Sergeant joked that we should detain every military-age male in the area and prevent problems from being problems. At least I think he was joking.*

---

1. The 2003 U.S. invasion of Iraq was the first U.S. combat operation where service members and the local population could access the internet, social media, and cell phones capable of taking pictures and filming videos, which created both opportunities and issues for the U.S. military. On the other hand, in the spring of 2003, Facebook would not be created for another year and YouTube not for another two years.

2. *See* PBS Frontline, *Truth, War, and Consequences* https://www.youtube.com/watch?v=0TDse_VAKlk (beginning at the 7:20 mark and continuing to the 8:40 mark depicts U.S. Army Soldiers during the 2003 invasion of Iraq encountering suspected Iraqi looters and crushing their civilian vehicle with an M1 tank).

I need you to get me up to speed on the law here. Our pre-deployment briefing, said the LOAC requires us to protect civilians. But what does that mean? Treat everyone the same? Including the Iranians? Are we just protecting people? What about their property? And what about Akram? I don't want to keep him, but if we cut him loose he's just going to try to steal again, or worse."

I. Introduction

As explained in several chapters of this book, one of the great developments in the *jus belli* was the rejection of the "total war" concept in favor of a more limited conception of war. Pursuant to the foundational principle of military necessity, only certain qualifying individuals, equipment, capabilities, and other objects that qualify as military objectives may be made the deliberate object of attack. By implication, this means that unlike earlier eras, armed conflict does not and cannot justify subjecting an entire population to the deliberate infliction of violence. Instead, civilians are protected from being made the deliberate object of attack. While this protection is not absolute, it nonetheless represents a profoundly important pillar in the framework of conflict regulation.

The legal protections the LOAC affords to civilians developed more slowly than those afforded to vulnerable military members: those wounded, sick, and captured. That's because extensive risk to the civilian population from the effects of war is a relatively recent occurrence. In 1864, when the first Geneva Conventions were adopted, wars were generally confined to limited geographic areas, normally removed from civilian population centers. As discussed in Chapter 3, the modern Red Cross movement began following Swiss businessman Henry Dunant, detailing the horrific aftermath of the 1859 Battle of Solferino in northern Italy.[3] Roughly 40,000 soldiers were wounded or killed, yet only one civilian died.[4] However, as the nature and capability of military weaponry evolved, both in range and effect, the protection temporal separation from armed conflict afforded civilians dissipated.

---

3. The Battle of Solferino was actually three separate battles fought *near* the town of Solferino. Contrast that with the 2017 battle for Mosul, Iraq, between Iraq and its coalition allies against the Islamic State, or ISIS. There, the "Battle of Mosul" means not near, but *in* the city, and amidst over 1 million civilian inhabitants.

4. "Civilians Bear Brunt of the Changing Nature of Hostilities," ICRC Interview with Pierre Krähenbühl, DICRC Director of Operations Jun. 23 2009
https://www.icrc.org/eng/resources/documents/interview/research-interview-240609.htm.

World War I claimed the lives of more civilians than soldiers.[5] That trend unfortunately not only continued, but exponentially worsened in World War II.[6] As a result, in drafting the 1949 Geneva Convention Relative to the Protection of Civilian Persons in Time of War (GCC),[7] the international community made a determined effort to improve humanitarian protections for civilians. But the drafters sought to address this issue through a specific context or lens: the civilian abuses that occurred when one country's military occupied the territory of another during the war. As a result, the GC focuses on enhancing protection for civilians under the authority of an enemy state, either as a result of an enemy occupation or being stranded in enemy territory during an international armed conflict (IAC). There is very little in the GCC that addresses death and injury of civilians or destruction or damage of their property resulting from combat operations. Such protections were not fully extant in the LOAC until the development of the Additional Protocols to the Geneva Conventions in 1977.

The vast majority of LOAC protections to civilians are found in IAC law, the law applicable to international armed conflicts like World War II. Yet the vast majority of armed conflicts occurring in the second half of the twentieth century and into this century have been non-international armed conflict (NIACs).[8] As the United Nations' Children's Fund stated:

> Modern warfare is often less a matter of confrontation between professional armies than one of grinding struggles between military and civilians in the same country, or between hostile groups of armed civilians. More and more wars are essentially low-intensity internal conflicts, and they are lasting longer. The days of set-piece battles between professional soldiers facing off in a field far from town are long gone. Today, wars are fought from apartment windows and in the lanes of villages and suburbs, where distinctions between combatant and non-combatant quickly melt away.[9]

---

5. While estimates vary depending on how directly one considers causation, one European Centre contends that there were roughly 20 million deaths in World I, approximately 9.7 million of which were military and roughly 10 million of which were civilians. *See* Robert Schuman Centre for Advanced Studies, *World War I Casualties* (2011) http://www.centre-robert-schuman.org/userfiles/files/REPERES%20%E2%80%93%20module%201-1%20-%20explanatory%20notes%20%E2%80%93%20World%20War%20I%20casualties%20%E2%80%93%20EN.pdf. Scholars continue to disagree over the ratio of civilians to soldiers killed. The ratio of civilians to soldiers killed remains in disagreement. *See*, e.g. COUNTING CIVILIAN CASUALTIES: AN INTRODUCTION (ed. Taylor B. Seybolt & Jay D. Aronson) (2013); Adam Roberts, *"Lives and Statistics: Are 90% of War Victims Civilians?"* 52 SURVIVAL 115 (2010) and Valerie Epps, *Civilian Casualties in Modern Warfare: The Death of the Collateral Damage Rule*, 41 GA. J. INT'L & COMP. L 307 (2013).

6. *See* Neil Halloran, *The Fallen of World War II* https://vimeo.com/128373915. This award winning animated data driven documentary depicts the "human cost of the Second World War." The discussion of civilian deaths begins at roughly the 7:30 mark.

7. Geneva Convention Relative to the Protection of Civilian Persons in Time of War, art. 3, Aug. 12, 1949, 6 U.S.T. 3516, 75 U.N.T.S 287 (hereinafter GC).

8. Uppsala Conflict Data Program, Armed Conflicts By Type and Year Armed Conflict By Type, 1946-2016 Uppsala Conflict Data Program (2017). Estimates are that over the past 50 years, over 90% of the armed conflicts have been NIACs.

9. United Nations Children Fund, "Patterns in Conflict: Civilians Are Now the Target" available at https://www.unicef.org/graca/patterns.htm.

I. Introduction

Civilian suffering in contemporary conflicts is due to more than just shifting from intrastate conflicts on open fields to interstate street battles. Parties to conflict are increasingly deliberating targeting civilians and their property *because* they are more vulnerable, and in an attempt to destabilize, demoralize, and in some cases to destroy ethnic or religious groups. In 1996, the United Nations Expert on the Impact of Armed Conflict on Children issued a report, writing that:

> In 1995, 30 major armed conflicts raged in different locations around the world. All of them took place within States, between factions split along ethnic, religious or cultural lines. The conflicts destroyed crops, places of worship and schools. Nothing was spared, held sacred or protected—not children, families or communities. In the past decade, an estimated two million children have been killed in armed conflict. Three times as many have been seriously injured or permanently disabled, many of them maimed by landmines. Countless others have been forced to witness or even to take part in horrifying acts of violence. These statistics are shocking enough, but more chilling is the conclusion to be drawn from them: more and more of the world is being sucked into a desolate moral vacuum. This is a space devoid of the most basic human values; a space in which children are slaughtered, raped, and maimed; a space in which children are exploited as soldiers; a space in which children are starved and exposed to extreme brutality. Such unregulated terror and violence speak of deliberate victimization. There are few further depths to which humanity can sink.[10]

Protecting the civilian population, and to lesser extent civilian property, is at the very core of the LOAC. Yet how can that be true while at the same time civilians are increasingly suffering the effects of armed conflict? Is the problem the result of gaps in the law, the inability of parties to conflicts to follow and enforce existing law, or maybe some combination of both?

To understand the LOAC's civilian protection regime, this chapter considers different functional areas of the law and their varied applications across the wide spectrum of situations in which civilians are the unintended recipients of derivative effects of armed conflict. This chapter reinforces concepts discussed in Chapter 4 (Classification and Status of Persons) and Chapter 10 (Occupation).

After explaining the concept and reiterating the definition of civilians in the LOAC, the first protection discussed is from the harmful effects of hostilities, meaning when parties to conflict are using force in or near civilian populated areas. Second is the protection from maltreatment at the hands of a party to the conflict. Third is the special protections the LOAC affords for especially vulnerable civilians, including children and the elderly. Fourth is protection from unlawful interference by a party to the conflict, whether restricting or

---

10. Note by the Secretary General, Promotion and Protection of the Rights of Children Impact of Armed Conflict on Children U.N. Doc. A/51/306 Aug. 26 1996 http://www.un.org/ga/search/view_doc.asp?symbol=A/51/306. The report argued that more children had been killed than soldiers in contemporary conflicts. Sadly, contemporary conflicts at the time of this writing in Syria, Mynamar, and Yemen, among other places, demonstrate that humanity can indeed sink lower.

requiring displacement and relocation or the seizure of private property. Fifth are a series of protections provided to civilians detained because their conduct posed a security threat. The chapter ends with a discussion on the relationship between LOAC and international human rights law.

A. The Concept of Civilian

"Civilian" is one of the broadest—and most misunderstood—terms in the LOAC. Its breadth stems from the ubiquitous presence of civilians amidst armed conflict, and the wide-ranging circumstances by which civilians come into contact with the effects of that conflict. That the U.S. military has formalized the process of planning for and managing issues related to civilians in the operational area—the CMOC—is an indication of just how prevalent the civilianization of the battlefield has become.[11]

From a practical perspective, ensuring compliance with LOAC provisions related to the protection of the civilian population involves a two-step methodology. First and most obviously, it is imperative to know which individuals are properly considered "civilian"—a term that, remained undefined until 1977. Second, a combination of factors must be assessed to determine the precise nature of the issue and the law applicable to its resolution. These factors include the type of the civilian (because, as will be explained below, some civilians receive more robust protections or shields than others), where the civilian is located, and the manner by which they are experiencing war's impacts. In contemporary conflicts, one need only consider the wide range of non-military actors connected to or impacted by the hostilities, including but certainly not limited to a wide range of contractors, journalists, non-governmental and humanitarian organizations, as well as the more traditional notion of the civilian population, citizens and non-citizens, living in or just trying to move through, or away from, the zone of conflict.

Civilian protection must begin with the clear and undisputed maxim: no civilian falls outside the LOAC protective shield. This, however, is merely the start-point of understanding civilian protections in armed conflict. That is because the extent of the protections afforded to civilians is not constant, but fluctuates based on the variables outlined in the preceding paragraph. Accordingly, it is useful to think of civilians as "beneficiaries" with the LOAC providing variable "benefit" packages or shields. While each civilian receives a shield from the LOAC, and some civilians receive several, not all shields are identical. Determining which shield applies to any individual civilian therefore is the key to understanding precisely how the LOAC protects the civilian population writ large, and how these protections impact the planning and execution of military operations. The complexity of this analysis, coupled with

---

11. For more information on how the U.S. Department of Defense views civil-military operations, *see* Department of Defense Joint Publication 3-57, CIVIL-MILITARY OPERATIONS (11 Sept. 2013)http://www.dtic.mil/doctrine/new_pubs/jp3_57.pdf.

the overlying policy considerations that often result in providing more robust benefits for civilians even when they are not required as a matter of law, reveals why factoring civilian relationship issues into the planning for military operations is so essential to mission accomplishment.

B. Who Is a Civilian within the Meaning of the LOAC?

As discussed in Chapter 4, no LOAC treaty defined "civilian" until the 1977 Additional Protocol I. According to Article 50 of this treaty, a civilian is any person who does not belong to one of the categories of persons referred to in Article 4 A (1), (2), (3), and (6) of the Prisoner of War Convention (GPW) or the modified definition of armed forces in Article 43 of AP I.[12] The end result is that "apart from members of the armed forces, everybody physically present in a territory is a civilian."[13]

Before discussing the LOAC protections that apply to civilians, the formulation of the terms civilian in the LOAC warrants some discussion.

The absence of a definition of "civilian" was the source of uncertainty regarding their protection. While a customary understanding certainly guided the treatment of individuals encountered during military operations, the lack of a clear definition invited parties to a conflict to develop justifications for excluding those who appeared to fall within the common sense and customary notion of civilian from the scope of LOAC protections. Nonetheless, as late as 1949, when the international community developed the GCC (the first LOAC treaty devoted exclusively to the protection of the civilian population), the term "civilian" remained undefined. This can be explained largely by the fact that this treaty did not focus on protecting civilians from the harmful consequences of hostilities, but instead on protecting civilians who fall under the authority of an enemy nation. It was not until the international community set about codifying rules related to the conduct of hostilities that it finally became necessary to define who was a civilian in order to give meaning to rules devoted to the protection of civilians.

As noted above, this definition was included in AP I. However, instead of attempting to define who was a civilian, Article 50 adopted a definition of exclusion. In so doing, the drafters implicitly recognized the difficulty of a comprehensive positive definition of every person considered a civilian. The ICRC Commentary associated with Article 50 explained this definitional methodology:

> In the course of history many definitions of the civilian population have been formulated, and everyone has an understanding of the meaning of this

---

12. Article 50(1), Protocol Additional to the Geneva Conventions of 12 August 1949, and Relating to the Protection of Victims of International Armed Conflicts (Protocol I), 8 June 1977, 1125 UNTS 3 (hereinafter AP I). Geneva Convention Relative to the Treatment of Prisoners of War, Aug. 12, 1949, 6 U.S.T. 3316, 75 U.N.T.S. 972 (hereinafter GPW).

13. International Committee of the Red Cross, Commentary on the Additional Protocols of 8 June 1977 to the Geneva Conventions of 12 August 1949, art. 50 (Yves Sandez et al eds. 1987) (hereafter ICRC Additional Protocols 1987 Commentary).

concept. However, all these definitions are lacking in precision, and it was desirable to lay down some more rigorous definition, particularly as the categories of persons they cover has varied. Thus the Protocol adopted the only satisfactory solution, which is that of a negative definition, namely, that the civilian population is made up of persons who are not members of the armed forces.[14]

While the broad, negative, definition of civilian has been generally followed by even States not bound to AP I, like the United States, the post September 11, 2001 military response to the threat of transnational terrorism exposed some limits the efficacy of the AP I approach.[15] Article 50's default civilian status rule became particularly problematic for the United States when U.S. armed forces captured individuals it considered to be belligerent operatives of an enemy organization who failed to qualify for POW status pursuant to Article 4 of the Prisoner of War Convention (GFW). The United States classified these detainees not as civilians posing a threat to U.S. armed forces, but as unlawful combatants (later re-designated as unprivileged belligerents). While the United States has never retreated from this approach, many other States assert that if a captive does not qualify as a combatant, he can only be a civilian, even if subject to security detention.

The interpretation that every individual who does not fall within one of the POW categories enumerated in the AP I definition of combatant is a civilian is the overwhelming majority view today, notwithstanding the U.S. approach. Ultimately, determining *who* is a civilian is generally not particularly complicated: for most States, it is anyone who does not qualify as a combatant as defined by AP I; for the United States, it is anyone who is not assessed as being a member of an organized armed group. Instead, the challenge is determining what protections apply to civilians impacted by an armed conflict. Accordingly, determining an individual's status as a civilian is only the start-point in identifying the protections the LOAC affords.

II. LOAC Shields of Protection for Civilians

As noted above, because the LOAC affords different protections — in type and degree — to different categories of civilians, it is useful to think of shields of protection. Each shield will be explained below, illustrating how the law operates to provide tailored protections in response to specific risks in order to mitigate the suffering inflicted upon civilians. Conceptualizing civilian protections

---

14. *Id.*
15. The United States is not a signatory to Additional Protocol I, but has accepted many of its provisions as customary international law. Michael J. Matheson, "The United States Position on the Relation of Customary International Law to the 1977 Protocols Additional to the 1949 Geneva Conventions," *Am. U. J. Int'l Law and Pol.*, 2 (1987).

as shields also facilitates understanding of how certain shields are superimposed on others, thereby adding protections in certain situations.

A. Shield From the Harmful Consequences of Attack

Protecting civilians from the harmful consequences of employing combat power is "the bedrock" of the LOAC.[16] As explained in the Targeting Chapter, LOAC regulation of the application of combat power evolved for the primary purpose of protecting the civilian population and civilian objects. While these protections are far from absolute (as the result of the reality that collateral damage and incidental injury to civilians and their property are an accepted aspect of armed conflict so long as that damage and injury is not considered excessive in relation to the anticipated advantage of launching an attack), the prohibition against deliberately attacking civilians and civilian property, when coupled with the proportionality and precautions principles, is an essential component in mitigating civilian suffering in armed conflict.

In the context of civilian protection law, LOAC targeting rules protect *all* civilians, *all* civilian property (that does not qualify as a military objective), during *all* types of armed conflict. As explained in Chapter 7, these rules protect against deliberate attack, indiscriminate attack, and excessive collateral damage resulting from an otherwise lawful attack. The requirement that belligerents limit their deliberate objects of attack to lawful military objectives, and that they forego otherwise lawful attacks when the anticipated harm to civilians and/or civilian property is excessive in relation to the concrete and direct military advantage anticipated, reveals that civilians are indeed the primary beneficiaries of these targeting rules. Although these rules are addressed comprehensively in the Targeting chapter, it is critical to bear in mind that when considering the range of LOAC protections provided to civilians, the rules and principles of targeting are especially significant because of the harm they are intended to avert, namely loss of life or severe physical injury.

B. Shield From Maltreatment at the Hands of a Party to the Conflict

Contemporary military operations almost inevitably involve close interaction between armed forces and civilians in situations not involving application of combat power. These situations trigger the most fundamental protection for civilians: the prohibition against subjecting civilians to cruel, inhumane, or degrading treatment.

This prohibition, or as stated in the affirmative the humane treatment mandate, is a baseline standard applicable to all civilians, at all times, during all armed conflicts. Accordingly, all civilians encountered during the operation

---

16. Prosecutor v. Kupreskic, IT-95-16T para. 52114 (Jan. 2000).

receive this shield of protection, which is a shield that applies *in addition to* other protections or shields that the LOAC provides (for example, the protections afforded by the targeting principles).

The prohibition against subjecting civilians to cruel, degrading, or inhumane treatment is reflected in a number of foundational LOAC treaty provisions. As early as 1899, the Hague Convention included within its preamble what is known as the Martens Clause (in recognition of the Russian diplomat Fyodor Fyodorovich Martens, who proposed the clause), which was again included in the 1907 Hague Convention with slight modification.[17] The 1907 version provides that:

> Until a more complete code of the laws of war is issued, the High Contracting Parties think it right to declare that in cases not included in the Regulations adopted by them, populations and belligerents remain under the protection and empire of the principles of international law, as they result from the usages established between civilized nations, from the laws of humanity and the requirements of the public conscience.

Versions of the Martens Clause also appear in the 1949 Geneva Conventions and the 1977 Additional Protocols. The International Court of Justice has indicated that protection afforded by this invocation of the principle of humanity is not merely precatory, but a substantive component of international law.[18] However, there is no universal consensus on either the scope or binding nature of this "Martens Clause" theory. Fortunately, the law has advanced since 1899 to provide this basic protection through other treaty provisions.

The most important such provision is Common Article 3 to the four Geneva Conventions of 1949, expressly mandating the humane treatment of any person not actively participating in hostilities during an NIAC. The importance of Common Article 3 is hard to overstate.[19] The article is considered a "mini Geneva Convention" for NIACs[20] and a "minimum yardstick" that reflects basic requirements of humanity.[21] And, while by its terms Common Article 3 applies only to NIACs the associated ICRC Commentary indicates that it was understood that an analogous mandate applies *a fortiori* to IACs.

---

17. *See* Rupert Ticehurst, *The Martens Clause and the Laws of Armed Conflict*, 317 INT'L REV. RED CROSS 125 (1997) and Jeff Kahn, '*Protection and Empire*': *The Martens Clause, State Sovereignty and Individual Rights*, 56 VA. J. INT'L L. 1 (2016).

18. *See* Legality of the Threat or Use of Nuclear Weapons Advisory Opinion, I.C.J. Reports, 1996, International Court of Justice, 8 July 1996 (hereinafter Nuclear Advisory Opinion).

19. *See* Jelena Pejic, *The Protective Scope of Common Article 3: More Than Meets the Eye*, 881 INT'L REV. RED CROSS 189 (2011).

20. Lindsey Cameron et al, *The Updated Commentary on the First Geneva Convention – A New Tool for Generating Respect for International Humanitarian Law*, 93 INT'L L. STUD. 157 (hereinafter Cameron) (2017 citing Diplomatic Conference for the Establishment of International Conventions for the Protection of War Victims, Final Record of the Diplomatic Conference of Geneva of 1949, Vol. II-B, p. 326.

21. *See* ICJ, Military and Paramilitary Activities in and against Nicaragua, Judgment, ICJ Reports 1986, paras 218–219 (hereinafter Nicaragua).

Indeed, the substantive mandate of Common Article 3 is now customarily recognized as applying in all armed conflicts, international or non-international.[22]

Common Article 3 not only prohibits cruel, inhumane, and degrading treatment of any person not taking an active part in hostilities. It also provides a non-exhaustive list of actions especially forbidden:

> (a) Violence to life and person, in particular murder of all kinds, mutilation, cruel treatment and torture;
> (b) Taking of hostages;
> (c) Outrages upon personal dignity, in particular humiliating and degrading treatment;[23]
> (d) The passing of sentences and the carrying out of executions without previous judgment pronounced by a regularly constituted court, affording all the judicial guarantees which are recognized as indispensable by civilized peoples.

Common Article 3 also requires that "[t]he wounded and sick shall be collected and cared for" and that impartial humanitarian organizations may offer their services. Unlike some of the protections discussed below, the humane treatment mandate of Common Article 3 applies irrespective of location, nationality, or the characterization of the armed conflict or occupation. Common Article 3 therefore is the most widely applicable benefit provided by the LOAC, protecting any person not taking an active part in hostilities, including from outrages committed by the armed forces of their own nation. However, with the exception of the affirmative obligation to collect and care for the wounded and sick,[24] the nature of the obligation imposed by Common Article 3 is primarily negative. While significant, Common Article 3 provides a quite limited benefit package to civilians, essentially protecting them from abusive treatment at the hands of a party to an armed conflict, including non-state actors and multinational forces.[25] As will be explained below, other LOAC provisions impose more extensive obligations requiring armed forces to take affirmative measures to reduce the suffering of certain civilians. Thus, Common Article 3 is extremely broad in application, but limited in its effect.

Today, it is universally accepted that Common Article 3 provides the baseline protection for civilians (and belligerents rendered *hors de combat*) in all armed conflicts however characterized. Nonetheless, Article 75 of AP I expressly extends the obligation to IACs. Titled "Fundamental Guarantees," Article 75 is a slightly more robust version of Common Article 3, included in AP I to ensure

---

22. *See id.* (Applying Common Article 3 to international armed conflict); Opinion and Judgment, Prosecutor v. Tadic, U.N. Doc. IT-94-1-T (May 7, 1997) (applying Common Article 3 to non-international armed conflict) and Hamdan v. Rumsfeld, 548 U.S. 557 (2006) (applying Common Article 3 to the United States in the transnational armed conflict against al Qaeda).

23. While the words "rape" or "sexual assault" do not appear in Common Article 3, such crimes are subsumed within the prohibition against outrages against personal dignity as well as that against violence to person. ICRC, Commentary on the First Geneva Convention, 2nd edition, paras 696-707 (hereinafter 2016 ICRC Commentary on the First Geneva Convention).

24. *Id.* at paras 768-778.

25. *Id.* at paras 503-517.

that no person is denied humane treatment for any reason, including disavowal of Common Article 3 applicability because the conflict is international in nature. Thus, while many consider Article 75 superfluous with the customary extension of Common Article 3 to IACs, it essentially provides a failsafe to confirm that all civilians receive the benefit of humane treatment. By adding weight to the customary nature of the humane treatment obligation, the significance of Article 75 extends beyond mere treaty obligation to bolster the universal nature of the mandate originally reflected in Common Article 3. This is reflected in the 2011 U.S. announcement that it considers Article 75 binding as customary international law.[26]

Humane treatment is therefore the foundation upon which the LOAC provides a host of other protections in both IAC and NIAC. However, because the additional protections built upon that foundation are more robust in IAC than NIAC, it remains important to distinguish the condition of civilians in these two types of armed conflicts. Is the conflict in question a NIAC or IAC? Or has the situation not even reached the level of armed conflict? The answer to these questions determines whether to even look to the LOAC for protections, and if so, to what extent between the types of conflicts and the varied protections the law provides to civilians in those conflicts.

For NIACs, Common Article 3 represents the primary benefit package provided by the LOAC.[27] Where applicable, AP II supplements this package by providing some proverbial flesh to the bones of Common Article 3.[28] These additional protections include respect for "convictions and religious practices"; a prohibition against terrorism directed against civilians; protections for individuals subjected to detention; and protections for individuals subjected to penal sanction. In other situations of internal disturbance that do not rise to the level of armed conflict, the LOAC is inapplicable (although in such situations international human rights law provides analogous protection against cruel, inhumane, and degrading treatment at the hands of state actors).

---

26. *See* White House, Fact Sheet: New Actions on Guantanamo and Detainee Policy, Mar.7,2011https://obamawhitehouse.archives.gov/the-press-office/2011/03/07/fact-sheet-new-actions-guant-namo-and-detainee-policy.

27. Additional Protocol II, which applies in some non-international armed conflicts, does provide some additional protections beyond those of CA 3. AP II. But these protections are nowhere near as robust as those provided through GC 4 and derivatively through AP I. Moreover, the trigger for AP II's applicability is daunting – requiring (1) an armed conflict which doesn't qualify as an international armed conflict; (2) between a party to the Geneva Conventions and a dissident armed group which exercises control over a part of territory such that the group may carry out sustained and concerned military action.

28. In 1987, President Reagan submitted AP II to the Senate in order to obtain the required advice and consent for the United States to ratify the treaty. In 2011, President Obama urged the Senate to act on AP II, but by the end of President Obama's second term in 2016, the treaty remained languishing on Capitol Hill. *See* https://obamawhitehouse.archives.gov/the-press-office/2011/03/07/fact-sheet-new-actions-guant-namo-and-detainee-policy.

C. General Shield of Protection for Civilian Populations

In addition to the customary humane treatment obligation applicable to all armed conflicts, a more comprehensive civilian protection regime applies during IACs. The two primary sources for these more comprehensive protections are the GCC, adopted for the specific purpose of enhancing the protection of civilians during international armed conflicts; and Additional Protocol I, which not only codified targeting rules intended to protect civilians from the effects of combat, but also supplemented the civilian protection regime of the GCC.

The GCC provides general protections for all civilians impacted by IACs. These protections, which benefit all civilians, include:

- Access for consignments of medical supplies, food, and clothing.
- The establishment of agreed upon hospital zones protected from attack.
- The establishment of agreed upon neutralized zones to shield civilians from the effects of hostilities.
- Feasible measures to protect the wounded and sick from suffering or abuse.

There are, however, legal and practical qualifications to these protections. In terms of legal qualifications, consider the requirement of access to medical supplies, food, and clothing. During an IAC between State A and State B, what do the protections mean in terms of a non-governmental organization that wishes to provide some combination of medical supplies, food, and/or clothing to civilians in need within the borders of State A? Article Ten of the GCC states that the GCC does not constitute an "obstacle to the humanitarian activities which the ICRC or any other impartial humanitarian organization, may, subject to the consent of the Parties to conflict concerned, undertake for the protection of civilian persons and for their relief."[29] Are there any limitations on State A withholding consent?[30] The 1952 Commentary to the GCC contended that "the decision whether to consent to humanitarian activities on their territory was entirely up to the belligerent Power and no reason needed to be given for refusing an offer or service."[31] The 2016 Commentary states that "such an offer of services may not be refused on arbitrary grounds."[32] The shift from no reason need be provided in withholding consent to the refusal may not be based on arbitrary grounds

---

29. GC, *supra*, note 7 at art. 10.
30. *See* John B. Bellinger & William J. Haynes II, *A US Government Response to the International Committee of the Red Cross Study Customary International Humanitarian Law*, 89 INT'L REV. RED CROSS 443 (2007) (discussing how the respect that humanitarian relief personnel are due depends in part on their acting within the terms of their mission and subject to the consent of the territorial State in which they operate).
31. Cameron, *supra*, note 20 at 169.
32. *Id*. In discussing the 2016 Commentary, ICRC authors wrote that "[s]ince 1949, international law in general, and IHL in particular, has evolved and it has not become accepted that the Party to the conflict whose concern is sought must assess an offer of services in good faith and in line with its international legal obligations in relation to humanitarian needs."

is not itself controversial. What is debatable is the ICRC's claim of a negative definition of arbitrary grounds, that "[i]f humanitarian needs cannot be met otherwise, the refusal of an offer of services from an impartial humanitarian organization would be arbitrary, and therefore in violation of international law."[33] And there is also the question of how to determine whether or not a humanitarian organization is impartial. Moreover, who makes that determination? Finally, is State A entitled to inspect the goods the humanitarian organization intends to bring into its territory?[34]

In terms of practical qualification for the establishment of hospital and neutral zones, the more parties to the conflict agree to the zones, the greater the likelihood that they will be respected. For example, in September, 2017, an Islamic State convoy of several fighters and their families was stranded in the Syrian desert.[35] The convoy was attempting to move to a location near the Syrian border with Iraq, pursuant to a safe passage agreement between the Syrian government, the Islamic State, and the organized armed group Hezbollah.[36] The international coalition fighting the Islamic State was not party to the agreement and proceeded to launch airstrikes to destroy the road in front of and behind the convoy, while not attacking the convoy itself. For two weeks the convoy was stranded in the Syrian desert and questions were raised over whether or not food and water was being delivered. A coalition spokesperson claimed that the convoy had been resupplied and that coalition was neither helping nor hindering such resupply efforts.[37]

---

33. Cameron, *supra*, note 33 at 169.

34. This issue, among others, was raised in the 2010 Gaza Flotilla Incident, in which Israeli Naval Forces, enforcing a blockade imposed on Gaza, directed a six-ship convoy to proceed to an Israeli port for inspection or be boarded. A Turkish group, the Turkish Foundation for Human Rights and Freedoms and Humanitarian Relief (IHH), organized the convoy. To some, the IHH is a humanitarian relief organization. To at least Israel and The Netherlands, the IHH is a designated terrorist organization. When the ships refused to proceed to the designated port, the Israeli Navy boarded the ships, encountering violent resistance on one ship, the Mavi Marmara. Nine passengers on the ship were killed, while ten Israeli sailors were injured. *See* Andrzej Makowski & Laurence Weinbaum, *The Mavi Marmara Incident and the Modern Law of Armed Conflict at Sea*, 7 ISRAEL J. FOR. AFF. 75 (2015). The nature of the armed conflict between Israel and several Palestinian groups is disputed, with Israel arguing for a NIAC and others claiming IAC. The incident generated considerable media attention and was the subject of Turkish, Israeli, and ultimately a United Nations investigation. *See* Report of the Secretary-General's Panel of Inquiry on the 31 May 2010 Flotilla Incident, Sept. 2011.

35. While it is clear that there is an armed conflict in Syria, and likely more than one, whether the conflict(s) are properly characterized as NIACs or IACs remains debated. The example is offered for the broader point on why obtaining agreement in establishing purported safe areas or safe passage areas is important.

36. Rod Nordlan, *No Relief for Islamic State Convoy Blocked in Syria*, NY TIMES, Sept. 7, 2017.

37. *Id.* While not helping or hindering relief efforts, the coalition purportedly did conduct air strikes, killing some 20 ISIS fighters who walked away from the convoy to urinate or defecate. Rod Nordland & Eric Schmitt, *Why the U.S. Allowed a Convoy of ISIS Fighters to Go Free*, NY TIMES, Sept. 15, 2017.

D. Shield of Special Protection for Especially Vulnerable Civilians

During IAC, the GCC affords a series of shields of protection to different categories of civilians especially vulnerable "against certain consequences of war."[38] These shields protect the wounded, sick and aged persons, children under 15, expectant mothers, and mothers of children under seven.[39]

Specifically, the GCC:

- Calls for parties to a conflict to agree to remove the "wounded, sick infirm, and aged persons, children and maternity cases....from besieged or encircled areas."[40]
- Requires that "civilian hospitals organized to give care to the wounded and sick, the infirm and maternity cases, may in no circumstances be the object of attack, but shall at all times be respected and protected by the Parties to the conflict."[41]
- Ensures that "children under fifteen, who are orphaned or are separated from their families as a result of the war, are not left to their own resources, and that their maintenance, the exercise of their religion and their education are facilitated in all circumstances."[42]

The GCC imposes a broad obligation on all parties to an armed conflict to protect the interests of these especially vulnerable categories of civilians. It is important to recognize that the applicability of these protections is in no way qualified by the nationality of the civilian or whose control the civilian is under. Indeed, the protections "cover the whole of the populations of the countries in conflict, without any adverse distinction based, in particular, on race, nationality, religion or political opinion, and are intended to alleviate the sufferings caused by war."[43]

E. Maximum Shield of Protection: Protected Persons

In contrast, *only* nationality and the belligerent power with control over a civilian is decisive in assessing whether the civilian qualifies for status as a protected person within the meaning of the GCC. This final shield, while not as comprehensive in coverage as those previously addressed, provides considerable

---

38. GC, *supra*, note 7 at Part II.
39. *Id.* at Part II.
40. *Id.* at art. 17.
41. *Id.* at art. 18. This protection afforded to civilian hospitals ceases if the facilities are "used to commit, outside their humanitarian duties, acts harmful to the enemy." *Id.* at art. 19. Even then, though, the protections afforded civilian hospitals cease only after "due warning has been given." *Id.* That a hospital may be rendering aid to sick or wounded combatants "shall not be considered to be acts harmful to the enemy."
42. *Id.* at art. 24.
43. *Id.* at art. 13.

protections to the civilians who qualify as protected persons. It is also the most difficult to understand and apply.[44]

Article 4 of the GCC details that protected persons are civilians "who, at a given moment and in any manner whatsoever, find themselves, in case of a conflict or occupation, in the hands of a Party to the conflict of Occupying Power of which they are not nationals."[45] Article 4 also, however, refines the definition by excluding certain civilians who appear to fall into this definition from protected person status.

First, "[n]ationals of a neutral State who find themselves in the territory of a belligerent State, and nationals of a co-belligerent State, shall not be regarded as protected persons while the State of which they are nationals has normal diplomatic representation in the State in whose hands they are."[46] Second, persons covered or protected by one of the other Geneva Conventions (wounded and sick on land; wounded, sick, or shipwrecked at sea; or prisoner of war) "shall not be considered as protected persons. . . ."[47] These two exclusions reveal that the essence of protected person qualification is the civilian's inability to avail herself to the protections of her state or some other source of protective treaty as the result of the armed conflict.

The 1958 ICRC Commentary to Article 4 confirms this when it explains "that there were two main classes of civilian to whom protection against arbitrary action on the part of the enemy was essential in time of war—[1] on the one hand, persons of enemy nationality living in the territory of a belligerent State, and [2] on the other, the inhabitants of occupied territories."[48] Stated more plainly, a protected person is a civilian who finds him/herself at the mercy of the military authorities of an enemy State.[49]

The significance of this qualification has come under increasing scrutiny as the LOAC has continued to evolve from a sovereignty focus to a focus on protection of the human person, what Professor Theodore Meron designated the "humanization of international humanitarian law." The International Criminal

---

44. Part of the difficulty stems from the different uses in the Geneva Conventions of the word "protected." "Protected person" is a term of art and "refers to persons who are protected by the GC in connection with international armed conflict or occupation." U.S. Department of Defense, Office of the General Counsel, Law of War Manual (revised ed., December 2016), para. 10.3.1 (DoD LOW Manual). As the DoD Law of War Manual explains, there are instances in the other three 1949 Geneva Conventions where the terms "protected persons" or "persons protected" are used, but those uses "refer to persons protected by that respective convention, as opposed to protected persons for purposes of the GC." *Id.*

45. GC, *supra*, note 7 at art. 4.

46. *Id.* at art. 4. "The persons must "find themselves" in the hands of a party to the conflict or Occupying Power, which suggests an element of happenstance or coincidence. For example, nationals of a neutral or non-belligerent State who travel to an occupied State to fight the Occupying Power cannot be said to have "found themselves" within that occupied territory within the meaning of Article 4 of the GC." DoD Manual, *supra*, note 44 at para. 10.3.2 *citing* Jack L. Goldsmith III, Assistant Attorney General, "Protected Person" Status in Occupied Iraq Under the Fourth Geneva Convention, Mar. 18, 2004, 28 Opinions of the Office of Legal Counsel 35, 51.

47. GC, *supra*, note 7 at art. 4.

48. IV Commentary, Geneva Conventions art. 4 (J. Pictet 1958) (hereinafter 1958 Commentary).

49. Gary D. Solis, THE LAW OF ARMED CONFLICT: INTERNATIONAL HUMANITARIAN LAW IN WAR *(2010)* (hereinafter Solis).

Tribunal for the Former Yugoslavia (ICTY) emphasized this in noting that "the nationality requirement [for determining protected person status] should not be given an overly strict or formal interpretation."[50] In the Blaskic Case, the ICTY examined allegations that members of the Croatian military committed a series of LOAC violations against Bosnian Muslims in Bosnia and Herzegovina, including that the Croats made Bosniak civilians the object of attack. Strictly speaking, both the Croats and Bosniaks were citizens of the former Yugoslavia, so the defense argued that Bosniaks (one state of Yugoslavia) could not, by definition, be in the hands of an enemy or occupying power (the Croats, another Yugoslav state), and thus could not be protected persons. In ruling that the protected person determination was not so formulaic or rigid, the ICTY held that, "in an inter-ethnic armed conflict, a person's ethnic background may be regarded as a decisive factor in determining the nation to which he owes his allegiance. . . . When it comes to determining nationality, ethnicity is more important than citizenship."[51]

Nonetheless, Article 4 of the GCC remains the controlling legal standard for determining protected person qualification. Whether applied strictly, or along the more pragmatic lines suggested by the ICTY (which is most likely how U.S. commanders would apply the treaty), this status is significant not only because of the protections it triggers, but because violations of the protections often qualify as a grave breach, the most serious violation of the Geneva Conventions, and that triggers a requirement that offenders be brought before the court of a high contracting party.[52]

The GCC, while allowing for the high contracting parties to conclude separate agreements, specifies that no special agreement shall adversely affect the situation of protected persons. But where such agreements benefit protected persons, they will receive whichever is more favorable to them: the agreement or the benefit package afforded to protected persons by the GCC. The shield of protection the GCC affords protected persons includes, *inter alia*, the following:

- Respect for their persons, their honor, their family rights, their religious convictions and practices, and their manners and customs;
- Women shall be especially protected against any attack on their honor;
- Access to the International Committee of the Red Cross;
- No physical or moral coercion used against them to obtain information;
- No collective punishment.[53]

---

50. The Prosecutor v. Tihomir Blaskic, Case No. IT-95-14-T, Mar. 3, 2000 at 3.
51. *Id.*
52. GC, *supra*, note 7 at art. 147 (defining the following acts, if committed against protected persons, as grave breaches): "willful killing, torture or inhuman treatment, including biological experiments, willfully causing great suffering or serious injury to body or health, unlawful deportation or transfer or unlawful confinement of a protected person, compelling a protected person to serve in the forces of a hostile Power, or willfully depriving a protected person of the rights of fair and regular trial prescribed in the present Convention, taking of hostages and extensive destruction and appropriation of property, not justified by military necessity and carried out unlawfully and wantonly."
53. *Id.* at arts. 27, 30, 31, and 33.

Those protections are certainly fundamental in nature, and generally analogous to those of Common Article 3 (it must be remembered, however, that in 1949 Common Article 3 was applicable exclusively to NIACs). However, these protections provide a humane treatment foundation upon which more robust protections are built. These additional protections are contingent on the characterization of the territory in which the protected person is located: either in the territory of their enemy, or in territory subject to belligerent occupation by an enemy armed force.

1. Protected Persons in the Territory of Their Enemy

Civilians "stranded" in the national territory of an enemy state during armed conflict are protected persons pursuant to Article 4. Indeed, these individuals exemplify the concept of the protected person civilian, for the initiation of armed conflict will normally result in termination of diplomatic relations between the state where they are located and their state of nationality. As a result, the GCC anticipates that these civilians will, as a consequence of the armed conflict, be deprived the benefit of diplomatic protection. Thus, the GCC designates them protected persons and provides a shield tailored to their needs to prevent arbitrary treatment by the authorities they find themselves at the mercy of, and provides for a protecting power to oversee compliance with the treaty (and as a result provide the protection normally provided through diplomatic intervention). Pursuant to Section II of the GCC, such civilians (imagine an Iraqi citizen living in the United States during the armed conflict between the two states) receive the following additional protection in addition to those applicable to all protected persons:

- Entitlement to leave the territory, and, where that request is denied, to have the refusal reconsidered by an appropriate court or administrative board;
- Entitlement to receive relief supplies;
- Right to receive medical care to the same extent as the nationals of the State concerned;
- Opportunity to find employment equal to that enjoyed by nationals of the State concerned;
- Compulsion to work only to the same extent as nationals of the State concerned.[54]

2. Protected Persons in Occupied Territory

The most common situation in which a civilian finds herself subjected to the authority of an enemy state is during belligerent occupation. While occupation law is specifically addressed in Chapter 10, territory is considered occupied

---

54. *Id.* at arts 35, 38, 39, 40.

when it is subjected to the firm control of an enemy armed force.[55] In such situations, the military commander assumes governing authority over the territory, to include the obligation to maintain control of the civilian population. The civilians subjected to occupation authority is obviously no longer capable of relying exclusively on her own government to protect her interests. Instead, they are at the true mercy of enemy armed forces. It was the protection of civilians in this difficult situation that served as the primary motivation for the GCC, for the unfortunate reason that abuses of such civilians were rampant during the Second World War.

Nationals of the occupied state are of course protected persons within the meaning of Article 4. However, for areas subjected to belligerent occupation, Article 4 also includes within the definition of protected persons all civilians except those of the occupying state or a co-belligerent. This is based on the assumption that normal diplomatic mechanisms will rarely be effective in areas subjected to belligerent occupation. Thus, civilians of a neutral state are included within the definition in the specific situation of belligerent occupation.

Section III of the GCC provides extensive rules for the conduct of belligerent occupation. Like Section II, it superimposes additional protections upon the protective foundation provided to all protected persons. Treatment of civilians in occupied territory (such as a protected person in Iraq subjected to the authority of an occupying U.S. military commander) is subject to the following additional rules:

- Protected persons who are *not* nationals of the occupied territory may leave (using the Iraq example, protected persons who are not Iraqi nationals may leave Iraq while it is occupied by the United States);
- Reprisals are prohibited;
- Individual or mass forcible transfers or deportations are prohibited;
- Civilians may not be compelled to serve in the occupying power's armed forces, or to engage in labor essential to the defense of those forces;[56]
- Civilian property may not be destroyed absent imperative military necessity;
- Deprivations of liberty are authorized only based on individual conduct and subjected to extensive treaty regulation (this is addressed in more detail in the Occupation Chapter).

Finally, in order to oversee compliance with obligations related to protected persons, the GC provides for the appointment of a protecting power. As with the other Geneva Conventions, this may be a neutral state agreed upon by the parties to the conflict. However, because in practice such agreements are rare,

---

55. For a contemporary discussion of occupation, *see* THE WRITING ON THE WALL: RETHINKING THE INTERNATIONAL LAW OF OCCUPATION (Aeyal Gross ed.) (2017).

56. GC, *supra*, note 7 at arts 48, 49, 51. Although individual or mass forcible transfers or deportations are prohibited, an occupying power "may undertake total or partial evacuation of a given area if the security of the population or imperative military reasons so demand." *Id.* at art. 49.

this function is often performed by the ICRC.[57] This is a critical component of the civilian protection regime, as access to the protecting power allows civilians to raise grievances related to their treatment at the hands of an enemy power. The amount and type of protective shields the LOAC affords different civilians in different points and places in the battlefield can be confusing. A reference chart of the protections is provided at the end of this chapter.

F. Shield of Protection for Private Property

When civilians encounter armed forces in the midst of hostilities or occupation, it is not only their physical well-being that may be placed in jeopardy. History unfortunately demonstrates that civilians are also often the victims of looting and plunder. However, it is also the case that there will be times when a military commander, based on genuine military necessity, may need to utilize civilian property, both public and private. Like so many other areas of the law, the LOAC includes rules that seek to balance the commander's authority to interfere with civilian property rights with the civilian interest in freedom from such interference.

The LOAC affords protections to property, both real and personal, belonging to civilians. These are in addition to the protections already discussed, for example that civilian objects may not be directly targeted, and that incidental damage to civilian property factors into the targeting proportionality analysis. The LOAC provides different levels of protection to property depending on whether the property is private or public. This section deals with the protections afforded civilian private property during armed conflict (as opposed to occupation) and when such property may be permissibly destroyed, seized, and requisitioned.

1. Destruction of Private Property

That the LOAC provides protection to civilian property is a relatively recent development. While medieval sieges of cities may be lost to all but the history books, the indiscriminate bombings and shelling of the Spanish Civil War and World War II were obviously twentieth century occurrences, and generally accepted as normative conduct during hostilities. In contrast, the contemporary (post-WWII) LOAC prohibits "[a]ny destruction . . . of real estate or personal property belonging individually or collectively to private persons." This prohibition is not, however, absolute. Instead, it is qualified by the caveat "except where such destruction is rendered absolutely necessary by military operations."[58] This evolving view of the propriety of destroying civilian property is also illustrated by a 1970 United Nations General Assembly Resolution entitled "Basic Principles for the Protection of Civilian Populations in Armed

---

57. For an example of the use of protecting powers, consider the Falklands War between the United Kingdom and Argentina, during which the two countries severed diplomatic relations. Switzerland became the protecting power for the United Kingdom, and for the duration of the conflict the British Embassy in Argentina became the British Interests Section of the Swiss Embassy. In similar fashion, Brazil became the protecting power for Argentina and the Argentine Embassy in London, transitioning to the Argentine Interests Section of the Brazilian Embassy.

58. *GC supra,* note 7, at art. 53.

Conflicts."[59] Adopted unanimously by the General Assembly (a relatively rare occurrence), one of the principles in the Resolution is that "dwellings and other installations that are used only by the civilian population should not be the subject of military operations."[60] But that, too, is a general proposition, and subject to a military necessity exception. The United Kingdom's LOAC manual provides a clear articulation of the balance between the interest of protecting civilian property and the dictates of military necessity:

> It may be permissible to destroy a house in order to clear a field of fire or because it is being used as an enemy military observation or sniper post. It would not be permissible to burn down a house simply to prevent its being inhabited by persons of a different ethnic group or religious persuasion.[61]

Similarly, there may be a legitimate military purpose to the destruction of "crops, foodstuffs, and water sources" including to deny their use by the enemy, but not to an extent that starvation of the civilian population is likely to result.

U.S. Army's Field Manual 27-10, The Law of Land Warfare (the Army's LOAC manual), also provides a useful frame of reference on the destruction of property:

> The measure of permissible devastation is found in the strict necessities of war. *Devastation as an end in itself or as a separate measure of war is not sanctioned by the law of war. There must be some reasonably close connection between the destruction of property and the overcoming of the enemy's army.* Thus the rule requiring respect for private property is not violated through damage resulting from operations, movements, or combat activity of the army; that is, real estate may be used for marches, camp sites, construction of field fortifications, etc. Buildings may be destroyed for sanitary purposes or used for shelter for troops . . . Fences, woods, crops, buildings, etc., may be demolished, cut down, and removed to clear a field of fire, to clear the ground for landing fields, or to furnish building materials or fuel if imperatively needed for the army.[62]

Accordingly, civilian property (like civilians themselves) is presumptively protected from destruction, subject to the dictates of military necessity. Importantly, while "[f]easible precautions should be taken to mitigate the burden on civilians, there is no obligation to compensate the owners of enemy property that is lawfully damaged."[63] The U.S. Foreign Claims Act establishes a process by which claims may be made against the U.S. government for damage the U.S. military may have caused to real or personal property. The statute excludes claims that "arise from any action by an enemy or result directly or

---

59. UNGAR 2675, Basic Principles for the Protection of Civilian Populations in Armed Conflicts, Dec. 9, 1970.
60. *Id.*
61. U.K. Ministry of Defense, JSP 383, The Joint Service Manual of the Law of Armed Conflict, 15.17.12 (2004).
62. U.S. Dep't of Army, Field Manual 27-10, The Law of Land Warfare (July 1956) para. 56 (emphasis added).
63. DoD LOW Manual, *supra*, note 44 at 5.17.

indirectly from an act of the armed forces of the United States in combat. . . ."[64] Thus, the LOAC does not require, and U.S. law does not allow, payment of claims for combat damage. Yet damage or destruction of private property, without compensation, while permissible subject to military necessity, is hardly the way to win the civilian "hearts and minds" crucial to success in counterinsurgency operations like those in Iraq and Afghanistan. As a result, Congress authorized funding for the "Commanders Emergency Response Program" (CERP) to "enable local commanders in Iraq and Afghanistan to respond to urgent humanitarian relief and reconstruction requirements."[65] Among the permissible uses of CERP funds is the "[r]epair, or payment for repair, of property damage that results from U.S. coalition, or supporting military operations and is not compensable under the Foreign Claims Act."[66] While CERP funds mitigate the problem of not being able to compensate for combat damage to civilian property, they are an exception, limited to only Iraq and Afghanistan. Moreover, the funds are provided through an authorization act requiring yearly approval. Absent CERP funds or something analogous, the baseline prohibition against paying for combat damage to civilian property from the Foreign Claims Act stands.

2. Taking Possession of Private Property

In addition to the risk of destruction, civilian property may be subjected to seizure and use by parties to a conflict. As a start point, pillaging, looting, or stealing private property is absolutely prohibited. Furthermore, the LOAC prohibits confiscation (meaning permanent appropriation of property without compensation) of private property.[67] The LOAC does however allow for seizure of private property and for its requisition.

Seizure is the temporary taking of property and is limited to property "susceptible for military use."[68] Illustrative examples include privately

---

64. *See* 10 U.S.C. 2734.

65. Under Secretary of Defense, Commander's Emergency Response Program (CERP) Guidance, May 9, 2007 http://comptroller.defense.gov/Portals/45/documents/fmr/archive/12arch/CERP_Guidance_May07.pdf (hereinafter CERP Guidance Memo) The start of CERP was U.S. funds hidden in Iraq by Saddam Hussein and other Bath Party officials. *See* Julian Coman, "*Troops Tempted by Saddam's $780m Hoard*" TELEGRAPH, Apr. 27, 2003.

http://www.telegraph.co.uk/news/worldnews/middleeast/iraq/1428506/Troops-tempted-by-Saddams-780m-hoard.html. The U.S. Army found and seized the funds and began using them for project to benefit the Iraqi population. *See* Heidi Lynn Osterhout, NO MORE "MAD MONEY" (2010). From there, the U.S. Congress began appropriating funds for CERP. By 2010, some $1.2 billion dollars of U.S. taxpayer funds were being used for CERP. Over time, considerable questions were raised concerning whether CERP is an alternative development program under the Department of Defense and how effectively the funds have been spent and even accounted for. *See* Special Inspector General for Iraq Reconstruction, Management of Iraq Commander's Emergency Response Program Needs to Be Improved, July 29, 2011 http://www.dtic.mil/dtic/tr/fulltext/u2/a546671.pdf

66. CERP Guidance Memo, *supra*, note 65.

67. Hague Convention No. IV Respecting the Laws and Customs of War on Land and Its Annex, Regulation Concerning the Laws and Customs of War on Land, 36 Stat. 2277, 205 Consol. T.S. 277, arts. 45-46 (hereinafter 1907 Hague IV).

68. FM 27-10, *supra*, note 62 para. 410.

owned communication devices (radios, TVs, phones), means of transport (cars), and weapons and ammunition.[69] Seized property must be returned to the owner and compensation provided when hostilities have concluded. The U.S. military's approach to seizures is that a receipt should be provided to the owner or at a minimum that a record is made of the nature and quantity of the items seized, if not from whom then at least from where, so that, again, the items may be returned and compensation provided to the owner.[70]

Requisition is the taking of private property necessary for the maintenance of an occupying armed force. This is a broader category of items than that eligible for seizure. Among the types of items which may be requisitioned are: fuel, food, clothing, machinery, tools, and space to billet or lodge troops.[71] With this broader grant comes additional restrictions. The requisitions "shall be in proportion to the resources of the country. . . ."[72] Not just anyone in the military may requisition civilian property—requisition requires the authority and approval of the local military commander. Finally, unlike seizure, which envisions compensation at some future date, the military that requisitions items shall "as far as possible" pay for the requisitioned items in cash. If that is not possible, the military shall provide a receipt and make payment "as soon as possible."[73]

Destruction of property in occupied territory is subject to a special rule: it is permissible only based on imperative military necessity. This heightened degree of necessity seems to require that the destruction be a genuine measure of last resort to accomplish a valid military purpose. The legality of such property destruction often arises in situations where an occupying force is retreating from the occupied territory and seeks to impede enemy pursuit by employing "scorched earth" tactics. The imperative military necessity standard reflects the standard applied by the post-World War II military tribunals. In one case, an international military tribunal acquitted a German General in command for employing scorched earth tactics during the German retreat from Finnmark. The tribunal concluded that the Commander reasonably believed Soviet forces were in close pursuit, and that destruction of property was the only available means to impede that pursuit. Interestingly, AP I adopts a more restrictive rule, imposing an absolute prohibition against scorched earth tactics in occupied territory, but permitting such tactics on the territory of the party employing the tactic.

As a general rule, military forces should avoid interfering with the property rights of civilians wherever they are encountered. However, where necessary, the LOAC permits interference with those rights. Commanders and their forces must understand the precise rules related to when such interference is

---

69. *Id.* para 410; 1907 Hague IV, *supra*, note 67 art. 53.
70. FM 27-10 *supra*, note 62 para. 409.
71. FM 27-10 *supra*, note 62 para. 412.
72. 1907 Hague IV, *supra*, note 67 art 52.
73. *Id.*

authorized, what procedures must be followed and how to compensate civilians for any resulting property loss.

G. Shield of Protection for Interned Civilians

Finally, in terms of shields, the GC provides a number of protections for interned or detained civilians. While the actual protections are in some ways very similar to those provided for POWs discussed in Chapter 5, the reasons for and duration of civilian detainment are both very different than the reasons for and duration of POW detainment.

1. Basis for Civilian Detention

The LOAC recognizes that civilians may pose a security threat such that the State may deprive them of their liberty, not as punishment but as "the severest 'measures of control' that may be taken by a State with respect to civilians whose activity is deemed to pose a serious threat to its security."[74] Thus, while POWs are detained because of their status, most often as members of the armed forces, civilian detention is individualized and cause-based (the result of the civilian's conduct).

Depending on where the civilian is located, the LOAC provides for slightly different permissible grounds for detention. If a State is detaining a civilian in that State's own territory, the standard under the GCC is that "the security of the Detaining Power makes it absolutely necessary." [75] Where a State is detaining a civilian in occupied territory, the standard under the GCC is that the detention be for "imperative reasons of security."[76]

But what constitutes a security threat? The Commentary to the GCC explains that it was "left very largely to Governments to decide the measure of activity prejudicial to the internal or external security of the State which justifies internment. . . ."[77] The Commentaries recognized that "subversive activity carried on inside the territory of a Party to the conflict or actions which are of direct assistance to an enemy Power" may constitute the requisite security threat, while "the mere fact that a person is a subject of an enemy Power cannot be considered as threatening the security of the country where he is living. . ."[78]

The decision to detain a civilian must be made on an individualized basis. Civilian detention is a last resort which requires that the State "have good reason to think that the person concerned, by his activities, knowledge

---

74. Internment in Armed Conflict: Basic Rules and Challenges International Committee of the Red Cross (ICRC) Opinion Paper, November 2014.
75. GC, *supra*, note 7 at art 24, 42(1). Additionally, a civilian may request to be interned. *Id.* at art. 42 (stating that "If any person, acking through the representatives of the Protecting Power, voluntary demands interment and if his situation renders this step necessary, he shall be interned by power in whose hands he may be").
76. *Id. 7* at art 78(1). Civilians who are citizens of an enemy state may also be detained in the home state of a nation of war if they voluntarily demand internment, presumably to be protected from the other residents of their state of domicile.
77. 1958 Commantary *supra*, note 48 at art. 42.(1).
78. *Id.*

or qualifications, represents a real threat to its present or future security."[79] Because civilian internment is an exception, the LOAC incorporates a range of protections.

2. Civilian Detention Treatment Protections

The GCC provides a template for treatment of civil internees, in either occupied territory of the nation's home territory, that is very similar to the one provided for POWs. The maintenance of civilian internees and the "medical attention required by their state of health" must be provided free of charge. Civilian internees should be accommodated according to nationality, language, and customs; and, wherever possible, families interned together are to be kept together (Art. 82). In addition, the detaining power is required to provide for the support of their dependents, if they are without adequate means of support, or are unable to earn a living (Art. 81). In practice, the approach has been to implement this obligation by ensuring that civilians in occupied territory have their basic needs provided for, either by local authorities or the occupying powers.

Requirements related to the places of civilian internee internment are similar to POW camps. They should not be exposed to the dangers of war, and be clearly marked as internment camps (Art. 83 and 88). Civilian internees should be administered separately from POWs and "from persons deprived of liberty for any other reasons" (e.g., criminal detainees) (Art. 84). Their quarters should provide "every possible safeguard, as regards hygiene and health, [and] provide efficient protection against the rigors of the climate and the effects of war"; their premises should be protected from dampness, adequately heated and lighted, spacious and well-ventilated; and they should be provided with blankets and bedding necessary to guard against the local climate, showers and toilet facilities to maintain a state of health and cleanliness, and sufficient laundry facilities (Art. 85). Food and clothing should be sufficient to maintain the health of civilian internees, accounting for their customary diet and the special needs of women, children, and working internees (Art. 89); both food and material may be provided to the detainees to prepare their own food and clothing, if feasible (Art. 90).

Although, like the GPW, the GCC includes a requirement to provide canteens for civilian internees, they normally receive their health and hygiene materials, as well as all food items, from the camp administration, rather than by purchasing them in canteens. Hygiene and medical attention for civilian internees should also be similar to that provided POWs, as well as "not inferior to that provided for the local population"; it should also be sufficient to prevent infectious diseases, and include all "dentures, appliances, and spectacles, free of charge to the internee," required to maintain them in good health (Art. 91). This medical attention also includes periodic health inspections and preventive medicine (Art. 92). Internees should also be provided religious facilities, including assistance of ministers of their faith (Art. 93). The detaining power

---

79. *Id.*

is obligated to "encourage intellectual, educational, and recreational pursuits, sports and games, amongst the internees," at their pleasure; and the education of children and young people should be ensured (Art. 94).

Like POWs, the detaining power may employ civilian internees. Inside the internment camp, civilian internees may be employed as doctors, dentists, and other medical personnel, administrative personnel, camp cooks, and maintenance workers. Outside the camp, they may be employed, in accordance with the wages, labor standards, and occupational health and safety standards of the local populace; their participation should be voluntary and they should not be employed in a manner that would threaten their health (Art. 95). They may not be required to work in support of military operations (Art. 40). Finally, their employment will remain under the supervision of the camp commandant, and subject to the periodic inspection of the protecting power or the ICRC (Art. 96).

The finances and personal property of civilian internees should be properly safeguarded, and property of personal or sentimental value should not be taken away. Civilian internees should receive a receipt for any money and personal property taken from them, and money and personal property should be returned upon their release. Also, women should only be searched by women (Art. 97). Civilian internees may receive allowances from their home nation, as well as wages from their employment outside the internment camp; the camp authorities must provide for the accounting and return of these funds to the internees upon release (Art. 98).

Rules related to discipline and penal sanctions for civilian internees are also similar to those provided by the GPW. The camp rules and procedures must be published, along with a copy of the Convention, in a language they understand, so that civilian internees know the rules in advance (Art. 99). Disciplinary sanctions for camp rule infractions must be consistent with "humanitarian principles," and avoid sanctions that impose dangerous physical exertion, like "prolonged standing and roll-calls, punishment drills, military drill and maneuvers, or the reduction of food rations" (Art. 100); in addition, they are limited to garnishment of wages, discontinuance of privileges, "fatigue duties" (work details), and confinement (Art. 119). Penal sanctions should apply the laws in force of the territory in which the civilian internees are detained, and no detainee may be punished for the same offense twice (Art. 117).

Internal communications and relations with the people and entities outside of the detention facility are also designed to maintain order in internment camps, while maintaining external oversight. Civilian internees are empowered to elect leadership of an internee committee and representatives to the camp officials (Art. 102); their duties include receiving supplies, organizing work details, and communicating with camp officials, the protecting powers, and/or the ICRC (Art. 103). Civilian internees may present petitions and complaints regarding the circumstances of their confinement to the camp officials, the protecting power, and the ICRC (Art. 101). Civilian internees are also allowed to prepare legal documents necessary for the management of their property

(Art. 113, 114) and must be allowed to assert themselves in civilian courts, with delays necessitated by their confinement (Art. 115).

Like POWs, the names and information regarding civilian internees must be provided, via a national reporting center, to the protecting power or the ICRC, for dispatch to the country of origin or local officials, for further notification to the family (Art. 106). Civilian internees may receive cards and letters, subject to some censorship for reasons of security, as well as relief shipments, including those provided by the ICRC or the protecting power (Art. 107-113); the detaining power and the ICRC may also provide modern electronic communication facilities. Unlike POWs, civilian internees must be allowed to receive frequent visits from close relatives and be permitted to visit their homes in urgent cases, like death or serious illness (Art. 116). Finally, like POWs, internees are entitled to visits by the protecting powers or the ICRC, in order to ensure appropriate treatment for civilian internees (Art. 143).

The rights afforded civilians who qualify as protected persons are subject to one qualification. Article 5 of the GC provides authority to deny civilians suspected of engaging or having engaged in activities hostile to the security of a detaining power the right "to claim such rights and privileges under the present Convention as would, if exercised in the favour of such individual person, be prejudicial to the security of such State." Article 5 also specifically addresses civilians suspected of espionage or sabotage operations, providing that "such person shall, in those cases where absolute military security so requires, be regarded as having forfeited rights of communication under the present Convention." However, Article 5 also emphasizes that even these civilians must be treated humanely (including being afforded fair and regular trial process if tried for their activities), and that they should be fully restored to protected person status at "the earliest date consistent with the security of the State or Occupying Power, as the case may be."

The authority to transfer civilian internees is more limited than for transferring POWs. "Individual or mass forcible transfers, as well as deportations of protected persons from occupied territory to the territory of the Occupying Power or to that of any other country, occupied or not, are prohibited, regardless of their motive." (Art. 49). Violation of this provision is a grave breach of the GCC, resulting in an obligation to prosecute the responsible individual. Civilian internees held in the territory of a party to the conflict may not be transferred without the civilian's consent, nor may they be transferred to a non-party that is unwilling to apply the provisions of the GCC. Finally, civilian internees who are released at the end of hostilities shall not be prohibited from returning to their home and state of residence (Art. 45). Transfers between camps within occupied territory are to be carefully controlled, in circumstances that would maintain the health, safety, and well-being of the internees (Art. 127). The transfer must be conducted in a civilized fashion, with a "change of address" notification to next-of-kin, an allowance to carry personal effects and parcels, and a provision to forward mail "without delay" (Art. 128).

3. Civilian Detention Review and Release Protections

The decision to detain a civilian is subject to an initial review "as soon as possible by an appropriate court or administrative board" designated by the detaining power and at least semi-annual review thereafter.[80] While judicial review is not required, "where the decision is an administrative one, it must be made not by one official but by an administrative board offering the necessary guarantees of independence and impartiality."[81] These periodic reviews are automatic and conducted "with a view to favourably amending the initial decision if circumstances permit."[82] If the armed conflict has ended, civilian internees will be released "as soon as possible after the close of hostilities."[83]

III. The Role of Human Rights Law

An area of ongoing complexity is the interrelationship between the LOAC and international human rights law.[84] The sources of LOAC were addressed in Chapter 2. International human rights law began in 1948 and was not originally developed to regulate armed conflict.[85] The two are "distinct but complimentary bodies of law. They are both concerned with the protection of the life, health, and dignity of individuals."[86]

There is widespread consensus that certain fundamental human rights norms—norms that protect civilians from arbitrary deprivations of life, liberty, and property at the hands of state actors—apply at all times, including during periods of armed conflict.[87]

---

80. GC, *supra*, note 7, art. 43. Technically the review process differs based on location. In a state party's own territory, the review is by an "appropriate court or administrative board", while in occupied territory, a "competent body" should utilize a "regular procedure." Internment in Armed Conflict: Basic Rules and Challenges International Committee of the Red Cross (ICRC) Opinion Paper, November 2014. Yet, "[d]espite these and other textual differences the rules are in essence the same." *Id.*

81. IV Commentary to the 1949 Geneva Convention Relative to the Protection of Civilian Persons in Time of War 260-262 (Jean Picet ed., 1958).

82. *Id.*

83. GC, *supra*, note 7, art. 133. Like POWs, however, civilian internees who are serving a sentence for crimes in violation of international or domestic law may be retained until completion of their sentence or extradition.

84. *See,* e.g. Darragh Murray et al. Practitioners' Guide to Human Rights Law in Armed Conflict (2016) and Ken Watkin, Fighting at the Legal Boundaries: Controlling the Use of Force in Contemporary Conflict, Oxford University Press (2016).

85. "The Universal Declaration of Human Rights [adopted in 1948] is generally agreed to be the foundation of international human rights law." United Nations, *The Foundation of International Human Rights Law,* http://www.un.org/en/sections/universal-declaration/foundation-international-human-rights-law/index.html.

86. ICRC, *IHL and Human Rights Law,* https://www.icrc.org/en/document/international-humanitarian-law-and-international-human-rights-law-similarities-and.

87. *See* International Court of Justice, Advisory Opinion of the Israeli Wall in Palestine, para. 106 (2004) (stating that "the protection of human rights conventions does not cease in case of armed conflict.").

But the specifics of which human rights law applies during armed conflict, when, and how remain very much debated.[88]

The United States' interpretation of the legal applicability of human rights law during armed conflict is quite different from other countries, and those differences may impact the conduct of military operations with coalition partners with different views.[89] First, the United States position is that absent plain language in the text of a human rights treaty, like the International Covenant on Civil and Political Rights (ICCPR), indicating that the treaty applies extraterritorially, it should not be construed as such.[90] Second, in resolving whether to apply human rights law or LOAC during an armed conflict, the United States draws from the legal maxim *"lex specialis"* that "[a]s a rule the special rule overrides the general law" and the United Nations International Law Commission conclusion that

> special law has priority over general law is justified by the fact that such special law, being more concrete, often takes better account of the particular features of the context in which it is to be applied than any applicable general law. Its application may also often create a more equitable result and it may often better reflect the intent of the legal subjects.[91]

As the LOAC is the more special rule or law, developed to regulate armed conflict, for any issue addressed by both LOAC and human rights law, the United States applies the LOAC. Where an issue is not addressed by LOAC but is covered by human rights law, the United States' view is that an applicable human rights treaty would control.[92]

---

88. *See* Francoise Hampson, The Relationship Between International Humanitarian Law and Human Rights Law from the Perspective of Human Rights Treaty Body 90 Int'l Rev. Red Cross 549 (2008) and Geoff Corn, Mixing Apples and Hand Grenades: The Logical Limit of Applying Human Rights Norms to Armed Conflict, __ J. of IHL Stud. __ (2009).

89. International Committee of the Red Cross, Intercross Joint Series: Guest Blogger Ken Watkin on the Overlap of IHL and IHRL (explain how "[t]he United States and Canada appear to look at the extra-territorial application of human rights obligations very differently than Europe." Watkin adds that "from a European perspective the exclusionary nature of the IHL/IHRL debate is grounded in the European Court of Human Rights approach of looking at international conflict exclusively through a human rights lens regardless of the intensity of the violence, or the nature of the conflict in question."

90. *See* DoD LOW Manual, *supra*, note 44 at 1.6.3.3 (noting that the ICCPR "creates obligations for a State with respect to any person within its territory and subject to its jurisdiction" and that "[t]he inclusion of the reference to 'within its territory' . . . .in the ICCP was adopted as a result of a proposal made by U.S. delegate Eleanor Roosevelt—specifically to ensure that a state party's obligations would not apply to persons outside its territories, such as in occupied territory and leased territory). *See also* Marko Milanoic, Extraterritorial Application of Human Rights Treaties: Law, Principles, and Policy (Oxford University Press (2011)).

91. DoD LOW Manual, *supra*, note 44 at 1.3.2.1 *citing* U.N. International Law Commission, Conclusions of the work of the Study Group on the Fragmentation of International Law: Difficulties arising from the Diversification and Expansion of International Law 2(7) (2006).

92. *Id*. at 1.6.3.1 (stating that

> [o]n the other hand, during armed conflict, human rights treaties would clearly be controlling with respect to matters that are within their scope of application and that are not addressed by the law of war. For example, a time of war does not suspend the operation of the ICCPR with respect to matters within its scope of application. Therefore, as an illustration, participation in a war would in no way excuse a State Party to the ICCPR from

Many other countries do not share the U.S. view that the ICCPR does not apply extraterritorially. And the ICJ has observed that "the protection of the International Covenant of Civil and Political Rights does not cease in times of war. . . ."[93] But how does the ICCPR's prohibition against the arbitrary deprivation of life apply during armed conflict? The ICJ's answer is that "[t]he test of what is an arbitrary deprivation of life, however, then falls to be determined by the applicable *lex specialis*, namely, the law applicable in armed conflict which is designed to regulate the conduct of hostilities."[94] Under this approach,

> what constitutes an 'arbitrary' deprivation of life during the conduct of hostilities is to be determined by reference to international humanitarian law. This law does not prohibit the use of force in hostilities against lawful targets (for example combatants or civilians directly participating in hostilities) if necessary from a military perspective. . . .[95]

In recognition of this divergence of interpretations of international law, U.S. forces routinely emphasize the symmetry between fundamental human rights norms and the obligations derived from Common Article 3 and Article 75 of AP I. Compliance with these LOAC provisions, as well as other rules related to the protection of the civilian population, will normally protect the force from accusations of indifference to the human rights of the civilians they encounter. There are, however, instances where the overlay of human rights norms might add important flesh to the bones of Common Article 3 and Article 75. For example, while Common Article 3 prohibits "the passing of sentences and the carrying out of executions without previous judgment pronounced by a regularly constituted court, affording all the judicial guarantees which are recognized as indispensable by civilized peoples," it does not indicate what procedures satisfy this obligation. Article 75 is slightly more instructive, but it is also useful to look to human rights treaties, such as the ICCPR, as a source of analogy to develop adequate procedures. This practice is not uncommon, even for U.S. forces.

Other situations are more complex. For example, do U.S. forces operating in the territory of a co-belligerent bear an obligation to intervene to protect civilians from imminent threats to life? This is especially problematic where the forces have the apparent capacity to do so with little to no risk. Such situations might arise where U.S. forces observe civilians subjected to unlawful violence, or where they encounter civilians in dire need of medical attention.[96] Technically, respect for the sovereign co-belligerent requires subordination to

---

respecting and ensuring the right and opportunity of every citizen to vote and to be elected at genuine periodic elections.)
93. *See* Nuclear Advisory Opinion, *supra*, note 18.
94. *Id.*
95. African Commission on Human and Peoples' Rights, General Comment no. 3, para. 32 (Nov. 2015). The African Commission goes on to say that "[a]ny violation of international humanitarian law resulting in death, including war crimes, will be an arbitrary deprivation of life." This claim raises interesting questions about how mens rea and causation operate in the LOAC vs. human rights law.
96. *See*, e.g., Joseph Goldstein, *U.S. Soldiers Told to Ignore Sexual Abuse of Boys by Afghan Allies*, NY TIMES, Sept. 20, 2015 (contending that U.S. troops deployed to Afghanistan were ordered to ignore sexual abuse by Afghan Security Forces of Afghan boys).

co-belligerent authorities. However, omission in such situations will almost certainly be considered inconsistent with respect for fundamental human rights. Such situations must therefore be contemplated by commanders, and response authorities ideally included in the rules of engagement.

The inescapable reality is that the conduct of U.S. forces during military operations, particularly the treatment of civilians, will be critiqued against the standards of international human rights law. Moreover, responding to allegations of human rights violations with the platitudes of legal inapplicability will ring increasingly hollow in the future.

Compliance with LOAC civilian protections rules will generally protect U.S. forces from allegations of human rights violations.[97] However, legal advisors should be prepared to consider human rights law as a source of useful analogy to add substance to general LOAC obligations. Doing so will enhance the credibility of U.S. operations, and facilitate interoperability with coalition partners bound to comply with human rights norms as a matter of law.[98]

IV. Conclusion

Dealing with civilians is an inevitable aspect of contemporary military operations. Planning for the range of issues related to interaction with the civilian population impacted by military operations is an essential aspect of accomplishing any mission. These challenges have only increased in number and complexity as the result of conflicts involving non-state actors fighting in major civilian population centers. Judge Advocates contribute to this process by providing expertise on the LOAC obligations and authorities related to civilians. While it is unrealistic to expect that no civilian suffering will occur during mission execution, knowledge of this law coupled with good faith compliance efforts will mitigate that suffering, which is the ultimate objective the law seeks to achieve.

Many of the distinctions between types of civilians and the laws applicable in certain contexts are in reality operationally antiquated. In the context

---

97. *But see* African Commission on Human and Peoples' Rights, General Comment no. 3, para. 32 (Nov. 2015) (claiming that "[a]ny violation of international humanitarian law resulting in death, including war crimes, will be an arbitrary deprivation of life.") This raises interesting questions about how mens rea and causation operate in the LOAC vs. human rights law.

98. For example, the vast majority of the United States' European allies are parties to the European Convention on Human Rights (ECHR), which most assuredly applies outside Europe and during armed conflict. In the United Kingdom there have been more than 2,000 compensation claims and lawsuits filed alleging British Military human rights violations in Afghanistan and Iraq. Tim Ross, £150m Legal Bill *For Troops Just Doing Their Duty*, THE TELEGRAPH, Oct. 17, 2015. While the 2016 "Brexit" does not implicate the ECHR, by some accounts the application of the Convention to British forces involved in combat operations outside the United Kingdom may be a significant, even primary, issue in the next general election, scheduled for 2020. *See* Christopher Hope, *Theresa May to Fight 2020 Election on Plans to Take Britain Out of European Convention on Human Rights After Brexit Completed*, THE TELEGRAPH, Dec. 28, 2016.

of contemporary military operations, exceeding the minimum legal requirements is increasingly the norm, and the overarching rule is that commanders must take all feasible measures to reduce the risk to civilians whenever possible. Nonetheless, remaining grounded in the LOAC's requirements is critically important as commanders seek to allocate limited resources and balance the demands of military necessity with the civilian protection imperative. As will be explained in Chapter 13, because the most severe violations of the Geneva Conventions are those committed against protected persons, the legal definition of that term is a critical aspect of imposing accountability for battlefield misconduct. Ultimately, while commanders are expected to understand the general obligation to limit civilian suffering as much as possible, Judge Advocates must be prepared to provide advice based on the law as it stands, with all the complexities that entails.

Study Questions

1. Immediately following the start of OPERATION IRAQI FREEDOM, the Iraqi government took the following actions within Iraq:
    a. Detained hundreds of Iraqi civilians with immediate family members living in the United States.
    b. Detained 20 members of "Aid Without Borders," a religious mission group seeking to establish aid networks to help Assyrian Christians living in Iraq. The detained members are from a variety of nations, including the United States, Canada, Australia, and New Zealand.
    c. Detained an American tour group on a "Wonders of the World Tour" while they were visiting the Hanging Gardens of Babylon. The tour group consisted of an extended family of 20 people from the Kansas City area, including 87-year-old Ed and Ethel, their 50-year-old son Fred and his wife Fran, and their three kids, Greg (27), pregnant Gemma (25), and Gavin (24). Greg's three children are with him: Sebastian (8), Alexandra (5), and Victoria (4).

What is the status of these individuals under the LOAC and what protections does the LOAC afford them?

1. Following the U.S. invasion of Iraq, which of the following are protected persons?
    a. A U.S. civilian working in Iraq.
    b. A wounded U.S. soldier in Iraq.
    c. An Iraqi civilian in Mexico.
    d. An Iraqi student attending college in the United States.
    e. An Iraqi soldier visiting Las Vegas in the United States.
    f. A Chinese civilian in Iraq.
    g. An Iraqi civilian in Iraq.

2. Returning to the questions Major Smith asked you at the outset:
   a. What are the U.S. military's LOAC obligations to the women, children, and elderly? Does it matter if they are Iraqi?
   b. What LOAC "talking points" would you provide Major Smith when she is answering questions about Iraqi civilians wounded or killed during the conflict?
   c. Assuming the report is correct, may the U.S. military permissibly destroy a family's home?
   d. What is the status of the Iranians in the camp?
   e. What does the LOAC allow Major Smith to do regarding Akram? Is that the same or different than what you advise Major Smith to do?
   f. Assume Major Smith tells you that some of the U.S. Army personnel at the CMOC have personal cell phones. She wants to know if she can, and if she should, limit or restrict their use while deployed to Iraq. What do you tell her?

GC IV Protections Analysis Flowchart

START HERE → 1. Is the Person Located in Occupied Territory or a State Party to an Armed Conflict?
- NO → GC IV DOES NOT APPLY
- YES (GO TO STEP 2)

2. Occupied Territory, Int'l Armed Conflict (CA2), or Non-Int'l Armed Conflict (CA3)?
- NIAC (CA3) → GC IV DOES NOT APPLY
- Occupied Territory or IAC (CA2) → GC IV, Part II protections apply (GO TO STEP 3)

3. National of a State Party to GC IV and NOT Covered by GC I, II, or III?
- NO → ONLY GC IV PART II PRO'S APPLY
- YES (GO TO STEP 4)

4. Located in?
- Territory of a Party to the Conflict ("Belligerent State") (GO TO STEP 5A)
- OR Occupied Territory (GO TO STEP 5B)

5A. Nat'l of the Belligerent State that has hands on?
- YES → ONLY GC IV PART II PRO'S APPLY
- NO (GO TO STEP 6A)

6A. Nat'l of Neutral or Co-belligerent (Ally) w/ Normal Dip. Rep. in Belligerent State?
- YES → ONLY GC IV PART II PRO'S APPLY
- NO → "Protected Person" Part III, Sec. I and II pro's apply (GO TO STEP 7A)

7A. Interned?
- If YES, Part III, Sec. IV pro's also apply

5B. Nat'l of Occupying State?
- YES → ONLY GC IV PART II PRO'S APPLY
- NO (GO TO STEP 6B)

6B. Nat'l of Co-belligerent (Ally of Occupying State) w/ Normal Dip. Rep. in Occupying State?
- YES → ONLY GC IV PART II PRO'S APPLY
- NO → "Protected Person" Part III, Sec. I and III pro's apply (GO TO STEP 7B)

7B. Interned?
- If YES, Part III, Sec. IV pro's also apply

GC IV Protections Analysis Flowchart

KEY: DIP. REP. = DIPLOMATIC REPRESENTATION; INT'L = INTERNATIONAL; NAT'L = NATIONAL; PRO's = PROTECTIONS; SEC. = SECTION

ALL GC IV PROTECTIONS ARE CUMULATIVE

7   Targeting

"Sir, I hate to interrupt your lunch, but I think you had better come in here." The commander put down his fork and looked up at his operations officer, Major Greaves. "It's OK. What have you got?"

They talked as they walked into the tactical operations center (TOC)[1] from the small tent where the commander had been eating his lunch. "Well, sir, we think we have intelligence regarding a meeting among key Iraqi Republican Guard leaders, potentially including Saddam Hussein, that is going to take place in about an hour. The meeting is going to take place in a school building in a residential neighborhood in Baghdad and we don't think it will last very long. If we are going to strike it, we need to get the wheels rolling now. We believe that portions of the school may also be used by the military after this meeting as a communication center, but we think that decision will not be made until after the meeting occurs."

By this time, the commander and Major Greaves were in the heart of the TOC, staring at the large map of the area for which they were responsible. "2,[2] tell me about the intel," the commander said, as he looked at the specific area where the school was located. "Sir, the information comes from a human intelligence source that we have used in the past. He has provided us actionable intelligence before and we rate him as very reliable. The information is less than six hours old," responded Captain Pindle. "What about the neighborhood?" the commander queried. "It is a middle- to lower-class neighborhood. Because the meeting is scheduled for 1500,[3] there will be plenty of people in their homes and moving around the area. Schools have been out since the invasion began, so we don't anticipate

---

1. The tactical operations center, or TOC, is the nerve center from which the commander and his primary advisors conduct the operation. It is usually run by a "watch officer" or "battle captain" and is staffed by representatives of all the major staff elements and representatives from the major units working for the commander.

2. A reference to the member of the commander's staff responsible for intelligence operations. In a normal tactical staff, the S1 is responsible for administration and personnel, the S2 for intelligence, the S3 for operations, the S4 for logistics, the S5 for civilian affairs, and the S6 for communications.

3. The military uses a 24-hour clock. 1500 is 3 P.M.

many civilians in the school, but there will certainly be some in the surrounding homes and streets."

"Do we have a predator drone up there yet?" the commander asked. "Not yet. We have talked with the Division[4] headquarters and warned them we may be asking for one, but the Division wanted to make sure you had given the 'OK' before they diverted the predator from current operations," answered Major Greaves. The commander pondered the information for a moment, then turned to the battle captain and ordered, "Get the armed Predator from Division there as soon as you can. I need to be able to see that target."

"Do we know where in the school the meeting is going to happen?" the commander asked. "The school is a big target. Are we going to have to destroy the whole place?" he continued. "We don't know that, sir," Captain Pindle answered. "Our source knew the meeting was going to happen at the school, but no further details."

"ALO,[5] what have you got?" asked the commander. "Sir, given the importance of this target, I think I can get you an F-16. The 2 and I have looked at avenues of approach and the burst radius of the munition. We think if we come in from the north and hit the school here," the ALO said, pointing to a larger picture of the school, "it will minimize the collateral damage to the surrounding civilian structures but still take out most of the building and almost certainly kill everyone inside." "When you say 'minimize,' what do you mean? Give me some details," the commander asked. "Here is the computer simulation of the effect of the munition if we attack from the north." Pointing to the chart he was handing to the commander, the ALO continued, "You can see the expected burst radius and the estimates of casualties given the time of day and the 2's best guess at the civilian activity in the area at the time. Civilian deaths, injury, and damage to civilian property will be minimal but there is the potential to be some."

"How does this compare with the hellfire missile from the Predator?" asked the commander. The ALO handed the commander another chart. "As you can see, the chance of civilian injury and damage decreases, but so does the chance of killing the targets."

"There is no way we can get in there on the ground? We could get some great information from them if we could capture them instead of kill them," queried the commander. "The neighborhood is full of militia and other sympathizers. There will also be some army units there at the time to provide local security," responded Captain Pindle. "If we tried to get in, there is no way we could do it without alerting the leaders to our approach, and there are too many exits out of the area to seal it off."

---

4. Army units are generally organized into units that, going from smallest to largest, include squad, platoon, company, battalion, brigade, division, corps, and army. The lower units combine to make up the higher unit so several squads compose a platoon, several platoons compose a company, and so on. In this scenario, the commander is the leader of a brigade and his unit, along with several other units, compose a division that is led by a division commander who would normally be a two star general.

5. The ALO is the air liaison officer who is a representative of the Air Force and works with an Army unit to allocate Air Force assets such as fighter aircraft to Army units when needed.

"OK," *the commander said as he stared at the map.* "JAG, what do you think?" *The commander turned to Captain Watts.*

I. Introduction

You have already read in Chapter 2 about some of the most fundamental principles of the law of armed conflict (LOAC). These principles, such as military necessity, humanity, distinction, and proportionality, deeply affect all military operations. The practical application of these principles is demonstrated most clearly in what is known as the "methods and means of warfare." The "methods" of warfare deal with how militaries go about fighting. This chapter on targeting will introduce you to how the law regulates the methods of warfare. Chapter 8 will discuss some tactics that are methods of warfare but will also introduce you to the means of warfare, generally encompassing the weapons of warfare.

Throughout this discussion of targeting, feel free to refer back to Chapter 2 to ensure that you understand the LOAC's fundamental principles. A thorough understanding of these principles is vital to applying military force in armed conflict. All four of these principles have significant impact on targeting decisions. The following sections will take those fundamental principles and apply them to the targeting process.

II. The Targeting Process

It is a simple reality of warfare that in order to defeat an enemy it is necessary to attack and destroy the enemy's combat capability, including its forces and equipment. This process, known as the targeting process, involves identifying a potential target or desired effect and determining whether it is a military objective; selecting the most appropriate capability, whether kinetic or non-kinetic, to achieve the desired operational effect; executing military operations to employ the combat capability; and assessing the effects achieved. Once the effects are assessed, that information is fed back into the targeting process, and the cycle continuously repeats itself.[6]

The targeting process occurs at all levels of military operations from tactical to national. President Lyndon Johnson famously said in the midst of the Vietnam War that no one bombed an outhouse without him approving it.[7] This national level control of operational level targeting decisions during the Vietnam War was unusual. One of the current means to exercise national level

---

6. U.S. Dep't of Army, Field Manual 6-20-10, Tactics, Techniques and Procedures for the Targeting Process, Chapter 2 (May 8, 1996).
7. *See* John T. Correll, *Rolling Thunder*, available at http://www.airforce-magazine.com/Magazine Archive/Pages/2005/March%202005/0305thunder.aspx (Mar. 2005).

control is through rules of engagement (ROE), which will be discussed below. As will be seen, some of the most problematic issues in armed conflict center on targeting decisions. Not only do these decisions and their results capture the news headlines, they also sway public opinion. No one can doubt the impact of pictures of dead civilian bodies spread across the front page of national newspapers in the aftermath of an attack.

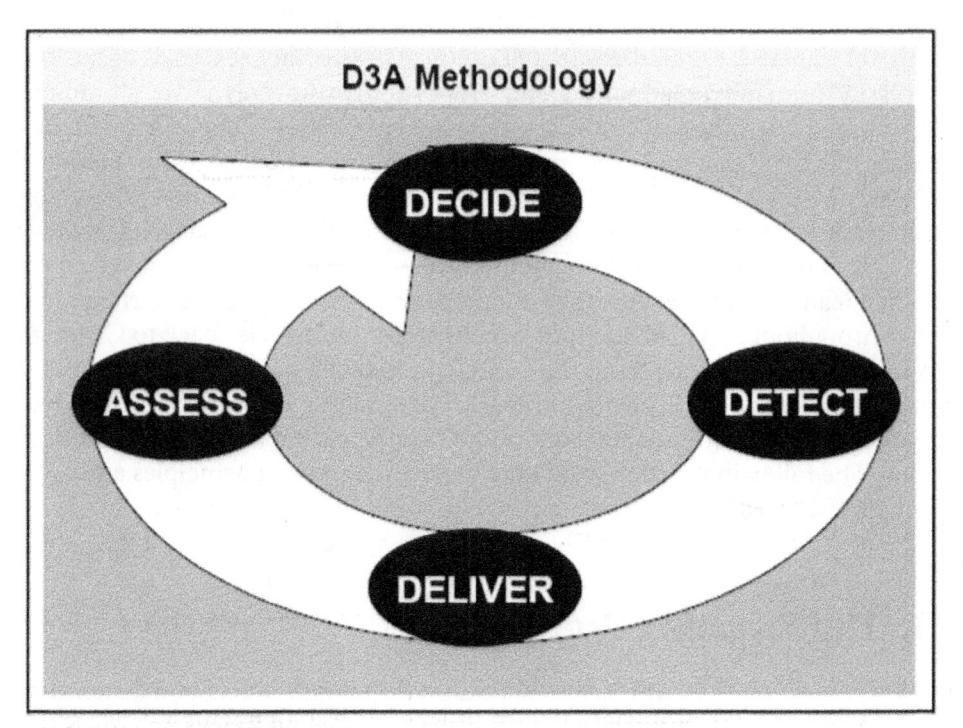

D3A Methodology

DECIDE → DETECT → DELIVER → ASSESS

Source: U.S. Army Field Manual 3-60, p. 2-1, 26 Nov. 2010.

Targeting in U.S. military doctrine is defined as "the process of selecting and prioritizing targets and matching the appropriate response to them, taking account of operational requirements and capabilities."[8] As mentioned in Chapter 2, targeting is centered on the effects that it will produce. Targeting is much more nuanced than merely blowing things up and killing the enemy; it involves influencing people to do things as well as to not do things.

At the earliest planning stages of an operation, military planners begin to consider targeting issues. Once the planners are given a potential military mission, they begin to determine what targets might need to be attacked to accomplish that mission. In the process, they also determine what things or places should not be targeted. This is known as a "no-strike list" and often contains buildings with special historical significance or infrastructure that would adversely affect the civilian population. Included in this process is reliance on

---

8. Chairman of the Joint Chiefs of Staff, JP 3-60, DOCTRINE FOR TARGETING I-1 (Jan. 31, 2013).

historical data, prevailing intelligence, satellite imagery, and every other source of up-to-date information. Failure to use the most current information can result in attacking the wrong target, such as when the United States mistakenly bombed the Chinese Embassy in Belgrade during military operations against Serbia in 1999.

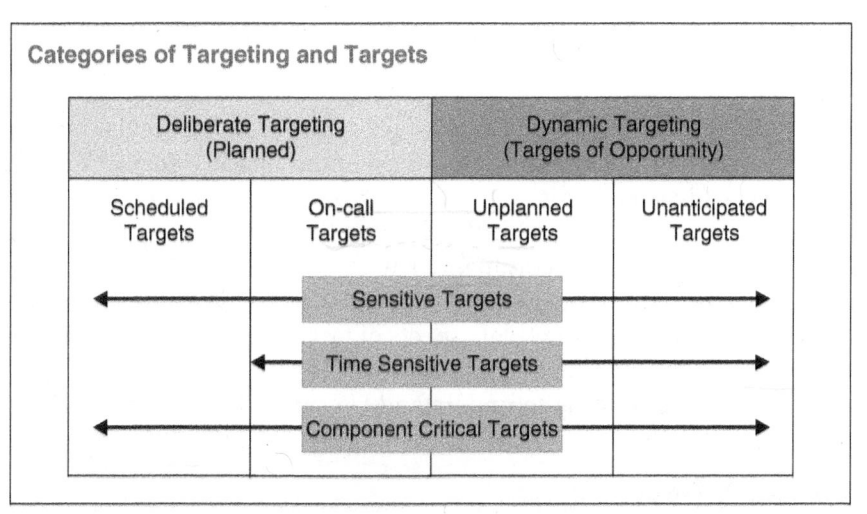

```
Categories of Targeting and Targets

| Deliberate Targeting        | Dynamic Targeting             |
| (Planned)                   | (Targets of Opportunity)      |
|-----------------------------|-------------------------------|
| Scheduled    | On-call      | Unplanned    | Unanticipated  |
| Targets      | Targets      | Targets      | Targets        |

              ←── Sensitive Targets ──→
              ←── Time Sensitive Targets ──→
              ←── Component Critical Targets ──→
```

Figure II-1. Categories of Targeting and Targets. Joint Publication 3-60 (Jan. 31, 2013), p. II-2.

This planning becomes the basis of the actual targeting process as the mission begins. During military operations, some targets can be scheduled hours or days in advance. Other targets appear suddenly and need to be attacked on little notice. The U.S. military has a process of scheduling attacks on targets that allows sufficient flexibility for both types of targets. The process starts with a targeting meeting where the commander and his staff review potential targets that have either been designated from the commander or have been nominated from subordinate units. At the targeting meeting, the various targets are prioritized and attack assets, such as aircraft or artillery, are allocated against those targets. For targets requiring air attack assets, an air tasking order (ATO) is produced that is a combined revolving 24-hour publication of the proposed allocation of attack assets. The process starts 72 hours before the intended attack and then is refined as the time for attack gets closer. The ATO also reserves some air assets for targets that were not anticipated but that may become important based on how the battle progresses.

The process is different at each level at which it occurs. For a large operation like the invasion of Iraq, there would likely be a Joint Air Operations Center that would coordinate the overall aircraft targeting for the entire operation. But at each level below that, there would also be a targeting group that would meet and discuss targeting issues. In each of these groups, from top to bottom, a military lawyer would be present to ensure all targeting operations were conducted in compliance with the LOAC. Just as the commander in the scenario at the beginning of the chapter turned to Captain Watts for his legal advice, lawyers are actively engaged in the targeting process from beginning to end and from the smallest unit to the largest.

III. Applying the General Principles in Targeting

Having briefly talked about the typical targeting process, let's return now to the scenario that opened this chapter. The commander had just turned to Captain Watts, his legal advisor, for his advice on the legal aspects of targeting. The following sections will walk through the analysis that Captain Watts would conduct in order to provide his commander with complete and appropriate legal advice. Among other documents that Captain Watts will certainly have access to and rely on when analyzing legal aspects of targeting will be the DoD Law of War Manual.[9] Chapter 5 specifically deals with this topic, and is an invaluable reference for anyone wanting to understand U.S. views on this topic.

A. Military Necessity

As you recall from Chapter 2, the principle of military necessity "justifies the use of all measures needed to defeat the enemy as quickly and efficiently as possible that are not prohibited by the law of war."[10] In a targeting analysis, invoking military necessity to target someone or something requires a military need to undertake the action, and the law of war must not forbid the action. Remember, military necessity is no defense to violating the LOAC, including the rules of targeting. As Captain Watts considers his response to the commander, he is going to have to weigh the necessity of the attack versus the legal harms associated with it. His first principle of analysis will likely be the principle of distinction.

1. Distinction

The principle of distinction is sometimes referred to as the "grandfather of all principles," and is the application of the balancing of humanity and military necessity in targeting. The essence of the principle is that military attacks should be directed at combatants and military targets, and not civilians or

---

9. U.S. DEPARTMENT OF DEFENSE, LAW OF WAR MANUAL (2015) (revised Dec. 2016), available at https://www.defense.gov/Portals/1/Documents/pubs/DoD%20Law%20of%20War%20Manual%20-%20June%202015%20Updated%20Dec%202016.pdf?ver=2016-12-13-172036-190 (hereinafter DoD LOW Manual (Dec. 2016)).

10. DoD LOW Manual (Dec. 2016), supra, note 9.

civilian property.[11] Additional Protocol I, Article 48 sets out the rule: "Parties to the conflict shall at all times distinguish between the civilian population and combatants and between civilian objects and military objectives and accordingly shall direct their operations only against military objectives."

In support of the principle of distinction, the LOAC creates certain presumptions. The first presumption is that military objects and combatants are targetable because of their status. The corollary presumption is that it is not militarily necessary to target civilians and civilian objects. These presumptions can be overcome by actions or events as will be explained below, but otherwise the presumptions carry great weight in targeting decisions. In the scenario at the beginning of the chapter, these presumptions alone do not provide a lot of clarity for Captain Watts. Under that general analysis, the military leaders are presumed to be targetable and the school in which they will meet is presumed to not be targetable. A more detailed analysis is clearly needed.

Commanders are required to "do everything feasible to verify that the objectives to be attacked are neither civilians nor civilian objects and are not subject to special protection but are military objectives."[12] In this case, "feasible" is a high, but not an absolute, standard. When formulating the convention, the delegates understood the term "feasible" to mean what was practicable under the existing circumstances. This includes gathering information in order to provide the commander with an accurate picture of the situation. In the words of the Office of the Prosecutor for the International Criminal Tribunal for the Former Yugoslavia (ICTY), "A military commander must set up an effective intelligence gathering system to collect and evaluate information concerning potential targets. The commander must also direct his forces to use available technical means to properly identify targets during operations."[13] If the commander does what is feasible to ensure proper distinction in targeting, then even when mistakes are made, he has not violated the law.

a. Persons

As was discussed in Chapter 4, many nations argue that every person on the battlefield falls into one of two categories, either a civilian or a combatant. The United States and a number of other countries believe that this third category of "unprivileged belligerents" exists and make targeting decisions accordingly. There are also certain persons who would otherwise be targetable but receive a

---

11. DoD LOW Manual (Dec. 2016), *supra*, note 9, § 5.2.

12. Protocol Additional to the Geneva Conventions of 12 August 1949, and Relating to the Protection of Victims of International Armed Conflicts, art. 57.2(a)(i); June 8, 1977, 1125 U.N.T.S. 17512 (hereinafter AP I); DoD LOW Manual (Dec. 2016), *supra*, note 9, § 5.2.3.

13. Final Report to the Prosecutor by the Committee Established to Review the NATO Bombing Campaign Against the Federal Republic of Yugoslavia, ¶29, *available at* http://www.icty.org/x/file/About/OTP/otp_report_nato_bombing_en.pdf.

protected status. These persons will be discussed at the end of this section. For Captain Watts, understanding these categories of persons is vital to his legal analysis of the proposed military operation.

(1) Combatants

The easiest category in targeting is combatants. These are persons who belong to one of the categories referred to in GPW, Article 4(A)(1), (2), (3), or (6).[14] Individuals are combatants based on a status granted to them by a state. Because only a State can grant combatant status to an individual, that person becomes an agent of the State and is targetable anywhere and anytime.[15]

For example, combatants need not be fighting or armed to be targeted. They may be retreating, hiding, or even eating, showering, or sleeping. They are targetable based on their status and remain targetable until their status changes. Their status can change either through their submission through surrender or by becoming *hors de combat* through wounds or sickness such that they are incapable of continuing the fight and cannot make their surrender known.

The targeting of combatants is also not limited to geography. A combatant need not be on an active battlefield to be targetable. If two combatants meet in a third country, they have a legal right under international law to target each other. They may be punished under the third nation's domestic law for murder, but they have not violated the LOAC by targeting each other at a geographic distance from the active battlefield.

(2) Civilians

In contrast to combatants, the rule for civilians is that "[t]he civilian population as such, as well as individual civilians, shall not be the object of attack."[16] As mentioned above, the general rule is that civilians and civilian property may not be the subject or sole object of a military attack. For the purposes of targeting, civilians are protected from attack unless and for such time as they take a direct part in the hostilities.

In the *Galic* case, the ICTY took up the issue of targeting of civilians. In that case, General Galic was in charge of the forces surrounding Sarajevo during the Bosnian conflict. He was charged with ordering a campaign of attacks that specifically targeted civilians in violation of the LOAC. The following excerpt from the judgment of the case provides a useful discussion of targeting civilians.

> The Defence's case is that civilian casualties were collateral to legitimate military activity. The casualties resulted as well from targeting errors and stray

---

14. Geneva Convention Relative to the Treatment of Prisoners of War, art. 4, Aug. 12, 1949, 6 U.S.T. 3316, 75 U.N.T.S. 972 (hereinafter GPW); DoD LOW Manual (Dec. 2016), *supra*, note 9, § 5.7.
15. DoD LOW Manual (Dec. 2016), *supra*, note 9, § 5.7.1.
16. AP I, *supra*, note 12, art. 51.2; DoD LOW Manual (Dec. 2016), *supra*, note 9, § 5.2.

bullets. According to the Defence, some casualties may have been the result of ABiH forces firing upon their own civilians.

. . .

The evidence demonstrates beyond reasonable doubt that Sarajevo civilians were indeed made the object of deliberate attack by SRK forces. The Trial Chamber heard from local witnesses who had experienced a multiplicity of attacks in their neighbourhoods. They were attacked while attending funerals, while in ambulances, trams, and buses, and while cycling. They were attacked while tending gardens, or shopping in markets, or clearing rubbish in the city. Children were targeted while playing or walking in the streets. . . .

The first sniping incident I shall discuss concerns the killing of Munira Zametica, a 48-year-old civilian woman on 11 July 1993.

Mrs. Zametica had gone to the Dobrinja river to fetch water. She remained for a while on the north-western side of the bridge. The bridge shielded her from sniping fire that had been on-going through that day. The half-dozen people standing with her hesitated to approach the river bank, for this would have meant leaving the shelter of the bridge. When Mrs. Zametica overcame her hesitation, and went down to the river to fill her bucket, she was struck by a bullet. The shooting continued. The bystanders and Mrs. Zametica's daughter, who had arrived in the meantime, could not approach the victim because of the danger. Mrs. Zametica was face down in the river, bleeding. She was finally pulled out of the water and taken to hospital, where she died. The Trial Chamber has concluded that she was deliberately shot from the area of the Orthodox church in Dobrinja, a well-known source of sniper fire under SRK control.

. . .

The exact number of civilian casualties from these attacks is not known. What is known is that hundreds of civilians were killed and thousands were injured in sniping and shelling incidents over the two-year period covered by the Indictment. A fraction of these, but no more than a fraction, may have been accidents.[17]

As the Court held in this case, the LOAC does not allow for targeting of civilians who are not taking part in hostilities. Civilians may be killed either incidental to operations or by accident, but where civilians who are not participating in hostilities are directly targeted, there is no excuse under the LOAC.

In addition to the general prohibition on targeting civilians, AP I provides for expanded protections of the civilian population from "indiscriminate" attacks. Article 51 states

> 4. Indiscriminate attacks are prohibited. Indiscriminate attacks are:
> (a) those which are not directed at a specific military objective;
> (b) those which employ a method or means of combat which cannot be directed at a specific military objective; or

---

17. ICTY Press Summary of Judgement in the Case of the Prosecutor v. Stanislav Galic, *available at* http://www.icty.org/sid/8148. The actual case is Prosecutor v. Stanislav Galić, Case No. IT-98-29-T, Summary of Judgement, 2-4 (Dec. 5, 2003) and is available at http://www.icty.org/x/cases/galic/tjug/en/031205_Gali_summary_en.pdf (last visited Feb. 22, 2011).

(c) those which employ a method or means of combat the effects of which cannot be limited as required by this Protocol; and consequently, in each such case, are of a nature to strike military objectives and civilians or civilian objects without distinction.[18]

Therefore, even if not specifically targeting civilians, if an attack is conducted indiscriminately, the attacker is still in violation of the LOAC because of the risk such attacks pose to civilians. In addition to ensuring the protection of civilians, Captain Watts will also have to make sure the attack is not an indiscriminate attack.[19]

As discussed in Chapter 4, the prohibition on targeting civilians is not absolute. AP I, Article 51(3) states that civilians enjoy protection from targeting "unless and for such time as they take a direct part in hostilities."[20] Those civilians who are directly participating in hostilities, or DPH-ing, lose their protection and can be targeted. They regain their protection once they are no longer DPH-ing, and can no longer be targeted. But remember, there are different views on how to interpret the meaning of both the actions that equate to DPH-ing, and the time element associated with DPH-ing.

Additionally, those nations who do not accept the doctrine of unprivileged belligerency discussed below would target members of organized armed groups (or at least those filling a military role) as DPH-ers. For those nations, the targeting criteria would correspond to their definition of when a civilian directly participates.

(3) Unprivileged Belligerents

As mentioned earlier in this book, this category is controversial and currently rejected by a majority of states. However, modern armed conflict is driving a reevaluation of this idea and even the ICRC seems to recognize the need to make special allowance for organized armed groups that are taking part in hostilities as structured participants.

Chapter 4 provided insight into the long history of the concept of unprivileged belligerents (or unlawful combatants as they are sometime termed). For the purposes of this chapter, the most important question is whether they should be targeted as civilians who are directly participating, with all the restrictive elements of that designation, or whether there is a broader authority to target them.

The ICRC argues that even organized armed groups who are involved in the conflict still should be treated as civilians unless they belong to a party to the conflict. The Interpretive Guidance states with respect to targeting:

---

18. AP I, *supra,* note 12, art. 51.4.
19. DoD LOW Manual (Dec. 2016), *supra,* note 9, § 5.12.
20. *See also* DoD LOW Manual (Dec. 2016), *supra,* note 9, § 5.8.

For the purposes of the principle of distinction in non-international armed conflict, all persons who are not members of State armed forces or organized armed groups of a party to the conflict are civilians and, therefore, entitled to protection against direct attack unless and for such time as they take a direct part in hostilities. In non-international armed conflict, organized armed groups constitute the armed forces of a non-State party to the conflict and consist only of individuals whose continuous function it is to take a direct part in hostilities ("continuous combat function").[21]

Again, many States, including the United States, take a contrary view and argue that membership in an organized armed group is sufficient for targeting.[22] These States argue by analogy that cooks, financiers, logistical personnel, and many others who are members of the State's regular armed forces who do not have a "combat function" are still targetable by the enemy because of their status and because they play a key role in the overall success of the organization. These States believe that members of organized armed groups should be treated similarly and be targetable simply due to membership in the group.[23]

Currently, this is an unresolved area of the law that is playing itself out on the modern battlefield.

(4) Other Protected Persons

There are other categories of persons that are specifically preserved from targeting, even though they might otherwise qualify as targetable.[24]

(a) Persons Who are *"Hors de Combat"*

Persons who are *"hors de combat"* are "out of the battle" and are no longer targetable, provided they refrain from hostile acts and do not attempt to escape.[25] Several categories of such persons exist:

i. Persons in the Power of an Adverse Party

This would include combatants and others who are in the power of opposing forces, including but not limited to those who are Prisoners of War.[26]

---

21. ICRC Interpretive Guidance on the Notion of Direct Participation in Hostilities Under International Humanitarian Law 1009 (Feb. 26, 2009) (prepared by Nils Melzer), *available at* http://www.icrc.org/eng/assets/files/other/irrc-872-reports-documents.pdf (last visited Feb. 22, 2011) (hereinafter ICRC Interpretive Guidance).
22. DoD LOW Manual (Dec. 2016), *supra*, note 9, § 5.6.2.
23. DoD LOW Manual (Dec. 2016), *supra*, note 9, § 5.7.3.
24. DoD LOW Manual (Dec. 2016), *supra*, note 9, § 5.5.2.
25. AP I, *supra*, note 12, art. 41; DoD LOW Manual (Dec. 2016), *supra*, note 9, § 5.9.
26. AP I, *supra*, note 12, art. 41.2.a; DoD LOW Manual (Dec. 2016), *supra*, note 9, § 5.9.2.

ii. Persons Who Have Clearly Expressed an Intention to Surrender

Once a person on the battlefield surrenders, they are no longer targetable.[27] However, they must genuinely desire to surrender, make that desire clear, and it must be feasible for the opposing forces to accept their surrender.[28]

iii. Persons Who Have Been Rendered Unconscious or are Otherwise Incapacitated by Wounds or Sickness, and Therefore are Incapable of Defending Themselves

Those soldiers who have fallen by reason of sickness or wounds and who cease to fight are to be respected and protected.[29] Civilians are included in the definition of wounded and sick ("who, because of trauma, disease . . . are in need of medical assistance and care and who refrain from any act of hostility").[30] Shipwrecked members of the armed forces at sea are to be respected and protected.[31] Shipwrecked includes downed passengers/crews on aircraft, ships in peril, and castaways.

In contrast to paratroopers, who are presumed to be on a military mission and therefore may be targeted,[32] parachutists who are crewmen of a disabled aircraft are presumed to be out of combat and may not be targeted unless it is apparent they are engaging in hostilities while in the process of parachuting to safety.[33] Parachutists, according to AP I, Article 42, "shall be given the opportunity to surrender before being made the object of attack" and are clearly treated differently from paratroopers.

(b) Medical Personnel

Medical personnel are considered out of combat if they are exclusively engaged in medical duties.[34] They may not be directly attacked so long as they remain exclusively engaged in medical duties. If medical personnel take part in hostilities, other than in self-defense against brigands or marauders, they lose their protection and may be targeted along with other combatants. Additionally, accidental killing or wounding of such personnel due to their proximity to military objectives "gives no just cause for complaint."[35] Medical personnel include medical personnel of the armed forces such as doctors, surgeons, nurses, chemists, stretcher-bearers, medics, corpsmen, orderlies, etc., who are "exclusively

---

27. AP I, *supra*, note 12, art. 41.2.b.
28. DoD LOW Manual (Dec. 2016), *supra*, note 9, § 5.9.3.
29. Geneva Convention for the Amelioration of the Condition of the Wounded and Sick in Armed Forces in the Field, art. 12, Aug. 12, 1949, 6 U.S.T. 3314, 75 U.N.T.S. 970 (hereinafter GWS); Geneva Convention for the Amelioration of the Condition of Wounded, Sick, and Shipwrecked Members at Sea, art. 12, Aug. 12, 1949, U.S.T. 3217, 75 U.N.T.S. 971 (hereinafter GWS Sea).
30. AP I, *supra*, note 12, art. 8(a).
31. GWS Sea, *supra*, note 29, art. 12; THE COMMANDER'S HANDBOOK ON THE LAW OF NAVAL OPERATIONS, NWP 1-14M, ¶11.6 (July 2007).
32. FM 27-10, *supra*, note 9, para. 30.
33. DoD LOW Manual (Dec. 2016), *supra*, note 9, § 5.9.5.
34. GWS, *supra*, note 29, art. 24; DoD LOW Manual (Dec. 2016), *supra*, note 9, § 5.5.2.
35. FM 27-10, *supra*, note 9, para. 225.

engaged" in the direct care of the wounded and sick, as well as administrative staffs of medical units (e.g., drivers, generator operators, cooks, etc.).

(c) Auxiliary Medical Personnel of the Armed Forces

To gain the protections from targeting, auxiliary medical personnel must have received "special training" and be carrying out their medical duties when they come in contact with the enemy.[36]

(d) Medical Transport

Though not "persons" as such, ground transports of the wounded and sick or of medical equipment shall not be attacked if performing a medical function.[37] Under the Geneva Conventions of 1949, medical aircraft were protected from direct attack only if they flew in accordance with a previous agreement between the parties as to their route, time, and altitude. AP I extends further protection to medical aircraft flying over areas controlled by friendly forces. Under this regime, identified medical aircraft are to be respected, regardless of whether a prior agreement between the parties exists. In "contact zones," protection can only be effective by prior agreement; medical aircraft "shall nevertheless be respected after they have been recognized as such."[38] Medical aircraft in areas controlled by an adverse party must have a prior agreement in order to gain protection.[39]

(e) Relief Societies

Personnel of National Red Cross Societies and other recognized relief societies as well as personnel of relief societies of neutral countries are protected from direct attack.[40]

(f) Chaplains

Chaplains and their assistants are also considered protected from direct targeting, though they do not wear distinctive insignia such as medical personnel wear, making them much more difficult to discern on the battlefield.[41]

(g) Civilian Medical and Religious Personnel

Article 15 of AP I requires that civilian medical and religious personnel shall be respected and protected. They receive the benefits of the provisions of the Geneva Conventions and their respective Additional Protocols concerning the protection and identification of medical personnel. Article 15 also dictates that

---

36. GWS, *supra*, note 29, art. 25.
37. *Id.*, art. 35; DoD LOW Manual (Dec. 2016), *supra*, note 9, § 5.5.2.
38. AP I, *supra*, note 12, art. 26(1).
39. *Id.*, art. 25-27; DoD LOW Manual (Dec. 2016), *supra*, note 9, § 5.5.2.
40. GWS, *supra*, note 29, art. 26-27.
41. *Id.*, art. 24.

any help possible shall be given to civilian medical personnel when civilian medical services are disrupted due to combat.

(h) Personnel Engaged in the Protection of Cultural Property

Article 17 of the 1954 Hague Cultural Property Convention[42] established a duty to respect (not directly attack) persons engaged in the protection of cultural property. The regulations attached to the Convention provide for specific positions as cultural protectors and for their identification.

(i) Journalists

Journalists are given protection as "civilians," even when accompanying military forces, provided they take no action adversely affecting their status as civilians.[43]

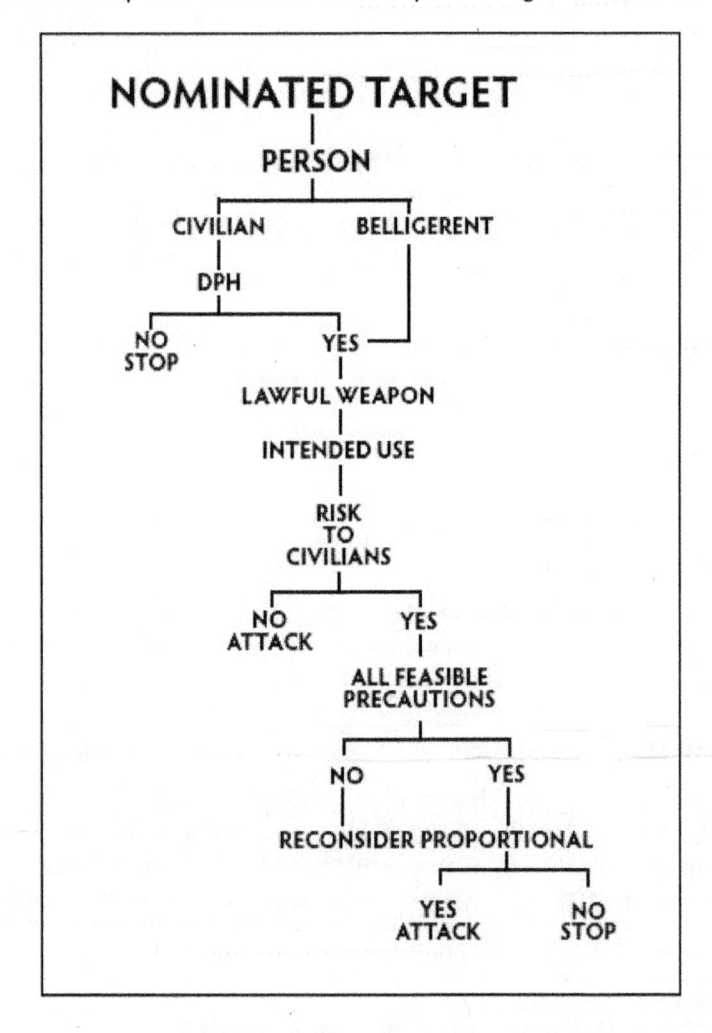

```
                    NOMINATED TARGET
                           |
                        PERSON
                     /          \
              CIVILIAN         BELLIGERENT
                 |                  |
                DPH                 |
              /     \               |
            NO      YES ————————————
            STOP     |
                  LAWFUL WEAPON
                     |
                  INTENDED USE
                     |
                    RISK
                     TO
                  CIVILIANS
                   /      \
                 NO        YES
               ATTACK       |
                       ALL FEASIBLE
                       PRECAUTIONS
                         /      \
                        NO      YES
                         |       |
                    RECONSIDER PROPORTIONAL
                         /      \
                       YES      NO
                     ATTACK    STOP
```

---

42. Convention for Protection of Cultural Property in Event of Armed Conflict, May 14, 1954, 249 U.N.T.S. 240 (hereinafter 1954 Cultural Property Convention).

43. DoD LOW Manual (Dec. 2016), *supra*, note 9, § 5.8.3.2.

The diagram on page 260 is a flow chart that is useful in analyzing decisions concerning the targeting of persons. If Captain Watts were to use this in his analysis of the proposed mission against the Iraqi generals, he would first conclude that the persons being targeted were belligerents because they are members of the opposing armed forces. He would then consider the lawfulness of the weapons to be used (which shall be discussed in more detail in Chapter 8), and if there was any risk to civilians. As the intelligence picture provides that there might be risk to civilians, Captain Watts would need to consider whether all feasible precautions have been taken, and then conduct a proportionality analysis (which will be discussed below).

b. Objects

In addition to persons, Captain Watts must also consider what objects are being targeted. The plan is to attack a school building, hoping that the destruction caused will also kill the Iraqi generals inside. While the real target is the Generals (and maybe Saddam Hussein), the school becomes an inseparable part of the attack and must also be analyzed. There are three categories of objects: military objectives, civilian objects, and protected objects or places. In compliance with the principle of distinction, the general rule is that "[a]ttacks shall be limited strictly to military objectives."[44] Civilian objects are immune from direct attack so long as they retain their civilian character and are not converted into military objectives. Some civilian objects are given special status or treated differently because of their role in civil society. These will be discussed at the end of this section.

(1) Military Objectives

Military objective is a component of military necessity. The methodology for determining that an object is a military objective assists the commander in applying the doctrine of military necessity to targeting. AP I contains a definition of military objective that is generally considered to be customary and is followed by the United States[45] as "those objects which by their nature, location, purpose or use make an effective contribution to military action and whose total or partial destruction, capture, or neutralization, in the circumstances ruling at the time, offers a definite military advantage."[46] This sets up a three-part test. First, the object to be targeted must meet one of the four criteria with respect to the military operation, and even if it does so, the commander must also determine that it makes, or could make, an effective contribution to military action. Finally, the commander must also determine that attacking the object will offer his forces a definite military advantage.[47] While these elements of the definition are most often considered in conjunction with one another (particularly the

---

44. AP I, *supra*, note 12, art. 52(2).
45. DoD LOW Manual (Dec. 2016), *supra*, note 9, § 5.6.3.
46. AP I, *supra*, note 12, art. 52(2).
47. *Id.*, art. 52.

nature, location, purpose, and use criteria), each of these elements of the definition deserves a more detailed analysis.

(a) Nature

The term "nature" is defined in the Commentary to API as "all objects directly used by the armed forces."[48] This would include objects such as weapons, tanks, transports, and materiel. The key to this category of targetable items is that the very nature of the object, the reason for which it was created, was to serve a military purpose. In a sense, this category is the object equivalent of a combatant. The object has a certain status because of its nature, not because of any other actions or uses. In the attack against Iraq, Iraqi military weapons, weapons storage areas, ammunition storage areas, military barracks, headquarters buildings, military communications facilities, and military transports such as ships, trucks, cars, and motorcycles are all military objectives by their nature.[49]

As Captain Watts does his analysis of the proposed attack on the school where the Iraqi generals are meeting, he will most likely determine that the school is not a military objective by its nature. He will have to continue through the other criteria to see if it meets this first element of the test for military objective.

(b) Location

Location is defined in the Commentary as "a site which is of special importance for military operations in view of its location."[50] This would include civilian objects such as a bridge, a road, a building, or a piece of ground that is otherwise a civilian object but that because of its location temporarily becomes a military objective and is targetable. The most common example where location makes a civilian objective targetable is a bridge. For example, assume there is a military base outside of Baghdad that is connected to Baghdad by a road. Along that road are several bridges that cross rivers. This road is used not only by the military but also by civilians and is one of the main access roads into Baghdad for residents who live outside the city. During the attack, U.S. forces may want to destroy that road or some of the bridges to prevent the movement of Iraqi forces from the military base into Baghdad. The location of that bridge along a known route of movement of military forces makes it a military objective.[51] Another example of location that is less interwoven with "use" or "purpose" is a beach where a military might conduct naval gunfire as part of a deception operation to convince the enemy that the beach is the location of an impending amphibious attack. The beach is not by its nature a military objective. The enemy is not currently "using" it, and may have no plans to do so in the future, but the location of the beach as somewhere other than the intended landing

---

48. Commentary, AP I, *supra*, note 16, ¶2020.
49. DoD LOW Manual (Dec. 2016), *supra*, note 9, §§ 5.6.4; 5.6.6.1.
50. Commentary, AP I, *supra*, note 16, ¶2021.
51. DoD LOW Manual (Dec. 2016), *supra*, note 9, § 5.6.6.1.

makes its location as the beach where the landing will not occur the key element in determining it a military objective.

As Captain Watts considers this aspect of the first element of the military objective test, he might think that the school qualifies, as it is the location selected for the meeting. However, that is not normally the analysis of location. Location is generally tied more to geographic location in relation to military operations than to a building's use.

(c) Purpose

Purpose is defined in the Commentary as "concerned with the intended future use of an object."[52] This would cover objects that are currently being used by civilians but, due to the circumstances, are projected to be used by the military forces in the future. For example, assume there is a factory near Colon that makes explosives for use in civilian mining operations. The U.S. commander could properly target that factory if he believed that those explosives were going to be redirected for military uses. Similarly, a shipment of civilian cars that is going to be redirected to military purposes could be targeted based on its future use, even before the vehicles had arrived at the military site and received their military markings.[53]

Captain Watts might argue that the school can be targeted, because after the meeting of the generals, it will potentially be transformed into a communications site—in other words, it can be targeted now based on its future use. However, because the generals are also targets, this analysis is unlikely to support to specific proposed attack.

(d) Use

Use is defined in the API Commentary as "concerned with [the object's] present function."[54] Recall the scenario that began this chapter. The commander was faced with the possibility of attacking a school building where a meeting of high-level military leaders was going to occur. A school is a civilian object and protected from attack. However, when it is put to a military use such as a meeting place, headquarters, or communications site, it temporarily loses its protections and becomes targetable as a military objective. This criterion of the first element of the military objective test is likely to be the one that Captain Watts relies on when he provides his legal advice to his commander.[55]

This category also includes what many people refer to as "dual-use" targets or targets that serve both civilian and military purposes, such as communications sites that can broadcast both civilian and military messages. In a literal sense, "dual-use" is an unhelpful designation because the objects civilians use have nothing to do with whether an object becomes a military objective. The

---

52. Commentary, on the Additional Protocol of 8 june 1977 to the Geneva Conventions of 1949 (API) 610 ¶2022 (S. Pictet et al, eds., 1987).
53. DoD LOW Manual (Dec. 2016), *supra*, note 9, § 5.6.6.1.
54. Commentary, AP I, *supra*, note 52, ¶2022.
55. DoD LOW Manual (Dec. 2016), *supra*, note 9, § 5.6.6.1.

use of a civilian object, however slight, for military purposes meets the first element of the military objective test. However, the analysis does not stop there. Rather, once the commander has established that something meets the first element of the military objective test based on its nature, location, purpose, or use, he must now consider part two of the targeting test.

(e) "Make an Effective Contribution to Military Action"

In theory, even if the object is clearly military in nature, such as a tank, it is not targetable if it does not meet this part of the test. For example, military hardware that is located in a museum in Baghdad is still by its nature a military objective, but is unlikely to be able to make an effective contribution to military action. Similarly, military hardware that has been abandoned would not meet the definition. In reality, such a target would be extremely low on a commander's prioritized target list anyway as it would not be considered an effective use of limited resources.[56]

Captain Watts must determine if the school, at the time of the proposed attack, would be making an effective contribution to the Iraqi military's efforts. Because the school provides a securable place for the meeting to occur, inside, where it cannot be monitored, it seems clear that the school meets this element of the military objective test.

(f) "Offers a Definite Military Advantage"

Part three of the test requires that attacking the objective would provide a definite military advantage to the attacking force. The Commentary states that "it is not legitimate to launch an attack which only offers potential or indeterminate advantages."[57] One of the interesting questions raised by this part of the test is the issue of whether the definite military advantage must be to the tactical commander doing the targeting or whether a strategic view of advantage may be applied. The United States takes the view that any military advantage, whether tactical or strategic, is sufficient for a commander to target a military objective.[58]

Attacking the school, particularly if it results in the deaths of the military leaders and potentially Saddam Hussein, would certainly provide U.S. forces a definite military advantage. While this is not a legal determination, the lawyer should look to the commander for his determination of this element. In this case, Captain Watts is likely to assume from the commander's interest in the attack that he believes he would experience a definite military advantage from the attack.

---

56. DoD LOW Manual (Dec. 2016), *supra*, note 9, § 5.6.6.2.
57. Commentary, AP I, *supra*, note 52, ¶2024.
58. DoD LOW Manual (Dec. 2016), *supra*, note 9, § 5.6.7.3.

III. Applying the General Principles in Targeting | 265

(g) Examples

In 1956, the ICRC drew up the following proposed list of categories of military objectives. They are rather uncontroversial and provide interesting insights into the types of objects that are readily accepted as military objectives.

> I. The objectives belonging to the following categories are those considered to be of generally recognized military importance:
>
> (1) Armed forces, including auxiliary or complementary organisations, and persons who, though not belonging to the above-mentioned formations, nevertheless take part in the fighting.
>
> (2) Positions, installations or constructions occupied by the forces indicated in sub-paragraph 1 above, as well as combat objectives (that is to say, those objectives which are directly contested in battle between land or sea forces including airborne forces).
>
> (3) Installations, constructions and other works of a military nature, such as barracks, fortifications, War Ministries (e.g. Ministries of Army, Navy, Air Force, National Defence, Supply) and other organs for the direction and administration of military operations.
>
> (4) Stores of army or military supplies, such as munition dumps, stores of equipment or fuel, vehicles parks.
>
> (5) Airfields, rocket launching ramps and naval base installations.
>
> (6) Those of the lines and means of communications (railway lines, roads, bridges, tunnels and canals) which are of fundamental military importance.
>
> (7) The installations of broadcasting and television stations; telephone and telegraph exchanges of fundamental military importance.
>
> (8) Industries of fundamental importance for the conduct of the war:
>
> (a) industries for the manufacture of armaments such as weapons, munitions, rockets, armoured vehicles, military aircraft, fighting ships, including the manufacture of accessories and all other war material;
>
> (b) industries for the manufacture of supplies and material of a military character, such as transport and communications material, equipment of the armed forces;
>
> (c) factories or plant constituting other production and manufacturing centres of fundamental importance for the conduct of war, such as the metallurgical, engineering and chemical industries, whose nature or purpose is essentially military;
>
> (d) storage and transport installations whose basic function it is to serve the industries referred to in (a)-(c);
>
> (e) installations providing energy mainly for national defence, e.g. coal, other fuels, or atomic energy, and plants producing gas or electricity mainly for military consumption.
>
> (9) Installations constituting experimental, research centres for experiments on and the development of weapons and war material.[59]

---

59. Final Report to the Prosecutor by the Committee Established to Review the NATO Bombing Campaign Against the Federal Republic of Yugoslavia, ¶39, *available at* http://www.icty.org/x/file/About/OTP/otp_report_nato_bombing_en.pdf (last visited Feb. 22, 2011) (hereinafter Final Report).

The commander is given the responsibility under the LOAC to make the determination of whether an object is a military objective or not. These decisions often raise great controversy, particularly if the decision proves to have been wrong or ill informed. One such controversial case was the bombing of the Radio and Television building during the North Atlantic Treaty Organization's (NATO) 1999 bombing campaign of Serbia and Kosovo. The NATO allies argued that it was being used for military purposes to transmit military communications.[60] After the bombing of the building, the ICTY Office of the Prosecutor (OTP) investigated this and a number of other incidents to determine if any of those decisions were in violation of the law and should be prosecuted.

After analyzing the situation, the OTP decided there were not sufficient grounds to prosecute based on any of the specific instances. The analysis of the OTP is instructive and a portion of the analysis is excerpted below.

> 75. NATO intentionally bombed the Radio and TV station and the persons killed or injured were civilians. The questions are: was the station a legitimate military objective and, if it was, were the civilian casualties disproportionate to the military advantage gained by the attack? For the station to be a military objective within the definition in Article 52 of Protocol I: a) its nature, purpose or use must make an effective contribution to military action and b) its total or partial destruction must offer a definite military advantage in the circumstances ruling at the time. . . . [T]he attack appears to have been justified by NATO as part of a more general attack aimed at disrupting the FRY Command, Control and Communications network, the nerve centre and apparatus that keeps Milošević in power, and also as an attempt to dismantle the FRY propaganda machinery. Insofar as the attack actually was aimed at disrupting the communications network, it was legally acceptable.
>
> 76. If, however, the attack was made because equal time was not provided for Western news broadcasts, that is, because the station was part of the propaganda machinery, the legal basis was more debatable. Disrupting government propaganda may help to undermine the morale of the population and the armed forces, but justifying an attack on a civilian facility on such grounds alone may not meet the "effective contribution to military action" and "definite military advantage" criteria required by the Additional Protocols. The ICRC Commentary on the Additional Protocols interprets the expression "definite military advantage anticipated" to exclude "an attack which only offers potential or indeterminate advantages" and interprets the expression "concrete and direct" as intended to show that the advantage concerned should be substantial and relatively close rather than hardly perceptible and likely to appear only in the long term. While stopping such propaganda may serve to demoralize the Yugoslav population and undermine the government's political support, it is unlikely that either of these purposes would offer the "concrete and direct" military advantage necessary to make them a legitimate military objective. . . . It appears, however, that NATO's targeting of the RTS building for propaganda purposes was an incidental (albeit complementary) aim of its primary goal of

---

60. *Id.* ¶¶72-73.

III. Applying the General Principles in Targeting | 267

disabling the Serbian military command and control system and to destroy the nerve system and apparatus that keeps Milošević in power.

...

78. Assuming the RTS building to be a legitimate military target, it appeared that NATO realised that attacking the RTS building would only interrupt broadcasting for a brief period. Indeed, broadcasting allegedly recommenced within hours of the strike, thus raising the issue of the importance of the military advantage gained by the attack vis-à-vis the civilian casualties incurred. The FRY command and control network was alleged by NATO to comprise a complex web and that could thus not be disabled in one strike. As noted by General Wesley Clark, NATO "knew when we struck that there would be alternate means of getting the Serb Television. There's no single switch to turn off everything but we thought it was a good move to strike it and the political leadership agreed with us." . . . With regard to these goals, the strategic target of these attacks was the Yugoslav command and control network. The attack on the RTS building must therefore be seen as forming part of an integrated attack against numerous objects, including transmission towers and control buildings of the Yugoslav radio relay network which were "essential to Milosevic's ability to direct and control the repressive activities of his army and special police forces in Kosovo." . . .

79. On the basis of the above analysis and on the information currently available to it, the committee recommends that the OTP not commence an investigation related to the bombing of the Serbian TV and Radio Station.[61]

(2) Civilian Objects

Civilian objects maintain their immunity from attack unless they are converted into military objectives. Until that happens, civilian objects are immune from direct attack. In accordance with the presumptions discussed earlier, unless the commander can establish that a civilian object is a military objective, he cannot target it. Therefore, if the planned meeting in the school never occurs and if it is never converted to a communication center, the school would maintain its protected status of a civilian object and not be a legitimate object of attack.

(3) Protected Objects or Places

There are a number of objects or places that have been singled out in the LOAC as deserving special protection. These are discussed below. It does not appear that any of these areas would influence Captain Watts's decision in this specific targeting scenario, but as a good legal advisor, he would routinely consider them to ensure he did not somehow overlook additional protections.[62]

---

61. *Id.* ¶¶75-79 (citations omitted).
62. DoD LOW Manual (Dec. 2016), *supra*, note 9, § 5.5.2.

(a) Undefended Places

The attack or bombardment of towns, villages, dwellings, or buildings that are undefended is prohibited.[63] An inhabited area may be declared an undefended place (and open for occupation) if the following criteria are met:

> all combatants and mobile military equipment are removed; no hostile use made of fixed military installations or establishments; no acts of hostility shall be committed by the authorities or by the population; and no activities in support of military operations shall be undertaken (presence of enemy medical units, enemy sick and wounded, and enemy police forces are allowed).[64]

(b) Hospitals or Safety Zones for the Sick or Wounded

The LOAC provides special protection for hospitals and other medical facilities and areas.[65] Fixed or mobile medical units shall be respected and protected and cannot be intentionally attacked unless they are used to commit "acts harmful to the enemy." Even in such a case, a warning is required before attacking the hospital, and the attacker must allow reasonable time to comply with the warning before attacking.

If a force receives fire from a hospital, there is no duty to warn before returning fire in self-defense. In several recent conflicts, including in Iraq and Afghanistan, U.S. forces were attacked from hospitals or other medical facilities. In such situations, the military forces are authorized to return fire until they are no longer in danger. Once out of immediate danger, the warning requirement would apply before any further military action could be taken against the hospital.

In all cases, all buildings and facilities used for medical care must be visibly marked to put potential attackers on notice. Additionally, misusing the medical markings is a grave breach of the Geneva Conventions. Currently, recognized markings include the Red Cross, Red Crescent, the Lion and Sun, the Red Star of David, and the new Red Crystal.

(c) Cultural Property

Cultural property is a category of civilian objects that receives special treatment and has been the source of separate international agreements. The 1954 Cultural Property Convention elaborates, but does not expand, the protections accorded cultural property found in other treaties. (This Convention has not been ratified by the United States and the United States asserts that the special protection regime does not reflect customary international law.) AP I, Article

---

63. Convention Respecting the Laws and Customs of War on Land, Oct. 18, 1907, art. 25, 1 Bevans 631, 36 Stat. 2277 (hereinafter 1907 Hague IV); DoD LOW Manual (Dec. 2016), *supra*, note 9, 276-281.

64. DoD LOW Manual (Dec. 2016), *supra*, note 9, § 5.5.2.

65. GWS, *supra*, note 29, art. 19; DoD LOW Manual (Dec. 2016), *supra*, note 9, § 5.5.2.

53, also contains provisions on the protection of cultural property. Cultural property includes buildings dedicated to religion, art, science, charitable purposes, historic monuments, hospitals, and places where the sick and wounded are collected.[66]

Articles 8 and 11 of the 1954 Hague Cultural Property Convention provide that certain cultural sites may be designated in an "International Register of Cultural Property under Special Protections." The Vatican, for example, and art storage areas in Europe have been designated under the Convention as "specially protected."

Misuse of cultural property will subject the areas or cultural property to attack. As with medical facilities, the party to the conflict has the duty to indicate the presence of such buildings with visible and distinctive signs. Cultural property also has a distinctive emblem: "A shield, consisting of a royal blue square, one of the angles of which forms the point of the shield and of a royal blue triangle above the square, the space on either side being taken up by a white triangle."[67]

(d) Works and Installations Containing Dangerous Forces

Under the Protocols, dams, dikes, and nuclear electrical generating stations shall not be attacked—even if they are military objectives—if the attack will cause the release of dangerous forces and cause "severe losses" among the civilian population.[68] The United States has not ratified these provisions and does not believe they reflect customary rules, but they should be considered because of the pervasive international acceptance of AP I and II. In the U.S. view, there is no preclusion to attacking these installations, though "additional precautions" may be necessary "in light of the increased potential magnitude of incidental harm."[69]

Military objectives that are near these potentially dangerous forces are also immune from attack if the attack may cause release of the forces (parties also have a duty to avoid locating military objectives near such locations). A military may attack works and installations containing dangerous forces only if they provide "significant and direct support" to military operations and attack is the only feasible way to terminate the support. The United States objects to this provision as creating a standard that differs from the customary definition of a military objective as an object that makes "an effective contribution to military action."

Parties may construct defensive weapons systems to protect works and installations containing dangerous forces. These weapons systems may not be attacked unless they are used for purposes other than protecting the installation.

---

66. DoD LOW Manual (Dec. 2016), *supra*, note 9, § 5.18.
67. 1954 Cultural Property Convention, *supra*, note 42, art. 16, 17.
68. AP I, *supra*, note 12, art. 56; Protocol Additional to the Geneva Conventions of 12 August 1949, and Relating to the Protection of Victims of Non-International Armed Conflicts, art. 15, June 8, 1977, 1125 U.N.T.S. 17513.
69. DoD LOW Manual (Dec. 2016), *supra*, note 9, § 5.13.

Three bright orange circles, of similar size, placed on the same axis, the distance between each circle being one radius is the protective emblem for works containing dangerous forces (AP I, Annex I, Article 16).

(e) Objects Indispensable to the Survival of the Civilian Population

Article 54 of AP I prohibits starvation as a method of warfare. It is prohibited to attack, destroy, remove, or render useless objects that are indispensable for survival of the civilian population, such as foodstuffs, crops, livestock, water installations, and irrigation works.[70]

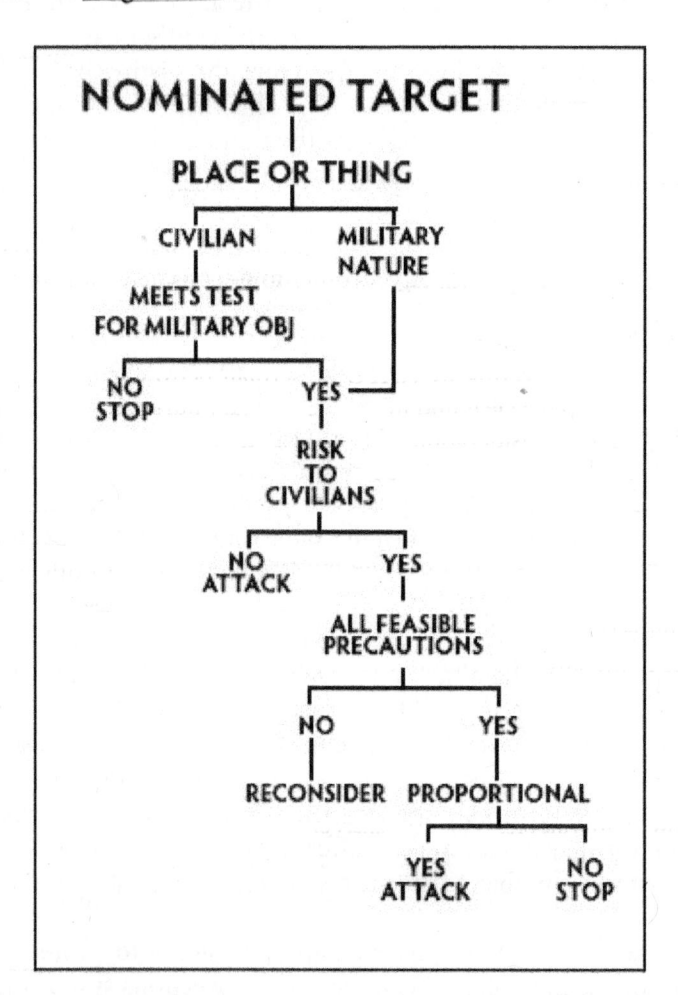

```
NOMINATED TARGET
        |
  PLACE OR THING
    |         |
 CIVILIAN   MILITARY
    |        NATURE
MEETS TEST      |
FOR MILITARY OBJ
  |       |
 NO      YES
STOP      |
        RISK
         TO
       CIVILIANS
        |      |
       NO     YES
     ATTACK    |
          ALL FEASIBLE
          PRECAUTIONS
           |       |
          NO      YES
       RECONSIDER PROPORTIONAL
                  |        |
                 YES       NO
               ATTACK     STOP
```

(f) Natural Environment

There has been a great deal of discussion lately about the natural environment in warfare. Several recent international law documents wrestle with the idea of how to treat the environment. At present there is not a common definition of

---

70. AP I, *supra*, note 12, art. 54; DoD LOW Manual (Dec. 2016), *supra*, note 9, § 5.20.

what the environment means, making it more difficult to determine what protections the environment should be afforded.

There is some limited law on the protection of the environment in times of armed conflict. For example, the environment cannot be intentionally used as a means of warfare,[71] or as the object of reprisals. In the course of normal military operations, care must be taken to protect the natural environment against long-term, widespread, and severe damage. These provisions are found generally in AP I[72] and not necessarily accepted as customary law.

The OTP opinion on the Kosovo bombing mentioned earlier took up the issue of the environment.

> 20. [T]he critical question is what kind of environmental damage can be considered to be excessive. Unfortunately, the customary rule of proportionality does not include any concrete guidelines to this effect.
>
> ...
>
> 22. Taken together, this suggests that in order to satisfy the requirement of proportionality, attacks against military targets which are known or can reasonably be assumed to cause grave environmental harm may need to confer a very substantial military advantage in order to be considered legitimate. At a minimum, actions resulting in massive environmental destruction, especially where they do not serve a clear and important military purpose, would be questionable. The targeting by NATO of Serbian petro-chemical industries may well have served a clear and important military purpose.
>
> 23. The above considerations also suggest that the requisite *mens rea* on the part of a commander would be actual or constructive knowledge as to the grave environmental effects of a military attack; a standard which would be difficult to establish for the purposes of prosecution and which may provide an insufficient basis to prosecute military commanders inflicting environmental harm in the (mistaken) belief that such conduct was warranted by military necessity....
>
> 25. It is therefore the opinion of the committee, based on information currently available to it, that the OTP should not commence an investigation

---

71. *See* Convention on the Prohibition of Military or Any Hostile Use of Environmental Modification Techniques, 10 December 1976; *available at* http://www.icrc.org/ihl.nsf/FULL/460?OpenDocument.
72. The applicable provisions of AP I are:

> Article 35
>
> 3. It is prohibited to employ methods or means of warfare which are intended, or may be expected, to cause widespread, long-term and severe damage to the natural environment.
>
> Article 55
>
> 1. Care shall be taken in warfare to protect the natural environment against widespread, long-term and severe damage. This protection includes a prohibition of the use of methods or means of warfare which are intended or may be expected to cause such damage to the natural environment and thereby to prejudice the health or survival of the population.
>
> 2. Attacks against the natural environment by way of reprisals are prohibited.

AP I, *supra*, note 12, art. 35, 55.

into the collateral environmental damage caused by the NATO bombing campaign.[73]

Currently, the environment—however it is defined—is protected both from intentional modification techniques designed to use the environment as a tool of warfare, and from those military actions that would cause long-term, widespread, and severe damage.

2. Proportionality

Despite the principle of distinction and the prohibition on attacking civilians and civilian objects, it is inevitable in armed conflict that in the process of attacking combatants and military objectives, some death to civilians and/or damage to civilian property will occur. Although this incidental damage is not prohibited *per se*, the principle of proportionality sets limits on how much incidental damage is acceptable. As Captain Watts and his fellow staff officers attempt to plan the attack in such a way as to minimize the risk to civilians and civilian objects, it is still possible that some civilian deaths or damage to civilian objects will occur. Such deaths or damages do not prevent the attack. Instead, they require the commander to take account of the possible deaths and damages, and conduct a proportionality analysis to determine if the attack should still be conducted.

The test to determine if an attack is proportional is found in AP I, Article 57.2(a)(iii). Commanders must "refrain from deciding to launch any attack which may be expected to cause incidental loss of civilian life, injury to civilians, damage to civilian objects, or a combination thereof, which would be excessive in relation to the concrete and direct military advantage anticipated." Note that this principle is only applicable when an attack has the possibility of affecting civilians. If the target is purely military with no known civilian personnel or property in the vicinity, no proportionality analysis is needed.

Incidental loss of life or injury and collateral damage is loss and damage that is considered unavoidable damage to civilian personnel and property incurred while attacking a military objective. The LOAC requirement is for the commander to weigh the expected death, injury, and destruction against the military advantage anticipated.[74] The question is whether such death, injury, and destruction is excessive in relation to the military advantage; not whether any death, injury, or destruction will occur. In other words, the prohibition is on the death, injury, and destruction being excessive; not on the attack causing such results.

This issue was also addressed in the OTP opinion.

> 48. The main problem with the principle of proportionality is not whether or not it exists but what it means and how it is to be applied. . . .

---

73. Final Report, *supra*, note 59, ¶¶ 20-23, 25.
74. DoD LOW Manual (Dec. 2016), *supra*, note 9, § 5.10.2.

III. Applying the General Principles in Targeting

49. The questions which remain unresolved once one decides to apply the principle of proportionality include the following:
   a) What are the relative values to be assigned to the military advantage gained and the injury to non-combatants and/or the damage to civilian objects?
   b) What do you include or exclude in totaling your sums?
   c) What is the standard of measurement in time or space? and
   d) To what extent is a military commander obligated to expose his own forces to danger in order to limit civilian casualties or damage to civilian objects?

50. The answers to these questions are not simple. It may be necessary to resolve them on a case by case basis, and the answers may differ depending on the background and values of the decision maker. It is unlikely that a human rights lawyer and an experienced combat commander would assign the same relative values to military advantage and to injury to noncombatants. Further, it is unlikely that military commanders with different doctrinal backgrounds and differing degrees of combat experience or national military histories would always agree in close cases. It is suggested that the determination of relative values must be that of the "reasonable military commander." Although there will be room for argument in close cases, there will be many cases where reasonable military commanders will agree that the injury to noncombatants or the damage to civilian objects was clearly disproportionate to the military advantage gained.[75]

In the scenario presented at the beginning of the chapter, the commander questioned his staff about possible civilian casualties and damage to civilian property. Once he has gathered the appropriate information, he must conduct a proportionality analysis and decide whether or not to conduct the attack. He may decide to conduct the attack but seek ways to alter the number of potential incidental civilian deaths or damage to civilian objects. Sometimes, by adjusting the weapon that is used to conduct the attack, or adjusting the direction of the attack or the way the attack will occur will help limit the number of civilian deaths and civilian damage. Also, in the case of the NATO attack on the Serbian radio and television building, the attack was carried out very early in the morning, a time when estimates had the fewest civilians in the area.

Commanders are charged to take into account such considerations. If there is a method of attack, such as attacking from the north as opposed to from the east, or a means of attack, such as using a hellfire missile launched from a UAV rather than attacking the military objective with artillery, the commander should take those precautions, if feasible.

Many technologically advanced nations now use computer modeling to assist them in conducting the proportionality analysis. Through computer modeling, a commander can predict the likely effects of a particular munition on a particular target. For example, as Captain Watts's commander contemplates attacking the school, he will have his staff run computer simulations to determine the various effects caused by different ordnance delivered from

---

75. Final Report, *supra*, note 59, ¶¶48-52.

different angles and directions. The simulations will take account of not only the proximity of various buildings and persons, but the materials out of which the buildings are made, and how they will react to the impact of the specific weapon system. Such computer modeling can greatly assist the commander when conducting the proportionality analysis and deciding whether or not to conduct a specific attack.

A topic of recent discussion that remains unresolved includes the question of whether States with advanced technologies incur a legal obligation to use those advanced technologies as opposed to other means of warfare. For example, the United States and other developed nations have precision-guided munitions capabilities. Because these munitions have very advanced guidance systems, they are extremely accurate—far more accurate than similar systems without precision guidance. Presumably, using these guidance systems would dramatically decrease the chance of a munition hitting somewhere other than the intended target. Does the fact that a nation possesses such capability give that nation an obligation to use the capabilities in every case? If a commander could have minimized incidental effects of an attack through using precision-guided munitions but chose not to in a particular situation, has he violated the law? The answers to these questions remain unclear, though the United States has clearly rejected such a notion.[76]

The importance of the principle of proportionality has been amply illustrated in recent military operations in Afghanistan and Iraq. The continuous outcry concerning the incidental deaths of civilians has applied immense political pressure on nations engaged in hostilities there. Some have argued for a numerical equation to determine compliance with the principle of proportionality, but militaries have resisted such a development, arguing that military targets have differing values, and relying on the commander's understanding of the situation at the time and his discretion to ensure the incidental death and damage is not excessive to the military advantage gained is the most effective test and what the law requires.

In response to public concern and to meet political objectives, the United States uses a collateral damage estimation methodology (CDEM) to provide guidance on the application of the principle of proportionality. The CDEM is contained in a publication by the Chairman of the Joint Chiefs of Staff[77] and mandates a process for identifying potential collateral damage in an operation, considering the method of attack (including an analysis of the critical effects radius of the weapon system proposed to be used), mitigating that damage, and where appropriate, seeking designated authority to conduct the attack if collateral damage cannot be avoided. It includes the application of technical data, such as weapons effects, the characteristics of the object of attack and the surrounding environment, and a host of other factors that help paint an accurate picture for the commander of exactly what the effects of the attack will be. With

---

76. DoD LOW Manual (Dec. 2016), *supra*, note 9, § 5.11.6.
77. Chairman, Joint Chiefs of Staff, INSTRUCTION 3160.01A, NO-STRIKE AND THE COLLATERAL DAMAGE ESTIMATION METHODOLOGY (12 October 2012).

this information, commanders are prepared to make well-informed decisions in compliance with both the LOAC and ROE.

In addition, President Obama issued an Executive Order 13732 announcing the United States Policy on Pre- and Post-Strike Measures to Address Civilian Casualties in U.S. Operations Involving the Use of Force[78] on July 1, 2016. The Executive Order codified current military practice in training, acquisition of weapons systems, development of targets, application of feasible precautions, and post-attack assessments. It highlighted the need to coordinate with the ICRC and other NGOs in order to ensure transparency in military operations, a point later confirmed in the Report on the Legal and Policy Frameworks Guiding the United States' Use of Military Force and Related National Security Operations.[79]

Captain Watts and his fellow staff members will have access to the CDEM and the useful information it provides to help him as he prepares his legal response to the commander. This will allow Captain Watts to ensure the commander has the necessary information to make the proportionality determination and ensure compliance with ROE and other constraints.

3. Current Controversy

Ongoing military operations, including active hostilities against the Taliban, al Qaeda, and ISIL have created a number of areas of controversy with respect to targeting. Two of the most significant involve the targeting of money and revenue-generating objects, and the targeting of individuals, including U.S. persons, outside "areas of active hostilities."

a. Money and Revenue-Generating Objects

The United States has long believed that certain "war-sustaining capabilities" meet the definition of military objective.[80] For example, the United States has attacked ISIS cash storage sites to destroy the actual money that was stored there, arguing that it was predominately being used to fund ISIL, and is not easily replaceable, as it would be for a State that has its own currency. Additionally, the United States has targeted both oil and natural gas generation facilities, refineries, pipelines, storage facilities, and transportation networks, including convoys of trucks. As a result of both of these types of attacks, the United States argues that ISIL has been forced to reduce operations, including the recruiting and funding of its fighters.[81]

---

78. Executive Order 13732, *United States Policy on Pre- and Post-Strike Measures to Address Civilian Casualties in U.S. Operations Involving the Use of Force*, 81 FEDERAL REGISTER 44485, 44485-86 (§2) (Jul. 1, 2016).

79. Office of the White House, Report on the Legal and Policy Frameworks Guiding the United States' Use of Military Force and Related National Security Operations 19-27 (Dec. 2016) at https://obamawhitehouse.archives.gov/sites/whitehouse.gov/files/documents/Legal_Policy_Report.pdf (hereinafter Transparency Report).

80. DoD LOW Manual (Dec. 2016), *supra*, note 9, § 5.6.8.5.

81. *See* Transparency Report, *supra*, note 79, 23-24.

Some coalition partners have agreed with the United States position and even participated in attacks, while others have not. The ICRC and other NGOs, as well as other governments, have taken a negative view on these attacks, arguing that they are predominately civilian targets and that justifying targeting economic targets is a slippery slope, whereby a large group of normally civilian objects suddenly becomes targetable.

A consensus has not emerged with respect to this issue, and it continues to be debated.

b. Targeting Individuals Who Are Outside "Areas of Active Hostilities"

There has also been a great deal of controversy recently surrounding the United States' decision to conduct targeted strikes with armed drones on individuals outside the area of active hostilities. Some of the controversy has been centered on legal issues associated with targeting. Harold Koh, then-legal advisor to the Department of State, spoke to the issue of targeting members of al Qaeda or other groups in a speech in 2010.[82] After clarifying that the United States was in an armed conflict with al Qaeda, Koh then stated that these targeting operations were reviewed to specifically ensure they complied with the LOAC, including the principles of distinction and proportionality. He then stated that neither targeting particular leaders of an enemy force, nor using advanced technologies to do so violated the LOAC.

Koh's successor as the legal advisor to the Secretary of State, Brian Egan, delivered an address in 2016, discussing the international law and the campaign against the terrorist organization known as the Islamic State, or ISIL.[83] One of the key points of the address was Egan's explanation of U.S. targeting of individuals outside the area of active hostilities. Such targeting is governed by a Presidential Policy Guidance, or PPG, which was issued in 2013. President Obama subsequently declassified and released the PPG in 2016.[84] The PPG contains a detailed accounting of the process for approving target selection of individuals who are not in the area of active hostilities but still present a threat to the United States. According to Egan, these procedures are designed, among other things, to ensure that the LOAC is applied, particularly the principle of proportionality.

Among other things, the PPG states a preference for capture, unless not feasible and no other effective alternatives exist. It also states that targeting outside areas of active hostilities requires, as a matter of policy, that the target poses a continuing and imminent threat to U.S. persons, and that there is "near certainty" that the target is at the proposed attack cite and that no civilians will

---

82. Harold Koh, American Society of International Law Session, (March 25, 2010) available at http://www.state.gov/s/l/releases/remarks/139119.htm.
83. Brian Egan, American Society of International Law Session (April 1, 2016) available at http://www.state.gov/s/l/releases/remarks/255493.htm.
84. Presidential Policy Guidance, U.S. Policy Standards and Procedures for the Use of Force in Counterterrorism Operations Outside the United States and Areas of Active Hostilities (May 22, 2013) (redacted) ("PPG"), available at https://www.justice.gov/oip/foia-library/procedures_for_approving_direct_action_against_terrorist_targets/download.

be injured or killed. All such operations go through an extensive interagency review and congressional notifications.

The clarity provided by the publication of the PPG is an attempt to provide transparency to U.S. military operations.[85] While its publication was broadly welcomed, discussion continues as to the legality of conducting such operations outside active areas of hostilities, and, even if legal, whether sufficient safeguards are in place.

c. Application of Targeting Principles to NIAC

In Egan's speech mentioned above, he discussed more generally the application of the law of targeting to NIACs. He clarified that the United States views this conflict with ISIL as a NIAC and applies common Article 3 as well as other treaty law and customary international law applicable to NIACs. He then states that the United States accepts the following targeting principles as binding under customary international law in NIACs:

> First, parties must distinguish between military objectives, including combatants, on the one hand, and civilians and civilian objects on the other. Only military objectives, including combatants, may be made the object of attack.
>
> Insofar as objects are concerned, military objectives are those objects which by their nature, location, purpose or use make an effective contribution to military action and whose total or partial destruction, capture or neutralization, in the circumstances ruling at the time, offers a definite military advantage. The United States has interpreted this definition to include objects that make an effective contribution to the enemy's war-fighting or war-sustaining capabilities.
>
> Feasible precautions must be taken in conducting an attack to reduce the risk of harm to civilians, such as, in certain circumstances, warnings to civilians before bombardments.
>
> Customary international law also specifically prohibits a number of targeting measures in NIACs. First, attacks directed against civilians or civilian objects as such are prohibited. Additionally, indiscriminate attacks, including but not limited to attacks using inherently indiscriminate weapons, are prohibited.
>
> Attacks directed against specifically protected objects such as cultural property and hospitals are also prohibited unless their protection has been forfeited.
>
> Also prohibited are attacks that violate the principle of proportionality—that is, attacks against combatants or other military objectives that are expected to cause incidental harm to civilians that would be excessive in relation to the concrete and direct military advantage anticipated.
>
> Moreover, acts or threats of violence the primary purpose of which is to spread terror among the civilian population are prohibited with respect to process in these types of attacks.

---

85. *See* Transparency Report, *supra*, note 79, 24-26.

While this speech has been praised for applying certain provisions of targeting law to NIACs, it has also generated some controversy in that it is unclear why certain other targeting provisions were not mentioned, and if their omission means that they are not considered applicable in NIACs. Additionally, these remarks provide limited clarity as to any geographic restraints, other than the justifications mentioned above.

B. Humanity and Unnecessary Suffering

As will be discussed in Chapter 8, article 22 of the Hague Conventions states that the right of belligerents to adopt means of injuring the enemy is not unlimited. Further, "it is especially forbidden . . . to employ arms, projectiles or material calculated to cause unnecessary suffering."[86] This concept limits targeting in two ways — it precludes certain types of weapons, making them illegal, and also precludes employing otherwise legal weapons in an illegal manner.

The prohibition on causing unnecessary suffering precludes targeting through the use of arms that are "calculated" to cause unnecessary suffering. This would include, for example, projectiles filled with glass (because they can't be discovered by x-ray), irregular shaped bullets, dum-dum rounds, lances with barbed heads, bullets laced with poison, and any other weapon designed or modified in order to increase the suffering of its victim. It would also preclude the use of any weapons specifically precluded by Treaty, such as expanding bullets, the use of biological and chemical agents, and blinding lasers.

This principle can also be violated by using otherwise lawful weapons in a way that will result in unnecessary suffering. This might include using a flamethrower — a lawful weapon designed to be used as a defoliant — against enemy combatants with the intent to "make them suffer," even though equally effective and more humane means are available.

The key to both prohibitions is the *mens rea* or intent element. To violate the unnecessary suffering provision, there is an intent requirement. Negligence is not enough. In most cases, States incorporate this principle through a weapons review. For U.S. reviews, this is specifically one of the issues that is considered in every weapons review.[87] Because those weapons reviews happen systematically in the Department of Defense, Captain Watts is unlikely to have to consider the legality of a weapon if it is in the current inventory of weapons. However, if it is not, he would have to at least conduct a review, and more likely argue against the weapon's use until an official review could be accomplished.

Assuming that the proposed attack only includes weapons that have been approved and are in the current inventory, Captain Watts still needs to ensure that the use of weapons in this specific mission is also not designed to cause unnecessary suffering.

---

86. Hague Regulations, *supra*, note 63, art. 23(e).
87. DoD LOW Manual (Dec. 2016), *supra*, note 9, § 6.2.

IV. Review of Targeting Decisions

Violating the principles discussed above can bring individual responsibility to the deciding commander. For example, it is a grave breach of AP I to launch an attack that a commander knows will cause excessive incidental damage in relation to the military advantage gained. The requirement is for a commander to act reasonably.

Those who plan or decide upon an attack, therefore, must take all reasonable steps to ensure not only that the objectives are identified as military objectives or defended places, but also that these objectives can be attacked without probable losses in lives and damage to property disproportionate to the military advantage anticipated.[88] Captain Watts's commander will be very careful to make sure that his staff has done all the preliminary intelligence gathering, analysis, and other planning, so that when he makes the targeting decision, he is doing so with as much information as possible.

In judging a commander's actions, one must look at the situation as the commander saw it in light of all circumstances.[89] In the aftermath of WW II, charges that German General Lothar Rendulic unlawfully destroyed civilian property via a "scorched earth" policy were dismissed by the International Military Tribunal because "the conditions, as they appeared to the defendant at the time were sufficient upon which he could honestly conclude that urgent military necessity warranted the decision made."[90] The same standard applies to targeting decisions today.

The question of reasonableness, however, ensures an objective standard that must be met as well. In this regard, two questions seem relevant. First, did the commander gather a reasonable amount of information to determine whether the target was a military objective and that the incidental damage would not be disproportionate? Second, did the commander act reasonably based on the gathered information? Of course, factors such as time, available staff, and combat conditions affecting the commander must also factor into the analysis.

An example from the 1991 Gulf War is instructive. During the armed conflict, planners identified a bunker, known as the Al Firdus Bunker, as a military objective. Barbed wire surrounded the complex, it was camouflaged, and armed sentries guarded its entrance and exit points. Intelligence estimates determined that this was a communications bunker. Unknown to coalition planners, however, Iraqi civilians used the shelter as nighttime sleeping quarters. The complex was bombed, resulting in 300 civilian casualties. Was there a violation of the law of war? The United States, in reviewing the decision, determined that it was not in violation of the LOAC. Based on information gathered by coalition planners, the commander made a reasonable assessment that the target was a military

---

88. DoD LOW Manual (Dec. 2016), *supra*, note 9, § 5.10.
89. DoD LOW Manual (Dec. 2016), *supra*, note 9, § 5.3.
90. *See* IX Nuremberg Military Tribunals, Trials of War Criminals Before the Nuremberg Military Tribunals 1113 (1950).

objective and that incidental damage would not outweigh the military advantage gained. Although the attack unfortunately resulted in numerous civilian deaths (and in hindsight, the attack might have been disproportionate to the military advantage gained had the attackers known of the civilians), there was no international law violation because the attackers, at the time of the attack, acted reasonably.[91]

V. Non-Lethal Targeting

Because of the many missions militaries are given on the modern battlefield, commanders have an increased need not only for lethal means and methods, but also for non-lethal means and methods of warfare. Such means and methods might include the use of military deception, psychological operations, information operations, and computer operations.

Additionally, with increases in technology, the commander also has at his disposal an increasing number of less than lethal weapon systems. These include rubber bullets, sticky foam, slippery foam, pepper spray and other riot control means and methods, microwave emitters, and other similar weapons discussed in Chapter 8. Although some of these technologies may actually result in death, they are not designed to do so and are, therefore, considered less than lethal and do not require the same analysis as lethal targeting.[92]

These resources provide a commander with valuable alternatives to the use of lethal force when targeting. The same considerations apply to non-lethal targeting that would result in "actual harm," even if not lethal harm.

VI. Rules of Engagement

Perhaps the most talked about targeting principle is the application of rules of engagement. As mentioned in Chapter 2, ROE are really control measures that commanders and the national command authorities apply to make sure the use of military force complies with political aims. ROE can never violate the LOAC, but may limit the use of force well beyond what the LOAC would allow.

When a commander and his staff begin the targeting process, they are not only constrained by the LOAC, but also by the ROE. If necessary, commanders can seek modification of the ROE from appropriate authorities in order to accomplish their proposed mission, but the ROE are considered lawful orders and commanders cannot legally violate them, even if the LOAC would allow it.

---

91. *See* Dep't of Defense, Conduct of the Persian Gulf War, Final Report to Congress 615-616 (1992).

92. *See generally* U.S. Dep't of Defense Directive (DoDD) 3000.3, Policy for Non-Lethal Weapons (July 9, 1996, certified as current as of Nov. 21, 2003).

VII. The Legal Advice

In the case set out at the beginning of this chapter, the planned attack does not appear to violate any specific LOAC provision. The generals are members of the enemy forces and are targetable. The school is being put to a military use. The military objective test seems to be met. The commander certainly will need to conduct a proportionality analysis, as there is a risk to civilians and civilian objects. Captain Watts will have to ensure that the commander understands what that analysis requires, and then provide any further assistance he needs in coming to his decision. It is important to note, as a practical matter, that Captain Watts' input should be given to the staff throughout the planning process to assist them in coming up with a fully developed recommendation to the commander.

Study Questions

1. Assume international armed conflict is under way between U.S. forces and Iraqi forces. Review the scenario at the beginning of the chapter. How would you advise the commander?
2. The commander of the U.S. forces in Iraq has received information that Iraqi forces may be planning an attack on several U.S. facilities using explosives to breach the perimeter. There is a factory used to make explosives for civilian construction operations on the outskirts of Mosul. U.S. satellite intelligence assets have provided pictures of Iraqi forces moving in and around the explosives factory. According to the new intelligence, the explosives factory employs approximately 250 workers. Several thousand civilians, many of them family members of the factory workers, reside in an area near the factory. The commander is considering attacking the factory. What factors should the commander consider in making his decision?
3. During ongoing operations, several questions come to the commander about engaging the following:
    a. A group of Iraqi soldiers have formed a defensive position in and around a major mosque. A U.S. force is now requesting the use of air-delivered munitions to destroy the building and the Iraqis within.
    b. A UAV has spotted a group of around fifty armed men moving toward an Iraqi military establishment. The targeting cell is requesting to fire hellfire missiles at the armed group because they believe that they are moving to join with the PDF.
    c. A U.S. infantry unit over-watching an Iraqi army location is prepared to call in artillery fires on the location but is reporting that there are 20 Lebanese advisors at the location.
    d. A Special Forces team in the desert has come across a camp of men armed with rifles and other personal weapons. They seem to

be preparing to move from the camp. The Special Forces team is requesting an air strike on the camp.
   e. A UAV feed is showing a group of armed civilians breaking into one of the major historical artifact museums in Baghdad. The commander does not have forces close enough to get to the site before he believes much of the looting will be completed. He is requesting the use of air-delivered munitions to stop the looting.
   f. While on patrol, a U.S. unit comes across a group of looters who have broken into local businesses and are stealing goods.
   g. The battle captain provides the following situation report: An Iraqi citizen is in a square in downtown Baghdad, armed with a rifle. He has been shooting into the air and yelling threats against anyone who tries to stop him. The civilians have been cleared from the area and the unit is requesting instructions.
   (Primary Research Sources: GPW, art. 4; AP I, art. 48, 51, 52, 54, 57)
4. Aerial photographs and other intelligence assets disclosed the following possible targets. Advise the targeting cell as it examines whether to add the particular item to the target list for attack.
   a. A large power plant located at the northeast edge of Tikrit, which serves not only the Iraqi military headquarters, but also all of the civilian hospitals and residential areas of the city.
   b. Troop billets (located in citizens' homes) in the southern part of Fallujah. A large church is located in the center of the billeting area.
   c. A barracks complex at the western edge of Baghdad, which is marked with the Red Cross emblem on all its buildings. Intelligence assets have not determined whether this barracks complex has actually been converted into a hospital.
   d. A 40-foot statue of Saddam Hussein located by itself in a large park.
   e. A railroad station located in the center of Bayji. A residential area surrounds the station. The station is located in such a manner that the rail line could be effectively interrupted at this point. The risk of coalition casualties is minimal. The railroad crosses several bridges outside the city. Destroying the railroad at the bridges would entail the use of the same amount of ordnance and would have the same effect as destroying the tracks at the rail station, but would also bring coalition aircraft within range of anti-aircraft missile sites and significantly increase the risk of friendly casualties. By the same token, this attack will significantly reduce the risk of civilian casualties. Does the law of war require U.S. forces to choose one target over the other?
   (Primary Research Sources: GPW, art. 4; AP I, art. 48, 51, 52, 54, 57)
5. While grabbing a bite to eat at the dining facility, you run into one of the signal officers on the joint staff who is very excited about a new mission he just received. In anticipation of an offensive maneuver further into Iraqi territory, the commander wants to jam all cell phone calls in and around the objective immediately before, during, and after the operation, by electromagnetically targeting the transmission towers in

the area. This proposed mission was not discussed at your latest targeting meeting. Should it have been? How would you analyze this mission under the law of war?
(Primary Research Sources: AP I, art. 48, 51, 52, 57)

6. You have been asked to review the ROE. The Brigade Combat Team's (BCT) assigned area of operations will contain few, if any, friendly forces or civilian populace. The commander seeks to incorporate the following language into the ROE for designated areas, such as the fields of fire around the BCT's nighttime perimeters. What do you think?

> SPECIFIED STRIKE ZONES: Areas designated by the commander in which there are no friendly forces or civilian populace and in which all targets may be attacked on the initiative of individual soldiers. There is no requirement for further clearance or coordination prior to the initiation of combat activity.

(Primary Research Sources: AP I, art. 48, 51, 52, 54, 57)

7. Assume coalition forces have stopped the Iraqi Army and have begun to gain momentum, pushing the retreating Iraqi Army farther north. Iraqi troops are flooding onto the highway that runs north. The commander is planning to allow the Iraqi forces to withdraw along the highway and then fix them in place utilizing air-dropped landmines. Once the Iraqi forces are fixed in place, air assets can then conduct massive aerial attacks against these forces, utilizing the full arsenal of weapons. The operation is called "Operation Turkeyshoot." Is this plan lawful?
(Primary Research Sources: AP I, art. 48, 51, 52, 54, 57)

8. While coordinating with the Service Judge Advocate (SJA) on changing the name of "Operation Turkeyshoot," the Public Affairs Officer (PAO) wants to discuss the following issue. Intelligence reports indicate a labyrinth of Iraqi-fortified tunnels in and around the outskirts of Tikrit that are probably impervious to airstrikes and indirect fire weapons. Therefore, the commander is considering utilizing blade tanks to employ the "plow tactic" made famous during Desert Storm. The PAO is concerned about the lawfulness of this tactic, not to mention the public affairs angle. What do you think?
(Primary Research Source: Hague Convention IV, art. 22)

9. Intelligence sources indicate that one of the most belligerent leaders of a local "militia" in Baghdad is a dual U.S./Iraqi citizen named Mohammad al-Qatar. The assessment is that he is inciting the militia and trying to get them to take a more active part in hostilities on the side of the Iraqi forces. Al-Qatar is currently on the border with Iran but is under surveillance by an armed drone. What should the commander consider before executing an attack?
(Primary Research Sources: AP I, art. 48, 51, 52, 54, 57)

8 | Weapons and Tactics

The Operational Law Attorney assigned to V Corps encountered a number of LOAC issues related to weapons and tactics before, during, and after the military operation.

While reviewing the operational plans, he discovered that the targeting cell was planning on using an experimental unmanned aerial vehicle (UAV) with a new warhead designed to create maximum fragmentation upon impact. The UAV was to be used during the initial entry, concentrating on the forward deployed units, and then shift to targets of opportunity during the stability operations phase, as coalition forces found themselves conducting counter-insurgency operations. One of the original targets was one of Saddam Hussein's residences, located in a suburb of Baghdad. Should that fail to get Saddam, Special Operations Forces, equipped with silencers, dum-dum bullets, and a special "knock-out drug," intend on capturing him at his house in Tikrit. The Special Forces want to know about the use of a "Trojan horse" tactic — entering Saddam's Tikrit compound dressed as Red Crescent workers, in an ambulance.

The Ops Law attorney also reviewed the targeting plans for the attack on the Ministry of Defense, which was located next to the heavily populated area of Al-Haram. Artillery units used white phosphorous as a marking round to ensure that the artillerymen could adjust fire to the target, which they were to engage from the outskirts of town during one of the armored "Thunder Runs" through Baghdad. The targeting cell is asking about what munitions to use on target – if they have precision munitions, like Excalibur (a GPS capability), are they required to use it? If not, the intention is to employ "dumb munitions," HE (high explosive). How about the use of cluster munitions and anti-personnel land mines? In addition, the operators in the G3 section want to know about the use of a "Trojan horse" virus against military computers controlling the air defense system and civilian computers that control the electrical system.

During the stability operations phase of the operation, when the primary mission is to maintain a secure and stable environment throughout Iraq, the Ops Law attorney spotted some other issues. The Military Police intend on bringing cayenne pepper spray to control prisoners at the Theater Detention Facility and rioters in Baghdad. And the Infantrymen manning checkpoints want to use "laser dazzlers" as a means to prevent escalation of force at their checkpoints.

What is your advice?

I. Introduction to Means and Methods of Warfare

Means and methods of warfare are regulated according to the Hague tradition, rather than the Geneva tradition of protection of victims of warfare. This area of the law addresses two inter-related areas: (1) the methods of warfare, or tactics, which describe how soldiers fight, and (2) the means of warfare, what instruments are used to fight. The regulation of weapons and tactics is governed by two major precepts. The first is the law of war principle of prohibiting superfluous injury or unnecessary suffering. The second is customary international law or treaty law dealing with specific tactics, weapons or weapon systems.

The principles of humanity, military necessity, and the underlying concept of chivalry are at the core of regulating weapons and tactics, also known as "means and methods" of warfare. And limitations on their employment flow from the basic principle of military necessity. As the 60-year-old Army Field Manual on the Law of Land Warfare, FM 27-10, states:

> The law of war places limits on the exercise of a belligerent's power. . . and requires that belligerents refrain from employing any kind or degree of violence which is not actually necessary for military purposes and that they conduct hostilities with regard for the principles of humanity and chivalry.[1]

The significance of these prohibitions cannot be overstated; they lie at the very core of conflict regulation and reflect the historical effort to strike an effective balance between necessity and humanity. According to the ICRC Commentary to Additional Protocol I:

> The principle contained in this paragraph [the right of the Parties to the conflict to choose methods or means of warfare is not unlimited] reaffirms the law in force. Whether the armed conflict concerned is considered by the protagonists to be lawful or unlawful, general or local, a war of liberation or a war of conquest, a war of aggression or of self-defence, limited or "total" war, using conventional weapons or not, the Parties to the conflict are not free to use any methods or any means of warfare whatsoever.
>
> . . .
>
> Contrary to what some might think or wish, in law there are no exceptions to this fundamental rule. If one were to renounce the rule, by which Parties to the conflict do not have an unlimited right, one would enter the realm of arbitrary behaviour, i.e., an area where law does not exist, whether this was intended or not. It is quite another matter to determine the actual scope of the

---

1. Para. 3(a), DEPARTMENT OF THE ARMY, FIELD MANUAL 27-10, THE LAW OF LAND WARFARE (1956) [FM 27-10].

principle, and the specific rules and practices implied by it, which may differ with the times, depending on the prevalent customs and treaties. These variations do not affect the principle itself but its application.[2]

A. Humanity

The principle of humanity provides the foundation for the prohibition against subjecting an opponent to superfluous injury or unnecessary suffering (injury or suffering beyond that which is necessary to bring about the opponent's prompt submission). The first articulation of this principle appeared in the 1868 St. Petersburg Declaration, which summarizes the connection between military necessity, humanity, and the limitation on certain weapons:

> Considering that the purpose of civilization should have the effect of alleviating as much as possible the calamities of war;
>
> That the only legitimate object which States should endeavour to accomplish during war is to weaken the military forces of the enemy;
>
> That for this purpose it is sufficient to disable the greatest possible number of men;
>
> That this object would be exceeded by the employment of arms which uselessly aggravate the sufferings of disabled men, or render their death inevitable;
>
> That the employment of such arms would, therefore, be contrary to the laws of humanity.[3]

The Regulations Annexed to the Hague Regulations of 1899 and 1907 included the original articulation of the current standard for prevention of unnecessary suffering. The text of each was identical, and prohibited "arms, projectiles, or material calculated to cause unnecessary suffering."[4] Article 35(2) of Additional Protocol I prohibits the employment of "weapons, projectiles and material and methods of warfare of a nature to cause superfluous injury and unnecessary suffering." This "of a nature to cause" standard appears to shift the analytical

---

2. Additional Protocol I COMMENTARY, pp. 390-391.

3. 1868 St. Petersburg Declaration [1868 St. Petersburg Declaration] Renouncing the Use, in Time of War, of Explosive Projectiles Under 400 Grammes Weight, *reprinted in* A. Roberts & R. Guelff, Documents on the Law of War (2001), at 55 [Documents on the Law of War].

4. Art. 23(e), 1907 Annex to the Hague Convention (IV): Regulations Respecting the Laws and Customs of War on Land [Hague Rules], Documents on the Law of War, at 77. Both *unnecessary suffering* and *superfluous injury* are inexact translations into English of the French phrase *mauxsuperflus*, which appears in the official French texts of the 1899 Hague Convention (II) 23(e) and Hague Rules, Article 23(e). The unofficial English text of the 1899 Hague Convention (II) translated *mauxsuperflus* to mean *unnecessary suffering*; the unofficial English translation of the successive 1907 text used the term *superfluous injury*. As both phrases have been used synonymously during the twentieth century, both were incorporated into the recodification of Hague Rules Article 23(e) as Additional Protocol I to the Geneva Conventions of 1949, and Relating to the Protection of Victims of International Armed Conflict [API], art. 35(2), Documents on the Law of War, at 442.

focus from the original "calculation" standard to more of an effects based standard. However, in U.S. practice, the phrases "calculated to" and "of a nature to," as well as the phrases "superfluous injury" and "unnecessary suffering," respectively, are viewed by the United States as synonymous[5] (although the ICRC and some other states consider the "of a nature" standard to be more easily violated than the "calculated" standard[6]). Together, they establish the test for determining the appropriate balance between humanity and military necessity.

B. Chivalry

Chivalry, also called honor, promotes good faith reliance on the standards of battlefield conduct established by customary law, and prior to the treaty codification of the LOAC was a primary source of regulation. Like the common law foundation of most contemporary criminal law codes in the United States, chivalry provided the foundation for much of the contemporary regulation of means and methods of warfare. The DoD Law of War Manual lists "honor" as a synonym of "chivalry," and defines it simply as "a certain amount of fairness in offense and defense and a certain mutual respect between opposing forces."[7] The Canadian Law of Armed Conflict Manual includes chivalry in its discussion of basic LOAC principles, and provides:

> The concept of chivalry is difficult to define. It refers to the conduct of armed conflict in accordance with certain recognized formalities and courtesies. An armed conflict is rarely a polite contest. Nevertheless, the concept of chivalry is reflected in specific prohibitions such as those against dishonourable or treacherous conduct and against misuse of enemy flags or flags of truce. The concept of chivalry makes armed conflict slightly less savage and more civilized for the individual combatant.[8]

Chivalry demands a certain mutual respect and trust between opposing forces. It denounces and forbids resort to dishonorable means, expedients, or conduct that would constitute a breach of trust.[9] There are certain elements of chivalry in the respect and protection components afforded prisoners of war and other individuals who are *hors de combat*, or no longer taking an active part in hostilities. But it is the former aspect of the chivalry principle that is operative in the prohibition against certain military tactics. Article 30 of the Lieber Code states in part that "the law of war imposes many limitations and restrictions on principles of justice, faith and honor," while Article 101 states:

---

5. *See* DoD LOWM, para. 6.6.1.
6. Add reference to the CIL study and/or the SIRUS Project.
7. *See* DoD LOWM, para. 2.6.
8. Canadian National Defence, Joint Doctrine Manual B-GJ-005-104/FP-021, Law of Armed Conflict at the Operational Level (2001), 2-1, available at www.fichl.org/fileadmin/_migrated/content_uploads/Canadian_LOAC_Manual_2001_English.pdf, last visited 22 Jun 2018.
9. DoD LOWM, para. 2.6.2.

While deception in war is admitted as a just and necessary means of hostility, and it is consistent with honorable warfare, the common law of war . . . [forbids] treacherous attempts to injure the enemy. . . .[10]

An example of this form of *chivalry* is the use of a white flag, which in land warfare represents a flag of truce. Its display is predicated upon good faith. Its misuse is prohibited, and constitutes a war crime.[11]

Like almost all aspects of the LOAC, these principles evolved into more explicit and specific regulatory obligations. The contemporary regulation of means and methods of warfare is effectuated through a number of modalities: legal review of weapons in the development phase; legal review of the employment of authorized weapons; treaties prohibiting or limiting the use of certain weapon systems; restrictions on certain battlefield conduct; and legal review of tactics and doctrine.

II. Legal Reviews of Weapons or Weapons Systems

A. The Requirement for Legal Review

In order to ensure that weapons comply with international law, art. 36 of Additional Protocol I requires that weapons be evaluated prior to acquisition:

> In the study, development, acquisition or adoption of a new weapon, means or method of warfare, a High Contracting Party is under an obligation to determine whether its employment would, in some or all circumstances, be prohibited by this Protocol or by any other rule of international law applicable to the High Contracting Party.

Very few states have actually translated this requirement into a process for the review of weapon systems; at last count only ten, mostly European states, actually apply this provision in a formal sense. The United States was among the first, having established such a program in 1974 (prior to Additional Protocol I coming into force). The current Department of Defense Directive for the Defense Acquisition System, Department of Defense Directive 5000.01, requires that an attorney appointed by the service (Army, Navy, or Air Force) involved, or the Department of Defense General Counsel's Office, review each weapon or weapon system for compliance with the law of war and relevant

---

10. Francis Lieber, art. 101, GENERAL ORDER NO. 100, INSTRUCTIONS OF THE GOVERNMENT OF ARMIES OF THE UNITED STATES IN THE FIELD (1863) [Lieber Code].

11. *See* discussion of perfidy, below. Under the laws of war on land, the white flag is a flag of truce, *not* a flag of surrender; it only signals an intent to initiate negotiations (although discussions regarding a desire to discuss terms of surrender may be a part of these negotiations). Misuse of, and refusal to recognize, a flag of truce are prohibited by HAGUE RULES, art. 23(f), and API, art.37(1). *See also* LIEBER CODE, arts. 114 and 117.

treaty obligations.[12] Accordingly, a LOAC compliance review is completed for every weapon and type of ammunition fielded for U.S. armed forces.[13]

B. Unnecessary Suffering

For weapons not expressly prohibited by treaty, there is the appearance of an incongruity in the LOAC: while it is legally permissible to kill an enemy combatant, a weapon cannot be used to inflict an injury (less than death) that causes unnecessary suffering. The prohibition of weapons calculated to cause superfluous injury or unnecessary suffering constitutes acknowledgement that the use of weapons in war causes suffering, including injury and loss of life. A weapon cannot be declared unlawful merely because it *may* cause severe injury or suffering. Nor is a State required to foresee or anticipate all possible uses or misuses of a weapon, for almost any weapon can be misused in ways that might be prohibited. The LOAC prohibits the design, modification, or employment of a weapon for the *purpose* of increasing or causing suffering beyond that required by military necessity.

When determining the legality of a weapon or munitions, each must be examined against comparable weapons in use on the modern battlefield, their effects on combatants, *and* the military necessity for the weapon or munitions under consideration. This determination should be made at the national level in the research, development, and acquisition process. This permits commanders to assume the legality of weapons, weapons systems, and munitions issued to them for battlefield use. Accordingly, U.S. practice is based on this assumption: once issued, weapons and munitions are considered consistent with this aspect of the prohibition on unnecessary suffering, that is, that those weapons and munitions are lawful for their intended purposes.

The standard of review is established by Art. 23(e) of the Hague Regulations, reinforced by Art.35(3) of Additional Protocol I. But the terms described above require some interpretation. "Calculated to cause" is interpreted to mean "developed with the specific intent to cause" unnecessary suffering. The unofficial ICRC commentary on Additional Protocol I was drafted by three prominent LOAC experts (who also contributed directly to the standards and the development of the protocols): Bothe, Partsch, and Solf. They noted that the analysis will focus on whether the employment of the weapon or munitions for its normal or expected use would inevitably cause injury or suffering manifestly disproportionate to its military effectiveness.[14] Pursuant to this understanding, U.S. legal experts who conduct weapons and munitions review for the U.S. military look at the intended use of the weapon, by examining the doctrine and

---

12. Para. E1.1.15, DEPARTMENT OF DEFENSE DIRECTIVE, THE DEFENSE ACQUISITION SYSTEM, DEPARTMENT OF DEFENSE DIRECTIVE 5000.01 (2003).
13. *See* DoD LOWM, para. 6.2.
14. Bothe, Partsch, & Solf, NEW RULES (1980), at 198.

instructions for its employment and the effects intended to be (and actually) produced.[15] The test cannot be conducted in isolation, but must be weighed in light of comparable, lawful weapons in use on the modern battlefield.[16] An example of such a review is found at Appendix 1.

In determining a weapon's legality, consideration must be given to the weapon's stated (primary) purpose, *i.e.*, its *intended use*, rather than its ancillary effect. The review then considers whether the suffering inflicted upon enemy personnel is needless, superfluous, or clearly disproportionate to the military advantage reasonably expected from the intended use of the weapon.[17] For example, while the intended purpose for a 30mm projectile would be to engage enemy aircraft, vehicles, and materiel, these munitions may (and often will) strike enemy personnel in the course of combat. The wounding effect on a single combatant is likely to be substantial and, in many cases, fatal. The same would be true were a single combatant to suffer the entire effect of, *e.g.*, a 155mm artillery shell or a 2,000-lb bomb. In each of these cases, the munitions are designed for, and employed against, armored or hardened targets. As a result, the effect on individuals is ancillary to the effect intended by use of weapons, and therefore the anticipated harm to individuals would not cause the munitions to be regarded as inconsistent with the object and purpose of Article 23(e).

Nor would engagement of enemy military personnel with such weapons or munitions be prohibited simply because the legality determination focused on a different intended use. Such employment may be necessary in certain tactical situations, but this is not the use *intended* when the munitions are developed. In fact, it is a general principle of tactical operations to employ weapons of similar character against enemy capabilities. Thus, the norm is to fight "rifles with rifles, tanks with tanks, artillery with artillery." This is often related to the intended use of a weapon during the developmental stage. It is this intent, and not all possible uses, that is the proper focus of the legal review. Any weapon can be used improperly; that is why the analysis focuses on the intended use of the weapon. But to violate the superfluous injury or unnecessary suffering provision by improper use, the use must result from a specific intent to cause unnecessary suffering, beyond what is required for military necessity (e.g., dipping field-expedient "booby traps" in excrement to cause infections).

C. Illegal Use in Customary Law and Treaty Law

Weapons may be illegal *per se*, by improper use, or by agreement in specific treaties. *Per se* illegality is established by treaties and the usage of states (customary international law).[18] For example, the Hague Regulations specifically

---

15. *See* DoD LOWM, para. 6.3.1.
16. Bothe, Partsch, and Solf, *supra*, note 14, at 200.
17. INT'L COMM. OF THE RED CROSS, CONFERENCE OF GOVERNMENT EXPERTS ON THE USE OF CERTAIN CONVENTIONAL WEAPONS CONVENTION: LUCERNE, SEPT. 24-OCT. 18, 1974, (Geneva, 1975). *See, e.g.*, BOTHE, PARTSCH & SOLF at 196. *See also* DoD LOWM, para. 6.6.
18. *See* DoD LOWM, para. 6.4.

recognized that it was "especially forbidden" to employ "poison or poisoned weapons."[19] Military doctrine also mentions lances with barbed heads, irregular shaped bullets, scored or intentionally marked bullets that deform in the human body, and projectiles filled with glass or any substance that would tend to unnecessarily inflame a wound inflicted by the projectile.[20] In addition to the Hague Regulations—and in large measure because of the amorphous nature of Hague prohibition—nations have also agreed to prohibit the use of certain weapons or munitions, or the manner in which they are used. These more specific prohibitions take the form of arms control treaties, such as the 1980 UN Convention on Prohibitions or Restrictions on the Use of Certain Conventional Weapons Convention Which May be Deemed to be Excessively Injurious or to Have Indiscriminate Effects.[21] Several provisions of this important treaty will be discussed below.

Weapons are also reviewed to determine if they are capable of being directed accurately at a military objective or combatant. The LOAC prohibits the use of indiscriminate attacks, to include employing weapons that "cannot be directed at a specific military objective."[22] For example, the "Scud" missiles used by Saddam Hussein during the first Gulf War to attack Israeli and Saudi Arabian cities violated this prohibition and were indiscriminate—they were incapable of being directed at a specific military objective. Use of this weapon was analogous to the German use of missiles against London in World War II, spreading terror amongst the civilian population. In addition, means or methods whose effects cannot be limited are prohibited.[23] This provision would arguably prevent the use of several types of weapons of mass destruction, like biological or chemical weapons, which cannot be limited to military objectives (although, as will be explained below, these weapons are today prohibited by specific treaties).[24]

Finally, weapons reviewers consider whether there are treaties or arms control agreements that prohibit the use of specific weapons or munitions.[25] Treaties intended to ban specific weapons were first introduced in the nineteenth

---

19. Art. 23(a), HAGUE RULES.
20. Para. 34, FM 27-10.
21. 1980 UN CONVENTION ON PROHIBITIONS OR RESTRICTIONS ON THE USE OF CERTAIN CONVENTIONAL WEAPONS CONVENTION WHICH MAY BE DEEMED TO BE EXCESSIVELY INJURIOUS OR TO HAVE INDISCRIMINATE EFFECTS (CONVENTIONAL WEAPONS CONVENTION), DOCUMENTS ON THE LAW OF WAR, at 515.
22. Art. 51(4)(b), AP I.
23. Art. 51(3)(c), AP I.
24. Although nuclear weapons might also fit in this category, the nuclear weapon states have been "persistent objectors" to the application of these provisions to nuclear weapons. *See, e.g.,* UK understanding, DOCUMENTS ON THE LAW OF WAR, at 510. *See also, generally,* 1996 ADVISORY OPINION OF THE INTERNATIONAL COURT OF JUSTICE ON THE LEGALITY OF THE THREAT OR USE OF NUCLEAR WEAPONS, DOCUMENTS ON THE LAW OF WAR, at 639. (The ICJ could not definitively conclude whether the threat or use of nuclear weapons would be lawful in an extreme circumstance, in national self-defense [when the fate of the nation was at stake].) Nuclear arms control agreements will be omitted from discussion in this chapter.
25. *See* DoD LOWM, para. 6.2.4.

century,[26] and have been pursued with varying success ever since.[27] This approach to limiting the use of specific weapon systems has become increasingly significant in the last several decades. These more recent prohibitions have been more successful in articulating specific weapons or munitions that should be controlled because of their presumed indiscriminate effects and/or their nature to cause superfluous injury or unnecessary suffering. In addition to arms control agreements limiting proliferation and testing of nuclear weapons, there are a series of agreements over the last forty years that have prohibited the use, manufacture, transfer, and export of certain types of weapons systems and munitions.

III. Specific Prohibitions on Weapons and Ammunition

A. Exploding Bullets

Except for the innovative language that established limits on the authority of belligerents to inflict suffering—the foundation for subsequent treaties—the 1868 St. Petersburg Declaration is obsolete. State practice reflects a longstanding use of tracer munitions (bullets with a phosphorus coating that "glows" upon firing so that the shooter can "trace" the trajectory and adjust fire), incendiary munitions, high-explosive munitions, or combinations thereof, weighing less than 400 grams for anti-materiel, anti-armor, and anti-aircraft purposes. The St. Petersburg Declaration has never, therefore, been applied to anti-materiel weapons.[28] Advances in technology have made the weight and size limitations of this treaty also obsolete, as munitions as small as .50 caliber have been developed to explode to produce an armor-piercing effect.

Furthermore, any high explosive or incendiary projectile, or combination thereof, designed exclusively for anti-personnel use would be prohibited, regardless of its weight. The intended effect of such a monition would violate the prohibition contained in Article 23(e) of the Hague Regulations prohibiting munitions calculated to cause superfluous injury. Nevertheless, although technological developments and national practice have rendered the technical specifications discussed in the 1868 St. Petersburg Declaration obsolete, the principles reflected in the Declaration permeate more contemporary LOAC treaty regimes. The Declaration itself remains important as the first multilateral agreement articulating the concept that munitions may not be intentionally

---

26. *See, e.g.,* 1868 ST. PETERSBURG DECLARATION, DOCUMENTS ON THE LAW OF WAR, at 1.
27. *See, e.g.,* KELLOGG-BRIAND PACT, 47 U.S. STAT. 2, at 2343 (27 Aug 1928), *available at* http://avalon.law.yale.edu/20th_century/kbpact.asp (last visited 25 Jul 2011).
28. BOTHE, PARTSCH & SOLF, *supra*, note 14, at 196.

designed to "uselessly aggravate" the injury caused combatants; this is the essence of the principle of avoidance of superfluous injury.

B. Expanding Bullets

The 1899 Hague Declaration 3 Concerning Expanding Bullets prohibited "bullets which expand or flatten easily in the human body, such as bullets with a hard envelope which does not entirely cover the core or is pierced with incisions."[29] This provision, a response to what is commonly called the "dum-dum bullet" is intended to prohibit use of bullets that are specifically designed to expand within the human body, or the intentional alteration of other bullets to achieve this effect. However, the prohibition does not apply to fragmentation of full metal jacket small arms ammunition, which is a common effect seen in high-velocity bullets utilized by most armed forces in the world. This treaty had very few participating States; only 34 nations ratified the treaty, not including the United States.

The current U.S. position is that the law of war does not prohibit the use of bullets that expand or flatten easily in the human body.[30] Like other weapons, such bullets are only prohibited if they are calculated to cause superfluous injury. The U.S. armed forces have used expanding bullets in counterterrorism and hostage rescue operations, some of which have been conducted in the context of armed conflict. A 2013 U.S. DoD review of expanding bullets concluded that the 1899 Hague Declaration does not reflect customary international law, as they are not inherently inhumane or needlessly cruel, and may provide effective incapacitation of enemy forces. In addition, such bullets are widely used by law enforcement throughout the world, and they provide significant humanitarian benefits by avoiding the collateral effects of ball ammunition (which may penetrate a wall or go through the intended target to injure innocent civilians).[31]

C. Convention on Certain Conventional Weapons

The regulation of specific weapon systems was the objective of the Convention on Certain Conventional Weapons (CCW). This treaty, negotiated in 1980 by 51 states, provides an umbrella for the negotiation of specific supplemental treaties (annexed protocols) to address specific weapons. Initially, CCW applied only to international armed conflicts. However, by supplemental agreement the treaty and annexed protocols were extended to apply to non-international armed conflicts. Future annexed protocols will ostensibly indicate their scope

---

29. 1899 HAGUE DECLARATION 3 CONCERNING EXPLODING BULLETS, DOCUMENTS ON THE LAW OF WAR, at 64.
30. *See* DoD LOWM, para. 6.5.4.4.
31. *Id.*

of applicability, although it is likely that this trend of applying the treaty provisions to any armed conflict will continue.[32]

The objective of the treaty is twofold: first, protect combatants from unnecessary suffering; second, prevent the incidental injury of civilians resulting from the effects of specifically regulated weapon systems. Entered into force in December 1983, the treaty's annexed protocols regulated the use of incendiary weapons, mines and booby-traps, and weapons designed to injure through very small fragments. Since that time, the number of states parties has more than doubled (today 103), and additional supplemental agreements now regulate the use of blinding lasers and the remnants of war (unexploded ordinance). The treaty establishes a framework for regulating other weapons in the future by adopting additional annexed protocols.

1. Plastic Fragments and Incendiaries

The Conventional Weapons Convention began with introduction of three annexed protocols to prohibit certain weapons or tactics.[33] These include the First Protocol on Non-Detectable Fragments, which prohibits the use of materials that, when fragmented, are undetectable by x-rays. It essentially codified the long-standing customary international law prohibition on glass fragments, updated for modern technology.[34] The Second Protocol, on the Use of Mines, Booby-Traps, and Other Devices, was substantially revised in 1996 and will be discussed below. The Third Protocol, on Prohibitions or Restrictions on the Use of Incendiary Weapons, the "Incendiary Protocol," does not ban a weapon or declare a specific weapon as "indiscriminate" by nature. Instead, this protocol prohibits the use of air-delivered incendiaries (munitions that destroy primarily by the use of fire) to attack military objectives in "concentrations of civilians," and bans the use of other incendiaries (delivered by artillery fire, for example), except when the military objective is "clearly separated" from concentrations of civilians and all feasible precautions are taken to prevent collateral damage.

It is important to note that the Incendiary Protocol does not prohibit the use of incendiaries against military objectives and combatants. It is also narrow in scope, defining incendiaries as distinct from munitions with a different primary purpose. Accordingly the Protocol does not apply to smoke or tracer munitions or munitions that have an incidental incendiary effect. Like several other Conventional Weapons Convention protocols, this protocol provides for strict, specific compliance with the discrimination and military objective (targeting) principles covered in Chapter 7. The Conventional Weapons Convention was amended to include non-international armed conflicts in 1995. The United States ratified the original version, and, in 2009, ratified the

---

32. *See* Convention on Certain Conventional Weapons (CCW) at a Glance, available at: http://www.armscontrol.org/factsheets/CCW.
33. DOCUMENTS ON THE LAW OF WAR, at 527-534.
34. This provision required weapons developers to add a radiopaque substance to rubber balls contained in "non-lethal" munitions, so that they could be detected if they became embedded in human flesh, for example.

1995 amendment. For U.S. forces, however, a "reservation" to this protocol permits the use of incendiaries in concentrations of civilians where it is judged that such use would cause fewer civilian casualties than conventional munitions.[35] Because this Protocol does not prohibit any weapon, *per se*, but instead limits the use of otherwise lawful weapons, compliance is contingent on legality assessments made during the targeting process.

2. Blinding Lasers

The 1995 Protocol (IV) on Blinding Laser Weapons bans certain lasers, another weapon system that, according to the treaty, is calculated to cause unnecessary suffering.[36] Protocol IV applies only to weapons "specifically designed, as their sole combat function or one of their combat functions, to cause permanent blindness." This provision has been especially important for reviewing "laser-dazzlers," or laser-based range finders. Both are required, under U.S. safety rules, to be listed with safe distances posted, so that they are not employed to blind soldiers or civilians on the battlefield. Blinding, "as an incidental or collateral effect," however, is specifically not prohibited by the protocol.[37]

3. Anti-Personnel Land Mines

Anti-personnel landmines have been used extensively in virtually every armed conflict since World War I. Inexpensive to manufacture, easy to employ, and devastating in effect, these weapons can offer significant military advantages. However, because they are incapable of distinguishing combatant from civilian, or even friend from foe, they are increasingly viewed as inherently indiscriminate. Furthermore, because it is often impossible to recover unexploded mines, use of this weapon contaminates former conflict areas, often inhibiting the ability of local inhabitants to work the land in their efforts to return to normalcy following conflict. It is therefore unsurprising that anti-personnel landmines have been the subject of significant regulatory efforts.

---

35. This provision eliminates White Phosphorous rounds and thermobaric munitions from consideration under the protocol. The United States ratified this protocol in 2009, including the following reservation:

> Reservation: The United States of America, with reference to Article 2, paragraphs 2 and 3, reserves the right to use incendiary weapons against military objectives located in concentrations of civilians where it is judged that such use would cause fewer casualties and/or less collateral damage than alternative weapons, but in so doing will take all feasible precautions with a view to limiting the incendiary effects to the military objective and to avoiding, and in any event to minimizing, incidental loss of civilian life, injury to civilians and damage to civilian objects.

The intent of this reservation is to permit engagement of targets, such as chemical weapons plants, which may be located in populated areas; use of incendiaries to destroy the plant would produce fewer casualties than if the chemicals were released with explosive munitions. *See also* DoD LOWM, para. 6.14,3,2.

36. Documents on the Law of War, at 535.
37. Art. 3, Protocol IV, *Id. See also* DoD LOWM, para. 6.15.

The 1996 amendment to the Conventional Weapons Convention's Protocol II, the Amended Protocol on Prohibitions or Restrictions on the Use of Mines, Booby-Traps, and Other Devices [Amended Protocol II],[38] was intended to eliminate the adverse humanitarian consequences of anti-personnel landmines. Amended Protocol II contains limitations on the manner in which these devices may be lawfully utilized. For example, claymore mines may only be used in a command-detonated mode, or when detonated by trip-wire very close to a military position where it can be observed. This limitation is intended to mitigate the risk that innocent civilians accidentally trip the device and fall victim to its devastating impact.

Due to their potential for harming innocent civilians, the Conventional Weapons Convention Amended Protocol II also prohibits the use of the following items as booby-traps: protected emblems or signs; the sick, wounded, or dead; medical equipment or facilities; children's toys; food or drink, except for military stores; kitchen appliances, except in military establishments; religious objects; historic monuments; and animals or their carcasses. Amended Protocol II also requires that mines be detectable by normal mine-detection equipment (thereby prohibiting non-detectable mines, such as mines made entirely of plastics). The protocol contains the previous requirements that anti-personnel minefields must be marked with signs indicating their emplacement, and that they be used only when subject to human over-watch. Like the restrictions on the use of claymore mines and booby-traps, these restrictions are intended to mitigate the risk that civilians will wander into mined areas during or after combat.

Furthermore, Amended Protocol II adds a prohibition on remotely delivered anti-personnel mines that do not contain self-destruct and self-neutralization devices. These are mines that are employed by firing them from artillery, rockets, or dispersing them from aircraft. This employment technique is highly effective in "seeding" minefields at short notice in response to actual or anticipated enemy and/or friendly battlefield maneuver. Using this employment technique enables commanders to "channel" the enemy into kill zones; to shield friendly forces from counter-attack or disruption attacks; or to disrupt enemy movement efforts. In order to balance these important legitimate uses with the protection of the civilian population, this provision was intended to ensure that remotely delivered anti-personnel mines are destroyed or neutralized after a conflict and do not cause an indiscriminate hazard to civilians returning to an area.

Despite the severity of wounds inflicted by landmines, booby traps, and other devices, the Conventional Weapons Convention Protocol II's regulation of these weapons indirectly indicates that such wounds do not constitute superfluous injury when inflicted against combatants, unless the mines contain an undetectable substance or poison, for example.[39] Nonetheless, the widespread belief that the inherent indiscriminate nature of anti-personnel landmines,

---

38. DOCUMENTS ON THE LAW OF WAR, at 536-548.
39. *See* DoD LOWM, para. 6.12.4.1.

along with the statistical reality that even the best self-neutralization technology cannot ensure that all mines become inert, motivated the development of a treaty (The Ottawa Convention[40]) to impose an absolute ban on the manufacture, stockpile, or use of anti-personnel landmines. The United States is not a party to the Ottawa ban, but has announced a policy (1) not to use anti-personnel landmines outside the Korean Peninsula; (2) not to assist, encourage, or induce anyone outside the Korean Peninsula to engage in activity prohibited by the Ottawa Convention; (3) to undertake to destroy anti-personnel landmine stockpiles not required for the defense of the Republic of Korea; and (4) not to produce or otherwise acquire any anti-personnel munitions that are not compliant with the Ottawa Convention. The United States also previously committed to not emplace new persistent anti-personnel or anti-vehicle landmines.[41] Because it applies to both type of mines and makes no exception for "marked and monitored" dumb minefields, this self-imposed policy constraint goes much further than either Amended Protocol II or the Ottawa Convention.

Explosive Remnants of War

The most recent addition to the Conventional Weapons Convention is Protocol V, the Explosive Remnants of War (ERW) Protocol. Protocol V contains no restrictions or prohibitions on weapons or munitions. It was, however, partially intended to respond to criticisms regarding the use of cluster munitions. The fragments from each sub-munition are effective against enemy personnel, vehicles with light armor, aircraft, and similar soft materiel targets, and the presence of unexploded cluster munitions on the battlefield after conflict termination.[42] It establishes obligations of parties to a conflict with respect to ERW that place civilians at risk and post-conflict remediation. Its focus is on pre-conflict preventative measures such as marking and self-neutralization technology and

---

40. Concurrent with the Conventional Weapons Convention adoption of Amended Conventional Weapons Convention Protocol II, and at the urging of the International Campaign to Ban Landmines (ICBL), the governments of Norway and Canada hosted conference sessions that produced the Ottawa Convention on the Prohibition of the Use, Stockpiling, Production and Transfer of Anti-Personnel Mines and on Their Destruction (September 18, 1997). The United States is not a party to this treaty, and does not regard it as a codification of customary international law. The Ottawa Convention does not conclude that anti-personnel land mines constitute a weapon calculated to cause superfluous injury.

As of 2017, 162 States have ratified the Ottawa Convention, which is clearly an arms control treaty. Most potential allies of the United States, including all other members of NATO, are parties to the Ottawa Convention. Australia, Canada, and the United Kingdom, for example, have all ratified the Ottawa Convention. Its Article 1 prohibits state parties from using, developing, producing, otherwise acquiring, stockpiling, retaining, or transferring to anyone, directly or indirectly, anti-personnel landmines, or from assisting, encouraging, or inducing, in any way, anyone to engage in any activity prohibited to a states party under the Convention. Australia and the United Kingdom have taken the position that its armed forces will not be guilty of violation of the Ottawa Convention merely by reason of taking part in joint operations with forces of an ally not bound by the Ottawa Convention that deploys anti-personnel mines. *See* UN DISARMAMENT AGENCY, OTTAWA CONVENTION, available at https://www.un.org/disarmament/geneva/aplc/states-parties-and-signatories/, last visited 7 March 2017.

41. *See also* DoD LOWM, para. 6.12,13.
42. *See* discussion of cluster munitions, below.

post-conflict corrective measures, such as removal or quarantine of contaminated areas. Its Technical Annex also suggests "best practices" that states parties are encouraged to follow on a voluntary basis in order to achieve greater munitions reliability. Obligations concerning clearance, removal, destruction, recording, precautions, and cooperation and assistance related to ERW apply only to ERW created after entry into force of Protocol V for the state party on whose territory the ERW are located. The obligations are not retroactive.[43]

D. Biological Weapons

Biological weapons, along with chemical weapons, were the subject of the 1925 Geneva Protocol, which prohibited the use of "asphyxiating, poisonous, or other gases and all analogous liquids, materials or devices," and extended its prohibition to the "use of bacteriological methods of warfare."[44] The United States, like many other states parties to this treaty, reserved the right to use chemical weapons in response to a first use by an enemy.[45] The 1972 Biological Weapons Convention,[46] an arms control agreement, sought to enhance the restriction against these weapons and prohibited the production, stockpiling, and use of microbial and other biological and toxin weapons. The United States is a party to this treaty, and renounced all use of biological and toxin weapons. Consistent with the treaty, the United States does lawfully retain sufficient quantities for research and prophylactic purposes, however.[47]

E. Chemical Weapons

The 1993 Chemical Weapons Convention (CWC)[48], another arms control agreement developed to enhance the prohibition established in the 1925 Gas Protocol, prohibits the production, stockpiling, and use of chemical agents. This method of banning all presence of this weapon in the battle-space was intended to avert the "lawful second use" qualification that essentially nullified the effect of the 1925 treaty. This also inspired the treaty drafters to include a provision prohibiting States from entering reservations to the treaty, thereby requiring them to accept the obligations in the treaty absolutely with no qualification. The CWC defines chemical agents as "any chemical which, through its

---

43. *See also* DoD LOWM, para. 6.20.
44. 1925 PROTOCOL FOR THE PROHIBITION OF THE USED IN WAR OF ASPHYXIATING, POISONOUS OR OTHER GASES, AND OF BACTERIOLOGICAL METHODS OF WARFARE, DOCUMENTS ON THE LAW OF WAR, at 158.
45. EXECUTIVE ORDER 11850, 40 FED. REG. 16187 (1975); para. 38c, FM 27-10.
46. 1972 CONVENTION ON THE PROHIBITION OF THE DEVELOPMENT, PRODUCTION AND STOCKPILING OF BACTERIOLOGICAL (BIOLOGICAL) AND TOXIN WEAPONS AND ON THEIR DESTRUCTION, available at http://www.opbw.org/ (last visited 28 Dec 2010).
47. *See also* DoD LOWM, para. 6.9.
48. 1993 CONVENTION ON THE PROHIBITION OF THE DEVELOPMENT, PRODUCTION AND STOCKPILING OF CHEMICAL WEAPONS AND ON THEIR DESTRUCTION, available at http://www.opcw.org/chemical-weapons-convention/ (last visited 28 Dec 2010).

chemical action on life processes, can cause death, temporary incapacitation, or permanent harm to humans or animals." This extensive arms control regime requires declarations of all chemical substances capable of creating chemical weapons and it allows inspection and verification of domestic chemical industries by other treaty member States. The United States, which is a party to the treaty, has retained sufficient quantities of chemical weapons for testing, training, and prophylactic purposes. It has, however, eliminated all chemical munitions from its operational inventory.[49]

F. Riot Control Agents

Riot control agents, another type of chemical controlled by the CWC, are defined as chemicals that will have a temporarily disabling effect. They are forbidden for use as a "method of warfare," primarily because they can be confused with more toxic chemical weapons in international armed conflict, and thereby cause rapid escalation of the conflict, should a party to a conflict retain a sub rosa reprisal capability. This provision proved particularly problematic when President Clinton sought Senate advice and consent so that he could ratify the treaty on behalf of the United States. However, because Article XXII of the CWC prohibits States from entering reservations to the treaty, the President was unable to modify the extent of the U.S. obligation. In a compromise, President Clinton agreed to an "understanding" with the Senate—essentially a statement of how the United States would interpret the treaty. Pursuant to this understanding, the President agreed that he would exclude from the meaning of the term "method of warfare" actions in context of military operations that do not involve armed conflict, to include use of riot control agents (RCA) in response to rioting prisoners, police actions in the rear areas, rescue of downed airmen, law enforcement, and peace-keeping operations.[50]

As part of this understanding, President Clinton promised to leave in effect Executive Order 11850, which provides authorization procedures for the use of RCA in these situations. As a result of this understanding and the retention of the Executive Order, the United States maintains stockpiles of both RCA and herbicides to control vegetation around defensive areas. While some critics contend this interpretation of the treaty is inherently inconsistent with its terms, it is unlikely the Senate would have given its consent to ratification had President Clinton insisted on a total renunciation of RCA use in all circumstances. Ultimately, the ability to use this less than lethal capability is perceived by many operational commanders as an important tool to avoid the necessity of using lethal force in response to these limited situations. RCA use is, however, strictly controlled and must be authorized in the rules of engagement.

---

49. *See also* DoD LOWM, para. 6.8.3.
50. *See* DoD LOWM, para. 6.16.2.

IV. Specific Weapons

A. Cluster Munitions

Cluster munitions are not yet the subject of a Conventional Weapons Convention protocol. As noted earlier, they are aerially or artillery-delivered sub-munitions intended to apply force uniformly over a small area, with each sub-munition acting much like a hand grenade. Their legality was considered by the original Certain Conventional Weapons conference (1979-1980) and subsequent review conferences (2001 and 2006). Many participants, including non-governmental organizations emboldened by the alleged use of cluster munitions that could not be relied on to self-neutralize by the Israelis in Lebanon (in 2005), argued that cluster munitions were indiscriminate, *per se*, because their unreliability left so many unexploded sub-munitions that they were a severe danger to civilians returning to the area.[51] However, despite this pressure, cluster munitions use was not prohibited, nor was it in any other way restricted. Conference participants did not conclude that the multiple-wounding risk to combatants constituted unnecessary suffering. The United States is not a party to any LOAC or arms control prohibition on the employment of cluster munitions against enemy personnel and material, and this weapon remains an important tool in the commander's arsenal.[52] Consideration may be given to their employment in the vicinity of populated areas, depending upon the target, delivery mechanism, and risk to the civilian population from other types of munitions reasonably available to the commander at the time. These are targeting decisions made by the commander and his or her staff based upon general law of war principles that are applied to all weapons. There is an international movement for a *per se* ban of cluster munitions. The Convention on Cluster Munitions, also known

---

51. Cluster munitions were the subject of consideration at the second (2001) and third (2006) Conventional Weapons Convention Review Conferences, as well as meetings of government experts within the Conventional Weapons Convention process between the two conferences, without conclusion. The 2009 Meeting of the High Contracting Parties extended the mandate to "continue its negotiations...to address urgently the humanitarian impact of cluster munitions, while striking a balance between military and humanitarian considerations." Current proposals include a ban of unreliable munitions and "opt-in" provisions that allow Oslo Convention (discussed below) members to ban weapons containing more than ten sub-munitions. For more information on this issue, *see* the web page for the UN Mission in Geneva, athttps://onug.ch/80256EE600585943/(httpPages)/4F0DEF093B4860B4C1257180004B1B30?OpenDocument (last visited 28 Dec 2010).

52. The United States is not a party to the Convention on Cluster Munitions (May 30, 2008), also known as the Oslo Convention. As a matter of policy, after 2018, the U.S. armed forces will only employ cluster munitions containing sub-munitions that, after arming, do not result in more than one percent unexploded ordnance (UXO). Until the end of 2018, use of cluster munitions that exceed the one percent UXO rate must be approved by the Combatant Commander. *See* Secretary of Defense Memorandum, DoD Policy on Cluster Munitions and Unintended Harm to Civilians, June 19, 2008. The intent of this policy is to minimize the potential unintended harm to civilians and civilian infrastructure due to cluster munitions employment. *See also* DoD LOWM, para. 6.13.3. But *see* Secretary of Defense Memorandum, DoD Policy on Cluster Munitions (Nov 30, 2017) (allowing continued use of cluster munitions while the U.S. develops new weapons to address area threats and minimize the potential for collateral damage).

as the Oslo Convention, bans the use, stockpiling, production, and transfer of cluster munitions. While 66 States are party to the Convention, and some proponents assert that it reflects customary international law, the United States has not ratified the Convention and does not recognize it as reflective of customary international law.[53]

B. Shotguns

Shotguns are lawful weapons. They have been used in combat as anti-materiel weapons, to guard prisoners, and as anti-personnel weapons, since the sixteenth century. Although the German government protested their use during World War I, due to their devastating effects in the trenches, the U.S. response emphasized that the weapon was lawful.[54] Shotguns remained in the U.S. arsenal ever since, and continue to be used by U.S. forces.[55]

C. Small Arms and Small Arms Ammunition

Small arms ammunition is the mainstay of the infantry and used by every modern military in the world. It includes all military small arms ammunition used in smaller caliber weapons. Since the 1899 Declaration, discussed above, most small caliber ammunition consists of lead or copper, covered by a "full-metal jacket." This ammunition often fired at high velocity and produces wound ballistics that have remained relatively consistent for most of the last century.[56] Most full-metal jacket ammunition changes trajectory, and often fragments to some degree in soft tissue.[57] When used as intended, and not altered by unlawful scoring or marking it has not been found by any nation to cause unnecessary suffering. Almost all of the small arms ammunition fielded for U.S. forces has been adopted by all other NATO militaries in an effort to standardize munitions in the event of needed cross-military resupply. Full-metal jacket ammunition for use by the United States, its allies, and its foes in pistols, sub-machineguns,

---

53. *See generally* http://www.clusterconvention.org.

54. On September 19, 1918, the United States was informed that Germany had protested shotgun use in combat by U.S. military forces. The German protest was rejected by the United States on September 28, 1918. U.S. Dep't of State, Papers Relating to the Foreign Relations of the United States, 1918, Supp. 2, The World War 785-786 (1933).

55. *See* DoD LOWM, para. 6.5.4.2.

56. This performance is illustrated in the wound profiles of the 7.62x51mm, 7.62x39mm, and 5.45x45mm projectiles in the Department of Defense's *Emergency War Surgery* (U.S. Department of Defense, Emergency War Surgery 23-25 (Thomas E. Bowen and Ronald Bellamy eds., 2d U.S. ed. 1988)).

57. The United States and most other nations who were signatories to the Conventional Weapons Convention rejected the International Committee of the Red Cross's SIrUS (Superfluous Injury or Unnecessary Suffering) Project, which attempted to quantify and qualify the damage caused by small arms ammunition, as it did not balance military necessity and provided no new information to the national authorities responsible for weapons reviews under art. 36, of Additional Protocol I. *See* ICRC Report on the Meeting of Government Experts (2001), available at http://www.icrc.org/eng/resources/documents/misc/57jr5z.htm (last visited 28 Dec 2010); *compare* Maj. Verchio, *Just Say No! The SIrUS Project: Well-Intentioned, but Unnecessary and Superfluous*, 51 A.F.L.Rev. 183 (2001).

rifles, or machineguns has included, and continues to include, ball, armor piercing, tracer, or incendiary bullets, or a combination thereof. The primary purpose for tracer ammunition is to aid directed fire, and armor piercing or incendiary ammunition is intended to serve as anti-materiel projectiles. It is inevitable that use of such ammunition will result in wounding or killing enemy personnel. There is, however, no evidence of any significant difference in terminal ballistics between full metal jacket, tracer, or armor-piercing small arms ammunition, or combinations thereof. Accordingly, although some of these rounds are intended for a more specific purpose, use of each against enemy personnel is historic and lawful.[58]

D. Edged Weapons

Knives and other edged weapons have also been in use by military forces for centuries. Military bayonets and knives have often been forged with a serrated edge, to assist the soldier in cutting barbed wire or small trees. As long as the serrated edge is not designed to aggravate a wound, like the "barbed lance" prohibited by U.S. Army doctrine,[59] the creation of a tool that is also used as a weapon is not a *per se* LOAC violation. Bayonets designed for the purpose of creating a vacuum wound, like the triangular bayonet fixed to the AK-50 assault rifle utilized by North Vietnamese forces in the Vietnam Conflict, are probably unlawful because they make treating the wounded combatant more difficult.[60]

E. .50 Caliber Rounds

Caliber .50 ammunition—a very large round—is multi-purpose, having been produced and employed historically on the battlefield for anti-personnel, anti-materiel, anti-armor, and anti-aircraft purposes. These rounds are lawful for all targets, as they are militarily necessary to engage targets at longer range, or to engage thin-skinned aircraft, armor, or other vehicles. This ammunition has included ball, tracer, armor piercing, incendiary, and explosive ammunition, or a combination thereof. The multi-purpose armor piercing, incendiary, and explosive rounds have been primarily employed as an anti-materiel weapon system; but enemy combatants inevitably have been, and will be, struck by caliber .50 multi-purpose ammunition, either due to their proximity to a legitimate target, or their occupancy of a legitimate target at the time it is attacked, such as an aircraft, ground, or water vehicle. The multi-purpose round has been designed to explode after contact with a hard surface and will not normally create any different wound profile than the M33 .50 caliber ball ammunition; it is, therefore, considered by the United States to comply with the explosive projectile provisions discussed earlier, even if fired at enemy personnel.[61]

---

58. *See* DoD LOWM, para. 6.5.4.
59. Para. 34, FM 27-10.
60. *See* DoD LOWM, para. 6.5.3.
61. *See* DoD LOWM, para. 6.5.4.7.

F. Explosive Munitions

Combat forces have employed explosive munitions of all calibers for many centuries, and these munitions remain an essential component of the combat arsenal. They are multi-fragmenting, high explosive munitions, designed for anti-personnel and anti-materiel uses. These munitions have and will inevitably continue to produce major casualties on the battlefield, either through fragmenting artillery shells, "grape shot," hand grenades, or more modern forms of pre-fragmented munitions. The purpose for multiple-fragmenting munitions is to increase the probability of wounding and disabling a number of enemy combatants within range of its fragments; not to aggravate the wounds of combatants.[62] Criticism of these weapons has been directed at the fact that they can cause gaping wounds or multiple injuries, simultaneously. More recently, non-governmental organizations have attacked the use of these munitions in populated areas, for their alleged "indiscriminate effect." Removing them from the combat arsenal would, however, be counter-intuitive from a military necessity standpoint. Indeed, the type of robust destructive capability provided by these munitions is a defining feature of armed hostilities.

Similarly, munitions that cause casualties through blast pressure, rather than fragmentation, are lawful weapons. Designed for specific targets, like bunkers or caves, these munitions offer commanders an important alternative to the hand-to-hand clearing of such defensive positions, one of the most dangerous missions in battle.[63] Finally, combined effects munitions that include incendiary, blast and fragmentation effects have substantial military utility for certain kinds of targets. All these munitions, if they are properly directed at lawful military objectives, civilians directly participating in hostilities, or combatants, are lawful weapons. Like any weapon, the user is required to comply with the general targeting principles discussed in Chapter 7, to ensure that any risk created to civilians is not feasibly avoided, and that the anticipated collateral effects to civilians and civilian objects is not *excessive* in relation to the concrete and direct military advantage gained.[64]

G. Depleted Uranium

Depleted uranium (DU) rounds are specialized munitions developed to penetrate the dense metal used by enemy armored forces (tanks and armored personnel carriers), used by armored forces to attack enemy armor. Radiological exposure to external sources of DU occurs through the proximity of personnel to munitions, armor, and contaminated equipment. These are low-level, low-dose-rate exposures that are within the current safety and health standards of the U.S. Nuclear Regulatory Commission (NRC). For all U.S. military DU munitions, the exposure is less than five percent of the NRC occupational worker exposure of 5,000 millirem

---

62. DoD LOWN, para. 6.5.6.
63. DoD LOWN, para. 6.55.
64. DoD LOWN, para. 6.19.

per year.[65] DU has been the subject of multiple national, international, and non-governmental organization studies with regard to its health and environmental effects.[66] None have found its properties to be a greater hazard to combatants, the general population, or the environment than other conventional munitions. The use of depleted uranium is in no way intended to aggravate or poison the wounds of enemy soldiers. DU munitions, therefore, are lawful weapons.[67]

H. Snipers

Military snipers are trained to deliver fire more accurately and against high-value targets on the battlefield. Their targets are often difficult to engage by the average military rifleman or other weapons, because of range, size, location, fleeting nature, or visibility. The military sniper complies with the fundamental LOAC principle of distinction through his or her direction of precision fire against lawful targets, whether enemy combatants or military materiel. The fact that a military sniper has the ability to engage enemy personnel at greater range than the average military rifleman, through the effective use of cover and concealment, or through the element of surprise, does not alter the legality of the military sniper and his or her mission. Nor is there anything inherently unlawful about targeting a specific enemy individual, such as a commander. Indeed, the principle of distinction mandates so called "targeted killings" in armed conflict—the alternative is utterly illogical. Identifying high value enemy personnel for deliberate attack has been a feature of armed hostilities for centuries, and snipers are simply an efficient method of achieving this objective. The sniper is neither an unlawful weapon nor normally guilty of perfidy, as discussed below.

I. Silencers

A silencer, or suppressor, is designed to silence or muffle the sound of the weapon being fired. It is intended to conceal the source of the attack. While it may be regulated under domestic law,[68] the silencer is a valid addition to military weaponry, as it enables an attack with stealth against military targets, particularly behind enemy lines in "capture or kill" missions conducted by special operations forces.[69] Care must be taken, however, to ensure the silencer does not improperly alter the fired ammunition. For this reason, it is common for U.S. commanders to prohibit the use of "field expedient" silencers — silencers

---

65. DEPARTMENT OF DEFENSE, SUMMARY REPORT TO CONGRESS. "HEALTH AND ENVIRONMENTAL CONSEQUENCES OF DEPLETED URANIUM USE BY THE U.S. ARMY" (June 1994).
66. See, for example, WORLD HEALTH ORGANIZATION, "DEPLETED URANIUM: SOURCES, EXPOSURE AND HEALTH EFFECTS" ¶ 15.2 (2001) and UNITED NATIONS ENVIRONMENTAL PROGRAMME, "DEPLETED URANIUM IN BOSNIA AND HERZEGOVINA: POST-CONFLICT ENVIRONMENTAL ASSESSMENT" 29-38 (May 2003).
67. See DoD LOWM, para. 6.5.7.
68. See, e.g., National Firearms Act, 26 U.S.C. §§ 5811, 5812, 5845 & 5861 (2006).
69. See DoD LOWM, para. 6.5.4.6.

created by troops in the field from available materials. U.S. forces utilize silencers fielded to the force after official procurement.

J. Non-Lethal Weapons

"Non-lethal" or "less-lethal" refers to the intention of the user; a non-lethal/less-lethal weapon, however, is less lethal than conventional means available to a military commander. Examples of non-lethal weapons used in this manner include, "laser dazzlers," stun grenades, acoustic hailers, the Active Denial System (ADS),[70] and caltrops or other barrier devices. Non-lethal weapons authorized for crowd control include Modular Crowd Control Munitions (grenades with rubber balls inside), RCA, and non-lethal 40mm ammunition with rubber bullets, sponge batons, and beanbags. None of these weapons are developed for the purpose of causing death; all of them implicate that risk, as there is no guarantee they will not result in fatalities. Like lethal weapons, non-lethal weapons are also reviewed for legal compliance pursuant to U.S. Department of Defense Directive, Department of Defense Directive 3000.3.[71] Military service attorneys who review these weapons apply the international law standard of review and ensure that the weapons also meet the standards of the Department of Defense Directive for lethal weapons review. The risk of serious injury or loss of life to persons in range of a non-lethal/less-lethal weapon is expected and intended to be substantially lower than the risk associated with lawful but lethal weapons.[72]

Where deadly force is justified, no legal obligation exists to resort to non-lethal/less-lethal weapons before resorting to lethal weapons.[73] Nonetheless, in today's complex operational environment, non-lethal weapons have been and will almost certainly continue to be indispensable to the soldier in the field, and to the commander's ability to achieve tactical, operational, and strategic objectives. They provide an invaluable capability to disable enemy personnel, or even civilians believed to be directly participating in hostilities. They also enable commanders to employ a graduated response when assessing the intent of a civilian who appears to be engaged in direct participation in hostilities or some other hostile act is uncertain. All non-lethal/less than lethal weapons in the U.S. inventory have been reviewed pursuant to the process described, *supra*, and authorized for military issue.

---

70. The ADS is a high-powered microwave device, recently approved for deployment, which heats the first 1/64th of an inch of the skin, causing the target to avoid the beam or flee. It can be used for checkpoints, fixed installation security, or crowd control.

71. Dep't of Defense, Dir. 3000.3, Policy for Non-Lethal Weapons ¶ 3.1 (July 9, 1996) (hereinafter Department of Defense Directive 3000.3).

72. *See* DoD LOWM, para. 6.5.10.

73. *See* Department of Defense Directive 3000.3 ¶ 4.5. A similar rule applies with respect to use of deadly force by police. *See, e.g.,* Scott v. Heinrich, 39 F.3d 912, 915 (9th Cir. 1994); Plakas v. Drinski, 19 F.3rd 1143, 1148, 1149 (7th Cir. 1994). *See also* Illinois v. Lafayette, 462 U.S. 640, 647 (1983) ("The reasonableness of any particular government activity does not necessarily or invariably turn on the existence of alternative, 'less intrusive' means.")

K. Cyber Weapons

Cyber weapons are the latest acquisition for the military arsenal. They may not be weapons at all—their status as a weapon depends on their use. If it is not used in armed conflict, the cyber capability may be a defensive device or used for intelligence collection. There is clearly no treaty law specifically directed at cyber capabilities. A weapon should be analyzed using standard principles—does it cause unnecessary suffering? Is it capable of being directed at a military objective? Some commentators have proposed using an "effects-based" analysis of the cyber capability to determine whether it is a weapon and employed in accordance with international law.[74] One method of determining this is to apply Article 49(1) of Additional Protocol I. Is it an "attack," a means of violence against the adversary, whether in attack or defense? If there is no violence, no "kinetic effects," there is nothing to analyze under the LOAC.[75] This is a rapidly developing area of the law, and like so many other new capabilities in the past, time and practice will ultimately define the regulatory framework applicable to this capability. It is clear, however, that the Department of Defense is taking this issue quite seriously, and has recently created a joint command devoted exclusively to cyber issues (U.S. Cyber Command).[76]

V. Employment of Weapons

Employment of a lawful weapon against enemy combatants, unprivileged belligerents, and military objectives does not violate the LOAC if the weapon is employed consistently with its intended purpose(s) and doctrine for its employment.[77] There is generally no obligation to employ the most precise weapon (unless, as explained in Chapter 7, there is no legitimate justification for selecting the less precise weapon when civilians are at risk from the attack); nor does the LOAC require the employment of weapons, munitions, or tactics that may place friendly personnel or forces at greater risk. The application of overwhelming force against enemy forces does not constitute unnecessary suffering. There is no LOAC requirement to employ the weapon that is likely to result in the least injury to enemy combatants, or to "shoot to disable or wound" rather than kill. In applying military power against enemy forces, a preponderance of destruction may be brought to bear, that is, there is no proportionality concept that limits the employment of the full range of lawful weapons against a legitimate

---

74. *See* Michael N. Schmitt, *Cyber Operations and the Jus in Bello: Key Issues,* Naval War College International Law Studies (2011).
75. *See generally* Eric T. Jensen, *Cyber Warfare and Precautions Against the Effects of Attacks,* Texas Law Review, Vol. 88 (2010).
76. http://www.securityfocus.com/brief/978; *see also* DoD LOWM, Chapter XVI.
77. *See, generally,* DoD LOWM, para. 6.3.

target, including individual enemy combatants or, for example, enemy troops in the open, where civilians are not present.

Nor does the infliction of injury or death upon enemy combatants by munitions designed primarily for anti-materiel purposes constitute a LOAC violation. Similarly, there is no use-of-force escalation continuum for engagement or attack of enemy combatants. The LOAC does not require that a combatant must hold his or her fire to avail an enemy an opportunity to surrender, nor does a combatant have an obligation to attempt to shoot to wound. The only LOAC restriction with respect to attack of enemy combatants or a civilian taking a direct part in hostilities is the prohibition on denial of quarter.[78] Attacking with a high probability of causing death does not violate the "no quarter" rule. Instead, that rule prohibits armed forces from declaring, prior to attack, that surrender will not be accepted. If enemy personnel place themselves under the control of attacking forces, or become *hors de combat* because of wounds or sickness, they must be spared from deliberate attack. However, it is important to emphasize that a white flag or raised hands does not indicate the conclusion of the surrender process, only the initiation of that process. The no quarter rule requires that *if and when* enemy personnel express their desire to surrender, they must not be denied a meaningful opportunity to do so. The ICRC Commentary to Article 40 provides:

> This article confirms in the first place the Hague rule, i.e., it would not be acceptable that "combatants who went on defending themselves to the limit of their strength and finally surrendered and laid down their arms, should be exterminated." It also prohibits the use of a threat to that effect to accelerate surrender. The demand of unconditional capitulation, which one Party to the conflict may make of the adversary, should never be a pretext for a refusal to give quarter, whether the demand is met or not. This even applies in the event that the 'jus ad bellum, 'the right to participate directly in hostilities, is contested. In other words, it is always prohibited to declare that the adversary is outside the law, or to treat him as such.[79]

In short, the prohibition against denial of quarter and attacking an enemy with overwhelming combat power with full knowledge that it will produce substantial casualties are mutually compatible.

VI. Methods of Warfare

Tactics, or methods of warfare, are governed by the principles of honor and chivalry, by relevant treaty provisions, and by customary international law. Perfidy — the exploitation of an opponent's fidelity to the LOAC in order to gain

---

78. *See* art. 40, Additional Protocol I, "It is prohibited that there shall be no survivors, to threaten an adversary therewith or to conduct hostilities on this basis."
79. ICRI Commentary to AP I, pp. 475-476.

a tactical advantage—is the most pernicious form of violation, the condemnation of which runs deep in the roots of the law. While "tricking" the enemy is permissible, the use of protected status or symbols to do so is not. The LOAC also prohibits, in whole or in part, assassination, espionage, and reprisals.

A. Ruses

Ruses are tactics that involve exploiting enemy recklessness produced by employing legitimate deception tactics.[80] An example in naval tactics includes the use of dummy funnels to trick the opponent into believing an armed raider was a merchant ship. In World War II, the British Navy employed the "Q-ship" tactic, where they outfitted merchant ships with extra, concealed armament and a cadre of Royal Navy crewmen disguised as merchant mariners; when attacked by German U-boats, they hoisted the battle ensign and engaged, sinking numerous U-boats.[81] In land warfare, lawful ruses involve the creation of fictitious units by planting false information, putting up dummy installations, making false radio transmissions, or using a smaller force to simulate a larger unit.[82] Perhaps the most famous example of this type of ruse occurred in World War II to support the allied deception operation to conceal the true location of the Normandy invasion. An entirely fictitious unit, the First U.S. Army Group, supposedly commanded by General George S. Patton, was created for this purpose. The ruse was intended to deceive the Germans into believing the unit, set up in Kent across from the Pas de Calais, was poised to attack there across the narrowest point of the English Channel.

A more common and far less elaborate type of lawful ruse involves using enemy equipment or uniforms. Enemy property may also be used to deceive the opponent. Combatants may wear enemy uniforms to infiltrate enemy lines, but the LOAC prohibits fighting in enemy uniforms. Because doing so violates the LOAC, if captured the soldier may be prosecuted for a war crime, or for violation of the law of the detaining power for conduct falling outside the scope of lawful combatant immunity. Thus, while use for infiltration is permissible, it is imperative that soldiers are able to quickly don their own uniforms if discovered and engaged by the enemy. Like uniforms, enemy colors (flags) may be employed as a ruse, as long as they are not employed during actual combat.[83] However, according to Article 39 of Additional Protocol I, the use of enemy flags, emblems, uniforms or insignia while engaging in attacks, or to "shield, favor, protect, or impede military operations" is prohibited.[84]

---

80. *See* DoD LOWM, para. 5.26.1.
81. *See* C. JOHN COLOMBOS, THE INTERNATIONAL LAW OF THE SEA, 454 (1962).
82. *See also* art. 37(2), Additional Protocol I, "The following are examples of ruses: the use of camouflage, decoys, mock operations, and misinformation."
83. Para's. 54 and 74, FM 27-10. *See also* DoD LOWM, para. 5.23.
84. Art. 39(2), Additional Protocol I.

B. Perfidy

Condemnation of perfidy is an ancient precept of the laws and customs of war, derived from the principle of chivalry. Perfidy degrades the protections and mutual restraints developed in the mutual interests of all parties to conflict, to include both combatants and civilians. In practice, the protections accorded to protected persons and objects is diluted when combatants experience perfidious conduct that causes them to believe or suspect that adversaries are abusing their claim to LOAC protections in order to gain a military advantage.[85] Thus, the perfidy prohibition is directly related to the protection of war victims. The practice of perfidy also inhibits the restoration of peace.[86] Perfidy includes acts "inviting the confidence of an adversary, by leading them to believe they are entitled to, or obliged to accord, protection under the rules of international law."[87] It is a betrayal of confidence by one side in the good faith compliance with the LOAC by the other. Perfidy includes use of protected symbols (the distinctive emblem of the red cross, for example),[88] feigning of intent to surrender, injured status, or non-combatant or civilian status.[89] Feigning, which is a grave breach in the context of international armed conflicts and a serious violation in non-international armed conflicts, is distinguished from misuse, a lesser violation of the law. Feigning is treachery that results in killing, wounding, or capture of the enemy; misuse is an act of treachery resulting in some other advantage over the enemy.

Furthermore, section 8(2)(b) of the Rome Statute of the International Criminal Court criminalizes certain acts of perfidy in international armed conflict, notably "making improper use of a flag of truce, of the flag or of the military insignia and uniform of the enemy or of the United Nations, as well as of the distinctive emblems of the Geneva Conventions, resulting in death or serious injury;"[90] and "killing or wounding treacherously individuals belonging to the hostile nation or army."[91]

C. Assassination

Assassination was first prohibited by the Lieber Code, which provides in art. 148:

> The law of war does not allow proclaiming either an individual belonging to the hostile army, or a citizen, or a subject of the hostile government, an outlaw,

---

85. *See* DoD LOWM, para. 5.22.1.
86. BOTHE, PARTSCH & SOLF *supra*, note 14 at 202.
87. Art. 37(1), Additional Protocol I.
88. Art. 38(1), Additional Protocol I.
89. Art. 37(1), Additional Protocol I. These are all breaches of faith, due to the obligation to protect an adversary who is *hors de combat*, per art. 41, Additional Protocol I.
90. Rome Statute of the International Criminal Court, § 8(2)(b)(vii).
91. *Id.* at § 8(2)(b)(xi).

who may be slain without trial by any captor. . . . Civilized nations look with horror upon offers of rewards for the assassination of enemies as relapses into barbarism.

A similar prohibition was included in The Hague Regulations: "[I]t is especially forbidden . . . to kill or wound treacherously individuals belonging to the hostile nation or army."[92]

These provisions are construed as prohibiting the hiring of assassins, putting a price on the enemy's head, and offering rewards for an enemy "dead or alive."[93] Assassination is also prohibited under U.S. domestic law by Executive Order 12333, which provides "No person employed by or acting on behalf of the United States Government shall engage in, or conspire to engage in, assassination."[94] Interestingly, the Executive Order does not define *assassination*, though traditionally, the term connotes a killing motivated by politics or religion.[95] However, it is essential to distinguish prohibited assassination from the deliberate killing of lawful combatants, including the head of the armed forces, or the "commander in chief" (even if he is a political figure). The status of such individuals renders them lawful targets at all times unless they are *hors de combat*. The LOAC provides legal authority for attacking such individuals and therefore such attack does not qualify as assassination.[96] For example, the houses of Saddam Hussein were targeted during the first days of the Second Gulf War. And recent U.S. practice has involved providing rewards for "information leading to the capture of an individual," taking advantage of the law enforcement aspects of counter-terrorism and counter-insurgency. These tactics share two common elements that distinguish them from assassination. They emphasize the use of lawful military force in warfare and they emphasize that "outlawry" is prohibited, since it encourages non-combatants or civilians to attack members of the opposing forces, and thus undermines the principle of distinction.[97] Deliberately attacking a protected person may be an unlawful assassination, but this is in large measure superfluous, as such an attack would also violate the LOAC principle of distinction and be unlawful for that reason alone.

---

92. HAGUE RULES, art. 23(b).
93. Para. 31, FM 27-10.
94. Exec. Order No. 12,333, 3 C.F.R. 200 (1981).
95. BLACK'S LAW DICTIONARY 47 (3d Pocket ed. 2006).
96. *See* W. Hays Parks, Memorandum of Law: Executive Order 12333 and Assassination, ARMY LAW (Dec. 1989), at 4.
97. A.P.V. ROGERS, LAW ON THE BATTLEFIELD (2004), at 47.

D. Espionage

Espionage involves acting clandestinely, or on false pretenses, to obtain information for transmission back to friendly territory.[98] Individuals who engage in espionage are "spies." Their conduct may violate domestic law, but it is not a LOAC violation to conduct or order espionage.[99] However, spies are not entitled to prisoner of war protections and cannot claim the benefit of combatant immunity to prevent prosecution by the detaining power. Art. 106 of the Uniform Code of Military Justice defines the offense of spying and vests U.S. military courts with jurisdiction to try such individuals. Art. 106 provides that:

> Any person who in time of war is found lurking as a spy or acting as a spy in or about any place, vessel, or aircraft, within the control or jurisdiction of any of the armed forces of the United States, or in or about any shipyard, any manufacturing or industrial plant, or any other place or institution engaged in work in aid of the prosecution of the war by the United States, or elsewhere, shall be tried by a general court martial or by a military commission and on conviction shall be punished by death.

Spying and espionage are also prohibited by a number of provisions in the U.S. criminal code.[100] Whether an individual suspected of spying in the context of an armed conflict against the United States is prosecuted in military or civilian court is a policy decision; either venue could assert lawful jurisdiction. However, it is important to distinguish spying and espionage from gathering intelligence while in uniform. The latter is not espionage, and is a common tactic employed by almost all militaries. Furthermore, Additional Protocol I provides that if spies are employed, returning to friendly lines upon completing a mission immunizes the spy for past espionage activities; therefore, if later captured as a lawful combatant, the former spy cannot be tried for past espionage.[101]

E. Reprisals

Reprisal involves engaging in action that normally violates the LOAC, taken in response to a prior enemy LOAC violation. Reprisal is a self-help LOAC enforcement action. The purpose of a reprisal is to sanction the enemy for their violations and compel the enemy to comply with the LOAC in the future.[102] Because reprisal always risks counter-reprisal and a spiraling erosion of LOAC

---

98. Art. 46(3), Additional Protocol I.
99. *See* DoD LOWM, para. 4.19.4.1.
100. http://www.justice.gov/usao/briefing_room/ns/counterespionage.html.
101. Art. 46(4), Additional Protocol I.
102. *See, generally,* DoD LOWM, para. 18.18.

protections, other means of securing LOAC compliance should normally be exhausted before resorting to reprisals.[103]

Reprisals against protected persons are prohibited by the Geneva Conventions.[104] According to the U.S. Army FM 27-10, reprisals are permitted by U.S. forces only when: timely; responsive to the enemy's violation; follow an unsatisfied demand to cease and desist; proportionate to the previous illegal act; and, authorized at the highest level of government.[105] Because of the almost instantaneous nature of modern communications, and the extreme political and policy risk associated with engaging in reprisal, it is almost inconceivable that any U.S. commander below the rank of General would ever authorize such action.

Additional Protocol I significantly enhanced the limitations on lawful reprisal, a provision the United States considered problematic. Additional Protocol I added several other categories of prohibited reprisal targets: the entire civilian populations, civilian property, cultural property, objects indispensable to the survival of the civilian population (food, livestock, drinking water), the natural environment, and installations containing dangerous forces (dams, dikes, and nuclear power plants).[106] The United States and several states parties objected to these additional restrictions, and it is doubtful that they reflect customary international law.[107] The practical effect of Additional Protocol I's expansion of individuals and objects protected from reprisal is to eliminate reprisals as viable options to respond to enemy noncompliance with the LOAC. In essence, compliance with Additional Protocol I would limit reprisals to enemy armed forces, their facilities, and equipment — an outcome that seems illogical as all of these targets are always subject to lawful attack. Reservations, declarations and objections of various parties in response to these restrictions, the persistent objection of nuclear states, and the reported threat of reprisal for any Iraqi use of chemical weapons made by Secretary of State James Baker to Iraqi Foreign Minister Tariq Aziz prior to the first Gulf War have kept the doctrine of belligerent reprisals alive (at least as a viable argument under international law, if not as a practically viable solution). While this may seem like a draconian measure, it is essential to recognize that prohibition of viable reprisal would also prohibit the *threat* of meaningful reprisal, which would deprive States of an important and historically effective tool to prevent anticipated LOAC violations by an enemy.

---

103. Para. 497, FM 27-10.
104. *See, e.g.*, art. 13, PRISONER OF WAR CONVENTION. *See also* DoD LOWM, para. 18.18.3.
105. Para. 497, FM 27-10.
106. Art's.51, 53-56, Additional Protocol I.
107. *See*, e.g., DOCUMENTS ON THE LAW OF WAR, at 511. *See also* DoD LOWM, para. 18.18.3.4.

Appendix 1

DEPARTMENT OF THE ARMY

**OFFICE OF THE JUDGE
ADVOCATE GENERAL
INTERNATIONAL AND OPERATIONAL
LAW DIVISION
1777 N. KENT STREET
ROSSLYN, VIRGINIA 22209-2194**

ATTENTION OF:

DAJA-IO   1 June 2005

MEMORANDUM FOR OFFICE OF THE PROJECT MANAGER, CLOSE COMBAT SYSTEM (SFAE-AMO-CSS), PICATINNY ARSENAL, NEW JERSEY 07806-5000

SUBJECT: Legal Review for the AT4 — Confined Space (AT4-CS (RS)).

1. **References.**

a. SFAE-AMO-CSS Memorandum (25 May 2005), Subject: Law of War Review for the U.S. Army Type Classification and Procurement of AT4 — Confined Space (AT4-CS (RS));
b. Department of Defense Memorandum (30 October 2002), Subject: Defense Acquisition.
c. Army Regulation 27-53 (1 January 1979), Subject: Review of Legality of Weapons under International Law.

2. **Purpose.**

Reference a. requests legal review of the AT4-CS (RS). This review is conducted pursuant to references b and c., which require a legal review of all weapons and munitions procured to meet a military requirement of the United States. The purpose of this review is to determine whether the AT4-CS (RS) and its intended use are consistent with the international legal obligations of the United States, including law of war treaties and arms control agreements to which the United States is a party, customary international law, and U.S. policy.

3. Summary Finding.

As more fully described below, the AT4-CS (RS) and its intended use in combat is consistent with the international legal obligations of the United States. (NOTE: This legal review of weapons under international law is entirely independent of any federal or state law enforcement authority to use such weapons within U.S. territorial jurisdictions.)

4. General Description and Mission of the AT4-CS (RS).

a. Current and emergent missions require U.S. forces to replenish aging stocks of M136 AT4 with a product improvement which will allow the AT4 to be safely fired from enclosed space. The AT4-CS (RS) has been developed to meet this requirement. The AT4-CS (RS) is a specially adapted, disposable 84mm light anti-armor shoulder fired weapon for close combat. The recoilless system is designed to support users needing the capability to defeat light and medium armored targets from an enclosure, typically associated with urban areas. Current shoulder launched weapons in the U.S. Army inventory do not allow the operator to fire the weapon from such an enclosed space, thereby limiting the employment capability in urban areas; depriving U.S. forces light anti-armor engagement capability in such areas; and increasing the risk of counter-fires after employment in any areas. The AT4-CS (RS) is a modified version of the current M136 AT4. Major design differences are in the composition and configuration of the liquid counter-mass and propellant charge that reduces the blast overpressure, signature, and toxic fumes, thereby allowing the operator to maximize survivability while engaging threat targets from confined spaces. The target engagement capability and effects of the AT4-CS (RS) are analogous to the current version of the AT4.

5. Law of War Considerations and Analysis.

a. General Considerations: The international law provisions relevant to this review are:

   (1) Hague Convention (IV) Respecting the Laws and Customs of War on Land of 18 October 1907 (36 Stat. 2277, TS 539, 1 Bevans 631). Article 23(e) of its Annexed Regulations prohibits the employment of "arms, projectiles, or material calculated to cause unnecessary suffering."
   (2) The customary international law prohibition against employing indiscriminate methods or means of warfare.

In determining the legality of a weapon or munition, appropriate consideration must be given to the legitimate military purpose of the munitions (*military necessity*) and the humanitarian interest of protecting the victims of conflict. With regard to combatants, this humanitarian interest is protected by the prohibition against the infliction of *unnecessary* suffering. With regard to other potential victims of conflict, this interest is protected by the prohibition against employing indiscriminate methods or means of warfare.

The prohibition of *unnecessary suffering* constitutes acknowledgement that *necessary suffering* to combatants is lawful, and may include severe injury or loss of life. There is no agreed definition as to what constitutes unnecessary suffering. However, as a general proposition, the suffering inflicted by a weapon or munition would be deemed unnecessary only if: it's use was calculated to cause unnecessary suffering; or the inevitable result of the normal use causes an injury the nature of which is considered by governments as excessive in relation to the military advantage anticipated from employment of the weapon or munition.

In determining whether a particular weapon is or is not consistent with the legal standards articulated above, it is essential that the reasonably anticipated effects of the weapon or munition be evaluated within the context of comparable, lawful weapons or munitions in use on the modern battlefield.[108]

A weapon cannot be declared unlawful merely because it *may* cause severe suffering or injury. The appropriate determination is whether a weapon's or munition's employment for its normal or expected use would be prohibited under some or all circumstances.[109] The correct criterion is whether the employment of a weapon for its normal or expected use inevitably would cause injury or suffering manifestly disproportionate to its military effectiveness. A State is not required to foresee or anticipate all possible uses or misuses of a weapon, for almost any weapon can be misused in ways that might be prohibited.

b. Analysis of the AT4-CS (RS). The purpose of the AT4 – CS (RS) is to provide U.S. forces with a light anti-armor capability adaptable to urban terrain and minimizing counter-fire risk associated with engagement signature. This capability will contribute to the ability of U.S. forces to kill or disable enemy combatants and other hostile forces engaged in conflict with U.S. forces, or to disable or destroy targets that satisfy the definition of military objective. This purpose is consistent with the principle of military necessity, which acknowledges the right of belligerents engaged in armed conflict to employ measures not forbidden by international law which are indispensable for securing the complete submission of the enemy as soon as possible. This munition is not otherwise prohibited by international law: it is not calculated to cause unnecessary suffering; the effect of employment will not be excessive in relation to the anticipated military advantage offered by such employment; there is

---

108. Law of war issues related to lawful targeting should be addressed at the time of employment, to be determined by the on-scene commander under the circumstances ruling at the time. These issues are not determinative of the lawfulness of a weapon or munition. The commander authorizing its use should consider its characteristics where innocent civilians are present in order to ensure consistency with mission rules of engagement and law of war proscriptions on the directing of attacks at civilians not taking an active part in hostilities, or who otherwise do not pose a threat to U.S. forces.

109. M. Bothe, K. Partsch, and W. Solf, New Rules for Victims of Armed Conflicts (1982), pp. 200-201.

nothing in the characteristics of this munition or its anticipated employment that lead to a conclusion that its effect will be indiscriminate. Each of these considerations will be addressed below.

(1) There is no indication that this munition is calculated to cause unnecessary suffering. The anticipated effect of this munition is analogous to that of the standard AT4 munition, a round used by a large number of nations and considered consistent with international law.

(2) The effect of employment of this munition will not be excessive in relation to the anticipated military advantage that will be gained by employment. The defeat or destruction of military objectives is an essential component for the success of U.S. forces. It is without dispute that such objectives could legally be engaged with existing light anti-armor capabilities. The AT4—CS (RS) will provide a more efficient and effective means of achieving the legitimate objective of attacking such military objectives. International law does not require that such an objective be achieved in an inefficient manner. Because the AT4—CS (RS) contributes to that purpose without effects that can be classified as excessive when compared to the effects of other available and legal methods and means of achieving this objective, there is no international legal objection based on this prong of the analysis.

(3) There is no basis to conclude that the AT4—CS (RS) is, by its nature, an indiscriminate weapon. Employment of this system must involve human decision-making and firing action. It is reasonable to presume that as a result, employment of the AT4—CS (RS) will be in accordance with the stated purpose: destroy or disable lawful military objectives. As noted above, it is not necessary to speculate on possible improper uses of this system in analyzing its legality. With regard to this conclusion, it is also noted that it is reasonable to conclude that the enhanced protection from enemy counter-fires and enemy suppression efforts offered by the ability to employ the AT4—CS (RS) from enclosed and quasi-protected locations will enhance the effectiveness of the target decision-making and engagement process, thus enhancing compliance with the law of war.

6. Conclusion.

The AT4—CS (RS) is consistent with the international law obligations of the United States, including the law of war, provided it is employed in accordance with the law of war.

Principal References:

AP I, Arts. 35-40
Hague Rules, Arts. 22-24
DoD LOW Manual, Chapters 5 and 6
Chemical Weapons Convention
Biological Weapons Convention
Certain Conventional Weapons Convention

Study Problems

You are the Operational Law attorney for V Corps. How do you address the following issues?

1. In reviewing the databases for weapons systems, available at the Center for Law and Military Operations (CLAMO) website, you discover that the experimental unmanned aerial vehicle (UAV), with a new warhead, has not been properly reviewed by the U.S. Army attorney responsible for doing so under Art. 35, Additional Protocol I. What needs to be reviewed? What information will the attorney need to review the UAV and its warhead? What issues do you anticipate he will need to resolve?
2. Is there anything wrong, per se, with the use of UAV's as a weapon or tactic? Is it perfidious or in any way dishonorable, as some Pakistani Taliban have suggested? How about the targeting of Saddam's home? Is that not an assassination of the head of state?
3. Some of those Special Forces weapons need a closer look. What about silencers, dum-dum bullets and the "knock-out drug"? How about their "Trojan horse" tactic — entering Saddam's Tikrit compound dressed as Red Cross workers, in an ambulance?
4. Fires in the Al-Haram area may have been caused by white phosphorous rounds. Is the use of white phosphorous prohibited? Isn't it an incendiary? How about its use in a densely populated area, like Al-Haram? What about other munitions, like high explosives (HE)? Are the gunners required to use precision munitions to limit civilian casualties? What about cluster munitions and the remotely delivered Family of Scatterable Mines (FASCAM) (including to attack and prevent the escape of the Republican Guard)? Or, on the flanks of the 101st Division's attack toward Najaf, is it permissible to use anti-personnel land mines? What kind?
5. Is the computer "Trojan Horse," targeting military computers controlling the air defense system and civilian computers that control the electrical system lawful? Any advice on their employment?
6. What about the non-lethal weapons proposed for stability operations phase of the operation? For instance, cayenne pepper spray to control prisoners at the Theater Detention Facility and rioters in Baghdad? And how about the "laser dazzlers" used by infantrymen to prevent escalation of force at their checkpoints?

9 | WOUNDED AND SICK

You are the Brigade Judge Advocate for a U.S. Army Stryker Brigade Combat Team in the midst of a combat deployment to Mosul, Iraq. Arriving at the tactical operations center one morning, you are accosted by the Brigade Executive Officer, who tells you that the commander, Colonel Brown, is looking for you. After you dutifully report, Colonel Brown tells you about a significant activity report that one of the battalion commanders, Lieutenant Colonel McCaffrey, recently submitted. The report deals with one of the Infantry companies, Alpha Company (also known as "Assassin Company"), and its engagement with enemy insurgents the night before, which resulted in seven enemy soldiers killed in action, and an estimated 18 enemies wounded, with no U.S. or coalition casualties. Colonel Brown tells you that upon seeing the report he contacted Lieutenant Colonel McCaffrey to congratulate him and discuss the tactics, techniques, and procedures that Assassin Company used. "McCaffrey said Assassin used a baited ambush," Colonel Brown informs you. "When I asked what he meant, he said that Assassin had been in a firefight with enemy insurgents, feigned that the Company was breaking contact and returning to the forward operating base. Instead, the Company left its third platoon in an overwatch position of the firefight engagement area. The platoon kept "eyes on," and waited for a couple of hours until the enemy returned to police up their dead and help their wounded. When they did, third platoon opened up on them." Rubbing his forehead with his hand, Colonel Brown closes with, "I don't know whether to recommend them for an award or start an investigation. What do you think?"[1]

---

1. Greg Jaffe, "Almost a Lost Cause": One of the Deadliest Attacks of the Afghan War Is a Symbol of the U.S. Military's Missteps, WASH. POST, Oct. 4, 2009, available at http://www.washingtonpost.com/wp-dyn/content/ article/2009/10/03/AR2009100303048.html?sid=ST2009100401053. The article describes how a U.S. Army unit deployed to Afghanistan purportedly called in artillery fire on insurgents who returned to the battlefield to collect their dead from an engagement hours earlier. Members of the unit filmed the artillery strike and can be heard laughing and cheering, which presents additional issues. *See also* Michael Yon, Adam Ray, MICHAEL YON ONLINE MAG., Feb. 18, 2010, http://www.michaelyononline.com/adam-ray.htm. In describing efforts by U.S. Army forces to counter the improvised explosive device (IED) threat in Afghanistan, Yon explains that the U.S. Army has deployed "small kill teams," or SKTs, to monitor culverts, small tunnels that run under roads and ideal IED emplacement areas. When insurgents approach the culverts, the SKTs call in artillery strikes that

Protection of the wounded and sick on the battlefield is the very foundation of the Geneva humanitarian tradition. No situation illustrates the concept of "victim of war" more than a wounded or sick soldier stranded on the field of battle, and no image better exemplifies the LOAC's humanitarian impact than the collection and care of such casualties by members of an enemy armed force.

The Geneva Convention for the Amelioration of the Condition of the Wounded and Sick in the Field (GWS) is the first of the four Geneva Conventions that today bind every nation in the world.[2] More importantly, this first Geneva Convention is the seed from which the Geneva tradition of protecting victims of war blossomed. As will be explained in this chapter, principles such as equality of treatment and the obligation to come to the aid of a wounded enemy in many ways provide the ultimate manifestation of the Geneva tradition: the dictates of humanity require *all* parties to endeavor to mitigate the suffering of *all* victims.

Implementing this humanitarian obligation, however, requires detailed rules to offset the natural instincts of belligerents engaged in mortal combat. The GWS perhaps more than any other Geneva Convention, reflects the time-tested implementation of the humanitarian obligation to spare, as much as possible, the suffering of the disabled belligerent. Countless wounded and sick belligerents survived their trauma because of the commitment—albeit in some cases marginal—to the proper treatment of the GWS. It should therefore be unsurprising that compliance with the obligations discussed in this chapter is absolutely essential for the execution of credible military operations.

I. Background

In the summer of 1812, the French Emperor Napoleon and his "Grande Armée" invaded Russia, fighting a massive battle against the Russian Army on 7 September at Borodino, roughly 75 miles west of Moscow. In the aftermaths, of what would prove to be the deadliest day of the Napoleonic Wars:

> Napoleon and his retinue were riding on ground so littered with corpses that it was impossible to avoid stepping on them, one of the horses trod on a dying soldier and drew a last moan of pain from him. The Emperor, until then as silent as his victory, terribly depressed by the sight of so many

---

kill the individuals who had come to emplace IEDs; when enemy forces arrive to collect the bodies, the SKTs engage them as well.

2. Geneva Convention for the Amelioration of the Condition of the Wounded and Sick in Armed Forces in the Field, Aug. 12, 1949, 75 UNTS 31 (hereinafter GWS). In 2012, South Sudan acceded to the 1949 Geneva Conventions. As a result "[a]ll the countries in the world have now signed the 1949 Geneva Conventions, making the treaties truly universal." ICRC News Release, South Sudan: world's newest country signs up to the Geneva Conventions, Jul. 7, 2012 https://www.icrc.org/eng/resources/documents/news-release/2012/south-sudan-news-2012-07-09.htm.

victims, suddenly exploded and relieved his feeling by cries of indignation and an exaggerated solicitude for the poor soldier. Someone, to appease him, remarked that after all, *it was only a Russian*. To which Napoleon replied, "[t]here are no enemies after a victory, but only men."[3]

While a noble sentiment, it was little more — at the time of the Battle of Borodino, there were no treaties that required military forces to provide relief to wounded and sick belligerents, protecting those who risk their lives to provide that relief, and ensuring respect for the dead. That all changed, but not for another 50 years, and not until another horrible battle, also involving the French Army, this time under the command of one of Napoleon's descendants.

In 1859, the Italian Kingdom of Piedmont-Sardinia formed an alliance with Napoleon III (Napoleon's nephew) to drive the Austrian Empire from northern Italy. The Second Italian War of Independence erupted in late April, and on June 4, Emperor Napoleon III led the French-Sardinian forces to victory against the Austrians at the Battle of Magenta. The Austrian Army retreated eastward whereupon Emperor Franz Joseph arrived and took command.

The Austrians turned to counterattack; at the same time, the allied French and Italians were in pursuit and unaware that the Austrians were no longer retreating. Due to faulty intelligence, the French-Piedmontese force had only expected to encounter the Austrian rearguard, while the Austrians only expected to clash with the French-Piedmontese vanguard. Both sides were shocked to encounter the entirety of the enemy army; the Austrians fielded around 160,000 soldiers against the French-Piedmontese force of 156,000. Beginning in the early morning of 24 June, for 15 hours across a 15-kilometer front in northern Italy, the two armies fought three battles in what became known as the Battle of Solferino. During the battles, some Austrian Army units refused to accept the surrender of wounded members of the French Army, while some French Army units "responded by beating wounded Austrian soldiers to death."[4] The battle ended in the early evening when the Austrian Army retreated, leaving the French-Piedmontese in possession of miles of battlefield carnage containing over 2,600 dead and 22,000 wounded from all sides, overwhelming the minimal, unorganized, military medical resources.[5] As a result, the wounded and dead remained on the battlefield largely without care or recovery.

As discussed in Chapter 2, Swiss businessman Henri Dunant arrived in Solferino the evening of the 24th and witnessed the battle's horrific aftermath. Dunant's presence in Italy was motivated purely by self-interest: he was seeking a meeting with Napoleon III to discuss issues related to Dunant's agriculture and trading company in French-controlled Algeria. Dunant had written a book

---

3. Matthew Milikowsky, "There Are No Enemies After Victory:" The Laws Against Killing the Wounded, 47 GEORGETOWN J. INT'L L 1221 (2016) (quoting from Philippe-Paul De Segur, DEFEAT: NAPOLEON'S RUSSIAN CAMPAIGN 80 – 81 describing the aftermath of the battle of Borodino) (emphasis in original) (hereinafter Milikowsky).
4. Id., at 1225.
5. *Id.*, citing Colonel H.C. Wylly, THE CAMPAIGN OF MAGENTA AND SOLFERINO 1859.

praising Napoleon III, intending to present it to him personally. Instead, he spent the next three days in the nearby town of Castiglione, helping the wounded and organizing aid. Dunant purchased medical supplies with personal funds and rallied the local civilian population to provide assistance and shelter to injured soldiers on both sides, without regard to their side in the conflict. Additionally, he convinced the French force to release a number of captured Austrian doctors. From Castiglione, Dunant traveled to Milan, where he spent five more days continuing to help the wounded from the battle.[6]

Upon returning to Geneva, Switzerland, Dunant recorded his experience in a book entitled *A Memory of Solferino*.[7] The book described not only the horrors of the battlefield but also Dunant's belief that a neutral organization was necessary to provide care to wounded soldiers. Dunant ended the book by asking: ". . . in an age when we hear so much of progress and civilization, is it not a matter of urgency, since unhappily we cannot always avoid wars, to press forward in a human and truly civilized spirit the attempt to prevent, or at least alleviate, the horrors of war?"[8] The answer, though several years in formulating, was yes.

Dunant promoted the book among the European political and military elite and *A Memory of Solferino* became an international best-seller. On February 9, 1863, the Geneva Society for Public Welfare met to discuss the topics in Dunant's book; ultimately, the Society created a committee to pursue Dunant's plan for a neutral humanitarian organization. The committee consisted of Genevan jurist and President of the Society for Public Welfare Gustave Moynier, General Henri Dufour of the Swiss Army, doctors Louis Appia and Theodore Manunoir, and Dunant.[9] The Committee met for the first time on February 17, 1863 in what was later considered the first meeting of the International Committee of the Red Cross (ICRC).

The ICRC recognized that it was "primarily the duty and responsibility of a nation to safeguard the health and physical well-being of its own people," but that there was a "need for voluntary agencies to supplement . . . the official agencies charged with these responsibilities in every country," especially in times of war.[10] Dunant's ideals came to fruition first in a 14-State conference to discuss methods of improving care for wounded soldiers in October 1863, and solidified on August 22, 1864, when 12 nations signed the Geneva Convention of 1864 for the Amelioration of the Condition of the Wounded in Armies in the

---

6. Milikowsky, *supra*, note 3, at 1226.
7. Henri Dunant, A MEMORY OF SOLFERINO, 127 (1862) available at https://shop.icrc.org/un-souvenir-de-solferino-2529.html.
8. *Id.*
9. Robert Kolb & Richard Hyde, AN INTRODUCTION TO THE INTERNATIONAL LAW OF ARMED CONFLICTS, 113 (2008).
10. Chandler P. Anderson, The International Red Cross Organization, 14 AM. J. INT'L L. 210 (1920).

Field (GWS).[11] The 1864 Convention provided treatment standards for medical personnel in the field, and "stipulated that wounded enemy soldiers were to be collected and cared for in the same way as members of friendly armed forces."[12] The GWS was amended in 1906,[13] when the Second Convention (for the Amelioration of the Condition of Wounded, Sick and Shipwrecked Members of Armed Forces at Sea) was added. Both the Wounded and Sick Convention and Wounded and Sick Convention Sea were amended again in 1929; in the same year, a separate Convention (GPW) regarding the treatment of prisoners of war (POW) was also adopted; yet when World War II began, several major nations were not parties to the three Geneva Conventions.[14]

After World War II, the focus of the LOAC evolved to address broader concerns of humanitarian protection, especially those related to civilian victims of war.[15] 1949 saw the revision of the three 1929 Geneva Conventions (including the GWS), and the creation of a new Fourth Convention aimed at protecting the civilians during wartime. Decades later, Additional Protocol I (AP I) would define basic wounded and sick terminology and expand the scope and beneficiaries of protection. Additional Protocol II (AP II) would extend basic protections to non-international armed conflict, while Additional Protocol III (AP III) would clarify the protective emblems available to mark personnel, facilities, and equipment devoted to medical aid.

Nonetheless, the GWS remains to this day the ultimate expression of the original humanitarian objectives of the Geneva tradition. The GWS establishes a comprehensive framework for the protection of the wounded and sick and the respect for the deceased. The treaty establishes basic obligations, defines special protections for the wounded and sick and those exclusively engaged in their collection and care, and provides special protected status for equipment and facilities devoted to their care. The overarching purpose of the GWS is to facilitate the prompt collection of and effective care for the wounded and sick.

---

11. The States that originally signed the Convention were Baden, Belgium, Denmark, France, Hesse, Italy, the Netherlands, Portugal, Prussia, Spain, Switzerland, and Württemberg. The United States ratified the Convention in 1882. Gary D. Solis, THE LAW OF ARMED CONFLICT: INTERNATIONAL HUMANITARIAN LAW IN WAR 49 (2010) (hereinafter Solis).

12. THE HANDBOOK OF INTERNATIONAL HUMANITARIAN LAW 22 (Dieter Fleck ed., 2d ed. 2008) (hereinafter Fleck).

13. The 1906 revision created provisions addressing the transfer of information between parties to a conflict; specifically, it required information transfer regarding wounded prisoners. Solis, *supra*, note 11, at 73.

14. *Id.* at 26. Japan and the USSR had not ratified the 1929 Conventions. *Id.*

15. Kolb & Hyde, *supra*, note 9, at 39-40. A major reason for this change was the large number of civilians killed during the First and Second World Wars (only one civilian was killed during the Battle of Solferino).

II. International Armed Conflict

Before delving into the specifics of the Wounded and Sick Convention, it is important to remember its scope. With the exception of common Article 3, each of the 1949 Geneva Conventions, including the GWS, only apply as a matter of law during an international armed conflict (IAC).[16] Common Article 3 applies during any armed conflict, however characterized. But even during an IAC, there are qualifications on who the GWS protects, when, and how.

A. Wounded and Sick

To qualify for protection, an individual must be wounded and/or sick as explained below, *and* belong[17] to one of the six categories of either members of the armed forces or associated forces listed in Article 13 of the GWS. These six categories are the same as those determining who qualifies for POW status[18] as described in Chapter 4: (1) members of the regular armed forces and members of militias or volunteer corps forming part of the armed forces; (2) members of other militias or volunteer groups that belong to a belligerent Party so long as certain conditions are met; (3) members of regular armed forces who claim allegiance to a government or authority not recognized by the detaining power; (4) those who accompany the regular armed forces of a Party without being members of the armed forces (correspondents, contractors, or members of labor units); (5) members of crews of the merchant marine and civil aircraft of the Parties to the conflict who do not receive more favorable treatment under any other treaty provision; and (6) members of a *levée en masse*—inhabitants of non-occupied territory who have spontaneously taken up arms to resist an invading force.[19]

---

16. The other ways law may apply is through custom or policy.

17. Protection under the Wounded and Sick Convention "does not require a wounded or sick person to have fallen into enemy hands in order to be protected. This means that the First Convention also applies to wounded and sick members of a Party's own armed forces, in addition to those of the adverse Party." ICRC, Commentary on the First Geneva Convention, 2nd edition, (2016) para. 1451 (hereinafter 2016 ICRC Commentary). In addition to defining protections, GWS also creates an absolute prohibition preventing protected persons from voluntarily relinquishing any of the protections bestowed upon them. *See* GWS, *supra,* note 2, art. 7 ("Wounded and sick, as well as members of the medical personnel and chaplains, may in no circumstances renounce in part or in entirety the rights secured to them by the present Convention [and by any existing special agreements]").

18. The Updated Commentary to the Wounded and Sick Convention notes that there are differences between Article 13 of the First Convention and Article 4 of the Third Convention, which details the categories of individuals qualifying for POW treatment. 2016 ICRC Commentary, *supra,* note 17, at para. 1444. The most significant of those differences is that for an individual to be covered by the Third Convention, they must be "in the hands of the enemy," which is not a requirement for the application of the First Convention.

19. GWS, *supra,* note 2, art. 5. While the captive is wounded, both the Wounded and Sick Convention and the Prisoner of War Convention apply; after the soldier has recovered from his injuries, the Prisoner of War Convention is the exclusive source of status and rights. Prisoners of war

Each of the six categories are fully protected by the GWS. Other than the civilians who fall under categories four and five, the Convention does not apply to civilians who are wounded and sick. But, as will be discussed later in this chapter, many of the obligations from the GWS require parties to the conflict to act before they would likely know whether an individual falls under one of the Article 13 categories. As the 2016 ICRC Commentary to the GWS states:

> Article 13 defines which persons, if they are wounded or sick, benefit from the protection of the First Convention. It must be emphasized, however, that all wounded and sick persons, including civilians, are entitled to respect, humane treatment, and the care which their condition requires. Anyone in need of medical attention is entitled to receive it. When a wounded or sick person falls into enemy hands, the priority must be to provide medical care with the least possible delay. The determination as to whether that person meets the conditions for being a prisoner of war can be made later, at an appropriate time and place. . . . At the Diplomatic Conference in 1949, it was emphasized that "it is of course clearly understood that those not included in this enumeration [of Article 13] still remain protected, either by other Conventions, or simply by the general principles of International Law." Thus, Article 12 cannot in any way entitle a Party to a conflict to fail to respect a wounded person, or to deny the requisite treatment, even where the person does not belong to one of the categories specified in it.[20]

In 1977, AP I reinforced many of the protections established by the GWS, and supplemented these with a number of new obligations. Perhaps most significantly, civilians were expressly protected within the AP I's wounded and sick definition: "[p]ersons, whether military or civilian, who, because of trauma, disease or other physical or mental disorder or disability, are in need of medical assistance or care and who refrain from any act of hostility."[21]

Overall, AP I reflects an attempt to address the needs of the wounded and sick more pragmatically with far less emphasis on limited categories of military wounded and sick, and is therefore an important advancement in the protection of all war victims.

---

retain their status until they are repatriated. *Id*, art. 14. *See* generally Geneva Convention Relative to the Treatment of Prisoners of War, Aug. 12, 1949, 6 U.S.T. 3316, 75 U.N.T.S. 972 (hereinafter GPW).

20. 2016 ICRC Commentary, *supra*, note 17, at paras. 1460-1461. Certainly in an era of intense scrutiny on the treatment of the civilian population by armed forces, commanders ignore civilian suffering at great peril. Accordingly, even absent express treaty obligations, it is increasingly common for commanders to attempt to anticipate civilian medical needs and to assist in meeting those needs in a manner that does not compromise the capacity to meet the primary mission of caring for military casualties.

21. Article 8(1), Protocol Additional to the Geneva Conventions of 12 August 1949, and Relating to the Protection of Victims of International Armed Conflicts (Protocol I), 8 June 1977, 1125 UNTS 3 (hereinafter AP I).

1. When are Individuals Wounded or Sick?

In order to maximize the coverage of the treaty and the beneficial effects of its provisions, the GWS did not include a definition for the term "wounded and sick." As the original Commentary to the 1949 GWS noted:

> No attempt has ever been made in the Geneva Convention to define what is meant by a "wounded or sick" combatant; nor has there ever been any definition of the degree of severity of a wound or sickness entitling the wounded or sick combatant to respect. That is as well; for any definition would necessarily be restrictive in character, and would thereby open the door to every kind of misinterpretation and abuse. The meaning of the words "wounded and sick" is a matter of common sense and good faith.[22]

The Department of Defense Law of War Manual provides that wounded and sick includes "combatants who have been rendered unconscious or otherwise have been incapacitated because of their wounds or sickness and combatants who have surrendered as a consequence of their health."[23] The key component to qualifying for protection under the GWS is *not* merely being wounded or sick. Rather it is being wounded or sick *and* out of the fight.[24] As a result, the Wounded and Sick Convention covers:

---

22. International Committee of the Red Cross, Commentary on the Geneva Convention (I) for the Amelioration of the Condition of the Wounded and Sick in Armed Forces in the Field 136 (Jean S. Pictet, ed., 1952) (hereinafter Pictet). The 2016 ICRC Commentaries to the GWS explain that there is no difference between the concepts of "wounded" and "sick." Qualifying as wounded or sick in the context of international humanitarian law requires the fulfillment of two cumulative criteria: a person must require medical care and must refrain from any act of hostility. 2016 ICRC Commentary, *supra*, note 17, at para. 1341.
23. US Department of Defense, Office of the General Counsel, Law of War Manual (revised ed., December 2016), para. 7.3.1.1 (hereinafter DoD LOW Manual).
24. Often referred to as "*hors de combat*," which is French for "out of the battle." The wording of the wounded and sick convention may unintentionally reinforce the incorrect view that any individual who falls under one of the Article 13 categories and is wounded or sick qualifies for protection and thus may no longer be made the object of attack. This misunderstanding has as its origin in the French words used in the original 1864 and subsequent 1906 and 1929 Wounded and Sick Conventions, as French was the official language of those treaties. In describing who should be protected, those conventions use the French word "*blesses*," which translates as wounded, or injured. Milikowsky, *supra*, note 3, at 1227. But clearly the drafters did not believe that merely being wounded qualified an individual for protection. The commentary to the 1864 Convention interchangeably uses "*blesses*" and "*hors de combat*," and the Memory of Solferino details the bravery of soldiers who continued to fight after being wounded, with no indication that Henri Dunant thought such belligerents were entitled to special protections unless and until they stopped fighting. As a prominent British commentator observed:

> Obviously, however, "wounded and sick" must be interpreted as "rendered helpless by wounds and sickness." If wounded men continue to fire while lying prostrate, as the Russians did, and they were perfectly entitled to do, at Inkerman (1854 battle during the Crimean war); or if they attack those who come to bring them succor, as the Dervishes did after Omdurman (1898 battle in Khartoum, Sudan); or if they act as a wounded Boer did at Vlakfontein (1901 battle in South Africa) . . . and crawl about the field of battle and shoot the enemy's wounded, they are not entitled to be "respected and taken care of." Such "wounded" as these I refer to . . . are enemy soldiers and nothing else. It is for the wounded and sick who ceased to resist that the Convention secures respect and care.

Id. at 1230 quoting J.M. Spaight, War Rights on Land 421 (1911). The official languages of the 1949 Wounded and Sick Convention are French and English, thus the continued use of the word *blesses* or wounded while meaning *hors de combat* or out of the fight.

Combatants who have fallen by reason of a wound or sickness of any kind, or who have ceased to fight and laid down their arms as a consequence of what they themselves think about their health. *It is the fact of falling or laying down of arms which constitutes the claim to protection. It is only the soldier who is himself seeking to kill who may be killed. The abandonment of all aggressiveness should put an end to aggression.*[25]

Additional Protocol I later offered some clarity to the wounded and sick terminology and expanded its reach. Under AP I, "'wounded' and 'sick' means persons, whether military or civilian, who, because of trauma, disease or other physical or mental disorder or disability, are in need of medical assistance or care and who refrain from any act of hostility."[26] AP I also explains that

> A person is hors de combat if:
> (1) he is in the power of an adverse Party;
> (2) he clearly expresses an intention to surrender; or
> (3) he has been rendered unconscious or is otherwise incapacitated by wounds or sickness, and therefore is incapable of defending himself. Provided that in any of these cases he abstains from any hostile act and does not attempt to escape.[27]

As the Commentary to AP I explains: "[i]t is a fundamental principle of the law of war that those who do not participate in the hostilities shall not be attacked. In this respect harmless civilians and soldiers '*hors de combat*' are a priori on the same footing."[28]

---

25. Pictet, *supra*, note 17. (emphasis added) "To merit respect and protection as "wounded" or "sick" under the law of war, combatants must abstain from hostile acts or attempts to evade capture." DoD LOW Manual, *supra*, note 23, at 7.3.1.1. "[A] combatant who is with his or her own forces and is recovering from a battle wound, still requires medical care and has not yet begun to engage in hostilities, but who, for example, performs weapons maintenance, can no longer be said to abstain from hostile acts and therefore does not qualify as wounded or sick in the legal sense of the term." 2016 ICRC Commentary, *supra*, note 17, at para 1346.

26. AP I, *supra*, note 21, art. 8. Notably, this definition includes mental disorders or disabilities as potentially rendering a belligerent *hors de combat*. While that addition was appropriate, even long overdue, how many mental disorders manifest themselves as overtly obvious to an opposing force? For example, a service member might be suffering from a mental disorder that has rendered him or her catatonic, which an opposing force would be very unlikely to recognize. Contrast that with behavior incorrectly recognized as manifestations of a mental disorder. During the 1944 "D-Day" allied invasion of mainland Europe, 21-year-old British Army Private Bill Millin marched up and down the beach playing the bagpipes in support of the Royal Army's First Special Service Brigade. Millin was following the orders of the Brigade Commander, Lord Lovat, the chief of a Scottish Clan, who thought the bagpipes would improve the morale of soldiers pinned down by German machine gun fire. Miraculously, Millin survived unscathed, while some 4,400 allied soldiers were killed all around him. After the war, Millin met German soldiers who had manned machine guns overlooking the beach and most certainly remembered the bagpipe player. The Germans said they didn't aim at Millin "because they thought [he] was crazy." *See* John F. Burns, Bill Millin, Scottish D-Day Piper, Dies at 88, NY Times Aug. 19, 2010.

27. AP I, *supra*, note 21, art.

28. *See also* International Committee of the Red Cross, Commentary on the Additional Protocols of 8 June 1977 to the Geneva Conventions of 12 August 1949 (Yves Sandoz et al. eds., 1987) at 224 (hereinafter Sandoz).

2. How are the Wounded & Sick Protected?

a. Respect and Protect

Under Article 12 of the GWS, qualifying wounded or sick persons "shall be respected and protected in all circumstances."[29] This obligation is considered a cornerstone of the LOAC. It is considered two distinct duties: "an obligation to respect, i.e., not to attack or otherwise harm the wounded and sick, and an obligation to protect, i.e., to take protective measures for the protection of the wounded and sick against various dangers arising in the context of an armed conflict."[30]

(1) Respect

The "respect" duty imposes an obligation of inaction: prohibiting any harmful action or attack directed against the wounded and sick.[31] Thus, the wounded and sick may never be considered lawful targets under the law regulating the conduct of hostilities."[32] The obligation to respect also prohibits other forms of harmful conduct towards the wounded and sick outside the conduct of hostilities. This would include any form of intentional ill-treatment of the wounded and sick.

(2) Protect

The "protect" duty imposes an obligation of action: coming to the defense of the wounded and sick, regardless of their side in the conflict,[33] and once collected, to care for the wounded and sick and defend them from further harm or

---

29. GWS, *supra*, note 17, art. 12.
30. 2016 ICRC Commentary, *supra*, note 17. at para 1352.
31. "There are many instances of violations of the respect principle. For example, North Vietnamese personnel shot wounded Americans on the Ia Drang Valley battlefield in November 1965. *See* Hal Moore & Joseph Galloway, WE WERE SOLDIERS ONCE. . . . AND YOUNG 298 (2002).
32. 2016 ICRC Commentary, *supra*, note 17, at para 1353-1354. While it is clear that the wounded and sick, as well as military medical personnel and facilities may not be made the object of attack, how they should factor into targeting analysis is unclear. *See* Geoffrey Corn & Andrew Culliver, Wounded Combatants, Military Medical Personnel, and the Dilemma of Collateral Risk, (2016) available at https://papers.ssrn.com/sol3/papers.cfm?abstract_id=2884854 (comparing the ICRC's approach in the revised commentary to the GWS, that such individuals factor into a proportionality analysis, and the approach of the DoD LOW manual, where they would not).
33. "The obligation to protect is complementary to the obligation to respect. It requires parties to the conflict to take active steps to protect the wounded and sick from harm. The obligation to protect is an obligation of conduct. The parties to the conflict are therefore obliged not only to refrain from attacking or otherwise harming the wounded and sick through their own organs (to respect), but also to exercise due diligence in preventing the wounded and sick from being harmed in other ways (to protect)." 2016 ICRC Commentary, *supra*, note 17, at para 1360. Fortunately, there are also many instances of the protect principle being respected. *See* The Judge Advocate General's Legal Center and School, 86th Law of War Course Deskbook E-5 (July 2006) (hereinafter Law of War Deskbook) (describing how, during the 1982 Falklands War between the United Kingdom and Argentina, "a British soldier came upon a gravely wounded Argentine whose brains were leaking into his helmet. The British soldier scooped the extruded material back into the soldier's skull and evacuated him. The Argentine survived.") (citation omitted).

victimization.[34] This fundamental obligation to care for the wounded and sick must be executed in a non-discriminatory manner.[35] Considerations must be made to ensure the continued protection of all wounded and sick, not simply those of one's own armed forces.[36]

The respect and protect obligations are broad: It is "unlawful for an enemy to attack, kill, ill-treat or in any way harm a fallen and unarmed soldier, while at the same time . . . the enemy [has] an obligation to come to his aid and give him such care as his condition require[s]."[37] The obligation to protect "arises at the instant the State learns of, or should normally have learned of, the existence of a serious risk" that harm to the wounded and sick may occur.[38]

b. Obligation to Search and Collect

Parties to a conflict are required to "take all possible measures to search for and collect" both the wounded and sick and the dead.[39] It is important to recognize that Parties must carry out this obligation before it is possible to determine whether those persons meet the criteria in Article 13.[40] This search and collection mandate applies to both friendly and enemy casualties.

The GWS suggests that the Parties should arrange "an armistice or a suspension of fire . . . to permit the removal, exchange and transport of the wounded left on the battlefield . . . [or] from a besieged or encircled area."[41] Such coordinated lulls in the conduct of hostilities are extraordinarily rare. That should not be taken to mean that the obligation is not followed, but rather that it must be balanced against risk. Indeed, it is critical to note that the search and collection obligation is qualified by feasibility considerations. Military personnel must assess the feasibility of search and collection efforts, and are not obligated to engage in those efforts when doing so will subject them to unnecessary risk.[42]

---

34. Armed Forces field manuals have generally adopted the definitions of GWS Commentary in defining their obligations. *See* Manual of the Law of Armed Conflict 7.3.1 (U.K. Ministry of Defense ed., Oxford, 2004) ("The duty of respect means that the wounded and sick are not to be made the target of attack. The duty of protection imposes positive duties to assist them") (hereinafter British LOAC Manual).

35. GWS, *supra*, note 2, art. 12.

36. See, e.g., id. (stating that humane treatment must be provided "without any adverse distinction founded on sex, race, nationality, religion, political opinions, or any other similar criteria" and that women among the wounded and sick population "shall be treated with all consideration due to their sex").

37. Pictet, *supra*, note 22, at 135.

38. 2016 ICRC Commentary, *supra*, note 17, at para. 1366.

39. GWS, *supra*, note 2, art. 15. This requirement is active "[at] all times, and particularly after an engagement." Id. The article seeks to prevent ill-treatment of the wounded and sick, presumably due to bandits, exposure, or the risk of infection, and to prevent the dead from being despoiled. *See id.*

40. 2016 ICRC Commentary, *supra*, note 17, at para 1460.

41. GWS, *supra*, note 2, art. 15.

42. "The obligation to act without delay is strict, but the action to be taken is limited to what is feasible, in particular in the light of security considerations. The military command must judge reasonably and in good faith, based on the circumstances and the available information, what is possible. . ." 2016 ICRC Commentary, *supra*, note 17, at para 1487. *See also* Law of War Deskbook, *supra*,

Further, the treaty drafters recognized that broad suspension-of-fire agreements to remove, transport, and exchange the wounded, sick, and dead are not always possible.[43] However, to offset these barriers to aiding the wounded and sick, the treaty sanctions "local arrangements": essentially, cease-fires arranged by local commanders to accomplish the same search-and-collection function on a smaller scale.[44] Local arrangements also might provide for removing wounded and dead from a besieged or encircled area, or permitting medical and religious personnel and relief supplies to enter the area.[45]

Civilians may assist in the collection and care of the wounded and sick.[46] A commander may request locals to do so, but civilian action must be voluntary; however, civilians are allowed to spontaneously provide care to the wounded and sick, without request from the military.[47] Civilians must respect the wounded and sick in the same manner as military care-providers. In fact, Article 12 is the only article of the GWS that directly applies to civilian conduct. At the same time, the military authority should grant civilians who have undertaken the task of caring for wounded and sick protection and facilities to support their efforts.[48] If an adverse Party takes control of the area, it must continue to grant the same protection and facilities to the civilians.[49] It should be noted, however, that this civilian support is merely an augment to the military obligation imposed by the GWS. Accordingly, allowing and facilitating civilian care for the wounded and sick does not relieve the Party of its "respect and protect" obligations.[50]

c. Obligation to Provide Medical Care

Article 12 of the GWS is perhaps the most important article in the treaty. It establishes the requirements of care, and defines the standard as one of humane treatment. The original ICRC Commentary notes that "each belligerent must treat his fallen adversaries as he would the wounded of his own army."[51]

---

note 33, at E-7 ("By way of example, US policy during Operation Desert Storm was not to search for casualties in Iraqi tanks or armored personnel carriers because of concern about unexploded ordnance").

43. GWS, *supra*, note 2, art. 17.
44. *Id.*
45. *Id.* Local arrangements were used to allow medical supplies into Sarajevo during the siege in 1992.
46. *Id.*, art. 18.
47. *Id.*
48. *Id.*
49. *Id.* Under no circumstances should a civilian or medical care-provider be molested or convicted for giving aid to the wounded or sick. The 1952 Commentary to this article describes that during and after World War II, several countries imposed harsh penalties on civilians or members of a Red Cross Society who treated or cared for enemies, as "laws . . . treated any form of service in an enemy army as high treason, and [care-providers] were regarded purely and simply as individuals who had taken up arms against their country." See Pictet, *supra*, note 22, at 192. Article 18 states that "medical treatment, even where given to enemies, is always legitimate, and does not constitute a hostile act. . . . This provision protects medical personnel in the strict sense of the word as well as civilians." *Id.* at 192-193.
50. *See* GWS, *supra*, note 2, art. 18.
51. Pictet, *supra*, note 22, at 137.

The obligation to care for the wounded and sick also includes other—similarly essential—forms of non-medical care, such as the provision of food, shelter, clothing and hygiene items. This is because exclusively medical treatment of a wound or sickness is not sufficient to ameliorate the condition of the wounded and sick. Indeed, it would be meaningless to provide medical care if adequate food, shelter, clothing and hygiene items were not provided simultaneously.[52]

Humane treatment prevents a Party in possession of wounded and sick from treating them adversely due to any "distinction founded on sex, race, nationality, religion, political opinions, or any other similar criteria."[53] Parties must safeguard the wounded and sick in their possession from any attempts on their lives, violence to their persons, and cruel punishment including torture or biological experimentation.[54] In the event that a Party in possession of wounded and sick must abandon them to the enemy, the Party must leave medical personnel and material to assist in caring for them.[55] However, the presence of personnel left behind does not obviate the adverse Party's duty to provide any additional assistance to the abandoned, wounded, and sick.

One of the most important aspects of Article 12 is that "[o]nly urgent medical reasons will authorize priority in the order of treatment to be administered" in a process called triage.[56] A commander may not prioritize allocation of medical care to his wounded soldiers above caring for captured enemy soldiers solely on the basis of the soldiers' national origins. Political and military considerations can play no role in determining priority of care; the determination

---

52. 2016 ICRC Commentary, *supra*, note 17, at para 1387. The Party in possession must provide shelter sufficient to prevent exposure to dangerous conditions, infection, or contagion. This requirement arose from practices during World War II, such as those of "the German[s] . . . at their main aircrew interrogation center . . . [where] [t]hey frequently delayed medical treatment until after interrogation. . . . [The Germans also] seal[ed] off Russian PW camps once typhus or tuberculosis was discovered." Law of War Deskbook, *supra*, note 33, at E-6 (citations omitted). Under Article 46, these practices are now expressly forbidden.

53. GWS, *supra*, note 2, art. 46.

54. *Id.*

55. *Id.*, art. 12. As noted by the Commentary to the 1929 Convention:

This obligation, natural and necessary as it is, may be a heavy charge if, for example, a retreating belligerent is compelled to abandon several groups of wounded in turn, leaving medical personnel and equipment with them each time. He runs the risk in such a case of having no medical personnel or equipment left for those of his troops who are the last to fall. That cannot be helped. It is his duty to provide for present needs without keeping back the means of relieving future casualties. If as a result he has no more medical personnel or equipment for subsequent casualties, he will have to do all he can to ensure that they receive relief, even appealing, in such a case, to the charity of the inhabitants, as he is entitled to do under Article 5 [Article 18 in the 1949 Convention].

Paul des Gouttes, Commentaire de la Convention de Geneve du 27 Juillet 1929 11 (Geneva 1930).

56. GWS, *supra*, note 2, art. 12. Triage principles are designed to "provide the greatest medical assets to those with significant injuries who may benefit from treatment, while those wounded who will die no matter what and those whose injuries are not serious are given lesser priority." Law of War Deskbook, *supra*, note 33, at E-6. For a discussion of American military triage categories, *see* id. at E-7 (classifying triage categories into the order of immediate, delayed, minimal/ambulatory, and expectant, and providing examples of injuries fitting into each classification).

must be made based on medical necessity and how best to allocate available medical supplies and services.[57] For example, a Party could provide the highest level of medical assets to those members of the enemy wounded and sick with significant injuries that might benefit from treatment and survive, while those who suffered mortal wounds and will die regardless of treatment may justifiably be given lesser priority.[58] While no adverse distinctions may be established in providing care, favorable distinctions may be made by taking certain attributes into account, such as age or pregnancy. Perhaps most importantly, medical personnel must make all decisions regarding priority on the basis of their expert knowledge and their medical ethics.[59]

d. Obligations to the Dead

There are "two distinct obligations regarding the dead, namely to search for them and to prevent their being despoiled. These obligations are important in ensuring respect for the dignity of the dead, which is crucial, not least because disrespect for the dead might set off a cycle of barbarity."[60] Parties to the conflict must look for the dead "with as much care as the wounded."[61]

Article 16 imposes a duty of examination of each body for the purpose of confirmation of death and identity as far as circumstances permit.[62] The dead should be examined and preferably given a full medical examination to confirm death, determine causation of death, and assist in identification of the body.[63] Examination should be followed by burial or cremation.[64]

---

57. For example, wounded Panamanian Defense Force personnel were provided "the same medical care and evacuated on the same aircraft as wounded American personnel during Operation Just Cause." Law of War Deskbook, *supra*, note 33, at E-7 (citation omitted). Another example of fairly applied triage principles occurred during the Falklands conflict, and scholars note that "the quality of medical care provided by the British to the wounded, without distinction between British and Argentine, was remarkable. More than 300 major surgeries were performed, and 100 of these were on Argentine soldiers." *Id*. (citation omitted).

58. This is very clearly what the LOAC requires. But its application on the battlefield can be exceedingly difficult. Consider a U.S. Army combat hospital in Iraq that has just received several trauma patients with gunshot wounds, including U.S. Army Sergeant Smith and an enemy insurgent, who were wounded in the same firefight, possibly by each other. Sergeant Smith has been shot in the abdomen and his liver is damaged. His care would require literally every unit of blood in the hospital and that still may not be enough blood, nor are the doctors optimistic about his survival even with the transfusion. The enemy soldier requires several units of blood and surgery, but doctors assess his chances of survival as very high. Under these circumstances, which have most certainly occurred during U.S. combat operations in Iraq and Afghanistan, care will be focused on the enemy insurgent who can be saved, while Sergeant Smith will die from his wounds.

59. *See* AP I, *supra*, note 21, art. 10.

60. 2016 ICRC Commentary, *supra*, note 17, at para 1508.

61. Pictet, *supra*, note 22, at 151.

62. GWS, *supra*, note 2, art. 17.

63. *Id*. "The examination serves to confirm death, establish identity and enable a report to be made." 2016 ICRC Commentary, *supra*, note 17, at para 1657. The Parties "do not have to undertake the examination themselves, referring it, for example, to a competent medical examiner outside the armed forces, they must make sure that the examination is carried out." Id. at 1658.

64. GWS, *supra*, note 2, art. 17.

Burial must be by honorable interment, preferably with individual graves (although mass graves are permitted when necessary for health or operational reasons), and should follow "the rites of the religion to which [the deceased] belonged"; graves should be grouped by nationality if possible, and must be marked and maintained so that they might be found.[65] Burial is the norm,[66] cremation should only occur for "*imperative* reasons of hygiene" and for "motives based on the religion of the deceased."[67] The hygiene concerns may threaten the health of the Party disposing of the dead body or civilians in the vicinity. The primary hygiene concern was fear of outbreak of disease, though understanding of that concern has changed since the drafting of the GWS in 1949.[68]

An Official Graves Registration Service, organized at the commencement of hostilities, notes the location of the graves and transmits that information to the Party on whom the deceased depends; this service also cares for the ashes of the cremated until the home country advises the Service about disposal.[69] The exchange of grave locations and information regarding the occupants of the graves should occur "[as] soon as circumstances permit, and at latest at the end of hostilities."[70]

e. Obligation to Provide Information

Under Article 16 of the GWS Parties must retain the following regarding the wounded, sick, and the dead: name, nationality, identification number, any

---

65. *Id.* "[F]or reasons of identification, one half of the double identity disc, or the identity disc itself if it is a single disc, should remain on the body at all times.... The effect of this provision is that no members of the armed forces, living or dead, may be deprived of their identity disc. The fact that military authorities may thus be certain of always being able to identify their own personnel again, unless in very exceptional circumstances, should encourage those of them who have not already done so to make universal use of the identity disc, preferably a double one." 2016 ICRC Commentary, *supra*, note 17, at para 1666. This is why U.S. service members wear two "dog tags."

66. The main reason why burial is favored over cremation today is that the latter is irreversible. Should the family of the deceased wish to cremate their loved one, it remains possible for them to do so, even if the deceased was previously buried. It is also easier for a Party to hide violations of the law by cremation than by burial. As happened in the Second World War, the traces of crimes under international law were effaced by cremation, a situation that was fresh in the minds of those attending the Diplomatic Conference. Confirmation of the identity of the deceased is also rendered impossible in the case of cremation and, therefore, unidentified individuals must in no circumstances be cremated. 2016 ICRC Commentary, *supra*, note 17, at para 1676.

67. GWS, *supra*, note 2, art. 17 (emphasis added). The qualifier "imperative" in this context indicates that the Party must be left with no other choice than to cremate.

68. 2016 Commentary, *supra*, note 22, at para 1678. "Today, it is recognized that [hygiene considerations] do not necessitate cremation rather than burial, as the risk to public health from dead bodies is negligible. Accordingly, based upon medical insights gained since 1949, the first situation justifying cremation rarely applies." *Id.*

69. Id. "The graves registration service has two sets of functions. The first set relates . . . to ensur[ing] respect for the graves, their grouping, and their proper maintenance and marking so that they may always be found....The second set of functions is . . . to allow subsequent exhumations, to ensure the identification of the bodies and to assist in the possible transportation to the home country. 2016 ICRC Commentary, *supra*, note 17, at paras 1704, 1706.

70. GWS, *supra*, note 2, art. 17. Additionally, the individual inhumation or cremation was considered important because "the idea of a common grave conflicts with the sentiment of respect for the dead, in addition to making any subsequent exhumation impossible or very difficult." *Id.*

particulars shown on the identity card or disk, date of birth, date and place of capture or death, and particulars concerning wounds, illness, or cause of death.[71] As soon as possible, the Party possessing the collected information should forward it to an Information Bureau, a designated office required by the GPW, that collects and forwards information relating to the identification, transfer, and health of POWs to the Party to whom the POW depends and his next-of-kin.[72] The Information Bureau also exchanges certificates of death or authenticated lists of the dead between the parties, as well as half of the double identity disk (or tag), wills or other important documents, and all articles of intrinsic or sentimental value found on the dead.[73] The goal of Article 16 is the free flow of information concerning the wounded, sick, or dead between Parties to a conflict, and ultimately, when possible to give information and possessions to the next-of-kin.

A. Care Providers, Equipment, and Facilities

Implementing the objectives of the GPW requires the presence of personnel, equipment, and facilities devoted exclusively to that purpose in areas of armed hostilities. These human and material resources cannot be effective in their missions if they are indistinguishable in the eyes of an enemy from the armed forces they are incorporated into. It is therefore necessary to distinguish them in a manner that indicates to an opposing armed force that they are both inoffensive and engaged in activities serving the humanitarian interests of all parties to the conflict.

If there is one LOAC norm that is understood well beyond the circles of professionals engaged in the study and implementation of the LOAC, it is the principle of protection for individuals bearing the distinctive emblems: the Red Cross, the Red Crescent, and now the Red Crystal. Each emblem, and the respect and protection they provide, is based on provisions of the GWS or the relatively new AP III. These treaties also define who may wear these emblems and what equipment and facilities may be marked with them. These definitions will be explained below. However, it is also important to note that in order to preserve the integrity of the protections accorded to persons, places, and things marked with these emblems, improper use of them is considered unlawful. Indeed, misuse of a protective distinctive emblem is one of the most serious violations of the LOAC, precisely because it compromises the trust and confidence afforded to other persons, places, or things properly marked.

---

71. *Id.*, art. 16. Pictet notes that "[w]hen picking up the wounded and dead, care should be taken to collect all their belongings (which may be scattered about); for such objects may inter alia be of assistance in establishing their identity." Pictet, *supra*, note 22, at 152.

72. GPW, *supra*, note 2, art. 122. The GPW states that "[u]pon the outbreak of a conflict and in all cases of occupation, each of the Parties to the conflict shall institute an official Information Bureau for prisoners of war who are in its power."

73. *Id.*

The GWS and AP III to the Conventions provide for this distinction in the form of special emblems of protection: the Red Cross, the Red Crescent, and now the Red Crystal.[74] Article 38 of the GWS describes the several recognized emblems that mark a person, vehicle, or facility as medical in nature.[75] The primary distinctive emblem is the Red Cross; authorized exceptions include the Red Crescent (used predominantly by Muslim nations), and the Red Crystal (in which some countries display a previously and effectively used symbol).[76]

Few symbols carry more profound significance or demand more universal respect than these distinctive emblems. Misuse of a distinctive emblem constitutes a war crime[77], and authorization to use the emblem by medical personnel is subject to "competent military authority."[78]

In order to be protected from attack, facilities, vehicles, and personnel must bear a distinctive medical emblem *and* be exclusively engaged in qualifying medical functions as described below.[79] Medical and religious personnel exclusively engaged in those duties must wear one of the distinctive emblems on their left arm.[80] They must also carry an identity disk[81] and an identity card that also bears the distinctive emblem.[82] These identifying markers indicate to the enemy that these individuals are protected from intentional attack and indicate entitlement to retained person status upon capture, which is explained below. Personnel may not be deprived of either their insignia or their identity cards, and may not be prevented from wearing the armlet.[83]

---

74. AP III entered force in 2005. *See* generally Protocol Additional to the Geneva Conventions of 12 August 1949, and Relating to the Adoption of an Additional Distinctive Emblem, Dec. 8, 2005.

75. *Id.*

76. The development of the Red Crystal was needed to counter the increasing risk of "symbol proliferation" and the attendant risks of degrading and undermining the universality of the Red Cross and its protect value. Thus, Israel may now use as its emblem a red Star of David inside the Red Crystal, and Iran may use the Red Lion and Sun — again, within the Red Crystal.

77. For example, in 2008, a member of the Colombian military participating in a deception operation that tricked rebels into freeing 15 hostages wore the insignia of the [ICRC] during the operation." Colombian Soldier Wore Red Cross Logo in Hostage Rescue, NY TIMES, Jul. 17, 2008. The Colombian government later apologized for the misuse of the emblem.

78. GWS, *supra*, note 2, art. 39. Sometimes it is in the commander's interest to withhold use of the emblem, especially dealing with enemy forces who do not respect the Geneva Conventions. "Israel directs its uniformed medical personnel to not wear any identifying protective sign in combat. On Iraq and Afghan battlefields, many U.S. corpsmen and medics forego red cross markings . . . because the enemy specially targets medical personnel." Solis, *supra*, note 11, at 139.

79. *See* GWS, *supra*, note 2, art. 39. "What is above all essential is to ensure the 'bonafides' [sic] of the wearer: the armlet must only be worn by those who are entitled to do so under the Convention. The brassard is not in itself sufficient evidence. . . . The armlet will have no protective value, and cannot be lawfully worn, unless it has been stamped and issued by the military authority." Pictet, *supra*, note 22, at 310-311.

80. GWS, *supra*, note 2, art. 40.

81. *Id.*, 2, art. 16, 40.

82. *Id.*, art. 40. The identification card must state the bearer's name, date of birth, rank and service number, bear a photograph of the owner and his signature and/or fingerprints, bear the stamp of the issuing military authority, and "shall state in what capacity he is entitled to the protection of [GWS]." *Id.*

83. *Id.*; *see also* Law of War Deskbook, *supra*, note 83, at E-23. Confiscation of either the ID card or the armlet would render determination of retained person status difficult or impossible. *Id.* "In

Medical units and establishments must fly both the flag of the Red Cross (or other distinctive emblem) and the national flag of the Party that owns the facility.[84] If a facility is captured, the adverse Party may not fly its flag; only the distinctive emblem flag may be flown.[85] Parties have an obligation to make the distinctive emblems clearly visible to enemy forces.[86] Neutral units assisting a Party to the conflict under Article 27 shall fly a flag bearing a descriptive emblem and the national flag of the belligerent Party they are assisting whenever that Party makes use of the neutral facility.[87] Neutral units may always fly their national flag, even if captured by an adverse Party.[88] For the United States, a military commander "may authorize the removal or obscuring of the distinctive emblem for tactical purposes, such as camouflage."[89]

1. Personnel Aiding the Wounded and Sick

Individuals authorized to wear the distinctive emblem of the Red Cross, Red Crescent, or Red Crystal are those exclusively engaged in the collection, evacuation, and care for the wounded and sick. The GWS establishes the rights and obligations of such personnel. Although they are normally members of the armed forces, according to the LOAC they are considered non-combatants because of their exclusive humanitarian function. This is a critical distinction. While the term "non-combatant" is routinely used pragmatically as a designation for civilians, in fact civilians are a different category of individuals within the meaning of the LOAC. This special non-combatant status of members of the armed forces exclusively engaged in the protection of the wounded and sick was originally established by the Hague Regulations of 1899 and 1907, both of which indicated that "the armed force of the belligerent parties may consist of combatants and non-combatants. In the case of capture by the enemy, both have a right to be treated as prisoners of war."[90] Thus, physicians, nurses, medics, and chaplains are properly considered non-combatant members of the armed forces.

The protections provided by the GWS and the effective collection and care of the wounded and sick it seeks to facilitate turn in large measure on

---

both world wars, medical personnel sometimes had their armlets and cards taken from them, which can be a way for the capturing State to attempt to evade its obligations.

This provision against confiscation is a result of routine denial of retained personnel protections during World War I and World War II." 2016 ICRC Commentary, *supra*, note 17, at para 2610.

84. GWS, *supra*, note 2, art. 42.
85. *Id.*
86. *Id.*
87. *Id.*, art. 43.
88. *Id.*
89. DoD LOW Manual, *supra*, note 23, at 7.15.2.1. This is generally controlled by a relatively high-level commander, meaning a colonel or higher.
90. Hague Convention with Respect to the Laws and Customs of War on Land and Its Annex: Regulations Concerning the Laws and Customs of War on Land, art. 3, July 29, 1899; Hague Convention No. IV Respecting the Laws and Customs of War on Land and Its Annex: Regulations Concerning the Laws and Customs of War on Land, art. 3, Oct. 18, 1907, 36 Stat. 2277, T.S. 539.

this special status. It would have been futile to cloak the wounded and sick with a respect and protect obligation without allocating accordant protections to those responsible for their collection and care. Accordingly, Article 24 provides:

> Medical personnel exclusively engaged in the search for, or the collection, transport or treatment of the wounded or sick, or in the prevention of disease, staff exclusively engaged in the administration of medical units and establishments, as well as chaplains attached to the armed forces, shall be respected and protected in all circumstances.[91]

The key to understanding this special status is the "exclusively engaged" requirement. In essence, the LOAC allows (or more appropriately encourages) parties to an armed conflict to field personnel, units, equipment, and facilities devoted exclusively to the amelioration of the suffering of the wounded and sick. Because Article 12 imposes an equality of care obligation for *all* wounded and sick irrespective of nationality, granting special status and protections to members of opposing armed forces exclusively engaged in the collection and care of casualties serves the interests of all parties to the conflict, because these members will act to protect all casualties. Accordingly, Article 24 status is contingent on the function assigned to a member of the armed forces: Each member is categorized based upon the role he or she plays in medical or relief efforts and is given rights accordingly. Medical personnel of the armed forces who are exclusively engaged in the practice of medicine receive the highest level of protection, along with chaplains and members of national relief organizations. Neutral personnel assisting a Party to the conflict with its medical needs receive similar protection, but are subject to different repatriation requirements than the medical personnel of a Party to the conflict. Auxiliary medical personnel receive a lessened degree of protection and lessened benefits if captured.

Medical personnel do not automatically lose their special protection merely by carrying light, individual weapons.[92] The GWS and AP I both contemplate circumstances in which it is proper for a medical facility to have an escort or guard, and in which medical personnel may be armed to provide for defense of the wounded and sick under their care. Permissible efforts are limited to defending "against unlawful violence directed either at medical personnel themselves or at the wounded and sick only."[93] As a result, "[t]he scope of defence would *not* cover cases of enemy military advances aimed at taking

---

91. GWS, *supra,* note 2, art. 24. "Exclusively engaged" is interpreted to mean that a person's assignment to the medical service is permanent. *See* 2016 ICRC Commentary, *supra,* note 17, at para 1980 & DoD LOW Manual, *supra,* note 23, at 4.9.2.3.

92. GWS, *supra,* note 2, art. 22(1).

93. *See* 2016 ICRC Commentary, *supra,* note 17, at para 1866. "The unlawful violence contemplated here may manifest itself, for example, in attacks by rioters or pillagers on in unlawful attacks by enemy soldiers against the medical establishment or units as such or against the wounded and sick, or other medical personnel, contained therein." Id.

control over the area where the medical establishments or units are located, nor would the use of force to prevent the capture of their unit by the enemy be permitted."[94]

United States policy authorizes medical personnel to defend themselves and their patients with individual small arms.[95] However, U.S. medical personnel may only use their weapons "in their personal defense and for the protection of the wounded and sick in their charge against marauders and other persons violating the law of war."[96] If medical facilities are guarded by combat units, they are also restricted to using force only to defend the facility from unlawful attack.[97]

a. Exclusively Engaged Medical Personnel and Staff of the Armed Forces, Chaplains, and Members of National Relief Organizations

As noted above, Article 24 describes the first category as permanent medical personnel: those exclusively engaged in the collection and care function. This category also includes staff of voluntary aid societies, such as national Red Cross, Red Crescent, or Red Crystal groups, so long as members of those groups are employed in the same manner as medical personnel described in Article 24, and so long as they are subject to military laws and regulations.[98] Permanent medical personnel as described by Articles 24 and 26 are entitled to full respect and protection at all times.[99] This status is central to treatment upon capture.

U.S. Army Regulation 190-8, which establishes the procedures for implementing obligations for captured and detained personnel, provides the following categorization of captured medical personnel who, in accordance with the GWS, are entitled to retained person (RP) status:

---

94. *Id.* at para. 1867.

95. *Id.* Military medical units and facilities may be armed to the extent necessary to enable them to defend themselves or their patients against unlawful attacks. For example, military medical and religious personnel may be equipped with weapons to meet internal security needs, to maintain discipline, to protect staff and patients from criminal threats of violence, and to prevent the theft of medical supplies. On the other hand, medical units or establishments should not be armed such that they would appear to an enemy military force to present an offensive threat.

DoD LOW Manual, *supra*, note 23, at 7.10.3.4. The kinds and types of weapons that could jeopardize protected status include: machine guns requiring a team of at least two people to operate, grenade launchers, hand grenades, and anti-tank weapons.

96. U.S. Dep't of Army, Field Manual 8-10-6, para A-4(b). Medical Evacuation in a Theater of Operations: Tactics, Techniques, and Procedures (Apr. 14, 2000).

97. *Id.* para. A-5(a).

98. GWS, *supra*, note 2, art. 26. During either peacetime or upon the commencement of hostilities, all Parties to the conflict must notify each other of which societies it has authorized to render assistance to the medical service of its armed forces. *Id.* This notification must occur before the Party actually utilizes the services of one of these societies. *Id.* A national Red Cross or similar society can both be recognized and authorized by the government of its home country. 2016 ICRC Commentary, *supra*, note 17, at para 2061.

99. GWS, *supra*, note 2, art. 24.

b. Enemy personnel who fall within any of the following categories, are eligible to be certified as RP:

    (1) Medical personnel who are members of the medical service of their armed forces.

    (2) Medical personnel who are exclusively engaged in:

        (a) The search for or the collection, transport, or treatment of the wounded or sick.

        (b) The prevention of disease.

        (c) Staffs exclusively engaged in administering medical units and establishments.

    (3) Chaplains.

    (4) The staff of the National Red Cross, Red Crescent, and other voluntary aid organizations. These organizations must be duly recognized and authorized by their governments. The staff of these organizations may be employed on the same duties as persons in (2) above, if such organizations are subject to military laws and regulations.[100]

The most important aspect of this protection provided to individuals qualifying as RPs by the GWS is that they may not be made the deliberate object of attack, even when they are caring for enemy casualties. Further, if captured, RPs are not classified as POWs, but as *retained* personnel.[101] While these personnel must be afforded all benefits provided by the GPW for the duration of their captivity, unlike POWs, they may only be retained "in so far as the state of health, the spiritual needs and the number of prisoners of war require."[102] In other words, captured personnel qualifying for RP status pursuant to Articles 24 and 26 are retained for the exclusive purpose of providing for the care of wounded and sick POWs. For U.S. armed forces, AR 190-8 implements this obligation:

> Retained medical personnel shall receive as a minimum the benefits and protection given to EPW and shall also be granted all facilities necessary to provide for the medical care of EPW. They shall continue to exercise their medical functions for the benefit of EPW, preferably those belonging to the armed forces upon which they depend, within the scope of the military laws and regulations of the United States Armed Forces. They shall be provided with necessary transport and allowed to periodically visit EPW situated in working detachments or in hospitals outside the EPW camp. Although subject to the internal discipline of the camp in which they are retained such personnel may not be compelled to carry out any work other than that concerned with their medical duties. The senior medical officer shall be responsible to the military

---

100. U.S. Dept' of Army, Army Regulation 190-8: Enemy Prisoners of War, Retained Personnel, Civilian Internees and Other Detainees § 3-15(b) (Oct. 1, 1997) (hereinafter AR 190-8).

101. *See* GWS, *supra*, note 2, art. 28. Retained personnel receive all of the benefits from the Prisoner of War Convention, including pay, monthly allowances, and correspondence privileges.

102. *Id.* In contrast, captured enemy combatants (POWs) are detained to prevent them from returning to hostilities, and therefore may be detained for the duration of the armed conflict.

authorities for everything connected with the activities of retained medical personnel.[103]

Retention is therefore an exception to the presumption of repatriation, and is justified for the exclusive purpose of providing for the care of captured enemy personnel. Thus, if there is no necessity for their services, the GWS obligates the retaining power to repatriate RPs.[104]

Further, consistent with this special RP status, RPs (unlike POWs) may not be required to perform any work aside from their regular medical or religious duties preferably ministering to the armed forces to which they themselves belong. They must also be allowed to periodically visit and be transported to POWs in labor units or hospitals outside of the camp.[105] While in the camp, the senior medical officer and the chaplains must have direct access to the military and medical authorities overseeing the camp.[106]

b. Auxiliary Medical Support Personnel of the Armed Forces

Auxiliary medical personnel are military personnel who have been specially trained in medical specialties, such as hospital orderlies or auxiliary stretcher-bearers.[107] Typically, auxiliaries perform other military duties, and only take up these medical duties as the need arises.[108] When acting in a medical capacity, they are entitled to the same respect and protection accorded to those meeting the qualification requirements of Article 24.[109] Auxiliary personnel must wear an armlet displaying a distinctive emblem in miniature, but only while carrying out medical duties, and their identification cards "should specify what special training they have received, the temporary character of the duties . . . engaged upon, and their authority for wearing the armlet."[110]

---

103. AR 190-8, *supra,* note 100, § 1-5(f).

104. Notably, this provision is one of the least honored. *See* Law of War Deskbook, *supra,* note 33, at E-14 ("US medical personnel in Korea and Vietnam were not repatriated, but were also denied retained person status") (citation omitted). Mukhtar Yahia Naji Al Warafi, a member of the Taliban detained at Guantanamo Bay, argued that he qualified as medical personnel under the GWS and that since the United States was not providing medical care for fellow detainees, he should be released. Both a U.S. District Court and a Federal Court of Appeals disagreed, finding that Al Warafi was not exclusively medical personnel within the meaning of Article 24 of the GWS. *See* Al Warafi v. Obama, 716 F.3d 627 (2013).

105. Article 24 or 26 personnel are still subject to the internal discipline procedures of the camp, but may not be forced to do labor aside from their medical or religious duties. *Id.* Medical personnel may only be retained to treat prisoners of war, though they may be required to treat POWs who are of different nationalities. Preferably, the retained persons will treat POWs of their own nationality, but this is not a strict requirement and as such, medical personnel may be retained to treat any POW. *See* GWS, *supra,* note 2, art. 30. Article 24 or 26 personnel may never be retained to treat enemy personnel.

106. *Id.* art. 28. The detaining Party is still bound to provide any medical attention required by POWs in the camp. *Id.*

107. *Id.,* art. 25.

108. *Id.*

109. *Id.*

110. *Id.,* art. 41. Notably, "if a military command should, without previous arrangement, send ordinary combatants to collect the wounded, it would be at their own risk," as such persons are not even considered auxiliary medical personnel, and therefore are bestowed no protection under the GWS. Pictet, *supra,* note 22, at 224.

Unlike dedicated medical or religious military personnel, or members of national aid societies, captured auxiliary medical personnel are considered POWs, not RPs.[111] Accordingly, the treatment of auxiliaries depends on the function they are providing at any given time, meaning they can effectively move back and forth between combatant and non-combatant roles.

Because of the inherent uncertainty resulting from Article 26 auxiliary status, the U.S. armed forces do not assert auxiliary status for their personnel.[112] While there are some members of combatant forces who perform emergency medical support functions when needed (in the Army these personnel are routinely designated as "combat lifesavers"), they are considered combatants at all times and are not provided with the special insignia entitling them to Wounded and Sick Convention protections. Nonetheless, other armed forces may opt for a different approach to their auxiliary medical personnel. When this is the case, upon capture these auxiliaries are not RPs, but are instead POWs in accordance with the GPW.[113] When not performing medical duties, they are treated as POWs in every manner.[114] When performing medical duties, they receive heightened benefits but are nevertheless not entitled to repatriation like their Article 24 RP qualified counterparts.

c. Members of Societies from Neutral Countries

In order to maximize the protections for the wounded and sick, Article 27 of the GWS establishes a mechanism whereby relief societies from neutral countries can lend their services to the parties to an armed conflict. However, before such a relief organization may lend assistance to a Party, it must obtain the consent of the organization's own government and (obviously) the authorization of the Party to the conflict to which the assistance will be provided.[115] Members of the relief organization must be furnished with identity cards in accordance with Article 40 of the GWS before leaving their neutral country, and are placed under the control of the Party authorizing their assistance. The neutral government must notify any adversaries of that Party to the conflict, and a neutral country that authorizes the activity is never considered to have interfered in the conflict by authorizing such activities.[116] The Party must also notify its adversaries before using neutral personnel.[117] If captured, persons designated under Article 27 may not be detained, and must be allowed to return to their country or, if that is not possible, to territory of the Party to

---

111. *See* GWS, *supra*, note 2, art. 29.
112. *See* Law of War Deskbook, *supra*, note 33, at E-15 ("The US Army does not have any personnel who officially fall into the category identified in Article 25. . . . Air Force regulations do provide for these personnel") (citations omitted).
113. *Id.* Further, auxiliary POWs shall be employed medically in the POW camp as the need arises. *Id.*
114. "Members of the personnel designated in Article 25 who have fallen into the hands of the enemy, shall be prisoners of war." GWS, *supra*, note 2, art. 30.
115. *Id.*, art. 27.
116. *Id.*
117. *Id.*, art. 27.

the conflict whose service they were in at the time of capture.[118] Return to the Party's territory may be constrained by availability of a route and by military considerations.[119] Pending release, neutral personnel must be allowed to continue their work assisting the adverse Party, preferably by caring for the wounded and sick of the Party whose service they were engaged in at the time of capture.[120] All Parties to the conflict should provide to neutral personnel the same food, lodging, allowances, and pay as are granted to corresponding personnel in their own armed forces.[121]

2. Medical Units, Establishments, and Transportation

The protections provided for the wounded and sick and those who collect and care for them would be of little meaning if the facilities in which they work or the means by which they transport casualties were subject to attack like any other lawful target on the battlefield. It is therefore self-evident that the objectives of the GWS can only be achieved by extending special protections to medical equipment and facilities.

a. Facilities and Vehicles

Article 38 defines the status of fixed and mobile facilities established for medical use and marked with one of the distinctive emblems. Such facilities are protected no differently than the wounded and sick they provide care for: They may not be attacked unless they abrogate their status.[122] This protection also extends to hospital ships covered by the Wounded and Sick Convention Sea; such ships may not be attacked from land.[123] However, in order to facilitate this protection, the GWS indicates that commanders should, when feasible, situate

---

118. *Id.*, art. 32. The explanation for the mandated return is that "[i]f [captured neutrals] cannot be retained, they cannot with even greater reason be regarded as prisoners of war; they should rather be treated as guests." Pictet, *supra*, note 22, at 268.

119. GWS, *supra*, note 2, art. 32.

120. *Id.*

121. *Id.* Note again that this is better treatment than that given even to RPs, as neutral personnel are governed neither by the GWS articles related to RPs, nor the general provision for pay and treatment of POWs from the GPW.

122. GWS, *supra*, note 2, art. 19. And yet hospitals, particularly those operated by nongovernmental organizations like Medecins sans Frontieres (MSF) are increasingly suffering the effects of armed conflict. Between July and October 2016, MSF reported 23 different attacks on hospitals in Syria. Eastern Aleppo: 23 Attacks on Hospitals since July; No Hospital Left Undamaged, Medecins sans Frontieres Press Release, Oct. 7, 2016. MSF facilities have also been damaged in Yemen on several occasions as the result of coalition airstrikes. Shuaib Almoswaw & Rob Nordland, Bombing of Doctors Without Borders Hospital in Yemen Kills at Least 15, NY Times, Aug. 15, 2016. In 2015, as the result of what the U.S. military called a "chain of errors", a U.S. warplane fired on an MSF facility for over half an hour, mistakenly believing it to be a Taliban occupied command post. Matthew Rosenbert, Pentagon Details Chain of Errors in Strike on Afghan Hospital, NY Times Apr. 29, 2016. The U.S. strike destroyed the MSF facility and killed some 42 individuals, both MSF personnel and patients. *Id.*

123. GWS, *supra*, note 2, art. 20.

medical units away from potential military objectives to ensure their safety.[124] If captured, medical units and personnel assigned to them must be permitted to continue caring for the wounded and sick.[125]

Under certain situations, a medical facility that would otherwise be protected from intentional attack may lose its protection. Protection is lost if the facility commits "acts harmful to the enemy" that fall outside the general humanitarian duties of the facility.[126] However, unlike any other potential object of attack, protection ceases only after a warning has been given and it remains unheeded after a reasonable amount of time to comply with the warning. Examples of harmful activities would include using a hospital as an ammunition storage point, command and control center, or vantage point to fire upon enemy personnel.[127]

Some conditions that may be interpreted as "harmful to the enemy" in some manner nevertheless do not cause a medical facility to abrogate its protected status.[128] The GWS enumerates the following as non-abrogating circumstances: (1) that personnel of the medical unit are armed and use their arms in their own defense or in the defense of the wounded and sick under their care; (2) in the absence of armed orderlies, the unit is protected by a picket, sentries, or an escort; (3) small arms and ammunition taken from the wounded and sick and not yet handed over to the proper service are found in the unit; (4) personnel and material of veterinary services are found in the unit without forming an integral part of the unit; or (5) the humanitarian activities of the medical unit or its personnel extend to caring for civilian wounded and sick.[129]

If captured, mobile medical units need not be returned, but may only be used in continuing care for wounded and sick.[130] Fixed medical establishments, including the material therein, must be used to care for the wounded and sick so long as a need exists.[131] An exception to this requirement is urgent

---

124. *See* GWS, *supra*, note 2, art. 19. Under no circumstances should medical units be used to shield military objectives from attack. *See Id.*, art. 12. The purpose of creating remoteness between military objectives and medical establishments is to protect the latter from attack against the former, and for medical units to be "situated [so] that attacks against military objectives cannot imperil their safety." Pictet, *supra*, note 22, at 198. While close proximity between a medical establishment and a lawful military target "would not weaken the legal protection enjoyed by a medical establishment . . . it would, in practice, endanger its security to some extent." *Id.* at 199.

125. GWS, *supra*, note 2, art. 19.

126. *Id.*, art. 21. "Examples of such use include firing at the enemy for reasons other than individual self-defence, installing a firing position in a medical post, the use of a hospital as a shelter for able-bodied combatants, as an arms or ammunition dump, or as a military observation post, or the placing of a medical unit in proximity to a military objective with the intention of shielding it from the enemy's military operations." *See* 2016 ICRC Commentary, *supra*, note 17, at para 1842.

127. GWS, *supra*, note 2, art. 21. Reasonable times vary depending on the circumstances; for example, no time limit would be required if fire was currently being taken from a hospital.

128. *See generally* GWS, *supra*, note 2, art. 22.

129. *Id.*

130. *Id.*, art. 33. This represents a departure from the 1929 Convention, which required mobile medical units to be returned.

131. *Id.* First priority for captured material in a medical unit must be any wounded and sick being treated in that unit at the time of capture. If the captured unit had no patients, the captured material may be used on other patients.

military necessity, but the capturing Party must ensure the continued welfare of any wounded and sick in a fixed medical establishment before converting it to another use.[132] It is also critical to distinguish captured medical supplies from other supplies captured from an enemy. Unlike the normal booty of war, under no circumstances may medical material and stores be intentionally destroyed.[133] If they cannot be used by the capturing force, they must be abandoned intact.

Vehicles devoted exclusively to medical purposes and properly marked with the distinctive emblem, such as ambulances, must be respected and protected in the same manner as mobile medical units.[134] Vehicles may be employed for medical duties either permanently or temporarily and need not be equipped specifically for medical purposes to be considered a medical vehicle.[135] If a vehicle is only temporarily employed as a medical vehicle, it must display one of Article 38's distinctive emblems while engaged in the medical mission to ensure protection. Temporary medical employment and the importance of the distinctive emblem is explained in the following manner:

> As ambulances are not always available, any vehicles may be adapted and used temporarily for transport of the wounded. During that time they will be entitled to protection, subject to the display of the distinctive emblem. Thus military vehicles going up to the forward areas with ammunition may bring back the wounded, with the important reservation the emblem must be detachable, e.g., a flag, so that it may be flown on the downward journey. Conversely military vehicles may take down wounded and bring up military supplies on the return journey. The flag must then be removed on the return journey.[136]

It is not uncommon to use vehicles for a non-medical mission when travelling in one direction and for a medical mission when travelling in the other direction. For example, troops or supplies may be transported to the "front lines," while the same transport assets may be used to "back-haul" casualties to the rear area. It is essential that armed forces strictly comply with the obligation to remove the distinctive emblem whenever the vehicle is not exclusively engaged in the medical function. Failing to do so will erode confidence in the protective effect of the emblem and invite attack on properly marked vehicles. If a medical vehicle is captured, the capturing Party must ensure the care of any wounded and sick therein.[137] Upon capture, medical vehicles may be treated as booty of war. This means the captor may use them for any purpose, and is not obligated to use them for medical purposes. However, the capturing Party is obligated to ensure that the wounded and sick in the vehicle are provided care and any that any distinctive medical emblems are removed prior to non-medical use.[138]

---

132. *Id.*
133. *Id.*
134. *Id.*, art. 35.
135. Nor does a human have to drive the vehicle for it to qualify for protection.
136. Giad Draper, THE RED CROSS CONVENTIONS OF 1949 87 (1958) (hereinafter Draper).
137. GWS, *supra*, note 2, art. 35.
138. *See id.*

The GWS does not require the use of the special emblem when transporting casualties. A Party to the conflict may use whatever assets that are available to transport casualties. Indeed, it may be necessary to mix casualties and non-medical personnel and/or equipment in transport assets. When doing so, the transport may not be marked with the special emblem because it is not "exclusively engaged" in the medical transport function. Further, tactical considerations may dictate the removal of special emblems. For example, during an infiltration mission, a commander may choose to remove or cover the Red Cross on a combat ambulance in order to mitigate the risk of enemy detection. However, it is important to note that whenever transport equipment is not marked, it will likely (and legitimately) be considered a lawful target by the enemy, even if it is in fact transporting the wounded and sick.

Within the limitations already discussed, the GWS permits medical personnel, units, and establishments to be armed and to use their weapons. The Convention is silent, however, as to whether medical transports may be armed. In its 2016 Commentary to the GWS, the ICRC addressed this ambiguity by analogy to the authority to use weapons to protect mobile medical units. Under this approach, light, individual weapons may be mounted on military medical transports.[139]

b. Medical Aircraft

Like vehicles, aircraft may be permanently dedicated to medical use or may be assigned temporarily to such use. Aircraft need not have been specially built for medical purposes to obtain protection as a medical aircraft; ordinary aircraft may be converted to medical use, and medical aircraft may be converted to other use provided that the converted aircraft no longer bears distinctive medical emblems.[140]

To remain protected during a relief mission, an aircraft must be used "exclusively" for medical purposes. Similar to medical transports, the GWS is silent on whether (1) medical aircraft and (2) medical personnel onboard may be armed. The answer, from both State practice and the 2016 ICRC Commentary to the GWS, is that both the medical aircraft and the medical personnel on board may be armed with light individual weapons "only used for the defense of the personnel on board and the wounded and sick in their charge."[141] If the emblem is removed, the helicopter may be armed and still perform medical evacuations, though foregoing the protection the emblem provides. That is the approach many countries take, creating hybrid armed medical evacuation (MEDEVAC) platforms that do not display the emblem. In contrast, the U.S. Army displays the emblem on its MEDEVAC helicopters, foregoing armament. Because many non-state actors do not respect the emblem and will target MEDEVAC

---

139. *See* 2016 ICRC Commentary, *supra*, note 17, at para 2396-2397.
140. *See* U.S. Dept. of Army, Field Manual 27-10, The Law of Land Warfare, para. 237(b) (July 1956) (hereinafter FM 27-10).
141. *See* 2016 ICRC Commentary, *supra*, note 17, at para 2449. Individual weapons fired from a helicopter will generally be of little use given their limited range and effects.

helicopters, the U.S. Army pairs them with heavily armed gunships that provide close air support.[142]

Unlike mobile or fixed units or vehicles, protection of medical aircraft is dependent on agreements entered into by the belligerent parties to a conflict. These agreements are intended to provide notice to the parties regarding the routes and times of medical aircraft activity. Accordingly, the GWS requires parties to respect medical aircraft "while flying at heights, times and on routes specifically agreed upon between the belligerents concerned."[143] If no such agreement is in place, medical aircraft fly at their own risk.[144] Furthermore, aircraft personnel may report information acquired incidentally to the aircraft's humanitarian mission; reporting such information does not cause the aircraft to lose its protection, and medical aircraft can search for the wounded and sick.[145] However, an aircraft on a humanitarian mission could not deviate from its mission to search for enemies.

The only way that an adverse Party can ensure that an aircraft bearing a distinctive medical emblem is not abusing the use of that emblem is by summoning the aircraft to land and inspecting its contents. Medical aircraft are obligated to obey any such enemy command to land.[146] The adverse Party decides whether or not an aircraft is allowed to continue after summoning it to land and conducting an inspection.[147] In the event of an involuntary landing in enemy territory, the personnel aboard the aircraft, and any wounded and sick aboard, are treated as POWs or RPs, depending on their status.[148] The adverse Party retains the obligation to care for any wounded and sick aboard the aircraft.[149]

Parties should be mindful of the territory their medical aircraft pass over. Aircraft should never fly over enemy territory without an agreement.[150] Medical aircraft of Parties to a conflict may generally fly over neutral Powers, land on

---

142. This policy can result in MEDEVAC helicopters having to wait for a gunship to be available, at least once costing a U.S. Army soldier his life. *See* David Martin, Did Military Rules Cost a Soldier His Life? CBS News, Jan. 19, 2012 https://www.cbsnews.com/news/did-military-rules-cost-a-soldier-his-life/. The U.S. Army contends that removing the emblem and arming the helicopters would not improve soldier survival rates, as any additional weight from the armament would reduce the medical equipment the helicopter could carry. Under the U.S. Army's policy of using the emblem on MEDEVAC helicopters and having gunships provide close air support, "a wounded soldier stands a 92 percent chance of surviving—the highest rate of any war." *Id.*

143. *Id.* Professor Draper notes that "the speed of modern aircraft makes identification by colour or markings useless. Only previous agreement could afford any real safeguard." Draper, *supra*, note 136, at 84.

144. *See* Law of War Deskbook, *supra*, note 33, at E-20 (noting that, absent an agreement, medical aircraft fly at their own risk and explaining "[t]his was certainly the case in Vietnam where 'any air ambulance pilot who served a full one year tour could expect to have his aircraft hit at least once by enemy fire.' 'Most of the Viet Cong and North Vietnamese clearly considered the air ambulances just another target'") (citations omitted).

145. Contra AP I, art. 28(4) ("[M]edical aircraft shall not, except by prior agreement with the adverse Party, be used to search for the wounded, sick and shipwrecked.").

146. GWS, *supra*, note 2, art. 36.

147. *See id.*

148. *See id.*

149. *See id.*

150. *Id.*, art. 36.

their territory in the case of necessity, or use neutral territory as a port of call.[151] Aircraft flying above neutral territory should give notice of their passage, obey all commands to land, and will only be immune to attack if traveling on routes, at heights, and at times agreed upon between the Parties.[152] If any wounded and sick disembark into a neutral's territory, the neutral must detain the wounded and sick in a manner preventing them from taking part in the operation of war.[153]

Additional Protocol I includes a number of provisions intended to update the law related to medical aircraft. The treaty added optional signals identifying medical aircraft[154] and amended the right of a medical aircraft to fly over territory of a neutral Power, requiring prior agreement to do so.[155] Additionally, AP I created three "overflight regimes" for medical aircraft, depending on the status of the terrain over which the aircraft is flying: friendly territory,[156] a contact zone,[157] or territory controlled by an adverse Party.[158]

Article 26 AP I addresses medical aircraft in contact zones, especially areas "physically controlled by friendly forces and in and over those areas the physical control of which is not clearly established."[159]

---

151. *Id.*, art. 37.

152. *Id.* Neutrals may place restrictions on medical aircraft, though the Wounded and Sick Convention advises that restrictions or conditions should apply to all Parties to the conflict. *Id.*

153. *Id.*

154. *See* generally AP I, *supra*, note 21, art. 18. In 1993, Annex I to AP I created a number of new signals to augment the distinctive emblems on an aircraft. These include the flashing blue light, radio signals, and use of a Secondary Surveillance Radar System, as well as special radio communications and recognized international codes. *See* Annex I (to AP I): Regulations Concerning IdenFelktification, art. 6-12, Nov. 30, 1993. These markings "are merely intended to facilitate identification, and do not themselves confer protected status." Fleck, *supra*, note 12, at 352. The Commentary to AP I states that the drafters recognized the limitations of pre-aircraft identification procedures, and stated that "adapting identification to modern combat techniques . . . was also of paramount importance, particularly for medical aircraft. . . . Merely to have the emblem . . . painted on an aircraft seemed insufficient to ensure effective protection, having regard to modern means of warfare." Sandoz, *supra*, note 28, at 224.

155. Compare AP I, *supra*, note 21, art. 31(1) ("[e]xcept by prior agreement, medical aircraft shall not fly over or land on the territory of a neutral or other State not a Party to the conflict") with GWS, *supra*, note 2, art. 37 ("medical aircraft of Parties to the conflict may fly over the territory of neutral Powers, land on it in case of necessity, or use it as a port of call," subject to conditions or restrictions placed by the neutral Powers).

156. AP I, *supra*, note 21, art. 25.

157. Id., art. 26(2). The Protocol defines "contact zone" as "any area on land where the forward elements of opposing forces are in contact with each other, especially where they are exposed to direct fire from the ground." *Id.*, art. 26(2). As noted in the Commentary, the language of "in and above the contact zone" means that medical aircraft are protected both on the ground of a contact zone and when flying above a contact zone. *See* Sandoz, *supra*, note 28, at 290.

158. AP I, *supra*, note 21, art. 27(1).

159. *Id.*, art. 26(2). The Protocol defines "contact zone" as "any area on land where the forward elements of opposing forces are in contact with each other, especially where they are exposed to direct fire from the ground." *Id.*, art. 26(2). As noted in the Commentary, the language of "in and above the contact zone" means that medical aircraft are protected both on the ground of a contact zone and when flying above a contact zone. *See* Sandoz, *supra*, note 28, at 290. Article 26 emphasizes that aircraft safety can only be ensured by an agreement between the Parties and that absent an agreement, the aircraft flies at its own risk. AP I, *supra*, note 21, art. 26(1). However, medical aircraft operating in the absence of an agreement "shall nevertheless be respected after they have been recognized as such."

An aircraft that either flies over an adverse Party's territory without an agreement or deviates from the agreement must immediately attempt to identify itself and inform the adverse Party of the circumstances, such as navigational error or emergency affecting the safety of the flight.[160] The adverse Party must attempt to recognize the aircraft as medical in nature; after that has occurred, the Party must either give the aircraft the order to land or to take other measures to protect its interests.[161] In all circumstances, an aircraft identified as bearing a medical emblem should be given time to comply with any order given before the adverse Party resorts to attack.[162] As a practical matter, such agreements are rare. Accordingly, overflight of enemy territory always involves substantial risk.

The Air and Missile Warfare Manual (AMWM) (a non-binding but highly authoritative statement of experts on LOAC obligations in relation to air and missile warfare), published in 2013, attempts to clarify the application of many of the rules related to medical aircraft. The AMWM explicitly provides that medical aircraft may be equipped with "deflective defenses" such as flares or chaff. However, equipping a heavy weapon such as a machine gun (which could be used either offensively or defensively) could either cause complete forfeiture of protection or, at the least, erosion of the status of the protective emblem.[163] While medical aircraft may be equipped to send or receive encrypted information for navigation, identification, and communication purposes "consistent with the execution of its humanitarian mission," it may not mount or use equipment to collect or transfer intelligence harmful to the enemy, as this would remove it from the category of exclusive use as a medical transport.[164] Carrying or using any such equipment may cause the medical aircraft to lose its specific protection.[165]

Id.; *see* Sandoz, *supra*, note 28, at 291 ("Obviously there is a risk that members of the armed forces of the adverse Party might fire before recognizing that the aircraft are 'medical' aircraft, but as soon as they have recognized them as such, they are under a strict obligation to respect the aircraft. . . . [B]y violating this obligation, they would commit a grave breach."). Sandoz continues to note that in areas where control is not clearly established, the enemy may order the aircraft to land (so long as landing is actually possible in the area); if the aircraft refuses to comply with such an order, it loses the right to respect and may be targeted. *Id.* at 292.

160. AP I, *supra*, note 21, art. 27(2).
161. *Id.*
162. *Id.* The purpose of Article 29(2) is "to prevent a tragic accident, i.e., the shooting down of a medical aircraft, while taking into account the legitimate fears of the Parties to the conflict with regard to their security." Sandoz, *supra*, note 28, at 296. While Article 29 is designed to provide all possible measures and time to prevent such an attack, a Party may resort to attack as a final solution to counter a perceived threat against its interests. *Id.*
163. Program on Humanitarian Policy and Conflict Research at Harvard University Manual on International Law Applicable to Air and Missile Warfare, Rule 82 (Cambridge University Press 2013) (hereinafter "Air and Missile Warfare Manual"); *see also* Program on Humanitarian Policy and Conflict Research at Harvard University Commentary to the HPCR Manual on International Law Applicable to Air and Missile Warfare Cambridge University Press (2013) (hereinafter "Air and Missile Warfare Manual Commentary").
164. The Air and Missile Warfare Manual Commentary emphasizes that merely possessing equipment designed to collect or transmit intelligence harmful to the enemy is "prohibited because it is difficult to prove in practice that an aircraft actually collected or transmitted such information." Air and Missile Warfare Manual Commentary, *supra*, note 163, at Rule 81 comment 2.
165. Air and Missile Warfare Manual, *supra*, note 163, at Rule 83.

Further, the AMWM draws a distinction between military-operated medical aircraft (engaged exclusively in the transport of the wounded and sick) and military aircraft on missions to search-and-rescue combatants.[166] The former receive all the protection accorded the distinctive emblem, but the latter do not, and may not bear the distinctive emblem. Medical aircraft are also forbidden from acting as search-and-rescue aircraft in combat areas; if they do so, they are treated as unprotected and fly at their own risk.[167]

III. Protecting the Wounded and Sick in Non-International Armed Conflicts

A number of articles are included in all four of the 1949 Conventions. These "Common Articles" represent provisions deemed so important and fundamental by the drafters that they bear repeating in each treaty. While the bulk of GWS provisions address the protection of the wounded and sick specifically during IACs, like its three other counterparts it also includes common Article 3. Through this common article, the GWS reinforces the broad humane treatment obligation applicable to any individual rendered *hors de combat* in non-international armed conflicts. This category includes all persons taken out of the fight by "sickness, wounds, detention, or any other cause."[168]

Common Article 3 imposes a humane treatment obligation for the protection of any such individual as well as "persons taking no active part in the hostilities, including members of armed forces who have laid down their arms."[169] Further, common Article 3 prohibits any adverse distinction affecting treatment based on race, religion, sex, wealth, or nationality.[170] Additionally, the *hors de combat* may not be assaulted, murdered, tortured, taken as hostages, humiliated or degraded, or subject to summary execution.[171] Most importantly for purposes of this chapter, common Article 3 explicitly requires that "the wounded and sick be collected and cared for."[172]

---

166. *Id.* at r. 86. Military aircraft on search-and-rescue missions are deemed to be engaged in combat activities. *See Id.* at r. 86(a) cmt. 1-2. Civilian aircraft engaged in such activities are generally protected in the same manner as other civilian aircraft, and do not gain the specific manner of medical aircraft. *Id.* at cmt. 3.

167. *Id.* at r. 86(b); *see also* AP I, *supra*, note 21, art. 28(4). This Rule is tempered by the Parties' ability to commit to an agreement authorizing medical aircraft to conduct search-and-rescue functions without losing their protected status. *See Id.*

168. GWS, *supra*, note 2, art. 3.

169. *Id.*

170. *Id.*

171. Interestingly, the English language version of Common Article 3 from the 1949 Geneva Conventions uses the French "*hors de combat.*" On the one hand, it is odd to have terms in a foreign language. On the other hand, the use of "*hors de combat*" avoids the potential misunderstanding from the *blesses*/wounded issue from the rest of the GWS. *See* Milikowsky, *supra*, note 3.

172. In 2016, the ICRC published updated commentary to the GWS, which included CA3. One important revision involved the offer of services by the ICRC or other humanitarian organizations. Whereas the previous commentary had stated that "the decision whether to consent to humanitarian activities on their territory and no reason needed to be given for refusing an offer of services, the new

While common Article 3 certainly provides important protections for the wounded and sick in non-international armed conflict (NIAC), its provisions are meager compared to the comprehensive regulatory framework established by the GWS. In order to compensate for this minimalism, AP II, the 1977 treaty supplementing the Geneva Conventions, substantially enhanced the rules related to the protection of the wounded and sick in NIAC. Additional Protocol II is far more modest than its IACs counterparts in the scope of the regulation it provides. However, it represents an important advancement in the regulation of NIAC by extending to these conflicts the special protections for those devoted to the collection and care of the wounded and sick.

Additional Protocol II builds on the foundation laid by common Article 3 for protecting victims of NIAC by ameliorating their suffering once they are rendered *hors de combat*. To that end, it explicitly extends a number of core rules established for the regulation of international armed conflict to NIAC. These include the obligation to respect and protect all wounded and sick; the equality of treatment rule; the obligation to respect and protect medical and religious personnel; the protection of medical transport equipment and medical facilities; the prohibition of attacking a medical facility being misused without first issuing a warning; and the protective effect of the distinctive emblem. Finally, the treaty expressly acknowledges the role of relief organizations in aiding the wounded and sick, a role that is increasingly central to non-international armed conflicts:

> Relief societies located in the territory of the High Contracting Party, such as Red Cross and Red Crescent organizations may offer their services for the performance of their traditional functions in relation to the victims of the armed conflict. The civilian population may, even on its own initiative, offer to collect and care for the wounded, sick and shipwrecked.[173]

Additional Protocol II also establishes several additional important safeguards for medical personnel, safeguards considered necessary because of the non-international nature of the armed conflict. First, medical personnel may never be punished for carrying out their duties compatible with medical ethics, regardless of the beneficiary (shielding such personnel from criminal prosecution by the State for activities in support of internal dissident forces). Second, they may not be forced to perform acts contrary to the rules of medical ethics, nor may they be prevented from performing acts required by rules of medical ethics.[174] Finally, medical personnel may not be penalized for refusing to give

---

Commentary concludes that, nowadays, such an offer of services may not be refused on arbitrary grounds." Lindsey Cameron, et al., The Updated Commentary on the First Geneva Convention — A New Tool for Generating Respect for International Humanitarian Law, 93 INT'L L. STUD. 157, 169 (2017).

173. Protocol Additional to the Geneva Conventions of 12 Aug. 1949, and Relating to the Protection of Victims of Non-International Armed Conflicts, art. 18(1), June 8, 1977, 1125 U.N.T.S. 17513 (hereinafter AP II). *See also* Sandoz, *supra*, note 28 ("Article 18 is aimed at permitting and facilitating humanitarian activities in non-international armed conflicts for the purpose of assisting victims wherever they are and assuring them the protection to which they are entitled").

174. AP II, *supra*, note 21, art. 10(2).

information concerning any of the wounded and sick under their care, even when such information is considered essential to the internal security of the State.[175]

IV. Violations

As noted in Chapter 13, violations of the Geneva Conventions are broadly divided into two categories: grave breaches and simple breaches. A simple breach is any violation that is not a grave breach.[176] The Wounded and Sick Convention describes grave breaches as certain acts directed against protected persons (individuals who qualify for that status pursuant to the treaty) such as the "wilful killing, torture or inhuman treatment, including biological experiments, wilfully causing great suffering or serious injury to body or health."[177] These violations trigger an obligation to prosecute or extradite the violator to a country that will prosecute. However, all violations of the GWS are serious, and may result in military criminal prosecution for U.S. personnel.

V. Conclusion

Protection of the wounded and sick is perhaps the most obvious manifestation of the principle of humanity. The history of warfare is replete with examples of the willingness of belligerents to come to the aid of their suffering comrades *and* enemies. The GWS establishes rules to facilitate this humanitarian action, rules that are among the most widely known and respected, and deeply woven into the fabric of the LOAC. Indeed, intentionally attacking personnel, facilities, or equipment marked with the emblems of special protection established by the LOAC would legitimately be considered *malum in se*, leaving virtually no room for doubt about the illegality of such attacks even for the most inexperienced soldier. The core of these protections applies today in all armed conflicts, and

---

175. *Id.*, art. 10(4).
176. *See* GWS, *supra*, note 2, art. 49 (stating that every "Party shall take measures necessary for the suppression of all acts contrary to the provisions of the present Convention other than the grave breaches defined in the following Article") (emphasis added). The purpose of defining non-grave breaches is "'repression of infractions other than 'grave breaches' for which administrative action may be taken." Solis, *supra*, note 11, at 94-95 (quoting Pictet, *supra*, note 22, at 367)).
177. GWS, *supra*, note 2, art. 50.
The notion of killing has been used interchangeably with causing death. Thus, this grave breach covers not only such acts as shooting a protected person to death, but also such conduct as reducing the food rations of protected persons, resulting in their starvation and ultimately their death. Wilful killing is prohibited, and amounts to a grave breach, irrespective of the motivation behind the act. "Mercy killings" intended to put wounded combatants "out of their misery" are prohibited. 2016 ICRC Commentary, *supra*, note 17, at para. 2953.

in many ways these protections establish a baseline, with parties often striving to enhance the protections for wounded and sick beyond that strictly required by the law.

It is therefore essential that military planners contemplate the scope of the obligations related to the wounded and sick, plan accordingly, and ensure personnel are properly trained and resourced to. Like so many other areas of the law, compliance will often become more challenging as operational situations mature. For the soldier on the front line, it is axiomatic that individuals marked with the Red Cross or similar protective emblem must not be subjected to attack. But issues related to collection, evacuation, interment, record keeping, equality of care, location of facilities, air evacuation, and dual use of equipment present far more complex issues. Commanders and medical officers will therefore invariably turn to legal advisors to assist them in resolving these issues. Competence in the law that guides resolution is therefore essential to the Judge Advocate, for few LOAC violations will be more corrosive to the credibility of the operation than those that compromise the protections of the wounded and sick.

Study Questions

1. You are a legal advisor in the planning cell for the 1st Calvary Division Current Operations Section. Your cell is in the final stages of preparing to invade Iraq. An issue arises regarding the planned location of the medical aid stations for each Brigade Combat Team, and for the Combat Support Hospital (CSH) designated to deploy with the Division. The plan calls for locating the aid stations within the Brigade Support Area (a cluster of support units located together to improve efficiency of support operations and to maximize defensibility of the area). The aid stations will be housed in tents marked prominently with the Red Cross. The CSH is a fully deployable full capability hospital that is composed of numerous interconnected tents. The Operations officer wants to know if the CSH should be included within the Division Support Area defensive perimeter, and if not, whether there should be any security forces detailed to the CSH. What would you advise?
2. As you are preparing to depart your assembly area in Kuwait for Iraq, you notice several medics sitting around cleaning their pistols. They are all wearing Red Cross armbands and have their aid bags with them. Your sergeant asks you, "Hey ma'am, are they allowed to carry weapons into combat while they wear the Red Cross?" How do you respond?
3. During the initial phase of the invasion, a U.S. unit overruns an Iraqi Army position. After securing the objective, 17 Iraqi prisoners of war are loaded onto a U.S. truck for transport back to the POW holding area. Several of the Iraqi soldiers are badly wounded, and the U.S. commander assigns a U.S. medic to travel with the group back to the POW camp to care for them. There is also an Iraqi medic among the captured soldiers,

and he assists in the care. During the drive to the holding area, the truck comes upon another group of Iraqi soldiers indicating a desire to surrender. There are about 30 of them on the side of the road, and their sergeant tells the U.S. squad leader in charge of the convoy that they have no desire to continue to fight and want to go to the POW facility. He also tells the U.S. squad leader that he has seven badly wounded troops, all of whom were hit during a U.S. airstrike. The squad leader knows that he cannot fit any more POWs on the truck, and so he plans on telling the Iraqi sergeant to wait on the road without any weapons until he can find another truck to be sent to collect them. What should he do with regard to the Iraqi casualties?

4. Iraqi Army members mustered a counter-attack on American forces occupying Baghdad. The Iraqi Army is accompanied by members of the Mahdi Army, a paramilitary organization. During this operation, elements of the U.S. Army's Task Force Bayonet captured approximately forty individuals, including several high-ranking Iraqi Army leaders, and four Mahdi Army members. Unfortunately, a group of the retreating Iraqi Army element managed to overwhelm and capture a U.S. infantry squad. Sergeant Daniel McKay, a member of the U.S. squad that was captured, escaped his captors and made his way back to friendly lines. As a Judge Advocate on the Task Force Bayonet legal staff, you have been asked to sit in on his debriefing to determine whether any violations of the Geneva Conventions have occurred. Assess the following questions and cite Convention articles you believe to have been violated.

   a. Sergeant McKay was kneeling by his wounded teammate and ready to apply a tourniquet when he was shot by an Iraqi Army soldier. The bullet grazed his temple and knocked him out. In response to your questions, Sergeant McKay stated that he had slung his M-4 over his shoulder in order to free his hands for first aid and that he did not have any special uniform markings since he was not a medic. Do these facts indicate a violation of the Geneva Conventions?

   b. When Sergeant McKay regained consciousness, he saw Iraqi Army soldiers tying up every soldier in the squad and throwing them into the backs of pick-up trucks, without checking to see whether they needed medical care. He saw them shoot one U.S. soldier in the head. His limited language skills enabled him to conclude that this soldier was shot after the captors decided he was too wounded to be worth taking along. Was this a violation of the Geneva Conventions?

   c. When the Iraqi force began to evacuate the area, Sergeant McKay looked back, and saw civilians stripping the bodies of the U.S. and Iraqi soldiers who had been killed during the engagement, and taking everything that they had on them. Was this a violation of the Geneva Conventions?

   d. After the Iraqi forces and the captured squad returned to the Iraqi Army base, an Iraqi soldier, apparently acting as a medic, began treating the wounded. An Iraqi Army officer stopped him from treating

any of the U.S. wounded until all of the Iraqi wounded had been cared for. Was this a violation of the Geneva Conventions?
   e. Sergeant McKay stated that shortly before his escape, the Iraqis detaining him brought another small group of captured American soldiers back to their base. One of the soldiers was in critical condition due to battlefield injury, but none of the newly captured Americans had first aid kits. Though the Iraqi commander on site relented and gave permission for Iraqi medics to treat the American soldiers, the medics discovered that they were completely out of medical supplies and painkillers, and had no feasible way to treat the newly arrived badly wounded captive. The wounded man spoke to the Iraqi commander in Arabic and Sergeant McKay was able to roughly discern what he said; the wounded soldier said that he was in a lot of pain, that he was slowly dying, and begged them to either give him morphine or put him out of his misery quickly. After consulting with his medic, the Iraqi commander removed his side-arm and shot the wounded U.S. soldier at point blank range in the head, killing him instantly. He then looked at Sergeant McKay and told him in perfect English, "I am sorry, but I could not allow him to continue to suffer. My medic assured me there was nothing we could do to save him, and that his agony would be prolonged if I did not act. I would hope that you would do the same for me if the tables were turned." Assuming that the killing of the soldier was, in fact, motivated by the Iraqi commander's desire to spare the victim from more suffering, would you report this as a violation of the Geneva Conventions?
5. After reading Sergeant McKay's debriefing, the Task Force Bayonet commander wants to send air assets to search for the rest of the squad. It is his intention to order UH-60 Black Hawk helicopters, marked with the Red Cross emblems, to conduct the search-and-rescue mission. The helicopters would be used to ferry supplies and troops to the front line units and then display the Red Cross emblem on the return trip while searching for wounded soldiers. The helicopters would also display the Red Cross while searching for troops. He wants to know whether the potential mixed mission is legal.
   a. If after the helicopter displays the Red Cross, the pilot sees unwounded U.S. soldiers hiding from Iraqi forces, can the helicopter land and pick them up?
   b. Can the helicopter crew be debriefed about the enemy position it sees while returning from this MEDEVAC mission?
6. During a counter-attack, U.S. forces capture several Iraqi Army and Mahdi Army casualties. All are evacuated to the nearest CSH via helicopter. During the flight, the helicopter (marked with the Red Cross) comes under small arms fire. The crew chief is able to see what appear to be civilians shooting at the helicopter from the rooftops of apartment buildings.

a. If U.S. forces are able to apprehend these civilians, may they be prosecuted for war crimes?
b. You learn that the crew chief returned fire with his M-16 rifle. Was this permissible?
c. When the helicopter arrives at the hospital, the casualties are all treated based on priority established during the triage process. One Iraqi casualty is assessed as "expectant" (death is inevitable, provide only pain medication). The Iraqi soldier is sedated but no further treatment is afforded. The soldier ultimately dies of his wounds. A local civilian observes the other soldiers being treated, but not the Iraqi soldier. The civilian is seen speaking to a CNN reporter, who soon thereafter approaches the hospital commander and asks, "If you let that Iraqi soldier die without trying to save him, wasn't that a war crime?" The commander refers the reporter to you. How would you respond to the question?
d. After all the other casualties are stabilized the Military Police officer assigned to the hospital asks you how to categorize the captured Iraqi Army and Mahdi Army personnel. What Geneva status do you advise to assign each casualty?
7. Returning to the hypothetical at the start of the chapter, what is your answer to Colonel Brown?

10 | Occupation, Termination of Hostilities, and Transition

It is early May 2003 and you are a U.S. Army Judge Advocate assigned to the U.S. Army's V Corps. V Corps forms part of the Joint Task Force that, following the invasion of Iraq that began on March 20, 2003, is expected to stabilize the country and quickly transition to the "end-state" envisioned by the Commander of U.S. Central Command:

> A stable Iraq, with its territorial integrity intact and a broad-based government that renounces WMD [weapons of mass destruction] development and use and no longer supports terrorism or threatens its neighbors.[1]

Initially, things seem to go well towards achieving these goals. On April 16, 2003, U.S. President George Bush offers a positive view of the progress of the invasion and its associated stability operations:

> By swift and effective military action, we avoided the massive flow of refugees that many had expected. By delivering food and water and medicine to the Iraqi people, even as coalition units engaged the enemy, we have helped to avert a humanitarian crisis. Emergency supplies are now moving freely to Iraq from many countries. Now that Iraq is liberated, the United Nations should lift economic sanctions on that country.
>
> We're also addressing Iraq's urgent medical problems — problems left by a regime that built palaces in a country that needed hospitals. Right now, hundreds of Iraqis are being treated at U.S. and British military facilities. Governments from Europe and the Middle East are moving field hospitals to Iraq. Coalition members and the United Nations and other international organizations are sending much-needed medical supplies. The Red Cross is working to keep water and electricity flowing to hospitals. And very soon our coalition will be making direct emergency payments to Iraqi doctors and nurses who will be providing desperately needed care to their fellow citizens. With all the hardships of this

---

1. *See* Catherine Dale, *Operation Iraqi Freedom: Strategies, Approaches, Results, and Issues for Congress* (CRS Report RL34387) CRS-9 n. 23 (March 28, 2008)(citing information she received from U.S. military planners while serving as political advisor to V Corps commander) [hereinafter *CRS Report on OIF*].

transition, the lives of the Iraqi people will be better than anything they have known for generations.

The journey from a totalitarian, brutal dictatorship to a free society is not easy. It will take time to build the institutions of democracy and the habits of freedom. Today, civil order is being restored in communities throughout Iraq, and Iraqis themselves are helping in the effort. Iraqis are leading coalition forces to caches of weapons and volunteering for citizen patrols to provide security. In Basra, British forces and Iraqis have formed joint patrols to maintain order. Just days after the fall of the dictator, just days after the people of Iraq realized they were free from the clutches of his terror, the Iraqi people are reclaiming their own streets, their own country, and their own future.[2]

On April 28, 2016, President Bush delivers a similarly upbeat report, noting, among other things, progress in restoring public services to the Iraqi population:

Rail lines are reopening, and fire stations are responding to calls. Oil — Iraqi oil, owned by the Iraqi people — is flowing again to fuel Iraq's power plants. In Hillah, more than 80 percent of the city now has running water. City residents can buy meats and grains and fruits and vegetables at local shops. The mayor's office, the city council have been reestablished.

In Basra, where more than half of the water treatment facilities were not working before the conflict — more than half weren't functioning — water supplies are now reaching 90 percent of the city. The opulent presidential palace in Basra will now serve a new and noble purpose. We've established a water purification unit there, to make hundreds of thousands of liters of clean water available to the residents of the city of Basra.

Day by day, hour by hour, life in Iraq is getting better for the citizens. Yet, much work remains to be done. I have directed [retired U.S. Army Lieutenant General] Jay Garner and his team to help Iraq achieve specific long-term goals. And they're doing a superb job. Congress recently allocated $2.5 — nearly $2.5 billion for Iraq's relief and reconstruction. With that money, we are renewing Iraq with the help of experts from inside our government, from private industry, from the international community and, most importantly, from within Iraq.

We are dispatching teams across Iraq to assess the critical needs of the Iraqi people. We're clearing land mines. We're working with Iraqis to recover artifacts, to find the hoodlums who ravished the National Museum of Antiquities in Baghdad. Like many of you here, we deplore the actions of the citizens who ravished that museum. And we will work with the Iraqi citizens to find out who they were and to bring them to justice.

We're working toward an Iraq where, for the first time ever, electrical power is reliable and widely available. One of our goals is to make sure everybody in Iraq has electricity. Already, 17 major power plants in Iraq are functioning. Our engineers are meeting with Iraqi engineers. We're visiting power plants throughout the country, and determining which ones need repair, which ones need to

---

2. *President Bush Outlines Progress in Operation Iraqi Freedom* (April 16, 2003) *available at* https://georgewbushwhitehouse.archives.gov/news/releases/2003/04/200304169.html (last visited Feb. 21, 2017).

be modernized, and which ones are obsolete, power plant by power plant. More Iraqis are getting the electricity they need.

We're working to make Iraq's drinking water clean and dependable. American and Iraqi water sanitation engineers are inspecting treatment plants across the country to make sure they have enough purification chemicals and power to produce safe water.[3]

A few days later, in a speech on the deck of the U.S. Navy aircraft carrier USS Abraham Lincoln, President Bush declares, "Major combat operations in Iraq have ended. In the battle of Iraq, the United States and our allies have prevailed. And now our coalition is engaged in securing and reconstructing that country."[4] He then lays out a vision for what is left to be done:

We have difficult work to do in Iraq. We're bringing order to parts of that country that remain dangerous. We're pursuing and finding leaders of the old regime, who will be held to account for their crimes. We've begun the search for hidden chemical and biological weapons and already know of hundreds of sites that will be investigated. We're helping to rebuild Iraq, where the dictator built palaces for himself, instead of hospitals and schools. And we will stand with the new leaders of Iraq as they establish a government of, by, and for the Iraqi people.

The transition from dictatorship to democracy will take time, but it is worth every effort. Our coalition will stay until our work is done. Then we will leave, and we will leave behind a free Iraq.[5]

However, you are aware that the conditions on the ground in Iraq are still uncertain. There is no clear plan for the transition. U.S. political leaders wanted to use "a streamlined force and a quick timeline,"[6] so the invasion force is not well-equipped to deal with civil disturbances or continued civilian resistance. An early example of the problem emerged in mid-April, when widespread looting began in Baghdad as the Hussein regime lost control. Among the looters' targets were priceless treasures at the Iraqi National Museum and weapons from government stockpiles.[7] A lack of adequate coalition troops to maintain order appears to have played a role in the chaos,[8] although the coalition was not yet in complete control of Baghdad at the time.

Now that Baghdad has been taken and the Iraqi military has been soundly defeated, a number of questions need to be addressed by the Commander of Central Command and the key units on the ground, including V Corps. These include:

---

3. President Discusses the Future of Iraq (April 28, 2003) *available at* https://georgewbushwhitehouse.archives.gov/news/releases/2003/04/200304283.html (last visited Feb. 21, 2017).

4. *President Bush Announces Major Combat Operations in Iraq Have Ended* (May 1, 2003) *available at* https://georgewbushwhitehouse.archives.gov/news/releases/2003/05/print/2003050115.html (last visited Feb. 21, 2017).

5. *Id.*

6. *CRS Report on OIF, supra,* note 1, at CRS-10.

7. *Id.* at CRS-23.

8. *Id.* at CRS-24.

- What obligations do U.S. military forces have to restore order and ensure services are provided to the population?
- What should be done with the Iraqi military? Should it remain an organized force, or be disbanded? If it is disbanded, should a new Army be formed?
- What about members of the Hussein regime—can they continue to be employed in government agencies, or should they be dismissed and replaced?
- What about the government itself? President Bush wants a "transition from dictatorship to democracy," but how far can the coalition go in changing the constitution and structure of Iraq's government?
- Who is going to pay for all the work that needs to be done to reconstruct Iraq? Does that fall on the United States and its allies, or can Iraqi funds be used? What about Iraqi oil? Can it be sold to pay for the costs of transition?

In January 2003, President Bush created the Organization for Reconstruction and Humanitarian Assistance (ORHA) in order to plan for the post-war transition, and then to deploy to Iraq. Retired Army Lieutenant General Jay Garner was appointed to lead ORHA. In early May 2003, however, President Bush appoints Ambassador L. Paul "Jerry" Bremer "to serve as Administrator of a new organization, the Coalition Provisional Authority ("CPA"), which would serve as the legal executive authority of Iraq—a much more authoritative mandate than ORHA had held."[9] On May 9, 2003, Ambassador Bremer arrived in Baghdad. Shortly thereafter, the headquarters of your unit—U.S. Army V Corps—assumed the coalition military leadership as part of a new organization called "Coalition Joint Task Force (CJTF) - 7," and served in direct support of CPA, as well as reporting to CENTCOM and through it to the Secretary of Defense.[10]

You are very experienced with the law applicable to combat operations, but you understand that the challenges ahead will be very different. Which law do you apply in these circumstances — the LOAC, international human rights law (HRL), Iraqi law, or U.S. law? You know that the ultimate objective is to withdraw forces and end the conflict, so you need to know more about what rules apply during the transition away from the conflict to a full return of sovereignty to Iraq. Where do you turn?

I. Introduction

The law of belligerent occupation is a branch of the law of armed conflict (LOAC) whose objective is to regulate the relationship between a State's military forces and the population and property in enemy territory, which, as a result of an international armed conflict, have come under the control of those forces. The foundation of this law is the modern concept that a State cannot

---

9. *Id.* at CRS-28.
10. *Id.*

acquire territory by military conquest. Rather, a State occupying another State's territory in armed conflict against that State only acquires a right to administer the conquered territory pending the restoration of peace, when the territory must be returned to the conquered State (unless, by terms of a peace agreement, the territory is transferred to the conquering State).

As an administrator, the occupying State is subject to a wide range of obligations intended to protect and preserve the enemy's population and property, subject to limitations required by military necessity, and in all cases consistent with broad humanitarian principles that mirror in many respects the principles of HRL. According to Professor Adam Roberts:

> This branch of [the LOAC] . . . seeks to strike a balance between the rights of the occupying power and those of the inhabitants; and it seeks to reduce the many points of friction and danger which arise when the armed forces of one power find themselves for a time in control of land and peoples beyond the existing frontiers of their state. It recognizes the occupant's right to administer territory and maintain order. It also requires an occupant to avoid extreme collective punishments, economic exploitation, and measures which would irreversibly alter the political or economic order in a territory. The assumption is that an occupant has a purely provisional role, pending a peace agreement.[11]

The law of belligerent occupation is, therefore, applicable to any mission in which military forces are likely to take control of enemy territory. Several LOAC treaties discussed in Chapter 2 provide the primary source of authority, rights, and obligations of the occupying State and the population of the occupied State. These treaties include the 1907 Hague Regulations Respecting the Laws and Customs of War on Land (1907 Hague IV),[12] the 1949 Geneva Convention Relative to the Treatment of Civilian Persons in Time of War (GCIV),[13] and the 1977 Protocol I Additional to the 1949 Geneva Conventions (AP I).[14] Customary international law (CIL) also provides norms relevant to the conduct of belligerent occupation. Finally, HRL is increasingly relevant in the conduct of any operation in which military forces exert control over the enemy or its population, including in particular the phase in which the occupier is seeking to transition the occupied territory to a more secure and stable post-conflict status. A State may view HRL as a source of obligation *vis à vis* the population of an occupied country, or it may turn to HRL to provide principles

---

11. Adam Roberts, *Decline of Illusions: The Status of the Israeli-Occupied Territories over 21 Years*, 64 INT'L AFF. 346-347 (1988) (hereinafter Roberts).

12. Convention Respecting the Laws and Customs of War on Land, Oct. 18, 1907, 1 Bevans 631, 36 Stat. 2277 (hereinafter 1907 Hague IV).

13. Geneva Convention Relative to the Protection of Civilian Persons in Time of War, Aug. 12, 1949, 6 U.S.T. 3516, 75 U.N.T.S. 973, (hereinafter GCIV).

14. Protocol Additional to the Geneva Conventions of 12 August 1949, and Relating to the Protection of Victims of International Armed Conflicts, June 8, 1977, 1125 U.N.T.S. 17512, (hereinafter AP I); *see also* U.S. DEP'T OF DEF., LAW OF WAR MANUAL para. 11.1.2 (2016) (hereinafter DoD LAW OF WAR MANUAL) (introducing these treaties as the bodies of law relevant to military occupation, and further discussing their application).

that can be followed, by analogy, in cases where the LOAC does not provide a clear rule or lacks details as to how a rule of the LOAC should apply.

Like all other LOAC issues, however, understanding when the law of occupation comes into force is the first step in issue analysis and resolution. Therefore, in this chapter, we turn first to the question of when the law is triggered.

II. Triggering the Law of Belligerent Occupation

Under applicable treaty law, the law of occupation is applicable only in the context of an international armed conflict. In fact, the commencement of a belligerent occupation, even if not preceded by actual armed conflict between the forces of the occupying and occupied States, itself triggers application of the LOAC applicable to international armed conflicts pursuant to common Article 2 of the four Geneva Conventions.[15] Accordingly, if a military operation will involve the introduction of troops into foreign territory, an initial question should be whether the introduction of those troops could result in the application of the law of belligerent occupation. As suggested above, the LOAC does not require hostilities in order to trigger the law of belligerent occupation. Instead, as long as the State into which another State's military forces are introduced did not consent to their introduction, the operation could result in an occupation under the LOAC if, as a result of the introduction of those forces, the territory "is actually placed under the authority of the hostile army."[16] Thus, in the Iraq war scenario described in this text, even if the Hussein regime had chosen not to resist the intervention, the coalition forces who invaded Iraq could be said to have occupied Iraqi territory as Hussein's (e.g., the Iraqi army) retreated or fled in the face of the invasion, and coalition forces were able to exercise authority over that territory.

A. Essential Criteria

The essential criterion for the law of belligerent occupation to apply is the ability of the invading forces to exercise authority over the occupied territory. The U.S. Department of Defense Law of War Manual provides the following explanation of the level of control required to meet this criteria:

---

15. For example, GCIV Article 2 provides, *inter alia*, that "[t]he Convention shall also apply to all cases of partial or total occupation of the territory of a High Contracting Party, even if the said occupation meets with no armed resistance." This same statement can be found in Article 2 of each of the Geneva Conventions, and is incorporated by reference in the clause of AP I that triggers application of AP I to an armed conflict.

16. *See* 1907 Hague IV, *supra*, note 12, art. 42.

[B]elligerent occupation must be both actual and effective, that is, the organized resistance must have been overcome and the force in possession must have taken measures to establish its authority.[17]

The U.S. Army's field manual on land warfare further provides that in an occupation "the invader has rendered the invaded government incapable of publicly exercising its authority, and . . . has successfully substituted its own authority for that of the legitimate government in the territory invaded."[18]

The presence of foreign troops in the territory of another State alone does not itself trigger this law. Instead, that presence must be the result of an armed conflict between States, meaning that the State into which foreign forces are introduced did not consent to their introduction. Thus, military bases that the United States has maintained in the United Kingdom for several decades, even though a legacy of World War II, are not subject to the law of belligerent occupation, but rather a matter of international agreement between two allies. Moreover, even where the presence began as a result of armed conflict, the basis of the presence may change over time so that the law of belligerent occupation no longer applies. For example, the continued presence of U.S. troops in Japan following the execution of peace treaties between Japan and the United States is not an extension of the post-World War II occupation of Japan, but rather a consensual presence supported by applicable stationing agreements between Japan and the United States.[19]

If the applicable criteria are met, the law of belligerent occupation will apply regardless of how the situation is characterized for political purposes. For example, characterizing a military intervention as a "liberation" does not limit the application of the law of belligerent application. If the legitimate government of the invaded territory has not consented, the intervention is still an occupation under the LOAC. In the classic example of Denmark in World War II, Denmark's decision not to resist invading German forces did not mean that Germany's takeover of Denmark was not an occupation under the LOAC.

B. Other Types of Operations

A belligerent occupation should be distinguished from operations in which one State's forces intervene in, and exert some level of control over, the territory and

---

17. DoD Law of War Manual, *supra*, note 14, para. 11.2.2.1 *citing* U.S. Dep't of Army, Field Manual 27-10; The Law of Land Warfare (July 18, 1956 with change 1 July 15, 1976), para. 356 (hereinafter FM 27-10). The U.S. Army field manual also points out that the foreign forces can exercise control in a variety of ways, including with "fixed garrisons or flying columns," and need not be present everywhere in the territory, "as long as the occupation is effective." *Id.*, para. 356.

18. FM 27-10, *supra*, note 17, para. 355.

19. Similarly, when, during World War II, Italy surrendered to the Allies, German forces who had previously been introduced into Italy when it was a German ally were no longer there with Italian consent, and, when they did not depart Italy, became an occupying force.

population of another State outside the scope of an armed conflict with that State. These operations include:[20]

- A consensual intervention, *i.e.*, a military intervention into the territory of another State undertaken at the request or with the consent of the legitimate government of the territory.
- An intervention authorized by the United Nations Security Council acting under its Chapter VII authority or by a regional security body implementing authority under Article 53 of the UN Charter.

A belligerent occupation also should be distinguished from a situation in which territory of an allied State is liberated from enemy forces. Pending the resumption of control by the ally's forces or government, the invading State will restore and maintain order, and may assume some governmental functions. Usually, this type of operation will be governed by an agreement between the invading force and its ally, but in the absence of such an agreement, the law of belligerent occupation may be applied by analogy.[21] If truly a "liberation," this operation does not involve the introduction of forces without the consent of the invaded State; instead, the invading State has introduced troops into another State's territory to expel foreign forces who are occupying that State (for example, the liberation of France following World War II). Of course, establishing that an exiled government actually is the legitimate authority with the ability to consent to an intervention can be controversial.

None of these operations are subject to the law of belligerent occupation, although much of the law of belligerent occupation often will be applied by analogy.[22] By using the law of belligerent occupation as a framework in these other operations, military forces have at their disposal a set of rules that may help provide greater legitimacy to the operation. At a minimum, these rules will ensure that the operation meets minimum standards

---

20. Another type of military occupation, not discussed here, occurs when territory of an allied State is liberated from enemy forces. Also not discussed here are military occupations where a national government liberates its own territory, or a rebel force takes control of territory in a struggle with a national government. The former case is generally a matter of domestic law, subject to obligations under HRL, while the law applicable in the latter case is not well defined in international law beyond the general humanitarian requirements applicable to non-international armed conflicts, such as Common Article 3 of the 1949 Geneva Conventions.

21. *See* DoD Law of War Manual, *supra*, note 14, para. 11.1.3.2 ("The law of belligerent occupation may provide appropriate rules to apply by analogy, pending an agreement with the lawful government."); Manual of the Law of Armed Conflict ¶11.1.2 (U.K. Ministry of Defense, ed., Oxford, 2004) (hereinafter British LOAC Manual) ("The rules of international law applying to occupied territory should, so far as possible, be applied by analogy until an agreement is concluded."). FM 27-10, *supra*, note 17, para. 354, also suggests that a military government, as described in paragraph 12 of that manual, may be established as a temporary measure pending conclusion of an agreement with the legitimate government of the liberated State.

22. For U.S. forces, the application of law by analogy is supported by the Department of Defense Directive 2311.01E, discussed in Chapter 2, which directs "[m]embers of the DoD Components comply with the law of war during all armed conflicts, however such conflicts are characterized, and in all other military operations. U.S. Dep't Defense, Dir. 2311.01e, DoD Law of War Program (May 9, 2006 with change 1 Nov. 15, 2010).

of protection for the population and property of the territory in which they have intervened.

C. Relationship to Non-International Armed Conflict

Belligerent occupation is a concept exclusive to international armed conflict and is wholly inapplicable in a non-international armed conflict. When a non-international armed conflict occurs within a single State, rebel forces may seize and hold territory, but no specific body of treaty law treats the exercise of territorial control by the non-state group as a belligerent occupation under the LOAC.[23] This is not altered by the intervention of the armed forces of another State to assist the lawful government resist the rebels.[24] Because such interventions are not the result of an armed conflict between the two States, there is no international armed conflict and therefore the occupation of territory as a result of such a conflict is not subject to the law of belligerent occupation. Even if the inviting State allows the intervening force to assume functional control over part of its territory, this is still not considered to be subject to the law of belligerent occupation as a legal matter (although, as noted above, the intervening forces may apply the law of belligerent occupation by analogy).

There is no body of treaty law that comprehensively addresses the rights and obligations of a non-state actor in a transnational conflict in which the non-state actor (such as the al Qaeda terrorist group) takes control of the territory of a State. An argument could be made that the same belligerent occupation standards that apply in an international armed conflict should apply to these situations, since the concerns at issue (standards for humane treatment

---

23. Language included in Article 1 of AP I treats as an international armed conflict conflicts against colonial domination, alien occupation, or racist regimes, which could occur within the territory of a single State or a colony or other territory of a single State. For countries that are party to AP I or that apply AP I's classification of conflicts against colonial domination, alien occupation, or racist regimes as international armed conflicts, the LOAC related to belligerent occupation discussed in this chapter would be applicable to the territory of a belligerent in such a conflict that is seized and held by the other belligerent, even if, that other belligerent is not a State. However, in the view of the U.S. government, these conflicts constitute non-international armed conflicts, and therefore the United States would not treat the law of belligerent occupation as applicable as a matter of law to territory seized in such a conflict. The U.S. position has merit: Where a conflict occurs solely in the territory or colony of one State, the LOAC analysis would be complicated where the belligerent seizing territory is in fact the existing government of that State, and thus its "occupation" of territory in the course of the conflict would merely be the recapture of its own territory. The problem with the U.S. position is that it creates a gap in LOAC coverage. AP I usefully affords protection to the population of a colony or other territory in a rebellion that may face repression or abuse (and indeed, such repression and abuse may have been one of the causes of the rebellion). At a minimum, applying provisions of AP I as a matter of customary law or by analogy would ensure that such a gap is not created.

24. The intervention of another State's armed forces on behalf of the rebels to resist the government of the State against which the rebels are fighting would result in an international armed conflict, but the control of the rebel government over territory would not be subject to the law of belligerent occupation, unless the intervening State's forces took over responsibilities for administering the territory or controlled the rebel forces' administration of the territory.

of the population under control of the transnational group and standards for preservation and appropriate use of public property and protection of private property in the occupied territory) are the same in any situation in which the existing government of a territory loses control over the territory as a result of an armed conflict. On the other hand, the law applicable to conflicts with transnational groups is far from clear, though generally such conflicts are treated as non-international armed conflicts. Accordingly, in the absence of any general consensus about how to characterize a conflict with a transnational actor such as al Qaeda, it is unlikely that a consensus could be found with respect to the law applicable to such an actor should it take effective control of territory.

The fact that the law of belligerent occupation is so narrowly focused on an occupation by State forces in an international armed conflict does not mean that armed forces of States or of non-state actors that achieve effective control over part of a State in a situation that is not clearly subject to the law of belligerent occupation may act with impunity. In such situations, other LOAC provisions (such as common Article 3 and AP II), as well as CIL, will protect the population of these areas from violations of basic human rights. Further, HRL could apply, either because the State whose forces take control of territory interpret it as being applicable (*e.g.*, in the case of European States) or, in the case of a non-state or transnational actor exercising control over territory, because HRL reflects universal principles of CIL regarding humanitarian treatment. However, neither the law applicable to non-international armed conflicts nor HRL is as comprehensive as the law of belligerent occupation. It is for this reason that States often apply the rules of the law of belligerent occupation by analogy (meaning that they apply it as a matter of policy, rather than legal obligation) when conducting operations that do not strictly fall under the law of belligerent occupation but involve the exercise by military forces of control over the territory of other States.

The chart that follows illustrates different types of military interventions and the primary law each type of intervention triggers.

Nature of Intervention	Triggering Event	Does Law of Belligerent Occupation Apply?
Internationally mandated, consensual presence to help restore order	Deployment of armed forces from one State into the territory of another State with an agreed international or regional mandate (e.g., pursuant to Security Council resolution)	No, but intervening forces are typically subject to mandates from the international or regional body authorizing the operation, and to agreements between the intervening and host States. These mandates and agreements may call for application of all or part of the law of belligerent occupation by analogy.

continued

Nature of Intervention	Triggering Event	Does Law of Belligerent Occupation Apply?
Consensual intervention to participate with another State in an internal armed conflict within the territory of the other State	Deployment of armed forces from one State into the territory of another State with consent to participate in a joint armed conflict against armed threat against the host State	No, but any territory seized from the non-state armed group will be subject to the receiving State's law (which should reflect HRL norms). The conflict would be subject to common Article 3 and possibly Additional Protocol II.[25] The law of belligerent occupation may be applied by analogy if the intervening State exercises a measure of control over territory of the inviting State.
Non-consensual intervention in another State to restore order pursuant to international or regional authority (e.g., Chapter VII of UN Charter)	Intervention against forces within another State to eliminate a threat to peace, restore order, and/or protect civilians. The opposing force may be the State being invaded or an armed group that the State either is not able to control or tolerates.	Yes, as augmented by provisions of any applicable international mandate (e.g., a UN Security Council resolution).
Non-consensual invasion of enemy State	International armed conflict between States	Yes

III. Terminating Hostilities: Transition to Occupation

The fact that one State's forces have been introduced into the territory of another State does not per se constitute a belligerent occupation, nor does the fact that the introduction was not consensual per se result in an occupation. Rather, the trigger for the law of occupation is the point at which the invading forces have seized sufficient control of the other State's territory for a belligerent occupation to commence. This is a question of fact.[26] Where an invasion is not opposed, identifying the point at which the necessary level of control was established may be comparatively straightforward. On the other hand, where the other State or

---

25. Protocol Additional to the Geneva Conventions of 12 August 1949, and Relating to the Protection of Victims of Non-International Armed Conflicts, June 8, 1977, 1125 U.N.T.S. 17513 (hereinafter AP II). If the intervening State is not a party to AP II, the host State nevertheless typically will require compliance with AP II if the host State is a party.

26. DoD LAW OF WAR MANUAL, *supra*, note 14, para. 11.2.

its population resists the invasion, this point may be more difficult to establish. Therefore, before turning to the rules applicable once an occupation is underway, it is important to first consider how commanders determine the point at which their operations transition to an occupation phase. Typically, this point will correspond with the point at which hostilities cease, although "an occupation may be effective despite the existence of areas in the enemy State that are temporarily controlled by enemy forces or pockets of resistance."[27]

In many cases, hostilities end when forces defending against an invasion simply cease to fight and melt into the population, leaving the invader in control of the invaded territory. In the 1989 U.S. invasion of Panama, for example, fighting in Panama City and Colon ended when Panamaniam soldiers traded in their uniforms for civilian clothes and mixed into the population. There was no formal transfer of power or capitulation of enemy forces; fighting simply stopped or transitioned to only sporadic resistance. In such a situation, there is no specific agreement to end hostilities — they simply end.[28]

In other cases, hostilities may terminate by prior agreement of the parties. Indeed, prior to 1949, both CIL (as reflected in the Lieber Code)[29] and treaty law (most prominently, 1907 Hague IV) envisioned a more formalized termination of hostilities. According to Article 36 of 1907 Hague IV, for example, an "armistice" can be signed to suspend military operations by mutual agreement between the belligerent parties.[30] If the duration of the armistice is not defined, either of the belligerent parties may resume operations at any time, provided always that the other party is warned prior to recommencement of hostilities or within a time agreed upon in the terms of the armistice.

According to Article 37 of 1907 Hague IV, an armistice may be general or local. A general armistice suspends hostilities between the belligerent States everywhere, while a local armistice suspends hostilities only between elements of the opposing forces within a fixed area. In either case, hostilities are suspended immediately after notification that the armistice has been signed, or they can be suspended on some future date fixed by agreement (as was the case with the armistice that ended fighting on the western front in World War I).

In theory, an armistice merely suspends hostilities. The parties to the armistice agreement can establish in their agreement that the terms only apply pending the resumption of hostilities. However, in historical practice, the armistice was typically used as a prelude to reaching agreement on a broader and

---

27. *Id.* para. 11.2.2.1.
28. In this connection, it is important to distinguish a unilateral of hostilities from a "cease-fire," which is generally a temporary suspension of hostilities for a specific purpose, such as the collection of the dead and wounded. A temporary suspension of hostilities for such a purpose does not fall into the category of termination of hostilities, although it may be a prelude to other measures to bring about such a termination. *See* BRITISH LOAC MANUAL, *supra*, note 21, ¶10.15.
29. War Dep't, Instructions for the Gov't of Armies of the United States in the Field, General Orders, No. 100 (1898) (reprint of 1863 original).
30. *See* DoD LAW OF WAR MANUAL, *supra*, note 14, para. 12.11-12.13; FM 27-10, *supra*, note 17, para. 479-494; BRITISH LOAC MANUAL, *supra*, note 21, ¶10.13-10.28 for more detailed descriptions of armistices. The footnotes to the sections of the British LOAC Manual provide several examples of instances in military history when armistices have been used.

more permanent peace (in which case, it is typically referred to as a "general armistice"). However, an armistice also can be used for more limited purposes, such as suspending hostilities while the wounded are removed from the field.[31] In modern practice, either the term "cease-fire" or "armistice" may be used to denote an agreement to suspend hostilities. For example, hostilities in the Korean War ended pursuant to an armistice, whereas hostilities in the first Gulf War terminated as the result of a cease-fire agreement. Although both effectively terminated each conflict, neither of these armistices led to formal peace agreements.

Like any agreement, an armistice can be violated. According to Article 40 of 1907 Hague IV, any serious violation of the armistice by one of the parties gives the other party the right to denounce it, and in cases of urgency, even of recommencing hostilities immediately. However, according to Article 41 of 1907 Hague IV, a violation of the terms of the armistice by private persons acting on their own initiative only entitles the injured party to demand the punishment of the offenders or, if necessary, compensation for the losses sustained.

When belligerent parties enter into an armistice or cease-fire, organized armed forces on both sides generally remain intact, though a broader peace may be sought that will result in disbanding of forces on one or both sides. If one side wishes to surrender, however, the LOAC provides for a "capitulation," which is an agreement entered into between commanders of belligerent forces for the surrender of units of troops, military positions, or a geographic theater of operations.[32] Of course, a force may surrender without resort to a capitulation, but a capitulation allows for an orderly surrender. There are numerous examples of capitulation agreements whereby commanders surrendered large numbers of forces to an enemy unrelated to an armistice, including, for example, the surrender of Argentine forces to the British at Port Stanley in the Falkland Islands in 1982.

Forces often are trained not to surrender, and, in the case of the U.S. military, it is a violation of the Uniform Code of Military Justice for a commander to surrender his forces when they still have a means to resist. However, even if soldiers or commanders surrender in violation of national laws or policies, the surrender is still valid under the LOAC, although a commander's surrender cannot extend beyond those forces under his or her control.[33] It is also clear that whether a commander surrenders or agrees to a capitulation or an armistice, its terms must be strictly honored. Feigning an offer or agreement to surrender,

---

31. *See, e.g.*, Geneva Convention for the Amelioration of the Condition of the Wounded and Sick in Armed Forces in the Field, Aug. 12, 1949, art. 15, U.S.T. 3114, 75 U.N.T.S. 970, (hereinafter GWS) ("Whenever circumstances permit, an armistice or a suspension of fire shall be arranged, or local arrangements made, to permit the removal, exchange and transport of the wounded left on the battlefield."). Rules governing armistices, including the terms typically included in armistices, are discussed in detail in DoD Law of War Manual, *supra*, note 14, para. 12.11-12.13; FM 27-10, *supra*, note 17, paras. 479-494.

32. 1907 Hague IV, *supra*, note 12, art. 35.

33. *See, generally* DoD Law of War Manual, *supra*, note 14, para. 12.8.2; FM 27-10, *supra*, note 17, paras. 470-478; British LOAC Manual, *supra*, note 21, ¶¶10.29-10.31.

armistice, or capitulation to gain a military advantage would be considered perfidy, which is a war crime.[34]

Whether as the result of surrender, cease-fire, armistice, flight, or simply a lack of initial resistance, the termination of effective enemy resistance to an invading force is the key factor in transitioning from hostilities to occupation. The critical question is not whether the enemy might attempt to regain control of the vacated or conquered territory, or engage in sporadic harassing operations, but whether friendly forces have effectively displaced enemy authority over the territory. Where displacement has occurred and the invading forces have taken effective control of the territory, the law of belligerent occupation operates to minimize disruption to the lives and property of the local population, preserve the area so that it can return to normal conditions following the end of hostilities, and balance the security interests of the occupying force with protection from the arbitrary deprivations of civilian lives, liberty, and property by the occupying forces.

IV. Features of Occupation

A. Commencement

Under the LOAC, when and whether an occupation has begun is a question of fact that focuses on whether two conditions are fulfilled:

> First, is the enemy government no longer capable of publicly exercising its authority; and
> Second, has the invading military force successfully substituted its own authority for that of the enemy government?[35]

---

34. FM 27-10, *supra*, note 17, para. 493; *see also* DoD Law of War Manual, *supra*, note 14, para. 5.22 for more on the crime of perfidy.

35. FM 27-10, *supra*, note 17, para. 355; *see also* DoD Law of War Manual, *supra*, note 14, para. 11.2.2 for a more intricate discussion. The British LOAC Manual describes the test for the commencement of occupation as follows:

> To determine whether a state of occupation exists, it is necessary to look at the area concerned and determine whether two conditions are satisfied: first that the former government has been rendered incapable of publicly exercising its authority in that area; and, secondly, that the occupying power is in a position to substitute its own authority for that of the former government.

British LOAC Manual, *supra*, note 21, ¶11.3. The Manual's description is somewhat imprecise, because it only speaks to whether the occupying forces are "in a position" to take control, while Article 42 of 1907 Hague IV makes clear that it is the fact of actual control that determines when occupation begins. However, in subsequent paragraphs, the British LOAC Manual is clearer on the point that actual control is required, and that merely defeating enemy forces, standing alone, is not sufficient. *Id.* ¶11.3.2 ("Occupation does not take effect merely because the main forces of the country have been defeated but depends on whether authority is actually being exercised over the civilian population.").

An occupying State does not need to maintain forces everywhere in enemy territory in order to exercise the necessary level of control, as long as control is actual and effective. Thus, an occupying power could use rapid response forces or other mobile units to respond to enemy resistance in order to ensure control over territory. The actual troops or units needed to maintain an effective occupation will depend on various considerations, such as the cooperation of the inhabitants, the size and density of the population, the nature of the terrain, and similar factors.[36] In Iraq in 2003, coalition forces lacked the numbers to establish a presence in every part of Iraq, but their ability to rapidly respond to threats or unrest in any part of the country indicated that they had achieved the type of effective control necessary to establish occupation authority, and indeed the period in which the Coalition Provisional Authority administered Iraq is considered to be an occupation under the LOAC.

The fact that a fort, enemy strongpoint, or isolated area within the occupied territory continues to hold out against attacks by the invader's forces does not mean the area in which that fort or isolated area is located has not been occupied. Rather, the question of whether the territory is occupied notwithstanding the presence of the fort, strongpoint, or isolated area depends on how effective it is to disrupting the ability of a State's forces to exercise control over the territory. If it is an isolated point of resistance within a broader territory that the State's forces control, the fort, strongpoint, or isolated area is not likely to be considered sufficient to deny control to the State's forces or to prevent the area from being subject to the law of belligerent occupation.[37]

The existence of a resistance movement also does not prevent a territory from being considered to be occupied. Indeed, the third Geneva Convention of 1949 relative to the treatment of prisoners of war recognizes as one category of combatant entitled to protection under the LOAC as a prisoner of war if captured during an international armed conflict, members of militias, volunteer corps, and "organized resistance movements, belonging to a Party to the conflict and operating in or outside their own territory, even if this territory is occupied," provided that they meet certain conditions.[38] On the other hand, while the LOAC recognizes that civilians may resist an invader,[39] once an occupation begins, resistance by the population who are not members of organized resistance groups that meet the conditions of the GPW must cease.

---

36. DoD Law of War Manual, *supra*, note 14, para. 11.2.2.1.
37. *Id.*
38. Geneva Convention Relative to the Treatment of Prisoners of War, Aug. 12, 1949, art. 4A, 6 U.S.T. 3316, 75 U.N.T.S. 972 (hereinafter GPW). These conditions are "(a) that of being commanded by a person responsible for his subordinates; (b) that of having a fixed distinctive sign recognizable at a distance; (c) that of carrying arms openly; (d) that of conducting their operations in accordance with the laws and customs of war." *Id.*
39. The categorization as prisoners of war of civilians who resist an invader as part of a so-called *levée en masse* is addressed in Article 4A of GPW and Article 2 of 1907 Hague IV. Both of these provisions make clear that the rights associated with a *levée en masse* only apply to inhabitants of a territory that has not been occupied.

As noted above, belligerent occupation need not be preceded by hostilities. Common Article 2 of the four Geneva Conventions of 1949 explicitly indicates that the Conventions apply "to all cases of partial or total occupation of the territory of a High Contracting Party, even if the said occupation meets with no armed resistance."

No matter how occupation begins, however, it must be maintained. Thus, if the occupying State evacuates all forces from a territory or is driven out, the occupation ceases. At that point, the occupying force's relationship with the inhabitants of the previously occupied territory reverts to the pre-occupation position. In contrast, if the occupying State's forces are simply moving forward in pressing their attacks, and leave behind only a small force to administer the areas previously conquered, this does not mean that occupation in those areas has terminated, so long as the smaller force has the ability to maintain effective control (which may involve calling upon forces outside of the occupied territory to support it militarily in order to defeat any challenge to control).[40]

It is often the case that an occupation will begin with a statement by the invader acknowledging that it has taken control of invaded territory, typically in the form of a proclamation of occupation issued by the senior military commander. The value of such a statement is that it gives notice to the population in the territory subjected to enemy military control of the commander's expectation that further resistance will cease. However, such a statement is not strictly required by the LOAC for an occupation to begin, nor does the statement by itself establish that there is an occupation. Rather, as the terms of Article 42 of 1907 Hague IV suggest, the commencement of occupation is a question of fact, and regardless of whether an invader declares that it is an occupying power, the occupation will begin once the invader has achieved the necessary level of control.[41]

B. Direct and Indirect Control

Control of occupied territory can be exercised directly through a military government that temporarily replaces the national government of the occupied territory (as in Germany after World War II), or the national government can remain in place and control can be exercised indirectly by the occupying forces acting through the national government (as in Japan after World War II, where the Allied military forces in the country worked through the existing Japanese bureaucracy in administering the occupation). In any case, the obligations and restrictions applicable to an occupying power cannot be avoided by using a puppet government to carry out acts that would be unlawful if performed directly by the occupying power. Acts induced or compelled by the occupying State are nonetheless its acts.[42]

---

40. DoD Law of War Manual, *supra*, note 14, para. 11.2.2. (the manual does note that "air superiority alone would not constitute an effective occupation.").
41. *Id.* para. 11.2.4.
42. *Id.* para. 11.8.3.

C. Is There an Obligation to Take Control?

Even if an invasion results in a widespread collapse of enemy forces that could give the invader sufficient control to qualify as occupation, is the invader obligated to assume the role of occupying State? The LOAC does not directly address this point. As noted above, Article 42 of 1907 Hague IV, which establishes the foundational principle of occupation law, provides simply that "[t]erritory is considered occupied when it is actually placed under the authority of the hostile army" and the DoD Law of War Manual indicates that "[t]erritory is considered occupied when it is actually placed under the authority of the hostile forces."[43]

None of the LOAC treaties specifically state that an invader must take control, however, and it would seem possible for an invader to simply withdraw after defeating the opposing army. In that case, the remnants of the defeated government or new forces emerging from the indigenous population might assume powers and seek to reconstitute a national government. However, while present in invalid territory, the invading force should not be permitted to avoid occupation obligations in an area subjected to effective control simply by disavowing the existence of occupation. For example, although, for various reasons, Israel never conceded the *de jure* applicability of the law of belligerent occupation to the West Bank and Gaza, while if administered these areas, it conceded the *de facto* occupied status of these areas and its commitment to comply with the law of belligerent occupation.[44]

In the modern era, there are several examples of interventions by State military forces, authorized by the United Nations or regional bodies, that are conducted for the express purpose of removing a repressive government or otherwise to address political or humanitarian problems in a country or territory that are considered to be threats to peace justifying international intervention. In these situations, it may be necessary to assume some of the responsibilities of government in order to correct the problems that led to the intervention. Moreover, a refusal to assume such responsibilities could delegitimize the use of military force from an international legal perspective.

In the initial phase of operations in Iraq in 2003 after U.S. and coalition forces entered Baghdad, hesitation in asserting occupation authority undermined international support for the operation because of the fear that the United States and its coalition partners were unprepared to address the instability in Iraq that the U.S. and coalition invasion had created. Such hesitation — whether motivated by political considerations, perceived capability limitations, or general uncertainty as to what the law actually requires — can also confuse, or even damage the morale of, friendly forces who may want to respond to the instability and help restore order, but feel constrained by a lack of clear guidance that their actions would be permitted. It is therefore imperative that where a State anticipates that its forces will take control of enemy territory, the State's

---

43. *Id.* para. 11.2.2.
44. *See* Roberts, *supra*, note 11, at 348-350.

forces have a clear understanding about the applicability of occupation law and develop plans in advance to meet their LOAC obligations.

D. Distinguishing Invasion from Occupation

It is important to distinguish occupation from invasion. Occupation may follow as a result of attacks on the territory of an enemy or an invasion of that territory, but the two are not synonymous (and, as noted above, an occupation actually may begin without any preceding hostilities at all). Instead, occupation does not commence until a State's forces establish effective control over an enemy State's territory.[45] For example, bombardment by land and sea forces does not establish effective control over territory and therefore such attacks, standing alone, would not constitute occupation. Of course, if such attacks result in surrender or evacuation of territory by the enemy State's forces, and the attacking forces take effective control of the territory, that territory would be considered to be occupied (as occurred at the end of World War II, when Japan, in response to the bombing of Hiroshima and Nagasaki, signed an armistice and allowed the Allies to enter Japan and take control of Japan). Similarly, a naval blockade of enemy territory is not, standing alone, an occupation, although an occupying power may use a blockade as one element of its control over enemy territory.

On the other hand, if there is an invasion, but it is effectively resisted so that the invader does not have control over the invaded territory, the contest for control of territory indicates that the invader does not yet have the degree of control required for a state of occupation to exist. Accordingly, contested territory is not considered occupied unless and until general organized military resistance has ended and the invader has taken effective control of the territory. For example, when U.S. and coalition forces invaded Iraq in March 2003, the resistance by Iraqi forces for the first few weeks indicated that, in the areas where the Iraqis were still putting up a broad and organized resistance, occupation had yet to commence. However, as organized Iraqi resistance was defeated, the zone of occupation gradually expanded to include the entire country, even though some guerrilla activity continued. This also explains why raids into enemy territory or reconnaissance missions that result in the defeat of enemy forces do not establish sufficient control for an occupation to commence, unless the raiding parties or reconnaissance teams seize territory and hold it to the exclusion of enemy forces.[46]

---

45. Gerhard von Glahn, The Occupation of Enemy Territory: A Commentary on the Law and Practice of Belligerent Occupation 28 (1957) ("Invasion as such does not ordinarily constitute occupation, although it precedes it and may coincide with it for a limited period of time.").

46. It is important to note, however, that Field Manual 27-10 indicates that U.S. Army units should look to occupation principles when dealing with civilians in areas not technically under sufficient control to qualify as occupied. See FM 27-10, supra, note 17, 352b ("The rules set forth in this chapter apply of their own force only to belligerently occupied areas, but they should, as a matter of policy, be observed as far as possible in areas through which troops are passing and even on the battlefield.").

E. Occupation vs. Annexation

The law of belligerent occupation recognizes that, as a matter of military necessity, the occupying State exercises control in the occupied territory only for the period of occupation. The right of the occupying State over occupied territory results from the military power of the occupying State and from the necessity of maintaining law and order, indispensable both to the inhabitants and to the occupying force. It is unlawful for a belligerent to annex occupied territory or to create a new State while hostilities are still in progress. A transfer of sovereignty can only occur by means of a peace treaty negotiated by both sides and recognized by the international community.[47]

V. Implications of Being an Occupying Power

As we will see in the balance of this chapter, the LOAC imposes significant responsibilities on the occupying State once the occupation begins. At its very core, the law of belligerent occupation establishes reciprocal obligations: The occupying State is obligated to maintain public order and provide for the essential needs of the occupied population (the duty of care); and the occupied population is obligated to refrain from any activity contrary to the security interests of the occupying State's forces (the duty of obedience). Taken collectively, the many treaty provisions related to belligerent occupation require the occupying State to restore and maintain public order, provide for the needs of the population, and ultimately return the occupied territory to the legitimate sovereign, subject to such damage or destruction of property or infrastructure as may be justified by military necessity. However, the fact that there may not be a "legitimate sovereign" who is available or capable of resuming control of the occupied territory can lead the occupying State to maintain control for an extended period after hostilities have ended, or even to engage in steps to create or reconstitute a "legitimate sovereign" to which control can be relinquished at a later date.

Fulfilling the obligations of an occupier can be complicated, costly, and time-consuming, and can have the effect of engaging the occupying State's military forces for a number of years. Therefore, an invader may want to avoid becoming an occupying State, and may try to characterize its control as something other than an occupation. This effort is unlikely to succeed, however, if, in the wake of the State's military operations in the territory of an enemy State, the central and local governments of that State collapse and the invader is the only authority remaining in the invaded territory that can ensure security and delivery of essential services. The international community may not tolerate

---

47. DoD Law of War Manual, *supra*, note 14, para. 11.3.1; FM 27-10, *supra*, note 17, para. 358; The Handbook of Humanitarian Law in Armed Conflicts para. 528 (D. Fleck ed., 1995).

abandonment of the conquered territory in such a case, particularly if there are significant risks that fundamental human rights and needs will not be met if the occupying State does not take or retain control.

There is no one-size-fits-all template for executing the complex occupation mission. However, over time certain aspects of occupation practice have emerged that will normally guide implementation of occupation obligations by the occupying State.[48]

First, it is generally considered preferable to retain as much of the occupied territory's domestic law as possible without compromising the legitimate security needs of the occupying force. Changes to this domestic law may be required to meet the requirements of the LOAC or other international law, however.[49]

Second, it is also considered preferable to maximize the continued use of the occupied territory's government services and personnel. While under the LOAC, the occupying State can suspend or replace domestic law in the occupied territory, and can disband or suspend the function of government services and agents, as long as public order is maintained and the needs of the population are met, the norm is to do so only when it is considered necessary to protect the security interests of the occupying forces. For example, an occupying State may decide it is necessary to suspend existing laws authorizing the local population to possess firearms or to impose a curfew or restrict certain areas from local access. The occupying State also may assess the willingness of local civil servants to continue to perform their duties (to include law enforcement personnel) and selectively remove some of these individuals from their duties. However, the wholesale termination or suspension of local government functions is fraught with risks as the occupying State will be obligated to provide a sufficient substitute for the functions fulfilled by the suspended employees.

The power of the occupying State to enact laws is recognized in GCIV Article 64, which provides, in part, as follows:

> The Occupying Power may, however, subject the population of the occupied territory to provisions which are essential to enable the Occupying Power to fulfil its obligations under the present Convention, to maintain the orderly government of the territory, and to ensure the security of the Occupying

---

48. The rights and obligations of the occupying State are generally exercised by the military commander of the occupying forces, but they are nonetheless the rights and obligations of that State and not the commander himself, who is an agent of the State that employs him or her. Further, the commander need not be a military officer. In addition, the occupying State may create a new organization or agency specifically to exercise the rights and obligations of the State under the law of belligerent. Indeed, following the invasion and occupation of Iraq in 2003 forces, a separate occupying authority with a civilian leader (the "Coalition Provisional Authority" led by Ambassador Paul Bremer) was created to fulfill the obligations of all the occupying nations.

49. *See, e.g.*, GCIV, *supra*, note 13, art. 64 (allowing for changes in the penal laws of the occupied territory where "they constitute . . . an obstacle to the application of the present Convention," which would include provisions such as GCIV Article 27 that guarantee members of the local population certain basic human rights). *See also* DoD LAW OF WAR MANUAL, *supra*, note 14, para. 11.9.2.

Power, of the members and property of the occupying forces or administration, and likewise of the establishments and lines of communication used by them.[50]

Although Article 64 describes the occupying State's power to enact "provisions" (*e.g.*, laws, directives, regulations, etc.) largely in terms of meeting its security concerns, Article 64 also mentions that such provisions can be used "to enable the Occupying Power to fulfil its obligations under the present Convention" (*i.e.*, GCIV). Therefore, an invading force that acknowledges that its occupation obligations include an obligation to protect the human rights of the local population, including women, ethnic minorities, and others who may be denied equal rights under existing local law, may feel compelled by the duty of care to implement changes in the domestic law of the occupied territory for reasons unrelated to its own security, but instead to improve the respect for human rights of such groups, or even to improve the human rights of the population as a whole (*e.g.*, by providing for greater political freedom).

The scope of an occupying State's power to enact such "provisions" is controversial, as nothing in GCIV or HR explicitly authorizes such actions, although GCIV does contain a number of provisions, such as Article 27, that require the occupying State to respect basic human rights. Nonetheless, even if the occupying State does not interpret its authority under GCIV very broadly, it may be politically difficult for that State to tolerate retaining domestic laws in the occupied territory that are considered inconsistent with fundamental HRL principles.

Where the occupation is the result of an action authorized by the UN Security Council, the Security Council's authorization itself may contain provisions that would suggest that ensuring respect for fundamental human rights is an implied (if not express) objective of the UN-authorized mission. These provisions may be interpreted as providing authority for the occupying State's forces to adopt provisions that expand the respect for human rights in the occupied territory. On the other hand, the occupying State needs to be mindful that such provisions may offend local sensitivities and must be aware of the cultural context for the existing law. Accordingly, provisions that direct change in local law for reasons other than protecting the security of the occupying forces and the local population should not be implemented without careful assessment and consultation with legal authorities, and approval from the occupying State's national leadership.

VI. Applicable Law

Once an occupation commences, two treaties—the 1907 Hague IV and the 1949 GCIV—provide the bulk of positive treaty law regulating the occupation,

---

50. GCIV, *supra*, note 13, art. 64.

although the 1954 Hague Convention on Cultural Property[51] and AP I also include provisions specifically addressed to the obligations of occupying States.

A. 1907 Hague IV

The regulations set out in Articles 42-56 of 1907 Hague IV deal specifically with the occupation of enemy territory by military forces. As noted in Chapter 2, while this treaty has not been ratified by all States, it is considered CIL. These regulations include general rules covering the rights and obligations of the occupying State with respect to the population and property of the occupied State. A key premise of 1907 Hague IV is that, while the occupying State is allowed to use the property of the occupied State in accordance with military necessity, the occupying State will return the occupied territory to the displaced sovereign after the conclusion of hostilities, with only limited changes. 1907 Hague IV does not include, for example, any express authorization to modify the laws of the occupied territory, although Article 43 does require the occupying State to "take all measures in his power to restore, and ensure, as far as possible, public order and safety, while respecting, unless absolutely prevented, the laws in effect in the country" — a broad mandate that can be interpreted to include the power to modify existing laws and enact new laws, where necessary to "restore, and ensure, as far as possible, public order and safety." Nonetheless, as a general matter, under 1907 Hague IV, the occupying State is a caretaker of the occupied territory, but without power to make any significant changes — even changes for the benefit of the population — unless such changes are required for "public order and safety."

Article 55 of 1907 Hague IV suggests that a kind of trustee relationship is established, at least with respect to real property:

> The occupying State shall be regarded only as administrator and usufructuary of public buildings, real estate, forests, and agricultural estates belonging to the hostile State, and situated in the occupied country. It must safeguard the capital of these properties, and administer them in accordance with the rules of usufruct.[52]

Whether the trusteeship concept under 1907 Hague IV also applies to the relationship of the occupying State with the population of the occupied territory is debatable.[53] An occupying State controls occupied territory on the basis of an actual or implied threat of coercion through the occupying State's military power. Thus, during an occupation, the occupying State remains at all times the enemy of both the former government of the territory and its people, and in fact 1907 Hague IV specifically forbids forcing the inhabitants of occupied terri-

---

51. Convention for the Protection of Cultural Property in the Event of Armed Conflict, May 14, 1954, 249 U.N.T.S. 240 (hereinafter 1954 Hague Convention).

52. 1907 Hague IV, *supra*, note 12, art. 55.

53. *See, e.g.*, Yoram Dinstein, The International Law of Belligerent Occupation 36 (2009) (hereinafter Dinstein).

tory to swear allegiance to the occupying State or to provide information about the army of the occupied State or its defense needs.[54] This is true even though its adherence to international legal obligations and perhaps a desire to pacify the occupied territory may lead an occupying State to adopt policies of greater benefit to the local population than the government that the occupying State displaced, and thereby arguably provide a "better" government for the people than what was in place prior to the occupation.[55]

B. 1949 Geneva Convention Relative to the Protection of the Civilian Population

The widespread abuses of civilians in occupied areas during World War II led the international community to adopt, as one of four post-World War II LOAC treaties, GCIV, which is devoted largely to the protection of civilians subjected to belligerent occupation. Accordingly, the provisions of GCIV regulate the relationship between the occupying State and the population of the occupied territory, in particular to ensure that the population is treated humanely.[56]

Individuals afforded the maximum benefits from GCIV are designated "protected persons" by the treaty, a legal term defined in Article 4(1) of GCIV as "[p]ersons protected by the Convention ... who, at a given moment and in any manner whatsoever find themselves, in case of conflict or occupation, in the hands of a Party to the conflict or occupying power of which they are not nationals."[57] GCIV includes a number of provisions that secure basic human rights for protected persons, including Article 27, which provides:

> Protected persons are entitled, in all circumstances, to respect for their persons, their honour, their family rights, their religious convictions and practices, and their manners and customs. They shall at all times be humanely treated, and shall be protected especially against all acts of violence or threats thereof and against insults and public curiosity.
>
> Women shall be especially protected against any attack on their honour, in particular against rape, enforced prostitution, or any form of indecent assault.
>
> Without prejudice to the provisions relating to their state of health, age and sex, all protected persons shall be treated with the same consideration by the Party to the conflict in whose power they are, without any adverse distinction based, in particular, on race, religion or political opinion.

---

54. 1907 Hague IV, *supra*, note 12, art. 44 and 45.

55. DINSTEIN, *supra*, note 53, at 36.

56. Despite its title, GCIV does not treat all civilians as protected persons. Instead, in addition to those who do not fall within the terms of Article 4 of GCIV, a careful reading of GCIV shows that the provisions of the Convention applicable to protected persons only apply in occupied territory and in the home territory of an enemy belligerent. Thus, while GCIV is relevant to the topic of this chapter, many of its provisions are not applicable to civilians in other situations, such as on a battlefield during active combat, although many of the protections afforded by GCIV may reflect customary law applicable to civilians generally.

57. GCIV, *supra*, note 13, art. 4(1).

However, the Parties to the conflict may take such measures of control and security in regard to protected persons as may be necessary as a result of the war.[58]

Like the other Geneva Conventions, GCIV provides for a "protecting Power" (a neutral State agreed upon by the parties to the conflict, or if no agreement is reached, the International Committee of the Red Cross (ICRC)) that is responsible for monitoring compliance with the Conventions and for ensuring that the rights of protected persons are respected. In essence, the protecting power interacts with the occupying State and its forces to ensure these forces respect their occupation obligations. Technically, the protecting power's role concerns only the interests of "protected persons," although in practice this distinction is increasingly irrelevant. Today, it is more likely that the protecting power (in most situations, the ICRC) will act to ensure compliance with all humanitarian obligations for all civilians affected by the armed conflict, irrespective of whether the interests of persons falling within the definition of "protected persons" are at stake.

The advocacy of the ICRC for the application of humanitarian standards with respect to all civilians is important, for not every civilian in occupied territory will be considered a "protected person" under GCIV (although all civilians benefit from the humane treatment obligations imposed by CIL and, where applicable, by Article 75 of AP I). For example, per the second paragraph of Article 4 of GCIV, nationals of the occupying State or of its co-belligerents are not protected persons, whereas nationals of a neutral State are. The logic here is revealed by the ICRC Commentary to Article 4, which indicates that these civilians are excluded from the "protected person" category because they do not need to rely on the protecting power to advocate for their interests as they are nationals of the occupying State who have rights under their own domestic law, or are nationals of co-belligerent States whose governments retain diplomatic relationships with the occupying State by virtue of which their rights can be protected.[59] On the other hand, for other civilians, including civilians of a neutral State, the existence of belligerent occupation disrupts their ability to call upon their government to protect their rights and interests, therefore necessitating the application of GCIV and the representation of the protecting power for that purpose.[60]

Further, individuals protected by the other Geneva Conventions also are not protected by GCIV. This includes primarily combatants who would qualify

---

58. As the paragraph at the end of the quoted language indicates, an occupying State may impose limitations on these rights, but only to the extent justified by military necessity.

59. *See* COMMENTARY, CONVENTION IV RELATIVE TO THE PROTECTION OF CIVILIAN PERSONS IN TIME OF WAR. Geneva, 12 August 1949 48-50 (Jean S. Pictet ed., 1960), at 48-50 (hereinafter Commentary, Convention IV).

60. *Id.* The Commentary adds: "The case of nationals of a co-belligerent State is simpler. They are not considered to be protected persons so long as the State whose nationals they are has normal diplomatic representation in the belligerent State or with the Occupying Power. It is assumed in this provision that the nationals of co-belligerent States, that is to say, of allies, do not need protection under the Convention." *Id.*

for treatment as prisoners of war under the GPW, civilians who accompany those forces, and civilians who resist the invasion as part of a *levée en masse*.[61] Therefore, during the occupation of Iraq, neither a U.S. human rights lawyer (who is a national of the occupying State (*i.e.*, the United States)) or a captured Iraqi soldier (a combatant protected by GPW) on whose behalf the lawyer might advocate would be considered protected persons under GCIV. On the other hand, the many nationals of neutral States in Iraq when U.S. forces took control and belligerent occupation commenced are protected by GCIV.

Protected person status under GCIV only applies from the point in time at which the occupation begins. Prior to that, the protection afforded to civilians during military operations (*e.g.*, during an invasion) is confined to a more limited set of articles in Part II of GCIV, dealing largely with (1) the protection of the wounded and sick, and of hospitals, medical transports, and medical personnel to treat the wounded and sick, and the delivery of relief supplies; (2) the protection of certain civilian groups considered to be more vulnerable (*e.g.*, children under 15); and (3) sharing of family information and reuniting families.

The general treatment standard applicable to protected persons is set forth in GCIV Article 27, quoted in full above, which, *inter alia*, provides that "[p]rotected persons are entitled, in all circumstances, to respect for their persons, their honor, their family rights, their religious convictions and practices, and their manners and customs. They shall at all times be humanely treated."[62] This provision is intended to guarantee protection of a protected person's physical safety and moral and intellectual integrity, as well as prohibiting arbitrary acts that interfere with marital and family ties or the support of the family. The latter is reinforced by GCIV Article 82, which requires that families be housed together in the case of internment (*see* discussion of internment below). Article 27 also prohibits arbitrary interference with religious observances, services, and rites, while Article 27's direction to respect for manners and customs is intended to protect practices that define a particular culture.

All acts of violence against protected persons, as well as inhumane treatment of protected persons, are prohibited by Article 27, all of which arguably also are prohibited by CIL or HRL, whether or not the victim qualified as a protected person. Attacks against women, including rape, enforced prostitution, and indecent assault and attacks on the honor of women also are specifically prohibited by Article 27. Further, no adverse distinctions are permitted with respect to protected persons. This prohibition extends to distinctions based on (although not limited to) race, religion, or political opinion. However, there is no prohibition on preferences that benefit protected persons that can be given, for example, in consideration of their health, age, or sex.

All of the protections of Article 27 are subject to the qualification that Parties to the conflict "may take measures of control and security in regard to protected

---

61. *See* discussion of *levée en masse*, *supra*, note 39. For more on *levée en masse*, *see* DoD Law of War Manual, *supra*, note 14, para. 4.7.

62. GCIV, *supra*, note 13, art. 27.

persons as may be necessary as a result of the war." Thus, restrictions, such as curfews, movement limitations, security screenings, and assembly limitations may be imposed if necessary to ensure the safety of the occupying State's forces.

GCIV provides a number of other key protections that apply in occupied territory,[63] including prohibitions against:

- Use of protected persons to shield a point or area immune from military operations (GCIV Art. 28);
- Physical or moral coercion, in particular to obtain information from protected persons or third parties (GCIV Art. 31);
- Any measure by a Party of a character to cause the physical suffering or extermination of protected persons in the hands of a Party, including murder, torture, corporal punishment, mutilation, medical or scientific experiments not required for medical treatment of the protected person, and any other measure of brutality by civilian or military agents (GCIV Art. 32);
- Any punishment for offenses the protected person did not commit, including any collective penalty or measure of intimidation or terrorism (GCIV Art. 33);
- Pillage (GCIV Art. 33);
- Reprisals against protected persons and their property (GCIV Art. 33);
- Taking of hostages (GCIV Art. 34);
- Forcing protected persons to serve in the occupying State's armed or auxiliary forces (GCIV Art. 51);
- Forcing protected persons to work unless they are over 18 years of age, and then only on work that is necessary either for the needs of the army of occupation, for the public utility services, or for the feeding, sheltering, clothing, transportation, or health of the population of the occupied country (GCIV Art. 51);
- Forcing protected persons to undertake any work that would involve them in the obligation of taking part in military operations (GCIV Art. 51); and
- Altering the status of public officials or judges, or in any way applying sanctions to them or taking any measures of coercion or discrimination against them, should they abstain from fulfilling their functions for reasons of conscience (although they may be removed from their duties) (GCIV Art. 54).

Moreover, the occupying State is responsible for the treatment accorded to protected persons by any of its agents, which could include local officials through whom the occupying State exercises its control of the occupied territory.

---

63. These rights are set forth in Section I of Part III of GCIV, and apply to all protected persons under GCIV, who include not only persons in occupied territory, but also citizens of the opposing side in a belligerent's home territory. The specific rules regarding these "enemies in the homeland," which are found in Section II of Part III of GCIV, are beyond the scope of this chapter, but mirror many of the rules applicable to occupied territory.

In addition, Article 30 of GCIV requires that all protected persons be permitted to communicate with countries and organizations that might assist them with respect to their rights under the Convention, including the "Protecting Powers" and the ICRC. Accordingly, under Article 30, the occupying State is required to facilitate visits to protected persons by organizations whose object is to give protected persons "spiritual aid or material relief."

Collectively, these provisions impose significant responsibilities on the occupying State to protect the physical and mental integrity of individual protected persons, and subject the occupying State to considerable oversight from the international community. In a number of respects, the structure established by GCIV parallels basic protections afforded under HRL to the occupying State's own citizens.

VII. Fundamental Obligations of the Occupying Power

A. Ensuring Public Order and Safety

As noted above, Article 43 of 1907 Hague IV embodies the core obligation of the occupying State:

> The authority of the legitimate power having in fact passed into the hands of the occupant, the latter shall take all the measures in his power to restore, and ensure, as far as possible, public order and safety, while respecting, unless absolutely prevented, the laws in force in the country.[64]

This duty to restore "public order and safety"[65] imposes on the occupying State the obligation to assume the responsibilities of government to the extent needed to provide essential security and public services. At the same time, the qualification that this responsibility applies "as far as possible" indicates that limitations resulting from mission, resources, and military necessity may influence the extent of the measures adopted by the occupying State. Included among these limitations is the need to ensure the safety of the forces of the occupying State and its allies. Further, continued operations by the occupying State's forces against the enemy forces may and often will consume significant resources, and there is no obligation to suspend or modify such operations in order to enhance resources devoted to the occupation mission. Thus, the obligation imposed by Article 43 is not absolute, but instead is balanced against the legitimate military

---

64. 1907 Hague IV, *supra*, note 12, art. 43.
65. It has been pointed out by experts that the phrase used in the authentic (and binding) French version of 1907 Hague IV is "*l'ordre et la vie publique*," which can be translated to mean "an even more comprehensive obligation than is indicated by "public order and safety." *See, e.g.*, DINSTEIN, *supra*, note 43, at 89.

considerations of the occupying State. The duty to restore order is discussed in greater detail, *infra*, in Section VIII.

An illustration of this reality occurred during the first Gulf War. According to then-Colonel Walter Huffman, Staff Judge Advocate for the U.S. VII Corps (who later became the Judge Advocate General of the U.S. Army), when hostilities terminated, the Corps commander he advised found himself in control of a small swath of territory in southern Iraq. Although the United States never formally acknowledged that the area was occupied, Colonel Huffman advised the Corps commander that U.S. forces must make all feasible efforts to provide for the security and essential needs of the local population. Because the forces had not necessarily planned to engage in a prolonged occupation, the resources available to accomplish this mission were constrained. Colonel Huffman likened the approach adopted by the Corps commander to an infantryman building a fighting position—start with whatever is available, but continuously improve the position. Such an approach to the challenge of conducting occupation operations was not only consistent with the plain text of Article 43 of 1907 Hague IV, but also manifested good faith on the part of the Corps commander and his legal advisors.[66]

B. Obligations Not Balanced with Military Necessity

While the obligations in Article 43 of 1907 Hague IV are subject to military necessity limitations, there are a number of non-derogable obligations imposed under 1907 Hague IV and GCIV upon the occupying State *vis à vis* the occupied territory and its population, as reflected in the absence of any language regarding military necessity in the text of these provisions. These rules provide the foundation of absolute requirements that an occupying State must comply with, irrespective of dictates of military necessity. Stated differently, the text of these provisions suggests that, under the LOAC, a deviation from these obligations can never be justified by necessity.

An example of such a provision is the prohibition, noted previously, against the use of an occupation in order to annex the occupied territory. Occupation is a temporary condition, whereas annexation is permanent, enabling the annexing State to impose its own sovereign authority over the territory and dispense with occupation obligations. According to the ICRC Commentary:

> [T]he occupation of territory in wartime is essentially a temporary, *de facto* situation, which deprives the occupied Power of neither its statehood nor its sovereignty; it merely interferes with its power to exercise its rights. That is what distinguishes occupation from annexation, whereby the Occupying Power acquires all or part of the occupied territory and incorporates it in its own territory.

---

66. For the Corps Commander's description of Colonel Huffman's advice and its impact, *see* Frederick M. Franks, Jr., *The Fourth Annual Hugh J. Clausen Leadership Lecture: Soldiering Today and Tomorrow*, 158 Mil. L. Rev. 130, 131-133 (Dec. 1998).

Consequently occupation as a result of war, while representing actual possession to all appearances, cannot imply any right whatsoever to dispose of territory. As long as hostilities continue the Occupying Power cannot therefore annex the occupied territory, even if it occupies the whole of the territory concerned. A decision on that point can only be reached in the peace treaty. That is a universally recognized rule which is endorsed by jurists and confirmed by numerous rulings of international and national courts.[67]

Reflecting this point, GCIV Article 47 expressly prohibits an occupying State from using a claim of annexation in order to deny the protections of GCIV to the population of an occupied territory. The ICRC Commentary explains the historical experience that led to the adoption of this treaty provision:

[T]he Second World War provides us with several examples of "anticipated annexation," as a result of unilateral action on the part of the victor to dispose of territory he had occupied. The population of such territories, which often covered a wide area, did not enjoy the benefit of the rules governing occupation, were without the rights and safeguards to which they were legitimately entitled, and were thus subjected to whatever laws or regulations the annexing State wished to promulgate.[68]

This prohibition was reinforced in 1977 in AP I Article 4, which states that "[n]either the occupation of a territory nor the application of the Conventions and this Protocol shall affect the legal status of the territory in question." Although the United States is not a party to AP I, the principle reflected in this provision is undoubtedly a rule of customary law binding on the United States and all other countries.[69]

Reflecting the prohibition on annexation, the law of belligerent occupation generally prohibits an occupying State from making permanent changes to the political system or economic structure of the occupied territory. To the extent that such changes have been implemented in connection with certain interventions (most recently, during the administration of the Coalition Provisional Authority following the invasion of Iraq in 2003), they have been introduced pursuant to alternate legal authority, *e.g.*, a mandate from the United Nations requiring the occupying State to implement political changes in order to facilitate restoration of sovereignty and international peace and security (although, beyond specific deviations that may be authorized by such mandates, the administration of an occupation pursuant to such a mandate still requires compliance with applicable provisions of 1907 Hague IV and GCIV). Further, during long-term periods of occupation, an occupying State may choose to implement changes to the economic structure of the occupied territory (to include infrastructure) in order to enhance the economic situation of the local

---

67. Commentary, Convention IV, *supra*, note 59, at 275.
68. *Id.*
69. Iraq's attempt to annex Kuwait following its invasion of that country in 1990 was rejected by the international community and treated instead as an occupation. *See* S.C. Res. 662, U.N. Doc. S/RES/0662 (Aug. 9, 1990) (in which the UN Security Council declared Iraq's annexation of Kuwait "null and void").

population. For example, the occupying power may modify tariffs and taxation in order to stimulate economic development.[70] These changes will be easier to justify under international law if there is an international mandate that provides greater authority than GCIV provides.

C. Protection of Basic Human Rights

One of the most fundamental obligations of an occupying State is to respect certain fundamental human rights guaranteed to the population under the applicable LOAC treaties. For example, Article 46 of 1907 Hague IV states one basic obligation—that "family honour and rights, the lives of persons, and private property, as well as religious convictions and practice, must be respected"[71]— while GCIV Article 27, quoted *supra*, as well as the other provisions of GCIV listed *supra* in Section VI, Applicable Law, provide an even more comprehensive articulation and protection of human rights. The rights in 1907 Hague IV Article 46 are, in the absence of any military necessity qualification in that article, non-derogable on the basis of military necessity, while, as noted above, the provisions of GCIV Article 27 are subject to "measures of control and security . . . as may be necessary as a result of the war."

D. Protection of Property

State property in occupied territory can be used by the occupying State to defray the costs of the occupation, but the occupying State cannot wantonly destroy such property or convert it to use for the benefit of its home economy. Further, the occupying party is obligated to respect private property. Thus, private property cannot be confiscated[72] nor can it be destroyed except as may be absolutely necessary in connection with military operations.[73] Indeed, "extensive destruction and appropriation of property, not justified by military necessity and carried out unlawfully and wantonly" is considered to be a grave breach of GCIV.[74] Rules related to respect for property, like all other aspects of occupation law, are intended to minimize the disruption of normal functioning of the occupied territory. Accordingly, occupying commanders must ensure that subordinate forces understand their obligations toward private and public property at the initiation of occupation. Failing to do so, risks violation of these obligations by forces more accustomed to permissible destruction of property in enemy territory.

---

70. *See* discussion *infra* in Section XIII, Transformational Occupation: Expanding the Permissible Scope of an Occupation.
71. 1907 Hague IV, *supra*, note 12, art. 46.
72. *Id.*; *see also* DoD Law of War Manual, *supra*, note 14, para. 11.18.2.
73. GCIV, *supra*, note 13, art. 53; *see also* DoD Law of War Manual, *supra*, note 14, para. 11.18.2 (making particular note that it does not matter whether the property is "real (immovable) or personal (movable) property belonging individually or collectively to private persons, to the State of the occupied territory, to other public authorities, or to social or cooperative organizations").
74. GCIV, *supra*, note 13, art. 147.

VIII. Restoring Order

As the terms of Article 43 of 1907 Hague IV suggest, the first responsibility of the occupying State is to restore order and security in the occupied territory. Typically, this will involve ensuring that local police forces continue to enforce law and order, and that water, electricity, and other essential public utilities, as well as medical and fire-fighting services, are restored as soon as possible. The occupying State can provide these services using its own resources, but typically does not have the necessary personnel or expertise for this purpose and, in any case, needs to conserve its manpower to protect its own security and to deal with any continuing resistance. Therefore, in practice, the occupying State often will try to provide these services using the indigenous personnel who provided these services prior to the occupation. Use of such personnel does not require them to swear any type of allegiance to the occupying State, and they need not be utilized should the occupying State determine that such personnel represent a security threat.

A. The Duty of Obedience

The relationship between local public officials and the occupying State reflects the difference between the duty of obedience and the duty of allegiance. While public officials must obey the lawful exercise of authority by the occupying State, they retain their allegiance to their national government. As the ICRC Commentary notes:

> [P]ublic officials and judges act under the superintendence and control of the occupant to whom legal power has passed in actual practice and to whom they, like any other protected person, owe obedience. But this duty of obedience does not cancel out the duty of allegiance which subsists during the period of occupation. The occupation authorities may not, therefore, compel judges or public officials to swear allegiance to them, nor demand that they should exercise their functions or pronounce their decisions and sentences in the name of the Occupying Power. There is not in general any inconsistency between the two ideas, provided that the Occupying Power, in exercising its authority, keeps strictly to the Convention and to other rules governing occupation and that it demands nothing of public officials and judges which might constitute an act of treason towards their country. The position is still, of course, a very delicate one in practice; for it is very difficult to avoid some conflict between these duties. It is for that reason that persons holding public posts are left free to abstain for reasons of conscience. In such cases the Occupying Power cannot hold it against them, nor apply sanctions or take any measures of coercion or discrimination.[75]

The lack of allegiance does not mean that there cannot be cooperation between local officials and the occupying State. Indeed, while it might seem unlikely that public officials would be willing to continue maintaining law and

---

75. Commentary, Convention IV, *supra*, note 59, at 305.

order under the authority of an occupying State, this has in fact been a common feature of occupations throughout modern history. During World War II, for example, German forces in Paris worked alongside members of the French Gendarmerie during the years of German occupation of that city. Similarly, during the German occupation of the Channel Islands in World War II, local British authorities continued to function and during the occupation of Japan after World War II, Japanese authorities worked under the control of Allied authorities.

B. Use of Existing Personnel to Continue Public Services

To facilitate the efficient maintenance of public services, GCIV Article 51 explicitly excludes individuals over 18 years of age who are needed "for the public utility services, or for the feeding, sheltering, clothing, transportation or health of the population of the occupied country" from the general prohibition against forcing the population of the occupied territory to work for the occupying State. However, these individuals can only be required to work in the occupied territory and so far as possible, at their usual place of work. They must be paid a fair wage and working conditions must be consistent with the occupied country's labor legislation.

One challenging area for an occupying State is restoring police and fire services. Often, the people employed by these services are prepared to remain on the job even during an invasion, but the quasi-military nature of their organizations as well as the fact that they may be armed can pose a dilemma for an occupying State. 1907 Hague IV and GCIV are silent concerning these types of personnel, although clearly the obligation of an occupying State to ensure public order and safety under Article 43 of 1907 Hague IV envisions that the occupying State could turn to local police and fire services to meet this obligation. Thus, how it implements that obligation is a matter of discretion for the occupying State and will depend on its perception of the security challenges it faces, and importantly, its available resources.[76]

AP I requires that parties to a conflict respect and protect civilian "civil defence" organizations and their personnel, meaning that they are not to be targeted and are to be allowed to perform their civil defense functions except in cases of "imperative military necessity."[77] Article 63 of AP I requires that, in occupied territories, civil defense organizations receive from the occupying State the facilities necessary for the performance of their tasks, and it specifically prohibits the occupying State from compelling these organizations to perform activities that would interfere with the performance of their primary tasks. The occupying State is not permitted to make any changes to these orga-

---

76. The ICRC Commentary to GCIV indicates that an occupying State has the right to compel civilian police to remain on the job, as long as they are not used in connection with military operations, such as actions against forces resisting the occupation. Commentary, Convention IV, *supra*, note 59, at 307.

77. AP I, *supra*, note 14, art. 62.

nizations that would jeopardize the efficient performance of their mission nor can it force these organizations to give priority to the nationals or interests of the occupying State. There appears to be no prohibition against compelling civil defense organizations to perform their functions, so long as they are not compelled, coerced, or induced to perform their tasks in any manner prejudicial to the interests of the civilian population.[78]

The term "civil defense" is broadly defined to include "humanitarian tasks intended to protect the civilian population against dangers, and to help it to recover from the immediate effects, of hostilities or disasters and also to provide the conditions necessary for its survival." It defines these tasks as:

(a) warning;
(b) evacuation;
(c) management of shelters;
(d) management of blackout measures;
(e) rescue;
(f) medical services, including first aid, and religious assistance;
(g) fire-fighting;
(h) detection and marking of danger areas;
(i) decontamination and similar protective measures;
(j) provision of emergency accommodation and supplies;
(k) emergency assistance in the restoration and maintenance of order in distressed areas;
(l) emergency repair of indispensable public utilities;
(m) emergency disposal of the dead;
(n) assistance in the preservation of objects essential for survival; and
(o) complementary activities necessary to carry out any of the tasks mentioned above, including, but not limited to, planning and organization.[79]

Police and public security functions, such as operating correctional facilities, are not listed and the ICRC's Commentary indicates that the definition of civil defense organizations was intended to exclude civilian police.[80] This does not mean that civilian police and public security personnel can be targeted.[81]

Civil defense organizations could be targeted or detained if they participate in hostilities against the occupying State, or commit, or used to commit, acts harmful to the enemy but AP I provides that the following shall not be considered as harmful acts:

---

78. Commentary on the Additional Protocols of 8 June 1977 to the Geneva Conventions of 12 August 1949, para. 2504 (Yves Sandoz et al., eds., 1987) (hereinafter AP I Commentary).
79. *Id.* para. 2389; *see also* AP I, *supra,* note 14, art. 63.
80. AP I Commentary, *supra,* note 68, para. 2389.
81. AP I, *supra,* note 14, art. 67(4). Note that the protection afforded by AP I is generally for civilians performing civil defense functions. Military personnel and military units generally fall within the definition of combatants, and therefore are targetable as such. However, AP I does provide for protection of military personnel and units who are assigned to civilian civil defense organizations and only perform civil defense functions. *Id.* art. 67(1). If captured, they are treated as prisoners of war, just like other soldiers. But, in occupied territory, they can be required to perform their civil defense functions so long as their tasks are not dangerous; if they are dangerous, they must volunteer. *Id.*

(a) that civil defense tasks are carried out under the direction or control of military authorities;
(b) that civilian civil defense personnel co-operate with military personnel in the performance of civil defense tasks, or that some military personnel are attached to civilian civil defense organizations; [or]
(c) that the performance of civil defense tasks may incidentally benefit military victims, particularly those who are hors de combat.[82]

An occupying State may disarm civilian civil defense organizations for reasons of security. However, the fact that civilian civil defense personnel bear light individual weapons for the purpose of maintaining order or for self-defense also is not considered a harmful act under AP I.[83]

Like civilian civil defense personnel, civilian police may continue to bear arms in order to perform their law enforcement function without losing their protection as civilians. Thus, an occupying State could choose to employ the civilian police or public security forces in implementing its obligation to restore public order and safety. Whether or not it chooses to do so would be a matter of discretion by the occupying State based on the facts prevailing on the ground.

IX. Addressing Threats to Security

A. Preventive Detention

As noted above, inhabitants of the occupied territory owe a duty of obedience to the occupying State. However, it would be naïve to expect all inhabitants to strictly comply with this obligation. In recognition of this reality, the LOAC allows the occupying State to take measures necessary to protect the security of its forces. Included among these measures is a form of preventive security detention known as internment, which is similar in most respects to the detention of prisoners of war. Internment is considered the most extreme deprivation of liberty for security purposes, and therefore may only be used when lesser forms of restraint would be ineffective, although if necessary, internment may be imposed for the duration of the occupation, subject to periodic review decribed below. In all cases, however, under GCIV Article 78, internment is only authorized "for imperative reasons of security."

A lesser form of detention is "assigned residence," which is similar to house arrest. GCIV does not define the term "assigned residence." According to the ICRC Commentary, it refers to forcing the protected person to live in a location away from his or her normal domicile where supervision is more easily

---

82. Further, even if they engage in harmful acts, they should not be targeted unless they are first given a warning to stop, and, after a reasonable time period, fail to heed the warning. *Id.* art. 65(1).
83. AP I indicates that, in order to distinguish them from combatants, civil defense personnel should be limited to carrying handguns, such as pistols or revolvers, and in any case, once recognized as civilian civil defense personnel, they should be respected and protected. *Id.* art. 65(3).

exercised for as long as the circumstances motivating such action continue to exist.[84] Internment is also a form of assigned residence, since internees are detained in a place other than their normal place of residence, but internment is a more severe deprivation of liberty, as it generally implies an obligation to live in a camp with other internees. Like internment, however, assigned residence is only supposed to be used when imperatively required for "reasons of security."

Neither internment nor assigned residence are intended to be punitive in nature, and therefore military legal advisors must ensure that commanders do not use either type of detention as a subterfuge to impose a punishment. The only legitimate use of these deprivations of liberty is to protect the occupying State from future threats to its security. In contrast, punitive incarceration may only be imposed pursuant to a conviction for violating the laws of the occupied territory, including violations of the rules established by the occupying State that are committed after those rules have been announced to the population in the occupied territory (see discussion, *infra*, in Section XI, Governing the Occupied Territory).

B. Procedural Requirements for Detention

GCIV Article 78 is a critical provision of the Convention, for it establishes the legal framework for imposing preventive detention measures. It provides that any decision to place a protected person in assigned residence or internment may only be made according to a regular procedure prescribed by the occupying State in accordance with the provisions of GCIV, that includes a right to appeal. Most importantly, if a decision is made to place a protected person in assigned residence or internment, the decision must be reviewed, if possible every six months, by a competent body set up by the occupying State.

Article 78 does not detail the process required for implementing a preventive detention regime. However, it is clear that at a minimum, the detainee must be provided notice of the basis for detention and a hearing before an impartial decision maker. This obviously provides occupying States with a certain amount of discretion in formulating the procedures for security detentions, and the United States has exercised this discretion in the form of Army Regulation 190-8 (AR 190-8) establishing these procedures. Although the Secretary of Defense has designated the U.S. Army as the executive agent for detentions by U.S. armed forces, this regulation is considered a "joint service" regulation, meaning that its provisions apply to detention operations conducted by any of the U.S. military services.

AR 190-8 is best understood as an attempt by the U.S. government to provide reasonable procedures for U.S. forces seeking to exercise detention authority in an armed conflict. It implements and supplements U.S. obligations with respect to detention under the LOAC and may add to (but not subtract from) the rights of detainees under international law.

---

84. Commentary, Conventiion IV, *supra*, note 59, at 256.

AR 190-8 permits an individual civilian to be ordered into internment in connection with an armed conflict or belligerent occupation only in the following circumstances:

(a) An internment order for imperative security reasons authenticated by a responsible commissioned officer of the United States Military specifically delegated such authority by the theater commander; or
(b) An order of an authorized commander approving and ordering into execution a sentence to internment pronounced by a properly constituted U.S. military court sitting in the occupied territory.[85]

An individual civilian who is interned for imperative security reasons (circumstance (a) quoted above) is accorded the right to appeal the order directing his or her internment to a board of officers.[86] If the appeal is denied, the internment should be reviewed again every six months, consistent with GCIV Article 78.

C. Treatment Standards for Internment

Once a civilian in occupied territory is subjected to any type of detention, including but not limited to assigned residence or internment, treatment standards become the predominant operational concern for the forces of the occupying State who will implement the detention. Under GCIV, all detainees in an occupation must be treated humanely, irrespective of the nature of detention, duration, justification, or status of the detainee. This humane treatment standard is reinforced by Article 75 of AP I which the Obama administration announced in 2011 reflects principles that the United States applies "out of a sense of legal obligation" to any person detained in an international armed conflict.[87] Article 75 requires the humane treatment of all persons detained in connection with an international armed conflict, including, but not limited to, detainees in an occupation. Article 75 explicitly mandates protection from physical and mental abuse, and also requires fundamental due process both with respect to the decision to detain and the prosecution of any charges against the detainee.

---

85. U.S. Dep't of Army, Army Regulation 190-8: Enemy Prisoners of War, Retained Personnel, Civilian Internees and Other Detainees (Oct. 1, 1997), para. 5-1c. The provisions of AR 190-8 discussed in this Chapter relate to "civilian internees" (defined in the regulation as "[a] civilian who is interned armed conflict or occupation for security reasons or for protection or because he has committed an offense against the detaining power") and not the internment of combatants subject to GPW. Implementation of U.S. legal obligations with respect to prisoners of war protected by GPW are covered by other provisions of AR 190-8. An internee can also request "compassionate internment" of his or her dependent children if they otherwise would be without parental care. *Id.* para. 5-1d.

86. *Id.* para. 5-1g (Appeals will be decided only on the grounds of the existence or nonexistence of imperative security.)

87. White House Office of the Press Secretary, Fact Sheet: New Actions on Guantanamo and Detainee Policy (Mar. 7, 2011), *available at* http://www.whitehouse.gov/thepress-office/2011/03/07/new-actions-guantanamo-bay-and-detainee-policy.

While more comprehensive treatment obligations apply to interned "protected persons" in an occupation, Article 75 makes clear that this does not justify deviating from the humane treatment standard for detainees who do not qualify for protected person status. Further, even if a distinction could be made on legal grounds, many of the treatment standards applicable only to protected persons under applicable LOAC treaties nonetheless may be extended to other detainees as a matter of national policy by the occupying State. Applying the same standard universally not only bolsters the perception that the detaining State is committed to humane treatment of detainees but also reduces uncertainty among detaining forces about which treatment standards apply to detainees. However, whenever such universal standards are applied, the lawyers advising the occupying State must ensure that the universal standard, never fall below the standards required by applicable treaties.

GCIV's treatment standards for individuals being held in internment are quite protective. These standards include:

- Protection of health and hygiene, with proper medical attention and monthly health inspections (GCIV Art. 81);
- Adequate housing, with proper heating and ventilation, blankets and bedding, and sanitation facilities, and separate quarters and facilities for men and women (with the exception of family quarters) (GCIV Art. 82 and 85);
- Adequate food and clothing, with canteens for purchase of foodstuffs and personal articles for everyday use and consumption at local market prices (GCIV Art. 87 and 89);
- Protection from air raids and other hazards of war, and protection against fire (GCIV Art. 88);
- "Complete latitude" in the exercise of religion and assistance from religious ministers to the extent available (GCIV Art. 93);
- Opportunities for intellectual, educational, and recreational pursuits, including sports and games (GCIV Art. 94);
- Paid employment if internees desire (medical personnel may be compelled to perform tasks in their professional capacity on behalf of other internees, while other internees can be detailed to perform administrative and maintenance tasks or to work in kitchens or other domestic tasks, in the places of internment, or to undertake duties to protect other internees, as long as they are physically suited for the work.) (GCIV Art. 95);
- The right to keep personal property (or, in the case of valuables, to have it held in accordance with an established procedure, subject to return upon release and a right to keep a certain amount of money to make purchases) (GCIV Art. 97);
- Money to pay for their personal items and the right to receive allowances from their home country or other outside sources (GCIV Art. 98);
- A right to send and receive correspondence and relief packages, to receive visitors and communicate with representatives of the ICRC, other humanitarian organizations, and the Protecting Power (if there is one) to

execute legal documents, such as wills, to otherwise manage their affairs and property, and to prevent the internee from being prejudiced in any court involving the internee (GCIV Arts. 106-116; 142-143).

Pursuant to GCIV Article 84, internees are also to be held separately from prisoners of war and from persons, such as those accused or convicted of crimes, who are deprived of liberty for reasons other than internment under the law of belligerent occupation.

While many of the rights of an internee are similar to those of a prisoner of war (POW) under GPW there are significant differences. For example, unlike a POW under the GPW, an internee under GCIV is permitted to be interned with his or her family if he or she has one. In addition, POWs are usually interned far from the battlefield and can be transported and detained in the home territory of the capturing State as a measure of ensuring that they do not return to the battle. In contrast, internees (as well as protected persons placed in assigned residence) must be detained in the occupied territory.[88] In fact, it may be considered a grave breach of GCIV to deport a civilian internee outside his national territory.[89]

Like POWs, civilian internees under the provisions of GCIV are presumptively entitled to communicate with individuals and organizations outside the place of internment.[90] However, GCIV Article 5 qualifies this right by providing that an occupying State may suspend a protected person's "rights of communication." Such suspension is justified only if the protected person is detained for security reasons as a spy, or saboteur, or is "definitely suspected of" or engaged in activity hostile to the security of the occupying State. The scope of these rights of communication is not well defined in GCIV, but appears to refer to suspension of a protected person's rights to communicate with the outside world, including possibly communication with the ICRC.[91] It also may imply a right to hold the detained person separately from other detainees in light of the security risk.

If the detainee is a protected person who has taken part in hostilities against the occupying State but is not entitled to POW status, Article 45 of AP I would prohibit suspension of the right to communication unless the person is being detained as a spy. However, because it is unclear whether this provision is binding as a matter of CIL on States, such as the United States, that have not signed AP I, it is unlikely such a non-signatory occupying State would agree that it cannot limit communications by such a detainee if the State believed the communications would compromise the security of its forces.

One issue intertwined with access to communication is notice of internment. As a general rule, any time a party to a conflict detains a protected person,

---

88. GCIV, *supra*, note 13, art. 49.
89. *Id.* art. 147 ("unlawful deportation or transfer or unlawful confinement of a protected person").
90. *See, e.g., id.* art. 107.
91. *See id.* art. 30. The ICRC Commentary notes the right of communication "may be suspended if seriousness of the circumstances so demands." ICRC Commentary, *supra*, note 59 at 214 (citing GC IV Article 5).

notice will be provided either to an official information bureau established by the detaining State, and the bureau will then notify a central agency established to maintain records of internment of protected persons (such as POWs, retained personnel, and civilian internees), or at a minimum, the ICRC. Article 136 of GCIV requires that the reporting to the national bureau take place within "the shortest possible period" and Article 137 requires the national bureau to report to the central agency "immediately."

GCIV articles governing reporting make no exception for internees whose access to communication is suspended for security reasons, and therefore there seems to be no legal basis to detain a protected person without providing notice in the required timeframe based on security concerns. Whether this same rule extends to detainees who are not protected persons is a more complicated question. It may be argued that notice of detention is an element of humane treatment. Such notice essentially makes the detaining State accountable for the disposition of the detainee at some future date, and therefore not only serves as an important check on potential abuse, but also reduces the detainee's sense of vulnerability or helplessness. However, failure to provide such notice is not included in the lists of specifically prohibited conduct in the core provisions of the LOAC dealing with humane treatment, such as common Article 3 of the Geneva Conventions or Article 75 of AP I, leading to a possible argument that secret detention as such is not *per se* inhumane. Nonetheless, the perception of impunity associated with secret detentions suggests that at the very least the decision to withhold notice of detention for any detainee should be made only after clearance by the most senior leadership of the detaining State.

All other rights, including the right to humane treatment and to a "fair and regular trial," enjoyed by protected persons under GCIV and AP I (for States who are party to AP I) remain applicable regardless of why the protected person was detained. Further, under Article 5 of GCIV, any rights of a protected person under GCIV that are suspended (such as the right to communication) must be restored at the earliest possible date consistent with the security interests of the occupying State.

D. Assigned Residence

None of the LOAC treaties detail the specific conditions of treatment for assigned residence, other than the requirement under GCIV Articles 39 and 78 that if a protected person is placed in assigned residence, and as a result is unable to support him- or herself (especially if assigned residence is imposed for reasons of security) because he or she is unable to find paid employment on reasonable conditions, the occupying State must ensure his or her support and that of his or her dependents. Presumably, however, assigned residence at least must meet the standards applicable to internment.[92]

---

92. The ICRC Commentary describes assigned residence as a less serious measure than internment. Commentary, Convention IV, *supra*, note 59, at 256.

E. Generally Applicable Treatment Standards

The comprehensive protections afforded to protected persons who are detained in the occupied territory may be viewed as disadvantageous to an occupying State, and consequently the occupying State may seek to find a basis to deny protected person characterization to a detainee. For example, a protected person may not be deported from the occupied territory, is subject to internment only as a measure of last resort, is afforded substantial procedural protections in relation to the internment decision, and is granted broad access to communication with the outside world. All of these rights may be perceived as problematic by an occupying commander contending with the ongoing threat of guerillas and other individuals who engage in hostilities against occupation forces but do not qualify for POW status (and hence would not be protected by the GPW (although, as noted below, they would be protected by Article 75 of AP I if the conflict is an international armed conflict under the LOAC and, in non-international armed conflicts, by common Article 3 of the 1949 Geneva Conventions and other treaty law and CIL applicable to non-international armed conflict)), especially when these individuals enter the occupied territory for the specific purpose of carrying on combat activities against the occupying State.

While the definition of protected person is intentionally broad to ensure the widest possible application, it would seem counterintuitive that persons who intentionally come to the occupied territory to engage in hostilities would be granted treatment equal or better than the treatment granted belligerents who are protected by GPW. Accordingly, arguments have been made that persons who infiltrate from other countries for the purpose of carrying on hostilities in the occupied territory should not qualify as protected persons because they do not "find themselves" in the hands of the occupying State. These arguments are controversial, particularly where they could lead to the conclusion that when detained, such individuals (who also fail to qualify for POW status and protections), fall outside of any LOAC treaty protection (other than Article 75 of AP I, where the detaining State has ratified that treaty or considers it to be CIL).

This "outside the law" problem may have been eliminated in U.S. operational practice by the Obama administration's pronouncement that the United States considers that the principles of Article 75 of AP I reflect binding legal obligations of the United States in an international armed conflict.[93] While there are other States also not bound by AP I, the Obama administration's announcement makes it more difficult for other nations to continue to hold to a position that all or part of Article 75 is not legally binding as CIL in an international armed conflict, thereby depriving them of an argument that there is no law applicable to combatants not protected by GPW who are directly participating in an international armed conflict.

---

93. *See supra,* note 87 and accompanying text.

F. Prohibited Treatment

One generally prohibited security measure is the deportation or forcible movement of protected persons, either collectively or individually, from the occupied territory.[94] However, the occupying State may order a total or partial evacuation of the occupied territory, if required for the security of the population or for "imperative reasons of military security," but persons who are evacuated have to be transferred back to their homes as soon as hostilities in the area have ceased. Further, when evacuating an area, the occupying State must ensure, to the greatest practicable extent, that the evacuees are provided proper accommodation, including satisfactory conditions of hygiene, health, safety, and nutrition, and that family members are not separated. In addition, the Protecting Power (*see* below) must be informed of the transfers and evacuations as soon as they take place.[95] Importantly, GCIV prohibits an occupying State from deporting or transferring parts of its own civilian population into the occupied territory.[96]

X. Meeting the Needs of the Civilian Population of the Occupied Territory

1907 Hague IV is silent on the specific obligations of the occupying State with respect to restoring public services, although arguably this obligation is implied in the requirement in Article 43 of 1907 Hague IV to "to restore, and ensure, as far as possible, public order and safety." Both GCIV and AP I contain a number of provisions intended to ensure that the civilian population has adequate food and medical supplies; the continued functioning of civilian medical and hospital establishments and services (with the cooperation of local and national authorities); the maintenance of public health and hygiene; and the continued provision of civilian medical services.[97] GCIV is supplemented by Article 69 of AP I, which obligates the occupying State to ensure "to the fullest extent available to it and without any adverse distinction" the provision of clothing, bedding, means of shelter, and other supplies essential to the survival of the civilian population, as well as objects necessary for religious worship.

In order to carry out these obligations with respect to the population of the occupied territory, the LOAC imposes both constraints and obligations on the occupying State. These protections are in addition to the general protections afforded civilians by the LOAC during military operations. For example, the

---

94. GCIV, *supra*, note 13, art. 49. On the other hand, protected persons who are not nationals of the occupied territory are permitted to voluntarily leave the occupied territory under a procedure to be established by the occupying State to consider requests to depart. *Id.* art. 48.
95. *Id.* art. 49.
96. *Id.*
97. *See, e.g.,* AP I, *supra*, note 14, art. 54, 69; GCIV, *supra*, note 13, art. 55, 56.

prohibition against using starvation of civilians as a method of warfare would continue to apply to the conduct of the occupation.[98]

The LOAC limits the authority of the occupying State to requisition for its own needs civilian medical and food supplies, and civilian medical units or their equipment or material, or the services of civilian medical personnel, if the needs of the civilian population would not be met as a result.[99] These limits circumscribe the broad authority granted to the occupying State under 1907 Hague IV to make use of property in the occupied territory (discussed *infra* in Section XII, Managing the Property of the Occupied Territory).

In addition to imposing limits on what the occupying State can requisition, the LOAC imposes affirmative obligations upon the occupying State to meet basic needs of the population. For example, Article 15 of AP I requires that:

> The Occupying Power shall afford civilian medical personnel in occupied territories every assistance to enable them to perform, to the best of their ability, their humanitarian functions. The Occupying Power may not require that, in the performance of those functions, such personnel shall give priority to the treatment of any person except on medical grounds. They shall not be compelled to carry out tasks which are not compatible with their humanitarian mission.[100]

As the first sentence of Article 15 indicates, some affirmative obligations are not absolute, but are qualified by recognition that they extend only to the best of the occupying State's ability. This language reinforces the overall pragmatic conception of the many occupation obligations that depend upon the resources of the occupying State. For example, under the first paragraph of GCIV Article 55:

> *To the fullest extent of the means available to it*, the Occupying Power has the duty of ensuring the food and medical supplies of the population; it should, in particular, bring in the necessary foodstuffs, medical stores and other articles if the resources of the occupied territory are inadequate.[101]

Accordingly, the tangible result of the obligation in a particular circumstance may differ depending upon the resources available to the occupying State. This does not automatically mean that a resource-rich State would be expected to provide more in the territories it occupies than an occupying State that has fewer resources. Rather, even the resource-rich State may be limited in its ability to provide resources in support of occupation obligations as the result of other demands. Further, a resource-limited occupying State may have an abundance of a particular resource necessary to enhance the situation of the occupied territory in some but not all respects (for example, a country might be able to provide robust medical support resources, but not fuel or food).

---

98. AP I, *supra*, note 14, art. 54(1).
99. *See* GCIV, *supra*, note 13, art. 55(2), 57; AP I, *supra*, note 14, art. 14.
100. In addition, pursuant to Article 18 of AP I, if fighting is continuing to take place in the occupied territory, the occupying State is obligated to provide civilian medical personnel and civilian religious personnel with a distinctive emblem and an identity card certifying their status, to ensure they are distinguishable from military personnel.
101. GCIV, *supra*, note 13, art. 27 (emphasis added).

X. Meeting the Needs of the Civilian Population of the Occupied Territory

To mitigate the effect that resource constraints could have on an occupying State's ability to meet the population's needs, the LOAC obligates the occupying State to endeavor to permit relief to be provided by outside sources, such as neutral States, international organizations, or even the authorities of the government that has been displaced by the occupying State, in cases where the population is inadequately supplied. If such relief is permitted, the occupying State is prohibited from diverting the shipments from their intended purpose, except where urgently necessary in the interests of the civilian population of the occupied territory. The occupying State can, however, impose reasonable regulations and procedures to ensure that relief is provided in an orderly manner, reaches the intended beneficiaries, and does not threaten the occupying State's security. This often involves inspecting relief supplies, and establishing strict transport and distribution protocols.[102]

GCIV also includes provisions to protect especially vulnerable groups in the civilian population, irrespective of whether they qualify as protected persons. For example, children (and particularly children adversely affected by hostilities) and certain mothers of children benefit from special protection in occupied territories under Article 50:

> The Occupying Power shall, with the cooperation of the national and local authorities, facilitate the proper working of all institutions devoted to the care and education of children.
>
> The Occupying Power shall take all necessary steps to facilitate the identification of children and the registration of their parentage. It may not, in any case, change their personal status, nor enlist them in formations or organizations subordinate to it.
>
> Should the local institutions be inadequate for the purpose, the Occupying Power shall make arrangements for the maintenance and education, if possible by persons of their own nationality, language and religion, of children who are orphaned or separated from their parents as a result of the war and who cannot be adequately cared for by a near relative or friend.
>
> A special section of the Bureau set up in accordance with Article 136 shall be responsible for taking all necessary steps to identify children whose identity is in doubt. Particulars of their parents or other near relatives should always be recorded if available.
>
> The Occupying Power shall not hinder the application of any preferential measures in regard to food, medical care and protection against the effects of war which may have been adopted prior to the occupation in favour of children under fifteen years, expectant mothers, and mothers of children under seven years.[103]

GCIV also includes provisions to enhance the spiritual assistance to the population of the occupied territory. Specifically, pursuant to Article 58, the occupying State "shall permit ministers of religion to give spiritual assistance

---

102. Relief shipments (which may be for the benefit of the general population or sent to specific individuals or groups) are covered in GCIV Articles 59-62 and 108-111, and Article 71 of AP I.

103. GCIV, *supra*, note 13, art. 50.

to the members of their religious communities" and "shall also accept consignments of books and articles required for religious needs and shall facilitate their distribution in occupied territory." These obligations are in addition to the special protections of religious practices afforded to detainees interned by the occupying State under the terms of GCIV.[104]

XI. Governing the Occupied Territory

In order to facilitate execution of its obligation under Article 43 of 1907 Hague IV to "restore, and ensure, as far as possible, public order and safety," the LOAC authorizes the occupying State to exercise a wide range of executive, legislative, and judicial authorities. However, consistent with the notion that the occupying State's control is only temporary, these powers are limited to what is necessary under the circumstances to fulfill the occupying State's military objectives (including execution of occupation obligations) while discharging the duties imposed by the LOAC with respect to protection of the population.

Consistent with these limitations, Article 43 of 1907 Hague IV provides that the occupying State is obligated to respect "unless absolutely prevented, the laws in force in the country." Similarly, GCIV Article 64 provides that the "penal laws of the occupied territory shall remain in force" except where the occupying State repeals them "where they constitute a threat to its security or an obstacle to the application of the present Convention [*i.e.*, GCIV]." Article 64 allows for the occupied territory's "tribunals" (*e.g.*, courts) to remain in place for "the effective administration of justice," albeit subject to the occupying State's security requirements and the need to eliminate any obstacle to implementing requirements of GCIV and to "the necessity of ensuring the effective administration of justice."

An occupying State may and normally will rely upon the local courts (to include judges) to enforce local laws, including those that prohibit common crimes such as murder, rape, and robbery. However, the occupying State may make changes to eliminate or suspend laws that violate the fundamental rights of the population guaranteed by GCIV and rules and procedures that may be inconsistent with minimum standards of due process.

Judges are not obligated to continue to serve if they believe, for reasons of conscience, that they cannot continue, nor can they be punished by the occupying State for making that choice. On the other hand, the occupying State is permitted to remove judges from their posts if it so wishes and can appoint other judges to replace them.[105] It may also appoint judges to replace those who leave the territory, retire, or die. In any case, judges who continue to serve must be

---

104. *See* GCIV, *supra*, note 13, art. 93.
105. DoD LAW OF WAR MANUAL, *supra*, note 14, para. 11.21 ("to prevent them from undermining the Occupying Power's administration" but not as a "measure[] of coercion or discrimination against them, should they abstain from fulfilling their functions for reasons of conscience.").

permitted to reach decisions independently, without coercion from the occupying State.[106]

An occupying State can promulgate penal laws and regulations to the extent "essential to enable the occupying power to fulfil its obligation under the present Convention [*i.e.*, GCIV], to maintain the orderly government of the territory, and to ensure the security of the occupying power, of the members and property of the occupying forces or administration, and likewise of the establishments and lines of communication used by them."[107] Thus, the occupying State can impose curfews and other restrictions if required for reasons of security, and can adopt laws that punish offenses against the occupying State's forces. However, any penal law or regulation adopted by the occupying State cannot be enforced until it is first published and brought to the knowledge of the population, in their own language.[108]

The occupying State may enforce this newly imposed penal law in its own "non-political military courts" provided that these courts are "properly constituted" and they sit in the occupied territory.[109] These are military courts, and thus the members of these courts would be members of the occupying State's military forces.[110] Courts to hear appeals from these military courts need not sit in the occupied territory, although "preferably" this would be the case.[111]

Military courts were used extensively by Israel in its occupation administration of the West Bank and Gaza, but it has been U.S. practice to rely on local courts. According to FM 27-10:

> The ordinary courts of justice should be suspended only if:
>   *a.* Judges and magistrates abstain from fulfilling their functions . . . ; or
>   *b.* The courts are corrupt or unfairly constituted; or
>   *c.* Local judicial administration has collapsed during the hostilities preceding the occupation and the occupant must set up its own courts to ensure that offenses against the local laws are properly tried.[112]

In the event that military courts are used, GCIV requires the procedure followed to provide for a "regular trial," including the rights of the accused to be informed of the particulars of the charges against him, to present evidence and call witnesses, to be assisted by qualified counsel of the accused's choosing (or to have one appointed), to receive the aid of an interpreter (both during the preliminary investigation and the trial), as to appeal a conviction and to seek a pardon or reprieve before the death penalty can be imposed. Importantly, the "Protecting Power" (discussed *supra*) may attend and assist in the proceedings

---

106. *Id.*; *see, generally* Commentary, Convention IV, *supra*, note 59, at 303-08.
107. *Id.*
108. *Id.* at 338-39.
109. *Id.* at 339-41.
110. In U.S. practice, these would be "provost courts," although such courts have not been used in recent conflicts. Eugene R. Fidell et al., *Military Commission Law*, Dec. 2005, ARMY LAW. 47, 50.
111. GCIV, *supra*, note 13, art. 66.
112. FM 27-10, *supra*, note 17, para. 373.

and must be notified of any penalty of death or imprisonment for two or more years. The death penalty may not be carried out until at least six months after notification to the Protecting Power, although with notice to the Protecting Power, this can be reduced in the event of "circumstances of grave emergency involving an organized threat to the security" of the occupying State or its forces.[113]

GCIV Article 67 provides that a protected person may only be prosecuted for violations of laws that were applicable prior to the offense, and that the provisions of law enforced must comply with "general principles of law, in particular the principle that the penalty shall be proportionate to the offense." The ICRC Commentary to this provision emphasizes that it ensures compliance with the general principle of *nulla poena sine lege*, which is a fundamental principle of international human rights law that bars punishment for an ex post facto law (*i.e.*, a law that criminalizes or punishes retroactively, and therefore would apply to any individual, even if the defendant did not qualify as a protected person).[114] However, the express terms of Article 67 do not limit its scope to only ex post facto offenses. Accordingly, this provision could also be invoked to prohibit prosecution for a law that existed at the time of the offense if it were determined the law was inconsistent with principles of HRL (for example, a discriminatory penal provision).

Article 68 of GCIV provides that offenses against the occupying State that (1) do not constitute attempts on life or limb of members of occupying forces, (2) do not pose a grave collective danger, or (3) do not seriously damage property of the occupying forces, should only be punished with internment or "simple confinement" and that the duration of the sentence should be "proportionate" to the offense committed. Of course, this does not preclude the imposition of fines and other penalties not involving deprivation of liberty.[115]

One clear objective of GCIV is to ensure that the death penalty is not imposed for comparatively minor offenses. Indeed, Article 68 provides that the death penalty may be imposed "only in cases where the person is guilty of espionage, of serious acts of sabotage against the military installations of the Occupying Power or of intentional offences which have caused the death of one or more persons, provided that such offences were punishable by death under the law of the occupied territory in force before the occupation began."[116] Further, before the death penalty is imposed, the attention of the court must be

---

113. See GCIV, *supra*, note 13, art. 71-75.
114. Commentary, Convention IV, *supra*, note 59, at 341. Consistent with this principle, an occupying State cannot arrest, prosecute, or convict any protected person for acts committed or opinions expressed prior to the occupation or during a temporary interruption of the occupation, unless those acts constitute breaches of the laws and customs of war. GCIV, *supra*, note 13, art. 70. While GCIV is not clear on this point, this would not appear to preclude the prosecution by local courts of common crimes committed prior to the occupation, as these are left to the ordinary jurisdiction of local courts. *See* FM 27-10, *supra*, note 17, para. 370.
115. *Id.* para. 438.
116. GCIV, *supra*, note 13, art. 68. The United States made a reservation to this qualification, and reserves the right to impose the death penalty for offenses that were not punishable by death under the law of the occupied territory.

drawn to the fact that the accused is not a national of the occupying State and does not owe it a duty of allegiance, and in any case, the death penalty cannot be imposed on a protected person under 18 years at the time of the offense.

In the event a protected person accused of offenses is detained or convicted, GCIV requires that he or she be held in the occupied territory and serve his or her sentence there. Individuals serving a sentence to confinement are to be separated "if possible" from other detainees (including security internees). Further, GCIV includes various guarantees regarding humane treatment, including the obligation to provide adequate food, hygiene, medical care, and spiritual assistance. Women and minors will receive appropriate special treatment, and all have the right to receive at least one monthly relief parcel as well as periodic visits by the Protecting Power and the ICRC.[117] Any time spent in confinement pending trial or punishment must be credited against any sentence imposed.[118]

The foregoing requirements explicitly apply to the proceedings and sentences imposed by any military courts established by the occupying State. However, there is no compelling reason why these obligations also should not extend to proceedings and sentences imposed by local courts operating under the overall authority of the occupying State. Further, because any individual subject to trial and punishment must be treated humanely, it would be difficult to deny extension of these protections to all defendants, even those not qualified as protected persons.

XII. Managing the Property of the Occupied Territory

While in control of the occupied territory, the occupying State is authorized to use property of the displaced national government for military purposes (including to prevent its use by hostile forces) and to support fulfilling its occupation obligations. This authority over moveable (*i.e.*, personal) property is derived from provisions in Article 53 of 1907 Hague IV that allow the occupying State to take the property for use in "operations of the war." With respect to immovable property (*e.g.*, real property), Article 55 of 1907 Hague IV provides that the occupying State only has a right to use such property as "administrator and usufructary." Given these qualifications, there are no longer "spoils of war" *per se*. Any use that does not fit these qualifications or violates other provisions of the LOAC could well be treated as a war crime.[119]

The LOAC includes some general rules and principles that protect property in any area of the battle-space, including occupied territory. For example, Article 23(g) of 1907 Hague IV establishes the general rule that a belligerent may not

---

117. These conditions of confinement are detailed in GCIV Article 76.
118. *Id.* art. 69.
119. Indeed, "extensive destruction and appropriation of property, not justified by military necessity and carried out unlawfully and wantonly" is a grave breach of GCIV under GCIV Article 147.

destroy or seize any private or public enemy property, "except as imperatively demanded by the necessities of war." This principle applies at all times in armed conflict. The use of the word "imperative" in this context is meaningful. Military necessity is always required for belligerent conduct that results in a deprivation of property, but the use of the word "imperative" suggests that the standard is higher where the deprivation will be uncompensated. Moreover, the standard is flexible, based on the level of hostilities and other factors. Thus, actions that might be justified on a battlefield may not be justified in an occupation in which active hostilities have ceased. In an occupation, destruction or damage of enemy property (such as military weapons and bases) in order to ensure that it will not subsequently fall into enemy hands would seem to meet this "imerative necessity" standard, as would damage or destruction of civilian public or private property incidental to attacks by or against resistance forces assuming, of course, that this damage or destruction by the occupying State was pursuant to attacks that otherwise comply with LOAC targeting rules. The likely damage to such civilian property is an element of the proportionality analysis that should precede such an attack.

In areas subject to belligerent occupation, GCIV Article 53 sets out an even more explicit limitation:

> Any destruction by the Occupying Power of real or personal property belonging individually or collectively to private persons, or to the State, or to other public authorities, or to social or cooperative organizations, is prohibited, except where such destruction is rendered absolutely necessary by military operations.[120]

The use of the term "absolutely" in GCIV Article 53 in lieu of "imperative" as used in Article 23(g) of 1907 Hague IV provides additional emphasis of the high level of military necessity required to comply with Article 53.

As is true in any battlefield situation, pillage or looting by occupation troops is strictly forbidden under both Article 47 of 1907 Hague IV and GCIV Article 33. Moreover, GCIV Article 147 provides that "extensive destruction and appropriation of property, not justified by military necessity and carried out unlawfully and wantonly" is a grave breach, if committed against protected persons or property protected by GCIV. As such, all parties to GCIV (which today includes all nations of the world) are obligated to either prosecute individuals suspected of violating this prohibition or hand them over to another State who will prosecute.

Certain property is subject to special protection. Thus, Article 56 of 1907 Hague IV treats "institutions dedicated to religion, charity and education, the arts and sciences" in the same category as the private property of protected persons, even if the institutions are owned by the occupied State; prohibits "seizure of, destruction or willful damage" to these institutions or to historic monuments or works of art and science; and provides that violation of the prohibition could be subject to legal proceedings for compensation. Under the 1954 Hague Convention on Cultural Property, an occupying State is required to prohibit, prevent, and put a stop to any form of theft, pillage, or misappropriation of,

---

120. GCIV, *supra*, note 13, art. 53.

and any acts of vandalism directed against, particularly significant categories of cultural property, and to assist the national authorities of the occupied territory to safeguard and preserve its cultural property. Should these national governments be unable to take measures to preserve cultural property damaged by military operations, the occupying State will have to take the "most necessary" measures of preservation.[121]

It must be emphasized that these prohibitions against needless destruction or damage to property — all of which must be scrupulously observed in the execution of the occupation mission — in no way deprive the occupying State of the authority to make use of all property of the occupied territory. Instead, this authority depends upon the type of property involved. An occupying State exercises its greatest authority with respect to property of the occupied State. Thus, Article 53 of 1907 Hague IV recognizes that the occupying State can take possession of all military and non-military moveable property of the occupied State, including "cash, funds, and realizable securities which are strictly the property of the State, depots of arms, means of transport, stores and supplies," but only to be used "for military operations." In practice, this authority has been interpreted to mean use to defray the costs of military operations in the occupied territory, including the costs of administering the occupied territory.[122] Under Article 55 of 1907 Hague IV, the occupying State can also take possession of, and use, real property of its enemy, including "public buildings, real estate, forests and agricultural estates belonging to the hostile State, and situated in the occupied country."

In the case of moveable property, Article 53 of 1907 Hague IV authorizes the occupying State to dispose of the property as it sees fit, consistent with the requirement that the property be used "for military operations." However, in the case of real property, while the occupying State is entitled to benefit from the fruits of these properties, Article 55 of 1907 Hague IV imposes on the occupying State an obligation to administer akin to the rights of a trustee, who must conserve the trust corpus, but can dispose of the fruits of the corpus for permitted purposes. This is because the occupying State is not the owner of the real property, but rather a temporary holder. Thus, while an occupying State can seize the cash of an occupied State and use it to defray the costs of occupation, where the property of the occupied State is real property (such as an oil field), Article 55 of 1907 Hague IV only allows the occupying State to sell the fruits of the real property (*e.g.*, the oil) but not the real property itself.[123]

The rules are more complex with respect to private property. Property considered private for LOAC purposes includes property of private persons (including legal persons such as companies and private institutions, like private universities) and property of municipal or other non-national governmental organizations. Also falling within this category is property of a religious,

---

121. 1954 Hague Convention, *supra*, note 51, art. 5.
122. *See, e.g.*, U.S. ex rel DRC Inc. v. Custer Battles, LLC, 376 F.Supp.2d 617, 643-44 (E.D. Va. 2005), *rev'd*, 562 F.3d 295 (4th Cir. 2009).
123. *See* FM 27-10, *supra*, note 17, para. 402.

charitable, educational, artistic or scientific organization, even if the organization is owned by the occupied State.[124] Also, property owned by the occupied State, but beneficially owned by private parties (*e.g.*, a pension fund for the benefit of State employees or deposits held in a bank owned by the occupied State) would be considered to be private in character. However, U.S. government practice is to treat property as public if the occupied State has assumed economic risk involved in holding and managing the property or if the owner is unknown.[125]

As a general rule, while property of the occupied State may be seized, private property may not,[126] although it may be requisitioned. A requisition is a demand for the surrender of property, and pursuant to Article 52 of 1907 Hague IV, such a demand should occur only when needed "for the needs of the army of occupation." Article 52 also provides that requisitions shall only be made "in proportion to the resources of the country, and of such a nature as not to involve the inhabitants in the obligation of taking part in military operations against their own country." The latter does not mean that property cannot be requisitioned if it will be used by the occupying State's forces in military operations, but rather that enemy civilians cannot be required to perform services in military operations (although civilians can be required to perform other services, such as operating public utilities, transportation services, etc., even if those services would benefit the occupying forces).

All requisitions for goods and services are only to be demanded on the authority of the commander in the locality occupied, although in State practice it often happens that requisitions are made on the spot by soldiers, but regardless of who makes the demand, such demands are only proper if there is an actual military need (otherwise, the property would be wrongfully appropriated, and such a taking may violate the LOAC). Further, compensation should be paid for requisitioned private property, in particular where the property is damaged while in possession of the occupying State. A receipt should be given to acknowledge that a requisition was made (in practice by the military unit making the requisition) and that the occupying State is obliged to return the property to its owner and/or pay compensation.[127]

Consistent with Article 23(g) of 1907 Hague IV, the terms of GCIV Article 53 would permit the destruction any property, including State and private property, where "rendered absolutely necessary by military operations." This would certainly be the case with respect to arms, munitions, and other property, regardless of ownership, that is susceptible of military use. It would be permissible to seize private stores of arms and ammunition from citizens and businesses and either hold them in a secure facility or (more likely) destroy them before they can fall into the wrong hands. If not destroyed, the property might be returned after hostilities end or, if the property is destroyed, compensation

---

124. 1907 Hague IV, *supra*, note 12, art. 56.
125. DoD Law of War Manual, *supra*, note 14, para. 11.18.4.3.
126. 1907 Hague IV, *supra*, note 12, art. 46.
127. The rules governing the requisition of private property can be found in 1907 Hague IV, *supra*, note 12, arts. 52-53; FM 27-10, *supra*, note 17, para. 412-417.

might be paid to private persons, but any return or compensation would be a matter dealt with in a subsequent peace settlement (if there were one).[128] GCIV Article 53 would also permit destruction of property where necessary to ensure the protection of friendly forces in the occupied territory. For example, it might be necessary to clear vegetation or crops from the side of roads used frequently by occupation forces in order to protect them from ambush by hostile forces using the vegetation for concealment; or to confiscate private residences in close proximity to military installations in order to prevent them from being used as staging points for attacks against the installation. In practice, the range of measures that would fall within this authority is extremely broad. What is essential, however, is that any occupying State exercising this authority makes a good faith determination that no alternative measure will satisfy the legitimate military need. In addition, a higher standard of military necessity will apply before destroying property that is subject to special protection under the LOAC (*e.g.*, cultural property protected by the 1954 Hague Convention).

While almost everything can be requisitioned, including fuel, food, clothing, building materials, machinery, tools, vehicles, furnishings for quarters, and quarters for billeting of troops, there are limits. First, as the terms of Article 52 of 1907 Hague IV make clear, requisitions can only be done "in proportion to the resources of the country," and thus cannot deprive the population of essential needs. Further, both GCIV and AP I restrict the requisitioning of certain essential items needed for protection of the population, including:

- Foodstuffs and medical articles and supplies (GCIV Art. 55);
- Civilian hospitals (GCIV Art. 57);
- Civilian medical units, including related equipment and material and the services of the units' personnel (AP I Art. 14); and
- Civil defense buildings and material (AP I Art. 63).

Thus, this property may be requisitioned only to the extent that doing so will not prevent meeting the needs of the civilian population in the occupied territory.[129]

Aside from requisitioning property, the occupying State may also compel the population to provide services in support of the occupation. This right is a traditional incident of war, as described in FM 27-10:

> The services which may be obtained from inhabitants by requisition include those of professional men, such as engineers, physicians and nurses and of artisans and laborers, such as clerks, carpenters, butchers, bakers, and truck drivers. The officials and employees of rail-ways, trucklines, airlines, canals, river or coastwise steamship companies, telegraph, telephone, radio, postal and similar services, gas, electric, and water works, and sanitary authorities, whether employed by the State or private companies, may be requisitioned to perform their professional duties only so long as the duties required do not directly concern the operations of war against their own country. The

---

128. *See, e.g.*, 1907 Hague IV, *supra*, note 12, art. 53.
129. *See, e.g.*, GCIV *supra*, note 13, art. 57.

occupant may also requisition labor to restore the general condition of the public works to that of peace, including the repair of roads, bridges, and railways, and to perform services on behalf of the local population, such as the care of the wounded and sick and the burial of the dead.[130]

The right to compel services is both explicitly and implicitly acknowledged in various provisions of 1907 Hague IV, GCIV, and AP I that limit the occupying State's exercise of the right to requisition services. There are a number of such limitations. First, the occupying State is prohibited from requiring inhabitants of the occupied territory to provide information about the military of the displaced sovereign, which would effectively require such inhabitants to commit treason.[131] Second, the occupying State may not compel protected persons to serve in its armed forces or auxiliary forces or to take part in military operations, nor can it exert pressure on them or use propaganda to persuade them to "voluntarily" enlist.[132] Third, the occupying State may not compel persons 18 years of age or under to provide services.[133] Further, protected persons can only be compelled to perform "work which is necessary either for the needs of the army of occupation, or for the public utility services, or for the feeding, sheltering, clothing, transportation or health of the population of the occupied country."[134]

All labor laws applicable to the performance and conditions of work under the laws of the occupied territory will continue to apply. Fair wages are to be paid, for example, and work is to be performed at the protected person's usual place of work, so far as possible, and in any case, the work will be performed "in the occupied territory where the persons whose services are requisitioned are [located]."[135] In addition, where a protected person is a public official or judge, he or she may elect to abstain from performance of his or her duties "for reasons of conscience," and the occupying State may not punish the public official for such abstention.[136] On the other hand, this does not permit the public official to exercise his or her duties in a subversive manner or a manner contrary to the occupying State's interests, and accordingly the occupying State may remove him or her from office in its discretion.[137]

An important consideration when utilizing the occupied population as a source of labor is the extent to which protected persons can provide security services in the occupied territory. Under GCIV Article 51, the occupying State cannot compel protected persons "to employ forcible means to ensure the

---

130. FM 27-10, *supra,* note 17, para. 419.
131. 1907 Hague IV, *supra,* note 12, art.
132. GCIV, *supra,* note 13, art. 51.
133. *Id.*
134. *Id.*
135. *Id.*
136. An occupying State may require public officials to take an oath to perform their duties conscientiously, and can remove them if they fail to take the oath. *See* FM 27-10, *supra,* note 17, para. 423. This is different than requiring them to take an oath of allegiance to the occupying State, which is forbidden by Article 45 of 1907 Hague IV.
137. GCIV, *supra,* note 13, art. 54.

security of the installations where they are performing compulsory labour." However, this does not preclude the possibility of requiring police and other security forces to continue to perform their public safety functions as long as they are not involved in providing security against guerillas or other resistance fighters who continue to engage in an armed conflict with the occupying State.

The LOAC does not, however, preclude an occupying State from recruiting workers to seek employment with the occupying State. On the other hand, the occupying State may not take measures to create unemployment or restrict employment opportunities offered to workers in an occupied territory, in order to induce them to work for the occupying State.[138] Further, regardless of whether a worker is compelled to provide services or volunteers, he or she shall always have the right to seek the assistance of the Protecting Power to request its intervention with the occupying State.[139]

In addition to requisitioning services, the occupying State may collect taxes and use state revenues to defray the costs of administering the occupied territory.[140] The basic right of the occupying State is set forth in Article 48 of 1907 Hague IV, which makes it clear that the right is an option and need not be exercised:

> If, in the territory occupied, the occupant collects the taxes, dues, and tolls imposed for the benefit of the State, he shall do so, as far as is possible, in accordance with the rules of assessment and incidence in force, and shall in consequence be bound to defray the expenses of the administration of the occupied territory to the same extent as the legitimate Government was so bound.[141]

Consistent with the notion that the occupying State is not to make fundamental changes in the occupied territory, taxes, dues, and tolls are to be collected in accordance with existing law and practice in the occupied territory "as far as possible." This U.S. government has interpreted this requirement flexibly. Thus, according to FM 27-10, "[i]f, due to the flight or unwillingness of the local officials, it is impracticable to follow the rules of incidence and assessment in force, then the total amount of taxes to be paid may be allotted among the districts, towns, etc., and the local authorities required to collect it," but "[u]nless required to do so by considerations of public order and safety, the occupant must not create new taxes."[142]

Aside from collecting taxes, the occupying State can also levy money contributions. However, such levies "shall only be for the needs of the army or

---

138. *Id.*
139. *Id.*
140. Consistent with the permitted uses of money contributions that can be levied under Article 49 of 1907 Hague IV, the U.S. government has broadly interpreted the purposes to which such revenues can be applied. FM 27-10, *supra*, note 17, paragraph 425b, provides that "[t]he first charge upon such taxes is for the cost of the administration of the occupied territory. The balance may be used for the purposes of the occupant."
141. 1907 Hague IV, *supra*, note 12, art. 48.
142. FM 27-10, *supra*, note 17, para. 426.

of the administration of the territory in question."[143] Contributions may only be collected pursuant to a written order, using "as far as possible" the rules of assessment and incidence of taxes then in force in the occupied territory and subject to the giving of receipts for all contributions.[144]

Counterbalanced against all these rights is a general prohibition in Article 50 of 1907 Hague IV against inflicting any general penalty, "pecuniary or otherwise" upon the population on account of acts of individuals for which they cannot be held jointly or severally responsible. Thus, an overly burdensome tax or any other requisition motivated by a desire to punish or otherwise harm the population in response to the armed resistance of the forces of the occupied territory or the actions of its displaced government would be prohibited. Ultimately, the objective of these LOAC authorities is to enable the occupying State's ability to maintain normal conditions in the occupied territory without permitting the punitive use of taxes, levies, or other collections. Whether an occupying State chooses to invoke this authority is always a complex policy decision; it may be that the occupying State prefers to fund its operations independently and hold collected taxes and other revenues in trust. However, for prolonged periods of occupation, the authority to administer a system to raise revenue to fund the provision of services to the population is critical, and fully provided for by the LOAC.

XIII. Transformational Occupation: Expanding the Permissible Scope of an Occupation

Despite the extensive authority granted to the occupying State to administer occupied territory, belligerent occupation is conclusively conceived to be a temporary condition. While changes to implement the LOAC protections established for the population of the occupied territory is permitted, the occupying State is not supposed to undertake significant reforms or changes. Accordingly, under the LOAC, the authority of the occupying State to make significant changes to the property or institutions of the occupied territory is intentionally limited.

Nevertheless, as the recent occupation of Iraq illustrates, more significant changes may be undertaken either on the basis of a liberal reading of the LOAC authority granted to the occupying State, or based on invocation of other legal authorities. One potential alternate source of authority is a United Nations mandate recognizing a broader scope of authorized measures for a particular occupation than the authority provided by applicable LOAC treaties. The most relevant contemporary example of this additional legal authority is UN Security

---

143. 1907 Hague IV, *supra*, note 12, art. 49.
144. *Id.* art. 51.

Council Resolution 1483, the resolution passed under Chapter VII of the UN Charter authorizing the post-invasion administration of Iraq.[145]

On May 8, 2003, the United States and the United Kingdom notified the Security Council that the United States, the United Kingdom, and the coalition partners intended to assist the Iraqi people "to take the first steps towards forming a representative government, based on the rule of law, that affords fundamental freedoms and equal protection and justice under law to the people of Iraq without regard to ethnicity, religion or gender."[146] To that end, the coalition partners declared their intention to facilitate "the establishment of representative institutions of government," "the responsible administration of the Iraqi financial sector," "humanitarian relief," "economic reconstruction," and the "transparent operation and repair of Iraq's infrastructure and natural resources," with the "progressive transfer of administrative responsibilities to such representative institutions of government, as appropriate . . . as early as possible," and invited the United Nations, its member states, and representative organizations to support and contribute in coordination with the Coalition Provisional Authority (CPA) established by the United States and the United Kingdom.

In response, the Security Council issued Resolution 1483 that included a call for the CPA, "consistent with the Charter of the United Nations and other relevant international law, to promote the welfare of the Iraqi people through the effective administration of the territory, including in particular working towards the restoration of conditions of security and stability and the creation of conditions in which the Iraqi people can freely determine their own political future." It also called for "all concerned to comply fully with their obligations under international law including in particular the Geneva Conventions of 1949 and the Hague Regulations of 1907," but it did not limit them to only the provisions of those treaties.

The resolution did not identify what "other law" was contemplated, but the reference to the UN Charter suggests that a broader scope of legal authority during the occupation of Iraq could be asserted. Thus, providing for "the establishment of representative institutions of government" might permit alterations in the form of government to include new elected bodies or the reconfiguration of political jurisdictions to allow minorities (or in the case of Iraq, the Shiite majority) greater representation in the government. The reference to "economic reconstruction" might permit the creation of new institutions in the economic sphere that would change the nature of the economy.

Another source of "other law" could be HRL, which would justify greater changes to the social and economic structure of the occupied territory. As noted in Chapter 2, there are various theories about the potential applicability and interrelationship of HRL with the LOAC in situations where the LOAC is

---

145. S.C. Res. 1483, U.N. Doc. S/Res/1483 (May 22, 2003).
146. Letter dated 8 May 2003 from the Permanent Representatives of the United Kingdom of Great Britain and Northern Ireland and the United States of America to the United Nations, addressed to the President of the Security Council, U.N. Doc. S/Res/538 (May 8, 2003).

unquestionably applicable. Belligerent occupation is arguably the most logical context for application of HRL. This is because HRL is the body of law intended to regulate the relationship between a government and its subjects. Although the occupying State is not the sovereign government of the occupied territory, it exercises many of the powers of a sovereign government on a temporary basis and could seek to rely on HRL to justify changes in the legal and economic structure of a country that otherwise might not be permitted by the LOAC. On the other hand, if active hostilities are continuing in the occupied territory, HRL principles normally controlling in peacetime may conflict with the military requirements of an occupation. For example, application of these principles would arguably give individuals preventively detained for security reasons in the occupied territory additional rights, beyond those provided in the LOAC, to challenge their detention or seek redress against the occupying State. Further, these principles may create uncertainty as to the scope of authority to use military force in response to organized resistance forces.

Notwithstanding these concerns, the role of HRL in the context of belligerent occupation is increasingly significant. As a result, HRL will almost certainly have a greater influence directly and indirectly in belligerent occupation, particularly where the level of resistance to the occupying force has declined and the duration of the occupation exceeds a brief period. Even for countries like the United States that continue to resist the full applicability of HRL during armed conflict, occupying commanders will invariably be scrutinized against HRL standards. Accordingly, the military lawyers who advise these commanders must be sensitive to this reality and prepared to rationally articulate why the occupation is consistent with these standards (even without conceding the binding nature of the standards).

XIV. Transition to Post-Conflict Phase and Termination of Occupation

A. Conflict Termination

Most LOAC obligations end when there is cessation of hostilities. However, delineating when exactly hostilities end is often difficult. Nevertheless, determination is of paramount importance, as certain new duties will arise. For example, the U.S. Department of Defense Law of War Manual provides the following:

> [T]he end of hostilities triggers obligations regarding the marking of minefields, demining, and clearance of unexploded ordnance. In addition, POWs and protected persons, in general, must be released and returned to the party to the conflict to which they belong.[147]

---

147. DoD Law of War Manual, *supra*, note 14, para. 3.83.

In addition to the imposition of new LOAC obligations, others that arose during the hostilities may continue:

> For example, POWs are protected by the GPW from the moment they fall into the power of the enemy until their final release and repatriation. Similarly, protected persons whose release, repatriation, or reestablishment may take place after the general close of military operations continue to benefit from the protection of the GC. In addition, duties under occupation law may continue after hostilities have ended.[148]

Generally, hostilities end when parties to the conflict decide to terminate their dispute, and actually do cease hostile action between their military forces. Cessation of hostilities is best understood by referring back to the test for determining the existence of an international armed conflict (IAC). To have an IAC, there must be both a dispute between two or more states, and actual use of military forces in relation to that dispute. Therefore, hostilities cease when both of these IAC existence prongs are severed.

Actual cessation of hostilities can be accomplished through several conflict termination methods, and visualizing each method on a spectrum is useful for conceptualizing their effectiveness. On one end of the spectrum is the existence of an armed conflict; on the other is the complete subjugation of one side to the conflict, therefore rendering the dispute finished and military forces incapacitated. Though each termination method provides some form of an end to hostilities, the closer one side of the conflict is to "complete subjugation," the closer the conflict is to a conclusive end.

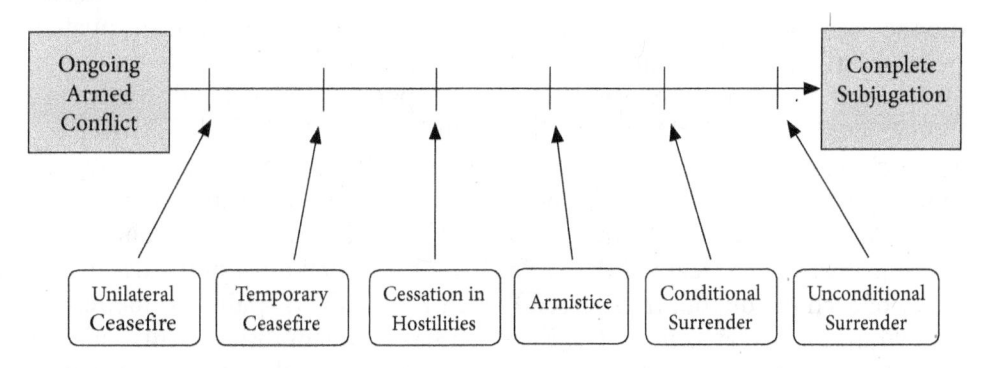

```
Ongoing Armed Conflict ────────────────────────→ Complete Subjugation

  Unilateral   Temporary   Cessation in   Armistice   Conditional   Unconditional
  Ceasefire    Ceasefire   Hostilities                Surrender     Surrender
```

Further analysis of each termination method's position on the spectrum will explain this.

A cessation in hostilities can occur with or without a formal written agreement between the parties to a conflict. However, where no agreement exists, the cessation is most fragile. This is the concern with the first conflict termination method, a unilateral ceasefire. In a unilateral ceasefire, one of the parties to the conflict makes the individual decision to sever its dispute with the enemy and remove its military forces from hostilities. To be effective, however, the other

---

148. *Id.* para. 3.8.2.

party must then meet the opponent with similar action, or minimally, recognize the act of the enemy and decline to lay chase to opposing forces.

The second method is a temporary ceasefire. Unlike unilateral ceasefires, temporary ceasefires are observed and often decided mutually by all parties to the conflict, but usually involve no formal written agreement. Temporary ceasefires can occur at a localized level, or over the entire field of hostilities. They are usually tolled for a specified duration as well. For example, during Christmas of 1914, British, French, and German troops across the Western Front engaged in localized ceasefires and even mild fraternization. The third method of informal conflict termination is the simple act of ceasing hostilities. Though reasons for this simplistic method are numerous, examples of it actually occurring are few.

Hostilities are often, and more effectively terminated through negotiated formal agreements, usually (but not always) taking the form of peace treaties. Herein arises the fourth method of conflict termination — armistice agreements — which are the more fragile of the formal termination methods. Armistices function similarly to complete temporary ceasefires,[149] but are supported by written agreements. Their intended function is to provide a temporary, but firm cessation in hostilities while a more lasting peace arrangement is negotiated. A notable example of an armistice is the ongoing Korean Armistice Agreement, which has halted hostilities on the Korean Peninsula since 1953.[150] In light of this example, it is important to distinguish that an armistice is not necessarily a conclusive end to a dispute, though it does function to stop fighting between parties.

The final two conflict termination methods are conditional and unconditional surrenders. Both types of surrender may take the form of negotiated treaties, but have historically been accomplished by other methods as well.[151] However, the level of negotiation between the parties may be fixed to the conditional or unconditional status of the surrender itself. A conditional surrender aligns closer to a negotiated settlement ending hostilities, and is historically the more common form of surrender used among nations. For example, the Seven Years' War was concluded by the conditional surrender of France and her allies to the British in the Treaty of Paris. The Treaty returned most of the home territory of each nation, but transferred French Louisiana to Spain and the rest of New France to Great Britain. On the contrary, an unconditional surrender is often non-negotiable, and includes no guarantees other than what is required by the Geneva and Hague Conventions. This is because unconditional surrenders usually occur on the precipice of the complete subjugation of a party to a conflict. The two most notable examples of unconditional surrender are that of Nazi Germany on May 7, 1945, in Reims, and of Japan on September 2, 1945, on the deck of the USS *Missouri*, docked in Tokyo Bay.

---

149. In fact, parties to a conflict will often arrange temporary ceasefires to allow for the negotiation of an armistice.

150. No further peace agreement has ever been reached on the Korean Peninsula, and the armistice is the sole source for the cessation of those hostilities.

151. During the Falklands War, the Argentine garrison commander in Port Stanley, General Mario Menéndez, negotiated an agreement for the surrender of Argentine forces. This was actually a violation of the Argentine Army code, as Menéndez's forces still had the requisite capacity to continue.

B. Cessation of Occupation

Occupation does not end upon cessation of hostilities, but continues until full sovereignty of the occupied territory is returned to the displaced sovereign, or until sovereignty is assumed by another government recognized by the international community.

The period required of occupation to cease varies, depending upon the situation on the ground in the occupied territory and the time required to restore sovereignty to the occupied territory. GCIV provides that "[i]n the case of occupied territory, the application of the present Convention shall cease one year after the general close of military operations . . .," but a number of provisions will continue to apply for so long as the occupying State "exercises the functions of government in such territory."[152] These provisions include those primarily intended to ensure that protected persons continue to be treated humanely, but without many of the limitations imposed on internment and other internal security measures (except that any persons who were still in security detention at the expiration of the one-year period will still benefit from the provisions of GCIV that apply to such detention (*e.g.*, the rules applicable to internment)).

In the occupation of Iraq in 2003-2004, a period of one year was sufficient for a transition to a national government that arguably was grounded on more than simply the law of military occupation. In practice, however, it may be unrealistic to expect that all occupations will terminate in one year. Accordingly, Article 3(b) of AP I replaces GCIV's termination provision by extending application of GCIV and AP I until "termination of the occupation." There is no definition of the phrase "termination of the occupation" and hence, like commencement of occupation, it will be a question of fact when the occupation has ended, turning on a pragmatic assessment of what authority actually administers the territory.

In any case, it is likely that extended occupations will transition to some type of hybrid civil/military arrangement based on international or domestic law. This will be the result of the perceived necessity to deal with the questions that inevitably emerge as the occupying State takes on long-term responsibility for the occupied territory, for example, as occurred in the case of Israeli occupation of the Palestinian territory, and the fact that civilian authority may be better placed (and more politically acceptable) to exercise government functions over the long term. Alternatively, the international community may require that a source of law additional to those provided by the LOAC, such as HRL, serve as the legal basis to deal with transition issues, as occurred in the case of the occupation of Iraq.[153]

---

152. GCIV, *supra*, note 13, art. 6.
153. What if the occupying power withdraws from the territory completely? In its 2016 update to its commentary on the First Geneva Convention (Convention (I) for the Amelioration of the Condition of the Wounded and Sick in Armed Forces in the Field or "GWS"), the International Committee of the Red Cross ("ICRC") stated:

[I]n some specific and exceptional cases — in particular when foreign forces withdraw from occupied territory (or parts thereof) while retaining key elements of authority or

These long-term transition issues are undoubtedly complex and fraught with strategic national security implications. However, they are generally beyond the scope of primary concern for military commanders and their legal advisors. For these individuals, a thorough knowledge of the LOAC rules and principles applicable to belligerent occupation is the essential professional requirement. No one in uniform can anticipate what the next day will bring, much less what issues will arise in the "next war." While the concept of belligerent occupation may be disfavored from a policy perspective because of the negative connotations it triggers, the tenets of that law reflect how the LOAC balances the legitimate needs of a military commander functionally responsible for enemy territory and population, against the humanitarian interests of that population. Accordingly, this law provides the best foundation for administration of territory by the military, regardless of the legal basis for the seizure or occupation of such territory.

---

other important governmental functions that are typical of those usually taken on by an Occupying Power—the law of occupation might continue to apply within the territorial and functional limits of those competences."

Int'l Comm. Red Cross, Commentary of 2016, Convention (I) for the Amelioration of the Condition of Wounded and Sick in Armed Forces in the Field Geneva, 12 August 1949, para. 307 (citation omitted), (hereinafter 2016 COMMENTARY, CONVENTION (I)). At issue here is whether Israel has continued obligations to protect the well-being of Palestinians in territories such as Gaza, from which Israel withdrew in 2005, but where it still maintains a considerable degree of control remotely from Israel, including over access to supplies such as fuel, and can easily reintroduce its forces, as it has since 2005, to deal with security threats. The Israeli government and the Israeli Supreme Court take the position that the occupation has ended because Israel does not have troops in Gaza; indeed there is a functioning government in Gaza. HCJ, 9132/07 Gaber Al-Bassiouni v. Prime Minister, Judgment of Jan. 30, 2008, para. 11, ("Israel no longer has effective control over what happens in the Gaza Strip. Military rule that applied in the past in this territory came to an end by a decision of the government, and Israeli soldiers are no longer stationed in the territory on a permanent basis, nor are they in charge of what happens there"), http://elyon1.court.gov.il/Files_ENG/07/320/091/n25/07091320.n25.pdf (unofficial translation). *See also* Yuval Shany, *The Law Applicable to Non-Occupied Gaza: A Comment on Bassiouni v. The Prime Minister of Israel*, 42 ISR. L. REV. 101 (2009). The ICRC, however, proposes a "functional approach" that would impose on a former occupying State, continuing obligations under the LOAC to protect the well-being of the inhabitants of the territory, noting that "[t]his test applies to the extent that the foreign forces still exercise within all or part of the territory governmental functions acquired when the occupation was undoubtedly established and ongoing." 2016 COMMENTARY, CONVENTION (I), para. 310. It also notes that "any geographical contiguity existing between the belligerent States might play a key role in facilitating the remote exercise of effective control, for instance by permitting an Occupying Power that has relocated its troops outside the territory to make its authority felt within reasonable time." *Id.*, para. 309.

Primary Authorities

Occupation Implementation Measure	Primary Legal Authorities	Special Considerations
General authority to administer occupied territory	1907 Hague IV art. 43	Grants occupying State broad authority to function as a temporary government
Protection of friendly forces from individuals posing a future security threat	GCIV art. 78	Authorizes preventive detention, but: • Internment only allowed when lesser restraint ineffective • Hearing and periodic review required
Protecting internees and other detainees from abusive treatment	GCIV arts. 5, 27, 31 & 32	• Requires the humane treatment of all detainees • Establishes special protections for security internees • Ensures provision of basic needs for all detainees
Permitting occupying State to enact legislation for effective occupation and security of occupying forces	GCIV arts. 64-65, 1907 Hague IV art. 43	• Encourages continued reliance on existing criminal law • Authorizes suspension and/or supplementation by occupation proclamations • Must be published in the indigenous language prior to taking effect
Maintenance of public security	1907 Hague IV art. 43, GCIV art. 51	• Can compel local population to continue providing essential services to fulfill obligations to restore public order • Cannot compel local population to provide security for occupation forces
Adjudication of criminal misconduct	GCIV arts. 54, 64 & 66	• Encourages continued use of local courts and judges • Authorizes removal but not sanction of public officials for refusing to serve based on conscience • Occupying State may establish military tribunals to enforce penal laws promulgated by occupying State

continued

Chapter 10 ■ Occupation, Termination of Hostilities, and Transition

Occupation Implementation Measure	Primary Legal Authorities	Special Considerations
Protecting the population from natural and man-made dangers	1907 Hague IV art. 43, AP I art. 63.	• Maintain existing civil defense and public service capabilities • Prohibits civil defense and public safety personnel from performing military-like functions
Utilization of public property necessary to support the occupation	1907 Hague IV arts. 23(g), 53 & 55	• Moveable public property may be confiscated • Real public property: limited to utilizing the fruits of the property • May be destroyed only based on imperative military necessity
Utilization of private property to extent necessary to support the occupation	1907 Hague IV arts. 23(g), 46 & 52	• May not be confiscated • May be requisitioned but replacement or compensation required • May be destroyed only based on imperative military necessity
Utilization of foodstuffs and medical resources to support the occupation	GCIV arts. 55-57	Only if needs of civilian population may still be met
Provision of basic needs of civilian population	GCIV arts. 55-56	• Obligates occupying State to provide for certain civilian needs (*e.g.*, medical, food) • AP I art. 69 expands the goods covered • Subject to "fullest extent of the means available to it" qualification
Facilitation of humanitarian assistance efforts	GCIV art. 59	• Obligates occupying State to endeavor to facilitate provision of humanitarian assistance • Authorizes imposition of security measures (such as screening shipments and monitoring distribution)
Defraying the cost of administration	1907 Hague IV arts. 48-49.	Authorizes the occupying State to collect and utilize public revenues and utilize revenues to offset the cost of occupation administration

Study Questions

1. On April 5 and 7, 2003, U.S. armored units make two "thunder runs" into Baghdad to test Iraqi defenses, but face only disorganized resistance. At about the same time, U.S. forces take a number of key objectives, including highway intersections, a key bridge, and a major Presidential palace, and demand that the Iraqi forces in Baghdad surrender. However, there is no response from the Iraqi government, because, by this time, it has largely disappeared or conceded defeat. At this point, has the occupation of Baghdad begun? If not, what more would be required for the occupation to begin? Be sure to cite your treaty sources.[154]

2. On April 9 2003, Saddam Hussein is seen greeting local citizens near his command bunker in northern Baghdad, but then he disappears (he is not seen publicly again until his capture months later). However, by this time, the Iraqi government has lost control of the city, and there is widespread looting and vandalism, including at the Iraqi National Museum. The statue of Saddam Hussein in Firdos Square in Baghdad is toppled by coalition forces that same day. At this point, U.S. forces have defeated organized Iraqi military units, though resistance continues in various parts of the city. You notice, however, that all the announcements coming from the U.S. forces avoid use of the term "occupation" to characterize the situation in Baghdad following submission of Iraqi's military forces. Assuming this is intentional, why do you think U.S. forces would want to avoid the use of the term "occupation"? What, in your view, is the legal significance of not using that term?[155]

3. You move forward with your unit to Baghdad to begin the process of implementing the occupation. On the way, you observe vandalism and are distressed to see priceless artwork being taken from the Iraqi National Museum. You speak to your commander about the vandalism and stress the need to restore order. He responds, in a somewhat irritated tone, by asking you a question: "Can you hear those explosions and weapons fire in the distance?" You nod affirmatively. He then says, "That's the sound of our guys fighting with the Iraqis out in the neighborhoods. This battle is not quite done, and we need all the forces we have to pacify this city. I don't really care about a bunch of looters right now. We'll take care of that later." Is the commander correct that U.S. forces can defer taking care of the vandalism? Please explain why or why not. If you did not want to use Coalition forces to deal with the vandalism, what other options might you have pursued?[156]

4. Assume it is early May 2003. The Coalition Provision Authority (CPA) is being established ("stood up"), and you are working in the CPA legal staff to organize the occupation. You receive a report that a school in one

---

154. *See* DoD Law of War Manual, *supra*, note 14, para. 11.2.
155. *See* FM 27-10, *supra*, note 17, paras. 351, 352, 355 & 356.
156. *See* DoD Law of War Manual, *supra*, note 14, para. 11.19.

of Baghdad's neighborhoods is on fire. The people in the neighborhood are doing what they can to put the flames out, but they don't have the equipment they need. Also, there is a real fear that those who try to go into the building to fight the fire at its source might be subject to smoke inhalation or other ailments. This would be a problem, because various hospitals and clinics near the fire are shuttered. Your commander, who received the same report, asks what the responsibility of U.S. forces is for these problems.[157]

5. After several months, there is organized violence in parts of the country, but Baghdad is generally quiet. The CPA has legal teams working on a variety of issues, and you have been assigned to a team considering changes to Iraqi court system and the adoption of laws to punish those who attack coalition personnel or coalition assets. Your team leader is a newly assigned civilian lawyer from the U.S. Department of Justice. She asks you to briefly describe what you are permitted to do under applicable LOAC rules, and in particular how far the team can go to reform Iraqi criminal law and court procedure. What do you tell her?[158] Can you draw on any law other than the LOAC in fashioning new rules for Iraq? Would applicable UN Security Council resolutions, such as Resolution 1483, influence your answer?

6. It is now six months after the invasion. There is an organized resistance group in several cities in Iraq. The group, which appears to have a connection with al Qaeda, includes (i) former members of the Republican Guard, (ii) newly radicalized Iraqi civilians who oppose the occupation, (iii) citizens of various nearby countries who are not part of the coalition, and who were living in Iraq at the time of the invasion, and (iv) citizens of various European countries, some of which are coalition countries, who came to Iraq after the invasion to "fight the infidels." Assume that a U.S. Army unit engages in a firefight with resistance fighters, and individuals in each of the categories (i) – (iv). How do you classify these individuals under the LOAC?[159] In what ways might the law applicable to each group differ for purposes of detention, treatment, and prosecution? What responsibility, if any, would the United States have for these individuals under international law if it turned them over to Iraq at the end of the occupation?

---

157. *See, e.g.,* 1907 Hague IV, *supra,* note 12, art. 43.
158. *See* DoD LAW OF WAR MANUAL, *supra,* note 14, paras. 11.10 & 11.11.
159. *See, e.g.,* GCIV, *supra,* note 13, art. 4. *See also* "Protected Person Status in Occupied Iraq under the Fourth Geneva Convention," Mar. 18, 2004, 28 OPINIONS OF THE OFFICE OF THE LEGAL COUNSEL 35.

11 NAVAL WARFARE AND NEUTRALITY

You are a young U.S. Navy Judge Advocate assigned to a group or "cell" of officers planning the invasion of Iraq. Commander Jones, one of the other members of the cell, approaches you with a rush request: "Judge, I really need your help. A number of maritime issues have popped up during our most recent walk-through of the invasion plan. I think we have solutions for all of them, but, of course, we need a legal concurrence ASAP to confirm that all of them comply with international law before we proceed. We do not have much time, so if you could just give me your 'OK' verbally, I think that will be sufficient."

"Well," you respond, "I will do the best I can, but I need to be careful because this is a particularly tricky issue, especially given the presence of international shipping in the Persian Gulf. Go ahead and walk me through your issues, and either I will give you an answer now or, if I need to research the matter, I will come back to you by 0900 tomorrow."

"Fine," growls Commander Jones, "but I need you to be as 'forward leaning' as you can because there are a lot of American lives in the balance, and we need to be sure we can do everything possible to protect our guys." Then he launches in with his list of issues:

"First, we know the Iraqis do not have a very strong navy and will not mount much resistance on water, but we have just learned that the Iraqis have been equipping fishing vessels with mines and torpedoes over the last year, so that they can be deployed against us if needed. Our naval forces have counter measures to deal with this type of threat, but we cannot take the risk that the Iraqis will get off a lucky shot and hit one of our ships. So we were thinking of either (1) a preemptive strike against Iraqi port facilities where these fishing vessels are moored so we can destroy the fishing fleet, or (2) seeding the waters in and around the port with mines so that the fishing vessels cannot leave. What do you think of all that?

"Second, we believe that North Korea is going to try to supply the Iraqis with additional weapons and military supplies on ships registered ("flagged") in third countries. We can establish a blockade of Iraq in Iraqi waters to intercept these ships. However, this operation poses a lot of risks, at least until the invasion begins. Further, we think the ships may actually off-load cargo in third country ports,

and then smugglers transship it to Iraq. We are not exactly sure which ports will be used, so we were thinking of various options to counter this flow of arms and supplies, including:

(i) We could set up a visit and search operation at the entrance to the Strait of Hormuz to search all ships coming into the Persian Gulf. If we find a ship with weapons and supplies that is not clearly documented to be destined for a country other than Iraq, we would seize the ship and its cargo.

(ii) Since the visit and search operation could be too resource-intensive, and in any case may lead to objections from third countries, we might instead just let merchant ships know that we may conduct random visit and search operations. Since no ship captain will know when we might intercept them, this could deter shipments to Iraq.

(iii) We also could institute a certification system, under which all merchant ships entering the Persian Gulf must have a certificate issued by the United States. Those that do not will be subject to visit and search by our ships. If a ship resists, we will sink it.

Let us know which of these options are legally permitted. If you don't think any of these options will work, then please let us know what we can do. We need to be sure these weapons and supplies don't get to the Iraqis."

"Third, after the invasion is underway, we will set up a naval blockade just outside of Iraqi territorial waters to block all trade going in and out of Iraq. Our intent is to put maximum pressure on Iraq and its population, in case the invasion is protracted. We recognize that we need to be careful about interfering with international shipping, so we will try to keep the blockade as close to Iraqi waters as possible, but our task force may not be able to cover all possible approaches to Iraq, so we have devised a plan to mine part of Iraq's waters. We also intend to set up a corridor through which third country ships that are passing near Iraqi waters on their way to other countries, such as Iran, can get through. This corridor will be established using mines to direct shipping in the route we have approved. I understand that, unlike antipersonnel mines on land, sea mines are not banned, but we would appreciate a summary of the rules that will apply to using mines in this way."

"Fourth, we really don't know what to expect from Iran and other countries in the region once the invasion begins. Will any of them take exception to an invasion of a Persian Gulf country by U.S. forces, and if so, will they attack our ships by sea or air? We also don't know if the Republican Guard or even terrorist groups might try to use civilian ships or even drones to launch attacks against our vessels. Our warships typically keep civilian ships and aircraft at a distance in any case, particularly when we are engaged in combat operations — it's the safest course for everyone — but the Persian Gulf is crowded and it's hard to keep everything away. We vaguely remember that during the Falklands War, the Argentinians set up some type of exclusion zone that allowed them to treat as hostile any vessel that entered the zone without their permission. That same approach might work for us here — we could set up a zone on the basis that any vessel or aircraft entering the zone would be presumed to be an enemy vessel or aircraft and subject to attack. Can we do this, and how large a zone do you think we can set up?"

"Finally, we know that the Iraqis have reflagged some of their tankers so that they can ship oil from their waters as "neutrals." These oil shipments are producing revenue for the Iraqi government. Until we are able to set up a blockade, we may not be able to stop these shipments, plus some of these shipments have already left. We cannot let the Iraqis continue to earn hard currency from this oil, so we plan to intercept oil shipments on the high seas, and where we find oil that we think is from Iraq, seize the ships and their cargo. To know we are serious, we will make clear to the international commercial shipping community that if ships don't stop when we intercept them, we will sink the ships. It is our understanding that we have a right to seize enemy merchant vessels and even destroy them under some circumstances. What are the legal rules precisely?"

You have written all this down as Commander Jones talked. You look over your notes quickly and then explain that you are going to defer answering until 0900 the next day. None of these questions is particularly easy and you need to do a little research before you answer. Once Commander Jones has left, you realize that the questions he asked touch on a number of key areas of the law of naval warfare so you will need to start with the basics and go from there.

I. Introduction

A State can exercise naval power in a variety of ways, each of which present different issues under international law. These include the use of naval forces to (1) defend national territory from military and other threats from the sea (including from under or over the sea); (2) ensure control of, and access to, resources in and under waters recognized as being part of a State's territory or to which it has special rights under international law; (3) protect shipping to and from the State's territory from various threats in territorial and international waters, including from attacks by the State's enemies, or from the belligerent acts of other States engaged in a conflict with each other; and (4) affirm customary rights and freedoms on the seas, including the freedom of navigation. A State may maintain a navy simply to protect their interests in the waters near their territory, or they may use their naval forces to project national power from the sea, such as by maintaining fleets that can travel to distant parts of the ocean to establish a military presence where needed; to conduct surveillance; to launch, or defend against, military attacks; to police international waters against pirates; or to intercept on the high seas ships engaged in activities of international or regional concern, such as the trafficking of weapons of mass destruction. A State also may use its naval forces to enforce laws against illegal drugs, illegal immigration, pollution, and other threats outside the context of armed conflict.[1]

---

1. *See generally* GEORGE P. POLITAKIS, MODERN ASPECTS OF THE LAWS OF NAVAL WARFARE AND MARITIME NEUTRALITY 1-3 (1998) (brief overview of tasks discharged by modern navies) (hereinafter POLITAKIS).

Regardless of the reasons that individual States use naval forces, international law regulates the conduct of States in maritime operations outside of their internal waters. In times of peace, the applicable rules are found principally in law of the sea treaties and customary international law.[2] In times of armed conflict, specialized rules of naval warfare will apply, but these do not negate the general law of the sea for peacetime that in any event continues to apply among those States not engaged in the armed conflict (including in the relations between warring and neutral States.) Accordingly, practitioners applying the law of naval warfare always must keep in mind the requirements of the law of the sea, particularly as it relates to the interaction between States involved in an armed conflict and those who are not.[3]

Like the law of land warfare, the law of naval warfare embodies the humanitarian obligations to respect and protect those individuals who are not participating in hostilities, or no longer participating due to, e.g., wounds, shipwreck, capture or surrender, and to minimize unnecessary suffering in attacks against those who do participate.[4] While some law of armed conflict (LOAC) treaties

---

[2]. The primary treaty in this regard is the United Nations Convention on the Law of the Sea, Dec. 10, 1982, 1833 U.N.T.S. 397 (hereinafter UNCLOS). The United States has not ratified UNCLOS, but accepts and follows its provisions regarding navigation in various maritime zones (such as the high seas). 19 Comp. Presid'l Doc. no. 10, at 383-385 (Mar. 14, 1983). Other relevant law of the sea treaties are the Geneva Convention on the High Seas, April 29, 1958, 450 U.N.T.S. 11 (hereinafter High Seas Convention) and the Geneva Convention on the Territorial Sea and the Contiguous Zone, April 29, 1958, 516 U.N.T.S. 205. The United States has ratified both of these older treaties and many of their provisions are also included in UNCLOS.

[3]. *See* POLITAKIS, *supra*, note 1, at 5-7, for a brief discussion of the intersection between the law of armed conflict in naval warfare and peacetime law of sea rules. The concept that belligerents must have "due regard" for the rights under international law of neutrals in ocean areas where armed conflict may occur is reflected, *inter alia*, in paragraph 12 of the San Remo Manual on International Law Applicable to Armed Conflicts at Sea. SAN REMO MANUAL ON INTERNATIONAL LAW APPLICABLE TO ARMED CONFLICTS AT SEA (Doswald-Beck ed., 1995) (hereinafter SAN REMO MANUAL). The purpose of the San Remo Manual is to "provide a contemporary restatement of international law applicable to armed conflicts at sea." *Id.* at 5. In a volume published by Cambridge University Press (relied upon in this book), the Manual consists of 183 "black letter" paragraphs, plus an extensive explanation. References in this book to a paragraph of the San Remo Manual also should be deemed to include the explanation of that paragraph included in the Cambridge University Press edition of the Manual.

[4]. The U.S. Department of Defense Law of War Manual includes one chapter (out of 19) dealing specifically with naval warfare. U.S. DEP'T OF DEF., DEPARTMENT OF DEFENSE LAW OF WAR MANUAL ch. XIII (2016) (hereinafter DoD LAW OF WAR MANUAL). One of the most useful surveys of the law of naval warfare can be found in THE COMMANDER'S HANDBOOK ON THE LAW OF NAVAL OPERATIONS, U.S. DEP'T OF NAVY ET AL., NAVAL WARFARE PUB. 1-14M. Prepared by the U.S. Naval War College and published as a tri-service manual for the U.S. Coast Guard, the U.S. Marine Corps, and the U.S. Navy, the Commander's Handbook provides a succinct overview of the law of the sea, the law of neutrality, and the law of armed conflict as applied to naval warfare. The most recent edition of the Commander's Handbook was issued in 2017 and is available to the public at http://usnwc.libguides.com/ld.php?content_id=38386466 (last visited Feb. 28, 2018), and is referred to in this book as COMMANDER'S HANDBOOK — 2017. However, in the late 1990s, the Naval War College published an extremely useful annotation of an earlier version of the Commander's Handbook, which includes helpful insights into the legal position of the Navy on a number of LOAC issues. This annotation, which is referred to in this book as ANNOTATED SUPPLEMENT TO COMMANDER'S HANDBOOK, was published in volume 73 of the U.S. Naval War College's INTERNATIONAL LAW STUDIES and is *available at* https://stockton.usnwc.edu/cgi/viewcontent.cgi?article=1556&context=ils (last visited Feb. 17, 2018).

are drafted to apply specifically to naval warfare,[5] the number of treaties focused on naval warfare is limited. However, the requirements in treaties for land warfare will apply where the sea is being used as a platform to launch attacks against land targets.[6] In addition, certain principles, such as the principles of humanity, military necessity, and proportionality that apply in land warfare apply equally to warfare on the seas (and over and under the seas).[7] Indeed, these principles apply to all forms of warfare. There are, however, certain rules, discussed in greater detail in this chapter, that apply explicitly and in at least one case, exclusively to naval warfare.[8] Such specialized rules reflect the particular challenges and requirements of operating in a maritime environment.

The sea presents some unique features not found in land warfare. For example, unlike the land, the sea is never stationary. Thus, weapons placed in the water in a belligerent zone, if not moored, can travel far away from the area of battle. Like weapons buried in the ground (e.g., anti-personnel landmines), underwater weapons (e.g., anti-ship mines) may persist for years after the war is over, but their removal may be more difficult than in the case of underground weapons because of the breadth of sea area over which they may be located, and the difficulty of locating them, particularly if they are not moored to the seabed.

The seas provide resources, including food, for many States, are used for international shipping of vast amounts of goods and significant numbers of people, and lie below the world's major air routes. Thus, all States have a stake in protecting the seas, as the condition of the seas and the creatures and plants that live in them, and the natural resources that the seas or the land underneath the seas contain, influence the quality of life around the world. Further, given the need to use the seas for shipping, all States have a great interest in ensuring that the seas remain available for use and exploitation, even during an armed conflict. Finally, the seas are a very dangerous place, in which lives and goods are likely to be lost if the vessels in which they are being carried are damaged. Accordingly international law expects all States to render aid when a vessel on the seas or its crew is in distress.[9]

In naval warfare, there is a great need at all times to be mindful of the rights of neutral States, because of the presence of neutral shipping on the naval battlefield and the maritime enviroment. Therefore, key elements of the law of naval warfare are intended to protect the rights of neutrals, even while belligerents engage in conflict at sea, and to ensure that neutrals are spared the effects

---

5. Geneva Convention for the Amelioration of the Condition of Wounded, Sick and Shipwrecked Members of the Armed Forces at Sea, Aug. 12, 1949, 6 U.S.T. 3217, 75 U.N.T.S. 971 (hereinafter GWS-Sea).

6. *See, e.g., id.*, art. 23.

7. SAN REMO MANUAL, *supra*, note 3, para. 4 ("[t]he principles of necessity and proportionality apply equally to armed conflict at sea . . . .").

8. *See infra*, Section IV.A (discussion of customary rule permitting naval warships to fly false colors).

9. *See* High Seas Convention, *supra*, note 2, art. 12; UNCLOS, *supra*, note 2, art. 98.

of the conflict.[10] Another goal of international law is to ensure that assistance is promptly provided to anyone (including the enemy) whose life is in danger at sea following any engagement among belligerents.[11]

The obligations imposed on a belligerent vessel are informed by the nature of the vessel and of the naval operations in which the vessel is engaged. For example, an undersea vessel (*i.e.*, a submarine) is small relative to many surface vessels, and shares with aircraft a limited ability to render aid to those who are *hors de combat* as a result of an attack. An undersea vessel also is extremely vulnerable to attack when surfaced. Thus, while the crew of an undersea vessel engaged in armed conflict is subject to all the obligations of the LOAC, the U.S. Navy takes the position that requirements arising from these obligations are informed by what the vessel can do in a practical sense to render aid to the wounded, sick, or shipwrecked.[12]

While undersea vessels have certain unique advantages in items of concealment from the enemy, the vessels that operate on the water, and the aircraft that operate over the water have little possibility of camouflaging themselves in the same manner as land forces (who may use paint or foliage to reduce their observability) and no possibility to shield themselves in the same manner as would land forces, which can use built-up areas, vegetation, or uneven terrain to shield themselves from observation. For this reason, it is essential for naval forces to be able to monitor and, where necessary, control all vessels and aircraft, including neutral vessels and aircraft, in the immediate vicinity of naval operations.[13] Further, the tenets of the LOAC that require land forces to distinguish themselves from civilians in all cases are relaxed at least in one respect in the case of naval forces in sea warfare, as discussed more fully below.[14]

II. Sources of the Law Applicable to Naval Warfare

In naval warfare, the legal practitioner must understand principles from three distinct but related areas of international law.

The first is the law of the sea, which is a broad and complex set of rules that govern the allocation of rights, obligations, and resources in respect of the

---

10. *See* SAN REMO MANUAL, *supra*, note 3, para. 12 ("In carrying out operations where neutral States enjoy sovereign rights, jurisdiction, or other rights under general international law, belligerents shall have due regard for the legitimate rights and duties of those neutral States.").

11. GWS-Sea, *supra*, note 5, art. 18. The International Committee of the Red Cross ("ICRC") contends that the obligation "to search for, collect and evacuate the wounded, sick and shipwrecked without adverse distinction" is a rule of customary international law applicable in both international and non-international armed conflicts. 1 JEAN-MARIE HENCKAERTS AND LOUISE DOSWALD-BECK, CUSTOMARY INTERNATIONAL HUMANITARIAN LAW 396 (2009) (Rule 109) (hereinafter "ICRC CIL STUDY").

12. *See* COMMANDER'S HANDBOOK, *supra*, note 4, para. 8.7; DoD LAW OF WAR MANUAL, *supra*, note 4, para. 13.7.2.

13. *See* SAN REMO MANUAL, *supra*, note 3, para. 108.

14. *See infra*, Section IV.A.

world's oceans and waters.[15] These rules apply at all times, including during times of armed conflict, because, even during armed conflict, the seas continue to be shared with States who are not in conflict, and who have rights to continued use of the oceans.

The second is the LOAC. The LOAC includes not only rules that apply specifically to naval weapons and operations, but also rules that apply to armed conflict generally, including belligerent rights, targeting, and protection of the sick and wounded. These general rules are relevant to all armed conflicts, including those occurring on, in or above the seas.

The third is the law of neutrality, which sets out the specific rights and obligations of States that wish to remain outside the scope of an armed conflict, and the rights and obligations of belligerents who conduct operations in a theater of war (the sea) in which neutrals and their property are regularly present. All States have the right to use the high seas, even during times when some States are engaged in conflict at sea, and the law of neutrality serves to protect vessels and aircraft of neutral States from the effects of the conflict, as long as these vessels and aircraft do not engage in acts harmful to a belligerent State.

Each of these areas of law is taken up in turn below.

III. The Law of Sea

To understand the law of naval warfare, one must understand, first, the division of the world's waters under international law, second, the freedoms that may be exercised in these waters under international law and, finally, the status under international law of vessels and aircraft operating on, in and over these waters. The following brief summary of the law of the sea relevant to naval operations is intended only to familiarize the student in broad terms with certain fundamental principles from the treaties on the law of the sea that are necessary to understand the LOAC applicable in naval warfare.[16] It is not a substitute for a more in-depth study of the subject, which is beyond the scope of this text.

A. The Division of the World's Waters

Under international law, the oceans, seas, and other waters of the earth can be divided into *national waters*, i.e., waters over which individual States enjoy exclusive sovereign rights and *international waters*, i.e., that portion of the world's waters over which no State has complete sovereignty, although, as noted

---

15. As stated in note 2, *supra*, the primary law of the sea treaty is UNCLOS. Although the United States is not a party to UNCLOS, it follows the provisions of UNCLOS related to the rights of navigation and overflight.

16. For example, GWS-Sea, *supra*, note 5, employs the term "warship" that is not defined in GWS-Sea but is defined in UNCLOS, *supra*, note 2.

below, international waters may include waters in which a coastal State enjoys some sovereign or economic rights.[17]

National waters include a State's *territorial sea*, which is a belt of ocean that is measured seaward from the baseline of a coastal State and over which it claims sovereignty,[18] and *internal waters*, which are all waters landward from the baseline from which the territorial waters are measured.[19] Thus, lakes, rivers, inland seas, and other waters that fall wholly within a State's territory or that define borders between States constitute internal waters. The calculation of baselines is beyond the scope of this book but depends on the geology of the State's coasts, including the impact of tides; the presence of bays, gulfs, and other geographic features; and whether the State's territory consists partially or completely of islands.

International waters are all ocean areas that are not subject to the territorial sovereignty of any State, and include *contiguous zones*, *exclusive economic zones*, and the *high seas*, all of which are defined, directly or indirectly, in applicable law of the sea treaties.[20] International waters can include waters that are not considered to be part of an ocean (*e.g.*, the Mediterranean Sea). In international waters, all States enjoy the traditional high seas freedoms of navigation and overflight,[21] and the right to conduct military operations in accordance with the LOAC during armed conflict. These freedoms are not limited by the fact that under modern law of the sea principles, coastal States are permitted to exercise certain rights in contiguous zones and exclusive economic zones.

A contiguous zone is an area extending seaward from a coastal State's territorial sea up to 24 nautical miles from its baseline. In its contiguous zone, the coastal State can exercise control to prevent or punish infringement of its customs, fiscal, immigration, and sanitary laws that occur within its territory or

---

17. The distinction between national and international waters is not found in UNCLOS, but is made in the Commander's Handbook and, in the opinion of the authors of this text, is a useful distinction for students. According to the Commander's Handbook:

> For operational purposes, the world's oceans are divided into two parts. The first includes internal waters, territorial seas, and archipelagic waters. These waters are subject to the territorial sovereignty of coastal States, with certain navigational rights reserved to the international community. The second part includes contiguous zones, waters of the EEZ, and the high seas. These are international waters in which all States enjoy the high seas freedoms of navigation and overflight.

COMMANDER'S HANDBOOK — 2017, *supra*, note 4, para. 1.5. *See also* DoD Law of War Manual, *supra*, note 4, para. 13.2.

18. UNCLOS *supra*, note 2, arts. 2-3. The United States and most States claim a territorial sea 12 nautical miles in width, while a few States claim territorial seas that are narrower or wider than 12 nautical miles. *See* ANNOTATED SUPPLEMENT TO COMMANDER'S HANDBOOK, *supra*, note 4, at 97-99 (Table A1-5). The United States does not recognize claims beyond 12 nautical miles, however. COMMANDER'S HANDBOOK — 2017, *supra*, note 4, para. 1.5.2.

19. UNCLOS, *supra*, note 2, art. 8.

20. *Id.*, art. 33 (contiguous zone), arts. 55-57 (exclusive economic zone), and art. 86 (high seas).

21. *Id.*, art. 87; SAN REMO MANUAL, *supra*, note 3, para. 10.

territorial sea.[22] However, the contiguous zone is not part of the coastal State's territory.[23]

An exclusive economic zone (also known as an EEZ) is an area adjacent to a coastal State's territorial waters and extending not more than 200 nautical miles from the coastal State's baselines.[24] In the EEZ, the coastal State can exercise certain economic and legal rights with respect to resources within the EEZ.[25] This includes exercising jurisdiction over exploration, exploitation, management, and conservation of natural resources in and under the EEZ; the use of the waters, currents, and winds in the zone to produce energy; the establishment of artificial installations in the zone having an economic purpose (e.g., oil drilling platforms); marine science research, marine environmental protection, and other resource-related matters affecting the zone.[26]

Waters beyond the EEZ are considered to be the high seas, in which all States enjoy equal rights.[27] Indeed, in areas where a coastal State has not claimed the right to an EEZ, the high seas begin at the seaward edge of that State's territorial sea.[28]

A State that consists wholly of one or more groups of islands, known as an "archipelagic" State, may draw straight baselines joining the outmost points of its outermost islands and thereby enclose waters that become "archipelagic waters."[29] Like internal waters, archipelagic waters are subject to the sovereignty of the archipelagic State, but subject to a right of "archipelagic sea lanes passage" by all States through the archipelagic waters.[30] The archipelagic State may designate the specific waters that will be used by the vessels and aircraft of other States to transit through its archipelagic waters, but if it does not, or if it only makes a partial designation, other States may exercise the right of archipelagic sea lanes passage through all the routes normally used for international navigation and overflight.[31]

---

22. UNCLOS, *supra*, note 2, art. 33.
23. DoD Law of War Manual, *supra*, note 4, para. 13.2.1.
24. Thus, the contiguous zone is included with the EEZ.
25. *Id.*, para. 13.2.3.3.
26. UNCLOS, *supra*, note 2, art. 57.
27. Id., art. 87 ("the high seas are open to all States").
28. Commander's Handbook — 2017, *supra*, note 4, para. 1.6.3 (stating this rule). Under UNCLOS, a coastal State has sovereign rights over the continental shelf for purposes of exploration and exploitation, UNCLOS, *supra*, note 2, art. 77, but these rights do not affect the legal status of the waters on top of the shelf, so that the width of the territorial waters, and the rights of navigation and overflight, are not determined by the continental shelf. *Id.*, art. 78.
29. The definition, rights, and obligations of archipelagic States can be found in Part IV of the UNCLOS.
30. The right of "archipelagic sea lanes passage" is substantially identical to the rights of "transit passage" through international straits, including rights of navigation and overflight (including submerged passage for submarines), for vessels that proceed in the sea lanes designated as such by the archipelagic State or that are normally used by international navigation. *See* Commander's Handbook — 2017, *supra*, note 4, para. 2.5.4.1. In other areas of archipelagic waters, the rules of "innocent passage" apply (including the prohibition of overflight and submerged passage). *Id.*, para. 2.5.4.2. Transit passage is discussed, *infra*, in this Section III.B.
31. UNCLOS, *supra*, note 2, art. 53(12).

B. The Exercise of Maritime Freedoms in National and International Waters

1. National Waters

A State's internal waters, like its land territory, are subject to its exclusive jurisdiction and control. Other States enjoy no more right to enter or operate in another State's internal waters than they do to enter or operate in that State's land territory, and entry into the internal waters of a State without its consent, except in certain emergency situations, would be considered a hostile act under international law that could justify an armed response by the State whose territorial waters were violated. Further, while a State may grant standing permission for foreign commercial vessels to enter internal waters (where, for example, commercial ports are located), another State's warships and auxiliary vessels[32] generally require specific and advance approval from a State in order to enter that State's internal waters.[33]

A State's territorial waters, by contrast, are subject to a limited right of "innocent passage," which, in peacetime, will allow any vessel, including foreign military vessels, to proceed through territorial waters continuously and expeditiously in order to travel from one part of international waters to another, or to reach the internal waters of the vessel's home country or of another country.[34] To constitute innocent passage, the vessel's transit through territorial waters must not be "prejudicial to the peace, good order, or security of the coastal State."[35] Acts that would disqualify the transit as innocent passage (absent consent of the coastal State) include:

- Any threat of use of force against the sovereignty, territorial integrity, or political independence of the coastal State, or in any manner that violates the international law principles embodied in the UN Charter;
- Any exercise or practice with weapons of any kind;
- Any act aimed at collecting information to the prejudice of the defense or security of the coastal State;
- Any act of propaganda aimed at affecting the defense or security of the coastal State;
- The launching, landing, or taking on board of any aircraft;
- The launching, landing, or taking on board of any military device;

---

32. For discussion of auxiliary vessels, *see infra* Section III.C.
33. COMMANDER'S HANDBOOK—2017, *supra*, note 4, para. 2.5.1 (noting that the rule also applies to aircraft, and may be modified if "other bilateral or multilateral arrangements have been concluded.")
34. UNCLOS, *supra*, note 2, art. 18. A ship in innocent passage may only stop and anchor "if incidental to ordinary navigation or rendered necessary by force majeure or distress or for the purposes of rendering assistance to persons, ships or aircraft in danger or distress." *Id. See also* COMMANDER'S HANDBOOK—2017, *supra*, note 4, para. 2.5.2.1 (description of innocent passage).
35. UNCLOS, *supra*, note 2, art. 19.

- The loading or unloading of any commodity, currency, or person contrary to the customs, fiscal, immigration, or sanitary laws and regulations of the coastal State;
- Any act of willful or serious pollution contrary to the UN Convention on the Law of the Sea;
- Any fishing activities;
- The carrying out of research or survey activities;
- Any act aimed at interfering with any systems of communications or any other facilities or installations of the coastal State; or
- Any other activity not having a direct bearing on passage.[36]

Notably, this list includes not only acts that are inconsistent with the security of the coastal State, but also acts contrary to its economic interests, which reflects the exclusive control that the coastal State exercises over its territorial seas.

Ships engaged in innocent passage must obey the laws and regulations enacted by the coastal State so long as these are consistent with international law.[37] Any ship failing to comply or otherwise violating the principles of innocent passage may be required by the coastal State to depart its territorial waters, and if the ship fails to do so, the coastal State may take all necessary action, including (with prior warning) military action to force the ship to depart or to neutralize the threat the ship poses.[38] This military action is an exercise of sovereignty and may be taken even in the absence of an armed conflict with the State to which the targeted ship belongs.

Innocent passage is limited in at least two respects. First, it does not include a right of overflight, meaning that, even though a vessel from a State may exercise the right of innocent passage through the territorial waters of another State, aircraft from the State to which the vessel belongs cannot also exercise the right of innocent passage. Thus, the vessel cannot be accompanied by aircraft in flight or, if aircraft are based on the vessel, they must remain on board throughout passage.[39] Second, the right of innocent passage does not include the right to transit submerged, so that submarines of other States must surface prior to entering a coastal State's territorial sea and remain on the surface throughout the passage.[40]

---

36. *Id.*
37. *Id.,* art. 21.
38. *Id.,* art. 25(1) ("[t]he coastal State may take the necessary steps in its territorial sea to prevent passage which is not innocent"); COMMANDER'S HANDBOOK — 2017, *supra,* note 4, para. 2.5.2.1 ("[i]f a foreign ship or aircraft enters the territorial sea or the airspace above it and engages in noninnocent activities, the appropriate remedy, consistent with customary international law, which includes the right of self-defense, is first to inform the ship or aircraft of the reasons the coastal nation questions the innocence of the passage, and to provide the vessel a reasonable opportunity to clarify its intentions or to correct its conduct in a reasonably short period of time.)
39. *See, e.g.,* UNCLOS, *supra,* note 2, art. 19(2)(e).
40. *Id.,* art. 20.

With advance notice during peacetime, a State can suspend the right of innocent passage through its waters temporarily to protect its security.[41] In armed conflict, it can be expected that each belligerent will engage in military operations against its enemy in the enemy's territory, including its territorial waters, and therefore its enemies will not enjoy the right of innocent passage through the belligerent's territorial waters. A belligerent also can suspend the right of neutrals to innocent passage through its territorial sea during armed conflict, except for those waters that fall within an international strait or archipelagic sea lane.[42]

A neutral State also can limit or suspend the right of passage through its waters during an armed conflict so long as it does so on a non-discriminatory basis, except that it may not suspend the right to innocent passage through waters that fall within an international strait or archipelagic sea lane.[43]

A regime of "transit passage" applies to international straits used by international navigation to travel from one part of international waters to another.[44] This specialized type of passage applies from shoreline to shoreline within the strait, and provides transiting vessels greater rights than in the case of innocent passage through a coastal State's territorial waters. So long as they proceed without delay through the strait; refrain from any threat or use of force against the sovereignty, territorial integrity, or political independence of States bordering the strait; and refrain from activities inconsistent with normal modes of continuous and expeditious transit (except as required by force majeure or distress), these vessels may engage in normal operations, including launching and recovery of aircraft; use of electronic detection, radar, sonar, and depth-sounding devices; submerging (in case of submarines); and so forth, as long as that is part of normal operations. Note that where an international strait does not consist entirely of overlapping territorial seas of bordering States, the portion outside of those territorial seas continues to be part of international waters where States can exercise their full rights of navigation and overflight.[45]

Transit passage can be regulated by the States bordering the strait in certain respects consistent with international law, but cannot be hampered or suspended.[46] In armed conflict, a belligerent is not permitted to launch attacks against its enemy in international straits and is to "refrain from any hostile actions or other activities not incident to their transit," but is allowed "to take

---

41. *Id.*, art. 25(3).

42. SAN REMO MANUAL, *supra*, note 3, para. 32.

43. *Id.*, paras. 19, 29, 31, and 33. In armed conflict, a neutral State also can permit "mere passage" by belligerent ships through its territorial waters without violating its neutrality. Convention Concerning the Rights and Duties of Neutral Powers in Naval War, Oct. 18, 1907, art. 10, 36 Stat. 2415, 1 Bevans 723 (hereinafter 1907 Hague XIII); SAN REMO MANUAL, *supra*, note 3, para. 20(a).

44. UNCLOS, *supra*, note 2, art. 38.

45. COMMANDER'S HANDBOOK — 2017, *supra*, note 4, para. 2.5.3.3. *See*, *id.*, para. 2.5.3, for a description of transit passage in international straits, including special rules that apply in straits that connect the high seas with a coastal State's territorial sea. *See also* DoD LAW OF WAR MANUAL, *supra*, note 4, para. 15.8.1 (passage of belligerent vessels and aircraft through international straits overlapped by neutral waters.).

46. UNCLOS, *supra*, note 2, arts. 42 and 44; SAN REMO MANUAL, *supra*, note 3, para. 29.

defensive measures consistent with their security."[47] The U.S. Navy's annotation of *The Commander's Handbook on the Law of Naval Operations*, notes, however, that a belligerent State that borders an international strait may attack enemy forces located in the portion of the strait overlapped by the belligerent State's coastal waters or in those portions of the strait that fall within the high seas or an EEZ.[48]

Note that an international strait should be distinguished from man-made canals that are used for international navigation, such as the Panama Canal. These canals typically fall within the territory of a single State, although not always (*e.g.*, the Suez Canal), and are subject to international agreements regarding their use that often seek to ensure that the canals remain neutral both in peacetime and war.[49]

2. International Waters

In international waters, including contiguous zones and EEZs, all ships and aircraft have complete freedom of movement and operation, including military vessels, auxiliary vessels, military aircraft, and State aircraft. This freedom permits the full range of military operations, including (i) during peacetime; intelligence gathering and training; and (ii) during armed conflict, offensive and defensive operations, as well as intelligence gathering and training. All activities, however, must be undertaken with due regard to the rights of other States and for the safe conduct and operation of other vessels and aircraft. These rights and obligations apply to activities on, under, and over international waters.[50]

States conducting dangerous operations in international waters (e.g., missile testing) can establish temporary warning zones to provide notice to other vessels and aircraft of the potential danger of proceeding into or through such zones, and there are various means by which notice of such zones can be provided. However, vessels and aircraft of other States are not obligated to remain outside these zones, as long as they do not interfere with the activities that are the subject of the zones.

In an armed conflict or other emergency, a State may claim the right to establish a security zone around its naval forces or around all or part of its territorial sea, based on its right of self-defense. Violation of the zone by a neutral is not justification *per se* for attack, and any use of force against the violator would be based upon the same standards of targeting that apply outside the zone.[51]

---

47. SAN REMO MANUAL, *supra*, note 3, para. 30. The Manual notes that the scope of this limitation has been debated among scholars: "The key point, in the minds of most, was a fair interpretation of the prohibition against using neutral waters as a base of operations." *Id.*, para. 30.3.

48. ANNOTATED SUPPLEMENT TO COMMANDER'S HANDBOOK, *supra*, note 4, para. 2.3.3.1 n. 42.

49. *See id.*, para. 2.3.3.1 n. 36 ("[m]an-made canals used for international navigation by definition are not 'straits used for international navigation,' and are generally controlled by agreement between the countries concerned. They are open to the use of all vessels, although tolls may be imposed for their use.")

50. *See, e.g.*, SAN REMO MANUAL, *supra*, note 3, para. 10.

51. SAN REMO MANUAL, *supra*, note 3, paras. 105 and 106.

C. Status of Vessels and Aircraft Under International Law

International law recognizes various categories of vessels and aircraft, with differing rights under the law. The rights of belligerents with respect to attack on, or capture of, these vessels and aircraft are defined by the LOAC, but the categories of vessels and aircraft are created by, or based upon, the peacetime law of the sea, which affords to every State the right "to sail ships flying its flag on the high seas"[52] and accords to each ship the nationality of the flag that it flies.[53]

All vessels and aircraft operating in, under, or over international waters should bear markings, and if possible, should be internationally registered, in a manner that will identify or "flag" them with a specific State. In times of armed conflict, all vessels and aircraft flagged to a belligerent on one side of the conflict will be treated as enemy vessels and aircraft by the belligerent or belligerents on the other side.[54] They may be captured[55] or, in certain cases (e.g., if an enemy warship or if a merchant vessel in a convoy protected by enemy warships) may be targeted and sunk.[56] On the other hand, vessels and aircraft flagged to a State that is not a belligerent, including warships, will be treated as neutral vessels or aircraft and are not subject to attack unless they take actions that deprive them of the right to be treated as a neutral under international law (see below).[57]

In times of armed conflict, the naval forces of each State are entitled to take reasonable measures to confirm the neutral status of vessels and aircraft except in cases where, under international law, the vessel or aircraft is exempt from being subjected to such measures. The measures typically involve stopping and boarding the vessel, examining its papers, and searching it where appropriate. Warships may only exercise this right of "visit and search" in an armed conflict and outside neutral waters, although there is a corresponding right in peacetime to approach on the high seas a vessel flagged by another State (other than a vessel owned or operated by a State and used only for government non-commercial service)[58] to verify its identity and to board it and examine its papers, where certain types of conduct are suspected (e.g., piracy).[59]

Warships are vessels (1) belonging to the armed forces of a State; (2) bearing external markings that distinguish the character and nationality of the vessels from civilian vessels and aircraft, including from State vessels and aircraft engaged in non-military government service; (3) under the command of an officer duly commissioned by the government of that State and duly listed as

---

52. UNCLOS, *supra,* note 2, art. 90.
53. *Id.,* art. 91.
54. *See, e.g.,* SAN REMO MANUAL, *supra,* note 3, para. 112.
55. *Id.,* para. 135.
56. *See, e.g., id.,* paras. 40 and 60.
57. *See, e.g., id.,* para. 67.
58. UNCLOS, *supra,* note 2, art. 96. According to this provision of UNCLOS, ships owned or operated by a State for non-government commercial purposes have "complete immunity" from the jurisdiction of any other State.
59. SAN REMO MANUAL, *supra,* note 3, para. 118. The conduct of peacetime "approach and visit" or maritime interception operations are beyond the scope of this chapter. *See* UNCLOS, *supra,* note 2, art. 110.

being in its military service; and (4) manned by a crew under regular armed forces discipline.[60] During an armed conflict, enemy warships are liable to attack, while neutral warships are protected from attack and exempt from any measures to verify their status, such as visit and search.[61]

Also exempt from visit and search measures are neutral "auxiliary vessels," which are vessels, other than warships, that are owned by or under the exclusive control of the armed forces of a State and used on government non-commercial service.[62]

Merchant vessels are vessels other than warships or non-commercial State vessels (including auxiliary vessels.) During an armed conflict, enemy merchant vessels are not subject to attack unless they engage in activities that render them military objectives,[63] but even if not military objectives, they can be captured and confiscated by an opposing belligerent State provided the capture occurs outside of neutral waters.[64] By contrast, neutral merchant vessels are not subject to attack or capture by a belligerent unless they violate their neutral status (e.g., by carrying contraband), which renders them subject to capture,[65] or take action (e.g., making an effective contribution to an enemy's military capabilities) that renders them a military objective subject to possible attack.[66] If a belligerent suspects a neutral merchant vessel of engaging in such activities, it may subject the vessel to a visit and search procedure to determine its status. Failure by a merchant vessel to submit to such visit and search itself can be treated as a hostile act and the vessel could be captured or attacked.[67]

There are corresponding categories of aircraft, including military aircraft, auxiliary aircraft, State aircraft, and civil aircraft.[68] Civil aircraft are subject to measures to verify their neutral status, but, due to the nature of air travel, the measures will involve requiring the aircraft to land for examination.

---

60. UNCLOS, *supra*, note 2, art. 30; SAN REMO MANUAL, *supra*, note 3, para. 13(g). There is a corresponding category of military aircraft. *Id.*, para. 13(j).

61. *See* COMMANDER'S HANDBOOK — 2017, *supra*, note 4, para. 7.6 (neutral warships are exempt from visit and search) and para. 8.6.1 (belligerent warships may be targeted).

62. SAN REMO MANUAL, *supra*, note 3, para. 13(h).

63. *Id.*, paras. 59 and 60.

64. *Id.*, para. 135. Certain categories of vessels are exempt from capture (e.g., vessels transporting the sick or wounded). *Id.*, para. 136.

65. *Id.*, para. 146.

66. *Id.*, para. 67.

67. *Id.*

68. An important subcategory of civil aircraft is civil airliners, which are presumed not to be making an effective contribution to military action, and are therefore not subject to attack. *See* PROGRAM ON HUMANITARIAN POLICY AND CONFLICT RESEARCH AT HARVARD UNIVERSITY, MANUAL ON INTERNATIONAL LAW APPLICABLE TO AIR AND MISSILE WARFARE, Rule 59 (2009) ("In case of doubt, civil airliners — either in flight or on the ground in a civilian airport — are presumed not to be making an effective contribution to military action.") The presumption is rebuttable, however. *See* PROGRAM ON HUMANITARIAN POLICY AND CONFLICT RESEARCH AT HARVARD UNIVERSITY, COMMENTARY ON HPCR MANUAL ON INTERNATIONAL LAW APPLICABLE TO AIR AND MISSILE WARFARE 157 (2010) ("The presumption is rebuttable, since the airliner may actually be used to carry combatants or otherwise make an effective contribution to military action.")

Hospital ships and medical aircraft are protected from attack under international law,[69] but measures may be taken to verify their protected status.

IV. The LOAC Applicable to Naval Warfare

The preceding section dealt with the laws applicable to peacetime navigation that are relevant background to the LOAC. In naval warfare, the conduct of hostilities between belligerents is also subject to a set of LOAC rules that in most respects is identical to the rules applicable to armed conflicts on land. For historical reasons or because of the special nature of naval operations, however, there are differences in certain respects between the LOAC at sea and the LOAC applicable on land, as the following discussion will show.

A. Sources

The first international treaty on naval warfare was the Paris Declaration Respecting Maritime Law of April 1856.[70] It abolished privateering, which was the practice of States of granting "letters of marque" to private vessels that authorized those vessels to capture merchant vessels of the granting State's enemy or to attack the enemy's warships. While privateering gave a State access to additional forces to wage war against its enemies, privateers bore in some respects the same traits as pirates, who were considered to be international criminals, and the use of privateers made it difficult to impose discipline on naval warfare. The Paris Declaration also established basic rules for blockades and provided for protection against seizure of enemy-owned goods being shipped on neutral vessels, except for contraband (see discussion of contraband, *supra*).

The international community did not agree upon any new treaties on naval warfare until 1907, with the adoption of a number of conventions dealing with naval subjects at the end of the Second Peace Conference at The Hague in the Netherlands (each referred to herein in shorthand form, such as 1907 Hague XIII). These conventions were:

(a) Hague Convention No. VI Relating to the Status of Enemy Merchant Ships at the Outbreak of Hostilities;

---

69. *See, e.g.,* GWS-Sea *supra,* note 5, art. 22 (hospital ships); Geneva Convention for the Amelioration of the Wounded and Sick in Armed Force in the Field, Aug. 12, 1949, art. 36 (medical aircraft), 6 U.S.T. 3114, 75 U.N.T.S. 31 (hereinafter GWS). The 1977 Additional Protocols I and 2 Protocol also include articles protecting medical transports of various types. Protocol Additional to the Geneva Conventions of 12 August 1949, and Relating to the Protection of Victims of International Armed Conflicts, June 8, 1977, arts. 21-31, 1125 U.N.T.S. 17512, (hereinafter AP I); Protocol Additional to the Geneva Conventions of 12 Aug. 1949, and Relating to the Protection of Victims of Non-International Armed Conflicts, June 8, 1977, art. 11, 1125 U.N.T.S. 609 (hereinafter AP II). The United States is not a party to either AP I or AP II. *See* Chapter 3 for a discussion of the U.S. position on AP I and AP II.

70. Declaration Respecting Maritime Law, April 16, 1856, *reprinted in* 1 AM. J. INT'L L. SUPP. 89 (1907).

(b) Hague Convention No. VII relating to the Conversion of Merchant Ships into Warships;

(c) Hague Convention No. VIII Relative to the Laying of Automatic Submarine Contact Mines;

(d) Hague Convention No. IX Concerning Bombardment by Naval Forces in Time of War;

(e) Hague Convention No. X for the Adaptation to Maritime Warfare of the Principles of the Geneva Convention;

(f) Hague Convention No. XI Relative to Certain Restrictions with Regard to the Exercise of the Right of Capture in Naval War; and

(g) Hague Convention No. XIII Concerning the Rights and Duties of Neutral Powers in Naval War.[71]

1907 Hague XIII, which bears on the rights and obligations of neutral States, is discussed, *infra,* in Section V of this Chapter. Of the remaining Conventions, 1907 Hague VIII is the most pertinent today, and is dealt with, *infra,* in Section IV.H.

The only other generally applicable treaties on naval warfare adopted since 1907 that are still in effect are a 1936 protocol dealing with submarine warfare[72] and the 1949 Geneva Convention for the Amelioration of the Condition of Wounded, Sick and Shipwrecked Members of Armed Forces at Sea.[73]

However, a great deal of the law of naval warfare has emerged as customary international law, as reflected in certain treaties that were never adopted but are widely cited, or international efforts among scholars and experts to define the principles of the law of naval warfare. The unadopted treaties include, most prominently, the 1909 London Declaration Concerning the Laws of Naval War,[74] while the efforts to define the legal principles include the Oxford Manual of the Laws of Naval War of 1913[75] and the 1994 San Remo Manual on International

---

71. The following are the citations for the conventions listed in the text: (i) Convention Relating to the Status of Enemy Merchant Ships at the Outbreak of Hostilities, Oct. 18, 1907, 205 Consol. T.S. 305, 3 Martens Nouveau Recueil (ser. 3) 533 (1907 Hague VI); (ii) Convention Relating to the Conversion of Merchant Ships into War-Ships, Oct. 18, 1907, 205 Consol. T.S. 319, 3 Martens Nouveau Recueil (ser. 3) 557 (1907 Hague VII); (iii) Convention Relative to the Laying of Automatic Submarine Contact Mines, Oct. 18, 1907, 36 Stat. 2332, 1 Bevans 669 (1907 Hague VIII); (iv) Convention Concerning Bombardment by Naval Forces in Time of War, Oct. 18, 1907, 36 Stat. 2351, 1 Bevans 681 (1907 Hague IX); (v) Convention for the Adaption to Maritime War of the Principles of the Geneva Convention, Oct. 18, 1907, 36 Stat. 2371, 1 Bevans 694 (1907 Hague X); (vi) Convention Relative to Certain Restrictions with Regard to the Exercise of the Right of Capture in Naval War, Oct. 18, 1907, 36 Stat. 2396, 1 Bevans 711 (1907 Hague XI); and (vii) Convention Concerning the Rights and Duties of Neutral Powers in Naval War, Oct. 18, 1907, 36 Stat. 2415, 1 Bevans 723 (1907 Hague XIII). Of these, the United States only ratified 1907 Hague VIII, IX, X, XI and XIII. The 1907 Hague Convention XII relative to the Creation of an International Prize Court never entered into force.

72. Procès-Verbal Relating to Rules of Submarine Warfare Set Forth in Part IV of the Treaty of London of 22 April 1930, Nov. 6, 1936, 3 Bevans 298, 173 L.N.T.S. 353 (hereinafter, 1936 London Protocol).

73. GWS-Sea, *supra,* note 5. 1907 Hague X, *supra,* note 71, is the predecessor of this 1949 Convention.

74. Declaration Concerning the Laws of Naval War, Feb. 26, 1909, *reprinted in* 3 AM. J. INT'L L. 179 (1909).

75. RESOLUTIONS OF THE INSTITUTE OF INTERNATIONAL LAW DEALING WITH THE LAW OF NATIONS 174-201 (James Scott ed., CARNEGIE ENDOWMENT FOR INTERNATIONAL PEACE) (1916).

Law Applicable to Armed Conflicts at Sea.[76] Together, these sources provide a wealth of guidance on the law of naval warfare that is reflected in military manuals, such as the U.S. Navy's Commander's Handbook on the Law of Naval Operations, which was most recently updated in 2017, and the DoD Law of War Manual, which was most recently updated in 2016.

It should be noted that, except where there is a special rule for naval warfare, all the treaties and conventions, as well as the principles of the LOAC, that deal with land warfare, as discussed in earlier chapters of this book, also will apply to naval warfare. Thus, just as in land warfare, parties to the conflict are obligated to distinguish between civilians and other protected persons, who are not subject to attack, and combatants, who are subject to attack. Further, in launching attacks from, over, or under the sea against any lawful targets, belligerents apply the same principles of humanity and proportionality as apply to attacks launched from the land.[77] Indeed, if the target is on shore, any treaty provision that explicitly applies to land-based targets would apply even though the attack is launched from the sea.

One of the few examples of a deviation from the law of land warfare is in the area of perfidy. Under the customary international law of naval warfare, it is permissible, and not considered perfidy, for a belligerent warship to fly false colors and disguise its outward appearance in other ways in order to deceive the enemy into believing the vessel is of neutral nationality or is other than a warship. This would not be permitted on land, where any disguise to feign civilian status to lure an enemy into an attack would be considered perfidy and prohibited. Note, however, that even in naval warfare, the use of neutral flags, insignia, or uniforms during an actual armed engagement at sea is forbidden and thus, even if disguised up to the point of engagement, it is unlawful for a warship to go into action against its enemy without first showing her true colors.[78]

Another example of differences in naval warfare is the treatment of merchant vessels. While in the conduct of operations on land, a belligerent armed force may use, and in some cases, destroy private property as required by military operations, there is no general right to seize and confiscate "unless such destruction or seizure be imperatively demanded by the necessities of war."[79] By contrast, the law applicable to naval warfare gives belligerents the general right to capture and potentially confiscate enemy merchant vessels and civil aircraft outside of neutral territory,[80] subject to certain exceptions.[81] Arguably, the law

---

76. SAN REMO MANUAL, *supra*, note 3.
77. *See, e.g.*, SAN REMO MANUAL, *supra*, note 3, para. 46; AP I, *supra*, note 69, art. 57(4).
78. For an interesting discussion of the rule, *see* C. Griggs, *False Colours in the Law of Naval Warfare*, 2003 N.Z. ARMED FORCES L. REV. 5.
79. Convention Respecting the Laws and Customs of War on Land, Oct. 18, 1907, art. 23, 1 Bevans 631, 36 Stat. 2277 (hereinafter 1907 Hague IV). The rule is discussed in FM 27-10, the U.S. Army's field manual on the law of land warfare. U.S. DEP'T OF ARMY, FIELD MANUAL 27-10, THE LAW OF LAND WARFARE (July 1956), paras. 58-59 and 405-411 (hereinafter FM 27-10).
80. *See* SAN REMO MANUAL, *supra*, note 3, paras. 135 and 141. Confiscation is subject to adjudication in a prize court, but a captured vessel also might be destroyed if military circumstances preclude sending it for adjudication. *See, e.g., id.*, paras. 138-140.
81. *See id.*, paras. 136-137 and 142-143.

in both land and naval warfare is based on the same principle — military necessity — but the application of the rule in naval warfare provides for greater scope for seizure and confiscation of enemy private property.

B. Rights to Engage in Warfare at Sea

As with land warfare, only States have a right to engage in armed conflict at sea. Any groups or individuals who engage in such conduct without State authority risk being characterized as pirates. Piracy is one of the oldest recognized crimes against international law and a pirate can be captured and prosecuted by any State, even if the pirate has not engaged in piratical activities against the capturing State — an early form of universal jurisdiction.[82]

A State may only wage war on the oceans against other States with warships and military aircraft.[83] These vessels are subject to attack or capture by the State's enemies in an armed conflict. Other ships and aircraft, even if operated by a belligerent State, are treated as civilian objects and are generally protected from attack, but not capture. If, however, such vessels and aircraft participate in hostilities or otherwise render themselves military objectives, they also may be attacked.[84]

As with land warfare, only certain categories of individuals enjoy the combatant's privilege in naval warfare, i.e., only these individuals can lawfully participate in hostilities.[85] The categories of individuals enjoying this privilege are the same as in land warfare:

> (a) Members of the armed forces of a Party to the conflict, as well as members of militias or volunteer corps forming part of such armed forces.
> (b) Members of other militias and members of other volunteer corps, including those of organized resistance movements, belonging to a Party to the conflict and operating in or outside the State's own territory, even if this territory is occupied, provided that such militias or volunteer corps, including such organized resistance movements, fulfill the following conditions:
>> (i) commanded by a person responsible for his subordinates;
>> (ii) wearing a fixed distinctive sign recognizable at a distance;
>> (iii) carrying arms openly; and
>> (iv) conducting their operations in accordance with the laws and customs of war.
>
> (c) Members of regular armed forces who profess allegiance to a government or an authority not recognized by the other Party to the conflict.

---

82. *See* UNCLOS, *supra*, note 2, arts. 100-105.
83. There is no generally accepted rule of naval warfare that requires a State to limit operations in a non-international armed conflict to State-registered warships. *See* DoD Law of War Manual, *supra*, note 4, para. 13.3.3.1. However, in any armed conflict, a State must ensure that its forces are distinguishable from civilians, and use of civilian ships to conduct combat operations against a non-State armed group could undermine a State's ability to fulfill this obligation.
84. *See* San Remo Manual, *supra*, note 3, para. 41.
85. *See* Commander's Handbook — 2017, *supra*, note 4, para. 5.4.1.

(d) Inhabitants of a non-occupied territory who, on the approach of the enemy, spontaneously take up arms to resist the invading forces, without having had time to form themselves into regular armed units, provided they carry arms openly and respect the laws and customs of war.

In naval warfare, the existence of resistance forces or militias at seas would be an exceptional occurrence, and therefore the individuals with combatant immunity who are likely to be encountered at sea generally are limited to officers and enlisted members of a belligerent's naval forces and uniformed armed forces accompanying them (e.g., naval infantry, such as U.S. Marines).

C. General Rules Regarding Attacks on, or Captures of, Vessels

Although 1907 Hague IX specifically deals with bombardment of land targets by naval artillery,[86] 1907 Hague IX has been subsumed within the general rules that govern targeting in armed conflict, as discussed more fully in Chapter 7 of this book. Attacks launched from the air, sea, or land against any target (whether the target itself is in, over, or under the land or sea) are subject to the same principles of necessity, proportionality, and humanity. Thus, as in land warfare, in naval warfare attacks are to be limited to strictly military objectives.

1. Vessels Subject to Attack

Enemy warships (including auxiliaries) generally are military objectives at all times, and subject to attack without warning, with the exception of (1) military vessels that also are exempt from capture (see the list below); (2) medical transports (whether or not needed for wounded, sick, and shipwrecked); (3) vessels that have surrendered; and (4) life rafts and life boats. It is particularly forbidden to target an enemy warship that in good faith unambiguously and effectively conveys a timely offer of surrender.

Enemy merchant vessels are subject to capture (see the discussion below) but not subject to attack unless by their nature, location, purpose, or use they become a military objective.[87] This is fundamentally the same standard as applies under Article 52 of AP I.

The San Remo Manual lists a number of ways in which an enemy merchant vessel may become a military objective and thereby subject to attack:

(a) engaging in belligerent acts on behalf of the enemy, e.g., laying mines, minesweeping, cutting undersea cables and pipelines, engaging in visit and search of neutral merchant vessels, or attacking other merchant vessels;

---

86. Article 2 of 1907 Hague IX is historically interesting because it is one of the few treaty provisions to list specific types of military targets for bombing, but today the same rules that apply to distinguishing military objectives from civilian objects apply to both land and sea warfare, as reflected in the San Remo Manual's paragraphs 38-46, which follow the general rules on targeting found in AP I.

87. SAN REMO MANUAL, *supra*, note 3, para. 59.

(b) acting as an auxiliary to an enemy's armed forces, e.g., carrying troops or replenishing warships;

(c) being incorporated into or assisting the enemy's intelligence gathering system, e.g., engaging in reconnaissance, early warning, surveillance, or command, control, and communications missions;

(d) sailing under convoy of enemy warships or military aircraft;

(e) refusing an order to stop or actively resisting visit, search, or capture;

(f) being armed to an extent that could inflict damage to a warship; this excludes light individual weapons for the defense of personnel, e.g., against pirates, and purely deflective systems such as 'chaff'; or

(g) otherwise making an effective contribution to military action, e.g., carrying military materials.[88]

Under these circumstances, no advance warning need be given to the vessel before it is attacked. Of course, where a merchant vessel is subject to attack, the rules governing the rescue of the shipwrecked and the treatment of the wounded or sick would apply to the merchant vessel under attack.[89] In addition, even where a merchant vessel is a military objective, the principles of proportionality and precautions would apply so that the attack should not be launched if the collateral casualties or damage to civilians and civilian objects would be excessive in relation to the concrete and direct military advantage anticipated from the attack as a whole.[90]

Certain vessels are exempt from attack, however. According to the San Remo Manual, these vessels include the following:

(a) hospital ships;

(b) small craft used for coastal rescue operations and other medical transports;

(c) vessels granted safe conduct by agreement between the belligerent parties, including:

(i) cartel vessels, e.g., vessels designated for and engaged in the transport of prisoners of war;

(ii) vessels engaged in humanitarian missions, including vessels carrying supplies indispensable to the survival of the civilian population, and vessels engaged in relief actions and rescue operations;

(d) vessels engaged in transporting cultural property under special protection;

(e) passenger vessels when engaged only in carrying civilian passengers;

(f) vessels charged with religious, non-military scientific or philanthropic missions, [however,] vessels collecting scientific data of likely military applications are not protected;

(g) small coastal fishing vessels and small boats engaged in local coastal trade, but they are subject to the regulations of a belligerent naval commander operating in the area and to inspection;

---

88. *Id.*, para. 60.
89. *See, e.g.*, ICRC CIL Study, *supra*, note 11, Rule 109.
90. San Remo Manual, *supra*, note 3, para. 61 (noting that attacks on merchant vessels are subject to the same "basic rules" that apply to attacks on warships.)

(h) vessels designated or adapted exclusively for responding to pollution incidents in the marine environment;
(i) vessels which have surrendered; and
(j) life rafts and life boats.[91]

The San Remo Manual provides that, to remain exempt from attack, the vessels must "(a) [be] . . . innocently employed in their normal role; (b) submit to identification when required; and (c) [not] . . . intentionally hamper the movement of combatants and obey orders to stop or move out of the way when required."[92] According to the San Remo Manual, however, a vessel that has lost its exemption may only be attacked if: "(a) diversion or capture is not feasible; (b) no other method is available for exercising military control; (c) the circumstances of non-compliance are sufficiently grave that the vessel has become, or may be reasonably assumed to be, a military objective; and (d) the collateral casualties or damage will not be disproportionate to the military advantage gained or expected."[93] Further, in the case of a hospital ship, a warning also must be given, along with a reasonable time to comply, before attacking the ship, and, like other vessels that have lost their exemption, the conditions in the prior sentence must be met.[94]

2. Vessels Subject to Capture

Even if the vessel is not subject to attack, a belligerent may capture the vessel if it has "enemy character." Enemy character can be acquired in a number of ways.

First, enemy warships (and auxiliaries (e.g., civilian vessels chartered to serve as military transports and military cargo ships), always have enemy character.

Second, any merchant vessel that flies the flag of a belligerent's enemy, or any civil aircraft that bears the marks of an enemy, is considered to have enemy character. Enemy character also can be determined by the registration, ownership, charter, or other criteria that indicate that the vessel or aircraft is under enemy control. The fact that a vessel or aircraft is not owned by the government of an enemy is not relevant for this purpose; it is sufficient if it is registered or chartered to, or owned by, an enemy citizen. The fact that the LOAC permits any merchant vessel to be subject to capture if owned by an enemy citizen may suggest a broader rule than in land warfare, where seizure is only permitted where militarily necessary, but given the utility of merchant vessels for military purposes, it is likely that a comparable land transport also would be subject to seizure under the LOAC.

Third, as discussed *infra*, merchant vessels from neutral States may acquire enemy character by carrying contraband or engaging in other hostile acts. Where a vessel is flagged to a neutral State or bears a neutral State's marks, it

---

91. *Id.*, para. 47.
92. *Id.*, para. 48.
93. Id., para. 52.
94. *Id.*, paras. 49-51.

will be presumed to be neutral but it is subject to visit and search to establish its true character.

In distinction from neutral vessels, no visit and search is required to capture an enemy vessel or the cargo on board the vessel. Capture must occur outside of neutral waters. Captured vessels are subject to "prize" proceedings in court, in which cargo owners from neutral States may seek to claim their non-contraband cargo or receive compensation for it (e.g., if the cargo was perishable and was rendered unfit for use due to the seizure). Cargo owned by enemy citizens, and the enemy merchant vessel itself, are subject to condemnation without compensation. The details of prize proceedings are outside the scope of this book.

Even where a merchant vessel is not a military objective but is only subject to capture, it nonetheless may be destroyed "as an exceptional measure" (according to the San Remo Manual) when military circumstances preclude taking or sending the vessel for adjudication as an enemy prize, but only if all the following criteria are met:

> (a) the safety of passengers and crew is provided for; for this purpose, the ship's boats are not regarded as a place of safety unless the safety of the passengers and crew is assured in the prevailing sea and weather conditions by the proximity of land or the presence of another vessel that is in a position to take them on board;
> (b) documents and papers relating to the prize are safeguarded; and
> (c) if feasible, personal effects of the passengers and crew are saved.[95]

These criteria are from the London Protocol of 1936, to which almost all of the belligerents of World War II expressly acceded.[96] The Protocol provides in part that:

> [E]xcept in the case of persistent refusal to stop on being duly summoned, or of active resistance to visit or search, a warship, whether surface vessel or submarine, may not sink or render incapable of navigation a merchant vessel without having first placed passengers, crew and ship's papers in a place of safety. For this purpose the ship's boats are not regarded as a place of safety unless the safety of the passengers and crew is assured, in the existing sea and weather conditions, by the proximity of land, or the presence of another vessel which is in a position to take them on board.[97]

---

95. *Id.*, para. 139. The San Remo Manual notes, however, that destruction at sea of enemy passenger ships which are carrying only civilian passengers is prohibited. *Id.*, para. 140. Instead, such ships should be diverted to a place where capture can be completed.

96. 1936 London Protocol, *supra*, note 72. The 1936 London Protocol continued in effect a 1930 treaty provision that prohibited the destruction of enemy merchant vessels unless the safety of the passengers, crew, and ship's papers were first assured. Under the 1936 Protocol, merely assuring that the passengers and crew could take to lifeboats is not considered to be sufficient unless their safety was assured given weather and sea conditions, the proximity of land, or the presence of another vessel that could rescue them.

97. During World War II, enemy merchant vessels were attacked and sunk by surface warships and submarines without prior warning and without first providing for the safety of passengers and crew. Various reasons were given by the belligerents to justify the failure to comply with the 1936 London Protocol, including reprisal for enemy acts in violation of international law. Later in the war, however, merchant vessels were incorporated directly or indirectly into each belligerent's war effort, including by being armed and convoyed, and participating in intelligence gathering. Consequently,

Various types of enemy vessels are exempt from capture. According to the San Remo Manual, these include:

> (a) hospital ships and small craft used for coastal rescue operations;
> (b) other medical transports, so long as they are needed for the wounded, sick and shipwrecked on board;
> (c) vessels granted safe conduct by agreement between the belligerent parties including:
> > (i) cartel vessels, e.g., vessels designated for and engaged in the transport of prisoners of war; and
> > (ii) vessels engaged in humanitarian missions, including vessels carrying supplies indispensable to the survival of the civilian population, and vessels engaged in relief actions and rescue operations;
>
> (d) vessels engaged in transporting cultural property under special protection;
> (e) vessels charged with religious, non-military scientific or philanthropic missions; vessels collecting scientific data of likely military applications are not protected;
> (f) small coastal fishing vessels and small boats engaged in local coastal trade, but they are subject to the regulations of a belligerent naval commander operating in the area and to inspection, and
> (g) vessels designed or adapted exclusively for responding to pollution incidents in the marine environment when actually engaged in such activities.[98]

A vessel's immunity from capture requires that it (i) is innocently employed in their normal role; (ii) does not commit acts harmful to the enemy (i.e., it has not engaged in activities that make it a military objective); (iii) immediately submits to identification and inspection when required; and (iv) does not intentionally hamper the movement of combatants and obeys orders to stop or move out of the way when required.[99]

D. Disposition of Crews and Passengers

Officers and crews of captured enemy warships and merchant ships and military and civilian aircraft may be detained. Personnel on board an enemy warship or airplane, including civilian technicians and others accompanying the military forces manning the warship or aircraft, are considered to be prisoners of war or, in the case of medical personnel and chaplains, retained personnel. GPW Article 4A(5) provides that "[m]embers of crews, including masters, pilots and apprentices, of the merchant marine and the crews of civil aircraft of the Parties

---

as the U.S. Navy's Commander's Handbook on the Law of Naval Operations notes, eventually "enemy merchant vessels were widely regarded as legitimate military targets subject to destruction on sight." COMMANDER'S HANDBOOK — 2017, *supra*, note 4, para. 8.6.2.2. While the 1936 London Protocol was largely violated in World War II, the Protocol's criteria continue to apply today. However, as noted in the Commander's Handbook, the rules have to be interpreted in light of "current technology" and the customary practice of belligerents in World War II and thereafter. *Id.*

98. San Remo Manual, *supra*, note 3, para. 136.

99. *Id.*, para. 137.

to the conflict, who do not benefit by more favorable treatment under any other provisions of international law" are entitled to treatment as prisoners of war under the GPW.[100] Other enemy nationals on board captured ships and aircraft as private passengers are subject to the discipline of the captor.[101]

Nationals of a neutral State on board captured enemy merchant vessels and civilian aircraft should not be detained unless they have participated in acts of hostility or resistance against the captor or are otherwise in the service of the enemy.

E. Blockade

A blockade is a military operation by which a belligerent's forces will deny all vessels and aircraft access to enemy territory, regardless of whether those vessels and aircraft are carrying contraband goods. As such, it is different than the right of a belligerent to visit and search neutral shipping and aircraft to determine if they are carrying contraband to enemy territory. Both blockade and visit and search operations are authorized by the customary law of war and recognized in treaty law,[102] but a blockade has potentially more far-reaching effects on the enemy's economy and its civilian population.

The traditional criteria for a lawful blockade are:

(a) A formal declaration of the blockade, including the duration, geographic limits, and grace period for neutral vessels to leave blockaded ports;

(b) Advance notification to neutrals (to ensure that they do not attempt to breach the blockade) of both the commencement and termination of the blockade, and its details;

(c) Effective enforcement of the blockade, i.e., not haphazard or unpredictable;

(d) Impartial enforcement against all shipping and aircraft attempting to enter the blockaded area (i.e., not just enemy merchant vessels and aircraft); and

(e) Reasonable geographic scope and enforcement to ensure the blockade does not interfere with third-country trade and does not block access to the ports and coasts of neutral States.[103]

---

100. An "other provision of international law" that might apply is 1907 Hague XI, *supra,* note 71, which stipulates that crew of captured vessels are not made prisoners of war under certain conditions.

101. COMMANDER'S HANDBOOK — 2017, *supra,* note 4, para. 8.6.2.1 (stating rule). The meaning of the phrase "subject to the discipline of the captor" is not clear, but it may only indicate that such persons may be detained until their status is determined, which is consistent with paragraph 167 of the San Remo Manual, *supra,* note 3 ("Persons on board vessels and aircraft having fallen into the power of a belligerent or neutral shall be protected and respected . . . [and] until determination of their status, they shall be subject to the jurisdiction of the State exercising power over them.") In any event, they are to be treated humanely. *Id.*, para. 167 (treatment of civilians as protected persons under the Fourth Geneva Convention).

102. The only treaty provisions that specifically address the international law requirements for a blockade can be found in the Paris Declaration Respecting Maritime Law of April 1856, *supra,* note 70.

103. *See* SAN REMO MANUAL, *supra,* note 3, paras. 93-101. These criteria are reflected in the discussion of blockades in the DoD Law of War Manual. DOD LAW OF WAR MANUAL, *supra,* note 4, para.

The latter element is particularly important, in that it ensures the blockade does not otherwise interfere with neutral States' fundamental rights of navigation on the high seas.

While the traditional rules of blockade permitted a total blocking of all trade with a blockaded country or area, modern LOAC treaties have imposed limitations on how far a blockade can go in terms of its effect of the civilian population. For example, AP I Article 54(1) specifically prohibits the use of starvation of civilians as a method of warfare. Thus, a blockade that has as its sole purpose the starvation of civilians clearly would be illegal. Even where the blockade does not have starvation as its sole purpose, it has been argued that, under the principles articulated in AP I Article 70, if the civilian population of the blockaded territory does not have adequate supplies of food or other objects essential for its survival, the blockading State must allow for free passage of neutral ships and aircraft delivering such supplies, subject to any necessary technical arrangements imposed by the blockading State to ensure that the supplies are given to the civilian population and not its enemy's armed forces (there being no prohibition under international law against the use of starvation as a weapon against the enemy's armed forces who are not *hors de combat*).[104]

The permissible geographic scope of a blockade can be controversial. As traditionally conceived, a blockade is imposed close to an enemy's ports, so as to minimize interference with neutral shipping. Today, weapons such as high performance military aircraft and submarines could make close-in blockades difficult to implement. In the Vietnam War, however, the United States successfully implemented a close-in blockade using underwater mines (though the operation was not referred to as a "blockade" at the time). [105]

A blockade is an act of war, against which a State would have the right of self-defense under the UN Charter, and also could trigger an international armed conflict for purposes of the application of LOAC under the rules discussed

---

13.10.2. The 1909 Declaration Concerning the Law of Naval War, *supra*, note 74, which was signed by the United States, contains these requirements but it never entered into force. The 1909 Declaration says that the blockade cannot extend beyond the ports and coasts of the enemy, which means that it cannot bar access to neutral ports or block international shipping lanes. The DoD Law of War Manual states that a blockade "must not bar access to, or departure from, neutral ports and coasts" and "must not be used for the purpose of starving the civilian population." DoD LAW OF WAR MANUAL, *supra*, note 4, para. 13.10.2.5 (citations omitted). The DoD Law of War Manual also requires a blockade to meet the proportionality test used in targeting, in regards to the incidental harm the blockade is expected to cause to the civilian population. *Id.*

104. SAN REMO MANUAL, *supra*, note 3, para. 103. The San Remo Manual derives this rule from Article 70 of AP I, which requires that "relief actions" be undertaken when the civilian population of territory under the control of a party to the conflict is not adequately supplied with essential items needed for survival. By its terms, however, this article is not directly applicable to a blockade, because a blockade does not place the civilian population of the blockaded territory under the control of the blockading States. Nevertheless, the San Remo Manual has derived from Article 70 the obligation stated in the text, although commentary to paragraph 103 of the San Remo Manual notes that "[t]he issue whether such an obligation exists under the Protocol, is still heavily debated." SAN REMO MANUAL, *supra*, note 3, para. 103.2.

105. COMMANDER'S HANDBOOK — 2017, *supra*, note 4, para. 7.7.5. For a description of the mining operation, *see* WILLIAM L. GREER, THE 1972 MINING OF HAIPHONG HARBOR: A CASE STUDY IN NAVAL MINING AND DIPLOMACY (1997).

in Chapter 3.[106] In the Cuban Missile Crisis, the U.S. government considered, but rejected, use of a blockade in fashioning a response to the construction of Soviet missile facilities in Cuba. Instead, pursuant to a recommendation by the Organization of American States authorizing all members States to take individual and collective action to ensure that Cuba could not continue to receive military material and supplies,[107] the United States imposed a "quarantine" on "cargoes of offensive weapons," bound for Cuba.[108] Instead of blocking all trade, the quarantine merely sought to interdict particular types of goods with a clear nexus to regional security. The U.S. position was that a quarantine, supported by the action of a regional body such as the OAS according to its procedures, was a use of force consistent with the UN Charter.[109]

A blockade similarly should be distinguished from embargoes, in which the international community agrees, typically through a UN Security Council resolution, to prohibit the shipment of certain goods to one or more targeted countries as an international sanction intended to compel these countries to comply with international law. For example, in response to the invasion of Kuwait in 1990, the Security Council imposed an economic embargo on Iraq in 1990[110] and requested naval forces of UN member States to enforce the embargo.[111] The embargo was enforced by a multinational Maritime Intercept Operation that searched vessels to ensure compliance with the embargo. This Maritime Intercept Operation was authorized under Article VII of the UN Charter, and was not part of an armed conflict with Iraq.

F. Zones and Control of Immediate Area of Naval Operations

Naval commanders must be concerned with the possibility that vessels or aircraft approaching their forces may pose a threat, even if those vessels or aircraft appear outwardly to be neutral or civilian in nature. Accordingly, it is standard naval practice in armed conflict to impose special restrictions on any vessels entering into the immediate area of naval operations during armed conflict, with such areas often reaching out several miles or even farther, depending

---

106. *See* Int'l Comm. Red Cross, Commentary of 2017, Convention (II) for the Amelioration of the Condition of Wounded, Sick and Shipwrecked Members of Armed Forces at Sea, Geneva, 12 August 1949, para. 245 ("the declaration, establishment and enforcement of an effective naval or air blockade, as an 'act of war,' may suffice to initiate an international armed conflict to which humanitarian law would also apply. . . .") (hereinafter 2017 COMMENTARY, CONVENTION (II)).

107. A. Chayes, *The Legal Case for U.S. Action on Cuba*, 47 DEP'T STATE BULL. 763, 764 (Nov. 19, 1962) (hereinafter, LEGAL CASE).

108. Radio and Television Report to the American People on the Soviet Arms Buildup in Cuba, 1962 PUB. PAPERS 806, 807 (President Kennedy speech announcing, *inter alia*, quarantine.)

109. LEGAL CASE, *supra*, note 107, at 765.

110. S.C. Res. 661, U.N. Doc. S/RESS/661 (Aug. 6, 1990), *available at* http://www.un.org/Docs/scres/1990/scres90.htm (last visited Feb. 17, 2018).

111. S.C. Res. 665, U.N. Doc. S/RESS/665 (Aug. 25, 1990), *available at* http://www.un.org/Docs/scres/1990/scres90.htm (last visited Feb. 17, 2018).

upon the military capabilities of the enemy. The U.S. Navy's Commander's Handbook on the Law of Naval Operations describes the practice as follows:

> The commanding officer of a belligerent warship may exercise control over the communication of any neutral merchant vessel or civil aircraft whose presence in the immediate area of naval operations might otherwise endanger or jeopardize those operations. A neutral merchant ship or civil aircraft within that area that fails to conform to a belligerent's directions concerning communications may thereby assume enemy character and risk being fired upon or captured. Legitimate distress communications should be permitted to the extent that the success of the operation is not prejudiced thereby. Any transmission to an opposing belligerent of information concerning military operations or military forces is inconsistent with the neutral duties of abstention and impartiality and renders the neutral vessel or aircraft liable to capture or destruction.[112]

As a means of warfare, a belligerent also may establish more extensive zones for imposing greater control over neutral shipping. This could be for the purpose of protecting neutral shipping from the effects of military operations, which would be a legitimate aim, or for the purpose of interfering with neutral shipping so that it cannot reach the belligerent's enemy, which, in the absence of a blockade, would not be legitimate. In some cases, belligerents have stated that any shipping entering the zone would be presumed to be non-neutral and subject to capture or destruction. Zones of this type were used in World War I and later conflicts and caused major disruptions to neutral shipping.

There is no treaty governing the use of zones, but it is widely accepted that belligerents, as a matter of customary law, must have due regard for the effects of their military operations on neutral shipping on the high seas or in neutral territorial waters, and that any interference must be limited to what is militarily necessary.[113] The San Remo Manual includes the following statement regarding the law governing zones established by a belligerent in an international armed conflict, which it refers to as an "exceptional measure":

> (a) the same body of law applies both inside and outside the zone;
> (b) the extent, location and duration of the zone and the measures imposed shall not exceed what is strictly required by military necessity and the principles of proportionality;
> (c) due regard shall be given to the rights of neutral States to legitimate uses of the seas;
> (d) necessary safe passage through the zone for neutral vessels and aircraft shall be provided:

---

112. COMMANDER'S HANDBOOK — 2017, *supra*, note 4, para. 7.8. The DoD Law of War Manual notes that the establishment of areas of control in the immediate area or vicinity on a belligerent State's naval forces is intended to "ensure proper battle space management and self-defense objectives." DoD LAW OF WAR MANUAL, *supra*, note 4, para. 13.8.1. For these purposes, the "immediate area or vicinity of naval operations is that area within which hostilities are taking place, or belligerent State forces are actually operating" and is based on the State's right to ensure the security of its forces and to conduct hostilities without interference of neutrals. *Id.* paras. 13.8.1 and 13.8.2.

113. SAN REMO MANUAL, *supra*, note 3, para. 106.

(i) where the geographical extent of the zone significantly impedes free and safe access to the ports and coasts of a neutral State;

(ii) in other cases where normal navigation routes are affected, except where military requirements do not permit; and

(e) the commencement, duration, location and extent of the zone, as well as the restrictions imposed, shall be publicly declared and appropriately notified.

In addition, the San Remo Manual notes that a belligerent cannot absolve itself of its duties under the LOAC by establishing a zone.[114] This means that the belligerent cannot declare a "free fire" zone, or otherwise engage in indiscriminate attacks or other types of activities in a zone that violate the LOAC or LOAC principles. Thus, if a merchant vessel enters a zone, it cannot be attacked unless it engages in actions that constitute the acquisition of enemy character, and it can only be seized if it is an enemy merchant vessel or if, after visit and search, it is determined to be carrying contraband. However, unauthorized entry into a zone may be evidence of a hostile intent, particularly if the vessel does not respond to directions to leave the zone or stay within lanes established for safe passage of vessels through the zone.[115]

Consistent with the position of the experts who drafted the San Remo Manual, the U.S. Navy considers zones outside of U.S. territorial waters to be an exceptional measure, subject to a number of restrictions to protect neutral shipping:[116]

> Because exclusion and war zones are not simply free fire zones for the warships of the belligerents, the establishment of such a zone carries with it certain obligations for belligerents with respect to neutral vessels entering the zone. Belligerents creating such zones must provide safe passage through the zone for neutral vessels and aircraft where the geographical extent of the zone significantly impedes free and safe access to the ports and coasts of a neutral state and, unless military requirements do not permit, in other cases where normal navigation routes are affected. For this reason, the Total Exclusion Zone announced by the United Kingdom and the Argentine declaration of the South Atlantic as a war zone during the Falklands/Malvinas conflict both were problematic in that they deemed any neutral vessel within the zone without permission as hostile and thus liable to attack. Likewise, the zones declared by both Iran and Iraq during the 1980s Gulf War appeared to unlawfully operate as "free fire zones" for all vessels entering therein.[117]

In short, the establishment of an "exclusion zone" does not mean that the belligerent can attack any vessel or aircraft that enters the zone. Instead, the belligerent must couple the heightened military readiness of its forces within the

---

114. *Id.*, para. 105.

115. *See* DoD LAW OF WAR MANUAL, *supra*, note 4, para. 13.9.2.

116. The DoD Law of War Manual notes that the authority of a belligerent State to establish a zone outside of waters under the State's sovereignty "may rely upon the belligerent State's: (1) right to interdict contraband; (2) right to control the immediate area of operations; or (3) right of blockade." *Id.*, para. 13.9.1.

117. COMMANDER'S HANDBOOK — 2017, *supra*, note 4, para. 7.9.

zone with a careful examination of each intrusion into the zone to ensure that only military objectives are targeted. The fact that a civilian ship or neutral ship entered the zone without permission does not, *per se*, justify targeting the ship without first ascertaining if it is a military objective.

G. Submarine Warfare

Naval submarines, like naval surface vessels, are warships, and thus the LOAC rules applicable to surface ships also apply to submarines. Submarines must follow the same targeting rules as surface ships in limiting attacks to lawful military objectives. In addition, following each engagement with an enemy vessel, submarines, like surface ships, are under an obligation pursuant to GWS-Sea Article 18 to

> without delay take all possible measures to search for and collect the shipwrecked, wounded and sick, to protect them from pillage and ill-treatment, to ensure their adequate care, and to search for the dead and prevent their being despoiled.

Of course, submarines have more limited capabilities to collect and care for the shipwrecked, sick, and wounded after an attack, and indeed an attempt by a submarine to collect and care for these individuals could expose the submarine to attack in a situation where it would be difficult to defend itself given that submarines generally do not travel with other vessels. Accordingly, as suggested by the phrase "all possible measures," international law recognizes that where discharge of the obligation under GWS-Sea Article 18 would subject a submarine to undue additional hazard or prevent it from accomplishing its military mission, it need not engage in rescue operations. Rather, it should alert a surface vessel or shore facility as soon as possible to provide assistance.[118]

Submarines are also subject to the London Protocol of 1936, which, as noted *supra*, provides that no warship "whether surface vessel or submarine," may sink or render incapable of navigation a merchant vessel without first securing the safety of the passengers, crew, and ship's papers, except where the merchant vessel persistently refuses to stop after being duly summoned, or actively resists

---

118. The ICRC's 1960 Commentary on GWS-Sea Article 18 states: "Generally speaking, one cannot lay down an absolute rule that the commander of a warship must engage in rescue operations if, by doing so, he would expose the vessel to attack. The 'possible measures' which may be taken by the belligerents to collect the shipwrecked are, on the other hand, many and varied and in nearly all cases they should enable the purpose of the present paragraph to be achieved." COMMENTARY, CONVENTION II FOR THE AMELIORATION OF THE CONDITION OF THE WOUNDED AND SICK IN ARMED FORCES IN THE FIELD. GENEVA, 12 August 1949 (Jean S. Pictet ed., 1960), at 28-37 (hereinafter 1960 COMMENTARY, CONVENTION II). The 2017 Commentary similarly notes that the rule is not absolute: "The obligation to act without delay is strict, but the action to be taken is limited to what is feasible, in particular in the light of security considerations. The military command must judge reasonably and in good faith, based on the circumstances and the available information, what is possible and to what extent it can commit its personnel. In all cases, the operation must be conducted in full compliance with the principle of non-discrimination." 2017 COMMENTARY, CONVENTION (II), *supra*, note 106, para. 1649.

visit or search. In addition, the ship's lifeboats are not considered to be a place of safety "unless the safety of the passengers and crew is assured, in the existing sea and weather conditions, by the proximity of land, or the presence of another vessel which is in a position to take them on board." The rule could be difficult for a submarine to implement in practice, but the U.S. view is that where a merchant vessel has become a valid military objective subject to attack (discussed in Section IV.C.1, *supra*), the rules in the London Protocol do not apply.[119]

H. Mines and Torpedoes

Anti-ship mines are an important part of naval warfare, as the widespread use of mines by Iran during the Iran-Iraq War of the 1980s demonstrated. However, early mines were indiscriminate weapons that did not differentiate between warships and civilian vessels, could come loose from their moorings and drift into civilian shipping lanes, and could remain active for many years after the conflict. In the modern era, more discriminate mines have been developed, including mines that detonate only when they detect the mechanical signature of specific types of vessels. Mines can be remote controlled or designed to activate or deactivate during specified periods. In addition, mines can be air-dropped as well as placed by surface vessels and submarines. As noted previously, mines delivered by air were used successfully to mine North Vietnamese ports in the early 1970s in order to pressure North Vietnam to complete peace negotiations to conclude U.S. involvement in the Vietnam War.

Notwithstanding their long history as a means of naval warfare, mines are only addressed in international law of war treaties by the 1907 Hague Convention (VIII) Relative to the Laying of Automatic Submarine Contact Mines.[120] 1907 Hague VIII was intended to address experiences with mines in the Russo-Japanese War of 1904-1905, in which offensive mines were used successfully by both parties, but in which mines damaged civilian shipping. As its name suggests, the Convention only addresses mines that are detonated on contact with a ship hull or other object. It focuses in particular on three types of underwater contact weapons — anchored mines, free-floating mines, and torpedoes (which are, essentially, self-propelled mines).

As to free-floating contact mines, the Convention does not prohibit the laying of such mines, but requires that they be constructed so that they will become harmless "one hour at most after the person who laid them ceases to control them."[121] Typically, such mines will be deployed off the deck of a ship into the path of an enemy ship, as a means of either attack or defense. The one-hour rule embodied in 1907 Hague VIII ensures that the mines do not persist as a threat to neutral shipping.

---

119. DoD Law of War Manual, *supra*, note 3, para. 13.5.2.
120. 1907 Hague VIII, *supra*, note 71.
121. *Id.*, art 1.

With respect to anchored automatic contact mines, 1907 Hague VIII requires only that such mines become harmless as soon as they have broken loose from their moorings.[122] The difference with free-floating contact mines is that the free-floating mines need to be "aimed" in some sense at a military target. They can only remain active for up to an hour after being released. Therefore, the free-floating mine has a very short useful life once it is deployed against an enemy. On the other hand, the anchored mine could remain active indefinitely, so long as it remains anchored (i.e., stationary).

Finally, torpedoes are not prohibited, but they must become harmless if they miss their mark.[123]

Regardless of type, all of these mines are automatic contact mines. 1907 Hague VIII specifically prohibits the laying of contact mines off the coast and ports of an enemy "with the sole object of intercepting commercial shipping."[124] Thus, it would be prohibited to set up a minefield solely to enforce visit and search and other practices affecting commercial shipping. However, a minefield that affects commercial shipping is not prohibited if there is a credible purpose for laying the minefield other than interfering with commercial shipping.

1907 Hague VIII requires the mine-laying State to take precautions to protect shipping (including notification to neutrals) and to render the mines harmless "within a limited time."[125] In addition, where the mines are no longer under the surveillance of the mine-laying State, that State must notify all States of the damage zones. Finally, and importantly, 1907 Hague VIII requires the party that laid the mines to do its utmost to remove the mines after the war.[126]

Belligerents are not the only States permitted to use naval mines. 1907 Hague VIII recognizes that neutral States also may lay mines off their coasts to protect their neutrality.[127] If a neutral State does this, it must comply with all precautions imposed on the belligerent armed forces regarding naval mines under 1907 Hague VIII. The neutral State also must inform ship owners, by means of a notice in advance through diplomatic channels, where the mines have been laid.

There are weaknesses with 1907 Hague VIII. First, as noted above, the only prohibition with respect to mining an enemy's ports and coast is that the mines cannot be placed with the "sole object of intercepting commercial shipping." A minefield that can be justified on other grounds, at least in part, arguably would be permitted, even if it interfered with commercial shipping, as long as that interference is not the sole purpose for the minefield.

Second, per the terms of Article 3 of 1907 Hague VIII, a State laying a minefield of anchored mines is only required to provide notice of the minefield "as soon as military exigencies permit" after it ceases to keep the minefield under

---

122. *Id.*
123. *Id.*
124. *Id.*, art. 2.
125. *Id.*, art. 3.
126. *Id.*, art. 5.
127. *Id.*, art. 4.

surveillance. The lack of a firm deadline for notice could result in significant delay before other States are made aware of the minefield.

Finally, while a minefield cannot be placed by belligerents in the territorial or internal waters of neutrals, they can be placed in international waters (other than areas subject to special regimes, such as international straits[128]), in addition to being placed in belligerent territorial or internal waters (including not only enemy waters, but also a belligerent's own waters[129]). However, a decision to place mines in international waters would be subject to the law of the sea obligation to exercise due regard for neutral shipping[130] and the law of war principle of discrimination, which would make it difficult to lawfully place mines in waters where they are likely to be encountered by civilian and neutral vessels.[131] With appropriate notification and only to the extent and for so long as required by military necessity, mines can be used to force neutral vessels to navigate away from areas of operations, provided that this does not preclude the vessels' use of international waters.

In consideration of the applicable treaty and customary law, the U.S. Navy's Commander's Handbook on the Law of Naval Operations sums up the rules regarding naval mines, as follows:

> Naval mines may be lawfully employed by parties to an armed conflict subject to the following restrictions:

---

128. "Armed mines may not be emplaced in international straits or archipelagic sea lanes during peacetime." COMMANDER'S HANDBOOK — 2017, *supra*, note 4, para. 9.2.2.

129. It is not unlawful for a State to emplace mines in its own internal waters at any time with or without notification, even in peacetime. *Id.* A State may also mine its own archipelagic waters (other than archipelagic sea lanes) and territorial sea during peacetime when deemed necessary for national security purposes, subject to (i) international notification if armed mines are emplaced and (ii) the right of other States to innocent passage. DoD LAW OF WAR MANUAL, *supra*, note 4, para. 13.11.2.1 (citations omitted). Because the right of innocent passage can be suspended only temporarily, armed mines placed in a State's territorial sea or archipelagic waters must be removed or rendered harmless as soon as the security threat is over. *Id* (citation omitted). However, emplacement of controlled mines in a State's own archipelagic waters or territorial sea is not subject to such notification or removal requirements. *Id.* Naval mines may not be emplaced in another country's internal waters, territorial seas, or archipelagic waters without that State's consent, except when in armed conflict against that State, but mines may not be emplaced off the enemy coasts and ports for the sole purpose of intercepting commercial shipping. *Id.*, para. 13.11.3.6 (citations omitted). Further, any emplacement of mines is subject to the LOAC obligation to take feasible precautions to avoid injury or damage to civilians and civilian objects. *See, e.g., id.* para. 13.11.3.1.

130. The U.S. position is also that armed mines may not be emplaced in international waters prior to the outbreak of armed conflict, except under the most demanding requirements of individual or collective self-defense, and in any case, prior notification and on-scene presence to give warning are required. *Id.* para. 13.11.2.

131. According to the Commanders' Handbook—2017, however, the U.S. position is that "[c]ontrollable mines may . . . be emplaced in international waters (i.e., beyond the territorial sea) if they do not unreasonably interfere with other lawful uses of the oceans." COMMANDER'S HANDBOOK—2017, *supra*, note 4, para. 9.2.2. For this purpose, "what constitutes an 'unreasonable interference' involves a balancing of a number of factors, including the rationale for their emplacement (i.e., the self-defense requirements of the emplacing nation), the extent of the area to be mined, the hazard (if any) to other lawful ocean uses, and the duration of their emplacement." *Id.*

International notification of the location of emplaced mines must be made as soon as military exigencies permit.[132]

Mines may not be emplaced by belligerents in neutral waters.

Anchored mines must become harmless as soon as they have broken their moorings.

Unanchored mines not otherwise affixed or imbedded in the bottom must become harmless within an hour after loss of control over them.

The location of minefields must be carefully recorded to ensure accurate notification and to facilitate subsequent removal and/or deactivation.

Naval mines may be employed to channelize neutral shipping, but not in a manner to deny transit passage of international straits or archipelagic sea lanes passage of archipelagic waters by such shipping.

Naval mines may not be emplaced off the coasts and ports of the enemy with the sole objective of intercepting commercial shipping, but may otherwise be employed in the strategic blockade of enemy ports, coasts, and waterways.

Mining of areas of indefinite extent in international waters is prohibited. Reasonably limited barred areas may be established by naval mines, provided neutral shipping retains an alternate route around or through such an area with reasonable assurance of safety.[133]

I. Protection of Persons *Hors de Combat* in Naval Operations

The Second Geneva Convention of 1949, also known as GWS-Sea, is devoted specifically to the protection, during armed conflict, of members of the armed forces, civilians who accompany the armed forces, and other specific categories of persons, who are at sea and are wounded, sick, or shipwrecked. The Convention is nearly identical to the First Geneva Convention or GWS, which protects the same categories of persons who are wounded or sick on land. Article 4 of GWS-Sea provides that, in engagements between forces on land and at sea, GWS-Sea applies to forces while on ship, but GWS applies to those forces once they are on land. In any case, the obligations effectively are the same, though GWS-Sea applies also to the shipwrecked (including crews and passengers of aircraft who crash into the sea or eject from their aircraft).

There are six categories of persons protected by GWS-Sea. These are the same categories of persons protected by GWS (which are also the categories of persons protected by the Third Geneva Convention or GPW, which deals with the protection of prisoners of war). The six categories include four categories (i.e., categories (1), (2), (3), and (6), as discussed, *supra* in Section IV.B) that have the privilege to lawfully participate in hostilities, plus two additional categories (i.e., categories (4) and (5)) that do not have that privilege but that

---

132. This is broader than the rule in Article 3 of 1907 Hague VIII, which only requires notification when the mines are not under surveillance.

133. COMMANDER'S HANDBOOK — 2017, *supra*, note 4, para. 9.2.3.

accompany or support forces at sea, and are entitled to protection under GWS, GWS-Sea, and GPW:

(1) Members of the armed forces of a Party to the conflict, as well as members of militias or volunteer corps forming part of such armed forces.

(2) Members of other militias and members of other volunteer corps, including those of organized resistance movements, belonging to a Party to the conflict and operating in or outside their own territory, even if this territory is occupied, provided that such militias or volunteer corps, including such organized resistance movements, fulfill the following conditions:

    (a) that of being commanded by a person responsible for his subordinates;
    (b) that of having a fixed distinctive sign recognizable at a distance;
    (c) that of carrying arms openly;
    (d) that of conducting their operations in accordance with the laws and customs of war.

(3) Members of regular armed forces who profess allegiance to a Government or an authority not recognized by the Detaining Power.

(4) Persons who accompany the armed forces without actually being members thereof, such as civilian members of military aircraft crews, war correspondents, supply contractors, members of labour units or of services responsible for the welfare of the armed forces, provided that they have received authorization from the armed forces which they accompany.

(5) Members of crews, including masters, pilots and apprentices, of the merchant marine and the crews of civil aircraft of the Parties to the conflict, who do not benefit by more favourable treatment under any other provisions of international law.

(6) Inhabitants of a non-occupied territory who, on the approach of the enemy, spontaneously take up arms to resist the invading forces, without having had time to form themselves into regular armed units, provided they carry arms openly and respect the laws and customs of war (also referred to as a *levée en masse*).

Some of these categories do not appear on their face likely to apply to naval warfare (e.g., category (6), the *levée en masse*), but the uniformity across the first three Geneva Conventions ensures that coverage of the Conventions for these categories of persons is seamless in armed conflicts to which the Conventions apply.[134]

The key provision of GWS-Sea is Article 12, which provides:

Members of the armed forces and other persons mentioned in the following Article [i.e., the six categories listed above], who are at sea and who are

---

134. In common with the other three Geneva Conventions, GWS-Sea, *supra*, note 5, includes an Article 3 that addresses humanitarian treatment of persons who are *hors de combat* in non-international armed conflicts. However, Article 3 by its terms is focused upon an armed conflict occurring in the territory of a Party to the Convention, and does not address conflicts occurring in international waters that fall outside the scope of the international armed conflicts described in Article 2 that is common to all of the Geneva Conventions. Similarly, Additional Protocol II, *supra*, note 69, which provides a set of rules for non-international armed conflicts occurring within the territory of a Party, does not expressly apply to conflicts occurring in international waters.

wounded, sick or shipwrecked, shall be respected and protected in all circumstances, it being understood that the term "shipwreck" means shipwreck from any cause and includes forced landings at sea by or from aircraft.

Such persons shall be treated humanely and cared for by the Parties to the conflict in whose power they may be, without any adverse distinction founded on sex, race, nationality, religion, political opinions, or any other similar criteria. Any attempts upon their lives, or violence to their persons, shall be strictly prohibited; in particular, they shall not be murdered or exterminated, subjected to torture or to biological experiments; they shall not wilfully be left without medical assistance and care, nor shall conditions exposing them to contagion or infection be created.

Only urgent medical reasons will authorize priority in the order of treatment to be administered.

Women shall be treated with all consideration due to their sex.

The obligations imposed on belligerents do not extend merely to providing this humanitarian treatment and care, but also includes an affirmative obligation to "take all measures to search for and collect the shipwrecked, wounded and sick to protect them against pillage and ill-treatment, to ensure their adequate care, and to search for the dead and prevent them from being despoiled."[135] The parties also may ask neutral craft, including yachts, to take on board and care for the wounded, sick, or shipwrecked persons.[136]

In addition to requiring that the sick, wounded, or shipwrecked falling within one of the foregoing six categories be protected and respected, GWS-Sea also protects (1) religious, medical, and hospital personnel on board ships who are assigned to provide medical or spiritual care to the sick, wounded, and shipwrecked persons falling in the categories above; (2) specially equipped and marked hospital ships, the crews of such ships, and the religious, medical, and hospital personnel on board such ships, dedicated to assisting and transporting the wounded, sick, and shipwrecked;[137] (3) ships chartered to transport equipment for treatment of the sick and wounded, or for the prevention of disease; and (4) medical aircraft "while flying at heights, at times, and on routes specifically agreed upon between the Parties to the conflict concerned."

Where it applies, the Convention imposes an obligation to "respect" and "protect." (The term "respect" means that the persons protected by the Convention are to be spared from the effects of military operations and not attacked, while the term "protect" means that they are to be provided assistance and care to treat their wounds and illnesses, and in the case of the shipwrecked, to be rescued.[138]) However, the protection is limited to just the categories of persons specified in the Convention; other persons, including civilians at sea who fall outside the six categories above, and medical and religious personnel who minister to these civilians, are not covered.

---

135. GWS-Sea, *supra*, note 5, art. 18.
136. *Id.*, art. 21.
137. Hospital ships typically are part of a State's navy, although GWS-Sea also provides for the protection of hospital ships operated by a humanitarian organization such as the Red Cross. *Id.*, art. 25.
138. The obligation to assist ships and persons in distress is a general obligation imposed by customary and treaty law on all vessels at sea.

The 1977 Additional Protocol I (AP I) to the four Geneva Conventions substantially expands the protection afforded by GWS-Sea, by extending it to cover both civilians and military personnel, and a wide variety of vessels and aircraft that rescue, assist, treat, and transport the wounded, sick, and shipwrecked at sea. It also relaxes GWS-Sea's rule that the protection of medical aircraft depends upon the agreement of all belligerents; instead, AP I only requires prior agreement of the parties where a medical aircraft flies over territory controlled by an enemy belligerent.[139] Accordingly, the full scope of the international regime for humanitarian protection of persons *hors de combat* at sea cannot be understood without consulting both GWS-Sea and AP I. The table at the end of this chapter summarizes the protections afforded to various categories of persons and objects under GWS-Sea and AP I in international armed conflict at sea.[140]

The United States and other States that have not ratified AP I are not bound by it as a matter of treaty law, and therefore any protection afforded to civilians and others not expressly covered by GWS-Sea would be based in large measure on applicable customary international law. In its recent study of customary international humanitarian law, the International Committee of the Red Cross asserted that the following rules regarding the wounded, sick, and shipwrecked at sea apply as a matter of customary international law in all types of conflicts, including non-international armed conflicts:

> **Rule 109.** Whenever circumstances permit, and particularly after an engagement, each party to the conflict must, without delay, take all possible measures to search for, collect and evacuate the wounded, sick and shipwrecked without adverse distinction.
>
> **Rule 110.** The wounded, sick and shipwrecked must receive, to the fullest extent practicable and with the least possible delay, the medical care and attention required by their condition. No distinction may be made among them founded on any grounds other than medical ones.
>
> **Rule 111.** Each party to the conflict must take all possible measures to protect the wounded, sick and shipwrecked against ill-treatment and against pillage of their personal property.[141]

Of course, the protection afforded by GWS-Sea, and where applicable, AP I, can be lost if the person or object protected directly participates in hostilities or takes other action harmful to the enemy. Before the person or object loses its protection, however, the enemy belligerent must provide due warning to the person or object to cease such activities, plus a time limit for compliance.[142]

---

139. AP I, *supra*, note 69, art. 27. The Fourth Geneva Convention, also referred to as GC IV, requires States engaged in an international armed conflict to "facilitate" measures to assist shipwrecked civilians and to protect and respect "specially provided" sea vessels carrying the civilian wounded and sick, but the details of GC IV's provisions on these matters fall short of the detail found in AP I. *See* Geneva Convention Relative to the Protection of Civilian Persons in Time of War, Aug. 12, 1949, arts. 16 and 21, 6 U.S.T. 3516, 75 U.N.T.S. 973.

140. Other than Article 3 of GWS-Sea, neither AP I nor GWS-Sea expressly apply to non-international armed conflicts, although customary international law would apply to such conflicts. *See* San Remo Manual, *supra*, note 3, para. 2.

141. ICRC CIL Study, *supra*, note 11, at 396-405.

142. GWS-Sea, *supra*, note 5, art. 34.

Only if the deadline passes without a response or compliance may protection be lifted when the time limit expires. GWS-Sea Article 35 also specifies that certain conditions, even if true, will not justify lifting of the protection:

> Art 35. The following conditions shall not be considered as depriving hospital ships or sick-bays of vessels of the protection due to them:
> (1) The fact that the crews of ships or sick-bays are armed for the maintenance of order, for their own defence or that of the sick and wounded.
> (2) The presence on board of apparatus exclusively intended to facilitate navigation or communication.
> (3) The discovery on board hospital ships or in sick-bays of portable arms and ammunition taken from the wounded, sick and shipwrecked and not yet handed to the proper service.
> (4) The fact that the humanitarian activities of hospital ships and sick-bays of vessels or of the crews extend to the care of wounded, sick or shipwrecked civilians.
> (5) The transport of equipment and of personnel intended exclusively for medical duties, over and above the normal requirements.[143]

A similar list is included in AP I Articles 12 and 13 to ensure that all the civilian and military persons, facilities, and conveyances to which AP I's expanded protection extends do not lose their protection due to these factors.

The wounded, sick, and shipwrecked persons who are within the six categories protected by GWS-Sea can be held as prisoners of war by an enemy belligerent if they fall into the enemy belligerent's hands (e.g., by being rescued by the enemy belligerent), subject, of course, to the obligation under GWS-Sea that the enemy belligerent must to provide care for them. Indeed, an enemy warship encountering a hospital ship can demand that the military wounded, sick, or shipwrecked persons on board the hospital ship be turned over to the warship to be held as prisoners of war, provided these wounded, sick, or shipwrecked persons are fit to move and the capturing warship has facilities to care for them.[144] Similarly, where wounded, sick, shipwrecked personnel of a belligerent, who would be prisoners of war in the hands of their enemy, are taken aboard neutral ships or neutral military aircraft, or are "landed" in neutral territory, the neutral State must take steps to ensure that such personnel cannot again take part in the armed conflict (e.g., they must be interned) if so required by international law.[145]

---

143. *Id.*, art. 35.
144. *Id.*, arts. 14 and 16.
145. *Id.*, arts. 15 and 17. The 1960 ICRC Commentary to Article 17 of GWS-Sea makes clear that "landed" means the situation where a ship elects to leave behind in neutral territory wounded, sick, or shipwrecked persons with the consent of the neutral. 1960 COMMENTARY, CONVENTION (II), *supra*, note 118, at 116-129. The Commentary also notes that the reference to international law in Article 17 renders the provision unclear about the situations in which such persons must be interned and when they must be set free. The Commentary offers some interpretations and discusses several situations that are not settled, but in general concludes that, when a belligerent leaves behind wounded, sick, or shipwrecked persons, the neutral should intern those persons who are of the same nationality as the belligerent ship (and presumably persons from States who are operating in coalition with the belligerent ship's State), while not interning others. The purpose of such a rule

V. The Law of Neutrality

In an armed conflict at sea, belligerents not only confront each other's vessels and aircraft, but also must take into account the vessels and aircraft of States who are not belligerents and who wish to remain outside the conflict.[146] Under international law, a belligerent in an armed conflict do not have the right to interfere with use of international waters by neutrals, except where the neutral is engaged in activities that contribute to the war-fighting capability of that belligerent's enemy, or where interference is a permissible incident of lawful naval operations (e.g., to protect the security of a naval force or to minimize the risk of collateral damage to neutral vessels as a consequence of a lawful attack on a State's enemy). In addition, international law permits a belligerent to set up a blockade of the ports of its enemy, which will interfere with the ability of neutral vessels to voyage to that enemy's ports, as long as the blockade is conducted in an orderly and discriminating way so as not to interfere (or not to unreasonably interfere) with the use of international waters for shipping unrelated to the conflict (e.g., shipping between two neutral States).

According to the U.S. Navy's Commander's Handbook on the Law of Naval Warfare:

> A principal purpose of the law of neutrality is the regulation of belligerent activities with respect to neutral commerce. For purposes of this publication, neutral commerce comprises all commerce between one neutral State and another not involving materials of war or armaments ultimately destined for a belligerent State, and all commerce between a neutral State and a belligerent that does not involve the carriage of contraband or otherwise contribute to the belligerent's war-fighting/war-sustaining capability.[147]

A. Sources of the Law of Neutrality

Customary international law contemplates that States have the option to refrain from participation in an armed conflict by declaring or otherwise assuming neutral status.[148] To implement this right, the LOAC imposes duties and confers rights upon neutral States and belligerents. The principal right of the neutral

---

would be to ensure that a belligerent did not take advantage of the rules governing "landed" persons in order to (1) leave its own personnel in the care of the neutral until such persons recovered and could then leave to rejoin the conflict (which would have occurred if the rule did not require that such personnel be interned), or (2) leave wounded, sick, or shipwrecked enemy prisoners in the neutral's care, with an obligation to keep those persons in internment (which would have occurred if the rule did not require that such personnel be given their freedom).

146. As stated in the U.S. Navy's Commander's Handbook, the law of neutrality "seeks to minimize the effects of armed conflict on States that are not party to the conflict, including by lessening the effect of war on neutral commerce." COMMANDER'S HANDBOOK — 2017, *supra*, note 4, para. 7.1.

147. *Id.*, para. 7.4.

148. *See* GREEN H. HACKWORTH, VII DIGEST OF INTERNATIONAL LAW § 656 (1943) (hereinafter HACKWORTH).

State is that of inviolability; its principal duties are those of abstention (from participation in hostilities) and impartiality (in dealing with each side of the conflict). Conversely, it is the duty of a belligerent to respect the inviolability of the neutral while at the same time insisting that neutrals strictly comply with their obligations of abstention and impartiality.[149] These duties and obligations are discussed below.

There are a number of sources that are directly relevant to the law of neutrality today. These include treaties that specifically set out the rights and obligations of neutrals as well as manuals and other sources that are not binding law, but are nonetheless persuasive as to what the law requires.

Also relevant are treaties that limit the areas where military operations can be conducted, such as the Antarctic Treaty (1959),[150] which requires that the Antarctic only be used for peaceful purposes. While not traditionally conceived as a source of the law of neutrality, these treaties create areas that are off limits to military operations during armed conflict and hence are to remain neutral in an armed conflict.

The principal treaty on the rights and obligations of neutrals in naval warfare is the 1907 Hague Convention XIII Respecting the Rights and Duties of Neutral Powers in Naval War, although the rights of neutral States are also addressed in the treaties governing the law of the sea, discussed above. A key provision is Article 1 of 1907 Hague XIII, which states:

> Belligerents are bound to respect the sovereign rights of neutral Powers and to abstain, in neutral territory or neutral waters, from any act which would, if knowingly permitted by any Power, constitute a violation of neutrality.[151]

A companion treaty, the 1907 Hague Convention IV Respecting the Rights and Duties of Neutral Powers and Persons in War on Land, is the primary source of rules concerning the rights and obligations of neutrals in land warfare.[152] Article 1 of 1907 Hague V states simply, "[t]he territory of neutral Power is inviolable."

In addition, there are sources that are not binding as treaties, but nonetheless reflect customary international law, and that address the rights and obligations of neutrals in an armed conflict. For naval warfare, these include the London Declaration Concerning the Laws of Naval War of 1909,[153] the Oxford Manual of the Laws of Naval War of 1913,[154] and the 1994 *San Remo Manual on International Law Applicable to Armed Conflicts at Sea of 1994*.[155] Indeed, the

---

149. *Id.*, § 657. *See also* FM 27-10, *supra*, note 79, para. 515.
150. Antarctic Treaty, Dec. 1, 1959, 12 U.S.T. 794, 402 U.N.T.S. 71.
151. 1907 Hague XIII, *supra*, note 71.
152. Rights and Duties of Neutral Powers and Persons in War on Land, Oct. 18, 1907, art. 3, 36 Stat. 2310, 1 Bevans 659 (hereinafter 1907 Hague V). While focused on land warfare, Article 3 of 1907 Hague V includes a prohibition against erecting equipment on neutral territory to communicate with belligerent forces at sea.
153. *See supra*, note 74.
154. *See supra*, note 75.
155. *See supra*, note 3. For a good summary of the evolution of the law of naval warfare, *see* J. Ashley Roach, *The Law of Naval Warfare at the Turn of Two Centuries*, 65 Am. J. Int'l L. 64 (2000).

San Remo Manual, which incorporates the principles from the earlier works, includes a comprehensive restatement of the law of neutrality as it relates to naval warfare.[156] Other works that provide restatements of the law of neutrality in armed conflict include the *Manual on International Law Applicable to Air and Missile Warfare*, and the *Tallinn Manual 2.0 on the International Law Applicable to Cyber Operations*.[157] Military manuals typically also provide summaries of this area of the law.[158]

B. Rights and Obligations of Neutral States

Under customary law, all States have the right to remain neutral in the event of an international armed conflict. Further, neutral status, once established, remains in effect unless and until the neutral State abandons its neutral stance and enters into the conflict. In addition, even without affirmatively joining the conflict, neutrals that violate their neutrality obligations in the conflict also risk losing their neutral status.

The customary right of neutrality arguably has been modified to some extent by the Charter of the United Nations.[159] Article 2(4) of the Charter provides that "[a]ll Members shall refrain in their international relations from the threat or use of force against the territorial integrity or political independence of any state, or in any other manner inconsistent with the Purposes of the United Nations." In the event of a threat to, or breach of, the peace or an act of aggression, the Security Council is empowered under Article VII of the UN Charter to take enforcement action on behalf of all member States, including the use of force, in order to maintain or restore international peace and security. Obligations pursuant to the UN Charter override other obligations. Therefore, all member States must comply with the terms of decisions taken by the Security Council under Chapter VII of the Charter.

Accordingly, where a State has taken an action inconsistent with Article 2(4), the United Nations may mount an international response to the violation (as, for example, occurred after Iraq invaded Kuwait in 1990). Article 2(5) of the Charter provides that "[a]ll Members shall give the United Nations every assistance in any action it takes in accordance with the present Charter, and shall refrain from giving assistance to any state against which the United Nations is taking preventive or enforcement action." Given the terms of Article 2(5), UN member States may be obliged to support a United Nations action at the expense of their pure neutrality, and States who provide support to the United Nations' "preventive or enforcement action" should not be considered to have abandoned their neutrality, but rather to be fulfilling their international

---

156. In addition to the DOD LAW OF WAR MANUAL and the COMMANDER'S HANDBOOK — 2017, both *supra*, note 4, FM 27-10, *supra*, note 79, also provides authoritative guidance on the law of neutrality.
157. Both of these manuals are discussed in greater detail in Chapters 2 and 12.
158. *See, e.g.*, DOD LAW OF WAR MANUAL, *supra*, note 4, chapter XV.
159. SAN REMO MANUAL, *supra*, note 3, para. 7; FM 27-10, *supra*, note 79, para. 513.

obligations.[160] Absent a binding decision of the Security Council or other international legal obligations that qualify the ability of the State to withhold support,[161] however, each State is free to determine whether to support the victim of an armed attack (invoking collective self-defense), or to remain neutral.

In any case, in order to maintain its neutrality, there are several key obligations that the neutral State must observe. The first is the obligation to abstain from taking any action that would contribute to the war-fighting capabilities of either side. This does not mean that the neutral State cannot favor one side or the other in a general political sense, but it cannot provide material support to either side's ability to pursue the armed conflict against the other. For example, a neutral State cannot permit belligerents to move troops and war materials across its territory, to use its territory for military operations or communications, or to recruit troops from its territory.[162] On the other hand, a neutral can

---

160. Relevant provisions of the UN Charter include Article 43(1), which provides:

The Security Council may decide what measures not involving the use of armed force are to be employed to give effect to its decisions, and it may call upon the Members of the United Nations to apply such measures. These may include complete or partial interruption of economic relations and of rail, sea, air, postal, telegraphic, radio, and other means of communication, and the severance of diplomatic relations.

Additionally, Article 48 of the UN Charter provides:

All Members of the United Nations, in order to contribute to the maintenance of international peace and security, undertake to make available to the Security Council, on its call and in accordance with a special agreement or agreements, armed forces, assistance, and facilities, including rights of passage, necessary for the purpose of maintaining international peace and security.

The action required to carry out the decisions of the Security Council for the maintenance of international peace and security shall be taken by all the Members of the United Nations or by some of them, as the Security Council may determine.

Such decisions shall be carried out by the Members of the United Nations directly and through their action in the appropriate international agencies of which they are members.

The DoD Law of War Manual explicitly acknowledges, that "[t]he Charter of the United Nations and decisions by the U.N. Security Council may, in certain circumstances, qualify rights and obligations under the law of neutrality. DoD LAW OF WAR MANUAL, *supra*, note 4, para. 15.2.

161. The U.S. Navy's Commander's Handbook notes the following regarding the impact of regional security arrangements on the right to remain neutral:

The possibility of asserting and maintaining neutral status under such arrangements depends upon the extent to which the parties are obligated to provide assistance in a regional action, or in the case of collective self-defense, to come to the aid of a victim of an armed attack. The practical effect of such treaties may be to transform the right of the parties to assist one of their number under attack into a duty to do so. This duty may assume a variety of forms ranging from economic assistance to commitment of armed forces.

COMMANDER'S HANDBOOK - 2017, *supra*, note 4, para. 7.2.3.

162. 1907 Hague V, *supra*, note 152, arts. 2 and 5. Under Article 14 of 1907 Hague V, a neutral may authorize passage through its territory of wounded and sick belonging to the armed forces of either side, on condition that the vehicles transporting them carry neither combatants nor materials of war. If passage of sick and wounded is permitted, the neutral State assumes responsibility for providing for their safety and control, as well as ensuring that they are not allowed to take part in military operations again. In addition, prisoners of war who have escaped their captors and made their way to neutral territory may be either repatriated or left at liberty in the neutral State. *Id.* art. 13. Finally,

permit "mere passage" of belligerent warships through its territorial waters, and can allow its licensed pilots to guide belligerent warships through its waters.[163]

Additionally, a neutral cannot supply "warships, ammunition, or war material of any kind" to belligerents,[164] although it can supply food and non-military goods and can continue to trade in non-contraband items (see discussion of contraband below). Indeed, one of the benefits of neutrality is the ability to preserve commercial relations with both sides to the conflict notwithstanding the armed conflict between them.

The second, related obligation is to be impartial in its dealings with belligerents. Thus, if a neutral State elects to open its ports to one belligerent, it must also open its ports to the other.[165] Similarly, if it elects to close its territorial seas to belligerents, it must close them equally to all belligerents. A failure to treat each side impartially could be deemed to be a violation of the State's neutrality. Again, the obligation to be impartial does not mean that a neutral State cannot support one belligerent diplomatically in terms of seeking a resolution of the armed conflict that favors one belligerent or supporting one belligerent's view that it is the victim of aggression, but it cannot contribute materially to the warfighting ability of either belligerent.

The third, related obligation of a neutral is to strictly enforce its neutral status. Thus, if a belligerent enters a neutral's territorial sea in a manner inconsistent with the "mere passage" permitted by 1907 Hague XIII (for example, by conducting offensive military operations in those waters), the neutral State must take action to put an end to the violation of its neutrality.[166] A failure to do so can be treated as acquiescence with the violation, which would give the other belligerent the right to take measures in its own right to respond to the violation.[167] This could result in military operations within the neutral State's territorial waters against the other belligerent, which could lead to responses and counter-responses by both sides of the conflict within the neutral State's territory that will further jeopardize the State's neutrality.[168] Moreover, a belligerent may treat a neutral State's acquiescence with violations of its neutral waters as actually an abandonment of neutrality, which could lead to the neutral State itself being treated as an enemy.[169]

---

if belligerent forces seek to take refuge in neutral territory, the neutral may allow them to do so, but must disarm and intern them. DoD LAW OF WAR MANUAL, *supra*, note 4, para. 15.6.

163. *Id.*, arts. 10 and 11. While "mere passage" is not defined in 1907 Hague XIII, it would appear to equate with "innocent passage" under UNCLOS.

164. *Id.*, art. 6. On the other hand, both 1907 Hague V and 1907 Hague XIII provide that a neutral is not obligated to prevent the export (presumably by private persons) "on behalf of one or other of the belligerents of arms, munitions of war, or, in general, anything which can be of use to an army or fleet." 1907 Hague V, *supra*, note 152, art. 7; 1907 Hague XIII, *supra*, note 71, art. 7.

165. *Id.*, art. 9.

166. *Id.*, art. 25. Belligerents may even employ a neutral's licensed ship pilots. *Id.*, art. 11. This rule is reflected in SAN REMO MANUAL, *supra*, note 3, arts. 31-33.

167. *See* DoD LAW OF WAR MANUAL, *supra*, note 4, para. 15.4.2.

168. For example, if belligerent troops come into neutral territory, they must be interned by the neutral. 1907 Hague V, *supra*, note 152, art. 11. A similar rule applies where a warship fails to leave a neutral port where it is not entitled to remain. 1907 Hague XIII, *supra*, note 71, art. 24.

169. *See* SAN REMO MANUAL, *supra*, note 3, para. 22.

Before taking any action inconsistent with a neutral State's neutrality, however, a belligerent must first demand that the neutral State eliminate the violation.[170] Following the September 11, 2001 attacks on the United States, for example, the United States demanded that the Taliban government then in power in Afghanistan surrender the al Qaeda terrorists operating within its territory.[171] When the Taliban did not do this, they also were treated as engaged in an armed conflict with the United States.

It should be recognized that any action taken by a neutral State consistent with its neutrality obligations cannot be treated as the abandonment of neutrality.[172] Thus, a neutral State's armed response to the conduct of offensive operations in its territorial waters by a belligerent in an armed conflict is not to be treated as an unneutral act; rather, the neutral State is simply complying with its international obligations. Similarly, the fact that a neutral State maintains itself in a high state of military readiness should not be treated as unneutral but rather as readiness to enforce its rights as a neutral should that be required. On the other hand, as noted above, obligations under the UN Charter may modify the neutrality obligations with respect to a UN Security Council response to the actions of one or both sides in a conflict, and any action taken within the scope of such response would not be abandonment of neutrality.

In short, the right to remain neutral in international armed conflict is not a passive right, but rather must be strenuously defended.

C. Rights and Obligations of Belligerents Regarding Neutrals

As the discussion above suggests, under the law of neutrality, belligerents in an armed conflict are obligated to respect the inviolability of the territory of neutral States, including the neutral's internal waters and territorial sea.[173] Thus, belligerents must abstain from belligerent acts in these areas, including the capture of enemy vessels and "visit and search" of vessels to determine if they have enemy character, and belligerents cannot use neutral territory or waters as a base of operations against other belligerents.[174]

The LOAC includes rules that regulate the access of belligerent ships to neutral ports during an international armed conflict. Article 13 of 1907 Hague XIII requires that upon learning of the outbreak of armed conflict, a neutral State must give belligerent warships 24-hour notice (or other time period as prescribed by local regulations) to depart from its ports, roadsteads,[175] and

---

170. *Id.*
171. Address Before a Joint Session of the Congress on the United States Response to the Terrorist Attacks of September 11, 37 WEEKLY COMP. PRES. DOC. 1347 (Sept. 20, 2001).
172. 1907 Hague V, *supra,* note 152, art. 10; 1907 Hague XIII, *supra,* note 71, art. 26.
173. 1907 Hague V, *supra,* note 152, art. 1; 1907 Hague XIII, *supra,* note 71, art. 1.
174. *See, e.g.,* 1907 Hague XIII, *supra,* note 71, art. 5.
175. A roadstead is a place outside a harbor where a ship can lie at anchor. It is an enclosed area with an opening to the sea, narrower than a bay or gulf.

territorial waters.[176] Any future visits of belligerent warships to the State's territory will be limited to those neutral ports and roadsteads that the neutral State may choose to leave open to them,[177] although all vessels, including belligerent vessels warships, "retain a right of entry in distress whether caused by *force majeure* or damage resulting from enemy action."[178]

In the absence of special provisions to the contrary in the laws or regulations of the neutral State,[179] belligerent warships are forbidden to remain in a neutral port or roadstead in excess of 24 hours.[180] This restriction does not apply to belligerent warships devoted exclusively to humanitarian, religious, or non-military scientific purposes, but belligerent warships engaged in the collection of scientific data of potential military application are not exempt.[181] Belligerent warships may be permitted by a neutral State to extend their stay in neutral ports and roadsteads on account of stress of weather or damage involving seaworthiness, but it is the duty of the neutral State to intern a belligerent warship, together with its officers and crew, that will not or cannot depart a neutral port or roadstead where it is not entitled to remain.[182]

Unless the neutral State has adopted laws or regulations to the contrary, no more than three warships of any one belligerent State may be present in the same neutral port or roadstead at any one time.[183] To mitigate the possibility of fighting breaking out between belligerents in neutral waters, not less than 24 hours must elapse between the departure of the warships of opposing belligerent States who are present in a neutral port or roadstead at the same time.[184] The order of departure is determined by the order of arrival unless an extension of stay has been granted. Similarly, to prevent the use of neutral waters for the capture of enemy shipping, a belligerent warship may not leave a neutral port or roadstead less than 24 hours after the departure of a merchant ship of its adversary.[185]

Belligerent warships may not make use of neutral ports, roadsteads, or territorial waters for replenishing or increasing "their supplies of war material or their armament, or for completing their crews."[186] Article 19 of 1907 Hague XIII also limits to "the peace standard" the amount of other supplies that a neutral State can provide to a belligerent warship. The meaning of this term and the scope of the limitation is uncertain, but Article 19 does permit a State to adopt,

---

176. 1907 Hague XIII, *supra*, note 71, arts. 12 and 13.
177. *See* SAN REMO MANUAL, *supra*, note 3, art. 19.
178. COMMANDER'S HANDBOOK — 2017, *supra*, note 4, para. 7.3.2.
179. "A neutral State may adopt laws or regulations governing the presence of belligerent warships in its waters provided that these laws and regulations are non-discriminatory and apply equally to all belligerents." *Id.*, para. 7.3.2.1.
180. 1907 Hague XIII, *supra*, note 71, art. 12.
181. *Id.*, art. 14. *See also* DoD LAW OF WAR MANUAL, *supra*, note 4, para. 15.7.3.
182. 1907 Hagus XIII *supra*, note 71, art. 24.
183. *Id.*, art. 15.
184. *Id.*, art. 16.
185. *Id.*
186. *Id.*, art. 18.

with respect to fuel, a rule that permits it to supply sufficient fuel to reach the nearest port in the belligerent warship's country.[187]

A prize (e.g., a captured enemy merchant vessel manned or under the direction of a crew of the capturing State) may only be brought into a neutral port or roadstead by a belligerent because of "unseaworthiness, stress of weather, or want of fuel or provisions," and must leave as soon as such circumstances are overcome or cease to prevail.[188] If it does not comply and does not leave when ordered, the neutral State is obligated to seize the prize, release it, and intern the capturing State's crew.[189]

D. Rules Governing Neutral Shipping

As noted above, neutral States may engage in trade with the belligerents. Accordingly, vessels flagged in a neutral State may transport and pick up cargo and persons (other than combatants) from a belligerent State for transportation to the neutral State, or to other destinations in accordance with international law. In doing so, however, these vessels must not acquire "enemy character." If a ship engages in acts that give it the character of an enemy merchant vessel, the vessel may be subject to capture, but if these acts entail making an effective contribution to military action, the vessel may be targeted as well.[190]

One means of acquiring the character of an enemy merchant vessel is to carry contraband. Contraband consists of goods destined for the enemy of a belligerent that may be susceptible to use in armed conflict.[191] Traditionally, contraband has been divided into two categories: absolute and conditional. Absolute contraband consisted of goods the character of which made it obvious that they are destined for use in armed conflict, such as munitions, weapons, uniforms, and the like. Conditional contraband consisted of goods equally susceptible to peaceful or warlike purposes, such as foodstuffs (other than essential foodstuffs intended for the civilian population), construction materials, and fuel.[192] Goods that are not on the contraband list are treated as "free goods"

---

187. According to the U.S. Navy's Commander's Handbook:

> Although they may take on food and fuel, the law is unsettled as to the quantities that may be allowed. In practice, it has been left to the neutral nation to determine the conditions for the replenishment and refueling of belligerent warships, subject to the principle of nondiscrimination among belligerents and the prohibition against the use of neutral territory as a base of operations.

COMMANDER'S HANDBOOK — 2017, *supra*, note 4, para. 7.3.2.2. This section of the Handbook also discusses the scope of repairs to belligerent warships that can occur in neutral ports.
188. 1907 Hague XIII, *supra*, note 71, art. 21.
189. *Id.*
190. *See* SAN REMO MANUAL, *supra*, note 3, paras. 67 and 146.
191. *Id.*, para. 148.
192. *See* COMMANDER'S HANDBOOK — 2017, *supra*, note 4, para. 7.4.1, for a discussion of contraband. The Handbook notes that during World War II, the belligerents of both sides tended to exercise governmental control over all imports and, as a result, "it became increasingly difficult to draw a meaningful distinction between goods destined for an enemy government and its armed forces and goods destined for consumption by the civilian populace; . . . [b]elligerents treated all imports directly

that are exempt from being treated as contraband.[193] Examples of "free goods" include goods not susceptible for use in armed conflict, such as medical supplies, religious articles, and clothing and essential foodstuffs intended for the civilian population.[194]

Belligerents are required to publish their lists of contraband, with sufficient specificity so that neutrals are aware of what is to be treated as contraband.[195] If a State's contraband list is particularly long, it may seek to meet its obligation by listing the goods that are not contraband, rather than providing a list of contraband goods.[196]

All neutral merchant vessels are subject to "visit and search" by belligerent warships to determine if they are subject to capture, e.g., by carrying contraband.[197] (A similar right exists with respect to neutral aircraft, although the right to visit and search is more cumbersome than visiting a vessel because it involves requiring the aircraft to land so that it can be inspected.[198]) If a neutral State vessel subject to visit and search is carrying contraband, it can be seized and condemned (i.e., taken as enemy property without compensation or destroyed). On the other hand, if a neutral State vessel subject to visit and search is engaged in legitimate neutral commerce and not carrying contraband, it may not be captured or destroyed by belligerent forces.

Under typical visit and search procedures, a neutral merchant vessel is ordered to "lie to" or "heave to," and if it fails to do so or resists, military force may be used to secure its submission. A naval officer and boarding team visits by boat or helicopter, and examines the vessel's papers to ascertain the ship's character, route, cargo, and so forth. If the papers are not in order or doubt exists, the officer or his higher command may order the search and questioning of the crew. If conducting the visit on the ocean is too complicated, the ship can be diverted to a non-neutral port or location where the visit can be conducted.

The risks to vessel owners are great, because a neutral vessel found to be carrying contraband may be condemned, although only after a hearing before the capturing State's prize court. Note that where it is uncertain whether goods

---

or indirectly sustaining the war effort as contraband without making a distinction between absolute and conditional contraband." *Id.*

193. SAN REMO MANUAL, *supra*, note 3, para. 150.

194. *Id.* Treatment of items such as food and clothing as free goods may lose this status if there is serious reason to believe that they might be diverted to other purposes or if there would be a definitive military advantage from substitution of the goods for enemy goods that would become available for military purposes. *Id.*

195. *Id.*, para. 149.

196. DoD LAW OF WAR MANUAL, *supra*, note 4, para. 15.12.1.3.

197. SAN REMO MANUAL, *supra*, note 3, para. 118. As noted *supra*, warships are not subject to visit and search. Neutral merchant vessels under convoy of neutral warships of the same nationality also are exempt from visit and search, although the convoy commander may be required to provide in writing to the commanding officer of an intercepting belligerent warship information as to the character of the vessels and of their cargoes, which could otherwise be obtained by visit and search. Should it be determined by the convoy commander that a vessel under his charge possesses enemy character or carries contraband cargo, he is obliged to withdraw his protection of the offending vessel, making it liable to visit and search, and possible capture, by the belligerent warship. DoD LAW OF WAR MANUAL, *supra*, note 4, para. 15.13.2.4.

198. SAN REMO MANUAL, *supra*, note 3, para. 125.

that could be contraband if shipped to a belligerent's enemy are intended for that enemy,[199] the goods will be presumed to be intended for the enemy under any of these circumstances:

>(a) The neutral vessel will call at the enemy belligerent's port before arriving at the neutral port where the vessel's documents say the goods are going;
>
>(b) The goods are documented to a neutral port known to serve as transit to the enemy belligerent's port(s); or
>
>(c) The goods are consigned to "order" or to an unnamed consignee, "but are destined to a neutral State in the vicinity of enemy territory."[200]

To provide greater certainty for neutral shipping, the international community may employ certificates of non-contraband carriage for neutral vessels and aircraft.[201]

As noted above, a belligerent may not conduct a visit and search in neutral waters, including the territorial seas of a neutral State. This prohibition extends to international straits overlapped by neutral territorial seas and archipelagic sea lanes.[202]

The carriage of contraband is not the only reason for which a neutral merchant vessel may be captured. It also can be captured if the vessel:

>(a) Is "especially undertaken" (e.g., chartered) to carry individuals who are part of the enemy's armed forces;
>
>(b) Is operating under enemy control, orders, charter, employment, or direction;
>
>(c) Presents to the visit and search boarding party, irregular or fraudulent documents, lacks necessary documents, or destroys, defaces, or conceals documents;
>
>(d) Violates regulations of a belligerent in immediate area of military operations; or
>
>(e) Engages in, or attempts to engage in, a breach of a blockade.[203]

Further, a neutral merchant vessel can be attacked or captured if it:

>(a) Is believed on reasonable grounds to be carrying contraband or breaching a blockade and, after warning, intentionally and clearly refuses to stop or intentionally and clearly resists visit and search;
>
>(b) Engages in belligerent acts on behalf of a belligerent's enemy, or is incorporated into, or assists, the enemy's intelligence system;
>
>(c) Acts as an auxiliary (e.g., as a transport) to the enemy's armed forces;

---

199. It is important to note that items not intended to be delivered to a belligerent would not be considered contraband and are not subject to capture. This would include military items intended for another neutral State. The fact that an armed conflict is ongoing does not preclude neutrals from engaging in trade in military equipment not otherwise subject to international rules banning trade in those items.

200. DoD Law of War Manual, *supra*, note 4, paras. 15.12.2.2 (stating the three bases for presumption of contraband).

201. San Remo Manual, *supra*, note 3, paras. 122 and 134.

202. DoD Law of War Manual, *supra*, note 4, para. 15.13.3.

203. San Remo Manual, *supra*, note 3, para. 146.

(d) Sails under convoy of enemy warships or enemy military aircraft; or

(e) Otherwise makes an effective contribution to the enemy's military action and it is not feasible to first place passengers and crew in a place of safety. A warning should be given if circumstances permit to allow the ship's crew to take precautions, or to divert to another route.[204]

Of course, any attack or capture of a neutral merchant vessel under these circumstances is subject to the same humanitarian rules as would apply to the attack or capture of enemy merchant vessels (see Section IV, *supra*, for a discussion of these rules).

E. Neutrality and Non-International Armed Conflicts

The rules of neutrality in armed conflict discussed in this chapter do not apply in non-international armed conflicts, as such conflicts do not involve belligerent States on both sides of the conflict. However, under general international law and as noted in Chapter 1, States are obligated to respect the sovereignty of other States, including the obligation not to intervene in the internal affairs of those other States. This non-intervention obligation, for example, would limit the type and amount of support that a State can provide to non-State parties to an armed conflict without becoming party to the non-international armed conflict or assuming responsibility for the acts of the non-State party to the conflict.[205]

As discussed in Chapter 1, there is a prohibition under the *jus ad bellum* (and the UN Charter) against the use of force by one State against the territorial integrity or political independence of other States. Thus, a State which provides material assistance or advice to a non-State armed group engaged in an armed conflict could — depending on the type of assistance provided or the extent of the State's involvement with, or control over, the non-State armed group's belligerent activities — be considered to be responsible for the acts of violence committed by the group, and thereby to have violated the prohibition on the use of force, or even to have launched an armed attack against the State engaged in the armed conflict against the non-State group.[206] This in turn could give the latter State a legal basis to take military action against the assisting State.

What if a State (the "territorial State") is not providing assistance to a non-State armed group in a conflict with another State, but instead, its territory is being used by the non-State armed group as a base of operations or safe haven? While under neutrality law, the failure by a neutral to put an end to a violation of its neutrality by one belligerent State may give an enemy belligerent State a "self-help" right to intervene in the neutral's territory to neutralize the threat posed by the violation,[207] there is no general right under international law for

---

204. *Id.*, para. 67.
205. Yoram Dinstein, Non-International Armed Conflicts in International Law 84-86. (2014).
206. *See* Military and Paramilitary Activities in and against Nicaragua (Nicar. v. U.S.). Judgment, 1986 I.C.J. Rep. 14 (June 27).
207. DoD Law of War Manual, *supra*, note 4, para. 15.4.2.

the State engaged in a non-international armed conflict with a non-State armed group to take action against that group in the territory of another State merely based on its presence in that other State. Of course, similar to the rule under neutrality law, the territorial State should respond to the use of its territory by a non-state armed group to prevent that group from threatening other States. Such response, even with military force, would not make the territorial State a party to the non-international armed conflict between that non-state group and other States, and this would be true whether the territorial State's efforts are successful or not, because its action against the non-State armed group would be merely an exercise of its sovereignty over its own territory. Nonetheless, a country threatened or attacked by a non-State armed group using another State's territory as a base of operations could demand that the territorial State eliminate the threat. If the territorial State is unwilling or unable to take effective action against the group, there is increasing State practice in support of an authority for the "victim" State to take self-help measures, including military action, against the non-State armed group or its operatives in the territorial State, either under authority obtained from the UN Security Council or, in the absence of such authority, in the exercise of its inherent right to self-defense under Article 51 of the UN Charter. Taking direct action in another State without Security Council authorization — even if characterized as only being directed against the non-State armed group and not the territorial State — is not, however, without legal and operational risk. When such action is taken without the territorial State's consent, the territorial State could claim that such action is a violation of the prohibition on the use of force under Article 2(4) of the UN Charter or an armed attack under Article 51 of the UN Charter. This in turn could lead the territorial State to respond militarily, resulting in an armed conflict between the two States.

Situations in which a State takes action against operatives of a non-State armed group located in another State, without that State's permission,[208] have increased in frequency in the post-9/11 era.[209] Particularly in the case of the conflict with the terrorist group known as the Islamic State in Iraq and Syria (ISIS),[210] claims that Syria is "unwilling or unable" to prevent attacks by ISIS on neighboring countries or against the United States or its allies, have been

---

208. As noted in Chapter 1, the territorial State's consent, however manifested, would provide a sufficient legal basis for direct action. Unlike in an international armed conflict to which neutrality law would apply, there is no limitation on the ability of one State to provide any level of support to another State engaged in a non-international armed conflict, up to and including combat support or intervention conducted in compliance with LOAC rules.

209. At the end of the Obama Administration, the White House issued a report that included the logic behind the use of the "unwilling and unable" theory to take direct action in the territory of other countries without their consent in the exercise of the United States' inherent right of self-defense. REPORT ON THE LEGAL AND POLICY FRAMEWORK GUIDING THE UNITED STATES' USE OF MILITARY FORCE AND RELATED NATIONAL SECURITY OPERATIONS 10 (Dec. 2016), *available at* https://tjaglcs-public.army.mil/2016-lptr (last visited Feb. 19, 2018).

210. This group has also been known as the Islamic State in Iraq and the Levant (ISIL) or the Islamic State (IS). *ISIS Fast Facts*, CNN.COM (December 12, 2017), https://www.cnn.com/2014/08/08/world/isis-fast-facts/index.html (last visited Feb. 17, 2018).

invoked to provide legal authority for coalition air strikes and even ground combat operations directed against ISIS military capabilities (this authority is distinct from the authority invoked by Russian military operations against ISIS, which is based on Syrian consent to support its efforts against ISIS).[211] These claims are not based on neutrality law, *per se*, but rather on the State's right of collective and individual self-defense. While this is not technically an invocation of neutrality's concept of self-help, these assertions of legal authority do follow a logic similar to the logic that a belligerent would use under neutrality law to justify action to eliminate a violation of neutral territory by another belligerent State where the neutral State does not eliminate the violation itself.

It is unsettled whether, when one State takes military action against operatives of a non-State armed group in the territory of another State, without the territorial State's consent, the operation against those operatives triggers an international armed conflict between the attacking State and the territorial State under the LOAC, even in the absence of any hostilities between the armed forces of the two States.[212] The ICRC takes the position that attacks by a State on forces of non-State armed groups in another State amount to an international armed conflict under the LOAC whenever the other State has not consented to the use of force in its territory, without regard to the participants in hostilities or the motive for the intervention.[213] This means that the full body of the LOAC

---

211. *See, e.g.*, Permanent Rep. of the United States of America, Letter dated 23 September 2014 from the Permanent Representative of the United States of America to the United Nations addressed to the Secretary-General, U.N. Doc. S/2014/695 (Sept. 23, 2014), http://www.un.org/en/ga/search/view_doc.asp?symbol=S/2014/695 (notifying the UN Secretary General of U.S. attacks on "ISIL sites and military strongholds in Syria" in the exercise of rights of individual and collective self-defense under Article 51 of the U.N. Charter and without Syrian consent, where "[t]he Syrian regime has shown that it cannot and will not confront these [ISIL] safe havens [in Syria] effectively itself."). Not all States invoke the "unwilling or unable" test directly, but instead cite to Syria's lack of control over areas of Syria in which ISIL operates. *See, e.g.*, Permanent Rep. of Germany, Letter dated 10 December 2015 from the Chargé d'affaires a.i. of the Permanent Mission of Germany to the United Nations addressed to the President of the Security Council, U.N. Doc. S/2015/946 (Dec. 15, 2015), http://www.un.org/en/ga/search/view_doc.asp?symbol=S/2015/946 ("ISIL has occupied a certain part of Syrian territory over which the Government of the Syrian Arab Republic does not at this time exercise effective control.")

212. Of course, in conducting an attack against the non-State armed group, the State must comply with the LOAC rules on targeting. A difficult question is what amount, if any, of incidental injury or death to citizens of the territorial State and incidental damage or destruction of property in the territorial State would be considered acceptable even under the LOAC's proportionality rule, where the individuals or property are not connected with the non-State armed group. While there is no clear rule, in 2013 President Obama adopted a policy regarding targeting "outside areas of active hostilities" that limited attacks to situations where, *inter alia*, there was "'near certainty' that non-combatants would not be killed or injured." White House Office of the Press Secretary, FACT SHEET: Executive Order on the US Policy on Pre & Post-Strike Measures to Address Civilian Casualties in the US Operations Involving the Use of Force & the DNI Release of Aggregate Date on Strike Outside of Area of Active Hostilities, (July 1, 2016), *available at* https://obamawhitehouse.archives.gov/the-press-office/2016/07/01/fact-sheet-executive-order-us-policy-pre-post-strike-measures-address (last visited Feb. 17, 2018).

213. 2017 COMMENTARY, CONVENTION (II), *supra*, note 106, para. 499. Moreover, the ICRC has cast doubt on the view that the LOAC applies where a State takes action against a non-State armed group's operatives in a territorial State located far from the country in which the conflict with the group is ongoing. Id., para. 500. Instead, the ICRC suggests that the LOAC could only apply to permit, under the principle of military necessity, attacks against the group's operatives in such a remote

would apply to any non-consensual military action in the territory of another State, and that the non-State armed group might assert its members are protected by these rules.

This ICRC interpretation is not necessarily reflective of emerging State practice. Since 2001, the United States, Israel, and other States involved in operations against ISIS in Syria and other terrorist groups have taken the position that military actions conducted under the "unable or unwilling" self-defense theory against non-State armed groups in another State's territory do not *ipso facto* result in an international armed conflict with that State.[214] How this aspect of conflict characterization law will evolve remains to be seen. In any case, aside from the parallel between neutrality law's authorization for one belligerent State to act against another belligerent State to put a stop to the use of neutral territory as a base of operations where the neutral fails or is unable to act, and the use of an "unwilling or unable" justification to strike non-State armed groups operating from third countries, none of the other features of neutrality law apply to non-international armed conflicts. For example, there is no right under the LOAC for a State engaged in a non-international armed conflict to "visit and search" third country merchant vessels or to seize contraband.

Study Questions

1. Commander Young's concerns about fishing vessels brings into play a customary law exemption for coastal fishing vessels discussed in a seminal U.S. Supreme Court case arising from the Spanish-American war.[215] In that case, the Court stated:

    > By an ancient usage among civilized nations, beginning centuries ago, and gradually ripening into a rule of international law, coast fishing vessels, pursuing their vocation of catching and bringing in fresh fish, have been recognized as exempt, with their cargoes and crews, from capture as prize of war.[216]

    The Court reversed a lower court decision holding that two fishing vessels seized by U.S. Navy ships off the coast of Cuba could be condemned (i.e., confiscated without compensation to their owners) by the United States as prizes of war. The Court held that "in the absence of any treaty or other public act of their own government in relation to the matter," customary international law exempted from capture coastal fishing vessels of an enemy State. According to the Court, the customary rule

---

territorial State where the threshold of organization and intensity of violence in the territorial State separately triggered a non-international armed conflict. *Id.* Otherwise, the operatives should be dealt with under the domestic law of the remote territorial State, including applicable human rights law and law enforcement rules for the use of force. *Id.*, para. 501.

214. *See* DoD Law of War Manual, *supra*, note 4, para. 17.18.2.
215. The Paquete Habana, 175 U.S. 677 (1900).
216. *Id.*, at 686.

... is an established rule of international law, founded on considerations of humanity to a poor and industrious order of men, and of the mutual convenience of belligerent states, that coast fishing vessels, with their implements and supplies, cargoes and crews, unarmed and honestly pursuing their peaceful calling of catching and bringing in fish, are exempt from capture as prize of war.[217]

Do you think this exemption would apply under the facts presented by Commander Young? If not, why not?[218]
2. Assume that you have concluded that the Iraqi fishing vessels do not fit within the exemption discussed in problem 1. Can U.S. forces launch a preemptive strike against the port where the vessels are moored? If not, why, and can you think of additional facts that, if true, might justify such a strike?[219]
3. What about the proposal to mine the port? Discuss the LOAC rules that would apply.[220]
4. In the scenario at the beginning of this chapter, Commander Jones has a number of proposals to deal with the possible shipment of weapons and military supplies to Iraq. Please evaluate each proposal based on what you learned in this Chapter.[221]
5. In the scenario at the beginning of this chapter, Commander Jones also proposed an exclusion zone to deal with potential threats to U.S. naval forces. Evaluate this proposal against the LOAC as discussed in this chapter.[222] If you do not think an exclusion zone would be permitted, can you alter the proposal to make it permissible under the LOAC or do you have any alternative ideas that the LOAC would permit U.S. forces to use?
6. Commander Jones proposes to seize Iraqi oil tankers, and even destroy them "under some circumstances." Which LOAC rules would apply in evaluating this proposal? If tankers are civilian objects, under which "circumstances" can he justify destroying them?[223]

---

217. The rule can be found in Article 3 of the 1907 Hague Convention (XI) on the Exercise of the Right of Capture in Naval War, *supra*, note 71, to which the United State is a party, and which likely is part of the customary law of naval warfare. Indeed, the San Remo Manual lists the following as one of the categories of vessels exempt from capture:

(f) small coastal fishing vessels and small boats engaged in local coastal trade, but they are subject to the regulations of a belligerent naval commander operating in the area and to inspection. . . .

SAN REMO MANUAL, *supra*, note 3, para. 136.
218. *Id.*, paras. 59 and 60.
219. *Compare id.*, paras. 135 and 136 *with* paras. 59 and 60.
220. *See id.*, paras. 80-92. *See also* COMMANDER'S HANDBOOK — 2017, *supra*, note 4, para. 9.2.
221. *Compare* SAN REMO MANUAL, *supra*, note 3, paras. 10-12, *with* paras. 14-22.
222. *See id.*, paras. 105-106. *See also* COMMANDER'S HANDBOOK — 2017, *supra*, note 4, para 7.9.
223. *See* DoD LAW OF WAR MANUAL, *supra*, note 4, para. 13.5.

Protected Person or Object	Nature of Protection in International Armed Conflict	Source
Sick, wounded, or shipwrecked falling within the six categories covered by Second Convention	(1) "shall at all times be respected and protected in all circumstances" (2) "shall be treated humanely and cared for by the Parties to the conflict in whose power they may be" (see discussion in text)	GWS-Sea, art. 12
Other wounded, sick, and shipwrecked (e.g., civilians not connected with armed forces and unprivileged combatants)	(1) "shall be respected and protected" (2) "in all circumstances shall be treated humanely and shall receive, to the fullest extent practicable and with least possible delay, the medical care and attention required by their condition" (see discussion in text)	AP I, art. 10 and 11
Religious, medical, and hospital personnel of hospital ships	(1) "shall be respected and protected" (2) "may not be captured during the time they are in the service of the hospital ship, whether or not there are wounded on board" (3) If they fall into the hands of the enemy, they may be retained to care for wounded, sick, and shipwrecked, but must be put ashore as early as possible, where they will be subject to the Third Convention (GPW) and treated as "retained personnel"	GWS-Sea, art. 36 and 37. See GWS-Sea, art. 42 for required distinctive emblem.
Civilian medical and religious personnel	(1) "shall be respected and protected" (2) civilian medical personnel: — shall be afforded all available help where combat activity has disrupted civilian medical services, and access to any place where their services are essential — shall not be punished for performing duties in conformance with medical ethics	AP I, art. 15 and 16 See AP I, art. 18 for required identification.

continued

V. The Law of Neutrality | 475

Protected Person or Object	Nature of Protection in International Armed Conflict	Source
Medical units, whether military or civilian, organized to search for, collect, transport, diagnose, or treat the wounded, sick, and shipwrecked and belong to a belligerent, are recognized and authorized by one of the belligerents (including officially recognized coastal rescue organizations) or are made available by a neutral, by a recognized and authorized aid society of a neutral, or by an impartial international humanitarian organization	"shall be protected and respected at all times and shall not be the object of attack"	AP I, art. 12 See AP I, art. 18 for required identification.
Military hospital ships (i.e., military ships built or equipped exclusively to assist, treat, and/or transport, the wounded, sick, and shipwrecked, which are notified to other belligerents)	(1) "shall at all times be respected and protected" (2) "may in no circumstances be attacked or captured"	GWS-Sea, art. 22 AP I, art. 22 extends protection to hospital ships that care for civilian wounded, sick, or shipwrecked. See GWS-Sea, art. 43 for required distinctive marking.
Authorized hospital ships used by National Red Cross Societies, by officially recognized relief societies or by private persons (if from a belligerent, must have commission from the belligerent State to which they belong; if from a neutral must have consent of the neutral State and authorization from the belligerent State)	Same as military hospital ships	GWS-Sea, art. 24 and 25 AP I, art. 22 extends protection to hospital ships that care for civilian wounded, sick, or shipwrecked. See GWS-Sea, art. 43 for required distinctive marking.

continued

Protected Person or Object	Nature of Protection in International Armed Conflict	Source
Small craft used by a belligerent or its officially recognized lifeboat institution for coastal rescue	"respected and protected, so far as operational requirements permit"	GWS-Sea, art. 27 AP I, art. 22 extends protection to coastal rescue craft that care for civilian wounded, sick, or shipwrecked. See GWS-Sea, art. 43 for required distinctive marking.
Sick-bays on board warships	(1) "respected and spared as far as possible" (2) Sick-bay and its equipment can be confiscated by the enemy belligerent, but not diverted from their purpose if needed to serve wounded and sick unless proper care is otherwise ensured	GWS-Sea, art. 28
Medical transports (ships chartered to transport equipment exclusively for wounded and sick members of armed forces, or for prevention of disease	Authorized if notified to, and approved by, the enemy: subject to "visit and search" by enemy, but enemy cannot capture them or seize the humanitarian cargo they carry	GWS-Sea, art. 38
Medical aircraft (aircraft exclusively employed to remove the wounded, sick, and shipwrecked persons, to transport medical personnel and equipment)	(1) "may not be the object of attack, but shall be respected by the Parties to the conflict, while flying at heights, at times and on routes specifically agreed upon between the Parties" (2) Can be summoned to land by enemy for inspection and in such a case, can continue on its flight, but if it lands involuntarily, all occupants including crew can be detained under GPW	GWS-Sea, art. 39 NB: Wounded, sick, or shipwrecked who are disembarked on neutral territory must be interned unless otherwise agreed with belligerents.
Other medical transports, whether by air or water AP I, art. 8 broadly defines "medical transports" to include any means of transport, whether civilian or military, permanent or temporary, assigned exclusively to medical transportation and under control of an authorized authority of a Party.	"respected and protected" subject to certain qualifications set out in AP I, arts. 23-31, including possible seizure if found to have operated in violation of certain treaty requirements	AP I, art. 23 ("other medical ships and craft" and art. 24 ("medical aircraft") NB: Persons disembarked temporarily in a neutral country can continue with voyage unless international law requires internment (e.g., under law of neutrality, belligerent soldiers and sailors would be detained).

12 | Air, Space, and Cyber Warfare

You are a civilian U.S. Air Force attorney sent to Saudi Arabia to help advise Central Command on "cutting edge" legal issues in air, space, and cyberwarfare. You have been selected for this job because the Air Force plans to use some new weapons and tactics in connection with the invasion. You formerly were an Air Force judge advocate, and served in targeting cells during various operations, so you are very familiar with the targeting rules discussed in earlier chapters. When you left active duty, you went to work on U.S. space and cyber policy, and never expected to be called in for advice on operations. Now that the United States is about to launch a major invasion, and recognizing the rapid proliferation of space and cyber capabilities among the nations of the world, you were quickly sent "downrange" to help judge advocates (JAGs) understand the law that applies to these new domains. Since you will be working primarily with Air Force military lawyers, you need to refresh your knowledge of the basics of air warfare as well.

You are assigned to the Central Command's "Advanced Tactics" planning group, led by Major Payne, a tough-minded pilot with lots of combat experience. The team consists of men and women from various military services, including JAGs, as well as technical experts from U.S. civilian agencies and even industry. At your first meeting, Major Payne lays down his vision for legal advice to be given to the team: "We are here to ensure the enemy does not get an unexpected advantage over us, by neutralizing our technological superiority. At the same time, we must ensure that all of our operations are fully compliant with the law and do not lead to mistakes that could embarrass us or undermine support for our operations. I am looking for you to help my JAGs understand the nuances of the law applicable to these operations, so that they can give me the best advice possible. I also want you to give them the freedom to be creative and flexible, within the confines of the law. I know this is tough because, as I recall, the rules are not exactly crystal clear."

You think to yourself: It is good to be back in the mix. However, your military experience was with operations against relatively unsophisticated armed groups. Here, the United States will be taking on a State that, while not an economic peer of the United States, nonetheless could have or obtain capabilities to challenge U.S. technological superiority. Therefore, it is not safe to assume that the Iraqis cannot take actions to shut down U.S. command and control, perhaps by using commercially available resources. In a widely diverse world, there are many potential threats and you can anticipate novel challenges. Therefore, your first order of business is to organize your thoughts on the applicable law.

I. Introduction

In this chapter, we consider three domains of warfare that are critically important in armed conflict today and are likely to be even more important in the future. As of the writing of this book, however, States have yet to agree on terms of a treaty to lay out the rules for conduct of hostilities in any of these domains. Thus, in the absence of treaties on the law of armed conflict (LOAC) directly applicable to these domains, operators and scholars are guided by LOAC rules from treaties devoted to other domains or from customary law.

Historically, warfare was confined to two domains—land and sea—and technology did not exist that would require other rules. During the nineteenth century, there were some possibilities for the use of the air to support military operations. In the American Civil War, for example, balloons were used for observation of enemy positions and movements, but they were not used as "engines of war" or weapons. While balloons were not widely used during the remainder of the nineteenth century, many, but not all,[1] States participating in the First Peace Conference at the Hague signed a declaration in 1899 prohibiting "for a term of five years, the launching of projectiles and explosives from balloons, or by other new methods of a similar nature,"[2] in anticipation of one possible future use of air power in warfare, but with little understanding of how important air power would become. The twentieth century witnessed a dramatic expansion of air warfare, including the use of aircraft to attack land and naval targets, to transport forces and equipment throughout the theater of

---

1. The United Kingdom did not sign the 1899 Declaration. The United States signed but did not ratify the 1899 Declaration.

2. Declaration Prohibiting for the Term of Five Years the Launching of Projectiles and Explosives from Balloons, and Other Methods of Similar Nature, Jul. 29, 1899, 32 STAT. 1839. The declaration was renewed in 1907 to impose the same prohibition until the close of the Third Peace Conference, which has never been held. Declaration (XIV) Prohibiting the Discharge of Projectiles and Explosives from Balloons, Oct. 18, 1907, 36 STAT. 2439. This declaration was ratified by 20 countries, including both the United States and the United Kingdom, and signed by 13 others who did not ratify. Other leading countries, including France, Germany, Italy, Japan, and Russia, did not sign or ratify it. The 1907 declaration technically is in force today but by its terms only applies to conflicts in which only parties to the Declaration are involved. It has not applied to any of the major international armed conflicts since 1907. In World War II, the United States took the position that the 1907 declaration was not binding. U.S. DEP'T OF DEF., DEPARTMENT OF DEFENSE LAW OF WAR MANUAL para. 19.8 (2016) *available at* https://www.defense.gov/Portals/1/Documents/pubs/DoD%20Law%20of%20War%20Manual%20-%20June%202015%20Updated%20Dec%202016.pdf?ver=2016-12-13-172036-190 (last visited Feb. 13, 2017) [hereinafter DoD LAW OF WAR MANUAL].

conflict, to evacuate the sick, wounded and others *hors de combat* (as well as civilians), to conduct surveillance, and to perform many other missions essential to the conduct of military operations. Aircraft have also engaged in combat with other aircraft and in recent years even have been used to attack targets in space. In the twenty-first century, it is inconceivable for any State to conduct military operations without relying to a greater or lesser degree on aircraft, and even some non-state armed groups have some air capability.[3] Yet, as will be discussed in Section II of this chapter, there are no binding treaties dealing exclusively with the LOAC applicable to air warfare, although a number of treaties do have provisions that are directed at military operations in the air or that apply to attacks from the air. Of course, the rules of customary law applicable to all conflicts, including the LOAC principles discussed in Chapter 2, the LOAC treaties applicable to warfare generally, and the law of neutrality (discussed in Chapter 11), all can be referred to in order to address LOAC issues in air warfare. In addition, an important study of the LOAC rules applicable to air and missile warfare was published in 2009, which is not binding as a matter of law, but is likely to be highly influential in the interpretation of how existing treaties and customary law should apply to issues connected with air warfare (which for this purpose includes operations involving both aircraft [manned and unmanned] and missiles).

During the last half of the twentieth century, outer space emerged as an important domain for warfare. While conflicts have not yet been fought in space, satellites now are critical to military operations of modern armed forces, for purposes of surveillance, communications, and navigation (i.e., global positioning system). In addition, anti-satellite (ASAT) weapons have been discussed, and, in a few cases, tested, and they could be deployed in a future conflict in which a State with ASAT capabilities engaged in hostilities with another State that employs space assets. A few treaties negotiated in the 1960s and 1970s to govern the use of space potentially restrain military operations in space, but there are no LOAC rules specifically designed for conflicts in space. Questions remain whether the customary rules of LOAC are sufficient to deal with the peculiar issues that are likely to arise in the future were objects in space targeted by parties to a conflict.

Finally, at the end of the twentieth century, cyberspace became another domain for armed conflict, with a myriad of new issues for the LOAC that have yet to be squarely addressed in treaty law. A study of the law applicable to cyber operations, published in 2012 and updated and expanded in 2017, along with parts of the 2009 air and missile warfare study mentioned above, seeks to resolve how the LOAC should apply to cyber warfare issues.

---

3. Further, as was demonstrated in the September 11, 2001 attacks in the United States, non-state groups can use aircraft as weapons of war and instruments of terror.

II. Air Warfare

A. Sources

1. General International Law

While there are no treaties devoted specifically to the LOAC applicable to air warfare, there are treaties, such as the 1944 Chicago Convention (the "Convention"),[4] that set out the general rules of international law applicable to civil aviation and are relevant to any discussion of military operations. The Convention, which has been ratified by nearly every nation in the world, recognizes the principle that "every State has complete and exclusive sovereignty over the airspace above its territory"[5] and that for this purpose, a State's territory includes "the land areas and territorial waters adjacent thereto under the sovereignty, suzerainty, protection or mandate of such State."[6] It also stipulates that the State of registration of an aircraft determines its nationality,[7] and that the aircraft engaged in international navigation must be marked "with appropriate nationality and registration marks"[8] and must carry, *inter alia*, registration papers.[9]

The Convention expressly states that it is not applicable to "State aircraft," which the Convention defines as aircraft used in military, customs, and police services, but there are provisions of the Convention that clearly do impact State aircraft:

- A prohibition against State aircraft of one State overflying or landing on the territory of another State without the permission of that State;[10]
- An undertaking by all States, "when issuing regulations for their state aircraft, that they will have due regard for the safety of navigation of civil aircraft";[11]
- A territorial State's right to intercept aircraft overflying its territory without authority or in a manner inconsistent with the Convention and to force the aircraft to land at a designated airport;[12] and

---

4. Convention on International Civil Aviation, Dec. 7, 1944, 61 Stat. 1180 (hereinafter, the "CONVENTION").
5. *Id.* art. 1.
6. *Id.* art. 2.
7. *Id.* art. 17.
8. *Id.* art. 20.
9. *Id.* art. 29.
10. *Id.* art. 3(c).
11. *Id.* art. 3(d).
12. *Id.* art. 3*bis*. While not explicitly required by the Convention, this right of interception likely would be exercised using State aircraft. Appendix 2 to Annex 2 to the Convention sets out standards to be used by States in drafting regulations to govern interception. These standards make clear that interception is to be used as a "last resort" and in a manner to ensure the safety of the intercepted aircraft and its occupants.

- The obligation, imposed on all States, to refrain from using weapons against civil aircraft and not to endanger the lives of persons on board aircraft intercepted in the exercise of the State's sovereignty.[13]

The Convention affords civil aircraft of its contracting parties certain essential rights, including the right to overfly the territory of other contracting States. This right permits civil aircraft to use the most direct route when traveling from one point to another. These rights are subject to the right of a State to restrict or prohibit overflight of certain areas of its territory "for reasons of military necessity or public safety," provided that the restriction is imposed "uniformly" and in a manner that does not "interfere unnecessarily with air navigation."[14] States also have the right to temporarily restrict or prohibit "with immediate effect" all or part of its territory "in exceptional circumstances or during a period of emergency," again subject to requirement that the restriction or prohibition be imposed "without distinction of nationality to aircraft of all states."[15] The Convention also prohibits "munitions of war or implements of war" (as defined in the territorial State's regulations) to be carried in or above the territory of a State without that State's permission.[16]

Article 89 of the Convention provides:

> In case of war, the provisions of this Convention shall not affect the freedom of action of any of the contracting States affected, whether as belligerents or as neutrals. The same principle shall apply in the case of any contracting State which declares a state of national emergency and notifies the fact to the Council.[17]

By virtue of this provision, the Convention would be subordinate to any provision of customary or treaty LOAC, applicable in an international armed conflict, or a non-international armed conflict (subject, in the latter case, to the requirement to notify the Council.)[18] Further, Article 3bis of the Convention, regarding the prohibition against the use of weapons against civil aircraft and the obligation not to endanger aircraft or those on board when conducting an interception, states that it "shall not be interpreted as modifying in any way the rights and obligations of States set forth in the Charter of the United Nations," which would include, *inter alia*, the "inherent right of individual or collective self-defence" of a State to respond to an armed attack against that State or another

---

13. *Id.*
14. *Id.* art. 9(a).
15. *Id.* art. 9(b).
16. *Id.* art. 35. Article 35 also permits a State to designate other articles that cannot be carried in or above its territory, as long as the prohibition is applied uniformly to the aircraft of all States.
17. The "Council" referred to here is a body of the International Civil Aviation Organization, which was created by the Convention.
18. Even in the event of an international or non-international armed conflict, however, the Convention and other international law related to international air navigation presumably would remain relevant in matters not regulated by the LOAC, such as in the navigation by belligerents over the territory of neutral States.

Member of the United Nations, including the right to use force to respond to actual or imminent threats of armed attack, as discussed in Chapter 1.[19]

2. Customary and Treaty LOAC

There is relatively little treaty law dealing specifically with air warfare. The Second Peace Conference in 1907 produced a declaration to prohibit "the discharge of projectiles and explosives from balloons or by other new methods of a similar nature" that technically remains in force among the small number of States that signed it (including the United States). The declaration was not ratified by Germany and therefore was not applicable in either World War. It also has not applied to any conflict since the end of World War II.

The regulation appended to the 1907 Convention (IV) Respecting the Laws and Customs of War on Land ("1907 Hague IV"), which did apply in World War I and were recognized as customary international law at the Nuremberg trials, included a prohibition against the "attack or bombardment, by whatever means, of towns, villages, dwelling or building which are undefended."[20] The phrase "by whatever means" was included in the treaty language to take account of aerial bombardment. However, the prohibition proved hard to apply because there was no agreed standard for determining when a town etc. was "undefended."[21]

1907 Hague IV includes provisions directed at "bombardment" generally that, while written originally to deal with artillery bombardment, also would apply to aerial bombardment. These include a requirement for a commander to "warn the authorities" before commencing a bombardment, "except in cases of assault,"[22] and an obligation to "spare, as far as possible" cultural and religious buildings, monuments, hospitals, collection points for sick and wounded, and places of worship, "provided they are not being used at the time for military purposes."[23]

After World War I, there was a concerted effort to draw up rules to regulate air warfare. A resolution adopted at the Washington Conference of 1922 on the Limitation of Armaments appointed a "Commission of Jurists" from France,

---

19. Another relevant treaty governing air navigation is the International Air Services Transit Agreement by which territorial States grant two key "privileges" or "freedoms" to civil aircraft on scheduled international air service (e.g., airliners): "the privilege to fly across its territory without landing" and "the privilege to land for non-traffic purposes" (e.g., not to take on or discharge passengers, cargo, or mail). International Air Services Transit Agreement, Dec. 7, 1944, art. 1, 59 Stat. 1693, 131 nations, including the United States, have ratified the Agreement. The Agreement provides that the two freedoms are not applicable with respect to "airports utilized for military purposes to the exclusion of any scheduled international air services." *Id.* Further, "[i]n areas of active hostilities or of military occupation, and in time of war along the supply routes leading to such areas, the exercise of such privileges shall be subject to the approval of the competent military authorities," again indicating that the Agreement, like the Convention, would be superseded by applicable treaty or customary LOAC. *Id.*

20. Convention (IV) Respecting the Laws and Customs of War on Land and Its Annex: Regulations concerning the Laws and Customs of War on Land, Oct. 18, 1907, art. 25, 1 Bevans 631, 36 Stat. 2277 (hereinafter 1907 Hague IV).

21. LASSA OPPENHEIM, INTERNATIONAL LAW: A TREATISE (7th ed., H. Lauterpacht ed.) §214a. (1952).

22. 1907 Hague IV, *supra*, note 20, art. 26.

23. *Id.* art. 27. Of course, any other provisions of the Hague Regulations that are generally applicable to the conduct of hostilities also could apply to air warfare.

Italy, Japan, the United Kingdom, and the United States to consider if existing rules of international law "adequately cover new methods of attack or defence resulting from the introduction or development, since the Hague Conference of 1907, of new agencies of warfare" and if not, to propose changes to international law.

From December 1922 to February 1923, the Commission drafted rules addressing wireless telegraphy and air warfare and produced a report that included both rules and commentary, hereinafter referred to as HRAW.[24] For various reasons, the rules were never adopted, but they were highly influential in the conduct of military operations in the following years. Among other things, the rules:

- Recognized the absolute sovereign right of States "belligerent or neutral" to control their airspace in the event of an armed conflict;[25]
- Defined the types of aircraft that could engage in belligerent activities, and how these aircraft and their crews were to be distinguished as lawful belligerents;[26]
- Established norms for (i) conducting hostilities from the air, including aerial combat and bombardment, (ii) distinguishing legitimate military objectives from civilians and civilian objects, and (iii) affording prisoner of war treatment to captured crews and passengers on military aircraft;[27]
- Outlined the rules for the interception, search and capture of enemy and neutral civil aircraft (including private and non-military public aircraft); the conditions under which such aircraft could be fired upon; and the treatment of crew and passengers of such aircraft;[28] and
- Set out the rights and duties of neutrals and belligerents in their relationship with one another during an armed conflict.[29]

Many of these rules have been accepted as customary law. This was evident in the articles and commentary resulting from two recent studies of customary LOAC—the 1994 San Remo Manual on International Law Applicable to Armed Conflicts at Sea (the "San Remo Manual")[30] and the 2009 Manual on International Law Applicable to Air and Missile Warfare (the "Air and Missile Warfare Manual").[31] Many of the provisions in the San Remo Manual and the Air and Missile Warfare Manual follow the HRAW.

---

24. The commission's report, including both the rules (in italics) and a commentary on the rules, can be found in volume 32 of the American Journal of International Law Supplement. 32 AM. J. INT'L L. SUPP. 1 (1938). This book uses the text of the rules as found in this report. The Commission met in the Hague and consequently, the rules are known as the Hague Rules of Air Warfare or "HRAW".
25. *Id.*, Part II, art. 12.
26. *Id.* Part II, arts. 3, 7, 9, 13-17.
27. *Id.* Part II, arts. 18-26, 36-38.
28. *Id.* Part II, arts. 30-35, 49-60.
29. *Id.* Part II, arts. 39-48.
30. SAN REMO MANUAL ON INTERNATIONAL LAW APPLICABLE TO ARMED CONFLICTS AT SEA (Doswald-Beck ed., 1995) (hereinafter SAN REMO MANUAL).
31. PROGRAM ON HUMANITARIAN POLICY AND CONFLICT RESEARCH AT HARVARD UNIVERSITY, MANUAL ON INTERNATIONAL LAW APPLICABLE TO AIR AND MISSILE WARFARE, (2009) (hereinafter

The San Remo Manual, prepared by a group of international lawyers and naval experts convened by the International Institute of Humanitarian Law in San Remo, Italy, was intended to be a "contemporary restatement" of the law of naval warfare. However, in connection with the preparation of the restatement, the group addressed in detail the law applicable to aircraft and air warfare, as it relates to the sea and naval operations. Therefore, the San Remo Manual contains an in-depth discussion of that law from a naval perspective.

The Air and Missile Warfare Manual was prepared by a group of experts convened by the Harvard Program on Humanitarian Policy and Conflict Research. Like the San Remo Manual, the Air and Missile Warfare Manual was intended to be a restatement of the customary international law. Unlike the San Remo Manual, however, the Air and Missile Warfare Manual is focused principally on air warfare itself, not just as an adjunct to a study of rules related to another domain of warfare.

Neither the San Remo Manual nor the Air and Missile Warfare Manual are binding law per se, but they do provide a good baseline for understanding the rules of air warfare that likely would be treated as customary law by international experts. Air warfare also is addressed in national military manuals, such as the U.S. Department of Defense's Law of War Manual (DoD Law of War Manual, which was published in 2015 and updated in 2016). These manuals can be consulted to determine what those nations who issued them believe to be the law.

While a treaty devoted exclusively to air warfare has not yet been signed, various LOAC treaties that have come into force since the end of World War II have included provisions that address the use of aircraft in connection with armed conflict. For example, the 1949 Geneva Conventions include provisions to protect "aircraft exclusively employed for the removal of wounded and sick and for the transport of medical personnel and equipment" from attack provided they are flying at heights, times, and on routes specifically agreed upon between the belligerents concerned, are clearly marked with the distinctive emblem (e.g., the red cross), and do not fly over enemy or enemy-occupied territory (unless the enemy agrees to such flights).[32]

The 1977 Additional Protocol I to the Geneva Conventions (AP I) includes provisions to further refine the 1949 Conventions' provisions on medical aircraft.[33] In addition, AP I's provisions on the conduct of hostilities, including

---

"AMW MANUAL"). A commentary on the Manual was published by Harvard University's Program on Humanitarian Policy and Conflict Research in 2010 that includes both the black letter rules from the Air and Missile Warfare Manual and comments on each rule by a subset of the experts who contributed to the Manual. In this chapter, citations to the commentary will be referred to as "AMW COMMENTARY".

32. Geneva Convention for the Amelioration of the Wounded and Sick in Armed Force in the Field, Aug. 12, 1949, arts. 36 and 37, 6 U.N.T.S. 3114, 75 U.N.T.S. 31 (hereinafter GWS); Geneva Convention for the Amelioration of the Condition of Wounded, Sick and Shipwrecked Members of the Armed Forces at Sea, Aug. 12, 1949, arts. 39 and 40, 6 U.S.T. 3217, 75 U.N.T.S. 971 (hereinafter GWS-Sea); and Geneva Convention Relative to the Protection of Civilian Persons in Time of War, Aug. 12, 1949, art. 22, 6 U.S.T. 3516, 75 U.N.T.S. 973 (hereinafter GCIV).

33. Protocol Additional to the Geneva Conventions of 12 August 1949, and Relating to the Protection of Victims of International Armed Conflicts, June 8, 1977, arts. 24-31, 1125 U.N.T.S. 3

the requirements to take precautions in planning and conducting attacks, were drafted to apply to attacks in all domains of warfare, including attacks from the air. Indeed, Article 49 of AP I states:

> The provisions of this Section ["General Protection Against Effects of Hostilities"] apply to any land, air or sea warfare which may affect the civilian population, individual civilians or civilian objects on land. They further apply to all attacks from the sea or from the air against objectives on land but do not otherwise affect the rules of international law applicable in armed conflict at sea or in the air.[34]

The last sentence of the quoted language suggests that the rules applicable to air warfare may be different when attacking targets at sea or in the air, as distinct from the rules applicable to attacks against targets on land. However, pursuant to the following provision of Article 49, it would appear that at least with respect to the protection of civilians and civilian objects, AP I's rules are intended to be additional protections in all domains and apply over and above the general protections already afforded by treaty and customary law:

> The provisions of this Section are additional to the rules concerning humanitarian protection contained in the Fourth Convention, particularly in Part II thereof, and in other international agreements binding upon the High Contracting Parties, as well as to other rules of international law relating to the protection of civilians and civilian objects on land, at sea or in the air against the effects of hostilities.[35]

Protocol III to the 1980 Convention on Prohibitions or Restrictions on the Use of Certain Conventional Weapons Which May be Deemed to be Excessively Injurious or to have Indiscriminate Effects prohibits attacking a military objective "located within a concentration of civilians" (e.g., within an urban area where civilians have not yet evacuated) with "air delivered incendiary weapons."[36] Such weapons would include napalm, for example. However, Protocol III is perhaps the only treaty rule in effect today that applies a prohibition based on the fact that a weapon is employed from the air.

In sum, while there is no treaty devoted to air warfare, there are treaties that deal with certain aspects of air operations in armed conflict. Further, consistent with the so-called Martens Clause (discussed in Chapter 2

(hereinafter AP I). A companion treaty to AP I applies a less detailed set of rules to certain non-international armed conflicts. Protocol Additional to the Geneva Conventions of 12 Aug. 1949, and Relating to the Protection of Victims of Non-International Armed Conflicts, June 8, 1977, 1125 U.N.T.S. 609 (hereinafter AP II).

34. AP I, *supra*, note 33, art. 49(3). The "Section" referred to in this provision includes Articles 48-67 of the Protocol, which are the Protocol's provisions dealing with the conduct of hostilities, including targeting.

35. *Id*. art. 49(4).

36. Protocol (III) on Prohibitions or Restrictions on the Use of Incendiary Weapons, Annexed to the Convention on Prohibitions or Restrictions on the Use of Certain Convention Weapons Which May be Deemed to be Excessively Injurious or to Have Indiscriminate Effects, Oct. 10, 1980, art. 2(2), 1342 U.N.T.S. 137.

of this book), customary law always applies. The HRAW, the San Remo Manual, and the Air and Missile Warfare Manual all are excellent sources of information regarding rules that international legal experts believe reflect customary law. In addition, national military manuals, such as the DoD Law of War Manual, are useful sources of information about the treaty and customary rules that nations believe apply to air warfare.

B. General Framework

1. Definition of Airspace

International law does not include an agreed treaty definition of "airspace." In the Air and Missile Warfare Manual, it is defined as "the air up to the highest altitude at which an aircraft can fly and below the lowest possible perigee of an earth satellite in orbit."[37] The Commentary to the Manual notes that an altitude of approximately 100 kilometers is generally agreed to be the limits of airspace, but this threshold has not achieved universal acceptance.[38] Indeed, in the DoD Law of War Manual, the U.S. Department of Defense states that "[t]he United States has expressed the view that there is no legal or practical need to delimit or otherwise define a specific boundary between airspace and outer space."[39]

Just as the law of the sea generally divides the world's waters into national and international waters,[40] the world's airspace can be categorized as *national airspace* and *international airspace*. The Air and Missile Warfare Manual distinguishes the two types of airspace, as follows: "Under international law, airspace is classified as either national airspace (that over the land, internal waters, archipelagic waters, and territorial seas of any State) or international airspace (that over contiguous zones, exclusive economic zones, the high seas, and territory not subject to the sovereignty of any State)."[41]

2. Types of Aircraft

The Air and Missile Warfare Manual defines an "aircraft" as "any vehicle—whether manned or unmanned—that can derive support in the atmosphere from the reactions of the air (other than the reactions of the air against the Earth's surface), including vehicles with either fixed or rotary wings."[42]

---

37. AMW Manual, *supra*, note 31, Rule 1(a).
38. AMW Commentary, *supra*, note 31, Rule 1(a), para. 5.
39. DoD Law of War Manual, *supra*, note 2, para. 14.2.2.
40. The concept of national and international waters is discussed in Chapter 11.
41. AMW Manual, *supra*, note 31, Rule 1(a). *See also*, DoD Law of War Manual, *supra*, note 2, para. 14.2.1. The reference in the Air and Missile Warfare Manual to "territory not subject to the sovereignty of any State" refers to parts of Antarctica or newly emerging islands, but in the case of Antarctica at least, other international law that precludes military use of that territory would preclude use of airspace over that territory for belligerent operations. *See* AMW Commentary, *supra*, note 31, Rule 107, para. 2.
42. AMW Manual, *supra*, note 31, Rule 1(d). Thus, a balloon, blimp, or dirigible is an aircraft. AMW Commentary, *supra*, note 31, Rule 1(d), para. 1. A glider also is an aircraft. *Id*. Missiles are not aircraft, however, though a cruise missile may exhibit the characteristics of an aircraft while cruising. *Id*., para. 4. Unless expressly stated in this chapter, the rules specifically applicable to aircraft do not

Under international law, all aircraft possess nationality. According to the U.S. Department of Defense, "State aircraft possess the nationality of the State that operates them. . .[and] [c]ivil aircraft possess the nationality of the State in which they are registered."[43]

Aircraft generally fall into two categories: State aircraft and civil aircraft[44] (also referred to as civilian aircraft).[45] Civil aircraft include all aircraft other than State aircraft (such as military, police, and customs aircraft) engaged in non-commercial service.[46] Thus, civilian airlines and cargo aircraft would be civil aircraft, as would private airliners, research craft, balloons, and pleasure craft. What is critical in the definition of State aircraft is that it is "operated by a government for sovereign, non-commercial purposes."[47] Thus, civil aircraft could include passenger aircraft of State-owned airlines used in commercial service.

Within the category of State aircraft, only military aircraft are entitled to engage in attacks in an international armed conflict.[48] The Air and Missile Warfare Manual defines "military aircraft" as "any aircraft (i) operated by the armed forces of a State; (ii) bearing the military markings of that State;

---

apply to missiles, *per se*, but missiles, when used as weapons, must be deployed in a manner that complies with all the LOAC rules applicable to weapons and attacks. *See, e.g.*, discussion of these rules in Chapters 7 and 8, as well as the rules on targeting discussed, *infra*, in this Chapter.

43. DoD Manual, *supra*, note 2, para. 14.3.2. The rules for registration of civil aircraft can be found in the Chicago Convention, which provides for registration in only one State, and requires that all aircraft "engaged in international air navigation shall bear its appropriate nationality and registration marks." Convention, *supra*, note 4, arts. 17-20. Since the Convention does not apply to State aircraft, registration is not required, per se, for these aircraft.

44. For this purpose, the Convention defines "State aircraft" as aircraft used in the "military, customs and police services." Convention, *supra*, note 4, art. 3(b). The Air and Missile Warfare Manual broadens the definition of "State aircraft" to mean "any aircraft owned or used by a State serving exclusively noncommercial government functions." AMW Manual, *supra*, note 31, Rule 1(cc). However, the Commentary to the Air and missile Warfare Manual notes that, for purposes of determining which aircraft can be seized as booty of war, a distinction can be made between military, police, and customs aircraft, which would be booty, and other government aircraft, which would be subject to prize proceedings. AMW Commentary, *supra*, note 31, Rule 1(cc), para. 6; AMW Manual, *supra*, note 31, Rule 136. The Air and Missile Warfare Manual's broader definition is relevant in establishing the category of neutral State aircraft that are immune from interception in international airspace (e.g., to determine if the aircraft is carrying contraband). AMW Manual, *supra*, note 31, Rule 137. However, the Department of Defense appears to take a broader position and considers all enemy State aircraft to be subject to capture as war booty. DoD Law of War Manual, *supra*, note 2, para. 14.5.3.

45. AMW Manual, *supra*, note 31, Rules 1(h) (civilian aircraft definition) and 1(cc) (State aircraft definition).

46. The AMW Manual defines a civil aircraft as "any aircraft other than military or other State aircraft." *Id.*, Rule 1(h).

47. DoD Law of War Manual, *supra*, note 2, para. 14.3.1 (citations omitted). The Defense Department notes that it does not consider aircraft contracted by the DoD to be State aircraft. *Id.* On the other hand, the San Remo Manual excludes from civil aircraft, "auxiliary aircraft," which it defines as "an aircraft, other than a military aircraft, that is owned by or under the exclusive control of the armed forces of a State and used for the time being on government non-commercial service." AMW Manual, *supra*, note 31, Rule 13(k). The "auxiliary aircraft" definition is not used in the Air and Missile Warfare Manual or in the DOD Law of War Manual.

48. AMW Manual, *supra*, note 31, Rule 17(a).

(iii) commanded by a member of the armed forces; and (iv) controlled, manned or preprogrammed by a crew subject to regular armed forces discipline."[49]

The definition is based on the HRAW,[50] which was never adopted as a treaty by States. Accordingly, while the Defense Department agrees with this type of definition as a general description of a military aircraft,[51] it notes that the "United States has not ratified a treaty that requires certain qualifications before an aircraft may be designated as military aircraft."[52] Therefore, in its view, military aircraft simply "may be understood as aircraft that are designated as such by a State that operates them."[53]

The requirement that the commander must be a member of the armed forces does not mean that the crew cannot include non-military personnel, nor does the fact that there may be civilians in the crew alter the status of the aircraft.[54] Indeed, it is not even necessary that there be a crew on board. By its terms, the Air and Missile Warfare Manual's definition does not require that a military aircraft be manned or even remotely piloted. Thus, an unmanned aerial vehicle or "drone" can be a military aircraft as long it is remotely piloted or programmed by members of a State's military.

The HRAW requires that all military aircraft "must carry an external mark indicating its nationality and military character"[55] and as shown above, the Air and Missile Warfare Manual describes a military aircraft as one "bearing the military markings" of the State whose armed forces are operating the aircraft.[56] On the other hand, the U.S. Defense Department does not view the marking requirement as mandatory in all cases: "[mi]litary aircraft are customarily marked to signify both their nationality and military character. Markings may help distinguish friend from foe and help preclude misidentification of aircraft as neutral or as civil. However, circumstances may exist where such markings are superfluous."[57]

The fact that the Air and Missile Warfare Manual's definition requires an aircraft to be operated by the armed forces of a State means that an aircraft operated by the non-military wing of a State would not qualify as a military aircraft. Nor could an aircraft operated by a non-State group qualify. However,

---

49. *Id.* Rule 1(x). The definition is similar to the definition in the San Remo Manual. SAN REMO MANUAL, *supra*, note 30, para. 13(j).

50. HRAW, *supra*, note 24, Part II, arts. 3 and 14.

51. DoD LAW OF WAR MANUAL, *supra*, note 2, para. 14.3.3 ("In general, military aircraft are operated by commissioned units of the armed forces of a State, bearing the military markings of that State, and commanded by a member of the armed forces of that State.")

52. *Id.*

53. *Id.*

54. AMW COMMENTARY, *supra*, note 31, Rule 1(x), para. 5. *See also* DoD Law of War MANUAL, *supra*, note 2, para. 14.3.3.3.

55. HRAW, *supra*, note 24, Part II, art. 3.

56. AMW MANUAL, *supra*, note 31, Rule 1(x).

57. DoD LAW OF WAR MANUAL, *supra*, note 2, para. 14.3.3.2 (citations omitted). By contrast, the requirement to mark military medical aircraft with the distinctive emblem (e.g., the red cross) is mandatory. *Id.*, para. 7.14.3.

depending on how the aircraft is deployed, it could become a military objective under the LOAC.[58]

Within the categories of civil and State aircraft (including military aircraft), there are special categories of aircraft that enjoy special protection under the LOAC. These include "medical aircraft," which are defined in the Air and Missile Warfare Manual as "any aircraft permanently or temporarily assigned—by the competent authorities of a Belligerent Party—exclusively to aerial transportation or treatment of wounded, sick, or shipwrecked persons, and/or the transport of medical personnel and medical equipment or supplies."[59]

In addition to being properly marked with the distinctive emblem required by applicable treaties,[60] the crucial requirements in this definition are that the aircraft is exclusively engaged in its medical mission and that it has been assigned that mission by a State. Under the applicable treaties, in order to enjoy protection, the aircraft must meet certain requirements intended to put the enemy belligerent on notice of its status as a medical aircraft.[61] Either State aircraft (including military aircraft) or civil aircraft may be employed as medical aircraft, provided they meet the terms of the definition.[62] Further, the fact that an aircraft may be employed on a non-medical mission during one leg of its flight, but is exclusively engaged in a medical mission on another leg (e.g., flying in food and flying casualties) does not disqualify it from being a medical aircraft during the leg on which it is exclusively engaged, but care needs to be taken to ensure that it is clear to the enemy that it is, in fact, exclusively engaged in the medical mission during that leg.[63]

Note that aircraft used for search and rescue of the crews of downed military aircraft in enemy territory are not medical aircraft. Despite its seemingly humanitarian purpose, the search and rescue mission is a combat mission, not a medical one, and medical aircraft should not be used for this purpose if they are to retain their protection from attack.[64] Medical aircraft also should not interfere with the capture of downed aircrew by the enemy.[65]

Another category of protected aircraft is a "cartel aircraft," which the Air and Missile Warfare Manual defines as "an aircraft granted safe conduct by

---

58. *See, e.g.*, AMW COMMENTARY, *supra*, note 31, Rule 1(x), para. 8.
59. AMW MANUAL, *supra*, note 31, Rule 1(u).
60. *See* GWS, *supra*, note 32, art. 38.
61. These requirements are discussed, *supra*, notes 32 and 33 and accompanying text, as well as in Chapter 8.
62. *See, e.g.*, AMW COMMENTARY, *supra*, note 31, Rule 1(u), para. 4.
63. *Id.*, para. 9. If an aircraft carries "able combatants" or non-medical equipment or supplies along with the wounded or sick or medical equipment or supplies, it risks falling outside the definition of a medical aircraft. *Id.*, para. 7.
64. AMW MANUAL, *supra*, note 31, Rule 86; DoD LAW OF WAR MANUAL, *supra*, note 2, paras. 7.14.2.2 and 14.4.3.3.
65. *Id.*, paras. 14.4.3.3.

agreement between the Belligerent Parties for the purpose of performing a specific function, such as the transport of prisoners of war or parlementaires."[66]

As with medical aircraft, any State aircraft (including a military aircraft) or any civil aircraft can be used as a "cartel aircraft." Further, while the definition mentions prisoners of war and parlementaires, the aircraft could be carrying anything agreed by the Belligerent Parties, including humanitarian aid. The aircraft can lose its protection if it fails to comply with the Parties' agreement or if it is not innocently employed in its role as a cartel aircraft and intentionally hampers the movement of combatants.[67] However, even if an aircraft fails to meet the requirement for protection as a cartel aircraft (or an aircraft otherwise granted safe conduct by agreement of the belligerent States), it may only be attacked if it is or has become a military objective (and the requirements described below are met). Thus, while a military aircraft would be a military objective if not granted special protection as a cartel aircraft, a civil aircraft would not automatically become a military objective merely by losing the special protection afforded by being a cartel aircraft.[68]

A category of civil aircraft granted special treatment is the civilian airliner, which the Air and Missile Warfare Manual defines as "civilian aircraft identifiable as such and engaged in carrying civilian passengers in scheduled or non-scheduled service."[69] Civilian airliners need to be distinguished from civil and military aircraft carrying military personnel of a belligerent States who are not *hors de combat*. Any passenger aircraft carrying enemy military personnel could be a military objective depending on the circumstances, including the number of military personnel on board and other factors.

The Air and Missile Warfare Manual does not afford special protection, *per se*, to civilian airliners. Rather, it calls for "particular care in terms of precautions."[70] These precautions (which the Manual also applies to any aircraft granted safe conduct, such as a cartel aircraft) include a presumption that the aircraft is not a military objective, and a requirement that all of the following be met before the aircraft is attacked:

> (a) Diversion for landing, inspection, and possible capture, is not feasible;
> (b) No other method is available for exercising military control;
> (c) The circumstances leading to the loss of protection are sufficiently grave to justify an attack; and

---

66. AMW MANUAL, *supra*, note 31, Rule 1(g). According to the Commentary, "a 'parlementaire' is a person who has been authorized by one of the Belligerent Parties to enter into communication with the enemy." AMW COMMENTARY, *supra*, note 31, Rule 1(g), para. 2.

67. Unless otherwise agreed by the Parties to an armed conflict, the fact that the aircraft is equipped with "purely defensive weapons (for example, chaff) and individual light weapons for the defence of the crew" is not a grounds, by itself, to withdraw protection from an aircraft granted safe conduct. *Id.*, Rule 65(ii), para. 5.

68. AMW MANUAL, *supra*, note 31, Rule 68.

69. *Id.*, Rule I(i).

70. *Id.*, Rule 58; AMW COMMENTARY, *supra*, note 31, Rule 1(i), para. 2. The Department of Defense Law of War Manual does not include special rules for airlines, but rather states simply that if an airliner is a military objective, any attack on the airliner must comply with applicable LOAC rules on targeting (e.g., proportionality). DoD LAW OF WAR MANUAL, *supra*, note 2, para. 14.8.3.

(d) The expected collateral damage will not be excessive in relation to the military advantage anticipated and all feasible precautions have been taken.[71]

Further, the Air and Missile Warfare Manual would require a warning to be issued to the aircraft as well as that any decision to attack the aircraft be taken at an "appropriate level of command."[72]

3. Rights and Obligations of Belligerents and Neutrals

a. Areas Open for Air Operations by Belligerents

International law permits a State to conduct belligerent air operations against another State over the same areas in which the State is permitted to conduct belligerent land and naval operations, i.e., in the airspace over (i) the belligerent State's own territory, (ii) the territory of the enemy State, and (iii) international airspace. However, in conducting operations against each other, States in an armed conflict must pay "due regard" for the rights of neutrals in international airspace. Among other things, the belligerents must refrain from hostile acts while exercising their rights to transit passage "through, under and over a neutral international strait" or archipelagic sea-lanes passage "through, under or over neutral archipelagic waters."[73] Additionally, because international airspace includes the airspace over the exclusive economic zones (EEZs) of neutral States and may be super adjacent to the waters above the continental shelf of neutral coastal States, the belligerents must have due regard to the right of these neutral coastal States in these areas under the U.N. Convention on the Law of the Sea ("UNCLOS"), including structures that they may have erected (e.g., oil drilling platforms).[74]

The concept of "due regard" is referred to in UNCLOS, as well as in the Chicago Convention, but is not defined in those treaties. According to the Commentary to the Air and Missile Warfare Manual, due regard means that "[b]elligerent Parties are called upon to balance the military advantages anticipated with the negative impact on the Neutral's rights in the respective airspace and sea areas."[75] However, the Commentary also notes that the "due regard" principle "imposes no absolute and affirmative obligation."[76] For its part, the

---

71. AMW Manual, *supra*, note 31, Rule 68.
72. *Id.*, Rules 69 and 70. The commentary to the Air and Missile Warfare Manual does acknowledge that an airliner itself could become a weapon, and hence a military objective, as was the case in the attacks on the United States on September 11, 2001. AMW Commentary, *supra*, note 31, Rule 58, para. 10.
73. San Remo Manual, *supra*, note 30, para. 30.
74. AMW Manual, *supra*, note 31, Rule 107(e). The concept of due regard is used, *inter alia*, in the provisions of UNCLOS dealing with the rights of a coastal State in the EEZ adjacent to its territorial waters, and with the freedom enjoyed by all States on the high seas. *See* United Nations Convention on the Law of the Sea, Dec. 10, 1982, arts. 56, 58, and 87, 1833 U.N.T.S. 397 (hereinafter UNCLOS). The United States has not ratified UNCLOS, but accepts and follows its provisions regarding navigation in various maritime zones (such as the high seas). 19 Comp. Presid'l Doc. no. 10, at 383-385 (Mar. 14, 1983).
75. AMW Commentary, *supra*, note 31, Rule 107, para. 2.
76. *Id.*

U.S. Defense Department notes that, among other things, "DOD policy has required that, in the event of combat operations during armed conflict, aircraft commanders, consistent with military necessity, take measures to minimize hazards to civil aircraft and surface traffic."[77] Note, however, that the reference to military necessity in the Department's statement indicates that application of the due regard principle is highly dependent on circumstances.[78]

b. Neutral Airspace

Under the Chicago Convention, "every State has complete and exclusive sovereignty over the airspace above its territory."[79] In the exercise of their sovereignty, the States that are party to the Chicago Convention have agreed on terms under which civil aircraft might fly into or over the territory of a State party,[80] but these terms do not apply to State aircraft. Accordingly, there is no right to conduct belligerent operations in the airspace of a neutral State, including over its territorial sea,[81] nor may belligerent aircraft or auxiliary aircraft enter neutral airspace.[82] Unlike under the law of naval warfare, there is not even a right to passage for State aircraft through the airspace over the territorial sea of other States,[83] although belligerent aircraft do retain the right of transit or archipelagic sea-lanes passage (but not a right to take hostile actions) over international straits and archipelagic sea-lanes that fall within a neutral's waters.[84]

To protect its neutrality, a neutral State must not allow its airspace to be used as a base of operations by a belligerent State engaged in an armed conflict, or to be overflown by a belligerent State in connection with operations against enemy State(s), nor may belligerents violate neutral airspace for this purpose.[85]

---

77. DoD Law of War Manual, *supra*, note 2, para. 14.1.1 (citation omitted).
78. *See* U.S. Dep't of Def, Inst. 4540.01, Use of International Airspace by U.S. Military Aircraft and for Missile and Projectile Firings, para. 3.e. (June 2, 2015) (detailing procedures to be followed when not practical to fly under international air traffic control rules, but reserving the right to suspend those procedures "[i]n time of war, armed conflict, national emergency, situations requiring self-defense, or similar military contingencies"; in those situations, "commanders must, *consistent with military necessity*, take measures to minimize hazards to all non-hostile air and surface traffic.") (emphasis supplied) (hereinafter DODI 4540.01).
79. Convention, *supra*, note 4, art. 1.
80. Under the Chicago Convention, each State party to the Convention (a "territorial State") agrees that, subject to the Convention's terms, civil aircraft (but not State aircraft) of other States that are not engaged in scheduled service, may overfly the territorial State and make stops in its territory "for non-traffic purposes" without obtaining prior permission, subject to the right of the territorial State to require landing. *Id*., art. 5. This includes the privilege of discharging and taking on passengers and cargo upon landing, subject to regulations and other requirements imposed by the State in which the aircraft is landing. *Id*. No scheduled air service to or over the territory of a State may be conducted without the territorial State's permission, *id*. art. 6, but in light of the robust passenger service that exists in the world today, it is obvious that such permission is frequently granted.
81. San Remo Manual, *supra*, note 30, para. 15; AMW Manual, *supra*, note 31, Rule 166.
82. HRAW, *supra*, note 24, Part II, art. 40 ("Belligerent military aircraft are forbidden to enter the jurisdiction of a neutral State."); San Remo Manual, *supra*, note 30, para. 18.
83. AMW Commentary, *supra*, note 31, Rule 167(a), para. 3.
84. San Remo Manual, *supra*, note 30, paras. 28 and 30; AMW Manual, *supra*, note 31, Rule 172(a)(ii).
85. AMW Manual, *supra*, note 31, Rules 167(a) and 168(a). Where a neutral is unwilling or unable to terminate a serious violation of its neutrality by a belligerent, the belligerent's enemy may

Further, should a belligerent State's air forces intrude into neutral airspace, the neutral State must take action to eliminate the violation, which would include the right to shoot down intruding belligerent aircraft that do not obey an order to leave neutral airspace.[86]

4. Methods of Warfare

a. Conduct of Hostilities

Only military aircraft are entitled to engage in hostilities under the LOAC, including launching of attacks against enemy military objectives or interception and capture of enemy aircraft.[87] Given that the definition of military aircraft requires that the aircraft be "operated by the armed forces of a State," the crew of a military aircraft typically will be members of the armed forces who fall within the category of lawful or privileged belligerents described in Chapter 5.[88] It is possible that civilians also may be part of the crew but the aircraft must be commanded by a member of a State's armed forces.[89]

Air warfare may occur in various ways, including the launching of attacks from the air against targets on land, sea, and even in space (i.e., ASAT weapons launched from aircraft). Land and at sea targets can be attacked by bombardment (e.g., the dropping of bombs from above), strafing, the launching of self-propelled munitions (e.g., missiles), or other means. It is also possible for aircraft to launch attacks against other aircraft. Further cyber means of warfare can be deployed from aircraft against targets on land or at sea or in space, or against other aircraft. At all times, however, the aircraft must be employed in a manner consistent with the principles of the LOAC discussed in Chapter 2 and other chapters of this book.

Other than the prohibition in Protocol III to the 1980 Convention on Prohibitions or Restrictions on the Use of Certain Conventional Weapons Which May be Deemed to be Excessively Injurious or to have Indiscriminate Effects, which prohibits attacking a military objective "located within a concentration of civilians" with air-delivered incendiary weapons (see discussion *supra*, in Section II.A.2), there are no LOAC treaty provisions narrowly applicable to air-delivered weapons.[90] It is clear, however, that all LOAC rules

---

use force to terminate the violation without violating the prohibition in the UN Charter on the use of force against the neutral. *Id.* Rule 168(b). However, as drafted by the experts in the AMW Manual, a belligerent State may only take action to terminate the violation "in the absence of any feasible and timely alternative." *Id.*

86. AMW Commentary, *supra*, note 31, Rule 170(c), para. 3.
87. AMW Manual, *supra*, note 31, Rule 17.
88. *See* Geneva Convention Relative to the Treatment of Prisoners of War, Aug. 12, 1949, art. 4A(1), 6 U.S.T. 3316, 75 U.N.T.S. 135 [hereinafter GPW].
89. All crew members would be treated as prisoners of war under GPW if captured in an international armed conflict. *Id.*, arts. 4A(1) (members of the armed forces) and 4A(4) (persons who accompany the armed forces). *See* DoD Law of War Manual, *supra*, note 2, para. 14.4.
90. Amended Protocol II to the CCW, *infra* note 204, does have a provision regulating "remotely delivered mines," which would apply to air-delivered landmines, but it also applies to mines that are remotely delivered by other means, such as in artillery shells. [Amended] Protocol on Prohibitions

of targeting apply to attacks from the air, as do those rules governing lawful means and methods of warfare. These LOAC rules include the requirement (discussed in earlier Chapters) to only direct attacks against combatants and military objectives and the prohibition against indiscriminate attacks or attacks that may be expected to cause collateral damage which would be excessive in relation to the concrete and direct military advantage anticipated.[91] Because aircraft can be used to attack targets located far away and even beyond the sight of the pilot, the obligation under the LOAC to take precautions before launching such attacks to ensure the requirements of the LOAC are met is particularly important in air warfare. This obligation is perhaps best summed up in Article 57(1) of AP I, which provides that "[i]n the conduct of military operations, constant care shall be taken to spare the civilian population, civilians and civilian objects."[92] The requirement to take precautions is a fundamental obligation under the LOAC and requires not only commanders, but also those who plan and execute attacks, including pilots, to ensure that the attack complies with the requirements of the LOAC, and to cancel the attack where facts change and it no longer appears that those requirements will be met.[93]

A key LOAC obligation when engaging in attacks is the requirement to take "feasible precautions" to reduce the risk of harm to the civilian population, civilians, and civilian objects.[94] The DoD Law of War Manual describes the obligation as "one of due regard or diligence, not an absolute requirement to do everything possible," adding that the precautions taken are "those that are practicable or practically possible, taking into account all circumstances ruling at the time, including humanitarian and military considerations."[95] However, the Manual does not offer any specific standard with respect to attacks against targets in the air. On the other hand, the Air and Missile Warfare Manual indicates that before an aircraft is attacked in the air, "all feasible precautions must be taken to verify that it constitutes a military objective," using "the best means available under the prevailing circumstances, having regard to the immediacy of any potential threat."[96] For this purpose, the Manual indicates that the following factors should be taken into account: (a) visual identification; (b) responses to oral warnings over radio; (c) infrared signature; (d) radar signature; (e) electronic signature; (f) identification modes and codes; (g) number and formation of aircraft; (h) altitude, speed,

---

or Restrictions on the Use of Mines, Booby-Traps and Other Devices, May 3, 1996, art. 6, 2048 U.N.T.S. 93.

The HRAW resolved a concern of that time that the St. Petersburg Declaration of 1868 (discussed in Chapter 2), which prohibits a certain type of munition that is "either explosive or charged with fulminating or inflammable substances," might limit the use of tracer munitions in attacks on or by aircraft. HRAW, *supra*, note 24, Part II, art. 18 ("The use of tracer, incendiary or explosive projectiles by or against aircraft is not prohibited.").

91. These rules are discussed in detail in Chapter 7.
92. AP I, *supra*, note 33, art. 57(1).
93. *Id.*, art. 57(2)(b).
94. DoD Law of War Manual, *supra*, note 2, para. 5.2.3.
95. *Id.*, para. 5.2.3.2.
96. AMW Manual, *supra*, note 31, Rule 40, (a)-(i).

track, profile and other flight characteristics; and (i) pre-flight and in-flight air traffic control information regarding possible flights.[97]

Given that military aircraft are entitled to engage in hostilities, they are, by nature, lawful military objectives in an armed conflict if operated by a party to the conflict,[98] unless they are medical aircraft or otherwise have been granted safe conduct.[99] Further, military aircraft are not limited to fighters and bombers, but may also include a variety of craft operated by a State's military, some of which may be unarmed.[100] As noted above, unmanned, remotely piloted aircraft (e.g., drones) or autonomous aircraft programmed for belligerent operations, also may be military aircraft, and hence are military objectives.

While military aircraft of a party to an armed conflict are by nature military objectives, other enemy aircraft, such as a party's civil aircraft and its State aircraft that are not military aircraft, only can be attacked if they engage in activities that render them "military objectives" under the LOAC.[101] Following Article 52 of AP I, the Air and Missile Warfare Manual defines a military objective in air warfare as an object (i) which by its "nature, location, purpose or use, make an effective contribution to military action" and (ii) "whose total or partial destruction, capture or neutralization, in the circumstances ruling at the time, offers a definite military advantage."[102] The Manual lists the following as activities that could make an enemy non-military State or civil aircraft into a military objective:

> (a) Engaging in hostile actions in support of the enemy, e.g., intercepting or attacking other aircraft; attacking persons or objects on land or sea; being used as a means of attack; engaging in electronic warfare; or providing targeting information to enemy forces.
> (b) Facilitating the military actions of the enemy's armed forces, e.g., transporting troops, carrying military materials, or refueling military aircraft.
> (c) Being incorporated into or assisting the enemy's intelligence gathering system, e.g., engaging in reconnaissance, early warning, surveillance or command, control and communications missions.
> (d) Refusing to comply with the orders of military authorities, including instructions for landing, inspection and possible capture, or clearly resisting interception.
> (e) Otherwise making an effective contribution to military action.[103]

---

97. *Id.* A Notice to Airmen (NOTAM) also may be used to warn neutral and civilian aircraft of belligerent operations. *See, e.g.,* SAN REMO MANUAL, *supra,* note 30, para. 75; DODI 4540.01, *supra,* note 78, Enclosure 3, para. 2.
98. DoD LAW OF WAR MANUAL, *supra,* note 2, para. 14.3.3.
99. *See* discussion, *supra,* of these types of aircraft in Section II.B.2.
100. DoD LAW OF WAR MANUAL, *supra,* note 2, para. 14.3.3. ("In addition to combat aircraft such as fighters and bombers, other types of aircraft operated by the armed forces of a State may also be designated as military aircraft, such as transport, reconnaissance, and meteorological aircraft.")
101. The definition of a military objective is found in Article 52(b) of AP I and is discussed in Chapter 7. Note that there is no right comparable to the customary rule of naval warfare for naval vessels that would permit a military aircraft to feign neutral or non-military status before engaging in attacks. THE COMMANDER'S HANDBOOK ON THE LAW OF NAVAL OPERATIONS, U.S. DEP'T OF NAVY ET AL., NAVAL WARFARE PUB. 1-14M, paras. 12-1 AND 12.-2 (2017) (hereinafter COMMANDER'S HANDBOOK-2017).
102. AMW MANUAL, *supra,* note 31, Rule 1(y).
103. *Id.*, Rule 27. *See also,* SAN REMO MANUAL, *supra,* note 30, para. 63.

The U.S. Department of Defense has adopted a similar set of activities that could render an enemy civil aircraft subject to attack:

(a) persistently refusing to comply with directions from intercepting aircraft;
(b) flying under convoy of enemy warships or military aircraft;
(c) armed with systems or weapons beyond that required for self-defense against terrorism, piracy, or like threats;
(d) incorporated into or assisting the enemy's military intelligence system; or
(e) otherwise integrated into the enemy's war-fighting or war-sustaining effort.[104]

A key difference between the two sets of examples is the Department of Defense's use of the phrase "the war-fighting or war-sustaining effort" in the residual category at the end of its set of examples. While the United States generally accepts the definition of military objective found in Article 52 of AP I, it interprets "contribution to military action" broadly to include contributions to an enemy's war-fighting or war-sustaining capability.[105] This broad interpretation would permit targeting of objects that provide economic support for an enemy's war effort, including exports of goods being sold by a party to the conflict to raise funds to support its forces.[106] As such, it is controversial and has been criticized for expanding the scope of potential targets to include objects whose connection with actual hostilities is remote or speculative.[107]

The threshold for withdrawing protection from attack for medical aircraft, civilian airliners, cartel aircraft and aircraft otherwise granted safe conduct is higher than for other aircraft.[108] For example, a military medical aircraft could only be attacked if it commits "acts harmful to the enemy." This phrase is not defined in treaty law, but the Commentary to the Air and Missile Warfare says "[t]he notion of 'acts harmful to the enemy' encompasses acts whose purpose or effect is to harm the enemy by facilitating or impeding military operations. Therefore, it does not only include acts inflicting harm on the enemy by direct attack, but also attempts at hindering its military operations in any way whatsoever (e.g., positioning a medical unit in a way that would impede a military attack or using a medical transport as a shelter for able-bodied combatants). 'Acts harmful to the enemy' may include intelligence gathering."[109] Thus, "[t]o lead to a loss of specific protection, acts harmful to the enemy must be 'committed outside of the humanitarian function' of the medical and religious personnel,

---

104. DoD Law of War Manual, *supra*, note 2, para. 14.8.3.2 (citations omitted). Presumably, State aircraft that are not military aircraft would only be targeted under these circumstances as well.
105. *Id.*, paras. 5.6.5 and 5.6.6.2.
106. *Id.*, para. 5.6.8.5.
107. AMW Commentary, *supra*, note 31, Rule 24, para. 2; *see also*, San Remo Manual, *supra*, note 30, para. 60.11 (specifically rejecting "integration into the enemy's war-fighting/war-sustaining effort" as a criterion for allowing direct attack of enemy merchant ships.)
108. *See* AMW Manual, *supra*, note 31, Rules 63 (airliners), 65 (aircraft granted safe conduct), 68 (airliners, cartel aircraft and aircraft granted safe conduct), and Rule 83 (medical aircraft.)
109. AMW Commentary, *supra*, note 31, Rule 74(a), para. 3.

medical units or medical transports may also be harmful to the enemy in some sense. This implies that certain acts harmful to the enemy may be compatible with the humanitarian function of the medical and religious personnel, medical units or transports (e.g., treating wounded soldiers so that they can return to combat). As such, such acts may be accomplished without entailing a loss of specific protection (e.g., the use of electronic equipment at a field hospital may interfere with the enemy's communication system)."[110]

Any neutral aircraft, including neutral State aircraft and civil aircraft, and any enemy civil aircraft can become a military objective if it takes on the character of enemy military aircraft. According to the U.S. Defense Department, this can happen where a neutral aircraft either takes a direct part in hostilities on the side of the enemy or acts as a naval or military auxiliary for the enemy's armed forces.[111] The Air and Missile Warfare Manual provides a more detailed list of actions that can make a neutral aircraft a military objective:

> (a) It is believed on reasonable grounds to be carrying contraband, and, after prior warning or interception, it intentionally and clearly refuses to divert from its destination, or intentionally and clearly refuses to proceed for inspection to a belligerent airfield that is safe for the type of aircraft involved and reasonably accessible.
> (b) Engaging in hostile actions in support of the enemy, e.g., intercepting or attacking other aircraft; attacking persons or objects on land or sea; being used as a means of attack; engaging in electronic warfare; or providing targeting information to enemy forces.
> (c) Facilitating the military actions of the enemy's armed forces, e.g., transporting troops, carrying military materials, or refueling military aircraft.
> (d) Being incorporated into or assisting the enemy's intelligence gathering system, e.g., engaging in reconnaissance, early warning, surveillance or command, control and communications missions.
> (e) Refusing to comply with the orders of military authorities, including instructions for landing, inspection and possible capture, or it clearly resists interception.
> (f) Otherwise making an effective contribution to military action.[112]

When an aircraft is downed in armed conflict, those who eject and parachute from the aircraft to save themselves are protected from attack, while descending to Earth and for so long as they do not seek to evade capture or otherwise engage in hostile activities.[113] Those who parachute into water, who

---

110. *Id.* para. 4.
111. DoD LAW OF WAR MANUAL, *supra*, note 2, paras. 14.8.3.2 and 15.14.2.1.
112. AMW MANUAL, *supra*, note 31, Rule 174. *See also*, SAN REMO MANUAL, *supra*, note 30, para. 70. The commentary to the Air and Missile Warfare Manual notes that, of these criteria, only (b), (c), (d) and (f) apply to neutral State aircraft, since these aircraft enjoy the sovereign immunity of the neutral State and therefore are not subject to interception, inspection, or capture, even if suspected of carrying contraband, and do not have to comply with the orders of a belligerent State, except in the case of an aerial blockade. AMW COMMENTARY, *supra*, note 31, Rule 174, para. 2.
113. AP I, *supra*, note 33, art. 42; DoD LAW OF WAR MANUAL, *supra*, note 2, para. 14.3.1; AMW MANUAL, *supra*, note 31, Rule 132. This rule does not apply to airborne troops parachuting as part of combat operations. *Id.*, Rule 133.

may survive a crash into water, or are otherwise forced to land at sea, are considered to be shipwrecked and protected from attack, and should be rescued when circumstances permit. The rules for the shipwrecked in an international armed conflict can be found in the provisions of the second Geneva Convention (GWS-Sea)[114] or the fourth Geneva Convention (GCIV), depending upon the status of the individuals involved.[115] There are similar rules in a treaty applicable to non-international armed conflict, but since the shipwrecked are *hors de combat*, at least the protection of the shipwrecked against attack, applies generally in all armed conflicts.[116]

b. Interception and Capture

i. Enemy Aircraft

Just as all vessels of an enemy are subject to capture by a belligerent State's warships in an international armed conflict, an enemy's civil and State aircraft other than (i) medical aircraft, (ii) cartel aircraft, and (iii) aircraft granted safe conduct[117] also are subject to capture by a belligerent State's military aircraft. Indeed, it would be permitted to capture an enemy State's civilian passenger airliners.[118] Typically, capture would be preceded by interception, in which the targeted aircraft is approached by a military aircraft of the belligerent States, for example, by "closing to visual range or to a distance where the target [aircraft] is within the range of weapons systems."[119] Interception serves to allow the intercepting aircraft to verify the status of the target aircraft and to direct the aircraft

---

114. GWS-Sea, *supra*, note 32, art. 12. This treaty generally applies only to specific categories of individuals who are part of, or associated with, a State's armed forces, militias, merchant marine, or State aircraft. Id., art. 13. However, Article 18 of GWS-Sea includes an obligation to search for, collect, and protect the shipwrecked that arguably applies to all persons in an international armed conflict, and not just those falling under Article 4 of GWS-Sea.

115. GCIV, *supra*, note 32, art. 33. This treaty provision applies to the civilian population of the parties to the conflict. Article 10 of AP I, *supra*, note 10, includes a general rule protecting all shipwrecked without distinction. Further, all States, including those that are not party to the conflict, are obligated to require every captain of a sea vessel to render assistance to those at distress at sea "in so far as he can do so without serious danger to the ship, the crew or the passengers." UNCLOS, *supra*, note 74, art. 98.

116. *See, e.g.*, GCIV, *supra*, note 32, art. 3. The 1977 Additional Protocols to the Geneva Conventions include a general rule protecting all shipwrecked without distinction. AP I, *supra*, note 33, art. 10; AP II, *supra*, note 33, art. 7. As noted, *supra*, in footnote 114, Article 13 of GWS-Sea includes an obligation to search for, collect, and protect the shipwrecked that arguably applies to all persons in an international armed conflict, and not just those falling under Article 4 of GWS-Sea. Article 8 of AP II extends this obligation to all persons in non-international armed conflicts to which AP II applies.

117. To retain their protection from capture, cartel aircraft and other aircraft granted safe conduct must (a) be innocently employed in their normal role (i.e. the role for which the aircraft is granted protection); (b) immediately submit to interception and identification when asked; (c) refrain from intentionally hampering the movement of combatants; (d) obey orders to divert from their flight path when required; and (e) comply with any agreement that gave the aircraft safe conduct. AMW MANUAL, *supra*, note 31, Rule 67. As for enemy medical aircraft, they lose their protection from capture if they engage in activities that are not consistent with their medical status, or if they have flown in breach of a prior agreement with the other belligerent or if there is no prior agreement. *Id.*, Rule 80(c).

118. According to the Air and Missile Warfare Manual, however, enemy airliners are subject to capture as prize as long as "all passenger and crew are safely deplaned and the papers of the aircraft are preserved." *Id.*, Rule 62.

119. DoD LAW OF WAR MANUAL, *supra*, note 2, para. 14.5.1.

to a place where it can land.[120] It also puts the intercepting aircraft in range to attack should the enemy aircraft refuse to cooperate.[121]

Inspection is not a required precondition for capture of enemy aircraft. Rather, the aircraft can simply be ordered to "a reasonably accessible belligerent airfield that is safe for the type of aircraft involved."[122]

Only military aircraft of a State can intercept or capture an enemy State's aircraft during armed conflict. Further, a belligerent State can only conduct interceptions and capture of aircraft outside of neutral territory.

All captured enemy military, law enforcement, and customs aircraft, and all property on board such aircraft, becomes the property of the capturing State as war booty, meaning that they do not need to be put through prize proceedings for the capturing State to take title to the aircraft and property.[123] On the other hand, other enemy State aircraft and all enemy civil aircraft (whether or not owned by the State) and the property on board such aircraft would be subject to prize proceedings in which the rights of ownership would be adjudicated by a prize court.[124]

With the exception of medical personnel who are entitled to be treated as retained personnel under the first Geneva Convention (GWS),[125] military and civilian members of the crew of any enemy aircraft captured in an international armed conflict are considered prisoners of war under the third Geneva Convention (GPW).[126] As for passengers, any member of the enemy's military forces on board the aircraft would be a prisoner of war or retained person if that was the status he or she would have if captured on land. Civilian prisoners also would have the status of either prisoner of war (if the civilian qualifies as such under GPW) or civilian internee under the fourth Geneva Convention (GCIV), unless the civilian is the citizen of a co-belligerent or neutral State and would be protected as such through the normal diplomatic relations between the civilian's home country and the belligerent State.[127]

An enemy medical aircraft may be intercepted to verify that it is exclusively engaged in its medical mission but the aircraft is not subject to capture to the extent it has complied with the terms agreed among the belligerents regarding flights of such aircraft. Accordingly, all crew, medical personnel, and sick and wounded on board the aircraft also are not subject to capture.[128] If, however,

---

120. AMW MANUAL, *supra*, note 31, Rule 134.
121. As noted, *supra*, in Section II.B.4.a., resisting interception can render any enemy aircraft a military objective.
122. *Id*.
123. *Id.*, para. 136(a).
124. *Id*. The U.S. Department of Defense takes a broader view, and treats all enemy State aircraft as subject to capture as war booty. DoD LAW OF WAR MANUAL, *supra*, note 2, para. 14.5.3.
125. GWS, *supra*, note 32, art. 28.
126. GPW, *supra*, note 88, art. 4A. Article 4A(5) specifically provides that "[m]embers of crews, including...the crews of civil aircraft of the Parties to the conflict" are prisoners of war, unless they benefit from more favorable treatment under any other provision of international law.
127. GCIV, *supra*, note 32, art. 4; AMW COMMENTARY, *supra*, note 31, Rule 131, para. 2.
128. Passengers who are not wounded and sick may be captured, including those who were shipwrecked. AMW COMMENTARY, *supra*, note 31, Rule 80(a), para. 4.

the medical aircraft does not comply with the agreed terms, it may be captured and the personnel on board held according to the status afforded to them under the applicable LOAC rules (e.g., prisoner of war, retained personnel, civilian internee, or other status.)[129]

A belligerent may determine that an aircraft is subject to capture in various ways, including, but not limited to, by interception followed by inspection upon landing where there is a reasonable basis to suspect that the aircraft is subject to capture.[130] Capture also may be based on intelligence about the aircraft as well as observations of the aircraft's behavior, without the necessity of inspection.[131] In any case, a belligerent State intercepting a civil aircraft must have due regard for safety of the aircraft and its crew and passengers.[132] Further, when capturing a civil aircraft, the capturing State must ensure the safety of the passengers and crew, and must safeguard documents and papers relating to the aircraft.[133]

An aircraft captured by a Belligerent will be sent to an airfield under the control of the belligerent or its co-belligerents, either for inspection or adjudication by a prize court. If the aircraft resists capture, it may be attacked.[134]

In lieu of capture, an aircraft can be diverted to a new destination.[135] A belligerent State can divert an enemy aircraft without the aircraft's consent, but a neutral aircraft must consent to diversion.[136]

It is possible for an enemy military aircraft to "surrender," and in the case of a valid surrender, it would be a violation of the LOAC—a denial of quarter—to attack the aircraft. Clearly, surrendering an aircraft in flight poses challenges, and there are no prescribed means in the LOAC for surrender of aircraft that might assure the capturing aircraft that the surrender is offered in good faith. At a minimum, an aircraft wishing to surrender must clearly communicate its intention to surrender, must refrain from any further hostile acts, and must not attempt to evade capture. Further, a State may dictate specific procedures for military aircraft to surrender to it, and a surrendering aircraft would be subject to attack if it failed to follow these procedures, which could include having to abandon the aircraft by parachute.[137]

ii. Neutral Aircraft

Neutral State aircraft, including neutral military aircraft, are not subject to capture "unless they are engaged in activities in support of the enemy's military actions."[138] Activities in support of the enemy's military actions, however,

---

129. *Id.*, Rule 80(c), para. 3.
130. *Id.*, Rule 137(b).
131. *Id.*, Rule 140, para. 1. *See also* DoD Law of War Manual, *supra*, note 2, para. 15.15.2.
132. AMW Commentary, *supra*, note 31, Rule 137(a), para. 3.
133. AMW Manual, *supra*, note 31, Rule 143.
134. *See* DoD Law of War Manual, *supra*, note 2, para. 15.15.2 and para. 15.15.2.1 (citations omitted).
135. AMW Manual, *supra*, note 31, Rule 137(c).
136. AMW Commentary, *supra*, note 31, Rule 137(c), para. 2.
137. AMW Manual, *supra*, note 31, Rules 125-131.
138. AMW Commentary, *supra*, note 31, Rule 137(a), para. 2.

also would make the aircraft a military objective subject to attack, as discussed, *supra*, in Section II.B.4.a.

According to the Air and Missile Warfare Manual, neutral civil aircraft are subject to capture where:

> (a) They are carrying contraband.
> (b) They are on a flight especially undertaken to transport individual passengers who are members of the enemy's armed forces.
> (c) They are operating directly under enemy control, orders, charter, employment or direction.
> (d) They present irregular or fraudulent documents, lack necessary documents, or destroy, deface or conceal documents.
> (e) They are violating regulations established by a Belligerent Party within the immediate area of military operations.
> (f) They are engaged in breach of an aerial blockade.[139]

A civil aircraft that does not bear any marks to indicate its nationality can be presumed to have enemy character and be captured.[140]

If a neutral civil aircraft is captured under one of the conditions in (a)-(f) above, the individuals on board the aircraft who are nationals of neutral countries should be released, while enemy nationals on board (if any) may be dealt with according to their status under the LOAC (e.g., those who may be members of the enemy's armed forces would be treated as prisoners of war under GPW). On the other hand, if a neutral aircraft is captured under circumstances that render it a military objective, the persons on board will be treated in the same manner as those found on board an enemy military aircraft.[141]

A belligerent State may intercept neutral civil aircraft (but not neutral State aircraft, however) outside of neutral airspace where the belligerent State reasonably believes the aircraft may be subject to capture. In such a case, the intercepting aircraft may require the neutral aircraft to land at a "reasonably accessible belligerent airfield" for inspection and to determine if capture is justified.[142]

Contraband found on board a neutral civil aircraft may be captured, but the validity of capture is subject to prize proceedings in a court.[143] The aircraft itself may be condemned as prize by the court if contraband represents more than one-half its cargo.[144] However, if the neutral civil aircraft is itself a military

---

139. *Id.* Rule 140. The Department of Defense offers a similar list: (a) carrying contraband; (b) carrying personnel in the military or public service of the enemy; (c) communicating information in the interest of the enemy; (d) breaching or attempting to breach a blockade; (e) violating regulations established by a belligerent within the immediate area of naval operations; (f) avoiding an attempt to establish identity, including visit and search; (g) presenting irregular or fraudulent papers; lacking necessary papers; or destroying, defacing, or concealing papers. DoD Law of War Manual, *supra*, note 2, para. 15.15.1.

140. AMW Manual, *supra*, note 31, Rule 145.

141. Commander's Handbook-2017, *supra*, note 101, para. 7.10.2.

142. AMW Manual, *supra*, note 31, Rule 137. To avoid capture, the intercepted aircraft may agree to divert away from its intended destination. *Id.*

143. *Id.*, Rule 141(a). Contraband is discussed in Chapter 11.

144. AMW Commentary, *supra*, note 31, Rule 141(a), para. 2.

objective subject to attack (see Section II.B.4.a., *supra*), both the aircraft and all property on board may be captured and condemned.

iii. Destruction of Captured Aircraft

Captured enemy State aircraft that qualify as war booty (see discussion, *supra*, of war booty may be destroyed at the option of the capturing State. On the other hand, other captured enemy aircraft and capture neutral aircraft only may be destroyed under certain circumstances. The Air and Missile Warfare Manual states that while destruction is "an exceptional measure," the aircraft and the property on board may be destroyed when "military circumstances preclude taking the aircraft for prize adjudication, provided that all persons on board have been placed in safety and documents relating to the prize have been preserved."[145] The DOD Manual adds that destruction of a neutral aircraft is a "much more serious responsibility than the destruction of an enemy prize, and thus a higher standard applies" before proceeding to destroy the aircraft.[146] Thus,

> Every reasonable effort should be made to avoid destruction of captured neutral vessels and aircraft. A capturing officer, therefore, should not order such destruction without being entirely satisfied that the prize can neither be sent to a belligerent State port or airfield nor, in his or her opinion, properly be released.
>
> Should it become necessary that the prize be destroyed, the capturing officer must provide for the safety of the passengers and crew. In that event, all documents and papers relating to the prize should be preserved. If practicable, the personal effects of passengers should also be safeguarded.[147]

c. Other Air Operations

Aircraft are used in many different ways in military operations that do not involve attacks or captures, including for surveillance, intelligence collection, telecommunications, and other activities. Except to the extent these activities have effects that would meet the threshold for an "attack" under the LOAC,[148] they are not specifically regulated by the LOAC, though they do fall under the general requirement in the LOAC to take "constant care" to protect civilians and the civilian population in all military operations.[149]

There are certain operations with a potential for violence that are called out for specific regulation in the Air and Missile Warfare Manual and the DoD Law of War Manual. These include (i) exclusion zones; (ii) no fly zones; and (iii) aerial blockades.

---

145. AMW Manual, *supra*, note 31, Rule 135.
146. DoD Law of War Manual, *supra*, note 2, para. 15.15.3.
147. *Id.*
148. AP I art. 49 defines "attacks" as "acts of violence against the adversary, whether in offence or in defence." AP I, *supra*, note 33, art. 49.
149. *See Id.*, arts. 51(a) ("[t]he civilian population and individual civilians shall enjoy general protection against dangers arising from military operations") and 57(1)("[i]n the conduct of military operations, constant care shall be taken to spare the civilian population, civilians and civilian objects.")

An exclusion zone is a zone established by a belligerent State to control or exclude aircraft within the zone. As noted by the Department of Defense, "[s]uch zones may be established for a variety of purposes, including to decrease the risk of inadvertent attack . . .[on] civil or neutral aircraft, to control the scope of the conflict, or to enhance the predictability and effectiveness of ongoing operations."[150] The Air and Missile Warfare Manual notes that the following rules apply to such a zone:

> (a) The same rules of the law of international armed conflict will apply both inside and outside the "exclusion zone".
> (b) The extent, location and duration of the "exclusion zone" and the measures imposed must not exceed what is reasonably required by military necessity.
> (c) The commencement, duration, location and extent of the "exclusion zone", as well as the restrictions imposed, must be appropriately notified to all concerned.
> (d) The establishment of an "exclusion zone" must neither encompass nor completely bar access to the airspace of neutral States.[151]

The authority to establish an exclusion zone depends on a number of factors, including the nature of the waters in and over which the zone applies, the military necessity for the zone, and the nature of the prohibition or regulation to be enforced in the zone. Thus, a zone established by a belligerent State in and over its territorial waters would be based on that State's sovereignty over those waters, while a zone established in and over international waters would be based on the State's right to conduct military operations on the high seas, subject to its obligation of due regard for neutrals and the requirement to limit any interference with the right of other States on the high seas to only that interference which can be justified by military necessity. An example of a zone justified by military necessity would be a zone established to preclude deliveries by air of cargo to an enemy in violation of a lawful naval blockade of the enemy's territory. An exclusion zone also might be used to control neutral air traffic near a State's naval forces as a matter of force protection or to ensure operational control and security.

The Department of Defense acknowledges that "[t]he establishment of a zone does not relieve the proclaiming belligerent State of its obligation under the law of war to refrain from attacking vessels and aircraft that do not constitute military objectives."[152] However, it also points out that "the fact that a vessel or aircraft enters a zone without authorization may be probative in assessing

---

150. DoD Law of War Manual, *supra*, note 2, para. 14.7. Another type of zone that is frequently established in peacetime is an "Air Defense Identification Zone" or "ADIZ," in which a State requires aircraft in airspace over international waters near the State's territorial waters to identify themselves. The zone itself is not a claim to sovereignty to the airspace or waters in which it is enforced and should not be used to interfere with the rights of other States in international airspace. *See id.*, para 14.2.4. Failure of an aircraft to identify itself does not, by itself, entitle the State maintaining the ADIZ to use force against the aircraft as long as the aircraft does not pose a threat to the State. *Id.*
151. AMW Manual, *supra*, note 31, Rule 107.
152. DoD Law of War Manual, *supra*, note 2, para. 13.9.2.

whether it is entitled to protection [from attack]" given that "the notification of the zone in advance may mean that most neutral or protected vessels and aircraft have departed the area."[153]

Of course, an exclusion zone has to be limited geographically to what can be justified by military necessity, taking into account the "due regard" obligation under UNCLOS. A zone cannot be used to deny essential food and supplies to the civilian population of the enemy, nor can the zone unreasonably burden neutral commerce.[154] Also safe passage through the zone for neutral vessels and aircraft must be provided if necessary to allow access to neutral water and ports, international straits, and archipelagic sea lanes.[155]

Another type of operation is a "no-fly zone." The Air and Missile Warfare Manual describes this type of zone as being established in either the home territory of a belligerent State or in the territory of its enemy, but not in international airspace.[156] In this zone, "aircraft entering . . . without specific permission are liable to be attacked."[157] Nonetheless, this is not a free fire-zone, in which every aircraft is subject to attack. Rather, those maintaining a no-fly zone must limit attacks to those aircraft that are military objectives and employ precautions in order to ensure that only military objectives are attacked. Further, the extent and duration of the zone must be notified to neutrals and civilians who could be affected by it.[158]

Finally, aircraft can be used to enforce an "aerial blockade." Such a blockade can be enforced using aircraft as well as naval vessels. The Air and Missile Warfare Manual describes an aerial blockade as "a belligerent operation to prevent aircraft (including UAVs/UCAVs) from entering or exiting specified airfields or coastal areas belonging to, occupied by, or under the control of the enemy."[159] This includes all aircraft, including aircraft that are not carrying cargo. Thus, an aerial blockade allows a belligerent to interfere with all trade and communication with its enemy even when it does not involve contraband.[160] Like a naval blockade, the aerial blockade must be effective (i.e., the belligerent State enforcing the blockade must deploy sufficient force to actually prevent trade with the blockaded area) but that does not require the belligerent State's aircraft to always be in the air, as long as the airspace is monitored and the belligerent can immediately address any attempted breach of the blockade.[161] Also like a naval blockade, notice of the blockade must be given to neutral States, the blockade cannot prevent access to neutral territory, and the blockade must be enforced impartially.[162]

---

153. *Id.*
154. *Id.*, para. 13.9.3.
155. *Id.*, para 13.9.4.
156. AMW MANUAL, *supra,* note 31, Rule 108.
157. *Id.*
158. *Id.*, Rule 109, first paragraph.
159. AMW MANUAL, *supra,* note 31, Rule 147. UAVs and UCAVs refer to unmanned aircraft.
160. AMW COMMENTARY, *supra,* note 31, Rule 147, para. 4.
161. *Id.*, Rule 151, para. 3.
162. AMW MANUAL, *supra,* note 31, Rules 149, 150, and 155.

II. Air Warfare

Like a naval blockade, an aerial blockade is not lawful if

(a) its sole or primary purpose is to starve the civilian population or to deny that population other objects essential for its survival, or
(b) the suffering of the civilian population as a result of the blockade is, or may be expected to be, excessive in relation to the concrete and direct military advantage anticipated from the aerial blockade.[163]

Additionally the blockading State must permit relief supplies to be brought in to meet the needs of the enemy's civilian population, subject to the right of the blockading State to impose specific technical conditions to ensure that the supplies are not diverted to the enemy's armed forces.[164]

5. Air Warfare in a Non-International Armed Conflict

There is no specific treaty governing air operations in a non-international armed conflict (NIAC), but the general treaty rules that apply to NIACs, such as found in common Article 3 to the 1949 Geneva Conventions and in Additional Protocol II would apply to air operations in the NIAC, as would customary international law and other bodies of international law, such as international human rights law (though the LOAC would be the *lex specialis*). The domestic law of the State in which the NIAC is occurring also would apply.

In a NIAC there is no strict treaty obligation that would require belligerent air operations to be conducted only using military aircraft. Thus, it is permissible for a State to use aircraft other than military aircraft (e.g., such as police or customs aircraft) to engage in attacks. Further, the aircraft of any non-State belligerent would not qualify as military aircraft or State aircraft, but instead would be civil aircraft. A non-State belligerent's aircraft would be subject to attack or capture under the LOAC if they constitute military objectives and any disposition of such aircraft if captured would be subject to the domestic law of the capturing State, not international law. There is no prize law applicable to a NIAC.

Non-state armed groups do not have a right to conduct belligerent operations under international law. Accordingly, the crews of their aircraft would not enjoy combatant immunity if captured, and could be prosecuted by the capturing State for violation of its domestic law. However, they would be entitled to be treated humanely in accordance with applicable treaty and customary law, such as common Article 3, including receiving appropriate medical care.

All sides of a non-international armed conflict would be obligated to conduct attacks in accordance with both treaty and customary international humanitarian law.[165] This includes the obligation of combatants to distinguish themselves from civilians and to respect (and not attack) civilians and civilian objects. Further, the aircraft used by either side must be deployed in a manner that does not feign a protected status. Thus, even though a non-State armed group's aircraft may be considered civil aircraft, the non-State group must not

---

163. *Id.*, Rule 157.
164. *See, id.*, Rule 158(a). *See also* GC IV, *supra*, note 32, art. 23, *supra*, note 33, art. 70.
165. AMW Commentary, *supra*, note 31, Rule17(a), para. 8.

intentionally seek to mislead its State enemy that the aircraft are civilian and protected from attack; such deception would be perfidious.[166]

Neutrality law does not apply in a NIAC and therefore, there is no right for any party to the NIAC to intercept or capture aircraft in international airspace in the same manner as a State might in an international armed conflict. There is no right in a NIAC to set up an aerial blocked or an exclusion zone in international waters. On the other hand, the State who is party to the NIAC can introduce measures to control or preclude access by air to its territorial waters and coastal areas as a method of warfare in the NIAC against its non-State enemy. However, the State "cannot exceed its sovereign rights and may not impose any restrictions relating to areas beyond the territory of the State."[167]

Medical aircraft of all sides to the conflict would be protected from attack, but should be properly marked with the distinctive emblem. Further, a medical aircraft operating over areas that are not controlled by friendly forces should secure the consent of the enemy in order to avoid the risk of attack.

III. Space Warfare

Although no armed conflicts have yet been fought directly in space, space today is extraordinarily important to the ability to project power on Earth for those nations that have the ability to use space assets.[168] For example, the unclassified summary of the "National Security Space Strategy" issued in 2011 by the U.S. Defense Department and the Office of the Director of National Intelligence, states:

> Space capabilities provide the United States and our allies unprecedented advantages in national decision-making, military operations, and homeland security. Space systems provide national security decision-makers with unfettered global access and create a decision advantage by enabling a rapid and tailored response to global challenges. Moreover, space systems are vital to monitoring strategic and military developments as well as supporting treaty monitoring and arms control verification.[169]

---

166. *Id.*, Rule 114(b), para. 9.
167. *Id.*, Section V, para. 7.
168. In fact, the 1991 Gulf War has been dubbed the first "space war" due to the importance of global positioning satellites and other satellite services to Coalition operations. Dale Stevens & Duncan Blake, *We're drafting a legal guide to war in space. Hopefully we'll never need to use it*, THE CONVERSATION (blog), Nov. 21, 2017, http://theconversation.com/we're-drafting-a-legal-guide-to-war-in-space-hopefully-we'll-never-need-to-use-it-86677 (last visited Mar. 18, 2018) (hereinafter, *Legal Guide*).
169. U.S. DEP'T. DEF. & U.S. OFC. DIR. NAT'L INTEL., NATIONAL SECURITY SPACE STRATEGY: UNCLASSIFIED EXECUTIVE SUMMARY i (2011) available at https://www.defense.gov/Portals/1/features/defenseReviews/NSSS/NationalSecuritySpaceStrategyUnclassifiedSummary_Jan2011.pdf) (last visited March 13, 2018).

Certainly, other States see military advantages in space as well. For example, according to a recent assessment of the Russian Federation military by the U.S. Defense Intelligence Agency:

> The Russian General Staff postulates that modern warfare is increasingly reliant on information, particularly from space, because of the expansion of the geographic scope of military action and the information needs of high-precision weapons. Russia has a significant constellation of satellites in orbit. According to Colonel Sergey Marchuk, chief of the Main Test Space Center, Russia has more than 130 spacecraft, civilian and military, performing communications, navigation, geodetic survey support, meteorological, reconnaissance, and intelligence gathering missions.[170]

Similarly, the People's Republic of China has acknowledged the importance of space in defense planning:

> Outer space has become a commanding height in international strategic competition. Countries concerned are developing their space forces and instruments, and the first signs of weaponization of outer space have appeared. China has all along advocated the peaceful use of outer space, opposed the weaponization of and arms race in outer space, and taken an active part in international space cooperation. China will keep abreast of the dynamics of outer space, deal with security threats and challenges in that domain, and secure its space assets to serve its national economic and social development, and maintain outer space security.[171]

The reliance on satellites to provide communications and intelligence for armed forces, and precision guidance for weapons, creates a vulnerability that can be exploited by adversaries. These adversaries need not have weapons that physically reach space, but instead may rely on cyber operations to take control of space assets or render them ineffective, or they may attack facilities on the ground that are needed to make use of space assets. As one U.S. expert noted in testimony to Congress in March 2018:

> Space capabilities enable the American way of warfare by making it possible for U.S. commanders and forces to see the battlespace more clearly, communicate with certainty, navigate with accuracy and strike with precision. However our adversaries and potential adversaries have noted these advantages and have moved aggressively to field forces that can challenge our space capabilities from the ground, through cyberspace, and in space. From simple GPS jammers in the hands of extremists to highly sophisticated anti-satellite (ASAT) weapons in the hands of near-peer competitors like Russia and China, today's

---

170. Def. Intel. Agency, Russia Military Power: Building a Military to Support Great Power Aspirations 35 (2017) *available at* http://www.dia.mil/Portals/27/Documents/News/Military%20Power%20Publications/Russia%20Military%20Power%20Report%202017.pdf (last visited Mar. 14, 2018).

171. The State Council Information Office of the People's Republic of China, *China's Military Strategy*, May 2015, http://eng.mod.gov.cn/Database/WhitePapers/index.htm.

military commanders are facing threats in a domain that is increasingly congested, contested and competitive.[172]

Given this background, we now turn to the legal rules that we have at present to apply to an armed conflict in space, recognizing that humanity—thankfully—has yet to truly experience warfare in that domain.

1. Space Warfare Legal Framework

a. Where Does Space Begin?

A threshold issue for the application of the LOAC to space warfare is the determination of where "outer space" begins. In the airspace from the subjacent land or sea areas up to the point where space begins, the law of air warfare described in the first part of this chapter would apply, including the sovereignty that each State has over the airspace over that State's land territory and national waters.

Logically, space would begin where airspace ends. The Air and Missile Warfare Manual defines "air" or "airspace" as "the air up to the highest altitude at which an aircraft can fly and below the lowest possible perigee of an earth satellite in orbit."[173] According to the Commentary to the Manual, "[a]t an altitude of approximately 100 km, a winged aircraft has to travel at about 8 km/sec. This is equal to orbital velocity, which means that the centrifugal force would prevent it from falling down, thus making the concept of winged flight meaningless."[174] Thus, 100 kilometers is "commonly accepted" as the difference between "aeronautical" flight and "astronautical" flight (space flight). The Commentary notes, however, that this threshold has not gained universal approval.[175] Indeed, the United States rejects a fixed definition of when space begins. Instead, while accepting that objects in orbit are in space, the "United States has expressed the view that there is no legal or practical need to delimit or otherwise define a specific boundary between airspace and outer space."[176]

The question of where outer space begins is critical because, as the next section shows, the law applicable to space warfare differs from the law applicable to air warfare. This textbook does not assume that any particular test for determining the boundary between airspace and outer space is correct, but rather highlights for students that the question remains unsettled.

b. Treaty Obligations Regarding Outer Space

There is no specific treaty regulating the use of space in hostilities. Rather, the treaties that do exist largely deal with issues regarding the nature of the space

---

172. Statement of General C. Robert Kehler, United States Air Force (Retired) before the House Armed Services Committee, 14 March 2018 *available* at http://docs.house.gov/meetings/AS/AS00/20180314/107973/HHRG-115-AS00-Wstate-KehlerR-20180314.pdf (last visited Mar. 14, 2018).
173. AMW Manual, *supra*, note 31, Rule 1(a).
174. AMW Commentary, *supra*, note 31, Rule 1(a) para. 5.
175. *Id.*
176. DoD Law of War Manual, *supra*, note 2, para. 14.2.2.

domain and State responsibility for objects and persons in space. The treaty most relevant to the question of what may constitute the LOAC applicable in outer space is the 1967 Outer Space Treaty (OST).[177] The OST is the key treaty governing the peaceful use of space, but it also includes a number of provisions that would be relevant to any armed conflict in space.

Article 1 of the OST provides that "[o]uter space, including the Moon and other celestial bodies, shall be free for exploration and use by all States without discrimination of any kind, on a basis of equality and in accordance with international law, and there shall be free access to all areas of celestial bodies."[178] Further, Article II of the OST states that "[o]uter space, including the Moon and other celestial bodies, is not subject to national appropriation by claim of sovereignty, by means of use or occupation, or by any other means."[179] Thus, no nation has the right to exclude other nations from accessing and using space, even in areas of space above a nation's territory. Further, all parties to the OST are obligated to "conduct all their activities in outer space, including the Moon and other celestial bodies, with due regard to the corresponding interests of all other States Parties to the Treaty."[180] Thus, the OST accords to outer space a status similar to international waters and international airspace, and imposes on all States an obligation, similar to that imposed on States using international waters and airspace, to respect the rights of other States, including neutral States during an armed conflict, to enjoy the use of space. However, the "due regard" obligation in space is more extensive than on the Earth, because, in the absence of any sovereign territory in space, spacefaring nations must observe the "due regard" obligation at all times in outer space.

Article III of the OST provides that "States Parties to the [Outer Space] Treaty shall carry on activities in the exploration and use of outer space, including the Moon and other celestial bodies, in accordance with international law, including the Charter of the United Nations, in the interest of maintaining international security and promoting international cooperation and understanding." Article III emphasizes the role of international law in the use of outer space, including the Moon. Arguably, international law for this purpose includes the LOAC[181] so that military operations in space must comply with the principles of distinction, proportionality, and precautions, which nations are bound to follow as a matter of customary law in all armed conflicts.[182]

The reference to the U.N. Charter in Article III of the OST indicates that the prohibition against "the threat or use of force against the territorial integrity or

---

177. Treaty on Principles Governing the Activities of States in the Exploration or Use of Outer Space, Jan. 27, 1967, art. I, 610 U.N.T.S. 205 (hereinafter "OST").

178. *Id.*, art. I.

179. *Id.*, art. II. A similar provision can be found in Article 11 of the Agreement Governing the Activities of States on the Moon and Other Celestial Bodies, Dec. 5, 1979, 1363 U.N.T.S. 3. Many countries, including the United States, did not ratify this treaty.

180. OST, *supra*, note 177, art. IX.

181. *See* TALLINN MANUAL 2.0 ON THE INTERNATIONAL LAW APPLICABLE TO CYBER OPERATIONS 271 (Michael N. Schmitt, ed., 2d ed., 2017) (hereinafter, TALLINN 2.0).

182. *See* discussion of these principles in Chapter 2.

political independence of any state" found in the Charter's Article 2(4) applies in space. While the terms of Article II of the OST indicate that States cannot exercise sovereignty over space, unlawful uses of force, including armed attacks, can be launched from and through space. Further, States do have sovereignty over their satellites and other craft in space, and those could be the target of unlawful uses of force. Thus, in the 2010 "National Space Policy," the United States adopted the following principle as one of five key principles that it would adhere to in space, and proposed that other nations recognize and follow these principles:

> As established in international law, there shall be no national claims of sovereignty over outer space or any celestial bodies. The United States considers the space systems of all nations to have the right of passage through, and conduct of operations in, space without interference. Purposeful interference with space systems, including supporting infrastructure, will be considered an infringement of a nation's rights.[183]

Moreover, States may identify their space assets as important to their national interests, and respond with force, including armed force, to interference with, or attacks on, those assets. For example, in its December 2017 "National Security Strategy," the United States cautioned others against interference with U.S. space objects and supporting facilities:

> Many countries are purchasing satellites to support their own strategic military activities. Others believe that the ability to attack space assets offers an asymmetric advantage and as a result, are pursuing a range of anti-satellite (ASAT) weapons. The United States considers unfettered access to and freedom to operate in space to be a vital interest. Any harmful interference with or an attack upon critical components of our space architecture that directly affects this vital U.S. interest will be met with a deliberate response at a time, place, manner, and domain of our choosing.[184]

The reference to the U.N. Charter in Article III of the OST also is helpful in interpreting the obligation under Article III to use outer space, including the Moon and other celestial bodies, "in the interest of maintaining international peace and security and promoting international cooperation and understanding." Some have argued that this peaceful use obligation precludes military use of space (or at least weaponization of space). However, many scholars, citing to State practice since the beginning of the Space age, instead believe that the peaceful use obligation relates only to use of space for offensive military purposes, without prejudice to a State's inherent right of individual or collective

---

183. Office of the President, National Space Policy of the United States of America 3 (June 28, 2010) (Presidential Policy Directive – 4), available at https://obamawhitehouse.archives.gov/sites/default/files/national_space_policy_6-28-10.pdf (last visited Mar. 14, 2018). On December 11, 2017, President Trump amended this policy to add guidance on manned exploration of space, but otherwise left the 2010 National Space Policy intact. Space Policy Directive-1 of December 11, 2017, Reinvigorating America's Human Space Exploration Program, 82 FED. REG. 59501 (Dec. 14, 2017).

184. Office of the President, National Security Strategy of the United States of America 32 (December 2017), *available at* https://www.whitehouse.gov/wp-content/uploads/2017/12/NSS-Final-12-18-2017-0905.pdf (last visited Mar. 14, 2018).

self-defense under Article 51 of the U.N. Charter, and does not preclude use of space by States in connection with conflicts on Earth.[185]

Article IV of the OST provides that "States Parties to the Treaty undertake not to place in orbit around the Earth any objects carrying nuclear weapons or any other kinds of weapons of mass destruction, install such weapons on celestial bodies, or station such weapons in outer space in any other manner."[186] Notably, this provision of the treaty only precludes the stationing of such weapons in space, but not the transit of missiles armed with such weapons through space, which is what occurs with intercontinental ballistic missiles launched from one point on Earth against a terrestrial target.[187] It also does not preclude the targeting of objects in space with nuclear weapons launched from Earth, nor does it preclude the stationing or use of non-nuclear weapons in space.[188]

Article IV of the OST also provides that "[t]he Moon and other celestial bodies shall be used by all States Parties to the Treaty exclusively for peaceful purposes"[189] and prohibits the "establishment of military bases, installations and fortifications, the testing of any type of weapons and the conduct of military manoeuvres on celestial bodies. . . ."[190] On the other hand, "the use of military personnel for scientific research or for any other peaceful purposes" is not prohibited on these bodies, nor is "[t]he use of any equipment or facility necessary for peaceful exploration of the Moon and other celestial bodies. . . ."[191]

In sum, Article IV on its face indicates that, if were there a military advantage to it, spacecraft could be armed with conventional weapons, conduct military operations (including both offensive and defense operations) in and from space and even be based in space (but not on celestial bodies). However, these armed spacecraft could not conduct military operations on celestial bodies nor could fortifications or armed bases be established on theses bodies. On the other hand, armed spacecraft could visit celestial bodies for peaceful purposes such as exploration. Of course, at this stage of human space travel, there has been no need to test the limits of Article IV as it relates to military forces in space. In the future, State practice will determine the exact contours of Article

---

185. Cassandra Steer, *Global Commons, Cosmic Commons: Implications of Military and Security Uses of Outer Space*, 18 GEO. J. INT'L AFF. 9, 11 (Winter/Spring 2017) (hereinafter Global Commons); Dale Stephens & Melissa de Zwart, *The Manual of International Law Applicable to Military Uses of Outer Space (MILAMOS)* 2 (RUMLAE Research Paper No. 17-12, 2017) (hereinafter MILAMOS). The U.S. government holds a similar view. *See* DOD LAW OF WAR MANUAL, *supra*, note 2, para. 14.10.4.

186. OST, *supra*, note 177, art. III.

187. While the lack of State sovereignty in space means that a State cannot object to the flight of a space object in outer space above its territory, it is not clear what rule applies if the object into space flies through the upper reaches of a State's airspace to reach space or return to space. Some, when launched states have claimed that there is a right of passage for this purpose, but even if this right exists, it may not apply in an armed conflict. Woff Heintschel von Heinegg, *Neutrality and Outer Space*, 93 INT'L L. STUD. 526, 538 (2017) (hereinafter von Heinegg).

188. DOD LAW OF WAR MANUAL, *supra*, note 2, para. 14.10.3.1.

189. OST, *supra*, note 177, art. IV.

190. The Earth is not a celestial body for this purpose, nor are man-made stations or craft.

191. OST, *supra*, note 177, art. IV.

IV, including how far the "peaceful purposes" limitation will restrict the use of military forces on celestial bodies.

Other provisions of the OST impose liability on States who launch or procure the launch of objects into space or to the Moon or other celestial bodies (or whose territory or facilities are used for such a launch), for damage done to another State or its citizens by those objects or their component parts on the Earth, in space, or in airspace.[192] Liability might not apply where damage is caused by a belligerent State to its enemy if the damage is justified by imperative military necessity,[193] but liability would apply where neutrals suffer damage from space objects launched by a belligerent State during hostilities. The OST also imposes liability on each State party to the Treaty for "national activities" in outer space, including activities of "non-governmental entities" and provides that any national activities carried on by non-governmental activities in outer space, on the Moon or on celestial bodies, will be subject to approval and supervision of the State who bears the liability to ensure compliance with the OST.[194] States retain jurisdiction and control over objects registered with that State, and anyone on board the object, even when in outer space or on a celestial object.[195]

Finally, under the OST, astronauts are considered "envoys of mankind in outer space," and all States are required to render them assistance in case of an accident, distress, or emergency landing, and they are promptly to be returned to the State in which their vehicle is registered.[196] Moreover, while in space, astronauts of one State are required to "render all possible assistance" to astronauts of other States.[197] How these obligations would apply in armed conflict is uncertain, but the obligation to render assistance appears to parallel the assistance to the shipwrecked required to be provided under the Geneva Conventions and

---

192. *Id.*, art. VII. The Convention on International Liability for Damage Caused by Space Objects, Mar. 29, 1972, 961 U.N.T.S. 187, allocates liability to the States who launch or procure the launch of space objects, or from whose territory the object is launched, based on strict liability (for damage on the surface of the Earth or to aircraft in flight) or on the basis of fault (in the case of damage to other space objects). Of particular relevance to the LOAC, there is no possibility of exoneration for strict liability where the damage results from activities not in conformity with the UN Charter. *Id.*, art. IV.

193. *See* 1907 Hague IV, *supra*, note 20, art. 23(g).

194. OST, *supra*, note 177, art. VI. Depending upon the scope of the definition of "national activities," a State conceivably could be liable, under Article VI, for space activities of non-State armed groups operating from the State's territory, and under Article VII, a State could be liable for an object launched by a non-State armed group from the State's territory without the State's participation or consent, but of course there has yet to be an instance where these theories of liability have been tested. The broader point, however, is that there potentially is a broad scope under the OST for State liability for damage caused in space by those under its jurisdiction, or by space objects launched from its territory.

195. *Id.*, art. VIII. Registration of space objects (which includes the launch vehicle as well as the object placed in space) is governed by Convention on Registration of Objects Launched Into Space, June 6, 1975, 1023 U.N.T.S. 15, which requires launching States (i.e., States that launch or procure the launch of a space object) to register the object in a registry maintained by the State, and to notify the U.N. Secretary-General of the registration. Where there are more than one launching State, they jointly determine which State will register the object.

196. OST, *supra*, note 177, art. V.

197. *Id.*

its Additional Protocols.[198] However, a State in an armed conflict may interpret the right to take prisoners of war to supersede, in time of war, the obligation to return an astronaut to the State of registry of his craft, in a case where the astronaut is a member of the enemy's armed forces.[199]

In addition to the OST and the treaties described in the footnotes to the discussion of the OST, there also are treaties banning the testing of nuclear weapons in space (but not their use in armed conflict)[200] as well as treaties governing commercial satellites that need to be considered. One such treaty is the constitution of the International Telecommunication Union (ITU). The ITU allocates global radio spectrum and satellite orbits for international communications. The provisions of the ITU's constitution do not preclude the use of space for military purposes, but they do require that radio stations established, operated, or authorized by States "be established and operated in such a manner as not to cause harmful interference to the radio services or communications of other Member States."[201] Further, while there is an exception for "military radio installations," the exception is subject to a requirement that "these installations must, so far as possible, observe statutory provisions relative to giving assistance in case of distress and to the measures to be taken to prevent harmful interference. . . ."[202] The provisions regarding prevention of harmful interference include the following condition, which States would need to consider before launching any operation (including not only attacks but also jamming) that would interfere with a communications satellite subject to the ITU:

> In using frequency bands for radio services, Member States shall bear in mind that radio frequencies and any associated orbits, including the geostationary-satellite orbit, are limited natural resources and that they must be used rationally, efficiently and economically, in conformity with the provisions of the [ITU's] Radio Regulations, so that countries or groups of countries may have equitable access to those orbits and frequencies, taking into account the special needs of the developing countries and the geographical situation of particular countries.[203]

In sum, the OST and the other treaties mentioned above are not directed expressly to the conduct of hostilities in space, and therefore cannot be said to

---

198. GWS-Sea, *supra*, note 32, art. 18; GCIV, *supra*, note 32, art. 16; AP I, *supra*, note 33, art. 10; AP II, *supra*, note 33, art. 7.

199. *See, e.g.*, DoD Law of War Manual, *supra*, note 2, para. 14.10.2.1 n. 153 (describing an instance in which the U.S. Department of Defense interpreted the law of armed conflict to supersede the general obligations of space law treaties). A distinction might be made between military astronauts who are engaged only in scientific or exploration duties, rather than military duties, and those who are directly involved in hostilities, with the former continuing to be treated as "envoys of mankind," while the latter could be treated as combatants.

200. Treaty Banning Nuclear Weapon Tests in the Atmosphere, In Outer Space and Under Water, Aug. 5, 1963, 480 U.N.T.S. 44. As its name implies, the ban does not apply to underground testing. The ban was intended to prevent explosions in peacetime that cause radioactive debris to be present outside the territorial limits of the State that conducts an explosion.

201. Constitution of the International Telecommunication Union, art. 45.1, Dec. 22, 1992, 1825 U.N.T.S., 331.

202. *Id.* art. 48.

203. *Id.* art. 45.2.

be LOAC treaties. However, any State proposing to use outer space, the Moon, or celestial bodies in connection with military operations in an armed conflict must consider these treaties, as they establish standards for use of the space domain, and the general obligation of all States, including those engaged in armed conflict, to respect the rights of all other States to use that domain.

c. LOAC Applicable to Hostilities Involving Outer Space

While none of the LOAC treaties discussed in this text expressly seek to regulate armed conflict in space, all LOAC treaties certainly should be applied in any armed conflict involving outer space except where the treaty provisions expressly applies to a specific domain other than space. LOAC treaties that could apply to military operations in space would include, for example, the protocols to the Convention on Conventional Weapons or CCW,[204] which prohibit or regulate certain weapons. Among those weapons are laser weapons designed, as one of their combat functions, to "cause permanent blindness to unenhanced vision."[205] These lasers are prohibited by Protocol IV to the CCW. Protocol IV also requires parties to an armed conflict to take "all feasible precautions to avoid the incidence of permanent blindness" as a result of the use of these weapons in armed conflict.[206] Given the potential for the use of lasers by or against space objects,[207] including to "blind" satellites, the requirements of Protocol IV would need to be followed were humans at risk of being exposed to the laser.[208]

A treaty, known as ENMOD, which prohibits States party to ENMOD from engaging in military or other hostile use of environmental modification techniques if the techniques will have "widespread, long lasting or severe effects as the means of destruction, damage or injury" to another State party, defines an "environmental modification technique" as "any technique for changing — through the deliberate manipulation of natural processes — the dynamics, composition or structure of the Earth, including its biota, lithosphere, hydrosphere and atmosphere, or of outer space." The threshold for application of the treaty is quite high, since it requires manipulation of natural processes and significant effects resulting from that manipulation. However, the fact the treaty regulates the manipulation of outer space as a means of warfare means that there is at least one rule of the LOAC expressly applicable to outer space. (Moreover, the treaty's acknowledgement that space could be manipulated as a means of

---

204. Convention on Prohibitions or Restrictions on the Use of Certain Conventional Weapons Which May Be Deemed to Be Excessively Injurious or to Have Indiscriminate Effects, Oct. 10, 1980, 1342 U.N.T.S. 137 (hereinafter CCW).

205. Protocol (IV) on Blinding Laser Weapons, Annexed to the Convention on Prohibitions or Restrictions on the Use of Certain Conventional Weapons Which May Be Deemed to Be Excessively Injurious or to Have Indiscriminate Effects, October 13, 1995, art. 1, 1380 U.N.T.S. 163 (hereinafter CCW Protocol IV).

206. *Id.*, art. 2.

207. *See* Joint Chiefs of Staff, Joint Pub. 3-14, Space Operations V-7 (May 29, 2013) (hereinafter JP 3-14) ("Space segments of a space system are vulnerable to attacks or interference such as direct-ascent antisatellite interceptors, laser blinding, and dazzling").

208. Blinding as a collateral effect of a lawful attack is not covered by Protocol IV, however. CCW Protocol IV, *supra,* note 205, art. 3.

warfare provides further evidence that the international community anticipates that States might conduct hostilities in space, or at least use space in connection with hostilities.)

Additionally, to the extent that LOAC treaties are not applicable to space operations, customary law could apply to fill in the gap, though this would require evidence of State practice out of a sense of legal obligation.[209] However, given that military space operations today are focused principally on enhancing the capabilities of armed force on Earth, one can certainly argue that operations in space with terrestrial effects should at least comply with the customary rules for terrestrial warfare, including the principles of the LOAC.[210]

There was an effort underway to draw up a manual on the international law applicable to military uses of outer space (MILAMOS). MILAMOS (also known as the "McGill Manual") was a joint project of the University of Adelaide in Australia, McGill University in Canada, and the University of Exeter in Great Britain. According to the leaders of the project, it was organized to use a process similar to that used for other "soft law" products, such as the Air and Missile Warfare Manual, in which experts, including government experts participating in their private capacity, meet to discuss and reconcile the various legal rules applicable to military operations in space and to develop a coherent restatement of the applicable law that can be set forth in the form of a manual that, according to its website, "will be relevant to States, militaries, private space actors, civil society, academics and other relevant stakeholders with an interest in the orderly conduct of space activities." The project has recently disbanded, breaking into separate projects because the experts involved could not come to agreement on the issues. This highlights the difficulty of determining the law governing armed conflict in outer space.

2. LOAC Issues in Space Warfare

While there are a number of legal issues related to military space operations of concern to scholars, we will focus on two that have drawn attention in recent years. The first relates to the widespread use of commercial space assets by State armed forces, and the question of when and how these assets could be targeted in an armed conflict. The second is the question of the collateral effects on an attack on a space object, including the potential for the creation of space debris that could damage other space objects and make commonly-used orbits risky to use, or even prevent the use of such orbits, and the potential for harmful effects on civilians and civilian objects on Earth from such an attack. To the extent foreseeable at the time the attack is planned and launched, these effects would

---

209. David A. Koplow, *ASAT-isfaction: Customary International Law and the Regulation of Anti-Satellite Weapons*, 30 MICH. J. INT'L L. 1187, 1222-1242, (2009) [hereinafter "ASAT-isfaction"].

210. For a lengthy and detailed analysis of the application of the LOAC to space warfare, *see* Robert A. Ramey, *Armed Conflict on the Final Frontier: The Law of War in Space*, 48 A.F. L. REV. 1 (2000). In his article, Ramey argues that "the near-total atmospheric vacuum characterizing outer space is matched by a similar legal vacuum with respect to the jus in bello for space warfare. Academicians and practitioners are left to making educated but uncertain guesses based on analogies with other legal regimes." *Id.*, at 155.

need to be considered in the proportionality analysis and feasible precautions taken to minimize the effects on civilians and civilian objects.

a. Dual Use Space Objects

It is a "cardinal principle" of the LOAC that belligerents distinguish between civilian objects and military objectives, and only direct attacks against the latter.[211] However, it may be difficult to comply with this principle where non-military commercial satellites and capabilities are used by State armed forces, or even non-State armed groups, to obtain imagery for use in the conflict, or to communicate within elements of a belligerent's forces or between one belligerent and a co-belligerent. The U.S. Joint Chiefs of Staff has noted that "[a]ccess to commercial space services has enabled even the smallest of nations to use GPS [global positioning system] commercial space imagery, SATCOM [satellite communications], and other services." As a consequence, "[s]pace capabilities are being used across the range of military operations by our multinational partners and have become a critical enabler for civil and military operations."[212]

Given the widespread use of commercial satellites, a belligerent in a future conflict will face the question of when a commercial satellite can be attacked. Any object can become a military objective under the definition in Article 52 of AP I, depending on whether its "nature, location, purpose or use makes an effective contribution to military action," and whether its "total or partial destruction, capture or neutralization" offers a definite military advantage.[213] However, if the satellite is also being used by civilians, the LOAC rules on precautions and proportionality discussed in earlier chapters of this book would need to be considered, to determine the effects that the attack on the satellite might have on civilians and civilian objects, and whether death or damage to civilians and the damage to, or loss of, civilian objects are anticipated to be excessive compared to the concrete and direct military advantage anticipated.[214]

What if the satellite is owned by a neutral State or its citizens, or there is multinational ownership? This does not immunize the satellite from attack if it is a military objective.[215] Of course, the fact that property is owned by the

---

211. Legality of the Threat or Use of Nuclear Weapons (Advisory Opinion), 1996 I.C.J. Rep. 226, ¶ 78 (July 8).
212. JP 3-14, *supra*, note 207, V-10.
213. AP I, *supra*, 33, art. 52. *See* discussion of military objectives generally in Chapter 7.
214. *Id.*, arts. 51 and 57. Proportionality and precautions in conducting attacks are discussed in chapters 2 and 7.
215. Given the provisions of OST Article VIII governing the continuing "jurisdiction and control" of a State over the space objects it has registered, the satellite might be considered an extension of the State's territory. Thus, if the State is a neutral in the conflict, an attack on the satellite might be considered an attack on neutral territory, which is prohibited by the law neutrality. However, leading scholars in this area have rejected this view. *See* von Heinegg, *supra*, note 187, at 531 ("With regard to belligerent attacks against neutral space objects and assets, it is certainly not correct to rely on the fundamental obligation of belligerents to respect the inviolability of neutral States. . . .The obligation is strictly limited to neutral territory; it does not protect objects and assets located outside neutral territory. . . .") Yet, given the excerpt from the U.S. government's December 2017 "National Security Strategy" in the text , it is clear that any attack on U.S. space assets and infrastructure could lead to an

citizens of a neutral State or by the neutral State itself, does not prevent it from being subject to attack, as we have seen in the discussion in this chapter of the situations in which neutral aircraft may lawfully be attacked, or the situations in which neutral ships may be attacked. However, there are no rules, either in treaty or customary law, specifically addressing the situations in which satellites registered in neutral States could be subject to attack in armed conflict. If one looks to the rules governing when a neutral aircraft is subject to attack or capture discussed *supra*, in Section II.B.4, one can see a few examples that might have a parallel to the situation in which a neutral commercial satellite is being used by an enemy, including (i) "facilitating the military actions of the enemy's armed forces," (ii) "being incorporated into or assisting the enemy's intelligence gathering system," or (iii) "otherwise making an effective contribution to military action." These criteria seem particularly apt if the satellite's operators are actively working with a belligerent to provide them the services needed to support the belligerent's forces, at a level that would be equivalent to participation in hostilities.

What if, however, the operator of a satellite is simply providing communications services to a party to an armed conflict on the same basis as it provides communications services to commercial customers, or is selling a party to an armed conflict satellite photographs or other data that the operator would be collecting anyways and selling to a broader set of customers, of which the party to the armed conflict is just one? Is this type of activity different and potentially protected, or does the fact that it "contributes to military action" subject the satellite to attack? Certainly, any provision to a belligerent party to an armed conflict of imagery or communications capacity from a neutral satellite could expose the satellite to attack by the belligerent's enemy,[216] if the satellite is actually making an effective contribution to the enemy's military action, by, for example, "the transmission of earth imaging data and/or of the information resulting from the processed data, which has either tactical or strategic value, in real time. . . ."[217]

Before targeting a commercial or neutral satellite, the United States likely would favor an approach that looks first to "diplomatic or economic means to deny an adversary access to these third party (commercial or foreign) space capabilities."[218] In any case, any attack would have to meet the LOAC principles of proportionality and precautions, which would require an assessment of the collateral harm from the attack (e.g., the damage that the attack could cause to the satellite itself and other space objects as well as the effects of the loss of services provided by the satellite to civilians or neutral States) and require

---

armed response, even in cases where the United States is a neutral. *See, supra,* note 184 and accompanying text.

216. Von Heinegg, *supra,* note 187, at 541.

217. Michel Bourbonnière, *The Ambit of the Law of Neutrality and Space Security,* 49 Proc. L. Outer Space 326, 333 (2006).

218. Curtis E. Lemay Center for Doctrine Development and Education, *Annex 3-1—Space Operations,* U.S. Air Force Doctrine, http://www.doctrine.af.mil/Doctrine-Annexes/Annex-3-14-Space-Ops/ (last visited Mar. 18, 2018).

consideration of ways in which such harm could be mitigated, including the use of non-kinetic means to disable the satellite, its supporting facilities, or the communications links between them.

b. Collateral Effects Resulting from Attacks on Space Objects

Collateral damage resulting from attacks on space objects has emerged as a significant concern among both policy makers and scholars in evaluating the lawfulness of ASAT attacks. One source of damage from such an attack would be the debris that the attack could leave in orbit around the Earth. This debris could result from the destruction of the satellite through a kinetic attack (either a direct collision or an explosion in proximity to the targeted satellite), with the satellite being torn apart into smaller pieces, each of which would become a piece of debris.[219] However, an attack might not be kinetic. Instead, the satellite could be rendered inoperable through, for example, cyber means or by use of lasers or other "directed energy" weapons.[220] In this case, the satellite would remain intact, but if it is no longer operable, the satellite itself would become debris, if it is no longer subject to control from Earth. In either case, the debris could persist for years in space, potentially threatening other space objects, both manned and unmanned, with damage, as long as the debris remains in space. Unless hardened against debris, space objects (satellites and spacecraft) colliding with even small-sized debris could suffer significant damage or even be destroyed. Moreover, while space is large, not all orbits have equal value, and therefore an accumulation of debris in a useful orbit could adversely impact the ability of many nations to make use of that orbit for years to come.[221]

The problems created by kinetic ASAT weapons were acutely demonstrated by an ASAT test by China in 2007. In that case, a Chinese interceptor missile was used to destroy an aging Chinese weather satellite while still in orbit. According to one scholar, the strike resulted in

> ...a miasma of 2600 pieces of trackable debris, and perhaps 150,000 smaller (but nonetheless hazardous) fragments careening in all directions. It created a swarm, moving through space like a high-speed lethal amoeba, stretching from 200 to 2350 kilometers in altitude, through which over 100 essential earth observation satellites must repeatedly pass in the years to come.[222]

---

219. ASAT-isfaction, *supra*, note 209, at 1201-1202.

220. *Id.* Other forms of attacks would include a temporary disabling of the satellite through a dazzling or jamming effect, or even a cyber operation that gives the attacker control of the satellite. Global Commons, *supra*, note 185, at 12. On their face, these other forms of attack appear to represent less of a problem under the principle of proportionality, and in fact may be a useful means of taking "feasible precautions" to minimize collateral damage from the attack.

221. Duncan P. Blake, The Laws of Star Wars—The Need for a "Manual of International Law Applicable to Space Warfare" 10 (Aug. 2013) (unpublished LL.M. thesis, McGill University), *available at* http://digitool.library.mcgill.ca/R/?func=dbin-jump-full&object_id=121467&local_base=GEN01-MCG02 (last visited Mar. 18, 2018) (hereinafter The Laws of Star Wars).

222. ASAT-isfaction, *supra*, note 209, at 1203.

The United States conducted its own ASAT operation a year later when it used an interceptor to destroy a satellite falling out of orbit. Because the satellite was in a very low orbit, most of the debris from the satellite entered the atmosphere quickly and disintegrated or fell harmlessly to the Earth's surface. This U.S. ASAT success served as a good example of how best to destroy space objects.[223] However, the United States, Russia, and other nations also share the blame for the debris problem, as many of their satellites have become space junk as they aged or collided with other space debris, and, while in orbit, this space junk must be tracked (and avoided) for years.[224]

Damage from space debris is not the only risk from an ASAT attack, however. Due to the dual use of many satellites, the services that they provide may benefit a large number of users, and in fact may be critical to services relied upon by the population of more than one country. A good example is the U.S. global positioning system (GPS), which has been made widely available and is used by civilians in a number of ways, including to manage air, sea, and land transportation. According to one writer, "[i]f the timing signal from the GPS constellation of satellites were partially disrupted, it may have unpredictable, perhaps even devastating effects on the communications systems necessary, for example, to banking, stock markets, travel sites, remote control of all manner of industrial sites, everyday commerce and communications."[225] Thus, as another writer has said, "[g]iven the dual use of many satellites, an armed conflict in space could be catastrophic to modern life."[226]

In light of these potential effects from an ASAT attack, the application of the LOAC principle of proportionality can be far more complex in space operations than on Earth. If an attack on a satellite could result in debris that could affect the ability of all nations to use certain orbits in space for years, is there any circumstance in which the anticipated damage to civilian objects (e.g., other satellites) and the potential loss of use of an orbit resulting from the attack would not be "excessive in relation to the concrete and direct military advantage anticipated" under Article 51(5)(b) of AP I?[227] Indeed, Bill Boothby, a military lawyer and retired Air Commodore in the U.K. Royal Air Force, recently observed that "the growing debris problem that is being experienced causes one to wonder for how long kinetic ASAT activities will continue to be acceptable among spacefaring nations."[228]

What of the damage that might be caused by the loss of the services provided by the satellite? Should the "ripple effect" of an ASAT attack on a satellite be factored in as well in evaluating the lawfulness of the attack? The experts involved in the drafting of the Tallinn Manual (discussed in the next section of

---

223. *Id.* at 1210.
224. *Id.* at 1204-1207.
225. The Laws of Star Wars, *supra*, note 221, at 17.
226. *Legal Guide, supra,* note 168.
227. *See* ASAT-isfaction, *supra,* note 209, at 1247 (arguing that under the customary LOAC principle of proportionality, "it seems clear that *many* possible ASAT operations would be ruled out, and even that *most* contemplated kinetic ASAT strikes would be of dubious legality") (emphasis in original).
228. Bill Boothby, *Space Weapons and the Law*, 93 INT'L L. STUD. 179, 2018 (2017).

this chapter) considered similar questions when looking at how the proportionality principle should be applied to an attack by cyber means. The commentary to the Tallinn Manual's rule on proportionality which tracks the language of AP I Article 51(5)(b) and AP Article 57(2)(a)(iii) notes that "[c]ollateral damage can consist of both direct and indirect effects."[229] Further, "[t]he collateral damage considered in the proportionality calculation includes any indirect effects that should be expected by those individuals planning, approving or executing a cyber attack."[230] Thus, according to the Tallinn Manual, in a proposed attack that blocks or disrupts GPS satellite data, "accidents involving transportation systems relying on the data can be expected in the short term, at least until adoption of other navigation aids and techniques."[231] Similarly, when evaluating an attack on space objects, their supporting infrastructure or the links between space objects and this infrastructure, one must consider the effects of the attack on the systems that rely on that space object and the data, imagery, or communications it provides, and the potential loss to civilians and civilian objects if those systems were disrupted.

One unanswered question is whether the effects of a series of ASAT attacks should be cumulated in assessing whether the attacks together might produce excessive collateral damage. There is no clear answer to this question, although the wording of AP I Article 51(5)(b) and AP Article 57(2)(a)(iii) might suggest that only the damage directly resulting from an individual attack is to be considered. However, it is interesting to note that in ratifying AP I, the United Kingdom and other States made declarations and reservations to the effect that, in reference to Articles 51 and 57, "the military advantage anticipated from an attack is intended to refer to the advantage anticipated from the attack considered as a whole, and not only from isolated or particular parts of the attack."[232] If the advantage should be considered from the attack as a whole, one might argue that the incidental damage to be included in the proportionality analysis also should consider the damage to civilians and civilian objects from the attack "as a whole", particularly where the attack is part of a larger set of attacks on an enemy's space objects and/or infrastructure.

The principle of precautions also must be carefully applied in the context of an ASAT attack. Not only must a careful evaluation be made of the potential harm to civilians or civilian objects that are anticipated to result from the attack (so as to properly apply the proportionality principle), but one also must consider the other elements of precautions set forth in AP I art. 57. These include (i) verifying that the space object is, in fact, a military objective (art. 57(2)(a)(i)); (ii) taking all "feasible precautions" to use means and methods of carrying out the attack to avoid or at least minimize incidental loss of civilian life, injury to civilians and damage to civilian objects (art. 57(2)(a)(ii)) resulting from an

---

229. TALLINN 2.0, *supra*, note 181, at 472.
230. *Id.*
231. *Id.*
232. United Kingdom of Great Britain and Northern Ireland, Ratifications (with Declarations and Reservations), Jan. 28, 1998, 2020 U.N.T.S. 75, 77.

attack on the space object, including not only minimizing space debris but also minimizing the anticipated losses from the disruption in the space object's services; and (iii) giving, to the extent permitted under the circumstances, an effective advance warning of the attack if the attack might affect the civilian population (art. 57(2)(c)). In all cases, it will be important to consider launching an attack that will not create space debris, including by attacking support facilities on the ground rather than in space where possible, or by disrupting the link with the space object.[233] Even if the space object is wholly military in nature, the possibility that, as space debris, it could threaten civilian space objects for years to come must be taken into account. In fact, given that space debris threatens all space objects — civilian and military — there would appear to be no attack on a space object in orbit that could not cause collateral damage. Therefore, *all* ASAT attacks against objects in orbit must be evaluated under the precautions principle.

Finally, a consideration not required by the LOAC, but certainly relevant to the decision to launch an ASAT attack, is the potential benefit to a belligerent of the situational awareness that the space object provides to its enemy. While the enemy can use that situational awareness for its strategic and tactical benefit, it may also be beneficial to allow the enemy to have at least some capabilities to understand and verify developments in the armed conflict, in order to avoid a miscalculation on the enemy's part, and to confirm LOAC compliance by the enemy's forces and those of other parties to the conflict. For example, as one writer has noted, the satellites that provide the "national technical means of verification" that one's enemy is complying with commitments not to use nuclear weapons are so essential to "maintaining a level of trust and confidence between nuclear-capable States that targeting them would be strategically foolish in almost all conceivable circumstances."[234]

IV. Cyber Operations

The internet began in the late 1950s as an Advanced Research Projects Agency (ARPA) project to help facilitate communications in response to the Soviet advances in space technology. The development of the ARPANET and its subsequent connection to other networks in the 1970s led to the development of the internet as we know it today.

As of the beginning of 2018, more than half of the world's population uses the internet, an increase of over 1,000 percent since 2000. The internet's

---

233. *See* ASAT-isfaction, *supra*, note 209, at 1248 (arguing that, where a State has both a kinetic ASAT weapon that would produce debris and a directed energy weapon that would not, and either weapon could fulfill a particular ASAT mission, customary LOAC rules would require that the directed energy weapon be used for that mission).

234. The Laws of Star Wars, *supra*, note 221, at 21. Satellites similarly may be essential to an armed forced ability to reliably identify eivilians and civilian objects in its targeting process.

penetration rate is over 85 percent in both Europe and North America.[235] There is no doubt that the internet is an ever-increasingly important part of life.

But, because of its origins, the internet was not built with security as a paramount interest. Rather, connectivity and ease of communication were the most important initial requirements. The infamous "Morris worm" that was released in 1988 was the first major public demonstration of the vulnerabilities inherent in the internet. Those architectural vulnerabilities continue today, and have led to the "weaponization" of the internet and the resulting national security risks.

1. Defining Cyberspace

Cyberspace is defined in the U.S. Joint Publication 1-02, Department of Defense Dictionary of Military and Associated Terms, as "[a] global domain within the information environment consisting of the interdependent network of information technology infrastructures and resident data, including the Internet, telecommunications networks, computer systems, and embedded processors and controllers." It is now being considered as a fifth domain for military activities, along with air, land, sea, and space.[236]

Because of its pervasive nature and its incredible importance to national security and military operations, nearly every nation is considering the internet's military implications, and an ever-increasing number of countries have issued cyber strategies to guide their military operations.[237] For example, the United States has issued a DoD Cyber Strategy,[238] and cyber activities and vulnerabilities play a large role in the 2018 National Security Strategy.[239]

2. Legal Paradigms

Both domestic and international law apply to the use of cyber tools. Most nations have laws that govern the use of cyber tools that apply to the government, as well as to the military and other government agencies.

a. Domestic Law

There are a number of U.S. domestic laws that govern the use of cyber tools by government agencies that also implicate actions by the U.S. Department of Defense. These include far-reaching legislation such as the Computer Fraud

---

235. *Internet Usage Statistics, The Internet Big Picture: World Internet Users and 2018 Population Stats*, INTERNET WORLD STATS, https://www.internetworldstats.com/stats.htm (last visited May 2, 2018).
236. DoD LAW OF WAR MANUAL, *supra*, note 2, para. 16.1.1.
237. *Cyber Security Strategy Documents*, NATO COOPERATIVE CYBER DEF. CTR. OF EXCELLENCE (CCDCOE), https://ccdcoe.org/cyber-security-strategy-documents.html.
238. *See* DEP'T. OF DEF. CYBER STRATEGY (2015), https://www.defense.gov/Portals/1/features/2015/
0415_cyberstrategy/Final_2015_DoD_CYBER_STRATEGY_for_web.pdf.
239. *See* NAT'L SECURITY STRATEGY OF THE UNITED STATES OF AMERICA (2018), https://www.whitehouse.gov/wp-content/uploads/2017/12/NSS-Final-12-18-2017-0905.pdf.

and Abuse Act[240] and the Electronic Communications Privacy Act[241] and also various National Defense Appropriations Acts (NDAA) such as the direction to turn United States Cyber Command into a unified combatant command in the 2017 NDAA.[242] While these laws, and similar laws in other countries, may not implicate the LOAC directly, they certainly affect how each nation prepares for and then approaches its use of cyber tools in armed conflict.

b. International Law

It is now also generally agreed that international law applies to cyber operations. In one of many official statements by U.S. government officials, then Secretary of State Legal Advisor Harold Koh stated in 2012 that "international law principles do apply in cyberspace."[243] This was echoed a year later when the United Nations Group of Governmental Experts on Developments in the Field of Information and Telecommunications in the Context of International Security (UN GGE) reported to the Secretary General that "[i]nternational law, and in particular the Charter of the United Nations, is applicable" to cyberspace.[244]

The international group of experts convened by the NATO Cooperative Cyber Defense Center of Excellence to write the Tallinn Manuals also agreed that international law applies to actions in cyberspace. And more specifically, the Tallinn Manual found that cyber operations were governed by the LOAC.[245] Additionally, the ICRC has made clear that it believes all uses of cyber tools in armed conflict are governed by the LOAC.[246]

However, concluding that international law, including the LOAC, applies is perhaps the easy part of the task. Determining *how* it applies is more challenging.

3. *Jus ad Bellum*

As detailed above, the UN GGE concluded that the *jus ad bellum* provisions of the UN Charter apply to cyber operations. While cyber operations are governed by the *jus ad bellum* in their own right, it seems most likely that such cyber operations will likely occur in conjunction with other military operations, rather than as discreet armed attacks.

Two examples illustrate the point. In 2007, Israel conducted a raid into Syria to destroy a nuclear facility at al-Kibar. The raid was carried out by military

---

240. Computer Fraud and Abuse Act of 1986, Pub. L. No. 99-474, 100 Stat. 1213 (1986).
241. Electronic Communications Privacy Act of 1986, Pub. L. No. 99-508, 100 Stat. 1848 (1986).
242. National Defense Authorization Act for Fiscal Year 2017, Pub. L. No. 114-328 § 923, 130 Stat. 2000 (2016).
243. Harold Hongju Koh, *International Law in Cyberspace: Remarks as Prepared for Delivery to the USCYBERCOM Inter-Agency Legal Conference*, 54 HARV. INT'L. J. ONLINE 1, 3 (2012).
244. U.N. Secretary-General, *Report of the Group of Governmental Experts on Developments in the Field of Information and Telecommunications in the Context of International Security*, ¶ 19, U.N. Doc. A/68/150 (June 24, 2013).
245. TALLINN 2.0, *supra*, note 181, at 375.
246. *Weapons: Statement of the ICRC to the United Nations, 2017*, INT'L COMM. OF THE RED CROSS, https://www.icrc.org/en/document/weapons-statement-icrc-united-nations-unag-2017 (last visited May 3, 2018).

fighter jet aircraft, but in the preparation to the raid, air defense systems were disabled to allow the aircraft to enter Syrian airspace. It is assumed that the air defense systems were disabled by a cyber operation.[247]

Similarly, in Russia's 2008 military action in South Ossetia, cyber operations were used in the build-up to and in conjunction with the attack.[248] Both government and non-government sites were targeted, and it appears that some of the cyber operations were carried out by military organizations and others by civilian "hacktivists."

What seems certain is that cyber operations, both in isolation from and in conjunction with other military operations, are now a regular part of armed conflict, and analysis of the law surrounding such operations is a valuable endeavor.

a. Armed Attack

The lack of clarity with respect to the definition of an armed attack previously discussed in Chapter 1 is only more pronounced with respect to cyber operations. This is confirmed by the Tallinn Manual experts who "noted that the law is unclear as to the precise point at which the effects of a cyber operation qualify as an armed attack."[249] Those experts concluded that "a cyber operation that seriously injures or kills a number of persons or that causes significant damage to, or destruction of, property would satisfy the scale and effects requirement."[250]

The Tallinn position reflected an earlier statement in a paper published by the U.S. Department of Defense Office of General Counsel (DoD OGC). In describing what scale and effects of cyber operations might amount to an armed attack, the paper (the "DoD Assessment") stated,

> if a coordinated computer network attack shuts down a nation's air traffic control system along with its banking and financial systems and public utilities, and opens the floodgates of several dams resulting in general flooding that causes widespread civilian deaths and property damage, it may well be that no one would challenge the victim nation if it concluded that it was a victim of an armed attack, or of an act equivalent to an armed attack.[251]

---

247. David A. Fulghum & Douglas Barrie, *Israel Used Electronic Attack in Air Strike Against Syria Syrian Mystery Target*, ABC NEWS, https://abcnews.go.com/Technology/story?id=3702807&page=1(last visited May 3, 2018); Joseph Trevithick, *Israel Details Long Secret Raid on Syrian Nuclear Reactor, Says It's Willing to Do It Again*, THE WARZONE, http://www.thedrive.com/the-war-zone/19492/israel-details-long-secret-raid-on-syrian-nuclear-reactor-says-its-willing-to-do-it-again (last visited May 3, 2018).

248. David J. Smith, *Russian Cyber Strategy and the War Against Georgia*, ATLANTIC COUNCIL: NATOSOURCE (Jan. 17, 2014), http://www.atlanticcouncil.org/blogs/natosource/russian-cyber-policy-and-the-war-against-georgia.

249. TALLINN 2.0, *supra*, note 181, at 341.

250. *Id.*

251. DEP'T OF DEF. OFF. OF GEN. COUNS., AN ASSESSMENT OF INTERNATIONAL LEGAL ISSUES IN INFORMATION OPERATIONS 18 (1999), http://www.au.af.mil/au/awc/awcgate/dod-io-legal/dod-io-legal.pdf [hereinafter DoD OGC Assessment].

While the sweeping breadth of the DoD OGC statement is perhaps not extremely helpful as a standard, it at least recognizes that a cyber operation alone could constitute an armed attack.

Two cyber operations potentially might be considered armed attacks. The first is the destruction of almost 1,000 centrifuges in an Iranian nuclear facility by the STUXNET malware.[252] Though no official government statements characterize it as an armed attack, some of the Tallinn Manual experts thought it might rise to that level.[253] The second potential cyber "armed attack" is the cyber operation against Saudi Aramco that has been attributed to Iran. The attack resulted in the destruction of around 30,000 computer systems and significantly degraded the state company's ability to operate.[254]

While the characterization of these two attacks is still undecided because no State has made a definitive statement on the subject, the operations provide some characteristics of what might approach the level of scale and effects necessary to trigger the right of self-defense under the *jus ad bellum*.

b. Use of Force

It seems clear that a cyber operation may amount to a use of force under the *jus ad bellum* even if conducted in isolation. As stated in the DoD Law of War Manual, "[c]yber operations may in certain circumstances constitute uses of force within the meaning of Article 2(4) of the Charter of the United Nations and customary international law."[255] The Tallinn Manual agrees. Rule 68 states that "[a] cyber operation that constitutes a threat or use of force against the territorial integrity or political independence of any State, or that is in any other manner inconsistent with the purposes of the United Nations, is unlawful."[256]

Though there appears to be general consensus on the point that a cyber operation can amount to a use of force, there is not universal agreement on what constitutes a cyber use of force. For example, rule 69 of the Tallinn Manual acknowledges that "[t]here is no authoritative definition of, or criteria for, 'threat' or 'use of force.'"[257] Although there is no authoritative definition, the rule points to a "scale and effects" analysis, including factors such as severity, immediacy, directness, invasiveness, measurability of effects, military character, state involvement, and presumptive legality.[258]

The DoD Law of War Manual adopts a similar approach, arguing that "if cyber operations cause effects that, if caused by traditional physical means, would be regarded as a use of force under *jus ad bellum*, then such cyber operations

---

252. Kim Zetter, *An Unprecedented Look at Stuxnet, the World's First Digital Weapon*, WIRED: SECURITY (Nov. 3, 2014, 6:30 AM), https://www.wired.com/2014/11/countdown-to-zero-day-stuxnet/.
253. TALLINN 2.0, *supra*, note 181, at 342.
254. Jose Pagliery, *The Inside Story of the Biggest Hack in History*, CNN MONEY: CYBER-SAFE (Aug. 5, 2015, 2:31 PM), http://money.cnn.com/2015/08/05/technology/aramco-hack/index.html.
255. DoD LAW OF WAR MANUAL, *supra*, note 2, para. 16.1.1.
256. TALLINN 2.0, *supra*, note 181, at 329.
257. *Id.* at 331.
258. *Id.* at 333–36.

would likely also be regarded as a use of force."[259] The DoD Law of War Manual also provides examples of cyber operations that would constitute a use of force under the *jus ad bellum*—"cyber operations that: (1) trigger a nuclear plant meltdown; (2) open a dam above a populated area, causing destruction; or (3) disable air traffic control services, resulting in airplane crashes."[260]

c. Prohibited Intervention

The vast majority of current cyber operations occur below the "use of force" threshold. This makes the doctrine of prohibited intervention all the more important with respect to cyber activities. As announced by the International Court of Justice (ICJ) in the *Nicaragua* case, States are precluded from taking actions that are coercive or dictatorial with respect to "the choice of a political, economic, social and cultural system, and the formulation of foreign policy."[261] The term often used to describe this "political, economic, social and cultural system, and the formulation of foreign policy" is *domaine réservé*.

The Tallinn Manual experts determined that the crux of prohibited intervention means "[a] State may not intervene, including by cyber means, in the internal or external affairs of another State"[262] and argued that "the matter most clearly within a State's *domaine réservé* appears to be the choice of both the political system and its organization, as these issues lie at the heart of sovereignty."[263] Therefore, actions targeting the political system, its organization, or other things clearly understood to be in a State's *domaine réservé* would violate international law.

As well as affecting the *domaine réservé*, the actions by the intervening State must be coercive in nature to amount to a legally prohibited intervention. With respect to this element of coercion, a majority of the Tallinn Manual experts thought "the coercive effort must be designed to influence outcomes in, or conduct with respect to, a matter reserved to a target State."[264]

An example of a potential prohibited coercive intervention would be the Russian hacks into the election systems of various Western nations, including the United States. From June through October of 2016, the Russians hacked into state election systems in at least 21 U.S. states. Hacking into the actual election systems to have the capability to either change the result of the election, or to cast doubt on the veracity of the election system, is likely a prohibited intervention. Again, no affirmative statement by a State has clearly identified a cyber intervention, but President Obama did call Russian President Putin in October of 2016 and warn him to stay out of the U.S. election systems.[265] The 2018

---

259. DoD Law of War Manual, *supra*, note 2, para. 16.3.1.
260. *Id.*
261. Military and Paramilitary Activities in and Against Nicaragua (Nic. v. U.S.), Judgment, 1986 I.C.J. Rep. 14, ¶ 205 (June 27).
262. Tallinn 2.0, *supra*, note 181, at 312.
263. *Id.* at 315.
264. *Id.* at 318.
265. William Arkin et al, *What Obama Said to Putin on the Red Phone About the Election Hack*, NBC News (Dec. 19, 2016, 4:30 PM), https://www.nbcnews.com/news/us-news/what-obama-said-

indictment of 13 Russians and three Russian companies in the U.S. "Mueller Investigation" may also provide some insight into how a domestic statement on the law can provide clarity as to what is included in the *domaine réservé*.[266]

d. Sovereignty

The most controversial question concerning cyber operation currently relates to how States consider sovereignty with respect to cyber operations and international law. Sovereignty is obviously a foundational principle that undergirds much of existing international law. The controversial question, on which well-informed and extremely intelligent international lawyers differ, is whether a violation of sovereignty by cyber means is a violation of international law and an unlawful act under the doctrine of state responsibility.

Sovereignty is a fundamental principle of international law and is considered a "basic constitutional doctrine of the law of nations. . . [involving] the collection of rights held by a State, first in its capacity as the entity entitled to exercise control over its territory and second in its capacity to act on the international plane, representing that territory and its people."[267] The ICJ in its *Corfu Channel* decision held that "[b]y sovereignty, we understand the whole body of rights and attributes which a State possesses in its territory, to the exclusion of all other States, and also in its relation with other States."[268]

The Tallinn Manual reads these provisions to create the following rule that, if violated, is an unlawful act: "[I]t is a violation of territorial sovereignty for an organ of a State, or others whose conduct may be attributed to the State, to conduct cyber operations while physically present on another State's territory against that State or entities or persons located there."[269] An alternate view is that "sovereignty is a baseline principle of the Westphalian international order undergirding binding norms such as the prohibition against the use of force in Article 2(4) of the UN Charter, or the customary international law rule of non-intervention, which States have assented to as an exercise of their sovereignty."[270] This "sovereignty as a principle" approach relies on the decision of the Permanent Court of International Justice (PCIJ) in the *Lotus* case which describes international law as a fundamentally permissive system and then states that "[r]estrictions upon the independence of States cannot therefore be presumed."[271] Therefore, unless there exists a conventional or customary norm prohibiting cyber operations below the level of a prohibited coercive intervention on the territory of another State, no restriction can be presumed.

---

putin-red-phone-about-election-hack-n697116.
 266. United States v. Internet Research Agency, L.L.C. (D.D.C. filed Feb. 16, 2018), https://www.justice.gov/file/1035477/download.
 267. JAMES CRAWFORD, BROWNLIE'S PRINCIPLES OF PUBLIC INTERNATIONAL LAW 447 (8th ed. 2012).
 268. Corfu Channel (U.K. v. Alb.), 1949 I.C.J. Rep. 4, 43 (Apr. 9) (separate opinion by Alvarez, J.).
 269. TALLINN 2.0, *supra*, note 181, at 19.
 270. Gary Corn, *Tallinn Manual 2.0—Advancing the Conversation*, JUSTSECURITY.ORG (Feb. 15, 2017), https://www.justsecurity.org/37812/tallinn-manual-2-0-advancing-conversation/.
 271. S.S. *Lotus* (Fr. v. Turk.), Judgment, 1927 P.C.I.J. (ser. A) No. 10, at 18 (Sept. 7).

A third view is that found in the 1999 DoD Assessment. The Assessment compares the different treatment of sovereignty across the air, sea, land, and space domains and then argues that "[a]n unauthorized electronic intrusion into another nation's computer systems may very well end up being regarded as a violation of the victim's sovereignty. It may even be regarded as equivalent to a physical trespass into a nation's territory, but such issues have yet to be addressed in the international community."[272]

In other words, sovereignty is a principle, subject to adjustment in interstate application, depending on the domain and the practical imperatives of States. It appears, based on State practice, that States are applying sovereignty with respect to cyber activities in a way that does not preclude cyber activities on the infrastructure and territory of another State, to include actions taken by one State that do not impinge on the inherently governmental functions of another State, unless those cyber activities rise to the level of a prohibited intervention. Where this will end up is unclear, but the discussion is of major importance given the transnational nature of cyber operations.

4. Jus in Bello

In addition to the *jus ad bellum*, it is the position of the United States that conduct of cyber operations in an armed conflict is governed by international law and the *jus in bello*, or LOAC, in particular.[273] The UN GGE was not able to come to agreement on this issue, but the Tallinn Manual experts had no trouble stating that "[c]yber operations executed in the context of an armed conflict are subject to the law of armed conflict."[274]

As with the *jus ad bellum*, the details of the application of the LOAC are the topic of important discussion. What cyber actions qualify as an attack, who can conduct cyber operations, what separates civilian from military objectives, and how to apply the doctrine of neutrality are all issues that require some thoughtful analysis with respect to cyber operations. In fact, the first Tallinn Manual[275] was written to specifically address these issues. The following paragraphs will provide an introduction to some of the issues presented by "cyber warfare," and to some of the answers.

a. LOAC General Principles

The general principles of the LOAC covered in Chapter 2 certainly apply to cyber operations. However, only the principles of distinction and proportionality will be dealt with here, as they seem to cause the most controversy.

---

272. DoD OGC Assessment, *supra*, note 251, at 19.
273. Koh, *supra*, note 243, at 4.
274. TALLINN 2.0, *supra*, note 181, at 375.
275. *See generally*, TALLINN MANUAL 1.0 ON THE INTERNATIONAL LAW APPLICABLE TO CYBER OPERATIONS (Michael N. Schmitt ed., 1st ed., 2013).

i. Distinction

The principle of distinction is one of the fundamental principles of the LOAC, and is codified in Article 48 of AP I. However, cyber operations cover such a vast array of options along the spectrum of "military operations" that it is unclear exactly which cyber operations are governed by the principle of distinction. For example, the Tallinn Manual argues that "[c]ertain operations directed against the civilian population are lawful. For instance, psychological operations such as dropping leaflets or making propaganda broadcasts are not prohibited even if civilians are the intended audience."[276] Another example would be a distributed denial of service, or DDoS, operation that denies civilians access to a website. Though inconvenient, a DDoS operation would not violate the principle of distinction. In trying to define where distinction does and does not apply to cyber operations, the Tallinn Manual ultimately concludes that "the practical application of the principle of distinction in the cyber context is dependent in great part on the position one takes with regard to the definition of 'cyber attack.'"[277]

"Attack" is defined in Article 49 of AP I as "acts of violence against the adversary, whether in offence or defence."[278] As will be discussed below, the cyber operations that are considered attacks have to comply not only with the principle of distinction, but also the other LOAC principles. The DoD Law of War Manual agrees with this proposition: "If a cyber operation constitutes an attack, then the law of war rules on conducting attacks must be applied to those cyber operations. For example, cyber operations must comport with the requirements of distinction and proportionality."[279]

With kinetic weapons, determining what is an "act of violence" seems fairly easy to discern. However, cyber attacks often lack the characteristic of heat, blast, and fragmentation that are traditionally equated with military violence. In answering this quandary, rule 92 of the Tallinn Manual states, "A cyber attack is a cyber operation, whether offensive or defensive, that is reasonably expected to cause injury or death to persons or damage or destruction to objects."[280] In other words, for a military cyber operation in armed conflict to be governed by the principle of distinction (and the other LOAC principles), it must be reasonably expected to cause injury or death to persons or damage or destruction to objects. Cyber operations that do not have these effects are not strictly subject to the distinction principle as a matter of law.

The principle of distinction also incorporates the obligation for combatants to distinguish themselves from the civilian population when conducting attacks. Yet, in the vast majority of cyber operations, the actual individual conducting the operation is far away and likely not even in the operational theater. Does distinction apply to the individual, the cyber tool, or both? Is masking a

---

276. TALLINN 2.0, *supra*, note 181, at 421.
277. *Id.* at 422.
278. AP I, *supra*, note 33, art. 49.
279. DoD LAW OF WAR MANUAL, *supra*, note 2, para. 16.5.1.
280. TALLINN 2.0, *supra*, note 181, at 415.

cyber exploit as coming from a civilian IP address good camouflage, or illegal perfidy?

Further, many cyber operations require civilian expertise rather than what uniformed personnel have been trained to do. Determining when such a civilian is directly participating in hostilities when engaged in cyber operations directed against an enemy in an armed conflict is an added difficulty.[281] Like other weapons, cyber tools require designers, programmers, and purchasers, as well as "shooters." None of this is new. But the nature of cyber tools, including their multiple purposes (intelligence gathering that may also do damage), adds a level of complexity that is different than most other weapons systems.

ii. Proportionality

Applying the principle of proportionality is also a topic of some debate in the cyber world. Both the Tallinn Manual[282] and the DoD Law of War Manual[283] agree that cyber operations must comply with proportionality, but they take different approaches to how proportionality might be applied in practice. For example, cyber operations have the potential to have cascading effects or cause remote harms. The DoD Manual is careful to say that "[i]n assessing incidental injury or damage during cyber operations, it may be important to consider that remote harms and lesser forms of harm, such as mere inconveniences or temporary disruptions, need not be considered in assessing whether an attack is prohibited by the principle of proportionality."[284]

In contrast, the Tallinn Manual argues that "indirect effects of a cyber attack comprise 'the delayed and/or displaced second-, third-, and higher-order consequences of action, created through intermediate events or mechanisms'. The collateral damage considered in the proportionality calculation includes any indirect effects that should be expected by those individuals planning, approving, or executing a cyber attack."[285] While these two approaches may end up at the same determination with respect to the proportionality analysis, the focus on attenuation (the DoD Law of War Manual approach) versus expectation (the Tallinn Manual approach) could also lead to different conclusions.

One of the potential indirect effects of cyber attacks that some have argued commanders must consider is the potential for reengineering and reuse of the cyber weapon employed in the attack. When a commander shoots or launches a kinetic weapon (e.g., a bullet or an artillery shell), nothing remains that is usable (assuming the weapon explodes and is not a dud). That is not true with cyber weapons. In fact, after the STUXNET malware discussed above was found on computer systems worldwide, enterprising individuals immediately began to reengineer the malware in order to figure out what made it work, and to see if they could reuse it. In fact, you can see people dissecting STUXNET

---

281. DoD Manual, *supra,* note 2, para. 16.5.5.
282. Tallinn 2.0, *supra,* note 181, at 470.
283. DoD Manual, *supra,* note 2, para. 16.5.1.1.
284. *Id.*
285. Tallinn 2.0, *supra,* note 181, at 472.

and reengineering it on YouTube. So, the question is whether a commander must consider the potential reuse of a cyber tool in her proportionality analysis. It seems clear, however, that both the Tallinn Manual view and the DoD view would consider these potential harms to be too speculative to be legally required to be considered as part of the proportionality analysis.

b. Precautions in the Attack

Cyber operations must comply with the principle of precautions in attack (discussed in Chapter 2), just as any other attack would. It is important, however, to recall the earlier discussion concerning "attacks." For the precautions to apply to cyber operations, the cyber operation must meet the definition of an attack. If it does, all the standard precautions apply, but if not, the "constant care" requirement described below would still apply.

i. Constant Care

While many cyber operations might not rise to the level of an "attack," it is important to note that Article 57(1) of AP I requires "constant care" in considering deleterious effects on civilians in all military operations, and not just those that qualify as an attack. While this provision does not act as a prohibition, it is nevertheless an important military consideration and an important baseline obligation in terms of civilian protection. As the Tallinn Manual states,

> The law admits of no situation in which, or time when, individuals involved in the planning and execution process may ignore the effects of their operations on civilians or civilian objects. In the cyber context, this requires situational awareness at all times, not merely during the preparatory stage of an operation.[286]

ii. Military Objective

Cyber capabilities significantly expand the list of potential means to attack military objectives. Prior to cyber capabilities, for example, if a commander wanted to cut off power to a command and control center, a bomb was basically the only option to do that, along with its potentially adverse physical impact on the civilian population and those civilians. Cyber operations open new and more discriminate options to the commander to accomplish the same goal, but with lower risk of collateral damage (e.g., physical injury to civilians or damage or loss of civilian property.)

Some have made the argument that because cyber tools have the potential to be more exacting and proportional, there may be a legal obligation to use them in certain circumstances. The United States flatly rejects this view. The DoD Law of War Manual states, "[a]s with other precautions, the decision of which weapon to use will be subject to many practical considerations, including

---

286. *Id.* at 477.

effectiveness, cost, and "fragility," i.e., the possibility that once used an adversary may be able to devise defenses that will render a cyber tool ineffective in the future."[287] In other words, the potential reduction in collateral damage is certainly a consideration with respect to the decision to use or not use cyber capabilities to launch an attack, but it is not the only consideration.

iii. Indiscriminate Attacks

The increased target set presented by cyber tools doesn't come without challenges, one being the potential effects of the attack. When a commander launches a missile or shoots a weapon, she is pretty confident what the "blast radius" of that weapon will be. For example, a hellfire missile has a particular radius that is within its lethal blast range. The determination of the lethal blast range associated with a weapon is subject to modification based on the surrounding situation, such as whether there are buildings in the targeted area and the materials those buildings are made of, but it is still possible to put an outer limit on the effects of the weapon. This is not necessarily so with cyber tools.

Cyber tools, even when very carefully crafted, can do unexpected things. And something like a worm, which is designed to propagate widely, will be found on large numbers of computers even if its "payload" doesn't trigger in all of them. For example, STUXNET only triggered its payload (that we know of) in the nuclear facility in Iran. However, the software was found on tens of thousands of computers in over 115 countries.

Assuming the definition of "attack" discussed above, the impacts of a malware such as STUXNET may not be governed by the LOAC prohibition against indiscriminate attacks. However, to the extent that it is (or could be) an attack, the prohibition applies.

c. Precautions Against the Effects of Attacks

The obligation of a defender to take precautions against the effects of attacks, as articulated, for example, in Article 58 of AP I, is understudied in modern armed conflict and undervalued as a means of providing meaningful protection to civilians. The obligation is in two parts, the first being the obligation to segregate military operations and objectives from the civilian population, and the second being the obligation to provide protection to civilians where segregation is not possible. As with many of the precautions in attack, the precautions against the effects of attacks are limited to doing that which is "feasible."

Emerging technologies in general, and cyber capabilities in particular, provide increased ability to both segregate and protect the civilian population and, therefore, should increase the discussion of what precautions are feasible.[288] For example, States seeking to defend themselves could use cyber capabilities to track civilian movements and even publish these movements to potential

---

287. DoD Law of War Manual, *supra*, note 2, para. 16.5.3.1.
288. Eric Talbot Jensen, *The Future of the Law of Armed Conflict: Ostriches, Butterflies, and Nanobots*, 35 Mich. J. of Int'l L. 253, 314–15 (2014).

attackers so that they can conduct their attacks in a manner that avoids adverse effects on civilians. Such a course of action would be a very feasible method of segregating the civilian population from military objectives.

Though failure to take feasible precautions in the attack has been the gravamen of many law of war prosecutions, failure to take feasible precautions against the effects of attacks has never been treated with such severity. Using cyber capabilities to elucidate the meaning of what is "feasible" should allow for a more meaningful enforcement of AP I, Article 58's standard.

d. Neutrality

The LOAC doctrine of neutrality is applicable only in an international armed conflict, but has significant impact on the conduct of cyber hostilities more generally. Unlike many other means and methods of war, the nature of the internet necessarily means that cyber communications of the parties to an armed conflict will travel through and reside on neutral States' cyber infrastructure. Though allowing infrastructure on neutral territory to be used by a party to a conflict would almost certainly amount to a breach of neutrality, the general consensus is that the transmission of communications on the internet through a neutral State's infrastructure does not amount to a violation of neutrality. The Tallinn Manual concludes that "[u]sing a public, internationally and openly accessible network such as the Internet for military purposes does not violate the law of neutrality. This is so even if it, or components thereof, is located in neutral territory."[289]

However, there are situations in which "[t]he use of communications infrastructure in neutral States may be implicated under the general rule that neutral territory may not serve as a base of operations for one belligerent against another. "[290] Thus, the Tallinn Manual is clear that "[t]he exercise of belligerent rights by cyber means directed against neutral cyber infrastructure is prohibited."[291] In this sense, "directed against" means "an operation intended to detrimentally affect neutral cyber infrastructure."[292] Equally, "[a] neutral State may not knowingly allow the exercise of belligerent rights by the parties to the conflict from cyber infrastructure located in its territory or under its exclusive control."[293]

Thus, if harmful cyber activities travel across the infrastructure of a neutral nation in the normal course of cyber transmission and in accordance with the normal packet allocation of web traffic, there is no violation of neutrality. However, if a belligerent State specifically uses neutral territory or if a neutral State knowingly allows its territory to be used, the doctrine of neutrality would be violated.

---

289. TALLINN 2.0, *supra*, note 181, at 556.
290. DoD LAW OF WAR MANUAL, *supra*, note 2, para. 16.4.1.
291. TALLINN 2.0, *supra*, note 181, at 555.
292. *Id.*
293. *Id.* at 558.

e. Non-State Actors

As alluded to above, one of the most challenging aspects of cyber operations is the pervasiveness of cyber capabilities and the devolution of State-level violence to non-state actors and even individuals. This is true both *ad bellum* and *in bello*.

With respect to the *jus in bello*, cyber hacktivists have already taken a direct part in armed hostilities, as in the case of Georgia discussed above. There is no doubt that this trend will continue. There is very little capacity to prevent or even stop ongoing actions by cyber "volunteers" who are participating in armed conflict. While direct targeting may be legal in many cases, it is often impractical, leaving the victim State to pursue historically ineffective criminal remedies. In response, some have argued for an enhanced application of the due diligence doctrine under the rules of State responsibility. Though there is little evidence that States are embracing such an enhanced version of the principle, the Tallinn Manual concluded that "[t]he principle of due diligence requires a State to take all measures that are feasible in the circumstances to put an end to cyber operations that affect a right of, and produce serious adverse consequences for, other States."[294] As non-state actors continue to take aggressive actions, particularly from States who are unable or unwilling to prevent those actions, it will be interesting to see how States respond.

f. Conclusion

Cyber operations are clearly going to be a mainstay of any armed conflict involving sufficiently modernized States. Both the *jus ad bellum* and the *jus in bello* are robust enough to deal with the vast majority of cyber issues currently contemplated. States will clarify what currently appear to be gaps in the application of the law through State practice. Particularly with respect to the LOAC, the world has not yet experienced an armed conflict between two cyber-capable, near peer adversaries. If that time comes, the LOAC will hopefully provide a sufficiently robust legal regime to constrain enemies and protect civilians.

V. Emerging Technologies

The development of modern technology is moving at a rate never before experienced in the history of mankind. This trend will likely continue, if not increase. And as then-Deputy Secretary of Defense William J. Lynn III once said, "Few weapons in the history of warfare, once created, have gone unused."[295] These advances in technology include increasing autonomous functions in weapon systems; the development and deployment of robotics; both internal and external, temporary and permanent human enhancement; the application of nano-

---

294. *Id.* at 43.
295. John D. Banusiewicz, *Lynn Outlines New Cybersecurity Effort*, U.S. DEPT. OF DEF. (June 16, 2011), http://archive.defense.gov/news/newsarticle.aspx?id=64349.

technology to a whole host of weapons and functions; the weaponization of virology and genetics with specific ties to an individual's or group's DNA; and the development of artificial intelligence.[296]

Some have raised the issue of whether the LOAC is responsive to the oncoming events or whether revisions need to be made. Opponents of this view argue that the Martens Clause[297] gives every country sufficient rights and responsibilities to ensure the law stays applicable in the face of emerging technologies. Under either view, it is important to contemplate what signaling role the LOAC can play in advance of the development of these weapons. In other words, can current LOAC standards act as a guide to States as they research and develop potential new weapons based on emerging technologies?

One way this signaling role might manifest itself is in a more widespread adoption by States of weapon reviews such as those mandated in AP I, Art. 36, discussed in Chapter 8. Such reviews will at least ensure compliance with existing law. Though there have been some calls for bans on some future weapons, the more historically sound view seems to be to take a cautious and deliberate approach to research and development, and to seek consensus among States through some process, such as the ongoing talks concerning autonomous weapons as part of the CCW process.[298]

Study Questions

1. Major Payne has located a cyber team operating from Iraqi territory. To date, it has launched some moderately successful operations hacking into U.S. military computers at bases in Saudi Arabia. No damage has been done, but it appears that the hackers are seeking to gain access to some non-secure commercial communications networks used by the U.S. military for sending administrative, medical, and logistical information to Department of Defense agencies in the United States supporting the U.S. forces in the Gulf.

    Major Payne's intelligence on the nature and location of the cyber operations is incomplete. The best information he has is that the signals from the cyber operations emanate from a laboratory at a university in Basra that, prior to the war, was cooperating with Western universities in marine biology research. It appears that the computer links developed for that research have now been adapted for cyber operations. He proposes to launch a cruise missile attack against the laboratory now, prior to the invasion, to ensure that the cyber team does not interfere with critical command and control during the invasion. Please comment on

---

296. *See generally*, Jensen, *supra*, note 288.
297. Go to Chapter 2 of this book for more information about the Martens Clause.
298. Hayley Evans, *Lethal Autonomous Weapons Systems at the First and Second U.N. GGE Meetings*, LAWFARE BLOG (Apr. 9, 2018, 9:00 AM), https://www.lawfareblog.com/lethal-autonomous-weapons-systems-first-and-second-un-gge-meetings.

the issues you see with this plan under the LOAC and other international law.
2. Assume Major Payne gets new intelligence that the cyber operation is being operated from an unmarked commercial aircraft in airspace just outside Iran's territorial sea. Major Payne wants the Commander to scramble a squadron of jets to shoot the aircraft down. Can the squadron do that under the LOAC? What if the aircraft ducks into Iranian airspace just as the squadron arrives? Can the squadron pursue the aircraft and shoot the aircraft down?
3. Major Payne says that an Indian commercial satellite in a geosynchronous orbit over Iraq and normally used for broadcasting television and other telecommunications has been "hijacked" by an enemy cyber team. The satellite is being used to provide real-time intelligence to the Iraqi Republican Guard about the location of U.S. forces in the Persian Gulf. Major Payne presents two options to neutralize the threat posed by the satellite. Please discuss the LOAC rules that you think might apply to each:
    a. Major Payne tells you that the U.S. Air Force can divert one of its military communications satellites to ram the Indian satellite and take it out of action. However, Ensign Newbee, who just graduated from the Naval Academy, where he took a short course on space law, says, "No Sir. You can't do that. That'll cause massive destruction, and the Outer Space Treaty bars weapons of mass destruction in space." How do you respond to Ensign Newbee, and how do you advise Major Payne?
    b. Major Payne also tells you that civilian experts working for Central Command can use cyber means to intercept the communications between the cyber team and the Indian satellite, and in Major Payne's words, he can "shut 'er down" (meaning that he can turn off the satellite temporarily). He also says that they can reverse the process once the invasion is over, and restore control over the satellite to its rightful owners. To turn off the satellite, however, Major Payne's cyber experts will need to route a signal through the headquarters of the Indian company that operates the satellite in order to mask who is conducting the operation. Any thoughts on LOAC rules that might apply?

13 WAR CRIMES

You are a Colonel in the U.S. Army and the Staff Judge Advocate for the 3rd Infantry Division, currently deployed to Baghdad, Iraq as part of Operation Iraqi Freedom. Sitting in the tactical operations center (TOC) late one afternoon, you are thinking that after the evening battlefield update briefing you may try to call home and talk to your spouse and children. The Chief of Staff abruptly interrupts your planning, yelling across the TOC, "Judge, go see the CG ASAP." The CG is the commanding general, Major General (MG) Smith. You began working with MG Smith about six months before the deployment. As is normally the case, he didn't pick you as the unit's head lawyer and you didn't pick him as a boss. You are a little uncertain as to where you currently stand with MG Smith. Back at your home station, Fort Stewart, Georgia. MG Smith told the entire staff that you and the legal office were "combat multipliers" because the Judge Advocates working for you were helping commanders deal with problem soldiers by administering non-judicial punishment, initiating administrative separation proceedings for significant misconduct, and prosecuting the offending soldiers at courts-martial. But since deploying to Iraq, MG Smith has acted as though legal actions are more a distraction than helping enable the unit to accomplish its mission.

As you walk into MG Smith's office, it's clear he is not in a good mood. "Judge, let me tell you about the day I planned to have and then the day I actually had. We have to 'secure and stabilize' a 50 mile wide ring surrounding Baghdad. Doctrinally, we don't have anywhere close to the number of soldiers and vehicles to accomplish that mission. So I have to know where and what our main effort should be and where we can accept risk. I had a day of key leader engagements scheduled around our area of responsibility. That plan didn't survive my first meeting. The 1st Brigade Commander told me that earlier this morning his partner Iraqi Army Brigade Commander told him that an Iraqi Army unit had been on patrol out east near the Iraqi town of Gassan and they found a village with over 20 people, including children, shot dead in the street. The Iraqi Army claims that the Ministry of Interior Police Commandos were responsible for the killings.

As soon as I left 1st Brigade, the Division Chaplain pulls me aside. He had several soldiers tell him that last week the 2nd Brigade Commander gave a pep talk before a mission during which he told the unit to kill all military-aged males on the objective. And during the mission, the soldiers said that several unarmed Iraqis were killed.

From there, the Corps Commander called me about the New York Times and "60 Minutes" stories about the Abu Ghraib prison scandal. Are you tracking this? Some U.S. Army Military Police unit was beating detainees, stripping them naked, putting women's underwear on them, walking them on dog leashes, you name it. I wouldn't believe it but they actually took pictures of what they were doing. The Corps Commander thinks we will have riots here if the pictures end up online. And he wants a review of our detention practices.

Next up was the Provost Marshall (PM). He told me that a detainee stabbed one of our military police guards, that we may have had a soldier break into an Iraqi home and rape a teenage girl, and last but not least was that a couple of civilian contractors claim that force protection concerns led them to drive the wrong way down a busy street, scaring the hell out of the villagers, plow into a local fruit stand, and take off without stopping. The PM was talking about joint U.S. and Iraqi investigations, whether we needed to contact the Federal Bureau of Investigation and the differences between U.S. military and federal court and also the Iraqi criminal system.

I need you to get me up to speed on what is happening, what we are required to do, where we have options, and what they are.

I. Introduction to War Crimes

It is important at the outset to highlight, and dispel, flawed conceptions about the relationship between the law and war as applied to both nations and the individuals participating in armed conflict. The concept of codifying and punishing war crimes can seem counterintuitive. We are all familiar with the phrase, "all's fair in love and war."[1] That expression suggests that when States resort to war, we throw out all the rules. Additionally, misinformed claims that fighting terrorism is somehow a new type of conflict[2] and one to which the LOAC either doesn't or shouldn't apply only reinforce this fundamental misunderstanding.

In terms of the individuals engaging in hostilities, there is also a tendency to conflate the tasks the military performs with the military's purpose and the role of combatant immunity. The purpose of the U.S. armed forces is to integrate with "other instruments of national power to advance and defend US values,

---

1. The expression originated from a sixteenth century "romantic intrigue" novel. In 1578, British author John Lyly wrote that "[t]he rules of fair play do not apply in love and war" in EUPHUES: THE ANATOMY OF WIT.

2. Terrorism traces back to at least 70 AD, where the Sicarii, a radical Jewish group opposed to Roman occupation of Judea, conducted an organized assassination campaign in which they would wear civilian clothes, blend in with the crowd, stab Roman officials at public events, then slip back into the crowd. The word "terrorism" dates to the eighteenth century French Revolution.

interests, and objectives."[3] To accomplish that purpose, the military engages in a wide range of activities or tasks, including training to kill people and destroy things. Where soldiers perform those tasks in the service of the State and in accordance with the LOAC, they enjoy combatant immunity. While the LOAC implicitly recognizes the inevitability of some amount of death and destruction in armed conflict, it nonetheless restrains conduct during war. Ultimately, the most efficient way for a military to achieve its mission in the shortest amount of time and using the least resources is by following, not violating, the LOAC.

A. Why Follow the LOAC?

Why even have a war crimes regime that punishes battlefield misconduct? Over time, combatants themselves recognize there are benefits in regulating their own battlefield conduct. In addition to legal requirements, there are a number of pragmatic reasons to implement and enforce the LOAC.

Most rules of humanitarian law reflect good military practice, and adherence by armed forces to those rules is likely to reinforce discipline and good order within the forces concerned. Similarly, the LOAC reinforces military effectiveness. "[V]arious military doctrines, such as accuracy of targeting, concentration of effort, maximization of military advantage, conservation of resources, avoidance of excessive collateral damage, and economy of force" are fully consistent with the LOAC.[4, 5] There are both practical and strategic offshoots of these points.

In a practical sense, at some point the war will be over and the conquering force might be taking or re-taking possession of lands and buildings, and control of people. If the conquering force has laid waste to the land and people, there may be nothing left to occupy. Similarly, militaries are uniquely hierarchical organizations where values like respect for authority and obedience to an established chain of command are at the heart of the military ethic. If soldiers are allowed to engage in completely lawless killing and destruction, and devolve into nothing more than an armed mob, respect for authority breaks down and there is little to prevent soldiers from turning against their own leaders.

Strategically, LOAC compliance helps maintain public support and political legitimacy. This point may be of even greater significance in counter-insurgency operations where the support of the local population is hugely important.[6]

---

3. DEP'T OF DEFENSE JOINT PUBLICATION 1 DOCTRINE FOR THE ARMED FORCES OF THE UNITED STATES 1-14 (25 Mar. 2013 incorporating Change 1 12 Jul. 2017).

4. DoD LOWM at 18.2.1. As a 1976 Air Force Pamphlet stated, "[u]se of excessive force is not only costly and highly inefficient—and to be avoided for those reasons—it may also be a waste of scare resources." *Id.* at fn 15.

5. *Id.* at fn 14 (citing Christopher Greenwood, *Historical Development and Legal Basis*, in Dieter Fleck, THE HANDBOOK OF HUMANITARIAN LAW IN ARMED CONFLICTS 33 (1999)).

6. *Id* at 18.2.3.

A related point is the desire for reciprocal LOAC compliance. If an army wants its forces treated well by the enemy, then it is incumbent on that army to treat enemy forces under its control with a basic level of protection. Similarly, if a State wants its enemies to surrender rather than fight to the last man, providing them an incentive to surrender rather than fight often hinges on how well they will be treated once they become prisoners. Additionally, [v]iolation of the LOAC committed by one side may encourage third parties to support the opposing side.

Additionally, supporting the existence of the LOAC and its enforcement helps mitigate the moral injury to members of the armed forces. As a former U.S. Army officer wrote of his experience as a platoon leader during the Vietnam war:

> I was making them kill, forcing them to commit the most uncivilized of acts, but at the same time I had to keep them civilized...War gives the appearance of condoning almost everything, but men must live with their actions for a long time afterwards.... War is, at its very core, the absence of order; and the absence of order leads very easily to the absence of morality.[7]

Complying with the LOAC is "necessary to diminish the corrosive effect of mortal combat on the participants."[8] Most soldiers will return from war and will have the rest of their lives to live and reflect on how they conducted themselves in battle.[9] If they hope to return to some sense of a normal life after war, they must maintain a sense of their moral agency and a belief they behaved appropriately in battle. Following the rules, the LOAC, can play an important role. For these and other pragmatic and moral reasons, stemming from the beginning of the twenty-first century, a war crimes regime which limits and governs the conduct of hostilities is a robust and necessary component of modern warfare.

---

7. James R. McDonough, PLATOON LEADER: A MEMOIR OF COMMAND IN COMBAT, 78 (1985).

8. Telford Taylor, NUREMBERG AND VIETNAM: AN AMERICAN TRAGEDY (1970).

9. For an example of the moral consequences of armed conflict, consider U.S. Army paratrooper Staff Sergeant Tom Blakely, who parachuted into France as part of Operation Overlord, the Allied forces' invasion of Nazi-controlled Europe in World War II. Blakely's unit was behind enemy lines and ordered to seize and hold a bridge to prevent the German military from reinforcing its positions at Normandy beach. While in defensive positions, Blakely's platoon leader ordered each U.S. soldier to identify not a direction to fire, but a specific German soldier. Blakely, later a docent at the World War II Museum in New Orleans, said: "I picked one out. I picked him out, got a site, hand on the trigger, and pulled it. I could see when the bullet hit him. He jumped in the air, raises his arms above his head, and dropped his rifle and fell backwards." This engagement was fully in compliance with the LOAC but it nonetheless took a moral toll on Blakely. The German soldier he shot and killed haunted him: "He came to me from that day on every so often. . . . There was never any rhyme or reason when he came and when he left. Sometimes he would do that three or court times, sometimes he'd only do it once. But it was always something'. He was always there. And he come vividly in my mind often. And this is a case where the service member followed the LOAC. See CBS News, "A 'Living Artifact' of WWII Shares His Story", 26 May 2013, available at: www.cbsnews.com/news/a-living-artifact-ofwwii-shares-his-story/.

B. What Is a War Crime?

As a general proposition, a war crime is an act or omission that remains criminal even in the context of armed conflict. But as a former war crimes prosecutor wrote:

> What is a "war crime"? To say that it is a violation of the laws of war is true, but not very meaningful.
>
> War consists largely of acts that would be criminal if performed in time of peace—killing, wounding, kidnapping, destroying or carrying off other people's property. Such conduct is not regarded as criminal if it takes place in the course of war, because the state of war lays a blanket of immunity over the warriors. . .
>
> But the area of immunity is not unlimited, and its boundaries are marked by the laws of war. Unless the conduct in question falls within those boundaries, it does not lose the criminal character it would have should it occur in peaceful circumstances. In a literal sense, therefore, the expression, "war crime" is a misnomer, for it means an act that remains criminal even though committed in the course of war, because it lies outside the area of immunity prescribed by the laws of war.[10]

The different understandings as to the meaning of the term "war crimes" depend on the context in which the term is being considered. First, there are different sources of law, including LOAC, domestic law, and the statutes of international criminal tribunals and courts. Depending on which source of law is being referred to, there may also be different understandings as to which violations constitute a war crime.[11] For example, one view is that any violation of the LOAC is considered a war crime,[12] while another is that minor violations would be excluded.[13]

Statutes and treaties defining war crimes are typically limited to serious violations of the laws and customs applicable in armed conflicts.[14] This "seriousness" component suggests that while any violation may technically be a war crime, prosecution and punishment of war criminals focuses on certain types of crimes. One point on which there is no disagreement is that war crimes are not limited to military personnel. Anyone, civilian or military, can commit a war crime. History and experience have shown this to be true.

The International Committee of the Red Cross separates war crimes into two categories. The first category is crimes that endanger protected persons or

---

10. Taylor, *supra*, note 8 at 19-20.
11. The easiest way to minimize confusion is to qualify the term "war crimes." For example, war crimes as defined by the Rome Statute of the International Criminal Court, or as defined by 18 U.S.C. 2441, or grave breaches of the 1949 Geneva Conventions.
12. *See* FM 27-10, Department of the Army Field Manual, The Law of Land Warfare, para 499, July 1956 (stating that "[e]very violation of the law of war is a war crime.").
13. DoD LOWM, *supra*, note, 4 at 18.9.5.2. The DoD Law of War Manual uses the example of military medical personnel wearing an armlet with the Red Cross or Crescent during an international armed conflict. Under the Geneva Conventions, the armlet is to be worn on the right arm, thus wearing it on the left arm would constitute a LOAC violation. But it is not reasonable to consider such a violation as a war crime.
14. *See, e.g.*, ICC, ICTY, ICTR definitions.

protected objects.[15] This includes crimes involving death, injury, destruction or unlawful taking of property.[16] The second broad category is crimes that breach important values. These include such things as abusing dead bodies and subjecting persons to humiliating treatment.[17]

Another important aspect of war crimes is that they include an individual responsibility component. While combatants are immune for their warlike acts when those acts were done in the service of the State, combatant immunity has its limits. Combatants are still moral agents; when their conduct, even in the service of the State, breaches important values or endangers protected persons or property, combatants can be held individually accountable as war criminals. Finally, there must be a nexus or connection between the act and an armed conflict. If no nexus exists, the act may certainly be a crime just not a war crime.

C. Historical Background

Regulation of battlefield conduct is not a new phenomenon. Throughout history, combatants developed rules and codes regulating the conduct of their forces, and placing limits on the use of certain weapons. One such example is the rules of chivalry, the warrior's code of ethical behavior that is both an important precursor to the modern LOAC but also a medium for contemporary compliance.[18] Some of these codes were generally accepted customs.

One of the first recorded war crimes trials was the trial of Peter von Hagenbach in 1474. Von Hagenbach was the appointed ruler of the town of Breisach, Austria. He was tried before a tribunal of 28 judges from the allied states of the Holy Roman Empire on charges of murder, rape, perjury, and other crimes against the "Laws of God." Von Hagenbach was convicted for failing to perform his duty as a knight to prevent these crimes from being committed by his soldiers, and sentenced to death.[19]

Other codes were written, one of the first dates is from the American Civil War in the 19th Century. Dr. Francis Lieber's *Instructions for the Government of Armies of the United States in the Field* inspired the contemporary treaty regulation of battlefield conduct. Among other things, the Lieber Code defined the concepts of military jurisdiction, military necessity, and retaliation. The Code

---

15. *See* Rule 156, Definition of War Crimes, Customary IHL, *available at* http://www.icrc.org/customary-ihl/eng/docs/v1_rul_rule156.
16. *Id.*
17. *Id.*
18. *See* DoD LOWM, *supra*, note 4 at 2.6.1 fn 107 (*citing* UNITED KINGDOM WAR OFFICE, MANUAL OF MILITARY LAW, CHAPTER XIV, THE LAWS AND USAGES OF WAR ON LAND, 234 (¶3) (1914) ("The development of the laws and usages of war is determined by three principles.... And there is, thirdly, the principle of chivalry, which demands a certain amount of fairness in offence and defence, and a certain mutual respect between the opposing forces.").
19. *See* Goerg Schwarzenberger, INTERNATIONAL LAW AS APPLIED BY INTERNATIONAL COURTS AND TRIBUNALS: THE LAW OF ARMED CONFLICT v. 2 462-466 (1968).

also created a category of protected persons and protected property. Under the Lieber Code:

> Military necessity, as understood by modern civilized nations, consists in the necessity of those measures which are indispensable for securing the ends of the war, and which are lawful according to the modern law and usages of war.
>
> Military necessity admits of all direct destruction of life or limb of armed enemies, and of other persons whose destruction is incidentally unavoidable in the armed contests of the war; it allows of the capturing of every armed enemy, and every enemy of importance to the hostile government, or of peculiar danger to the captor; it allows of all destruction of property, and obstruction of the ways and channels of traffic, travel, or communication, and of all withholding of sustenance or means of life from the enemy;....
>
> Military necessity does not admit of cruelty—that is, the infliction of suffering for the sake of suffering or for revenge, nor of maiming or wounding except in fight, nor of torture to extort confessions. It does not admit of the use of poison in any way, nor of the wanton devastation of a district. It admits of deception, but disclaims acts of perfidy; and, in general, military necessity does not include any act of hostility which makes the return to peace unnecessarily difficult.[20]

Necessity imposes express limits on justified wartime conduct and provides a legal basis for the prosecution of battlefield misconduct. As a reflection of customary norms, the Lieber Code served as the legal basis for the prosecution of Confederate captives, such as Captain Henry Wirtz, the commander of the infamous Sumter Prisoner of War Camp near Andersonville, Georgia.[21]

Historically, Nation states punished their own soldiers for misconduct in war, although these proceedings were not necessarily characterized as war crimes prosecutions. One such example involved the court-martial of Army Brigadier General Jacob A. Smith, commander of U.S. forces in the Philippines during the Philippine insurrection in 1901. During the insurrection, Brigadier General Smith ordered his subordinate officer, Major L.W.T. Waller, as follows: "I want no prisoners and I wish you to kill and burn. The more you kill and burn, the more you will please me, and the interior of Samar must be made a howling wilderness." Brigadier General Smith was convicted of conduct prejudicial to the good order and discipline of the military for issuing this order and for the killings that followed.[22]

---

20. *See* Francis Lieber, GENERAL ORDER NO. 100, INSTRUCTIONS FOR THE GOVERNMENT OF ARMIES OF THE UNITED STATES IN THE FIELD (Apr. 24, 1863) (hereinafter Lieber Code). Originally issued as General Orders No. 100, Adjutant General's Office, 1863, Washington 1898: GPO, available at http:// avalon.law.yale.edu/19th_century/lieber.asp.

21. United States. 40th Congress, 2d Session. 1867-1868. House Executive Document No. 23, December 7, 1867 (summarizing the military commission proceedings against Captain Wirz) https://www.loc.gov/rr/frd/Military_Law/Wirz_trial.html.

22. *See* Elihu Root, *Trials or Courts-Martial in the Philippine Islands in Consequence of Certain Instructions*, S. Doc. No. 213, at 1-17 (2d Sess. 1903). Smith's only punishment was admonishment, and he was forced to retire.

An important development in the law of war came near the conclusion of World War I. The allies formed a commission entitled *The Commission on the Responsibility of the Authors of the War and on Enforcement of Penalties*.[23] This commission initially proposed the creation of an international criminal court to try those charged, including Kaiser Wilhelm. The proposal resulted in Article 228[24] of the Treaty of Versailles (the treaty that formally ended the war), in which Germany recognized the right of the Allied powers to try Germans for violations of the laws and customs of war; and Article 229, which provided for the creation of an international military tribunal for such trials when the defendant committed war crimes against victims of more than one Allied power.[25]

The effort to try Germans by Allied military tribunals never came to fruition; German resistance and a lack of Allied determination ultimately resulted in a compromise: Germany would be permitted to try its own personnel for alleged war crimes committed against Allied victims. The Leipzig Trials, as they were called, proved largely incapable and demonstrated an unwillingness to establish accountability or impose serious sanctions on offenders. Nonetheless, the Treaty of Versailles and the Leipzig Trials provided the foundation for the modern concept of individual criminal responsibility for war crimes. It was perhaps because of the failures of these trials that there was far greater international resolve to establish an effective accountability framework at the conclusion of World War II, which led to adoption of the London Charter for the creation of international military tribunals "for the just and prompt trial and punishment of the major war criminals of the European Axis."[26]

The trials by international military tribunals, military commissions, national military tribunals, and national domestic criminal courts following World War II solidified the doctrine of individual criminal responsibility for violations of the laws and customs of war. These trials also provided a rich jurisprudential foundation for the further evolution of war crimes liability. The

---

23. 14-1 AM. J. INT'L L. 95-154 (Jan.-Apr. 1920) published by the American Society of International Law, available at http://www.jstor.org/stable/2187841.

24. Treaty of Versailles, Article 228

> The German Government recognises the right of the Allied and Associated Powers to bring before military tribunals persons accused of having committed acts in violation of the laws and customs of war. Such persons shall, if found guilty, be sentenced to punishments laid down by law. This provision will apply notwithstanding any proceedings or prosecution before a tribunal in Germany or in the territory of her allies. The German Government shall hand over to the Allied and Associated Powers, or to such one of them as shall so request, all persons accused of having committed an act in violation of the laws and customs of war, who are specified either by name or by the rank, office or employment which they held under the German authorities.

25. Treaty of Versailles, Article 229.

> Persons guilty of criminal acts against the nationals of one of the Allied and Associated Powers will be brought before the military tribunals of that Power. Persons guilty of criminal acts against the nationals of more than one of the Allied and Associated Powers will be brought before military tribunals composed of members of the military tribunals of the Powers concerned. In every case the accused will be entitled to name his own counsel.

26. *See* http://www.loc.gov/rr/frd/Military_Law/NT_major-war-criminals.html (located in vol. I, at 10).

International Military Tribunal at Nuremberg, or "IMT" conducted what are certainly the best known post-war trials of war criminals. However, it is important to note that they were certainly not the only tribunals. Senior Japanese military and civilian defendants were tried by the Far East counterpart to the IMT, known as the Tokyo Trials.

Both of these tribunals focused exclusively on the highest-level Axis defendants, leaving accountability for the thousands of lower-level defendants to other tribunals. As a result, many thousands of other international and national tribunals adjudicated these cases. Other tribunals, established by Allied occupying powers to hear cases in their respective sectors, continued the process of holding war criminals accountable for their misconduct.

For example, in Europe, the United States Army judge advocate was made responsible for the prosecution of crimes committed against American troops, or in Nazi concentration camps that had been overrun and "liberated" by American forces. Under this authority, some 1,600 German war crimes defendants (as compared with 200 at Nuremberg) were tried before Army military commissions and military government courts, and over 250 death sentences (as compared with 25 at Nuremberg) were carried out. About an equal number were tried by British, French, and other military courts established by the countries that had been occupied by Germany.

Precise figures are lacking, but by the spring of 1948 some 2,500 individuals had been tried on war crimes charges in Europe and 2,800 in the Far East, taking no account of trials held by the Soviet Union or China. It would be a conservative estimate that some 10,000 persons were tired on such charges from 1945-1950.[27]

Finally, national criminal tribunals—including the criminal courts in post-war Federal Republic of Germany—provided their contribution to the accountability process. Indeed, civilian trials of World War II war criminals continued into the 21st Century.[28] This international commitment to prosecuting war criminals was a landmark development in the doctrine of individual criminal responsibility for violations of international law and established the procedural and substantive foundation for modern-day war crimes prosecutions.

II. Sources of Contemporary War Crimes

There is no single source that codifies all of the acts that could constitute a war crime. There is no super-legislature with the authority to either promulgate a criminal code or impose such a code on sovereign States. There is also no

---

27. Jan E. Aldykiewicz & Geoff Corn, *Authority to Court-Martial Non-U.S. Military Personnel for Serious Violations of International Humanitarian Law* 167 MIL. L. REV. 74 (2001) (quoting Telford Taylor) (hereinafter Aldykiewicz).

28. *See* Eliza Gray, *Nazi Trials: The Case of Auschwitz Guard Reinhold Hanning*, TIME (describing efforts to prosecute a 94-year-old former SS guard 70 years after his alleged crimes).

general agreement on all the kinds of conduct that should be criminalized and what the elements of particular offenses should be. Because the evolution and development of the law of war over the centuries has not proceeded in a linear, organized way, it should not be surprising that there is no clarifying document describing what the specific war crimes are or should be. Nevertheless, there are several sources that do provide important and arguably binding guidance as to what conduct constitutes a war crime, and what a State's obligations are for preventing war crimes and punishing war criminals.

A. Geneva Conventions and Grave Breaches

Treaty law is the most definitive and most important source for war crimes in the post-World War II era. The 1949 Geneva Conventions are the most important treaties within this category. These treaties included, for the first time in the history of conflict regulation, provisions explicitly establishing both war crimes and obligations of States to respond to such crimes. Equally significant with respect to war crimes was the creation or recognition of a category of war crimes characterized in the treaties as "grave breaches." Each Convention includes an article defining those articles of the treaty that, when breached, qualify as grave breaches—the most serious violations of the treaties. In that sense, the concept of a grave breach is common to all four Conventions. However, these grave breaches are not common in the same way Article 3 is common to all four Conventions, because they are found in different articles and the language is not identical within each Convention.[29] Article 130 from the Third Geneva Convention on the treatment of prisoners of war is representative of these various grave breach articles. It defines grave breaches as:

> [A]ny of the following acts, if committed against persons or property protected by the Convention: willful killing, torture or inhuman treatment, including biological experiments, willfully causing great suffering or serious injury to body or health, compelling a prisoner of war to serve in the forces of the hostile Power, or willfully depriving a prisoner of war of the rights of fair and regular trial prescribed in this Convention.[30]

Because this Convention relates to the treatment of prisoners of war, the "grave breach" conduct is understandably focused on prisoners of war. By contrast, the grave breaches article on treatment of civilians in time of war

---

29. The grave breaches articles are located within each Convention as follows: Geneva Convention for the Amelioration of the Condition of the Wounded and Sick in Armed Forces in the Field, Aug. 12, 1949, 6 U.S.T. 3114, 75 U.N.T.S. 970, art. 50, (hereinafter GWS); Geneva Convention for the Amelioration of the Condition of Wounded, Sick and Shipwrecked Members of the Armed Forces at Sea, Aug. 12, 1949, 6 U.S.T. 3217, 75 U.N.T.S. 971, art. 51, (hereinafter GWS Sea); Geneva Convention Relative to the Treatment of Prisoners of War, Aug. 12, 1949, 6 U.S.T. 3316, 75 U.N.T.S. 972, art. 130 (hereinafter GPW); Geneva Convention Relative to the Protection of Civilian Persons in Time of War, Aug. 12, 1949, 6 U.S.T. 3516, 75 U.N.T.S. 973, art. 147 (hereinafter GCC).

30. GPW, *supra*, note 31, Art. 130.

stemming from the Fourth Convention is focused on the harms that combatants can impose on civilians. Article 147 of the Fourth Convention reads:

> Grave breaches to which the preceding Article relates shall be those involving any of the following acts, if committed against persons or property protected by the present Convention: willful killing, torture or inhuman treatment, including biological experiments, willfully causing great suffering or serious injury to body or health, unlawful deportation or transfer or unlawful confinement of a protected person, compelling a protected person to serve in the forces of a hostile Power, or willfully depriving a protected person of the rights of fair and regular trial prescribed in the present Convention, taking of hostages and extensive destruction and appropriation of property, not justified by military necessity and carried out unlawfully and wantonly.[31]

Any observer familiar with domestic concepts of criminal law should be struck by the fact that these grave breach articles do not provide specific elements for offenses nor do they set out what punishments should be imposed for committing the various grave breaches. This makes these articles very different than what one would typically see in a criminal code, where the elements of specific crimes and authorized punishments are enumerated, or at least easily distilled. Instead, the purpose of these articles was to identify in very broad terms the provisions of each treaty considered so critically important that violation could never be treated as minor or insignificant; in short, a consensus identification of the most serious battlefield misconduct.

1. Duties of Signatory States

Rather than define specific elements or impose specific punishments, the Conventions impose three affirmative obligations on the party States (which today includes all States in the world) with respect to grave breaches. First, each State must enact legislation to provide "effective penal sanctions for persons committing, or ordering to be committed, any of the grave breaches...."[32] Rather than impose a treaty-based criminal code, the Conventions bind each party State to implement the treaty obligation through domestic legislation. This structure creates two sources of law for grave breaches. The first source is the Conventions themselves, which set out in broad terms what qualify as grave breaches. The second source is the criminal code of the State where the prosecution will take place (U.S. implementation of this obligation will be examined below).

In addition to imposing an obligation on party States to implement the grave breach regime through domestic penal law, the Conventions also impose a duty on party States to "search for persons alleged to have committed, or have ordered to be committed, such grave breaches, and ... bring such persons, regardless of their nationality, before its own courts."[33] This is a broad

---
31. GCC, *supra*, note 32, Art. 147.
32. *See* GWS, *supra*, note 32, Art. 49; GWS Sea, *supra*, note 32, Art. 50; GPW, *supra*, note 32, Art. 129; GCC, *supra*, note 32, Art. 146.
33. *See id.*

obligation. The Conventions do not dictate any particular methodology States must use to search for alleged violators nor do they inform the States on how diligently they must search or what resources they must dedicate to this search. Because of the broad and unspecified nature of this obligation, compliance by States varies greatly. Often, it is only in high profile cases or perhaps politically motivated prosecutions that States will act on this obligation.[34]

Finally, in an often overlooked manifestation of the Conventions' prioritization of individual protection over that of State interest, each Convention includes an article prohibiting party States from absolving themselves or other States of responsibility for grave breaches ("No High Contracting Party shall be allowed to absolve itself or any other High Contracting Party of any liability incurred by itself or by another High Contracting Party in respect of breaches referred to in the preceding Article.").

Note that there is no requirement that the State exercising jurisdiction over an individual alleged to have committed a grave breach have any nationality connection to the defendant, the victim, or even to have been a participant in the conflict. This is a manifestation of the international criminal law concept of universal jurisdiction. The gravity of such a breach of the Conventions justified subjecting violators to this broadest of all jurisdictional concepts. In essence, a grave breach is so serious an offense against international law that it offends all States, thereby vesting all States with an interest in prosecution.

Transfer of war criminals to other countries for prosecution reflects the third affirmative obligation imposed by the Conventions with respect to grave breaches. States that choose not to prosecute alleged violators under their own laws (or that are unable to do so because they have not enacted effective implementing legislation) may, in the alternative, "hand such persons over for trial to another High Contracting Party concerned. . . ."[35] There are numerous reasons why a party State might prefer this "extradition" course of action. It may be that the State that apprehends the alleged violator lacks the laws, resources, or the political will to conduct the prosecution. It may also be that the apprehending State cannot, under its own laws, legally prosecute the alleged perpetrator. For example, because the United States did not enact implementing legislation criminalizing grave breaches until 1996,[36] extradition was the exclusive remedy until that date. The Constitution's ex post facto provisions might also prevent the United States government from prosecuting Nazi war criminals in U.S. federal courts for their conduct during World War II. Since the 1996 enactment of the War Crimes Act, (WCA) the United States is able to prosecute individuals who commit grave breaches in federal court (although only if the defendant or

---

34. Since 1979, the U.S. Department of Justice Office of Special Investigations is responsible for identifying and bringing perpetrators of crimes against humanity to justice. The focus of their work has primarily been identifying Nazi war criminals who reside in the United States, denaturalizing them and then extraditing them to Israel for criminal prosecution. *See* the bulletin describing their work at http://www.justice.gov/criminal/hrsp/archives/2006/01-06USABulletin.pdf.

35. *See* GWS, *supra*, note 32, Art. 49; GWS Sea, *supra*, note 32, Art. 50; GPW, *supra*, note 32, Art. 129; GCC, *supra*, note 32, Art. 146.

36. 18 U.S.C. § 2441.

the victim is a U.S. national). Nonetheless, political, diplomatic, or resources considerations might still lead to use of the extradition option in such cases.[37]

Why did the Convention drafters adopt this method to highlight and single out grave breaches from other treaty violations? Why did the Conventions opt for broad definitions, leaving the details for the States to work out? The Commentary to the Geneva Conventions notes that in 1947, a conference of experts convened under the auspices of the ICRC suggested there was the need to identify grave breaches. In order to distinguish these breaches from lesser forms of battlefield misconduct and ensure their universal repression, it was necessary to define in the Conventions what constituted a grave breach.[38] But why leave it to States to define the elements and punishments for these breaches? Although not explained in the Commentary, this was likely due to the political and cultural impossibility of creating specific offenses and punishments to which all the party States could agree.

Unfortunately, what is gained in political and cultural expedience is lost in clarity and precision. As exposed by the United States' efforts following the September 11 attacks, leaving terms such as "torture and inhuman treatment" undefined allows States to define and manipulate these terms in ways likely unintended by the treaty drafters.[39] However, practice has added significant clarity to many of the provisions of the Conventions falling within the grave breach category. Further, the general nature of the grave breach provisions facilitated positive evolutions in the law (for example, through the decisions of international criminal tribunals established to address war crimes in the Balkans and Rwanda). Ultimately, achieving universal agreement that the LOAC does in fact include a core category of offenses that qualify as so serious that prosecution is an essential response, and that all States share an equal interest in holding violators accountable, was a profoundly significant development in international law that continues to contribute to preventing impunity.

An example of the evolution that followed the establishment of the Geneva Convention grave breach regime is found in the 1977 Additional Protocol I. (AP I) That treaty, developed to supplement the four Geneva Conventions, added to the violations qualifying as grave breaches. According to Article 11(4):

> Any willful act or omission which seriously endangers the physical or mental health or integrity of any person who is in the power of a Party other than the one on which he depends and which either violates any of the prohibitions in

---

37. Debbie Cenziper & Scott Nover, *Inside the Race to Deport a 94-year-old Nazi Guard*, WASH. POST, Dec. 16, 2017 (describing the 14-year-long process to deport the last known Nazi collaborator living in the United States). According to the article, since 2005, nine Nazi collaborators died on U.S. soil, while efforts to deport them either to their native country or to Germany were ongoing.

38. *See* Commentary, Convention (III) Relative to the Treatment of Prisoners of War. Geneva, 12 August 1949 (Jean S. Pictet, ed., 1960), at 19-20 (hereinafter Commentary, Convention III).

39. *See, e.g.*, the memo from the Office of Legal Counsel to the White House General Counsel setting out the standards for conducting interrogations of suspected terrorists, available at http://dspace.wrlc.org/doc/bitstream/2041/70964/00355_020801_001display.pdf.

paragraphs 1 and 2 or fails to comply with the requirements of paragraph 3 shall be a grave breach of this Protocol.[40]

In addition, Article 85 of AP I enumerates the following grave breaches:

3. In addition to the grave breaches defined in Article 11, the following acts shall be regarded as grave breaches of this Protocol, when committed willfully, in violation of the relevant provisions of this Protocol, and causing death or serious injury to body or health:

    (a) making the civilian population or individual civilians the object of attack;

    (b) launching an indiscriminate attack affecting the civilian population or civilian objects in the knowledge that such attack will cause excessive loss of life, injury to civilians or damage to civilian objects, as defined in Article 57, paragraph 2(a)(iii);

    (c) launching an attack against works or installations containing dangerous forces in the knowledge that such attack will cause excessive loss of life, injury to civilians or damage to civilian objects, as defined in Article 57, paragraph 2(a)(iii);

    (d) making non-defended localities and demilitarized zones the object of attack;

    (e) making a person the object of attack in the knowledge that he is hors de combat;

    (f) the perfidious use, in violation of Article 37, of the distinctive emblem of the red cross, red crescent or red lion and sun or of other protective signs recognized by the Conventions or this Protocol.

4. In addition to the grave breaches defined in the preceding paragraphs and in the Conventions, the following shall be regarded as grave breaches of this Protocol, when committed willfully and in violation of the Conventions or the Protocol:

    (a) the transfer by the occupying Power of parts of its own civilian population into the territory it occupies, or the deportation or transfer of all or parts of the population of the occupied territory within or outside this territory, in violation of Article 49 of the Fourth Convention;

    (b) unjustifiable delay in the repatriation of prisoners of war or civilians;

    (c) practices of apartheid and other inhuman and degrading practices involving outrages upon personal dignity, based on racial discrimination;

    (d) making the clearly-recognized historic monuments, works of art or places of worship which constitute the cultural or spiritual heritage of peoples and to which special protection has been given by special arrangement, for example, within the framework of a competent international organization, the object of attack, causing as a result extensive destruction thereof, where there is no evidence of the violation by the adverse Party of Article 53, subparagraph (b), and when such historic

---

40. Protocol Additional to the Geneva Conventions of 12 August 1949, and Relating to the Protection of Victims of International Armed Conflict, June 8, 1977, 1125 U.N.T.S. 17512, art. 11(b).

monuments, works of art and places of worship are not located in the immediate proximity of military objectives;

(e) depriving a person protected by the Conventions or referred to in paragraph 2 of this Article of the rights of fair and regular trial.[41]

Even though the United States is not a party to AP I, there is no indication the United States considered this enumeration objectionable. This is not conclusive evidence that the United States considers Article 84 a reflection of customary international law, but it does provide an important indication of the broader international understanding of the scope of contemporary grave breach liability. It is particularly important to note that unlike the 1949 Geneva Conventions, AP I includes within the category of grave breaches certain unlawful attacks, an addition that was made possible by AP I's inclusion of rules regulating the targeting process (rules that were not included in the 1949 Conventions).

2. IAC Trigger

As explained in Chapter 2, the provisions of the Geneva Conventions (with the exception of common Article 3) come into force when triggered by a common Article 2 international armed conflict (IAC). Or the partial or total occupation of the territory of a High Contracting Party. Because of this, the grave breach provisions of the Conventions apply only during IACs or occupation. As explained below, this does not mean that the underlying conduct prohibited by these provisions cannot be the basis for war crimes allegations in the context of a non-international armed conflict (NIAC) (for example, abusive treatment of a detainee or deliberate attack on civilians). But as a matter of law, such violations are grave breaches only when committed in the context of a common Article 2 conflict. That is likely to strike someone new to this subject matter as both arbitrary and ill-considered. Nonetheless, this seemingly strange result stems from the law triggering paradigm of the Conventions.

Nor is this the only limitation on properly alleging a grave breach. First, even in the context of a common Article 2 IAC, not every crime is a war crime. There must be some nexus between battlefield operations, the crime, the offenders, and the victims. Determining the existence of a nexus between a criminal offense and armed conflict can be challenging. International criminal tribunal decisions have developed a number of factors to aid in this analysis. To start, the armed conflict must have "played a substantial part in the perpetrator's ability to commit [the offense], his decision to commit it, the manner in which it was committed or the purpose for which it was committed." [42] The nexus is established where the accused "acted in furtherance of or under the guise of the armed conflict."[43] It is not established where all that is proven is that the crime was committed "at the same time as an armed conflict" or "in any circumstances

---

41. *Id.*, art. 85.
42. Prosecutor v. Kunarac, Case No. IT-96-23 & IT-96-23/1-A, Appeals Chamber Judgment, ¶ 58 (Int'l Crim. Trib. for the Former Yugoslavia June 12, 2002), http://www.icty.org/x/cases/kunarac/acjug/en/kun-aj020612e.pdf.
43. *Id.*

created in part by the armed conflict."[44] Additional factors to consider in determining whether a nexus exists include: the status of the perpetrator; the status of the victim; whether the act advanced a military purpose; whether the act was committed in the context of the perpetrator's official duties; and whether the crime was committed under the guise of military authority.[45] If no nexus exists, then the crime in question is not a war crime. Second, not every LOAC violation qualifies as a grave breach. As noted above, only those violations included within the treaty definition fall within that category.

Additionally, there are many conflicts and military operations that do not fall strictly within the definition of an IAC. When U.S. forces are conducting peacekeeping operations pursuant to United Nations authorization in Bosnia, for example, and a U.S. solider kills an unarmed prisoner, does that mean he has not committed a war crime because the operation is not an IAC? Of course, he has committed a crime, and depending on the context and surrounding factors, he may have committed a war crime. He has not, however, committed a grave breach of the Conventions because he is not engaged in an IAC. As will be discussed below, two important judicial opinions arising from the International Tribunals for the Former Yugoslavia have expanded significantly the application of the Conventions beyond strictly IAC, making the limits set out in the Conventions less clear.

3. "Simple Breaches"

Response obligations for violations of the 1949 Geneva Conventions and AP I that do not fall within the grave breach definition are less specific. These lesser breaches are often referred to as "simple breaches," although the term is not found in the Conventions, and is somewhat misleading by suggesting LOAC violations can be simple. All violations are problematic, and dealing with them is rarely simple. Nonetheless, the only obligation imposed on state parties to the Geneva Conventions for any violation that does qualify as a grave breach is to "take measures necessary for [their] suppression."[46] States can and

---

44. Rutaganda v. Prosecutor, Case No. ICTR-96-3-A, Appeals Chamber Judgment, ¶ 570 (May 26, 2003), http://unictr.unmict.org/sites/unictr.org/files/case-documents/ictr-96-3/appeals-chamber-judgements/en/030526.pdf.

45. *Id.* at ¶¶ 569-70 (quoting Kunarac, at ¶¶ 58-59). Tribunals have also indicated that establishing the nexus does not require evaluating whether the conduct took place during actual combat or hostilities, was part of a policy or practice officially endorsed or tolerated by one of the parties to the conflict, or was in furtherance of a policy associated with the conduct of war or in the interest of a party to the conflict. Prosecutor v. Delalić, Case No. IT-96-21-T, Trial Chamber Judgment, ¶¶ 193-97 (Int'l Crim. Trib. for the Former Yugoslavia Nov. 16, 1998), http://www.icty.org/x/cases/mucic/tjug/en/981116_judg_en.pdf; Prosecutor v. Tadic, Case No. IT-94-1-T, Trial Chamber Judgment, ¶ 573 (Int'l Crim. Trib. for the Former Yugoslavia May 7, 1997), http://www.icty.org/x/cases/tadic/tjug/en/tad-tsj70507JT2- e.pdf; Prosecutor v. Akayesu, Case No. ICTR-96-4 Appeals Chamber Judgment, ¶¶ 430-46 (June 1, 2001), http://unictr.unmict.org/sites/unictr.org/files/case-documents/ictr96-4/appeals-chamber-judgements/en/010601.pdf.

46. *See* GWS, *supra*, note 32, Art. 49; GWS Sea, *supra*, note 32, Art. 50; GPW, *supra*, note 32, Art. 129; GCC, *supra*, note 32, Art. 146.

do have laws criminalizing simple breach violations, though it is not required by the Conventions. Necessary measures can include administrative sanctions, additional training of soldiers, or other actions intended to prevent or suppress this conduct. Likewise, for these simple breaches, the State has no duty to bring violators found within their territory to justice. Finally, because grave breaches are limited to situations of IAC, all LOAC violations occurring in NIAC must, by necessity, fall within the "simple breach" category. This does not mean they are insignificant or beyond the scope of war crimes jurisdiction, as will be explained in the next section.

B. Common Article 3 as a Source of War Crimes

The operation and applicability of Common Article 3 of the four Geneva Conventions is set out in Chapter 2. This article, common to all four Conventions, is often referred to as a "mini-convention" because it creates a baseline set of humanitarian protections that are applicable in NIACs.

The effect of Common Article 3 is significant. It pierces the veil of State sovereignty and imposes specific minimum obligations on a State fighting to suppress an internal insurrection or a civil war, on non-state belligerent groups fighting the State or each other, and arguably on transnational non-state actors, such as international terrorist groups engaged in armed conflicts with States. As explained in Chapter 2, it is a complicated task to determine when civil unrest or acts of banditry reach the point of a NIAC. The insurgent force will normally be quick to claim it is fighting an armed conflict, not only to gain the protections that Common Article 3 may provide, but also to obtain international recognition and increased internal and external support. The State, on the other hand, will normally characterize the conflict as sporadic internal violence, actions of a criminal band, or criminal terrorism (such as the Turkish response to the Kurdistan Workers' Party). Characterizing the struggle as a criminal internal action allows the State to deal with the insurgents through its domestic criminal laws and criminal courts unconstrained by Common Article 3. In the latter case, the State's sovereignty is unaffected by the LOAC (although many of the basic protections of Common Article 3 would nonetheless apply pursuant to international human rights obligations).

When situations of violence between States and non-state groups, or between multiple non-state groups do trigger application of Common Article 3, a question arises as to whether this limited LOAC regulation includes a war crimes component. Unlike Convention provisions applicable to IACs, Common Article 3 does not specify any grave breaches, nor does it even indicate violations must be sanctioned; Common Article 3 does not refer to individual criminal liability at all. Instead, the article protects individuals who do not take an active part in the conflict, are armed forces who have laid down their arms, or those who have become hors de combat (outside of combat) for any other reason. Common Article 3 prohibits certain acts against these protected persons. Specifically, the article provides:

> In the case of armed conflict not of an international character occurring in the territory of one of the High Contracting Parties, each Party to the conflict shall be bound to apply, as a minimum, the following provisions: (1) Persons taking no active part in the hostilities, including members of armed forces who have laid down their arms and those placed "hors de combat" by sickness, wounds, detention, or any other cause, shall in all circumstances be treated humanely, without any adverse distinction founded on race, colour, religion or faith, sex, birth or wealth, or any other similar criteria. To this end, the following acts are and shall remain prohibited at any time and in any place whatsoever with respect to the above-mentioned persons:
>
>> (a) violence to life and person, in particular murder of all kinds, mutilation, cruel treatment and torture;
>> (b) taking of hostages;
>> (c) outrages upon personal dignity, in particular humiliating and degrading treatment;
>> (d) the passing of sentences and the carrying out of executions without previous judgment pronounced by a regularly constituted court, affording all the judicial guarantees which are recognized as indispensable by civilized peoples. (2) The wounded and sick shall be collected and cared for.[47]

These proscriptions are today recognized as providing a valid basis for war crimes liability in a NIAC. Any conduct inconsistent with these humanitarian obligations by a participant in the hostilities triggers individual criminal responsibility, although unlike a grave breach prosecution is not mandatory. However, similar to grave breaches, Common Article 3 avoids the specific details typically found in a criminal code. There are no elements enumerated in common Article 3 and no punishment structure is mentioned. Common Article 3 was not intended to provide a basis for war crimes responsibility, even though it has evolved to that effect.

The only clear obligation is that in the context of an internal armed conflict within the territory of a High Contracting Party, neither the State nor the insurgent force should engage in the prohibited conduct against protected persons. Recently, courts have held that the basic protections outlined in Common Article 3 have broader applicability, and are not limited to internal armed conflicts. These protections are generally recognized as the "minimum yardstick of rules of international humanitarian law" applicable across the entire spectrum of armed conflict.[48] This suggests that any violation of the baseline humanitarian obligations established by Common Article 3 provides a legitimate basis for war crimes prosecution in any armed conflict. Indeed, at this point in history this interpretation of the relationship between Common Article 3's humanitarian mandate and war crimes liability is virtually axiomatic.

---

47. Common Article 3.
48. Delalic, *supra*, note 47.

C. Customary Law

Customary international law (CIL) provides the foundational source of authority for determining what constitutes war crimes. The International Court of Justice describes customary international law as "a general practice accepted as law."[49] The existence of CIL "requires the presence of two elements, namely State practice (*usus*) and a belief that such practice is required, prohibited or allowed, depending on the nature of the rule, as a matter of law (*opinio juris sive necessitates*)."[50]

Given the vagaries of the CIL development and recognition process, determining what specific war crimes are part of CIL is no easy task. This can often be a situation where "beauty is in the eye of the beholder." The State or entity seeking to impose criminal accountability might claim the practice in question is a violation of well-established CIL rules, while the one accused of the violation claims that the rule does not meet the CIL test. A claim that killing unarmed prisoners of war is not a violation of customary LOAC is not likely to have much success. However, the validity of prosecution based on novel theories of CIL or newly developed offenses might indeed be tenuous (whether a defendant will prevail in challenging the allegation is a very different question, often dependent on the quality and legitimacy of the judicial process).

The treaty codification of many contemporary war crimes has alleviated the difficulties associated with reliance on CIL. In contemporary practice, the primary value of CIL, like the common law, is to fill in the gaps that exist in this increasingly comprehensive treaty law. Even though a number of treaties governing war crimes were developed in an effort to clarify the scope of war crimes liability (particularly after World War II), these treaties do not cover all situations and all contingencies. Additionally, not all States are bound by all of these treaties. Without CIL to fill in these gaps, a State might claim its armed forces are not bound by the law, and are therefore functionally immune from war crimes liability. CIL helps reduce the situations where such claims are meritorious.

The ICRC recently developed a database of what it believes to be CIL LOAC rules.[51] In the war crimes category, this database includes such offenses as violence to life; rape; torture and cruel, inhuman, or degrading treatment; forced labor; and several other offenses. In the years since World War II, there has been significant convergence of war crimes under CIL and war crimes defined by treaty. Often, treaty law is deemed to represent emerging CIL norms—treaty rules that "blossom" into new CIL norms. Similarly, modern treaty war crimes provisions are often understood as simply codifying preexisting customary norms. These distinctions between pure treaty obligation and treaty provisions that reflect CIL norms are extremely important, because they suggest obligations extending to

---

49. Statute of the International Court of Justice art. 38, ii l (b).
50. Assessment of Customary International Law, ICRC, https://ihl-databases.icrc.org/customary-ihl/eng/docs/vl_rul_in_asofcuin#Fn_l6_10. As the ICRC notes, "[t]he exact meaning of these two elements has been the subject of much academic writing." *Id.*
51. The database can be found at http://www.icrc.org/customary-ihl/eng/docs/home.

non-signatory states. The line is often obscure between pure treaty-based war crimes liability and CIL war crimes reflected in treaty provisions. But the existence of uncodified war crimes under CIL remains an important concept.

D. Other Sources and Other Laws

While CIL and the Geneva Conventions are the most important universal sources for what constitutes war crimes, they are not the only sources. A number of statutes detail and specifically codify war crimes. Perhaps this codification is due in large part because of the vagueness of the Conventions and the inability or unwillingness of individual States to codify crimes and prosecute offenders. Before discussing some examples of these codification efforts, there are three other offenses, not war crimes *per se*, but they often have a significant role in war crimes prosecutions. These crimes are: aggression, genocide, and crimes against humanity.

1. Aggression

The first of these is crimes against peace also referred to as crimes of aggression. The Charter for the IMT, defined crimes against peace as "planning, preparation, initiation or waging of a war of aggression, or a war in violation of international treaties, agreements or assurances, or participation in a common plan or conspiracy for the accomplishment of any of the foregoing."[52] This offense was intended to hold accountable those senior military and civilian leaders within the Third Reich responsible for starting World War II. Sixteen members of the Third Reich were charged with crimes against peace; twelve were convicted.[53]

This offense did not exist prior to its inclusion in the IMT Charter and it has never been charged outside of the IMT. Crimes against peace or crimes of aggression are not strictly war crimes because no battlefield nexus is required. Because the focus of this crime is to impose criminal liability on those senior political and military leaders who waged aggressive war in the first instance, requiring a battlefield nexus makes no sense, particularly when those who are most culpable are often far removed from the battlefield. Nonetheless, this offense is closely related to war crimes and may likely be prosecuted in a war crimes tribunal.[54]

In 1974, the United Nations General Assembly adopted a definition of aggression that comprised eight articles and listed a number of specific acts of aggression. This definition was primarily intended to assist the Security

---

52. Agreement by the Government of the United States of America, the Provisional Government of the French Republic, the Government of the United Kingdom of Great Britain and Northern Ireland and the Government of the Union of Soviet Socialist Republics for the Prosecution and Punishment of Major War Criminals of European Axis, 59 stat. 1544, Article 6(a) (1945).

53. "Nuremberg Trials." Genocide and Crimes Against Humanity. Ed. Dinah L. Shelton. Gale Cengage, 2005. eNotes.com. 2006. 17 Mar, 2011, *available at* http://www.enotes.com/genocide-encyclopedia/nuremberg-trials.

54. International Criminal Court, RC/Res. 6, The Crime of Aggression, adopted at the 13th plenary meeting, on 11 June 2010, available at http://www.icc-cpi.int/iccdocs/asp_docs/Resolutions/RC-Res.6-ENG.pdf.

Council in determining aggression by States. While it has not been used for that purpose, the definition has been used by the International Criminal Court (ICC) to create the crime of aggression. Article 8 of the Rome Statute defines aggression as:

> [T]he planning, preparation, initiation or execution, by a person in a position effectively to exercise control over or to direct the political or military action of a State, of an act of aggression which, by its character, gravity and scale, constitutes a manifest violation of the Charter of the United Nations.[55]

In December, 2017, the Assembly of States Parties to the Statute of the International Criminal Court adopted a resolution which activated the jurisdiction of the Court over the crime of aggression as of 17 July, 2018.[56]

2. Genocide

The second offense, the crime of genocide, is not a war crime but is often associated with war crimes prosecutions. Genocide is not strictly a war crime for the same reason that crimes against peace are not war crimes; there is no battlefield nexus required to commit genocide. Genocide can be committed outside the context of any armed conflict. Genocide could also occur in an international armed conflict or a NIAC. Many of the modern conflicts where the international community is involved from Yugoslavia, to Rwanda, to Cambodia involved acts of genocide.[57]

The International Tribunal for the former Yugoslavia (ICTY) defined genocide as committing acts such as torture or murder with the "intent to destroy, in whole or in part, a national, ethnic, racial, or religious group."[58] Under this definition, the specific intent requirement to destroy a national, ethnic, racial, or religious group distinguishes genocide from other crimes. While civilians and those far removed from the battlefield could be guilty of this offense, soldiers too could be guilty of genocide. Because genocide is often accomplished at the hands of military, genocide has a close association with war crimes prosecutions. The ICC defines genocide as:

> [A]ny of the following acts committed with intent to destroy, in whole or in part, a national, ethnical, racial, or religious group, as such:
>
> (a) Killing members of the group;
> (b) Causing serious bodily or mental harm to members of the group;

---

55. Rome Statute of the International Criminal Court, July 17, 1998, 2187 U.N.T.S. 3 (hereinafter Rome Statute).
56. The crime of aggression was adopted as the result of the Kampala Amendments to the Rome Statute, which not all states parties have agreed to. There remain questions as to whether the ICC has jurisdiction over aggression committed by nationals of non-ratifying states.
57. Daniel M. Greenfield, *The Crime of Complicity in Genocide: How the International Criminal Tribunals for Rwanda and Yugoslavia Got It Wrong, and Why It Matters*, 98 J. CRIM. L. & CRIMINOLOGY No. 3, 92-93 (2008), *available at* http://www.law.northwestern.edu/jclc/symposium/Greenfield.pdf.
58. ICTY, S.C. Res. 827, (May 25, 1993), available at http://www.icty.org/x/file/Legal%20Library/Statute/statute_827_1993_en.pdf.

(c) Deliberately inflicting on the group conditions of life calculated to bring about its physical destruction in whole or in part;
(d) Imposing measures intended to prevent births within the group;
(e) Forcibly transferring children of the group to another group.[59]

3. Crimes Against Humanity

Crimes against humanity, the third offense, has a close relationship to war crimes but is not technically a war crime. This offense first appeared as part of the IMT Charter, and was later used in other post World War II tribunals in the Far East and Germany. Article 6(c) defined crimes against humanity as:

> Murder, extermination, enslavement, deportation, and other inhumane acts committed against civilian populations, before or during the war; or persecutions on political, racial or religious grounds in execution of or in connection with any crime within the jurisdiction of the Tribunal, whether or not in violation of the domestic law of the country where perpetrated.[60]

More recent international tribunals expanded this definition to include offenses such as rape and torture.[61] Historically, crimes against humanity have a close nexus to armed conflict and fit more within the traditional definition of a war crime. However, more contemporary international tribunals have not required a close nexus with armed conflicts. More recent definitions of crimes against humanity have the following features in common: first, they refer to specific acts of violence irrespective of whether these acts are committed in time of war or peace, and second, these acts must be the product of persecution against an identifiable group of persons.[62] Crimes against humanity committed during an armed conflict are no longer strictly considered war crimes because customary law no longer seems to require that characterization. Like aggression and genocide, crimes against humanity often occur in the context of an armed conflict or other military operations and are often closely related to war crimes prosecutions. The ICC defines crimes against humanity as:

> [A]ny of the following acts when committed as part of a widespread or systematic attack directed against any civilian population, with knowledge of the attack:
>
> (a) Murder;
> (b) Extermination;
> (c) Enslavement;
> (d) Deportation or forcible transfer of population;
> (e) Imprisonment or other severe deprivation of physical liberty in violation of fundamental rules of international law;

---

59. Rome Statute, *supra*, note 54, art. 6.
60. Agreement by the Government of the United States of America, the Provisional Government of the French Republic, the Government of the United Kingdom of Great Britain and Northern Ireland and the Government of the Union of Soviet Socialist Republics for the Prosecution and Punishment of Major War Criminals of European Axis, 59 stat. 1544, Article 6(c) (1945).
61. *See* ICTY and ICTR.
62. M. Cherif Bassiouni, CRIMES AGAINST HUMANITY (2011).

(f) Torture;
(g) Rape, sexual slavery, enforced prostitution, forced pregnancy, enforced sterilization, or any other form of sexual violence of comparable gravity;
(h) Persecution against any identifiable group or collectivity on political, racial, national, ethnic, cultural, religious, gender as defined in paragraph 3, or other grounds that are universally recognized as impermissible under international law, in connection with any act referred to in this paragraph or any crime within the jurisdiction of the Court;
(i) Enforced disappearance of persons;
(j) The crime of apartheid;
(k) Other inhumane acts of a similar character intentionally causing great suffering, or serious injury to body or to mental or physical health.[63]

Aggression, genocide, and crimes against humanity, along with war crimes, have been codified in a number of statutes and treaties over the years. These statutes incorporate terms and definitions found in the Geneva Conventions as well as from other treaties and international documents. Some of these statutes list certain violations of the laws or customs of war. They provide additional important sources of what constitutes a war crime.

4. War Crimes Codified by Specialized Tribunals

Even though the Geneva Conventions continues to play an important role in war crimes prosecution, the landscape has changed significantly in the past several years. The Geneva Conventions establish universal jurisdiction for a very finite number of grave breaches, and impose a duty on states to suppress all other war crimes. Today there are several statutes and treaties that have a vastly expanded list of serious war crimes. In addition, there are many different forums for prosecuting this expanded list of war crimes. In some cases the jurisdiction of these forums is limited to a specific conflict or geographic region. The tribunals for the former Yugoslavia and Rwanda are the most significant examples of these specialized tribunals. The ICC has more plenary war crimes jurisdiction, as will be discussed below.

In response to widespread LOAC violations in the civil wars in the former Yugoslavia and Rwanda, the United Nations Security Council, exercising its Chapter VII authority, authorized the creation of ad hoc international criminal tribunals for the ICTY and Rwanda (ICTR).[64] The Security Council Resolutions for each of these tribunals enumerated specific war crimes falling within their jurisdiction.[65] Among the offenses punishable by the ICTY are grave breaches of the Geneva Conventions, genocide, crimes against humanity, and violations of the laws or customs of war. Included in the non-exclusive list of violations of the laws and customs of war are weapons calculated to cause unnecessary suffering; wanton destruction of cities, towns, or villages; attack,

---

63. Rome Statute, *supra*, note 54, art. 7.
64. For Yugoslavia (ICTY), *see* S.C. Res. 827 (May 25, 1993), available at http://www.icty.org/x/file/Legal%20Library/Statute/statute_827_1993_en.pdf. For Rwanda (ICTR), *see* S.C. Res. 955 (Nov. 8, 1994), *available at* http://www.unictr.org/Portals/0/English/Legal/Resolutions/English/955e.pdf.
65. *Id.*

or bombardment, by whatever means, of undefended towns, villages, dwellings, or buildings; seizure of, destruction or willful damage done to institutions dedicated to religion, charity and education, the arts and sciences, historic monuments, and works of art and science; and plunder of public or private property.[66]

The offenses themselves are defined broadly with no attempt to create specific elements for each offense. These violations of the laws provided a basis for criminal responsibility only in the context of the conflict in the former Yugoslavia. However, imposition of criminal responsibility for these offenses is an important indication that they fall within the category of internationally recognized war crimes, and therefore the jurisprudence of both these ad hoc tribunals provides additional useful indicia of what might constitute war crimes in other conflicts. The ICTY operated for 24 years, dissolving in 2017.[67]

The Security Council Resolution creating the statute for the ICTR followed a similar approach. Because the conflict in Rwanda was not an international armed conflict, the grave breach offenses of the Geneva Conventions were not incorporated into the Rwandan tribunal statute. Instead, common Article 3 and Additional Protocol II violations were incorporated into the enumeration of the crimes within the tribunal's jurisdiction. Some of these listed common Article 3 offenses include violence to life, health and physical or mental well-being of persons; collective punishments; taking of hostages; acts of terrorism; outrages upon personal dignity; pillage; the passing of sentences and the carrying out of executions without previous judgment pronounced by a regularly constituted court, affording all the judicial guarantees that are recognized as indispensable by civilized peoples.[68]

In addition, the statute lists genocide and crimes against humanity as offenses punishable by the tribunal. However, violations of the laws and customs of war are not specifically listed as offenses. Like the statute for the ICTY, the ICTR statute was contextualized for that specific conflict, but it too provides additional indicia of what are internationally accepted as war crimes, particularly in the context of non-international armed conflicts. The ICTR operated for 21 years, dissolving in 2015.[69]

5. War Crimes Codified by the ICC

The ICC was established in 1998 as "a permanent institution and shall have the power to exercise its jurisdiction over persons for the most serious crimes of international concern, as referred to in this Statute, and shall be complementary to

---

66. See ICTY, *supra*, note 63, art. 3.
67. During that 24 years, the ICTY was in session for "10,800 days, hear[d] 4,650 witnesses and digest[ed] 2.5 million pages of transcript" in the process of indicting 161 people, 90 of whom were found guilty for crimes including genocide and crimes against humanity. Owen Bowcott, *Yugoslavia Tribunal Closes, Leaving a Powerful Legacy of War Crimes Justice*, THE GUARDIAN, Dec. 20, 2017.
68. See ICTR, *supra*, note 63, art. 4.
69. During that 21 years, the ICTR indicted 93 people, sentencing 62, for serious LOAC violations. The ICTR was the first international tribunal to deliver "verdicts against persons responsible for committing genocide . . . [and] was also the first institution to recognize rape as a means of perpetrating genocide." United Nations Mechanism for International Criminal Tribunals Legacy Website of the International Criminal Tribunal for Rwanda.

national criminal jurisdictions."[70] The authorizing statute for the ICC is the Rome Statute. The Rome Statute codifies both war crimes and criminal law doctrines that are applicable in war crimes prosecutions. Like the ICTY and ICTR, the ICC is having a profound influence on both the genesis of war crimes and their prosecution.

The Rome Statute, like the ICTY, incorporates grave breaches as punishable offenses. It codifies genocide and crimes against humanity with some variations from the ICTY and the ICTR definitions. It also codifies war crimes, and lists 26 specific acts that constitute war crimes in addition to the grave breaches of the Geneva Conventions. These 26 crimes are:

(i) Intentionally directing attacks against the civilian population as such or against individual civilians not taking direct part in hostilities;

(ii) Intentionally directing attacks against civilian objects, that is, objects which are not military objectives;

(iii) Intentionally directing attacks against personnel, installations, material, units or vehicles involved in a humanitarian assistance or peacekeeping mission in accordance with the Charter of the United Nations, as long as they are entitled to the protection given to civilians or civilian objects under the international law of armed conflict;

(iv) Intentionally launching an attack in the knowledge that such attack will cause incidental loss of life or injury to civilians or damage to civilian objects or widespread, long-term and severe damage to the natural environment which would be clearly excessive in relation to the concrete and direct overall military advantage anticipated;

(v) Attacking or bombarding, by whatever means, towns, villages, dwellings or buildings which are undefended and which are not military objectives;

(vi) Killing or wounding a combatant who, having laid down his arms or having no longer means of defence, has surrendered at discretion;

(vii) Making improper use of a flag of truce, of the flag or of the military insignia and uniform of the enemy or of the United Nations, as well as of the distinctive emblems of the Geneva Conventions, resulting in death or serious personal injury;

(viii) The transfer, directly or indirectly, by the Occupying Power of parts of its own civilian population into the territory it occupies, or the deportation or transfer of all or parts of the population of the occupied territory within or outside this territory;

(ix) Intentionally directing attacks against buildings dedicated to religion, education, art, science or charitable purposes, historic monuments, hospitals and places where the sick and wounded are collected, provided they are not military objectives;

(x) Subjecting persons who are in the power of an adverse party to physical mutilation or to medical or scientific experiments of any kind which are neither justified by the medical, dental or hospital treatment of the person concerned nor carried out in his or her interest, and which cause death to or seriously endanger the health of such person or persons;

---

70. Rome Statute, *supra*, note 54, art. 1.

(xi) Killing or wounding treacherously individuals belonging to the hostile nation or army;

(xii) Declaring that no quarter will be given;

(xiii) Destroying or seizing the enemy's property unless such destruction or seizure be imperatively demanded by the necessities of war;

(xiv) Declaring abolished, suspended or inadmissible in a court of law the rights and actions of the nationals of the hostile party;

(xv) Compelling the nationals of the hostile party to take part in the operations of war directed against their own country, even if they were in the belligerent's service before the commencement of the war;

(xvi) Pillaging a town or place, even when taken by assault;

(xvii) Employing poison or poisoned weapons;

(xviii) Employing asphyxiating, poisonous or other gases, and all analogous liquids, materials or devices;

(xix) Employing bullets which expand or flatten easily in the human body, such as bullets with a hard envelope which does not entirely cover the core or is pierced with incisions;

(xx) Employing weapons, projectiles and material and methods of warfare which are of a nature to cause superfluous injury or unnecessary suffering or which are inherently indiscriminate in violation of the international law of armed conflict, provided that such weapons, projectiles and material and methods of warfare are the subject of a comprehensive prohibition and are included in an annex to this Statute, by an amendment in accordance with the relevant provisions set forth in articles 121 and 123;

(xxi) Committing outrages upon personal dignity, in particular humiliating and degrading treatment;

(xxii) Committing rape, sexual slavery, enforced prostitution, forced pregnancy, as defined in article 7, paragraph 2 (f), enforced sterilization, or any other form of sexual violence also constituting a grave breach of the Geneva Conventions;

(xxiii) Utilizing the presence of a civilian or other protected person to render certain points, areas or military forces immune from military operations;

(xxiv) Intentionally directing attacks against buildings, material, medical units and transport, and personnel using the distinctive emblems of the Geneva Conventions in conformity with international law;

(xxv) Intentionally using starvation of civilians as a method of warfare by depriving them of objects indispensable to their survival, including willfully impeding relief supplies as provided for under the Geneva Conventions;

(xxvi) Conscripting or enlisting children under the age of fifteen years into the national armed forces or using them to participate actively in hostilities.[71]

Like the Geneva Conventions of 1949, the Rome Statute also maintains the distinction between international armed conflicts and non-international armed

---

71. *Id.*, Art. 8.

conflicts. The Rome Statute lists a separate category of crimes that can be committed in a non-international armed conflict. This category includes violations of common Article 3. It also includes twelve other serious violations of the laws and customs applicable in armed conflicts not of an international character. These violations are:

(i) Intentionally directing attacks against the civilian population as such or against individual civilians not taking direct part in hostilities;

(ii) Intentionally directing attacks against buildings, material, medical units and transport, and personnel using the distinctive emblems of the Geneva Conventions in conformity with international law;

(iii) Intentionally directing attacks against personnel, installations, material, units or vehicles involved in a humanitarian assistance or peacekeeping mission in accordance with the Charter of the United Nations, as long as they are entitled to the protection given to civilians or civilian objects under the international law of armed conflict;

(iv) Intentionally directing attacks against buildings dedicated to religion, education, art, science or charitable purposes, historic monuments, hospitals and places where the sick and wounded are collected, provided they are not military objectives;

(v) Pillaging a town or place, even when taken by assault;

(vi) Committing rape, sexual slavery, enforced prostitution, forced pregnancy, as defined in article 7, paragraph 2 (f), enforced sterilization, and any other form of sexual violence also constituting a serious violation of article 3 common to the four Geneva Conventions;

(vii) Conscripting or enlisting children under the age of fifteen years into armed forces or groups or using them to participate actively in hostilities;

(viii) Ordering the displacement of the civilian population for reasons related to the conflict, unless the security of the civilians involved or imperative military reasons so demand;

(ix) Killing or wounding treacherously a combatant adversary;

(x) Declaring that no quarter will be given;

(xi) Subjecting persons who are in the power of another party to the conflict to physical mutilation or to medical or scientific experiments of any kind which are neither justified by the medical, dental or hospital treatment of the person concerned nor carried out in his or her interest, and which cause death to or seriously endanger the health of such person or persons;

(xii) Destroying or seizing the property of an adversary unless such destruction or seizure be imperatively demanded by the necessities of the conflict.[72]

The Rome Statute is unique not only because it represents the most comprehensive listing to date of what constitutes a war crime, but also because the statute provides much greater detail and precision as to what these offenses

---

72. *Id.*

are, what their elements include,[73] what punishments can be imposed[74] and the defenses that may be applicable.[75] Indeed much of the Rome Statute reads like a traditional criminal code and it is quite different from the broad and general language found in the Geneva Conventions and other international treaties and statutes. The Rome Statute is probably the most valuable single source based on its coverage and specific detail for what battlefield misconduct constitutes a war crime.

E. *Nulla Crimen sine Lege*

A criticism frequently raised against prosecuting war crimes is that the alleged misconduct frequently involves offenses that were made up by the victorious forces after the fact. In U.S. constitutional parlance, the argument is that these so called "war crimes" are ex post facto laws, and are invalid because the conduct in question was not a crime at the time it was committed. The alleged perpetrators had no knowledge of the offenses and therefore were unable to conform their conduct to a non-existent law. This criticism is frequently mentioned in reference to the IMT. Justice Douglas said of these trials:

> No matter how many books are written or briefs filed, no matter how finely the lawyers analyzed it, the crime for which the Nazis were tried had never been formalized as a crime with the definiteness required by our legal standards, nor outlawed with a death penalty by the international community. By our standards that crime arose under an ex post facto law. Goering et al deserved severe punishment. But their guilt did not justify us in substituting power for principle.[76]

The IMT was the first time in modern history that senior civilian and military leaders were brought to account for their conduct by an international tribunal. Prior to their inclusion on the London Charter, crimes against humanity and crimes against peace had not previously been defined, let alone prosecuted. Other criminal concepts, like obedience to orders as a defense and the doctrine of command responsibility, did have some basis in preexisting practice. However, they were expanded or applied differently in many post-World War II war crimes tribunals than those concepts had previously been understood. There is no doubt that many of the criminal offenses and other legal concepts used in these tribunals were either cobbled together or created out of whole cloth.

---

73. While the statute is much more specific in its definition of what constitutes war crimes, the statute itself does not define the elements of specific offenses. However, pursuant to Article 9 of the Rome Statute, in 2002 specific elements of each of the crimes listed was adopted by the ICC. These elements are to assist the Court in the interpretation and application of Articles 6, 7, and 8 (war crimes articles). *See* http://www1.umn.edu/humanrts/instree/iccelementsofcrimes.html.
74. *See* Rome Statute, *supra,* note 54, Arts. 77 and 78.
75. *See* Id. at Arts. 30-33.
76. U.S. Supreme Court Justice William O. Douglas, Kennedy, *Profiles in Courage,* (New York: Harper & Row, 1964), p.190.

Whether this is an exercise in interpretive evolution necessary due to the amorphous nature of international proscriptions in war, or a violation of the nulle crimen principle, is a debate that continues to this day. Indeed, defendants have leveled this nulle crimen criticism against contemporary war crimes tribunals. For example, defendants in both the ICTY and ICTR have claimed that the crimes alleged against them are new and were not previously recognized as war crimes.[77] Some defendants have also challenged the extension of individual criminal responsibility to the context of NIAC as a violation of the nulle crimen principle, or that the very creation of the tribunal violated this principle.[78]

The enumeration of grave breaches in the Geneva Conventions and the codification of other crimes have substantially blunted these criticisms. As the substance of war crimes jurisdiction continues to gain clarity as the result of tribunal jurisprudence and especially the Rome Statute, the risk that the vagaries of the law invite manipulation and ex post facto application is diminished. Efforts by the ICC to provide more comprehensive and specific definitions of exactly what constitutes war crimes is a welcome and important development in the LOAC. The creation of ad hoc tribunals to prosecute war crimes in a specific conflict establishes an important precedent and helps to refute future nulle crimen criticisms. While this law will almost certainly continue to evolve, the existence of a permanent international court vested with jurisdiction over war crimes, and the embedded process for revising its treaty-based jurisdiction, should transform what has previously been a very generalized development process to one akin to the development of domestic criminal law.

III. Jurisdiction

Defining what constitutes war crimes is only part of the accountability equation. As with any criminal system, one of the most fundamental questions in a war crimes prosecution is determining jurisdiction over the offense and over the offender. In most criminal codes, criminal jurisdiction is based on the location of the crime. How does such a territorially based jurisdiction work when the persons alleged to have committed the war crimes did so outside of the State that now seeks to prosecute the offender? For war crimes, this question is often answered through the doctrine of universal jurisdiction.

The notion of universal jurisdiction is not new to international law or the LOAC. The rationale for universal jurisdiction is that some crimes, like crimes against humanity, genocide, and certain war crimes, are so serious that they offend all humanity and all States have not only a right but a responsibility to

---

77. Prosecutor v. Tadic, Case No. IT-94-1, Decision on Defence Motion on Jurisdiction (Aug. 10, 1995), available at http://www.icty.org/x/cases/tadic/tdec/en/100895.htm.
78. *Id.*

bring the perpetrators to justice. Although the United States has historically supported the prosecution of serious war criminals, it has also demonstrated its unease with assertions of universal jurisdiction. This is based on the concern that universal jurisdiction may be a political tool to be misused against American officials and military personnel. Indeed, this concern led Congress to limit the WCA (the criminal statute implementing our grave breach obligation) jurisdiction over grave breaches of the Geneva Conventions to only those involving a nationality connection to the United States.[79]

Regardless of the United States' misgivings, the 1949 Geneva Conventions establish a precedent for universal jurisdiction. Recall that the High Contracting Parties to the Geneva Conventions are obligated to search for persons alleged to have committed grave breaches and bring these persons, regardless of their nationality, before their own courts. There is no territorial or nationality jurisdictional requirement. Instead, the Conventions require each State to create laws that will allow it to assert jurisdiction to try grave breaches. This is certainly one illustration of universal jurisdiction. A majority of States have enacted implementing legislation that vests their courts with the ability to exercise universal jurisdiction in order to meet their Geneva Convention obligations and to ensure that they do not become a safe haven for war criminals.

The ad hoc tribunals for the former Yugoslavia and Rwanda have also exercised universal jurisdiction. These tribunals were created by the broader international community. The ICTY has the power to "prosecute persons responsible for serious violations of international humanitarian law committed in the territory of the former Yugoslavia since 1991. . . ."[80] However, this limitation on temporal and geographic jurisdiction reflects the tribunal's origins as a measure authorized by the UN Security Council to restore international peace and security in the former Yugoslavia, not a limitation on universal jurisdiction. The mere fact that this tribunal is composed of judges from States with no territorial or nationality link to that conflict is a manifestation of the tribunal's underlying universal jurisdiction. By vesting the ICTY with jurisdiction over all serious violations of the laws and customs of war, the Security Council certainly indicated its invocation of universal jurisdiction.

The ICTR reflects a similar invocation of universal jurisdiction. Like the ICTY, its jurisdiction is limited to persons responsible for serious violations of international humanitarian law committed in the territory of Rwanda and over Rwandan citizens responsible for such violations committed in the territories of neighboring States between 1 January 1994 and 31 December 1994.[81] However, it also is composed of judges from UN member States with no connection whatsoever to that conflict.

The jurisdiction of the ICC is offense-based. Article 5 of the Rome Statute provides:

---

79. 18 USC 2441
80. ICTY, *supra*, note 63, at art. 1.
81. ICTR, *supra*, note 63, at Article 1.

The jurisdiction of the Court shall be limited to the most serious crimes of concern to the international community as a whole. The Court has jurisdiction in accordance with this Statute with respect to the following crimes:

(a) The crime of genocide;
(b) Crimes against humanity;
(c) War crimes;
(d) The crime of aggression.[82]

The terms of the statute suggest the ICC has a more expansive universal jurisdiction than the ICTY, the ICTR, the Nuremberg and other World War II tribunals. The United States is not a party to the ICC, not necessarily because of this expansive assertion of universal jurisdiction, but because of the plenary authority of the ICC prosecutor to assert this jurisdiction with no UN Security Council check. The United States has asserted since the inception of ICC negotiation efforts that this authority is too prone to political manipulation, and places U.S. personnel at risk. However, the United States has supported assertions of ICC jurisdiction through the alternate process of Security Council referral. In fact, the ICC's jurisdiction may not be as expansive as Article 5 suggests. A key feature of the ICC is the principle of complementarity. The ICC party States are still required to investigate and prosecute serious crimes subject to their own domestic criminal jurisdiction (to include grave breaches when the perpetrator is found within the State's jurisdiction). Only if a party State is unwilling or unable to investigate and prosecute these offenses should the ICC assert jurisdiction.

That said, the United States has been skeptical that this complementary design will offset the risk of politicizing ICC prosecutions. In November, 2017, the ICC prosecutor requested that a pre-trial chamber investigate allegations that war crimes had been committed in Afghanistan by Afghan military and security forces, the Taliban, and other organized armed groups, and by the U.S. armed forces and the Central Intelligence Agency.[83] In December, 2017 the United States made an intervention at the Assembly of States Parties to the Rome Statute, claiming that any attempt by the ICC to assert jurisdiction over U.S. personnel would be "illegitimate".[84]

The United States' opposition toward the ICC and its concern over the Court's universal jurisdiction authority raises another common criticism of war crimes prosecutions. Like the creation of seemingly ex post facto laws, the creation of universal jurisdiction not specifically tied to nationality or territorial principles of jurisdiction also risks a perception of victor's justice. Universal

---

82. Rome Statute, *supra*, note 54, art. 5.
83. *See* International Criminal Court Office of the Prosecutor, Situation in the Islamic Republic of Afghanistan, Request For Authorization of an Investigation Pursuant to Article 15, 20 November 2017, ICC-02/17-7-Conf-Exp.
84. Statement of Behalf of the United States of America, 16th Session of the Assembly of State Parties December 8, 2017. Some commentators questioned the validity of the U.S. claims that any ICC exercise of jurisdiction over U.S. personnel would be invalid. *See* Kevin Jon Heller, The Puzzling US Submission to the Assembly of States Parties, Opinio Juris Dec. 13, 2017 http://opiniojuris.org/2017/12/13/the-puzzling-us-submission-to-the-asp-about-aggression/.

jurisdiction also places a significant limitation on individual State sovereignty. If any State may assert universal jurisdiction, there is concern that war crimes prosecutions will be used for political purposes. In spite of these concerns, the concept of universal jurisdiction is very deliberately more expansive than traditional nationality or territorial principles of jurisdiction. While this does increase the risk that States will assert jurisdiction over cases they have no meaningful connection to in order to advance a political agenda, it also represents what many believe is a positive response to the historic impunity many war criminals exploited to avoid accountability. How this doctrine will evolve, and how the United States will interact with the ICC, are important issues in the future development of international criminal responsibility.

IV. Recent Developments in War Crimes Prosecutions

This chapter makes several references to the ICTY and the ICTR, the ad hoc tribunals for the former Yugoslavia and Rwanda. These and other specialized tribunals are a relatively recent development in the history of war crimes prosecutions. These ad hoc tribunals were established pursuant to United Nations Security Council authorization.[85] Other specialized war crimes tribunals have been established pursuant to agreement between States and the United Nations, such as the special tribunals for Sierra Leone, Cambodia, and Lebanon. While the creation of the ICC may displace the need for such ad hoc and specialized tribunals, they are making important contributions to the development of war crimes today.

A. Use of Specialized Tribunals

These specialized tribunals have proven to be effective in bringing war criminals—both soldiers and senior military and civilian leaders—to justice. But why did the international community use these mechanisms to prosecute war crimes instead of creating the ICC much earlier? The answer boils down to State sovereignty. The simple reality is that States have been much more willing to establish tribunals to prosecute war crimes in specific locations because of the distinct geographic and temporal limits on the jurisdiction of these tribunals.

States not involved in the Yugoslavian war did not directly surrender any portion of their own sovereignty by agreeing to create an ad hoc tribunal for that specific conflict (although NATO States ultimately faced a bit of a surprise when the ICTY investigated the air campaign conducted against Serbia in 1998).[86] States were simply more willing to support such prosecutions when

---

85. *See specifically* Chapter VII of the Charter of the United Nations; both resolution-documents in *supra,* note 63 state expressly that they receive their authority from Chapter VII.
86. *See* http://www.icty.org/sid/7846. International Criminal Tribune for the Former Yugoslavia Prosecutor's Report on the NATO Bombing Campaign (June 13, 2000).

their own sovereignty was not at stake. In the views of many, the ICC is therefore an important step forward in the evolution of accountability for war crimes, although the U.S. position reflects this traditional aversion to surrendering sovereignty over such offenses.

The Special Tribunal for Lebanon opened in 2009, seven years after the ICC was created. Whether the international community will continue to press for the use of such specialized ad hoc tribunals in the future is yet to be seen. It is possible that the ICC will become the primary forum for addressing future war crimes allegations not effectively addressed by States. This is certainly the intent of the States that created the ICC. Even when the individual is beyond the consensual jurisdiction of the ICC (not a national of a party State; crime not committed in the territory of a party State), referral of the case to the ICC by the UN Security Council seems like a more logical response than Security Council creation of an entirely new tribunal. In short, the ICC jurisdictional scheme facilitates its use as what is in essence a permanent venue for the Security Council to use as an ad hoc tribunal. There still, however, may be a need for hybrid tribunals, such as the ones established in Sierra Leone and Cambodia, when the recovering State seeks an international participation in its accountability efforts but the Security Council is not interested in elevating the issue to its level.[87]

B. Blurring the Lines of IAC and NIAC

These specialized tribunals have proven to be an effective way to bring individuals to justice in specific conflicts. However, their existence and decisions have also been profoundly significant because of their broader impact on the law of war generally. In some instances, the rulings in these cases have clarified or even changed CIL. Arguably the most significant impact has come from ICTY decisions that blur or even remove distinctions between IAC and NIACs, and the law that applies in both these conflict categories. It is clear that the Geneva Conventions law triggering paradigm created separate legal regimes applicable for IAC and NIACs. Grave and simple breaches of the Conventions only apply in cases of international armed conflicts. If the conflict is an NIAC, the "mini-convention" provisions of Common Article 3 apply. Two cases from the ICTY challenged this regulator compartmentalization, and initiated a merger of the law applicable to both categories of armed conflicts that continues to this day.

The first case, Prosecutor v. Tadic, involved the alleged mistreatment of Bosnian Muslims and Croats by Serb forces at Camp Omarska. The defendants were charged, inter alia, with grave breaches of the Geneva Conventions and violations of the laws and customs of war. The defendants challenged the ICTY's jurisdiction to hear these charges, because the offenses only exist in an IAC and the armed conflict in Bosnia was NIAC. The Trial Chamber ruled that the existence of an IAC was not required because Articles 2 and 3 of the ICTY statute referencing grave breaches and war crimes were declaratory of

---

87. Karma Nabulsi, Jus ad Bellum/Jus in Bello, Crimes of War A-Z Guide.

customary international law applicable even in NIACs. The concern of the tribunal was, of course, that if these offenses did not apply to non-international armed conflicts, some of the most serious misconduct would go unpunished simply because it did not take place in a context satisfying the technical requirements of the Geneva Conventions.[88]

The ICTY Appellate Chamber (an appeals bench composed of ICTY member judges) took a different approach. It did not adopt the trial chamber's rationale. Instead, the Appellate Chamber maintained the distinction between IAC and NIAC, rejecting the "one-size-fits-all" approach of the trial chamber. The Appellate Chamber ruled that because of Serbia's support for the breakaway Serb enclave in Bosnia, in some areas the armed conflict might be of an international character, while in other areas strictly non-international. The question of fact for the trial chamber to determine was whether the situation at Camp Omarska was related to an international or an internal armed conflict. The resolution of this factual issue would determine if the defendants could be charged with grave breaches of the Geneva Conventions and certain other war crimes. However, one of the Chamber's most important conclusions was that the law applicable to NIAC was not restricted to common Article 3 and AP II. Instead, laws developed for and applicable to an IAC had "migrated" to the realm of internal armed conflicts. The Chamber reasoned that "principles and rules of humanitarian law reflect elementary considerations of humanity widely recognized as the mandatory minimum for conduct in armed conflicts of any kind."[89] This conclusion, along with the Appeals Chamber decision upholding the jurisdiction to try Tadic for a range of war crimes, indicated a merger of regulatory norms for both IAC and NIAC, thereby blurring the war crimes distinctions between these two categories of armed conflict. While this merger did not allow extending the formal concept of grave breach to non-international armed conflict, it did permit the prosecution of other violations of the laws and customs of war related to the conduct of hostilities.[90]

The second case, the ICTY Appeals Chamber Celebici decision, further eroded the distinction between the law that applies to an international versus an internal armed conflict. The defendants in this case were charged with grave breaches of the Geneva Conventions and other war crimes for their alleged murder, torture, and sexual assault of detainees at the Celebici Camp. The issue again arose as to what law should apply, a determination that depended on whether this was an international or an internal armed conflict. The Appeals Chamber noted that common Article 3, which constitutes a mandatory minimum code applicable to internal conflicts, had gradually become part of customary law.[91] In doing so, the Chamber asserted that these principles are so

---

88. *Tadic, supra*, note 47, para. 51.
89. *Id.* 129 (*see* http://www.icty.org/case/tadic/4#tdec for search of this document).
90. *Tadic*, Appeals Chamber Judgment, 74-75 at http://www.icty.org/x/cases/tadic/acjug/en/=tad-aj990715e.pdf.
91. *See* Prosecutor v. Delalic et al., Celebici: Case No. IT-96-21-T at 1 140 (Nov. 16, 1998), *available at* http://www.un.org/icty/celebici/trialc2/judgement/cel-tj981116e.pdf.

fundamental that they govern both international and internal conflicts.[92] The Chamber also ruled that maintaining a legally binding distinction between the two legal regimes and their criminal consequences would ignore the very purpose of the Geneva Conventions.[93]

The Tadic and Celebici decisions have important consequences. By eroding the traditional distinction between the law applicable to the two distinct categories of armed conflicts, the ICTY significantly expanded the scope and applicability of war crimes jurisdiction. The limited piercing of the sovereignty veil initiated by common Article 3 has, as a result of these decisions, been expanded not only by including an individual criminal responsibility component, but also by extending offenses not contemplated by common Article 3 to the non-international armed conflict context. Likewise, the ICTY affirmed that the protections of common Article 3 now apply to all armed conflicts. This represents a remarkable shift. Prior to these decisions, the law of NIAC focused almost exclusively on the protections of individuals who were not participating in hostilities. Now, the protections extend well beyond, to include the regulation of means and methods of warfare previously limited to international armed conflicts. As a result of these decisions, "the fundamental norms applicable to both types of armed conflict have become in large measure synonymous, and it is the disparities between the applicable laws that have become minor."[94]

V. The U.S. Approach to War Crimes Prosecution

Historical background and contemporary international practice provide the essential foundation for all war crimes prosecutions. For U.S. commanders and the Judge Advocates who advise them, however, unique aspects of U.S. practice are equally important. How does the United States prosecute war crimes committed by its enemies, or by its own forces? What law does the United States normally apply as the basis for these prosecutions? How does the United States assert jurisdiction over those whom it chooses to try in its own courts? This section examines these questions.

A. A Subject Matter Jurisdiction

1. Uniform Code of Military Justice Structure

The Uniform Code of Military Justice (UCMJ) was enacted in 1950 pursuant to the authority vested in Congress by the U.S. Constitution "to make Rules for the Government and Regulation of the land and naval Forces."[95] As the title

---

92. *Id.* at para. 141.
93. *Id.* at para. 172.
94. Geoff Corn et al., The War on Terror and the Laws of War: A Military Perspective 167-168 (2009).
95. U.S. Const., art. I, § 8, cl. 14.

suggests, the UCMJ serves as the criminal code of all of the armed forces. The UCMJ codifies common law crimes and military-specific offenses, as well as other enumerated violations of good order and discipline and other service discrediting conduct. Pursuant to Article 36 of the UCMJ, Congress delegated to the President the primary, but not exclusive responsibility for creating rules of procedure. To the extent practicable, these rules should follow the principles of law recognized in criminal cases in the United States district courts.[96]

Since its enactment, the UCMJ has evolved into a fully developed and highly credible system. The criminal code and the rules of procedure and evidence are today engrained in the U.S. military ethos. Further, the system has proven to be an effective means of maintaining military justice and discipline while respecting and protecting the rights of individual service members. The UCMJ has also proven functional and effective during times of peace and war. A wealth of case law surrounding the code and the corresponding procedural rules has also developed over the years

a. Punitive Articles

The UCMJ's codification of crimes is the "punitive articles" of the code, which provide the primary source of proscription enabling the United States to meet its obligation under the Geneva Conventions. These crimes are sufficiently comprehensive to bring U.S. military personnel alleged to have committed grave breaches to justice before military courts. Unlike the laws creating the ICC, the ICTY, the ICTR, or other similar international statutes, the UCMJ punitive articles do not incorporate by reference either grave breaches or violations of common Article 3. In fact, the punitive articles make no direct reference to the Geneva Conventions. These punitive articles read much more like a typical criminal code. The articles define specific criminal conduct, list specific elements of each offense, and set out the punishments that can be imposed for violation of the code.

The punitive articles do not incorporate by reference grave breaches of the Geneva Conventions. The code instead enumerates and penalizes common law and military-specific crimes that are counterparts to the Conventions' grave breaches. The UCMJ's punitive articles that most directly correspond to grave breaches and other war crimes include Article 93 Cruelty or Maltreatment; Article 97 Unlawful Detention; Article 116 Riot; Article 118 Murder; Article 119 Manslaughter; Article 120 Rape; Article 124 Maiming; Article 128 Assault; Article 134 Kidnapping; and Article 134 Negligent Homicide.[97]

Assuming that a U.S. solider was accused of killing an unarmed prisoner under his charge, that solider would most likely face murder charges under the UCMJ. U.S. military case law is replete with examples of war crimes that were charged utilizing this approach, instead of an express allegation of a war crime.

---

96. *See* Uniform Code of Military Justice, art. 36 (hereinafter UCMJ).
97. *See* UCMJ, *supra*, note 93, § 897 art. 97, § 916 art. 116, § 918 art. 118, § 919 art. 119, § 924 art. 124, § 928 art. 128, and § 934 art. 134, *reprinted in* MANUAL FOR COURTS-MARTIAL UNITED STATES. at A2-26, A2-29, and A2-31–A2-32 (2016).

In fact, the United States has a policy of not prosecuting its own forces for violations of the law of war. Violations of the law of war committed by U.S. forces will usually constitute violations of the UCMJ and will be prosecuted under that code.[98] Because UCMJ crimes, defenses, and process are firmly established and understood, relying on the code simplifies the criminal process and ultimately facilitates efficient and effective criminal accountability for battlefield misconduct.

One recent high profile prosecution involved detainee abuse at the Abu Ghraib prison during the Iraq war. One of the alleged ringleaders, Corporal Charles Graner, was alleged to have engaged in a number of acts of abuse. Several pictures emerged depicting Graner and his fellow soldiers abusing detainees. Because the detainees were civilian internees during a period of U.S. occupation, it is almost certain that at least some of this conduct constituted grave breaches of the Fourth Geneva Convention and possibly other war crimes. Corporal Graner was, however, not charged with grave breaches or any express war crime. Instead, he was charged and ultimately convicted of maltreatment, conspiracy to commit maltreatment, and assault in violation of enumerated UCMJ offenses. The charge sheet from his case illustrates this commonly utilized charging methodology (see pages 574-575).

b. Article 18 Jurisdiction over War Crimes

Prosecuting soldiers for violations of the punitive articles is not the only way that the United States can prosecute individuals alleged to have committed war crimes. In addition to courts-martial prosecutions for punitive article violations, Article 18 of the UCMJ grants court martial jurisdiction over war crimes. The article states that "general courts-martial also have jurisdiction to try any person who by the law of war is subject to trial by a military tribunal and may adjudge any punishment permitted by the law of war."[99] This provision allows the United States to prosecute persons, including not only its own soldiers but any other individual, for law of war violations.

Two important points should be kept in mind with this alternate basis of jurisdiction. First and foremost, if the United States decides to prosecute someone under this provision of Article 18, jurisdiction demands that the prosecution allege an offense that qualifies as a valid war crime. Conduct not recognized as a war crime does not fall within the jurisdiction of Article 18, even if it occurs in the context of a military operation (for example, the abuse of a U.S. soldier by a local national in the context of a peace operation). This requires proof not only that the conduct is recognized as a war crime, but that it occurred in the context of an armed conflict (and perhaps a specific type of armed conflict).

---

98. *See* R.C.M. 307(c) (2) Discussion (stating that "[o]rdinarily persons subject to the [UCMJ] should be charged with a specific violation of the [UMCJ] rather than a violation of the law of war.").

99. *See* UCMJ, *supra,* note 93, art. 18.

CHARGE SHEET

I. PERSONAL DATA

1. NAME OF ACCUSED (Last, First, MI)	2. SSN	3. GRADE OR RANK	4. PAY GRADE
GRANER, Charles A., Jr.		SPC	E-4

5. UNIT OR ORGANIZATION	6. CURRENT SERVICE	
Headquarters and Headquarters Company, 16th Military Police Brigade (Airborne), III Corps, Victory Base, Iraq APO AE 09342	a. INITIAL DATE: 20 Dec 01	b. TERM: 8 years

7. PAY PER MONTH			8. NATURE OF RESTRAINT OF ACCUSED	9. DATE(S) IMPOSED
a. BASIC	b. SEA/FOREIGN DUTY	c. TOTAL	None	N/A
$1,891.50	$100.00	$1,991.50		

II. CHARGES AND SPECIFICATIONS

10. CHARGE I VIOLATION OF THE UCMJ, ARTICLE 81

SPECIFICATION 1: In that Corporal Charles A. Graner, Jr., U.S. Army, did, at or near Baghdad Central Correctional Facility, Abu Ghraib, Iraq, on or about 23 October 2003, conspire with Staff Sergeant Ivan L. Frederick, II, and Private First Class Lynndie R. England, to commit an offense under the Uniform Code of Military Justice, to wit: maltreatment of subordinates, and in order to effect the object of the conspiracy the said Corporal Graner did photograph a detainee being dragged by Private First Class England with a leash wrapped around the neck of the detainee.

SPECIFICATION 2: In that Corporal Charles A. Graner, Jr., U.S. Army, did, at or near Baghdad Central Correctional Facility, Abu Ghraib, Iraq, on or about 8 November 2003, conspire with Sergeant Javal S. Davis, Specialist Jeremy C. Sivits, Specialist Sabrina D. Harman, Specialist Megan M. Ambuhl and Private First Class Lynndie R. England, to commit an offense under the Uniform Code of Military Justice, to wit: maltreatment of subordinates, and in order to effect the object of the conspiracy the said Corporal Graner posed for a photograph with the said Specialist Harman behind a pyramid of naked detainees.

(SEE CONTINUATION SHEETS)

III. PREFERRAL

11a. NAME OF ACCUSER (Last, First, MI)	b. GRADE	c. ORGANIZATION OF ACCUSER
EDENFIELD, Phillip F.	O-3	HHC, 16th MP Bde (Abn) APO AE 09342

d. SIGNATURE OF ACCUSER e. DATE: 20 MAR 04

AFFIDAVIT: Before me, the undersigned, authorized by law to administer oaths in cases of this character, personally appeared the above named accuser this 20th day of March, 2004, and signed the foregoing charges and specifications under oath that he/she is a person subject to the Uniform Code of Military Justice and that he/she either has personal knowledge of or has investigated the matters set forth therein and that the same are true to the best of his/her knowledge and belief.

JOHN M. McCABE	HHC, XVIII Abn Corps
Typed Name of Officer	Organization of Officer
O-3	Trial Counsel
Grade	Official Capacity to Administer Oath (See R.C.M. 307(b) – must be a commissioned officer)

DD FORM 458, MAY 2000   PREVIOUS EDITION IS OBSOLETE.

CONTINUATION SHEET 1 of 3, DD Form 458, GRANER, Charles A. Jr., SPC, ▮▮▮▮▮▮▮, HHC, 16th MP Bde (Abn), III Corps, Victory Base, Iraq APO AE 09342

Item 10 (continued):

CHARGE II: VIOLATION OF THE UCMJ, ARTICLE 92

THE SPECIFICATION: In that Corporal Charles A. Graner, Jr., U.S. Army, who knew of his duties at or near Baghdad Central Correctional Facility, Abu Ghraib, Iraq, from on or about 20 October 2003 to on or about 1 December 2003, was derelict in the performance of those duties in that he willfully failed to protect detainees from abuse, cruelty and maltreatment, as it was his duty to do.

CHARGE III: VIOLATION OF THE UCMJ, ARTICLE 93

SPECIFICATION 1: In that Corporal Charles A. Graner, Jr., U.S. Army, at or near Baghdad Central Correctional Facility, Abu Ghraib, Iraq, on or about 8 November 2003, did maltreat several detainees, persons subject to his orders, by placing naked detainees in a human pyramid and photographing and being photographed with the pyramid of naked detainees.

SPECIFICATION 2: In that Corporal Charles A. Graner, Jr., U.S. Army, at or near Baghdad Central Correctional Facility, Abu Ghraib, Iraq, on or about 8 November 2003, did maltreat several detainees, persons subject to his orders, by ordering the detainees to strip, and then ordering the detainees to masturbate in front of the other detainees and soldiers, and then placing one in a position so that the detainee's face was directly in front of the genitals of another detainee to simulate fellatio and photographing the detainees during these acts.

SPECIFICATION 3: In that Corporal Charles A. Graner, Jr., U.S. Army, at or near Baghdad Central Correctional Facility, Abu Ghraib, Iraq, on or about 8 November 2003 did maltreat a detainee, a person subject to his orders, by being photographed with one arm cocked back as if he was going to hit the detainee in the neck or back.

SPECIFICATION 4: In that Corporal Charles A. Graner, Jr., U.S. Army, at or near Baghdad Central Correctional Facility, Abu Ghraib, Iraq, on or about 23 October 2003 did maltreat a detainee, a person subject to his orders, by encouraging Private First Class Lynndie R. England to drag a detainee by a leash wrapped around said detainees neck, and photographing said misconduct.

Second, determining and defining specific offenses under the law of war is not an easy task. As noted earlier, other than the Rome Statute, most international treaties and statutes give only general definitions rather than clear and specific elements of particular war crimes. This lack of clarity presents particular challenges in prosecuting U.S. soldiers or other individuals for general violations of the law of war. Undoubtedly, these prosecutions would raise constitutional challenges of vagueness and overbreadth. This provision could, however, still prove critically important to assert U.S. military jurisdiction over a captured or detained individual believed to have violated the law of war.

Because such individuals are not subject to the punitive articles of the UCMJ prior to capture (unlike U.S. service members and other U.S. persons associated with the military command), Article 18 provides the exclusive jurisdiction to prosecute before U.S. courts-martial (although use of military commission is also an option).[100]

As explained above, the distinctions between the law applicable to IAC and NIAC has become less significant in recent years. Further, because it is the policy of the United States to prosecute its own forces for violations of the UCMJ rather than for war crimes, this distinction has even less significance for a U.S. commander who perceives the need to criminally prosecute a soldier for misconduct in the context of any military operation.

2. The War Crimes Act

The UCMJ is not the only means by which the United States prosecutes war crimes and meets its Geneva Convention obligations. In 1996, the United States implemented (although as explained above, not fully) the "repress and punish" obligation of the Geneva Conventions with enactment of the WCA.[101] The WCA establishes federal criminal jurisdiction to punish any person who commits a war crime as defined, if either the perpetrator or the victim is a member of the U.S. armed forces or a "national of the United States."[102]

a. Punishable Offenses

Rather than listing specific war crimes, the WCA incorporates by reference the grave breaches of the four Geneva Conventions, conduct prohibited by certain articles of the Hague Convention IV of 1907, violations of common Article 3 of the Geneva Conventions, and violations of the Convention Restricting the Use of Mines, Booby-Traps, and Other Devices. According to the Act:

> (c) Definition.—As used in this section the term "war crime" means any conduct—
> (1) defined as a grave breach in any of the international conventions signed at Geneva 12 August 1949, or any protocol to such convention to which the United States is a party;
> (2) prohibited by Article 23, 25, 27, or 28 of the Annex to the Hague Convention IV, Respecting the Laws and Customs of War on Land, signed 18 October 1907;
> (3) which constitutes a grave breach of common Article 3 (as defined in subsection (d)) when committed in the context of and in association with an armed conflict not of an international character; or
> (4) of a person who, in relation to an armed conflict and contrary to the provisions of the Protocol on Prohibitions or Restrictions on the

---

100. Geoffrey S. Corn, *Authority to Court-Martial Non-U.S. Military Personnel for Serious Violations of International Humanitarian Law Committed During Internal Armed Conflicts*, 74 Mil. L. Rev. 167 (2001).
101. 18 U.S.C. § 2441 (2006).
102. *Id.*

Use of Mines, Booby-Traps and Other Devices as amended at Geneva on 3 May 1996 (Protocol II as amended on 3 May 1996), when the United States is a party to such Protocol, willfully kills or causes serious injury to civilians.

(d) Common Article 3 Violations.—

(1) Prohibited conduct.—In subsection (c)(3), the term "grave breach of common Article 3" means any conduct (such conduct constituting a grave breach of common Article 3 of the international conventions done at Geneva August 12, 1949), as follows:

(A) Torture.—The act of a person who commits, or conspires or attempts to commit, an act specifically intended to inflict severe physical or mental pain or suffering (other than pain or suffering incidental to lawful sanctions) upon another person within his custody or physical control for the purpose of obtaining information or a confession, punishment, intimidation, coercion, or any reason based on discrimination of any kind.

(B) Cruel or inhuman treatment.—The act of a person who commits, or conspires or attempts to commit, an act intended to inflict severe or serious physical or mental pain or suffering (other than pain or suffering incidental to lawful sanctions), including serious physical abuse, upon another within his custody or control.

(C) Performing biological experiments.—The act of a person who subjects, or conspires or attempts to subject, one or more persons within his custody or physical control to biological experiments without a legitimate medical or dental purpose and in so doing endangers the body or health of such person or persons.

(D) Murder.—The act of a person who intentionally kills, or conspires or attempts to kill, or kills whether intentionally or unintentionally in the course of committing any other offense under this subsection, one or more persons taking no active part in the hostilities, including those placed out of combat by sickness, wounds, detention, or any other cause.

(E) Mutilation or maiming.—The act of a person who intentionally injures, or conspires or attempts to injure, or injures whether intentionally or unintentionally in the course of committing any other offense under this subsection, one or more persons taking no active part in the hostilities, including those placed out of combat by sickness, wounds, detention, or any other cause, by disfiguring the person or persons by any mutilation thereof or by permanently disabling any member, limb, or organ of his body, without any legitimate medical or dental purpose.

(F) Intentionally causing serious bodily injury.—The act of a person who intentionally causes, or conspires or attempts to cause, serious bodily injury to one or more persons, including lawful combatants, in violation of the law of war.

(G) Rape.—The act of a person who forcibly or with coercion or threat of force wrongfully invades, or conspires or attempts to invade, the body of a person by penetrating, however slightly, the anal or genital opening of the victim with any part of the body of the accused, or with any foreign object.

(H) Sexual assault or abuse.—The act of a person who forcibly or with coercion or threat of force engages, or conspires or attempts to engage, in sexual contact with one or more persons, or causes, or conspires or attempts to cause, one or more persons to engage in sexual contact.

(I) Taking hostages.—The act of a person who, having knowingly seized or detained one or more persons, threatens to kill, injure, or continue to detain such person or persons with the intent of compelling any nation, person other than the hostage, or group of persons to act or refrain from acting as an explicit or implicit condition for the safety or release of such person or persons.[103]

The primary purpose of the WCA is twofold. First, the statute was enacted to provide a legal mechanism to prosecute former soldiers who may have committed enumerated war crimes, but whose violations were only discovered after the soldier left the service and no longer subject to military jurisdiction.[104] The second purpose was outward looking: to prosecute those outside the United States who committed war crimes against U.S. citizens and soldiers. To date, no one has been prosecuted under the WCA.

b. Modifications by the DTA and MCA

After the Supreme Court's opinion in Hamdan v. Rumsfeld ruling that common Article 3 protections apply to the United States' fight against al Qaeda, concern arose that the WCA could be used to prosecute members of the armed forces and other government agents because of their aggressive interrogations and harsh treatment of terrorist suspects. To prevent this from happening, Congress amended the WCA to limit its applicability. These amendments were incorporated into the Detainee Treatment Act (DTA) of 2005 and the Military Commissions Act (MCA) of 2006.

First, the DTA created statutory immunity for U.S. personnel who were engaging in specific operational practices that had been authorized by government officials. The immunity does not apply to senior government officials or to unauthorized conduct, and was designed to protect those at the operational level who were conducting interrogations that might, in retrospect, be determined to have violated common Article 3 as referenced in the WCA, but did so pursuant to apparent lawful authority. This is in a sense a statutory-based mistake of law defense.[105]

The next, and more dramatic modification to the WCA came with the passage of the 2006 MCA. The 2006 MCA was enacted to resurrect military commission prosecutions in response to the Supreme Court's invalidation of the military commission system established by President Bush's Military Order Number 1 in October 2002. The 2006 MCA also sought to provide broad retroactive protection to operators and senior government officials who either

---

103. *Id.*
104. *See* H.R. Rep. No. 104-689 (1996).
105. *See* http://www.dtic.mil/cgi-bin/GetTRDoc?Location=U2&doc=GetTRDoc.pdf&AD=ADA479062.

ordered or were involved in interrogation and treatment practices that might run afoul of the WCA.[106]

The 2006 MCA did this by first narrowing the violations of common Article 3 that would be punishable under the WCA. The United States created a new category of "grave breaches" of common Article 3; only those grave breaches could be prosecuted under the WCA. These grave breaches included torture, cruel treatment, performing biological experiments, murder, and other serious offenses. The 2006 MCA then significantly narrowed the definitions of torture, cruel treatment, serious pain and suffering, and other similar terms. These definitions are arguably now much narrower than how these same terms are defined in various treaties and other international agreements and statutes, or generally understood internationally. This does not mean that other violations of common Article 3 are authorized. Instead, it segregates the broad scope of common Article 3 prohibitions from those qualifying for criminal prosecution pursuant to the WCA (although any violation could still be prosecuted in a military court).[107]

Finally, the 2006 MCA expanded significantly the statutory immunity created by the DTA. The statutory immunity protections now apply not only to operators on the ground, but also to more senior officials who developed or sanctioned aggressive interrogation and harsh treatment. The statutory immunity period applies specifically to conduct that occurred between September 11, 2001 and December 30, 2005 (the date the DTA was enacted). Even after the passage of the DTA and the 2006 MCA, it was the position of the Bush administration that certain interrogation techniques, such as water boarding and sleep deprivation, did not violate common Article 3. Further, it was posited that even if the military was precluded from using such techniques under its policies, other government agencies, specifically the CIA, could lawfully continue to use those techniques.[108]

When President Obama came into office in 2009 he issued an Executive Order barring anyone in U.S. custody in an armed conflict from being subject to any interrogation technique that is not authorized by the Army's Interrogation Manual. Additional amendments in the 2009 Military Commissions Act (MCA) have clarified and closed some of the gaps in the admissibility of statements obtained by cruel, inhumane, and degrading treatment. The 2009 amendments did not change the statutory immunity for U.S. officials created in the 2006 MCA.

What does this recent history tell us about the WCA as a mechanism for prosecuting suspected war criminals? While the passage of the Act might partially satisfy the United States' obligations under the Geneva Conventions to establish laws to bring those suspected of committing grave breaches to justice, the practical impact of the WCA has been insignificant. This is so for several reasons. First, as this recent history demonstrates, the WCA was modified and manipulated when it looked like the WCA might actually be enforced against U.S. personnel and senior government officials. Second, the limitations now placed on the WCA and the narrowness of the definitions mean that only the most serious offenses would be prosecuted. Additionally, because no one has

---

106. *Id.*
107. *Id.*
108. *Id.*

ever been prosecuted under the Act, if there are alternatives available, like the UCMJ and military commissions, those alternatives will continue to be the preferred method for prosecution. Finally, the statutory immunities that now exist because of the DTA and MCA's amendments create an obvious inequality. Non-U.S. personnel can be prosecuted for the conduct while U.S. personnel might be immune from prosecution for that same conduct. That inequity is not likely to go unnoticed by the courts were a case to arise under the statute.

VI. Personal Jurisdiction

A. Jurisdiction over Soldiers

Members of the armed forces obviously engage in conduct that can result in war crimes allegations. The primary means to prosecute soldiers is the UCMJ. Jurisdiction over soldiers is based not on the location of the crimes but on the status of the soldier. Article 2 of the UCMJ defines individuals subject to the UCMJ (and most importantly, the punitive articles of the Code). Included within this personal jurisdiction are members of the regular components of the armed forces; members of the reserve when activated; and members of the National Guard when in federal service.[109] The extraterritorial reach of the UCMJ over soldiers is fairly straightforward. The jurisdictional question of fact is whether the person being prosecuted was a member of the armed forces at the time the offenses were alleged to have been committed and whether the person is still a member of the armed forces at the time he or she is facing court-martial.[110]

While this is a fairly straightforward question of fact, status-based jurisdiction creates some difficulties. For example, the alleged perpetrator must be a member of the armed forces at the time court-martial charges are leveled against him or her. Therefore, if a soldier's service was terminated before the crimes were discovered, or before a prosecution was initiated, there is no authority under the UCMJ to bring that former soldier back into military service. This can create a loophole where the former soldier is beyond the reach of the military jurisdiction for crimes committed as a soldier. Perhaps the most notorious example of this loophole was related to the My Lai massacre. During the Vietnam War, U.S. Army soldiers, massacred hundreds of civilians near the village of My Lai. Several months passed before military officials investigated the massacre and by the time criminal prosecutions were initiated, a number of the soldiers implicated in the crimes had been discharged from military service. Because of the gap created by status-based jurisdiction, these former soldiers were never prosecuted for their involvement in this war crime, even though some of them candidly admitted their participation in multiple murders.

---

109. *See* UCMJ, art. 2.
110. *See* 10 U.S.C. § 802(a)(1); Solorio v. United States, 483 U.S. 435 (1987); Holland, Instructor, The Judge Advocate General's School, Military Status: Not Necessarily Equivalent to Subject Matter Jurisdiction, March 1990 Army Law. 38 (Westlaw).

Other than the UCMJ, two other statutes can be used to extend extraterritorial application of U.S. law to members of the armed forces. The first is the WCA. As explained above, the WCA can apply to current or former members of the armed forces. No member of the armed forces has yet been prosecuted under this statute. The next section discusses how the extraterritorial reach of the WCA extends beyond active duty soldiers and is therefore broader than the UCMJ.

The third statute that has the extraterritorial jurisdiction to reach members of the armed forces is the Military Extraterritorial Jurisdiction Act (MEJA). As will be seen in the next section, the MEJA is intended primarily as a gap filler to provide for U.S. prosecution of civilians associated with the armed forces abroad who were not subject to military jurisdiction. One provision of the MEJA provides that members of the armed forces subject to the UCMJ can be prosecuted instead under the MEJA if the indictment or information charges that the member committed the offense with one or more other defendants, at least one of whom is not subject to the UCMJ.[111]

B. Jurisdiction over Former Soldiers

As noted above, former soldiers may engage in misconduct while in uniform that is not discovered until after their discharge from military service. In these situations, the United States would want to assert criminal jurisdiction over their extraterritorial misconduct. If the suspect is truly a former soldier with no current legal connection to the military, the UCMJ cannot be used to assert jurisdiction. However, there are some former service members who may still have a legal connection to the military; for example, military retirees (individuals entitled to and receiving retirement pay) are within the jurisdiction of Article 2 of the UCMJ. These retirees may be involuntarily recalled to active duty where they can face court-martial prosecution for crimes that they may have committed while previously an active member of the armed forces.[112]

Another closely related category of former service member subject to recall to active duty is one who is no longer on active duty but still retains some legal connection to the military. Frequently, a soldier's contract includes service for a period of time on "inactive" status after completing an active duty obligation. Article 3(d) of the UCMJ provides that those soldiers who are on inactive status can be activated and face court-martial prosecution for offenses that they were alleged to have committed while previously on active duty. If a former soldier still maintains some legal connection to the military, however slight that connection might be, he or she is still under UCMJ jurisdiction for offenses committed while on active duty.

If, on the other hand, the legal connection between the former service member and the military is completely severed, the UCMJ cannot be used to prosecute the suspect for war crimes that he may have committed while on active duty. It is here that the MEJA and the WCA attempt to bridge the jurisdictional gap. The MEJA extends federal jurisdiction to U.S. armed forces who committed felonies while overseas and who are no longer subject to UCMJ jurisdiction. With respect

---

111. *See* MEJA § 3261(d).
112. Retired members are subject to be called back to active duty under 10 U.S.C. § 802(a)(4).

to military personnel, the MEJA was specifically intended to address the problem identified in the My Lai case and establish a means of prosecuting former soldiers who are alleged to have committed war crimes but who are no longer subject to military jurisdiction. The MEJA is a fairly new law and there have been only a few cases where former soldiers were prosecuted under its terms.

An example of such a prosecution is the case against a former soldier, Steven Green, who was convicted in 2009 of the rape of a 14-year-old girl and the murder of her and her family in a village south of Baghdad. Green was discharged from the Army before the allegations came to light and he was prosecuted in U.S. District Court, in Paducah, Kentucky. The government used the MEJA to assert jurisdiction over former Private Green, who was convicted and sentenced to life in prison (his military counterparts were all court-martialed). Prosecution under the MEJA can itself present a number of definitional challenges, and it is likely that the MEJA will be used for only the most serious cases that would justify the time and resources such a prosecution would require, such as those against Green.

The WCA is the other means available for prosecuting former soldiers who committed either a grave breach of the Conventions or a "grave breach" of common Article 3, or one of the other enumerated offenses. As noted above, jurisdiction to try former soldiers under the WCA is based on the Act's provision granting jurisdiction over persons suspected of war crimes committed while on active duty, or someone otherwise a national of the United States. Under these terms, even if the person is not a member of the armed forces at the time of the prosecution, so long as he or she was a national of the United States at the time of the offense (or the victim was a U.S. national), and are a national of the United States at the time of prosecution, WCA jurisdiction is valid. Note that the scope of the WCA is far more limited than the MEJA or even the UCMJ. Prosecution under the WCA is limited to enumerated war crimes. Further, for the purposes of asserting jurisdiction, the prosecution would have to prove that the offense was committed during either an armed conflict.[113]

C. Jurisdiction over Civilians

Civilians comprise the next category of potential war criminals. The same three mechanisms, the UCMJ, the MEJA, and the WCA may be used to assert U.S. jurisdiction over civilians who are alleged to have committed war crimes while overseas. The most limited of the three options is the UCMJ. Supreme Court case law from the 1950s holds that the military does not have jurisdiction over civilian dependents stationed overseas with their military spouses.[114] Since that time, UCMJ jurisdiction over civilians was limited to those civilians who were serving with or accompanying the force in time of war.[115] Military case law defines the term "in time of war" to mean a formally declared war. Since the United States has not formally declared war since World War II, this interpretation proved to be a significant limitation on UCMJ jurisdiction over civilians.

---

113. 18 U.S.C. § 2441.
114. *See* Reid v. Covert, 354 U.S. 1 (1957).
115. *See* pre-2006 UCMJ, art. 2(10).

In 2006, Congress amended Article 2(10) of the UCMJ to expand jurisdiction "in time of declared war or contingency operation, [to] persons serving with or accompanying an armed force in the field." The added language "contingency operation" encompasses more situations than just declared wars, and could arguably include the full spectrum of military operations. Note, however, that the scope is still limited to civilians serving with or accompanying the force. This fact suggests that not just any civilian serving overseas, or even in a combat environment, would fall within the UCMJ's jurisdiction. However, with the U.S. military's expansive use of civilian contractors to perform what were once traditional military jobs, such as detainee interrogation, it is quite possible that a civilian contractor accused of detainee abuse could face a military court-martial.[116]

The MEJA may also extend jurisdiction to civilians overseas. Like the UCMJ, not all civilians who committed what would qualify as a federal felony overseas fall within the MEJA's jurisdiction. The MEJA's scope is limited to those civilians who committed a felony overseas while employed by or accompanying the armed forces. It does seem, however, that the MEJA is evolving into the statute of choice for federal prosecutors focused on civilian misconduct associated with U.S. military operations.[117]

The WCA presents a third means for extending jurisdiction. The WCA is in some ways broader and in some ways narrower in scope than the previously discussed options. It is broader in scope because it is not limited to civilians accompanying the armed forces or civilians employed by the armed forces; the WCA applies to any national of the United States. The WCA is narrower than the MEJA and the UCMJ with respect to civilians because it is limited to only those war crimes enumerated in the statute, which by implication includes an "armed conflict" limitation.[118] Finally, if a civilian does commit an offense that qualifies as an established law of war violation in the context of an armed conflict, Article 18(2) of the UCMJ ostensibly would permit trial by a general court-martial, although the likelihood of asserting such jurisdiction seems highly improbable considering the range of more traditional criminal response options.

D. Jurisdiction over Enemies and Former Enemies

There is one final category of individuals the United States may seek to prosecute for war crimes: captured enemies and former enemies.

Article 2(a)(9) of the UCMJ establishes jurisdiction over prisoners of war in the custody of the armed forces.[119] This means that once captured, the POW is subject to the criminal proscriptions of the UCMJ's punitive articles. If a

---

116. In 2007, Alaa "Alex" Mohammad Ali, a civilian and former Army translator in Iraq, was prosecuted by the military after an altercation in Iraq during which he allegedly stole a U.S. soldier's knife and used it to stab another translator. He pleaded guilty to lesser charges. This was the first, and as of the end of 2017, the only prosecution of a civilian under the new Article 2(10) of the UCMJ.

117. In fact, the Department of Justice has expressed support for a new statute proposed by Senator Leahy to improve upon the MEJA and more specifically address misconduct by civilian employees and contractors. *See* http://www.justice.gov/criminal/pr/testimony/2011/crmtestimony-110525.html.

118. 18 U.S.C. § 2441.

119. *See* UCMJ, § 897, art. 2(a)(9).

POW engages in conduct in violation of this military code, the U.S. military commander may dispose of the case by any method authorized in the UCMJ, including trial by general courts-martial.[120]

In addition, POWs do not enjoy combatant immunity for pre-capture LOAC violations. Assume that a prisoner of war is alleged to have raped a civilian during military operations prior to his capture. Article 18 provides that if the prisoner could be tried by a military tribunal for the alleged rape as a violation of the law of war, he may be tried by general courts-martial. Article 18 thereby extends court-martial jurisdiction over POWs who committed war crimes before their capture. It is important to note that prosecution under this provision would not be for violations of the UCMJ's punitive articles, it would be for violations of the law of war.

The United States can also prosecute its enemies and former enemies by military commissions or other military tribunals (such as provost courts) if these enemies are unprivileged belligerents. Article 21 of the UCMJ states that courts-martial jurisdiction is not exclusive and the UCMJ does not preclude using military commissions or other military tribunals to prosecute violators of the law of war. Use of military commissions to try enemies and former enemies for law of war violations has a long tradition in the United States. The vast majority of war crimes tribunals following World War II were not international tribunals, but military tribunals convened by the United States or other Allied States. Most recently, the United States used military commissions to try captured al Qaeda and Taliban operatives (unlawful enemy combatants or unprivileged belligerents) for alleged violations of the law of war.

In addition to the UCMJ and military commissions and tribunals, the WCA also provides valid jurisdiction to try captured enemies for violations of the enumerated war crimes. WCA jurisdiction is triggered when the victim of the war crime is either a member of the armed forces or a United States national, even if the offense was committed outside of the United States, irrespective of the defendant's nationality or whether the United States is a party to the conflict.[121]

VII. Defenses to War Crimes

Defenses to war crimes allegations can be as varied and fact dependent as the actual crimes themselves, and it is impossible to set out in specific detail all potential defenses and how they might apply to a specific set of facts. In recognizing the factual nature of possible defenses, the Rome Statute states, "[T]he Court shall determine the applicability of the grounds for excluding criminal responsibility provided for in this Statute to the case before it."[122] If a defendant is prosecuted for violation of the UCMJ's punitive articles, the defenses generally available to any

---

120. For example, in 1945 the U.S. Army executed 14 German prisoners of war following their courts-martial for killing other German POWs suspected of collaborating with the United States.
121. 18 U.S.C. § 2441(a), (b).
122. Rome Statute, *supra*, note 63.

other military defendant would be applicable. The fact that the allegations may also support charging as war crimes does not preclude the suspect from asserting these defenses. However, there are some general defenses that arise frequently in war crimes prosecutions, and it is useful to briefly consider them.

A. Obedience to Superior Orders

Obedience to orders was a particularly controversial defense theory asserted during the IMT. The IMT are frequently cited in support of the international legal invalidity of this defense. However, while obedience to orders was generally rejected at Nuremberg, it is incorrect to assume that obedience to superior orders is never a viable defense to a war crime. It is a narrow defense in the law of war. If the defendant was required to obey the order, the defendant did not know the order was unlawful, and the order on its face was not manifestly unlawful, this remains a viable defense theory to an allegation of criminal misconduct. Accordingly, invalidity of this defense will almost always turn on the manifest illegality of the order.

The obedience to orders defense has been codified in a number of different forms. For example, Rule for Courts-Martial 916(d) provides: "[I]t is a defense to any offense that the accused was acting pursuant to orders unless the accused knew the orders to be unlawful or a person of ordinary sense and understanding would have known the orders to be unlawful."[123] Similarly, the Rome Statute's defense of obedience to superior orders has the following elements: "(a) The person was under a legal obligation to obey orders of the Government or the superior in question; (b) [t]he person did not know that the order was unlawful; and (c) [t]he order was not manifestly unlawful." The Rome Statute notes that orders to commit genocide or crimes against humanity are manifestly unlawful.[124]

These examples show just how narrow this defense is likely to be. It is difficult to imagine how an order that constitutes a grave breach of the Geneva Conventions would fail to satisfy the manifest illegality requirement, or that a person of ordinary understanding—even the most inexperienced soldier—would not know the order is unlawful. Additionally, soldiers in the United States military and the militaries of many other countries receive periodic training on the requirements of the Geneva Conventions, which makes prevailing on such a defense even more difficult.

B. Duress

Duress, or choice of evils, is a closely related and similarly narrow defense. Traditional common law principles of duress state that it is not a defense to murder, and a valid assertion of the defense requires a reasonable apprehension that the defendant or another person would immediately be killed or seriously injured

---

123. Rule for Courts-Martial 916(d).
124. Rome Statute, *supra*, note 54, at art. 33.

to excuse serious physical abuse.[125] The defendant must also have no reasonable opportunity to avoid committing the unlawful act. In the law of war context, a suspect might not be able to claim the defense where he voluntarily joined a unit known to routinely commit war crimes (such as al Qaeda or some of the more brutal paramilitary groups in the Bosnian Civil War). The elements of the duress defense in the Rome Statute are similar to this common law formulation.

A close examination of the elements of this defense reveals why it is a narrow defense. It would not be enough for a soldier to claim that he felt compelled to commit a war crime because otherwise he would have faced ostracism, ridicule, or hazing by other members of his unit. Nor would it be a defense to claim that the command would have subjected the soldier to unspecified punishments or abuse if he did not commit the crimes. This is not to say it could never be a viable defense theory. For example, a conscript in a military unit confronted with a demand to physically abuse a detainee or else suffer summary execution, with no way to avoid this choice of evils, might prevail on such a defense. Of course, in such cases, the individual imposing the unlawful compulsion should also be prosecuted, irrespective of the efficacy of the defense.

C. Self-Defense

The legal justification of self-defense may apply similarly to war crimes as to any other common law crime. To be effective, the defense must be a response to an imminent and unlawful threat. Additionally, the response must be proportional to the threat. In contrast to its common law counterpart, the Rome Statute includes the following caveat regarding self-defense: "[T]he fact that the person was involved in a defensive operation conducted by forces shall not in itself constitute a ground for excluding criminal responsibility."[126] In other words, the national level self-defense legal justification for using military force in response to an unlawful threat or act of aggression does not justify LOAC violations in the execution of military operations to achieve this self-defense objective.

Self-defense could potentially apply to a number of war crimes, such as both murder and assault. However, because self-defense is a necessity-based theory, and because absolute LOAC prohibitions foreclose the legitimate assertion of military necessity as a justification for violation, the defense should not be viable in such cases (recall that military necessity is defined as "all measures,

---

125. In 1996, an ICTY appellate chamber rejected the duress claim of a Croatian, Erdemovic, who admitted to participating in the execution of some 1,200 Muslim men in Srebenica. Erdemovic claimed he only participated in the executions because after he initially refused he was told "if you don't wish to do it, stand in line with the rest of them and give others your rifle so that they can shoot you" and that he had "witnessed the commander ordering someone else to be killed for refusing to obey orders." Sarah J. Heim, *The Applicability of the Duress Defense to the Killing of Innocent Persons*, 46 CORNEL INT'L L.J. 165, 172-173 (2013). The appellate chamber ruled three to two that duress could not provide "a complete defense to a soldier who participated in the killing of innocent civilians." *Id* at 173. In a dissenting opinion, noted international law scholar Antonio Cassese contended that duress should be available where "it is highly probable. . . . that if the person acting under duress had refused to commit the crime, the crime would in any event have been carried out by persons other than the accused." *Id* at 176.

126. *See* id., art. 31.

not otherwise prohibited by international law, necessary for bringing about the prompt submission of an enemy"). For example, because the law presumes it is never necessary to kill an individual who is hors de combat, or to torture a POW, a defendant should not be permitted to raise self-defense in response to an allegation of such war crimes.

D. Lack of Mental Responsibility

If the crime in question requires that the suspect act with a certain mental state or mens rea, evidence that negates that mental state could serve as a defense. This could include claims of insanity or lack of mental responsibility. The Rome Statute also recognizes involuntary intoxication, mistake of fact, and a limited mistake of law defense.[127] It is not clear if or to what extent these defenses are recognized as customary international law.

E. Head of State and Official Acts Immunity

Whether immunity from prosecution by current and former heads of state and high ranking state officials is a defense to war crimes is an open question under international law. Historically, immunity for heads of state and other senior officials was a complete defense. Modern developments have significantly eroded this immunity. The Charter for the Nuremberg Tribunal specifically rejected head of state immunity for crimes against humanity. The Charter states: "[T]he official position of defendants, whether Heads of State or responsible officials in Government Departments, shall not be considered as freeing them from responsibility or mitigating punishment."[128] The statutes for the ICTY, the ICTR, the Special Court for Sierra Leone, and the ICC contain similar provisions. On their face, these statutes seem to reject immunity for heads of state and other senior government officials for genocide, crimes against humanity, and serious war crimes.[129]

In spite of these provisions, it is not clear that head of state immunity is entirely rejected under customary international law. In the case of the Democratic Republic of Congo v. Belgium, the ICJ quashed an arrest warrant by a Belgium judge against the DRC's then-Minister of Foreign Affairs, Abdoulaye Yerodia Ndombasi. In 1998, Mr. Ndombasi publicly encouraged the Congolese population to kill members of a rebellion against the government, primarily ethnic Tutsis. With respect to the arrest warrant, the ICJ was unable to find "any form of exception to the rule according immunity from criminal jurisdiction and inviolability to incumbent ministers for foreign affairs, where they are suspected of having committed war crimes or crimes against humanity."[130] The

---

127. *See id.*, art. 31 and 32.
128. *See* IMT, *supra*, note 51, art. 7.
129. The Rome Statute, in article 27, states that official conduct immunity does not bar the ICC from exercising jurisdiction. Does that article apply the same to nationals of states parties to the Rome Statute as to nationals of non-states parties? *See generally* Dapo Akande & Sangeeta Shah, *Immunities of State Officials, International Crimes and Foreign Domestic Courts*, 21 Eur. J. I'ntl L. 815 (2011).
130. Opinion available at http://www.icj-cij.org/docket/files/121/8126.pdf.

opinion, however, might not be as far reaching as it seems. The ICJ noted that there was no treaty or similar provision that disposed of the defense. Had there been a head of state immunity provision similar to the language in the ICTY, the outcome might have been different. Also, the arrest warrant was sought pursuant to an investigation being conducted by Belgium officials. Had an international organization (such as the ICC) been conducting the investigation, the outcome might have been different. Finally, the ICJ noted that the official's immunity was limited to the time that he was in office. The court suggested that once he was no longer in office, Belgium could renew its warrant.[131]

In 2009, the ICC (acting following a referral of the matter from the UN Security Council) issued an arrest warrant for Sudanese President Omar al-Bashir. Al-Bashir is charged with war crimes and crimes against humanity. This is the first time the ICC has issued an arrest warrant for a sitting head of state. The Sudanese government claims that the ICC has no jurisdiction over the matter and has refused to hand over al-Bashir for prosecution. While head of state immunity might still be a limited defense under international law, the more significant practical limitation for the ICC is an unwillingness to recognize the authority of an outside organization to prosecute sitting heads of state (not only has Sudan refused to cooperate with the ICC, other States in Africa have permitted al-Bashir to visit with no risk of action on the arrest warrant).[132] This practical limitation is likely to present a greater impediment to prosecution than any legally recognized head of state immunity. More recently, in 2018, the American Journal of International Law Unbound devoted an entire volume to the present and expected future of foreign official immunity.[133]

VIII. Emerging LOAC Issues

Like any law or legal system, the LOAC is not stagnant. Indeed, much of this chapter is devoted to explaining the evolution of war crimes liability. There is always a challenge when applying law or norms of a legal system developed for certain situations to new and emerging circumstances. Not surprisingly, the law does not always fit the new circumstance with precision, and at times it may seem like the square peg of an old law is being shoved into the round hole of a new problem. Among the emerging and developing LOAC issues, the question that has most vexed the United States in the past decade is how the LOAC applies to the fight against international terrorism.

---

131. All case documents related to the Arrest Warrant of 11 April 2000 (Democratic Republic of the Congo v. Belgium) are available at http://www.icj-cij.org/docket/index.php?p1=3&p2=3&k=36&case=121&code=cobe&p3=4, and the final judgment is available at http://www.icjcij.org/docket/files/121/8126.pdf.

132. *See* Stephanie van den Berg, *South Africa Defends Decision to Ignore ICC's Bashir Arrest Warrant*, REUTERS, Apr. 7, 2017.

133. *See* AJIL Unbound, Symposium on the Present and Future of Foreign Official Immunity Vol. 112 (2018).

A. Applicability of the Law of War to Non-State Actors

The fight against international terrorist organizations may seem to occupy a type of legal no man's land. This is not a purely domestic matter because often terrorists operate outside a State's territory, and thus escape domestic criminal justice. However, this is not a pure situation of armed conflict because terrorists are non-state actors whose actions are not restricted to the territory of a single State. This law applicability dilemma is further complicated because the intensity of any conflict may be sporadic, and the organization of terrorist groups is normally dispersed and irregular.

When it comes to bringing international terrorists to justice, what paradigm should be invoked? One argument is that the United States should rely exclusively on the domestic criminal justice paradigm. Under this paradigm, terrorist suspects would be prosecuted and punished in U.S. criminal courts. Terrorists would be treated like any other criminal. Many federal criminal laws, including laws directed against terrorists, have an extraterritorial component that would allow these criminal laws to reach terrorist activity outside the territorial United States. U.S. counter-terrorism laws and the U.S. judicial system are fully developed and well respected internationally. For proponents of this view, this enables the United States to bring these perpetrators to justice in a way that does not erode their fundamental freedoms and protections and preserves U.S. credibility.

The other approach is to address terrorist prosecutions under a war fighting paradigm. This is based on the premise that the threat of terrorism is different in nature than the threat posed by ordinary criminals. Terrorists' reach is greater and the scope of their activity is broader, and the United States must respond to this distinct threat by resorting to the use of armed force. An important part of an armed response is to try terrorist operatives not as ordinary criminals, but as war criminals. This in turn requires use of special tribunals that are better suited for such trials because terrorists are not entitled to the protections afforded lawful combatants. Also, military tribunals can best respond to the sensitive nature of these cases and the need to protect national security information, so they are the appropriate forum to adjudicate misconduct committed by international terrorists.

One of President Bush's first actions in response to the terrorist attacks of September 11 was the order to create a military commission system to try captured and detained terrorist suspects. To say that the Bush administration faced significant challenges in using military commissions would be an understatement. It was not until Congress ultimately passed the 2006 MCA, a portion of which the Supreme Court later found unconstitutional. During this same period, the Bush administration continued to prosecute terrorist suspects, not in military commissions, but in federal court. Hundreds of "terrorist cases" between 2001 and 2008 were effectively prosecuted as criminal cases.[134]

---

134. James J. Benjamin & Richard B. Zabel, In Pursuit of Justice: Prosecuting Terrorism Cases in the Federal Courts (Human Rights First) (May 2008), at 5. (*See* http://www.amazon.com/Pursuit-Justice-Prosecuting-Terrorism-Federal/dp/0979997542.)

After taking office in 2008, President Obama continued this hybrid approach. The Obama administration pushed for and obtained a number of amendments to the Military Commissions Act. These amendments passed in 2009.[135] While the Obama administration pursued a few military commission prosecutions, the vast majority of terrorist prosecutions were handled in federal court. But in early 2018, President Trump revoked an Executive Order President Obama had issued to close the detention facility at Guantanamo.

In order to deal with the unique situation posed by non-state terrorist groups, the United States has clearly adopted a hybrid approach. This approach raises a number of questions. For example, what cases are best suited for trial by military commissions as opposed to federal courts? What principles should govern this choice? Do military commissions formulated to try terrorist suspects comply with Common Article 3? In other words, are the trials conducted by regularly constituted courts affording the essential judicial guarantees recognized as indispensable by civilized peoples?[136]

In addition to these questions, there is the fundamental question of what crimes can be tried by military commissions. Historically, military commissions have been used by the United States to try violations of the laws and customs of war. Does or should the law of war apply to these non-state actors? What makes them war criminals? Is it their actions? Is it their status? Is it because the United States classifies them as "unlawful enemy combatants" and "unprivileged belligerents"? Assuming the United States is engaged in an armed conflict with al Qaeda triggering the LOAC, what war crimes apply in this conflict? How much of a battlefield nexus must there be? Where is the battlefield? Do your answers change if instead of al Qaeda, the U.S. is engaged in an armed conflict with ISIS? What if the non-state actor, and member of al Qaeda or ISIS is a U.S. citizen?[137]

The MCA enumerated what Congress determined are "offenses that have traditionally been triable by military commissions."[138] Included in this list of offenses are such crimes as "conspiracy" and "material support for terrorism." Many critics contend that these are not traditional war crimes; they certainly have no basis in the war crimes history explored throughout this chapter. Should military commissions have the authority to try crimes not traditionally recognized as war crimes?[139]

---

135. Signed into law by President Obama on October 28, 2009, Pub. L. No. 111-84 (*See* http://www.govtrack.us/congress/bill.xpd?bill=h111-2647).

136. For an interesting discussion of whether non-state armed groups have the capacity under the LOAC to establish courts and impose penal sanctions, see ICRC, Sweden/Syria, Can Armed Groups Issue Judgments https://casebook.icrc.org/case-study/swedensyria-can-armed-groups-issue-judgments.

137. United States citizenship adds several different challenges in terms of available approaches. This challenges include that while U.S. citizens may be detained at Guantanamo, per U.S. law they may not be subject to trial by military commission. Additionally, U.S. citizens have the right to challenge their detention through habeas corpus (assuming that it is the U.S. that is detaining), a right that non U.S. citizens detained outside the U.S. do not have. Now consider you are the legal advisor to a U.S. Special Operations unit engaged in combat operations against ISIS in Syria and your unit has just captured two ISIS fighters, one of whom is a U.S. citizen. What do you advise? *See* CNN, US Wants to Leave This American in Syria with $4,200 and No Passport.

138. 10 U.S.C. § 950p.

139. Is conspiracy a war crimes? In a 163 page per curiam opinion, the U.S. Court of Appeals for the District of Columbia Circuit, answered yes, though the four concurring opinions convey very

In the midst of this debate it is useful to keep broader themes in mind. Not every crime is a war crime and not every use of force is an armed conflict. Because the LOAC operates on a law triggering paradigm, the basic questions of the type of person, the type of conflict, and the specific context in which the alleged offense arises all matter when extending war crimes liability to this context. If the LOAC is not triggered, there is no legitimate basis to invoke war crimes jurisdiction to deal with alleged criminal misconduct. Instead, the matter remains the exclusive focus of domestic criminal law.

This section raises these questions not to provide answers but to illustrate the complexity of the contemporary extension of war crimes liability to the "war on terror." For many (if not most) of these questions there are no clear answers. Regardless, the information provided in this chapter should provide the foundation needed to effectively examine these issues and propose intelligent and thoughtful responses.

B. Accountability Norms

In addition to the challenges posed by non-state actors engaging in transnational NIACs, contemporary conflicts are yielding if not LOAC accountability issues than at least emerging questions.[140] This section briefly highlights two such areas, technology and coalition warfare.

In terms of technology, advances in computing power have led to corresponding advances in, and reliance on, the cyber domain, computers or information networks. Think for a moment how much of your day to day life is facilitated by computer networks and the internet. Just like civil society, the military has incorporated technology to help improve effectiveness and efficiency. While traditionally armed conflicts were, and of course still are, fought on land, sea, and in the air, cyberspace has become a battlespace domain onto itself. Aspects of the military are now devoted to both cyber defense, defending one's network from intrusion and hacking but also on offensive cyber capabilities. The LOAC principles discussed throughout this book apply to cyber operations during armed conflict the same way they apply to all military operations. Consider for a moment how the principle of distinction applies in cyber space and when then principle has been violated. What about proportionality?

---

different ways of reaching that answer. *See* Bahlul v. United States, No. 11-1324 (D.C. Cir. 2016). The U.S. Supreme Court subsequently declined to review the case, leaving in place the D.C. Circuit opinion. Similarly, what about material support to terrorism? Is that a war crime?

140. Even the concept of what constitutes a war crime is under examination. Specifically, where a member of a State armed forces commits a crime during an armed conflict against another member of that same State's armed forces, can that be considered a war crime? Consider U.S. Army Sergeant Smith, who allegedly sexually assaults U.S. Army Private Jones at a combat outpost in Afghanistan. Smith has committed an offense under the UCMJ, but should that offense be considered a war crime? In its update to the Geneva Conventions Commentaries, the ICRC claims that Jones is entitled to the protection of Common Article 3 from not just the enemy but, in this case, other members of the U.S. 2016 ICRC Commentaries, *supra*, note ____ paras 544-549. The validity of this interpretation is unclear. Regardless, would you think differently in hearing that a U.S. Army soldier was being prosecuted for raping another U.S. Army soldier vs that a U.S. Army soldier was being prosecuted for a war crime of rape of another U.S. Army soldier? Why?

It is just a matter of time before the question of "cyber war crimes" receive more attention.

As technology advances and more and more functions or tasks are delegated to machines and computers some worry that an accountability gap results. It does not. The LOAC imposes obligations on people, not weapons. Inanimate objects, even sophisticated ones, lack agency and assume obligations. So while weapon systems may factual determinations based on their programming, the legal determinations (and responsibilities) remain where they have always been, on and with the humans who ordered and employed the use of weapons, whether that weapon is a rock or a robot.

How militaries fight is not only changing due to technology but also as a result of global strategic or political reasons. Contemporary conflicts are increasingly fought by coalitions, groups of States. For example, the coalition to fight the Islamic State or ISIS is comprised of over 70 States. Different states provide different kinds and types of support to the coalition, funding, supplies, personnel, and equipment. While there are a number of advantages to and benefits from coalition operations, accountability is harder to operationalize in practical terms. Consider the following scenarios: First, a U.S. Army unit conducts an operation near the Iraq/Syria border. The operation is commanded by a U.S. Army officer, relies on intelligence from U.S. Army sources, and the ground force is limited to a U.S. Army unit. Second, a coalition airstrike occurs near the Iraq/Syria border. Two British war planes participated in the strike, which was controlled by an operations center commanded by an American and which relied on intelligence analysis produced by Australian and Italian military intelligence personnel. As a result of both operations, allegations arise that civilians were killed and the question about whether those deaths amounted to a LOAC violation is also being discussed. Battlefield investigations are challenging under any circumstances, and causation and intent can be particularly difficult to establish. The identity of who investigates the first operation and under what rules and procedures is straightforward enough as the operation was solely conducted by the U.S. Army. But who should investigate the coalition airstrike? And what rules and procedures should be utilized? There are not clear answers to those questions. But if the trend of coalition operations continues, the need for, if not standardized rules then agreed upon best practices will become even more pronounced.

Conclusions

If the primary purpose of having a war crimes regime is to give meaning to the limitations on permissible battlefield conduct in order to better protect those not participating in the conflict, it might be justifiable to conclude that the war crimes regime has been a failure. Even after the very public Nuremberg Trials, the last half of the twentieth century was characterized by conflicts where the civilian casualties far exceeded military casualties and where misconduct related to concentration camps, genocide, biological experiments, and other egregious crimes seems to have been committed with impunity. If anything, it might seem that the war crimes regime has been more honored in the breach than in the observance.

The Conventions, the broader LOAC, and the war crimes regime developed to effectuate this law have, however, had positive and increasingly quantifiable impact on the regulation of hostilities. While it cannot be known how many unnecessary deaths have been prevented by training soldiers to abide by the laws of war, it is fair to say that enough of the rules have been followed enough of the time to prevent a certain level of unnecessary death and destruction. Even countries that systematically violate the LOAC may conform to some minimum level of humane conduct. Senator John McCain was a prisoner of war held and systematically tortured by the North Vietnamese for over eight years. None of his tormentors ever faced criminal accountability, and it is highly unlikely they were in any way deterred by concern over such an eventuality. However, despite breaches of the Geneva Conventions, he credits the LOAC with preventing his captors from killing him and other POWs.[141] Further, ad hoc tribunals, the ICC, and the ever-increasing number of States willing to exercise universal jurisdiction indicates that no commander, soldier, or statesman can today act with a sense of absolute impunity; the contemporary risk of accountability is genuine, and a result of this evolutionary journey.

A war crimes regime is also necessary to "diminish the corrosive effect of mortal combat on the participants."[142] "War does not entitle combatants to kill any person at any time for any reason. Soldiers must be trained to draw the distinction between lawful and unlawful killing and maintain a respect for the value of life."[143] It is enormously difficult for soldiers to maintain a moral compass in war. Without a war crimes regime, the task would likely be impossible. Francis Lieber stated, "[M]en who take up arms against one another in public war do not cease on this account to be moral beings, responsible to one another and to God."[144] That ideal is the very foundation for a war crimes regime and the guiding principle behind the LOAC's attempt to regulate conduct during times of both international and non-international armed conflicts. While war crimes prosecutions are not and cannot be the primary method of achieving this goal, it is an increasingly significant component in the compliance mosaic.

Study Questions

1. Subsequent investigation by U.S. and Iraqi forces into the killings of villagers in Gassan confirmed that the Ministry of Interior Special Police Commandos were responsible for the killings. The evidence is based on

---

141. Senator John McCain, Speech to the American Red Cross Promise of Humanity Conference (May 6, 1999), available at http://www.senate.gov/mccain/index.cfm?fuseaction=Newscenter.View pressrelease&Content_id=820.
142. *See* NUREMBERG AND VIETNAM, *supra,* note 8, at 40.
143. Id. at 41.
144. Lieber Code, *supra,* note 20, Section 1, art. 15.

forensic examinations and interrogations of some of the police commandos, who claimed to be present in Gassan during the killings, and that a secret "kill squad" within the special commandos unit shot the unarmed villagers based on their religious and tribal affiliations. Assume that at the time of the killing the armed conflict in Iraq is considered a NIAC.
   a. Are the killings by these police officers war crimes?
   b. If so, what kind of breach is it?
   c. What obligations does the United States have with respect to these crimes?
   d. If these soldiers were taken into custody by U.S. forces, what options would the United States have for prosecuting them? What option would you recommend? Why?
   e. What obligations does the newly instituted government of Iraq have?
2. Investigation into the conduct of the 2nd Brigade during their mission has confirmed that a U.S. Army sergeant shot and killed three unarmed military-aged males, whose hands and legs had been bound with flex cuffs when they were shot.
   a. How is the United States likely to prosecute this case, assuming the evidence warrants a prosecution? Is the sergeant in question a "war criminal"?
   b. What if the sergeant in question had left active military service before the incident was discovered? Would the United States still be able to prosecute him? How? For what offenses?
3. Following the Corps Commander's direction that detention practices be reviewed, an investigation reveals detainee abuse had been occurring within unit detention facilities similar to that committed at Abu Ghraib. Is this abuse a war crime? Does it matter if this conflict is characterized as a non-international armed conflict? Why or why not?
4. Questions from the Provost Marshall:
   a. "A detainee stabbed one of our military police guards." Is this a war crime? In what forum could the detainee be prosecuted?
   b. "It looks like we may have had a soldier break into an Iraqi home and rape a teenage girl." Is this a war crime? Why or why not?
   c. "A couple of civilians claim that force protection concerns led them to drive the wrong way down a busy street, scaring the hell out of the villagers, plow into a local fruit stand, and take off without stopping. Is this a war crime? If so, what sort of breach or breaches have these civilians committed? Does the United States have jurisdiction to prosecute these civilians? If so, under what grounds? Would it matter if the civilians were local nationals?

14 | Command Responsibility and Compliance Mechanisms

Two nights ago, a platoon of coalition soldiers was sent to a local village within their Area of Responsibility (AOR); their assignment: to check on reports of small arms and automatic weapons fire emanating from the village. The Republican Guard had been operating in that village for the past few days. The villagers were thought to be sympathetic to U.S. forces. The patrol reported finding 50-60 unarmed villagers, including several women and small children shot and their bodies disposed in a ravine near the village. The report reached the JTF headquarters later that same day. Investigation of the report continues by both coalition and U.S. forces in the area.

Earlier today the chaplain assigned to the 193rd Infantry Brigade met with the Brigade Commander. The chaplain reported that he was hearing rumors from soldiers in one of the battalions; last week a company commander in the battalion gave his company a pep talk before they left on their mission. The commander allegedly told his soldiers to "deal with" anyone they captured from the Republican Guard, and they could not let enemy prisoners slow them down. The chaplain said a soldier who attended the briefing later reported that he saw a first sergeant shoot a captured member of the Republican Guard execution-style. The Brigade Commander ordered an investigation into the allegation.

Recently, the ICRC representative completed a visit to the U.S. detention facility at Empire Prison. This is a makeshift tent city where the U.S. is holding about 300 Iraqi Army detainees. The ICRC's report to the JTF commander includes allegations by several detainees of being forced to sleep naked and without shelter. Other detainees report being hit and kicked by their military guards during interrogation sessions. One detainee reported being choked, slapped, and struck with a rifle butt during questioning. The ICRC's report is sealed and marked "For JTF Commander Only." The JTF Commander has not yet read the report although his staff has had the report for two days, and his Chief of Staff alerted him of the reports existence.

I. Introduction

Chapter 13 addresses the role of criminal sanctions for LOAC violations. The focus of war crimes is the imposition of penalties for violations of the law. Obviously, war crimes prosecutions are intended to produce a deterrent effect, but ultimately such prosecutions respond to compliance failures. Such failures, and the prosecutions in response, should, however, be the exception and not the rule. Ideally, the combination of deterrence, training, leadership, and swift disciplinary reaction to minor LOAC infractions will ensure LOAC compliance and avert the need to conduct war crimes prosecutions. This chapter focuses on this aspect of the equation: understanding the broader range of mechanisms available to encourage respect for the law and help ensure LOAC compliance. The chapter focuses first on the military commander and the role that the commander plays in ensuring LOAC compliance. What legal structure and incentives exist for the military commander to ensure LOAC compliance by the forces under his command? The chapter also discusses LOAC training programs, war crimes reporting requirements, and protocols used by U.S. forces to investigate war crimes allegations.

A. The Role of the Commander

The LOAC is a unique legal regime. It seeks to inject humanitarian regulation into the brutal endeavor of warfare. No person who has not experienced war can truly understand demands placed on warriors and the officers and non-commissioned officers responsible for their leadership. Military training involves developing a genuine killer instinct—a willingness to take life on order and without hesitation. However, professional warriors must be able to essentially suspend that instinct at a moment's notice in order to exercise humanitarian constraint and preserve the critically important line between legitimate and illegitimate violence, the ultimate objective of the LOAC.

The brutality, intensity, and sheer terror of warfare therefore stresses the ability of military leaders to ensure their subordinates respect LOAC obligations. Commanders, staff officers and their legal advisors are expected and required to understand these obligations and to correctly apply the law in the context of ongoing military operations. This is not easy. Beyond the commander's responsibility to know the law and conform operational decisions to the dictates of the LOAC, commanders also bear the additional and critical responsibility to prepare their subordinates to respect these obligations and to establish a command culture that prioritizes fidelity to the law.

The individual responsible for molding a group of individuals into an efficient and effective military unit is the commander. The commander holds a unique position in a military organization. Primarily through the use of positive leadership and example, the commander sets the tone for the unit. He ensures the soldiers under his command are well trained and prepared to conduct military operations and achieve the unit's objectives. The commander is the focal point of military discipline and order within the unit. He is responsible for maintaining command and control over his subordinate forces. The commander stands on the line that separates a disciplined military unit from a lawless mob. Through the use of all available resources, to include moral authority, law, and collective purpose, the military commander makes sure his forces effectively execute military operations—which often involves the decisive application of deadly combat power—in a manner that fully complies with the LOAC. When military units fail to do so, it is in large measure attributable to the commander's failings.

B. A Commander's Involvement or Complicity in LOAC Violations[1]

A commander can fail in this most vital responsibility in any number of ways. There are situations when the commander's actions are directly responsible for the LOAC violations committed by his forces. For example, if a commander participates with his forces in the unlawful targeting and killing of civilians, he is directly and criminally liable under LOAC for the resulting harm. Likewise, a commander who orders his forces to attack a protected place is, as a result of ordering unlawful conduct, responsible for the subsequent LOAC violation as if he had executed the attack himself. Similarly, a commander who encourages his forces to kill or otherwise mistreat prisoners of war, or a commander who assists his subordinates covering up evidence of a past war crime, is criminally liable for those LOAC violations.

In these examples, the commander's complicity with LOAC violation is direct—a mere application of accomplice liability theory. However, even if the commander's involvement is not direct, it is easy to see how his encouragement and assistance can contribute to LOAC violations, rendering him equally culpable.

There are numerous possible scenarios where a commander's action or inaction can have a close and direct nexus to the war crimes committed by subordinates. Even if a commander did not directly order forces under his command to engage in conduct in violation of the LOAC, he may have permitted or acquiesced in those violations. This can include situations where the commander has firsthand knowledge of the offenses and allows those offences to occur or to continue to occur over time.

In these situations the nexus between commander inaction and a subordinate's war crime exists because soldiers frequently and unquestionably interpret the commander's inaction and acquiescence as approval and permission. This risk is even more significant where the commander passes on manifestly illegal orders from higher commands to his subordinates. The act of passing them down the chain of command suggests to subordinates endorsement of those

---

1. Many of the liability principles discussed here apply not only to military commanders, but also to others in positions of superior authority.

orders by their immediate commander. In such a situation, a claim of obedience to orders will provide no defense for the subordinates; nor will the commander prevail on a defense theory that he was merely passing along the orders from a superior, precisely because of the risk that doing so indicates implicit endorsement.

One of the most important components of the LOAC, therefore, are the mechanisms that evolved to hold commanders accountable in these instances where the commander's direct participation, encouragement, incitement, involvement, knowledge and/or acquiescence in the LOAC violations is either direct, or where the nexus between the commander's actions and the crime is clear. Even if the commander's involvement was less direct, such as ordering his forces to commit unlawful killings but not directly participating in those killings, the doctrine of accomplice liability would provide a solid basis for criminal accountability. If a commander ordered, encouraged, or otherwise supported his forces in committing war crimes, and if the commander shared in the criminal purpose or design of the perpetrators and takes some action or fails to perform a legal duty and this action or failure to act aids, abets, counsels, or commands the perpetrator to commit the offense, the commander could be guilty as a principal.[2]

Similarly, in U.S. practice, if a commander aided or assisted his subordinates in covering up evidence of a war crime, he may be liable as an Accessory After the Fact. To be liable, the commander must know that the perpetrator committed a criminal offense, and must assist the perpetrator for the purpose of hindering or preventing the apprehension, trial, or punishment of the perpetrator.[3] These doctrines have been codified in the Uniform Code of Military Justice (UCMJ).

None of this is in any way remarkable. It is merely an application of traditional accomplice liability principles to the war crimes context, whether the offense is charged as a war crime or a violation of the U.S. military code. Because the LOAC implicitly relies so heavily on commander's executing their responsibilities, it should be apparent why legal mechanisms facilitate holding commanders accountable when evidence establishes the commander is either directly involved in LOAC violations or if he acceded as an accomplice or an accessory. Without such legal mechanisms, LOAC principles would be largely ineffective and unenforceable. These mechanisms also provide powerful incentives for the commander to fulfill his responsibilities to ensure compliance with LOAC obligations.

This legal structure would be incomplete, however, if these were the only mechanisms available to establish command responsibility for LOAC violations. Direct liability, accomplice liability, and the liability of an accessory only address situations of commander complicity; where the evidence establishes the commander has some independent or shared intent to commit war crimes

---

2. UNIF. CODE OF MILITARY JUSTICE §877 art. 77, *reprinted in* MANUAL FOR COURTS-MARTIAL UNITED STATES A2-24 (2005).
3. MANUAL FOR COURTS-MARTIAL UNITED STATES para. 2b. at IV-2 (2005).

or prevent their detection. Punishing commanders in these situations will certainly deter such complicity, but will not necessarily incentivize the creation of a command culture that emphasizes LOAC compliance and condemns violations. How then does the law address situations where a commander's dereliction of duty—negligence in supervising the forces under his command—contributes to subordinate LAOC violations? What about a commander who remains willfully ignorant of battlefield reports indicating LOAC violations, or who upon receiving such reports fails to take appropriate remedial action? In these instances, it is the lack of action that contributes to subordinate violations, often times without any intent to violate the LOAC by the commander himself. And yet, in such instances, the commander's failings may set the conditions for the commission war crimes by the forces under his command. As the individual in the critical position directly responsible for ensuring LOAC compliance within a military unit, should commanders bear responsibility when the risk becomes reality?

II. Command Responsibility

The doctrine of command responsibility developed under customary international law. Its purpose was to align the scope of a commander's criminal accountability for war crimes committed by subordinates with the full extent of the commander's obligation to ensure subordinate compliance with the law. Accordingly, the doctrine accounts for two situations. First, where a commander's responsibility for war crimes is established by traditional complicity principles; second, where the commander may not have been complicit in the war crimes in the traditional sense, but rather was derelict in his duties to ensure respect for the law by the forces under his command. Extending a commander's legal responsibility for subordinate misconduct beyond situations of traditional complicity ultimately provides a necessary incentive to train, monitor, supervise, and correct subordinates, and in so doing to establish a command culture of commitment to compliance with the law of armed conflict.

A clear understanding of what is meant by command responsibility, the liability it imposes, and precisely what conduct falls within the scope of the doctrine is critically important for commanders and the JAGs who advise them. Unfortunately, much of the discussion within legal literature has actually complicated this understanding by confusing the doctrine. While relatively narrow at inception, today the doctrine is applied to a broad range of situations, and scholars often disagree on the exact meaning of command responsibility. Understanding its relationship to U.S. military operations will be the focus of this chapter.

A. Definition

To understand what we mean by "command responsibility," it is helpful to understand what it is not. Command responsibility in U.S. practice does not refer to a commander's direct criminal responsibility for war crimes. In cases where evidence establishes that a commander is an accomplice to a subordinate's war crimes, criminal responsibility need not rely on the command responsibility doctrine. The criminal law doctrines of accomplice liability, accessory liability, and perhaps co-conspirator liability adequately link the commander to the criminal misconduct.

Nor does command responsibility impose strict vicarious liability. This extreme concept of liability would attribute responsibility to the commander for a subordinate's misconduct based exclusively on his command position. Strict vicarious liability would, therefore, require no proof the commander was in any way derelict in his duties. Nor would there be a requirement to prove the commander knew or even could have known about the crimes being committed by his subordinates. The commander is liable simply by virtue of the position he holds. This type of vicarious liability is common in civil tort law and is often referred to as respondeat superior, but is not properly associated with the doctrine of command responsibility.

Some legal scholars conclude this vicarious liability standard of command responsibility emerged from World War II war crimes tribunals.[4] This conclusion is erroneous. Every post-World War II international tribunal that has addressed the issue of command responsibility has specifically rejected strict vicarious liability as a basis for imposing criminal responsibility on military commanders.[5] Strict vicarious liability has subsequently been rejected by every international criminal code and treaty addressing command responsibility.

Accordingly, command responsibility is neither direct liability nor strict liability. It is instead a principle of derivative imputed liability. The commander's liability is derived from his relationship to his subordinates and the link between his act or omission and the crimes committed by those subordinates. If this derivative relationship can be established, the criminal misconduct by the subordinate can be imputed to the commander.

The key distinction between vicarious liability and true command responsibility is that derivative imputed liability requires proof of a mens rea and an actus reus. The mens rea component focuses on what the commander was aware of, or failed to be aware of, regarding crimes about to be committed,

---

4. Scholars have associated the term "command responsibility" with concepts of direct liability, liability as a principal, and derivative liability. *See* Yuval Shany & Keren R. Michaeli, The Case Against Ariel Sharon: Revisiting the Doctrine of Command Responsibility, 34 N.Y.U. J. INT'L L. & POL. 797, 883 (2002) (stating that Article 43 of the Hague Relations should be construed as a direct liability form of command responsibility); Allison Marston Danner & Jenny S. Martinez, Guilty Associations: Joint Criminal Enterprise, Command Responsibility, and the Development of International Criminal Law, 93 CAL. L. REV. 75, 120 (2005). For use of the term "command responsibility" when discussing liability as a principal (Conspiracy), *see* Richard P. Barrett & Laura E. Little, Lessons of Yugoslavia Rape Trials: A Role of Conspiracy Law in International Tribunals, 88 MINN. L. REV. 30, 32 (2003).

5. *See* 12 U.N. WAR CRIMES COMMISSION, LAW REPORTS OF TRIALS OF WAR CRIMINALS Case 72: *The German High Command Trial: Trial of Wilhelm Von Leeb and Thirteen Others*, at 76-77 (Jan. 1949) (*prepared by* Mr. Aars Rynning); *see also* 8 U.N. WAR CRIMES COMMISSION, LAW REPORTS OF TRIALS OF WAR CRIMINALS Case 47: *The Hostage Trial: Trial of Wilhelm List and Others*, at 75-76 (Nov. 1948) (*prepared by* Mr. Brand).

being committed, or that had been committed by forces under his command. The actus reus component focuses on the commander's failure to execute his duty to act to prevent subordinates from committing future war crimes, stop subordinates from committing ongoing war crimes, or to punish subordinates for commission of past war crimes. This, of course, assumes the commander is capable of executing his duty. However, if evidence establishes these mens rea and actus reus requirements, criminal responsibility is imputed to the commander for the war crimes committed by his soldiers; in other words, the commander is punished *as if he had committed* those crimes, not merely for dereliction of duty.

B. Pre-World War II History of Command Responsibility[6]

Command responsibility was firmly established as a legal doctrine in the war crimes tribunals following World War II. However, the idea of holding a commander responsible for his subordinates' criminal and law of war violations has much earlier origins in foreign, domestic, and international law. Military codes on occasion included provisions imposing what was in effect command responsibility. One of the most frequently cited examples is the Ordinance of Orleans, issued in 1439 by Charles the VII of France. The ordinance provided:

> The King orders that each Captain or lieutenant be held responsible for the abuses, ills and offenses committed by members of his company, and that as soon as he receives any complaint concerning any such misdeed or abuse, he bring the offender to justice so that the said offender be punished in a manner commensurate with his offence, according to these Ordinances. If he fails to do so or covers up the misdeed or delays taking action, or if, because of his negligence or otherwise, the offender escapes and thus evades punishment, *the Captain shall be deemed responsible for the offense as if he had committed it himself and shall be punished in the same way as the offender would have been.*[7]

During the American Civil War, Article 71 of Dr. Francis Lieber's Code—General Order 100 [8]—established that:

> Whosoever intentionally inflicts additional wounds on an enemy already wholly disabled, or kills such an enemy, or *who orders or encourages* soldiers to do so, shall suffer death, if duly convicted, whether he belongs to the Army of the United States, or is an enemy captured after having committed his misdeed.[9]

---

6. *See,* Victor Hansen, *What's Good for the Goose Is Good for the Gander—Lessons from Abu Ghraib: Time for the United States to Adopt a Standard of Command Responsibility Towards its Own*, 42 Gonz. L. Rev. 335 (2007).

7. Theodor Meron, *Reflections on the Prosecution of War Crimes by International Tribunals*, 100 Am. J. Int'l L. 551, at 149 n.40 (2006). (emphasis added).

8. Francis Lieber, General Orders No. 100 (1863) *reprinted in* Richard Shell, Hartigan Lieber's Code and the Law of War 45 (Transaction Publishers 1995) (1983).

9. Richard Shell, Hartigan Lieber's Code and the Law of War 45, art. 71 (Transaction Publishers 1995) (1983). (emphasis added).

The Fourth Hague Convention of 1907 respecting the laws and customs of war on land[10] was the first modern treaty to impose a form of command responsibility as a matter of express international legal obligation. Article 3 states, "[a] belligerent party which violates the provisions of the said Regulations shall, if the case demands, be liable to pay compensation. *It shall be responsible for all acts committed by persons forming part of its armed forces.*"[11] The underlying premise of the modern command responsibility doctrine is also reflected in Chapter 1, Article 1, which established what is recognized as a key characteristic of an army or other organized militia: the military organization is "commanded by a person *responsible* for his subordinates."[12]

There are a number of commonalities among these historical antecedents to the contemporary command responsibility doctrine. First, they all recognize the unique position a commander holds in a military organization. Second, they all reflect the axiom that command authority includes both the legal authority and the legal obligation to control subordinate conduct in order to achieve military objectives while respecting the then existing humanitarian limits on the conduct of hostilities. Third, all of these antecedents implicitly recognize that imposing responsibility on the commander for the conduct of subordinates enhances the probability of such respect. These antecedents also recognize that a commander can be held accountable for his subordinates' law of war violations if he was directly involved, or even in some cases if the commander's involvement was less direct or obvious. From this foundation, the modern doctrine of command responsibility emerged at the end of World War II.

C. World War II War Crimes Tribunals: The Doctrine Evolves

At the Moscow Conference in October 1943, the United States, the Soviet Union, and the United Kingdom agreed that German officers who were responsible for "atrocities" committed throughout the occupied areas would be "delivered to their accusers in order that justice may be done."[13] Then, toward the end of the war in Europe, the United States, the Soviet Union, France, and the United Kingdom signed the London Charter[14] which established the International Military Tribunal ("IMT") for the trial of German war criminals. In several of the cases before the IMT, the doctrine of command responsibility served as a mechanism for imposing criminal liability on senior commanders for the

---

10. Hague Convention Respecting the Laws and Customs of War on Land, Oct. 18, 1907, 36 Stat. 2277.
11. *Id.* at 2277, 2290.
12. *Id.* at 2277, 2295.
13. THE TRIPARTITE CONFERENCE IN MOSCOW: DECLARATION OF GERMAN ATROCITIES (Nov. 1, 1943), *reprinted in* 9 DEP'T STAT. BULL 305, 311 (1943).
14. PROSECUTION AND PUNISHMENT OF MAJOR WAR CRIMINALS OF EUROPEAN AXIS (Aug. 8, 1945), *reprinted in* 3 TREATIES AND OTHER INTERNATIONAL AGREEMENTS OF THE UNITED STATES OF AMERICA 1776-1949, at 1238 (Charles I Bevans, ed., 1969).

many atrocities that inspired the Moscow declaration and the creation of the IMT. A similar process took place in the Far East. The victorious allies agreed to establish an IMT for the Far East. In that tribunal, as well as numerous other subordinate international and national military trials conducted in both theaters, commanders were criminally sanctioned for their command failings when those failings led to widespread violations of the laws and customs of war. However, the following four cases provide the most significant insight into the doctrine's development.

1. The Yamashita Military Tribunal

The most well-known case involving the command responsibility doctrine was the trial of General Yamashita.[15] At the end of World War II, General Yamashita was the Commanding General of the Fourteenth Army Group of the Imperial Japanese Army in the Philippine Islands. The Japanese government placed General Yamashita in command of these forces just ten days before the American forces landed in the Philippines. General Yamashita was in command during a desperate time for the Japanese forces fighting a delaying action all across the Philippines. In Manila, Japanese army and naval forces turned the city into a battlefield, and were responsible for the death of an estimated 100,000 Filipino civilians. These forces also committed other atrocities including thousands of rapes and other serious war crimes.

On September 3, 1945, General Yamashita surrendered his command to U.S. forces and became a prisoner of war. On September 25, 1945, General MacArthur initiated a war crimes prosecution for General Yamashita based on the following charge:

> Tomoyuki Yamashita, General Imperial Japanese Army, between 9th October, 1944 and 2nd September, 1945, at Manila and at other places in the Philippine Islands, while a commander of armed forces of Japan at war with the United States of America and its allies, unlawfully disregarded and *failed to discharge his duty as commander to control the operations of the members of his command, permitting them to commit* brutal atrocities and other high crimes against people of the United States and of its allies and dependencies, particularly the Philippines; and he, General Tomoyuki Yamashita, thereby violated the laws of war.[16]

---

15. The trial of General Yamashita was not an international military tribunal. General Yamashita was tried by a United States military commission established under the provisions of the Pacific Regulations of September 24, 1945, governing the trial of war criminals. The commission acted under the authority of General MacArthur, Commander-in-Chief, United States Army Forces, Pacific Theatre and, General Styer, Commanding General, United States Army Forces, Western Pacific. *See* 4 U.N. War Crimes Commission, Law Reports of Trials of War Criminals Case 21: *The Trial of General Tomoyuki Yamashita*, 2-3 (Feb. 17, 1948) (*prepared by* G. Brand). The commission was convened on October 8, 1945. The members of the tribunal were American military general officers, none of whom were judges or lawyers.

16. 4 U.N. War Crimes Commission, Law Reports of Trials of War Criminals Case 21: *The Trial of General Tomoyuki Yamashita*, at 3-4 (Feb. 17, 1948) (*prepared by* G. Brand).

The prosecution theory was that these violations were so flagrant and enormous that they must have been known to General Yamashita if he had made any effort to fulfill his responsibilities as a commander.[17] If General Yamashita did know of these offenses, he was complicit in them for his failure to stop them; if he did not know of these acts it was because he "took affirmative action not to know." In either case, he bore individual criminal responsibility for them.

General Yamashita did not deny the commission of widespread atrocities by the forces under his command. Instead he argued he had never ordered the commission of any crime or atrocity; he never gave permission to anyone to commit any crimes or atrocities; he had no knowledge of the commission of the alleged crimes or atrocities; and perhaps most importantly, he had no actual control over the perpetrators of the atrocities at the time the atrocities were committed. Additionally, the defense attempted to show General Yamashita was executing his command responsibilities as best he could under extremely difficult circumstances, with inadequate support, and under constant attack from U.S. forces.

In response to the prosecution's expansive theory of derivative liability, the defense claimed the United States had never recognized war crimes responsibility based solely upon the defendant's status as a commander. According to the defense, a commander who did not order, authorize, encourage, or even know of the war crimes committed by a subordinate could not be criminally responsible for their conduct.[18] In short, the defense asserted that unless the prosecution could establish a traditional accomplice link between General Yamashita and the atrocities, he could not properly be held criminally accountable for that misconduct.

The military commission that tried General Yamashita rejected the assertion that he took no part in the crimes committed by his troops, and that he did not know what was occurring. According to the commission, the evidence showed the "crimes were so extensive and widespread, both as to time and area, that they must either have been willfully permitted by [Yamashita], or secretly ordered by [him]."[19] However, the commission did not rest its judgment solely on the conclusion that General Yamashita was lying about his role in the atrocities. With respect to General Yamashita's dereliction of duty, the president of the commission (the senior military officer on the 'jury') stated:

> [W]here murder and rape and vicious, revengeful actions are widespread offences, and there is no effective attempt by a commander to discover and control the criminal acts, such a commander may be held responsible, even criminally liable, for the lawless acts of his troops, depending upon their nature and the circumstances surrounding them.[20]

Accordingly, the commission concluded:

> (1) That a series of atrocities and other high crimes have been committed by members of the Japanese armed forces under your command against people

---

17. *Id.* at 17.
18. *Id.* at 29.
19. *Id.* at 34.
20. *Id.* at 35.

of the United States, their allies and dependencies throughout the Philippine Islands; that they were not sporadic in nature but in many cases were methodically supervised by Japanese officers and non-commissioned officers; (2) That during the period in question you failed to provide effective control of your troops as was required by the circumstances.[21]

The commission applied the doctrine to hold Yamashita accountable not for his direct complicity, but based on his failings as a commander. Some contend the Yamashita holding creates a strict liability standard. Others contend that Yamashita's standard for command responsibility is that if the commander knew or should have known of the commission of war crimes by his forces and failed to prevent or suppress them, he is equally responsible. Still others contend the Yamashita standard is that liability should attach to the commander if the commander knew or must have known of the war crimes being committed by his forces.

Given the commission's confusing and somewhat contradictory language, it is impossible to conclude definitively which if any of the aforementioned interpretations is completely valid. Regardless of the lack of clarity in the commission's decision, key elements of the command responsibility doctrine did emerge from the case. A commander's responsibility and liability is predicated on: (1) a command relationship between the superior and subordinate; (2) information or knowledge that triggers the commander's duty to act; (3) if the duty to act is triggered, the commander must take some action regarding the ongoing or anticipated law of war violations by subordinates; (4) a causal relationship between the commander's omission and the war crimes committed by the subordinates. Ultimately, Yamashita resulted in a critically important precedent: if all of the above elements are met, criminal liability can be imputed to the commander for the war crimes committed by the subordinate forces.

a. Scope of Authority

The scope of a commander's responsibilities for purposes of the doctrine of command responsibility is broad. In the Yamashita decision, General Yamashita's claim that he had only operational control over many of the forces under his command, without the ability to discipline them or assign their officers, was of no consequence to the commission. So long as the commander is in a position that carries the responsibility to maintain the good order and discipline of subordinates, this element is met.

b. Mens Rea of Command Responsibility

The law of armed conflict imposes a duty on the commander to act to prevent or suppress war crimes. Inaction by the commander where action is required is no defense. But it is unclear as to what triggers this duty to act. Must the commander actually know of the war crimes being committed by his subordinates before he is required to take action? Can knowledge be imputed to

---

21. *Id.* at 35.

a commander and if so, in what circumstances? What of a commander who either failed to become aware or consciously disregarded the violations being committed by his forces? Does the law require a commander to act if the commander did not know but should have known of his subordinate's war crimes? What if the commander did not know but had the means and the opportunity to discover the law of war violations?

Irrespective of these questions, most of which were not addressed by the Yamashita decision, what does seem clear is that the standard is not one of strict liability. However, it is equally clear that pursuant to the Yamashita standard, a commander cannot remain willfully blind to the conduct of his troops and then claim that as a result of his ignorance his duty to act was never triggered. Between these two ends of the spectrum, the Yamashita case left the question unanswered as to when the law imputes criminal responsibility to a commander who fails to intervene effectively to halt or prevent subordinate war crimes.

c. Actus Reus of Yamashita Command Responsibility

Even assuming the information available to a commander is sufficient to trigger the duty to act, what action is required by the commander? What is the actus reus of command responsibility? The Yamashita commission did not address this point directly, other than to say that during the period in question General Yamashita failed to provide effective control of his troops as was required by the circumstances. Failing to provide effective control under the circumstances is a broad standard for command responsibility, susceptible to varying interpretations considering that the commission did not indicate specifically what a commander in Yamashita's position could or should have done.

This lack of clarity raises several additional questions. How much effort and how many resources must he devote to the detection, prevention, and prosecution of war crimes? At what point in the conflict must the commander take action? Does he have a duty to investigate and punish past war crimes? If so, must he cease all other combat operations in order to prevent or stop subordinates from committing war crimes, or can he continue to execute combat operations and address alleged war crimes at a later time? Does he have the duty to prevent future war crimes before they occur? By what standard are his efforts to be judged? The Yamashita decision may have established an obligation to act, but failed to provide precise guidance on these important aspects of the doctrine.

d. Causation

The Yamashita decision does not directly address the question of what causal link, if any, must be established between the commander's failures and the war crimes committed by subordinates. Must the government establish both cause-in-fact and proximate cause in order to impute liability on the commander? Can causation be assumed by the mere fact that the subordinates engaged in war crimes? If a commander has a duty to punish past violations but fails to do so, should liability be imposed for the underlying offense even though no causal link can be established?

e. Imputed Liability

The imputed liability element of the command responsibility doctrine was clearly applied against General Yamashita. If the prosecution can meet its burden and establish liability, the commander can be punished as though he actually engaged in the war crimes committed by his forces. The commission found General Yamashita guilty for widespread atrocities and sentenced him to death by hanging.

2. In re Yamashita

General Yamashita appealed this decision to the U.S. Supreme Court in a petition for a writ of habeas corpus.[22] The petition attacked the military commission on three grounds. First, he contended that the military commission was not lawfully created. Second, he claimed that the charges he was convicted of failed to state law of war violations. Third, he argued that the commission lacked the authority and jurisdiction to try the offenses.[23] The second ground relates to the doctrine of command responsibility applied by the commission.

The Supreme Court noted that in order for the commission to have jurisdiction to properly try General Yamashita, the charges against him had to state violations of the law of war. The Court then framed the issue as follows:

> [T]he gist of the charge is an unlawful breach of duty by petitioner as an army commander to control the operations of the members of his command by "permitting them to commit" the extensive and widespread atrocities specified. The question then is whether the law of war imposes on an army commander a duty to take such appropriate measures as are within his power to control the troops under his command for the prevention of the specified acts which are violations of the law of war and which are likely to attend the occupation of hostile territory by an uncontrolled soldiery, and whether he may be charged with personal liability for his failure to take such measures when violations result.[24]

In assessing this issue, the majority had little difficulty concluding that the law of war does impose an affirmative duty on the commander to control his forces, and because of this the charges against General Yamashita stated an offense under the law of war. The Court cited to language from Article I of the Annex to the Fourth Hague Convention of 1907, noting that the first criteria of any armed force is that it is under the command of someone who is responsible for his subordinates. Likewise, the Court noted that Article 43 of the Annex to the Fourth Hague Convention of 1907 requires that commanders of occupied

---

22. In re Yamashita, 327 U.S. 1, 4 (1946). Because this was a petition for habeas corpus, the Court did not evaluate the evidence on which General Yamashita was convicted. Id. at 17. The Court also did not consider any efforts that General Yamashita may have undertaken to prevent the war crimes and whether these measures would have been sufficient under the circumstances. Id. According to the Court, these issues fell within the preview and expertise of the military officers of the commission. Id.
23. Id.
24. Id. at 14-15.

territory take all measures within their power to restore and ensure public safety and order. Having considered these treaties, the Court concluded that the law of war imposed an affirmative duty on General Yamashita to control his forces in order to prevent or stop them from committing war crimes.[25]

Justices Murphy and Rutledge wrote impassioned dissents. Justice Murphy said of the charge against General Yamashita, "The recorded annals of warfare and the established principles of international law afford not the slightest precedent for such a charge."[26] Justice Murphy also said the charges against General Yamashita amount to this:

> We, the victorious American forces, have done everything possible to destroy and disorganize your lines of communication, your effective control of your personnel, your ability to wage war. In those respects we have succeeded. We have defeated and crushed your forces. And now we charge and condemn you for having been inefficient in maintaining control of your troops during the period when we were so effectively besieging and eliminating your forces and blocking your ability to maintain effective control.[27]

Justice Rutledge, in his dissent, pointed to the "vagueness" and "vacuity" of the commission's findings.[28] According to Justice Rutledge, the commission's finding was unclear as to whether General Yamashita was convicted for a willful and intentional failure to restrain his forces, known by him to be committing war crimes, or if he was convicted of a negligent failure to discover what his forces were doing and to take appropriate action. This lack of clarity, it was argued, both undermined the majority's opinion and was an insufficient basis on which the commission could impose a capital sentence.[29]

The opinions of Justices Murphy and Rutledge have been criticized as emotion-laden responses that have more to do with their frustrations with the lack of due process afforded to General Yamashita, rather than a thoughtful critique of the doctrine of command responsibility that emerged from the case.[30] This criticism, however, is misplaced. The dissenting opinions do highlight the inconsistencies in the commission's holding and in the Supreme Court's majority opinion. The dissents further highlight the fact that the doctrine of command responsibility that emerged from Yamashita was to some degree cobbled together from a variety of international sources and that it was not based on the long established criminal law doctrines of personal responsibility and accountability.

3. Other World War II Tribunals

Other war crimes tribunals from the European and Far East Theaters also applied and developed the doctrine of command responsibility. One such case,

---

25. *Id.* at 16.
26. *Id.* at 28.
27. *Id.* at 34.
28. *Id.* at 51.
29. *Id.* at 53.
30. William H. Parks, Command Responsibility for War Crimes, 62 Mil. L. Rev. 1, 36 (1973).

the "High Command Case" involved the trial of Wilhelm von Leeb and 13 other high-ranking German officers who executed and passed on orders that were clearly inconsistent with the laws and customs of war. These orders called for the extermination of "Bolshevist Commissars" and "Communist intelligentsia," subjecting civilians in occupied areas to subjective punishment, refusing quarter for captured commandos, and issuing death sentences for civilians in occupied areas by the use of summary and arbitrary proceedings.

In the High Command Case, the subordinate war crimes were committed in large part "at the insistence of [the] higher military and Reich authorities."[31] The tribunal held that a commander has certain obligations under international law that he cannot set aside or ignore by reason of his own state's activities or orders. The scope of this commander's responsibility is broad, and the commander cannot avoid that responsibility by claiming he was merely passing on or obeying the orders issued to him from a higher command authority.

Like Yamashita, the High Command Case recognized that commanders have a duty to act. However, the High Command tribunal was much more precise in defining the amount of information available to the commander to trigger this duty. To establish criminal responsibility for the transmittal of an unlawful order, the commander must have "passed the order to the chain of command and the order must be one that is criminal upon its face, or one which he is shown to have *known was criminal*."[32] With respect to a commander's supervisory responsibility, the result of the commander's personal dereliction must establish that "his failure to properly supervise his subordinates constitutes criminal negligence on his part."[33] Dereliction alone is insufficient; it must be a personal neglect "amounting to a wanton, immoral disregard of the action of his subordinates amounting to acquiescence."[34]

The application of these standards is exemplified in the case against General von Kuechler relating to the execution of Russian prisoners of war. According to the High Command tribunal, there was insufficient proof that von Kuechler transmitted illegal orders from the German High Command regarding the execution of these prisoners. However, regardless of the lack of transmission of the orders, the tribunal did find sufficient evidence that subordinate units relayed several reports of these executions to General von Kuechler's command post. The tribunal also found the General visited all prisoner of war camps within his command, and admitted he was aware of Russian prisoner executions. Based on this evidence, his failure to take action, according to the tribunal, amounted to criminal neglect. However, the High Command Tribunal, like in Yamashita, did not expressly define terms such as criminal neglect. Therefore, the terminology of command responsibility must be understood in the context of each respective case.

---

31. 12 U.N. War Crimes Commission, Law Reports of Trials of War Criminals Case 72: *The German High Command Trial: Trial of Wilhelm Von Leeb and Thirteen Others*, (January, 1949) (*prepared by* Mr. Aars Rynning).
32. *Id.* at 74 (emphasis added).
33. *Id.* at 76.
34. *Id.*

The High Command cases also provide important examples of commanders who met their duty to act. According to the tribunal's judgment, General von Leeb fulfilled his duty with respect to the orders to execute Bolshevist commissars. Upon receipt of the order, General von Leeb expressed to his superiors his opposition to the order. When he passed the order to his subordinate commanders, General von Leeb expressed his disagreement with the order and reminded his subordinates of the importance of maintaining discipline and order. Based on this evidence, Von Leeb was acquitted of some of the charges.[35]

Another important series of war crimes trials from the European Theater are known as the Hostage Case. These trials involved the prosecution of 12 senior German military officials by the United States.[36] The defendants were charged, inter alia, with four counts alleging that they willfully and knowingly committed war crimes against the populations of Greece, Yugoslavia, Norway, and Albania. There was evidence showing the defendant commanders' headquarters received regular reports regarding the illegal treatment of civilians and other war crimes being committed by subordinate forces. In their defense, many of the commanders claimed they did not know of the reports received, and as a result had no duty to act. On this point, the tribunal stated:

> Want of knowledge of the contents of reports made to him is not a defense. Reports to commanding generals are made for their special benefit. Any failure to acquaint themselves with the contents of such reports, or a failure to require additional reports where inadequacy appears on their face, constitutes a dereliction of duty which he cannot use in his own behalf.[37]

The tribunal's judgment adopts a knowledge standard similar to the High Command cases. When evidence establishes a commander clearly had information regarding the commission of subordinate war crimes, knowledge of that information is imputed to him, even if he chose to ignore this information. This imputation of knowledge is known in contemporary criminal law as the doctrine of willful blindness. Willful blindness satisfies the knowledge element of an offense when a defendant willfully avoids becoming aware of facts a reasonable person would have investigated. In short, it transforms ignorance resulting from a reckless disregard of information to knowledge. Bolstering this willful blindness theory, the tribunal's judgment imposed a "should have known" standard. The tribunal stated that a commander would ordinarily not be permitted to deny knowledge of happenings within the area of his command while he was present therein. This judgment is premised on an implicit command duty to know what is occurring within the command's operational area, especially when he was physically present in that area when the events occurred. In short, ignorance will rarely provide a viable defense to command responsibility when it is the result of a failure to maintain operational situation

---

35. 12 U.N. War Crimes Commission, Law Reports of Trials of War Criminals, 1, 27 (William S. Hein & Co. 1997).
36. 8 U.N. War Crimes Commission, Law Reports of Trials of War Criminals, Case 47: *The Hostage Trial: Trial of Wilhelm List and Others,* 34 (November, 1948) (*prepared by* Mr. Brand).
37. *Id.* at 70.

awareness—precisely the type of awareness inherent in the effective execution of command responsibilities.

The doctrine of command responsibility was also considered in the post-World War II tribunal in Japan, known as the Tokyo Trials. This tribunal considered charges against 28 former Japanese civilian and military leaders for crimes against the peace, murder, conspiracy to commit murder, war crimes, and crimes against humanity.[38] Defining the leaders' duties owed to prisoners of war, the tribunal addressed the mens rea and actus reus elements of command responsibility. On the mens rea element, the tribunal concluded that defendant is responsible for the mistreatment of prisoners of war if he:

> (1) ... had knowledge that such crimes were being committed and having such knowledge they failed to take such steps as were within their power to prevent the commission of such crimes in the future, or
>
> (2) They are at fault in having failed to acquire such knowledge ... [I]t is not enough for him to show that he accepted assurances from others more directly associated with the control of prisoners if having regard to the position of those others, to the frequency of reports of such crimes, or any other circumstances he should have been put on further enquiry as to whether those assurances were true or untrue.[39]

This articulation added significant depth to the requisite mens rea standard for command responsibility. The duty to act is clearly triggered by a commander who knows his subordinates are committing war crimes. In addition, commanders must actively seek out information to obtain knowledge. A commander who negligently failed to obtain information, or a commander who relies on questionable information without further inquiry when the circumstances called for it, cannot avoid his duty to act. Thus, in many ways this standard reflects an amalgamation of the various standards applied by the European war crimes tribunals.

C. International Developments after the World War II Tribunals

These post-World War II tribunals provided a critical foundation for the further evolution of the command responsibility doctrine. However, while many armed forces incorporated the doctrine into their manuals and laws, there was virtually no evolution of the doctrine during the four decades of Cold War that followed. For almost 30 years the international legal community did not make further attempts to codify, refine, or clarify points of the command responsibility

---

38. The Tokyo Major War Crimes Trial xxvi (R. John Pritchard, ed., 1981).

39. *See* The Official Transcript in 101 The Tokyo Major War Crimes Trial: The Judgment, Separate Opinions, Proceedings in Chambers, Appeals and Reviews of the International Military Tribunal for the Far East with an Authoritative Commentary and Comprehensive Guide 48,444 (R. John Pritchard, ed., 1981).

doctrine. This changed in 1977 with the promulgation of Additional Protocol I to the 1949 Geneva Convention (Protocol I), which included the first express treaty provision establishing individual criminal command responsibility.[40] The evolution process gained substantial additional momentum following the end of the Cold War and in response to the armed conflicts in the former Yugoslavia and Rwanda. The United Nations response to the widespread war crimes in both these conflicts led to two tribunals with jurisdiction over criminal command responsibility. Each tribunal was based upon a charter document called a statute: the Statute for the International Criminal Tribunal for the Former Yugoslavia ("ICTY"),[41] and the Statute for the International Criminal Tribunal for Rwanda ("ICTR").[42] These statutes, and the tribunal jurisprudence resulting therefrom, ultimately culminated with inclusion of a command responsibility provision in the Rome Statute for the International Criminal Court ("ICC").[43]

1. Additional Protocol I

The doctrine of command responsibility is central to Additional Protocol I's accountability framework. Articles 86 and 87 made significant contributions to the command responsibility doctrine via the articulation of the specific duties for a commander to ensure law of war compliance. Under Article 86, paragraph 2, the commander has the duty to prevent and repress breaches of the Protocol and Conventions. Article 87, paragraph 1 imposes a duty on commanders to prevent, suppress, and report breaches to the Convention. Article 87, paragraph 3 requires a commander to prevent violations; otherwise take penal or disciplinary actions in response to past violations if that commander is aware that his forces are going to commit, or have committed a breach. Collectively, the commander's duties are to (1) prevent future war crimes, (2) suppress or stop ongoing crimes, and (3) report and punish past crimes. Articles 86 of Protocol I addresses the omission component of the doctrine, and provides:

> Article 86.-Failure to Act
> 1. The High Contracting Parties and the Parties to the conflict shall repress grave breaches, and take measures necessary to suppress all other breaches, of the Conventions or of this Protocol which result from a failure to act when under a duty to do so.
> 2. The fact that a breach of the Conventions or of this Protocol was committed by a subordinate does not absolve his superiors from penal or

---

40. Diplomatic Conference on Reaffirmation and Development of International Humanitarian Law Applicable in Armed Conflicts, Protocol additional to the Geneva Conventions of 12 August 1949, and Relating to the Protection of Victims of International Armed Conflicts (Protocol I), 72 AM. J. INT'L L. 457 (1978).
41. S.C. Res. 995, U.N. Doc. S./RES/955 (November 8, 1994), *reprinted in* 2 THE INTERNATIONAL CRIMINAL TRIBUNAL FOR RWANDA at 3 (Virginia Morris & Michael P. Scharf, eds., 1998).
42. S.C. Res. 808, U.N. Doc. S./RES/808 (May 3 1993), *reprinted in* 2 THE INTERNATIONAL CRIMINAL TRIBUNAL FOR RWANDA at 504 (Virginia Morris & Michael P. Scharf, eds., 1998).
43. THE ROME STATUTE OF THE INTERNATIONAL CRIMINAL COURT (July 17, 1998), *reprinted in* THE ROME STATUTE OF THE INTERNATIONAL CRIMINAL COURT: MATERIALS, at 3 (Antonio Cassese, Paola Gaeta, and John R.W.D. Jones, eds., 2002).

disciplinary responsibility, as the case may be, if they knew, or had information which should have enabled them to conclude in the circumstances at the time, that he was committing or was going to commit such a breach and if they did not take all feasible measures within their power to prevent or repress the breach.

Article 87 then explicitly establishes the scope of a commander's duty to act:

> 1. The High Contracting Parties and the Parties to the conflict shall require military commanders, with respect to members of the armed forces under their command and other persons under their control, to prevent and, where necessary, to suppress and to report to competent authorities breaches of the Conventions and of this Protocol.
> 2. In order to prevent and suppress breaches, High Contracting Parties and Parties to the conflict shall require that, commensurate with their level of responsibility, commanders ensure that members of the armed forces under their command are aware of their obligations under the Conventions and this Protocol.
> 3. The High Contracting Parties and Parties to the conflict shall require any commander who is aware that subordinates or other persons under his control are going to commit or have committed a breach of the Conventions or of this Protocol, to initiate such steps as are necessary to prevent such violations of the Conventions or this Protocol, and, where appropriate, to initiate disciplinary or penal action against violators thereof.[44]

Article 86, paragraph 1 affirms the proposition that liability for a failure to act is predicated on a duty to act. Paragraph 2 of Article 86 defines those circumstances in which the duty to act is triggered. Protocol I does not define who qualifies as a superior or commander, leaving that definition to the national law of the contracting state. The associated ICRC commentary does, however, state that a command relationship is not dependent upon rank. This indicates the intent of the Protocol: assess liability based on a pragmatic, as opposed to formalistic, conception of command and superior responsibility.

In sub-paragraphs 1 and 3, Article 87 defines the broad scope of command responsibility. It notes commanders have authority for "forces under their control" and "other persons under their control." It is important to note that the term "other persons under their control" recognizes that a command relationship and a duty to act are not necessarily limited subordinates formally assigned to a unit, nor even to members of the armed forces. Instead, the commander is responsible for any individual under her *de facto* authority.

Article 86, paragraph 2, sets forth the mens rea of command responsibility. A commander's duty to act is triggered either by direct knowledge or by "information which should have enabled them [the superior] to conclude" that subordinate forces were committing or about to commit violations of the Conventions or the Protocol. At first blush, this standard may seem identical to the "should have known" standard applied in the Hostage Case and the Tokyo

---

44. Cite to Articles 86 & 87.

Trials. However, it is not. In fact, the ICRC proposed the language "knew or should have known," but this proposal was rejected, as was the United States' proposed language of "knew or should have reasonably known."[45] The language adopted in Article 86, "information which should have enabled them to conclude," suggests that the Protocol I mens rea requirement for command responsibility is either actual knowledge or something very close to it. It is certainly narrower than the "known or should have known" standard applied in the Hostage Cases, the Tokyo Trials, and arguably in Yamashita.

Not only do the foregoing articles of Protocol I delineate a commander's duties, they define what is required of the commander to accomplish these duties. This specific guidance helps to close the gap between general legal requirements in the abstract, and the actual conduct of commanders in the field and the subordinates they are obligated to control. Furthermore, Article 87, paragraph 2, imposes on commanders the general obligation to "ensure that members of the armed forces under their command are aware of their obligations under the Conventions and this Protocol."[46] This duty has no specific triggering mechanism. However, it is intended to enhance the likelihood of compliance by requiring that subordinates be educated on their individual legal obligations. Commanders have a general responsibility to disseminate information about their obligations under the Protocol and Conventions regardless of whether the commander has information that his forces are about to engage in or are engaging in breaches of the Conventions.

Article 87 paragraph 3 sets out additional requirements on what a commander must do to fulfill his duties. If a commander is aware his forces are going to breach the Protocol or Conventions, he must "initiate steps as are necessary to prevent such violations." The text does not clarify what measures satisfy this obligation. However, when read in conjunction with Article 86, paragraph 2, it becomes clear: the commander must take all feasible measures or steps within his power to prevent the breach. This "all feasible measures" obligation is responsive to the concerns raised by the Yamashita defense: commanders are expected to do what is necessary and possible, and not held to a standard of strict liability for actions they could never take.

For past breaches, Article 87 requires commanders to "initiate disciplinary or penal action against violators" where necessary. This requirement should be read in conjunction with the commander's duty to report past breaches set forth in Article 87, paragraph 1. This disciplinary obligation may also extend to a successor in command. If the violations occurred under a former commander's watch, and the current commander only learns of the breaches after taking command, there is no plausible reason why the current commander would be excused from the Article 87 obligation. Whether a failure to initiate disciplinary

---

45. COMMENTARY ON THE ADDITIONAL PROTOCOLS OF 1977 TO THE GENEVA CONVENTIONS OF 1949, para. 3545 n. 31, at 1013.

46. Diplomatic Conference on Reaffirmation and Development of International Humanitarian Law Applicable in Armed Conflicts, Protocol additional to the Geneva Conventions of 12 August 1949, and Relating to the Protection of Victims of International Armed Conflicts (Protocol I), 72 AM. J. INT'L L. 457, 497 (1978).

action for violations that occurred under a prior commander's authority subjects the new commander to liability for those violations is unlikely; such an outcome would amount to an extreme version of strict liability. However, such a failure would be an important factor linking the successor commander to *subsequent* subordinate misconduct as it would indicate the current commander was aware of information satisfying the notice element of Article 87 command responsibility.

2. Implementing Command Responsibility: Contemporary International Criminal Tribunals

The proceedings of the International Criminal Tribunal for the former Yugoslavia (ICTY) and the International Criminal Tribunal for Rwanda (ICTR) initiated the contemporary evolution of the command responsibility doctrine. The command responsibility provision in the statutes for each tribunal, promulgated in 1993 and 1994 respectively, are virtually identical. Article 7(3) of the ICTY states:

> The fact that any of the acts referred to in articles 2 and 5 of the present Statute [Grave Breaches of the Geneva Conventions of 1949 and Crimes Against Humanity] was committed by a subordinate does not relieve his superior of criminal liability if he knew or had reason to know that the subordinate was about to commit such acts or had done so and the superior failed to take the necessary and reasonable measures to prevent such acts or to punish the perpetrators thereof.[47]

Article 6(3) of the ICTR states:

> The fact that any of the acts referred to in articles 2 and 4 of the present Statute [Genocide and Violations of Article 3 Common to the Geneva Conventions and Additional Protocol II] was committed by a subordinate does not relieve his or her superior of criminal liability if he or she knew or had reason to know that the subordinate was about to commit such acts or had done so and the superior failed to take the necessary and reasonable measures to prevent such acts or to punish the perpetrators thereof.[48]

The liability established in both statutes is not limited in application to only military commanders. The term "superior" extends liability to both military and civilian leaders.[49] Indeed, many ICTY and ICTR decisions extensively addressed application of command responsibility to civilian leaders who exercised *de*

---

47. S.C. Res. 808, U.N. Doc. S./RES/808 art. 7 (3) (May 3, 1993), *reprinted in* 2 THE INTERNATIONAL CRIMINAL TRIBUNAL FOR RWANDA at 515 (Virginia Morris & Michael P. Scharf, eds., 1998).

48. S.C. Res. 995, U.N. Doc. S./RES/955 art. 6 (3) (November 8, 1994), *reprinted in* 2 THE INTERNATIONAL CRIMINAL TRIBUNAL FOR RWANDA at 5 (Virginia Morris & Michael P. Scharf, eds., 1998).

49. Celebici: Case No. IT-96-21 A (Prosecutor v. Delalic *et al.*) para. 196 (Feb. 20, 2001), *reprinted in* 2L GLOBAL WAR CRIMES TRIBUNAL COLLECTION at 57 (S. De. Haardt & W. Van Der Wolf, eds., 2001).

facto command and control of military subordinates. However, neither statute adopted Protocol I's mens rea standard. Instead, the statute drafters adopted the term "know or had reason to know" as the command responsibility mens rea standard. Exactly what this language meant was, however, uncertain; uncertainty exacerbated by the disparate interpretations of the language by tribunals applying the doctrine.

Perhaps the most significant ICTY treatment of the scope of command responsibility pursuant to the statute is the Celebici case.[50] This case involved the prosecution of four individuals for various grave breaches and crimes against humanity relating to the mistreatment of prisoners of war at the Celebici prison camp. Prison survivors said soldiers entered at night and beat prisoners. Several prisoners died from the beatings and maltreatment. Each of the defendants—all members of the Bosnian armed forces—occupied different positions: Landzo was a camp guard, Mucic was the camp commander, Delic was the camp's deputy commander, and Delalic was the coordinator of the Bosnian Muslim and Bosnian Croat forces in the area and later a commander in the Bosnian Army. Delalic, Mucic, and Delic were charged under the command responsibility doctrine, and Delic and Landzo were charged with individual responsibility.

On the issue of command responsibility, the prosecution conceded that it was not possible to establish that every defendant had actual knowledge of the abuses. However, the prosecution asserted that where actual knowledge could not be established, when the crimes committed by the subordinates are widespread, prolonged, or received public notoriety, command knowledge of those crimes should be presumed by the tribunal because such evidence indicates the commander "had reason to know" of the offenses. The ICTY rejected this argument that "had reason to know" equated to "should have known." The tribunal instead held "had reason to know" meant that a commander's duty to act is triggered only when he has specific information available placing him on notice that subordinates would violate the law. This information need not explicitly establish that war crimes were being committed so long as it put the commander on notice that such offenses were likely, thereby indicating the need for further inquiry.[51]

The Blaskic decision offered a different ICTY interpretation of the term "had reason to know."[52] General Blaskic commanded the HVO [the Croatian Defense Council] armed forces headquarters in central Bosnia. While in command he was accused of planning, instigating, ordering or otherwise aiding in the planning, a number of very serious war crimes. Included among these were preparation or execution of unlawful attacks on civilians and civilian objects, willful killing and serious bodily injury, destruction and plunder of property,

---

50. *See* Celebici: Case No. IT-96-21-T (Prosecutor v. Delalic *et al.*) (November 16, 1998), *available at* http://www.un.org/icty/celebici/trialc2/judgement/cel-tj981116e.pdf.
51. *Id.* at para. 393.
52. Prosecutor v. Blaskic para. 332 (March 3, 2000), *reprinted in* 2J GLOBAL WAR CRIMES TRIBUNAL COLLECTION at 90 (S. De. Haardt & W. Van Der Wolf, eds., 2001).

destruction of institutions dedicated to religion or education, inhumane treatment, taking of hostages, and use of human shields.

The Blaskic tribunal reviewed a number of sources to determine the appropriate command responsibility standard. These included the post-World War II decisions discussed above, Protocol I, and the Celebici opinion. From these sources, the tribunal concluded "ignorance cannot be a defense where the absence of knowledge is the result of negligence in the discharge of his [the commander's] duties." Accordingly, the tribunal held that ordinary negligence was the customary international law mens rea standard applicable to the ICTY, and that this mens rea was more akin to a "know or should have known" standard rejected by the Celebici judgment.[53]

Tribunals of the ICTR also reached differing conclusions about the mens rea standard for command responsibility. In one case, Jean-Paul Akayesu, a mayor of Tuba commune, was charged with assisting in the killings of ethnic Tutsis. In this case the tribunal failed to clearly differentiate between a commander's duty to obtain information and a commander's duty to act on that information. The tribunal instead tied both duties together, ruling that "it is certainly proper to ensure that there has been malicious intent, or, at least, ensure that negligence was so serious as to be tantamount to acquiescence or even malicious intent."[54]

The ICTR took a different view of the term "had reason to know" in the Bagilishema case.[55] Ignace Bagilishema was a mayor in Rwanda also accused of committing genocide against ethnic Tutsis. The Bagilishema tribunal focused its opinion primarily on the mens rea required to trigger a superior's duty to act to prevent, suppress, or punish war crimes. The tribunal stated that the mens rea element could be met in one of three ways: 1) if the defendant had actual knowledge that subordinates were about to commit, were committing, or had committed, a crime; or, 2) the defendant had information that put him or her on notice of the risk of such offences by indicating the need for additional investigation in order to ascertain whether such offences were about to be committed, were being committed, or had been committed, by subordinates; or, 3) the absence of such knowledge is the result of negligence in the discharge of the superior's duties.[56] According to this judgment, the mens rea standard can be met if the commander or superior's lack of knowledge was the result of negligence. Thus, in this case the term "had reason to know" equates to the standard of "should have known."

---

53. *Id.*

54. Prosecutor v. Akayesu, Case No. ICTR-96-4-I para. 471-91 (Sept. 2, 1998), reprinted in 1B GLOBAL WAR CRIMES TRIBUNAL COLLECTION 312-17 (S. De. Haardt & W. Van Der Wolf, eds., 2000).

55. The Bagilishema Trial: Case No. ICTR 96-IA-T (Prosecutor v. Bagilishema) para. 131, reprinted in 1E GLOBAL WAR CRIMES TRIBUNAL COLLECTION at 18 (S. De. Haardt & W. Van Der Wolf, eds., 2001).

56. The Bagilishema Trial: Case No. ICTR 96-IA-T (Prosecutor v. Bagilishema) para. 131, reprinted in 1E GLOBAL WAR CRIMES TRIBUNAL COLLECTION at 18 (S. De. Haardt & W. Van Der Wolf eds., 2001).

As these cases from the ICTY and ICTR illustrate, even among these tribunals, there is no controlling meaning of the critical terminology "know or had reason to know." This uncertainty extends beyond these tribunals to the broader international community. When the mens rea standards applied by the ICTY and ICTR are compared with the Protocol I standard, it is clear there is no universal international agreement on the requisite mens rea to establish command responsibility.

The impact of this uncertainty has been mitigated by the most recent international codification of command responsibility doctrine in the Rome Statute for the International Criminal Court ("ICC").[57] The Rome Statute sets forth ICC's authority, vesting the court with jurisdiction for cases involving genocide, crimes against humanity, war crimes, and the crime of aggression.[58] Article 28 of the Rome Statute is entitled "Responsibility of Commanders and Other Superiors" and provides:

> (a) A military commander or person effectively acting as a military commander shall be criminally responsible for crimes within the jurisdiction of the Court committed by forces under his or her effective command and control, or effective authority and control as the case may be, as a result of his or her failure to exercise control properly over such forces, where:
>
> > (i) That military commander or person either knew or, owing to the circumstances at the time, should have known that the forces were committing or about to commit such crimes; and
> >
> > (ii) That military commander or person failed to take all necessary and reasonable measures within his or her power to prevent or repress their commission or to submit the matter to the competent authorities for investigation and prosecution.
>
> (b) With respect to superior and subordinate relationships not described in paragraph (a), a superior shall be criminally responsible for crimes within the jurisdiction of the Court committed by subordinates under his or her effective authority and control, as a result of his or her failure to exercise control properly over such subordinates, where:
>
> > (i) The superior either knew, or consciously disregarded information which clearly indicated, that the subordinates were committing or about to commit such crimes;
> >
> > (ii) The crimes concerned activities that were within the effective responsibility and control of the superior; and
> >
> > (iii) The superior failed to take all necessary and reasonable measures within his or her power to prevent or repress their commission or to submit the matter to the competent authorities for investigation and prosecution.[59]

---

57. THE ROME STATUTE OF THE INTERNATIONAL CRIMINAL COURT (July 17, 1998), reprinted in THE ROME STATUTE OF THE INTERNATIONAL CRIMINAL COURT: MATERIALS, at 3 (Antonio Cassese, Paola Gaeta, and John R.W.D. Jones, eds., 2002).

58. THE ROME STATUTE OF THE INTERNATIONAL CRIMINAL COURT (July 17, 1998), *reprinted in* THE ROME STATUTE OF THE INTERNATIONAL CRIMINAL COURT: MATERIALS, at 3 (Antonio Cassese, Paola Gaeta, and John R.W.D. Jones, eds., 2002).

59. Rome Statute.

Article 28 uses the terms "military commander" and a person "effectively acting as a military commander" to describe the applicability of the statute,[60] and defines subordinates as "forces under his or her effective command and control, or effective authority and control as the case may be."[61] These definitions are consistent with prior command responsibility jurisprudence, establishing an expansive scope of a commander's responsibility. The statute also recognizes the possibility of a *de facto* commander based on the idea that the actions and responsibilities of the officer are more important than the officer's rank or title when determining who is subject to command responsibility liability. Consistent with prior cases and statutes, ICC liability is premised on the important relationship between the defendant and his ability to control subordinates under his authority.

The ICC mens rea standard is a "know or should have known" standard. The specific rejection of the more limited standard of Article 86 of Protocol I, as well as the language used in the ICTY and ICTR statutes, was undoubtedly intentional. The term "should have known" is more akin to a negligence standard used in the Hostage Case and the Tokyo Trials. ICC command responsibility requires consideration of the circumstances that existed at the time the war crimes were committed when determining what the commander should have known.

The Rome Statute is the first codification of command responsibility that draws a clear distinction between the application of the mens rea standard as applied to civilian and military leaders. The Statute established a higher mens rea standard for civilian superiors. For civilians, the standard is "knew, or consciously disregarded information which clearly indicated, that the subordinates were committing or about to commit such crimes." This standard requires proof of actual knowledge. However, the Statute allows proof of willful blindness to satisfy this knowledge requirement: actual knowledge will be imputed if the civilian superior remained willfully blind to information regarding war crimes committed by subordinates.

If a commander knows or should know that his subordinates are about to commit, are committing, or have committed war crimes, the obligation imposed by the ICC Statute is to take all necessary and reasonable steps to prevent, suppress, or report and punish such crimes. This language is identical to the requirements in the ICTY and the ICTR. The terms "necessary and reasonable" connote a flexible approach to this obligation, recognizing a commander should not be required to do the impossible. Use of the term "reasonable" in the Statute also creates an objective standard by which to judge the sufficiency of a commander's response to such situations, accounting for the type of situation Justice Murphy believed existed in the Yamashita case.

The Rome Statute explicitly provides that a culpable commander "shall be criminally responsible for crimes within the jurisdiction of the Court committed by forces under his or her effective command and control . . . ." This is

---

60. THE ROME STATUTE OF THE INTERNATIONAL CRIMINAL COURT, at 17.
61. *Id.*

merely a reflection of the traditional scope of command responsibility, holding the commander accountable not merely for a dereliction, but for the offenses caused by that dereliction. Since Yamashita, this concept has been a key component of the doctrine, however the Rome Statute is the first specific codification of this imputed liability theory under international law.

III. U.S. Practice and the Accountability of Responsible Commanders

Protocol I, the ICTY and ICTR, and the Rome Statute all influenced the evolution of the command responsibility doctrine, adding clarity to its scope and elements. The mens rea element is still a matter of varying formulations and interpretation. Nevertheless, the doctrine continues to mature, and is regularly applied in various international tribunals. Given that the United States was one of the leading proponents of this doctrine after World War II, it would seem logical that the U.S. military law would fully embrace the doctrine. That is not the case. To date, the United States has not expressly included the doctrine of command responsibility in its military code. Instead, other provisions of the code are used to hold U.S. commanders accountable when the commander has either directly committed war crimes, or when a close nexus exists between the commander's acts or omissions and war crimes committed by subordinate forces.

A. Accountability of U.S. Commanders

Several punitive articles (the section of the military code enumerating offenses) in the UCMJ prohibit conduct that if committed would also qualify as war crimes. These articles include: Article 93 Cruelty or Maltreatment; Article 97 Unlawful Detention; Article 116 Riot; Article 118 Murder; Article 119 Manslaughter; Article 120 Rape; Article 124 Maiming; Article 128 Assault; Article 134 Kidnapping; and Article 134 Negligent Homicide.[62] The UCMJ also includes what is known as a "general article," allowing prosecutors to craft offenses when conduct is prejudicial to good order and discipline and/or of a nature to bring discredit upon the armed forces. If conduct that would qualify as a war crime pursuant to international law does not fall within the definition of one of the foregoing specific articles, the general article could provide an alternate basis for charging the responsible service-member. If a commander was directly involved in the commission of any of these offenses, his criminal liability is clear.

---

62. *See* UNIFORM CODE OF MILITARY JUSTICE §897 art. 97, §916 art. 116, §918 art. 118, §919 art. 119, §924 art. 124, §928 art. 128, and §934 art. 134, *reprinted in* MANUAL FOR COURTS-MARTIAL UNITED STATES A2-26, A2-29, A2-31, A2-32 (2005).

Even if a commander did not directly engage in these offenses, the accomplice liability provision of the Uniform Code of Military Justice, Article 77 can be used to impose criminal responsibility.[63] Article 77 provides an umbrella-like function, applying the accomplice liability doctrine to other punitive articles within the code.[64] If a commander ordered, encouraged, or otherwise supported his forces in committing a violation of the code corresponding to a war crime, the commander would be liable as a principal. Article 77 liability would be based on the commander's shared criminal purpose or design. Like traditional common law accomplice liability, the commander must take some action or fail to perform a legal duty, with the purpose to aid, abet, counsel, or command, or encourage the perpetrator to commit the offense.[65]

Similarly, if a commander aided or assisted his subordinates in covering up evidence of a war crime, the commander could be liable as an accessory to the crime. Article 78 of the UCMJ establishes the elements for an accessory liability. Like Article 77, Article 78 applies these elements to all punitive articles in the code. To be guilty as an accessory, the commander must (1) know the perpetrator committed a criminal offense under the code and (2) assist the perpetrator for the purpose of hindering or preventing the apprehension, trial, or punishment of the perpetrator.[66] However, unlike Article 77 accomplice liability, being an accessory is a distinct offense, and does not result in conviction for the offense committed by the subordinate.

There are legal and practical hurdles to overcome before convicting a commander as a principle, accomplice, or accessory after the fact to war crimes. In a case of direct involvement or participation by the commander, there are challenges of proof. The battlefield is a chaotic and confusing environment where the collection and preservation of evidence needed to build a criminal case might be difficult, if not impossible, to accomplish. However, if such proof is available, the commander would be guilty as a principle (for example, if the proof established that a commander ordered a subordinate to execute a prisoner of war, the commander would likely be convicted of murder in violation of Article 118 of the UCMJ).

To establish a commander's liability as an accomplice or an accessory, the most difficult legal obstacle is proving the commander shared the criminal purpose or design. The evidence must establish both that the commander's act or omission "set the conditions" for subordinate war crimes, and also that the acts or omissions resulted from the commander's purpose to facilitate the commission of the crime or to prevent the detection of past crimes committed by his forces. It is unlikely that a commander who shares such an illicit mens rea with his subordinates will be careless enough to explicitly indicate that intent; it is more likely that the shared illicit intent will have to be inferred from equivocal

---

63. UNIFORM CODE OF MILITARY JUSTICE §877 art. 77, *reprinted in* MANUAL FOR COURTS-MARTIAL UNITED STATES A2-24 (2005).
64. MANUAL FOR COURTS-MARTIAL UNITED STATES para. 1b(1) at IV-1 (2005).
65. UCMJ Article 77. UNIFORM CODE OF MILITARY JUSTICE §877 art. 77, *reprinted in* MANUAL FOR COURTS-MARTIAL UNITED STATES A2-24 (2005).
66. MANUAL FOR COURTS-MARTIAL UNITED STATES para. 2b. IV – 2 (2005).

or veiled language and conduct by the commander. Ultimately, because a commander suspected of complicity in subordinate war crimes benefits from a presumption of innocence, only when the evidence is sufficient to meet the demanding standard of proof beyond a reasonable doubt will this shared intent be established, a proof challenge exacerbated by the nature of armed hostilities.

1. My Lai and Command Responsibility

A serious and highly publicized incident during the Vietnam War illustrates these proof difficulties. The incident, most commonly referred to as the My Lai Massacre, involved the killing of several hundred unarmed non-combatants by members of Charlie Company, Task Force Barker of the 11th Brigade of the Americal Division.[67] Among those prosecuted for the murder of these civilians was the Charlie Company Commander, Captain Ernest Medina.[68] The evidence put Captain Medina within a few hundred yards of the village where his subordinates were killing these unarmed and inoffensive victims.[69] He was at this location for some three hours during the time of the killings. There was no evidence that Captain Medina either took part in the killings or issued direct orders to his soldiers to kill unarmed civilians.[70]

The U.S. government charged Captain Medina with intentional murder under Article 118 of the UCMJ.[71] The government's theory was that Captain Medina knew exactly what his soldiers were doing; he had the means to stop or prevent the killing, and he chose not to do so. Accordingly, his knowledge of the crimes being committed, his ability to stop or prevent the crimes, and his unwillingness to do so, made him a principal to the murders under Article 77 of the UCMJ. The military judge, however, rejected the prosecution's theory on the grounds it was not supported by the facts or the law.[72] The military judge then reduced the charges to involuntary manslaughter under Article 119 of the UCMJ, and provided the following instruction to the military panel (military jury):

> In relation to the question pertaining to the supervisory responsibility of a Company Commander, I advise you that as a general principle of military law and custom a military superior in command is responsible for and required, in the performance of his command duties, to make certain the proper performance by his subordinates of their duties assigned by him. In other words,

---

67. *See* William R. Peers, THE PEERS REPORT Ch. 2 (March 14, 1970), *reprinted in* THE MY LAI MASSACRE AND ITS COVER-UP: BEYOND THE REACH OF LAW? 44-46 (Joseph Goldstein, Burke Marshall & Jack Schwartz eds., 1976).
68. Medina v. Resor et al., 43 C.M.R. 243, 244 (C.M.A. 1971).
69. *See* Peers Report on Mai Lai.
70. There is evidence that the evening before the operation, Captain Medina gave his troops a "pep talk," but nothing in that evidences orders or directions to kill unarmed civilians. *Id.* at 95-99. The Peers Report states that although he did not say kill all civilians after the pep talk, all the soldiers knew to kill anything that moved.
71. Medina v. Resor et al., 43 C.M.R. 243, 244 (C.M.A. 1971).
72. *See* Editor's notes of Kenneth Howard, *Command Responsibility for War Crimes*, 21 J. PUB. L. 7, 8 (1972).

after taking action or issuing an order, a commander must remain alert and make timely adjustments as required by a changing situation. Furthermore, a commander is also responsible if he has actual knowledge that the troops or other persons subject to his control are in the process of committing or are about to commit a war crime and he wrongfully fails to take the necessary and reasonable steps to insure compliance with the law of war. *You will observe that these legal requirements placed upon a commander require actual knowledge plus a wrongful failure to act. Thus, mere presence at the scene without knowledge will not suffice.* That is, the commander-subordinate relationship alone will not allow an inference of knowledge. While it is not necessary that a commander actually see an atrocity being committed, it is essential that he know that his subordinates are in the process of committing atrocities or are about to commit atrocities [emphasis added].[73]

Captain Medina was acquitted because the prosecution failed to prove his actual knowledge of the massacre.

In Captain Medina's case, the judge's instruction for actual knowledge given on the involuntary manslaughter charge is similar to the kind of actual knowledge instruction that would apply to someone charged as accomplice or an accessory. Considering in most instances direct evidence of a commander's complicity may not exist, knowledge or shared intent by the commander in the commission of war crimes must be proven circumstantially. Such proof will often be difficult to muster, and as Medina's acquittal indicates, even if presented it may not convince a panel of military officers that this evidence established actual knowledge and shared purpose. This is especially true in the context of the confusion and chaotic environment of the battlefield. That a jury would give a commander charged with such complicity the benefit of the "fog of war" is unsurprising; trial by military jury is intended to inject genuine appreciation of the challenges of the operational environment into the adjudication process.

In cases where a commander cannot be charged either as a direct participant, or as an accomplice or an accessory, evidence might show the commander was derelict in his duties by failing to prevent, suppress, or punish subordinate war crimes. Dereliction of duty is the essence of the command responsibility doctrine that emerged from the World War II tribunals. It is not, however, analogous to command responsibility as a theory of criminal responsibility.

2. Article 92 Dereliction of Duty

Article 92 of the UCMJ defines the elements for dereliction of duty as follows: (a) that the accused had certain duties; (b) that the accused knew or reasonably should have known of the duties; and (c) that the accused was (willfully) (through neglect or culpable inefficiency) derelict in the performance of those duties.[74] The Manual for Courts-Martial (MCM) sets out the key aspects and definitions of Article 92. According to the MCM and established military case

---

73. Id at 8, 10-11.
74. *See* UNIFORM CODE OF MILITARY JUSTICE §892 art. 92, *reprinted in* MANUAL FOR COURTS-MARTIAL UNITED STATES at A2-26 (2005).

law, the source of the legal duty can come from a "treaty, statute, lawful order, standard operating procedure, or custom of the service."[75] Even though the elements and explanation does not explicitly mention the special legal duties imposed on a commander, this definition is certainly broad enough to include a commander's law of armed conflict-based duties and responsibilities to supervise subordinates.

Article 92 adopts a mens rea of "know or reasonably should have known" standard in order to trigger a commander's duty to act; however, military appellate decisions interpreting Article 92 have frequently imposed a higher mens rea standard. For example, in *United States v. Ferguson*,[76] the Navy-Marine Court of Military Review held that in order to prove that a service member's dereliction was willful; the prosecution had the burden of proving the accused had actual knowledge of his duty. The court reasoned that because a charge of willful dereliction carries with it a higher punishment, a higher mens rea standard was required than is defined in Article 92.[77]

Article 92 defines dereliction as willful, negligent, or culpably inefficient conduct.[78] Under this formulation, to avoid liability, a commander must avoid willful failures and achieve a level of competency that is somewhere above simple negligence or culpable inefficiency. One could argue that a commander who has the ability to prevent or suppress law of war violations by his forces but fails to do so is the very embodiment of dereliction. However, even if a commander is successfully prosecuted for a violation of Article 92, he will not be held accountable for the war crimes his dereliction facilitated. Instead, he will be subject to a much less significant range of permissible punishments. Thus, in its current form, the Uniform Code of Military Justice will only permit conviction and punishment for the war crimes committed by subordinates when the evidence meets the demanding requirements of principal liability, *not* when it is sufficient to meet the requirements of the international standards of "should have known" command responsibility.

3. Gap in U.S. Military Law

In cases of very serious command responsibility failures (like those related to the massacre by Charlie Company at My Lai) occurring today, UCMJ prosecution options remain limited. Without proof of direct complicity, dereliction of duty is the only viable offense in the punitive articles to allege against the responsible commander. One possible alternative approach would be to prosecute the U.S. commander not for a violation of an offense enumerated by the UCMJ punitive articles, but instead for an actual law of war violation. Article 18 of the UCMJ establishes jurisdiction for the general court-martial. Article 18 obviously vests those courts with jurisdiction to try allegations of violation of crimes enumerated by the Code (such as dereliction of duty and murder).

---

75. MANUAL FOR COURTS-MARTIAL UNITED STATES para. 16c(3)(a) at IV-24 (2005).
76. United States v. Ferguson, 40 M.J. 823, 833-34 (N.M.C.M.R. 1994).
77. *Id.*
78. MANUAL FOR COURTS-MARTIAL UNITED STATES para. 16b(3)(c) at IV-23 (2005).

However, Article 18 also vests the general court-martial with jurisdiction to try "any person who by the law of war is subject to trial by a military tribunal and may adjudge any punishment permitted by the law of war."[79]

Accordingly, Article 18 authorizes trial by general court-martial for offenses enacted by Congress in the U.S. military code, *and* for offenses established by international law subject to trial by military courts—war crimes. Because the doctrine of command responsibility provides an international legal basis to prosecute commanders for the war crimes committed by their subordinates with an established history of applying the doctrine in military tribunals, Article 18 vests general court-martial with authority to try U.S. commanders for command responsibility offenses.

This option is, however, purely theoretical. First, it has never been used; second, there are several problems with this approach. If the U.S. military were to use this alternate Article 18 jurisdiction as the basis for prosecuting a U.S. commander, the government would be limited to prosecuting only law of war violations. The punitive articles enumerated under the UCMJ and the accompanying case law would not apply. The elements, definitions, and applications associated with law of war offenses are less precise, raising vagueness and ex post facto concerns. In addition, it is against U.S. policy to try our own service members for law of war violations. Rather, it is policy to try service members for UCMJ punitive article violations only.[80] These constitutional, practical, and policy reasons make this alternate approach unlikely. As a result, the United States is now in the awkward position of being one of the earliest and strongest proponents of the command responsibility doctrine, but without a meaningful and viable mechanism for implementing the doctrine in response to the misconduct of its own military commanders. Considering this has been the state of U.S. military law since the time of the Yamashita trial, it is unlikely the defect will be cured in the foreseeable future.[81]

B. Accountability of Enemy Commanders

How would the United States prosecute commanders of enemy forces for violations under the command responsibility doctrine? Article 2(a)(9) of the UCMJ subjects prisoners of war to courts-martial jurisdiction. This establishes personal jurisdiction and it only becomes applicable at the point the enemy is captured. However, Article 2(a)(9) does not establish subject matter jurisdiction over pre-capture crimes. Accordingly, unlike the U.S. soldier or commander, pre-capture war crimes could not be tried as violations of the UCMJ punitive articles. However, this is where the alternate grant of subject matter

---

79. *See* UNIFORM CODE OF MILITARY JUSTICE §818 art. 18, *reprinted in* MANUAL FOR COURTS-MARTIAL UNITED STATES A2-6 (2005).
80. *See* DEPARTMENT OF THE ARMY, FM 27-10 DEPARTMENT OF THE ARMY FIELD MANUAL: THE LAW OF LAND WARFARE, para. 507(b) at Appendix A – 120 (1956).
81. Victor Hansen, *What's Good for the Goose Is Good for the Gander—Lessons from Abu Ghraib: Time for the United States to Adopt a Standard of Command Responsibility Towards its Own*, 42 Gonz. L. Rev. 335 (2007).

jurisdiction in Article 18 becomes critical. As noted, Article 18's grant of court-martial jurisdiction over any person who by the law of war is subject to trial by military commission would vest the general court-martial with authority to try the captured enemy commander for pre-capture violations of international law, including applying the doctrine of command responsibility.

This is a broad jurisdictional grant; any enemy commander who becomes a prisoner of war comes within the jurisdiction of the UCMJ, and misconduct committed while a prisoner of war will be addressed through the punitive articles (for example, if a prisoner of war orders the murder of a U.S. prison guard, or even of a fellow POW, he would be charged with a violation of Article 118 of the UCMJ). Therefore, similar to a U.S. commander, an enemy commander can be punished for his direct involvement in LOAC violations. Also, like a U.S. commander, an enemy commander can be punished as an accomplice or an accessory for less direct but complicit conduct, and could be punished for derelictions that lead to or contributed to LOAC violations by his subordinates.

For pre-capture war crimes exposed while the prisoner of war is in U.S. custody, trial and punishment by general court-martial would be a viable option pursuant to the second clause of Article 18. This allows utilization of the doctrine of command responsibility for command failures by an enemy commander. Ironically, this may be a more viable option for the enemy commander than his U.S. counterpart. For example, constitutional concerns over the vagueness of the command responsibility standard may be less significant when prosecuting an enemy commander than when prosecuting a U.S. commander. Also, unlike with U.S. forces, there is no policy preference for trying enemy forces under the UCMJ. Nor is the general court-martial the only forum available for prosecuting enemy commanders for war crimes. Article 21 of the UCMJ makes clear that courts-martial jurisdiction runs concurrent with military commissions, provost courts, and other military tribunals that also have jurisdiction to try law of war violations. Indeed, trying captured enemy personnel by military commission for their pre-capture war crimes is an historically valid use of such tribunals; it was a military commission that tried General Yamashita.

The most recent use of the military commission for such prosecutions is the military commissions system established to try members of al Qaeda and other "unprivileged belligerents" for violations of the laws of war. This military commissions system has undergone a number of revisions since it was first established by presidential order.[82] The most recent revisions are reflected in the Military Commissions Act of 2009.[83] While the jurisdiction of this military commission is limited to "alien unprivileged enemy belligerents for violations of the law of war and other offenses triable by military commission," the President,

---

82. "Military Order—Detention, Treatment and Trial of Certain Non-Citizens in the War Against Terrorism," Executive Order dated November 13, 2001, 66 Fed. Reg. 57833 (Nov. 16, 2001).
83. http://www.defense.gov/news/2009%20MCA%20Pub%20%20Law%20111-84.pdf.

acting in his capacity as Commander in Chief or with congressional support, could certainly establish other military commissions or broaden the scope to apply to other contexts. If the United States were to try an enemy commander either by court-martial or military commission, what mens rea standard for command responsibility would apply?

There are two sources that suggest the answer. The first answer comes from Army Field Manual 27-10, The Law of Land Warfare.[84] This field manual represents the U.S. Army's view of the customary and treaty law applicable to the conduct of warfare.[85] On the doctrine of command responsibility, paragraph 501 of FM 27-10 states:

> In some cases, military commanders may be responsible for war crimes committed by subordinate members of the armed forces, or other persons subject to their control. Thus, for instance, when troops commit massacres and atrocities against the civilian population of occupied territory or against prisoners of war, the responsibility may rest not only with the actual perpetrators but also with the commander. Such a responsibility arises directly when the acts in question have been committed in pursuance of an order of the commander concerned. *The commander is also responsible if he has actual knowledge, or should have knowledge,* through reports received by him or through other means, that troops or other persons subject to his control are about to commit or have committed a war crime and he fails to take the necessary and reasonable steps to insure compliance with the law of war or to punish violators thereof.[86]

The second is the Military Commissions Act of 2009, which codifies a version of command responsibility that applies to unprivileged belligerents. The act includes in the definition of principals "a superior commander who, with regard to acts punishable by this chapter, knew, had reason to know, or should have known, that a subordinate was about to commit such acts or had done so and who failed to take the necessary and reasonable measures to prevent such acts or to punish the perpetrators thereof."[87]

These sources suggest the United States would apply the actual knowledge, constructive knowledge, or "should have known" mens rea standard to enemy commanders whose subordinates commit war crimes, where the commander failed to take necessary action to prevent, suppress, or punish that misconduct. This is essentially the standard codified by the ICC and applied in Yamashita and the Hostage Cases.

---

84. Army Field Manual 27-10 "The Law of Land Warfare" (FM 27-10) published in July of 1956, is still the current manual in publication and includes an explanation of the doctrine of command responsibility. DEPARTMENT OF THE ARMY, FM 27-10 DEPARTMENT OF THE ARMY FIELD MANUAL: THE LAW OF LAND WARFARE (1956).
85. *Id.* para. 501 at Appendix A – 117.
86. Army Field Manual 27-10 "The Law of Land Warfare" (FM 27-10).
87. Military Commissions Act of 2009, Sec. 950q(3).

IV. Other Compliance Mechanisms

Thus far, this chapter has focused on the doctrine of command responsibility and how that doctrine provides a legal incentive to commanders to ensure that their forces comply with the law of armed conflict obligations. Beyond this doctrine, there are other obligations and mechanisms that influence compliance with the law and the conduct of disciplined military operations. This section focuses on the U.S. commander's obligation to investigate possible war crimes and to ensure subordinates are trained to respect the LOAC.

A. Investigating War Crimes

The Geneva Conventions require party states to "search for persons alleged to have committed, or have ordered to be committed, such grave breaches, and . . . bring such persons, regardless of their nationality, before its own courts."[88] The Conventions do not create a particular methodology States must use to satisfy this obligation. A recent fact finding mission ordered by the Human Rights Council of the United Nations examined violations of international human rights law and international humanitarian law that might have been committed in military operations in Gaza in 2008-2009. The report of this fact finding mission, known as the Goldstone Report,[89] concluded that international law requires that investigations of war crimes allegations "should comply with standards of impartiality, independence, promptness and effectiveness."[90] How does the United States military meet its obligation to investigate and punish war crimes in a manner that indicates credible outcomes?

The U.S. military does not have a separate investigative regime solely for war crimes allegations. As noted above, the policy of the U.S. military is to prosecute war crimes committed by U.S. forces as violations of the UCMJ. There are a number of offenses under the UCMJ that criminalize conduct that could also be defined as a war crime. Consistent with this policy, the U.S. military's system for investigating alleged war crimes is to investigate them as it would any other alleged violation of the UCMJ.

However, war crimes often adversely impact the military's mission in a way that other crimes may not. Because of this, incidents where there is credible information indicating a suspected or alleged violation of the law of war are defined by Department of Defense Directive 2310.01A, the Law of War Program, as "reportable incidents."[91] Reportable incidents that occur in war or other contingency operations must be reported through the chain of command for ultimate transmission to appropriate U.S. agencies. This same directive

---

88. *See* GC I, Art. 49; GC II, Art. 50; GC III, Art. 129; GC IV, Art. 146.
89. http://www2.ohchr.org/english/bodies/hrcouncil/specialsession/9/docs/UNFFMGC_Report.PDF.
90. Goldstone Report page 36.
91. *See* Department of Defense Directive 2311.01E, May 9, 2006.

instructs commanders to report these incidents promptly, to investigate thoroughly, and where appropriate, take corrective action. On-scene commanders are also instructed to take measures to preserve evidence pending transfer of the investigation to the appropriate authority. While this directive sets out some specific procedures with respect to reportable incidents, it does not create a separate investigative procedure.

Criminal investigations in the military can be a fluid and sometimes overlapping process. It is not unusual in sensitive or high profile cases—often the case for war crimes investigations—for multiple investigations to be occurring simultaneously. One overriding principle in these investigations and possible subsequent prosecutions is the primacy of the military commander. Unlike the civilian criminal justice system, the unit commander plays a central role in all phases of the military justice system. In the investigation context, the military commander has the authority to initiate investigations within his command, to appoint investigating officers, to approve or disapprove the results of an investigation, to request an outside agency or a higher level commander to investigate allegations of misconduct, and to take or initiate disciplinary actions based on the results of an investigation. The central role of the commander reflects the U.S. military's policy that the military criminal justice system is primarily a tool of the commander to maintain good order and discipline within the military unit.[92]

Because in most cases the commander does not have any formal legal training, an important feature in military investigations and military justice system is the role of the commander's legal advisor, or Judge Advocate General's Corps officer (JAG). JAG officers can be found at every level of command. These JAGs are responsible for advising military commanders on all aspects of military justice, including investigations. In certain situations the commander cannot take specific actions without first consulting his JAG officer and obtaining that officer's advice.[93] In practice, JAGs play a very active part in military investigations.

1. Investigation Procedures: The Army Example

All U.S. services have established process for conducting investigations. The Army model is illustrative. In the Army there are three primary kinds of investigations into allegations of misconduct, including war crimes allegations. They are commonly referred to as commander's inquiries, 15-6 investigations, and criminal investigations. There is also a fourth type of investigation conducted by the Army's Inspector General which can, in some instances, investigate crimes, including war crimes.

---

92. Victor Hansen, *Changes in Modern Military Codes and the Role of the Military Commander: What Should the United States Learn from this Revolution?*, 16 Tul. J. Int'l & Comp. L. 419 (2008).

93. Joint Publication 1-04 Legal Support to Joint Operations, http://www.dtic.mil/doctrine/new_pubs/jp1_04.pdf.

a. Commander's Inquiry

The first and most basic kind of investigation is a commander's inquiry. Commanders at every level of command have the inherent authority to investigate misconduct that is alleged to have occurred within the command. Rule for courts-martial 303 directs the commander to make preliminary inquiries into charges or suspected offenses if the commander receives information that a member of the command has committed an offense under the UCMJ. These commander's inquiries can take two primary forms. The commander can conduct the inquiry personally, and this is sometimes done for very minor allegations. The commander can also appoint someone within the command to conduct the investigation and report the findings and recommendations back to the commander.

Commander's inquiries typically involve interviewing witnesses, taking sworn statements, collecting and reviewing relevant documentary evidence, and examining physical evidence that may exist. At the conclusion of the investigation, the investigating official prepares a report of the factual findings. The investigating official can also make legal conclusions and recommendations as to what actions the commander should take. The findings, conclusions, and recommendations are not binding on the commander. The commander is free to accept or reject them. Before taking any action on the investigation, commanders often seek advice from their JAG officer.[94]

The commander's inquiry is used frequently within the military. The benefits of this type of investigation are that it can be done expeditiously and it allows the commander to get a quick assessment of the facts and issues involved. If the allegations prove to be unfounded or relatively minor, the matter can be disposed of quickly with little disruption to the unit's mission. The drawbacks of this informal investigation are that the investigation is often conducted by officers without any formal training in investigations, evidence collection, witness interviewing, evidence preservation and other investigation techniques. As a result, these investigations can be cursory, incomplete, or lead to inaccurate results. In addition, if the commander personally conducted the investigation and later wants to take disciplinary action against a soldier, he may be precluded from taking such actions because of his direct involvement in the investigation. Because of these drawbacks, commander's inquiries are not frequently used for allegations of serious misconduct such as serious war crimes. However, because it is often unclear how serious an incident may be at the time of initial report, commander's inquiries often evolve into more formal investigations when information developed from a commander's inquiry reveals more serious misconduct than was initially suspected. In such instances, the commander can initiate more formal investigations.

---

94. See RULES FOR COURTS-MARTIALS Rule 303, reprinted in MANUAL FOR COURTS-MARTIAL UNITED STATES at II-1(2009).

b. Investigations Under Army Regulation 15-6

A more formal investigation than a commander's inquiry is frequently referred to as 15-6 investigation. Procedures for conducting these investigations are set out in Army Regulation 15-6.[95] There are two general types of investigations pursuant to this regulation, informal and formal inquiries. It is typically the commander who decides the type of investigation to be conducted. Because it is often a military commander who orders these 15-6 investigations, they are in many cases a more formalized commander's inquiry. In addition to the commander, any flag officer, any principal staff officer, and certain Department of the Army civilians are also authorized to initiate 15-6 investigations.[96]

Before deciding on whether to use formal or informal procedures, the appointing authority consults with the JAG legal advisor. Informal investigations can be conducted by one officer or a board of officers. Investigating officers are selected to serve based on the officer's qualifications, education, training, experience, length of service, and temperament. Frequently the investigating officer will receive advice on conducting the investigation from a JAG officer. To ensure the independence of the investigation this advice will come from a different JAG officer than the JAG officer who advises the appointing commander. The investigating officer can use whatever method determined most efficient to conduct the investigation. The most common method is to appoint a single officer who will interview witnesses, collect evidence, make findings of fact, conclusions of law, and make specific recommendations to the appointing authority. As with commander's inquiries, these recommendations are not binding on the appointing authority.

The second type of 15-6 investigation is a formal investigation. Formal investigations are a type of administrative hearing, conducted by a board of officers appointed by the officer ordering the investigation. Because these investigations are a type of hearing, a recorder and legal advisor are also required, but these are non-voting members of the investigation. In addition, a respondent is identified, notified, and has a right to be represented by counsel and to be present during the presentation of the evidence. Formal 15-6 investigations are used primarily for serious accidents and for termination of military service (firing a soldier); they are almost never used when investigating criminal misconduct. However, it is not uncommon for criminal misconduct to be exposed during the course of such investigations.

Before an appointing authority can take action in response to the findings and recommendations of either a formal or informal 15-6 investigation, the investigative report must receive a legal review. This review determines whether the investigation complied with the regulatory requirements, whether there is sufficient evidence to support the findings, and whether the recommendations are consistent with the findings. The standard of proof is a "more probable

---

[95]. *See* ARMY REGULATION 15-6 PROCEDURES FOR INVESTIGATING OFFICERS AND BOARDS OF OFFICERS.

[96]. *See* ARMY REGULATION 15-6 PROCEDURES FOR INVESTIGATING OFFICERS AND BOARDS OF OFFICERS, paragraph 2-1 (2006).

than not" standard. These investigations can take place concurrently with other investigations, including criminal investigations or possibly even other 15-6 investigations conducted by another command.

While the regulation encourages cooperation and coordination between investigations, nothing precludes multiple investigations occurring simultaneously. It is not unusual, particularly in complex investigations or investigations of sensitive matters, for a 15-6 investigation to take place while a criminal investigation is underway. For example, there were multiple and simultaneous investigations into the allegations of abuse by U.S. forces at Abu Ghraib prison in Iraq. However, if a 15-6 investigation proceeds concurrently with a criminal investigation, the 15-6 investigation might have a different focus.

A criminal investigation is primarily focused on the conduct at issue and the extent of criminal liability. A simultaneous 15-6 investigation might be more focused on such things as the underlying causes of the misconduct, steps taken by the chain of command to prevent the misconduct, and the adequacy of solider training and support. This was the case with the multiple investigations into the Abu Ghraib abuse allegations. Even though the primary focus of the 15-6 investigation might be on issues other than the specifics of criminal misconduct, nothing precludes evidence developed as part of the investigation from being used in subsequent criminal proceedings. Likewise, evidence and information initially developed as part of a 15-6 investigation can be the basis for opening or expanding a criminal investigation.

c. Criminal Investigations

The third type of investigation is a criminal investigation. These investigations are conducted by military police and/or agents of the Army's Criminal Investigation Division (CID). The Army CID is a separate military organization with its own chain of command that is independent of other military chains of command, with specific responsibility for investigating serious crimes including war crimes and serious maltreatment or abuse of detainees.[97] Criminal investigations by CID can be initiated at the request of a commander, or independently by CID, or at the request of senior military or civilian officials within the Department of Defense. The Army CID's obligation to investigate crimes continues in deployed environments and active theaters of combat.

CID investigations are conducted by special agents trained in law enforcement, witness questioning, evidence development, evidence collection, and evidence preservation. CID agents have the authority to secure crime scenes and exclude access to those crime scenes in order to preserve evidence. CID also maintains a crime lab that conducts various types of forensic testing on evidence, including ballistic testing. CID agents have the authority to collect evidence and submit it for testing.

---

97. *See* ARMY REGULATION 195-2, CRIMINAL INVESTIGATION ACTIVITIES, paragraph 3-3(a)(6) (2009).

Because war crimes allegations frequently involve serious violations of the UCMJ, and because these allegations require timely and thorough investigations, CID will most often be the agency conducting investigation into such allegations. The criminal investigations into the Abu Ghraib abuse allegations, for example, were conducted by the Army's CID. During the course of the investigation CID agents may consult with legal advisors within CID as well as military prosecutors who would ultimately be responsible for prosecuting cases at court-martial. In many cases the command may begin initiating criminal proceedings against an accused soldier before a CID investigation is completed. This is particularly true in serious cases. In such cases the unit's military prosecutor will work closely with both the commander responsible for initiating the criminal trial process, and the CID agents in preparing the case for possible court-martial.

While Army CID has the independent authority to initiate and conduct criminal investigations, CID does not have the authority to initiate criminal charges or court-martial proceedings. Only the soldier's military commander has the authority to initiate court-martial proceedings. Usually the commander's decision to initiate criminal proceedings for serious offenses will be based in part on information contained in the CID report. The commander makes decisions on the prosecution of a soldier after consultation with his JAG legal advisor and in serious cases, after the recommendation of an independent investigating officer. A criminal report may also give a commander reason to initiate a commander's inquiry or a 15-6 investigation into aspects of the case that were not part of the criminal investigation. Reports of criminal investigations are in writing and the reports are filed and maintained centrally by the Army CID.

d. Inspector General Investigations

A fourth type of investigation that can include an investigation of war crimes is an Inspector General's (IG) investigation. IG investigations into misconduct can be initiated by certain senior military officials or on the initiative of the Inspector General.[98] The decision to initiate an investigation can be based on reports or allegations of misconduct from any number of sources, to include commander's inquiries, 15-6 investigations, and even anonymous reports. Generally, IG investigations are limited to investigating misconduct of a non-criminal nature. However, the Chief of Staff of the Army can direct the IG to investigate criminal allegations and the results of those investigations can serve as the basis for disciplinary actions, to include criminal sanctions. This is most often done when the IG is tasked with investigating allegations of misconduct against senior military officers. On occasion, allegations investigated by the IG may include war crimes.

---

98. Army Regulation 20-1, Inspector General Activities and Procedures, Chapter 8.

2. Investigation Oversight and Review

There are both formal and informal oversight mechanisms of military investigations. Most investigations, other than some very informal commander's inquiries, receive a legal review on the sufficiency and accuracy of the investigation by a JAG officer before the investigation is final. Additionally, the officer who appointed or directed the investigation must review the report and can approve the report, disapprove all or part of the report, or order additional investigation into the matter. The commander will make these decisions after consulting his JAG officer.

The definition of a war crime as a "reportable incident" by the Department of Defense Law of War Directive is intended to ensure war crimes allegations are passed quickly up the chain of command in order to prevent the allegations from remaining buried at the lower levels. Of course, no system is perfect and there are incidents where information about suspected war crimes has been suppressed. One such example involved allegations of unlawful killings by U.S. Marines in Haditha, Iraq. Once the incident was brought to light, members of the chain of command, including the unit legal advisor were investigated for dereliction of duty for failing to take initial action on the allegations. The reporting obligation established by the Law of War Directive established the duty the participants were derelict in executing.

One issue that is scrutinized in the legal review process is the independence of the investigation and whether the officer who appointed the investigation can act in a neutral and detached fashion. If, for example, an investigation reveals evidence that might implicate the officer who appointed the investigation, the investigating officer should forward the matter to a higher level of command so that the investigation can be conducted by someone outside of the unit. Failure to appoint an independent investigation would render any report legally inadequate.

Many times the consequence of an investigation will not result in a criminal prosecution. Nevertheless, the investigation may serve as the basis for taking some other administrative and/or disciplinary action, such as relief from command, reprimand, corrective training, or separation from service. In those instances as well, if the investigation serves as the basis for the adverse action, the respondent soldier is entitled to review the investigation. Soldiers may challenge the accuracy, fairness, completeness, or independence of the investigation. In most cases, a JAG officer is detailed to assist the soldier in this review/challenge process, and to represent the solider in any administrative or disciplinary proceedings.

There are a number of statutory and constitutional rights that must be afforded to soldiers subject to war crimes investigations. While the rights that soldiers enjoy may be more limited than those rights enjoyed by the civilian population, service members are afforded significant protections by the U.S. Constitution, the UCMJ, and military regulations. These include the statutory (UCMJ) and constitutional right to remain silent and to be informed of that right. In addition, at some stages of the investigation both the constitutional and statutory right to be represented by counsel and to consult with counsel will be applicable. There are also privacy rights afforded by the UCMJ and the

Fourth Amendment to the U.S. Constitution that protect soldiers from unreasonable searches and seizures. Investigators must be mindful of these protections. Failure to respect these rights can result in legally flawed and inadequate investigations and the exclusion of evidence from a courts-martial proceeding, among other consequences.

In addition to these internal mechanisms for challenging investigation results, media and other public interest and attention in high profile cases, including war crimes allegations, will often subject the military process to scrutiny. This outside attention can often be the catalyst for additional investigation. The best recent example of this is the Abu Ghraib detainee abuse allegations. Several months before the photos of detainee abuse were made public by media organizations, Army CID was conducting a criminal investigation. There was also a 15-6 investigation being conducted into the systemic causes and command failings that led to the abuse.

When the detainee abuse photographs became public, members of Congress, interest groups, the media, and the general public all became intensely interested in what had happened and why it had happened. There were a number of congressional hearings held in both the House and the Senate. At those hearings, officials who conducted the initial investigation, several senior commanders, and the senior legal advisor to the command in Iraq testified. This led to additional investigations by the Army, and by the Department of Defense. The scope of these investigations focused on internal and external causes of the detainee abuse. There was no set process that required these additional investigations. Their creation and direction was as an ad hoc response to the situation at Abu Ghraib. These additional investigations came about primarily because of public scrutiny and Congress's responsibility for governing of the armed forces. This process serves as an important reminder of the necessity of timely, transparent, and credible investigations into war crimes allegations. Any commander who attempts to cover up incidents of misconduct or manipulate the investigatory process in such cases does so at great peril, and may ultimately exacerbate the negative impact of the war crimes.

As noted above, the policy of the United States is to prosecute alleged war crimes by U.S. service members as violations of enumerated punitive articles of the UCMJ. As such, the military does not have a separate war crimes investigation process and does not apply separate or different investigating standards for war crimes allegations. In addition, because U.S. policy is to apply the law of war to the full spectrum of military operations, the investigation procedures are the same whether the allegation arises in the context of an international armed conflict or a non-international armed conflict.

B. Ensuring Compliance with the LOAC

Article 87 of Additional Protocol I provides that:

> In order to prevent and suppress breaches, High Contracting Parties and Parties to the conflict shall require that, commensurate with their level of

responsibility, commanders ensure that members of the armed forces under their command are aware of their obligations under the Conventions and this Protocol.[99]

The command responsibility doctrine also obliges commanders at all levels to prevent LOAC violations by the forces under their command. In addition, the 1949 Geneva Conventions require the High Contracting Parties to:

> disseminate the text of the present Convention as widely as possible in their respective countries, and, in particular, to include the study thereof in their programmes of military and, if possible, civil instruction, so that the principles thereof may become known to the entire population, in particular to the armed fighting forces, the medical personnel and the chaplains.[100]

The U.S. military meets this obligation primarily through the Department of Defense Law of War Program.

Department of Defense Directive 2311.01E not only establishes war crimes reporting obligations, it also outlines other responsibilities related to the training of forces and repression of violations.[101] The directive imposes obligations on all levels of command to prevent law of war violations. The directive makes clear that these obligations apply to "all armed conflicts, however such conflicts are characterized, and in all other military operations."[102]

The directive requires that all Department of Defense components "institute and implement effective programs to prevent violations of the law of war, including law of war training and dissemination." It also requires that qualified legal advisors are available at all levels of command to provide advice about law of war compliance during planning and execution of exercises and operations. Military contractors and contractor work statements must also comply with these obligations.

To meet these requirements, JAG officers routinely conduct periodic training to service members on the LOAC and rules of engagement. This training covers all key aspects of operational compliance. Perhaps most importantly, LOAC training is increasingly adapted and focused to the respective audience and embedded within tactical training. Soldiers typically receive an annual lecture on these issues. However, as soldiers prepare to deploy to combat, LOAC review and critique is embedded into many aspects of their training process. While the sophistication of the training will vary among levels of command, it has become a hallmark of contemporary LOAC training to rely far more heavily on experiential learning than on the classroom lecture.[103]

In addition to training, JAG officers play an important role during operational planning and execution. Uniformed JAG officers are at the forefront of

---

99. Id.
100. *See* Geneva Convention (I) Article 47.
101. http://www.dtic.mil/whs/directives/corres/pdf/231101e.pdf.
102. http://www.dtic.mil/whs/directives/corres/pdf/231101e.pdf.
103. Major Mark Martins, *Rules of Engagement for Land Forces: A Matter of Training, Not Lawyering*, 143 Military Law Review 1 (1994).

the U.S. military's law of war programs. These JAG officers are the recognized experts in LOAC obligations and compliance. As two experienced commentators noted:

> In contemporary US operations, judge advocates are fully integrated members of military staffs. The senior judge advocate assigned to a unit serves as a personal advisor to the commander, ensuring that the commander receives sufficient timely and accurate advice to conduct operations in accordance with law and policy. To perform these functions, judge advocates must have a thorough grasp of the applicable law, US policy, the unit's mission, his commander's intent, enemy objectives and tactics, the capabilities of weapons systems, and the staff planning processes.[104]

As illustrated throughout this text, JAG officers are part of a unit's planning and targeting cells and they provide input on LOAC obligations and ensure that operational plans and targets comply with LOAC requirements. In addition, JAG officers play a critical role in creating and reviewing rules of engagement to ensure that these rules comply with LOAC while giving the military commander the necessary tools to accomplish the assigned mission.

There is little doubt that the command responsibility doctrine serves as an important and necessary incentive for commanders to set the conditions for subordinate compliance with the LOAC. However, the positive obligations created in the Geneva Conventions and under international law for commanders to prepare and train their units for legally compliant operational execution is in actuality of greater and more practical import. The United States meets these obligations through the Department of Defense Law of War Program, the UCMJ the uniformed military lawyers who play a vital role in the compliance process, and the thousands of commanders committed to executing their obligations in good faith and accomplishing their combat missions in full compliance with the law.

Further Reading

> Victor Hansen, What's Good for the Goose Is Good for the Gander—Lessons from Abu Ghraib: Time for the United States to Adopt a Standard of Command Responsibility Towards its Own, 42 Gonz. L. Rev. 335 (2007).
> William H. Parks, Command Responsibility for War Crimes, 62 MIL. L. REV. 1, 36 (1973).
> In re Yamashita, 327 U.S. 1 (1946).

---

104. Michael L. Kramer & Michael N. Schmitt, Lawyers on Horseback? Thoughts on Judge Advocates and Civil-Military Relations, 55 UCLA L. REV. 1407 (2008).

Study Questions

1. Subsequent investigations by U.S. and Iraqi forces into the killings of villagers identified members of the Republican Guard to be responsible for the killings. The evidence is based on forensic examinations and interrogations of captured Republican soldiers. Captured soldiers who claimed to be present at the village during the killings alleged that a secret unit within the Republican Guard rounded up the villagers, shot them, and dumped their bodies into the ravine. This special force is alleged to be under the direct command of Colonel Hassan. Captured soldiers claim that these kinds of killings took place in other jungle villages near the Syrian border. Colonel Hassan was recently captured by U.S. forces while attempting to cross into Syria.
    a. If evidence can establish that Colonel Hassan's forces were responsible for the killings of these villagers, what criminal liability could be imposed on Colonel Hassan if he participated in the killings?
    What if he did not directly participate in these killings but he ordered forces under his command to kill the unarmed villagers?
    What if Colonel Hassan was simply passing along orders from a higher command to kill these villagers?
    b. Assume the evidence shows the killing of these villagers was not an isolated incident; that in three other villages, civilians were killed by these Republican Guard forces. Assume also that there is no evidence directly linking these killings to any officials outside of Colonel Hassan's special unit. In order to impose criminal liability on high ranking military officials outside of this special unit, what evidence or information would be relevant? What legal standard should be used to impose criminal liability on these senior officials? Be prepared to fully justify and explain what standard you adopted and why.
    c. Assume the evidence shows the civilian mayor of the village invited and encouraged the Republican Guard forces to come to his village at a time when no U.S. or other allied forces would be in the area. Could the mayor be held responsible for the killing of these villagers even if he claims he did not order or even know that this would happen? What standard of accountability should apply? What evidence would be relevant to meet that standard?
2. Investigation into the killing of the captured POW by a first sergeant from the 193rd revealed that the POW was killed while in the first sergeant's custody. The POW's hands and legs had been bound with flexi-cuffs when he was shot. The investigation also shows that the company commander did meet with his soldiers on the evening before their mission. Several soldiers who were at the meeting said that the company commander was fired up because one of his best friends in another company was killed earlier that day while on a patrol. The soldiers said the commander told his soldiers they would need to travel light and fast on

their mission and that any POWs should be dealt with. Evidence also suggested that the killing of the POW was reported up the chain of command to the battalion commander and that orders came down from the battalion not to discuss the matter with anyone outside of the company. The killing was not reported by the battalion commander to the Brigade even though reporting was required by regulation and standard operating procedure.
   a. Assume the commander's pep talk did in fact take place as the soldiers reported. What liability could be imposed on the company commander under U.S. military law for the unlawful killing of the POW?
   b. Under U.S. military law, what options are available for holding the battalion commander accountable for failing to report the killing of the POW? Would it matter whether the battalion commander knew the full circumstances of the killing when he failed to report it to higher headquarters? Why or why not?
3. The ICRC's report to the JTF commander on the conditions at Empire Prison includes allegations by several detainees of being forced to sleep naked and without shelter. Other detainees report being hit and kicked by their military guards during interrogation sessions. One detainee reported being choked, slapped, and struck with a rifle butt during questioning. The ICRC's report is sealed and marked "For JTF Commander Only." The JTF Commander has not yet read the report although his staff has had the report for two days, and his Chief of Staff alerted him of the report's existence.
   a. How would the U.S. military likely investigate these allegations of abuse?
   b. Could the JTF commander be held criminally liable for any past incidents of prisoner abuse at Empire Prison under international law? If so, under what theory?
   c. If further prisoner abuse takes place at Empire Prison over the next several days, can the JTF commander be held criminally liable for that abuse if he never reads the ICRC report? What if his Chief of Staff reads the report and fails to inform the JTF commander of its contents? What if the JTF commander reads the report and takes no action?

Glossary of Terms

The following terms reflect terminology used in the text that may be unfamiliar to students. Terms are drawn from the military experience of the authors as well as from publications such as Joint Publication 1-02, DOD Dictionary of Military and Associated Terms *(2010, as amended), the* San Remo Manual, *and the U.N. Convention on the Law of the Sea.*

Air Defense Missiles: Ground launched missiles used to destroy enemy aircraft. This is the primary asset used to defend against air attack.

Air Tasking Order: A centralized list that is created by a targeting committee and approved by the commander that allocates air assets to subordinate units and/or against specific targets.

Archipelagic Sea Lanes Passage: Navigation and overflight in the normal mode in sea lanes and air routes designated by an archipelagic State, solely for the purpose of continuous, expeditious, and unobstructed transit between one part of the high seas or an exclusive economic zone and another part of the high seas or an exclusive economic zone.

Archipelagic Waters: Waters enclosed by archipelagic baselines joining the outermost points of the outermost islands and drying reefs of the archipelago provided that within such baselines are included the main islands and an area in which the ratio of the area of the water to the area of the land, including atolls, is between 1 to 1 and 9 to 1. An archipelago is a group of islands, including parts of islands, interconnecting waters and other natural features which are so closely interrelated that such islands, waters, and other natural features form an intrinsic geographical, economic, and political entity, or which historically have been regarded as such.

Armistice: A suspension or temporary cessation of hostilities by agreement between belligerents.

Artillery: Equipment, supplies, ammunition, and personnel involved in the use of cannon, rocket, or surface-to-surface missile launchers. Field artillery cannons are classified according to caliber as follows: Light—120 mm and less. Medium—121-160mm. Heavy—161-210mm. Very heavy—greater than 210mm. All military units are able to call for "fire support" from artillery assets, and all Brigades are provided their own artillery assets to support operations.

Auxiliary Aircraft: An aircraft, other than a military aircraft, that is owned by or under the exclusive control of the armed forces of a State and used for the time being on government non-commercial service.

Auxiliary Vessel: A vessel, other than a warship, that is owned by or under the exclusive control of the armed forces of a State and used for the time being on government non-commercial service.

Battalion: A military unit of an army typically consisting of approximately four companies and commanded by an officer with approximately 12-15 years' experience. This is the first level of command where the commander is provided with a planning "staff."

Blockade: A belligerent operation to prevent vessels and/or aircraft of all nations, enemy as well as neutral, from entering or exiting specified ports, airfields, or coastal areas belonging to, occupied by, or under the control of an enemy nation. A belligerent's purpose in establishing a blockade is to deny the enemy the use of enemy and neutral vessels or aircraft to transport personnel and goods to or from enemy territory.

Brigade: A military unit of an army typically consisting of approximately three or more battalions or two or more regiments and commanded by a senior officer with approximately 17-20 years' experience. This is the first level of command where the commander's staff routinely includes a legal officer. This is the first level of command capable of conducting independent operations and sustaining those operations with internal capabilities.

Campaign: A series of related major operations aimed at achieving strategic and operational objectives within a given time and space.

Chemical Munition: An artillery or rocket delivered warhead that contains gas or other chemicals intended to cause death or disability.

Civil Aircraft: An aircraft other than a military, auxiliary, or State aircraft such as a customs or police aircraft that is engaged in commercial or private service.

Civil Airliner: A civil aircraft that is clearly marked and engaged in carrying civilian passengers in scheduled or non-scheduled services along Air Traffic Service routes.

Civil War: An internal conflict, typically between a State and one or more rebel forces within that State, either for control of the entire State or to determine the political independence of a portion of a State. It may also include a conflict between two or more factions within the same State battling for control of the State.

Civilian Internee: A civilian who is interned during armed conflict, occupation, or other military operation for security reasons, for protection, or because he or she committed an offense against the detaining power.

Close Air Support: Air action by military aircraft against hostile targets that are in close proximity to friendly forces and that require coordination of each air mission with the fire and movement of those forces.

Coalition: An arrangement between two or more States for common action, which may involve use of their armed forces.

Collateral Casualties or **Collateral Damage:** The loss of life of, or injury to, civilians or other protected persons, and damage to or the destruction of the natural environment or objects that are not in themselves military objectives but instead are the result of an attack on a military objective.

Combat Air support: Air operations directly supporting the ground combat forces.

Combat Engineering: Engineering capabilities and activities that closely support the maneuver of land combat forces.

Combatant Commander: A commander of one of the regional or functional commands established by the President. Examples of regional commands include Southern Command, which is generally responsible for military missions in South America, or Pacific Command, which is responsible for military missions in the Pacific Rim countries. Examples of functional commands include Space Command.

Combined Arms: The integration and application of two or more arms or elements of one military Service into an operation (for example, an operation involving both infantry and aviation units).

Command: The authority that a commander in the armed forces lawfully exercises over subordinates by virtue of rank or assignment, which includes the authority and responsibility for effectively using available resources to plan and accomplish assigned missions and tasks. Command includes responsibility for health, welfare, morale, and discipline of assigned personnel. The term also refers to orders given by a commander and to the specific unit or units, organization, or area under the command of one individual.

Command and Control: The exercise of authority and direction by a properly designated commander over assigned and attached forces in the accomplishment of an assigned mission.

Command Post: A unit headquarters where the commander and staff perform their activities.

Company: A military unit typically consisting of approximately 3 or more platoons commanded by an officer with approximately 3-4 years' experience.

Computer Network Attack: Actions taken through the use of computer networks to disrupt, deny, degrade, or destroy information resident in an enemy's computers and computer networks, or the computers and networks themselves.

Continental Shelf: The seabed and subsoil of the submarine areas that extend beyond the territorial sea of a coastal State throughout the natural prolongation of its land territory to the outer edge of the continental margin, or to a distance of 200 nautical miles from the baselines from which the breadth of the territorial sea is measured where the outer edge of the continental margin does not extend up to that distance.

Contractors authorized to accompany the force: Employees of private companies, who are specifically authorized through their contract with a State (or with a prime contractor that has a contract with a State) to accompany the force and who have protected status in accordance with the Geneva conventions, including but not limited to, GPW.

Convoy: In naval warfare, a number of merchant ships and/or naval auxiliaries usually escorted by warships and/or aircraft, or a single merchant ship or naval auxiliary under surface escort, assembled and organized for the purpose of passage together; in land warfare, a group of vehicles organized for the purpose of control and orderly movement with or without escort protection that moves over the same route at the same time and under one commander.

Corps: A military unit of an army typically consisting of two or more Divisions and commanded by a senior general officer with extensive experience and a robust planning staff. This level of command will include a senior legal officer and a legal staff.

Counterattack: A deliberate attack launched to recover an area of objective recently captured by enemy forces.

Detainee: Any person captured or otherwise detained by a State during armed conflict, occupation, or other military operation. (Can also include persons captured or detained by an armed force of a State in other contexts not covered by this text.)

Division: A military unit typically consisting of approximately three or more brigades and commanded by a general officer with extensive experience and a robust planning staff. This level of command will include a senior legal officer and a legal staff.

Engineer: The military specialty responsible for constructing and clearing battlefield obstacles, such as minefields, bridges, tank traps, etc. Each unit from the Company level higher will normally include a contingent of engineers.

Exclusive Economic Zone: An area beyond and adjacent to the territorial sea in which the rights and jurisdiction of the coastal State are subject to rights and freedoms of other States as set forth in the U.N. Convention on the Law of the Sea.

Field Artillery: Equipment, supplies, ammunition, and personnel involved in the use of cannon, rocket, or surface-to-surface missile launchers.

Fire support: Fires (see definition below) that directly support land, maritime, amphibious, and special operations forces to engage enemy forces, combat formations, and facilities in pursuit of tactical and operational objectives.

Fires: The use of weapon systems to create specific lethal or nonlethal effects on a target.

High Seas: All parts of the sea that are not included in the exclusive economic zone, the territorial sea, the internal waters of a State, or the archipelagic waters of an archipelagic State.

ICRC: International Committee of the Red Cross. The Non-Government Organization vested with special responsibility to oversee implementation of the Geneva Conventions.

ICTR: International Criminal Tribunal for Rwanda.

ICTY: International Criminal Tribunal for the Former Yugoslavia.

Indirect Fire: Fire delivered on a target that is not itself used as a point of aim for the weapons or the director.

Infiltrate: To cross through or over enemy lines and into enemy controlled territory surreptitiously.

Innocent Passage. Continuous and expeditious navigation by ships of other States through a State's territorial sea solely for the purpose of traversing that sea without entering internal waters or calling at a roadstead or port facility outside internal waters; or proceeding to or from internal waters or a call at such roadstead or port facility. Innocent passage includes stopping and anchoring, but only in so far as they are incidental to ordinary navigation or are rendered necessary by force majeure or distress or for the purpose of rendering assistance to persons, ships, or aircraft in danger or distress.

Interdict: To cut off or sever.

Internal Waters: Generally, waters on the landward side of the baseline of the territorial sea form part of the internal waters of the State.

International Strait: Straits used for international navigation in which all ships and aircraft enjoy a right of transit passage.

Iran Hostage Crisis: The foreign policy crisis between the United States and Iran that occurred when Iranian students stormed the U.S. Embassy in Tehran and took all the personnel at the Embassy hostage. When the U.S. demanded that the government of Iran intervene to free the hostages and restore the diplomatic sanctity of the Embassy, the Iranian government refused and essentially endorsed the action. U.S. personnel were held hostage by Iran for 444 days, until finally released by the Iranian government.

Joint Force: A general term applied to a force composed of significant elements of two or more Military Departments (e.g., Air Force, Army, and Navy elements) operating under a single joint force commander.

Joint Force Commander: A general term applied to a commander authorized to exercise combatant command (command authority) or operational control over a joint force.

Joint Staff: In the U.S. military, the staff of a commander of a command that includes personnel from more than one Military Department.

Logistics: Planning and executing the movement and support of forces. It includes those aspects of military operations that deal with: (i) design and development, acquisition, storage, movement, distribution, maintenance, evacuation, and disposition of materiel; (ii) movement, evacuation, and hospitalization of personnel; (iii) acquisition or construction, maintenance, operation, and disposition of facilities; and (iv) acquisition or furnishing of services.

M-16: A standard issue rifle used by some U.S. forces. It is capable of firing in single shot mode, in three shot bursts, and in full automatic fire. This was the weapon used in the Panama invasion in 1989, but active units of the U.S. Army now employ a more modern variant, the M-4 carbine.

Maneuver: A movement of ships, aircraft, or land forces to gain advantage over the enemy, typically in combination with direct and indirect fires.

Merchant Vessel: A vessel, other than a warship, an auxiliary vessel, or a State vessel such as a customs or police vessel, that is engaged in commercial or private service.

Military Aircraft: An aircraft operated by commissioned units of the armed forces of a State having the military marks of that State, commanded by a member of the armed forces and manned by a crew subject to regular armed forces discipline.

Mortar: A muzzle-loading, indirect fire weapon with either a rifled or smooth bore. It usually has a shorter range than a howitzer (cannon) and employs a higher angle of fire.

Neutralize: To render ineffective or unusable. With respect to enemy personnel or materiel, it means rendering them incapable of interfering with a particular operation.

Occupied Territory: Territory under the authority and effective control of a belligerent armed force in an international armed conflict. The term is not applicable to territory being administered pursuant to peace terms, treaty, or other agreement, express or implied, with the civil authority of the territory.

Operational Planning: The process of planning future military operations.

Operations Officer: The officer on a Commander's staff responsible for planning and coordinating all of the unit operations. This includes coordinating the efforts of all assets assigned to the unit.

Perfidy: Acts inviting the confidence of an adversary to lead it to believe that it is entitled to, or is obliged to accord, protection under the rules of international law applicable in armed conflict, with intent to betray that confidence. One example of perfidy would be to use the white flag to trick enemy combatants to cease offensive operations and then exploiting the pause to launch operations against them.

Platoon: A military unit consisting of approximately 40 persons led by one junior officer and one senior enlisted soldier (typically a sergeant) and subdivided into smaller units (e.g., squads).

Prisoner of War: A person who falls within one of the categories in Article 4A of the Geneva Convention Relative to the Treatment of Prisoners of War (GPW), and in connection with an international armed conflict, is captured by the armed forces of the enemy. Also called EPW, POW, or PW.

Rapid Response Force: A force (usually a battalion or smaller) that can deploy on short notice to provide an immediate or emergency response to a threat.

Regiment: A military unit typically consisting of two or more battalions and commanded by a senior officer below a general with approximately 17-20 years' experience. This level of command may include a legal officer.

Retrograde: A tactical withdrawal from one fighting position to a position more removed from the enemy, typically in response to an attack or threat of attack by the enemy.

Scatterable Minefield: A minefield delivered with remote capability, normally fired by artillery into designated areas. The minefields can be anti-personnel, anti-tank, or a mixture of both. The range of mines falling into this category is known by the acronym FASCAM: Family of Scatterable Mines.

Security Council Resolution: Term used to describe actions taken by the Security Council that can bind the members of the United Nations.

Supply Depot: A location where military supplies are stored for future distribution.

Tactical Operations Center: The headquarters area from which a commander and his staff and advisors conduct the military operation.

Targeting Officer: The officer on a Commander's staff responsible for planning and managing the use of unit assets to achieve the Commander's tactical objectives.

Task Force (TF): A temporary grouping of units, under one commander, formed for the purpose of carrying out a specific operation or mission; also can mean (i) a semi-permanent organization of units, under one commander, formed for the purpose of carrying out a continuing specific task or (ii) a component of a naval fleet organized for the accomplishment of a specific task or tasks.

Territorial Sea: A belt of sea, adjacent to the land territory of a State, over which a State exercises sovereignty. (U.N. Convention on the Law of the Sea art. 2).

Transit Passage: The freedom of navigation and overflight solely for the purpose of continuous and expeditious transit of a strait between one part of the high seas or an exclusive economic zone and another part of the high seas or an exclusive economic zone.

Unmanned Aircraft: An aircraft or balloon that does not carry a human operator. The aircraft may be flown under remote control or by autonomous programming.

Visit and search: Procedures by which a State's forces conduct maritime interception operations of merchant vessels in order to determine the true character of vessels, cargo, and passengers in an armed conflict.

Warship: A ship belonging to the armed forces of a State bearing the external marks distinguishing the character and nationality of such a ship, under the command of an officer duly commissioned by the government of that State and whose name appears in the appropriate service list or its equivalent, and manned by a crew which is under regular armed forces discipline.

Table of Cases

Akayesu; Prosecutor v., 553n47, 617n54
Al-Bassiouni v. Prime Minister, 416n153
Al-Bihani v. Obama, 156, 157, 157n72, 175n10
Al-Skeini v. United Kingdom, 75n172, 188n50
Al Warafi v. Obama, 340n104
Armed Activities on the Territory of the Congo. *See* Democratic Republic of the Congo v. Uganda

Bagilishema; Prosecutor v., 617, 617nn55–56
Belsen Trial, 149n37
Blaskic; Prosecutor v., 229, 229n50, 616-617, 616n52
Boldt. *See* Lieutenants Dithmar & Boldt, Case of
Boskoski; Prosecutor v., 111n55
Boumediene v. Bush, 155, 155n65, 187, 187n45, 188

Case of. *See name of party*
Celebici. *See* Delalic; Prosecutor v.
Corfu Channel (U.K. v. Alb.), 527, 527n268

Dachau Concentration Camp Trial, 149n37
Delalic; Prosecutor v., Celebici: Case No. IT-96-21-A (Feb. 20, 2001), 555n50, 615n49
Delalic; Prosecutor v., Celebici: Case No. IT-96-21-T (Nov. 16, 1998), 553n47, 570n88, 616n50
Democratic Republic of the Congo v. Belgium, 588, 589nn128-129

Democratic Republic of the Congo v. Uganda, 14-15, 32
DRC Inc., United States ex rel. v. Custer Battles, LLC, 405n122
Dulag Luft Trial, 149n37

Ex parte. *See name of party*
Ex rel. *See name of party*

Ferguson; United States v., 624, 624n76
France v. Turkey. *See* Lotus

Galic; Prosecutor v., 255n17
Guantanamo Bay Detainee Litigation, In re, 156n66, 175n9

Hamdan v. Rumsfeld, 2, 2n10, 118, 118nn83-84, 120n90, 132n140, 133, 133n143, 133n147, 135n157, 135n159, 157n73, 174, 174n6, 175, 186, 187, 208, 208n112
Hamdi v. Rumsfeld, 51n40, 67n124, 155, 155n64
Haradinaj; Prosecutor v., 111, 111n56
High Command Case, 149n38, 609-610, 609n31, 660n5
Homma, In re, 149n37
Hospital Ship "Dover Castle." *See* Neumann, Commander Karl, Case of
Hospital Ship "Llandovery Castle." *See* Lieutenants Dithmar and Boldt, Case of
Hostage Case, 52n46, 610, 610n36, 613, 614, 619, 627

Illinois v. Lafayette, 306n70
In re. *See name of party*
Internet Research Agency, LLC; United States v., 527n266

Killinger, Erich. *See* Dulag Luft Trial
Kramer and 44 Other (Belsen Trial), 149n37
Krupp Case, 52n46
Kunarac; Prosecutor v., 552n44
Kupreskic; Prosecutor v., 221n16

Legal Consequences of the Constr. of a Wall in the Occupied Palestinian Territory, 7n25, 15, 32, 76n174, 83n207
Legality of the Threat or Use of Nuclear Weapons, 7n25, 50, 50n36, 83n205, 188n48, 222n8, 292n24, 516n211
Lieutenants Dithmar & Boldt, Case of: Hospital Ship "Llandovery Castle," 82n196
Limaj; Prosecutor v., 111n55
Lindh; United States v., 147n23

S.S. Lotus (France v. Turkey), 527, 527n271

Maqaleh v. Gates, 188, 188n51
Medina v. Resor, 622n68, 622n71, 622-623
Military and Paramilitary Activities in & Against Nicaragua. *See* Nicaragua v. United States
Mohamadali & Another v. Public Prosecutor, 146n21
Muhammed v. Sec'y of State for Defence, 51n43

Neumann, Commander Karl, Case of: Hospital Ship "Dover Castle," 82n196
Nicaragua v. United States, 14, 14n59, 26, 26n92, 83n206, 129, 129n119, 200, 200n76, 201, 222n21, 223n22, 469n206, 526n261
Noriega v. Pastrana, 193, 195, 195n60
Noriega; United States v., 115, 115n73
North Sea Cont'l Shelf, Judgment, 76n177

The Paquete Habana, 472n215
Plakas v. Drinski, 306n70
Prosecutor v. *See name of opposing party*
Public Comm. against Torture in Israel v. Government of Israel, 83n208

Quirin, Ex parte, 146n21, 154, 154n56

Reid v. Covert, 583n111
Rutaganda; Prosecutor v., 111n55, 552n46

Scott v. Heinrich, 306n70
Skorzeny & Others, Trial of, 147n24
Solorio v. United States, 580n107

Tadic; Prosecutor v., 11, 12, 12n53, 16n63, 83n203, 111, 111n53-54, 113n61, 130, 131n129, 164n101, 553n47, 565n76, 569, 570n85
Tokyo Major War Crimes Trial, 611, 611nn38-39, 613-614, 619
Trial of. *See name of defendant*

United States v. *See name of opposing party*
United States ex rel. *See name of relator*

von Leeb et al., 149n38, 600n5

Weiss and Thirty-Nine Others, Trial of (Dachau Concentration Camp Trial), 149n37

Yamashita, In re, 327 U.S. 1 (1946), 607-608, 607n22, 637
Yamashita, Trial of (Feb. 17, 1948), 603-606, 603nn15-16
Youngstown Sheet & Tube Co. v. Sawyer, 2n9

Index

Abu Ghraib, 202-203, 207, 209, 573, 632, 635
Abu Nidal, 21
Accessory liability, 598, 600, 621, 623
Accomplice liability, 597-598, 600, 621, 623
Actus reus of command responsibility, 606
Additional Protocols (1977)
    air warfare, 484-485, 494-496
        civilians, 216, 219-220, 222-225, 235, 242
    classification of persons, 147, 151-152, 157, 161, 163
    combatants, 145
    command responsibility, 612-615, 617
    compliance mechanisms, 635-636
    customary international law, 77-79
    cyber warfare, 529, 531-533
    detainees, 176-177, 179, 185-186, 197-198
    distinction, 57, 253, 255-256, 258-263, 268-271
    emerging technologies, 535
    humanity, 54-55
    IAC, 69
    interrogation, 201, 208-209
    naval warfare, 440, 446, 457-458
    NIAC, 68
    occupation, 361, 365n23, 385, 388-390, 392-398, 407-408
    overview, 68-69
    proportionality, 272
    "soft law," 86
    space warfare, 512-513, 516, 520-521
    triggering of LOAC, 120-127
    unlawful combatants, 152-155
    war crimes, 550-553, 570
    weapons and tactics, 286-287, 289-290, 307-309, 313
    wounded and sick, 323, 325, 327, 337, 347, 350-351
Administrative Review Board, 189
Advanced Research Projects Agency (ARPA), 521
Afghanistan, 8, 20, 114, 128, 136, 158, 172, 182, 184, 187-189, 196-197, 204, 206-207, 234, 464, 567
    Detention Review Boards, 184
    Taliban. *See* Taliban
Aggression, 4n16, 556-557
Air and Missile Warfare Manual (AMWM). *See* Manual on International Law Applicable to Air and Missile Warfare
Aircraft for medical transport. *See* Medical aircraft
Air defense missiles, 641
Air tasking orders, 641
Air warfare, 480-506
    Additional Protocols, 484-485, 494-496
    air operations, 502-505
    airspace defined, 486
    belligerents, areas open for air operations by, 491-492
    cartel aircraft, 498
    Common Article 3, 505
    First Geneva Convention, 499
    Fourth Geneva Convention, 498-499
    Geneva Conventions, 484
    Hague Conventions, 478, 482-483
    law enforcement, 499
    medical aircraft, 498
    neutral airspace, 492-493
    in NIAC, 505-506
    overview, 478-479
    Second Geneva Convention, 498

Air warfare (cont'd)
  sources of law, 480-486
    customary international law, 482-486
    general international law, 480-482
    treaty law, 482-486
  state aircraft vs. civil aircraft, 487-488
  tactics, 493-502
    conduct of hostilities, 493-498
    destruction of captured aircraft, 502
    enemy aircraft, interception and capture of, 498-500
    neutral aircraft, interception and capture of, 500-502
    Third Geneva Convention, 499
  types of aircraft, 491
Akayesu, Jean-Paul, 617
Albania, 610
al-Bashir, Omar, 589
Albright, Madeline, 22
Alexander II (Russia), 46, 61
Al Firdus Bunker, 279
al-Maliki, Nouri, 19
al Qaeda
  classification of persons, 152, 155-156, 159
  command responsibility, 626
  detention of belligerents, 172, 175, 182
  drones, 33
  interrogation, 203, 208
  neutrality, 464
  targeting, 275-276
  triggering of LOAC, 116-119, 128, 132-135
  war crimes, 578, 585
Al Qahtani, Mohammed, 206
Al Warafi, Mukhtar Yahia Naji, 340n104
American Civil War, 44, 96, 153, 478, 601
American Revolutionary War, 148
Ammunition. See Weapons
AMWM (Air and Missile Warfare Manual). See Manual on International Law Applicable to Air and Missile Warfare
Annexation, occupation compared, 375
Antarctica, 74
Antarctic Treaty (1959), 460
Anticipatory self-defense, 24
Anti-personnel land mines, 296-299
Anti-satellite weapons (ASAT), 507, 510, 518-521
AP I, AP II, and AP III. See Additional Protocols (1977)
Appia, Louis, 322
Archipelagic sea lane passage, 429, 641
Archipelagic waters, 429, 641
Argentina, 369
Armed conflict. See specific topic

Armistice, 641
Army Field Manual 2-22.3, 88n238, 208
Army Field Manual 3-60, 250
Army Field Manual 27-10
  civilians, 233
  command responsibility, 627
  detention of belligerents, 173
  military doctrine, 88
  occupation, 363, 374n46, 401, 407-409
  weapons and tactics, 286
"Army in exile," 146
Army of Serbian Republic of Bosnia and Herzegovina (VRS), 131
Army Regulation 15-6, 629, 631.632
Army Regulation 190-8, 87-88, 181, 196, 201-202, 338-340, 391-392
ARPA (Advanced Research Projects Agency), 521
ARPANET, 521
Article 5 tribunals, 180-183
Artillery, 641-642
The Art of War (Sun Tzu), 42
ASAT. See Anti-satellite weapons
Ashburton, Lord, 24
Assassination, 310-311
Assigned residence during occupation, 395
Australia, 32, 49
Austria, 321
Authorization for the Use of Military Force (2001), 32, 156, 175
Auxiliary aircraft, 642
Auxiliary medical personnel, 259
Auxiliary vessels, 435, 642

Bagilishema, Ignace, 617
Bagram Air Base, 206-207, 209
Battalions, 642
Battle of ___. See name of specific battle
Baxter, Richard, 154-155
Bayonets, 303
Belgium, 32
Belligerents. See Combatants
Bible as historical foundation for rules of conduct of hostilities, 42
Biological agents, 278
Biological weapons, 299
Biological Weapons Convention (1972), 299
Blakely, Tom, 540n9
Blaskic, Tihomir, 616-617
Blinding lasers, 278, 295, 296
Blockades, 445-447, 642
Booby-traps, 291, 295
Boothby, Bill, 519
Borodino, Battle of (1812), 320-321

Bosnia and Herzegovina
    civilians, 229
    command responsibility, 616-617
    detention of belligerents, 172
    triggering of LOAC, 111, 130-131, 136
    war crimes, 569-571
Bothe, Michael, 290
Brazil, 17
Bremer, Jerry, 360
Brigades, 642
Brussels Declaration (1874), 61-62
Bulge, Battle of the (1944), 147n24
Bunker Hill, Battle of (1775), 89
Bush, George H.W., 22, 115
Bush, George W., 25, 114, 117, 132-133, 171, 182, 186, 203, 208-209, 585, 590

Cambodia, 557, 568, 569
Campaigns, 642
Camp Omarska, 569-570
Canada, 49, 52, 288
Capitulation, 368-370
Caroline affair, 24
Cartel aircraft, 498
Carter, Jimmy, 123
Casualties. *See* Wounded and sick
CAT (Convention Against Torture), 74
Causation, command responsibility, 606
CCW. *See* Convention on Certain Conventional Weapons
Cease-fire, 368-370
Celebici Case, 570-571, 616-617
CERP (Commanders Emergency Response Program), 234
Chaplains, 259
Charles VII (France), 601
Chemical agents, 278, 299-300
Chemical munitions, 642
Chemical weapons, 299-300
Chemical Weapons Convention (CWC), 299-300
Chicago Convention (1944), 480-482, 491-492
China, 7, 507, 518
Chivalry, 288-289
Chklaver, Georges, 70
CIL. *See* Customary international law
Civil aircraft, 487-488, 642
Civil airliners, 435n68, 642
Civil defense, 389-390
Civilian internees, 642
Civilian objects, 267
Civilians, 213-245
    Additional Protocols, 216, 219-220, 222-225, 235, 242
    civilians accompanying force, 150
    classification of persons, 144-145
    Common Article 3, 222-224, 230
    concept of, 218-219
    defined, 218-220
    degrading treatment, 221, 223
    detention of
        basis for detention, 236-237
        detention review and release protections, 240
        direct participation in hostilities (DPH), 166
        POWs compared, 175-177
        protections, 236-240
        standard of treatment, 196-197
        treatment protections, 237-239
    direct participation in hostilities (DPH), 161-166
        alternative definition, 164-165
        detention, 166
        human shields, 165-166
        ICRC, 162-164
    distinction, 254-256
    Geneva Conventions, 66, 144-145, 216, 222
    Hague Conventions, 222
    IAC, 216-217, 224
    IHRL, 240-243
    interned civilians, 236-240
        basis for detention, 236-237
        detention review and release protections, 240
        treatment protections, 237-239
    within meaning of LOAC, 219-220
    NIAC, 216-217, 224
    during occupation
        meeting needs of, 397-400
        protection of, 230-232
    overview, 215-218, 243-244
    POWs compared, 237-239
    private property, 232-236
        destruction of, 232-234
        taking possession of, 234-236
    protected persons, 227-232
        in enemy territory, 230
        in occupied territory, 230-232
    rape, 223n23
    shield of protection, 220-240
        especially vulnerable civilians, 227
        general protection for civilian populations, 226-227
        harmful consequences of attack, 221
        interned civilians, 236-240

Civilians (cont'd)
  maltreatment at hands of party to conflict, 221-225
  private property, 232-236
  protected persons, 227-232
  Third Geneva Convention, 219-220
  war crimes, 583-584
Civilians Convention. *See* Fourth Geneva Convention
Civil war, 643
Classification of persons, 141-168
  Additional Protocols, 147, 151-152, 157, 161, 163
  civilians, 144-145. *See also* Civilians
  combatants, 145-147. *See also* Combatants
  definitional problem, 143-144
  First Geneva Convention, 150
  Fourth Geneva Convention, 144
  Geneva Conventions, 157, 161
  NIAC, 157-158
  organized armed groups, 158-161
  overview, 142-143, 166-167
  POWs, 143-144
  presumptions, 147-148
  Third Geneva Convention, 144, 149-150
  unlawful combatants, 152-157. *See also* Unlawful combatants
Clinton, Bill, 126, 300
Clinton, Hillary, 186
Close air support, 642
Cluster munitions, 301-302
Cluster Munitions Convention (Oslo Convention) (2008), 301-302
Coalitions, 643
Codification of LOAC, 38
Collateral casualties, 643
Collateral damage estimation methodology (CDEM), 274-275, 643
Collective self-defense, 26
Colombia, 158
"Colonial domination, alien occupation, or a racist regime," 122-123, 151
Combat air support, 643
Combatant commanders, 643
Combatants
  Additional Protocols, 145
  classification of persons, 145-147
  detention. *See* Detention of belligerents
  distinction, 254
  Geneva Conventions, 144, 145
  POWs compared, 145-147
Combatant Status Review Tribunals (CSRTs), 187, 189
Combined arms, 643

Command, 643
Command and control, 643
Commanders Emergency Response Program (CERP), 234
Commander's Handbook on the Law of Naval Operations (U.S. Navy), 88, 433, 438, 448, 453-454, 459
Command posts, 643
Command responsibility, 595-627
  accessory liability, 598, 600, 621, 623
  accomplice liability, 597-598, 600, 621, 623
  actus reus of, 606
  Additional Protocols, 612-615, 617
  causation, 606
  compliance mechanisms, 628-637. *See also* Compliance mechanisms
  defined, 599-601
  derivative liability, 600n4
  direct liability, 600n4
  Hague Conventions, 601, 607-608
  historical background, 601-602
  ICTR, 615-620
  ICTY, 615-620
  imputed liability, 607
  involvement or complicity in violations, 597-599
  law enforcement, 632
  mens rea of, 605-606
  overview, 596
  post-World War II developments, 611-620
  role of commander, 596-597
  U.S. practice, 620-627
    Article 92 dereliction of duty, 623-624
    enemy commander accountability, 625-627
    gaps in law, 624-625
    My Lai Massacre, 622-623
    U.S. commander accountability, 620-625
  vicarious liability, 600-601
  willful blindness, 610, 619
  World War II war crimes tribunals, 602-611
    "High Command Case," 608-610
    Hostage Case, 610-611, 613-614, 619, 627
    Tokyo Trials, 611, 613-614, 619
    Yamashita Tribunal, 603-608. *See also* Yamashita Tribunal
Committee of the Green Cross, 194
Common Article 1, 66-67
Common Article 2, 66
  detention of belligerents, 171n1
  occupation, 362, 372
  triggering of LOAC, 99-103
  war crimes, 552

Common Article 3, 67-68
  air warfare, 505
  civilians, 222-224, 230
  detention of belligerents, 178, 184-185, 197-198
  interrogation, 199-201, 203, 208-209
  occupation, 395-396
  principles of LOAC, 54
  triggering of LOAC, 99-103
  war crimes, 554-555, 569-572
  wounded and sick, 324, 349-350
Companies, 643
Compliance mechanisms, 628-637
  Additional Protocols, 635-636
  Geneva Conventions, 636-637
  principles of LOAC, 635-637
  war crimes, investigation of, 628-635
    Army Regulation 15-6, 631-632
    commander's inquiry, 630
    criminal investigations, 632-633
    Inspector General investigations, 633
    oversight and review, 634-635
    procedures, 629-633
Computer Fraud and Abuse Act of 1986, 522-523
Computer network attacks, 643
Computers. *See* Cyber warfare
Conflict classification paradigm, 95-99
Congo, Democratic Republic of
  ICJ, 14-15
  Security Council, 10-11
  United Nations Organization Mission in the DRC (MONUC), 10-11
  United Nations Organization Stabilization Mission in the DRC (MONUSCO), 11
  war crimes, 588-589
Consent, use of force, 18-19
Constitution, 2, 571, 634-635
Contiguous zones, 428-429
Continental shelf, 644
Contractors authorized to accompany the force, 644
Convention Against Torture (CAT) (1985), 74
Convention on Certain Conventional Weapons (CCW) (1980), 292
  air warfare, 485, 493
  blinding lasers, 296
  explosive remnants of war, 298-299
  incendiaries, 295-296
  overview, 72-73
  plastic fragments, 295-296
  prohibited weapons, 296-299
  space warfare, 514

Convention on Cluster Munitions (Oslo Convention) (2008), 301-302
Convention on International Liability for Damage Caused by Space Objects, 512n192
Convention on the Law of the Sea (UNCLOS) (1982), 74, 424n2, 432, 491, 504
Convention on the Prevention and Punishment of the Crime of Genocide (1948), 74
Convoys, 644
Corps, 644
Côte d'Ivoire, 8
Counterattacks, 644
Counterinsurgency, 48, 88
Courts and tribunals. *See specific court or tribunal*
Courts-martial, 573
Crimes against humanity, 558-559
Criminal Investigation Division (U.S. Army), 632-633, 635
Croatia, 8, 229
Crops, 270
Cruel treatment, 199-200
CSTRs (Combatant Status Review Tribunals), 187, 189
Cuba, 447
Cuban Missile Crisis (1962), 447
Cultural property
  distinction, 258-259
    personnel protecting, 260
  Hague Conventions, 70
  treaties protecting, 70-72
Customary international law (CIL), 76-81
  Additional Protocols, 77-79
  air warfare, 482-486
  Hague Conventions, 77
  neutrality, 459
  NIAC, 80
  occupation, 361, 366, 378, 381, 394, 396
  treaty law compared, 76n175
  U.S. practice, 78-79n186
  weapons in, 291-293
CWC (Chemical Weapons Convention), 299-300
Cyber Command, 523
Cyber warfare, 521-534
  Additional Protocols, 529, 531-533
  cyberspace defined, 522
  cyber weapons, 307
  denial of service (DDoS) operations, 529
  domestic law paradigm, 522-523
  international law paradigm, 523

Cyber warfare (cont'd)
  jus ad bellum, 523-528
    armed attack, 524-525
    prohibited intervention, 526-527
    sovereignty, 527-528
    use of force, 525-526
  jus in bello, 528-534
    constant care, 531
    distinction, 529-530
    effects of attacks, precautions against, 532-533
    indiscriminate attacks, 532
    military objective, 531-532
    neutrality, 533
    non-state actors, 534
    overview, 534
    precautions, 531-533
    proportionality, 530-531
  overview, 478-479, 521-522
  use of force in, 34-35, 525-526
Cyprus, 8-9

Daesh. *See* Islamic State in Iraq and Syria
Dams, 269-270
Dangerous forces, works and installations containing, 269-270
Dead, obligations to, 319-320n1, 332-333
Declaration on Principles of International Law Concerning Friendly Relations and Co-operation Among States in Accordance with the Charter of the United Nations (1970), 16
Declaration Renouncing the Use, in Time of War, of Explosive Projectiles Under 400 Grammes Weight (St. Petersburg Declaration) (1868), 46, 48, 287, 293
De facto authority or commander, 115, 613, 619
De facto nature of conflict, 98, 100-101, 103, 110, 113, 134, 136, 373, 384
De facto vs. *de jure* war, 99, 153
Defense Department. *See specific topic*
Defense Department Directive 2310.01A, 628-629
Defense Department Directive 2311.01E, 87, 636
Defense Department Directive 3000.3, 306
Defense Department Directive 5000.01, 289
Defenses to war crimes, 585-589
  duress, 586-587
  head of state immunity, 588-589
  lack of mental responsibility, 588
  obedience to superior orders, 586
  official acts immunity, 588-589
  self-defense, 587-588
Degrading treatment
  civilians, 221, 223
  detention of belligerents, 197
  interrogation, 199, 202
  war crimes, 546, 579
De jure war, 99, 100-101, 153
Delalic, Zejnil, 616
Democratic Republic of Congo. *See* Congo, Democratic Republic of
Denial of service (DDoS) operations, 529
Depleted uranium, 304-305
Dereliction of duty, 623-624
Derivative liability, 600n4
Detainees, 644
Detainee Treatment Act of 2005, 189, 207-209, 578-580
Detention of belligerents, 169-212
  Additional Protocols, 176-177, 179, 185-186, 197-198
  authority for, 173-175
  civilians
    basis for detention, 236-237
    detention review and release protections, 240
    direct participation in hostilities (DPH), 166
    POWs compared, 175-177
    protections, 236-240
    standard of treatment, 196-197
    treatment protections, 237-239
  Common Article 2, 171n1
  Common Article 3, 178, 184-185, 197-198
  degrading treatment, 197
  due process, 180-190
    Additional Protocols, 185-186
    Article 5 tribunals, 180-183
    contemporary U.S. practice, 186-189
    Geneva Conventions, 180-185
    in NIAC, 184-186
    ongoing enhancement, 189-190
    procedural safeguards, 183-184
    supplemental standards, 186-189
  Fourth Geneva Convention, 176-177, 183-184, 196-197
  Geneva Conventions, 171-173, 175-176, 180-185
  habeas corpus, 187-188
  interrogation, 198-211. *See also* Interrogation
  in NIAC, 178-179
    due process, 184-186
    interrogation, 199, 211
    standard of treatment, 197-198

during occupation, 390-397
   assigned residence, 395
   generally applicable treatment
     standards, 396
   preventive detention, 390-391
   procedural requirements, 391-392
   prohibited treatment, 397
   treatment standards for internment,
     392-395
overview, 171-172
POWs, 175-177
   standard of treatment, 190-196
rape, 197
standard of treatment, 190-198
   civilians, 196-197
   in NIAC, 197-198
   POWs, 190-196
Third Geneva Convention, 173, 175-177, 180-183, 190-196
torture, 172, 198-200, 204, 207, 209
unprivileged belligerents, 177-178
Dinstein, Yoram, 24-25, 96, 152, 155
Direct liability, 600n4
Direct participation in hostilities (DPH), 161-166
   alternative definition, 164-165
   detention, 166
   human shields, 165-166
   ICRC, 162-164
Distinction
   Additional Protocols, 57, 253, 255-256, 258-263, 268-271
   auxiliary medical personnel, 259
   chaplains, 259
   civilian objects, 267
   civilians, 254-256
   combatants, 254
   cultural property, 268-269
     personnel protecting, 260
   cyber warfare, 529-530
   Geneva Conventions, 259, 268
   journalists, 260-261
   medical personnel, 258-259
     civilians, 259-260
   medical transport, 259
   military objectives, 261-267
     examples, 265-267
     location, 261-263
     "make and effective contribution to military action," 264
     nature, 261
     "offers a definite military advantage," 264
     purpose, 263
     use, 263-264
   objects, 261-272
   persons, 252-261
   persons *hors de combat,* 257-258
     persons clearly expressing intent to surrender, 258
     persons in power of adverse party, 257
     unconscious, wounded, or sick persons, 258
   as principle of LOAC, 55-57
   protected objects or places, 267-272
     cultural property, 268-269
     dangerous forces, works and installations containing, 269-270
     hospitals, 268
     natural environment, 270-272
     objects indispensable to survival of civilian population, 270
     safety zones, 268
     undefended places, 268
   relief societies, 259
   religious personnel, 259-260
   targeting, 252-272
   Third Geneva Convention, 254
   unprivileged belligerents, 256-257
   wounded and sick, 268
Divisions, 644
Douglas, William O., 564
DPH. *See* Direct participation in hostilities
DRC. *See* Congo, Democratic Republic of
Drones, use of force, 33-34
D3A methodology, 250
Dual use space objects, 516-518
Due process, 180-190
   Additional Protocols, 185-186
   Article 5 tribunals, 180-183
   contemporary U.S. practice, 186-189
   Geneva Conventions, 180-185
   in NIAC, 184-186
   ongoing enhancement, 189-190
   procedural safeguards, 183-184
   supplemental standards, 186-189
Dufour, Henri, 322
"Dum-dum bullets," 294
Dunant, Jean-Henri, 44, 64, 215, 321-322
Duress as defense to war crimes, 586-587

Edged weapons, 303
Egan, Brian J., 22, 80, 128n118, 276-278
Electrical generating stations, 269-270
Electronic Communications Privacy
   Act of 1986, 523
Elisha, 42
El Salvador, 14, 26-27, 129-130, 200-201

Emerging technology, 534-535
Enemy character, 442-443
Engineers, 644
England, Gordon, 208
"Enhanced interrogation techniques," 207-208
Environmental Modification Convention (ENMOD) (1977), 514-515
Eritrea, 8
Espionage, 312. *See also* Spies and spying
Estonia, 35
Ethiopia, 8
European Convention on Human Rights, 243n98
European Court of Human Rights, 75
Exclusive economic zones, 428-429, 644
Executive orders, 81, 87
Expanding bullets, 294
Exploding bullets, 293-294
Explosive munitions, 304
Explosive remnants of war, 298-299
Explosive Remnants of War (ERW) Protocol, 298-299

Falklands War, 232n57, 369
FARC (Revolutionary Armed Forces of Colombia), 158
Fay, George, 207
Field artillery, 644
Field Manual on the Law of Land Warfare (U.S. Army), 39
.50 caliber rounds, 303
Fighting at the Legal Boundaries (Watkin), 107-108
Fires, 645
Fire support, 645
First Geneva Convention (1949), 64-65
 air warfare, 499
 classification of persons, 150
 naval warfare, 454
First Gulf War, 279, 384
Flag of truce, 289, 310
Flamethrowers, 278
"Fog of war," 623
Foodstuffs, 270
Force, use of. *See* Use of force
Foreign Claims Act of 1942, 233-234
Fourth Amendment, 634-635
Fourth Geneva Convention (1949), 66. *See also* Civilians
 air warfare, 498-499
 classification of persons, 144
 detention of belligerents, 176-177, 183-184, 196-197
 interrogation, 199-200
 occupation. *See* Occupation
 Third Geneva Convention compared, 237-239
 war crimes, 547-548, 573
France
 air warfare, 482
 command responsibility, 602
 occupation, 387, 414
 in Security Council, 7
 use of force, 32
 wounded and sick, 320-321
French Revolution, 43

Gas Protocol (1925), 299
Gaza. *See* Occupied Palestinian Territory
Gaza Flotilla, 226n34
General Assembly
 private property, 232-233
 Resolution 3314 on the Definition of Aggression, 17
 Uniting for Peace Resolution, 6
 use of force, 5-7
Geneva Convention for the Amelioration of the Condition of the Wounded, Sick and Shipwrecked Members of Armed Forces at Sea (1906), 64-65, 323. *See also* Wounded and sick
Geneva Convention for the Amelioration of the Condition of the Wounded in Armies in the Field (1864), 64, 215, 320, 322-323. *See also* Wounded and sick
Geneva Convention Relative to the Treatment of Prisoners of War (1929), 65, 323
Geneva Conventions (1949)
 Additional Protocols. *See* Additional Protocols
 air warfare, 484
 CCW compared, 73
 civilians, 66, 144-145, 216, 222
 classification of persons, 157, 161
 combatants, 144, 145
 Common Article 1, 66-67
 Common Article 2. *See* Common Article 2
 Common Article 3. *See* Common Article 3
 compliance mechanisms, 636-637
 detention of belligerents, 171-173, 175-176, 180-185
 distinction, 259, 268
 First Geneva Convention. *See* First Geneva Convention
 Fourth Geneva Convention. *See* Fourth Geneva Convention

humanity, 54-55
IAC, 68
laws, 87
occupation, 361, 411, 414
overview, 64-68
POWs, 41, 65-66, 144, 145-146, 149-150, 152
Second Geneva Convention. *See* Second Geneva Convention
"soft law," 86
space warfare, 512-513
Third Geneva Convention. *See* Third Geneva Convention
triggering of LOAC, 99-120. *See also* Triggering of LOAC
  duration and intensity of conflict, 111-112
  existence of armed conflict, 103-113
  nature of armed conflict, 113-120
unlawful combatants, 152-155
war crimes. *See* War crimes
War Crimes Act, 576, 580
weapons and tactics, 313
wounded and sick, 44, 64-66, 323, 351
Geneva Protocol (1925), 299
Geneva Society for Public Welfare, 322
Genocide, 557, 565, 586, 588, 592, 617-618
Genocide Convention (1948), 74
Georgia, 8, 35, 534
Germany
  civilians, 235
  command responsibility, 602, 610
  international tribunals, 82
  Joint Services Regulation (ZDv) 15/2, 88
  occupation, 387, 414-415
  POWs, 149
  Spanish Civil War, 97
  unlawful combatants, 153-154
  use of force, 32
  war crimes, 544, 556
  weapons and tactics, 292, 302
Global War on Terror, 171-172, 202-209
Glossary, 641-648
Goldstone Report, 628
GPW. *See* Third Geneva Convention (1949)
Graner, Charles, 573
"Grave breaches," 547-553
Graves, 333
Greece, 610
Greek Civil War, 100
Green, Steven, 582
Green Cross, 194
Grenada, 29
Grotius, Hugo, 43

Guantanamo Bay
  classification of persons, 155
  detention of belligerents, 175, 182, 186-187, 189-190, 196-197
  interrogation, 204-206, 209
  war crimes, 591
GWS-Sea. *See* Second Geneva Convention (1949)

Habeas corpus
  detention of belligerents, 187-188
  unlawful combatants, 155-157
Hague Convention for the Protection of Cultural Property in the Event of Armed Conflict (1954), 71-72
Hague Conventions (1899/1907)
  air warfare, 478, 482-483
  civilians, 222
  command responsibility, 601, 607-608
  cultural property, 70
  customary international law, 77
  humanity, 278
  Martens Clause, 77, 222, 485-486, 535
  military necessity, 50
  naval warfare, 436-437, 440, 451-453
  neutrality, 460, 463, 464-466, 473n217
  occupation. *See* Occupation
  overview, 61-64
  POWs, 145, 149
  "soft law," 86
  use of force, 3
  War Crimes Act, 576
  weapons and tactics, 287-288, 290-294, 311
Hague Cultural Property Convention (1954), 260, 268-269
Hague Rules of Air Warfare (HRAW) (1922-1923), 483, 486
Haiti, 20
Hamdan, Salim Ahmed, 118
Hamdi, Yaser, 186-187
Harmful consequences of attack, protection of civilians from, 221
Harvard Program on Humanitarian Policy and Conflict Research, 484
Harvard University, 84
Head of state immunity as defense to war crimes, 588-589
Hezbollah, 114-115, 134, 158, 226
"High Command Case," 608-610
High seas, 428-429, 645
Hill, Tom, 41
Historical background of LOAC, 38-46
Holy Roman Empire, 42-43, 542

Index

Hors de combat. *See* Persons who are *hors de combat*
Hospitals, 268-269, 277
Hospital ships, 342, 436, 441, 442, 458
Hostage Case, 52n46, 610-611, 613-614, 619, 627
Hostile intent, 160, 449
Huffman, Walter, 384
Humanitarian intervention, use of force, 29-31
Humanitarian missions, 343, 348, 441. *See also* Wounded and sick
Humanity
   Additional Protocols, 54-55
   Geneva Conventions, 54-55
   Hague Conventions, 278
   as principle of LOAC, 53-55
   targeting, 278
   weapons and tactics, 287-288
Human shields, 165-166
Hussein, Saddam, 10, 264, 292, 311

ICC. *See* International Criminal Court
ICCPR. *See* International Covenant on Civil and Political Rights
ICRC. *See* International Committee of the Red Cross
ICTR. *See* International Criminal Tribunal for Rwanda
ICTY. *See* International Criminal Tribunal for the Former Yugoslavia
IHRL. *See* International human rights law
ILA (International Law Association), 104-106
Immunity
   head of state immunity, 588-589
   official acts immunity, 588-589
Imputed liability, command responsibility, 607
IMT. *See* International Military Tribunal
Incendiaries, 295-296
India, 9
Indirect fire, 645
Infiltrate, 645
Information Bureau, 334
Inhumane treatment, 74, 111, 222, 381, 617
Innocent passage, 430-432, 645
Insignia requirement, 146-147
Inspector General, 629, 633
Institute of International Law, 61, 84
Interceptive self-defense, 24-25
Interdict, 645
Internal armed conflicts, external intervention in, triggering of LOAC, 127-132

Internal waters, 428, 645
International Air Services Transit Agreement, 482n19
International armed conflict (IAC)
   Additional Protocols, 69
   civilians, 216-217, 224
   cultural property, 72
   Geneva Conventions, 68
   interrogation in, 210
   principles of LOAC, 39, 53-54
   rules of engagement, 91
   triggering of LOAC
      Additional Protocols, 121-123, 125
      external intervention in internal armed conflict, 127-128, 130
      nature of armed conflict, 113-115, 119
      transnational armed conflicts, 135
   war crimes, 552-555, 569-571
   wounded and sick in, 324-349. *See also* Wounded and sick
International Campaign to Ban Landmines, 298n40
International Commission on Intervention and State Sovereignty, 30
International Committee of the Red Cross (ICRC), 215
   civilians, 219-220, 222, 225-226, 228, 231-232, 238-239
   classification of persons, 143-145, 158-159, 162-164
   command responsibility, 613-614
   customary international law, 79
   defined, 645
   detention of belligerents, 173, 181, 192-196
   distinction, 256-257, 265-267
   emblems of protection, 198, 268, 335
   historical background of LOAC, 44
   interrogation, 199
   naval warfare, 450n118, 457-458
   neutrality, 471-472
   occupation, 380, 384-385, 387, 389-391, 394-395, 403, 415-416n153
   origins of, 322-323
   "soft law," 85
   Superfluous Injury or Unnecessary Suffering (SIrUS) Project, 302n57
   targeting, 276
   triggering of LOAC, 98
      Additional Protocols, 120-121, 124-125, 134
      Geneva Conventions, 99, 101, 103, 106-110, 112, 116-120
      transnational armed conflicts, 134

war crimes, 542, 546, 549-550
weapons and tactics, 286-287, 290, 308
wounded and sick, 330-331, 345, 349-350n172
International Court of Justice (ICJ)
Advisory Opinions, 7, 13-15
civilians, 222, 242
command responsibility, 618-620
customary international law, 76-77
cyber warfare, 526-527
detention of belligerents, 188n48
IHRL, 75-76
interrogation, 200-201
principles of LOAC, 49-50
self-defense, 26-27
as source of LOAC, 83
Statute, 13-14
triggering of LOAC, 129-130
use of force, 13-15, 32
war crimes, 588-589
weapons and tactics, 310
International Covenant on Civil and Political Rights (ICCPR), 74, 188, 241-242
International Criminal Court (ICC)
aggression, 4n16
Rome Statute, 310, 556-557, 560-564, 566-567, 585, 587, 618-620
UCMJ compared, 572
war crimes, 556-559, 560-564, 566-569, 589
weapons and tactics, 310
International Criminal Tribunal for Rwanda (ICTR)
command responsibility, 615-620
defined, 645
jurisdiction, 566-567
UCMJ compared, 572
war crimes, 559-560, 565, 568-571
International Criminal Tribunal for the Former Yugoslavia (ICTY), 11-12, 612
civilians, 228-229
command responsibility, 615-620
defined, 645
distinction, 253-255, 266-267, 271-272
jurisdiction, 566-567
proportionality, 272-273
as source of LOAC, 83
triggering of LOAC, 111, 113, 130-131
UCMJ compared, 572
use of force, 15-16
war crimes, 557, 559-560, 565, 568-571, 586-587n123
International Declaration concerning the Laws and Customs of War (Brussels Declaration) (1874), 61-62
International humanitarian law (IHL), 49-50
International human rights law (IHRL)
civilians, 240-243
occupation, 361-362, 366, 381, 386, 411-412, 415
treaties, 74-76
triggering of LOAC, 94-95
International Law Association (ILA), 104-106
International Law Commission, 241
International Military Tribunal (IMT), 544-545, 556, 558, 564, 588, 602-603
International Telecommunication Union (ITU), 513
International waters
exercise of maritime freedoms in, 433
national waters contrasted, 428n17
Interned civilians, 236-240
basis for detention, 236-237
detention review and release protections, 240
treatment protections, 237-239
Internet. *See* Cyber warfare
Internment. *See* Detention of belligerents
Interpretive Guidance on Direct Participation in Hostilities Under International Humanitarian Law, 84-85
Interrogation, 198-211
Additional Protocols, 201, 208-209
Common Article 3, 199-201, 203, 208-209
degrading treatment, 199, 202
"enhanced interrogation techniques," 207-208
Fourth Geneva Convention, 199-200
in Global War on Terror, 202-209
historical limitations, 200-202
in IAC, 198-199, 210
in NIAC, 199, 211
Third Geneva Convention, 198-200, 208
Intervention
cyber warfare, prohibited intervention, 526-527
humanitarian intervention, 29-31
internal armed conflict, external intervention in, 127-132
third-party interventions, 127-128
Invasion, occupation compared, 374
Investigation of war crimes, 628-635
Army Regulation 15-6, 631-632
commander's inquiry, 630
criminal investigations, 632-633
Inspector General investigations, 633
oversight and review, 634-635
procedures, 629-633

Iran, 451, 525, 532
Iran hostage crisis, 645
Iran-Iraq War, 451
Iraq
  civilians, 234
  Coalition Provisional Authority (CPA), 184, 360, 371, 385, 411
  detention of belligerents, 172, 181, 182, 184, 187, 196-197
  interrogation, 202-203
  Multi-National Force Review Committee, 184
  naval warfare, 447, 451
  occupation, 371, 373-374, 411, 415
  Organization for Reconstruction and Humanitarian Assistance (ORHA), 360
  Security Council, 10, 19
  self-defense, 21-22, 25
  targeting, 251-252
  use of force, 19
  weapons and tactics, 292
Iraq War, 214n1
Irrigation, 270
Islamic State in Iraq and Syria (ISIS)
  civilians, 226
  neutrality, 470-472
  targeting, 275
  triggering of LOAC, 115, 128, 134
  use of force, 19, 32
Israel
  CCW, 73
  civilians, 226n34
  cyber warfare, 523-524
  occupation, 401
  self-defense, 25
  triggering of LOAC, 114-115, 134
  use of force, 6-7
  weapons and tactics, 292
Italy, 97, 483

Japan, 82, 149, 387, 414-415, 483, 603
Jehoram (Israel), 42
Jesus, 42
JNA (Yugoslavia People's Army), 131
Johnson, Lyndon, 249
Joint Doctrine Manual on the Law of Armed Conflict (Canada), 49, 288
Joint force commander, 646
Joint forces, 645
Joint staff, 646
Journalists, 260-261
Jurisdiction over war crimes
  Geneva Conventions, 566
  ICTR, 566-568
  ICTY, 566-568
  overview, 565-568
  UCMJ, 573, 575-576
  War Crimes Act, 566, 580-585
Jus ad bellum, 3, 11, 43, 74
  cyber warfare, 523-528
    armed attack, 524-525
    prohibited intervention, 526-527
    sovereignty, 527-528
    use of force, 525-526
  neutrality, 469
Jus in bello, 3, 35, 43, 74
  cyber warfare, 528-534. *See also* Cyber warfare
Jus militare, 153
Just War Theory, 3, 42-43, 153

Kellogg-Briand Pact (1928), 4, 15
Koh, Harold, 27, 276, 523
Korean War, 195-196
Kosovo, 20, 29-31, 127-128, 136, 163-164
Kosovo Liberation Army (KLA), 128
Kurdistan Workers' Party (PKK), 158
Kuwait, 10, 19, 21-22, 181, 447

Lack of mental responsibility as defense to war crimes, 588
Land mines, 296-299
Landzo, Esad, 616
Lasers, 296
Law enforcement
  air warfare, 499
  command responsibility, 632
  occupation, 390
  proportionality, 58
  tactics, 311
  triggering of LOAC, 94-95, 119, 132, 136
  weapons, 294, 300
Law of armed conflict (LOAC). *See specific topic*
Law of the Sea, 427-436. *See also* Convention on the Law of the Sea (UNCLOS)
  division of world's waters, 427-429
  exercise of maritime freedoms, 430-433
    in international waters, 433
    in national waters, 430-433
  status of vessels and aircraft, 434-436
Law of War Manual (DoD), 88
  air warfare, 484, 486-488, 491-492, 494, 496-497, 502-504
  classification of persons, 157
  compliance mechanisms, 634
  cyber warfare, 525-526
  naval warfare, 424-425n4, 438

occupation, 362-363, 373, 412
principles of LOAC, 47, 49, 51-53, 59
targeting, 252
treaties, 75
use of force, 32
weapons and tactics, 288
wounded and sick, 326
Laws as source of LOAC, 87
Laws of Manu (Hindu), 42
League of Nations, 3-4
Lebanon, 114-115, 134, 136, 158, 568, 569
Leipzig Trials, 544
Letters of marque, 436
Leveé en masse, 145, 161, 324, 381, 455
Lex specialis, 187-188, 241
Liberation of territory, 364n20
Libya, 21, 31
Lieber, Francis, 44, 542, 593
Lieber Code
  classification of persons, 148-150
  command responsibility, 601
  customary international law, 77
  historical background, 44-46
  interrogation, 209
  war crimes, 542-543
  weapons and tactics, 288-289, 310-311
Lincoln, Abraham, 44
Lion and Sun, 268
LOAC (Law of armed conflict). *See specific topic*
Logistics, 646
London Charter (1945), 544, 602
London Declaration Concerning the Laws of Naval War (1909), 437, 445-446n103, 460
London Protocol (1936), 443, 450
Lynn, William J. III, 534

MacArthur, Douglas, 603
Macedonia, 104
Magenta, Battle of (1859), 321
Maltreatment at hands of party to conflict, protection of civilians from, 221-224
Maneuvers, 646
Manual for Courts-Martial (MCM), 623-624
Manual of the Laws and Customs of War. *See* Oxford Manual on the Laws of Naval War Governing the Relations Between Belligerents
Manual on International Law Applicable to Air and Missile Warfare (2009), 84
  neutrality, 461, 483-484, 486-491, 494-497, 501-504
  space warfare, 508
  wounded and sick, 348-349

Manual on International Law Applicable to Military Uses of Outer Space (MILAMOS) (2016), 515
Manunoir, Theodore, 322
Maritime freedoms, 430-433
  in international waters, 433
  in national waters, 430-433
Maritime Intercept Operation, 447
Marque, letters of, 436
Martens, Fyodor, Fyodorovich, 222
Martens Clause (1907), 77, 222, 485-486, 535
Matheson, Michael, 78
McCain, John, 592
McGill Manual, 515
Medecins sans Frontieres, 342n122
MEDEVAC helicopters, 345-346
Medical aircraft
  air warfare, 498
  protected from attack, 259-260
  wounded and sick, 345-349
Medical personnel, protection of, 258-260. *See also* Medical aircraft
  auxiliary medical personnel, 259
  civilians, 259-260
Medical transport, 259
Medina, Ernest, 622-623
A Memory of Solferino (Dunant), 44, 64, 322
Mens rea of command responsibility, 605-606
Mental responsibility, lack of as defense to war crimes, 588
Merchant vessels, 435, 443-444n97, 646
Meron, Theodore, 228
Methods of warfare. *See* Tactics
Milikowsky, Matthew, 320-321
Military aircraft, 646
Military commissions, 625-627
Military Commissions Act of 2006, 87, 152, 155, 578-580, 590-591
Military Commissions Act of 2009, 87, 152, 155, 626-627
Military courts, 401-402
Military deception, 280
Military doctrine, 87-88
Military Extraterritorial Jurisdiction Act of 2000 (MEJA), 581-584
Military necessity
  Hague Conventions, 50
  occupation, 384-386
  as principle of LOAC, 49-53
  targeting, 252-278
    distinction, 252-272. *See also* Distinction
    proportionality, 272-275
Military objectives, 55-56n61

Military Order Number 1 (2002), 117, 203, 208
Mines, naval warfare, 451-454
Miranda warnings, 198-199
Mohammad Ali, Alaa, 583n113
Money, targeting of, 275-276
MONUC (United Nations Organization Mission in the DRC), 10-11
MONUSCO (United Nations Organization Stabilization Mission in the DRC), 11
Mora, Alberto, 205
Mortars, 646
Moscow Conference (1943), 602
Moses, 42
Moynier, Gustave, 322
M-16, 646
Mucic, Zdravko, 616
Mueller, Robert, 527
Murphy, Frank W., 608
My Lai Massacre (1968), 581, 622-623

Naco, Battle of (1913), 89-90
Napoleon, 51, 320-321
Napoleon III, 44, 321-322
Napoleonic Wars, 43
National Defense Authorization Act of 2017, 523
National relief societies, 259
National Security Council, 189
National waters
  exercise of maritime freedoms in, 430-433
  international waters contrasted, 428n17
NATO. *See* North Atlantic Treaty Organization
Natural environment, 270-272
Naval warfare, 421-476
  Additional Protocols, 440, 446, 457
  applicability of LOAC, 436-458
  applicable law, 426-427, 474-476
  blockade, 445-447
  crews and passengers, disposition of, 444-445
  First Geneva Convention, 454
  Hague Conventions, 436-437, 440, 451-453
  Law of the Sea, 427-436
    division of world's waters, 427-429
    exercise of maritime freedoms, 430-433
    status of vessels and aircraft, 434-436
  maritime freedoms, exercise of, 430-433
    in international waters, 433
    in national waters, 430-433
  mines, 451-454
  neutrality, 459-472. *See also* Neutrality
  overview, 423-426
  persons *hors de combat,* protection of, 454-458
  right to engage in warfare at sea, 439-440
  Second Geneva Convention, 437, 450, 454-458
  sources of LOAC, 436-439
  submarine warfare, 450-451
  Third Geneva Convention, 444-445
  torpedoes, 451-454
  vessels, 440-444
    attack, vessels subject to, 440-442
    capture, vessels subject to, 442-444
    Law of the Sea, status of vessels and aircraft, 434-436
  zones and control of immediate area of naval operations, 447-450
Navy-Marine Court of Military Review, 624
Ndombasi, Abdoulaye Yerodia, 588-589
Necessity, self-defense, 21-22
Negroponte, John, 9
Netherlands, 148
Neutral airspace, 492-493
Neutrality, 459-472
  belligerents, rights and obligations of, 464-466
  customary international law, 459
  cyber warfare, 533
  Hague Conventions, 460, 463, 464-466, 473n217
  neutral shipping, rules governing, 466-469
  neutral states, rights and obligations of, 461-464
  in NIAC, 469-472
  sources of law, 459-461
Neutralize, 646
Nicaragua, 14, 26-27, 83, 129-130, 200-201
9/11 attacks, 203
Nobel Peace Prize, 44
Non-combatants, 150-151. *See also* Civilians
Non-international armed conflict (NIAC)
  Additional Protocols, 68
  air warfare in, 505-506
  civilians, 216-217, 224
  classification of persons, 157-158
  cultural property, 72
  customary international law, 80
  detention of belligerents in, 178-179
    due process, 184-186
    interrogation, 199, 211
    standard of treatment, 197-198
  international tribunals, 83
  neutrality in, 469-472
  occupation law, relationship to, 365-367

principles of LOAC, 39, 53-54
triggering of LOAC
   Additional Protocols, 122-130
   existence of armed conflict, 107-108, 110-113
   nature of armed conflict, 115-117, 119
   transnational armed conflicts, 134, 136
war crimes, 569-571
weapons and tactics, 72-73
wounded and sick in, 349-351
Non-lethal targeting, 280
Non-lethal weapons, 306
Non-state actors
   cyber warfare, 534
   use of force, 31-33
   war crimes, 590-592
Noriega, Manual, 115, 193
North Atlantic Treaty Organization (NATO), 26
   Cooperative Cyber Defense Center of Excellence, 35, 85, 523
   humanitarian intervention, 29-30
   proportionality, 273
   triggering of LOAC, 127-128
   use of force, 31
   weapons and tactics, 302
North Korea, 195
Norway, 610
"No-strike list," 250-251
Nuclear power plants, 269-270
Nuclear Regulatory Commission (NRC), 304
Nuclear weapons, 292n24
Nulla crimen sine lege, 564-565
Nulla poena sine lege, 402
Nuremberg Charter (1945), 4
Nuremberg Tribunal. *See* International Military Tribunal

Obama, Barack, 81, 156, 189, 275, 396, 471n212, 526, 579, 585, 591
Obedience to superior orders as defense to war crimes, 586
Occupation, 357-420
   Additional Protocols, 361, 365n23, 385, 388-390, 392-398, 407-408
   applicable law, 377-383
      chart, 417-418
      Fourth Geneva Convention, 379-383
      Hague Conventions, 378-379
   civil defense, 389-390
   civilians
      meeting needs of, 397-400
      protection of, 230-232
   Common Article 2, 362, 372
   Common Article 3, 395-396
   customary international law, 361, 366, 378, 381, 394, 396
   detention during, 390-397
      assigned residence, 395
      generally applicable treatment standards, 396
      preventive detention, 390-391
      procedural requirements, 391-392
      prohibited treatment, 397
      treatment standards for internment, 392-395
   expanding scope of, 410-412
   features of, 370-375
      annexation compared, 375
      commencement, 370-372
      direct and indirect control, 372
      invasion compared, 374
      obligation to take control, 373-374
   Fourth Geneva Convention, 361, 379-383
      civilians, 397-400
      detention, 390-397
      governing of occupied territory, 400-403
      implications of, 376-377
      obligations of, 386
      overview, 379-383
      private property, 404, 406-409
      restoring order, 388
      termination of, 415
   Geneva Conventions, 361, 411, 414
   governing territory during, 400-403
   Hague Conventions, 361
      applicable law, 378-379
      civilians, 397
      features of, 372-373
      governing of occupied territory, 400
      obligations of, 383-387
      overview, 378-379
      private property, 403-410
      restoring order, 388
      termination of hostilities, 368-369
      termination of occupation, 414
      transformational occupation, 411
   hostilities, termination of, 367-370
      continued occupation after cessation of hostilities, 415-416
   IHRL, 361-362, 366, 381, 411-412, 415
   implications of, 375-377
   law enforcement, 390
   military courts, 401-402
   obligations of, 383-386
      human rights, 386
      military necessity, 384-386
      protection of property, 386
      public order and safety, 383-384

Occupation (cont'd)
  overview, 360-362
  post-conflict phase, transition to, 412-416
    conflict termination, 412-415
    continued occupation after cessation of hostilities, 415-416
  private property
    management of, 403-410
    protection of, 386
  rape, 381, 400
  restoring order, 387-390
    duty of obedience, 387-388
    use of existing personnel, 388-390
  termination of, 412-416
    conflict termination, 412-415
    continued occupation after cessation of hostilities, 415-416
  Third Geneva Convention, 371, 380-381, 394, 396
  transformational occupation, 410-412
  transition to, 367-370
  triggering law of, 362-367
    essential criteria, 362-363
    NIAC, relationship to, 365-367
    other types of operations, 363-365
Occupied Palestinian Territory, 226n34
  compliance mechanisms, 628
  ICJ, 15, 83
  occupation, 401
Occupied territory, 646
O'Connor, Sandra Day, 174-175, 186-187
Official acts immunity as defense to war crimes, 588-589
Official Graves Registration Service, 333
Omar, Mullah, 33
On the Law of War and Peace (Grotius), 43
On War (von Clausewitz), 43
Operational lawyering, 95
Operational planning, 646
Operation Desert Storm, 181
Operation El Dorado Canyon, 21, 23
Operation Just Cause, 115, 181, 193-194
Operations officers, 646
Oppenheim, L.F.L., 96-98
Ordinance of Orleans (1439), 601
Organization for Reconstruction and Humanitarian Assistance (ORHA), 360
Organized armed groups, 158-161
Oslo Convention (2008), 301-302
Ottawa Convention (1997), 297-298
Outer Space Treaty (1967), 509-514
Oxford Manual on the Laws of Naval War Governing the Relations Between Belligerents (1913), 48-49, 61-62, 84, 86, 437, 460

Pakistan, 9, 33
Panama, 115, 172, 181, 193, 368
Panama Canal, 433
Panama Defense Force (PDF), 181
Pappas, Thomas, 207
Parachutists, 258
Paratroopers, 258
Paris, Treaty of (1763), 414
Paris Declaration Respecting Maritime Law (1856), 436
Parks, W. Hays, 51-52n45, 104n31
Partsch, Karl Josef, 290
Patton, George S., 309
Perfidy, 310, 646-647
Periodic review boards, 189-190
Permanent Court of International Justice (PCIJ), 527
Persons who are *hors de combat*, 257-258
  persons clearly expressing intent to surrender, 258
  persons in power of adverse party, 257
  unconscious, wounded, or sick persons, 258
  wounded and sick, 326n24
Philippines, 543, 603
Piedmont-Sardinia, 321
Piracy, 439
PKK (Kurdistan Workers' Party), 158
Plastic fragments, 295-296
Platoons, 647
POWs. *See* Prisoners of war
Precautions
  cyber warfare, 531-533
    constant care, 531
    effects of attacks, against, 532-533
    indiscriminate attacks, 532
    military objective, 531-532
  as principle of LOAC, 59-61
Prescott, William, 89
Presidential Policy Guidance (PPG), 276-277
Preventive detention during occupation, 390-391
Preventive self-defense, 25-26
Principles of LOAC, 46-61
  Common Article 3, 54
  defining, 49-61
  distinction, 55-57. *See also* Distinction
  humanity, 53-55. *See also* Humanity
  importance of, 47-49
  military necessity, 49-53. *See also* Military necessity
  overview, 46-47
  precautions, 59-61
    cyber warfare, 531-533. *See also* Cyber warfare

proportionality, 57-59. *See also* Proportionality
Prisoner of War Convention. *See* Third Geneva Convention
Prisoners of war (POWs), 148-151. *See also* Third Geneva Convention
   civilians accompanying force, 150
   civilians compared, 237-239
   classification of persons, 143-144
   combatants compared, 145-147
   defined, 647
   detention of, 175-177
      standard of treatment, 190-196
   Geneva Conventions, 41, 65-66, 144, 145-146, 149-150, 152
   Hague Conventions, 145
   historical background, 148-149
   retained personnel, 150-151
   triggering of LOAC, 103-104
   wounded and sick compared, 324, 341
Privateering, 436
Private property
   civilians, 232-236
   destruction of, 232-234
   during occupation
      management of, 403-410
      protection of, 386
   protection of property, obligations of occupation, 386
   taking possession of, 234-236
Program on Humanitarian Policy and Conflict Research, 84
Proportionality
   Additional Protocols, 272
   cyber warfare, 530-531
   law enforcement, 58
   military necessity, 272-275
   as principle of LOAC, 57-59
   self-defense, 22
   targeting, 272-275
Protected objects or places, 267-272
   cultural property, 268-269
   dangerous forces, works and installations containing, 269-270
   hospitals, 268
   natural environment, 270-272
   objects indispensable to survival of civilian population, 270
   safety zones, 268
   undefended places, 268
Protected persons, 227-232
   in enemy territory, 230
   in occupied territory, 230-232
Protection of nationals, use of force, 28-29
Protracted hostilities, 111

Prussia, 148
Psychological operations, 280
Public order and safety, obligations of occupation, 383-384
Putin, Vladimir, 526

Qaddafi, Muammar, 21, 31
Qur'an as historical foundation for rules of conduct of hostilities, 42

Rape
   civilians, 223n23
   detention of belligerents, 197
   occupation, 381, 400
   war crimes, 546, 558, 582, 584-585
Rapid response forces, 647
Reagan, Ronald, 21, 23, 123, 125-126, 224n28
Reciprocity, 13, 49, 67, 171-172, 192
Red Crescent, 198, 268, 335-336, 338
Red Cross. *See* International Committee of the Red Cross
Red Crystal, 268, 335-336, 338
Red Star of David, 268
Regiments, 647
Relief societies, 259
Religious personnel, 259-260
Remnants of war, 298-299
Rendulic, Lothar, 179
Reprisals, 312-313
"Respect and protect," wounded and sick, 328-329
Responsibility to protect (R2P), use of force, 29-31
Restatement of the Law (Third) of Foreign Relations of the United States, 76
Restoring order, 388
Retained personnel, 150-151
Retrograde, 647
Revenue-generating objects, targeting of, 275-276
Revolutionary Armed Forces of Colombia (FARC), 158
Riot control agents, 300
Roberts, Adam, 361
Roerich, Nicholas, 70
Roerich Pact, 70
Rome Statute. *See* International Criminal Court
Roosevelt, Eleanor, 188
Rule for Courts-Martial 916(d), 586
Rules Concerning the Control of Wireless Telegraphy in Time of War and Air Warfare, 84
Rules of engagement (ROE)
   as source of LOAC, 89-91
   targeting, 249-250, 280

Rumsfeld, Donald, 206, 209
Ruses, 309
Russia
   CCW, 73
   cyber warfare, 524, 526-527
   in Security Council, 7
   space warfare, 507, 519
   wounded and sick, 320-321
Russo-Japanese War, 451
Rutledge, Wiley B., 608
Rwanda, 83, 557, 559, 617. *See also* International Criminal Tribunal for Rwanda

Saboteurs, 153-155, 176, 196, 394
Safety zones, 268
St. Petersburg Declaration (1868). *See* Declaration Renouncing the Use, in Time of War, of Explosive Projectiles Under 400 Grammes Weight
San Remo Manual on International Law Applicable to Armed Conflicts at Sea (1994)
   air warfare, 483-484, 486
   naval warfare, 437-438, 440-442, 444, 446n104, 448-449, 460-461
   as "soft law," 84-85
Saudi Arabia, 292
Scatterable minefields, 647
Schlesinger Report (2004), 207
Schmitt, Michael, 35
Searches and seizures, 634-635
Second Geneva Convention (1949), 63, 66. *See also* Naval warfare
   air warfare, 498
   naval warfare, 437, 450, 454-458
   Third Geneva Convention compared, 454-455
   wounded and sick, 342
Second Gulf War, 311
Second Italian War of Independence, 321
Security Council
   Chapter VI actions (Pacific Settlement of Disputes), 7-9
   Chapter VII actions (Action with Respect to Threats to the Peace, Breaches of the Peace, and Acts of Aggression), 9-13
   neutrality, 461-462, 464, 470
   occupation, 364, 377, 410-411
   Resolutions, 647
   self-defense, 27-28
   use of force, 7-13, 19-20, 63n94
   war crimes, 560

Self-defense, 20-28
   armed attack, 26-27
   collective self-defense, 26
   "inherent right," 23-26
      anticipatory self-defense, 24
      interceptive self-defense, 24-25
      no action before armed attack, 24
      preventive self-defense, 25-26
   overview, 20-21
   principles of, 21-23
      necessity, 21-22
      proportionality, 22
      timeliness, 22-23
   "until the Security Council has taken measures," 27-28
   war crimes, as defense to, 587-588
September 11, 2001 terrorist attacks, 203
Serbia
   humanitarian intervention, 29-30
   proportionality, 273
   targeting, 251
   triggering of LOAC, 104, 127-128, 130-131
   war crimes, 568-571
Seven Years' War, 414
Sexual assault, 570
Shipping, neutrality, 466-469
Shipwrecked persons. *See* Second Geneva Convention (1949)
Shotguns, 302
Sick. *See* Wounded and sick
Sierra Leone, 29, 568, 569
Silencers, 305
"Simple breaches," 553
Skorzeny, Otto, 147n24
Sleep deprivation, 206, 579
Small arms, 302-303
Smith, Jacob A., 543
Snipers, 233, 255, 305
Sofaer, Abe, 14
"Soft law," 84-86
"Soldiers' rules," 47
Solf, Waldemar A., 290
Solferino, Battle of (1859), 44, 215, 321
Somalia, 21, 114, 136, 172
Sources of LOAC, 82-91
   decisions of courts and tribunals, 82-83
   executive orders, 87
   laws, 87
   military doctrine, 87-88
   rules of engagement (ROE), 89-91
   "soft law," 84-86
South Korea, 298
Sovereignty, cyber warfare, 527-528
Soviet Union, 97, 602. *See also* Russia

Space Objects, Convention on International Liability for Damage Caused by, 512n192
Space warfare, 506-521
   Additional Protocols, 512-513, 516, 520-521
   anti-satellite weapons (ASAT), 507, 510, 518-521
   applicability of LOAC, 514-515
   collateral effects resulting from attacks on space objects, 518-521
   dual use space objects, 516-518
   Geneva Conventions, 512-513
   overview, 478-479, 506-508
   space defined, 508
   treaty law, 508-514
Spain, 148, 414
Spanish Civil War, 65, 97, 100
Specialized tribunals, war crimes and crimes codified by, 559-560
   use of, 568-569
Special Tribunal for Lebanon, 569
Spies and spying, 61-62, 154, 310, 312
"Spoils of war," 403
Stalin, Josef, 97
Standing Rules of Engagement (U.S.), 160
State aircraft, 487-488
Status of persons. *See* Classification of persons
STUXNET malware, 525, 530-532
Submarine warfare, 450-451
Sub-munitions, 301
Subordinates. *See* Command responsibility
Sudan, 589
Sumter Prisoner of War Camp, 543
Sun Tzu, 42
Superfluous Injury or Unnecessary Suffering (SIrUS) Project, 302n57
Superior orders, obedience to as defense to war crimes, 586
Supply depots, 647
Suppressors, 305
Switzerland, 84
Syria, 32, 103-105, 128, 226, 470-472, 523-524

Tactical operations centers, 647
Tactics, 308-313. *See also* Weapons
   air warfare, 493-502
      conduct of hostilities, 493-498
      destruction of captured aircraft, 502
      enemy aircraft, interception and capture of, 498-500
      neutral aircraft, interception and capture of, 500-502
   assassination, 310-311
   chivalry, 288-289
   espionage, 312
   Hague Conventions, 287-288, 311
   humanity, 287-288
   law enforcement, 311
   overview, 286-289, 308-309
   perfidy, 310
   proportionality, 286-287, 308-309, 313
   reprisals, 312-313
   ruses, 309
Taguba, Antonio, 207
Taliban
   classification of persons, 152, 155-156, 158
   detention of belligerents, 172, 175, 182
   drones, 33
   interrogation, 203
   neutrality, 464
   targeting, 275
   triggering of LOAC, 117, 128, 133
   war crimes, 567, 585
Tallinn Manuals
   cyber warfare, 35, 523-526, 528-531, 533-534
   neutrality, 461
   as "soft law," 85-86
   space warfare, 519-520
Targeting, 247-283
   categories of, 251
   current controversies, 275
   defined, 250
   distinction, 55-57, 252-272. *See also* Distinction
   D3A methodology, 250
   humanity, 278
   individuals outside "areas of active hostilities," 276-277
   legal advice, 281
   military necessity, 252-278
      distinction, 252-272. *See also* Distinction
      proportionality, 272-275
   money and revenue-generating objects, 275-276
   NIAC, 277-278
   non-lethal targeting, 280
   overview, 249
   process, 249-251
   proportionality, 272-275
   review of decisions, 279-280
   rules of engagement, 249-250, 280
   unnecessary suffering, 278
Targeting officers, 647
Task forces, 647

Termination of hostilities
  continued occupation after cessation of hostilities, 415-416
  overview, 367-370
Territorial seas, 428, 647
Terrorism. *See also specific entity*
  Global War on Terror, 171-172, 202-209
  non-state actors
    cyber warfare, 534
    use of force, 31-33
    war crimes, 590-592
  use of force, 31-33
Thermobaric munitions, 296n35
Third Geneva Convention (1949), 41, 66. *See also* Prisoners of war
  air warfare, 499
  civilians, 219-220
  classification of persons, 144, 149-150
  detention of belligerents, 173, 175-177, 180-183, 190-196
  distinction, 254
  Fourth Geneva Convention compared, 237-239
  interrogation, 198-200, 208
  naval warfare, 444-445
  occupation, 371, 380-381, 394, 396
  Second Geneva Convention compared, 454-455
  war crimes, 547, 584
Third-party interventions, 127-128
Threats to security during occupation, 390-397
  assigned residence, 395
  generally applicable treatment standards, 396
  preventive detention, 390-391
  procedural requirements, 391-392
  prohibited treatment, 397
  treatment standards for internment, 392-395
Timeliness, self-defense, 22-23
Tokyo Trials, 545, 611, 613-614, 619
Torpedoes, 451-454
Torture
  detention of belligerents, 172, 198-200, 204, 207, 209
  treaty law, 74-75
  war crimes, 546, 557-558, 570, 579, 588
  wounded and sick, 331
Torture Convention (CAT) (1985), 74
"Torture Memorandum," 204-205
Tracer munitions, 293, 295, 303
Tradition of LOAC, 38-41
Training in LOAC, 47

Transformational occupation, 410-412
Transit passage, 432-433, 648
Transnational armed conflicts, triggering of LOAC, 132-137
Treaty Banning Nuclear Weapon Tests in the Atmosphere, In Outer Space and Under Water, 513n200
Treaty law, 61-76. *See also specific Treaty or Convention*
  Additional Protocols, 68-69. *See also* Additional Protocols
  air warfare, 482-486
  cultural property, 70-72
  customary international law compared, 76, 76n175
  Geneva Conventions, 64-68. *See also* Geneva Conventions
  Hague Conventions, 61-64. *See also* Hague Conventions
  space warfare, 508-514
  torture, 74-75
  treaties outside scope of LOAC, 73-76
  weapons and tactics, 72-73, 291-293
Treaty of Friendship (1785), 148
Treaty of Paris (1763), 414
Treaty of Versailles (1919), 82, 544
Triggering of LOAC, 93-139
  Additional Protocols, 120-127
  belligerency doctrine, 96
  Common Article 2, 99-103
  Common Article 3, 99-103
  conflict classification paradigm, 95-99
  de jure vs. *de facto* nature of conflict, 100-101
  Geneva Conventions, 99-120
    duration and intensity of conflict, 111-112
    existence of armed conflict, 103-113
    nature of armed conflict, 113-120
  IAC
    Additional Protocols, 121-123, 125
    external intervention in internal armed conflict, 127-128, 130
    nature of armed conflict, 113-115, 119
    transnational armed conflicts, 135
  IHRL, 94-95
  internal armed conflict, external intervention in, 127-132
  law enforcement, 94-95, 119, 132, 136
  NIAC
    Additional Protocols, 122-130
    existence of armed conflict, 107-108, 110-113
    nature of armed conflict, 115-117, 119

transnational armed conflicts, 134, 136
occupation law, 362-367
    essential criteria, 362-363
    NIAC, relationship to, 365-367
    other types of operations, 363-365
overview, 94-95, 137
transnational armed conflicts, 132-137
Truce, flag of, 289, 310
Turkey, 158
Turkish Foundation for Human Rights and Freedoms and Humanitarian Relief, 226n34

UAVs. *See* Unmanned aerial vehicles
UNCLOS. *See* Convention on the Law of the Sea
Unconditional surrender, 414-415
Undefended places, 268
Unexploded ordnance, 298-299
Uniform Code of Military Justice (UCMJ)
    Article 18 jurisdiction, 573, 575-576
    charge sheet, 574-575
    command responsibility, 598, 620-627
    compliance mechanisms, 628, 630, 633-635, 637
    courts-martial, 573
    detention of belligerents, 192, 200
    ICC compared, 572
    ICTR compared, 572
    ICTY compared, 572
    occupation, 369
    punitive articles, 572-573
    war crimes, 571-576
    War Crimes Act compared, 576, 580-585
    weapons and tactics, 312
Uniform requirement, 146-147
United Kingdom
    air warfare, 483
    civilians, 233
    command responsibility, 602
    detention of belligerents in, 51n43
    Manual of the Law of Armed Conflict, 46-47, 49, 88
    Ministry of Defence, 88
    occupation, 369, 370n35, 387, 411, 414
    principles of LOAC in, 46-47, 49
    in Security Council, 7
    use of force, 32
    weapons and tactics, 292, 309
United Nations. *See also specific Convention*
    Charter. *See* United Nations Charter
    Children's Fund, 216
    Economic and Social Council, 5
    Expert on the Impact of Armed Conflict on Children, 217

General Assembly
    private property, 232-233
    Resolution 3314 on the Definition of Aggression, 17
    Uniting for Peace Resolution, 6
    use of force, 5-7
Group of Governmental Experts on Developments in the Field of Information and Telecommunications in the Context of International Security, 523, 528
High Level Panel on Threats, Challenges and Change, 30
Human Rights Committee, 75-76
Human Rights Council, 628
ICJ. *See* International Court of Justice
A More Secure World: Our Shared Responsibility, 30
Secretariat, 5
Security Council. *See* Security Council
Trusteeship Council, 5
United Nations Organization Mission in the DRC (MONUC), 10-11
United Nations Organization Stabilization Mission in the DRC (MONUSCO), 11
United Nations Charter
    Chapter VI (Pacific Settlement of Disputes), 7-9
    Chapter VII (Action with Respect to Threats to the Peace, Breaches of the Peace, and Acts of Aggression), 9-13
    LOAC, 73-74
    naval warfare, 446-447
    neutrality, 461-462, 470
    occupation, 364, 411
    overview, 4-5
    space warfare, 509-511
    use of force, 4-15
        General Assembly, 5-7
        ICJ, 13-15
        Security Council, 7-13
Universal Declaration of Human Rights, 188
Unlawful combatants, 143-144
    Additional Protocols, 152-155
    classification of persons, 152-157
    gap in coverage, 154-155
    Geneva Conventions, 152-155
    habeas corpus litigation, 155-157
    historical background, 152-154
Unmanned aerial vehicles (UAVs), 163-164, 273, 504, 648
Unnecessary suffering
    targeting, 278
    weapons, 290-291

Unprivileged belligerents
   detention of, 177-178
   distinction, 256-257
Use of force, 1-36
   in cyber warfare, 34-35, 525-526
   drones, 33-34
   Hague Conventions, 3
   historical background, 3-4
   legal bases for, 15-31
      consent, 18-19
      humanitarian intervention, 29-31
      protection of nationals, 28-29
      responsibility to protect (R2P), 29-31
      Security Council authorization, 19-20
      self-defense, 20-28. *See also*
         Self-defense
   non-state actors, 31-33
   overview, 1-3
   terrorism, 31-33
   UN Charter paradigm, 4-15
      General Assembly, 5-7
      ICJ, 13-15
      Security Council, 7-13. *See also*
         Security Council

Vehicles, wounded and sick, 342-345
Versailles, Treaty of (1919), 82, 544
Vessels, naval warfare and, 440-444
   attack, vessels subject to, 440-442
   capture, vessels subject to, 442-444
   Law of the Sea, status of vessels and
      aircraft, 434-436
Vicarious liability, command responsibility, 600-601
Vietnam War, 249, 303, 451, 540, 592
Visit and search, 648
von Clausewitz, Karl, 43
von Hagenbach, Peter, 542
von Kuechler, Georg, 609
von Leeb, Wilhelm, 608-610
VRS (Army of Serbian Republic of Bosnia and Herzegovina), 131

Waller, L.W.T., 543
War crimes, 537-594
   Additional Protocols, 550-553, 570
   aggression, 556-557
   applicability of LOAC, 539-540
   Common Article 2, 552
   crimes against humanity, 558-559
   customary international law, 545-546
   defenses to, 585-589
      duress, 586-587
      head of state immunity, 588-589
      lack of mental responsibility, 588
      obedience to superior orders, 586
      official acts immunity, 588-589
      self-defense, 587-588
   defined, 541-542
   degrading treatment, 546, 579
   Geneva Conventions
      Common Article 3, 554-555, 569-572
      crimes against humanity, 559
      defenses to, 586
      duties of signatory states, 548-552
      Fourth Geneva Convention, 547-548, 573
      "grave breaches," 547-553
      in IAC, 569-570
      IAC trigger, 552-555
      jurisdiction, 566
      in NIAC, 569-570
      nulla crimen sine lege, 565
      "simple breaches," 553
   genocide, 557
   historical background, 542-545
   in IAC, 552-555, 569-571
   ICC, codified by, 560-564
   investigation of, 628-635
      Army Regulation 15-6, 631-632
      commander's inquiry, 630
      criminal investigations, 632-633
      Inspector General investigations, 633
      oversight and review, 634-635
      procedures, 629-633
   jurisdiction
      Geneva Conventions, 566
      ICTR, 566-568
      ICTY, 566-568
      overview, 565-568
      UCMJ, 573, 575-576
      War Crimes Act, 566, 580-585
   in NIAC, 569-571
   non-state actors, 590-592
   nulla crimen sine lege, 564-565
   overview, 538-539
   rape, 546, 558, 582, 584-585
   sources of, 545-565
   specialized tribunals
      crimes codified by, 559-560
      use of, 568-569
   Third Geneva Convention, 547, 584
   torture, 546, 557-558, 570, 579, 588
   UCMJ, 571-576
   value of prosecuting, 592-593
   War Crimes Act, 549, 576-585
      civilians, jurisdiction over, 583-584
      enemies, jurisdiction over, 584-585

former soldiers, jurisdiction over,
    581-582
  jurisdiction, 566
  modifications, 578-580
  punishable offenses, 576-578
  soldiers, jurisdiction over, 580-581
World War II war crimes tribunals,
    602-611
  "High Command Case," 608-610
  Hostage Case, 52n46, 610-611,
    613-614, 619, 627
  Tokyo Trials, 545, 611, 613-614, 619
  Yamashita Tribunal, 603-608. *See also*
    Yamashita Tribunal
War Crimes Act of 1996, 87, 549
  Geneva Conventions, 576, 580
  Hague Conventions, 576
  jurisdiction, 566, 580-585
  UCMJ compared, 576, 580-585
  war crimes, 549, 576-585
    civilians, jurisdiction over, 583-584
    enemies, jurisdiction over, 584-585
    former soldiers, jurisdiction over,
      581-582
    jurisdiction, 566
    modifications, 578-580
    punishable offenses, 576-578
    soldiers, jurisdiction over, 580-581
War Powers Resolution of 1973, 2
Warships, 434-435, 648
Washington, George, 148
Washington Conference on the Limitation of
    Armaments (1922), 482-483
Water boarding, 205, 579
Watkin, Kenneth, 107-108
Weapons, 289-308. *See also* Tactics
  bayonets, 303
  chivalry, 288-289
  cluster munitions, 301-302
  in customary international law, 291-293
  cyber weapons, 307
  depleted uranium, 304-305
  edged weapons, 303
  employment of, 307-308
  explosive munitions, 304
  .50 caliber rounds, 303
  Hague Conventions, 287-288, 290-294
  humanity, 287-288
  illegal use, 291-293
  law enforcement, 294, 300
  legal review, 289-290, 314-317
  NIAC, 72-73
  non-lethal weapons, 306
  nuclear weapons, 292n24

overview, 286-289
prohibited weapons
  anti-personnel land mines, 296-299
  biological weapons, 299
  blinding lasers, 296
  chemical weapons, 299-300
  "dum-dum bullets," 294
  expanding bullets, 294
  exploding bullets, 293-294
  explosive remnants of war, 298-299
  incendiaries, 295-296
  plastic fragments, 295-296
  riot control agents, 300
proportionality, 286-287, 289-290,
    307-308
shotguns, 302
silencers, 305
small arms, 302-303
snipers, 305
suppressors, 305
thermobaric munitions, 296n35
treaties regarding, 72-73
treaty law, 72-73, 291-293
unnecessary suffering, 290-291
white phosphorous rounds, 296n35
Webster, Daniel, 24
West Bank. *See* Occupied Palestinian
    Territory
Whitaker, Rich, 40-41
White phosphorous rounds, 296n35
Wilhelm II (Germany), 544
Willful blindness, command responsibility,
    610, 619
Wirz, Henry, 543
Works and installations containing dangerous
    forces, 269-270
World War I, 149, 216, 302, 448
World War II, 146, 292, 309, 379, 388
  war crimes tribunals, 602-611
    "High Command Case," 608-610
    Hostage Case, 52n46, 610-611,
      613-614, 619, 627
    Tokyo Trials, 545, 611, 613-614, 619
    Yamashita Tribunal, 603-608. *See also*
      Yamashita Tribunal
Wounded and sick, 319-355
  Additional Protocols, 323, 325, 327, 337,
    347, 350-351
  categories of, 324-325
  Common Article 3, 324, 349-350
  distinction, 268
  emblems of protection, 268, 335-336
  Geneva Conventions, 323, 351
  historical background, 320-323

Wounded and sick (cont'd)
   in IAC, 324-349
      auxiliary medical support personnel, 340-341
      care providers, equipment, and facilities, 334-349
      dead, obligations to, 332-333
      determination of "wounded and sick," 326-327
      exclusively engaged medical personnel, 338-340
      facilities and vehicles, 342-345
      information, obligation to provide, 333-334
      medical aircraft, 345-349
      medical care, obligation to provide, 330-332
      medical units, establishments, and transportation, 342-349
      members of societies from neutral countries, 341-342
      methods of protection, 328-334
      overview, 324-325
      personnel aiding, 336-342
      protection, 328-329
      respect, 328
      retained person (RP) status, 338-340
      search and collect, obligation to, 329-330
   in NIAC, 349-351
   overview, 320, 351-352
   persons *hors de combat*, 326n24
   POWs compared, 324, 341
   Second Geneva Convention, 342
   torture, 331
   violations, 351
Wounded and Sick Convention. *See* Geneva Convention for the Amelioration of the Condition of the Wounded in Armies in the Field

Yamashita, Tomoyuki, 603-608
Yamashita Tribunal, 603-608, 619-620, 626-627
   actus reus of command responsibility, 606
   causation, 606
   imputed liability, 607
   mens rea of command responsibility, 605-606
   overview, 603-605
   scope of authority, 605
   Supreme Court case, 607-608
Yemen, 21
Yoo, John, 204-205
Yugoslavia (former), 83, 131, 557, 559, 568-569, 610. *See also* International Criminal Tribunal for the Former Yugoslavia
Yugoslavia People's Army (JNA), 131